P9-CQQ-015

lonely planet

# Malaysia, Singapore & Brunei

**Chris Rowthorn**
**Sara Benson**
**Russell Kerr**
**Christine Niven**

LONELY PLANET PUBLICATIONS
Melbourne • Oakland • London • Paris

# PENINSULAR MALAYSIA & SINGAPORE

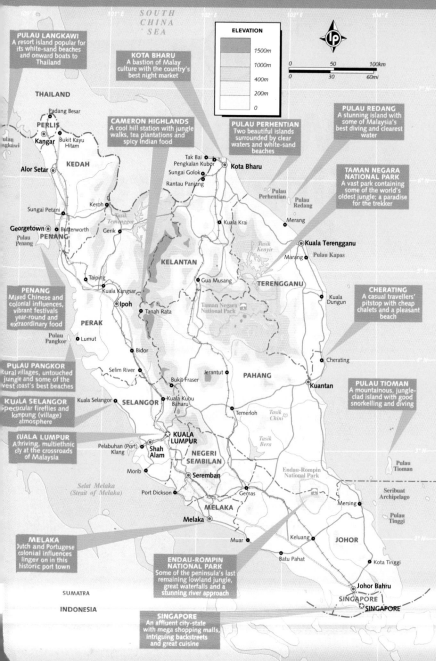

SOUTH CHINA SEA

**ELEVATION**

1500m
1000m
400m
200m
0

0    50    100km
0    30    60mi

**PULAU LANGKAWI**
A resort island popular for its white-sand beaches and onward boats to Thailand

**KOTA BHARU**
A bastion of Malay culture with the country's best night market

**PULAU REDANG**
A stunning island with some of Malaysia's best diving and clearest water

THAILAND

Padang Besar

**PERLIS**

Kangar   Bukit Kayu Hitam

Alor Setar

**KEDAH**

Pulau angkawi

**CAMERON HIGHLANDS**
A cool hill station with jungle walks, tea plantations and spicy Indian food

**PULAU PERHENTIAN**
Two beautiful islands surrounded by clear waters and white-sand beaches

Tak Bai
Pengkalan Kubor
Sungai Golok
Rantau Panjang

Kota Bharu

**TAMAN NEGARA NATIONAL PARK**
A vast park containing some of the world's oldest jungle; a paradise for the trekker

Keroh

Sungai Petani

Gerik

Georgetown ⊙ ● Butterworth

**PENANG**

Pulau Penang

Tasik Temenggor

Kuala Krai

Pulau Perhentian

Pulau Redang

Merang

Tasik Kenyir

◉ Kuala Terengganu

**PENANG**
Mixed Chinese and colonial influences, vibrant festivals year-round and extraordinary food

Taiping

Kuala Kangsar

◉ Ipoh

Tanah Rata

**KELANTAN**

Gua Musang

Taman Negara National Park

**TERENGGANU**

Marang   Pulau Kapas

Kuala Dungun

**CHERATING**
A casual travellers' pitstop with cheap chalets and a pleasant beach

**PERAK**

Pulau Pangkor

Lumut

Bidor

Selim River

Jerantut

Bukit Fraser

Cherating

**PAHANG**

Kuantan

**PULAU TIOMAN**
A mountainous, jungle-clad island with good snorkelling and diving

**PULAU PANGKOR**
Rural villages, untouched jungle and some of the west coast's best beaches

**KUALA SELANGOR**
Spectacular fireflies and kampung (village) atmosphere

Kuala Selangor

**SELANGOR**

Kuala Kubu Baharu

Temerloh

Tasik Chini

Tasik Bera

**KUALA LUMPUR**
A thriving, multiethnic city at the crossroads of Malaysia

Pelabuhan (Port) Klang

Shah Alam

◉ **KUALA LUMPUR**

**NEGERI SEMBILAN**

Morib

◉ Seremban

Port Dickson

Selat Melaka (Strait of Melaka)

Gemas

Endau-Rompin National Park

Pulau Tioman

Seribuat Archipelago

Pulau Tinggi

**MELAKA**

Melaka ◉

Muar

Keluang

Mersing

**JOHOR**

Batu Pahat

Kota Tinggi

**MELAKA**
Dutch and Portugese colonial influences linger on in this historic port town

**ENDAU-ROMPIN NATIONAL PARK**
Some of the peninsula's last remaining lowland jungle, great waterfalls and a stunning river approach

SUMATRA

INDONESIA

Johor Bahru

**SINGAPORE**

◎ **SINGAPORE**

**SINGAPORE**
An affluent city-state with mega shopping malls, intriguing backstreets and great cuisine

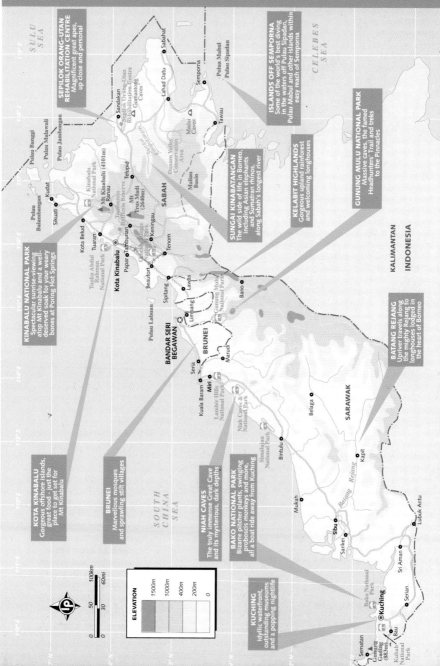

# MALAYSIAN BORNEO & BRUNEI

**SEPILOK ORANG-UTAN REHABILITATION CENTRE**
Magnificent great apes, up close and personal

**ISLANDS OFF SEMPORNA**
Some of the world's best diving in the waters off Pulau Sipadan, Pulau Mabul and other islands within easy reach of Semporna

**GUNUNG MULU NATIONAL PARK**
Massive caves, the famed Headhunters' Trail and treks to the Pinnacles

**KELABIT HIGHLANDS**
Gorgeous upland rainforest and welcoming longhouses

**SUNGAI KINABATANGAN**
The wild side of life in Borneo, including Asian elephants and Sumatran rhinos, along Sabah's longest river

**KINABALU NATIONAL PARK**
Spectacular sunrise-viewing atop Mt Kinabalu and a well-deserved soak for your weary bones at Poring Hot Springs

**BATANG REJANG**
Upriver travels along the mighty Rejang to longhouses lodged in the heart of Borneo

**KOTA KINABALU**
Gorgeous offshore islands, great food – just the set for Mt Kinabalu

**BRUNEI**
Marvellous mosques and sprawling stilt villages

**NIAH CAVE**
The truly immense Great Cave and its mysterious, dark depths

**BAKO NATIONAL PARK**
Bizarre pitcher plants, swinging, proboscis monkeys and more, all a boat ride away from Kuching

**KUCHING**
Idyllic waterfront, outstanding museums and a popping nightlife

SULU SEA

CELEBES SEA

SOUTH CHINA SEA

SABAH

SARAWAK

BRUNEI

KALIMANTAN
INDONESIA

Kota Kinabalu

BANDAR SERI BEGAWAN

Kuching

ELEVATION
1500m
1000m
400m
200m
0

100km
60m
50
30
0

Malaysia, Singapore & Brunei
8th edition – March 2001
First published – May 1982

Published by
Lonely Planet Publications Pty Ltd  ABN 36 005 607 983
90 Maribyrnong St, Footscray, Victoria 3011, Australia

Lonely Planet Offices
Australia Locked Bag 1, Footscray, Victoria 3011
USA 150 Linden St, Oakland, CA 94607
UK 10a Spring Place, London NW5 3BH
France 1 rue du Dahomey, 75011 Paris

Photographs
All of the images in this guide are available for licensing from
Lonely Planet Images.
email: lpi@lonelyplanet.com.au

Front cover photograph
Sea Turtle, Pulau Sipadan, Sabah, Malaysia (Mark Daffey)

Malaysia title page photograph
Participant of drum festival, Kuala Lumpur, Malaysia (Richard I'Anson)

Singapore title page photograph
Raffles Hotel, Singapore (Veronica Garbutt)

Brunei title page photograph
Omar Ali Saifuddien Mosque, Brunei (Jane Sweeney)

ISBN 1 86450 188 X

text & maps © Lonely Planet 2001
photos © photographers as indicated 2001

Printed by SNP Offset Sdn Bhd
Printed in Malaysia

All rights reserved. No part of this publication may be reproduced,
stored in a retrieval system or transmitted in any form by any means,
electronic, mechanical, photocopying, recording or otherwise, except
brief extracts for the purpose of review, without the written permission
of the publisher and copyright owner.

LONELY PLANET and the Lonely Planet logo are trade marks of Lonely
Planet Publications Pty Ltd.

**Although the authors
and Lonely Planet try
to make the informa-
tion as accurate as
possible, we accept
no responsibility for
any loss, injury or
inconvenience sus-
tained by anyone
using this book.**

# Contents – Text

## 2  Contents – Text

## SINGAPORE

## BRUNEI

## LANGUAGE

## GLOSSARY

## INDEX

## MAP LEGEND

## METRIC CONVERSION TABLE

# Contents – Maps

## MAP LEGEND    back page

# MAP INDEX

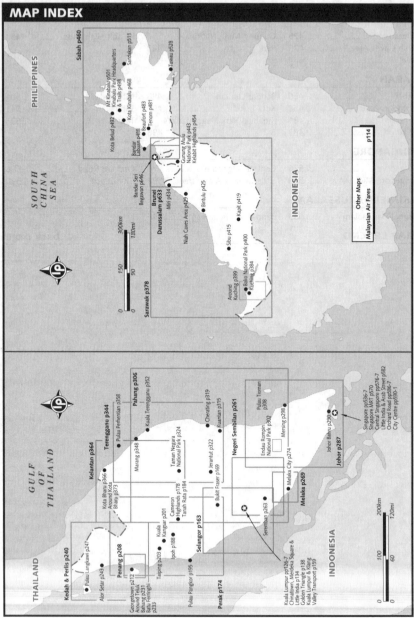

# The Authors

### Chris Rowthorn

Chris has been travelling ever since he crossed the Atlantic at the age of two aboard an ocean liner bound for New York. After graduating from college he lived for eight years in Kyoto, Japan, working first as an English teacher and then as a regional correspondent for the Japan Times. He's worked on a total of 10 books for Lonely Planet, including *Malaysia, Singapore & Brunei; Tokyo, Hiking in Japan; South-East Asia on a shoestring* and *Asia & India: Read This First.* When he's not travelling the world for Lonely Planet, he's usually travelling for himself, and he considers himself one of the world's foremost authorities on cheap hotel rooms. Chris was the coordinating author of this book and also wrote the East Peninsular Malaysia chapters.

### Sara 'Sam' Benson

Having begun a love affair with Asia at age 16, Sam still finds herself mesmerised by the tropical splendours and hidden backwaters of South-East Asia. After graduating with a futile Liberal Arts degree from university in Chicago, she rotated through several jobs as a writer, editor, graphic designer and teacher both in the USA and Japan. With some luck and sedikit Bahasa Malaysia, Sam updated the West Peninsular Malaysia chapters of this book and returned home to the San Francisco Bay area, thankfully in one piece.

### Russ Kerr

Russ wrote the Sabah, Sarawak and Brunei chapters of this book. Raised in Kamloops, Canada, he studied in Finland and Russia after finishing high school. After university, a trip on the Trans-Mongolian Railway led to seven years of wandering around the north-east of Asia. A few years of teaching convinced him he'd rather be a student, so Russ moved to Melbourne in 1995 to finish his PhD in political philosophy. There he met Sam, an encounter that soon produced son James and the need for a steady job, which is where Lonely Planet first came in. Russ is now a freelance writer and editor, while Sam builds straw-bale houses and James runs a railway.

### Christine Niven

Christine first began working for Lonely Planet as an editor. It wasn't long before the allure of travel proved too much, and she abandoned office life for life on the road as a Lonely Planet writer. So far her travels have taken her to India, Sri Lanka, New Zealand and, now, Singapore.

# FROM THE AUTHORS

## Chris Rowthorn

I would like to thank Zurina Susan Binti Abdullah, Bruno Fehrenback, Alex and Jo'an Lee YP, Omar Bentris, Rudy Noordin, Yvonne Oh, Will Le', Mayee, Hoon Tai Chee, Chandra Sehgaran, Mohd Nasaruddin Abdullah, the uncle of Wei Sien, Jenny Daneels and all the folks who were kind enough to write to Lonely Planet with information about Malaysia. I would also like to thank my co-authors Sam Benson, who kept going when most others would have quit, and Russ Kerr, who kept me entertained with emails from Borneo.

## Sara 'Sam' Benson

Big thanks to my KL oniisan for late-night rojak pinang and telling me honestly everything I needed to know. Julia Bell, 'Sunway' Stuart Mayotte, forest fanatics Tanya and Daniel (KL), and Ollie & Co (LGK) supplied reports from the field. Ms Khoo Siew Wah of the Penang Tourist Guides Association, and the Melaka tourist office, gave much-needed support on the road, as did Chris Rowthorn. Without endgame editing by Tracy Hodson and my mom, my work on this book would never have been completed – thank you.

## Russ Kerr

Thanks to the helpful staff of tourist offices in Kuching, Sibu, Miri, Kota Kinabalu and Labuan. Wayne Tarman and Mike Reed of Travelcom Asia showed me the best of Borneo hospitality and generosity, hangovers and all. Many thanks also to Philip Yong and Michael Hawkins of Borneo Adventure, Christina Mazzei and Rob Lanham of Borneo Action; Cede Prudente of the WWF Wetlands Project in Sabah; Uncle Tan, the lone ranger of the Kinabatangan; January Kohli of the Royal Mulu Resort; Erin Anderson and Helga of Jasra Harrisons in BSB; and Datuk Verus Aman Sham of KRK Mai Aman and Lee Kim Shah of Innoprise Jungle Lodge in Sabah. Jarman Riboh and his wife, and Gerewat Gala, show why the Kelabit are such respected people in Sarawak. My thanks also to Mike Cadman for his great reports from Sabah, Dave Andrew, and Chris Rowthorn and the Lonely Planet staff working on this book for their patience, as I discovered the joys of giardia while writing my chapters. Finally, special thanks to Sam and James for not only putting up with me and the bugs when I got back, but for hanging in there while I was on the road.

## Christine Niven

Many thanks to Geraldene who generously set aside a day to show me around Chinatown. Thanks to Melvyn who came up with all sorts of helpful information. Thanks too to the staff of Perak Lodge for whom nothing was too much trouble. And, lastly, thanks to the people at Lonely Planet who hammered the maps and manuscript into shape.

# This Book

The 1st edition of this guide was written by Geoff Crowther and Tony and Maureen Wheeler. Mark Lightbody handled the research for the 2nd edition. The 3rd edition was the joint effort of Sue Tan and Joe Cummings. Hugh Finlay and Peter Turner updated the 4th and 5th editions. The 6th edition was researched and written by Peter Turner and Chris Rowthorn. Chris Rowthorn, David Andrew, Paul Hellander and Clem Lindenmayer teamed up on the 7th edition. This 8th edition was coordinated by Chris Rowthorn, who updated the introductory Malaysia chapters and East Peninsular Malaysia chapters. Sara 'Sam' Benson updated the West Peninsular Malaysia chapters, Russ Kerr covered Malaysian Borneo and Brunei, and Christine Niven updated the Singapore chapters.

## From the Publisher

This 8th edition of Malaysia, Singapore & Brunei was produced in Lonely Planet's Melbourne office. Barb Benson took charge of the design and mapping and Jane Thompson coordinated the editing. Barb was assisted by Kusnandar, Jack Gavran, Chris Love and Chris Thomas. Jane had help from Joanne Newell, Kristin Odijk, Sally O'Brien, Rachael Antony, Hilary Ericksen, Anne Mulvaney and Bruce Evans. Kusnandar whipped up the climate charts, Matt King organised the illustrations, and Glenn Beanland and Brett Pascoe were the friendly photogenic faces of Lonely Planet Images. Kathleen Brand lent a hand with the colour wraps, Pablo Gastar created the niftiest chapter-end we could have hoped for, and Daniel New worked his magic with the cover. Quentin Frayne wrote the language chapter. Kristin Odijk, Chris Love, Jocelyn Harewood and Jane Hart cast eagle eyes over the layout, and Tim Uden and Lisa Borg made good use of their Quark XPress-pertise. Special thanks go to Mark Hamman for telling us all about sea turtles.

---

**THANKS**
Many thanks to the travellers who used the last edition and wrote to us with helpful hints, advice and interesting anecdotes. Your names appear in the back of this book.

# Foreword

## ABOUT LONELY PLANET GUIDEBOOKS

The story begins with a classic travel adventure: Tony and Maureen Wheeler's 1972 journey across Europe and Asia to Australia. Useful information about the overland trail did not exist at that time, so Tony and Maureen published the first Lonely Planet guidebook to meet a growing need.

From a kitchen table, then from a tiny office in Melbourne (Australia), Lonely Planet has become the largest independent travel publisher in the world, an international company with offices in Melbourne, Oakland (USA), London (UK) and Paris (France).

Today Lonely Planet guidebooks cover the globe. There is an ever-growing list of books and there's information in a variety of forms and media. Some things haven't changed. The main aim is still to help make it possible for adventurous travellers to get out there – to explore and better understand the world.

At Lonely Planet we believe travellers can make a positive contribution to the countries they visit – if they respect their host communities and spend their money wisely. Since 1986 a percentage of the income from each book has been donated to aid projects and human rights campaigns.

**Updates** Lonely Planet thoroughly updates each guidebook as often as possible. This usually means there are around two years between editions, although for more unusual or more stable destinations the gap can be longer. Check the imprint page (following the colour map at the beginning of the book) for publication dates.

Between editions up-to-date information is available in two free newsletters – the paper *Planet Talk* and email *Comet* (to subscribe, contact any Lonely Planet office) – and on our Web site at www.lonelyplanet.com. The *Upgrades* section of the Web site covers a number of important and volatile destinations and is regularly updated by Lonely Planet authors. *Scoop* covers news and current affairs relevant to travellers. And, lastly, the *Thorn Tree* bulletin board and *Postcards* section of the site carry unverified, but fascinating, reports from travellers.

**Correspondence** The process of creating new editions begins with the letters, postcards and emails received from travellers. This correspondence often includes suggestions, criticisms and comments about the current editions. Interesting excerpts are immediately passed on via newsletters and the Web site, and everything goes to our authors to be verified when they're researching on the road. We're keen to get more feedback from organisations or individuals who represent communities visited by travellers.

Lonely Planet gathers information for everyone who's curious about the planet – and especially for those who explore it first-hand. Through guidebooks, phrasebooks, activity guides, maps, literature, image library, TV series and Web site we act as an information exchange for a worldwide community of travellers.

**Research** Authors aim to gather sufficient practical information to enable travellers to make informed choices and to make the mechanics of a journey run smoothly. They also research historical and cultural background to help enrich the travel experience and allow travellers to understand and respond appropriately to cultural and environmental issues.

Authors don't stay in every hotel because that would mean spending a couple of months in each medium-sized city and, no, they don't eat at every restaurant because that would mean stretching belts beyond capacity. They do visit hotels and restaurants to check standards and prices, but feedback based on readers' direct experiences can be very helpful.

Many of our authors work undercover, others aren't so secretive. None of them accept freebies in exchange for positive write-ups. And none of our guidebooks contain any advertising.

**Production** Authors submit their raw manuscripts and maps to offices in Australia, USA, UK or France. Editors and cartographers – all experienced travellers themselves – then begin the process of assembling the pieces. When the book finally hits the shops, some things are already out of date, we start getting feedback from readers and the process begins again ...

## WARNING & REQUEST

Things change – prices go up, schedules change, good places go bad and bad places go bankrupt – nothing stays the same. So, if you find things better or worse, recently opened or long since closed, please tell us and help make the next edition even more accurate and useful. We genuinely value all the feedback we receive. Julie Young coordinates a well travelled team that reads and acknowledges every letter, postcard and email and ensures that every morsel of information finds its way to the appropriate authors, editors and cartographers for verification.

Everyone who writes to us will find their name in the next edition of the appropriate guidebook. They will also receive the latest issue of *Planet Talk*, our quarterly printed newsletter, or *Comet*, our monthly email newsletter. Subscriptions to both newsletters are free. The very best contributions will be rewarded with a free guidebook.

Excerpts from your correspondence may appear in new editions of Lonely Planet guidebooks, the Lonely Planet Web site, *Planet Talk* or *Comet*, so please let us know if you *don't* want your letter published or your name acknowledged.

Send all correspondence to the Lonely Planet office closest to you:

**Australia:** Locked Bag 1, Footscray, Victoria 3011
**USA:** 150 Linden St, Oakland, CA 94607
**UK:** 10A Spring Place, London NW5 3BH
**France:** 1 rue du Dahomey, 75011 Paris

Or email us at: talk2us@lonelyplanet.com.au

**For news, views and updates see our Web site: www.lonelyplanet.com**

## HOW TO USE A LONELY PLANET GUIDEBOOK

The best way to use a Lonely Planet guidebook is any way you choose. At Lonely Planet we believe the most memorable travel experiences are often those that are unexpected, and the finest discoveries are those you make yourself. Guidebooks are not intended to be used as if they provide a detailed set of infallible instructions!

**Contents** All Lonely Planet guidebooks follow roughly the same format. The Facts about the Destination chapters or sections give background information ranging from history to weather. Facts for the Visitor gives practical information on issues like visas and health. Getting There & Away gives a brief starting point for researching travel to and from the destination. Getting Around gives an overview of the transport options when you arrive.

The peculiar demands of each destination determine how subsequent chapters are broken up, but some things remain constant. We always start with background, then proceed to sights, places to stay, places to eat, entertainment, getting there and away, and getting around information – in that order.

**Heading Hierarchy** Lonely Planet headings are used in a strict hierarchical structure that can be visualised as a set of Russian dolls. Each heading (and its following text) is encompassed by any preceding heading that is higher on the hierarchical ladder.

**Entry Points** We do not assume guidebooks will be read from beginning to end, but that people will dip into them. The traditional entry points are the list of contents and the index. In addition, however, some books have a complete list of maps and an index map illustrating map coverage.

There may also be a colour map that shows highlights. These highlights are dealt with in greater detail in the Facts for the Visitor chapter, along with planning questions and suggested itineraries. Each chapter covering a geographical region usually begins with a locator map and another list of highlights. Once you find something of interest in a list of highlights, turn to the index.

**Maps** Maps play a crucial role in Lonely Planet guidebooks and include a huge amount of information. A legend is printed on the back page. We seek to have complete consistency between maps and text, and to have every important place in the text captured on a map. Map key numbers usually start in the top left corner.

Although inclusion in a guidebook usually implies a recommendation we cannot list every good place. Exclusion does not necessarily imply criticism. In fact there are a number of reasons why we might exclude a place – sometimes it is simply inappropriate to encourage an influx of travellers.

# Introduction

Malaysia, Singapore and Brunei are three independent South-East Asian nations offering the visitor a taste of Asia at its most accessible. These countries are among the richest in Asia and are relatively forward-looking. Transport facilities are good, accommodation standards are high and there are few problems for visitors.

Yet, even with these high standards, these are not expensive countries to visit. Singapore can offer all the air-conditioned comforts your credit cards can handle; hiring a Mercedes may help you to blend in Brunei; and Malaysian Borneo may at times be a little pricey due to its jungle-frontier situation; but in Peninsular Malaysia costs can be very cheap, especially if you hire a bike to get around and use the local markets for provisions.

More important than simple ease of travel, this region offers amazing variety – both geographically and culturally. If you want beaches and tropical islands, it's hard to beat the east coast of Peninsular Malaysia. If it's mountains, parks and wildlife, you can climb Mt Kinabalu, stroll through Brunei's Wasai Kandal forest, explore the rivers of Sarawak or trek the trails of the huge Taman Negara National Park on the peninsula. Dive or snorkel your way around Pulau Sipadan, off the coast of Sabah, to observe the tropical fish and sea turtles in clear warm water. If you're after a taste of the region's city life, bargain for kites in Kota Bharu, try the historic old port of Melaka, the easy-going backstreets of Georgetown in Penang, the quiet streets of Bandar Seri Begawan or

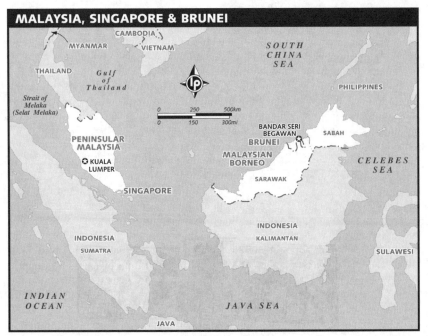

the modern-as-tomorrow city of Singapore with, of course, the famous Raffles Hotel.

When it comes to people, you've got Malays, Chinese, Indians, and a host of indigenous tribes in Sabah and Sarawak. In every town or city you will find markets with local produce, arts and crafts, and a gathering of folk you'll not see anywhere else.

The food brings people back to the region again and again; for many people there's no question that Singapore is the food capital of Asia.

So, whether you want to experience the tropical climate by pounding city streets, traipsing through jungle in a national park, meandering through steamy food markets or by relaxing on islands where the water is warm and the beach is a pristine white, Malaysia, Singapore and Brunei offer a travel experience unlike any other.

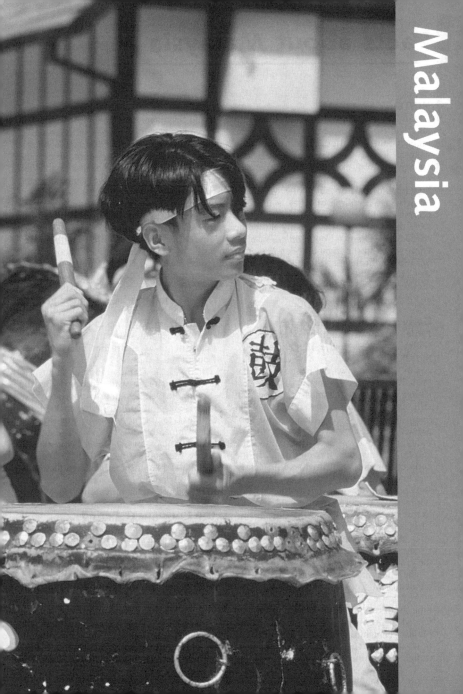

Malaysia

# Facts about Malaysia

## HISTORY

It is only since WWII that Malaysia, Singapore and Brunei have emerged as separate, independent countries. Prior to that they were all loosely amalgamated as a British colony, Sarawak excepted, and earlier still they may have been independent Malay kingdoms or part of the greater Majapahit or Srivijaya Empires of what is now Indonesia. In the dim mists of time it's possible that Malaysia was actually the home of the earliest known *Homo sapiens* in Asia. Discoveries in the gigantic Niah Caves of Sarawak indicate that Stone Age humans were present there, and in other caves of northern Borneo and the Malay Peninsula, as long ago as 40,000 years.

### Early Trade & Empires

Little is known about the Stone Age Malaysians, but around 10,000 years ago the aboriginal Malays – the Orang Asli – began to move down the peninsula from a probable starting point in South-West China. Remote settlements of Orang Asli still live in parts of Malaysia, but 4000 years ago they were already being supplanted by the Proto-Malays, ancestors of today's Malays, who at first settled the coastal regions, then moved inland. In the early centuries of the Christian era, Malaya was known as far away as Europe. Ptolemy showed it on his early map, with the label 'Golden Chersonese'. It spelt gold not only to the Romans but also to the Indians and Chinese, whose traders arrived not long after in search of that most valuable metal. Hindu mini-states began to spring up along the great Malay rivers.

The Malay people were basically similar ethnically to the people of Sumatra, Java and even the Philippines, and from time to time various South-East Asian empires extended their control over all or part of the Malay Peninsula. Funan, a kingdom based in what is now Cambodia, at one time controlled the northern part of the peninsula.

From the 7th century the great Sumatran-based Srivijaya Empire, with its capital in Palembang, held the whole area and even extended its rule into Thailand. A significant Malay trading kingdom, under the suzerainty of Srivijaya, became established at the Bujang Valley in today's Perak state. Its Hindu temples remain the most significant reminder of the Hindu-Buddhist period that held sway over much of the peninsula for nearly a millennium.

Srivijaya eventually fell to the Java-based Majapahit Empire, and then in 1403 Parameswara, a Sumatran prince, established himself at Melaka, which soon became the most powerful city-state in the region. At this time the spice trade from the Moluccas was beginning to develop and Melaka, with its strategic position on the strait that separates Sumatra from the Malay Peninsula, was a familiar port for ships from the east and west.

In 1405 the Chinese admiral Cheng Ho arrived in Melaka with greetings from the 'Son of Heaven' and, more importantly, the promise of protection from the encroaching Siamese to the north. With this support from China, the power of Melaka extended to include most of the Malay Peninsula. At about the same time, Islam arrived in Melaka and soon spread through the country (see Islam in Malaysia under Religion later in this chapter for details).

### The Portuguese Period

For the next century Melaka's power and wealth expanded to such an extent that the city became one of the wealthiest in the east – so wealthy, in fact, that the Portuguese began to take an active interest in the place. After a preliminary skirmish in 1509, Alfonso de Albuquerque arrived in 1511 with a fleet of 18 ships and overpowered Melaka's 20,000 defenders and their war elephants. The sultan of Melaka fled south with his court to Johor, from where the Portuguese were unable to dislodge him. Thus

Melaka came to be the centre of European power in the region, and Johor grew to be the main Malay city-state, along with other Malay centres at Brunei in northern Borneo and Aceh in the north of Sumatra.

The Portuguese held Melaka for over 100 years, but they were never able to capitalise on the city's fabulous wealth and superb position. Portuguese trading power and strength was never great enough to take full advantage of the volume of trade that used to flow through Melaka, and, more importantly, the Portuguese did not develop the complex pattern of influence and patronage upon which Melaka had based its power and control. Worse, their reputation for narrow-mindedness and cruelty had preceded them, and they gained few converts to Christianity and little support for their rule.

Thus the other Malay states were able to grow into the vacuum created by the Portuguese takeover of Melaka – and although they squabbled and fought among themselves, they also had the strength to make attacks on Melaka. Gradually Portuguese power declined, and after long skirmishes with the Dutch, who supported the rulers of Johor, Melaka eventually fell to the Dutch, after a long and bitter siege, in 1641.

## The Dutch Period

Like the Portuguese, the Dutch ruled Melaka for over a century but, also like the Portuguese, they failed to recognise that Melaka's greatest importance was as a centre for entrepôt trade. To an even greater extent than their predecessors, the Dutch tried to keep Melaka's trade totally to themselves, and as a result Melaka continued to decline. The greatest Dutch interest was reserved for Batavia (now Jakarta), so Melaka was always the poor sister to the more important Javan port.

## The Arrival of the British

By the late 18th century the British had begun to eye Malaysia, having previously been tied up with their Indian possessions. In 1786 Captain Francis Light docked at Pulau Penang (Penang Island) and occupied it. Light instituted a free trade policy at Penang, a clear contrast to the monopolistic intentions of the Portuguese and then the Dutch in Melaka. Penang soon became a thriving port, and by 1800 the population of the island, virtually uninhabited when Light took over, had reached 10,000.

Meanwhile, events far away in Europe were conspiring to consolidate British influence on the Malay Peninsula. When Napoleon overran the Netherlands in 1795, the British East India Company took over the administration of Melaka and other Dutch possessions in the region. In 1814, with Napoleon defeated, an agreement was reached on the return of these possessions, and by 1818 Melaka and Java had been returned to Dutch control.

Nevertheless, Britain's brief spell at the helm prompted some British figures to argue for more influence on the peninsula, particularly given that Malaysian ports made access to major trading destinations (such as China) easier. The calls of Sir Thomas Stamford Raffles to supplant the Dutch in Malaya had largely fallen on deaf ears. But in 1818, with the re-establishment of Dutch control in the region, Raffles was told to go ahead and establish a second British base farther south than Penang. In early 1819 Raffles decided on Singapore. In 1826 Singapore became part of the British Straits Settlements, governed with Melaka and Penang from Bengal in India; by then its population was approaching 100,000.

## The British Period

Despite existing cultural ties between disparate groups of Malays on the peninsula, it was under the British that the Malaysia of today came into being as a distinct geographic unit. In 1824 the British and the Dutch signed a treaty that divided the peninsula into 'spheres of influence'. The kingdom of Johor was split into the Dutch-administered Riau Lingga Islands and the British administration on the peninsula. In 1826 the formation of the British Straits Settlements under the British brought together Singapore, Melaka, Pulau Penang and Province Wellesley (the mainland part of what is now Penang state). In 1874 the

Pangkor Treaty brought the Malay state of Perak into the ambit of British rule via a British Resident, who was to be consulted on all matters 'other than those touching upon Malay religion and custom'.

As was the case in India, the British Residential system allowed colonial influence to prosper without Britain ever having to go to war. The system preserved the prestige of local rulers, while at the same time providing the British with indirect control over matters – chiefly economic – that interested them most. In 1896 the states of Perak, Selangor, Negeri Sembilan and Pahang became the Federated Malay States (FMS), each governed indirectly by a British Resident. Johor held out until 1913; and Kelantan, Terengganu, Perlis and Kedah were controlled by the Thais until 1909, when they became known as the Unfederated Malay States (UMS), again under the British Residential system.

British influence in Malaya brought enormous economic and social changes. A communications infrastructure was established to allow the smooth transportation of rubber and tin to ports. A colonial legal and administrative system was put in place, providing an environment in which free enterprise could flourish. But it was on the social front that the British administration was to have the greatest long-term effects.

Raffles, and later other British administrators, argued in favour of an ethnic division of labour. A British-educated Malay elite would have a place in the administration system, while ordinary Malays would continue fishing and farming. Immigrants from China's coastal provinces of Fujian (Hokkien) and Guangdong were imported as traders and workers in tin mines. Later, Indians were brought over to work in the bureaucracy, on the rubber estates and as labourers in public works. By the turn of the 19th century, Malaya's economy had been revolutionised, but so had its social make-up. The once predominantly Malay peninsula was emerging as an ethnic melting pot (see Population & People later in this chapter for details).

## Meanwhile, in Borneo...

Across the South China Sea, in the steamy jungles of northern Borneo, events were unfolding with the implausibility of high Victorian melodrama. In 1838 James Brooke, a British adventurer, arrived in Borneo in his armed sloop to find the Brunei aristocracy facing rebellion by dissatisfied inland tribes. He quelled the rebellion and in gratitude was given power over part of what is today Sarawak. Appointing himself 'Raja Brooke', he successfully tamed the fractious tribes, suppressed head-hunting, eliminated the dreaded Borneo pirates and founded a personal dynasty that was to last for over 100 years. The Brooke family of 'white rajas' were still empire building, bringing more and more of Borneo under their power, when the Japanese arrived in WWII.

The extension of British influence into Sabah took a less romantic complexion. In 1865 the American consul to Brunei managed to acquire a lease for most of what is now Sabah. He sold it in Hong Kong, after which it was sold again to the Austrian consul there, Count Von Overbeck. Overbeck had no success interesting his government in a new territory, and finally Sabah ended up in the hands of an Englishman, Alfred Dent. Dent established the British North Borneo Company, and from 1881 the land the company governed became known as British North Borneo.

## WWII Period

By 1913 all of Peninsular Malaysia and north-western Borneo was united in a loose federation known as British Malaya. The colony prospered, though overwhelmingly the economy was dependent on tin and rubber – by the time WWII broke out in Europe, Malaya supplied nearly 40% of the world's rubber and 60% of its tin.

At the same time – encouraged by the British – Chinese and Indian immigrants arrived in such numbers that they eventually outnumbered indigenous Malays. A 1931 census revealed that the Chinese alone numbered over 1.7 million, the Malays 1.6 million.

The arrival of WWII was sudden and devastating. A few hours before the first

Japanese aircraft was sighted over Pearl Harbor, the Japanese landed at Kota Bharu in the north of Malaya and started their lightning dash down the peninsula. British confidence that they were more than a match for the Japanese soon proved to be sadly misplaced, and it took the Japanese little over a month to take Kuala Lumpur (KL) and a month more to reach the doorstep of Singapore. North Borneo had fallen to the Japanese with even greater speed.

The Japanese were unable to form a cohesive policy in Malaya, since there was not a well-organised Malay independence movement they could harness to secure their goals. Furthermore, many Chinese were bitterly opposed to the Japanese, who had invaded China in the 1930s. Remnants of the British forces, together with the predominantly Chinese Communist Malayan People's Anti-Japanese Army, waged a guerrilla struggle against the Japanese throughout the war.

Resistance in Borneo was organised in a different fashion, as there was a much smaller Chinese population on hand. Since the Japanese only had control of the coastal areas, the vast inner regions of Borneo were ripe for the planning and resourcing of armed resistance. However, the problem of supplying and organising such resistance was almost insurmountable until the allies were able to capture islands close enough to Borneo to permit airdrops into the interior.

After securing an airstrip on the island of Moratai in 1944, a primarily Australian force known as Z Special Unit parachuted into the Kelabit Highlands and succeeded in winning over the Kelabit to their cause. Armed mostly with traditional blowpipes, the Kelabit, led by the Australian commandos, scored a number of daring victories over the Japanese. For more information on Borneo history, see the Sabah and Sarawak chapters.

## Postwar & the Emergency

When the Japanese surrendered on 15 August 1945, the British inherited a troubled country. The ethnic divide between indigenous Malays and the Chinese had polarised around the issues of wartime resistance to the Japanese and the future of Malaya. The mainly Chinese Malayan Communist Party (MCP) maintained that many Malays and their leaders had capitulated to and cooperated with the Japanese, and in some cases the MCP meted out punishment to the guilty parties.

The British response was a plan to form a Malayan Union under the sovereignty of the British crown, in which citizenship was to be extended to all with equal rights. There was an outcry from native Malays, who feared the growing wealth and influence of the Chinese, and in March 1946 the United Malays National Organisation (UMNO) formed to fight the proposal. The British backed off, and in February 1948 they formed the Federation of Malaya, under which the sultans maintained their sovereignty and Malays were granted special privileges denied to the non-native inhabitants of Malaya – the Indians and Chinese.

Meanwhile the MCP, which had fought against the Japanese throughout the war, launched a guerrilla struggle to end British colonial rule. In 1948 the British declared the Emergency and put the country on a war footing. The communist threat was eventually declared over in 1960, although there were sporadic outbreaks of violence until 1989. The communists never enjoyed a broad spectrum of support. They were always a predominantly Chinese group, and while the Malays might have wanted independence from Britain they certainly did not want rule by the Chinese. Nor were all Chinese in favour of the party; it was mainly an uprising of the peasantry and lower classes.

Despite the diminished threat of communist takeover, guerrillas were still resident in the jungle around the Thai border until the last remaining faithful accepted the government's long-standing offer of amnesty in 1989.

## Independence

In 1955 Britain agreed that Malaya would become fully independent within two years. Elections held in 1955 swept the Alliance

## Malays, Malaya & Malaysia

Malays are the indigenous people of Malaysia, although they are not the original inhabitants. Malaya is the old name for the country which, prior to 1963, consisted only of the states on the peninsula. With the amalgamation of Malaya, Sarawak and Sabah, the title Malaysia was coined for the new nation; the peninsula is now referred to as Peninsular Malaysia, while Sarawak and Sabah are referred to as East Malaysia, or Malaysian Borneo.

Party, a union of the Malayan Indian Congress (MIC), UMNO and the Malayan Chinese Association (MCA), into power. Nevertheless, when Malaya achieved *merdeka* (independence) on 15 August 1957, the resulting Merdeka Constitution enshrined special privileges for indigenous Malays, while at the same time offering citizenship to all. The unequal rights granted by the new constitution were to bedevil the country in years to come. Tunku Abdul Rahman was the leader of the new nation, which came into existence with remarkably few problems.

In Singapore things went nowhere near as smoothly and politics became increasingly radical. The election in 1959 swept Lee Kuan Yew's People's Action Party (PAP) into power, but it faced a series of major problems. When the Federation of Malaya was formed in 1948, the Malay leaders were strongly opposed to including Singapore because this would have tipped the racial balance from Malay dominance to a Chinese majority. Furthermore, while politics in Malaya was orderly, upper class and gentlemanly, in Singapore it was anything but controlled.

Nevertheless, to Singapore, merging with Malaya seemed to be the only answer to high unemployment, a soaring birth-rate and the loss of its traditional trading role with the growth of independent South-East Asian nations. Malaya was none too keen to inherit this little parcel of problems, but when it seemed possible that the moderate PAP might be toppled by its own left wing, the thought of a moderate Singapore within

Malaysia became less off-putting than the thought of a communist Singapore just outside the country. Accordingly, in 1961 Tunku Abdul Rahman agreed to work towards the creation of a Malaysia that would include Singapore. To balance the addition of Singapore, discussion also commenced on adding Sarawak, Sabah and Brunei to the union, a move welcomed by Britain, which faced the problem of what to do with its North Borneo possessions.

## Confrontation

Accordingly, in 1963 the Federation of Malaysia came into existence, although at the last moment Brunei, afraid of losing its oil wealth, refused to join. No sooner had Malaysia been created than problems arose. First of all the Philippines laid claim to Sabah, which had been known as North Borneo prior to the union. More seriously, Indonesia laid claim to the whole of Borneo. Achmed Soekarno, the Indonesian autocrat who seized power in 1957, in an effort to oust the Malaysians, began his ill-starred 'Confrontation'. Indonesian guerrilla forces crossed the borders from Kalimantan (Indonesian Borneo) into Sabah and Sarawak, and landings were also made in Peninsular Malaysia and even in Singapore. British troops, having just recently quelled the Emergency, now found themselves back in the jungle. While it took three years to quell the threat, the Malaysian states on the island of Borneo were never seriously threatened.

## Singapore Departs

At the same time, relations between Singapore and the rest of Malaysia soured almost as soon as the country was formed. The main stumbling block to a happy union lay in Singapore's refusal to extend constitutional Malay privileges to Malays in Singapore. In August 1965, exactly two years after Malaysia was created, Singapore was kicked out.

## Racial Problems

With Singapore and Brunei out of the union, Malaysia was an independent country. One niggling problem that remained, however, was that the country was far from integrated. Naturally, the Alliance Party looked to education and language as the cornerstones of national identity. But what it had not counted on was the fierce opposition of other ethnic groups to what many saw as the extension of Malay privileges into the education system.

Privileges or no, Malays had a very weak hold on the economy. In 1969 only 1.5% of company assets in Malaysia were owned by Malays, and the average per capita income among Malays was less than 50% of other citizens. But attempts to make Bahasa Malaysia the one national language, along with the privileges Malays had in land ownership, business licences, educational opportunities and government positions, resulted in resentment from non-Malays. Their opposition to such moves resulted in the Alliance Party losing its two-thirds majority in the May 1969 federal elections. Victorious opposition parties took to the streets in celebration. The next day, on 13 May, a UMNO rally took to the streets in KL and interracial riots broke out. Hundreds of people, mostly Chinese, were killed.

Following these riots the government moved to improve the position of Malays in Malaysia with greater speed. The title *bumiputra* (sons of the soil), was created to denote the indigenous Malay people: this included not only Malays but also the aboriginal inhabitants and the indigenous peoples of Sarawak and Sabah. New guidelines were instituted stipulating how much of a company's share must be held by the bumiputra, and in other ways enforced a Malay share in the nation's wealth.

Although many Chinese realised that Malaysia could never attain real stability without an equitable distribution of the country's wealth, there was also much resentment, and many talented people either left the country or simply withdrew their abilities and their capital. Fortunately, Malaysia's natural resources enabled it to absorb this flight of talent and wealth, but the problem of bringing the Malays to an equal position in the nation, economically as well as politically, is one that is still not fully resolved.

After 1969, government policy aimed to integrate economic development and ethnic policy. A series of five-year plans have been undertaken, with the ultimate objective of transforming Malaysia into a developed country in which race no longer has any bearing on economic function. On the political front, the Alliance Party has expanded, drawing in other parties, to become the National Front (Barisan Nasional).

## Malaysia & Islam
While promotion of Bahasa Malaysia has been the main focus of the drive to forge a national identity, Islam has also been an important rallying point. The Malaysian Islamic Youth Movement was formed in 1971 with the aim of promoting Islamic values and even implementing Islamic law *(syariah)* in Malaysia. In November 1993 the most Islamic of Malaysia's states, Kelantan, attempted to do just that. The new laws would have required federal constitutional changes, and among other things stipulated that thieves have their right hands amputated and that adulterers be stoned to death. The federal government stepped in to prevent these changes from taking effect in the state.

Islam presents the national government with a prickly problem. On the one hand, UMNO is bound to represent Malay and Islamic interests. On the other, a full-blown Islamic revival would run counter to the government's economic aims. Kelantan, for example, remains a poor state, a quarter of its population lives below the poverty line, and local policies have caused foreign investment to dwindle.

The other issue to consider is that an Islamic resurgence is potentially even more destabilising to ethnic unity than the problems associated with promotion of Bahasa Malaysia and with Malay domination of politics. Efforts by Islamic groups to outlaw alcohol, lotteries, unisex hairdressers and even to enforce conservative Islamic dress standards go down badly with Malaysia's pork-eating, gambling-mad ethnic Chinese.

## Asian Values

Malaysia's Prime Minister Mahathir Mohamad has whipped up passion in his own country and inflamed tempers in the West with his talk of 'Asian Values'. While it's not always clear what Asian Values are, it's very clear what they are not – they are the opposite of Western values.

As Dr Mahathir puts it in his recent book *The Voice of Asia:*

Western societies are riddled with single-parent families, which foster incest, with homosexuality, with cohabitation, with unrestrained avarice, with disrespect for others and, of course, rejection of religious teachings and values.

When Mahathir and other Asian leaders speak of Asian Values it's clear that they are talking about a kind of neo-Confucianism, which places a strong emphasis on filial piety, education, hard work and clearly defined social hierarchies.

In the months prior to the Asian currency crisis of 1997, Mahathir fulminated regularly on Asian Values, predicting the decline of the West and the dawn of an 'Asian Century'.

However, now that the entire Asian region is mired in recession, the worth of these much-ballyhooed Asian Values has been called into question. Indeed, countries like Japan are quickly rushing in the opposite direction and adopting American business practices. Likewise, countries like Korea and Indonesia didn't mind accepting an International Monetary Fund (IMF) bailout when Asian Values alone were not enough to boost their sagging economies.

The bigger irony in Malaysia, of course, is that the true practitioners of Asian Values, the Malaysian Chinese, suffer under Apartheid-like discriminatory laws designed to hold them back economically. Apparently, the Malaysian Chinese have taken this whole Asian Values thing far too seriously – they're too successful!

**Chris Rowthorn**

## Recent History

Ethnic problems aside, Malaysia's economy expanded rapidly in the decades following its independence. Much of this was due to the government's centralised economic planning and diversification of an economy that was once almost entirely reliant on rubber, tin and logging. Riding the wave of economic success, UMNO, by far the majority faction of the National Front coalition, steadily consolidated its power during this time.

Much of UMNO's success can be attributed directly to Dr Datuk Seri Mahathir Mohamad, Malaysia's charismatic and occasionally controversial prime minister. Since coming to power in 1981, Mahathir has become the country's longest serving prime minister. Mahathir, a man of strong opinions and near-visionary ambitions for Malaysia, has been keen to raise his stature on the world stage as a pan-Asian leader. He fulminates regularly on the subject of Western colonialist attitudes and decadence, and promotes 'Asian Values' as the ethical basis of Asian economic success. See the boxed text 'Asian Values' in this chapter. Mahathir's grand plan for Malaysia, known as Wawasan 2020, is intended to make Malaysia a fully industrialised country by the year 2020.

By the mid-1990s, it looked as if Malaysia was right on track to achieving this goal. Then, in August of 1997, a currency crisis that started in Thailand quickly spread to the rest of South-East Asia, plunging Malaysia into a recession from which it has yet to fully recover (see the Economy section later in this chapter for details).

In the wake of the currency crisis, Malaysia was swept up in a political crisis that drew world attention. In September 1998, Mahathir sacked Deputy Prime Minister Anwar Ibrahim, the man whom most assumed was next in line for Mahathir's position. Analysts blamed their falling out on disagreements over Mahathir's handling of the currency crisis and Anwar's call for greater transparency in Malaysian government. Two weeks after being sacked, Anwar was arrested under the Internal Security Act and charged with corruption (the charge of sodomy was later added).

Many Malaysians felt that Anwar had been falsely arrested and took to the streets of KL under the banner of *reformasi* (reformation). The ensuing riots were the worst the country had seen since the interracial riots of 1969. On 14 April 1999, Anwar was convicted of corruption and sentenced to six years in prison. He is presently appealing that verdict and standing trial for sodomy. With his most visible opponent locked away in jail, it looks as though Mahathir's grip on power in Malaysia will remain unchallenged in the near future.

Just as the furore over the arrest of Anwar was dying down, Malaysia found itself in world headlines once again when Canadian journalist Murray Hiebert was jailed for contempt of court after writing an article about the Malaysian court system. Both domestic and foreign analysts were quick to decry the act as a blatant infringement of the freedom of the press. Released after four weeks in jail, Hiebert quickly left the country but his case remains up for appeal in the Malaysian courts.

In spite of all this turmoil, the Malaysian economy quietly improved in 1998 and 1999 and, at the time of writing, things are largely back to normal in the country, economically, if not politically.

## GEOGRAPHY

Malaysia consists of two distinct regions. Peninsular Malaysia is the long finger of land extending south from Asia as if pointing towards Indonesia and Australia. Much of the peninsula is covered by dense jungle, particularly its mountainous, thinly populated northern half. On the western side of the peninsula there is a long, fertile plain running down to the sea, while on the eastern side the mountains descend more steeply and the coast is fringed with sandy beaches.

The other part of the country, comprising more than 50% of its area, is Malaysian Borneo – the northern part of the island of Borneo (the larger, southern part is the Indonesian state of Kalimantan). Malaysian Borneo is divided into the states of Sarawak and Sabah, with Brunei a small enclave between them. Both states are covered by dense jungle, with many large river systems, particularly in Sarawak. Mt Kinabalu (4101m) in Sabah is the highest mountain between the Himalayas and New Guinea.

## CLIMATE

Malaysia has a typically tropical climate – it's hot and humid year-round. The temperature rarely drops below 20°C even at night and usually climbs to 30°C or more during the day. The tropics can take some adjusting to. Take it easy when you first arrive and try to avoid running around in the heat of the mid-day sun (see the Environmental Hazards section under Health in Malaysia's Facts for the Visitor chapter).

Rain tends to arrive in brief torrential downpours and is soon replaced by more of that ever-present sunshine. At certain times of the year it may rain every day, but it rarely rains all day. Although the region is monsoonal, it's only the east coast of Peninsular Malaysia that has a real rainy season – elsewhere it's just a time of year when the average rainfall is heavier than at other times of year.

Throughout the region the humidity tends to hover around the 90% mark, but on the peninsula you can always escape from heat and humidity by retreating to the delightfully cool hill-stations.

### Peninsular Malaysia

The peninsula is affected by the monsoon winds blowing from the north-east between October and April, and from the south-west the rest of the year.

The October–April monsoon brings rain to most of the peninsula, but the east coast bears the full brunt, with the heaviest rain falling from November to January. For the rest of the year the east coast is relatively dry.

Rainfall on the west coast is much more variable and comes throughout the year. Much of the west coast is sheltered from the worst of the October–April rains by the central mountains, but it also gets some rain from the less-pronounced May–October monsoon.

MALAYSIA

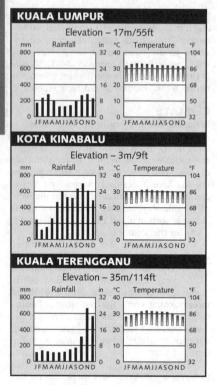

**KUALA LUMPUR**
Elevation – 17m/55ft

**KOTA KINABALU**
Elevation – 3m/9ft

**KUALA TERENGGANU**
Elevation – 35m/114ft

months, peaking in December and January. Sabah's north-east coast also gets high rainfall at this time, while its west coast gets most of its rainfall from May to November. Sabah receives less rainfall than Sarawak.

## ECOLOGY & ENVIRONMENT

Malaysia attracts more than its fair share of criticism on the environmental front, and it is an issue that the government is particularly sensitive about. Dr Mahathir, Malaysia's long-serving prime minister, and his government, maintain the line that Western concern about environmental issues in developing countries is a form of hypocrisy. And there is some truth in this. After all, logging (and this is where foreign criticism is loudest) was started in earnest in Sabah and Sarawak during the 1930s by the British Borneo Timber Company.

Nonetheless, preserving something of Malaysia's environmental heritage before it is all shipped overseas as logs is of utmost importance. Probably more than 60% of Peninsular Malaysia's rainforests have been logged, and similar figures apply to Malaysian Borneo. Government initiatives and the formation of national parks has slowed down logging on the peninsula, but it continues at a great rate in Sabah and Sarawak, despite international and domestic pressure.

In addition to logging, Malaysia has been attacked for undertaking several large dam-construction projects, which critics claim are both economically and environmentally unsound. The most controversial of these is the Bakun Dam project in Sarawak. As well as drowning hundreds of square kilometres of virgin rainforest, construction of the dam will force thousands of indigenous peoples from their homes. Fortunately, the current economic slowdown has put this and some of the other projects on hold indefinitely.

More recently, Malaysia's environment has been threatened by a force completely beyond its control – the so-called 'haze' from fires burning in the Indonesian states of Kalimantan and Sumatra. While some of these fires are of natural origin, most are set by Indonesian farmers to clear land for

The flat south of the peninsula around Johor and Singapore gets rainfall all year, slightly more from November to February. Farther north, rainfall is fairly even year-round, with January and February and especially June and July being the drier months. The north-west around Alor Setar and Langkawi receives less rainfall and has a more distinct wet season from April to October, and the rest of the year is quite dry. Penang seasons are similar but not as pronounced and it gets high rainfall in September and October.

## Malaysian Borneo

Malaysian Borneo also gets the north-east and south-west monsoons. Sarawak has high rainfall year-round, especially around Kuching, with October to March being the wettest agricultural purposes. Although this problem occurs to some extent every year, the last half of 1997 saw unprecedented levels of air pollution – at times the smoke was so thick that airplanes couldn't land at airports in Sabah and Sarawak.

The summer of 2000 saw a repeat of hazy conditions in Malaysia, although not quite on par with those of 1997. Because this is a yearly problem in the region, it pays to check the web for up-to-date reports before heading to Malaysia, particularly Malaysian Borneo.

## FLORA

Malaysia boasts a staggering range of trees, plants and flowers. The tropical climate and high rainfall promote the growth of dense rainforests and both the peninsula and Borneo once had extensive stands. Much of this forest cover has been cleared to make way for vast plantations of oil palms and other cash crops, but near-pristine forests are preserved in national parks and other reserves. Even where the original vegetation has been replaced by concrete and bricks, the climate favours quick plant-growth; any cleared patch of land is invaded by creepers, vines and grasses, followed by shrubs and, if left long enough, the rainforest trees from seeds dropped by monkeys or birds. Buildings left derelict soon grow a mantle of ferns, moss and even orchids.

Rainforest is often referred to as dipterocarp forest. These rainforest communities are extremely complex and many species of trees can grow in a single hectare, unlike the great forests of temperate regions, which are dominated by only a few species, such as pine, eucalypt or oak. Malaysian rainforests are categorised according to the type of seeds the trees produce: despite the diversity of species, most produce seeds of a similar structure – dipterocarp roughly translates from Latin as 'five seeds'. Dominated by tall trees, these forests nonetheless support a vast diversity of other plants, including many thousands of species of orchids, fungi, ferns and moss.

Another term used in reference to rainforest plant communities is 'epiphyte', which simply means any plant growing on another, for example a cluster of ferns growing high in the fork of a tree. Epiphytes use their hosts for support only, and themselves often provide shelter to other organisms, such as insects and tree frogs.

Other important vegetation types include mangroves, which fringe coasts and estuaries, and provide nurseries for fish and crustaceans; the stunted rhododendron forests of Borneo's high peaks, which also support epiphytic communities of orchids and hanging lichens (beard moss); and the kerangas of Sarawak, which grows on dry, sandy soil and can support many types of pitcher plants.

### Rafflesia

Probably the most famous of Malaysia's plants, the rafflesia produces the largest flower in the world; large specimens can measure up to 1m across. There are about 12 species of rafflesia, all confined to the rainforests of Sumatra (Indonesia), Peninsular Malaysia and Borneo. The rafflesia lives most of its life as an underground parasite, living off the root systems of select plants.

There is no apparent flowering season and rafflesias are extremely difficult to locate until they flower. The bud starts as a nondescript, brown growth; within a few days it swells to the size of a football, then gradually opens to reveal bright red petals. The flower continues to mature over a few days but gradually loses colour and withers. Rafflesias are probably most easily seen at Gunung Gading National Park, near Kuching in Sarawak, but they are also reasonably common in Sabah.

### Pitcher Plants

Growing as unobtrusive vines in poor, often well-drained soils, these unusual plants feature a modified leaf-type that forms a well, filled with liquid. Insects attracted to the plants fall into the well and drown, then are digested as part of the plant's nutrient intake. There are many species, whose pitchers can range from pipe- to pint-glass-sized. They reach their greatest diversity in Borneo;

several species are unique to the Mt Kinabalu and Gunung Mulu regions, and at least four are common in Bako National Park.

## FAUNA

An incredibly diverse and unusual array of mammals, birds, reptiles and insects make their home in the region. Although vast areas of forests have been cleared, some magnificent stands remain and the range of life forms that can still be seen with a bit of patience is astonishing. Most of the best wildlife-viewing is to be had in the excellent system of reserves and national parks – see the relevant chapters for details.

In the following section on mammals, the Malay name for each is given in brackets after the English name.

## Mammals

**Orang-Utan** *(orang hutan)* The Malay name for this great, fiery-red haired ape means 'man of the forest'. The orang-utan is Asia's only representative of the great ape family and the only one that spends most of its life in the trees. The orang-utan is rare and found only on the islands of Sumatra and Borneo. It was once said that an orang-utan could swing from one end of Borneo to the other without touching the ground; sadly, this is no longer true. This inoffensive creature and its habitat are disappearing fast.

Unlike many primates, orang-utans are generally solitary animals; they are also unusual because they build a nest of sticks and branches in which to sleep each night. Young orang-utans are appealing and amusing animals that show all the mischievous traits of their human counterparts; they stay with their mothers for up to the age of five. Adult males are massive: they can weigh up to 100kg, stand up to 1.5m tall and can have an arm-span of nearly 3m. In contrast, females are of far more delicate build and seldom weigh more than 50kg.

**Gibbons** *(ungka)* More closely related to apes than monkeys, gibbons dwell strictly in the trees, where they feed on fruits such as figs. Gibbons are superbly adapted to their lifestyle: they have small, slender bodies,

and like other apes have no tail. They have incredibly long arms for swinging effortlessly through the trees, their short legs dangling as they swing. Gibbons make an appalling racket in the predawn hour – a far-carrying, raucous hooting that is one of the most distinctive sounds of the Malaysian jungle. The calls help gibbons establish territories and find mates. Several species inhabit large stands of forest on Peninsular Malaysia and in Borneo, but they are generally shy of people.

**Monkeys** *(monyet)* Malaysia has 10 species of monkeys, divided by biologists into langurs and macaques. Langurs (or leaf monkeys) are mostly tree-dwelling, and generally have black palms and soles and grey faces. Macaques have pale palms and soles, and brown- or red-coloured faces; they spend a great deal of time on the ground, although they are also agile climbers. Monkeys usually live in loose groups comprising one or more families; a large group can number up to 50 individuals.

The long-tailed macaque *(kera)* is the most common and widespread of Malaysia's monkeys, and can even be a nuisance when troupes raid orchards and plantations. It is a small animal, and greyish-brown in colour with a long, slender tail. Family groups, usually with a dominant male in attendance, forage on the forest floor and in trees for fruit, leaves and insects. This species occasionally feeds on crabs along the shoreline.

The pig-tailed macaque *(beruk)* is slightly bigger, with golden brown fur; its tail is reduced to a dangling stump. This species is sometimes trained to pick coconuts.

Malaysia's various species of langurs are far more retiring than macaques and some are very attractively marked. The silver leaf monkey's black fur is frosted with grey tips; this beautiful animal can be observed at Kuala Selangor Nature Park in Peninsular Malaysia and at Bako National Park in Sarawak. The upper body of the banded langur *(cenaka)* is usually a black or dark grey colour; the spectacled langur *(cenkung)* has white rings around its eyes; and the maroon langur of Malaysian Borneo has reddish fur similar to that of the orang-utan.

The fantastic proboscis monkey *(orang blander)* is a type of langur and is probably Malaysia's second-most famous animal, after the orang-utan. The male proboscis monkey is an improbable-looking creature with a pendulous nose and bulbous belly; females and youngsters are more daintily built with quaint, upturned noses. When European traders reached the region locals saw a resemblance and the Malay name for this monkey literally means 'Dutchman'. Proboscis monkeys inhabit only the forests of Borneo, where they live almost entirely on leaves. Nowhere are they common, but they are usually encountered in forests near water, including mangroves. Proboscis monkeys occasionally enter the water and have even been seen to swim. The Sungai (River) Kinabatangan in Sabah is the best place to look for these monkeys, although there are also colonies in Bako National Park in Sarawak and in Brunei.

The slow loris *(kongkang)* is thought to be related to the monkeys and apes, although its main similarities are its grasping hands and long toes, with which it moves about in trees. Otherwise, the slow loris is a bizarre creature: It is small (about 30cm in length), has no tail and has enormous, bulbous eyes that help it locate and catch insects and other small animals at night. The slow loris is a solitary creature, found in forests, plantations and even gardens. As its name suggests, it moves with painful deliberation.

**Cats** *(kucing)* Malaysia has many species of wild cats, including the largest and some of the smallest. Several species are no longer common because of the pressures of hunting and, more recently, the trade in body parts for their supposed medicinal qualities.

The magnificent tiger *(harimau)*, largest of the great cats, was once widespread in South-East Asia and common in Peninsular Malaysia. Hunting and habitat destruction have taken their toll, although they are still rumoured to be present in Taman Negara National Park. Tigers are generally nocturnal and solitary, feeding on wild pigs and small

animals such as frogs and fish. An adult tiger can measure 3m from nose to tail tip and a fully grown male can weigh up to 200kg.

The leopard *(harimau bintang)* is still occasionally reported on the peninsula, although it is a secretive animal and may actually be relatively common. The black form of the leopard – often called black panther – is more common in Malaysia than the spotted variety. Neither leopard nor tiger has been recorded in Borneo.

Several smaller species of cats hunt birds and small mammals in forests and adjoining plantations, although one – the bay cat *(kucing hutan)* – is a specialised fish-eater. The leopard cat *(kucing batu)* is a widespread species a bit larger than a domestic cat; as its name suggests, it has spotted fur. The marbled cat *(kucing dahan)* is similar in size, with less-distinct markings. The clouded leopard *(harimau dahan)* is Borneo's biggest cat, although it is also found on the peninsula. This beautiful predator measures only 1.5m from head to tail; its spots are blurred in subtle shades of yellow and fawn. Danum Valley in Sabah is probably the best place to look for wild cats, although the bay cat is seen regularly along Sabah's Sungai Kinabatangan at night.

**Civets** *(musang)* Members of this diverse, sometimes attractive group of mainly carnivorous animals bear a superficial resemblance to cats. However, they differ in that they usually have long, pointed snouts, and move about at night with an ambling gait as they sniff out prey such as frogs, insects, nestlings and fruit. The common palm civet *(musang pulut)* is found throughout Malaysia, even straying into the outskirts of urban areas (including Singapore); it measures about 1m from its nose to the end of its tail. The Malay civet *(tangalung)* is slightly larger and attractively patterned, with a ringed tail and spotted or striped coat. The binturong is the largest of the civets; it has a shaggy black or dark-brown coat that helps keep it dry in its damp forest habitat. Also known as the bearcat, the binturong can measure almost 2m in length and is equally at home in trees or on the ground.

**MALAYSIA**

**Sun Bear** *(beruang)* Malaysia's only bear is found throughout the South-East Asian region, including Peninsular Malaysia and Borneo. As bears go this is a small one, measuring only up to 1.5m in length and weighing 50kg to 60kg. It is black with white or pale-yellow chest markings, and feeds on fruit, vegetation and small animals. Sun bears also raid bee hives for honey, and eat grubs. Sun bears are rarely encountered and are generally not a bother to humans. However, they can behave unpredictably – especially females with young – and should be treated with caution.

**Asian Elephant** *(gajah)* Although the Asian elephant is a familiar beast of burden that has been domesticated for thousands of years, wild elephants still roam the forests of Malaysia. No fossil records have been found, so Borneo's elephants are believed to have been introduced by traders hundreds of years ago. An adult male elephant can grow to 2.5m tall and weigh up to 3000kg, with tusks up to 1.5m in length; females are smaller and usually have small tusks or none at all. Adult males tend to be solitary; females and young usually form small groups, but these may join to form groups of 50 to 100 animals. When these groups invade plantations or crops they can be very destructive. Wild elephants can be dangerous and should not be approached.

**Sumatran Rhinoceros** *(badak berendam)* The two-horned rhino was once common in South-East Asia, but its numbers have declined dramatically and it is now extremely rare. In Malaysia it is known to exist only in Endau-Rompin National Park on the peninsula and in remote parts of Sabah, such as Danum Valley. An adult rhino can be up to 2.5m in length and weigh up to 900kg. Rhinos eat only plants, and are inoffensive and extremely shy; the chances of seeing one in the wild are virtually nil.

**Tapir** *(tapir* or *tenuk)* An extraordinary animal that looks like a cross between a wild pig and a hippo, the Malaysian tapir's only living relative inhabits the jungles of Amazonian South America. Tapirs can grow up to 2m in length and weigh some 300kg; they are vegetarian and are sometimes seen at the salt licks in the farther reaches of Taman Negara. Adult tapirs have a two-tone colour scheme, almost black in the foreparts, changing to a white hindquarters. Young tapirs are striped and look somewhat like animated watermelons.

**Squirrels** *(tupai)* Malaysia has more than 20 species of squirrels, of which several are common; most are active during the day and are readily seen in parks, gardens and patches of forest. Squirrels climb and jump with agility, and generally feed on fruits and leaves. Palm squirrels are small, and brown or greyish with cream-coloured stripes down their back; they are common in plantations. One of the most attractive species is Prevost's squirrel *(tupai gading)*, which is variable in colour, but generally has bright chestnut belly-fur, grey or silver haunches and a black body.

The giant squirrel *(kerawak)* is most easily distinguished by its enormous size – it reaches almost 1m in length and has a very bushy tail. Flying squirrels *(tupai terbang)* are also large; some measure nearly 1m, of which about half is tail. They don't literally fly – they glide from tree to tree by extending a flap of loose skin that stretches between each front and back leg. Flying squirrels are generally active at night and can be difficult to observe because they tend to feed high in the canopy.

**Pangolin** *(tenggiling)* Also known as the scaly anteater, the pangolin feeds exclusively on ants and termites. It is a small, nonthreatening animal, measuring only 1m in length. It's covered in broad scales like a pine cone, and uses its powerful claws to dig open ant and termite mounds. Its method of self defence is to roll up into a ball to protect itself. Pangolins are found throughout Peninsular Malaysia and Borneo, often straying into gardens and plantations.

**Bats** *(kelawar)* Malaysia has more than 100 species of bats, most of which are tiny, insectivorous (insect-eating) species that live in caves, and under eaves and bark. All bats are nocturnal; most insectivorous bats have poor eyesight and navigate by emitting a constant stream of high-pitched squeaks that bounce off objects like radar. This extraordinary adaptation is sensitive enough to locate small insects in flight.

Fruit bats, or flying foxes, are only distantly related to insectivorous bats; unlike them they have well developed eyes and do not navigate by echolocation. Fruit bats roost in great, noisy colonies and sally forth at dusk in search of fruiting trees such as figs; they also raid orchards and can become a pest to farmers. There are fruit bats in Taman Negara, and the great cave systems of Borneo host a famous bat spectacle: The best place to witness this is at Deer Cave in Mulu National Park in Sarawak, where several million insectivorous bats stream out at dusk in wave after chittering wave.

## Birds

Bird-watchers are drawn from all over the world in search of Malaysia's hundreds of unusual, colourful and unique bird species. Most towns and villages host at least a few species, and you won't have to go far into the countryside to see a whole lot more. Even in large cities there are usually a few species to see in parks and gardens, including bulbuls, starlings and, wheeling overhead in endless movement, house swifts.

On Peninsular Malaysia, there's excellent bird-watching within a day's reach of KL; prime locations include:

**Taman Negara** Malaysia's most famous national park hosts a great variety of species, sometimes in abundance; those particularly sought here include various hornbills and pheasants. Walk along the jungle trails in the early morning and wait for 'bird waves' – noisy, frenetic parties of mixed species (sometimes a dozen or more) moving through the forest.

**Bukit Fraser** A short trip from KL, Bukit Fraser (Fraser's Hill) features a great selection of lowland and highland species, including many migrants. Among those particularly sought by bird-watchers are the brown bullfinch, rusty-naped pitta and the rare Malaysian peacock-pheasant. One of the best strategies is to walk down the access road in the early morning (be careful of traffic), bird-watching as you go, and catch a lift back up by late morning, when it gets hot and bird activity slows down.

**Kuala Selangor Nature Park** About 60km from KL, this pleasant little park is home to a variety of migratory wading birds such as sandpipers, stints and shanks from about September to March every year. Other birds seen year-round include herons, the secretive mangrove pitta, the stately crested serpent-eagle and various species of kingfishers.

The great island of Borneo hosts a slightly different range of birds to the peninsula, including some 38 species found nowhere else, and is well worth a visit. Both Sabah and Sarawak have great bird-watching, although sites in Sabah are probably slightly better and easier to reach. Good locations for bird-watching include:

**Gunung Mulu National Park** This park in Sarawak features near-pristine forest with well-marked trails along which you can see trogons, jungle-flycatchers and several species of bulbuls and babblers. Birds of prey are another attraction here, and include the bat hawk, which picks off bats emerging from the park's great caves at dusk.

**Mt Kinabalu** Sabah's most popular attraction also has great bird-watching. Follow any of the jungle trails that radiate from the park accommodation complex, or simply walk around the gardens in the early morning to see laughing-thrushes, drongoes, bulbuls, Bornean treepies, green magpies and various flycatchers. The climb to the summit features several species not seen around park HQ, including the dainty mountain black-eye, mountain blackbird and mountain serpent-eagle.

**Sungai Kinabatangan** A narrow corridor of forest along Sabah's longest river hosts all eight of Borneo's hornbill species, at least three pittas (including the endemic blue-headed and black-and-crimson pittas), rarities such as Storm's stork, and blue and paradise-flycatchers.

**Danum Valley** Superb, towering and untouched, the rainforest of Danum Valley in Sabah is famous for its wildlife, although some work may be required to search it out. Pheasants and hornbills are still relatively common, and a bizarre endemic species, the Bornean bristlehead, is often seen in this area.

Waterbirds you may see include various herons and storks. One of the best places to see them is Kuala Selangor Nature Park near KL, although a good variety of herons and egrets can usually be seen near rice paddies and estuaries around the region.

Both Peninsular Malaysia and Borneo are home to a number of beautiful pheasants, although they are more-often heard than seen. The most spectacular of these is the argus pheasant; the striking male has a long showy train that trails 1m or more behind him. Silvery-grey in colour, its tail, which it raises in courtship displays, has numerous eye-shaped markings.

Kingfishers usually live near waterways, where they hunt for fish, crabs and other small animals. The stork-billed kingfisher is a large, common species found along rivers and mangroves. It is coloured blue and fawn, and has a massive red bill from which it takes its name.

Hornbills are one of the bird attractions of Malaysia; nine species have been recorded and various species are important in the folklore of Borneo tribes. Hornbills are large – up to 1m in length – and generally patterned black and white. All have large, downward-curving bills, and some have a bushy crest, colourful face and bill markings or other adornments. Despite their great size, they can be difficult to spot in the rainforest canopy and are best seen when they fly. The great hornbill is the largest species in the region and is found only on the peninsula. The rhinoceros hornbill is one of the most spectacular species, because of its huge red-and-yellow bill with a casque on top.

Pittas are the jewels of the rainforest. These medium-sized birds are brilliantly coloured and seem to glow in the gloom of the forest floor, where they hunt insects and spiders. No fewer than eight species inhabit the rainforests of Borneo, of which two – the blue-headed and the black-and-crimson pittas – are particularly beautiful and found nowhere else. Others are found also on the peninsula – the rusty-naped pitta can be spotted at Bukit Fraser and the rare mangrove pitta can sometimes be seen at Kuala Selangor.

Broadbills are related to pittas, and like them can be brightly coloured. Unlike pittas,

they spend much time in the forest canopy, where they often perch then sally forth after insects. The aptly named black-and-red broadbill has a bulbous, bright-blue bill to offset its already colourful livery; it makes untidy nests of dried grass and is usually seen along rivers – look for it at Taman Negara or along the Sungai (River) Kinabatangan in Sabah.

Malaysia's many species of babblers and bulbuls can pose a perplexing identification problem – most are rather drab in colouration and many species look very similar to each other. Babblers in particular may skulk in the undergrowth and be difficult to see – if not hear. Bulbuls are among the most common birds seen by visitors and at least one or two species usually inhabit parks or gardens.

Other small birds that may be seen in gardens and patches of forest include leafbirds, which are all active little insect-hunters with bright-green colouration; the iridescent sunbirds, whose sharp, downward-curving bills are used for extracting nectar; and a bewildering array of flycatchers – including monarchs, jungle-flycatchers and blue-flycatchers. The Asian paradise-flycatcher is one of the most attractive examples of the latter: The female is a rich chestnut colour but the male is mainly white and sports two trailing tail-streamers, which are many times its own body length.

## Other Animals

There are far too many forms and species to name here, but a few groups stand out for their interest, beauty or – too often – for their rarity. Some 250 species of reptiles have been recorded, including 100 of snakes, 14 of tortoises and turtles, and three of crocodiles.

Most snakes are inoffensive, but all should be treated with caution, because if you are bitten by a dangerous one you may find yourself far from help. Cobras and vipers are the most dangerous, although the chances of encountering them are low. Pythons are sometimes seen in national parks and one, the reticulated python, is reputed to grow to 10m in length. Several species of flying snakes

Nine species of hornbill call Malaysia home.

JOHN BORTHWICK
Taking a walk with a rhinoceros beetle.

JEAN-BERNARD CARILLET
Cameron Highlands, a-flutter with butterflies.

ANDERS BLOMQVIST

MARK DAFFEY
A chameleon-esque lizard on the lookout.

ANDERS BLOMQVIST
A long-tailed macaque does its thing.

MARK DAFFEY
Orang-utan, the great ape of Borneo.

SIMON BRACKEN

Bird of paradise

MARK DAFFEY

Pitcher plants, insect soup.

SUSAN STORM

Heliconia

DAVID ANDREW

Rafflesia, the world's largest flower.

MICHAEL AW

Hibiscus

inhabit the rainforests; they don't literally fly, but glide from trees by extending a flap of loose skin along either side of their bodies. There are also flying lizards and frogs. Sea turtles may be seen near off-shore islands, particularly Pulau Sipadan in Borneo. See the boxed text 'The Disappearing Turtles of the East Coast' in the Terengganu chapter for information on the plight of these beautiful creatures.

The reptile you're most likely to see is the monitor lizard, which can be found in both Peninsular Malaysia and on Borneo. These carrion-eaters are especially easy to spot on island beaches – Pulau Perhentian Besar is home to several monsters close to 2m in length. Although they look scary, they generally shy away from humans, unlike their close relative, the Komodo Dragon.

Insects in Malaysia are abundant, to say the least, and number upwards of 150,000 species. Most spectacular and beautiful are the many hundreds of species of butterflies, including the large birdwings, which may have a wingspan of 20cm. The moon moth is a large, attractive green moth with long tail-streamers.

## NATIONAL PARKS

The British established the first national park in Malaysia in 1938 and it is now included in Taman Negara, Malaysia's major national park, which crosses the borders of Terengganu, Kelantan and Pahang on the peninsula. Malaysian Borneo has several national parks, which form a valuable and growing network.

For those who wish to experience the primeval world of the ancient rainforests, Taman Negara offers a spectacular introduction. However there are other parks you can visit in Peninsular Malaysia, and a trip to Malaysian Borneo is recommended, if only to see (and perhaps climb) Mt Kinabalu.

Accommodation is not a problem when visiting most national parks. Various categories are available, from hostel to chalet. Transport and accommodation operations are increasingly being handled by private tour companies, and you have to book in advance and pay a deposit. The best times to

visit are April to September (east coast, including Taman Negara), October through March (west coast) and April to September for Malaysian Borneo.

## Marine Parks

Malaysia's marine parks range from inaccessible islands with no tourist facilities to tourist meccas like Pulau Tioman. In order to protect their fragile underwater environments, no potentially destructive activities like fishing or motorised watersports are allowed. This makes these parks ideal for activities such as snorkelling, diving or just lazing around on the beach.

Some of the more-accessible marine parks are Pulau Payar (Kedah), Pulau Tioman (Pahang), the Seribuat Archipelago (Johor), Pulau Kapas (Terengganu), Pulau Redang (Terengganu), and Pulau Perhentian (Terengganu) in Peninsular Malaysia; and Tunku Abdul Rahman and Turtle Island national parks in Sabah. Some of the parks have also been gazetted as national parks. See the relevant chapters and the 'Diving & Snorkelling' special section in the Terengganu chapter for more information.

There is a RM5 entry fee for all marine parks. However, collection of this fee is inconsistent at best (if you're asked to pay it, be sure that the person collecting the fee is actually a marine park official).

## GOVERNMENT & POLITICS

Malaysia is a confederation of 13 states and the federal districts of Kuala Lumpur and Pulau Labuan. It is a constitutional monarchy and the head of state is the *yang dipertuan agong* (king), elected every five years by the sultans who head nine of the peninsular states.

The country has two houses of parliament. The lower house is the Dewan Rakyat (People's Council), consisting of 180 members elected every five years, and it is this house that forms the government and holds the real power. The senate, or Dewan Negara (States' Council), consists of 70 members, 40 of whom are appointed by the yang di-pertuan agong on the basis of their experience or wisdom, or to represent interest groups or minorities. The remaining 30 are elected by the state legislatures.

Each state has its own government, and members are elected to the unicameral state legislatures every five years. States have wide powers to pass laws. Each state also has a head of state, and in the case of the peninsula the hereditary sultans, who exist in all states except Melaka and Penang, are appointed. The states of Sabah and Sarawak in Malaysian Borneo are rather different from the Peninsular Malaysian states, since they were separate colonies, not parts of Malaya, prior to independence. The four states without sultans have a *yang di-pertuan negeri*, or governor, appointed by the federal government for a term of four years.

The judiciary is composed of the Supreme Court, High Courts and magistrates courts. Penghulu courts were set up to hear cases at a village level, but they can only try disputes worth no more than RM50, so cases are very rarely heard. The *penghulu* (village chief) acts on an informal level. In Sabah and Sarawak native courts exist to try breaches of native law or custom, acting in much the same way as Islamic courts, which are there to try breaches of syariah, or Islamic law, by Muslims.

## Sultans

The sultans' positions are enshrined in the constitution, but their power is largely ceremonial. The yang di-pertuan agong must approve all acts of parliament and can refuse the appointment of a prime minister, but acts on the advice of parliament and the cabinet. Sultans, who are heads of their respective states, have the same powers and responsibilities.

The political process is very similar to the institutions of governors and governors-general as found in other British Commonwealth countries.

The first great sultanate was that of Melaka, which rose to prominence in the 15th century. It began life as a Hindu kingdom, but with the conversion to Islam the raja, or king, took on the title of sultan. Hindu traditions and court customs continued in the courts of the sultans despite the rise of Islam and are

still evident today. After European intervention and the defeat of Melaka, the peninsula fragmented into several small sultanates and by the 19th century the Malay sultanates were in disarray, many of them involved in internal wars, while the Siamese controlled the north of the peninsula.

The British stepped in, using military force to resolve some disputes and appointing British Residents to the sultans as 'advisers'. The British exerted their influence by shoring up the sultanates, which may well have disappeared otherwise. The British increasingly assumed power from the traditional monarchs. But the sultanate system was maintained, along with the rights and privileges of the sultans, which were enshrined in the constitution after independence from Britain.

For Malays, the sultans are the upholders of Malay tradition and the symbolic heads of Islam. They command great respect, especially in rural areas and the more traditional east-coast states. The royal families have emerged as a modern elite and are very active in government and business. Scandals involving assault, abuse of privilege and corruption have helped to undermine their position, but they still exert a great deal of influence in modern Malaysia.

## ECONOMY

Malaysia is one of the economic success-stories of the postwar period. Since independence it has moved away from its reliance on tin and rubber and diversified its economy by aggressively attracting investment, both foreign and domestic. After Singapore and Brunei, it is the most developed country in South-East Asia, with the highest standard of living.

Malaysia's push to become a manufacturing centre has seen it become a major supplier of electronic components and equipment, and along with other products such as textiles and footwear, manufactured goods now account for over half of all exports. Important primary exports are petroleum and petroleum products, logs, timber, and palm oil. Rubber now accounts for less than 2% of exports, tin barely half of 1%.

## Sultans, Fast Cars & the Law

Like England, Malaysia has royalty and nobility – but there are nine royal families in Malaysia, not just one. Like Britain's House of Windsor, they come in for plenty of criticism – but you won't hear it, because criticising Malaysia's royalty can put you in prison on a charge of sedition. In part this relates back to Malaysia's early history as an independent state, when politicians often had royal connections, notably the first prime minister, Tunku Abdul Rahman.

Nine of the states of Malaysia are ruled by sultans, who are totally exempt from the law. They take it in turn to assume the title of *yang di-pertuan agong*, effectively the 'king' of Malaysia. Although they're not inclined towards prancing around half-naked or indulging in anguished marital separations, the Malaysian nobility does have its own colourful scandals.

The funniest in recent years has been that concerning the sultan of Kelantan and his penchant for expensive toys. Each sultan is allowed to own seven imported cars without paying import duties and taxes. This rule has customarily been treated with some flexibility – 10 is near enough to seven if your maths isn't too good. Unfortunately for the sultan of Kelantan, it was finally decided that 20 was definitely more than seven, and when a brand new Lamborghini Diablo arrived in an air-freight consignment at Kuala Lumpur International Airport (KLIA) the sultan was informed he would have to pay import duties before he was allowed to take it home. 'Let me at least sit in my new toy', implored the sultan, who then proceeded to screech out of the hangar and burn rubber all the way back to the palace in Kelantan!

More serious than mere evasion of customs duty are outright cases of law breaking. In 1976 one member of the Johor royal family was actually convicted of manslaughter, then pardoned by his father, the sultan at the time. The Malaysian parliament was informed that the sultan of Johor and his son had been involved in 23 cases of assault.

Although the Malaysian government would quite like to bring the sultans to heel, their popularity in rural areas and their image as protectors of Malay culture and history make the government reluctant to meddle with the status quo. The Malaysian constitution also makes it difficult to institute changes, as it specifically states that no alteration can be made to the sultans' 'privileges, position, honours or dignities' without their agreement!

**Tony Wheeler**

Major imports are machinery and equipment, chemicals, food and petroleum products. Major trading partners are Japan, the USA and Singapore.

Malaysia's rapid increase in manufacturing has been achieved by modernising the country's transport, communications and energy infrastructures, developing industrial zones and offering substantial tax breaks for investors in export-oriented industries.

The government has promoted a relatively open, market-oriented economy and has instituted significant reforms by dismantling many state-run enterprises and encouraging private enterprise to undertake many of the country's development projects. Though promoting a free market in some areas, the government is also an investor in the economy (usually as a minority partner) and controls prices on some key commodities, such as fuel and rice.

## The Currency Crisis

Until August 1997, it seemed as though the Malaysian economy could do no wrong. In the 11 years from 1985 to 1996 the country had an average annual growth rate of more than 8%. Exports were booming, the nation's infrastructure was rapidly developing and standards of living were approaching those of more-developed nations. The economy was growing so fast that Malaysia couldn't keep up with its labour requirements and had to import workers from countries such as Indonesia, Thailand, the Philippines, Bangladesh and elsewhere.

Emboldened by success after success, the Mahathir government embarked on the construction of several well-publicised megaprojects. The projects included the new high-tech capital city of Putrajaya (US$8 billion), the Bakun Dam (US$6 billion), a new airport and freeway links (US$7.6 billion), the city of Gelang Patah in Johor (US$12.8 billion), KL's Light Rail Transit (LRT; US$2 billion), power plants (US$4.8)…the list goes on.

Then, in July 1997, a currency crisis in nearby Thailand quickly spread to the neighbouring countries of South-East Asia and the region was plunged into a recession. The ringgit, which had been one of the region's strongest and most stable currencies, plunged in value from RM2.5 to US$1 to almost RM5 to US$1.

Prime Minister Mahathir, never one to pull punches, quickly blamed international currency speculators for the disaster, singling out in particular American billionaire George Soros. Soros, he maintained, was trying to punish the member countries of the Association of South-East Asian Nations (Asean) for its inclusion of Myanmar, with its record of human rights abuses. It was also whispered by some that religious prejudices were at work, since Soros is Jewish and the majority of Malaysians are Muslim. Needless to say, these claims were coldly received in the West, and many commentators both inside and outside the country observed that Malaysia was to blame for a lot of its economic woes.

Unlike Indonesia, Malaysia did not accept an International Monetary Fund (IMF) tendered bail-out program. Instead, Mahathir recalled foreign holdings of the ringgit and pegged its value at RM3.8 to the US dollar. He also passed legislation preventing foreign investors from repatriating profits earned in Malaysia for one year. At the time, most analysts predicted that such measures would lead to a mass exodus of foreign capital, and deeper recession. Miraculously, however, the measures seemed to work and the economy began to claw its way back, recording 5.4% growth in 1999 with forecasts of continuing growth.

## POPULATION & PEOPLE

Malaysia's population is currently around 21.38 million, but the government's Wawasan 2020 national development program gives a target population of 70 million by the year 2020!

The people of Malaysia come from a number of different ethnic groups – Malay, Chinese, Indian, indigenous Orang Asli and the various tribes of Sarawak and Sabah. Approximately 85% of the population lives in Peninsular Malaysia and the remaining 15% in the much more lightly populated states of Sabah and Sarawak.

It's reasonable to say that political power is controlled by Malays, while the Chinese control the economic sphere. The old images of Malays being a rural, traditional people and Chinese being an urban, capitalist class can still be applied, but the stereotypes are slowly breaking down. Malays dominate the countryside, but the number of urban Malays is growing, attracted by the new wealth and jobs of the cities.

The Indians, the next-largest group, are less easy to categorise and are divided by religion and linguistic background. A small, English-educated Indian elite has always played a prominent role in Malaysian society, and a significant merchant class exists, but a large percentage of Indians, imported as indentured labourers by the British, remain a disadvantaged labouring class.

Malaysia is very much a multiracial society, something that has figured prominently and not always happily in its development. From the ashes of the interracial riots of 1969, when distrust between the Malays and Chinese peaked, the country has managed to forge a more tolerant, multicultural society. Though ethnic loyalties remain strong, the emergence of a single 'Malaysian' identity is now a much-discussed and lauded concept, even if not yet really embraced.

Much of the improvement in race relations is due, paradoxically, to the government's bumiputra policy. This policy of positive discrimination in favour of Malays, largely responsible for events in 1969, was accelerated after the riots to concentrate on

Malay economic advancement. Through awarding government contracts to bumiputra groups, requiring bumiputra involvement in economic projects and targeting Malay areas for economic development, the government has increased Malay involvement in the economy, albeit largely for an elite, and helped defuse Malay fears and resentment of Chinese economic dominance.

A widespread backlash from the Chinese community has not emerged, because the government has given the country a booming economy, benefiting Chinese entrepreneurs and delivering jobs to Chinese and Malays alike. Mahathir's government is also careful to show even-handedness in cultural issues and keep the Chinese community on side. Nonetheless, the Chinese remain excluded from political control, and are disadvantaged by bumiputra policies. However, the government has promised that the races will compete on an equal footing when the development goals of Wawasan 2020 are achieved – a promise almost no one in the country believes.

The once-bitter issue of the promotion of Bahasa Malaysia, the national language, has also ultimately helped unify the country as the proficiency and use of the language has spread among all races. The government has also allayed Chinese and Indian concerns at attempts to introduce it as the sole language of instruction in all levels of education and is again promoting English, for business and practical reasons.

Malaysia has made enormous strides in promoting racial harmony, but old divisions exist. Moves such as those by the Kelantan government to introduce Islamic law applying to all its citizens, including the Chinese, has the potential to open old wounds, but the federal government is keen to put a lid on any threats to the largely peaceful multicultural balance in today's Malaysia.

## Peninsular Malaysia

**Malays** The Malays are the majority indigenous people of the region, although they were preceded by aboriginal people, small pockets of whom still survive. The overwhelming majority of Malays are Mus-

### The Minangkabau

The Minangkabau people from Sumatra (Indonesia) migrated to Peninsular Malaysia in quite large numbers from the 17th century. They were attracted by the rich tin mines of the peninsula, and many also became successful merchants and farmers, particularly in the sparsely settled interior. The Malay sultans had no objections to the Minangkabau immigrants, as they brought Islam to the interior with them and also went a long way towards offsetting the large influxes of Chinese.

Although the Minangkabau were related ethnically and linguistically to Malays on the peninsula, there was a marked difference in their social organisation in that it was matrilineal – descent and inheritance are traced through the female line.

While property is vested in the clan, or *suku*, ownership of it passes from mother to daughter. Upon marriage the husband enters his new wife's suku. Traditionally, the husband would continue to live with his mother after marriage and only visit his wife in her suku!

lim and, despite major changes in recent decades, are still to some extent 'country' rather than 'city' people.

Despite the fact that they account for only 55% of the population of Peninsular Malaysia (much less in Borneo), they are largely responsible for the political fortunes of the country, in part because of the failure of minority groups to unite into an effective opposition party.

**Chinese** Although some Chinese have been here since the time of Admiral Cheng Ho's visit to Melaka in 1405, the vast majority of the region's Chinese settlers have arrived since the beginning of the 19th century.

Most arrived from southern provinces of China but belong to different dialect groups, the major ones being Hakka, Hokkien, Teochew, Cantonese and Hainanese. Although all Chinese use the same written language, the dialects are not mutually comprehensible. Most Malaysian Chinese nowadays speak Mandarin; if they don't, a Hokkien-speaker and a Hakka-speaker may well have to resort to English or Malay to communicate.

The Baba Chinese, or Peranakan, of Melaka speak a Malay dialect but are still culturally Chinese.

The Chinese comprise about 35% of the population in Peninsular Malaysia, 30% in Sarawak and 16% in Sabah. They are generally traders and merchants.

**Indians** The region's Indian population arrived later still and in a more organised fashion. Whereas the Chinese flooded in of their own volition, the Indians were mainly brought in to provide plantation labour for the British colonists. Usually landless labourers, they were enticed under indentured labour schemes of three to five years, though later arrivals were free labourers who paid their own passage. Most of the Indian population is made up of Tamils, the rest are mainly Malayalis from the other South Indian state of Kerala, with a smattering of Punjabis, Gujeratis, Telugus and Bengalis. They account for 10% of the population on the peninsula, and are mainly concentrated in the west coast's larger towns.

**Orang Asli** There are still small scattered groups of Orang Asli (Original People), in Peninsular Malaysia. They number over 80,000 according to the latest census, and are the descendants of the people who inhabited the peninsula before the Malays arrived. Although most have given up their nomadic or shifting-agriculture techniques and some have been absorbed into modern Malaysian society, there are still a number of Orang Asli settlements in the forests and rural areas of the interior. There are many Orang Asli tribes, but the three main racial groups are the Negrito, the Senoi and the Proto-Malays.

The Negrito are thought to be the oldest inhabitants of the Malay Peninsula and are the smallest group of Orang Asli people, numbering less than 3000. They resemble Melanesians but are small in stature and have intermarried with other Orang Asli such as the Senoi. Some suggest they are more closely related to the tribal people of India and the Andaman Islands. Traditionally nomadic hunters, the Negrito inhabit the inland forest areas of the peninsula, primarily in Kelantan and Perak. The largest tribes are the Jahai and the Batek.

The Senoi are the most numerous Orang Asli (46,000), and were the second wave of immigrants to inhabit Peninsular Malaysia. Their language is related to the Mon-Khmer hill tribes of Cambodia, and for the most part they resemble Malays. Traditionally they are shifting agriculturists, forming permanent settlements, but today many Senoi have integrated into modern Malaysian society. Senoi villages are found mostly in Perak, Pahang and Kelantan, and the largest tribes are the Semai and the Temiar.

The Proto-Malays (35,000) are the third group of immigrants to the peninsula. It is thought that they came from Sumatra and the Riau Archipelago of Indonesia; they closely resemble the Malays and nowadays speak Malay. Proto-Malays are most numerous in Pahang, but live also throughout Johor, Negeri Sembilan and Selangor. The largest tribes are the Jakun, who can be visited at Tasik Cini; the Temuan; and the Semelai, centred mostly on Tasik Bera in Pahang.

Although some Orang Asli are Muslim (most notably the Proto-Malay Orang Laut of south-western coastal Johor), the majority have resisted conversion and retain their animist religions. Orang Asli are classified as bumiputra and are therefore eligible for the same economic advantages as Malays, but they are still the most economically disadvantaged group. While wage-earners do contribute to village economies, many Orang Asli communities still rely on traditional crops and hunting, and some still live a traditional, nomadic life in the jungles. The government is keen to promote development but also to foster Islam in some areas.

## Malaysian Borneo

The population make-up of the Malaysian Borneo states of Sabah and Sarawak is far more complex than in Peninsular Malaysia, with around 25 different ethnic groups in the two states.

**Malays** The indigenous Malays, who make up around 20% of the population, are descended from local people who converted to Islam and adopted Malay customs around 400 years ago.

The Melanie, who number approximately 100,000 in Sarawak, are also native Malays but are ethnically different from the Malays – they have different physical characteristics and speak different dialects. Most of the Melanie are followers of Islam, while the rest have converted to Christianity.

**Chinese** The Chinese minority in the Malaysian Borneo states is smaller than on the mainland but is no less important; they are basically the merchants and have a large influence on the economy.

**The Dayak** Dayak is the term used to cover the non-Muslim people of Borneo. These people migrated to Borneo at times and along routes that are not clearly defined. It is estimated that there are more than 200 Dayak tribes in Borneo.

**Ethnic Groups in Sarawak** The largest ethnic group in Sarawak is the Iban, numbering around 395,000. The early Europeans in the area named them Sea Dayaks, as they used to make forays down the rivers and out to sea. They were fierce headhunters and gave the Europeans a bad time along the coasts. Today the Iban are largely longhouse-dwellers, living along the Rejang and Baram rivers in Sarawak.

Another important group is the Bidayuh people, numbering about 107,000 in Sarawak. These people live along the rivers in Sarawak's First Division, which is the area around Kuching including the Sungai Skrang.

The other, much smaller, tribes, including the Kenyah, Kayan, Kelabit, Lun Bawang, Kajang, Kedayan, Bisaya and Punan, make up around 5% of Sarawak's total population. It's these small tribal communities of Sarawak that are worst hit by the logging that

is currently destroying the rainforests at an incredible rate. The Penan (Punan) are particularly hard hit, as they lead a purely hunter-gatherer existence, relying totally on the forest for food and shelter. The other communities practice much-maligned (by the government) slash-and-burn agriculture and so, while they are less devastated by the loss of forest, still find their land, lifestyle and customs under siege from the disruption.

**Ethnic Groups in Sabah** The people of Sabah are different again. While there are significant minorities of Chinese (16%) and the Bajau (10%), the major ethnic group is the Kadazan, who account for around 25%. Other smaller groups include the Murut (5%), Malays, the Orang Sungai (River People), Sulu, Tidong and Bisaya. There are also significant numbers of refugees and immigrants from the Philippines and Indonesia, residing mostly in the eastern towns of Sandakan, Lahad Datu and Tawau.

The Kadazan are traditionally agriculturists and longhouse-dwellers who live mainly in the west of the state. These days there have been large-scale conversions to Christianity and Islam, and many Kadazan have moved to the cities.

The Bajau live mainly in the north-west of the state, and around Semporna in the south-east. They were originally Sulu Sea pirates but these days pursue the much more prosaic practices of agriculture and animal husbandry.

The only other group of any size is the Murut, who number around 40,000 and live in the south-west in the Tenom area. They are agriculturists who used to occupy a much larger area of Sabah but were pushed south by the migrating Kadazan.

## EDUCATION

The Ministry of Education runs most schools in Malaysia. The Malaysian educational system is similar to the British system; children attend pre-school, kindergarten, primary (elementary) school and secondary (high) school. Upon graduating from secondary school, eligible students may continue on to university.

Children start primary school at the age of seven and instruction is in Bahasa Malaysia. English is also taught, as is Chinese in Chinese-run primary schools, and Tamil in Tamil-run primary schools. Upon completion of six years of schooling, children take an exam that determines whether or not they can enter secondary school. Eligible students may enter government-run secondary schools, most of which are Malay but some of which are Chinese; or private secondary schools, which are predominantly Chinese.

There are both public and private universities in Malaysia. The public universities are government supported and admissions policies heavily favour bumiputra students over students of Chinese or Indian descent. For this reason, many of these students attend private universities, either in Malaysia or overseas.

The adult literacy rate in Malaysia is 83.5% according to the *CIA World Factbook*.

## ARTS
It's along the east coast of Peninsular Malaysia, the predominantly Malay part of the country, that you'll find Malay arts and crafts, culture and games at their liveliest and most widely practised. Most modern art activity is in and around KL (see Modern Arts later in this section).

### Wayang Kulit
Similar to the shadow-puppet performances of other South-East Asian societies, in particular Java in Indonesia, the *wayang kulit* (shadow play) retells tales from the Hindu epic the *Ramayana*.

The Tok Dalang, or 'Father of the Mysteries', sits behind a semi-transparent screen and manipulates buffalo-hide puppets, whose images are thrown onto the screen. Characters include heroes, demons, kings, animals and, ever favourites, clowns.

Performances can last for many hours and throughout that time the puppeteer has to move the figures, sing all the voice parts and conduct the orchestra – it's a feat of some endurance. There are two forms of wayang kulit – the *wayang siam* and

Wayang kulit tells stories from the *Ramayana*.

*wayang melayu*. Performances often take place at weddings or after the harvest.

The wayang kulit used to be an immensely popular form of entertainment, but it was all but killed off with the advent of TV. Fifty years ago there were well over 100 wayang kulit masters; these days there are fewer than half a dozen. The tourism industry has been something of a saviour for wayang kulit performers, and the art form is unlikely to disappear completely.

### Dance
There are a variety of dances and dance-dramas performed in Malaysia. Though disco dancing is the most popular dance-form these days, traditional dance troupes perform for special occasions.

*Menora* is a dance-drama of Thai origin performed by an all-male cast dressed in grotesque masks.

*Mak yong* is a similar traditional form of theatre, but the participants are female. These performances often take place at Puja Ketek, Buddhist festivals held at temples in Kelantan, near the Thai border.

The *joget* is an upbeat dance of Portuguese origins. It is danced by couples who move quickly and never touch. It is the most popular traditional dance in Malaysia today and is often performed at Malay weddings by professional dancers. In Melaka it is better known as *chakunchak*.

*Rebana kercing* is a dance performed by young men to the accompaniment of tambourines. Other dances, not all of which are from the east coast, include the *tari piring, hadrah* and *zapin*.

The *rodat* is a dance from Terengganu and is accompanied by the *tar* drum.

## Silat

Also known as *bersilat*, this is the Malay martial art that originated in Melaka in the 15th century. Today it is a highly refined and stylised activity. Demonstrations are often performed at ceremonies and weddings, accompanied by music from drums and gongs.

## Music

Much Malay music has heavy Islamic and Chinese influences and takes different forms. The major types include:

**Dondang sayang** Chinese-influenced romantic songs accompanied by an orchestra, mainly in Melaka

**Hadrah** Islamic chants, sometimes accompanied by dance and music

**Ghazal** Female singers with orchestra, mainly in Johor

**Zikir** A type of religious singing

**Musical Instruments** Traditional Malay music is based largely on the *gendang* (drum), of which there are more than a dozen types. The four most-commonly used are:

**kompang or rebana kercing** Used widely at official functions

**rebana besar** Used at major festivals and on religious occasions

**rebana ubi** The long drums of Kelantan, made from hollowed-out logs

**tar** Used as an accompaniment to the rodat (see Dance earlier)

Other percussion instruments include the gong, *cerucap* (made of shells), *raurau* (coconut shells), *kertuk* and *pertuang* (both made from bamboo), and the wooden *celampang*.

Wind instruments include a number of types of flute (such as the *seruling* and *serunai*) and the trumpet-like *nafiri*.

Stringed instruments are also an important component of a traditional ensemble, and include the *biola, gambus* and *sundatang*.

The *nobat* is an exclusive royal orchestra of four or five players performing on drums, flute, trumpet and gong. They play only on ceremonial occasions and are found these days only in the states of Kedah, Terengganu, Johor and Perak.

The *gamelan*, a traditional Indonesian gong orchestra, is also found in the state of Kelantan, where a typical ensemble will comprise four different gongs, two xylophones and a large drum.

## Crafts

**Batik** Originally an Indonesian craft, batik has made itself equally at home in Malaysia. You'll find it in Penang on the west coast, but Kelantan and Terengganu are its true homes.

Batik is produced by drawing a pattern on fabric with wax and then dyeing the material. The wax is then melted away by boiling the cloth, and a second wax design is drawn in. After repeated waxing, dyeing and boiling processes, an intricate and beautifully coloured design is produced.

Batik can be found as clothes, cushion covers, tablecloths, placemats or simply as works of art. Malay designs are usually less traditional than those found in neighbouring Indonesia. The wax designs can either be drawn on a one-off basis or printed with a stencil.

**Kain Songket & Other Weaving** A speciality of Kelantan and Terengganu, *kain songket* is a hand-woven fabric with gold and silver threads through the material. Clothes made from this beautiful fabric are usually reserved for the most important festivals and occasions. *Mengkuang* is a far more prosaic form of weaving using pandanus leaves and strips of bamboo to make baskets, bags and mats.

**Silver & Brasswork** Kelantan is famed for its silversmiths, who work in a variety of

## Traditional Malay Houses

Gaily coloured and handsomely proportioned, traditional Malay houses are perfectly adapted to the hot, humid conditions of the region. Built on stilts, with high, peaked roofs, they take advantage of even the slightest breeze to cool the interior. Further ventilation is achieved by full-length windows, a lack of internal partitions, and lattice-like grilles in the walls. Not only are these houses relatively cool, they are also cheap to build, taking advantage of local materials like *atap* (jungle thatch) for roofing and jungle hardwood for framing.

The layout of a traditional Malay house reflects Muslim sensibilities. Notably, there are separate areas for men and women, as well as distinct areas where guests of either sex may be entertained. Some common features include:

**anjung** (covered porch) – A perfect refuge from the heat on the hottest days, this is where the men of the house relax and greet visitors. Between the anjung and the house is the *serambi gantung*, a covered veranda where more-intimate male visitors are entertained.
**rumah ibu** (main room) – This is the heart of the house, doubling as a living room and sleeping area. Reflecting the closeness of Malay families, there are no partitions and everyone sleeps in the same room. The only time outsiders may enter this room is during ceremonies like the marriage ceremony.
**rumah tengah** (kitchen area) – Separated from the main house, this is where meals are prepared and dishes washed. It is the domain of the women of the house.
**selang** (passageway) – This passageway connects the main house with the kitchen area. Usually outfitted with a stairway, the selang doubles as a social area for the women of the house, and is a place where they may entertain female guests.

Of course, there are regional variations in the architecture of traditional Malay houses (see the boxed texts 'The Minangkabau House' in the Negeri Sembilan chapter, 'The Melaka House' in the Melaka chapter and 'The East Coast House' in the Kelantan chapter).

Sadly, traditional Malay houses are quickly being replaced by concrete-block structures or simpler, characterless wood-frame houses. Perhaps the best place to see some remaining examples of Malay houses is in the *kampung* (villages) of Kelantan, outside Kota Bharu.

**Chris Rowthorn**

ways and specialise in filigree and repoussé work. In the latter, designs are hammered through the silver from the underside. Kampung Sireh at Kota Bharu is a centre for silverwork. Brasswork is an equally traditional skill in Kuala Terengganu.

**Arts & Crafts of Malaysian Borneo** The indigenous peoples of Malaysian Borneo have a rich legacy of arts and crafts. Perhaps the most famous Malaysian Borneo art is *pua kumbu*, a colourful weaving technique used to produce both everyday and ceremonial items decorated with a wide range of patterns. A special dyeing process known as *ikat* is used to produce the colours for pua kumbu. Ikat dyeing is performed while the threads of the pattern are already in place on the loom, giving rise to its English name, warp tie-dyeing.

Woodcarving is a prized art among the peoples of Malaysian Borneo, and the most skilled carvers of all are held to be the Kenyah and Kayan peoples. In these societies, enormous burial columns carved from tree trunks were used to bury the remains of headmen. These columns, known as *kelirieng* sometimes reached 2m in diameter and 10m in height and were covered with detailed carvings from top to bottom. Decaying remnants of kelirieng are still uncovered in the rainforest of Sarawak, and an example can be seen in Kuching Municipal Park. Less formidable, but equally beautiful, the Kenyah and Kayan also produced smaller wooden hunting-charms and ornate wooden knife-hilts known as *parang ilang*.

The baskets of the Iban, Kayan, Kenyah and Penan are among the most highly regarded in Borneo. The most common material for basket building is rattan, but bamboo, swamp nipah grass and pandanus palms are also used. In addition to baskets, sleeping mats, seats and materials for shelters were all produced by related techniques. While each ethnic group has certain distinctive patterns, hundreds, or even thousands of years of trade and interaction has led to an intermixing of patterns. Some ethnic groups still produce baskets and other goods in the traditional way and these can be found in some of the markets of Malaysian Borneo. Others may be offered for sale upon a visit to a longhouse.

### Modern Arts

The modern art scene in Malaysia is based in KL. There are active theatre, music, film and literary happenings for those with the patience to seek them out. Merdeka Square in KL (see Entertainment in the Kuala Lumpur chapter) is the de facto centre of the KL arts scene and is a good place to get a sense of what's out there. While you're in Merdeka Square, be sure to check out Dama House, a bookshop/music library with a good collection of Asian music, including lots of Chinese-Malaysian offerings. Check out the excellent online magazine *Kulture* at www.kulture.com.my for information on the Malaysian arts scene and listings of upcoming events. For more information, see the Kuala Lumpur chapter.

**Cinema** The Malaysian film industry dates back to the 1930s. Many of the Malay-language films made in this period were adaptations of the popular Chinese films of the time. WWII brought a halt to Malaysia's nascent film industry. After the war, most popular Malaysian films were directed by Indian-born directors, who continued to adapt foreign plots for Malayan audiences.

The 1950s marked the golden age of Malay films and the first acting and directorial efforts of the king of Malaysian cinema: P Ramlee. Ramlee's directorial debut was *Penarik Becha*, a commercial success released in 1955. Ramlee also acted in some 70 films in his lifetime. Some of his most famous films include the dramas *Anakku Sazali* and *Ibu Mertua Ku* and the comedy *Madu Tiga*.

During the 1960s, production of Malay-language films moved from Singapore to KL, and Malays began to take control of more aspects of film production. At present, between 10 and 15 films are produced in Malaysia each year, most of them heavily influenced by Hollywood and Hong Kong action films. In Malaysia, these films are screened in Bahasa Malaysia with Chinese subtitles.

## SOCIETY & CONDUCT
### Malay Customs

That Malays are Muslim is a tautology. Most follow Islam devoutly, and the religion is the social fabric of Malay society. When Islam came to Malaysia it supplanted existing spiritual beliefs and systems of social law, or *adat*; however, conversion to Islam did not mean a total abolition of existing customs and beliefs. Many aspects of adat are still a part of everyday life in the *kampung* (village), and indeed in the suburbs of the cities, though Islam and modern life have seen the passing of many older beliefs and customs.

Adat, with its roots in the Hindu period and earlier, is customary law that places great emphasis on collective rather than individual responsibility. It is very much a village-based social system and its principles still affect everyday life for many Malays. *Adat temenggong* defines the authoritarian, patriarchal system of the sultans and still influences court ritual in some areas. It owes its existence to the Hindu state, with ultimate power placed in the hands of the raja, or king.

The kampung and its obligations of kinship are at the heart of the Malay world. It is mutually supportive and places great emphasis on maintaining harmony. In principle, villagers are of equal status, though a headman is appointed on the basis of his wealth, greater experience or spiritual knowledge. Traditionally the founder of the village was appointed village leader (penghulu or *ketua kampung*), and often members of the same family would also become leaders. A penghulu is usually a *haji*, one who has made the pilgrimage to Mecca – a position of great importance.

As a religious leader, the *imam* holds a position of great importance in the community as the keeper of Islamic knowledge and the leader of prayer. The *pawang* and the *bomoh* are keepers of a spiritual knowledge that is part of an older tradition. A pawang possesses skills and esoteric knowledge about such things as the rice harvest, rain making and fishing and knows the rituals needed to ensure their success and appease the necessary spirits. The bomoh is a spiritual healer who has not only learned the knowledge of curative plants but can contact the spirit world and harness its power. The bomoh's chants, or *mantra*, may contain Sanskrit words but will more often contain passages from the Quran and invoke the power of Allah. The bomoh, or at least their imitators, are still occasionally seen in the markets as they put on their magic shows and then bring out their cure-all medicines for sale. Though the bomoh is a dying tradition that flies in the face of orthodox Islam, it is widely held that prominent members of UMNO (the ruling political party) consult bomoh for political guidance.

Islamic fundamentalism and Western rationalism have helped to undermine the role of the pawang and the bomoh, but spirits, magic and such things as *keramat* (saint) worship still survive in the village, despite such ideas being at odds with Islamic teachings. Many traditional beliefs and adat customs have adapted to Islam, rather than having been destroyed by it.

**Ceremonies** Adat is most noticeable in the important ceremonies of birth, circumcision and marriage. Customs of everyday life are known as *adat resam*, while customs and traditions relating to the courts of the sultans are known as *adat istiadat diraja*.

Traditionally in a birth attended by the midwife, a baby is spat on to protect it from the spirits of disease and the Muslim call to prayer is whispered in the baby's ear. On the seventh day the baby's first hair-cutting *(bercukur)* is performed and the baby is named. If it is later decided that the name doesn't suit the baby or is hampering its development, the name can be changed.

The Malay wedding tradition is quite involved and there are a number of rituals to be observed. The prospective husband despatches an uncle or aunt to his wife-to-be's house to get the family's permission to marry *(hantar tanda)*. Once this is given, the couple are engaged *(bertunang)*, and then the ceremony *(akad nikah)* takes place.

The bride and groom, dressed in traditional kain songket – silk with gold thread – have henna applied to their palms and fingertips *(berinai)* and then, in a ceremony with significant Hindu influence *(bersanding)*, they 'sit in state' on a dais and are surrounded by modern gifts and traditional offerings, such as a bouquet of folded paper flowers in a vase made of bath towels, ringed by quail eggs in satin ribbons. The couple are showered with *bunga rampai* (flower petals and thinly shredded pandanus leaves) and sprinkled with *air mawar* (rose water).

Important ceremonies in family life are accompanied by a feast known as *kenduri*. Guests can number in the hundreds and preparations take days, as many traditional dishes such as *nasi minyak* (spicy rice) and *pulut kuning* (sticky saffron rice) have to be prepared. The cost of these feasts can be a burden on poorer families.

The most important festival is Hari Raya Puasa, the end of the fasting month. New clothes are bought, families are reunited and, of course, there is much kenduri-style feasting when an 'open house' is offered for family, friends and neighbours, and everyone goes visiting.

**Traditional Pastimes** Top spinning *(main gasing)* may not seem like an activity for grown-ups to engage in, but *gasing,* Malaysian tops, are not child's play. A top can weigh up to 7kg and it takes a good deal of strength to whip the 5m cord back and spin the top competitively. The top is hurled on to a polished mud slab, then scooped up with a thin wooden paddle and placed to spin on a small, metal-tipped wooden post.

Top-spinning contests are held in east-coast villages during the slack time of year when the rice is ripening. Contests are usually between teams of fighting tops, where the attackers attempt to dislodge the defenders from a prearranged pattern. There are also contests for length of spin – the record spinning time approaches two hours!

Flying kites is another child's game that takes on adult-size proportions on the east coast. Kite-flying contests include events for greatest height reached, and competitions between fighting kites.

The kites, which can be up to 2.5m wide, are real works of art. There are cat kites, bird kites and, most popular, the *wau bulan* (moon kite). An attachment to the front of the kite makes a humming noise and in favourable conditions a kite may be left flying, humming pleasantly, all night. Kites are popular souvenirs of Malaysia, and a stylised Kelantan kite is the symbol of Malaysia Airlines.

*Sepak raga* is one of the most popular kampung games. The equipment needed to play the game is simplicity itself – a lightweight ball made of strips of rattan. Drawn up in a circle, the opposing teams must keep the ball continuously in the air, using legs, head and shoulders. Points are scored for each time a team member hits the ball.

*Sepak takraw* is a version of the same game where the players hit the ball back and forth over a net, as in volleyball – but again without using hands. It's a popular sport in a number of South-East Asian countries and the Thais are the champions.

Bird-singing competitions are a popular pastime, particularly on the east coast. *Merbuk* and *tekukur* dove birds are suspended in highly decorative cages from 8m-high poles, supposedly because this is the height at which the birds feel most relaxed. Apparently each bird has its own unique song.

It's all taken very seriously and competition is fierce – at a large contest there may be as many as 300 birds, and champion tweeters can be worth anything up to RM50,000! Kota Bharu is one of the best places to see a bird-singing contest as they take place fairly regularly. Larger local and national competitions are also held annually.

## Chinese Customs

The Chinese are born into a very different cultural tradition from that of the Malays. Chinese culture has evolved over 3000 years, and for much of that time it was the centre of Asia – indeed, as far as the Chinese themselves were concerned, the whole world. It's not surprising that the Chinese are proud of such a distinguished past, and most Chinese in Malaysia and Singapore can tell you the village, town or at least the province in China from which their ancestors emigrated.

At the heart of the Chinese sense of cultural continuity is the family. Most Chinese families and family businesses have a small family shrine adorned with photographs of grandparents and usually plaques engraved with the names of ancestors stretching as far back as it is possible to trace them. Even distant ancestors, long removed from the petty troubles of everyday life, take a keen interest in their family's daily tribulations. It is important to pay respect to them by lighting incense and bowing with the hands clasped in prayer *(bai-bai)* at least once a day, and particularly when making decisions that may affect family fortunes.

Chinese families are patrilineal. Only male children are able to continue the family name – and it is the name that is all important in one's connection with one's ancestors. Women traditionally had very low status in the Chinese familial scheme of things. Married off at a young age, girls were considered a drain on family resources. Such attitudes are much less common nowadays.

The theoretical and ethical backbone of Chinese family relationships is found in the teachings of China's most famous sage, Confucius. Confucianism provides a hierarchical structure of respect within the family that extends into society as a whole. It also places great emphasis on scholarship. Most Chinese parents will spare nothing to ensure their children get a good education.

Many Chinese customs are undergoing great changes these days. Marriages, for example, are now rarely arranged by matchmakers or by agreements between families, as they were in the past. An astrologer may be consulted, however, to determine an auspicious date for the wedding.

Funerals remain much more traditional, elaborate affairs (though in Singapore they are generally much lower key than in Malaysia). The body is dressed in best clothes and sealed in the coffin along with a few valuables. The coffin is placed in front of the ancestral altar in the house, and joss-sticks and candles are burnt. Mourning and prayers may go on for three days before the funeral, which is an expensive affair involving professional mourners and musicians who clash cymbals and gongs to drive away the evil spirits. Traditionally, children would mourn the death of a father for three years and black would be worn during this period, but modern life has seen the mourning period greatly reduced. Whatever changes in tradition have occurred, the importance of the grave and its upkeep remains, and most Chinese pay respects to their elders on All Souls' Day.

Chinese New Year is the major festival, and even Chinese who profess no religion will celebrate it with gusto. It is a time for clearing out the old and bringing in the new. The house is given a spring clean and all business affairs and debts are brought up to date before the new year. It is a time for family, friends and feasting, and *ang pow* (red envelopes of money) are given to children. Chap Goh Meh is the last day of the Chinese New Year and is the peak of celebrations.

## Indian Customs

Most Malaysian and Singaporean Indians are Hindus from South India, so the customs and festivals that are important in the south of India, especially Chennai (Madras), are the most popular Hindu festivals celebrated in Malaysia and in Singapore.

Traditionally, the *namakarana* (name-giving ceremony), is held about 10 days after the birth of a baby. An astrologer will be called upon to give an auspicious name, often the name of a god. Boys are very much favoured, as only males can perform certain family rituals and the dowry system in India can mean financial ruin for a family with too many daughters.

The major ceremony in the life of a boy of higher caste (especially for the highest caste, Brahmin), is the initiation involving receiving the sacred threads. The boy is bathed, blessed by priests and showered with rice by guests. Then three strands of thread, representing Brahma, Vishnu and Shiva, are draped around the boy's left shoulder and knotted underneath the right arm, and the boy has officially been initiated into his caste.

Arranged marriages are still common, though the bride and groom have an increasing say in their choice of partner. The day, hour and minute of the wedding are the preserve of the astrologer. The marriage is usually held at the house of the bride's family. The couple are seated on a dais and a sacred flame is placed in the centre of the room. The final ceremony involves the bridegroom placing the *thali* necklace around the bride's neck, and then the couple proceeds around the fire seven times.

Deepavali (Festival of Lights), is the major Indian festival in Malaysia, when homes are decorated with oil lamps to signify the victory of light over darkness. The spectacular Thaipusam is the most exciting festival, when pilgrims perform extraordinary feats at temples across the country (see the boxed text in the 'Places of Worship' special section).

## Dos & Don'ts

As in many Muslim countries, Islam in Malaysia has seen a significant revival over the past 15 years or so. It's wise for visitors to be appropriately discreet in dress and behaviour, particularly on the more-strictly Muslim east coast of the peninsula.

For women, topless bathing is definitely not acceptable, and away from the beaches you should cover as much as possible. Take your cue not from fellow travellers but from Malaysian women. For men, shorts are considered odd attire for adults but they are not offensive. Bare torsos are not acceptable in the villages and towns.

Unfortunately, women may encounter unwanted attention from Malaysian men who consider Western women to be of loose morals. Dressing conservatively will help to alleviate problems. See Women Travellers in the Facts for the Visitor chapter for details.

As in most Asian countries, it is very impolite to use the left hand to give or receive something, as the left hand is used for washing after going to the toilet. Pointing or beckoning with the forefinger is considered rude, and Malaysians will motion towards something with the thumb atop a loose fist; hailing someone is done by waving the fingers downwards from an open hand. Shoes must be removed before entering a mosque and are also usually removed before entering someone's house. See the 'Places of Worship' special section for more information on the etiquette of entering religious buildings.

For advice on correct etiquette in a Dayak longhouse, see the 'Longhouse Visits' boxed text in the Sarawak chapter.

## RELIGION

The variety of religions found in Malaysia is a direct reflection of the diversity of races living there. Although Islam is the state religion of Malaysia, freedom of religion is guaranteed. Hinduism has been practised in Malaysia for at least 1500 years; Islam became dominant in the mid-14th century but the arrival of Indian contract labourers in the 20th century brought an increase in the followers of Hinduism.

The Malays are almost all Muslims. The Chinese embrace an eclectic brew of Taoism, Buddhism and ancestor worship, though some are Christians. The majority of the region's Indian population come from South India and are mainly Hindu, though some are Muslims or Sikhs.

Although Christianity has made no great inroads into Peninsular Malaysia it has had a much greater impact upon Malaysian Borneo, where many of the indigenous people have converted to Christianity, although others still follow their animist traditions.

## Islam

In the early 7th century in Mecca, Mohammed received the word of Allah (God) and called on the people to turn away from pagan worship and submit to the one true God. His teachings appealed to the poorer levels of society and angered the wealthy merchant class. By AD 622 life had become sufficiently unpleasant to force Mohammed and his followers to migrate to Medina, an oasis town some 300km to the north. This migration – the *hijrah* – marks the beginning of the Islamic calendar, year 1 AH, or AD 622. By AD 630 Mohammed had gained a large enough following to return and take Mecca.

With boundless zeal the followers of Mohammed spread the word, using force where necessary, and by 644 the Islamic state covered Syria, Persia, Mesopotamia, Egypt and North Africa; in following decades its influence would extend from the Atlantic to the Indian Ocean.

Islam is the Arabic word for submission, and it is the duty of all Muslims to submit themselves to Allah. This profession of faith (the *Shahada*) is the first of the Five Pillars of Islam, the five tenets in the Quran which guide Muslims in their daily life:

**Shahada** 'There is no God but Allah and Mohammed is his prophet.' This profession of faith is the fundamental tenet of Islam. It is to Islam what the Lord's Prayer is to Christianity, and it is often quoted (eg, to greet the newly born and to farewell the dead).

**Salah** The call to prayer. Five times a day – at dawn, noon, mid-afternoon, sunset and nightfall – Muslims must face Mecca and recite the prescribed prayer. *Kiblat*, the Malay word for the direction of Mecca, accompanies an arrow in many hotel rooms.

**Zakat** This was originally the act of giving alms to the poor and needy. The amount given was fixed at 5% of one's income. It has been

MALAYSIA

developed by some modern states into a land tax that goes to help the poor.

**Ramadan** This is the ninth month of the Muslim calendar, when all Muslims must abstain from eating, drinking, smoking and sex from dawn to dusk. It commemorates the month when Mohammed had the Quran revealed to him; the purpose of the physical deprivation is to strengthen the will and forfeit the body to the spirit.

**Hajj** The pilgrimage to Mecca, the holiest place in Islam. It is the duty of every Muslim who is fit and can afford it to make the pilgrimage at least once in their life. On the pilgrimage, the pilgrim *(haji)* wears two plain white sheets and walks around the *kabbah*, the black stone in the centre of the mosque, seven times. Other ceremonies, such as sacrificing an animal and shaving the pilgrim's head, also take place.

According to Muslim belief, Allah is the same as the God worshipped by Christians and Jews. Adam, Abraham, Noah, Moses, David, Jacob, Joseph, Job and Jesus are all recognised as prophets by Islam. Jesus is not, however, recognised as the son of God. According to Islam, all these prophets partly received the word of God but only Mohammed received the complete revelation.

In its early days Islam suffered a major schism that divided the faith into two streams: the Sunnis (or Sunnites) and the Shi'ites. The Prophet's son-in-law, Ali, became the fourth caliph following the murder of Mohammed's third successor, and he in turn was assassinated in 661 by the governor of Syria, who set himself up as caliph. The Sunnis, who comprise the majority of Muslims today, are followers of the succession from this caliph, while the Shi'ites follow the descendants of Ali. The Shi'ites live mostly in Iran, Iraq, Syria, India and Yemen. The Malaysian government actively discourages Shi'ite sects, which it regards as extremist.

**Islam in Malaysia** Islam came to Malaysia with the Indian traders from South India and was not of the more-orthodox Islamic tradition of Arabia. It was adopted peacefully by the coastal trading ports of Malaysia and Indonesia, absorbing rather than conquering existing beliefs.

Islam was established in northern Sumatra by the end of the 13th century, but did not become dominant until the third ruler of Melaka adopted it in the mid-14th century. Melaka's political dominance in the region saw the religion spread throughout Malaysia and Indonesia. By the time the Portuguese arrived in the 16th century, Islam was firmly established and converting the people to Christianity was difficult.

Islamic sultanates replaced Hindu kingdoms, though the Hindu concept of kings remained. The traditions of adat continued, but Islamic law dominated, while the caste system, never as entrenched as in India, had no place in the more egalitarian Islamic society.

Women had great influence in pre-Islamic Malay society; there were women leaders in Malay societies, and the descendants of the Sumatran Minangkabau in Negeri Sembilan still have a matriarchal society. The arrival of Islam weakened the position of women in Malaysia. Nonetheless, women were not cloistered or forced to wear full purdah as in the Middle East, and Malay women today still enjoy more freedom than their counterparts in many other Muslim societies.

Malay ceremonies and beliefs still exhibit pre-Islamic traditions, but most Malays are ardent Muslims and to suggest otherwise to a Malay would cause great offence. With the rise of Islamic fundamentalism, the calls to introduce Islamic law and purify the practices of Islam have increased, but while the federal government of Malaysia is keen to espouse Muslim ideals, it is wary of religious extremism. Syariah, Islamic law, is the preserve of state governments, as is the establishment of Muslim courts of law, which since 1988 cannot be overruled by secular courts.

Only Muslims are tried in Islamic courts. Kelantan state is the country's hotbed of Islamic fervour, and the state government is keen to apply syariah to all of its citizens, as it has demonstrated by outlawing alcohol in restaurants and nightclubs and banning snooker halls. In the same spirit, the Kelantan state government has also renamed the Beach of Passionate Love (Pantai Cinta Berahi) Moonlight Beach (Pantai Cahaya Bulan).

*(Continued on page 57)*

Mosque in Semporna, Sabah

Christ Church, Melaka

Buddhist temple, Penang

Amoy St temple, Singapore

Steps to the Batu Caves main temple, north of Kuala Lumpur.

# PLACES OF WORSHIP

Places of worship in Malaysia, Singapore and Brunei are as diverse as the populations in those countries. While mosques might be the most obvious, in terms of both sight and sound, you'll also find plenty of Chinese and Hindu temples scattered around, particularly in Peninsular Malaysia and Singapore. There are even a handful of Sikh temples, including Sri Guru Singh Sabha in Singapore.

Visitors are welcome at most places of worship, but it's important to follow certain etiquette to avoid causing offence. This section gives guidelines for behaviour and lists some of the most impressive examples of religious architecture in the region.

## MOSQUES

Along with much of the region's public architecture, many older mosques, which have one minaret, follow Indian rather than Middle Eastern style. Some newer mosques, however, are modern showpieces of extraordinary design.

### Design & Function

The community gathers for prayer on Friday (Islam's holy day) at the *masjid jamek* (main mosque). Smaller, local mosques are used for prayer on other days of the week.

Despite their sometimes astounding beauty and the great variety of designs, mosques are essentially simple buildings that provide a large space for communal prayer. Many mosques have domes, which are the best architectural devices for enclosing large spaces that don't have columns. Larger mosques may have a school attached.

**Title Page:** Kek Lok Si Temple, Penang (Photograph by Richard I'Anson).

**Right:** The Malabar Muslim Jama-Ath Mosque is on the corner of Jalan Sultan and Victoria St, Singapore.

JENNY BOWMAN

## Etiquette for Visitors

Always remove your shoes before entering a mosque and make sure you dress appropriately. Men and women must cover their arms, legs and shoulders; women should cover their heads. A few larger mosques have robes for visitors who are not appropriately dressed. Some mosques don't admit women visitors and prayer times are often off-limits for sightseers. When inside do not walk in front of any praying person and remember, non-Muslims must not touch the Quran.

## Mosques to See

One of the oldest surviving mosques in Kuala Lumpur is the pictur-esque Masjid Jamek overlooking Merdeka Square. In contrast, Kuala

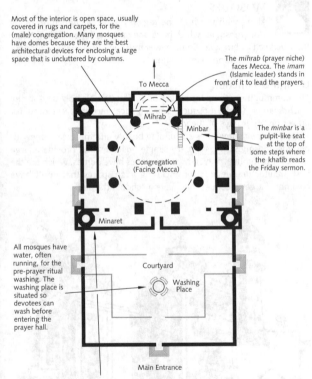

Most of the interior is open space, usually covered in rugs and carpets, for the (male) congregation. Many mosques have domes because they are the best architectural devices for enclosing a large space that is uncluttered by columns.

The *mihrab* (prayer niche) faces Mecca. The *imam* (Islamic leader) stands in front of it to lead the prayers.

To Mecca

Mihrab

Minbar

The *minbar* is a pulpit-like seat at the top of some steps where the khatib reads the Friday sermon.

Congregation (Facing Mecca)

Minaret

All mosques have water, often running, for the pre-prayer ritual washing. The washing place is situated so devotees can wash before entering the prayer hall.

Courtyard

Washing Place

Main Entrance

Most mosques have a minaret, usually a tower, which the *muezzin* (the official of the mosque) climbs five times a day to call the faithful to prayer. Increasingly, the muezzin's call is tape-recorded and booms out over loudspeakers. Most older Malaysian mosques are based on Indian designs, so there is usually one minaret rather than several.

Lumpur's enormous Masjid Negara (National Mosque) is an example of modern design. Singapore's large Sultan Mosque is the focus for its Muslim community, and Brunei's Omar Ali Saifuddin Mosque is a stunning modern structure.

## HINDU TEMPLES

Most of the region's Hindus originally came from South India, so Hindu temples in Malaysia and Singapore adopt design elements from that area.

### Design & Function

For Hindus, the square is the perfect shape (a circle isn't perfect because it implies motion), so temples are always based on a square

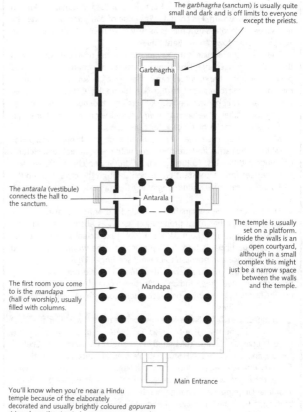

The *garbhagrha* (sanctum) is usually quite small and dark and is off limits to everyone except the priests.

Garbhagrha

The *antarala* (vestibule) connects the hall to the sanctum.

Antarala

The temple is usually set on a platform. Inside the walls is an open courtyard, although in a small complex this might just be a narrow space between the walls and the temple.

The first room you come to is the *mandapa* (hall of worship), usually filled with columns.

Mandapa

Main Entrance

You'll know when you're near a Hindu temple because of the elaborately decorated and usually brightly coloured *gopuram* rising above the street. A gopuram surmounts the gateway(s) in the walls surrounding the temple.

ground-plan. Extremely complex rules based on numerology, astronomy, astrology and religious law govern the location, design and construction of each temple. These are so complicated and so important that it's customary for each temple to harbour its own set of calculations as though they were religious texts.

Each temple is dedicated to a particular god in the vast Hindu pantheon. The temple is used exclusively for religious rites. However, because Hinduism has so many rites and festivals, there's always something happening and the temple is a defacto community centre.

## Thaipusam

Each year in the Hindu month of Thai (January/February), when the constellation of Pusam is in its ascendancy, up to a million devotees and onlookers flock to the Batu Caves, in KL, to honour Lord Muruga, also known as Lord Subramaniam. His chariot takes pride of place and is attended by thousands of devotees as it makes its way from the Sri Mahamariamman Temple in Chinatown to the Batu Caves.

The greatest spectacle is the *kavadi* carriers, the devotees who subject themselves to seemingly masochistic acts as fulfilment for answered prayers. Many of the devotees carry offerings of milk in *paal kudam*, or milk pots, often connected to the skin by hooks. Others pierce their tongues and cheeks with hooks, skewers and tridents. Couples whose prayers for children have been answered carry their babies on their shoulders in saffron cradles made of sugar-cane stalks.

Most spectacular are the *vel kavadi*, great cages of spikes that pierce the skin of the carrier and are decorated with peacock feathers, pictures of deities and flowers. To the beating of drums and chants of 'Vel, Vel' the devotees form a constant procession through the caves and up the 272 steps to the main shrine, beginning their arduous journey as early as 3 am.

The festival is the culmination of around a month of prayer, a vegetarian diet and other ritual preparations, such as abstinence from sex, or sleeping on a hard floor. While it looks excruciating, a trance-like state stops participants from feeling pain; later the wounds are treated with lemon juice and holy ash to prevent scarring. Like firewalking, only the truly faithful should attempt the ritual. It is said that insufficiently prepared devotees keep Indian doctors especially busy over the Thaipusam festival period with skin lacerations, or by collapsing after the strenuous activities.

Originating in Tamil Nadu and now banned in India, this is the most spectacular Hindu festival in Malaysia, celebrated with the greatest gusto in Kuala Lumpur. It is also celebrated in Penang at the Nattukotai Chettiar Temple and the Waterfall Hilltop Temple, and in Johor Bahru at the Sri Thandayuthabani Temple. Ipoh attracts a large number of devotees, who follow the procession from the Sri Mariamar Temple in Buntong to the Sri Subramaniar Temple in Gunung Cheroh. In Singapore, Hindus march in a procession from the Sri Srinivasa Perumal Temple on Serangoon Rd to the Chettiar Hindu Temple.

## Etiquette for Visitors

Dress conservatively, remove your shoes before entering and do not attempt to enter the sanctum.

## Hindu Temples to See

The Sri Mahamariamman Temple in Kuala Lumpur dates from 1873 and is large and ornate. Two Sri Mariamman temples, one in Singapore and the other in Georgetown on Pulau Penang, are also elaborately sculpted and painted.

## CHINESE TEMPLES

Taoism, Buddhism and Confucianism have blended in Chinese religion, and although many temples are theoretically Buddhist or Taoist it takes an extremely sharp eye to tell the difference. You'll often find statues of Buddha next to statues of Taoist deities. You may also see a statue of Confucius, but a temple devoted entirely to Confucius will be quieter and less colourful than other Chinese temples.

## Design & Function

An elaborate 'Chinese-style' roof distinguishes most Chinese temples. Some temples are built to a multistorey pagoda design, but many are simpler single-storey buildings.

A screen often separates the entrance from the main hall. The hall is a riot of carved and gilded wood, bright cloth and various antiquities such as ceremonial chairs and swords. The lighting of joss sticks (incense) accompanies all prayer. For good fortune, people burn prayers written on paper, and to appease evil spirits they burn 'ghost money'. Food is offered to ghosts – luckily, they don't eat much, and the food is shared later among the living.

There are priests, but religious life is an individual's responsibility. There are no set times for prayers and no communal services except for funerals, but the community gathers to celebrate popular holidays. In Malaysia and Singapore, many Chinese participate in Buddhist and Taoist festivals, and visit a temple on special days such as Wesak, a triple holy-day celebrating the Buddha's birth, death and enlightenment (usually in May). Noise, colour and a lot of burning incense (sometimes emanating from incense sticks bigger than baseball bats) are features of religious holidays. At other times, people pray for success and the basics of life.

## Etiquette for Visitors

It is customary to remove your shoes before entering a temple, although this may not be mandatory at some temples. Because people are constantly coming and going, often praying for deceased relatives, you should be careful not treat temples as the superb art galleries they often appear to be. Loud talking, smoking and taking photographs with a flash are definitely not appreciated.

## Chinese Temples to See

There are fascinating Chinese temples throughout the region. In Kuala Lumpur you'll find many Chinese temples, including the ornate Chan See Shu Yuen Temple. The Kuan Yin Teng Temple in Georgetown in Penang is especially popular among devotees, as are Singapore's Kuan Yin and Siong Lim Temples. Thian Hock Keng Temple, also known as the Temple of Heavenly Happiness, was built in 1841 and is Singapore's oldest and most colourful Chinese place of worship.

In the north of Peninsular Malaysia there are some Buddhist temples (such as Wat Chayamangkalaram in Penang) that are Thai-style Theravada Buddhist temples. The Temple of 1000 Lights in Singapore is a Thai-style temple, but features technicolour Chinese decorations.

There is sometimes a separate room where the funerary tablets (small blocks of wood inscribed with characters) of deceased members of the community are displayed. Offerings are left for the spirits. The local community's 'dragon' may be stored in the temple.

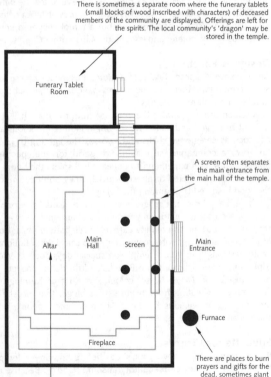

Funerary Tablet Room

A screen often separates the main entrance from the main hall of the temple.

Altar

Main Hall

Screen

Main Entrance

Furnace

Fireplace

There are places to burn prayers and gifts for the dead, sometimes giant iron 'furnaces' standing outside the temple.

At the back of the hall is a large and elaborately decorated altar, usually containing an image of the deity (or person) to whom the temple is dedicated. In front of the altar is some sort of bench or table where devotees light their incense and pray.

## SIKH TEMPLES

Sikhism doesn't recognise caste or class, so everyone is involved in ceremonies. As communal meals are a feature of temple activities, every temple has a large and colourful kitchen.

### Design & Function

A Sikh temple is called a *gurdwara*. Outside, a flagpole, called a *nishan sahib,* flies a triangular flag with the Sikh insignia. There are no special requirements for the buildings' design, but most use some elements from Punjabi gurdwaras. Sikhs worship only one god and are opposed to idol worship. You'll probably see pictures of the Gurus (the spiritual leaders who founded Sikhism), especially the first, fifth and 10th (last)

Sikhism differs from Hinduism in that there are no caste-related taboos in the preparation and cooking of food. This is an important community ritual, and every *gurdwara* (Sikh temple) has a large and cheerful kitchen.

Food prepared in the temple is eaten as a communal meal in the dining hall.

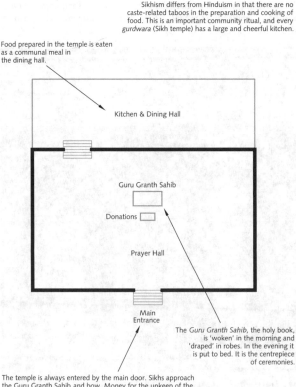

Kitchen & Dining Hall

Guru Granth Sahib

Donations

Prayer Hall

Main Entrance

The *Guru Granth Sahib*, the holy book, is 'woken' in the morning and 'draped' in robes. In the evening it is put to bed. It is the centrepiece of ceremonies.

The temple is always entered by the main door. Sikhs approach the Guru Granth Sahib and bow. Money for the upkeep of the temple is usually placed in a box in front of the holy book.

Gurus. The wisdom of the Gurus is contained in the *Guru Granth Sahib*, a book written by Arjun, the fifth Guru, in the early 17th century. It has become an object of veneration and is regarded as the 'living' Guru. This holy book, the centrepiece of ceremonies, is 'woken' in the morning and 'draped' in robes. In the evening it is put to bed.

## Etiquette for Visitors

Sikhism is an egalitarian religion and everyone is welcome to enter the temple. However, you should remove your shoes and cover your head.

## Sikh Temples to See

Sikh temples in this region are generally quite modest buildings, such as the Sri Guru Nanak Sat Sangh Sabha on Wilkinson St in Singapore. Unlike almost all other places of worship, there has been little attempt to reproduce the architectural styles of Sikhism's birthplace. However, the increasing wealth of the Sikh community has seen some impressive new temples built recently, such as the Gurdwara Sahib Yishun, also in Singapore.

RICHARD I'ANSON

**Left:** Detail from the Sri Krishnan Temple, Singapore

*(Continued from page 48)*

The Quran is the main source of religious law for Malays, and though few are proficient in Arabic, all Malay children aresent to learn to read the Quran. Malaysia has an annual Quran-reading competition, and passages are read in Arabic at many Malay ceremonies. However, the main language of religious instruction is Jawi, the Malay language written in the Arabic script. Kitab Jawi (Jawi books written by Malay religious scholars) are widely read in the mosques and pondok (religious schools). For centuries these books have been the main source of Islamic thought for Malays, and while they express the same beliefs and tenets held by Muslims worldwide, they do so with a Malay perspective.

There is no Malaysia-wide head of Islam. The sultans of the various states are the Islamic heads of their respective states, while the yang di-pertuan agong is head of Islam in his own state as well as in Melaka, Penang, Sabah and Sarawak.

## Chinese Religion

The Chinese religion is a mix of Taoism, Confucianism and Buddhism. Taoism combines with animistic beliefs to teach people to maintain harmony with the universe. Confucianism takes care of the political and moral aspects of life, while Buddhism takes care of the afterlife. But to say that the Chinese have three religions is too simple a view of their traditional religious life. At the first level Chinese religion is animistic, with a belief in the innate vital energy in rocks, trees, rivers and springs. At the second level people from the distant past, both real and mythological, are worshipped as gods. Overlaid on this are popular Taoist, Mahayana Buddhist and Confucian beliefs.

On a day-to-day level the Chinese are much less concerned with the high-minded philosophies and asceticism of Buddha, Confucius or Lao Zi than they are with the pursuit of worldly success, the appeasement of the dead and the spirits, and the seeking of knowledge about the future. Chinese religion incorporates elements of what Westerners might call 'superstition' – if you want your fortune told, for instance, you go to a temple. The other thing to remember is that Chinese religion is polytheistic. Apart from Buddha, Lao Zi and Confucius there are many divinities, such as house gods and gods and goddesses for particular professions.

The most popular gods and local deities, or *shen*, are Kuan Yin, the goddess of mercy, and Toh Peh Kong, a local deity representing the spirit of the pioneers and found only outside China. Kuan Ti, the god of war, is also very popular and is regarded as the god of wealth. Sam Po Shan, the spirit of the Chinese Admiral Cheng Ho, who visited Melaka in the 15th century, is worshipped as the patron saint of travellers.

Joss sticks and fruit are offered at temples but most homes also have their own altars.

Integral parts of Chinese religion are death, the afterlife and ancestor worship. At least as far back as China's Shang Dynasty, funerals were lavish ceremonies involving the interment of horses, carriages, wives and slaves. The more important the person, the greater their requirements for the next world, and the more possessions and people were buried with them. The deceased had to be kept happy because people's powers to inflict punishments or to grant favours greatly increased after their death. Even today, a traditional Chinese funeral can be a lavish event (see Chinese Customs under Society & Conduct earlier).

While ancestor worship plays an important role, it is not as extensive as in China. Malaysian Chinese generally only honour the ancestors of two or three generations, that is, going as far back as their immigrant forefathers.

The most important word in the Chinese popular religious vocabulary is *joss* (luck), and the Chinese are too astute not to utilise it. Gods have to be appeased, bad spirits blown away and sleeping dragons soothed to keep joss on one's side. Feng shui (literally, windwater) is the Chinese technique of judging or manipulating the environment. Feng shui uses unseen currents that swirl around the surface of the earth and are caused by dragons that sleep beneath the ground.

If you want to build a house, high-rise hotel or find a suitable site for a grave, then you call in a feng shui expert; the wrath of a dragon who wakes to find a house on his tail can easily be imagined!

## Hinduism

On first appearances, Hinduism is a complex religion. Its basic premise is simple enough, though: we all go through a series of rebirths and reincarnations that eventually lead to *moksha*, the spiritual salvation which frees one from the cycle of rebirths. With each rebirth you can move closer to or farther from eventual moksha; the deciding factor is your karma, which is literally a law of cause and effect. Bad actions during your life result in bad karma, which leads to lower reincarnation. Conversely, if your deeds and actions have been good you will reincarnate on a higher level and be a step closer to eventual freedom from rebirth. *Dharma*, or the natural law, defines the total social, ethical and spiritual harmony of your life.

Hinduism has three basic practices: *puja*, or worship; the cremation of the dead; and the rules and regulations of the caste system. Although still very strong in India, the caste system was never significant in Malaysia, mainly because the labourers brought here from India were mostly from the lower classes.

Westerners often have trouble understanding Hinduism, principally because of its vast pantheon of gods. You can look upon all these different gods simply as pictorial representations of the many attributes of a god. The one omnipresent god usually has three physical representations: Brahma, the creator; Vishnu, the preserver; and Shiva, the destroyer or reproducer. All three gods are usually shown with four arms, but Brahma has the added advantage of four heads to represent his all-seeing presence. The four Veda, the books of 'divine knowledge' which are the foundation of Hindu philosophy, are believed to have emanated from his mouths.

Hinduism is not a proselytising religion, since you cannot be converted. You're either born a Hindu or you are not – you can never become one.

Hinduism in Malaysia dates back at least 1500 years and there are Hindu influences in cultural traditions, such as the wayang kulit (see Arts earlier) and the wedding ceremony (see Society & Conduct earlier). However, it is only in the last 100 or so years, following the influx of Indian contract labourers and settlers, that it has again become widely practised.

## Religions of Indigenous Peoples

The religions of indigenous peoples of Malaysia, both on the peninsula and on the island of Borneo, are as diverse as the peoples themselves. Despite their differences, they can generally be grouped together as animism. While animism does not have a rigid system of tenets or codified beliefs, it can be said of animist peoples that they perceive natural phenomena to be animated by various spirits or deities, and a complex system of practices are used to propitiate these spirits.

Ancestor worship is also a common feature of animist societies and departed souls are often considered to be intermediaries between this world and the next. Some examples of elaborate burial rituals can still be found in some parts of Sarawak in Malaysian Borneo, where the remains of monolithic burial markers and funerary objects still dot the jungle around Kelabit longhouses. However, most of these are no longer maintained and they're being rapidly swallowed up by the fast-growing jungle.

The religions of the indigenous peoples of Malaysia are disappearing as fast as the rainforest. A major cause of the decline of these religions is evangelical Christianity, which is being spread through large areas of Sabah and Sarawak by competing denominations of the Christian faith. Some of the peoples of Borneo have accepted the Muslim faith, and scandals have erupted when cash bonuses were offered for those willing to convert to Islam.

However, it is clear that even without the influence of proselytising world religions, the animist religions of Malaysia would slowly disappear, as more and more indigenous peoples abandon their ancient ways and join modern technological society.

## LANGUAGE

The official language of the region is Bahasa Malaysia, an Austronesian language also known as Bahasa Melayu (language of the Malays) or simply Malay. English is widely understood throughout Malaysia and, although it isn't the official language, it's often the only language various ethnic groups have in common, especially among the middle classes. When a Tamil wants to speak to a Chinese or a Chinese to a Malay, it's likely they'll speak English.

Other languages of the region include the Chinese dialects like Cantonese, Hakka and Hokkien. The majority of the region's Indians speak Tamil, although there are also groups who speak Malayalam, Hindi or other Indian languages. Many different dialects are spoken by the Dayak peoples of Sabah and Sarawak in Malaysian Borneo (see the Batang Rejang section in the Sarawak chapter for Iban words and phrases).

One peculiarity of written Bahasa Malaysia is its endlessly evolving spelling. On Peninsular Malaysia, for example, you will find the word for 'new' spelled at least three different ways: *bharu* (as in Kota Bharu), *bahru* (as in Johor Bahru) and *baharu* (as in Wakaf Baharu). For this reason, if you see a word spelled slightly differently from the way it appears in this book, you can usually assume that it refers to the same thing.

For a guide to Malay and a list of useful words and phrases, see the Language chapter at the back of this book. For a more comprehensive guide to the language get a copy of Lonely Planet's *Malay phrasebook*.

# Facts for the Visitor

## SUGGESTED ITINERARIES

Malaysia is easily divided into Peninsular Malaysia and the Borneo states of Sabah and Sarawak. To get a good look at both halves of Malaysia will take well over a month, but each half of the country can be covered separately in a few weeks.

Travel around Peninsular Malaysia is easy, so you can see a lot in a relatively short time without being hampered or exhausted by transport connections. Travel in Sarawak and Sabah is more time-consuming and requires more planning but can be much more rewarding in terms of exotic vistas and off-the-beaten-track destinations.

Your own itinerary depends very much on personal interests and budget. We've outlined the major routes and main destinations to help in planning, but you'll find many more places of interest in this book.

### Peninsular Malaysia

Travel on the peninsula is often divided into west and east coasts, and you can do a tour down one side and up the other for an overall look. The mountainous jungle area of the centre, containing Taman Negara National Park, is usually included in an east-coast itinerary but many visit it as a diversion from the west coast.

If time is limited to a week or two, it is best to concentrate on just one coast. The west coast has the main historical and cultural attractions, while the east coast is popular mainly for beaches and islands. In three or four weeks you can sample both sides, and in two months you can explore the whole peninsula in depth.

The well-worn tourist route, starting from Singapore, is up the west coast via Melaka, Kuala Lumpur (KL) and the Cameron Highlands to Penang. Then over to Kota Bharu and down the east coast via Kuala Terengganu and Kuantan, stopping at the beach resorts of the Pulau Perhentian (Perhentian Islands), Pulau Tioman and others in between. Then it's back to KL or Singapore, with perhaps a stop at Taman Negara on the way.

The main travel routes for each coast follow.

**West Coast** The west coast is the dominant half of the peninsula, containing the major cities and industries of Malaysia. Historically it is the most interesting and has the greatest colonial influence. Culturally the west coast is also the more diverse, and the cities are a vibrant Chinese-Malay-Indian mix. The west coast is more modern than the east, both in terms of economic development and people's attitudes.

The main highlights of the west coast, included in almost everyone's itinerary, are KL, Penang and historic Melaka, and the hill station and tea plantations of the Cameron Highlands. The west also has a couple of decent beach resorts, and other hill stations and interesting cities.

Melaka–KL–Cameron–Highland–Penang is possible in a week but is rushed, unless you drop one destination or just transit through KL. Two weeks is more comfortable, allowing time for a few more destinations, such as the islands and beaches of Pulau Pangkor and Langkawi or the hill station of Bukit Fraser (Fraser's Hill). If you want to see the back roads, you can take indirect routes along this well-beaten trail. From KL start by following the Klang Valley to Kuala Selangor, a rural town with natural attractions, then continue by local bus to Pulau Pangkor. Between the Cameron Highlands and Penang, you can detour to the cave temples at Ipoh, the old royal town of Kuala Kangsar and the colonial town of Taiping on your way up or down the peninsula.

**East Coast** The less-developed states of Kelantan, Terengganu and Pahang are a Malay stronghold, with much less Chinese and Indian influence. The cities are bustling but small, and it is still primarily a rural area. Although the east coast provides insight into Malay culture, the main attractions are the beach resorts along the coast.

Inland in Pahang state is Taman Negara National Park, Malaysia's most-visited and extensive area of protected jungle.

In a week you can take in a couple of beaches, though with limited time many people prefer to choose just one and take it easy. Pulau Tioman – off Johor state, the southern gateway to Peninsular Malaysia – is a popular destination if coming from KL or Singapore. From Thailand, you can head to Kota Bharu for a day or two and then go to Pulau Perhentian. In two weeks you can go right along the coast, though three weeks or more is preferable if you want to take in all the beaches and relax.

Taman Negara requires at least four or five days, and from KL or Kuantan getting in and out of the park will take the best part of a day's travel in each direction, usually with an overnight stop in Jerantut. To do one of the longer walks, count on at least a week.

## Malaysian Borneo

**Sarawak** Sarawak is one of the least-visited parts of Malaysia, and this is a pity. Longhouse visits are popular but expensive; Kuching is an engaging city and Sarawak has some of Malaysia's best national parks.

In a week you can see Kuching's fine museums and sample the nightlife, make day trips to Bako and Kubah National Parks, and drop by the Sarawak Cultural Village; then head off for a couple of days on a longhouse tour up a nearby river, or stay longer at Bako. If a rafflesia (the world's largest flower) is in bloom, take a jaunt to Gunung (Mt) Gading National Park.

An upriver trip from Sibu to Kapit or Belaga on the Batang (River) Rejang will take at least four days (you could fly back from Belaga), but the longhouse visits are special around here. The Niah Caves can be seen in a day but you'll need two days to include travel from Sibu to Miri before and after your visit. Allow a couple of days at Mulu if caves are your thing, and five days to a week if you go trekking in the park. A trip to the Kelabit Highlands definitely warrants the three to five days needed to make it worthwhile.

A month is probably needed to cover Sarawak's main attractions, though three weeks will do in a pinch.

**Sabah** Sabah's main attractions are Kinabalu National Park and the Sungai (River) Kinabatangan; the orang-utans at Sepilok are a delight, and divers will find joy on the islands off Semporna. Unless you're driving, getting around takes a bit longer in Sabah – connections between towns can require careful timing.

If you have a week you can spend a day or two on the islands of Tunku Abdul Rahman National Park near Kota Kinabalu, then head up Mt Kinabalu – a climb normally done over two days. Spend a day relaxing afterwards at Poring Hot Springs; If you have time left, head down to Sepilok just outside Sandakan for an overnight stay.

With two weeks you can also visit the Tambunan Rafflesia Reserve and see eastern Sabah's main sights, including the Gomantong Caves, and spend a few days up the Kinabatangan. Divers will find five-day trips to be a common package for Pulau Mabul, Sipadan and the rest, though three-day trips are also available.

Additional possibilities include a two-day trip to Turtle Islands National Park, plus an excursion to Tenom and its nearby Orchid Centre; the Sunday morning market at Kota Belud is also popular. If you have the cash, three days in the Danum Valley is paradise. In three weeks you can easily cover the state's highlights, including some diving or snorkelling; two weeks is enough if you stay on dry land.

## PLANNING
## When to Go

Rain occurs fairly evenly throughout the year in Malaysia and the differences between the main October-to-April rainy season and the rest of the year are not that marked, so travel is possible year-round. The exception is the east coast of the peninsula, which receives heavy rain from November to mid-February. During these months many east-coast resorts close and boat services dwindle or stop altogether.

Travel along the west coast is not affected. The states of Sabah and Sarawak receive high rainfall throughout the year, but it is heaviest from October to March.

With such a wide ethnic diversity, celebrations of one kind or another are held throughout the year. Public holidays in Malaysia are not a good time to travel (see Public Holidays & Special Events later in this chapter). Malaysians like to get away at these times, so transport is crowded and hotel prices rise in the resorts. The peak times are Chinese New Year, Hari Raya and Christmas. If you're in the country at these times, it's best to wait until the holiday rush is over. The main beach- and hill-resorts also get crowded on weekends but are often deserted during the week.

The Muslim fasting month of Ramadan is generally not a problem for travel. Some services may be cut back, especially in the east-coast states of Kelantan and Terengganu, but transport, hotels, restaurants and many businesses function as normal.

## Maps

The most useful overall map for Peninsular Malaysia is the 1:650,000 *West Malaysia* map produced by Nelles Verlag. It has most of the major and minor roads and shows some topographical features. Nelles also produces *Malaysia,* a decent map that shows both Peninsular Malaysia and Malaysian Borneo. Periplus produces an excellent series of Malaysia city and state maps, including *Johor; Kuala Lumpur; Melaka; Penang; Sabah;* and *Sarawak.*

It may be difficult to find some of these maps outside of KL (see Bookshops in the Kuala Lumpur chapter) – you may even have difficulty finding them in KL. In fact, the best place to buy maps of Malaysia is in Singapore or in your home country.

It's worth picking up Tourism Malaysia's *The Map of Malaysia,* which has useful distance charts, facts about the country and inset maps of many major cities.

If you're intent on getting accurate maps of rural areas, you'll have to visit the National Survey & Mapping Department (Ibu Pejabat Ukur Dan Pemetaan Malaysia;

☎ 03-296 2628), Jalan Semarak, 50578, Kuala Lumpur. You'll have to apply for permission to purchase maps here and you may need a Malaysian national to vouch for you.

## What to Bring

Don't worry if you've forgotten to pack a few items – for the most part, you should have no trouble finding your favourite toothpaste or even common medicines in Malaysia. But as is the case anywhere, you will only find a good selection of products in the bigger cities, and the peninsula is a little ahead of Malaysian Borneo in terms of availability of goods.

Print film is usually not a problem, but you may want to bring slide film from home, as the selection in Malaysia is not very good and storage techniques are often inadequate. If it's camera equipment you want, again, it's best to bring what you need, as the selection in even the biggest cities is fairly limited. Quality video-film is available in major centres but hard to find in other places.

Clothes are readily available and very reasonably priced. The best advice is to bring as little with you as possible; travelling light is the only way to go (see also the 'Considerations for Jungle Trekking' boxed text later in this chapter). In any case, you don't need too much to start with, as the weather is perpetually of the short-sleeve variety. However, if you're planning to head up to the hill stations, you may appreciate a sweater or light jacket in the evenings. More importantly, if you're planning to climb Mt Kinabalu, it is essential to bring some warm and waterproof outerwear, a pair of gloves and a hat. A headlamp will also come in handy and is useful for exploring caves like those found in Gunung Mulu National Park.

Sensible accessories include sunglasses, a hat, a water bottle/canteen, a pocket knife, a day pack, a basic first-aid kit and a money belt or pouch.

If you're going to be staying primarily in budget accommodation, you should consider bringing an insect net as many of the cheaper places do not have netting on the windows.

## RESPONSIBLE TOURISM

Travel in Malaysia is not fraught with the sorts of issues that come into play when visiting more-remote regions of Asia. Even in Malaysian Borneo, it is unlikely that your presence will have a destabilising effect on indigenous peoples. Those peoples who might be adversely affected by contact with outsiders are usually inaccessible to foreign tourists. The environment is another matter, however, and you should take sensible precautions to minimise your impact when venturing into wilderness areas. Following are some basic guidelines:

- Produce as little garbage as possible by using recyclable containers. If your garbage won't be disposed of properly, carry it out yourself.
- If possible, use environmentally friendly methods of transportation or walk from place to place.
- Stick to designated trails and camping spots.
- Avoid polluting water sources – use established toilets, or go at least 50m from rivers or lakes.
- Support environmentally friendly tour operators and locally owned businesses, and buy locally produced goods.
- Never buy products made from endangered species.

See Considerations for Responsible Diving in the 'Diving & Snorkelling' special section for information on responsible marine practices.

## TOURIST OFFICES

Malaysia's national tourist body, Tourism Malaysia, has an efficient network of overseas offices, which are useful for pre-departure planning. Unfortunately, its domestic offices are less helpful and are often unable to give specific information about destinations and transportation. Nonetheless, they do stock some decent brochures as well as the excellent *The Map of Malaysia*. You can visit its Web site at www.tourism.gov.my or send email to ℮ tourism@tourism.gov.my.

Within Malaysia there are also a number of state tourist-promotion organisations, such as the Penang Tourist Association, which often have more-detailed information about specific areas.

Where there are representatives, Tourism Malaysia and state tourism offices are listed in individual destination entries. The head office of Tourism Malaysia (☎ 03-293 5188, fax 293 5884) is on the 17th floor of Menara Dato Onn, Putra World Trade Centre, 45 Jalan Tun Ismail, 50480, Kuala Lumpur.

### Tourist Offices Abroad

Tourism Malaysia maintains the following offices overseas:

**Australia**
*Sydney:* (☎ 02-9299 4441) Ground floor, 65 York St, Sydney, NSW 2000
*Perth:* (☎ 08-9481 0400) 56 William St, Perth, WA 6000
**Canada**
(☎ 604-689 8899) 830 Burrard St, Vancouver, BC V6Z 2K4
**France**
(☎ 01-42 97 41 71) 29 rue des Pyramides, 75001 Paris
**Germany**
(☎ 069-28 37 82) Rossmarkt 11, 60311 Frankfurt-am-Main
**Japan**
*Tokyo:* (☎ 03-3501 8691) 5F Chiyoda Biru, 1-6-4 Yurakucho, Chiyoda-ku, Tokyo 100
*Osaka:* (☎ 06-6444 1220) 10F Cotton Nissay Biru, 1-8-2 Utsubo-Honmachi, Nishi-ku, Osaka 755
**Singapore**
(☎ 02-532 6321) 10 Collyer Quay, 01–06 Ocean Bldg, Singapore 049315
**Sweden**
(☎ 08-824 99 00) Klarabergsgatan 35, 2 tr, 11121 Stockholm
**Thailand**
(☎ 02-631 1994), Unit 1001 Liberty Square, 287 Silom Rd, Bangkok 10500
**UK**
(☎ 020-7930 7932) 57 Trafalgar Square, London WC2N 5DU
**USA**
*Los Angeles:* (☎ 213-689 9702) 818 West 7th St, Suite 804, Los Angeles, CA 90017
*New York City:* (☎ 212-754 1113) 120 East 56th St, Suite 804, New York, NY 10022

## VISAS & DOCUMENTS
### Passport

Visitors must have a valid passport or internationally recognised travel document valid for at least six months beyond the date of entry into Malaysia.

## Visas

**Malaysian Visas** Commonwealth citizens (except those from India, Bangladesh, Sri Lanka and Pakistan), and citizens of the Republic of Ireland, Switzerland, the Netherlands, San Marino and Liechtenstein do not require a visa to visit Malaysia.

Citizens of Austria, Belgium, the Czech Republic, Denmark, Finland, Germany, Hungary, Iceland, Italy, Japan, Luxembourg, Norway, Slovak Republic, South Korea, Sweden, the USA and most Arab countries do not require a visa for a visit not exceeding three months.

Citizens of France, Greece, Poland, South Africa and many South American and African countries do not require a visa for a visit not exceeding one month. Most other nationalities are given a shorter stay-period or require a visa. Citizens of Israel cannot enter Malaysia.

Nationals of most countries are given a 30- or 60-day visa on arrival, depending on the expected length of stay. As a general rule, if you arrive by air you will be given 60 days automatically, though coming overland you may be given 30 days unless you specifically ask for a 60-day permit. It's possible to get an extension at an immigration office in Malaysia for a total stay of up to three months. This is a straightforward procedure that is easily done in major Malaysian cities (immigration offices are listed under Information in the relevant destination chapters).

Sabah and Sarawak are treated in some ways like separate countries. Your passport will be checked on arrival in each state and a new stay-permit issued. You are usually issued with a 30-day permit on arrival in Sarawak or Sabah. Travelling directly from either Sabah or Sarawak back to Peninsular Malaysia, however, there are no formalities and you do not start a new entry period, so your 30-day permit from Sabah or Sarawak remains valid. You can then extend your initial 30-day permit, though it can be difficult to get an extension in Sarawak.

Note that holders of dual citizenship should use only one passport for entering and leaving Malaysia. Declaration of dual citizenship will probably result in refusal of entry, as holding two passports is technically illegal in Malaysia.

Lastly, when you go through Malaysian passport control, make sure your passport has been properly stamped. Some travellers have reported that they did not get a stamp on their way into Malaysia and then had to pay fines for illegal entry into the country.

**Thai Visas** You can get Thai visas from the embassies in Singapore and KL or the consulates in Penang and Kota Bharu. The consulates are quick and convenient.

There are two main types of Thai visa: If you have an onward air ticket and will not be staying in Thailand for more than four weeks, you do not need to prearrange a visa and can get a free entry-permit (which cannot be extended) on arrival by air or land; otherwise a two-month tourist visa from a Thai consulate or embassy costs RM33. Two photos are required.

**Indonesian Visas** For nationals of most Western countries no visa is required on arrival in Indonesia, as long as you have a ticket out (this is not always rigidly enforced) and do not intend to stay more than 60 days. The only catch is that the 'no visa' entry only applies if you enter and leave Indonesia through certain recognised gateways. These entry and exit points include all the usual airports and seaports, but there are some places, such as Jayapura in Irian Jaya, not on the list. If you intend to arrive or leave Indonesia through one of the oddball places, get a visa in advance.

## Travel Insurance

A travel insurance policy to cover theft, loss and medical problems is strongly recommended. Though Malaysia is generally a healthy and safe country in which to travel, sickness, accidents and theft do happen. There are a wide variety of policies, and travel agents have recommendations. Check the small print to see if it covers potentially dangerous sporting activities, such as diving or trekking, and make sure that it adequately covers your valuables. A few credit cards offer limited, sometimes full, travel insurance to the holder.

## Other Documents

Major Malaysian car-hire agencies will rent a car on the production of a valid home drivers licence with a photo, and don't require an International Driving Permit. Though not required, an International Driving Permit is good to have if stopped by overly officious police looking for any dubious reason to extract 'fines' – a rare occurrence, but it happens. International Driving Permits can be obtained through motoring associations in your home country. Bring your home driver's licence even if you don't intend to drive – you might decide to use it, and it can occasionally be good for identification purposes.

A Hostelling International (HI) card is of limited use in Malaysia, as only KL, Melaka and Port Dickson have HI hostels, though it can also be used to waive the small initial membership fee at some YMCAs and YWCAs. Bring it if you have one.

An ISIC international student card is worth bringing. Many student discounts, such as on the trains, are only available for Malaysian students, but some places do offer discounts for international students.

You're officially required to have been vaccinated against yellow fever before entering Malaysia, but in practice this is only enforced if you're travelling from an infected area such as South America or parts of Africa. If you do get vaccinations, it is a good idea to have them recorded on an International Certificate of Vaccination, for your own record if nothing else (see the Health section later in this chapter for more information).

## Copies

All important documents (passport data page and visa page, credit cards, travel insurance policy, air/bus/train tickets, driving licence etc) should be photocopied before you leave home. Leave one copy with someone at home and keep another with you, separate from the originals.

## EMBASSIES & CONSULATES
## Malaysian Embassies & Consulates

Visas can be obtained at Malaysian diplomatic missions overseas, including:

**Australia** (☎ 02-6273 1543) 7 Perth Ave, Yarralumla, ACT 2600
**Brunei** (☎ 02-345652) 27 & 29 Simpang 396–39 Kampung Sungai Akar, Jalan Kebangsaan, BC 4115, Bandar Seri Begawan
**Canada** (☎ 613-241 5182, fax 241 5214) 360 Boteler St, Ottawa, ON K1N 8Y7
**France** (☎ 01-45 53 11 85) 2, bis rue Benouville, Paris 75116
**Germany** (☎ 0228-38 80 30) Mittelstrasse 43, 53175 Bonn
**Indonesia**
 *Jakarta:* (☎ 021-522 4947) Jalan HR Rasuna Said Kav X/6, Kuningan, Jakarta Selatan
 *Kalimantan:* (☎ 561-36060, 36061) 42 Jalan A Yani, Pontianak, Kalimantan
 *Medan:* (☎ 061-531342) 11 Jalan Diponegoro, Medan
 *Riau:* (☎ 761-25944) 59 Jalan Diponegoro, Pekanbaru, Riau
**Japan** (☎ 03-3476 3840) 20–16, Nanpeidai-cho, Shibuya-ku, Tokyo 150 0036
**Netherlands** (☎ 070-350 6506) Rustenburgweg, 22517 KE, The Hague
**New Zealand**
 (☎ 04-385 2439) 10 Washington Ave, Brooklyn, Wellington
**Philippines** (☎ 02-817 4581) 107 Tordesillas St, Salcedo Village, Makati, Metro Manila
**Singapore** (☎ 02-235 0111, fax 733 6135) 02-26, 268 Orchard Rd
**Thailand**
 *Bangkok:* (☎ 02-248 8350) 35 South Sathorn Rd, Bangkok 10120
 *Songkhla:* (☎ 74-311 072) 4 Sukhom Rd, Songkhla
**UK** (☎ 020-7235 8033) 45 Belgrave Square, London SW1X 8QT
**USA** (☎ 202-328 2700, fax 483 7661) 2401 Massachusetts Ave NW, Washington DC 20008

## Embassies & Consulates in Malaysia

The following countries are among nations with diplomatic representation in Malaysia. You'll find these embassies and consulates in KL (area code ☎ 03) unless otherwise noted:

**Australia** (☎ 246 5555) 6 Jalan Yap Kwan Sweng
**Brunei** (☎ 261 2800) 8th and 9th floors, Wisma Sin Heap Yee, Jalan Tun Razak
**Canada**
 (☎ 2718 3333) MBF Plaza, 172 Jalan Ampang
**France** (☎ 249 4122) 192 Jalan Ampang;
 *Consulate in Penang:* (☎ 04-262 8816), Wisma Rajab, 82 Bishop St, Georgetown, Penang

**Germany** (☎ 242 9666) 3 Jalan U Thant
**Indonesia** (☎ 242 1151) 233 Jalan Tun Razak
  *Consulate in Penang:* (☎ 04-227 4686) 467
  Jalan Burma, Georgetown, Penang
  *Consulate in Sabah:* (☎ 088-219110) Jalan
  Karamunsing, Kota Kinabalu, Sabah; (☎ 089-
  772052) Jalan Apas, Tawau, Sabah
  *Consulate in Sarawak:* (☎ 082-241734) 5A
  Pisang Rd, Kuching, Sarawak
**Ireland** (☎ 2161 2963) Ireland House, Amp
  Walk, 218 Jalan Ampang
**Japan** (☎ 242 7044) 11 Persiaran Stonor
  *Consulate in Johor:* (☎ 07-221 7621) Menara
  Ansar, Jalan Abdullah Ibrahim, Johor Bahru,
  Johor
  *Consulate in Penang:* (☎ 04-226 8222) 2 Jalan
  Biggs, Georgetown, Penang
  *Consulate in Sabah:* (☎ 088-254669) Wisma
  Perindustrian, Jalan Istiandat, Kota Kinabalu,
  Sabah
**Laos** (☎ 451 1118) Persigran Madge, Off Jalan
  Ampang Hilir
**Netherlands** (☎ 248 5151) 4 Jalan Mesra, off
  Jalan Damai
**New Zealand** (☎ 238 2533) Level 21 Menara
  IMC, Jalan Sultan Ismail
**Philippines** (☎ 248 4233) 1 Jalan Changkat Kia
  Peng
**Singapore** (☎ 1261 6277) 209 Jalan Tun Razak
**Thailand** (☎ 248 8222) 206 Jalan Ampang
  *Consulate in Kelantan:* (☎ 09-744 0867) 4426
  Jalan Pengkalan Chepa, Kota Bharu
  *Consulate in Penang:* (☎ 04-226 9484) 1 Jalan
  Tunku Abdul Rahman, Georgetown, Penang
**UK** (☎ 248 2122) 185 Jalan Ampang
**USA** (☎ 2168 9011) 376 Jalan Tun Razak

Note that at the time of research, telephone
numbers in KL were changing from seven to
eight digits. Some of the embassy and consulate phone numbers may have changed. If
you reach a wrong number, don't give up –
call ☎ 1050 for information in Malaysia.

### Your Own Embassy

As a tourist, it's important to realise what
your own embassy can and can't do. Generally speaking, it won't be much help in
emergencies if the trouble you're in is re-
motely your own fault. Remember that you
are bound by the laws of the country you
are in. Your embassy won't be sympathetic
if you end up in jail after committing a
crime locally, even if such actions are legal
in your own country.

In genuine emergencies you might get
some assistance, but only if other channels
have been exhausted. For example, if you
need to get home urgently, a free ticket home
is exceedingly unlikely – the embassy would
expect you to have insurance. If you have all
your money and documents stolen, it might
assist with getting a new passport, but a loan
for onward travel is out of the question.

### CUSTOMS

The following can be brought into Malaysia
duty free: 1L of alcohol, 225g of tobacco
(200 cigarettes or 50 cigars) and souvenirs
and gifts not exceeding RM200 (RM500
when coming from Labuan or Langkawi).
Cameras, portable radios, perfume, cosmetics and watches do not incur duty.

The list of prohibited items includes:
counterfeit currency, weapons (including
imitations), fireworks, drugs and 'obscene
and prejudicial articles' (pornography, for
example, and items that may be considered
inflammatory, or disruptive to Malaysia's
ethnic harmony).

Visitors can carry only RM1000 in rin-
git in and out of Malaysia; there is no limit
on foreign currency. When you enter
Malaysia, you must fill out a Currency Declaration Form on which you are required to
declare the amount of ringgit notes you are
carrying if the figure exceeds RM1000, and
any amount of foreign currency you are
carrying. Keep this in your passport as you
must produce it when leaving Malaysia.

### MONEY
### Currency

The local currency is the Malaysian ringgit
(RM), which is divided into 100 sen. It took
a beating in the 1997 South-East Asian currency crisis but has since recovered much of
its value. It is fairly stable and fully transferable. However, following the currency
crisis, certain restrictions have been placed
on the ringgit (see the boxed text 'Changes
to the Ringgit' later in this chapter).

Notes in circulation are RM2, RM5,
RM10, RM20, RM50 and RM100; the
coins in use are 1, 5, 10, 20 and 50 sen, and
RM1. Old RM1 notes are occasionally seen.

Malaysians habitually refer to ringgit as 'dollars', the old name for the country's currency. Unless someone makes clear that they are talking about US dollars, you can be sure they mean ringgit.

Be sure to carry plenty of small bills with you when venturing outside cities – people often cannot change bills larger than RM20.

Banks are efficient and there are plenty of moneychangers. Banks usually charge commission (around RM5 per transaction), whereas moneychangers have no charges but their rates vary more – so know what the current rate is before using moneychangers. You'll generally get a better rate for cash at a moneychanger than from a bank – it's usually quicker too. Away from the tourist centres, moneychangers' rates are often poorer and they may not change travellers cheques.

## Exchange Rates

The following table shows exchange rates at the time this book went to press:

| country | unit | | ringgit |
| --- | --- | --- | --- |
| Australia | A$1 | = | RM2.06 |
| Brunei | B$1 | = | RM2.17 |
| Canada | C$1 | = | RM2.55 |
| euro | €1 | = | RM3.33 |
| France | 10FF | = | RM4.97 |
| Germany | DM1 | = | RM1.70 |
| Indonesia | Rp1000 | = | RM0.43 |
| Japan | ¥100 | = | RM3.51 |
| New Zealand | NZ$1 | = | RM1.56 |
| Singapore | S$1 | = | RM2.17 |
| Thailand | 100B | = | RM8.89 |
| UK | UK£1 | = | RM5.52 |
| USA | US$1 | = | RM3.80 |

## Exchanging Money

**Travellers Cheques & Cash** Travellers cheques are always the safest way to carry money, though it doesn't hurt to have some cash (say US$100 to US$200) carried separately for emergencies. You'll need it if your cheques are stolen or you have to change money after hours at a moneychanger or large hotel.

All major brands of travellers cheques are accepted in Malaysia. Cash in major

### Changes to the Ringgit

In September 1998 Malaysia fixed the ringgit at RM3.8 to US$1 (the rate for other currencies remains variable) and recalled foreign holdings of ringgit in an attempt to protect the economy from currency speculators.

It is now technically illegal to trade the ringgit outside Malaysia; in practice, you can (usually) buy and sell ringgit in southern Thailand, Singapore and Brunei. US dollars can still be exchanged for ringgit at banks and moneychangers inside Malaysia.

Because of the fixed rate, it pays to make some calculations before deciding where to change your money. If you're travelling to Malaysia from Thailand, for example, work out whether changing your dollars into baht there, then changing baht into ringgit in Malaysia, will earn you more for your dollar. You could also calculate whether exchanging another currency for ringgit would be more profitable than the US dollar.

currencies is also readily exchanged, though like everywhere else in the world the US dollar has a slight edge.

**Credit Cards & ATMs** If you use them correctly, credit cards are a viable and very convenient way to carry money. They are readily accepted for purchases in many establishments – airline offices, car-hire agencies, major hotels, better restaurants, large shops etc. MasterCard and Visa are widely accepted and are the best to carry in Malaysia.

Banks all over the country accept credit cards for over-the-counter cash advances, or through ATMs if you have your PIN. Many banks in Malaysia are also linked to international banking networks such as Cirrus (the most common), Maestro and Plus, allowing withdrawals from overseas savings accounts.

Maybank, Malaysia's biggest bank with branches everywhere, accepts both Visa and MasterCard. Hongkong Bank accepts Visa, and the Standard Chartered Bank accepts MasterCard. If you have any questions about whether your cards will be accepted in Malaysia, ask your home bank about its reciprocal relationships with Malaysian banks.

## Costs

Though one of the more-expensive countries in South-East Asia, Malaysia is still cheap by world standards and caters well to all budgets. At the time of writing, the ringgit still had not regained all the value it lost in the 1997 South-East Asian currency crisis, meaning that travel in Malaysia is still a bargain.

You can easily find a spartan double room in an old hotel for as little as US$5, but if you want to spend US$100 a night that's no problem either. Though still plentiful, the older cheap hotels are diminishing in number, but new travellers' guesthouses are springing up in the tourist centres and offer dormitory beds for around US$2.50, as well as cheap rooms. The mid-range is well catered for and hotel rooms with air-con and attached bathroom start at around US$12.

Food is quite cheap. There's a good variety in the cities and you can usually get away with between US$1 and US$2 for a simple meal. A full meal at a food centre with a couple of drinks and dessert will come closer to US$3. At the other end of the scale, fancy hotels and restaurants in the main cities offer international cuisine at international prices.

Alcoholic drinks are usually quite expensive, particularly in the conservative areas of the east coast or on islands. Beer costs about US$2 a can, almost double in isolated areas. Spirits are even more expensive – about 50% more than beer.

Transportation is generally a real bargain in Malaysia. There are plenty of reasonably priced trishaws and taxis for local travel. Drivers are fairly honest and prices are either fixed or there are meters. Most drivers will turn on the meter without being asked, but some have to be reminded – keep in mind that drivers are legally required to use their meters. For long-distance journeys, Malaysia has excellent buses, trains and long-distance taxis, all at very reasonable prices.

On top of these travel essentials – food, accommodation and transport – you'll also find nonessentials and luxuries are moderately priced, even downright cheap.

## Tipping & Bargaining

Tipping is not normally done in Malaysia. The more-expensive hotels and restaurants have a 10% service charge, while at the cheaper places tipping is not expected. Taxi and rickshaw drivers will naturally not refuse a tip should you decide to give one but it's not expected as a matter of course.

Bargaining is not usually required for everyday goods, unlike in some Asian countries. But you should always bargain for souvenirs, antiques and other tourist items, even if prices are displayed. In tourist outlets prices are rarely fixed and can be grossly inflated. Other major purchases, such as cameras and electronics, also usually require bargaining, except in department stores. In outdoor markets, bargaining is standard procedure, especially for durable goods (as opposed to food).

Bargaining should be conducted with equanimity – aggression will only force both parties to lose face, and will push prices up.

Transport prices are most often fixed but negotiation is required for trishaws and unmetered taxis around town or for charter. Hotels may be willing to bend their prices, especially if business is slack. Expensive hotels are most likely to drop prices, and you should always inquire about their 'promotional rates'.

## POST & COMMUNICATIONS
### Post

Malaysia has an efficient postal system with good poste restante at the major post offices. Post offices are open daily from 8 am to 5 pm and closed on Sunday and public holidays (closed on Friday and public holidays in Kedah, Kelantan and Terengganu).

Aerograms and postcards cost 50 sen to send to any destination. Letters weighing 10g or less cost 55 sen to Asia, Australia or New Zealand, 90 sen to the UK and Europe, and RM1.10 to North America.

It's easy to send parcels from any major post office, although the rates are fairly high (from around RM20 to RM35 for a 1kg parcel, depending on the destination).

Main post offices in larger cities have POS2020 stores, which sell packaging materials and stationary.

## Telephone

**Local Calls** Making domestic telephone calls in Malaysia is usually a simple matter, provided you can find a working payphone (at least one-third seem to be out of order). You can direct-dial long-distance calls between all major towns in Malaysia. Local calls cost 10 sen for three minutes.

All over the country you'll come across card telephones operated by Telekom Malaysia and a private communications company, Uniphone. These telephones take coins or plastic cards, but you need different cards for each company. Telekom cardphones are the most reliable and convenient for most calls, but you'll have to use Uniphone phones for 1-800 calls. In the larger cities, you'll also find Cityphone card telephones, but since these are only found in the cities it makes little sense for travellers to buy one of these cards.

Uniphone cards can be bought from 7-Elevens and some other shops. They come in denominations of RM3, RM5, RM10, RM30 and RM50 (international calls only). Telekom cards are available from Telekom offices, post offices and some shops (news sellers in particular). They come in similar denominations.

Phone calls to Singapore are STD (long-distance) rather than international calls. Area codes for Malaysia include:

| town/region | area code |
| --- | --- |
| Cameron Highlands | ☎ 05 |
| Ipoh | ☎ 05 |
| Johor Bahru | ☎ 07 |
| Kota Bharu | ☎ 09 |
| Kota Kinabalu | ☎ 088 |
| Kuala Lumpur | ☎ 03 |
| Kuala Terengganu | ☎ 09 |
| Kuantan | ☎ 09 |
| Kuching | ☎ 082 |
| Labuan | ☎ 087 |
| Langkawi | ☎ 04 |

| town/region | area code |
| --- | --- |
| Melaka | ☎ 06 |
| Miri | ☎ 085 |
| Penang | ☎ 04 |
| Sandakan | ☎ 089 |
| Singapore | ☎ 02 |

Dial ☎ 999 to call the police or ambulance. Dial ☎ 994 to call the fire brigade, and ☎ 103 for domestic directory assistance.

**International Calls** Making international calls from Malaysia can be an exercise in frustration. In addition to the legion of broken pay phones, the traveller is beset by a bewildering number of mutually exclusive services and phone cards.

International direct dial (IDD) calls and operator-assisted calls can be made from any private phone. The access code for making international calls to most countries is ☎ 00. For information on international calls dial ☎ 103. For operator-assisted calls dial ☎ 108.

To make an IDD call from a pay phone, you'll have to find a Telekom pay phone marked 'international' (with which you can use coins or Telekom phone cards; dial the international access code, 00, and then the number). A more-convenient option is to buy a TIME phone card from a newsagent and dial from a small coin phone of the type found in most guesthouses or from the occasional Uniphone pay phone that accepts international calls. The third option is to go to a Telekom office, where you can make IDD or operator-assisted international calls. These days, there are very few regular pay phones that allow IDD calls, apparently because of a rash of counterfeit phone cards.

For calls to a number of countries, it's possible to make Home Country Direct calls, which allow you to deal directly with an operator in your home country (who can arrange reverse charge calls etc). These can be made from participating Uniphone pay phones for the cost of a local call (10 sen for three minutes); from private phones there is no charge. The Home Country Direct table later in this section lists the countries hooked up to this service and the numbers to call.

If you're making a call to Malaysia from outside the country, dial ☎ 60, drop the 0 before the Malaysian area code, then dial the number you want. See the list in the Local Calls entry earlier in this section for area codes for Malaysia's major cities and destinations.

**eKno Communication Service** Lonely Planet's eKno global communication service provides low-cost international calls – for local calls you're usually better off with a local phone card. eKno also offers free messaging services, email, travel information and an online travel vault, where you can securely store all your important documents. You can join online at www.ekno .lonelyplanet.com, where you will find the local-access numbers for the 24-hour customer-service centre. Once you have joined, always check the eKno Web site for the latest access numbers for each country and updates on new features.

### Fax
Fax facilities are available at Telekom offices in larger cities and at some main post offices. You can also send and receive faxes at travel agencies, but the rates are usually pretty steep. Large hotels also have fax machines but these are generally only for the use of guests.

### Email & Internet Access
In spite of the government's well-publicised campaign to promote information technology, there are only two major Internet Service Providers (ISPs) in the country and connections tend to be very slow. Rates at Internet cafes range from RM2 to RM12 per hour, with the cheaper rates in rural areas.

If you plan to log on with your own machine, you'll find that most phone jacks in Malaysia accept standard-wired RJ11 plugs. Most modems also seem to work fine in Malaysia, but if you've got any concerns, you can always get a global modem. See Electricity later in this chapter for information on Malaysia's power supply.

Only the largest international ISPs have POPs in Malaysia, and most of these charge

| Home Country Direct Access Codes | |
| --- | --- |
| Australia | |
|    Telstra | ☎ 1 800 80 0061 |
|    Optus | ☎ 1 800 80 0068 |
| Canada | ☎ 1 800 80 0017 |
| Hong Kong | ☎ 1 800 80 0085 |
| Italy | ☎ 1 800 80 0039 |
| Japan | ☎ 1 800 80 0081 |
| Netherlands | ☎ 1 800 80 0031 |
| New Zealand | ☎ 1 800 80 0064 |
| South Korea | ☎ 1 800 80 0082 |
| Taiwan | ☎ 1 800 80 0088 |
| UK | |
|    BT | ☎ 1 800 80 0044 |
|    Mercury | ☎ 1 800 80 0048 |
| USA | |
|    AT&T | ☎ 1 800 80 0011 |
|    MCI | ☎ 1 800 80 0012 |
|    Sprint | ☎ 1 800 80 0016 |

a surcharge for logging on in Malaysia. Before leaving, you may want to download a list of your ISP's dial-up numbers in Malaysia.

### INTERNET RESOURCES
There's no better place to start your Web explorations than the Lonely Planet Web site, at www.lonelyplanet.com. Here you'll find succinct summaries on travelling to most places on earth, postcards from other travellers and the Thorn Tree bulletin board, where you can ask questions before you go or dispense advice when you get back. You can also find travel news and updates to many of our most popular guidebooks, and the subWWWay section links you to the most useful travel resources elsewhere on the Web.

Additional sites to check include the following:

**Cari.com** Malaysia's first search engine, useful for pre-trip planning, but you'll have to put up with some annoying ads.
www.cari.com.my/
**Cyber Malaysia** Online mag about Malaysia, mostly aimed at Malaysians, with some useful event listings and features.
www.cybermalaysia.com

**KTM** The official site of Malaysia's national train company, KTM, with up-to-date schedules, fares and ways to order and reserve tickets outside Malaysia etc. Very useful.
www.ktmb.com.my

**Malaysia.net** Background on major ethnic groups, religions, customs, history, environment (ecology), states plus links to government and business homepages, some in Bahasa Malaysia.
www.mymalaysia.net.my/knowmsia

**Malaysia Airlines** Up-to-date schedules, fare information and links to regional office sites.
www.malaysiaairlines.com.my

**News Malaysia.com** Straightforward search engine site with links to Web discussion forums, news, job listings, classifieds, and categorised links for travel, arts etc.
www.newmalaysia.com

**New York Office of the Malaysia Tourism Promotion Board Official Site** Attractive, slickly designed site with some general information on destinations in Malaysia and aspects of Malay culture – good crafts information.
www.visitmalaysia.com

**Tourism Malaysia** The best overall site on Malaysia, with events calendars, regional links, background information and listings of domestic and international tourist offices.
www.tourism.gov.my/

**University of Michigan's Malaysia Page** Factual list of links for news, weather, Net discussion groups, general Malaysia sites and selected travel sites.
www.umich.edu/~umimsa/Malaysia/

## BOOKS

Most of the books in this section should be available on the Web. Some of the more current titles may also be found in the bigger bookshops of KL or Singapore (see Bookshops in those chapters). Because books are published in different editions by different publishers in different countries, we don't list publishers for most of the books in this section. You should be able to find these books by searching under title or author.

### Lonely Planet

*South-East Asia on a shoestring* is our overall guidebook to the region. For those travelling further afield, there are LP guides to most South-East and North-East Asian countries, including *Singapore*. LP also publishes the *Malay phrasebook,* an introduction to the Malay language; and the

*South-East Asia phrasebook. Travel Photography: A Guide to Taking Better Pictures* is written by internationally renowned travel photographer, Richard I'Anson. It's full colour throughout and designed to take on the road.

### Guidebooks

*Mountains of Malaysia – A Practical Guide and Manual* by John Briggs is essential reading for anyone intending to do a lot of mountain walking in Malaysia. Most of the climbs listed are in Borneo, but a few of the peninsula's major climbs are also covered. By the same author, *Parks of Malaysia* is a slightly dated but still useful guide to the trails of Malaysia's many national parks.

### Travel

*Tales from the South China Seas,* edited by Charles Allen, is the South-East Asian version of *Plain Tales from the Raj.* It recounts the stories of the British colonial experience, mostly in Malaya.

*A Malaysian Journey* by Rehman Rashad is an excellent introduction to Malaysia. Written by an expatriate Malaysian journalist who returns to travel right around his home country, it is peppered with affectionate and critical insights, and touches on Malaysia's history and current issues.

### History & Politics

*A Short History of Malaysia, Singapore & Brunei* by C Mary Turnbull is straightforward and a good introductory volume on Malaysia's long history, from early civilisation to modern politics. *A History of Malaya* by R Winstedt is a standard history with a colonial perspective.

*A History of Malaysia* by Barbara Andaya & Leonard Watson is one of the best histories with a post-independence slant.

A number of books deal with the fall of Malaysia and Singapore, the subsequent Japanese occupation, and the internal and external struggles of the 1950s and 1960s. *The Jungle is Neutral* by F Spencer Chapman tells of the hardships and adventures of a British guerrilla force that fought on in the jungles of Malaya after the Japanese overran Malaya and took Singapore. Noel Barber's *The War of the Running Dogs – Malaya 1948–1960* recounts the events of the long-running Communist insurrection in the country.

*The Undeclared War – The Story of the Indonesian Confrontation* by Harold James & Denis Sheil-Small tells the story of the strange and disorganised confrontation with Indonesia that arose immediately after the Communist struggle.

## People & Society

*Kampong Boy* by Lat (Straits Times Publishing) provides a delightful introduction to Malay life. It's a humorous autobiographical cartoon series on growing up in a *kampung* (village) and then moving to the town of Ipoh in Perak. Lat has many other excellent cartoon collections in print.

*Culture Shock Malaysia* by JoAnn Craig explains the customs, cultures and lifestyles of Malaysia's polyglot population to expatriates working there.

*An Analysis of Malay Magic* by KM Endicott is a scholarly look at Malay folk-religion and the importance of spirits and magic in the world view of Malays.

*Chinese Beliefs & Practices in South-East Asia* edited by Cheu Hock Tong is an excellent introduction to Chinese religion and society, with special reference to variations from mainland Chinese customs.

Malaysia's prime minister, Dr Mahathir Mohamad, is a prolific writer. What his books lack in scholarship is made up for by Dr Mahathir's lively, controversial style. *The Malay Dilemma,* written before he became prime minister, is an interesting polemic of racial stereotyping that makes the case for the preferential treatment of Malays in Malaysia. It was banned for a number of years. *The Voice of Asia* (1995), co-authored by Tokyo's controversial mayor Ishihara Shintaro, outlines Dr Mahatir's notions of 'Asian Values' (see the boxed text in the Facts About Malaysia chapter), stressing the need for Asia to assert its own identity in the face of Western arrogance and decadence.

Ian Buruma's *God's Dust* looks critically at the 'Westernisation' of Asia, and in a long chapter on Malaysia and Singapore searchingly examines the idea of Asian Values. It is a fascinating read by one of the most astute commentators on all things Asian.

## Fiction

Singapore and Malaysia have always provided a fertile setting for novelists, and Joseph Conrad's *The Shadow Line* and *Lord Jim* use the region as a location. Somerset Maugham also set many of his classic short stories in Malaya – look for the *Borneo Stories*.

*The Long Day Wanes* is a reissue in one volume of Anthony Burgess' classic *Malayan Trilogy.* It's well worth picking up a copy – it has some of the finest English-language fiction set in South-East Asia. Burgess' depiction of a variously alcoholic, set-upon, bewildered and valiant collection of Brits attempting to carry the flickering torch of empire against a backdrop of Malay nationalism bristles with superbly realised characters and fascinating insights.

*The Consul's File* by Paul Theroux is a very readable collection of short stories set in, of all places, Ayer Hitam near KL. Theroux's *Saint Jack* is set in Singapore.

*Turtle Beach* by Blanche d'Alpuget is set in Australia and Malaysia during the racial tensions of 1969 and focuses on the plight of Vietnamese boat people. The subsequent film, and its portrayal of Malay racial hatred, outraged Malaysia, and both the book and the film have been banned.

## Borneo

*Nineteenth Century Borneo – A Study in Diplomatic Rivalry* by Graham Irwin is a good book on the fascinating history of Sarawak, Sabah and Brunei.

*Rajah Charles Brooke – Monarch of all He Surveyed* by Colin N Criswell tells more about the white rajas, as does *The White Rajahs of Sarawak* by Robert Payne.

The Norwegian explorer Karl Lumholtz recounts a journey he made through Sabah and Sarawak between 1913 and 1917 in *Through Central Borneo.*

*In Borneo Jungles* by William Krohn is a fascinating account of the author's experiences with Dayak head-hunters in the 1920s.

*Vanishing World, the Ibans of Borneo* by Leigh Wright has some beautiful colour photographs.

*A Stroll Through Borneo* by James Barclay is a delightful tale of a long walk and river trip through Sarawak, Sabah and Indonesian Kalimantan. The contrasts between Malaysian bureaucracy and the Indonesian variety are enlightening, with the Malaysians coming off as distinctly second best.

*Into the Heart of Borneo* by Redmond O'Hanlon is a humorous, classic adventure of two foreigners as they journey by foot and boat into Borneo.

Another good read is *Stranger in the Forest* by Eric Hansen, about the author's experiences trekking right across Sarawak and Kalimantan. Or try *The Day Nothing Happened* by Terence Clarke, an entertaining novel about an American engineer who comes to Sarawak to build a road through the jungle.

*Sarawak Crafts – Methods, Material and Motifs* by Heidi Munan is a good introduction, but if you can afford it, buy *Hornbill and Dragon* by Bernard Sellato, a superbly illustrated large-format bible of Borneo crafts.

## Nature

Periplus Editions puts out a great series of field guides to the plants and animals of Malaysia. Titles include: *Tropical Marine Life of Malaysia & Singapore, Tropical Birds of Malaysia & Singapore, Tropical Fruits of Malaysia & Singapore* and *Tropical Plants of Malaysia & Singapore.*

For those travelling to Borneo, *A Field Guide to the Mammals of Borneo* by Junaidi Payne, Charles M Francis & Karen Phillipps is a must. The illustrations are excellent. The definitive guide to birds is Smythies' *Birds of Borneo,* but the World Wide Fund for Nature (WWF) and the Sabah Foundation have condensed this weighty volume into the *Pocket Guide to the Birds of Borneo*, which is brilliantly illustrated and ideal for the field.

## Bookshops

The best bookshop-chains in Malaysia are MPH and Times. Only in big cities like KL will you find an adequate selection of books, maps and periodicals, so it makes sense to stock up before heading out to other areas. If you happen to be in Singapore, you'll find a much wider selection of English-language books than in Malaysia. For details on bookshops, see the Bookshops sections in each chapter.

## NEWSPAPERS & MAGAZINES

Malaysia has newspapers in Malay, English, Chinese and Tamil. The *New Straits Times* is the most popular offering in English. Other English-language papers include the the *Star* and the *Malay Mail*; in Malaysian Borneo there are locals such as the *Borneo Post* and the *Sarawak Tribune.*

The main newspaper in Bahasa Malaysia, and Malaysia's most-circulated paper, is the *Berita Harian; Utusan Malaysia* is a second-string paper.

In Malaysia, as in Singapore, freedom of the press is tightly controlled. The main newspapers tend to parrot the government line, sometimes publishing articles that amount to little more than government propaganda. Nonetheless, small opposition papers are tolerated and these tend to enjoy a fair amount of editorial freedom. Interested travellers should look out for *Aliran* and *Harakah,* both of which run occasional articles in English.

Though 'anti-Malaysian' stories in the foreign press occasionally provoke the ire of the government, Asian and Western magazines are readily available in Malaysia.

## RADIO & TV

Radio and TV are equally cosmopolitan in their languages and programming. Malaysia has two government TV channels, TV1 and TV2, and three commercial stations. Programs range from local productions in various languages to imports from the USA and UK. TV censorship is strict – all kissing and nudity is cut. Check the *New Straits Times* for details on upcoming programs.

Radio Malaysia runs six domestic channels broadcasting in all the major languages and there are a number of commercial stations. The three main ones are HITZ FM

(92.9 FM; top 40), MIX FM (94.5 FM; adult contemporary) and Light & Easy FM (105.7 FM; easy listening). Note that the frequencies given are for the KL area and may differ in other parts of Malaysia. These stations are not available in Malaysian Borneo. For details on the latest programming, check the *New Straits Times*.

## PHOTOGRAPHY & VIDEO
Malaysia is a delightful country to photograph. There's a lot of natural colour and activity and the people usually have no antipathy to being photographed. However, it is, of course, polite to ask permission before photographing people or taking pictures in mosques or temples. If you're looking for tips, *Travel Photography: A Guide to Taking Better Pictures* is written by travel photographer Richard I'Anson. It's designed for taking on the road and is full colour throughout.

Print film is commonly available at good prices – a 36-exposure roll averages RM10. Slide film is a little harder to come by and more expensive – a 36-exposure roll of Fuji Velvia averages RM29 and a 36-exposure roll of Sensia averages RM18. Professional slide film can only be found in the biggest cities – if you're a serious photographer, you may want to bring your own slide film, especially since most available in Malaysia show signs of improper storage.

Colour film can be developed quickly and competently in Malaysia. Processing prices for a 36-exposure roll of slide film range from RM15 to RM18 (mounted) and 60 sen to 70 sen per exposure for print film. In bigger cities like KL, you'll find photo shops with a decent range of equipment at reasonable prices, but Malaysia isn't really the place to buy camera equipment (try Singapore or Hong Kong).

Malaysia uses the PAL video system. You'll find high-quality video tapes for sale in the major cities. You'll also find a limited selection of video equipment, but, as is the case with cameras, you'll probably be better off shopping for video equipment in Singapore.

## TIME
Malaysia is 16 hours ahead of US Pacific Standard Time (San Francisco and Los Angeles), 13 hours ahead of US Eastern Standard Time (New York), eight hours ahead of GMT/UTC (London) and two hours behind Australian Eastern Standard Time (Sydney and Melbourne). Thus, when it is noon in KL, it is 8 pm in Los Angeles and 11 pm in New York (the previous day), 4 am in London and 2 pm in Sydney and Melbourne.

## ELECTRICITY
Electricity supplies are reliable throughout Malaysia. Supply is 220–240V, 50 cycles. Power sockets are almost always of the three-square-pin type found in the UK, although some older places have the three-round-pin sockets. Universal adaptors are widely available at electronics shops in Malaysia for around RM3.

## WEIGHTS & MEASURES
Malaysia uses the metric system. For readers more familiar with the imperial system, there's a conversion table at the back of this book.

Some addresses refer to *batu* (literally, stone), the mileposts that are still found on a few roads. So an address might be 'Batu 10, Jalan Ipoh', which means at the 10-mile mark on the Ipoh road, even though the 10-mile marker may have long been replaced by a 16km post. You may come across other ancient measurements such as the *kati* (about 600g), but these are rare.

Fruit may be sold by the *biji*, eg, 'three biji RM1'; the biji is not a unit of weight, but a classifier for fruit and roughly translates as 'piece'. In Malay, it is poor usage to say 'tiga rambutan' (three rambutan) – the proper usage is 'tiga biji rambutan' (three 'pieces' of rambutan), just as in English 'three pieces of paper' is correct, not 'three papers'.

## TOILETS
Malaysian toilets are not nearly as horrifying as those in other South-East Asian countries. You will find both Western-style and Asian squat-style toilets, the former rapidly replacing the latter. In places with squat-style toilets,

toilet paper is not usually provided. Instead, you will find a hose which you are supposed to use as a bidet, or in cheaper places, a bucket of water and a tap. If you do not find this to your liking, make a point of taking packets of tissues or toilet paper wherever you go.

## HEALTH

Travel health depends on your predeparture preparations, your daily health care while travelling and how you handle any medical problem that does develop. While the potential dangers can seem quite frightening, in reality few travellers experience anything more than an upset stomach.

Malaysia enjoys a good standard of health and cleanliness. It is one of the healthiest countries in South-East Asia, but the usual rules for healthy living in a tropical environment apply. Ensure that you do not become dehydrated, particularly before you have become acclimatised, by keeping your liquid intake up. Wear cool, lightweight clothes and avoid prolonged exposure to the sun. Treat cuts and scratches with care, since they can easily become infected.

If you do experience health problems, you'll find the quality of hospitals and clinics in Malaysia to be quite high. Most doctors and nurses speak English. Pharmacies (chemists) are of similarly high quality and can be found in the bigger cities. A prescription is not required for most medications.

### Predeparture planning

**Immunisations** Plan ahead for getting your vaccinations: some of them require more than one injection, while some vaccinations should not be given together. Note that some vaccinations should not be given during pregnancy or in people with allergies – discuss with your doctor.

It is recommended you seek medical advice at least six weeks before travel. Be aware that there is often a greater risk of disease with children and during pregnancy.

Record all vaccinations on an International Certificate of Vaccination, available from your doctor or government health department.

The only vaccination required to enter Malaysia is yellow fever if coming from an infected area (parts of Africa and South America). Discuss other requirements with

## Medical Kit Check List

Following is a list of items you should consider including in your medical kit – consult your pharmacist for brands available in your country.

☐ **Aspirin or paracetamol (acetaminophen in the USA)** – for pain or fever
☐ **Antihistamine** – for allergies, eg, hay fever; to ease the itch from insect bites or stings; and to prevent motion sickness
☐ **Cold and flu tablets, throat lozenges and nasal decongestant**
☐ **Multivitamins** – consider for long trips, when dietary vitamin intake may be inadequate
☐ **Antibiotics** – consider including these if you're travelling well off the beaten track; see your doctor, as they must be prescribed, and carry the prescription with you
☐ **Loperamide or diphenoxylate** –'blockers' for diarrhoea
☐ **Prochlorperazine or metaclopramide** – for nausea and vomiting
☐ **Rehydration mixture** – to prevent dehydration, which may occur, for example, during bouts of diarrhoea; particularly important when travelling with children
☐ **Insect repellent, sunscreen, lip balm and eye drops**
☐ **Calamine lotion, sting relief spray or aloe vera** – to ease irritation from sunburn and insect bites or stings
☐ **Antifungal cream or powder** – for fungal skin infections and thrush
☐ **Antiseptic (such as povidone-iodine)** – for cuts and grazes
☐ **Bandages, Band-Aids (plasters) and other wound dressings**
☐ **Water purification tablets or iodine**
☐ **Scissors, tweezers and a thermometer** – note that mercury thermometers are prohibited by airlines
☐ **Sterile kit** – in case you need injections in a country with medical hygiene problems; discuss with your doctor

your doctor, but vaccinations you should consider for this trip include the following (see later entries in this section for more details on some of the diseases listed here):

**Cholera** The current injectable vaccine against cholera is poorly protective and has many side effects, so it is not generally recommended for travellers.

**Diphtheria & Tetanus** Vaccinations for these two diseases are usually combined and are recommended for everyone. After an initial course of three injections (usually given in childhood), boosters are necessary every 10 years.

**Hepatitis A** Hepatitis A vaccine (eg, Avaxim, Havrix 1440 or VAQTA) provides long-term immunity (possibly more than 10 years) after an initial injection and a booster at six to 12 months.Alternatively, an injection of gamma globulin can provide short-term protection against hepatitis A – two to six months, depending on the dose given. It is not a vaccine, but is ready-made antibody collected from blood donations. It is reasonably effective and, unlike the vaccine, it is protective immediately, but because it is a blood product, there are current concerns about its long-term safety. Hepatitis A vaccine is also available in a combined form, Twinrix, with hepatitis B vaccine. Three injections over a six-month period are required, the first two providing substantial protection against hepatitis A. Ask your doctor about a combined hepatitis/typhoid vaccination.

**Hepatitis B** Travellers on a long trip to Malaysia should consider vaccination against hepatitis B, although there is not a high rate of infection. Vaccination involves three injections, with a booster at 12 months. More-rapid courses are available if necessary.

**Japanese B Encephalitis** Consider vaccination against this disease if spending a month or longer in Malaysia, making repeated trips or visiting during an epidemic. It involves three injections over 30 days.

**Polio** Everyone should keep up to date with this vaccination, which is normally given in childhood. A booster every 10 years maintains immunity.

**Rabies** Vaccination should be considered by those who will spend a month or longer in Malaysia, especially if they are cycling, handling animals, caving or travelling to remote areas, and for children (who may not report a bite). Pretravel rabies vaccination involves having three injections over 21 to 28 days. If someone who has been vaccinated is bitten or scratched by an animal,

they will require two booster injections of vaccine; those not vaccinated require more.

**Tuberculosis** The risk of TB to travellers is usually very low, unless you will be living with or closely associating with local people in high-risk areas such as Asia, Africa and some parts of the Americas and Pacific. Vaccination against TB (BCG) is recommended for children and young adults living in these areas for three months or longer.

**Typhoid** Vaccination against typhoid may be required if you are travelling for more than a couple of weeks in most parts of Asia, Africa, Central and South America and Central and Eastern Europe. It is now available either as an injection or as capsules to be taken orally. A combined hepatitis/typhoid vaccine was launched recently but its availability is still limited – check with your doctor to find out its status in your country.

**Yellow Fever** A yellow fever vaccination is now the only vaccination legally required for entry into Malaysia for travellers over one year of age; it is usually only enforced if you're coming from an infected area such as parts of Africa and South America.

## Malaria Medication

Antimalarial drugs do not prevent you from being infected but do kill the malaria parasites during a stage in their development and significantly reduce your risk of becoming very ill or dying. Expert advice on malaria medication should be sought, as there are many factors to consider, including the area to be visited, the risk of exposure to malaria-carrying mosquitoes, the side effects of the available medication, your medical history and whether you are a child or an adult or pregnant. Travellers to isolated areas in high-risk countries may like to carry a treatment dose of medication for use if symptoms occur.

## Health Insurance

Make sure that you have adequate health insurance. See Travel Insurance under Visas & Documents earlier in this chapter for details.

## Travel Health Guides

Lonely Planet's *Healthy Travel: India & Asia* is a handy pocket-size and packed with useful information, including pretrip planning, emergency first aid, immunisation and disease information and what to do if you get sick on the road. *Travel with Children* from Lonely Planet also includes advice on travel health for younger children. If you are planning to be away or travelling in remote areas for a long period of time, you may like to consider taking a more-detailed health guide.

There are also many excellent travel-health sites on the Internet. Lonely Planet's home page has links at www.lonelyplanet.com/weblinks/wlprep.htm#heal to the World Health Organisation and the US Centers for Disease Control & Prevention.

**Other Preparations** Make sure you're healthy before you start travelling. If you are going on a long trip make sure your teeth are OK. If you wear glasses take a spare pair and your prescription. It's relatively easy to get replacements made in Malaysia.

If you require a particular medication take an adequate supply, as it may not be available locally. Take part of the packaging showing the generic name rather than the brand, which will make getting replacements easier. It's a good idea to have a legible prescription or letter from your doctor to show that you legally use the medication, to avoid any problems at customs.

## Basic Rules

**Food** Standards of food preparation in Malaysia are high and subject to government health controls, but that doesn't mean that standards of hygiene are always acceptable. Food stalls are generally safe places to eat but some are definitely on the grotty side. If a place looks clean and well run and the vendor also looks clean and healthy, then the food is probably safe. In general, places that are packed with travellers or locals will be fine, while empty restaurants are questionable. The food in busy restaurants is cooked and eaten quite quickly with little standing around and is probably not reheated.

Be particularly careful with some food. Shellfish such as mussels, oysters and clams should be avoided, as well as undercooked meat, particularly in the form of mince. Steaming does not make shellfish

safe for eating. Vegetables and fruit should be washed with purified water or peeled where possible. Beware of ice cream sold in the street or anywhere it might have been melted and refrozen; if there's any doubt (for example a power cut in the last day or two) steer well clear.

**Water** In the major towns and cities in Malaysia you can drink tap water, but it is still wise to ensure that water has been boiled if you're in a kampung or off the beaten track. If you don't know for certain that the water is safe, always assume the worst. A wide variety of bottled water is available in Malaysia. Reputable brands of bottled water or soft drinks are generally fine, although in some places bottles may be refilled with tap water. Only use water from containers with a serrated seal – not tops or corks.

Take care with fruit juice, particularly if water may have been added. Milk should be treated with suspicion as it is often unpasteurised, though boiled milk is fine if it is kept properly. Tea or coffee should also be OK, since the water should have been boiled.

**Water Purification** The simplest way of purifying water is to boil it thoroughly. Vigorous boiling should be satisfactory; however, at high altitude water boils at a lower temperature, so germs are less likely to be killed. Boil it for longer in these environments.

Consider purchasing a water filter for a long trip. There are two main kinds of filter. Total filters take out all parasites, bacteria and viruses and make water safe to drink. They are often expensive, but they can be more cost-effective than buying bottled water. Simple filters (which can even be a nylon mesh bag) take out dirt and larger foreign bodies from the water so that chemical solutions work much more effectively; if water is dirty, chemical solutions may not work at all. It's very important when buying a filter to read the specifications, so that you know exactly what it removes from the water and what it doesn't. Simple filtering will not remove all dangerous organisms, so if you cannot boil

## Nutrition

If your diet is poor or limited in variety, if you're travelling hard and fast and therefore missing meals or if you simply lose your appetite, you can soon start to lose weight and place your health at risk.

Make sure your diet is well balanced. Cooked eggs, tofu, beans, lentils (dhal in India) and nuts are all safe ways to get protein. Fruit you can peel (bananas, oranges or mandarins, for example) is usually safe and a good source of vitamins. Melons can harbour bacteria in their flesh and are best 'avoided. Try to eat plenty of grains (including rice) and bread. Remember that although food is generally safer if it is cooked well, overcooked food loses much of its nutritional value. If your diet isn't well balanced or if your food intake is insufficient, it's a good idea to take vitamin and iron pills.

In hot climates make sure you drink enough – don't rely on feeling thirsty to indicate when you should drink. Not needing to urinate or voiding small amounts of very dark yellow urine is a danger sign. Always carry a water bottle with you on long trips. Excessive sweating can lead to loss of salt and therefore muscle cramping. Salt tablets are not a good idea as a preventative, but in places where salt is not used much, adding salt to food can help.

water it should be treated chemically. Chlorine tablets will kill many pathogens, but not some parasites like giardia and amoebic cysts. Iodine is more effective in purifying water and is available in tablet form. Follow the directions carefully and remember that too much iodine can be harmful.

### Medical Problems & Treatment

Self-diagnosis and treatment can be risky, so you should always seek medical help. An embassy, consulate or five-star hotel can usually recommend a local doctor or clinic. Although we do give drug dosages in this section, they are for emergency use only. Correct diagnosis is vital. In this section we have used the generic names for medications – check with a pharmacist for brands available locally.

Note that antibiotics should ideally be administered only under medical supervision. Take only the recommended dose at the prescribed intervals and use the whole course, even if the illness seems to be cured earlier. Stop immediately if there are any serious reactions and don't use the antibiotic at all if you are unsure that you have the correct one. Some people are allergic to commonly prescribed antibiotics such as penicillin; carry this information (eg, on a bracelet) when travelling.

### Environmental Hazards

**Altitude Sickness** Lack of oxygen at high altitudes (over 2500m) affects most people to some extent. In Malaysia the only place you're likely to get it is on Mt Kinabalu in Sabah. The effect may be mild or severe and occurs because less oxygen reaches the muscles and the brain at high altitude, requiring the heart and lungs to compensate by working harder. Symptoms of acute mountain sickness (AMS) usually develop during the first 24 hours at altitude but may be delayed up to three weeks. Mild symptoms include headache, lethargy, dizziness, difficulty sleeping and loss of appetite. AMS may become more severe without warning and can be fatal. Severe symptoms include breathlessness, a dry, irritative cough (which may progress to the production of pink, frothy sputum), severe headache, lack of coordination and balance, confusion, irrational behaviour, vomiting, drowsiness and unconsciousness. There is no hard-and-fast rule as to what is too high: AMS has been fatal at 3000m, although 3500 to 4500m is the usual range.

It is compulsory to take a guide up Mt Kinabalu. If you develop symptoms, you should tell your guide. Treat mild symptoms by resting at the same altitude until recovery, usually a day or two. Paracetamol or aspirin can be taken for headaches. If symptoms persist or become worse, however, *immediate descent is necessary;* even 500m can help. Drug treatments should never be used to avoid descent or to enable further ascent.

The drugs acetazolamide (Diamox) and dexamethasone are recommended by some doctors for the prevention of AMS, however, their use is controversial. They can reduce the symptoms, but they may also mask warning signs; severe and fatal AMS has occurred in people taking these drugs. In general we do not recommend them for travellers.

To prevent acute mountain sickness:

- Ascend slowly – have frequent rest days, spending two to three nights at each rise of 1000m. If you reach a high altitude by trekking, acclimatisation takes place gradually and you are less likely to be affected than if you fly directly to high altitude.
- It is always wise to sleep at a lower altitude than the greatest height reached during the day, if possible. Also, once above 3000m, care should be taken not to increase the sleeping altitude by more than 300m per day.
- Drink extra fluids. The mountain air is dry and cold and moisture is lost as you breathe. Evaporation of sweat may occur unnoticed and result in dehydration.
- Eat light, high-carbohydrate meals for more energy.
- Avoid alcohol as it may increase the risk of dehydration.
- Avoid sedatives.

**Heat Exhaustion** Dehydration and salt deficiency can cause heat exhaustion. Take time to acclimatise to high temperatures, drink sufficient liquids and do not do anything too physically demanding.

Salt deficiency is characterised by fatigue, lethargy, headaches, giddiness and muscle cramps; salt tablets may help, but adding extra salt to your food is better.

Anhidrotic heat exhaustion is a rare form of heat exhaustion that is caused by an inability to sweat. It tends to affect people who have been in a hot climate for some time, rather than newcomers. It can progress to heatstroke. Treatment involves removal to a cooler climate.

**Heatstroke** This serious, occasionally fatal, condition can occur if the body's heat-regulating mechanism breaks down and the body temperature rises to dangerous levels. Long, continuous periods of exposure to high temperatures and insufficient fluids can leave you vulnerable to heatstroke.

The symptoms are feeling unwell, not sweating very much (or at all) and a high body temperature (39° to 41°C or 102° to 106°F). Where sweating has ceased, the skin becomes flushed and red. Severe, throbbing headaches and lack of coordination will also occur, and the sufferer may be confused or aggressive. Eventually the victim will become delirious or convulse. Hospitalisation is essential, but in the interim get victims out of the sun, remove their clothing, cover them with a wet sheet or towel and then fan continually. Give fluids if they are conscious.

**Hypothermia** Too much cold can be just as dangerous as too much heat. If you are trekking at high altitudes or simply taking a long bus trip over mountains, particularly at night, be prepared. Sarawak's Kelabit Highlands and Sabah's Mt Kinabalu are the only places in Malaysia where there is a risk of hypothermia.

Hypothermia occurs when the body loses heat faster than it can produce it and the core temperature of the body falls. It is surprisingly easy to progress from very cold to dangerously cold due to a combination of wind, wet clothing, fatigue and hunger, even if the air temperature is above freezing. It is best to dress in layers: silk, wool and some of the new artificial fibres are all good insulating materials. A hat is important, as a lot of heat is lost through the head. A strong, waterproof outer layer (and a 'space' blanket for emergencies) is essential. Carry basic supplies, including food containing simple sugars to generate heat quickly and fluid to drink.

Symptoms of hypothermia are exhaustion, numb skin (particularly toes and fingers), shivering, slurred speech, irrational or violent behaviour, lethargy, stumbling, dizzy spells, muscle cramps and violent bursts of energy. Irrationality may take the form of sufferers claiming they are warm and trying to take off their clothes.

To treat mild hypothermia, first get the person out of the wind and/or rain, remove their clothing if it's wet and replace it with dry, warm clothing. Give them hot liquids – not alcohol – and some high-kilojoule, easily digestible food. Do not rub victims: instead, allow them to slowly warm themselves. This should be enough to treat the early stages of hypothermia. The early recognition and treatment of mild hypothermia is the only way to prevent severe hypothermia, which is a critical condition.

**Jet Lag** Jet lag is experienced when a person travels by air across more than three time zones (each time zone usually represents a one-hour time difference). It occurs because many of the functions of the human body (such as temperature, pulse rate and emptying of the bladder and bowels) are regulated by internal 24-hour cycles. When we travel long distances rapidly, our bodies take time to adjust to the 'new time' of our destination, and we may experience fatigue, disorientation, insomnia, anxiety, impaired concentration and loss of appetite. These effects will usually be gone within three days of arrival, but to minimise the impact of jet lag:

- Rest for a couple of days prior to departure.
- Try to select flight schedules that minimise sleep deprivation; arriving late in the day means you can go to sleep soon after you arrive. For very long flights, try to organise a stopover.
- Avoid excessive eating (which bloats the stomach) and alcohol (which causes dehydration) during the flight. Instead, drink plenty of non-carbonated, nonalcoholic drinks such as fruit juice or water.
- Avoid smoking.
- Make yourself comfortable by wearing loose-fitting clothes and perhaps bringing an eye mask and ear plugs to help you sleep.
- Try to sleep at the appropriate time for the time zone you are travelling to.

**Motion Sickness** Eating lightly before and during a trip will reduce the chances of motion sickness. If you are prone to motion sickness try to find a place that minimises movement – near the wing on aircraft, close to midships on boats, near the centre on buses. Fresh air usually helps; reading and cigarette smoke don't. Commercial motion-sickness preparations, which can cause drowsiness, have to be taken before the trip commences. Ginger (available in capsule form) and peppermint (including mint-flavoured sweets) are natural preventatives.

**Prickly Heat** Prickly heat is an itchy rash caused by excessive perspiration trapped under the skin. It usually strikes people who have just arrived in a hot climate. Keeping cool, bathing often, drying the skin and using a mild talcum or prickly heat powder or resorting to air-conditioning may help.

**Sunburn** In Malaysia's tropics, the desert or at high altitude you can get sunburnt surprisingly quickly, even through cloud. Use a sunscreen, a hat, and a barrier cream for your nose and lips. Calamine lotion or a commercial after-sun preparation are good for mild sunburn. Protect your eyes with good-quality sunglasses, particularly if you will be near water, sand or snow.

## Infectious Diseases

**Diarrhoea** Simple things like a change of water, food or climate can all cause a mild bout of diarrhoea, but a few rushed toilet trips with no other symptoms is not indicative of a major problem.

Dehydration is the main danger with any diarrhoea, particularly in children or the elderly as dehydration can occur quite quickly. Under all circumstances *fluid replacement* (at least equal to the volume being lost) is the most important thing to remember. Weak black tea with a little sugar, soda water, or soft drinks allowed to go flat and diluted 50% with clean water are all good. With severe diarrhoea a rehydrating solution is preferable to replace lost minerals and salts. Commercially available oral rehydration salts (ORS) are very useful; add them to boiled or bottled water. In an emergency you can make up a solution of six teaspoons of sugar and a half-teaspoon of salt to a litre of boiled or bottled water. You need to drink at least the same volume of fluid that you are losing in bowel movements and vomiting. Urine is the best guide to the adequacy of replacement – if you have small amounts of concentrated urine, you need to

## Everyday Health

Normal body temperature is up to 37°C (98.6°F); more than 2°C (4°F) higher indicates a high fever. The normal adult pulse rate is 60 to 100 per minute (children 80 to 100, babies 100 to 140). As a general rule the pulse increases about 20 beats per minute for each 1°C (2°F) rise in fever.

Respiration (breathing) rate is also an indicator of illness. Count the number of breaths per minute: Between 12 and 20 is normal for adults and older children (up to 30 for younger children, 40 for babies). People with a high fever or serious respiratory illness breathe more quickly than normal. More than 40 shallow breaths a minute may indicate pneumonia.

drink more. Keep drinking small amounts often. Stick to a bland diet as you recover.

Gut-paralysing drugs such as loperamide or diphenoxylate can be used to bring relief from the symptoms, although they do not actually cure the problem. Only use these drugs if you do not have access to toilets, eg, if you *must* travel. Note that these drugs are not recommended for children under 12 years.

In certain situations antibiotics may be required: diarrhoea with blood or mucus (dysentery), any diarrhoea with fever, profuse watery diarrhoea, persistent diarrhoea not improving after 48 hours and severe diarrhoea. These suggest a more serious cause of diarrhoea and in these situations gut-paralysing drugs should be avoided.

In these cases, a stool test may be necessary to diagnose what bug is causing your diarrhoea, so you should seek medical help urgently. Where this is not possible the recommended drugs for bacterial diarrhoea (the most likely cause of severe diarrhoea in travellers) are norfloxacin 400mg twice daily for three days or ciprofloxacin 500mg twice daily for five days. These are not recommended for children or pregnant women. The drug of choice for children would be co-trimoxazole with dosage dependent on weight. A five-day course is given. Ampicillin or amoxycillin may be given in pregnancy, but medical care is necessary.

Two other causes of persistent diarrhoea in travellers are giardiasis and amoebic dysentery.

**Giardiasis** is caused by a common parasite, *Giardia lamblia*. Symptoms include stomach cramps, nausea, a bloated stomach, watery, foul-smelling diarrhoea and frequent gas. Giardiasis can appear several weeks after you have been exposed to the parasite. The symptoms may disappear for a few days and then return; this can go on for several weeks.

**Amoebic dysentery**, caused by the protozoan *Entamoeba histolytica*, is characterised by a gradual onset of low-grade diarrhoea, often with blood and mucus. Cramping abdominal pain and vomiting are less likely than in other types of diarrhoea, and fever may not be present. It will persist until treated and can recur and cause other health problems.

You should seek medical advice if you think you have giardiasis or amoebic dysentery, but where this is not possible, tinidazole or metronidazole are the recommended drugs. Treatment is a 2g single dose of tinidazole or 250mg of metronidazole three times daily for five to 10 days.

**Fungal Infections** Fungal infections occur more commonly in hot weather and are usually found on the scalp, between the toes (athlete's foot) or fingers, in the groin and on the body (ringworm). You get ringworm (which is a fungal infection, not a worm) from infected animals or other people. Moisture encourages these infections.

To prevent fungal infections wear loose, comfortable clothes, avoid artificial fibres, wash frequently and dry yourself carefully. If you do get an infection, wash the infected area at least daily with a disinfectant or medicated soap and water, and rinse and dry well. Apply an antifungal cream or powder like tolnaftate. Try to expose the infected area to air or sunlight as much as possible and wash all towels and underwear in hot water, change them often and let them dry in the sun.

**Hepatitis** Hepatitis is a general term for inflammation of the liver. It is a common disease worldwide. There are several different viruses that cause hepatitis, and they differ in the way that they are transmitted. The symptoms are similar in all forms of the illness, and include fever, chills, headache, fatigue, feelings of weakness and aches and pains, followed by loss of appetite, nausea, vomiting, abdominal pain, dark urine, light-coloured faeces, jaundiced (yellow) skin and yellowing of the whites of the eyes. People who have had hepatitis should avoid alcohol for some time after the illness, as the liver needs time to recover.

**Hepatitis A** is transmitted by contaminated food and drinking water. You should seek medical advice, but there is not much you can do apart from resting, drinking lots of fluids, eating lightly and avoiding fatty foods. Hepatitis E is transmitted in the same way as hepatitis A; it can be particularly serious in pregnant women.

There are almost 300 million chronic carriers of **hepatitis B** in the world. It is spread through contact with infected blood, blood products or body fluids, for example through sexual contact, unsterilised needles and blood transfusions, or contact with blood via small breaks in the skin. Other risk situations include having a shave, tattoo or body piercing with contaminated equipment. The symptoms of hepatitis B may be more severe than type A and the disease can lead to long-term problems such as chronic liver damage, liver cancer or a long-term carrier state. Hepatitis C and D are spread in the same way as hepatitis B and can also lead to long term complications.

There are vaccines against hepatitis A and B, but there are currently no vaccines against the other types of hepatitis. Following the basic rules about food and water (hepatitis A and E) and avoiding risk situations (hepatitis B, C and D) are important preventative measures.

**HIV/AIDS** Infection with the human immunodeficiency virus (HIV) may lead to acquired immune deficiency syndrome (AIDS), which is a fatal disease. Any exposure to blood, blood products or body fluids may put the individual at risk. The disease is often transmitted through sexual contact or dirty needles – vaccinations, acupuncture, tattooing and body piercing can be potentially as dangerous as intravenous drug use. HIV/AIDS can also be spread through infected blood transfusions; in Malaysia this is generally not a problem.

If you do need an injection, ask to see the syringe unwrapped in front of you, or take a needle and syringe pack with you.

Fear of HIV infection should never preclude treatment for serious medical conditions.

To avoid infection through sexual contact, make sure you practise safe sex. Condoms are available throughout Malaysia, but they are of varying quality and may be hard to find in rural areas – take your own to be safe.

**Intestinal Worms** These parasites are most common in rural, tropical areas. The different worms have different ways of infecting people. Some may be ingested on food such as undercooked meat (eg, tapeworms) and some enter through your skin (eg, hookworms). Infestations may not show up for some time, and although they are generally not serious, if left untreated some can cause severe health problems later. Consider having a stool test when you return home to check for these and determine the appropriate treatment.

**Sexually Transmitted Infections** HIV/AIDS and hepatitis B can be transmitted through sexual contact – see relevant entries earlier in this section for more details. Other STIs include gonorrhoea, herpes and syphilis; sores, blisters or rashes around the genitals and discharges or pain when urinating are common symptoms. In some STIs, such as wart virus or chlamydia, symptoms may be less marked or not observed at all, especially in women. Chlamydia infection can cause infertility in men and women before any symptoms have been noticed. Syphilis symptoms eventually disappear but the disease continues and can cause severe problems in later years. While abstinence from sexual contact is the only 100% effective prevention, using condoms is also effective. The treatment of gonorrhoea and syphilis is with antibiotics. Different sexually transmitted infections require specific antibiotics.

**Typhoid** Typhoid fever is a dangerous gut infection caused by contaminated water and food. Medical help must be sought.

In its early stages sufferers may feel they have a bad cold or flu on the way, as early symptoms are a headache, body aches and a fever that rises a little each day until it is around 40°C (104°F) or more. The victim's pulse is often slow relative to the degree of fever present – unlike a normal fever where the pulse increases. There may also be vomiting, abdominal pain, diarrhoea or constipation.

In the second week the high fever and slow pulse continue and a few pink spots may appear on the body; trembling, delirium, weakness, weight loss and dehydration may occur. Complications such as pneumonia, perforated bowel or meningitis may occur.

### Insect-Borne Diseases

Chagas' disease, filariasis, leishmaniasis, Lyme disease, sleeping sickness, typhus and yellow fever are all insect-borne diseases, but they do not pose a great risk to travellers in Malaysia.

**Malaria** This serious and potentially fatal disease is spread by mosquito bites. It is endemic in Malaysian Borneo, but apart from occasional, isolated outbreaks, it is not found in Peninsular Malaysia. It crops up every now and then in the Cameron Highlands, but the risk is low. Unless you are planning on spending extended periods in the Cameron Highlands, malarial prophylactics are unnecessary. For Sabah and Sarawak, they are recommended – malaria is prevalent throughout Sabah.

If you are travelling in endemic areas it is extremely important to avoid mosquito bites and to take tablets to prevent this disease. Symptoms range from fever, chills and sweating, headache, diarrhoea and abdominal pains to a vague feeling of ill-health. Seek medical help immediately if malaria is suspected. Without treatment malaria can rapidly become more serious and can be fatal.

If medical care is not available, malaria tablets can be used for treatment. You need to use a malaria tablet that is different from the one you were taking when you contracted malaria. The standard treatment dose of mefloquine is two 250mg tablets and a further two six hours later. For Fansidar, it's a single dose of three tablets. If you were previously taking mefloquine and cannot obtain Fansidar, then other alternatives are Malarone (atovaquone-proguanil; four tablets once daily for three days), halofantrine (three doses of two 250mg tablets every six hours) or quinine sulphate (600mg every six hours). There is a greater risk of side effects with these dosages than in normal use if used with mefloquine, so medical advice is preferable. Be aware also that halofantrine is no longer recommended by the World Health Organization (WHO) as emergency standby treatment, because of side effects, and should only be used if no other drugs are available.

Travellers are advised to prevent mosquito bites at all times. The main messages are:

- Wear light-coloured clothing.
- Wear long trousers and long-sleeved shirts.
- Use mosquito repellents containing the compound DEET on exposed areas (prolonged overuse of DEET may be harmful, especially to children, but its use is considered preferable to being bitten by disease-transmitting mosquitoes).
- Avoid perfumes or aftershave.
- Use a mosquito net impregnated with mosquito repellent (permethrin) – it may be worth taking your own.
- Impregnate clothes with permethrin – this effectively deters mosquitoes and other insects.

**Dengue Fever** This viral disease is transmitted by mosquitoes and is fast becoming one of the top public-health problems in the tropical world. It is present in both East and West Malaysia. Unlike the malaria mosquito, the *Aedes aegypti* mosquito (which transmits the dengue virus) is most active during the day, and is found mainly in urban areas, in and around human dwellings.

Signs and symptoms of dengue fever include a sudden onset of high fever, headache, joint and muscle pains (hence its old name, 'breakbone fever') and nausea and vomiting. A rash of small red spots sometimes appears three to four days after the onset of fever. In the early phase of illness, dengue may be mistaken for other infectious diseases, including malaria and influenza. Minor bleeding such as nose bleeds may occur in the course of the illness, but this does not necessarily mean that you have progressed to the potentially fatal dengue haemorrhagic fever (DHF). This is a severe illness, characterised by heavy bleeding, which is thought to be a result of second infection due to a different strain (there are four major strains) and usually affects residents of the country rather than travellers. Recovery even from simple dengue fever may be prolonged, with tiredness lasting for several weeks.

You should seek medical attention as soon as possible if you think you may be infected. A blood test can exclude malaria and indicate the possibility of dengue fever. There is no specific treatment for dengue. Aspirin should be avoided, as it increases the risk of haemorrhaging. There is no vaccine against dengue fever. The best prevention is to avoid mosquito bites at all times by covering up, using insect repellents containing the compound DEET, and mosquito nets – see the Malaria entry earlier for more advice on avoiding mosquito bites.

**Japanese B Encephalitis** This viral infection of the brain is transmitted by mosquitoes. Most cases occur in rural areas, as the virus exists in pigs and wading birds. Symptoms include fever, headache and alteration in consciousness. Hospitalisation is needed for correct diagnosis and treatment. There is a high mortality rate among those who have symptoms; of those who survive many are intellectually disabled.

## Cuts, Bites & Stings

See Less-Common Diseases later in this section for details of rabies, which is passed through animal bites.

**Cuts & Scratches** Wash well and treat any cut with an antiseptic such as povidone-iodine. Where possible avoid bandages and Band-Aids, which can keep wounds wet. Coral cuts are notoriously slow to heal and if they are not adequately cleaned, small pieces of coral can become embedded in the wound.

**Bedbugs & Lice** Bedbugs live in various places, but particularly in dirty mattresses and bedding, evidenced by spots of blood on bedclothes or on the wall. Bedbugs leave itchy bites in neat rows. Calamine lotion or a sting-relief spray may help.

All lice cause itching and discomfort. They make themselves at home in your hair (head lice), your clothing (body lice) or in your pubic hair (crabs). You catch lice through direct contact with infected people or by sharing combs, clothing and the like. Powder or shampoo treatment will kill the lice and infected clothing should then be washed in very hot, soapy water and left in the sun to dry.

**Bites & Stings** Bee and wasp stings are usually painful rather than dangerous. However, in people who are allergic to them severe breathing difficulties may occur and require urgent medical care. Calamine lotion or a sting-relief spray will give relief and ice packs will reduce the pain and swelling. There are some spiders with dangerous bites but antivenenes are usually available. Scorpions often shelter in shoes or clothing; their stings are notoriously painful. Certain cone shells can sting dangerously or even fatally. There are various fish and other sea creatures that can sting or bite dangerously or that are dangerous to eat – seek local advice.

**Leeches & Ticks** Leeches may be present in damp rainforest conditions; they attach themselves to your skin to suck your blood. Trekkers often get them on their legs or in their boots. Salt or a lit cigarette end will make them fall off. Do not pull them off, as the bite is then more likely to become infected. Clean and apply pressure if the point of attachment is bleeding. An insect repellent may keep them away.

You should always check all over your body if you have been walking through a potentially tick-infested area as ticks can cause skin infections and other more-serious diseases. If a tick is found attached, press down around the tick's head with tweezers, grab the head and gently pull upwards. Avoid pulling the rear of the body as this may squeeze the tick's gut contents through the attached mouth parts into the skin, increasing the risk of infection and disease. Smearing chemicals on the tick will not make it let go and is not recommended.

**Snakes** To minimise your chances of being bitten always wear boots, socks and long trousers when walking through undergrowth where snakes may be present. Don't put your hands into holes and crevices, and be careful when collecting firewood.

Snake bites do not cause instantaneous death and antivenenes are usually available. Immediately wrap the bitten limb tightly, as you would for a sprained ankle, and then attach a splint to immobilise it. Keep the victim still and seek medical help, if possible with the dead snake for identification. Don't attempt to catch the snake if there is a possibility of being bitten again. Tourniquets and sucking out the poison are now comprehensively discredited.

## Women's Health
**Gynaecological Problems** Antibiotic use, synthetic underwear, sweating and contraceptive pills can lead to fungal vaginal infections, especially when travelling in hot climates. Thrush or vaginal candidiasis is characterised by a rash, itch and discharge. Nystatin, miconazole or clotrimazole pessaries are the usual treatment, but some people use a more traditional remedy involving vinegar or lemon-juice douches, or yoghurt. Maintaining good personal hygiene and wearing loose-fitting clothes and cotton underwear may help prevent these infections.

Sexually transmitted diseases are a major cause of vaginal problems. Symptoms include a smelly discharge, painful intercourse and sometimes a burning sensation when urinating. Medical attention should be sought and male sexual partners must also be treated. For more details see the entry on Sexually

Transmitted Infections, under Infectious Diseases, earlier. Besides abstinence, the best thing is to practise safer sex using condoms.

**Pregnancy** It is not advisable to travel to some places while pregnant as a few vaccinations normally used to prevent serious diseases are not advisable during pregnancy (eg, yellow fever). In addition, some diseases are much more serious for the mother (and may increase the risk of a stillborn child) in pregnancy (eg, malaria).

Most miscarriages occur during the first three months of pregnancy. Miscarriage is not uncommon and can occasionally lead to severe bleeding. The last three months should also be spent within reasonable distance of good medical care. A baby born as early as 24 weeks stands a chance of survival, but only in a good modern hospital. Pregnant women should avoid all unnecessary medication, although vaccinations and malarial prophylactics should still be taken where needed. Additional care should be taken to prevent illness and particular attention should be paid to diet and nutrition. Alcohol and nicotine, for example, should be avoided.

## Less-Common Diseases
The following diseases pose a small risk to travellers in Malaysia, and so are only mentioned in passing. Seek medical advice if you think you may have any of these diseases.

**Cholera** This is the worst of the watery diarrhoeas and medical help should be sought. Outbreaks of cholera are generally widely reported, so you can avoid such problem areas. *Fluid replacement is the most vital treatment* – the risk of dehydration is severe as you may lose up to 20L a day. If there is a delay in getting to hospital, then begin taking tetracycline. The adult dose is 250mg four times daily. It is not recommended for children under nine years nor for pregnant women. Tetracycline may help shorten the illness, but adequate fluids are required to save lives.

**Filariasis** This is a mosquito-transmitted parasitic infection found in many parts of

Africa, Asia (including Malaysia), Central and South America and the Pacific. Possible symptoms include fever, pain and swelling of the lymph glands; inflammation of lymph drainage areas; swelling of a limb or the scrotum; skin rashes; and blindness. Treatment is available to eliminate the parasites from the body, but some of the damage already caused may not be reversible. Medical advice should be obtained promptly if the infection is suspected.

**Rabies** This fatal viral infection is found in many countries, including Malaysia. Many animals can be infected (such as dogs, cats, bats and monkeys) and it is their saliva that is infectious. Any bite, scratch or even lick from an animal should be cleaned immediately and thoroughly. Scrub with soap and running water, and then apply alcohol or iodine solution. Medical help should be sought promptly to receive a course of injections to prevent the onset of symptoms and death.

**Tetanus** This disease is caused by a germ that lives in soil and in the faeces of horses and other animals. It enters the body via breaks in the skin. The first symptom may be discomfort in swallowing, or stiffening of the jaw and neck; this is followed by painful convulsions of the jaw and whole body. The disease can be fatal. It can be prevented by vaccination.

**Tuberculosis (TB)** TB is a bacterial infection usually transmitted from person to person by coughing but which may be transmitted through consumption of unpasteurised milk. Milk that has been boiled is safe to drink, and the souring of milk to make yoghurt or cheese also kills the bacilli. Travellers are usually not at great risk as close household contact with the infected person is usually required before the disease is passed on. You may need to have a TB test before you travel as this can help diagnose the disease later if you become ill.

**Typhus** This disease is spread by mites in Malaysia. It begins with fever, chills, headache and muscle pains followed a few days later by a body rash. There is often a large painful sore at the site of the bite and nearby lymph nodes are swollen and painful. Typhus can be treated under medical supervision.

## WOMEN TRAVELLERS
The following information unfortunately reflects the experiences of a growing number of women travellers in Malaysia, including Lonely Planet authors. Solo women can often (and unfairly) become lightning rods for trouble once in Malaysia, an especially rude awakening for those travelling overland from gentler Thailand or Singapore. While we don't suggest that women shouldn't travel here, we do think it's important to be aware of safety issues you might encounter.

Foreign women travelling in Malaysia can expect hassles ranging from minor verbal aggravation to full-on physical assault. What you run into really depends on where in Malaysia you are. In general, it's easier-going in Borneo, especially in Sarawak, and worse on both coasts of Peninsular Malaysia.

Hard as it is to say, the truth is that the closer you get to conservative Muslim areas, the more aggressive Malay men tend to be towards women who look obviously foreign. In contrast, you are unlikely to be hassled too much in the Indian-populated highlands resorts or the Little Indias of major west-coast cities. You're even safer in Malaysia's many Chinatowns, where harassment of foreign women is just about unheard of.

In Peninsular Malaysia, the farther you go off the well-beaten routes, the greater your chances of being groped, fondled, flashed, masturbated on, followed or having the unspeakable pleasure of several men simultaneously beating down your hotel-room door at 2 am. On the west coast, the cities of Alor Setar and Ipoh, as well as the backpacker resorts on Pulau Pangkor, are especially unsafe for women; on the east coast, exercise caution in the states of Kelantan and Terengganu, particularly in rural areas. After dark, travellers of both sexes should take care not to wander beaches alone.

All this is not to say 'don't go', but be proactive about your own safety. Treat overly friendly strangers, both male and female, with a good deal of caution. Many travellers have reported the existence of small peep-holes in the walls and doors of cheap hotels, some of which operate as boarding houses or brothels (often identified by their advertising 'day use' rates). You could always plug the holes with tissue paper or try asking to change rooms, but if you're on a budget, you may not have much of a choice in some towns. This is especially true in Sarawak, where if there's a cage around the reception desk, you can bet it's probably a brothel and/or gambling den. When you have a choice, stay in a Chinatown, or at least in a Chinese-operated hotel. On island resorts, stick to crowded beaches and choose a chalet close to reception and other travellers.

No matter how limited your budget, it sometimes pays to upgrade – pay for taxis after dark or in seedy areas of town and treat yourself to a mid-range hotel if all your other options are brothels. You won't regret it.

Keep in mind that the majority of Malaysians are Muslim and modesty in dress is culturally important. In conservative Muslim areas, you can cut your hassles in half just by tying a bandanna over your hair (a minimal concession to the headscarf worn by most Muslim Malay women). When visiting mosques, you must cover all limbs and either borrow a headscarf at the mosque entrance or buy one of the cheap silk ones (RM3) available on the street. At the beach, most Malaysian women swim fully clothed in T-shirts and shorts, so don't go topless – cover up.

Tampons and pads are widely available in Malaysia, especially in the big cities, and over-the-counter medications for common gynaecological health problems (like yeast infections) are also fairly easy to find.

## GAY & LESBIAN TRAVELLERS

Malaysia attracted worldwide attention with the October 1998 launch of Pasrah, the People's Anti-Homosexual Voluntary Movement. The group, which contains at least one high-ranking member of the ruling UMNO party, calls for a crackdown on homosexuality and the closing of gay clubs in Malaysia.

This story isn't exactly new; conservative political parties make a regular habit of denouncing gays and lesbians in Malaysia, a country where homosexuality is punishable by imprisonment and caning. Fortunately, Pasrah and its ilk remain on the political fringe and outright persecution of gays and lesbians is rare. Nonetheless, gay and lesbian travellers (particularly the former) should avoid behaviour that attracts unwanted attention while in the country.

In light of all this, you may be surprised to hear that there is actually a fairly active gay scene in KL. The lesbian scene is less obvious but, naturally, exists for those willing to seek it out. The best place to look for information on Malaysia's gay and lesbian scene is Utopia's Travel & Resources Web site at www.utopia-asia.com/tipsmala.htm.

## DISABLED TRAVELLERS

For the mobility impaired, Malaysia can be a nightmare. In most cities and towns there are often no footpaths; kerbs are very high; construction sites are everywhere; and crossings are few and far between. On the up-side, the modern urban rail lines being built in KL are at least reasonably accessible.

Both Malaysia Airlines and KTM (the national rail service) offer 50% discounts on travel for disabled travellers.

Three travel-information sources for the mobility-impaired are Mobility USA (☎ 1-541 343 1284), PO Box 1076, Eugene, OR 97440, USA; Holiday Care Service (☎ 01293-774535, fax 784647), Imperial Buildings, Victoria Road, Horley, Surrey, RH6 7PZ, England; and the Global Access Disability Travel Network, on the Web at www.geocities.com/Paris/1502/.

## SENIOR TRAVELLERS

Senior travellers get a variety of discounts on admission at most cultural attractions. The usual eligible age for seniors is 65 years. Malaysia Airlines does not offer discounts for foreign seniors, but KTM does offer a 50% discount on all travel for foreign seniors over 65 years of age.

Senior travellers will find plenty of useful travel information on the Web. Two sites to

try are the Senior Travel Links at http\\.
webfanatix.com/senior_travel_resources.htm
and the Senior Travel page at www.travel
health.com/seniors/seniors.phtml.

## TRAVEL WITH CHILDREN

Like many places in South-East Asia, travelling with children in Malaysia can be a lot
of fun as long as you come with the right attitudes and the usual parental patience.
*Travel with Children* by Maureen Wheeler
and others contains useful advice on how to
cope with kids on the road and what to
bring along to make things go more
smoothly, with special attention paid to
travel in developing countries.

There are discounts for children for most
attractions and for most transport in
Malaysia. Many beach-resorts have special
family chalets that average RM70 per night.
Chinese hotels are also a good bargain as
they charge by the room rather than the
number of people. Cots, however, are not
widely available in cheap accommodation.
Public transport is comfortable and relatively well organised.

Baby formula, baby food and nappies
(diapers) are widely available in Malaysia.
However, it makes sense to stock up on
these items before heading to remote destinations or islands.

For the most part parents needn't worry
too much about health concerns, though it
pays to lay down a few ground rules – such
as regular hand-washing – to head off potential problems. All the usual health precautions apply (see the Health section
earlier for details); children should especially be warned not to play with animals,
as rabies occurs in Malaysia.

Some beach destinations suitable for
families with younger children include
Pulau Perhentian (Besar), Pulau Kapas and
Tunku Abdul Rahman National Park. Those
with older children might enjoy some of the
jungle parks of the country, including
Taman Negara National Park.

## DANGERS & ANNOYANCES

We've received a number of letters and
emails, especially from women, complaining

about UBAT Adventure Tours. We suggest
you check the details of its tours very carefully. Other operators mentioned in this book
have been personally checked by the authors
and should be reliable. However, you should
always check terms and conditions carefully.

### Theft

Malaysia is not a theft-prone country – in
fact, compared with Indonesia or Thailand
it is extremely safe. Nevertheless, it pays to
keep a close eye on your belongings, especially your travel documents (passport,
travellers cheques etc), which should be
kept with you at all times.

A small, sturdy padlock is well worth
carrying, especially if you are going to be
staying at any of the cheap chalets found on
Malaysia's beaches, where flimsy padlocks
are the norm.

### Violence

While Malaysia is generally safe for travellers of both sexes, physical attacks have
been known to occur, particularly after
hours and in dangerous neighbourhoods. In
particular, keep your wits about you in the
town of Sibu in Sarawak. See the Women
Travellers section earlier in this chapter.

### Scams

When in KL beware of scams. Many of
these involve card games or the purchase of
large amounts of gold jewellery. Still others
involve people who claim to have a relative
studying abroad; these always start with the
scammer asking you where you come from
– the best answer is none at all.

The scam-of-the-day may have changed
by the time this book is published, but if you
use common sense and avoid deals that seem
too good to be true, you should be all right.

## LEGAL MATTERS
### Drugs

In Malaysia, the answer is simple – don't.
Drug trafficking carries a mandatory death
penalty. In almost every village in Malaysia
you will see anti-*dada* (drugs) signs por-
traying a skull and crossbones and a noose.
No one can say they haven't been warned!

MALAYSIA

Under Malaysian law all drug offenders are considered equal, and being a foreigner will not save you from the gallows. A number of foreigners have been executed in Malaysia, some of them for possession of amazingly small quantities of heroin.

The penalties are severe and the authorities seem to catch a steady stream of unsuccessful peddlers, smugglers and users. Mere possession can bring down a lengthy jail sentence and a beating with the *rotan* (a cane).

## BUSINESS HOURS

Government offices are usually open from 8 am to 4.15 pm weekdays. Most close for lunch from 12.45 to 2 pm, and on Friday the lunch break is from 12.15 to 2.45 pm for Friday prayers at the mosque. The offices are open from 8 am to 12.45 pm on Saturday.

Bank hours are generally 10 am to 3 pm on weekdays and 9.30 to 11.30 am on Saturday. Shop hours are variable, although a good rule of thumb for small shops is that they're open from 9 am to 6 pm from Monday to Saturday. Major department stores, shopping malls, Chinese emporiums and some large stores are open from around 10 am until 9 or 10 pm seven days a week.

Most of Malaysia follows this working week – Monday to Friday with Saturday a half-day. But in the more Islamic-minded states of Kedah, Perlis, Kelantan and Terengganu, government offices, banks and many shops are closed on Friday and on Saturday afternoon. They have declared Friday the holiday, and their working week is from Sunday to Thursday with Saturday a half-day. However, federal government offices follow the same hours as the rest of the country.

## PUBLIC HOLIDAYS & SPECIAL EVENTS

With so many cultures and religions in Malaysia, there is quite an amazing number of occasions to celebrate. Although some of them have a fixed date each year, the Hindus, Muslims and Chinese all follow a lunar calendar, so the dates for many events vary each year. Tourism Malaysia puts out bi-annual *Calendar of Events* sheets with specific dates and venues of various festivals

and parades, but state tourist offices have more-detailed listings.

## Public Holidays

In addition to national public holidays, each state has its own holidays, usually associated with the sultan's birthday or a Muslim celebration. Muslim holidays move back 10 or 11 days each year, and dates given here may vary by one day. Hindu and Chinese holiday dates also vary but fall roughly within the same months each year. National holidays in the following list of Malaysia's mind-boggling number of public holidays are marked with an asterisk (*).

### January–February
**New Year's Day** 1 January (National except Johor, Kedah, Kelantan, Perlis and Terengganu)
**Thaipusam** Variable (7 February 2001; Johor, Negeri Sembilan, Perak, Penang and Selangor)
**Federal Territory Day** 1 February (KL and Labuan)
**Sultan of Kedah's Birthday** 7 February (Kedah)
**\*Chinese New Year** Variable, two days (24 & 25 January 2001; one day only in Kelantan and Terengganu)

### March
**\*Hari Raya Haji** Variable (6 & 7 March 2001; the following day is also a holiday in Kedah, Kelantan, Perlis and Terengganu)
**Sultan of Selangor's Birthday** 2nd Saturday of March (Selangor)
**Anniversary of Installation of Sultan of Terengganu** 21 March (Terengganu)
**\*Awal Muharram (Muslim New Year)** Variable (26 March 2001)
**Sultan of Kelantan's Birthday** 30 & 31 March (Kelantan)

### April
**Sultan of Johor's Birthday** 8 April (Johor)
**Good Friday** Variable (13 April 2001; Sarawak and Sabah)
**Melaka Historical City Day** 15 April (Melaka)
**Sultan of Perak's Birthday** 19 April (Perak)
**Sultan of Terengganu's Birthday** 29 April (Terengganu)

### May
**\*Worker's Day** 1 May
**Hol Day** 7 May (Pahang)
**Raja of Perlis' Birthday** Variable (April/May; Perlis)

**\*Wesak Day** Variable (7 May 2001)
**Harvest Festival** 30 & 31 May (Sabah and Labuan)

**June**
**\*Yang di-Pertuan Agong's (King's) Birthday** 1st Saturday in June
**Dayak Festival** 1 & 2 June (Sarawak)
**\*Prophet's Birthday** Variable (4 June 2001)

**July**
**Governor of Penang's Birthday** 2nd Saturday in July (Penang)
**Governor of Negeri Sembilan's Birthday** 19 July (Negeri Sembilan)

**August**
**\*National Day** 31 August

**September**
**Malaysia Day** 16 September (Sabah)

**October–November**
**Governor of Melaka's Birthday** 2nd Saturday in October (Melaka)
**Hol Day (Sultan Ismail)** Variable (October or November; Johor)
**Sultan of Pahang's Birthday** 24 October (Pahang)
**Israk & Mikraj** Variable (15 October 2001; Kedah and Negeri Sembilan)
**Deepavali** Variable (14 November 2001; national except Sarawak and Labuan)
**Awal Ramadan (Beginning of Ramadan)** Variable (17 November 2001; Johor and Melaka)

**December**
**Nuzul Al-Quran** Variable (3 December 2001; Kelantan, Pahang, Perak, Perlis, Selangor and Terengganu)
**\*Hari Raya Puasa** Variable (16 December 2001)
**\*Christmas Day** 25 December

## Festivals & Events

Public holidays mark many major festivals, but numerous other events are celebrated with temple offerings or chanting of the Quran.

The major Islamic events each year are connected with Ramadan, the month during which Muslims do not eat or drink from sunrise to sunset.

Fifteen days before the start of Ramadan, it is believed the souls of the dead visit their homes on Nisfu Night. During Ramadan Lailatul Qadar, the 'Night of Grandeur', Muslims celebrate the arrival of the Quran on earth before its revelation by Mohammed. A Quran-reading competition is held in KL (and extensively televised) during Ramadan.

Hari Raya Puasa marks the end of the month-long fast with two days of joyful celebration. This is the major holiday of the Muslim calendar and it can be difficult to find accommodation in Malaysia, particularly on the east coast. During this time everyone wears new clothes, homes are cleaned and redecorated and everyone seems to visit everyone else.

Hari Raya Haji is the day when pilgrims mark the successful completion of the *hajj* (pilgrimage to Mecca). It is a two-day holiday in many of the peninsula states and is marked by the consumption of large amounts of cakes and sweets.

The major Chinese event is Chinese New Year; the major Indian celebration is Deepavali, though Thaipusam is the most spectacular, celebrated with a painful-looking spectacle in some states of the peninsula. See the 'Thaipusam' boxed text in the 'Places of Worship' special section for details.

There are also other special events, ranging from fun runs and Grand Prix events to kite-flying and fishing competitions.

**January–February**
**Thai Pongal** A Hindu harvest-festival marking the beginning of the Hindu month of Thai, considered the luckiest month of the year. Celebrated by Tamils.
**Chinese New Year** Dragon dances and pedestrian parades mark the start of the new year. Families hold open house, unmarried relatives (especially children) receive *ang pow* (money in red packets), businesses traditionally clear their debts and everybody wishes you a *'kong hee fatt choy'* (a happy and prosperous New Year).
**Birthday of the Jade Emperor** Nine days after New Year, this Chinese festival honours Yu Huang, the supreme ruler of heaven, with offerings at temples.
**Ban Hood Huat Hoay** A 12-day celebration for the Day of Ten Thousand Buddhas is held at the Kek Lok Si Temple in Penang.
**Chap Goh Meh** On the 15th day after Chinese New Year, the celebrations officially end.

Chingay In Johor Bahru, processions of Chinese flagbearers balancing bamboo flagpoles 6m- to 12m-long can be seen on the 22nd day after New Year.

Thaipusam One of the most dramatic Hindu festivals (now banned in India), in which devotees honour Lord Subramaniam with acts of amazing physical resilience. In KL they march in a procession to the Batu Caves carrying *kavadi,* heavy metal frames decorated with peacock feathers, fruit and flowers. The kavadi are hung from their bodies with metal hooks and spikes driven into the flesh. Other devotees pierce their cheeks and tongues with metal skewers, or walk on sandals of nails. Along the procession route, the kavadi carriers dance to the drum beat while spectators urge them on with shouts of *'Vel, Vel'.* In the evening the procession continues with an image of Subramaniam in a temple car. In Penang, Thaipusam is celebrated at the Waterfall Hilltop Temple. See the information on Thaipusam in the 'Places of Worship' special section.

Kwong Teck Sun Ong's Birthday Celebration of the birthday of a child deity at the Chinese temple in Kuching in late February.

## March–April
Tua Peck Kong Paper money and paper models of useful things to have with you in the afterlife are burnt at the Sia Sen Temple in Kuching.

Easter On Palm Sunday a candlelight procession is held at St Peter's in Melaka. Good Friday and Easter Monday also see colourful celebrations at St Peter's and other Melaka churches.

Panguni Uttiram The marriage of Shiva to Shakti and of Lord Subramaniam to Theivani is celebrated on the full-moon day of the Tamil month of Panguni.

Birthday of the Goddess of Mercy Offerings are made to the very popular Kuan Yin at her temples in Penang and KL.

Cheng Ming On Cheng Ming, Chinese traditionally visit the tombs of their ancestors to clean and repair them and to make offerings.

Sri Rama Navami A nine-day festival held by the Brahmin caste to honour the Hindu hero of the *Ramayana,* Sri Rama.

Birthday of the Monkey God The birthday of T'se Tien Tai Seng Yeh is celebrated twice a year. Mediums pierce their cheeks and tongues with skewers and go into trances during which they write special charms in blood.

## April–May
Songkran Festival A traditional Thai Buddhist New Year in which Buddha images are bathed.

Chithirai Vishu The start of the Hindu New Year.

Puja Pantai A large three-day Hindu-inspired Malay festival held 5km south of Kuala Terengganu.

Birthday of the Queen of Heaven Ma Cho Po, the queen of heaven and goddess of the sea, is honoured at her temples.

Wesak Day Buddha's birth, enlightenment and death are celebrated with various events, including the release of caged birds to symbolise the setting free of captive souls.

Turtle season From May until September giant turtles come ashore each night to lay their eggs along the beach at Rantau Abang, on the east coast of the peninsula.

## June
Gawai Dayak Annual Sarawak Dayak Festival on 1 and 2 June to mark the end of the rice season, with war dances, cockfights and blowpipe events.

Festa de San Pedro Christian celebration in honour of the patron saint of the fishing community on 29 June, particularly celebrated by the Eurasian-Portuguese community of Melaka.

Birthday of the God of War Kuan Ti, who has the ability to avert war and to protect people during war, is honoured on his birthday.

Dragon Boat Festival Commemorating the death of a Chinese saint who drowned himself. In an attempt to save him, the local fishing community paddled out to sea, beating drums to scare away any fish that might attack him. To mark the anniversary, this festival is celebrated from June to August with boat races in Penang and other places.

## July
Birthday of Kuan Yin The goddess of mercy has another birthday!

Feast of St Anne A Roman Catholic festival celebrated at St Anne's Church in Penang.

Prophet Mohammed's Birthday Muslims pray and religious leaders recite verses from the Quran.

## July–August
Sri Krishna Jayanti A 10-day Hindu festival celebrating popular events in Krishna's life is highlighted on day eight with celebrations of his birthday. The Laxmi Narayan Temple in KL is a particular focus.

Lumut Sea Carnival Boat races, swimming races and many other events are held at Lumut, the port for Pulau Pangkor.

## August–September
Festival of the Seven Sisters Chinese girls pray to the weaving maid for good husbands.

**Festival of the Hungry Ghosts** The souls of the dead are released for one day of feasting and entertainment on earth. Chinese operas and other events are laid on for them and food is put out. The ghosts eat the spirit of the food, but thoughtfully leave the substance for mortal celebrants. Mainly in Penang.

**National Day (Hari Kebangsaan)** Malaysia celebrates its independence on 31 August with events all over the country, but particularly in KL, where there are parades and a variety of performances in the Lake Gardens.

**Vinayagar Chathuri** During the Tamil month of Avani (around August and September), prayers are offered to Vinayagar, another name for the popular elephant-headed god Ganesh.

**Feast of Santa Cruz** A month-long pilgrimage season in September at the Church of Santa Cruz at Malim, Melaka.

**Papar Tamu Besar** This annual market festival is held from 15 to 20 September in Papar, an area of Sabah renowned for its beautiful Kadazan girls.

**Moon Cake Festival** The overthrow of the Mongol warlords in ancient China is celebrated by eating moon cakes and lighting colourful paper lanterns. Moon cakes are made with bean paste, lotus seeds and sometimes a duck egg.

### September–October

**Thimithi (Fire-Walking Ceremony)** Hindu devotees prove their faith by walking across glowing coals at the Gajah Berang Temple in Melaka.

**Navarathri** In the Tamil month of Purattasi, the Hindu festival of 'Nine Nights' is dedicated to the wives of Shiva, Vishnu and Brahma. Young girls are dressed as the goddess Kali.

**Festival of the Nine Emperor Gods** Nine days of Chinese operas, processions and other events honour the nine emperor gods. Fire-walking ceremonies are held on the evening of the ninth day at the Kau Ong Yah Temples in KL and Penang.

**Puja Ketek** Offerings are brought to Buddhist shrines, or *ketek,* in the state of Kelantan during this festival in October. Traditional dances are often performed.

### October–November

**Kantha Shashithi** Subramaniam, a great fighter against the forces of evil, is honoured during the Hindu month of Aipasi.

**Deepavali** Later in the month of Aipasi, Rama's victory over the demon king Ravana is celebrated with the Festival of Lights, when tiny oil-lamps are lit outside the homes of Hindu people, as it's

believed that Lakshmi, the goddess of wealth, will not enter an unlit home. For business people, this is the time to start a new financial year, and for the family a pre-dawn oil bath, new clothes and lots of sweets is the order of the day. It's bad luck to sweep the house, as this would sweep away good fortune; it is also bad luck to break anything on this day.

**Birthday of Kuan Yin** The birthday of the popular goddess of mercy is celebrated yet again.

**Kartikai Deepam** Huge bonfires are lit to commemorate Shiva's appearance as a pillar of fire following an argument with Vishnu and Brahma. The Thandayuthapani Temple in Muar is a major site for this festival.

**Guru Nanak's Birthday** The birthday of Guru Nanak, founder of the Sikh religion, is celebrated on 22 November.

### December

**Pesta Pulau Penang** A two-month carnival on Pulau Penang in November and December featuring many water events, including dragon-boat races towards the end of the festival.

**Winter Solstice Festival** A Chinese festival to offer thanks for a good harvest.

**Christmas Day** On 25 December Christians celebrate the birth of Jesus Christ.

## ACTIVITIES

The following is a brief list of some of Malaysia's more-popular activities. For details on the locations listed, please see individual entries later in this book.

## Diving & Snorkelling

With its tropical location and wealth of islands, it's not surprising that Malaysia has some great snorkelling and diving. The main centres include Pulau Perhentian, Pulau Redang, Pulau Tioman, the Seribuat Archipelago and Pulau Sipadan. See the 'Diving & Snorkelling' special section for more information.

## Mountain Climbing

Mt Kinabalu is an obvious choice for those interested in mountain climbing (see the 'Climbing Kinabalu' special section in the Sabah chapter for details). However, this is not the only mountain worth climbing in Malaysia. Gunung Mulu, in Sarawak's Gunung Mulu National Park, is a challenging four-day climb. On the peninsula, there are several good climbs in Taman Negara National Park. There are also a few lesser peaks scattered around that make pleasant day-outings. Keen mountain-climbers should be sure to pick up a copy of *Mountains of Malaysia – A Practical Guide and Manual* by John Briggs (see Books earlier).

### Jungle Trekking
Despite the pressures of logging, Malaysia is still home to some of the world's most impressive stands of virgin tropical jungle. Almost all of Malaysia's national parks offer excellent jungle-trekking, including Taman Negara on the peninsula and Gunung Mulu in Malaysian Borneo. There are treks to suit all ability levels, from 20-minute jaunts to 10-day expeditions. The 'Trekking in Sarawak' special section has more information on some of the best routes in Sarawak.

### Caving
Malaysia's limestone hills are riddled with caves to lure spelunkers. Some of these are easily accessible and can be visited without any special equipment or preparation while others are strictly the terrain of the experienced caver. There are caves on the peninsula – Gua Charas (Charas Caves), Gua Musang and in Taman Negara, among others – and dotted around Malaysian Borneo, including one of the world's premier caving destinations: Gunung Mulu National Park.

### Bicycle Touring
Malaysia is one of the best places in South-East Asia for bike touring. Perhaps the most popular route is the one up the east coast of Peninsular Malaysia, with its relatively quiet roads. However, if you're fit and energetic, you may prefer the hillier regions of the peninsula's interior or Malaysian Borneo. Refer to the boxed text 'By Bicycle – Peninsular Malaysia and Singapore' in the Getting Around chapter for details of routes.

### Handicraft Classes
Several of Malaysia's cultural centres offer classes in traditional Malaysian handicrafts. Kota Bharu and Cherating are perhaps the best places to get a hands-on feel for batik, puppet making and kite making.

---

### Considerations for Jungle Trekking

Jungle trekking can be one of the true highlights of a trip to Malaysia. To the uninitiated, however, it can be something of a shock – like marching all day in a sauna with a heavy pack strapped to your back. The following guidelines will help to make the experience as painless as possible:

- On overnight trips, bring two sets of clothing, one for hiking and one to put on at the end of the day (keep your night kit in a plastic bag so that it stays dry). Within minutes of starting out, your hiking kit will be drenched and it will stay that way throughout your trip. If you'll be travelling through dense vegetation, wear long trousers and a long-sleeved shirt. Otherwise, shorts and a T-shirt will suffice. Whatever you wear, make sure that it's loose fitting.
- Drink plenty of water. If you're going long distances, you'll have to bring a water filter or a water purification agent like iodine (most people opt for the latter to keep weight down).
- Get in shape long before coming to Malaysia and start slowly – try a day hike before setting out on a longer trek.
- Take a guide if you're setting off on a longer and/or lesser travelled trek.
- Bring talcum powder to cope with the chafing caused by wet undergarments. Wearing loose underwear (or better yet, no underwear at all) will also help prevent chafing.
- If you wear glasses, be sure to treat them with an anti-fog solution (ask at the shop where you buy your glasses). Otherwise, you may find yourself blinded by fog within not long after setting out.

Serious jungle-trekkers should pick up a copy of John Briggs' *Mountains of Malaysia – A Practical Guide and Manual* for more tips, and details of popular routes.

**Chris Rowthorn**

## Bird-Watching

Malaysia's tropical jungles and islands are home to a tremendous variety of bird species. On the peninsula, Taman Negara, Kenong Rimba and Endau-Rompin all offer excellent bird-watching. In Malaysian Borneo, Kinabalu, Gunung Mulu, Simalajau and Gunung Gading are similarly rich in bird species. See the Birds entry under Flora & Fauna in the Facts About Malaysia chapter for information on Malaysia's bird species and some more spots for bird-watching.

## WORK

Being neither extremely poor nor extremely rich, Malaysia lacks some of the work and volunteer opportunities of its Asian neighbours. However, there are possibilities for those who seek them out. At the upper end of the scale, there are professional-level jobs in finance, journalism and the oil industry. Likewise, those with teaching credentials can find English-teaching jobs in Malaysia, though pickings are slim compared to Japan and Korea. On the other end of the scale, temporary jobs can be found at some guesthouses and dive centres in popular resort areas.

The Web is the best place to start your search. JobStreet.com advertises a wide variety of jobs at www.jobs.com.my. Teachers can check some of the many TEFL sites, including the TEFL Job Centre, at www.jobs.edunet.com. Those looking for volunteer work should contact the major volunteer organisations in their home country.

Depending on the nature of your job, you'll need either an Expatriate Personnel Visa or Temporary Employment Visa. For details and requirements, check the Immigration Department of Malaysia's Web site at www.imi.gov.my.

## ACCOMMODATION

Malaysia has a very wide range of accommodation possibilities – you can still find places to stay for US$4 per person per night; at the other end of the scale, more-luxurious 'international standard' hotels can charge over US$100 a night for a room. Note that most hotels quote similar prices for single and double (sometimes even triple) rooms so it is a lot cheaper to travel with another person or two.

### Taxes & Service Charges

In Malaysia there's a 5% government tax that applies to all hotel rooms. On top of this there's a 10% service charge in the more expensive places. You are not expected to tip in addition to this. Expensive places sometimes quote prices exclusive of tax and service charge – this is represented as ++ (called plus-plus), for example $120++ for a double. Nett means that tax and service charges are included. Tax and service charges are also applied to food, drinks and services in the more expensive hotels and restaurants.

Cheap Malaysian hotels, however, generally quote a price inclusive of the 5% government tax.

### International Hotels

There are modern, multistorey, air-con, swimming pool, all-mod-cons hotels of major international chains – Hyatt, Holiday Inn, Hilton – all over Malaysia. In these hotels, nightly costs are generally from RM120 and up for a double. Malaysia has not suffered the price hikes of neighbouring Singapore, but KL and Penang have seen climbing occupancy rates and higher prices.

### Traditional Chinese Hotels

At the low end of the price scale are the traditional Chinese hotels found in great numbers all over Malaysia. They're the mainstay of budget travellers and backpackers, and in Malaysia you can generally find a good fan room for RM12 to RM25 and a good air-con room for RM25 to RM40.

Chinese hotels are generally fairly spartan – bare floors and just a bed, a couple of chairs and a table, a wardrobe and a sink. The showers and toilets (which will sometimes be Asian squat-style) may be down the corridor. A point to watch for: couples can sometimes economise by asking for a single, since in Chinese hotel language 'single' means one double bed, and 'double' means two beds. Don't think of this as being tight; in Chinese hotels you can pack as many into one room as you wish.

The main catch with these hotels is that they can sometimes be terribly noisy. They're often on main streets, and the bottom rung of the Chinese-hotel ladder has a serious design flaw – the walls rarely reach the ceiling. The top is simply meshed or barred in. This is great for ventilation but terrible for acoustics. Every noise carries throughout the hotel, and guests all awake to a terrible dawn chorus of hawking, coughing and spitting.

## Resthouses
Some of the old British-developed resthouses are still operating. These were set up during the colonial era to provide accommodation for travelling officials, and later provided excellent shelter for all types of travellers. Many of the resthouses are still government owned but are now privately operated. Some have been turned into midrange resorts, but many retain traditional style. The average price for a room in a resthouse is RM70, and this usually includes air-con and attached bathroom.

## Guesthouses
At beach centres and in the major tourist cities you will find a variety of cheap accommodation that can be grouped together under the term 'guesthouses'. These may be huts on the beach or private homes or rented houses divided by partition walls into a number of rooms. Dormitory accommodation is usually available. Rooms are spartan, but this is the cheapest accommodation around and often the nicest, with a real family atmosphere. These places often cater only to foreign travellers and offer their customers lots of little extras to outdo the competition, such as free tea and coffee, bicycles and transport. A dorm bed will cost RM6 to RM10, and rooms will cost from RM12, up to RM40 for a hotel-style room with air-con.

## Homestays
A homestay is a private home with a few rooms set aside for travellers. They are not nearly as common as they once were, but you can still find them in KL, Kota Bharu and Johor Bahru. Some of the bigger homestays offer both dorm rooms (RM5 to RM15 per bed) and private rooms (from RM12 to RM20 per double). Many homestays also serve breakfast and/or dinner and this is often a good chance to sample authentic Malaysian food.

## Longhouses in Malaysian Borneo
Longhouses are the traditional dwellings of the indigenous peoples of Borneo. These communal dwellings may contain up to 100 individual family 'apartments' under one long roof. The most important area of a longhouse is the common veranda, which serves as a social area. These days there are two main types of longhouse: 'tourist longhouses' and 'authentic longhouses'. While a visit to a tourist longhouse is easily enough arranged it is unlikely to be of much interest. A visit to an authentic, living longhouse can be a magical experience, but it is easier said than done – one does not merely show up on the veranda with a carton of cigarettes and expect to be welcomed inside. Indeed, there is a very specific etiquette to visiting a longhouse. For details, see the 'Longhouse Visits' boxed text in the Sarawak chapter.

## Camping
Camping is a good, cheap option in Malaysia. Many of the national parks have official camping grounds and will permit camping in nondesignated sites once you are into the back country. There are also many lonely stretches of beach, particularly on the east coast of the peninsula, which are ideal for camping. Likewise, it is possible to camp on uninhabited bays on many of Malaysia's islands. If you do decide to camp in Malaysia, a two-season tent with mosquito netting is ideal. A summer-weight sleeping bag is okay, but the best choice is a lightweight bag-liner, since even the nights are warm in Malaysia.

## FOOD & DRINKS
While travelling around some parts of Asia is as good as a session with Weight Watchers, Singapore and Malaysia are quite the opposite. The food is simply terrific, the variety unbeatable and the costs pleasantly low. Whether you're looking for Chinese

food, Malay food, Indian food, Indonesian food or even a Big Mac, you'll find happiness! There's also a good range of non-alcoholic and alcoholic drinks. For a complete description, see the special section 'Tastes of Malaysia, Singapore & Brunei' following this chapter, and the Food section in the Glossary at the end of this book.

## ENTERTAINMENT

Entertainment in Malaysia is much the same as in Western countries, though Asian Values apply (see the 'Asian Values' boxed text in the Facts About Malaysia chapter). The traditional pastimes of *wayang* (Chinese opera) puppet theatre and traditional dance have all but disappeared, except for special occasions or tourist recreations. The main cities have discos, clubs, pubs and bars, usually fairly tame with high bar-prices. KL has a very lively and extensive nightlife scene – if you are looking for a place to rage, this is it. Almost every town has a karaoke bar if you are desperate for something to do. In small towns, Chinese coffee-shops and restaurants double as nightspots, since they're the only places that serve alcohol.

Cinemas generally show B-grade adventure movies and Hong Kong kung fu flicks, either dubbed or with multiple subtitles covering all the major languages. The latest Hollywood blockbusters are occasionally shown, though movies are heavily censored. Various cultural organisations in KL and Penang, such as Alliance Française and the Goethe Institut, have regular screenings of their foreign-language films.

## SPECTATOR SPORTS

The main spectator sports in Malaysia are football, badminton, squash and track and field. In the smaller kampung you may also be able to observe *sepak takraw,* a game similar to volleyball in which players use only their head and feet to propel a ball over a net. To find out about upcoming sporting events look in the *New Straits Times* or check with Tourism Malaysia.

## SHOPPING

Every tourist centre has a selection of shops and stalls selling souvenirs but because of high wages, handicrafts are not a big item in Malaysia. Many of the 'Malay' handicrafts on sale are imported from Indonesia and elsewhere. Nevertheless, there are many attractive souvenirs and handicrafts around, but bargain hard for tourist-oriented items.

Malaysian kites *(wau)* are readily available and are a colourful and typical souvenir from Malaysia – Kota Bharu is a good place to find them. The distinctive Kedah pottery – hand-painted, bulb-shaped pots with long necks – is another Malaysian craft, as is pewterware, most of which comes from Selangor, and wavy-bladed *kris* knives, many of which come from Indonesia. Some fine Dayak weavings and woodcarvings can be found in Sarawak, but prices are very high. The east coast of the peninsula has attractive *songket* (weaving with gold thread) and Malaysia also produces batik, usually with floral motifs though the work is not always high quality.

Antiques are readily available in Melaka and to a lesser extent Penang. Everything from lion-head door knockers to marble-topped tables are on sale, but prices are often very high and hard bargaining is required. Chinese pottery and jewellery is available everywhere.

Malaysia is reasonably priced for electronics, though the range is not great and prices are slightly higher than in Singapore, which has a much better range. Portable radios and cameras are duty-free in Malaysia. Cameras and accessories are available, but selection and prices are at least as good in Singapore.

Copies of brand-name goods can be found – you can outfit yourself with Nike, Lacoste and Rolex for a fraction of the cost of the real thing; the real thing is also on sale in many places.

Depending on your country of origin you may find clothes and shoes a reasonable buy. The range and styles are good, and larger sizes are available. Cheap cotton beachwear is available at beach centres.

Pick and choose: nasi kampur on offer at Kuching market, Sarawak.

Raw fish. Well. That looks like fun.

Stacks of sticks of chicken satay.

Ceremonial buns cooling in the street.

# TASTES OF MALAYSIA, SINGAPORE & BRUNEI

## FOOD

Malaysia, Singapore and Brunei are renowned for their diverse cuisines and great food. The region's ethnic mix means you can eat Malay food for breakfast, Chinese for lunch and Indian for dinner! And you can snack on deliciously fresh tropical fruit between meals. Many types of Chinese food are available, particularly in Singapore; don't forget to try the cuisine of the Straits Chinese, or Peranakan (Baba-Nyonya), people. There's good-quality food to suit all budgets and tastes, ranging from the popular hawker centres and coffee shops to fine dining at exclusive restaurants. This section will help you negotiate your way around the array of culinary options in the three countries, identify the variety of tasty tropical fruits and know which alcoholic drinks to watch out for! See also the Food section in the Glossary at the end of this book.

### WHERE TO EAT

In Malaysia you'll probably wind up eating a lot of your meals in *kedai kopi* (coffee shops), which generally serve a variety of beverages as well as a selection of light meals and snacks – usually a *nasi kampur* (rice buffet) and dishes such as *nasi goreng* (fried rice) and *mee goreng* (fried noodles). Chinese- or Indian-run kedai kopi serve more-varied ethnic cuisine reflective of their ownership. Coffee shops are called *kopi tiam* in Singapore (*tiam* is Hokkien for 'shop'). These range from spartan restaurants with open fronts and two or three stalls to restaurant-like shops offering a greater range of dishes.

You'll also find a variety of hawker stalls in Malaysia, Singapore and Brunei, particularly in the night markets of the bigger cities. While some of these are generalist, serving the standard noodle and rice favourites, you will also find specialist stalls selling dishes like Thai *tom yam kum* soup (spicy-and-sour seafood soup), Indian *murtabak* (paper-thin dough filled with egg and minced mutton and lightly grilled with oil), Chinese chicken-rice, various seafood specialities. Some carts specialise only in drinks. Most travellers find that the food from hawker stalls is superior to that served by kedai kopi. These two types of places to eat are often the only options outside large cities.

Without a doubt, Singapore is the world capital of hawker food and the city is packed with sprawling hawker centres where you can put together delicious, varied meals for around S$7. Indeed, many travellers visit Singapore precisely to enjoy the wonderful food on offer in its hawker centres.

**Title page:** Central Market, Kota Bharu (Photograph by Richard I'Anson).

In Malaysia's cities, and in Singapore and Brunei, you will also find a range of ethnic restaurants. These primarily serve Chinese and Indian

## A Typical Kedai Kopi Menu

America has diners, Britain has pubs and Malaysia has *kedai kopi* (literally, coffee shops). While travelling in Malaysia, you'll probably be eating half your meals in kedai kopi and the other half in outdoor hawker centres. For this reason, it's a good idea to familiarise yourself with some of the common dishes you'll find on offer in a typical kedai kopi.

The common denominator at kedai kopi is *nasi kampur* (sometimes written *nasi campur* or *nasi padang*). The nasi kampur counter is often the first thing you'll see when you walk into a kedai kopi. It's basically a buffet – grab a plate, pile on some rice and help yourself from a range of curried vegetable, meat and fish dishes. You'll be charged according to how much you take – count on spending about RM5 for a good feed.

Other dishes and all drinks at kedai kopi must be ordered from a menu. While there is variation between Malay-, Indian- and Chinese-run kedai kopi, many of the most-common dishes are universal. Some of these include:

**Drinks**

| | |
|---|---|
| *kopi* | hot coffee (comes with sweet condensed milk) |
| *teh* | hot tea (comes with sweet condensed milk) |
| *teh tarik* | very sweet milky tea (literally, pulled tea) |
| *teh-o* | tea without milk |
| *teh-o ais* | iced tea without milk |
| *teh-o ais limau* | iced tea with lime (or lemon) |

food. Ironically, Malay restaurants are the hardest to find. Complementing these places, the big cities also have the inevitable fast-food restaurants, with KFC leading the way. Those who want to self-cater will find supermarkets in the cities, and outdoor markets in the smaller towns.

## CUISINES

The most prominent cuisines in Malaysia and Singapore are Chinese and Indian, in all their regional variations, and Malay. You'll also find Indonesian and Peranakan dishes, so make the most of the eating options.

### Chinese

**Chinese or Cantonese?**  When people in the West speak of Chinese food, they're usually talking about Cantonese food. It's the best-known and most popular style of Chinese cooking – even in Singapore, where the majority of Chinese are not Cantonese. Cantonese food is noted for the variety and freshness of its ingredients. It is usually stir-fried with just a touch of oil to ensure that the result is crisp and fresh. All those best-known 'Western Chinese' dishes fit into this category – sweet-and-sour dishes, won ton soup, chow mein and spring rolls, for example.

## A Typical Kedai Kopi Menu

**Food**

| | |
|---|---|
| roti | thin, fried bread |
| roti canai | thin, fried bread with a curry sauce for dipping |
| roti telor | thin, fried bread made with egg |
| nasi lemak | rice boiled in coconut milk with side dishes |
| nasi goreng | fried rice |
| mee goreng | fried noodles |
| mee rebus | Javanese fried noodles served in a sweet sauce |
| murtabak | fried roti dough cooked with assorted fillings |
| nasi puteh | white rice |
| mee sup | noodle soup |
| rojak | fried tofu, greens & fruit with a sweet peanut sauce |

**Other Useful Terms**

| | |
|---|---|
| ayam | chicken |
| daging lembu | beef |
| garam | salt |
| goreng | fried |
| gula | sugar |
| ikan | fish |
| kambing | lamb |
| nasi | rice |
| sayur | vegetables |
| sotong | squid |
| susu | milk |

**Chris Rowthorn**

TRUDI CANAVAN

Ginger is a basic ingredient in Chinese dishes.

With Cantonese food, the more people you can muster for the meal the better, because dishes are traditionally shared so that everyone manages to sample the greatest variety. A corollary of this is that Cantonese food should be balanced: Traditionally, all foods are said to be either *yin* (cooling), like vegetables, most fruits and clear soups; or *yang* (heating), like starchy foods and meat. A 'cooling' dish should be balanced by a 'heating' dish: Too much of one or the other is not good for you.

Another Cantonese speciality is dim sum, or 'little heart'. Dim sum is usually eaten at lunchtime or as a Sunday brunch. Dim sum restaurants are often large, noisy affairs and the dim sum – little snacks that come in small bowls – are whisked around the tables on individual trolleys or carts. As they come by, you simply ask for a plate of this or a bowl of that. At the end of the meal your bill is toted up from the number of empty containers on your table.

Cantonese cuisine can offer real extremes – shark's-fin soup or bird's-nest soup are expensive delicacies, while *mee* (noodles) or *congee* (rice porridge) are cheap basics.

## The Hawkers' Variety

Singapore's popular hawker centres offer a huge variety of the cheapest meals in town. Eating at these huge food centres is an essential part of a visit to Singapore, and you'll be experiencing the food of average Singaporeans.

Some typical hawker food you may come across includes carrot cake, or *chye tow kway*, usually sold for S$2 to S$3. Also known as radish cake, it's a vegetable-and-egg dish, which tastes something like a potato omelette, and is totally unlike the Western health-food idea of carrot cake.

Indian biryani (basmati rice and meat, seafood or vegetables) costs around S$3 or you can buy *murtabak* (roti filled with pieces of mutton, chicken or vegetables) for around S$2. Naturally, chicken-rice and *char siew* (roast pork) are always available in food centres (S$2 to S$3). All the usual Cantonese dishes like fried rice (S$1.50 to S$3), fried vegetables (S$3), beef and vegetables (S$5), and sweet-and-sour pork (S$3 to S$5) are available, as well as other dishes like fish heads with black beans and chilli from S$3 to S$5.

There will often be Malay or Indonesian stalls with satay from 30c to 35c a stick, *mee rebus* (Javanese fried noodles served in a sweet sauce) for S$2 and *mee soto* (noodle soup with shredded chicken) at similar prices. *Won ton mee*, a substantial soup dish with shredded chicken or braised beef, costs from S$2 to S$3. You could try *chee chong fun*, a type of stuffed noodle, which costs from S$2 to S$4 or more, depending on whether you want the noodles with prawns, mushrooms, chicken or pork. *Hokkien fried prawn mee* costs around S$2 to S$4, as does *prawn mee soup*. *Popiah* (unfried spring rolls) and *laksa* (spicy coconut-based soup) are other regulars, but there's also a whole variety of other dishes and soups. You can even opt for Western food such as sausages, egg and chips, burgers or fish and chips.

Drinks include a large bottle of beer for S$8; soft drinks from 80c; *ais kacang* (local dessert made from ice shavings, red beans, *attap* and jelly, topped with syrups and evaporated milk) for 80c; and sugar-cane juice from 50c to S$1, depending on the size. Fruit juices such as melon, papaya, pineapple, apple, orange or starfruit range from 80c to S$2. To finish up you might try a fruit salad for S$2 or a *pisang goreng* (fried banana) for 50c.

**Hokkien** It is quite easy to find a number of regional styles of Chinese food, particularly since so many of the region's Chinese are Hokkien or Hakka. One of the best-known of southern Chinese dishes comes from the island of Hainan. Around Malaysia one of the most widely available and economical meals is Hainanese chicken-rice, known in Singapore and Malaysia as *nasi ayam* or *nasi ayam hainan*. It's one of those dishes whose very simplicity ensures its quality. Chicken-rice is simply steamed chicken, rice boiled or steamed in chicken stock, a clear soup and slices of cucumber. You can flavour this delicate dish with soy or chilli sauce and have yourself a delicious meal for around RM3. The Hainanese also produce steamboat, a sort of Oriental variation on a Swiss fondue, where you have a boiling stockpot in the middle of the table, into which you dip pieces of meat, seafood or vegetables.

The Hokkien come from China's Fujian province and make up the largest dialect group in Singapore. Although Hokkien food is rated way down the Chinese gastronomic scale, it has provided the unofficial national dish of Singapore – *hokkien fried mee*, or Singapore noodles. It's made of thick egg noodles cooked with pork, seafood and vegetables and a rich sauce. Hokkien *popiah* (unfried spring rolls) are also delicious.

TRUDI CANAVAN

Star anise features in Chinese five-spice.

**Szechuan** The fiery food of China, peppers really get into the act in Szechuan (or Sichuan) food. Whereas the tastes of Cantonese food are delicate and understated, in Szechuan food the flavours are strong and dramatic – garlic and chillies play their part in dishes like diced chicken, and hot-and-sour soup.

**Beijing** The famous Beijing duck is the best-known dish in this cuisine. The specially fattened ducks are basted in syrup and roasted on a revolving spit. The skin is served as a separate first course. Like the other northern cuisines, Beijing food is less subtle than Cantonese food. Because rice does not grow in the cold Beijing region, in China Beijing food is usually eaten with noodles or steamed buns. In Singapore and Malaysia, however, it's equally likely to come with rice.

**Teochew** From the area around Swatow in China, Teochew is another style noted for its delicacy and natural flavours. Teochew cuisine is famous for seafood, and a popular food-centre dish is *char kway teow* – broad noodles, clams and eggs fried in chilli and black bean sauce.

**Hakka** Simple ingredients are a feature of Hakka food. The best-known Hakka dish, again easily found in food centres, is *yong tau foo*, bean curd stuffed with minced meat.

**Shanghai** Food from Shanghai is, to some extent, a cross between northern and Cantonese cuisines, combining the strong flavours of the north with the ingredients of Canton. It is not easy to find, however, in Singapore or Malaysia.

## Indian

Indian food is one of the region's greatest delights. Indeed, some people say it's easier to find really good Indian food in Singapore or Malaysia than in India! Very approximately, you can divide Indian food into southern, Muslim and northern styles.

Common to all Indian food are the spices, or *masala;* the lentil soup known as *dhal;* the yogurt-and-water drink known as *lass;* and the sauces or condiments called chutneys.

**South Indian** Food from southern India tends to be hot, with the emphasis on vegetarian food. The typical South Indian dish is a *thali* (rice plate), but if you ask for one in a vegetarian restaurant you won't get a plate at all but a large *daun pisang* (banana leaf). On this leaf is placed a large mound of rice, then scoops of a variety of vegetable curries, and a couple of pappadams for good measure. With your right hand (South Indian veg-etarian food is never eaten with utensils), knead the

TRUDI CANAVAN

Cardamon is an important flavour in Indian food.

curries into the rice and eat away. Use the tips of your fingers, without the food passing your middle knuckles. When your banana leaf starts to look empty you'll suddenly find it refilled – the rice plate is always an all-you-can-eat meal. When you've finished, fold the banana leaf in two, with the fold towards you, to indicate that you've had enough.

Other vegetarian dishes include the popular *masala dosa*, a thin pancake which, when rolled around spiced vegetables with some *rasam* (spicy soup) on the side, is about the cheapest light meal you could ask for. An equivalent snack meal in Indian halal restaurants is murtabak, made from paper-thin dough filled with egg and minced mutton and lightly grilled with oil. A *roti canai* – made from murtabak dough, which you dip into a bowl of dhal or curry – is a very popular and filling breakfast eaten throughout the region. A samosa is a veg-etable- or meat-filled pastry.

**Muslim Indian** Indian halal food tends to be more subtly spiced and uses more meat than cuisines from South India. It is a mixture of south-ern and northern Indian influences and has developed a distinctly Malaysian style. A favourite Indian halal dish, and one that is cheap, easy to find and of excellent standard, is biryani. Served with a chicken or mutton curry, the dish takes its name from the saffron-coloured rice it is usually served with.

**North Indian** A particular favourite is the north Indian *tandoori* food, which takes its name from the clay tandoor oven in which meat is cooked The meat is marinated overnight in a complex yogurt-and-spice mixture. Tandoori chicken is the best-known tandoori dish.

Although rice is also eaten in northern India, it is not the ubiquitous staple it is in the south. North Indian food makes wide use of the de-licious Indian breads like naan (leavened bread baked inside a clay oven), chapati (griddle-fried wholewheat bread), *paratha* (bread made with ghee and cooked on a hotplate) and roti (thin, wheat-flour pan-cakes). The rich Mogul dishes of northern India are not so common and are generally only found in more expensive restaurants.

## Malay

Surprisingly, Malay food is not as easily found in Malaysia as Chinese or Indian food, although many Malay dishes, like satay, are everywhere. Satay is delicious tiny kebabs of chicken, mutton or beef dipped in a spicy peanut sauce. Some Malay dishes you may have a chance to try include *tahu goreng* – fried soya bean curd and bean sprouts in a peanut sauce; *ikan bilis* – anchovies fried whole; *ikan assam* – fried fish in a sour tamarind curry; and *sambal udang* – fiery curried prawns. *Ayam goreng* is fried chicken and *rendang* is a sort of spiced curried meat in coconut marinade. Nasi goreng (fried rice) is widely available, but it is as much a Chinese and Indian dish as Malay, and each style has its own flavours. *Nasi lemak* is coconut rice served with fried ikan bilis, peanuts and a curry dish.

## Indonesian

Indonesian food is very similar to Malay, and you'll find Malaysian regional dishes that have been influenced by Indonesian cuisine, as well as a number of Indonesian restaurants scattered around. In Sumatra the Indonesian food bends much more towards curries and chillies. The popular Sumatran food is *nasi padang,* from the Minangkabau region of West Sumatra, and consists of a wide variety of hot curries served with rice. The Malaysian equivalent is found in the state of Negeri Sembilan, which was originally peopled by Minangkabau settlers from Sumatra. *Mee rebus,* noodles in a rich soya-based sauce, is a Javanese dish that has been adopted as a local favourite in Johor.

TRUDI CANAVAN

Cinnamon tree bark is ground and used in curry powders.

## Nyonya

The Baba-Nyonya, or Peranakan, people are descendants of Chinese-Malay intermarriage. Nyonya cooking is a local variation on Chinese and Malay food, using Chinese ingredients and local spices such as lemon grass and coconut cream.

Nyonya cooking is essentially a home skill rather than a restaurant one, but there are a number of Nyonya restaurants around. *Laksa lemak,* a spicy coconut-based noodle soup, is a classic Nyonya dish that has been adopted by all Malaysians and is found everywhere. *Laksa penang* is the more sour variety from Penang that uses fish paste for the stock.

## DESSERTS

Although desserts are not a really big deal in the region, you can find some interesting after-dinner snacks, such as *pisang goreng* (banana fritters) or *ais kacang* and *cendol*. Halfway between a drink and a dessert, ais kacang is rather like an old-fashioned 'snowcone', but the shaved ice is topped with syrups and evaporated milk and it's all piled on top of a foundation of beans and jellies. It sounds gross and looks lurid but tastes terrific! Cendol is similar – it consists of coconut milk with brown sugar syrup and greenish noodle-like things topped with shaved ice. (It also tastes terrific.)

## TROPICAL FRUIT

Once you've tried rambutans, mangosteens, jackfruit and durians, how can you ever go back to boring old apples and oranges? If you're already addicted to tropical fruit, Singapore and Malaysia are great places to indulge the passion. If you've not yet been initiated, there could hardly be a better place in the world to develop a taste for these exotic flavours.

For an easy introduction, head for the fruit stalls, which you'll find in food centres or even just on the streets. Slices of a whole variety of fruits (including those dull old apples and oranges) are laid out on ice in a colourful and mouth-watering display from which you can make a selection for just 30 sen and up. You can also have a fruit salad made up on the spot from as many fruits as you care to choose. Some tastes to sample include:

**Rambutan** *(Nephelium lappaceum)*
The Malay name means 'spiny', and that's just what they are. Rambutans are the size of a large walnut or small tangerine and they're covered in soft red spines. You peel the skin away to reveal a very close cousin to the lychee, with cool and mouthwatering flesh around a central stone. The main rambutan season is from June to September.

**Mangosteen** *(Garcinia mangostana)*
One of the finest tropical fruits, the mangosteen is the size of a small orange or apple. The dark-purple outer skin breaks open to reveal pure white segments shaped like orange segments – but with a sweet-sour flavour that has been compared to a combination of strawberries and grapes. Queen Victoria, so the story goes, offered a considerable prize to anybody able to bring a mangosteen back intact from the east for her to try. The main season is from June to September.

**Durian** *(Durio zibethinus)*
The region's most infamous fruit, the durian is a large, oval fruit about 20cm to 25cm long, although it may often grow much larger. The durian is renowned for its phenomenal smell, a stink so powerful that first-timers are often forced to hold their noses while they taste. In fact, durians emanate a stench so redolent of open sewers that in season you'll see signs in hotels all over Malaysia and Singapore warning that durians are expressly forbidden entry. It's definitely an acquired taste – the nearest approximation is onion-flavoured ice cream.

When the hard, spiny shell is cracked open, pale white-green segments are revealed with a taste as distinctive as their smell. Durians are so highly esteemed that great care is taken over their selection and you'll see gourmets feeling them carefully, sniffing them reverently and finally demanding a preliminary taste before purchasing.

Durians are expensive and, unlike other fruits that are generally yin (cooling), durians are yang (heating) – so much so that the durian is said to be a powerful aphrodisiac. It's no wonder that durians are reputed to be the only fruit craved by tigers!

There are two seasons: from June to August and November to February.

### Jackfruit *(Artocarpus hetero-phyllus)*
This enormous watermelon-sized fruit, otherwise known as *nangka*, hangs from trees, and, when opened, breaks up into a large number of bright orange-yellow segments with a slightly rubbery texture. The nangka is covered by a green pimply skin – it's not worth buying a whole one, because it's too big and too messy to eat. From street fruit-stalls you can often buy several nangka segments skewered on a stick. Nangka is available year-round, but is most prolific from June to December.

### Papaya *(Carica papaya)*
The papaya, or pawpaw, originated in Central America but is now quite common throughout South-East Asia and is very popular at breakfast time: A slice of papaya served with a dash of lemon or lime juice is the perfect way to start the day. The papaya is about 30cm or so in length; the bright-orange flesh is somewhat similar in texture and appearance to pumpkin, but it is related in taste to a melon. The numerous black seeds in the centre of a papaya are said to have a contraceptive effect if eaten by women. The fruit is available year-round.

### Starfruit *(Averrhoa carambola)*
The starfruit (also known as *carambola* or *belembing*) takes its name from its cross-sectional star shape. A translucent green-yellow in colour, starfruit has a crisp, cool, watery taste similar to an apple. It is available year-round.

### Custard Apple *(Annona muricata)*
Sometimes known as soursop or white mango, the custard apple has a warty green outer covering and is ripe and ready to eat when it begins to look slightly off – the fresh green skin begins to look black-ish and the feel becomes slightly squishy. Inside, the creamy white flesh has a deliciously thirst-quenching flavour with a hint of lemon.

### Pomelo *(Citrus grandis)*
The pomelo looks like a huge orange or grapefruit, although the skin is generally more green than yellow. The flesh often has a purplish tinge, and the flavour is similar to a grapefruit, although the texture is tougher and drier. A single fruit can weigh as much as 1.5kg.

### Mango *(Mangifera indica)*
There are many types of mango found in Malaysia; some are specifi-cally for cooking while others are for eating. Ask before you buy.

## Other Fruit

Coconuts, lychees, *jambu* (guavas), *duku, chiku, jeruk,* and even strawberries up in the Cameron Highlands, are among the other fruits available. There are also temperate-climate fruits imported from Australia, New Zealand and farther afield.

Malaysia is a major producer of *pisang (bananas); musa* and more than 40 varieties are grown here. Some, such as the *pisang embun* and *pisang mas,* are eaten raw, while others, such as plantain *(pisang abu)* and *pisang awak,* must be cooked.

# DRINKS
## NONALCOHOLIC DRINKS

Life can be thirsty in the tropics so you'll be relieved to hear that drinks are excellent, economical and readily available. For a start, water can be drunk straight from the taps in Singapore and in most larger Malaysian cities (which is a far cry from many other Asian countries, where drinking water without elaborate sterilisation preparations is foolhardy).

There is a wide variety of soft drinks, from Coca-Cola, Pepsi, 7-Up and Fanta to a variety of more unusual flavours like sarsaparilla (for root beer fans). Soft drinks generally cost around RM1.30.

You can also find those fruit-juice-in-a-box drinks all over the region in normal fruit flavours and also oddities like chrysanthemum tea.

Sipping a coffee or tea in a Chinese coffee shop or restaurant is a time-honoured pursuit at any time of day or night. If you want your tea, which the Chinese and Malays make very well, without the added thickening of condensed milk, then ask for *teh-o.* Shout it out – it's one of those words that cannot be said quietly. If you don't want sugar either, you have to ask for *teh kosong,* but you're unlikely to get it – they simply cannot believe anyone would drink their tea that way!

Fresh fruit juices are very popular and very good. With the aid of a blender and crushed ice, delicious concoctions like watermelon juice can be whipped up in seconds. Old-fashioned sugar-cane crushers, which look like grandma's old washing mangle, are still used.

The milky white drink in clear plastic bins at street drink-stalls is soya bean milk, which is also sold in a yogurty form. Soya bean milk is also available in soft-drink bottles. Medicinal teas are very popular with the health-minded Chinese.

## ALCOHOLIC DRINKS

Beer drinkers will probably find Anchor, Tiger or Carlsberg beer to their taste, although the minimum price for a large bottle of beer in Malaysia is at least RM9, and its hard to find in some states. Irish travellers may be surprised to find that Guinness has a considerable following in Malaysia – in part because the Chinese believe that it has a strong medicinal value. Royal Stout is a cheaper local equivalent of the black brew. Singapore is known for its cocktail, the Singapore Sling (see the boxed text in this section).

Beware of the only really cheap alcohol in Malaysia, the dreaded *samsu*. Sold in small bottles of around 150ml and costing only RM2, this firewater has an alcohol content of 20% to 70%. Some claim tonic properties, curing everything from rheumatism to indigestion, but make no mistake: This is cheap, deadly booze.

Or at least it used to be deadly, especially in the Indian plantation areas where contaminated, home-distilled samsu regularly killed half a village. Though illegal distilling still goes on, many brands of samsu are legally manufactured under brand names such as Three Snakes, Horse Brand, Tiger and other descriptive labels. Many are also named after Indian warriors, for samsu is typically a product of the South Indian brewing tradition, where villagers produce a variety of 'toddy' from fermented coconut and stronger rice-wine brews.

Samsu drinking is a problem not just among the poor, rural Indian community but also in the cities and among Malays and foreign workers. Though only licensed outlets are allowed to sell it, most of it is sold under the counter through general shops and private houses.

## The Singapore Sling

A visit to Singapore is considered by many to be incomplete without sampling Singapore's famous cocktail, the Singapore Sling. This colourful and refreshing drink was created at Raffles Hotel in 1915 by a Hainanese-Chinese bartender called Ngiam Tong Boon.

Originally, the Singapore Sling was meant to be a woman's drink, hence the attractive pink colour. Today it is very definitely a drink enjoyed by all. Raffles makes a killing by selling rather overpriced, commercially prepared versions of the cocktail in the Bar & Billiard Room and the Long Bar. However, if you can't make it to the hotel to enjoy this national cocktail, go ahead and make your own.

### Ingredients
½ measure of gin
¼ measure of cherry brandy
¼ measure of mixed fruit juices (orange, lime or lemon and pineapple)
a few drops of Cointreau & Benedictine
a dash of Angostura Bitters
a cherry and a slice of pineapple to garnish

Mix all the above, pour into a long glass, find a comfy cane chair on a sunny veranda, grab a Somerset Maugham novel and sip away, making believe that you're in the tropics under a swishing ceiling fan back in the heyday of Singapore's colonial past.

# Getting There & Away

## AIR

Kuala Lumpur (KL) is the major gateway to Malaysia, handling almost all international flights with the exception of a few regional flights from Asia, which may come via Penang, Johor Bahru, Kota Kinabalu and a few other cities. Many airlines service Malaysia, but the country's international airline, Malaysia Airlines, is the major carrier.

When shopping for a ticket, be sure to compare the costs of flying into Malaysia versus flying into Singapore – you'll often find it's much cheaper to fly into Singapore (see Singapore's Getting There & Away chapter for details). From Singapore, you can travel overland to almost any place in Peninsular Malaysia in less than 18 hours.

KL, Penang (see Getting There & Away in the Penang chapter) and Singapore are good places to buy tickets for onward travel from Malaysia, but if you're really in search of bargains, you'll almost always do better in Bangkok (just a train ride away).

### Departure Tax

Malaysia levies airport taxes on all flights. The fee is RM40 on international departures and RM20 for flights to Singapore and Brunei. If you buy your tickets in Malaysia, the departure tax is included in the price.

### The USA

It's possible to find fares from the US west coast to Malaysia for around US$900 return, with Malaysia Airlines offering some of the cheapest. Other airlines to check include Singapore Airlines, Air China and Cathay Pacific. From New York, fares start at US$1100. Some cheap fares may include a stopover in Hong Kong.

San Francisco consolidators (discount travel agents) have some of the cheapest fares, although good deals can also be found in Los Angeles, New York and other big cities. The *San Francisco Examiner,* the *New York Times*, the *Los Angeles Times* and

### Warning

The information in this chapter is particularly vulnerable to change: Prices for international travel are volatile, routes are introduced and cancelled, schedules change, special deals come and go, and rules and visa requirements are amended. Airlines and governments seem to take a perverse pleasure in making price structures and regulations as complicated as possible. You should check directly with the airline or a travel agent to make sure you understand how a fare (and ticket you may buy) works. In addition, the travel industry is highly competitive and there are many lurks and perks.

The upshot of this is that you should get opinions, quotes and advice from as many airlines and travel agents as possible before you part with your hard-earned cash. The details given in this chapter should be regarded as pointers and are not a substitute for your own careful, up-to-date research.

the *Chicago Tribune* all produce weekly travel sections in which you'll find any number of travel agents' ads. Council Travel, America's largest student travel organisation, has around 60 offices in the USA; its head office (☎ 800-226 8624) is at 205 E 42 St, New York, NY 10017. Visit its Web site at www.ciee.org. STA Travel (☎ 800-777 0112) has offices in major cities; its Web site is at www.statravel.com.

### Canada

Low-season return fares from Vancouver average CA$1400; from Toronto they're closer to CA$2200. Malaysia Airlines and Canadian Airlines International are two carriers to check. The *Globe & Mail*, the *Toronto Star*, the *Montreal Gazette* and the *Vancouver Sun* carry travel agents' ads. Travel CUTS (☎ 800-667 2887) is Canada's national student travel agency; visit its Web site at www.travelcuts.com.

## Australia

Discounted fares from Melbourne or Sydney to KL cost around A$819 return in the low season, rising to A$1179 in the high season (December to February). Flying from Brisbane is about A$100 cheaper, from Perth A$200 cheaper.

Malaysia Airlines, Singapore Airlines, Ansett Australia and Qantas Airways all offer good deals; also check some of the Middle-Eastern airlines that fly between Europe and Australia.

The travel sections of weekend newspapers such as the *Age* in Melbourne and the *Sydney Morning Herald* are good places to look for air-fare deals.

STA Travel (☎ 03-9349 2411) has offices in all major cities. Call ☎ 131 776 Australiawide for the location of your nearest branch or visit its Web site at www.statravel.com.au. Flight Centre (☎ 131 600 Australiawide) has dozens of offices throughout Australia. Its Web site is at www.flightcentre.com.au.

## New Zealand

Malaysia Airlines, Singapore Airlines, Air New Zealand and Qantas Airways fly between New Zealand and Malaysia. Lowseason return tickets start at NZ$1314; high-season return fares start at NZ$1500. Round-the-World (RTW) and Circle Pacific fares for travel to/from Malaysia are often a good value.

The *New Zealand Herald* has a travel section in which travel agents advertise fares. Flight Centre (☎ 09-309 6171) has a large office in Auckland and many branches throughout the country. STA Travel (☎ 09-309 0458) has offices in all major towns and cities. Its Web site is at www.statravel.com.au.

## The UK

London has the best deals for flights to Malaysia and Singapore. You can take your pick from a wide range of carriers, but the cheapest are Aeroflot, Pakistan International Airlines and Air Lanka. Low-season discount tickets start from UK£400.

Other airlines such as Lufthansa Airlines, Virgin Atlantic and Malaysia Airlines have return fares from around UK£565, but there are seasonal fluctuations of around UK£100. One-way flights start at around UK£240.

Advertisements for many travel agents appear in the travel pages of the weekend broadsheets, such as the *Independent* on Saturday and the *Sunday Times*. Look out for free magazines such as *TNT*.

Popular travel agencies in the UK include STA Travel (☎ 020-7361 6161), which has an office at 86 Old Brompton Rd, London SW7 3LQ, and other offices in London and Manchester. Visit its Web site at www.statravel.co.uk.

Usit Campus (☎ 0870-240 1010), 52 Grosvenor Gardens, London SW1WOAG, has branches throughout the UK. Its Web site is at www.usitcampus.com.

Other recommended travel agents include: Trailfinders (☎ 020-7938 3939), 194 Kensington High St, London W8 7RG; Bridge to the World (☎ 020-7734 7447), 4 Regent Place, London W1R 5FB; and Flightbookers (☎ 020-7757 2000), 177–178 Tottenham Court Rd, London W1P 9LF.

## Continental Europe

Prices for low/high-season return tickets from Belgium start at around FB27,400/29,600. Return tickets from Paris to KL cost from FF3250/3600. Also, check with Nouvelles Frontières (☎ 08 03 33 33 33) to see if it's offering spring/autumn specials on Gulf Air.

Return flights from Frankfurt to KL start at around DM1460/1665. Prices for return tickets from Switzerland start at around FS1038/FS1156. Return flights from Amsterdam to KL start at around G1768/2380.

## Hong Kong

Hong Kong is not the discount-flight centre it once was. The cheapest one-way flights to Malaysia cost around US$200. In addition to KL, it is possible to fly from Hong Kong to Penang, Langkawi and Kota Kinabalu.

Tsim Sha Tsui is Hong Kong's budget travel-agency centre. Most of the operators nowadays are reliable. One of the best is Phoenix Services (☎ 2722 7378), 6th floor,

MALAYSIA

## Air Travel Glossary

**Cancellation Penalties** If you have to cancel or change a discounted ticket, there are often heavy penalties involved; insurance can sometimes be taken out against these penalties. Some airlines impose penalties on regular tickets as well, particularly against 'no-show' passengers.

**Courier Fares** Businesses often need to send urgent documents or freight securely and quickly. Courier companies hire people to accompany the package through customs and, in return, offer a discount ticket which is sometimes a phenomenal bargain. However, you may have to surrender all your baggage allowance and take only carry-on luggage.

**Full Fares** Airlines traditionally offer 1st class (coded F), business class (coded J) and economy class (coded Y) tickets. These days there are so many promotional and discounted fares available that few passengers pay full economy fare.

**Lost Tickets** If you lose your airline ticket an airline will usually treat it like a travellers cheque and, after inquiries, issue you with another one. Legally, however, an airline is entitled to treat it like cash and if you lose it then it's gone forever. Take good care of your tickets.

**Onward Tickets** An entry requirement for many countries is that you have a ticket out of the country. If you're unsure of your next move, the easiest solution is to buy the cheapest onward ticket to a neighbouring country or a ticket from a reliable airline which can later be refunded if you do not use it.

**Open-Jaw Tickets** These are return tickets where you fly out to one place but return from another. If available, this can save you backtracking to your arrival point.

**Overbooking** Since every flight has some passengers who fail to show up, airlines often book more passengers than they have seats. Usually excess passengers make up for the no-shows, but occasionally somebody gets 'bumped' onto the next available flight. Guess who it is most likely to be? The passengers who check in late.

**Promotional Fares** These are officially discounted fares, available from travel agencies or direct from the airline.

**Reconfirmation** If you don't reconfirm your flight at least 72 hours prior to departure, the airline may delete your name from the passenger list. Ring to find out if your airline requires reconfirmation.

**Restrictions** Discounted tickets often have various restrictions on them – such as needing to be paid for in advance and incurring a penalty to be altered. Others are restrictions on the minimum and maximum period you must be away.

**Round-the-World Tickets** RTW tickets give you a limited period (usually a year) in which to circumnavigate the globe. You can go anywhere the carrying airlines go, as long as you don't backtrack. The number of stopovers or total number of separate flights is decided before you set off and they usually cost a bit more than a basic return flight.

**Transferred Tickets** Airline tickets cannot be transferred from one person to another. Travellers sometimes try to sell the return half of their ticket, but officials can ask you to prove that you are the person named on the ticket. On an international flight tickets are compared with passports.

**Travel Periods** Ticket prices vary with the time of year. There is a low (off-peak) season and a high (peak) season, and often a low-shoulder season and a high-shoulder season as well. Usually the fare depends on your outward flight – if you depart in the high season and return in the low season, you pay the high-season fare.

Milton Mansion, 96 Nathan Rd, Tsim Sha Tsui.

## Japan
Return flights from Japan to KL or Penang cost between ¥50,000 and ¥70,000. One-way tickets are expensive, averaging around ¥50,000. It's usually around ¥10,000 cheaper to fly to/from Tokyo rather than Osaka/KIX. The best agency to deal with is STA Travel, which has branches in Tokyo (☎ 03-5485 8380) and Osaka (☎ 06-262 7066). A'Cross Travel is another reliable agency that is used to dealing with foreigners; it has branches in Tokyo (☎ 03-3340 6741), Osaka (☎ 06-6345 0150) and Kyoto (☎ 075-255 3559).

For information on the latest discount prices, pick up a copy of *Tokyo Classified* or, if you're in the Kansai region, get hold of *Kansai Time Out*. The four English-language newspapers also run advertisements from the major travel agents.

## Thailand
The place to buy tickets to Malaysia or Singapore in Bangkok is Khao San Rd. The agents here deal in discounted tickets; rip-offs do occur from time to time, so take care. Flights from Bangkok to KL cost from B4800/6500 one way/return and flights from Bangkok to Penang cost from B3600/6800.

## Indonesia
There are several interesting possibilities for travel from Indonesia to Malaysia.

The short hop from Medan in Sumatra to Penang costs around US$60 to US$140 (depending on discounts); from Penang it's RM231. There are also weekly flights between Kuching in Sarawak and Pontianak in Kalimantan (the Indonesian part of the island of Borneo) for RM296. Similarly, at the eastern end of Borneo there is a weekly connection between Tawau in Sabah and Tarakan in Kalimantan.

To get to Java, the cheapest connections are from Singapore, for as little as S$120. However it's worth remembering that Malaysia Airlines also has competitively priced flights from Johor Bahru to Jakarta.

(Note that the prices we've mentioned here are for one-way tickets.)

The travel agencies on Jalan Jaksa, Jakarta's budget accommodation area, are good places to look for international flights. Indo Shangrila Travel (☎ 021-625 6080), Jalan Gajah Mada 219G, is a large ticketing agent and often has good deals.

## Singapore
See the Getting There & Away chapter of the Singapore section for details on flying between Singapore and Malaysia.

## India & Other Places in Asia
Although Indonesia and Thailand are the two usual places to travel to/from Malaysia, there are plenty of other possibilities, including India, Sri Lanka and the Philippines. Check prices in Singapore and Penang – the two discount airline-ticket centres.

## LAND
## Thailand
You can cross the border by land at Padang Besar (road or rail), Bukit Kayu Hitam (road) or Keroh-Betong (road) in the west; or at Rantau Panjang–Sungai Golok or Pengkalan Kubor in the east. For information on Thai visas, refer to the Visas & Documents section in Malaysia's Facts for the Visitor chapter.

**West Coast Road** Although there are border points at Padang Besar and Keroh, most travellers cross by road at Bukit Kayu Hitam on the Lebuhraya (North-South Highway) for Hat Yai. The easiest way to cross here is to take a bus from Georgetown (see the Penang chapter) to Hat Yai for around RM20. Buses also run from Alor Setar to the large border-post complex at Bukit Kayu Hitam, from where you walk a few hundred metres to the Thai checkpoint. On the other side, buses and taxis run to Sadao and Hat Yai. Buses and trains run from Hat Yai to Phuket, Krabi, Surat Thani, Bangkok and other places.

The alternative is to cross at Padang Besar, where it is an easy walk across. The only reason to go this way by road is if you're heading to/from Langkawi. Buses run from Kuala Perlis to Padang Besar via Kangar. The train from Alor Setar all the way to Hat Yai is the easiest way to cross this border.

**East Coast Road** The Thai border is at Rantau Panjang (Sungai Golok on the Thai side), 1½ hours by bus from Kota Bharu. From Rantau Panjang walk across the border, and it's about 1km to the station, from where trains go to Hat Yai, Surat Thani and Bangkok. Buses also take this route. See Kota Bharu in the Kelantan chapter for more details.

An alternative route into Thailand is via Pengkalan Kubor on the coast. It's more time-consuming and very few travellers go this way. See Around Kota Bharu for more details.

**Train** The rail route into Thailand is on the Butterworth–Alor Setar–Hat Yai route, which crosses into Thailand at Padang Besar. You can take the *International Express* from Butterworth all the way to Bangkok with connections from Singapore and KL. From Hat Yai there are frequent train and bus connections to other parts of Thailand (see the *International Express* table in this chapter for train fares and schedules). One train a day also goes from Alor Setar to Hat Yai (see Alor Setar in the Kedah & Perlis chapter for details).

A variation on the *International Express*, the *Eastern & Oriental Express* makes the 1943km journey from Singapore to Bangkok once a week and caters to the well-heeled. See the Singapore Getting There & Away chapter for more information.

## Singapore

The Causeway linking Johor Bahru with Singapore handles most traffic between the countries. Trains and buses run from all over Malaysia straight through to Singapore, or you can take a bus to Johor Bahru and get a taxi or one of the frequent buses from JB to Singapore.

There is also a new causeway linking Tuas, in western Singapore, with Geyland

## International Express Fares & Schedules

**Fares (2nd class):**

|  | Singapore | Kuala Lumpur | Butterworth |
|---|---|---|---|
| Hat Yai | S$64.20 | RM43.50 | RM14.90 |
| Bangkok | S$91.70 | RM70.30 | RM44.90 |

**Schedule:**

| Train No 36 | | Train No 35 | |
|---|---|---|---|
| (International Express from Butterworth – runs daily) | | (International Express from Bangkok – runs daily) | |
| Butterworth | 14:10 | Bangkok | 13:20* |
| Alor Setar | 16:15 | Hat Yai | 6:55* |
| Hat Yai | 18:50* | Alor Setar | 11:06 |
| Bangkok | 11:00* | Butterworth | 12:55 |

* Thai time (one hour behind Malaysian time).

There is an express surcharge on the *International Express* of RM13.60 for air-con and RM8.10 for non-air-con, plus RM7.20 for the Thai leg of the journey. Sleeping berths in 2nd class cost an additional RM22.30 for an upper berth and RM28.50 for a lower berth. Surcharges may also apply to fares in Singapore dollars; check with KTM or visit its Web site at www.ktmb.com.my.

Patah. This is known as the Second Link, but it's of little use to travellers without their own transport. If you do have a car, tolls on the Second Link are much higher than the charge on the main Causeway.

See the Singapore Getting There & Away chapter and the Johor Bahru section of the Johor chapter.

## Indonesia

It is easy to cross the land border between Malaysia and Indonesia, which is between Pontianak in Kalimantan and Kuching in Sarawak. A daily express bus (10 hours) runs between Pontianak and Kuching. The bus crosses at the Tebedu/Entikong border, a visa-free entry point into Indonesia. See the Kuching Getting There & Away section for details.

## SEA
## Thailand

Regular daily boats run between Langkawi and Satun in Thailand. There are customs and immigration posts here, so you can cross quite legally, although it's an unusual and rarely used entry/exit point. Make sure you get your passport stamped on entry. See the Langkawi section in the Kedah & Perlis chapter for details.

In the main tourist season (around Christmas) yachts run irregularly between Langkawi and Phuket in Thailand, taking in Thai islands on the way. The trip usually takes five days and costs around US$70 per person, per day. The best way to find a boat is to ask around the travellers' bars and restaurants in either Langkawi or Phuket. Otherwise, check with the owners of Terengganu's Kapas Island Resort (☎ 010-984 1686, 04-899 4325).

## Singapore

There are a number of ways to cross the Strait of Johor, but most people cross on the main Causeway, either by train or by road.

The main ferry crossing is between Changi Village (Singapore) and Tanjung Belungkur (Johor, Malaysia), and exists mainly for Singaporeans holidaying in Desaru on the Malaysian coast. High-speed catamarans run between the Tanah Merah ferry terminal in Singapore and Pulau Tioman in Pahang state, again, primarily for Singaporean holiday-makers. Small boats also ply between Pengerang in Johor and Changi Village in Singapore.

The Singapore Getting There & Away chapter has full details.

## Indonesia

The three main ferry routes between Malaysia and Indonesia are Penang-Medan and Melaka-Dumai connecting Peninsular Malaysia with Sumatra, and Tawau-Tarakan linking Sabah with Kalimantan in Borneo.

The popular crossing between Penang and Medan is handled by two companies that between them have services most days of the week. The boats actually land in Belawan in Sumatra, and the journey to Medan is completed by bus (included in the price). See the Penang chapter for details.

Twice daily high-speed ferries run between Melaka and Dumai in Sumatra. Dumai is now a visa-free entry port into Indonesia for citizens of most countries. See the Melaka chapter for details.

Boats also operate most days from Tawau in Sabah to Nunukan in Kalimantan and then on to Tarakan in Kalimantan (see Tawau in the Sabah chapter for details).

Another possibility is to take a boat from the Bebas Cukai ferry terminal in Johor Bahru. Boats go direct to Batu Ampar and Tanjung Pinang, both in Sumatra. See Johor Bahru in the Johor chapter for details on these boats. You can also take a ferry from Kukup, in Johor, to Tanjung Balai in Sumatra. See the Kukup section in the Johor chapter for details.

## Philippines

Passenger ferries now run between Sandakan and Zamboanga in the Philippines. The trip takes 18 hours and costs from RM60 – see the Sandakan section in the Sabah chapter.

# Getting Around

## AIR

Malaysia Airlines is the country's main domestic operator. The Malaysian Air Fares map in this chapter details some of the main regional routes and the standard one-way fares in Malaysian ringgit. Malaysia Airlines has many other regional routes in Sarawak and Sabah. It operates Airbuses, Boeing 737s and Fokker F50s/F70s on its main domestic routes, plus 18-seater Twin Otters on most of the more-remote Sarawak and Sabah routes.

There are lots of local flights in Malaysian Borneo, where many communities rely on air transport as the only quick way in or out. These flights are very much dependent on the vagaries of the weather. In the wet season (October to March in Sarawak and on Sabah's north-east coast; May to November on Sabah's west coast), places like Bario in Sarawak can be isolated for days at a time, so don't venture into this area if you have a very tight schedule. These flights are completely booked during school holidays. At other times it's easier to get a seat at a few days' notice, but always book as far in advance as possible.

Malaysia Airlines is very accommodating about changes in travel plans and will alter any ticket on the spot, in any of its offices. If the value of the new ticket is less than the old one, it will issue vouchers for the difference.

The other main domestic carrier is Pelangi Air. It offers far fewer flights but covers a few destinations that Malaysia Airlines doesn't, including some routes to Ipoh and Langkawi. Pelangi reservations should be made through Malaysia Airlines. The tiny Berjaya Air has flights between Pulau Tioman (Tioman Island) and Kuala Lumpur (KL).

### Discounts & Special Flights

A variety of worthwhile discounts are available, especially for groups and for travel between Peninsular Malaysia and Malaysian Borneo. Student discounts are available, but

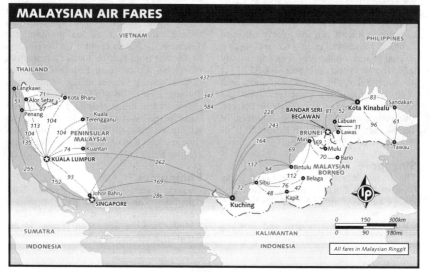

MALAYSIAN AIR FARES

All fares in Malaysian Ringgit

only for students enrolled in institutions in Malaysia.

The following discounts apply for families or groups (a group must comprise at least three people) on regular Malaysia Airlines return economy air fares. The minimum stay requirement is four days, the maximum stay is 30 days, and tickets must be booked and paid for at least seven days in advance.

• 50% between Peninsular Malaysia and Malaysian Borneo, and between Sabah and Sarawak
• 25% within Peninsular Malaysia, Sabah or Sarawak
• 25% anywhere in Malaysia for families (a couple with or without children), provided one spouse pays full fare. Children receive the 25% discount on the applicable child's fare.
• 20% for groups of 10 or more travelling between Malaysia and Singapore or Brunei
• 50% for escorted disabled passengers (25% for the escort)

Malaysia Airlines also has special seven-day advance-purchase one-way tickets (YOX fares) and apex 30-day return tickets (YEE30 fares) for the following flights from Johor Bahru (JB) and KL:

| flight | fare (RM) YOX/YEE30 |
| --- | --- |
| JB-Kuching | 144/305 |
| JB–Kota Kinabalu | 295/624 |
| JB-Penang | 150/318 |
| KL-Kuching | 227/425 |
| KL–Kota Kinabalu | 372/689 |
| KL-Miri | 359/679 |
| KL-Labuan | 372/656 |
| KL-Sibu | – /510 |

There are also a few economy night-flights between Kuala Lumpur and Kota Kinabalu (RM306), Kuching (RM187), Alor Setar (RM74) and Penang (RM73), and between JB and KK (RM260).

## Flying from Malaysia vs Flying from Singapore
You can save quite a few ringgit if you are flying to Sarawak or Sabah by flying from Johor Bahru rather than Kuala Lumpur or

Singapore. The regular economy fare is RM169 from Johor Bahru to Kuching against RM262 from KL and S$199 from Singapore. To Kota Kinabalu, the respective fares are RM347, RM437 and S$403. To persuade travellers to take advantage of these lower fares, Malaysia Airlines offers a bus service directly from its office at the Novotel Orchid Hotel, 214 Dunearn Rd, in Singapore to the Johor Bahru airport for S$12.

It is worth bearing in mind that fares on flights between Singapore and Malaysia cost almost the same in ringgit/dollar terms whether bought in Malaysia or Singapore, making Singapore tickets much more expensive when the exchange rate is taken into account.

## TRAIN
Malaysia has a modern, comfortable and economical railway service, although there are basically only two lines. One runs from Singapore to Kuala Lumpur, to Butterworth and on into Thailand. The other branches off from this line at Gemas and runs through Kuala Lipis up to the north-eastern corner of the country near Kota Bharu. Often referred to as the 'jungle train', this line is properly known as the 'east-coast line'. Other lines are just minor branches off these two routes and are not much used.

In Sabah there's a small narrow-gauge railway line that can take you through the Sungai Pegas gorge from Tenom to Beaufort. Unfortunately, the line has fallen into disrepair and accidents are common.

Malaysia's first railway line was a 13km route from Taiping to Port Weld that was laid in 1884, but it's no longer in use. By 1903 you could travel all the way from Johor Bahru to near Butterworth; the line was extended to the Thai border in 1918 and across the Causeway to Singapore in 1923. In 1931 the east-coast line was completed, effectively bringing the railway system to its present state.

## Train Passes
The privatised national railway company, Keretapi Tanah Melayu (KTM), offers a

MALAYSIA

# Train Fares & Times in Malaysia

## Train Fares from Butterworth (RM)

| destination | express | | | local | | |
|---|---|---|---|---|---|---|
| | 1st class | 2nd class | 3rd class | 1st class | 2nd class | 3rd class |
| Padang Besar | 34.00 | 20.00 | 11.00 | 25.50 | 11.10 | 6.30 |
| Taiping | 23.00 | 15.00 | 8.00 | 14.40 | 6.30 | 3.60 |
| Ipoh | 36.00 | 21.00 | 11.00 | 27.80 | 12.10 | 6.90 |
| Tapah Road | 44.00 | 24.00 | 13.00 | 36.00 | 15.60 | 8.90 |
| Kuala Lumpur | 67.00 | 34.00 | 19.00 | 58.50 | 25.40 | 14.40 |
| Tampin | 85.00 | 42.00 | 23.00 | 76.50 | 33.20 | 18.90 |
| Johor Bahru | 122.00 | 58.00 | 33.00 | 114.00 | 49.40 | 28.10 |
| Singapore | 127.00 | 60.00 | 34.00 | 118.50 | 51.40 | 29.90 |

## Train Fares from Kuala Lumpur (RM)

| destination | express | | | local | | |
|---|---|---|---|---|---|---|
| | 1st class | 2nd class | 3rd class | 1st class | 2nd class | 3rd class |
| Padang Besar | – | – | – | 81.00 | 35.10 | 20.00 |
| Butterworth | 67.00 | 34.00 | 19.00 | 58.50 | 25.40 | 14.40 |
| Taiping | 53.00 | 28.00 | 16.00 | 45.00 | 19.50 | 11.10 |
| Ipoh | 40.00 | 22.00 | 12.00 | 31.50 | 13.70 | 7.80 |
| Tapah Road | 32.00 | 19.00 | 10.00 | 23.30 | 10.10 | 5.80 |
| Tampin | 27.00 | 17.00 | 9.00 | 18.80 | 8.20 | 4.70 |
| Johor Bahru | 64.00 | 33.00 | 18.00 | 55.50 | 24.10 | 13.70 |
| Singapore | 68.00 | 34.00 | 19.00 | 60.00 | 26.00 | 14.80 |
| Jerantut | 48.00 | 35.00 | 15.00 | – | – | – |
| Kuala Lipis | 56.00 | 36.50 | 18.00 | – | – | – |
| Wakaf Baharu | 78.00 | 45.50 | 28.00 | – | – | – |
| Tumpat | 80.00 | 46.50 | 29.00 | – | – | – |

## Train Fares from Singapore (S$)

| destination | express | | | local | | |
|---|---|---|---|---|---|---|
| | 1st class | 2nd class | 3rd class | 1st class | 2nd class | 3rd class |
| Padang Besar | – | – | – | 139.50 | 60.50 | 34.40 |
| Butterworth | 127.00 | 60.00 | 34.00 | 118.50 | 51.40 | 29.20 |
| Taiping | 112.00 | 53.00 | 30.00 | 103.50 | 44.90 | 25.50 |
| Ipoh | 100.00 | 48.00 | 27.00 | 91.50 | 39.70 | 22.60 |
| Tapah Road | 92.00 | 45.00 | 25.00 | 84.00 | 36.40 | 20.70 |
| Kuala Lumpur | 68.00 | 34.00 | 19.00 | 60.00 | 26.00 | 14.80 |
| Tampin | 50.00 | 27.00 | 15.00 | 42.00 | 18.20 | 10.40 |
| Johor Bahru | 13.00 | 10.00 | 6.00 | 4.20 | 1.90 | 1.10 |
| Kuala Lipis | 76.00 | 31.00 | 21.00 | – | 29.30 | 16.70 |
| Wakaf Baharu | 119.00 | 41.00 | 32.00 | – | 48.10 | 27.40 |
| Tumpat | 121.00 | 57.00 | 32.00 | – | 48.80 | 27.70 |

Supplementary berth charges for Malaysian services are as follows: RM70 for 1st-class lower berth; RM50 for 1st-class upper berth; RM14 for 2nd-class air-con lower berth; RM11.50 for 2nd-class air-con upper berth. Supplementary charges may also apply to ex-Singapore fares.

*(Continued next page)*

MALAYSIA

## Train Fares & Times in Malaysia

### Timetables for Main West-Coast Services
ES & SM trains are limited express services, all others are express.

|  | R/1 | XSP/3 | EL/7 |
|---|---|---|---|
| Hat Yai | – | – | 1510 |
| Alor Setar | – | – | 1907 |
| Butterworth | 0750 | 1520 | 2059 |
| Taiping | 0931 | 1714 | 2341 |
| Ipoh | 1105 | 1900 | 0140 |
| Kuala Lumpur | 1437 | 2235 | 0605 |

|  | XSP/4 | ER/2 | EL/8 |
|---|---|---|---|
| Kuala Lumpur | 0735 | 1455 | 2100 |
| Ipoh | 1008 | 1838 | 0129 |
| Taiping | 1244 | 2016 | 0341 |
| Butterworth | 1440 | 2115 | 0602 |
| Alor Setar | – | – | 0827 |
| Hat Yai | – | – | 0950 |

|  | XSP/5 | ER/1 | SM/11 |
|---|---|---|---|
| Kuala Lumpur | 0740 | 1450 | 2230 |
| Tampin | 0929 | 1643 | 0034 |
| Gemas | 1013 | 1727 | 0133 |
| Johor Bahru | 1252 | 2016 | 0537 |
| Singapore | 1345 | 2105 | 0642 |

|  | ER/2 | ES/64 | XSP/6 | ES/61 | SM/12 |
|---|---|---|---|---|---|
| Singapore | 0800 | 1815 | 1455 | 1045 | 2200 |
| Johor Bahru | 0900 | 1902 | 1545 | 0932 | 2305 |
| Gemas | 1152 | – | 1844 | 0540 | 0214 |
| Tampin | 1239 | – | 1934 | – | 0329 |
| Kuala Lumpur | 1442 | – | 2145 | – | 0628 |

### Timetables for Main East-Coast Services
XW trains are express services; 91 & 92 are local trains.

|  | 91 | XW/17 |  | 92 | XW/16 |
|---|---|---|---|---|---|
| Tumpat | 0545 | 1945 | Singapore | – | 2000 |
| Wakaf Baharu | 0606 | 2001 | Johor Bahru | – | 2045 |
| Kuala Lipis | 1343 | 0032 | Gemas | 0745 | 2333 |
| Jerantut | 1525 | 0128 | Jerantut | 1139 | 0245 |
| Gemas | 1935 | 0445 | Kuala Lipis | 1310 | 0338 |
| Johor Bahru | – | 0734 | Wakaf Baharu | 2047 | – |
| Singapore | – | 0840 | Tumpat | 2120 | 0840 |

For details on train types and services, see the Train section of this chapter. Train schedules may change but departure times can be checked on the KTM Web site, at www.ktmb.com.my.

Tourist Railpass for 30 days (US$120/60 for adults/children under 12) or 10 days (US$55/28). This pass entitles the holder to unlimited travel on any class of train but does not include sleeping-berth charges. Railpasses are available only to foreigners and can be purchased at KL, Johor Bahru, Butterworth, Pelabuhan (Port) Klang, Padang Besar, Wakaf Baharu and Penang train stations. You have to do an awful lot of train travel to make them worthwhile.

## Services & Classes

Malaysia has three main types of rail services: express, limited express and local trains. Express trains are air-conditioned and generally 1st and 2nd class only, and on night trains there's a choice of berths or seats. Limited express trains may have 2nd and 3rd class only but some have 1st, 2nd and 3rd class with overnight sleepers. Local trains are usually 3rd class only, but some have 2nd class (see the train fares and schedule tables in this chapter).

Express trains stop only at main stations. Limited express trains stop at a few more stations but still provide a quick service; however, these are being gradually phased out. These two options are much faster than the local trains, and in most respects are definitely the ones to take. The local services, which operate mostly on the east-coast line, are colourful experiences for short journeys. They stop everywhere, including the middle of the jungle, to let passengers and their goods on and off, but they take more than twice as long as the express trains and run to erratic schedules.

For more information on KTM schedules and fares call ☎ 03-273 8000 or ☎ 275 7269, access KTM's Web site, www.ktmb.com.my, or email them at ✉ passenger@ktmb.com.my. Train schedules are reviewed biannually so check before you make detailed plans.

## BUS

Malaysia has an excellent bus system. There are public buses on local runs and a variety of privately operated buses on the longer trips. Transnasional is the largest

---

### Maybe 30%, Maybe Less

We're sure it wasn't intentional, but it wasn't until this book was well into production that Malaysian transport officials announced a nation-wide bus-fare hike of up to 30%. Fare increases affect all buses in Peninsular Malaysia and Malaysian Borneo, including local, minibus, minivan and intercity services. It's always a good idea to check prices before planning your route from A to B, but we suggest you be especially diligent in checking current bus fares with local operators.

---

private bus company with a huge fleet plying most routes on the peninsula.

In larger towns there may be a number of bus stations; local/regional buses often operate from one station and long-distance buses from another; in other cases, KL for example, bus stations are differentiated by the destinations they serve.

Buses are fast, economical and comfortable and seats can be reserved. There are so many buses on major runs that you can often turn up and get a seat on the next bus. On main routes most buses have air-con and cost only a few ringgit more than regular buses. They make travel a sweat-free activity, but you should take note of one traveller's warning: 'Malaysian air-conditioned buses are really meat lockers on wheels with just two settings: cold and suspended animation.'

Getting off the beaten track is only marginally more difficult. Small towns and *kampung* (villages) all over the country are serviced by public buses, usually non-air-con rattlers. Unfortunately, they are often poorly labelled; sometimes the only way to find your bus is to ask a local. These buses are invariably dirt cheap and are great for sampling rural life. In most towns there are no ticket offices – buy your ticket from the conductor after you board.

## CAR

Driving in Malaysia is a breeze compared to most Asian countries; the roads are generally of a high quality, there are plenty of new cars available and driving standards are not too hair-raising.

The Lebuhraya, or North-South Highway, is a new six-lane expressway that runs virtually the whole length of the peninsula from the Thai border in the north to Johor Bahru in the south. There are toll charges for using the expressway, and these vary according to the distance travelled. It's not all that cheap, the result being that the normal highways remain crowded while traffic on the expressway is light. As an example, the trip from KL to Johor Bahru costs RM39.90. Many other highways are in excellent condition and many are under construction.

Driving in the big cities, especially KL, is confusing, chaotic and not much fun, but once out in the countryside driving is relatively easy and a car gives you a great deal of flexibility.

Petrol is inexpensive at around RM1.10 a litre; diesel fuel costs RM0.75 per litre. Wearing safety belts *is* compulsory, although they are fitted to the front seats only.

The Automobile Association of Malaysia (☎ 03-262 5777, fax 262 5358), 25 Jalan Yap Kwan Seng, 50450 Kuala Lumpur, will let you join its organisation if you have a letter of introduction from your own automobile association.

## Road Rules

Basically, driving in Malaysia follows much the same rules as in Britain and Australia – cars are right-hand drive and you drive on the left side of the road. The only additional precaution you need to take is to remain constantly aware of the possible road hazards of stray animals and the large number of motorcyclists. And take it easy on the back roads through the kampung.

Although most drivers in Malaysia are relatively sane, safe and slow, there are also a fair few who specialise in overtaking on blind corners and otherwise trusting in divine intervention. Malaysian drivers also use a curious signalling system, where a flashing left indicator means 'you are safe to overtake', or 'I'm about to turn off', or 'I've forgotten to turn my indicator off', or 'look out, I'm about to do something totally unpredictable'. Giving a quick blast of the horn when you're overtaking a slower vehicle is common practice and helps alert otherwise sleepy drivers to your presence.

## ROAD DISTANCES FOR PENINSULA MALAYSIA (KM)

| | Alor Setar | Bukit Fraser | Butterworth | Ipoh | Johor Bahru | Klang | Kota Bharu | Kuala Lumpur | Kuala Terengganu | Kuantan | Melaka | Mersing | Pelabuan (Port) Klang | Port Dickson | Seremban | Taiping |
|---|---|---|---|---|---|---|---|---|---|---|---|---|---|---|---|---|
| Alor Setar | --- | | | | | | | | | | | | | | | |
| Bukit Fraser | 443 | --- | | | | | | | | | | | | | | |
| Butterworth | 93 | 350 | --- | | | | | | | | | | | | | |
| Ipoh | 257 | 186 | 164 | --- | | | | | | | | | | | | |
| Johor Bahru | 830 | 467 | 737 | 573 | --- | | | | | | | | | | | |
| Klang | 495 | 132 | 400 | 236 | 401 | --- | | | | | | | | | | |
| Kota Bharu | 409 | 406 | 386 | 391 | 689 | 507 | --- | | | | | | | | | |
| Kuala Lumpur | 462 | 99 | 369 | 205 | 368 | 33 | 474 | --- | | | | | | | | |
| Kuala Terengganu | 521 | 453 | 498 | 503 | 521 | 488 | 168 | 455 | --- | | | | | | | |
| Kuantan | 684 | 253 | 591 | 427 | 325 | 292 | 371 | 259 | 209 | --- | | | | | | |
| Melaka | 606 | 243 | 513 | 349 | 224 | 177 | 607 | 144 | 508 | 292 | --- | | | | | |
| Mersing | 815 | 436 | 722 | 558 | 134 | 386 | 568 | 353 | 401 | 191 | 255 | --- | | | | |
| Pelabuan (Port) Klang | 503 | 140 | 410 | 246 | 409 | 8 | 515 | 41 | 496 | 300 | 185 | 394 | --- | | | |
| Port Dickson | 552 | 189 | 459 | 295 | 318 | 115 | 564 | 90 | 503 | 291 | 94 | 321 | 123 | --- | | |
| Seremban | 526 | 163 | 433 | 269 | 304 | 97 | 538 | 64 | 471 | 259 | 80 | 289 | 105 | 32 | --- | |
| Taiping | 183 | 272 | 90 | 86 | 659 | 322 | 369 | 291 | 481 | 513 | 435 | 644 | 332 | 387 | 355 | --- |

## By Bicycle – Peninsular Malaysia & Singapore

Bicycle touring from Singapore, around Malaysia and on to Thailand is an increasingly popular activity.

### Equipment

A well-maintained bike with good tyres is essential. Road conditions are good enough for touring bikes but many people prefer hybrids or mountain bikes with medium-width tyres.

Essential tools include: Allen keys, spoke key, tyre levers and a small Swiss army knife.

Accessories include: helmet, gloves, panniers, front pack with map-holder, rear-view mirror that attaches to the right handlebar, sunglasses, spare tube and patch kit, pump, bungee cord, two large water bottles, insect repellent and sunscreen.

Pack lightly, with everything in waterproof plastic bags. Warm-weather clothes, a pullover (for high altitudes) and a rain shell are recommended.

### Shipping

Bikes are carried free in lieu of luggage on most scheduled international flights. Charter carriers have their own rules. You can purchase a box from the airlines or supply your own. When boxes are unavailable, handlers are often more careful with the unboxed bikes. Take the pedals off (tape them to the back rack), secure the pump with tape and turn the handlebars. Place your panniers in the dead space of the shipping box to protect the gears.

### Planning

Nelles' *West Malaysia* (scale 1:650,000) is the best map around; it's available abroad and in big cities in Malaysia. Weather and wind will either hasten or slow your progress, so a flexible overall plan is best. The equatorial climate has high temperatures, and it's wet all year round (see Climate in Malaysia's Facts for the Visitor chapter). The winds are north-east from November to February and south-west from April to September. March and October are the changeover months, when winds are light and variable. Due to the seasonal headwinds, ride north on the west coast from November to February and south on the east coast from April to September. There are no organised bicycle tours to Singapore or Malaysia.

### Road Rules

*Ride on the left.* Third-world rules apply: the right of way belongs to the larger vehicle. Use a rear-view mirror.

### Practical Information

The main road system is well engineered with good surfaces. The secondary road system is limited. Sealed shoulders are lacking on all but the largest roads, which can make for dangerous riding, especially on busy roads.

Singapore has many bicycle shops. Minor repairs can be handled throughout Malaysia, but try Triathlon Sports Centre (☎ 03-982 6633) in Kuala Lumpur (KL) for major repairs on foreign bikes. The Kuala Lumpur Bike Hash Web site, at www.bikehash.freeservers.com/ has lists of KL and Singaporean bike shops and other useful information.

A major concern when riding in a tropical climate is dehydration. Drink at least half a litre of water before riding and keep drinking fluids all day. Drink *before* you feel thirsty.

### Alternative Transport

In general, buses do not take bicycles, although some express buses might if their luggage compartments are empty – good luck! Trains take bikes, but they must be shipped ahead with freight. Hitching in small trucks is always an excellent option, but rides are tougher to get here than in the

## By Bicycle – Peninsular Malaysia & Singapore

rest of Asia. Pick-up trucks are best. Keep the panniers on to protect the gears when putting bikes in trucks.

### Routes

**Changi Airport to Singapore (25km)** There is no way to take your bike on public transport. You'll have to ride – it's officially illegal on the East Coast Parkway, but you'll have to take this road to get to the East Coast Parkway Service Rd. The alternative is to put your bike in the boot of a taxi or take the bicycle track along the east-coast beach. Turn left onto the East Coast Parkway Service Rd and follow this to the 13km road marker, then turn right onto Fort Rd. Turn left onto Mountbatten Rd, pass Stadium Rd and then turn left onto Nicoll Hwy into the city.

**Singapore to Johor Bahru (27km)** There are multiple options on city streets through Singapore to the Causeway to Johor Bahru. The most direct route is along Bukit Timah Rd to Woodlands Rd to the bridge. It is also possible to take bicycles on the ferries that leave from Changi Village, going to Pengerang for Desaru in Johor state.

**West Coast Peninsular Malaysia** This route is through rolling hills and flat country, with interesting cities to visit. From Johor Bahru follow the coast west to Hwy 1 (four lanes with shoulder) and turn onto a secondary road (Route 5) to Pontian Kecil (61km) on the coast. Follow Hwy 5 along the coast to Batu Pahat (73km), then Muar (53km) and Melaka (45km). There are some views of the Selat Melaka (Straits of Melaka) from the road. Port Dickson is another 94km and from there to Banting it's 83km.

After Banting the traffic becomes treacherous on this narrow highway to Klang (32km), where there is a turn-off to KL (32km). There are some designated bicycle lanes in KL.

From KL to Butterworth (Penang), the best route is via the coast and inland roads to Taiping, and then along secondary roads to Butterworth. From Butterworth, take the ferry to Pulau Penang (Penang Island; bikes are not allowed on the bridge). There is some good riding on the island along the beaches.

**Cross-Peninsula Route** This route has very light traffic. From Butterworth to Baling (91km) there are multiple routes with few signposts. Ask for Baling or Gerik and note that there are hills between these towns (62km). Gerik has facilities and hotels, and you can also stay at Pulau Banding. Hwy 4 (East-West Highway) is a well-engineered road with good surfaces. There are some long climbs through the interior mountains; facilities are sparse and there are no hotels, but the views are often excellent. Gerik to Jeli is 124km, and it's 97km from Jeli to the crossroads of Hwy 4 and Hwy 3. Alternatively, you can take Hwy 8 north to Kota Bharu. Expect rain.

**East Coast Peninsular Malaysia** This is the most popular route for cycling through the peninsula. Although, as on all highways, traffic is increasing, there is less traffic on this route than on the west-coast route, and it's flat and follows the coast for long stretches.

Hwy 3 from Kota Bharu (168km) south to Kuala Terengganu has light traffic but fast-moving buses and trucks. About 80km before Kuala Terengganu you can cut into the beach (14km) and enjoy a quiet ride into the city. Hwy 3 runs along the coast to Kuala Dungun (78km). From Kuala Dungun to Kuantan (131km) there are lots of beach hotels (most are closed in the off season).

Take the passenger ferry across the river from Kuantan and follow another quiet coastal road south to Pekan (47km). Continue from Pekan to Mersing back on Hwy 3 (144km). Follow Hwy 3 to Kota Tinggi (92km). The busy highway is wider from here to Johor Bahru (41km).

**Peter & Sally Blommer** from *Cycle Singapore/Malaysia* – **Blommer**

## Rental

Rent-a-car operations are well established in Malaysia. Major rental companies include Avis, Budget, Mayflower, Hertz, National and Thrifty; there are many others, though, including local operators only found in one city. Unlimited distance rates for a 1.3L Proton Saga, the cheapest and most popular car in Malaysia, are posted at around RM150/900 per day/week, including insurance and collision-damage waiver. The Proton Wira is a step up in standard and a bit more expensive. The Proton is basically a Mitsubishi assembled under licence in Malaysia. Charges for a Ford Laser are around RM200/1200 per day/week.

These are the standard rates from the major car-hire companies but you can often get better deals, either through smaller local companies or when the major companies offer special deals. Rates drop substantially for longer rentals and you can get a Proton Saga for as little as RM2000 per month, including unlimited kilometres and insurance, if you shop around by phone. The main advantage of dealing with a large company is that it has offices all over the country, giving better backup if something goes wrong and allowing you to pick up in one city and drop off in another (typically for a RM50 surcharge). Mayflower is one local company with offices all over and some competitive rates.

KL is the best place to look for car hire and Penang is also good (see Getting There & Away in those chapters for details). In Sabah and Sarawak there is less competition and rates are higher, partly because of the condition of the roads.

A valid overseas licence is needed to rent a car. An International Driving Permit is usually not required by local car-hire companies but it is recommended that you bring one (see Other Documents under Visas & Documents in Malaysia's Facts for the Visitor chapter). Age limits apply, and most companies require that drivers are at least 23 years old.

## LONG-DISTANCE TAXI

Long-distance taxis make Malaysian travel, already easy and convenient even by the best Asian standards, a real breeze. In almost every town there will be a 'teksi' stand where the cars are lined up and ready to go to their various destinations.

Taxis are ideal for groups of four, and are also available on a share basis. As soon as a full complement of four passengers turns up, off you go. Between major towns you have a reasonable chance of finding other passengers to share without having to wait too long, but otherwise you will have to charter a whole taxi, which is four times the single-fare rate (in this book we generally quote the rate for a whole taxi). As Malaysia becomes increasingly wealthy, and people can afford to hire a whole taxi, the share system is becoming less reliable. Early morning is generally the best time to find people to share a taxi, but you can inquire at the taxi stand the day before to see when is the best time.

Taxi rates to specific destinations are fixed by the government and are posted at the taxi stands; usually the rate for a whole taxi is listed. Air-con taxis cost a few more ringgit than non-air-con taxis. Taxi fares generally work out at about twice the comparable bus fares. If you want to charter a taxi to an obscure destination, or by the hour, you'll probably have to do some negotiating. As a rule of thumb, you should pay around 50 sen per kilometre.

Taxi drivers often drive at frighteningly high speeds. They don't have as many head-on collisions as you might expect, but closing your eyes at times of high stress certainly helps! You also have the option of demanding that the driver slow down, but, this is met with varying degrees of hostility. Another tactic is to look for aging taxis and taxi drivers – they must be doing something right to have made it this far!

## HITCHING

Malaysia has long had a reputation for being an excellent place for hitchhiking and it's generally still true, though with the ease of the buses most travellers don't bother.

On the west coast of Malaysia, hitching is generally quite easy but it is not possible on the main Lebuhraya expressway. On the east coast, traffic is lighter and there may be long waits between rides. Hitching in Malaysian Borneo also depends on the traffic, although it's quite possible.

Keep in mind that hitching is never entirely safe in any country in the world, and we don't recommend it. Travellers who decide to hitch should understand that they are taking a small but potentially serious risk. People who do choose to hitch will be safer if they travel in pairs and let someone know where they are planning to go.

Women travellers considering hitching in Malaysia should have a look at the Women Travellers section in Malaysia's Facts for the Visitor chapter.

## BOAT

There are no services connecting the peninsula with Malaysian Borneo. On a local level, there are boats and ferries between the peninsula and offshore islands, and along the rivers of Sabah and Sarawak – check the relevant chapters for details. Note that some ferry operators are notoriously lax about observing safety rules and local authorities are often nonexistent. If a boat looks overloaded or otherwise unsafe, *do not board it* – no one else will look out for your safety.

## LOCAL TRANSPORT

Local transport varies widely from place to place. Large cities in Malaysia have local taxis (as opposed to long-distance taxis).

These taxis usually have meters but there are exceptions to this rule (usually in smaller towns like Kuantan in Pahang). For metered taxis, rates are as follows: flagfall (first 2km) – RM2; 10 sen for each 200m or 45 seconds thereafter; 20 sen for each additional passenger over two passengers; RM1 for each piece of luggage in the boot (trunk); plus 50% between midnight and 6 am. Drivers are legally required to use meters if they exist – insist that they do so.

In major cities there are also buses – in KL the government buses are backed up by private operators. Where they exist, these buses are extremely cheap and convenient, provided you can figure out which one is going your way. KL also has new commuter trains and LRT (Light Rail Transit).

Some towns have bicycle rickshaws. While they have died out in KL and have become principally a tourist gimmick in many Malaysian cities, they are still a viable form of transport. Indeed, in places like Georgetown, with its convoluted and narrow streets, a bicycle rickshaw is probably the best way of getting around.

In the bigger cities of Malaysian Borneo, like Kuching and Kota Kinabalu, you will find taxis, buses and minibuses. Once you're out of the big cities, though, you're basically on your own and must either walk or hitch. If you're really in the bush, of course, riverboats and aeroplanes are the only alternatives to lengthy jungle treks.

# Kuala Lumpur

☎ 03

In its 120 years, Kuala Lumpur has grown from a wild-west tin-mining town, harassed by civil war, fires and floods, into an affluent modern Asian capital of over 1.5 million people. Today the city's skyline and its gleaming skyscrapers, including the skyscraping twin Petronas Towers in the city's glittering Golden Triangle district, are a reflection of the short-lived Malaysian economic boom of the 1990s.

KL (as it's almost universally known) is a federal territory, directly under the control of the Malaysian federal government. The city's urban sprawl extends well beyond the boundaries of the territory into surrounding Selangor state, particularly along the Klang Valley – the powerhouse of the Malaysian economy, where much of the city's workforce and industry resides.

Greater KL sees many of the country's extravagant megaprojects. Work is well advanced on Putrajaya, a US$8 billion 21st-century city for administration and government on Kuala Lumpur's southern periphery. An adjoining ultra-high-tech 'multimedia supercorridor' dubbed Cyberjaya is also taking shape, although one of Cyberjaya's major projects – the construction of the world's longest building – has been postponed.

Despite all the recent development, KL retains plenty of character – old colonial buildings and modern Islamic masterpieces stand proudly right in the centre of town. Chinatown, with its street vendors and old shophouses, in the heart of the city, is as vibrant as any you'll encounter. To complete the cultural mix, a bustling Little India and the Malay-dominated Chow Kit Market area are north of the city centre.

At first glance, many visitors see KL as just another noisy, Westernised Asian city, but if you're prepared to delve a bit deeper it more than repays any time spent. It still has the colour that has been so effectively wiped out in Singapore, yet lacks the pollution and congestion of Bangkok.

## HIGHLIGHTS

- **Architecture** – a vibrant 'new Asian' city stretching from the gleaming Petronas Towers to the low-lying palm trees of Masjid Jamek (Friday Mosque) and Merdeka Square

- **Chinatown and Little India** – colourful street markets in a hectic crush of Chinese herbalists and steamboat stalls, sari shops and sweet-sellers

- **Lake Gardens** – a peaceful garden district near the distinguished Islamic Arts Museum on the city's edge

## HISTORY

Kuala Lumpur came into being in 1857, when a band of prospectors in search of tin landed at the meeting point of the Klang and Gombak rivers and imaginatively named the place Kuala Lumpur – Muddy Confluence. More than half of those first arrivals died of malaria and other tropical diseases, but the tin they discovered in Ampang attracted more miners and KL quickly became a brawling, noisy, violent boom-town.

As in other parts of Malaysia, the local sultan appointed a 'Kapitan China' to bring the unruly Chinese fortune-seekers and their secret societies into line – a problem that Yap Ah Loy jumped at with such ruthless relish that he became known as the founder of KL.

In the 1880s successful miners and merchants began to build fine homes along Jalan Ampang. British Resident Frank Swettenham pushed through a far-reaching new town-plan, which transferred the central government here from Klang.

In 1881 the entire town was destroyed by fire and a subsequent flood, but it quickly got back on its feet: By 1886 a railway line linked KL to Klang; by 1887 several thousand brick buildings had been built; and in 1896 the city became the capital of the newly formed Federated Malay States.

KL has never looked back. After occupation by Japanese forces during WWII (during which many Chinese were tortured and killed and many Indians sent to work on Burma's 'Death Railway'), the British temporarily returned, only to be ousted when Malaysia finally declared its independence here in 1957 in Dataran Merdeka (Freedom Square). The city officially became the Federal Territory of Kuala Lumpur when it was ceded by the sultan of Selangor state in 1974.

Today KL is not only Malaysia's political and commercial capital, but also its most populous and prosperous city.

## ORIENTATION

The traditional heart of KL is Merdeka Square, not far from the confluence of the two muddy rivers from which KL takes its name. The square is easily spotted because of its 100m-high flagpole – claimed to be the world's tallest – and it's in the heart of the old colonial district. To the south-east across the river, the banking district merges into the older Chinatown, a bustling area with a range of accommodation and a lively night market.

The main post office is just south of Merdeka Square. A little farther on is Masjid Negara (National Mosque) and the historic KL train station. Farther west are the peaceful attractions of the Lake Gardens and the Malaysian Parliament House.

East of the Merdeka Square area is Masjid Jamek, at the intersection of the Star and Putra Light Rail Transit (LRT) lines. Jalan Tun Perak, a major trunk road, leads east to the long-distance transport hub of the country, the Puduraya bus station.

To the east of Puduraya bus station, around Jalan Ampang and Jalan Sultan Ismail, the Golden Triangle is the modern heart of the new KL, crammed with mid-range and luxury hotels, shopping centres and office towers.

Running north of Merdeka Square is Jalan Tunku Abdul Rahman (Jalan TAR). It runs one way southbound through Little India and Chow Kit. Jalan Raja Laut runs almost parallel to Jalan TAR and takes the northbound traffic. Both roads are horrendously noisy during peak hours, and late at night, when gangs of local teenagers drag-race up and down on scores of motorbikes.

Jalan Tun Sambanthan runs south-west from the main train station through the lower-income Brickfields area. Although something of a backwater compared to other parts of inner KL, Brickfields may liven up once the city's new public-transport hub of KL Sentral (Grand Central) station is ever completed. On the other side of the tracks, Bangsar makes for a posh night out in the city, with dozens of upmarket bars and restaurants catering to wealthier citizens and expats.

KL is relatively easy to find your way around, although getting from place to place on foot can be frustrating. Distances are short, but footpaths are often missing. When in doubt, the slick LRT system is quicker and easier, and taxis are dirt cheap.

## INFORMATION
### Tourist Offices

KL has many tourist offices but they are of only limited use to travellers. The sleepy staff rouse themselves to hand out brochures, but are reluctant to go out of their way to help independent travellers. An often-heard response to a query about public transport is

# KUALA LUMPUR

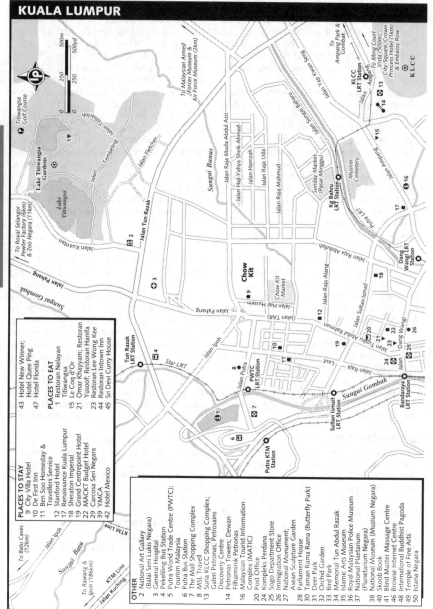

## PLACES TO STAY
9  City Villa Hotel
10  De First Inn
11  Ben Soo Homestay &
    Travellers Service
12  Stanford Hotel
17  Renaissance Kuala Lumpur
18  Sheraton Imperial
19  Grand Centrepoint Hotel
22  MACKT Budget Hotel
29  Carcosa Seri Negara
39  YMCA
42  Hotel Mexico
43  Hotel New Winner;
    Hotel Quee Ping
47  Hotel Florida

## PLACES TO EAT
1  Restoran Nelayan
   Titiwangsa
15  Le Coq d'Or
21  Omar Khayyam; Restoran
    Yusoof; Restoran Hanifa
23  Restoran Lee Wong Kee
44  Restoran Intown Inn
45  Sri Devi Curry House

## OTHER
2  National Art Gallery
   (Balai Seni Lukis Negara)
3  General Hospital
4  Pekeliling Bus Station
5  Putra World Trade Centre (PWTC);
   Tourism Malaysia
6  Putra Bus Station
7  MSL Travell
8  The Mall Shopping Complex
13  Suria KLCC Shopping Complex;
    Galeri Petronas; Petrosains
    Discovery Centre
14  Petronas Towers; Dewan
    Filharmonik Petronas
16  Malaysian Tourist Information
    Complex (MATIC)
20  Post Office
24  Kompleks Perdana
25  Sogo Department Store
26  Immigration Office
27  National Monument;
    Asean Sculpture Garden
28  Parliament House
30  Taman Rama Rama (Butterfly Park)
31  Deer Park
32  Orchid Garden
33  Bird Park
34  Memorial Tun Abdul Razak
35  Islamic Arts Museum
36  Royal Malaysian Police Museum
37  National Plaetarium
    (Planetarium Negara)
38  National Museum (Muzium Negara)
40  Skoob Book
41  Blind Master Massage Centre
46  Browse Internet Centre
48  International Buddhist Pagoda
49  Temple of Fine Arts
50  Istana Negara

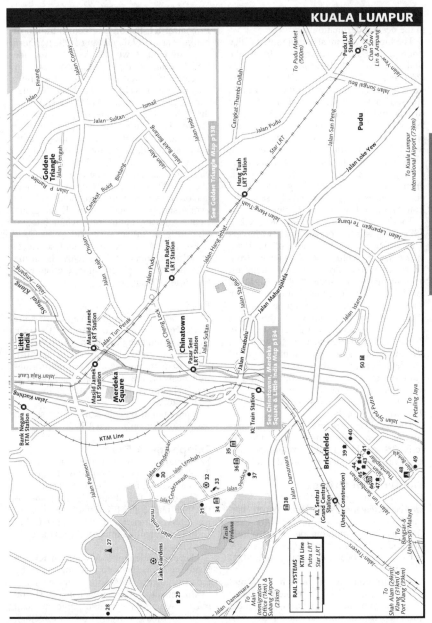

# KUALA LUMPUR

PENINSULAR MALAYSIA

To Pudu Market (500m)

Pudu LRT Station

To Chan Sow Lin & Ampang

Jalan Lumpur

Jalan Sungai Besi

Cangkat Thambi Dollah

Jalan Pudu

Jalan San Peng

Pudu

Jalan Loke Yew

To Kuala Lumpur International Airport (73km)

Star LRT

Hang Tuah LRT Station

Jalan Hang Tuah

Jalan Lapangan Terbang

Jalan Conlay

Jalan Bukit

Pinang

Jalan

Ismail

Jalan Sultan

Golden Triangle

Jalan Tengah

Jalan P Ramlee

Jalan Imbi

Cangkat Bukit Bintang

Jalan Alor

Jalan Bukit Bintang

See Golden Triangle Map p138

Chulan

Jalan Raja

Jalan Pudu

Plaza Rakyat LRT Station

Jalan Hang Jebat

Jalan Sin

Jalan Maharajalela

Jalan Istana

Sungai Klang

Jalan Ampang

Little India

Masjid Jamek LRT Station

Jalan Tun Perak

Jalan Cheng Lock

Chinatown

Pasar Seni LRT Station

Jalan Sultan

Jalan Kinabalu

50

See Chinatown, Merdeka Square & Little India Map p134

Jalan Raja Laut

Masjid Jamek LRT Station

Merdeka Square

KL Train Station

To Petaling Jaya

Jalan Syed Putra

Jalan Kuching

Bank Negara KTM Station

KTM Line

Brickfields

39

40

44

42

41

43

Jalan Thambipillai

45

46

48

49

47

Jalan Tun Sambanthan

Jalan Parlimen

Jalan Cenderasari

30

Jalan Lembah

35

36

37

38

KL Sentral (Grand Central) Station (Under Construction)

To Bangsar & Universiti Malaya

Jalan Cenderawasih

32

33

Jalan Perdana

Jalan

34

31

Tasik Perdana

Jalan Tembusu

Jalan Damansara

27

Lake Gardens

RAIL SYSTEMS

KTM Line

Putra LRT

Star LRT

29

28

To Main Immigration Office (1km) & Subang Airport (23km)

Jalan Damansara

To Shah Alam (24km), Klang (31km) & Port Klang (39km)

Jalan Travers

'Take a taxi', even if there are several buses to the desired destination.

The biggest and most useful tourist office (though that's not saying much) is the Malaysia Tourist Information Complex (MATIC; ☎ 2164 3929, fax 2162 1149), 109 Jalan Ampang, north-east of the city centre. Housed in the former mansion (later the British and then Japanese army headquarters) of a Malaysian planter and tin miner, it's almost a tourist attraction in its own right. As well as a tourist information counter, there are a couple of national-park travel agencies and an express bus counter. The complex is open from 9 am to 6 pm daily, and cultural performances are staged regularly (see under Entertainment later in this chapter).

Tourism Malaysia (☎ 293 5188, fax 293 5884, ✆ tourism@tourism.gov.my) has its head office on the 17th floor of the Putra World Trade Centre (PWTC), not far from Chow Kit Market. For basic travel inquiries, its information counter (☎ 441 1295) on level two of the same building is open from 9 am to 6 pm Monday to Saturday.

Smaller Tourism Malaysia information centres are located underground in Plaza Putra (☎ 293 6664, open 10 am to 6 pm, closed Sunday) on the southern side of Merdeka Square; on the eastern side of KL train station (☎ 274 6063, open 9 am to 6 pm daily); and at Kuala Lumpur International Airport (KLIA; ☎ 8787 4212, open 9 am to 10 pm daily).

The weekly magazine *Day & Night* has hot tips on entertainment, eating and leisure activities in KL and the surrounding areas. It is available for free at top-end hotels.

## Immigration Offices

The main immigration office (☎ 255 5077) for visa extensions is at Block I, Pusat Bandar Damansara, about 1km west of the Lake Gardens. Take Intrakota bus No 18 from along Jalan Raja Laut in the Chow Kit area, or No 21 from Jalan Tun Perak just north of Chinatown.

A more-convenient branch (☎ 2698 0377, fax 2698 0068) is located on Jalan Dang Wangi in the Kompleks Wilayah, near Sogo department store on Jalan TAR.

## Money

In central KL the biggest concentration of banks is around Jalan Silang at the northern edge of Chinatown. Banks here include HSBC Bank, Citibank and Maybank for foreign exchange (cash and travellers cheques) and ATM transactions. Smaller exchange counters and ATMs are sprinkled throughout the city, especially in shopping centres. Banks are generally open from 9 or 10 am to 3.30 or 4.30 pm weekdays, until noon on Saturday, and are closed Sunday.

Moneychangers offer better rates for changing cash and (sometimes) travellers cheques. They are usually open later hours and on weekends. You'll see them in almost every shopping mall, as well as along Lebuh Ampang and near the Klang bus station on Jalan Sultan.

For American Express client services, Mayflower Tours (☎ 2163 5909) is on the 18th floor of The Weld shopping centre in the Golden Triangle.

## Post

The gigantic main post office is across the river from the Central Market. It's open from 8.30 am to 6 pm Monday to Saturday (closed the first Saturday of the month). Poste restante mail is held at the information desk on the 2nd floor. Packaging is available for reasonable rates at the post office store.

International parcels can also be sent at the post office on Jalan TAR.

## Telephone & Fax

For international calls and faxes, the Telekom office (☎ 239 6025) on Jalan Raja Chulan is open from 8.30 am to 9 pm daily.

There are a few shops offering competitive Net-phone and fax services in the Central Market area, including Adamz Cyber Cafe (see Email & Internet Access later in this chapter).

Currently telephone numbers in KL are changing from seven to eight digits, so by the time you read this, phone numbers listed in this chapter may have changed. If you reach a wrong number, don't give up – call ☎ 1050 for the new Kuala Lumpur directory.

Kuala Lumpur's Petronas Towers.

Quick and easy: KL's slick LRT system.

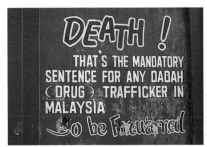
Dancers in traditional costume.

Crowds, noise and atmosphere: festivities in KL.

DEATH!
THAT'S THE MANDATORY SENTENCE FOR ANY DADAH (DRUG) TRAFFICKER IN MALAYSIA
So be Forewarned

A little reminder. In case you forget.

Independence Day celebrations in KL.

CLEM LINDENMAYER

ROSS BARNETT

Kellie's Castle, Perak

Sungai Palas tea estate, Cameron Highlands

CLEM LINDENMAYER

Cocoons at a butterfly farm, Cameron Highlands.

VERONICA GARBUTT

Dried flowers for sale, Cameron Highlands.

## Email & Internet Access
Big-city rates for Internet access start at RM5 per hour and rise to RM12 for state-of-the-art connections in air-con surrounds.

The enormous Master World Surfnet Café on Jalan Cheng Lock in Chinatown has super-fast connections and charges RM6 per hour, or RM3 after paying an RM40 membership fee. Master World is open from 9 am to 2 am daily. Adamz Cyber Cafe in the Central Market Annexe charges the same rates and offers Net-phone and fax services; it's open from 10 am to 10 pm daily.

On Jalan Melayu, near the Masjid Jamek LRT stations, the hole-in-the-wall HMI Multimedia Network has the cheapest rates in central KL (RM3 per hour). Several back-packer guesthouses also offer Internet access, though it's not especially cheap or fast.

In the Golden Triangle, you have plenty of places to choose from: E@sy Access Internet Centre (RM6 per hour) on Jalan Bukit Bintang; Surfnet (RM5, one hour minimum) in BB Plaza; and IT@Sungei Wang (RM4, one hour minimum) on the 3rd floor of Sungei Wang Plaza, where the interactive games are deafening.

## Internet Resources
Tourism Malaysia's official homepage, at www.tourism.gov.my, has an overview of KL and regional attractions, including an annual calendar of major festivals and events. You can also download traditional Malaysian music, search for accommodation or link to the more-colourful www.visitmalaysia.com, maintained by the US-based Tourism Malaysia offices.

For up-to-the-minute listings of restaurants and entertainment venues in KL and Klang Valley go to www.klangvalley.com.my. Its business directory lists bookshops, Internet cafes and even acupuncture clinics. The entertainment listings at www.mnet.com.my/klonline are just as fresh. But far and away the most detailed guide to the performing arts in Kuala Lumpur is at www.kulture.com.my, the insider's 'kulture webzine' with snappy reviews of everything from pop to classical dance, current events, news and hot cafe and bookshop recommendations.

The Star newsagency's Web site, at www.Metro.thestar.com.my, has great news-coverage of the KL metro area, including current events, hotel promotions and classified ads for employment and housing.

## Travel Agencies
For discount airline tickets, two long-running and reliable student-travel agencies are MSL Travel (☎ 442 4722), 66 Jalan Putra, in the Chow Kit area; and STA Travel (☎ 248 9800, fax 248 3046), 128 Jalan Pudu on the 5th floor of Plaza Magnum, above the Multi-Purpose Bank.

## Bookshops
Malaysia's three best book-shop chains, Times, Popular and MPH, are well represented in KL. Times has branches in The Weld and Star Hill shopping centres. Popular and MPH have branches on the lower levels of Sungei Wang Plaza and BB Plaza.

On the lower ground floor of the Suria KLCC shopping complex, Magstore has a good selection of imported magazines.

The Minerva Bookstore on Jalan TAR stocks mainly technical literature, but it also has a good range of magazines and a few English books.

## Cultural Centres & Libraries
You'll find the following libraries in KL:

**Alliance Française** (☎ 294 7880, 292 5929, ✉ afkuala@tm.net.my) 15 Lorong Gurney
**Australian Information Library** (☎ 246 5555, ✉ austh@po.jaring.my) 6 Jalan Yap Kwan Seng
**British Council** (☎ 298 7555, ✉ arts@britishcouncil.org.my) Jalan Bukit Aman
**Canadian Education Information Library** (☎ 248 2548) 9 Jalan Sejantera
**Goethe Institut** (☎ 242 2011) 1 Langgak Golf
**The Japan Foundation** (☎ 2161 2104, ✉ jcc@jfkl.org.my) Suite 3001, Level 30, Menara Lion, 165 Jalan Ampang
**Lincoln Resource Center** US Embassy, 376 Jalan Tun Razak
**National Library of Malaysia** (☎ 294 3488) Jalan Tun Razak
**New Zealand Education Centre** (☎ 238 4612) Menara IMC, Jalan Sultan Ismail

PENINSULAR MALAYSIA

## Left Luggage
There is 24-hour left-luggage storage at KLIA on levels 3 and 5, but it's expensive, starting at RM9 per day for a small bag (35cm x 1.2m, or 1.1 feet x 2.7 feet) and up to RM27 for larger items.

There are inexpensive left-luggage offices inside Puduraya bus station (8 am to 10 pm daily, RM1.50 per item per day) and at Klang bus station in Chinatown (7 am to 10 pm daily, RM2 per day).

## Dangers & Annoyances
You're unlikely to feel threatened at night in Chinatown or the Golden Triangle, where there's plenty of foot traffic until late.

The stretch of Jalan TAR north of Masjid Jamek to Little India is deserted after dark; it's better to take a taxi than to walk.

The Chow Kit area, once (and arguably still) KL's red-light district, gets hairy at night when heroin pushers, transvestite prostitutes and bar girls all come out to play.

## WALKING TOURS
With new six-lane roads and fly-overs dividing KL up into sections unconnected by footpaths, it's no pedestrian's paradise.

However, the city is surprisingly compact and all the main areas of interest are close together. Walking from Little India and Jalan TAR down through Merdeka Square to Chinatown takes only 20 to 30 minutes – if you know where to find the pedestrian crossings, that is. The walking tours in this section will take you to all the major sights (and a few off-beat places) in KL's old colonial district around Merdeka Square and Chinatown. The tours are marked on the Chinatown, Merdeka Square & Little India map.

If you really want to explore, KL has recently designated Heritage Trails covering Merdeka Square, Market Square, Chinatown and Jalan TAR. These detailed do-it-yourself walking tours focus on pre-war architecture and early city history, pointing out odd buildings and temples you might otherwise overlook.

Tourism Malaysia offices usually stock the trail brochures, which are also available directly from Badan Warisan Malaysia

(Heritage of Malaysia Trust; ☎ 244 9273), 2 Jalan Stonor, 50450, Kuala Lumpur.

## Colonial District
This walking tour begins in the same place as many travellers do – KL's magnificent train station. Built in 1911, this delightful example of colonial whimsy designed by British architect AB Hubbock is a Moorish fantasy of spires, minarets, towers, cupolas and arches. It couldn't look any better if it had been built as a set for some Hollywood extravaganza. It also contains the atmospheric Heritage Station Hotel (see the Train Station & Brickfields section under Places to Stay – Mid-Range later in this chapter).

For the best views of the train station, take the pedestrian tunnel outside the station's west Pintu (Exit) D underneath Jalan Sultan Hishamuddin and stand in front of the superb Malayan Railway Administration building opposite.

Walk north and turn the corner onto Jalan Perdana. A short distance west you'll find the equally impressive **Pusat Islam Malaysia** (Islamic Centre) and, on the other side of the street, the **Masjid Negara**. Situated in five hectares of landscaped gardens, this modern mosque is one of the largest in South-East Asia. A 73m-high minaret stands in the centre of a pool, and the main dome is an 18-pointed star, symbolising the 13 states of Malaysia and the five pillars of Islam. Forty-eight smaller domes cover the courtyard; their design is said to be inspired by the Grand Mosque in Mecca. Visitors must remove their shoes before entering and be properly attired – they'll lend you a robe and a headscarf (for women). It's open to non-Muslims outside of prayer times.

Backtrack to the train station and exit Pintu B on the eastern side. Turn left and walk alongside the fenced-in train platforms underneath a covered footpath until you reach the Pejabat Pos Besar (Main Post Office). Take the car ramp heading upward and skirt the east side of the post office until you reach the small **Petronas Fountain**, with its globe highlighting the world's petroleum-producing countries (including Malaysia, of course).

Immediately to your right is the impressive high-rise **Kompleks Dayabumi**, with its multiple sides that appear covered in metal filigree. Note the Islamic arches and recurring motifs.

Continue left (clockwise) around the tower. As you cut back to the riverside, look for the stunning **skyline view** of the Menara Kuala Lumpur (KL Tower) and the twin Petronas Towers framed by palm trees.

Continue walking north alongside the river until the promenade comes to a dead end. Turn left and descend the stone staircase. After passing under a grand brick archway, the steps empty out onto Lebuh Pasar Besar. Here you'll find the old City Hall, now housing a **Textile Museum** (currently under renovation).

Walk west across Jalan Sultan Hishamuddin to the **National History Museum**. Dating from 1910, this building originally housed KL's first bank, then a Japanese telecommunications base during WWII, and then one of the early administration offices after independence. The exhibits on Malaysia's Stone Age, Buddhist and colonial periods are unsatisfyingly scant, but there are better displays upstairs on the Malacca sultanate and foreign intervention in Sabah and Sarawak. The museum is open from 9 am to 6 pm daily (free). Next door is the **Kuala Lumpur Memorial Library**.

Cross Jalan Raja to the southern side of **Merdeka Square**, once at the heart of colonial KL, and part of the open field formerly known as the Padang. It was here that Malaysia's British administrators engaged in that curious English rite known as cricket. It's no coincidence that in 1957 Malaysia's independence was proclaimed here, and dignitaries still gather on National Day to watch the parades (see Special Events later in this chapter).

From the flagpole, walk counter-clockwise around the perimeter of the square. The **Royal Selangor Club**, a social centre for KL's high society in the tin-boom days of the 1890s, is across the field to your left. It's still a gathering place for the KL elite.

East of the square across Jalan Sultan Hishamuddin you can see the **Sultan Abdul Samad Building**. Its blend of Victorian and Moorish architecture is typical of the colonial buildings that give the city much of its character. Designed by AC Norman (of KL train station fame) and built between 1894 and 1897, it was once the Secretariat building for the British administration and is now Malaysia's Supreme Court. Its 43m-high clock tower is overshadowed by the financial skyscrapers of Chinatown (Citibank, HSBC, Oriental Bank and Maybank), which appear all squeezed together from this angle.

Continue walking north towards the **memorial arches** inscribed with 'Dataran Merdeka' (Freedom Square). Farther north be careful crossing over Jalan Raja from the square to another of AC Norman's creations, **St Mary's Cathedral**, dating from 1894 and housing a fine pipe-organ.

As there are no crossings here, you'll have to head north up Jalan Raja Laut to the spectacularly ugly **treehouse fountain**. Make a U-turn via the lengthy pedestrian crossings and head back south along the east side of Jalan Sultan Hishamuddin. You can cut through the Supreme Court grounds, past rushing clerks and lawyers shielding their high-profile clients from the press, to the quieter riverside.

Turn left and walk alongside the river until you reach the entrance to **Masjid Jamek** (Friday Mosque), the most delightful of all KL's mosques and the end of this walking tour. Built in 1907, it's located at the confluence of the Klang and Gombak rivers, where KL's founders first set foot and where supplies for the tin mines were shipped. Set in a grove of palm trees, the mosque's onion domes and minarets of layered pink and cream bricks look best at sunset.

Properly attired visitors (covered limbs and headscarves for women) are admitted 8.30 am to 12.30 pm and 2.30 to 4 pm daily, except during Friday prayers (11 am to 2.30 pm).

## Chinatown

South of Masjid Jamek are the teeming streets of KL's Chinatown. This crowded, colourful area is the usual melange of

PENINSULAR MALAYSIA

PENINSULAR MALAYSIA

Chinese signs and shops, activity and noise, and is bounded by Jalan Cheng Lock, Jalan Hang Kasturi and by Jalan Sultan (on two sides). The central section of **Jalan Petaling** is closed to traffic and is a frantically busy market, at its most vivid at night when brightly lit.

All the activity may distract you from the area's historic Chinese shophouses. Local conservation groups are making efforts to protect these buildings from city development and to restore them to their former glory.

Starting from Masjid Jamek, cross over to the northern side of Jalan Tun Perak and walk one block east to **Lebuh Ampang**. A short detour up this narrow street reveals a South-Indian Chettiar community, full of moneychangers and street vendors selling Indian sweets and flower garlands. Note the striking **old shophouses** at Nos 16 to 18 and Nos 24 to 30 and the ceramic peacock-tiles on the **Chettiar house** at No 85.

Backtrack across Jalan Tun Perak and follow the path along Jalan Benteng until the street splits at the clock tower. This is **Medan Pasar** (Market Square), the site of the city's original market and gambling sheds set up for early tin miners. On your right is a row of **painted shophouses** at Nos 2 to 8, all designed by the same Chinese architect in 1906.

Head south to where Medan Pasar meets Lebuh Pasar Besar. On the south-eastern corner is the **OCBC Building**, an imposing Art Deco structure built in 1938 for the Overseas Chinese Banking Company.

Turn east along this street, passing the whimsical, white **Federal Stores**, dating from 1905 and taking up an entire side of the block on your left. Opposite is the rose-pink and white **MS Ally Company**, one of KL's longest-running and most venerable pharmacies.

Turn south at the next block onto Jalan Tun HS Lee. A few hundred metres down on your right is the yellow-green **Bank Simpanan Building**, constructed during WWII in grand Palladian style. It was originally a printing press and KL's first Chinese newspaper was produced here.

At the end of this block, cross Lebuh Pudu and, after 100m, duck right into the alleyway with dragon designs painted on the ground. It leads to the small Taoist **Sze Yah Temple**, which is set at an angle to Jalan Tun HS Lee and Lebuh Pudu in harmony with feng shui principles. 'Kapitan China' Yap Ah Loy himself organised its construction in 1864, and there is a photograph of him on an altar at the back. The hall on the left is dedicated to the god of wealth, Choi Sen, and the one on the right to Kuan Yin, goddess of mercy.

Exiting the western side of the temple, cross the street and walk through the alley opposite the enormous **Central Market**. Previously the city's produce market, this Art Deco building was saved by preservationists and refurbished as a centre for handicraft, antique and art sales. It is surrounded by pedestrian areas, providing a welcome break from Chinatown's choking traffic. Rotating art exhibitions and cultural shows are regularly held here (see Entertainment later), and you can get your palm read for fortune, fame and happiness, by Master Chin upstairs.

At the southern end of the market, turn left onto Jalan Cheng Lock, then right onto Jalan Tun HS Lee and head south, passing the Hotel Malaya and a bright-red **Chinese temple** with carved and painted animal figures on the rooftop. Farther down, also on your left, is a covered alleyway of **noodle shops**.

Cross over to the eastern side of the street to No 163, the **Sri Mahamariamman Temple**, a large and ornate South-Indian Hindu temple dating from 1873. Still looking fresh and colourful, it houses a large **silver chariot** that is taken out and paraded to the Batu Caves during the Thaipusam festival, in January or February each year.

Walk to the end of the block and turn left onto Jalan Sultan. You can detour to the **Chinese tea shops** on the southern side of the street leading back along Jalan Penggong and Jalan Balai Polis. Then continue east and look for an alleyway on your left that's filled with hawker stalls. At the end of the alley, hidden away on your right, is perhaps the last original **gas lamp** from KL's early days. It's now fronted by the family-run **Restoran Hoi Nam Choi**, a food stall selling inexpensive *mee goreng* (fried noodles) and an excellent place to rest your feet and refuel – *sila duduk* (please sit down).

Later you can finish by walking south to the end of Jalan Petaling, where you'll find two late-19th-century Chinese temples: the ornate **Chan See Shu Yuen Temple**, one of KL's largest, and, across Jalan Stadium, the Hokkien-Chinese **Khoon Yam Temple**, which also houses a local Chinese clan-association.

## LAKE GARDENS

As in many planned, colonial cities in Malaysia, this garden district lies at the edge of the central city area, around landscaped hills. Here the British elite built their fine houses, away from the hurly burly of downtown commerce and people of other races. The official residence of British Resident Frank Swettenham is now the Carcosa Seri Negara, Malaysia's most expensive hotel (see Places to Stay – Top End later).

At the centre of the 92-hectare gardens is **Tasik Perdana** (Premier Lake). You can rent boats on weekends and watch t'ai chi practitioners in the early mornings.

The gardens contain a host of expensive attractions, which often cost double for foreign tourists. You can take a leisurely, if sweaty, stroll around them, or hop on the shuttle bus that does a loop of the gardens 9 am to 7 pm daily (except Friday, when it stops from noon to 3 pm) for 20/50 sen for children/adults. Intrakota bus No 21C from the Sultan Mohammed bus stop, or bus Nos 21B, 22, 48C or F3 from in front of Kota Raya shopping complex in Chinatown will take you to the gardens.

Out on Jalan Cendarasari, **Taman Rama Rama** (Butterfly Park; RM5/9 for children/adults) claims to be the largest in South-East Asia, but is rather disappointing. The adjacent **insect museum** is slightly more interesting. The park is open from 9 am to 6 pm daily.

Other sights are all clustered together. One of the highlights is the **Bird Park**, an enormous walk-in aviary with 160 (mostly South-East Asian) species of birds (RM1/3 for children/adults). Opposite is **Taman Orkid** (Orchid Garden) and the adjacent **Taman Bunga Raya** (Hibiscus Garden), both open from 9 am to 5 pm daily (RM5/10 for children/adults).

The nearby **Memorial Tun Abdul Razak** has memorabilia of Malaysia's second prime minister. To the north, the **Deer Park** has a number of tame species, including the tiny kancil. Entry is free.

The massive **National Monument** overlooks the Lake Gardens from the northern side. Sculpted in bronze in 1966 by Felix de Weldon, the creator of the Iwo Jima monument in Washington DC, this memorial commemorates the Communist defeat during the Emergency (1950).

On the southern side, the **National Planetarium** has a small space-exhibition. It also puts on audiovisual science demonstrations in English (RM2/3 for children/adults) and IMAX films on a 20m domed screen (RM4/6). The planetarium is open from 11 am to 4 pm (closed Monday).

## MUSEUMS

Museums are scattered around the city, though most visitors only bother taking in the National Museum and maybe the Islamic Arts Museum or the National Art Gallery – the rest are for those with special interests.

### Islamic Arts Museum

Just outside the Lake Gardens, and a short walk from the National Mosque, is the impressive new Islamic Arts Museum (Muzium Kesenian Islam Malaysia). The spacious, dazzlingly white building incorporates a dome and other Islamic architectural features and the extensive collections are well labelled. On the 3rd level are scale models of the world's most famous mosques and a full-scale interior reproduction of a typical Muslim room of the Ottoman Empire. Upstairs are exhibits of religious calligraphy, textiles, armour, metalwork and carpets. The museum shop sells beautiful Islamic crafts of higher quality (and at higher prices) than elsewhere in KL.

PENINSULAR MALAYSIA

# CHINATOWN, MERDEKA SQUARE & LITTLE INDIA

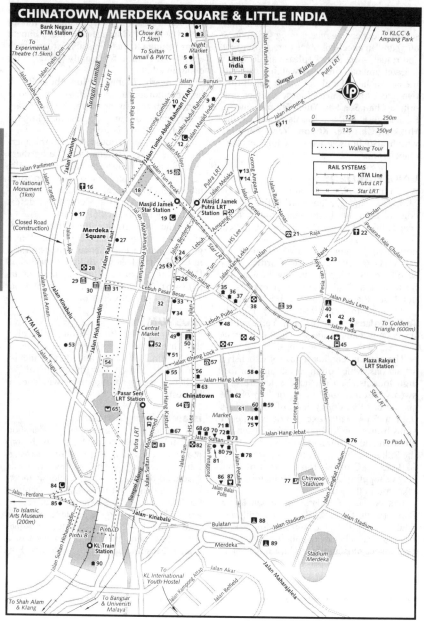

## CHINATOWN, MERDEKA SQUARE & LITTLE INDIA

**PLACES TO STAY**
2   Kowloon Hotel
3   Hotel Noble
6   Coliseum Hotel
7   Hotel Champagne
8   Garden City Hotel
9   Palace Hotel; Hotel Empire
35  Travellers Moon Lodge
36  Twin Happiness Inn
37  The Odyssey Backpacker
41  KL City Lodge
42  Anuja Backpackers Inn
43  Hotel Katari
56  Backpackers Travellers
    Lodge
59  Hotel Furama
61  Swiss-Inn
62  Hotel China Town Inn
63  Hotel Malaya
67  Starlight Hotel
68  Mandarin Hotel
69  Wan Kow Hotel
71  Hotel Excel Inn
72  Chinatown Guest House
73  Chinatown Lodge
74  Backpackers Travellers Inn
76  YWCA
78  Golden Plaza Hostel
79  Hotel Lok Ann
90  Majestic Hotel

**PLACES TO EAT**
4   Govinda's Vegetarian
    Restaurant
10  The Bangles
13  The Kapitan's Club
14  Bilal Restoran

34  Meidi-ya
48  Restoran Wilayah Baru
51  Restoran Yusoof
70  Restoran Kam Lun Tai; Fatt
    Yon Vegetarian Restaurant
75  Pandamania Comics & Cafe
80  West Lake Restoran
86  Old China Cafe

**OTHER**
1   Globe Silk Store
5   Minerva Bookstore
11  Citibank
12  Masjid Little India
15  HMI Multimedia Network
16  St Mary's Cathedral
17  Royal Selangor Club
18  Supreme Court
19  Masjid Jamek
20  Lebuh Ampang Bus Stop
21  Telekom Office; Muzium
    Telekom
22  St Andrew's Presbyterian
    Church
23  KL Stock Exchange
24  HSBC Bank
25  Citibank
26  Medan Pasar Bus Stop
27  Sultan Abdul Samad Bldg
28  Plaza Putra Tourism Malaysia;
    Actors' Studio Theatre;
    Restoran Sri Putra
29  Kuala Lumpur Memorial
    Library
30  National History Museum
31  Textile Museum (Old City
    Hall)

32  Central Market Annexe;
    Adamz Cyber Café
33  OCBC Bldg
38  Metrojaya Department Store
39  Muzium Numismatik
    Maybank
40  Court Hill Ganesh Temple
44  Tourist Police
45  Puduraya Bus Station;
    Hotel Puduraya
46  Kota Raya Shopping
    Complex
47  S&M Shopping Arcade
49  Soon Hing Cheong
    Ginseng
50  Sze Yah Temple
52  Bull's Head
53  British Council
54  Kompleks Dayabumi
55  Peter Hoe Evolution
57  Master World Surfnet Café
58  Popular Bookstore
60  King's Confectionary
64  Sri Mahamariamman Temple
65  Main Post Office
66  Jalan Sultan Mohammed
    Bus Stop
77  Swimming Pool
81  Purple Cane Tea Art Centre
82  UDA Ocean Plaza
83  Klang Bus Station
84  Masjid Negara
85  Pusat Islam Malaysia
    (Islamic Centre)
87  Halo Rock Cafe
88  Koon Yam Temple
89  Chan See Shu Yuen Temple

**PENINSULAR MALAYSIA**

The museum is open from 10 am to 6 pm but is closed Monday (RM2/4 students/ adults). It's a 15-minute walk west of the KL train station, at the south-eastern edge of the Lake Gardens.

### National Museum
South of Tasik Perdana, at the edge of the Lake Gardens, the National Museum (Muzium Negara) was built on the site of the old Selangor Museum, which was destroyed during WWII. A mixture of Malay architectural styles, the museum opened in 1963, and it looks as if nothing has changed since then. Various dusty exhibits on Malaysia's history, economy, arts, crafts, cultures and traditions are getting rather tacky and could do with a

facelift. The *wayang kulit* (shadow puppets) and traditional Malay *kris* (weapons) and musical instruments are still worth a look, though. One intriguing exhibit is an 'amok catcher', an ugly barbed device used to catch and hold a person who has run amok.

Outside the museum, antique machinery, including an original Penang Hill Railway car, is on display. The last of KL's infamous pink minibuses, now retired from service, has found its final parking place in front of the main entrance. The museum is open from 9 am to 6 pm daily (RM1).

### National Art Gallery
The National Art Gallery (Balai Seni Lukis Negara) has a permanent collection of work

by contemporary Malaysian artists, and rotating exhibitions of Asian and international art, including photography. The gallery (☎ 4025 4990) also conducts symposiums and art classes for kids. It's open from 10 am to 6 pm daily (free).

The Malaysian kite-shaped **National Theatre** (Istana Budaya) next door, with its Langkawi marble and tropical-hardwood doors, is a work of art in and of itself. The costume gallery on the 2nd floor is open from 10 am to 6 pm Monday to Saturday.

Both the National Art Gallery and National Theatre are outside the Lake Titiwangsa Gardens, north of the city centre. Take any Len Seng bus from Lebuh Ampang or from along Jalan Raja Laut and get off at the hospital stop.

### Other Museums

The **Muzium Numismatik Maybank** houses an interesting collection of coins and notes (open 10 am to 6 pm daily, free). It's in the Maybank building on Jalan Tun Perak, near Puduraya bus station.

The talking mannequins at the small **Telekom Museum** on Jalan Raja Chulan expound the history of telecommunications in Malaysia from the Stone Age to the IT era (open 9.30 am to 5 pm, closed Sunday, free).

A few kilometres north-east of the city, inside the Ministry of Defence complex on Jalan Padang Tembak, the **Malaysian Armed Forces Museum** displays weapons, paintings, uniforms and other military paraphernalia, and cannons and tanks rest outside (open 10 am to 4 pm Saturday to Thursday, free). In the same area, the **Air Force Museum** is just a hangar containing a few light planes and similar memorabilia. It's open from 8 am to 4 pm Monday to Thursday and from 10 am to 5 pm weekends (free).

The **Royal Malaysian Police Museum**, on Jalan Perdana in the Lake Gardens, has its fair share of weaponry and anti-Communist memorabilia (open 10 am to 6 pm daily, free).

### JALAN TUNKU ABDUL RAHMAN (JALAN TAR)

Originally called Batu Road, Jalan TAR was once a dusty track leading north out of the city to the caves and tin mines at Batu village (see Batu Caves under Around Kuala Lumpur later in this chapter). Despite cars whizzing by and motorbike drag-racing at night, the modern Jalan TAR leads through an historic section of the city, passing Little India.

Named for its South Indian-style mosque, the main street of **Little India** is Jalan Masjid India, which is crammed with Indian sari-shops and halal restaurants. Little India has all the feel of a Middle Eastern bazaar, especially during the Saturday night *pasar malam* (night market).

Farther north along Jalan TAR many of the buildings are modern, but one surviving colonial relic is the **Coliseum Hotel** (see Hotels under Places to Stay – Budget later in this chapter). Enter through the saloon doors to the bar, where you can relax and sip your drink in a planter's chair where Somerset Maugham once sat. The Coliseum's wealthy owner began his business empire here in 1921 and the hotel hasn't changed in decades – for good luck, it is said in the Chinese tradition.

Jalan TAR is good for shopping during the day, and you can browse in the long-running Globe Silk Store for cheap clothes or drop in at the historic Lee Wong Kee restaurant, which has served Chinese banquet-style meals since 1926. It's tucked behind the former Odeon Cinema, now a shopping arcade but still a striking example of 1930s Art Deco style.

Farther north is Chow Kit, once (and arguably still) KL's famed red-light district. Though attempts have been made to clean the area out, it's still fairly seedy, especially at night. The **Chow Kit Market** has a gaggle of roadside vendors, and all manner of goods are on sale (see Shops & Markets under Shopping later in this chapter). The area around the City Villa Hotel is crammed with hawker stalls, good for satay and *nasi lemak* (boiled rice in coconut milk).

### GOLDEN TRIANGLE

Filled with postmodern high-rises, the Golden Triangle is central KL's flashy business, shopping and entertainment district.

## The Petronas Towers

Rising some 451.9m above the flat plain of Kuala Lumpur, the Petronas Towers have quickly become a symbol of the new Malaysia. Once arguably the tallest buildings in the world, they were completed in 1998 at a cost of $US1.9 billion, a monument to the overreaching ambitions of an economy that soon became mired deep in a national recession. Some critics have even suggested that it is megaprojects like the towers that led to the economic slowdown.

All economic considerations aside, the 88-storey towers (the number 88 symbolises prosperity in Chinese geomancy) are an arresting sight. Unique in design, the twin towers' floor plan is based on an eight-sided star that echoes the arabesque patterns of Islamic art. Islamic influences are also evident in each tower's five tiers, representing the five pillars of Islam; and in the 63m masts that crown them, calling to mind the minarets of a mosque and the Star of Islam.

The design of the Petronas Towers was the result of lengthy dialogue between the American architectural firm of Cesar Pelli & Associates and the government of Malaysia, including Dr Mahathir. The towers were constructed simultaneously, though the tower contracted to a Japanese firm was finished first while the Korean side lagged behind. However, the Koreans successfully built the bridge linking the two towers, the most technically difficult aspect of the entire structure.

It was the masts that caused so much controversy. As soon as they were installed, the government of Malaysia jubilantly announced that the Petronas Towers were the tallest buildings in the world. This claim was quickly disputed by critics who argued that it was unfair to count the masts in the overall measurement. In an effort to resolve the issue, the US-based Council on Tall Buildings and Urban Habitats announced new standards for determining the world's tallest building, according to which the Petronas Towers qualified as the tallest in only one of four categories. When the new office building being raised in Shanghai surpasses the Petronas Towers by a full 10m, the point will be moot.

The Petronas Towers are privately owned: 49% belongs to the Petronas corporation, 48.5% to a local tycoon and the remaining 2.5% to local shareholders, mainly the exclusive Penang Turf Club. In June 2000, the towers were opened to the public for the first time. If you want to see KL's skyline from on high, visitors are now permitted to climb to the 42nd-floor skybridge between 9 am and 5 pm. Admission and tours were free at the time this book went to press.

Encompassing an area of several square kilometres, it extends north from its base along Jalan Imbi to its apex at the landmark **Petronas Towers**, formerly the world's tallest office-buildings (see 'The Petronas Towers' boxed text). These graceful twin skyscrapers rise up from the spacious landscaped gardens of the Kuala Lumpur City Centre (KLCC).

Jalan Sultan Ismail has most of KL's luxury hotels and nightspots spaced out along it. It intersects with Jalan Bukit Bintang, the most lively pedestrian area, which has the biggest concentration of shopping malls, mid-range hotels and eating establishments in Kuala Lumpur.

At the western edge of the Golden Triangle is the impressive 421m **Menara Kuala Lumpur** (KL Tower), the fourth-highest telecommunications tower in the world. Visitors can ride the lift to the viewing deck (RM3/8 children/adults) for a superb panorama of the city, or dine in style at the Seri Angkasa revolving restaurant (see Malay & Nyonya under Places to Eat later).

Off Jalan Raja Chulan, the high-rise **Stock Exchange** is a curious amalgam of postmodern and neoclassical styles. Downhill towards Jalan Pudu is the tiny, busy **Court Hill Ganesh Temple**.

At the northern edge of the Golden Triangle, **Jalan Ampang** was built up by early tin millionaires and is lined with impressive mansions. Many of these stately buildings have become embassies or consulates, so the street is nicknamed 'Embassy Row'.

PENINSULAR MALAYSIA

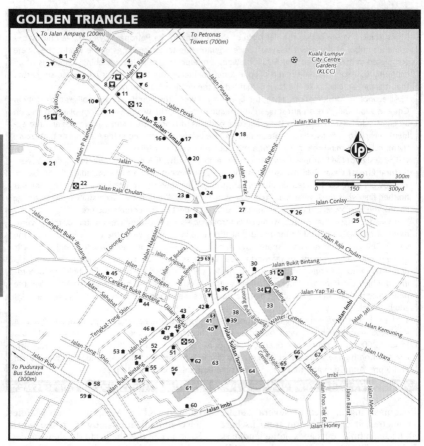

## GOLDEN TRIANGLE

## INTERNATIONAL BUDDHIST PAGODA

In the Brickfields area south of KL train station, the shrine at this modern pagoda was built in the 1800s by Sinhalese Buddhists from Sri Lanka. There's a bodhi tree on the grounds.

The International Buddhist Pagoda is a centre for Buddhist teaching and meditation in KL (see the Language & Cultural Courses section later in this chapter for more information on courses offered here). Bus No 12 from Klang bus station will take you there.

## ART GALLERIES

Conveniently located on the 3rd floor of Suria KLCC mall, near KLCC LRT station in the Golden Triangle, the impressive **Galeri Petronas** (☎ 207 7770) has fresh, thought-provoking exhibitions of contemporary photography, paintings, etc. It's free and is open from 10 am to 8 pm daily (closed Friday and during installations).

In the City-Square shopping complex on Jalan Ampang, you'll find cutting-edge interior-design shops and, on the 3rd level, the **ArtFolio** and **ArtCase** galleries, selling contemporary Malaysian art.

## GOLDEN TRIANGLE

**PLACES TO STAY**
1 Concorde Hotel; Hard Rock Cafe
9 Shangri-La
13 Hotel Equatorial; Chalet
19 Hilton Kuala Lumpur; Avis
23 The Lodge Hotel
28 Hotel Istana; Ristorante Bologna
30 The Regent; Edo
32 JW Mariott Hotel; Shook!
42 Agora Hotel
43 Hotel Imperial; Restoran Easy-OK
44 Park Inn International
45 Pondok Lodge; Ziño Kafe
46 Budget Inn
47 Hotel Seasons View
49 Bintang Warisan Hotel
51 Malaysia Hotel
53 Hotel Nova
54 Cardogan Hotel
55 Federal Hotel
57 Century Kuala Lumpur Hotel
59 Swiss-Garden Hotel
60 Meliá Kuala Lumpur
64 Parkroyal Kuala Lumpur; Delaney's

**PLACES TO EAT**
2 Bierkeller
3 Afternoon Hawker-Food Stalls
4 The Talk; Galleriwan
6 Sri Perak Hawker Centre
26 Restoran Seri Melayu
27 Restoran Eden Village
35 Dontaku Restoran Jepun; E@sy Access
37 Sushi King; Toku Toku
40 Super Noodle House
48 Restoran Best Thai Cuisine
52 Restoran Ramzan
56 BB Park
62 Restoran Instant
65 Restoran Overseas
66 Fong Lye Restaurant
67 Restoran Sakura

**OTHER**
5 Modesto's
7 Kafe Emporium
8 Gloria Jean's
10 Menara UBN; Cathay Pacific; Royal Brunei
11 Wisma Tong Ah; Aeroflot
12 Life Centre; The Warp
14 H Mui Plaza; KAL, China Southern Airlines

15 The Backroom
16 Malaysia Airlines
17 Pernas International Building
18 Wisma UOA I & II; Hawk Rent-a-Car
20 Kompleks Antarabangsa; Hertz
21 Menara Kuala Lumpur (KL Tower); Seri Angkasa
22 The Weld Shopping Centre; Mayflower Tours
24 Wisma Genting
25 Kompleks Budaya Kraf
29 HSBC Bank
31 Star Hill Centre
33 KL Plaza; Tower Records Metrojaya Plaza; Marks & Spencer
34 Sol Pub
36 Nam Lee Cheong Wine Shop
38 Lot 10 Shopping Complex; Isetan
39 Blues Cafe
41 Maybank
50 Bukit Bintang (BB) Plaza
58 STA Travel
61 Low Yat Plaza
63 Sungei Wang Plaza

The exclusive **Galleriwan** often deals in antique Peranakan slippers, majestic Malaysian kites, fine pottery and contemporary fine arts. It's on the 1st floor of the Crown Regency apartments, behind The Talk bistro, in the Golden Triangle.

Other galleries for contemporary art (as well as South-East Asian antiques and crafts) are located south of the city centre in the up-and-coming area of Bangsar.

## MARKETS

KL's streets are the scene of busy pasar malam, with hawker-food stalls and vendors selling souvenirs and household goods.

In Kampung Bahru, north-east of the city centre, Jalan Raja Muda comes alive on Saturday night for the **Pasar Minggu (Sunday Market)**, so-called because it continues until Sunday morning. It's mainly a food and produce market.

Little India's **Saturday-night market**, along Lorong TAR, is another of the city's best.

Open day and night, **Jalan Petaling** in Chinatown is a bustling street-market where you can have a Chinese alfresco meal or snack, bargain for clothes, or pick up a kilogram of lychees or mangoes.

North of the city centre, **Chow Kit Market** is incredibly busy from early morning until late at night. During the day vendors sell all manner of bits and pieces; after 6 pm the food stalls take over.

The predominantly Chinese-run **Pudu Market**, 3km south-east of the city centre, is the largest wet (produce) market in KL. It's definitely a *wet* market – it's a good idea to wear shoes rather than thongs or sandals. Here you can get every imaginable type of fruit, vegetable, fish and meat – everything from a foot from a chicken slaughtered and butchered on the spot, to a stingray fillet or a pig's penis. Pudu Market is five minutes' walk from Pudu Star LRT station; go north along Jalan Pudu, right onto Jalan Pasar, then right down Jalan Pasar Baharu.

## ACTIVITIES

There are public swimming pools next to the Chinwoo and Commonwealth Stadiums, and at the Bangsar Sports Complex (☎ 254 605) on Jalan Bangsar, which also has tennis courts, squash and badminton facilities.

You can knock down a few pins at the Arena Bowl inside the City-Square shopping complex on Jalan Ampang.

Close to the YMCA in Brickfields, Blind Master Massage Centre (☎ 273 0188), 17A Jalan Tun Sambanthan 4, is open from 11 am to 11 pm daily.

In Bangsar, Planet Scuba (☎ 287 2822) dive shop and PADI-IDC academy fulfils all your aquatic needs, with scuba equipment rental/purchase, beginner and intermediate dive-classes and certification for dive instructors.

For horse riding, escape to the Awana Golf & Country Resort (☎ 211 2026) in the Genting Highlands (see the Selangor chapter).

In Selangor you can also go white-water rafting; contact Tracks Outdoor for more information (☎ 777 8363, ✉ tracks@mol .net.my).

Truly adventurous souls should talk to Wilayah Sky Divers (☎ 984 0063, 408 3648) or check out its Web site at www .mnet.com.my/klonline/mypage/skymaster/ welcome.html.

## LANGUAGE & CULTURAL COURSES

In Brickfields, the community YMCA (☎ 2274 1439, fax 2274 0559) offers a variety of short- and long-term language classes in Bahasa Malaysia, Hindi, Thai, Mandarin/Cantonese, and Japanese, as well as courses in martial arts and even ballroom dancing.

Also in Brickfields, at 123 Jalan Berhala, the Buddhist school at the International Buddhist Pagoda is over 70 years old. Meditation sessions are held at 8 pm on Monday and Thursday and chanting classes at 7.30 pm on Tuesday and Friday. Dharma talks are given at 8 pm on Friday.

Across from the pagoda, The Temple of Fine Arts (☎ 2274 3709), 114 Jalan Berhala,

offers classes in classical Indian dance and music.

The Actors Studio Academy (☎ 297 2797), in the underground Plaza Putra at Merdeka Square, has workshops in everything from modern choreography and classical Indian dance to Chinese orchestral music, to name a few.

The Kapitan's Club restaurant (see Malay & Nyonya under Places to Eat later) hosts Chinese calligraphy and painting classes. RM300 covers eight two-hour weekend sessions, including three-course dinners. For registration, contact Mr Lim on ☎ 201 0242 or fax 201 0637.

At the Kompleks Budaya Kraf (☎ 2162 7533) in the Golden Triangle, you can try your hand at batik (RM15 for a quick lesson) or sign up for a basic batik course.

## ORGANISED TOURS

Ecstasy Travel (☎ 442 5688, fax 441 9864), 3rd floor, Jalan 14/48A, Sentul Raya, off Jalan Sentul, organises half-day city tours that briefly touch on the Lake Gardens, Merdeka Square and the National Museum and National Palace. Half-day stop-and-shop 'country tours' visit a pewter factory, insect farm, batik factory and a kampung house, finishing at the Batu Caves (see Around Kuala Lumpur later in this chapter). Both tours run twice daily and cost RM25 (excluding minimal entry fees), but neither is very in-depth.

Ecstasy Travel also runs longer tours to Melaka, Selangor and other destinations, which usually require a minimum of two adults.

## SPECIAL EVENTS

The capital is a good venue for Malaysia's major holidays and festivals like Thaipusam, Chinese New Year and Deepavali – see Public Holidays & Special Events in the Facts for the Visitor chapter earlier, and the 'Thaipusam' boxed text in the 'Places of Worship' special section.

City Day is 1 February, when KL commemorates its becoming a federal territory. Celebrations take place at Tasik Perdana and Lake Titiwangsa gardens in the north of the city.

## A Drinking Club for People with a Running Problem

The internationally known Hash House Harriers was established in 1938 in KL, by a group of British colonials who found themselves drinking too much and needing exercise. 'Hash house' was the nickname for their dining room at the Selangor Club. The harrier idea of a group of runners chasing papers along trails set by an appointed member (the 'hare') was not altogether new – groups had existed in KL, Ipoh, Johor Bahru and Melaka. However, the original 1938 Hash House Harriers (HHHs) institutionalised the chase to such an extent that it became an expat tradition all over Asia.

A few hours in advance of a hash run, the hare goes to the run site – usually in secondary jungle areas, or rubber and palm-oil estates – and lays an irregular trail (sometimes including false trails) using paper markers. The point is to allow faster runners to scout for the next bit of trail while slower harriers catch up. The run begins with a call of 'On, on' – the slogan of all HHHs – and when looking for paper markers, runners shout out 'Are you?', to which runners ahead reply 'Checking' to help in trail-finding. A typical run lasts one to 1½ hours and is followed by beer drinking at the end of the trail and a meal at a local restaurant.

Until 1961 there was only the KL Hash, but in the following year a chapter opened in Singapore, followed by others in Brunei, Kuching, Kota Kinabalu, Ipoh and Penang. The first group outside South-East Asia opened in Perth in 1967 and there are now around 500 HHHs in 70 countries. Annual international interhash meetings are held at a different place each year (Malaysia hosted in 1998).

The Hash welcomes guest participants. Currently, there are several groups in the KL area, including one for men only (the original tradition) and one for women only (the Hash House Harriettes). The rest are mixed, and all have local members. There's even a KL Mountain Bike Hash – see the insanity at the Web site, at www.bikehash.freeservers.com. Most larger Malaysian towns have their own HHH groups; there are listings on the Internet at www.gthhh.com/database/counsrch .asp?srchcoun=Malaysia.

For further information, contact the Kuala Lumpur Hash House Harriers (☎ 2282 9798, fax 2242 9796), PO Box 13603, 50816 Kuala Lumpur.

In July, KL goes flower-crazy during the **Flora Fest**, with exhibitions and the international Floral Parade.

At midnight on 30 August, revellers crowd Merdeka Square (like Times Square on New Year's Eve) to celebrate **National Day**, the anniversary of Malaysia's independence in 1957. There are parades and festivities the next morning, usually at Commonwealth Stadium, but ask the tourist information office (☎ 2164 3929, fax 2162 1149) to be sure.

For two weeks in September KL celebrates **Malaysia Fest** (also called the Colors of Malaysia) with exhibits of traditional arts and special cultural performances around town. The October **Shopping Carnival** follows on its heels.

### PLACES TO STAY

The main area for cheap accommodation is Chinatown, near Puduraya bus station. It is noisy, traffic-clogged and grotty, but always lively. Most of KL's backpackers' guesthouses are here, as well as a handful of mid-range hotels.

Chinatown is very central, but don't feel limited to staying here, as other neighbourhoods are within easy reach by public transport or on foot – KL actually feels smaller than it appears on maps.

North of Chinatown, colourful Little India has quite a few cheap and mid-range hotels. Although fewer travellers stay here, it's a valid alternative, though the stretch of Jalan TAR between Masjid Jamek and Little India between Jalan Tun Perak and Jalan Bunus is deserted at night – take a taxi.

Farther north along Jalan TAR, the Chow Kit area has plenty of cheaper accommodation, though some with less-than-desirable reputations.

The main area for mid-range and top-end hotels is the Golden Triangle district, east of Puduraya bus station, where you'll find most of KL's shopping malls and some nightlife. Busy Jalan Bukit Bintang is a good hunting ground for mid-range hotels. Luxury hotels are scattered nearby on Jalan Sultan Ismail.

## PLACES TO STAY – BUDGET

Budget accommodation in KL consists of a variety of ever-dwindling (and crumbling) Chinese hotels and cookie-cutter guesthouses; the truly worthwhile budget places are rare.

As a rule, hotels with 'Rumah Tumpangan' signs written in Malay are long-term boarding houses or offer a different type of – ah – customer service.

### Guesthouses

KL has quite a number of guesthouses that cater exclusively to budget travellers. Competition generally keeps prices down, but don't expect more than a bed in a box or (in the case of dorms) too many beds in a box. Rooms usually lack windows and are partitioned by thin plywood. Most guesthouses offer washing facilities and a noticeboard, and sometimes Internet access.

The better places in Chinatown tend to fill up quickly. If you arrive late at night or early in the morning, you should call ahead to the smaller guesthouses before just turning up and expecting someone to let you in when you ring the bell at 4 am.

**Chinatown** On the edge of Chinatown and only a few minutes' walk from Puduraya bus station is *Travellers Moon Lodge* (☎ 230 6601, 36B Jalan Silang). It's roomier than other Chinatown hostels and offers singles/ doubles for RM18/25, and average dorm beds for RM9 to RM10. Just a few doors along at No 46C is *The Odyssey Backpacker* (☎ 206 6337), run by the same people. It's smaller and quieter, but extremely hospital-like. Dorm beds cost RM10 to RM12 and basic rooms are RM22/28, but the kindly, informative manager counts for a lot. Nearby *Twin Happiness Inn* (☎ 238 7667) is actually

a hotel, not a hostel, though it offers similar guesthouse-rates for impersonal lodgings. Fan rooms with common bath cost RM20/25; air-con triples cost RM40.

*Backpackers Travellers Inn* (☎ 238 2473, 60 Jalan Sultan) is another popular place. Though a little cramped, with typically windowless rooms, it's relatively clean and well run. It shows nightly movies and has a rooftop bar. Air-con dorm beds cost RM10, fan rooms RM22/30, and rooms with air-con cost RM40/50.

At the more-spacious *Backpackers Travellers Lodge* (☎ 201 0889, 158 Jalan Tun HS Lee) there's a good, if spartan, TV lounge and the usual variety of facilities. Very basic windowless doubles start at RM22; somewhat-better rooms with fan and window are RM30; and rooms with air-con and shower cost RM50. Dorm beds cost RM8 each.

Close by, the scruffier *Chinatown Guest House* (☎ 232 0417, Wisma BWT, 103 Jalan Petaling) is right on the pasar malam in the middle of Chinatown. Dorm beds cost RM10 each in four-bed rooms, and rooms cost RM20/23.

On the next block south, *Golden Plaza Hostel* (☎ 206 8559, 106 Jalan Petaling) is cramped and hot, but gets good reports from travellers for its amicable staff and cleanliness. This secure hostel locks its outer grate, for which guests are given a key. Dorm beds cost RM10, bunk-bed twins RM25 and singles/doubles RM25/35.

Across from the West Lake Restoran, *Chinatown Lodge* (☎ 230 7027, 111 Jalan Sultan) is not as popular but has passable rooms without/with window for RM20/35 with fan, and RM40/45 with air-con.

**Chow Kit** Just off Jalan Raja Laut, near Chow Kit opposite the Wilayah Hotel, is the very friendly, family-run *Ben Soo Homestay & Travellers Service* (☎ 2691 8096, 019-332 7013, 2nd floor, 61B Jalan Tiong Nam). It offers rare value in budget accommodation with secure, spacious and clean singles/doubles for only RM25/32 with fan, RM35/40 with air-con, including a light breakfast. The homestay is a 10-minute walk from both Sultan Ismail and PWTC Star LRT stations. For a minimal fee, the owner will pick you up from the train or bus stations, and can also help arrange tours and air tickets.

**Golden Triangle** A jewel of a guesthouse, the hospitable *Pondok Lodge (☎ 242 8449, fax 452 4127, @ pondok@tm.net.my)* is at 20 Jalan Cangkat Bukit Bintang (Jalan Hicks). This spacious, beautifully decorated and (for now) undiscovered retreat has airy common lounges and a rooftop sitting area. Bright Western- or Malay-style rooms with fan cost RM30 to RM40, RM45 with air-con. Reasonable four- or six-bed dorms cost RM12/15 with fan/air-con. The guesthouse is on the 3rd floor above Ziño Kafe, just a 10-minute walk from Jalan Bukit Bintang.

**Puduraya** The ultra-convenient *Anuja Backpackers Inn (☎ 206 6479, fax 201 3725, @ anujainn@tm.net.my, 28 Jalan Pudu)* is opposite Puduraya bus station. It has a brisk turnover of travellers arriving early and late – you may see its touts when you step off the bus. Rooms are pretty basic, but relatively secure and OK for a quick stay. Single/doubles cost RM22/28 without windows, slightly more with windows. Air-con singles/doubles/triples cost RM30/40/50.

**Train Station** At KL's historic old train station, up a staircase beside KFC and the Tourism Malaysia office, *The Traveller's Station (☎ 2272 2237, @ station1@tm.net.my)* is not dirt-cheap at RM15 for air-con dorm beds, but many backpackers favour its convenience, spacious common rooms, good facilities (including kitchen, laundry and Internet access) and easy-going staff. Simple singles cost RM20/25/30, depending on size, and air-con doubles are RM45.

**Other Areas** A 15-minute walk south-east of the train station, the fully air-conditioned *KL International Youth Hostel (☎ 273 6870, 21 Jalan Kampung Attap)* is often deserted. Dorm beds cost RM15 each.

Finally, there are the Ys. In Brickfields, the *YMCA (☎ 274 1439, fax 274 0559, 95 Jalan Padang Belia)* is a centre of local community activity, but out of the way for sightseeing. Simple singles/doubles with fan cost RM38/50 (triples/quads RM65/75). Better air-con rooms with bathroom are RM68/78.

East of Chinatown, the *YWCA (☎ 230 1623, 12 Jalan Hang Jebat)* is extremely quiet and tucked away. It has plain but acceptable rooms for women/married couples at RM30/50 with fan and bathroom. Family rooms are available for RM80.

### Hotels
In Chinatown, the cheapest of the Chinese cheapies is the well-camouflaged *Wan Kow Hotel (☎ 238 2909, 16 Jalan Sultan)*. Very basic rooms with fan and common bathroom cost RM27. *Starlight Hotel (☎ 238 9811, 90 Jalan Hang Kasturi)*, opposite the Klang bus station, is more expensive. Air-con singles/doubles with bathroom and hot water start at RM50/60. The rooms are large but sparsely furnished, and some cop the noise from the bus station across the road.

*KL City Lodge (☎ 230 5275, 16 Jalan Pudu)* is opposite Puduraya bus station. This scruffy hotel still draws a few travellers. Air-con dorm beds cost RM12 each, while simple rooms are RM20/30 with fan, RM25/35 with air-con.

Along Jalan TAR and its side streets there are quite a few basic, cheap hotels but many either have 'health centres' or rent by the hour, so choose carefully.

In Little India your cheapest option is *MACKT Budget Hotel (☎ 294 7422, 29 Jalan Medan Tuanku)*. Carpeted air-con rooms with TV and hot water cost RM35/45; superior rooms cost RM55.

North of Jalan TAR's junction with Jalan Bunus, there's the *Coliseum Hotel (☎ 292 6270, 100 Jalan TAR)*, with its famous old planters' restaurant and bar downstairs. All rooms share bathrooms and cost RM25/40 for fan singles/doubles, RM35/40 with air-con. The rooms are dilapidated, but large and quiet, and this atmospheric hotel is a KL institution; consequently, it's often full.

PENINSULAR MALAYSIA

## PLACES TO STAY – MID-RANGE

In the past few years new mid-range hotels have cropped up and more are being built. Increased competition in an already teeming market means that promotional discounts are often given, especially at the more-expensive places. Attached bathroom, air-conditioning and TV are standard facilities at these hotels.

### Chinatown

Right in the thick of things is *Hotel Lok Ann* (☎ *238 9544, 113A Jalan Petaling)*, which has large rooms for RM60. Unfortunately, they all front noisy Jalan Sultan, though things usually quieten down by about 11 pm. A discreet refuge on this lively market lane is *Hotel Excel Inn* (☎ *201 86210, 89 Jalan Petaling)*, offering windowless but clean rooms at RM50 for up to two people, and triples/quads at RM60/70.

Far better value, and thoroughly recommended, is the *Hotel China Town Inn* (☎ *238 4034, fax 238 4033, 52–54 Jalan Petaling)*, where spotless, hotel-quality rooms (with hot water!) cost just RM50/65/70 for singles/twins/doubles.

You'll find many more-luxurious hotels in this price range. The respectable *Hotel Malaya* (☎ *232 7722, fax 230 0980)*, on the corner of Jalan Tun HS Lee and Jalan Hang Lekir, has good singles/doubles from RM140/165 before discount. There's a 24-hour restaurant and coffee shop downstairs.

Another place right in the heart of Chinatown is *Swiss-Inn* (☎ *232 3333, fax 201 6699, @ sikl@sgihotels.com.my, 62 Jalan Sultan)*, catering to wealthier European and Japanese tourists. Comfortable rooms start at RM150, but promotional discounts knock off as much as 35%. The hotel has two entrances; the one on Jalan Sultan is closer to reception. On the side fronting busy Jalan Petaling, the outdoor coffee-shop has set menus, as well as high teas and evening steamboat meals.

On Jalan Sultan, diagonally opposite, is the high-rise *Hotel Furama* (☎ *230 1777, fax 230 2110)*, where rooms start at RM100, including breakfast. *KL Mandarin Hotel* (☎ *230 3000, 2–8 Jalan Sultan)* is a similar hotel with standard/deluxe rooms for RM70/86, but some don't have windows.

The high-rise *Hotel Puduraya* (☎ *232 1000, fax 230 5567)* is on top of Puduraya bus station. Faded but well-appointed doubles cost RM115, or RM88 after discount. It's ideal for an overnighter, but the hot and chaotic station downstairs does not offer a welcoming face to KL for longer stays. Along with a few pubs, it has a good coffee shop with an inexpensive breakfast buffet.

Opposite Puduraya bus station is the modern *Hotel Katari* (☎ *201 7777, fax 201 7911, @ katari@tm.net.my, 38 Jalan Pudu)*, where standard business-style rooms cost RM138.

### Golden Triangle

Lively Jalan Bukit Bintang, just east of the city centre at the edge of the Golden Triangle, has a large selection of mid-range hotels and the competition means that discounts are often available. Many of the cheaper hotels rent by the hour, however, so you may want to be choosy. Unless otherwise stated, the following hotels do not engage in these practices.

*Malaysia Hotel* (☎ *242 8033, fax 242 8579, 67–69 Jalan Bukit Bintang)* is looking a little down-at-heel, but standard rooms are comfortable for RM92, including breakfast. Across the street, the business-style *Cardogan Hotel* (☎ *244 4883/56, fax 244 4865)* at No 64 has ageing but OK standard rooms for RM70, including breakfast.

Another average mid-range place is *Bintang Warisan Hotel* (☎ *248 8111, fax 248 2333)* at No 68, with singles/doubles from RM150/170. Neighbouring *Sungei Wang Hotel* (☎ *248 5255, fax 242 4576)*, with its bright lobby, offers more luxury at similar rates, with rooms for RM99/110.

*Agora Hotel* (☎ *242 8133, fax 242 7815, 106–110 Jalan Bukit Bintang)* is an older hotel that has undergone a major facelift. Standard rooms cost RM130/150.

At the other end of Jalan Bukit Bintang, but more desirable than any of the preceding places, *Century Kuala Lumpur Hotel* (☎ *243 9898, fax 468 0880)* has quality rooms for RM150/170.

One street west of Jalan Bukit Bintang at Nos 42, 74 and 82 Jalan Alor is the seedy **Budget Inn** (☎ 248 4732), where air-con rooms with bathroom are cheap at RM45/55. There are plenty of other cheap hotels nearby, but they also accept by-the-hour rentals.

The new **Hotel Seasons View** (☎ 245 7577, fax 243 3532, 59–61 Jalan Alor) is better-lit and welcoming; economy singles cost RM73, and standard single/doubles are RM84, including breakfast at the downstairs cafe. Also new, the snazzy **Hotel Nova** (☎ 243 1818, fax 242 9985, ❷ novahtl@ tm.net.my, 16–22 Jalan Alor) is exceptional value, with rooms for RM90/95, including breakfast.

At the top of Jalan Alor on Jalan Cangkat Bukit Bintang (Jalan Hicks), **Hotel Imperial** (☎ 248 1422) has acceptable rooms for one or two people at RM69/92 without/with windows, though the staff are unwelcoming. Farther west, but in a much quieter area, **Park Inn International** (☎ 2715 3888, fax 2715 1888) has rooms starting at RM118 after discount, including breakfast and use of the rooftop swimming pool.

Hidden among the top-end hotels off Jalan Sultan Ismail, the unassuming **The Lodge Hotel** (☎ 242 0122, fax 242 0122, 2 Jalan Tengah) is very convenient. This retro '60s-style motel has a small outdoor pool. Annexe rooms without TV cost RM92, and fully equipped standard/deluxe rooms are RM115/138.

### Jalan TAR Area

The infamous **Kowloon Hotel** (☎ 293 4246, 142–146 Jalan TAR) is one of the older breed of hotels. It's reputation rests on its 2nd-floor 'health club', but guests aren't much disturbed. Singles/doubles costing from RM80/95 could do with an upgrade but are otherwise clean and large.

Little India, just off Jalan TAR, has quite good mid-range options. The plush **Hotel Noble** (☎ 925 7111), around the corner from the Kowloon, has rooms for RM145, or RM98 after discount.

**Garden City Hotel** (☎ 925 7777, fax 925 7717, ❷ gdcity@pd.jaring.my, 213–214 Jalan Bunus), off Jalan Masjid India, is recommended for its cleanliness, friendly service and the 1st-floor Indian tandoori restaurant. Promotional rates for rooms start at RM80, including breakfast.

Though not as shiny and new, **Hotel Champagne** (☎ 298 6333, 14 Jalan Bunus) is a popular place where air-con rooms with bathroom cost RM73.50.

The nearby **Palace Hotel** (☎ 298 6122, 40–46 Jalan Masjid India) is definitely a step up, though only marginally more expensive at RM95/115 for singles/doubles, before discount. **Hotel Empire** (☎ 293 6890) next door offers much less for far fewer ringgit.

Midway between Little India and Chow Kit, **Grand Centrepoint Hotel** (☎ 293 3988, 316 Jalan TAR) offers one of the best mid-range deals in KL. Rooms well-insulated from traffic noise cost RM85, including breakfast. It's a five-minute walk from Sultan Ismail LRT station.

At the top end of Jalan TAR, near the Chow Kit Market, is the eminently respectable **Stanford Hotel** (☎ 291 9833, fax 291 3103, 449 Jalan TAR). Room prices start at RM155/166, but promotional discounts of 40% may apply. On nearby Jalan Raja Laut, the new **De First Inn** (☎ 445 2323, fax 445 2939) has very comfortable rooms starting at RM90/120, before discount.

### Train Station & Brickfields

**Heritage Station Hotel** (☎ 2273 5588, fax 2273 2842) is housed in the magnificent neo-Moorish KL train station. The renovated building has some fine old touches although most rooms have modern decor. The cheapest single/double rooms cost RM90, but grander colonial-style suites are available for RM220. Sometimes 20% discounts are available.

Although Brickfields is out of the way and not especially recommended for women travellers, the vibrant Indian community is a draw. There are a few mid-range places on Jalan Thambapillai. **Hotel Florida** (☎ 2260 1111), at 71–73 is head and shoulders above the rest, charging RM60/75 for good rooms.

Not far away at No 11, *Hotel New Winner* (☎ 2273 3766) offers fading air-con rooms with bathroom for RM77. *Quee Ping Hotel* (☎ 2274 3505) next door is better value at RM50 for an air-con room. *Hotel Mexico* (☎ 2274 0235), at No 1, is overpriced at RM86/97 for fully-equipped rooms.

## PLACES TO STAY – TOP END

Kuala Lumpur has a profusion of luxury hotels catering primarily to business travellers. All of these hotels have a swimming pool and a host of restaurants and bars. Many offer promotional discounts (up to 50%) off regular rates quoted here, which include 5% tax and 10% service charge.

Most luxury hotels are found in the Golden Triangle district. At the top end of Jalan Sultan Ismail, the *Sheraton Imperial* (☎ 486 9821, fax 486 9955) is one of KL's most luxurious establishments, with rooms starting at RM500. The equally opulent *Renaissance Kuala Lumpur* (☎ 2162 2233, fax 2163 1122), at the corner of Jalan Sultan Ismail and Jalan Ampang, has room rates that vary seasonally but dip as low as RM230, including breakfast for two. Both these hotels are removed from the main action.

Farther south, where things start to get lively, the excellently located *Concorde* (☎ 244 2200, fax 244 1628, 2 Jalan Sultan Ismail) is a luxury hotel with personality and style. Standard/deluxe rooms regularly cost RM250/300, but spectacular promotional deals can include a standard room, a limo from the airport, breakfast and a complimentary drink for RM198.

Halfway down the next block, the classy *Hotel Equatorial* (☎ 261 7777, fax 261 9020) attracts a mostly Asian clientele. Singles/twins start at RM340/360, including use of the fitness centre. Nearby, the ever-popular *Hilton Kuala Lumpur* (☎ 248 2322, fax 244 2157) has rooms from RM350.

At the intersection of Jalan Sultan Ismail and Jalan Raja Chulan, *Hotel Istana* (☎ 241 9988, fax 244 0111) has one of KL's most impressive lobbies and is favoured by visiting dignitaries. Singles/doubles start at RM495/525. At the bottom end of Jalan

Sultan Ismail, *Parkroyal Kuala Lumpur* (☎ 242 5588, fax 241 5524) is next to Lot 10 and is handy to other shopping plazas. Standard/deluxe rooms are RM460/495, but 50% promotional discounts may be available.

Set among the mid-range hotels on Jalan Bukit Bintang, *Federal Hotel* (☎ 248 9166, fax 248 2877, 35 Jalan Bukit Bintang) was the first modern luxury hotel in KL, dating from Malaysia's independence in 1957. It's smaller and slightly less expensive, with singles/twins from RM290/320 before discount.

At the north-eastern end of Jalan Bukit Bintang, the impressive Four Seasons hotel *The Regent* (☎ 241 8000, fax 242 1441, 160 Jalan Bukit Bintang) has gorgeous rooms from RM575 in the superluxury category. Almost directly opposite, the equally sumptuous *JW Mariott Hotel* (☎ 2715 9000, fax 2715 7000) has deluxe rooms starting at RM345/195 for weekends/weekdays, which is a steal. It's attached to the Star Hill shopping centre and has an excellent restaurant, called Shook!

On Jalan Imbi, south of Jalan Bukit Bintang, *Meliá Kuala Lumpur* (☎ 242 8333, fax 242 6623) is a classy choice; superior/deluxe rooms start at RM322/391.

At the south-western edge of the Golden Triangle, *Swiss-Garden Hotel* (☎ 241 3333, fax 241 5555, 117 Jalan Pudu) has rooms from RM350, but offers up to 50% off during promotions.

The eastern end of Jalan Ampang, past the Petronas Towers and the KLCC shopping centre, also has a few top-end hotels, and more are being built. This area doesn't have much atmosphere or foot traffic, however. A few hundred metres south of Ampang Park LRT station, *Mi Casa Hotel Apartments* (☎ 2161 8833, fax 2161 1186, 386B Jalan Tun Razak) has apartment-style suites costing from RM238 to RM890. North of the station on Jalan Tun Razak, *Crown Princess* (☎ 262 5522, fax 262 4492, ❻ crown princess@fhikl.com.my) is adjacent to the City-Square shopping complex. Promotional rates at this very elegant hotel start at RM168/188 for singles/doubles, including breakfast – a very good deal.

In the Chow Kit area, *The Legend Hotel* (☎ *442 9888, fax 443 0700, 100 Jalan Putra)* is next to The Mall. Standard/deluxe rooms start at RM380/RM430, apartments from RM450 (ask about monthly rates). The reception lobby is on the 9th floor.

For colonial style, *Carcosa Seri Negara* (☎ *282 1888, fax 282 6868, Taman Tasik Perdana)* comprises two magnificent colonial mansions in tranquil gardens at the western edge of the Lake Gardens. Carcosa was the residence of British Resident Sir Frank Swettenham, and Seri Negara was the official guesthouse. Each of the 14 exclusive luxury suites costs between RM1100 and RM2400, including airport transfers.

*Pan Pacific KLIA* (☎ *8787 3333)*, a top-end hotel linked by sky bridge to the main terminal, has published rates of RM560/590 for singles/doubles, but ask at its airport reservation desk about promotional discounts (up to 50% off). See Air under Getting There & Away later for information on napping-accommodation at KLIA.

## PLACES TO EAT
### Hawker Food
KL has plenty of indoor and outdoor hawker venues all around the city.

In **Chinatown**, Jalan Petaling is closed to traffic between Jalan Cheng Lock and Jalan Sultan. Tables are set up in the evenings outside Chinese restaurants on Jalan Hang Lekir between Jalan Petaling and Jalan Sultan.

The stall on the corner of Jalan Sultan and Jalan Hang Lekir serves steamboat. The food on skewers is laid out on the table, so you just cook what you want and pay according to the number of empty skewers you've collected. There are also stalls in this area selling satay, peanut pancakes, sweets, ice drinks and fruit.

Other night markets for Malay food include the *Sunday Market* out at Kampung Bahru and the *Chow Kit Market*, just off Jalan TAR. Night owls head to Chow Kit for the all-night nasi lemak stalls.

Little India's *Saturday night market* along Lorong TAR has many food vendors and a great atmosphere. Most stalls sell takeaway snacks, but a few also set up tables for eating there. *Jalan Masjid India* is almost as good any evening of the week for Indian fare.

*Jalan Alor*, one street north-west of Jalan Bukit Bintang in the Golden Triangle district, has some of the best Chinese hawker stalls and coffee shops in KL, serving excellent *ikan bakar* (grilled fish). It starts after dark around 7 pm and closes late. Off Jalan Sultan Ismail, the small *Sri Perak*, just back from Modesto's, and the lane of hawkers beside Gloria Jean's are both busy places.

But the best outdoor hawker-centre in the Golden Triangle is *BB Park*, squeezed next to BB Plaza in front of Low Yat Plaza, where a delicious variety of stalls sell just about everything from tandoori to Western grills and satay.

Most shopping malls have food courts for slightly more expensive hawker food in air-con surrounds. One of the best is in The Mall shopping complex, opposite the PWTC in the Chow Kit area. The top-floor *Medan Hang Tuah* is a re-creation of an old city street, complete with mock shophouses, and has an excellent selection of cheap Malay, Chinese and Indian favourites.

Shopping malls in the Golden Triangle also have hawker food. For something a little different, the *Chili Food Court* in the basement of the Isetan department store in Lot 10, has a wide range of Asian food including Korean, Vietnamese and Japanese – there's even a desserts-only branch of the Barn Thai restaurant here. The 2nd-floor Suria KLCC food court also has good selections.

The *Central Market* in Chinatown has an average selection of hawker food upstairs on the 2nd level.

### Chinese
You'll find Chinese restaurants everywhere, but particularly in Chinatown and around Jalan Bukit Bintang in the Golden Triangle.

In Chinatown, the long-running *West Lake Restoran (15 Jalan Sultan)* is a local favourite for *yong tau foo* (fried tofu, vegetables etc in gravy). Directly opposite, the equally favoured *Restoran Kam Lun Tai* has dim sum (before noon), and *Fatt Yon Vegetarian Restaurant* sells, among other things, cheap takeaway steamed buns from a rack at the front.

The atmosphere that these places lack can be found on the other side of the swinging wooden doors of *Old China Café (11 Jalan Balai Polis)*. Inside what feels like a Shanghai teahouse, complete with quaint 1920s crooner music, try the incredible coffee and generous servings of Nyonya (Straits Chinese) fare. It's open from 11 am to 11 pm daily.

Outside the entrance to Sungei Wang Plaza on Jalan Sultan Ismail is the cheap and popular *Super Noodle House*. At the back entrance, near Low Yat Plaza, *Restoran Instant* dishes up a variety of regional Chinese noodle specialities very cheaply. Another Cantonese fast-food place is *Restoran Easy-OK*, adjacent to the Hotel Imperial.

There are two good options at Low Yat Plaza: *Beijing Wok*, where you can order large Chinese lunch-sets for RM10; and *Tuck Sang Herbal Food*, with its eccentric menu of pricey Chinese herbal concoctions including Gecko Kidney Consolidating Soup (RM35) and expensive ginseng dishes for developing that special potency. There's another branch on the 3rd floor of the City-Square shopping complex.

Another local speciality is *bah kut teh*, which supposedly originated in Klang. It's a very popular meal of pork ribs with white rice and Chinese tea. There are stalls in the Chinatown night market selling this dish for a few ringgit, as well as several along Jalan Raja Laut in Chow Kit.

There are some outstanding Chinese restaurants along Jalan Imbi just north-east of Jalan Sultan Ismail, with banquet-style meals for groups and all the Chinese favourites from shark's fin to *belacan* (prawn paste). These places include the *Fong Lye Restaurant*, the Malaysian-Chinese *Restoran Sakura* and the popular *Restoran Overseas*, which dishes up mainly Cantonese food. Just look for all the Mercedes parked outside.

## Indian

Little India is obviously a good hunting ground for Indian food. Plenty of coffee shops can be found in the Jalan Masjid India/Jalan TAR area, and food stalls specialise in cheap tandoori chicken, naan, dosas and chapatis. One good tip is the excellent upstairs *Govinda's Vegetarian Restaurant*, near the end of Jalan Bunus 6, which has simple vegetarian lunch buffets for RM5 per person (11.30 am to 3.30 pm) plus delicious lassi (RM2). A la carte dinner options are made from soy fake meat and include Indian, Malay and Chinese dishes, even rendang from Negeri Sembilan!

For more-upmarket North Indian fare, try *Garden City Hotel* or head south to *The Bangles (60A Jalan TAR)*. Farther north of Little India, on Jalan Medan Tuanku off Jalan TAR, the upmarket *Omar Khayyam* serves North Indian food in air-con surrounds. Next door are two competing cafeteria-style Indian halal places, *Restoran Yusoof* and *Restoran Hanifa*, both specialising in fish-head curry. In Sogo department store, the air-con *Bombay Express* has yummy tandoori in its RM23 lunch buffet.

Facing the Central Market on the Jalan Hang Kasturi pedestrian mall there's another branch of *Restoran Yusoof* at No 36, a popular place for roti, biryani, *murtabak* (roti filled with mutton, chicken or vegetables) and *rojak singapura* (batter-fried egg, tofu, vegies and shrimp with spicy dipping sauce). North of Chinatown, *Bilal Restoran (33 Jalan Ampang)* is a KL institution for South Indian halal food at reasonable prices.

In the Golden Triangle, *Restoran Ramzan* has an excellent range of murtabak, biryani, curry and naan at cheap prices.

For fiery, authentic South Indian food, head to the Brickfields area, a couple of kilometres south of the city centre, where there are several *daun pisang* (banana leaf) restaurants serving rice with vegetarian, fish, chicken and mutton curries. *Sri Devi Curry House*, on Jalan Tun Sambanthan, specialises in spicy, tropical Chettinad cookery. The slightly more upmarket *Restoran Intown Inn*, on Jalan Thambapillai, has a bar at the back.

## Malay & Nyonya

There are Malay *warung* (small eating-stalls) and *kedai kopi* (coffee shops) throughout KL, but especially along and just off Jalan TAR.

*Restoran Wilayah Baru (29 Lebuh Pudu)* in Chinatown has excellent, cheap Malay food. One of the house specialities is *rojak pinang,* a Malay salad served with a spicy dipping sauce.

One of Kuala Lumpur's classic old eating dens, *The Kapitan's Club (☎ 201 0242, 35 Jalan Ampang)* is in an old Peranakan shophouse. Kapitan chicken curry is a speciality, as are 30 other Nyonya creations, like creamy Cincalok chicken (RM11.50) and spicy Manggo Kerabu salad (RM7.50). Although similar to Melaka's classic Nyonya cafes, it's nevertheless a bit cheesy at night, when the disco ball flashes.

In BB Plaza on Jalan Bukit Bintang, the 2nd-floor *Nyonya Wok* has Nyonya specialities at moderately high prices. On the lower ground level of adjacent Sungei Wang Plaza, *Rasa Utara* specialises in inexpensive Malay cuisine from Kedah state.

*Restoran Eden Village (☎ 241 4027, 260 Jalan Raja Chulan),* a huge, elaborate Malay-style building, is a megarestaurant serving so-so Western and Malay seafood during nightly cultural shows (see Entertainment later in this chapter).

*Restoran Nelayan Titiwangsa (☎ 422 8400),* set in the Lake Titiwangsa Gardens in northern KL, is in an enormous hut built over the water. It picks up in the evenings, when tours groups roll in for live performances (see Entertainment later in this chapter). Main dishes start at RM12, but the seafood is ominously unpriced.

The rather exclusive *Seri Angkasa (☎ 208 5055),* a revolving restaurant high up in the KL Tower, offers more exhilarating scenery as you dine, but you must book well in advance – ask for sunset time.

## Japanese

In Chinatown, the hole-in-the-wall *Pandamania Comics & Cafe* has cheap Japanese fare (even okonomiyaki!) for around RM4 and large ice-blend juices and coffees (RM4.50). You'll be surrounded by Hello Kitty and Japanese *manga* (comics) while noir Japanese action-flicks (subtitled in Chinese) play on the TV overhead.

On the top floor of The Mall, near PWTC LRT station, *Restaurant Hoshigaoka* is a peaceful retreat, although service is brusque. The noodles (RM8) and *donburi* (rice dishes; RM10) taste authentic.

In the Golden Triangle, *Sushi King* on Jalan Sultan Ismail has reasonably priced self-serve sushi at the conveyor-belt-bar. A few doors along, *TokuToku* is more atmospheric yet affordable – you can eat for around RM20 per person. Across from Lot 10, *Dontaku Restoran Jepun* is an authentic-looking *izakaya*-(Japanese pub) style place, where a group can order several small dishes (averaging RM5 to RM15) and share.

Pricier, but more stylish, is *The Talk*, a Japanese bistro, cigar and wine bar on Jalan P Ramlee in the Golden Triangle, and at 22 Jalan Telawi 3 in Bangsar. Lunch sets are a good bargain (RM15), and ramen noodles will only set you back RM10.

*Edo*, in the Regent Hotel on Jalan Bukit Bintang, has excellent Japanese food, at suitably breathtaking prices.

## Thai & Other Asian

Thai-food possibilities range from tom yam soup at food centres to expensive meals in Thai restaurants at top-end hotels.

Though not strictly Thai, *Ginger*, upstairs in the Central Market, has good food (including Malaysian and Indonesian fare) and a tiny indoor waterfall, hardwood tables and soothing lighting. The apple fried-rice with prawns (RM8) is mouthwatering; vegetarian and noodle dishes start at RM6.

In the Golden Triangle, the long-running *Restoran Best Thai Cuisine (74 Jalan Bukit Bintang)* is favoured for its outstanding cooking and very reasonable prices.

*Tamnak Thai*, on the 6th floor of Sogo department store on Jalan TAR, has a less-extensive menu of equally classic (and hot) Thai dishes, but prices are higher (mains start at RM12). *Vietnamhôuse* next door is under the same management as The Kapitan's Club (see Malay & Nyonya earlier in

PENINSULAR MALAYSIA

this section). From its wide menu of Vietnamese food, starters cost RM8 to RM10 and mains from RM20; the springs rolls and fish soup are especially good.

The 4th floor of Suria KLCC mall has many upmarket Asian restaurants, including *Chakri Palace* for Royal Thai cooking, and *House of Sundanese Food*. The affordable, attractive *rain nudle house* has rice- and noodle-dishes from RM12, plus good desserts (try the pumpkin custard).

## International

Central KL has a surprising variety of Western restaurants, although most of the innovative and authentic places are in Bangsar, south of the city centre.

**Central KL** *Coliseum Hotel* on Jalan TAR is far from hygienic, although people still come for the passable sizzling steaks (RM28). The place is quite a colonial experience and has scarcely changed over the years, with indifferent service and stained tablecloths at no extra charge. You're better off just having a drink at the bar.

*Be My Friend Deli*, on the 1st floor of the Central Market Annexe, has a terrace overlooking the river, healthy home-cooked fare and some vegetarian options, as well as great coffee.

*Le Coq d'Or (121 Jalan Ampang)*, a restaurant in a fine late-19th-century mansion, is not as expensive as the elegant surroundings might indicate. Which is good, since it's not uncommon for diners to see rats scuttling through the dark, cavernous interior. If you want to soak in the atmosphere, with its faded touches of the raj, come just for drinks.

The elegant *Scalini's (19 Jalan Sultan Ismail)* has authentic Italian food, as does *Ristorante Bologna* in the Hotel Istana.

Opposite the Hard Rock Cafe in Menara Haw Par, *Bierkeller* (☎ 201 3313) is full of expat Central Europeans savouring their bratwurst and sauerkraut (RM15.50), gulping imported brews (from RM13) and perusing the selection of recent German newspapers and magazines. The bar is open until 1 am, but the kitchen closes at 11 pm.

Most hotels have fine-dining options, but nothing beats the sleek style of *Shook!* (☎ 926 8535) on the lower level of Star Hill shopping complex, adjoining the JW Mariott. The bar with its silver fountains looks like a contemporary art installation and the impressive restaurant offers three separate, but equally appetising menus: Japanese, Chinese and Western grill. Entrees hover around RM30 to RM40 and imaginative, tempting desserts are less than RM10. Reservations are advised.

In the Hotel Equatorial, *Chalet* serves gourmet Swiss cuisine. Yes, it has fondue.

**Bangsar** This favourite haunt of expats and KL's wealthier citizens has almost all of the city's stylish, innovative restaurants and a lot of foreigner-friendly pubs. To get there, take the Putra LRT to Bangsar station, then a feeder bus to the main strip around Jalan Telawi.

At *The Red Chamber*, you can dine on red velvet couches on pan-Asian and fusion cuisine, including dumplings and noodle dishes, and take advantage of a full bar. Another inviting restaurant-bar is *La Bodega (16 Jalan Telawi 2)*, serving Spanish tapas (even for vegetarians) starting at RM8 per plate.

*Lucerne*, on Jalan Telawi 3, does sinfully rich chocolate fondue. Try the nearby *Brasserie Gusto* for Italian, or *The White Raja* on Jalan Telawi for East-West fusion cuisine. *Ronnie Q's*, which is also on Jalan Telawi 3, serves up Nyonya Chinese food and Saturday-afternoon jazz.

Finally, there's the top-end *q\*doz*, with the most adventurous menu in town – and the most exorbitant prices.

## Bakeries & Cafes

Two inexpensive sit-down bakeries in Chinatown are *Meidi-ya*, across from the Central Market, and *King's Confectionery*, under the Backpackers Travellers Inn.

Outside on the ground level of Lot 10 shopping centre, *Secret Recipe* has unbelievable treats for RM6: cherry cheesecake, banana-chocolate layer cake and even brownies.

PENINSULAR MALAYSIA

Other cafes for hot croissants and real coffee include *Malayan Aromas* in the City-Square shopping complex, serving delicious regional Malay coffees that certainly aren't cheap at RM9 per cup. On the concourse level of Sungei Wang Plaza, *West 57th St. Cafe* serves great cakes and coffee, as well as main dishes, right in the middle of a clothing boutique. Finally, there is *Four Leaves* in the Sogo shopping complex, and *Delifrance*, which is virtually everywhere.

## Self-Catering

You can find supermarkets in Chinatown at the S&M Shopping Arcade on Jalan Cheng Lock, and at UDA Ocean Plaza on the corner of Jalan Sultan and Jalan Tun HS Lee.

On Jalan TAR, Sogo department store has a well-stocked basement supermarket. Many of the shopping malls and department stores in the Golden Triangle also have supermarkets; there's one in the basement of the Isetan department store on Jalan Sultan Ismail.

## ENTERTAINMENT
### Bars & Discos

Most of KL's nightlife was once found in the Golden Triangle, and Jalan Sultan Ismail is still the centre of the universe for KL's middle class, as well as for some ravingly bored youth.

However, most expats head to Bangsar, south of the city centre, to see and be seen. The most popular is the three-storey *The Roof (2 Jalan Telawi 4)*, with wrought-iron balconies perfect for people-watching while you drink imported wine and nibble on oysters. Uphill on Jalan Telawi 5 are a line-up of three loud, crowded bars: *Planet Scuba*, *Finnegan's* and *House Frankfurt*. Many of Bangsar's restaurants also encourage lounging at their bars.

Back in the Golden Triangle, *Hard Rock Cafe* in the Concorde Hotel on Jalan Sultan Ismail has the usual blend of food-and-rock memorabilia, and live bands from 11 pm. There is a cover charge of RM23, but this includes your first drink.

On Jalan P Ramlee, a short stroll behind the Hard Rock Cafe, is *Modesto's*, a bar chain popular among trendy KL-ites, where better-than-average Italian food is served.

Around the corner from the Shangri-La in the basement of the Menara Pan Global are a few rave discos that change hands every few months. For now the name to give is *The Backroom (☎ 382 2988)*. Just look for the flashing lights and keep an ear out for the techno beat booming onto Lorong P Ramlee. For the same crowd and more techno, check out *The Warp* in the Life Centre on Jalan Sultan Ismail. The older R&B crowd goes to *Kafe Emporium* disco across the street. Standard cover charges hover around RM25 on weekends, usually including one drink.

A restaurant-cum-pub, *Blues Cafe* is outside the ground level of the Lot 10 shopping centre. It features anything from tropical jazz to reggae and Latin rock every night (except Sunday) with no cover charge. The bar is small and the volume is cranked up high but the open-air terrace facing the street offers a respite and serves grills. Happy hours are 3 to 9 pm, and all day on Sunday.

Across the street *Sol Pub* has Corona, a few decent wines and equally generous happy hours from 5 to 8 pm weekdays.

Nearby in the Parkroyal Hotel is *Delaney's (☎ 241 5195)*, an Irish-style pub with live sports satellite-TV. Happy hours from 6 to 9 pm are heavily patronised by older expats and businessmen.

Chinatown is quiet at night, but the Central Market has a few laid-back places for a drink. Facing the river on the western side of the market, *Bull's Head* is an English-style pub. Despite the decor, it's Eagles on the jukebox and Anchor on tap; you can sit outside and snack on excellent curries and breads from a tandoori hawker.

### Cultural Shows

The *Malaysian Tourist Information Complex (MATIC; ☎ 2164 3929)* on Jalan Ampang has traditional dance and music performances at 3.30 pm on Tuesday, Thursday, Saturday and Sunday (RM2).

The *Central Market (☎ 2274 6542)* has a regular program of events including Indian dancing and *pencak silat* martial arts

PENINSULAR MALAYSIA

performances, wayang kulit and Malay comedy nights, starting at 7.45 pm every weekend (free). Pick up a monthly calendar from the information desk.

Hotels and restaurants also have dinner cultural shows, but most are fairly tacky. In Plaza Putra below Merdeka Square, the large *Restoran Sri Putra* (☎ 294 3411) has shows at 7.15 pm every evening for RM25.

At Lake Titiwangsa in the north of KL, *Restoran Nelayan Titiwangsa* (☎ 422 8400) has shows at 8.30 pm daily except Monday. Other regular venues include *Seri Melayu* (☎ 245 1833, 1 Jalan Conlay), close to the Kompleks Budaya Kraf, and the nearby *Restoran Eden Village* (☎ 241 4027).

## Classical Music

*Dewan Filharmonik Petronas* (☎/fax 207 7007, ✉ dfp_boxoffice@petronas.com.my) on level 2 of the Petronas twin towers has classical music performances by the Malaysian Philharmonic Orchestra and international ensembles. Ticket prices vary, but Sunday matinees are cheapest.

At Lake Titiwangsa Gardens, *The National Theatre* (☎ 4025 2525) is the home of the National Symphony and National Choir. Occasional drama and dance performances are also held.

## Cinemas

There are plenty of cinemas in the city centre. Check the *New Straits Times* or other dailies for listings. Hollywood features are now widely shown (in English with Malay/Chinese subtitles), while Hong Kong action extravaganzas, Indonesian dramas and Indian musicals also draw crowds.

## Theatre

The *Actors Studio Theatre* (☎ 294 5400/5927) in the underground Plaza Putra, below Merdeka Square, has performances of contemporary dance, comedy and new plays (often in English) most nights; tickets cost RM20 to RM35. The theatre also runs a small cafe and bookshop inside the mall.

The *Experimental Theatre* (☎ 294 3022, 464 Jalan Tun Ismail), north of the Lake Gardens, has modern theatre performances in Bahasa Malaysia and English.

## SHOPPING

KL promotes itself as a shopping haven. Clothes and shoes are inexpensive, though not as cheap as neighbouring Thailand and Indonesia – still, the range is better. Singapore has a much wider selection of electronics at lower prices, but KL is very competitively priced for camera gear, film, and computer software and hardware.

KL may be the best place to buy handicrafts in Malaysia, but higher wages mean that Malaysia produces fewer handicrafts these days. Traditional Malay batik cloth and kites can be found, but not cheaply, and almost everything else is imported from Indonesia, Thailand or elsewhere.

## Shops & Markets

The crowded Central Market (formerly a wet market) is housed in a cavernous Art Deco building beside the river in Chinatown. It's easy to spend an hour or more wandering around the various craft outlets, which sell souvenirs, clothes and jewellery, expensive Asian artefacts and antiques. They're often shockingly overpriced for the quality of the goods on offer. Bargain hard. As a general rule, the higher the price, the more you should bargain. Some of the antique shops are interesting for old bric-a-brac, and Wau Tradisi at shop M51 has a good collection of Malaysian kites.

Just south of the Central Market, the small shop Peter Hoe Evolution (☎ 206 0722), 2 Jalan Hang Lekir, has tastefully arranged Malaysian and imported Asian goods, including true (not machine-printed) batik and silks and contemporary pottery and jewellery; prices are saner than at the Central Market.

The City-Square shopping complex on Jalan Ampang also has reasonably priced Asian art and crafts (see Shopping Malls later in this section).

Jalan Petaling in the heart of Chinatown is one of the most colourful shopping streets in KL, particularly at night. This streetside market has cheap clothes, copy watches, pirated

CDs and a smattering of crafts. Hard bargaining is definitely in order.

Also in Chinatown, the unique National Geographic Back Issues shop (☎ 201 9905, fax 245 9488), on the lower ground floor of the S&M Shopping Arcade, carries imported *National Geographic* magazines dating back to the 1930s. Current issues cost RM10, and prices are RM100 or more for the earliest issues.

The Kompleks Budaya Kraf (☎ 2162 7459), on Jalan Conlay east of Jalan Raja Chulan, is a large handicrafts complex with a variety of locally produced batiks, carved wooden artefacts, pewter utensils, woven baskets, rattan furniture, glassware, glazed ceramics and more. There is a small museum and craft demonstrations are given between 9.30 am and 12.30 pm and again from 2 to 3.30 pm weekdays; the complex is open from 10 am to 6 pm daily. You can also try batik here (see Language & Cultural Courses earlier in this chapter).

The stalls at the Chow Kit Market sell everything – cheap clothes, basketware and leather goods are good buys if you bargain hard. Shops in the lanes around the market, particularly Jalan Haji Hussein, specialise in made-to-order *songkok,* the traditional Malay male headdress.

In Little India, Jalan Masjid India is the place to shop for saris, Indian silks, carpets and other textiles. You can also find great deals on carpets on the upper floors of the City-Square complex in the north-east of KL.

Pewterware, made from 97% high-quality Malaysian tin, is an important local craft. Royal Selangor Pewter is the main manufacturer and its pewter is available in department stores and shops around town. Its factory (☎ 4022 1000), at 4 Jalan Usahawan Enam, is located 8km north-east of central KL in the suburb of Setapak Jaya. Free 15-minute tours of the factory (which has the world's largest pewter tankard at 1557kg) are conducted between 8 am and 4.45 pm daily. Take Len Seng bus W12 from Jalan Ampang, or ride the Putra LRT to Wangsa Maju station and take a Putra feeder bus (50 sen) to the factory. A direct metered taxi from central KL should cost RM6.

## Shopping Malls

KL has plenty of shopping malls catering to affluent Malaysians. If it's clothes, shoes, electronics, cameras and everyday goods you're after, the Golden Triangle has the biggest selection. Shopping malls are generally open from 10 am to 10 pm, but smaller shops close earlier.

Sungei Wang Plaza on Jalan Sultan Ismail and BB Plaza on Jalan Bukit Bintang adjoin to form one of KL's biggest and best complexes. The Metrojaya and Parkson Grand department stores combine with hundreds of small shops to sell just about everything. Sungei Wang is especially good for camera gear and, as all the computer shops from Imbi Plaza have moved here, for cheap (but possibly pirated) copies of software and hardware components.

Two nearby shopping malls are Lot 10 and Star Hill, both on Jalan Bukit Bintang. These new, upmarket centres sell genuine designer-label clothes, shoes and perfume. Squeezed between them is KL Plaza, housing Tower Records and Planet Hollywood.

The Mall shopping centre on Jalan Putra, opposite the Pan Pacific Hotel in Chow Kit, is another good place for brand-name goods. The Yaohan department store has a reasonable selection of electronics in the basement – it's a good place to go to get an

Beautiful, elaborately decorated kris are popular souvenirs.

PENINSULAR MALAYSIA

idea of current prices before bargaining elsewhere.

On the northern outskirts of the Golden Triangle, on Jalan Ampang, Hankyu department store is inside the Ampang Park mall, which also has cheaper clothes and jewellery shops and moneychangers offering very competitive rates. It's linked by a pedestrian bridge to the classier City-Square shopping complex on Jalan Tun Razak, which has interesting upmarket interior-design stores and art galleries. Shops here have a better selection of Asian crafts and carpets than the Central Market, and at fairer prices.

On Jalan TAR in Little India, Globe Silk is a KL institution. This long-running, small department store has cosmetics, textiles and clothes at some of the cheapest prices in town. The modern Sogo department store farther north carries designer clothes, household goods and a few electronics. The Pertama Complex across the street sells cheaper clothes and shoes. On the ground floor is a camera shop, Selangor Photographers (☎ 291 7745), recommended for great deals on new equipment, reliable camera-repair services and on-site photo developing.

Chinatown has a few busy shopping centres, including the crammed S&M Shopping Arcade on Jalan Cheng Lock, and the more-upmarket Kota Raya next door. Both have a good selection of clothes, shoes, music tapes and CDs, as well as outdoor sports gear and backpacks.

KL's newest shopping complex is the flashy Suria KLCC, at the foot of the Petronas Towers. Anchored by the Isetan and Parkson Grand department stores, the mall has several bookshops, designer clothes and shoe stores, and gourmet restaurants. It even has the Petrosains Discovery Centre (☎ 581 8181) to amuse the kids with the wonders of petroleum through high-tech wayang kulit parables. On the ground floor is the FotoSuria pro lab and every fast food outlet you might've been missing, even the Japanese chain Mos Burger. Near Galeri Petronas on the 3rd floor are some arts and crafts shops: Pucuk Rebung has antiques and fine Malay items.

## GETTING THERE & AWAY

Kuala Lumpur is Malaysia's principal international arrival gateway and the crossroads for domestic bus, train and taxi travel.

### Air

In 1999, 13.1 million passengers passed through the colossal new Kuala Lumpur International Airport, 75km south of the city centre at Sepang. State-of-the-art terminal facilities include an airport information desk, a Tourism Malaysia office (☎ 8787 4212) that is open from 9 am to 10 pm daily, and several fast-food outlets. At Eden Seafood Restaurant, dim sum is served all day long. Note that phonecards used with the airport's TimeReach phones don't work anywhere else in Malaysia.

At the Airside Transit Hotel (☎ 8787 4040), near Gate C5 in the Satellite Building, you can crash for six hours (RM100). See the Pan Pacific KLIA entry under Places to Stay – Top End, earlier in this chapter.

KLIA now takes all scheduled international flights to and from Kuala Lumpur. At the time of writing, Terminal 3 at the old airport in Subang still handled some domestic Air Asia, Berjaya Air and Pelangi Air flights, though these will eventually be transferred over to KLIA when Subang becomes a trade-convention centre.

In spite of the RM9-billion expense of building KLIA, airport departure taxes are steady at RM40 for international flights and RM5 for domestic.

Some airlines with offices in KL include:

**Aeroflot** (☎ 2161 0231) Wisma Tong Ah, 1 Jalan Perak
**Air Asia** (☎ 745 7777) Level 6 Wisma Hicom, 2 Jalan Usahawan U1/8, Shah Alam
**Air India** (☎ 242 0166) Angkasa Raya Bldg, Jalan Ampang
**Berjaya Air** (☎ 746 8228) Terminal 3, Subang Airport
**British Airways/Qantas** (☎ 2167 6188) 8th floor, West Wing, Rohas Terkasa, 8 Jalan Perak
**Cathay Pacific Airways** (☎ 238 3377) Menara UBN, 10 Jalan P Ramlee
**China Airlines** (☎ 242 7344) Amoda Bldg, 22 Jalan Imbi

**Eva Air** (☎ 2161 7500) Suite 1205, Kenanga International, Jalan Sultan Ismail
**Garuda Indonesia Airlines** (☎ 2162 2811) 3rd floor, Menara Lion, Jalan Ampang
**Japan Airlines** (☎ 2161 1722) 20th floor, Menara Lion, Jalan Ampang
**Lufthansa** (☎ 261 4666) 3rd floor, Kenanga International, Jalan Sultan Ismail
**Malaysia Airlines** (☎ 2161 0555, 24-hour reservations ☎ 746 3000) Bangunan MAS, Jalan Sultan Ismail; Kompleks Dayabumi, Jalan Sultan Hishamuddin; and 3rd floor The Mall, 100 Jalan Putra
**Pakistan International Airlines** (☎ 242 5444) Angkasaraya Bldg, Jalan Ampang
**Pelangi Air** (☎ 755 5557) 17th floor, PKNS Tower, Jalan Yong Shook Lin, Petaling Jaya
**Royal Brunei Airlines** (☎ 230 7166) Menara UBN, 10 Jalan P Ramlee
**Singapore Airlines** (☎ 292 3122) Wisma SIA, 2 Jalan Dang Wangi
**Thai Airways International** (☎ 201 2900) Wisma Gold Hill, 67 Jalan Raja Chulan

KL is the hub for Malaysia Airlines' domestic network, with nonstop flights to:

| destination | flights daily | fare (RM) |
| --- | --- | --- |
| Alor Setar | 2 | 113* |
| Ipoh | 2 | 66 |
| Johor Bahru | 6 | 93* |
| Kota Bharu | 4 | 104* |
| Kota Kinabalu | 12 | 437* |
| Kuala Terengganu | 3 | 104 |
| Kuantan | 3 | 74 |
| Kuching | 10 | 262* |
| Labuan | 6 | 437 |
| Langkawi | 5 | 135 |
| Miri | 7 | 422 |
| Penang | 11 | 104* |
| Singapore | 12 | 152 |

* Cheaper night fares and 7-day advance-purchase fares are applicable on some flights on these routes.

Malaysia Airlines and Singapore Airlines operate a joint shuttle-service between KL and Singapore on a stand-by basis (RM207, including departure tax). Simply turn up at the shuttle counter at the airport, take a number and wait for the next available flight, usually no more than an hour.

For other destinations in Peninsular Malaysia and in Malaysian Borneo, see individual destination entries in the appropriate chapters.

## Bus

KL's main bus station is Puduraya, just east of Chinatown. From here buses go all over Peninsular Malaysia, including the east coast, and to Singapore and Thailand.

The Pekeliling and Putra bus stations in the north of the city handle a greater number of services to the east coast. Buses at these stations often have seats available when Puduraya buses are fully booked. The only long-distance destinations that Puduraya doesn't handle are Kuala Lipis and Jerantut, which leave only from Pekeliling bus station.

Alternatively, to Taman Negara, a direct shuttle minibus (RM25) to the Kuala Tembeling jetty leaves at 8 am daily from the Hotel Istana in the Golden Triangle. The ticket office (☎ 245 5585, fax 245 5430) is across the street in the Kompleks Antarabangsa, next to the Hilton.

**Puduraya Bus Station** This hot, confusing, clamorous bus-and-taxi station is centrally located on Jalan Pudu. A few travellers have reported being robbed late at night, so stay alert. The Tourist Police office is inside the main entrance, and, opposite, is an information counter (☎ 230 0145).

Inside are dozens of bus company ticket-windows. A large signboard in front lists which destinations are served by which ticket windows. As you walk down the row of ticket counters, staff will shout out destinations, but check to be sure the departure time suits you, as they sometimes try to sell tickets for buses that aren't leaving for many hours. Buses leave from numbered platforms in the basement, and note that you'll have to look for the name of the bus company rather than your destination.

On the main runs, services are so numerous that you can sometimes just turn up and get a seat on the next bus. However, tickets should preferably be booked at least the day before, and a few days before during peak holiday periods, especially to the Cameron Highlands and other east coast destinations.

PENINSULAR MALAYSIA

Transnasional Express (☎ 238 4670) has the largest office inside the terminal and has buses to almost all major destinations. It also has a ticket outlet (☎ 202 2813) on the ground floor of the Central Market Annexe, open from 9 am to 9 pm daily. Transnasional buses are often slower than private companies', but that's because they're safer and more reliable.

Outside the terminal, on Jalan Pudu, there are at least another dozen private companies handling tickets for buses to Thailand, Singapore and some Malaysian destinations. Though not the most reliable bunch of operators, they are currently the only ones selling tickets to the Cameron Highlands.

There are only a few daily services to the Cameron Highlands and east-coast destinations, but quite-frequent departures to most other places during the day, and at night to the main towns. For the latter, try to leave as late as possible; otherwise, shortened travel times on the Lebuhraya tollway mean you'll arrive at your destination too early in the morning.

Typical fares and journey times from KL are:

| destination | fare (RM) | duration (hrs) |
| --- | --- | --- |
| Alor Setar | 22 | 6 |
| Butterworth | 18 | 4 |
| Cameron Highlands | 13 | 4 |
| Ipoh | 9.50 | 2½ |
| Johor Bahru | 16 | 4 |
| Kota Bharu | 22.60 | 6½ |
| Kuala Kedah | 21 | 6 |
| Kuala Terengganu | 21.50 | 7 |
| Kuantan | 12 | 5 |
| Lumut | 15 | 4 |
| Melaka | 8 | 2½ |
| Mersing | 16.60 | 5½ |
| Penang | 20 | 5 |
| Singapore | 23 | 5½ |
| Sungai Petani | 18 | 5 |
| Taiping | 13 | 3½ |

You can get to Puduraya bus station by taking the Star LRT to Plaza Rakyat station.

**Putra Bus Station** Though Puduraya handles buses to the east coast, there are also a number of large coach services leaving from the more-manageably-sized Putra bus station, opposite PWTC. Buses leave between 8 and 10 am, and 8 to 10 pm. There are services to Kota Bharu (RM21), Kuantan (RM12) and Kuala Terengganu (RM21.50).

Putra bus station is easily reached by taking the Star LRT to PWTC station, or a KTM Komuter train to Putra station.

**Pekeliling Bus Station** Buses to Jerantut, the jumping off point for Taman Negara National Park, and Kuala Lipis (Endau-Rompin National Park) operate only from Pekeliling bus station in the north of the city, just off Jalan Tun Razak.

Transnasional Express has departures to Kuala Lipis (seven daily, four hours, RM8) and Raub (five daily, RM5.30). Park May has six buses a day to Kuantan (4½ hours, RM11.70).

Perwira Ekspres and Bulau Restu each has several buses to Jerantut via Temerloh (3½ hours, RM9.40). Alternatively, Perkasa Ekspres and Transnasional have departures roughly every two hours between 8.30 am and 7 pm to Temerloh (RM6.10), from where regular buses run to Jerantut.

Buses run from Pekeliling to the Genting Highlands (RM2.60) every half-hour from 6.30 am to 9 pm.

Pekeliling bus station is close to Tun Razak Star LRT station.

**Klang Bus Station** From the Klang bus station in Chinatown, at the southern end of Jalan Hang Kasturi, frequent buses include No 47 to Subang airport, No 222 to Shah Alam, No 710 to Klang and Nos 58 and 793 for Pelabuhan (Port) Klang.

### Train

Kuala Lumpur is the hub of the KTM (national railway) system. Long-distance trains depart from the historic KL train station, 1km north of the unfinished KL Sentral station. The competent KTM information office (☎ 2275 7357) in the main hall can advise on schedules and check seat availability; it's open from 6.30 am to 10.30 pm daily. There's also a KTM ticket booth (☎ 245

6902) on the concourse level of Sungei Wang Plaza, near the Parkson Grand department store entrance. It's open from noon to 2.30 pm and from 3.30 to 7 pm daily.

There are daily departures for Butterworth, Wakaf Baharu (for Kota Bharu), Johor Bahru, Thailand and Singapore. Most express-train seats can be booked up to 60 days in advance. See the Malaysia Getting Around chapter for fare and schedule information. KTM Komuter trains also link KL with the Klang Valley and Seremban (see City Trains in the Getting Around section later in this chapter).

### Taxi
Long-distance taxis depart from upstairs at Puduraya bus station. They often do not make a journey much faster than buses. If you turn up early in the morning, chances are reasonable of finding other passengers waiting to share on the main west-coast runs to Johor Bahru, Melaka, Ipoh and Penang. But it's always a matter of luck and sometimes there's a long wait to get a full complement of four passengers. Otherwise, you'll have to charter a whole taxi.

Fixed whole-taxi fares include: Cameron Highlands (RM140), Genting Highlands (RM42), Ipoh (RM96), Bukit Fraser (Fraser's Hill; RM80), Johor Bahru (RM180), Lumut (RM140), Melaka (RM96) and Penang (RM220). These prices are for non-air-con – add about RM12 to RM20 for air-con, depending on the distance. Prices should include toll charges, but some taxi drivers, especially those on the Johor Bahru run, insist on charging extra. Drivers may be reluctant to take on other long-haul east-coast destinations, and fares must be bargained for.

### Car
Navigating the city's complex (and mostly one-way) traffic system will only frustrate you, but KL is the best place to hire a car for touring the peninsula. Rates start at around RM155 a day for a recent-model small car. The best deals are for longer rentals – as low as RM240 for a long weekend (Friday noon to Monday noon), or RM900 per week, including insurance and unlimited kilometres.

All the major companies have offices at the airport as well as the following city offices, which are generally open from 9 am to 6 pm weekdays, and sometimes on weekends. The best deals are usually with Orix and Hawk. There are also dozens of small hire-companies listed in the *Yellow Pages*.

**Avis** (☎ 241 7144) 40 Jalan Sultan Ismail
**Budget** (☎ 242 4693) Zasyah Travel & Tours, Wisma SPS, 32 Jalan Imbi
**Hawk** (☎ 2164 6455) Ground floor, Wisma UOA, 19 Jalan Pinang
Web site: www.hawkrac.com
**Hertz** (☎ 248 6433) Kompleks Antarabangsa, Jalan Sultan Ismail
**Mayflower Tours** (☎ 6252 1888/2163 5000) 13th floor, Wisma UOAII, 21 Jalan Pinang
**National** (☎ 248 0522) 9th floor, Menara Boustead, 69 Jalan Raja Chulan
**Orix** (☎ 242 3009) Ground floor, Federal Hotel, 35 Jalan Bukit Bintang
Web site: www.orix.com.my
**Pacific Rent-a-Car** (☎ 244 0268) Ground floor, Menara Shahzan Insas, 30 Jalan Sultan Ismail
**Thrifty** (☎ 248 8877) 14 Jalan Inai

## GETTING AROUND
Kuala Lumpur's public transport system is changing from slow, chaotic and crowded to speedy, comfortable and uncomplicated. Efforts to ease the city's chronic traffic congestion have seen massive investment in new infrastructure, including the construction of new expressways.

In future years, KL Sentral station, in the Brickfields area 1km south of the historic old train station, will be the hub of a new sophisticated rail-based urban network of KTM Komuter, LRT and Monorail (PRT) systems (see the following entries). Construction drastically slowed during the Asian economic setbacks of the late 1990s, and has yet to pick up again. Combined ticketing to facilitate passenger interchange between the various rail systems is planned, but for now the systems remain unintegrated.

### To/From KLIA
From Hentian Duta terminal on the northern outskirts of KL, Airport Coach (☎ 653 3154)

PENINSULAR MALAYSIA

buses leave for KLIA every 30 minutes from 5.30 am to 10.15 pm (one to 1½ hours, RM20/34 one way/return). At KLIA, these buses depart from the lower terminal levels from 6.45 am to 12.30 am. As Hentian Duta is not connected to KL by public transport, Airport Coach minibuses do pick-ups and drop-offs at selected downtown hotels, taking somewhat longer (RM25/45).

Airport Coach buses also run between KLIA and Chan Sow Lin Star LRT station, about 20 minutes from Masjid Jamek Star LRT station north of Chinatown (RM1.80). From Chan Sow Lin, airport buses depart every half-hour from 6.30 am to 8.30 pm (45 minutes to one hour, RM12/20). In the reverse direction, buses depart from the airport between 7.30 am and 9.30 pm.

There are plans for a train to connect KLIA and the new KL Sentral train station being built at Brickfields, but this is years away.

Taxis from KLIA operate on a fixed-fare coupon system. Purchase a coupon from a counter at the arrival hall and use it to pay the driver. Standard taxis cost RM66 and luxury taxis or family-sized minivans RM91; return tickets are significantly discounted. It's best to buy your taxi coupon before you exit arrivals to avoid the aggressive pirate taxis that hassle you to pay a few hundred ringgit for the same ride.

Going to the airport, flag down any city taxi but make sure that the agreed fare includes tolls, typically RM65 after bargaining from Chinatown.

## To/From Subang Airport
The old airport at Subang is 25km west of the city centre. Take bus No 47 (RM2) from the Jalan Sultan Mohammed bus stop opposite the Klang bus station. The trip takes 45 minutes, though it's a good idea to allow more time since traffic can be heavy.

Special taxis from the airport operate on a coupon system and the fare is RM29.50 to Chinatown or the Golden Triangle, rising to RM44.20 after midnight until 6 am. Purchase a coupon from a booth as you leave the arrivals hall and pay the driver with it.

Going to the airport, take any city taxi and negotiate a price of around RM25 to

RM30, comparable to what you'd be charged if you could actually convince the driver to use the meter.

## Bus
The two main companies are Intrakota (☎ 707 7771) and Park May Cityliner (☎ 782 6904). Intrakota's (grey with blue stripes) and Park May Cityliner's (white with red stripes) modern air-con buses run along key routes throughout the city, although the already baffling bus system has been further confused by the renumbering of some routes. Thankfully, both companies have helpful information booths, conveniently located on the northern side of Klang bus station (Cityliner) and at Jalan Sultan Mohammed bus stand (Intrakota). If you're stuck, call the English Info-line on ☎ 230 0300.

Local buses leave from many of the bus terminals around the city, including the huge Puduraya bus station on Jalan Pudu, the Klang bus station, the Jalan Sultan Mohammed bus stop south of the Central Market, and from along Medan Pasar and Lebuh Ampang near the Masjid Jamek LRT stations. The maximum fare is usually 90 sen or RM1 for destinations within the city limits; try to have correct change ready when you board, especially during rush hours or if you're boarding somewhere other than a terminal.

Since KL's inexpensive taxis and reliable LRT systems are more efficient, not to mention air-conditioned, there's little point in trying to come to grips with the bus system unless you're going to be in KL for some time. You'll only really need the bus for trips to outlying areas, such as the Batu Caves.

## City Trains
The KTM Komuter service (☎ 2272 2828) runs along existing long-distance railway lines, stopping at KL train station. The service is primarily designed for those who commute from the vast, outlying urban sprawl. It is of limited use to visitors since it does not connect central KL with any of the city's attractions, but it may still be

# KUALA LUMPUR & KLANG VALLEY TRANSPORT

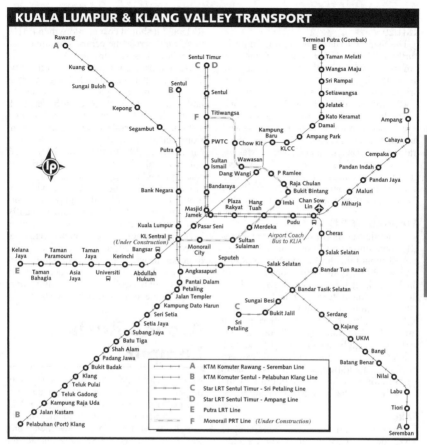

| | | A | KTM Komuter Rawang - Seremban Line |
| | | B | KTM Komuter Sentul - Pelabuhan Klang Line |
| | | C | Star LRT Sentul Timur - Sri Petaling Line |
| | | D | Star LRT Sentul Timur - Ampang Line |
| | | E | Putra LRT Line |
| | | F | Monorail PRT Line *(Under Construction)* |

useful for day trips to Selangor and Negeri Sembilan states.

The main north-south service runs from Sentul, just north of the city centre, to Pelabuhan Klang via Klang and Shah Alam in Selangor. The other line runs from Rawang, 20km north-west of the city centre, to Seremban in Negeri Sembilan, 66km south-east of KL.

Trains run every 15 to 20 minutes between approximately 6 am and 11 pm. Ticket dispensing machines are installed at stations – select your destination and the price is displayed. An RM5 'go anywhere' day-ticket allows unlimited travel on KTM Komuter trains after 9 am.

## Light Rail (LRT)

KL's pride and joy is the Light Rail Transit (LRT), a fast, frequent and inexpensive 'metro'. The mostly elevated LRT network is not integrated, however; transfers between the privately run Star and Putra LRT lines can only be made at Masjid Jamek, by leaving one system and walking across the street to the other station. An electronic control system for each checks tickets as you enter and exit via turnstiles. The minimum

PENINSULAR MALAYSIA

fare is 50 to 70 sen, and most trips cost about RM1.20.

The Star LRT runs from Sentul Timur in northern KL via Masjid Jamek to Chan Sow Lin station, where it splits into two separate lines, heading east to Ampang and south to Sri Petaling. Star LRT trains run every six to 10 minutes from 6 am to 11 or 11.30 pm.

The Putra LRT runs from Terminal Putra (Gombak) in north-eastern KL via Masjid Jamek, then south via the unfinished KL Sentral station to Bangsar and Universiti Malaya, terminating at Kelana Jaya on KL's western outskirts. The Putra LRT runs about every 10 minutes from 6 am to midnight, and from 8 am to 11 pm on Sunday and holidays.

## Monorail (PRT)

KL's public transport infrastructure will really come into its own once a new 16km elevated monorail, the People-Mover Rapid Transit (PRT), is finished. Construction of the PRT, like the incomplete KL Sentral station, has almost stopped due to the late-1990s economic downturn.

When finished, the PRT will run south from Jalan Tun Razak (near Pekeliling bus station) through the Golden Triangle to Kampung Pasir on the city's south-western outskirts. In addition, a 1km branch line in Brickfields will link the monorail to the (hopefully finished) KL Sentral station.

## Taxi

KL has plenty of taxis, and fares start at RM2 for the first kilometre, with an additional 10 sen for each 200m. From midnight to 6 am there's a surcharge of 50% on the metered fare, and extra passengers (more than two) are charged 20 sen each. RM1 is charged for luggage placed in the boot.

At these rates taxis are very cheap – perhaps, as the drivers claim, too cheap. KL's traffic problems being as they are, many drivers don't want to sit in a traffic snarl for just a couple of ringgit, and may be unwilling to go to out-of-the-way destinations from where it is hard to get a fare back. In these cases they are sometimes unwilling to use the meter (even though the law mandates it). Get out and hail another, or if you

have to bargain, fares around town start at RM5 and it should cost no more than RM10 to go right across the central city area.

Taxis at bus stations refuse to use the meter and prey on new arrivals to the city. They will ask at least double the going rate. It is always better to go down the street and hail a taxi from there, or even better, look for the closest LRT station. At the KL train station, taxis operate on a coupon system from outside platform 4. It costs RM5 to Chinatown, RM7 to the Jalan TAR/Chow Kit area and RM9 to the Golden Triangle (including RM2 luggage surcharge).

Be aware that legitimate taxis will usually only stop at officially signposted 'Perhentian Taxi' stands. You can't usually wave one down just anywhere, which is very inconvenient. When you do finally get a taxi, it may seem to head in the opposite direction to what you'd expect, simply because in KL the quickest route between two points is not necessarily the most direct one, thanks to the system of one-way streets.

# Around Kuala Lumpur

Numerous attractions lie just outside the city proper in Selangor state, although they are still inside the urban bounds of Greater KL. Many attractions farther afield in Selangor can also be visited as day- or weekend-long trips from KL. See the Selangor chapter for details.

## BATU CAVES

The huge Batu Caves are the best-known attraction near KL. They're just 15km north of the capital, a short distance off the Ipoh road. The caves are in a towering limestone formation and were little known until about 100 years ago, when an American naturalist stumbled across them. Later a small Hindu shrine was built in the vast open space, later known as Temple Cave. Each year in February almost a million pilgrims come to the caves during the Thaipusam festival in February to watch the spectacular, masochistic-looking feats of devotees (see the 'Thaipusam' boxed text in the 'Places of Worship' special section).

The main cave is reached by a straight flight of 272 steps. There are several other caves in the same formation, including a small one at the base of the outcrop, reached by crossing over a turtle pond. This cave contains an 'art gallery' (RM1) of elaborately painted sculptures of various Hindu gods. Lord Subramaniam takes centre stage as the dancing Shiva, and other deities such as the fearsome Durga, Shiva's female half, are arranged to tell parables from the Bhagavad Gita and other Hindu scriptures.

The caves are open from 7 am to 6 pm daily and can be reached by Intrakota bus No 11D (30 minutes, 90 sen) or Cityliner bus No 69 (RM1) from Medan Pasar, near the Central Market. No 11D also stops along Jalan Raja Laut in the Chow Kit area. During Thaipusam special trains and buses carry devotees and onlookers to the caves.

## ZOO NEGARA

About 13km north-east of KL, Zoo Negara (National Zoo) is laid out over 62 hectares around a central lake. The collection has a sampling of native Malaysian wildlife, as well as other animals from Asia and Africa. Though a good zoo by Asian standards, some of the animal enclosures are still sadly cramped. Elephant and pony rides (RM2) are available around lunchtime and there are elephant shows in the morning and afternoon. A shuttle takes visitors around the landscaped grounds.

The zoo is open from 9 am to 5pm daily (RM2/6 children/adults). On Sunday and holidays it's open until 6 pm and admission costs RM2 extra. Take a No 170 bus from Lebuh Ampang in Chinatown or from along Jalan Raja Laut in Chow Kit, from where you could also catch bus No 17 to the zoo.

## FORESTRY RESEARCH INSTITUTE (FRIM)

The Forestry Research Institute of Malaysia (☎ 634 2633) maintains a jungle park at Kepong, 15km north-west of the city centre, the closest park to KL and popular on weekends. It is a centre for research into forest regeneration, and though not aimed at tourists, displays roughly outline the work done by FRIM and explain the rainforest habitat and its renewal. Visitors can view close to 30 species of local and exotic bamboo, traditional medicinal-herb gardens and Malaysia's rainforest flora up close, but not much is labelled. On the grounds there is also a traditional Chengal wood house from the Terengganu region of east Peninsular Malaysia.

The main interest is the variety of short to strenuous jungle trails. For a closer inspection of the rainforest canopy, you can book a canopy walk by phoning ☎ 635 9578 in advance.

The park is open from 8 am to 6.30 pm daily. There is no public bus service from KL; a metered taxi direct to FRIM costs RM12 to RM14.

## TEMPLER PARK

Beside Hwy 1, 22km north of KL, Templer Park (☎ 691 0022) is a 1200-hectare tract of primary jungle named after the last British high commissioner of Malaysia. There are a number of marked jungle paths, swimming lagoons, an artificial lake and several waterfalls within the park boundaries.

Just north of the park is a 350m-high limestone formation known as Bukit Takun, and nearby is the smaller Anak Takun, which has many caves for exploring.

Templer Park is a half-hour ride on Tanjung Malim bus No 66 from the Puduraya bus station, on the way to Kuala Kota Bharu (for Bukit Fraser).

# Selangor

Selangor state surrounds the Federal Territory of Kuala Lumpur (KL) city. Its major borders are aquatic: the Selat Melaka (Strait of Melaka) to the west, Sungai (River) Sepang to the south, Sungai Bernam to the north and the Banjaran Titiwangsa mountain range watershed to the east.

Selangor's focus is the busy, industrial Klang Valley, which runs from KL down to the coast at Pelabuhan (Port) Klang, once Malaysia's busiest port. Shah Alam has a few modern architectural glories and Klang has reminders of the old sultanate, but it is not until you reach Kuala Selangor on the coast that you finally leave the traffic and urban sprawl behind.

Many of the state's attractions – such as the Batu Caves, Zoo Negara and Templer Park on the northern outskirts of KL – are best visited on day trips and are included at the end of the KL chapter. However, Selangor also has rewarding, off-beat stopovers in Bukit Fraser (Fraser's Hill), which straddles the state's border with Pahang; and Kuala Selangor with its wildlife watching and *kampung* (village) atmosphere.

## History

In the 15th century, Selangor was under the control of Melaka's great *bendahara* (chief minister) Tun Perak. Once Melaka fell to the Portuguese, control of Selangor was hotly contested, partly because of its rich tin reserves. The Minangkabau settlers, who had migrated to the area from Sumatra only about 100 years earlier, were displaced by Buginese immigrants from Celebes (present-day Sulawesi), who aided Dutch colonisation by hiring themselves out as mercenaries. Meanwhile, the Dutch made some fairly ineffective moves to establish control over the tin trade by overtaking, and then losing again, the forts at Kuala Linggi and Kuala Selangor. By the middle of the 18th century, the Buginese had established the current sultanate, based

## HIGHLIGHTS

- **Kuala Selangor** – spectacular fireflies and *kampung* (village) atmosphere
- **Bukit Fraser** – old-fashioned hill station with colonial charm
- **Shah Alam** – the awe-inspiring 'Blue Mosque'

at Kuala Selangor, and their sphere of influence spread as far as western Sumatra and the Riau Archipelago.

The 19th century saw an influx of Chinese merchants and miners, drawn by the rapidly growing and lucrative tin trade. Many attained powerful positions – in 1857 two Chinese merchants went into partnership with two Selangor chiefs and opened tin mines at Ampang, out of which grew the city of Kuala Lumpur.

The success of the tin trade and the growing wealth of the Chinese communities led to conflicts among the Selangor chiefs and between the miners. The outcome was a prolonged civil war, which began as a conflict only between chiefs, but before long

PENINSULAR MALAYSIA

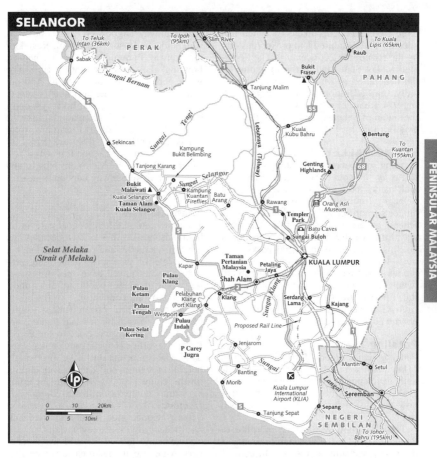

SELANGOR

the Chinese miners were dragged into the conflict. As the miners belonged to different secret societies, they fought not only against and in alliance with the chiefs but also among themselves. KL, which had been effectively controlled by 'Kapitan China' Yap Ah Loy, was captured in 1872 and razed to the ground. Its recapture in 1873 brought about an end to the civil war.

By this time the colonial British were keen to impose some order on the chaos, especially as tin production had dropped to a fraction of its former volume just when industrial Europe's demand for raw materials

was high. In 1874 the sultan was forced to accede to the installation of a British Resident at Klang, and for the next 25 years the state prospered, largely on the back of another boom in tin prices.

Perhaps the most famous of all of the British Residents was Frank Swettenham who, evincing more tolerance and cultural insight than his colleagues, smoothed relations among the sultan and the local chiefs. He cajoled the sultans of four states (Perak, Selangor, Negeri Sembilan and Pahang) into an alliance that eventually became the Federated Malay States in 1896.

PENINSULAR MALAYSIA

The federation was centrally adminis-tered from a phoenix-like KL, which had become a well-ordered and prosperous city by the turn of the 20th century. The Feder-ated Malay States led to the formation of the Federation of Malaya in 1948 and, fi-nally, the Federation of Malaysia in 1963. In 1974 Kuala Lumpur city was ceded by the sultan of Selangor and became the Fed-eral Territory.

## KLANG VALLEY

Heading south-west of KL along the Klang Highway, the **Kota Darul Ehsan** ceremonial arch marks the boundary between KL and Selangor. It memorialises the sultan of Se-langor's 'sacrifice' of Kuala Lumpur to the federal government. Apart from the arch-way, little else distinguishes this corridor of housing estates and industrial parks. Just over the boundary, Petaling Jaya (PJ) blends into Shah Alam, the state capital, which blends into Klang, the old royal cap-ital. Efficient transport connections to and from KL make for easy day trips, but there's not a whole lot to see.

### Petaling Jaya

Petaling Jaya is a modern suburb of KL, just 11km south-west of the city centre. Origi-nally developed as a dormitory town, PJ has grown so successfully and rapidly that it is now a major industrial centre in its own right.

The **Universiti Malaya** is en route to Petaling Jaya. On the university grounds is the musty **Muzium Seni Asia** (Museum of Asian Arts). It houses an overflowing col-lection of Asian ceramics, Islamic calligra-phy and a few Orang Asli carvings, but there is little labelling in English. The mu-seum is open from 9 am to 5 pm Monday to Saturday (closed from noon to 2.45 pm on Friday); admission is free. Also on the sprawling campus grounds are a **botanical garden** and a small **biomedical museum**. Take the Putra LRT from KL to the Univer-siti stop (RM1.20), then a shuttle bus (50 sen) or a metered taxi to the campus.

PJ is well supplied with shopping malls and amusement places popular with well-to-do KL residents. Malaysia's first theme park, **Sunway Lagoon** (☎ 735 8000), has waterslides and a surf-wave pool. Next door the Sunway Pyramid mall has a cineplex, bowling alley and ice skating rink. The water park is open from noon to 7.30 pm weekdays (closed Tuesday) and 10 am to 7.30 pm on weekends and holidays; entry costs RM18/29 for children/adults. Take the Putra LRT to Kelana Jaya terminus, from where shuttle bus No 900 runs every 30 minutes to Sunway Lagoon (50 sen). City-Liner bus No 51 and Metro bus Nos 10 and 11 go directly to Sunway Lagoon from KL's Klang bus station.

### Shah Alam

The new capital of Selangor state is an hour's drive west of KL. Two decades ago it was just a rubber-and-palm plantation, but in the late 1970s a massive building pro-gram spawned a well-developed infrastruc-ture, some enormous public buildings and a rapidly growing population.

The new Dahrul Ehsan Tourist Centre (☎ 553 6266) is at Shah Alam Square, op-posite the Holiday Inn close to the PKNS Plaza. The office is open from 9 am to 7 pm daily. The competent staff have surprisingly helpful brochures and can answer queries on the entire state of Selangor, including agro-tourism opportunities at **Banghuris Homestay** (☎ 7874 0825, fax 7874 0108) in Sepang. Good-value handicrafts and cul-tural videos are on display upstairs.

Like many planned cities, Shah Alam has very wide streets and great distances be-tween parts of the city, making it very dif-ficult to get around. Most sights, however, are at or near the attractive central **Lake Gardens**. The showpiece is **Masjid Sultan Salahuddin Abdul Aziz Shah**, nicknamed the 'Blue Mosque' for its blue aluminium dome centred in a rosette of verses from the Quran. This huge, gleaming mosque is Malaysia's largest and accommodates up to 24,000 worshippers; its four minarets are the tallest in the world at over 140m.

Millions of ringgit have been lavished on the **State Museum**, a short walk from the mosque through the Lake Gardens. The museum is an impressive structure, both inside and out. After a couple of hours here you'll know everything there is to know about Selangor and the sultan. The museum's Web site, at www.selangor.gov.my/muzium, has in-depth descriptions of the collections and state history. The museum is open from 10 am to 5.30 pm, 12.15 to 2.45 pm on Friday (closed Tuesday); entry is free.

Four kilometres north of the lake garden is **Taman Pertanian Malaysia** at Bukit Cahaya Seri Alam. This 'agroforestry theme park' is a popular weekend escape for KL families. It's a curious blend of landscaped gardens, rice paddies, rubber and native fruit trees, cocoa and coffee plants, orchid and cactus gardens, a fishing lake and an aviary; it also has forest trails and a canopy walkway. It's open from 8.30 am to 6 pm daily (closed Monday).

**Places to Stay & Eat** The luxurious *Concorde Hotel* (☎ 552 2200, 3 Jalan Tengku Ampuan Zabedah C9/C, Section 9) offers rooms from RM280, and also has a pool. *Raku* (☎ 552 2233) restaurant and contemporary art gallery, open from 11 am until midnight, is also situation here. You'll need to take a taxi to the hotel from the Lake Gardens, as it's too far to walk.

On the ground floor of the central *PKNS Plaza* are a number of fast-food places. At the Holiday Inn on Shah Alam Square, the *Gardenia Food Court* offers a lunch buffet for RM20 per person.

**Getting There & Away** A No 222 Shah Alam bus from KL's Klang bus station will drop you in front of PKNS plaza, from where it's a short walk to all the sights; the bus continues on to the Taman Pertanian Malaysia (RM1.60). Alternatively, you could take a frequent Komuter train from KL to Shah Alam station, but from there it's another bus or taxi ride to the Lake Gardens.

## Klang

Klang (sometimes still spelt Kelang) is the old royal capital of Selangor, where the British installed their first Resident in 1874.

Its few attractions are in the old city, south of the bus station and across the river, nearer to the train station.

**Masjid Di Raja Sultan Suleiman**, 1km south of the train station along Jalan Raya Timur, is a blend of Art Deco and Middle Eastern influences. Behind the mosque, on Jalan Istana, is **Istana Alam Shah**, the main palace of the sultan before the capital was moved to Shah Alam. There are other mosques and minor palaces scattered about, and all are signposted from the intersection in front of the train station.

Klang's bus station is opposite the My Din shopping complex, on the northern side of the river. There are several buses every hour to KL's Klang bus station (RM2) or Kuala Selangor (RM2). Express buses between KL and Pelabuhan Klang also stop in Klang. Klang's taxi station is one block east, behind the bus station.

Coming from KL, KTM Komuter trains are more convenient as the train station, a 10-minute walk over the bridge from the bus station, is closer to the sights.

## Pelabuhan Klang

Some 41km south-west of KL, 8km past Klang, is Pelabuhan Klang (formerly Port Swettenham). It's hard to believe, but Pelabuhan Klang was KL's main seaport until the establishment of a major new harbour at Westport on Pulau Indah. Though not a particularly attractive place, Pelabuhan Klang is renowned for its excellent seafood, particularly chilli crabs (about RM35 per plate).

The 30-minute ferry trip to **Pulau Ketam** (Crab Island) is a popular weekend excursion for KL residents. The island has a stilt fishing village and Chinese seafood restaurants. Public ferries leave from the wharf every one to two hours between 9.40 am and 5.30 pm (until 7 pm on Saturday); the last ferry back from Pulau Ketam is at 4.30 pm (5.50 pm on Saturday).

One of the few places to stay in Pelabuhan Klang is *Embassy Hotel* (☎ 368 6901, 2 Jalan Kem), about 600m towards the town centre from the port. Air-con doubles with bathroom cost RM52, but you may as well press on to Kuala Selangor or KL instead.

PENINSULAR MALAYSIA

PENINSULAR MALAYSIA

**Getting There & Away** Buses from KL's Klang bus station run to Pelabuhan Klang via Klang, but they only stop in town about a kilometre from the port. KTM Komuter trains also run to/from the capital and Klang, and the station is just a stone's throw from the wharf.

Ferries to Tanjung Balai (Asahan) in Sumatra depart from Pelabuhan Klang every day except Monday at 11 am (3½ hours, RM90/170 one way/return). Doyan Shipping & Forwarding (☎ 365 3073) and NTV Times Travel & Tours (☎ 365 5406) have ticket counters inside the passenger-ferry terminal, opposite the KTM station at the end of Persiaran Raja Muda Musa. As Tanjung Balai is not a visa-free entry point you must have an Indonesian visa before boarding.

## KUALA SELANGOR

Where Sungai Selangor meets the sea is the old royal capital of Kuala Selangor. This small town was conquered by the Dutch when they invaded Selangor in 1784, then became the scene of ongoing battles and civil disturbances, even after British intervention in 1874.

Well off the beaten tourist track, Kuala Selangor has an enjoyable kampung atmosphere and a few notable points of interest. It's well worth a stopover for those venturing along this rewarding back route to Perak state.

### Bukit Malawati

The flat coastal plain along this stretch of coast is broken by Bukit Malawati, the hill overlooking the town. It is a pleasant walk through landscaped parklands and forest to the top, with views across the mangrove coastline.

Bukit Malawati was an ideal site for monitoring shipping in the Straits of Melaka, first for the sultans of Selangor, then for the Dutch and British. The hill was previously the site of two forts, one built by Malays during the reign of Selangor's second sultan (1778–1826). The Dutch destroyed it during their invasion in 1784, then rebuilt and named it Fort Atlingsburg after their governor-general. The fort was quickly recaptured by the sultan in 1785, repeatedly changing hands and being fought over – all that remains are some sections of wall and cannons presided over by wild monkeys at the hilltop lighthouse. Farther downhill, the second fort became **Makam Di Raja Kota Malawati**, the mausoleum of the local raja. Scattered around are some fine colonial bungalows, now the preserve of government officials.

The road up Bukit Malawati starts one block behind the shops facing the old bus station in the town centre. It does a clockwise loop of the hill; you can walk up and around in about an hour.

### Taman Alam Kuala Selangor

This 240-hectare nature park is on the estuary of Sungai Selangor, 2km outside town towards the new bus station. The turn-off to the park is at Jalan Klinik, set back a few hundred metres from the highway. This park of mangroves and some secondary forest is noted for its **birdlife**, especially mangrove waders such as the rare spoonbilled sandpiper and Nordmann's greenshank, best seen at dusk. Around 150 species have been sighted. The park is also home to silver leaf monkeys, and you may be lucky enough to spot otters, nocturnal leopard cats and civets.

To aid in bird-watching, two watchtowers and several hides have been constructed, and two boardwalks lead through the mangroves to the sea. Tame nature trails, which take 25 minutes to 2½ hours to complete, radiate from the visitors' centre. The main trails are dirt roads – the side trails are more interesting.

Entry to the park costs RM2 and the visitors' centre is open daily. Be advised that the park may be deserted except for local men on motorbikes who seem to have nothing better to do than hassle travellers, especially women.

### Fireflies

Of the 130-odd species of firefly (*kelip kelip* in Bahasa Malaysia), those of South-East Asia are the most spectacular, noted for their displays of synchronised flashing. The folded-wing fireflies *(Pteroptyx tener)* gather in particular berembang trees along the banks of Sungai Selangor. Some of these mangrove-type trees are ablaze with flashes, while others fail to attract any. When large numbers gather (sometimes in the thousands) their flashing becomes synchronised at about three flashes per second.

This natural light show can be seen at a few places, notably Kampung Kuantan, 10km east of Kuala Selangor. Malay-style wooden boats row out on the river to the show trees and their dazzling displays. Boats take four people at RM10 each for the 45-minute trip, and leave on demand throughout the evening from around 8 until 10.30 pm. The trips are not recommended on full-moon or rainy nights, when the fireflies are not at their luminous best. Take mosquito repellent.

To reach the village take the turn-off to Batang Berjuntai, 2km south of Kuala Selangor. A taxi from Kuala Selangor costs RM30 for the return trip. This is a very popular excursion for tour groups and KL residents. One reliable operator is Ecstasy Travel (☎ 442 5688, fax 441 9864) in KL – see Organised Tours in the Kuala Lumpur chapter.

You can also see fireflies by motorboat at Kampung Bukit Belimbing; the owner of the Melawati Ria Hotel in Kuala Selangor has more information on how to arrange this. See the following entry for details.

### Places to Stay & Eat

Kuala Selangor is just one long block of shops next to the old bus station. Directly opposite is *Hotel Kuala Selangor (☎ 889 2709, 90B Jalan Stesen)*, with spotless fan/air-con rooms for RM25/38; rooms with air-con and bathroom cost RM43. One street back towards Bukit Malawati, *Melawati Ria Hotel (☎ 889 1268, 15 Jalan Raja Jalil)* is an older hotel with air-con rooms from RM40. The helpful, English-speaking owner takes good care of her guests and can suggest day trips and places to see the fireflies.

Another attractive option, but a long walk from town, is right in the nature park.

*Taman Alam Kuala Selangor (☎ 889 2294)* has small, simple A-frames for RM25, and larger four-person chalets with bathroom for RM45. A kitchen is available but cooking utensils must be hired.

In town, *Seri Kampong* restaurant *(36 Jalan Raja Jalil)* and *Waterfall Restaurant* next to the Hotel Kuala Selangor come recommended by travellers. Several kilometres outside town on the way to Kampung Kuantan, *New River View* restaurant serves fresh seafood on the riverbank – follow the lobster signs.

### Getting There & Away

Buses run roughly hourly between Kuala Selangor and KL's Puduraya bus and taxi station (two hours, RM5.50). Air-con buses run every 15 minutes between Kuala Selangor and Klang (1¼ hours, RM2). Heading north from Kuala Selangor to Perak state, first take one of the old rattlers to Tanjong Karang for connections to Teluk Intan.

Many bus services originate from the new bus station, 2km outside the town centre. If you're headed to KL or Teluk Intan, it's best to start there; take a local bus (60 sen) from the old bus station, or it's a 20-minute walk from town.

Approximate fares for a taxi from Kuala Selangor are: KL (RM40), Klang (RM20) and Teluk Intan (RM52).

### KAJANG

This town, 22km south of KL on the KL-Seremban route, is said to have the best satay in Malaysia. If your meal time is approaching, stop off at the row of food stalls on the main street for a taste.

Frequent KTM Komuter trains between KL and Seremban all stop in Kajang.

### ORANG ASLI MUSEUM

Built in 1995, this small museum has extensive exhibits that give insight into the life and culture of Peninsular Malaysia's 80,000 indigenous inhabitants. Highlights include Mah Meri carved spirit masks, musical instruments (including 'nose flutes' that imitate bird and insect noises) and blowpipes. The museum's positive eco-philosophy aims to show that the Orang Asli have something to teach mainstream Malaysia about how to live in harmony with nature.

The museum is open from 9 am to 5 pm Saturday to Thursday; donations are requested (RM5 or better would be reasonable). It is 24km north of KL, set back across from the Hospital Orang Asli Gombak on the Old Pahang road. Take the hourly Len Seng bus No 174 from Lebuh Ampang in KL (one hour, RM1).

## GENTING HIGHLANDS

Genting Highlands is a thoroughly modern hill station designed for the affluent citizens of KL, just 50km to the south. While the style of other Malaysian hill stations is Old English, concrete high-rise blocks dominate Genting's landscape. At the older hill stations the entertainment is jungle walks, but here it's nightclubs – and Malaysia's only casino, offering all the usual Las Vegas–style games and Eastern favourites like *tai sai*.

Instead of waterfalls and mountain views, Genting's four-hectare artificial lake has boating facilities and is encircled by a miniature railway in the outdoor kiddie theme-park (there's an indoor one, too). Naturally there's a golf course, 700m below, near the lower cable-car station. There's also a bowling alley; a cinema; and Chin Swee Temple, a cave temple on the road up to the highlands. Genting has cooler weather like any other hill station; the main part of the resort is almost 2000m above sea level.

### Places to Stay

There are four upmarket hotels on the Highlands proper, and all are run by *Genting Highlands Resort* (☎ 2162 3555, ☻ room rsv@genting.com.my). The KL office of Resorts World Berhad (☎ 2162 3555, fax 2161 6611), in Wisma Genting on Jalan Sultan Ismail, also accepts reservations. Rates vary enormously over low, shoulder (school holidays and June), peak (Saturday nights and November to January) and super-peak (Chinese and Western New Year's) seasons. The resort's flash Web site, at www.genting.com.my, has comprehensive listings of promotional discounts, recreational facilities and current events.

*Theme Park Hotel* has the least expensive rooms, starting from RM120/220 in low/super-peak season, while *Resort Hotel* charges RM160/290 low/peak for somewhat preferable rooms. *Genting Hotel* and *Highlands Hotel* have every facility imaginable, from saunas and swimming pools to tennis courts. Rooms from RM190/350 low/peak at Genting are better bang for your ringgit – the aging rooms at the Highlands are overpriced at RM210/370 low/peak.

A few kilometres below the bus and lower cable-car station, *Awana Golf & Country Resort* (☎ 211 3015) has doubles for RM120/200 low/peak, and offers swimming, tennis, squash, golf and horse riding.

### Getting There & Away

Buses leave from KL's Pekeliling bus station every 30 minutes for Genting Highlands (1½ hours, RM2.60). From Puduraya bus and taxi station, Bas Ekspres runs equally frequent services to the Highlands (RM2.30); a taxi will cost RM52. There are also direct bus services from Kuala Lumpur International Airport (KLIA) via Hentian Duta to the Highlands (RM22, including the Skyway).

From the Genting Highlands bus station, the precipitous 3.4km-long Genting Skyway cable car hums up past kitsch sculptures scattered in the rainforest below to the main resort, 700 vertical metres above, in 15 minutes (RM6 return, or RM3 with an in-bound Pekeliling bus stub). The cable car operates from 7.30 am to 11 pm daily (until 2 am on Saturday). After hours, the Awana Skyway will take you up or down (hourly).

## BUKIT FRASER
☎ 09

Bukit Fraser is named after Louis James Fraser, a reclusive ore-trader and mule train operator who lived here at the turn of the 20th century. It's said he ran gambling-and-opium dens, but these had vanished (along with Fraser himself) by 1910, when Bishop Ferguson-Davie of Singapore came looking for Fraser and recognised the area's potential as a hill station.

Of all the hill stations, Fraser's retains the most colonial charm. The station, set at a cool 1524m altitude, is too quiet and relatively undeveloped to attract the high-rollers drawn to Genting Highlands or the hundreds of backpackers spotted in the Cameron Highlands. There is relatively little to do besides relax in the cool and enjoy a jungle stroll and the views.

Bukit Fraser deserves more visitors than it sees. It can be done as a (long) day trip from KL, but it's best to gather a few people and descend upon one of the charming state-run stone bungalows for an overnight stay. Though a family destination, it also has a reputation as a resort for illicit liaisons, but old-fashioned service prevails at Fraser's and discretion is assured.

## Information

The tiny village at the western end of the golf course is the centre of Bukit Fraser. Here you'll find the post office and, under the Puncak Inn, the Bukit Fraser Development Corporation (FHDC) information office (☎ 362 2201). It's open from 8 am to 10 pm daily, but closes for lunch. The office staff have a few maps and brochures and can book all FHDC accommodation in Bukit Fraser.

A few minutes' walk uphill is the WWF Nature Education Centre (☎/fax 362 2517), with a library and small museum on local flora and fauna. Up-to-date and detailed hiking trail guides and maps are available here. The excellent, knowledgeable staff can answer queries and organise guided jungle walks.

Maybank has a small branch at the Quest resort, open from 9.30 am to 4.30 pm weekdays and until 11 am on Saturday. Back in Kuala Kota Bharu (KKB), the turn-off to Bukit Fraser from Hwy 1, there is a Maybank with ATMs opposite the bus station.

Like the Genting Highlands, Bukit Fraser is right on the Selangor-Pahang state border.

PENINSULAR MALAYSIA

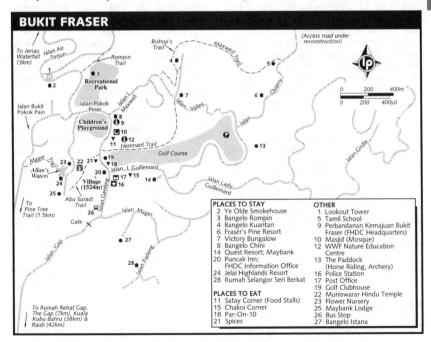

**BUKIT FRASER**

To Jeriau Waterfall (3km)
Jalan Air Terjun
Bishop's Trail
Maxwell Trail
Rompin Trail
(Access road under reconstruction)
Jalan Bukit Pokok Pain
Jalan Pokok Pines
Recreational Park
Jalan L Maxwell
Jalan Valley
Quarry
Children's Playground
Jalan Maxwell
Hemnant Trail
Golf Course
Jalan Girdle
Mager Trail
Allan's Waters
Village (1524m)
Jalan L Guillemard
Jalan Genting
Jalan Lady Guillemard
Abu Suradi Trail
To Pine Tree Trail (1.5km)
Gate
Jalan Mager
Jalan Gap
Jalan Padang
To Rumah Rehat Gap, The Gap (7km), Kuala Kubu Bahru (38km) & Raub (42km)

0   200   400m
0   200   400yd

**PLACES TO STAY**
2 Ye Olde Smokehouse
3 Bangelo Rompin
4 Bangelo Kuantan
6 Fraser's Pine Resort
7 Victory Bungalow
8 Bangelo Chini
14 Quest Resort; Maybank
20 Puncak Inn;
   FHDC Information Office
24 Jelai Highlands Resort
28 Rumah Selangor Seri Berkat

**PLACES TO EAT**
11 Satay Corner (Food Stalls)
15 Chakoi Corner
18 Par-On-10
21 Spices

**OTHER**
1 Lookout Tower
5 Tamil School
9 Perbandanan Kemajuan Bukit
   Fraser (FHDC Headquarters)
10 Masjid (Mosque)
12 WWF Nature Education
   Centre
13 The Paddock
   (Horse Riding, Archery)
16 Police Station
17 Post Office
19 Golf Clubhouse
22 Muniswarar Hindu Temple
23 Flower Nursery
25 Maybank Lodge
26 Bus Stop
27 Bangelo Istana

Though it's usually claimed by Pahang, almost all visitors come through Selangor, and the state border actually cuts right through the town.

## Things to See & Do

As in the Cameron Highlands in Perak state, there are many **wild flowers**, dense **jungle** and impressive towering trees, though walks are mostly limited to quick strolls off and on the quiet paved roads.

One of the only real trails of note is the 2½-hour walk from the children's playground (complete with go-karts and minigolf) to the small Tamil school. The walk is strenuous and the trail is muddy in parts. For less-vigorous walkers, the **Hemmant Trail**, which takes only 20 minutes, leads from the side of the WWF office to Victory Bungalow. More rewarding, but also more difficult, the **Pine Tree Trail** starts a few kilometres west of town near the Admiralty and High Pines bungalows. The steep 6km trail takes four hours to scramble to the peak of Pine Tree Hill; check in at the WWF office for a detailed trail guide before setting out.

Bukit Fraser is a bird-watcher's delight, with 265 species sighted, included 100 resident **birds**. Native species include the rare cutia, mountain peacock-pheasant, rusty-naped pitta and Malaysian whistling-thrush.

At the picturesque nine-hole **golf course**, where dusky leaf monkeys wander, a game costs RM30/40 on weekdays/weekends, plus RM15 for club rental. Table tennis, snooker, a gym and sauna are available at the clubhouse. At the Paddock to the east of the golf course, you can go **horse riding** or practice **archery**. Aquatic enthusiasts can hire a paddle boat or do some fishing at **Allan's Waters**, a small lake next to the flower nursery and Muniswarar Hindu temple.

About 5km north-west of the town centre is **Jeriau Waterfall**, with a swimming pool fed from the falls. It's easily reached via Jalan Air Terjun, passing a **lookout tower** along the way.

## Places to Stay

Most of the accommodation is run by the FHDC, a government-contracted *bumiputra*

(indigenous Malaysian) organisation, and there are no real budget options. Rates at FHDC lodgings are slightly lower during the week; the 'peak season' is on weekends and public holidays, when bookings (☎ 362 2201) are strongly recommended. All have bathrooms and showers, but rooms are usually musty due to the cool, damp climate at Fraser's.

**Places to Stay – Mid-Range** Above the little shopping centre close to where the bus stops is *Puncak Inn (☎ 362 2201)*. Although it's convenient and looks inviting from the outside, rooms with TV and hot shower are rather ordinary and expensive from RM38.50 to RM61.60 on weekdays, RM55 to RM88 on weekends.

The FHDC also has *bangelo* (bungalows) – well worth the extra money. They are stone buildings with pleasant gardens, good views, large lounge areas and plenty of colonial grace. Many of the dozens of bungalows scattered around Bukit Fraser are privately leased out by the FHDC. Availability to the public changes, so ask in advance at the information office under the Puncak Inn.

At the time of research, available bungalows were the Kuantan, Rompin and Chini. *Bangelo Kuantan* has a pleasant hillside aspect but is almost 3km from the centre. *Bangelo Rompin* is only 1km north-west of the centre; *Bangelo Chini* is the nearest, up on a hillside above the FHDC headquarters, although the views are partly obscured. Most FHDC bungalows are a fair way from the bus stop, but once you get your gear there, it is a pleasant walk around the roads. All the bungalows cost RM88 for large rooms, and food is provided by the caretakers if there is enough demand; negotiate the price beforehand, as the caretakers usually expect to be paid much more than the set price (RM28).

Another option is *Rumah Selangor Seri Berkat*, the Selangor government resthouse on Jalan Padang, across the state line on the south side of Bukit Fraser. Book through the District Office (☎ 03-804 1026) in KKB. This two-storey colonial edifice built in 1926 has large rooms with high ceilings for RM65, and even larger VIP rooms for RM85.

The Selangor government also runs the wonderfully old-fashioned **Rumah Rehat Gap** (☎ 362 2227), at the Gap turn-off from the main road 8km below Bukit Fraser. Spacious rooms cost RM62 with bathroom and they're big enough for three people, with room to spare.

**Places to Stay – Top End** Most of the top-end hotels offer discounts of around 30% on weekdays and in the low season.

Overlooking the golf course is the modern **Quest Resort** (☎ 362 2300, fax 362 2284), with rapidly aging rooms from RM99/109 on weekdays/weekends. **Jelai Highlands Resort** (☎ 362 2600, fax 362 2604), on the south side of Allan's Waters, has spacious if slightly damp doubles overlooking the lake for RM80/140 for deluxe/family rooms, plus RM20 on weekends.

Popular with families and NGO types, the bland **Fraser's Pine Resort** (☎ 362 2122, fax 362 2288, ❷ frasershill@hotmail.com; in KL ☎ 03-704 3422) has well-kept one/two/three bedroom apartments for RM288/330/440 during peak periods. There is a reasonable coffee house in the main lodge.

Fraser's classiest lodging is **Ye Olde Smokehouse** (☎ 362 2226, fax 362 2035, ❷ yoshfh@tm.net.my), a mock-Tudor building in the same style as the Smokehouse in the Cameron Highlands. With its exposed beams, log fires, stained-wood armchairs and the lingering smell of roasts, it has all the charm of a country manse. Standard twins/doubles cost from RM308 including full English breakfast, and more-luxurious rooms are also available.

Other privately owned bungalows and condominiums are sometimes available for rent, but advance bookings are necessary. The FHDC can help and the restaurants below the Puncak Inn sometimes advertise space on their bulletin boards.

**Places to Eat**
The small shopping centre at the Puncak Inn is a scale model of Malaysia's multiethnic community. At one end is the Chinese **Hill View**, and at the other is the Malay **Arzed**, both serving simple meals and snacks. Between the two is the **Restoran Puncak**, serving roti canai (flat bread dipped in dhal or curry) for 60 sen any time of day.

Across the road, **Par-On-10** terrace restaurant at the golf club has more-varied Western and Malaysian dishes at moderate prices. In the evening it turns up the music and becomes a disco/karaoke lounge. Just uphill, **Spices** serves Western food like fish and chips (RM11.50) and sirloin steaks (RM17.50). Farther uphill, just below the WWF office, **Satay Corner** has basic, delicious hawker fare.

The simple **Chakoi Corner** Malay restaurant is below the Quest Resort, which also has its own glass-enclosed restaurant with great views. A Devonshire tea in an English garden at **Ye Olde Smokehouse** is a pleasant if somewhat expensive experience at RM14.50.

**Getting There & Away**
Bukit Fraser is 103km north of KL and 240km from Kuantan on the east coast. The usual access is via Kuala Kubu Bahru (KKB), 62km north of KL, just off Hwy 1 and the KL-Butterworth railway line.

From platform 20 or 21 of KL's Puduraya bus station, take a No 66 Tanjung Malim bus to KKB (1¾ hours, RM3.90). These buses run roughly every 30 minutes (via the old Ipoh road, not the freeway), but to ensure connections to Bukit Fraser you must take one no later than either 6.30 am or 12.30 pm. Otherwise, a taxi from KKB to Bukit Fraser is RM50. A direct taxi all the way from KL's Puduraya bus station costs around RM80; in the reverse direction it'll cost nearly double.

Buses to Bukit Fraser run via the Gap, a mountain pass on the KKB-Raub road. The 11km-long road up the back side of Bukit Fraser via the Tamil school and Fraser's Pine Resort was washed out, though it's now under reconstruction. For the time being the old 8km-long road, which descends directly from Bukit Fraser village centre, has an alternating one-way traffic

PENINSULAR MALAYSIA

system, with fixed times for uphill and downhill traffic.

From KKB buses depart for Bukit Fraser at 8.30 am and 2 pm, returning from Fraser's to KKB shortly after 10 am and 4 pm (1½ hours, RM2.30). If you don't want to wait until 4 pm for the last bus from Bukit Fraser back to KKB, you can walk down the Gap in about 1½ hours (8km) and catch the KKB-bound bus from Raub that passes by the Gap around 3.30 pm. If you're coming from Raub via that bus, wait at the Gap turn-off for the next bus up to Bukit Fraser. If you plan to head east after visiting Fraser's, the 4 pm bus back to KKB can drop you off on the main road beneath the Gap to meet the Raub-bound bus that passes by at around 5 pm. From Raub you can continue to Jerantut and Kuala Lipis, though maybe not the same day.

Bukit Fraser is open to private vehicles, but drivers are warned that there's no fuel station in Fraser's; the nearest places with fuel are Raub and KKB.

# Perak

Perak is the second-largest state on the peninsula at 21,000 sq km and has a population of just over two million. For centuries the state's fame rested on its rich tin deposits; in fact, it gained its name from the ore (*perak* means 'silver' in Malay). Perak also gave birth to the rubber industry, another mainstay of the Malaysian economy.

For the visitor, the main attractions of Perak are the island of Pangkor, which lies just off the southern coast; the historic town of Kuala Kangsar; and the cave temples outside the capital city of Ipoh, all of which are highlighted on-line at www.perak.gov.my. Perak is also the access point for the Cameron Highlands, Malaysia's premier hill station and one of the country's most justifiably popular tourist destinations.

## History

The current sultanate of Perak dates back to the early 16th century, when the eldest son of the last sultan of Melaka, Sultan Muzaffar Shah, established his own dynasty on the banks of the Sungai (River) Perak. Being so rich in tin, the state was regularly threatened.

Dutch efforts in the 17th century to monopolise the tin trade had little result, but remains of their forts can still be seen on Pulau Pangkor (Pangkor Island) and at the mouth of the Sungai Perak. In the 18th century the Buginese from the south and the Siamese to the north made concerted attempts to dominate Perak; if it weren't for British assistance in the 1820s, the state would have come under Siam's domination.

The British had remained reluctant to intervene in the peninsula's affairs, but growing investment from the Strait Settlements, along with the burgeoning rubber industry and rich tin mines of Perak, committed their interest. The mines also attracted a great influx of Chinese immigrants, who soon formed rival clan groups allied with local Malay chiefs, all of whom battled to control the mines.

## HIGHLIGHTS

- **Cameron Highlands** – cool heights of lush rainforest surrounding tea plantations and strawberry fields
- **Pulau Pangkor** – a rural island with lovely beaches, untouched jungle and bustling villages
- **Kuala Kangsar** – the magnificent Masjid Ubudiah, set in a graceful, riverside royal town

**PENINSULAR MALAYSIA**

The Perak sultanate was in disarray, and fighting among successors to the throne gave the British their opportunity to step in, making the first real colonial incursion on the peninsula in 1874. The governor, Sir Andrew Clarke, convened a meeting at Pulau Pangkor at which Sultan Abdullah was installed on the throne in preference to Sultan Ismail, the other major contender. The Pangkor Treaty that ensued required that the sultan accept a British Resident, to be consulted on all issues other than those relating to religion or Malay custom.

Though the Resident had no executive authority, this foot in the door soon helped

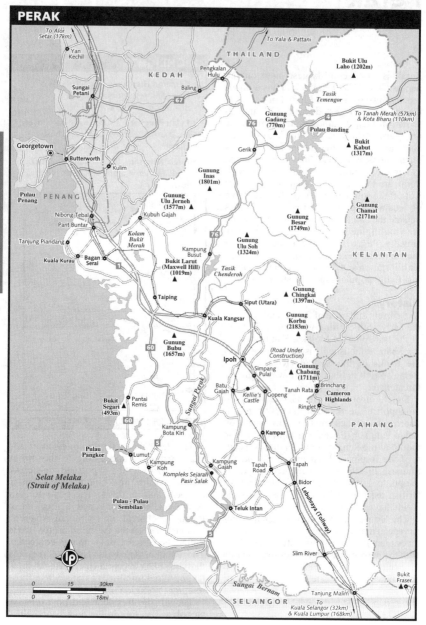

PERAK

To Alòr Setar (17km)
To Yala & Pattani
THAILAND

Yan Kechil
Pengkalan Hulu
KEDAH
Baling
Sungai Petani
Bukit Ulu Laho (1202m)
Tasik Temengor
Gunung Gadang (770m)
To Tanah Merah (57km) & Kota Bharu (110km)
Pulau Banding
Gerik
Georgetown
Butterworth
Kulim
Bukit Kabut (1317m)
Gunung Inas (1801m)
Pulau Penang
PENANG
Gunung Chamat (2171m)
Gunung Ulu Jerneh (1577m)
Nibong Tebal
Parit Buntar
Kubuh Gajah
Kolam Bukit Merah
Tanjung Piandang
Gunung Besar (1749m)
Kampung Busut
Bagan Serai
Kuala Kurau
Bukit Larut (Maxwell Hill) (1019m)
Gunung Ulu Soh (1324m)
KELANTAN
Tasik Chenderoh
Taiping
Siput (Utara)
Kuala Kangsar
Gunung Chingkai (1397m)
Gunung Korbu (2183m)
Gunung Bubu (1657m)
(Road Under Construction)
Ipoh
Gunung Chabang (1711m)
Simpang Pulai
Batu Gajah
Kellie's Castle
Gopeng
Tanah Rata
Brinchang
Cameron Highlands
Bukit Segari (493m)
Pantai Remis
Ringlet
PAHANG
Kampung Bota Kiri
Kampar
Pulau Pangkor
Lumut
Kampung Koh
Kampung Gajah
Kompleks Sejarah Pasir Salak
Tapah Road
Tapah
Selat Melaka (Strait of Melaka)
Sungai Perak
Bidor
Pulau - Pulau Sembilan
Teluk Intan
Lebuhraya (Tollway)
Slim River
Bukit Fraser
0  15  30km
0  9  18mi
Sungai Bernam
SELANGOR
Tanjung Malim
To Kuala Selangor (32km) & Kuala Lumpur (168km)

PENINSULAR MALAYSIA

to escalate British rule. In 1875, only one year after the Pangkor Treaty, Sultan Abdullah was forced, under threat of deposition, to accept administration by British officials on his behalf. Various Perak chiefs united in their desire to get rid of the Resident, JWW Birch, who was assassinated at Pasir Salak in November 1875.

Colonial troops were called in to fight what proved to be a short-lived war, Sultan Abdullah was exiled to the Seychelles, and a new British-sanctioned sultan was installed. Hugh Low, well-versed in Malay affairs and language, became the next British Resident in Kuala Kangsar and proved to be a much more able administrator. He assumed control of taxes from the tin mines and practised greater intervention in state affairs, while the sultans maintained their status but were increasingly effete figureheads, bought out with stipends. The first railway in the state, from Taiping to Port Weld, was built in 1885, to transport the wealth of tin; the result was rapid development in Taiping and Ipoh.

In 1896 Perak, along with Selangor, Pahang and Negeri Sembilan, became part of the Federated Malay States. The Resident system persisted, however, even after the Japanese invasion and WWII, ending only when Perak became part of the Federation of Malaya in 1948.

## TANJUNG MALIM TO IPOH

The road north from Kuala Lumpur (KL) crosses the state border from Selangor into Perak at Tanjung Malim. If you have your own transport, you can get off the Lebuhraya (East-West Highway) tollway and take the old Hwy 1 through a number of diverting towns. The first of these is Slim River, where British forces made an unsuccessful last-ditch attempt to halt the Japanese advance through the peninsula during WWII.

The first main town is Bidor, famous for its guava and smelly *petai* beans, where you can turn off for Teluk Intan (see that section, following), 42km to the west. Kampung Pasir Salak, 25km north of Teluk Intan, is a small village of some historical interest (see the Kompleks Sejarah Pasir Salak entry later). From this village you can follow the valley of the Sungai Perak to Kampung Bota Kiri. This river valley was the original home of the Perak sultanate and is dotted with royal graves. From Kampung Bota Kiri you can take the road to Lumut on the coast or travel north-east through the *kampung* (villages) to Ipoh.

On the highway north of Bidor is Tapah, the gateway to the Cameron Highlands. Farther north is Kampar, famous for its pomelo orchards; many pomelo stalls line the highway.

### Teluk Intan

Once known as Teluk Anson, after the early colonial planner who developed the town, the name Teluk Intan was reinstated after Malaysia's independence. There is no pressing reason to visit Teluk Intan, its only gazetted tourist attraction being a leaning clock tower, but it's a pleasant, lazy town at the junction of the Sungai Perak and Sungai Bidor.

The town's striking pagoda-style **jam besar** (clock tower) appears to have eight storeys (though there are only three levels inside) and is the town's answer to the Leaning Tower of Pisa. Local lore has it that it was built, in the manner of the Taj Mahal, by a mourning Chinese merchant in 1885 as a memorial to his wife; cynics say that it was only designed as a potable-water storage tank. The clock tower is officially closed, though its image was featured everywhere as a symbol of the Visit Perak 2000 state tourist campaign.

Teluk Intan also has a few fine colonial buildings and old Chinese shophouses standing around, most looking as ready to topple over as the tower. The **Istana Raja Muda Perak** is the crumbling palace of the next in line to the sultanate of Perak.

**Places to Stay & Eat** The *Kok Min Hotel* (☎ *622 1529, 1605A Jalan Sekolah*) is a well-kept old villa with simple singles/doubles from RM18/23. With your back to the clock tower, walk south from the bus station to the main road, turn left (east) and the hotel is a block or so down on your left.

Five minutes farther along, *Hotel Anson* (☎ *622 6166*) is the best in the town centre (that's not saying much), with air-con rooms from RM60/70.

Daytime and night *hawker-food stalls* line the streets around the clock tower and bus station. The interesting, old-style covered market north of the clock tower has an endless selection of Malaysian, Indian and Chinese favourites.

**Getting There & Away** The central bus station is just south of the clock tower. There are frequent direct buses to/from Ipoh (RM3.50) and KL's Puduraya bus station (RM8.40), as well as express buses to Lumut (five daily, RM4.20). Local buses to Lumut (hourly, RM4) and Klang in Selangor depart from the side street next to the post office, just west of the clock tower.

## Kompleks Sejarah Pasir Salak

The Kompleks Sejarah Pasir Salak (Pasir Salak Historical Complex) stands in the sleepy riverside Kampung Pasir Salak – best-known as the village where the first British Resident of Perak, James WW Birch, was slain in 1875 while bathing at a raft-house on the river. Birch is widely characterised as an intolerant man, insensitive to Malay customs and known to lecture Sultan Abdullah in public. However, his murder was as much a reaction to the colonial government's decision to assume direct control in Perak as it was to any shortcomings in Birch's personality. A memorial to Birch marks the exact spot of the assassination.

His executioners, Maharaja Lela (a local chief), Dato Sagor and Pandak Indut were arrested by British troops and later hanged. They have since been enshrined as national heroes, and the memorial dedicated to them here is in the shape of a traditional *sundang* knife, widely used in rebellions against the British. Replicas of Maharaja Lela's fort and house are nearby.

Of greater interest are the restored traditional houses, *rumah kutai,* on the grounds of the historical complex at Pasir Salak. They show all the features of Perak houses, with carved eaves, shuttered windows, and

walls of wood and woven bamboo to allow for breezes. One house, reputed to be 120 years old, is a museum that describes the events of 1875 dramatically heightened by a few blood-thirsty paintings, traditional swords and other old weapons. Another displays traditional Malay wedding customs and a few native musical instruments. The largest house has been transformed into a 'Time Tunnel' of 42 historical dioramas depicting Perak from prehistoric times through independence, complete with a full-scale model of Birch's assassination and screaming soundtracks (RM5).

This surprisingly peaceful complex is open from 9 am to 5 pm daily (closed 11.30 am to 2.30 pm on Friday); entry costs RM2.

**Getting There & Away** Pasir Salak is 4km by road across the Sungai Perak bridge from the nearest town, Kampung Gajah. A chartered taxi from Teluk Intan to Pasir Salak costs about RM35 return.

## Tapah

The small town of Tapah has no attractions, but is the main transit point for bus connections for the Cameron Highlands.

**Places to Stay** If you get stuck, Tapah has well-priced hotels on Jalan Stesen; take the street directly opposite the bus station for two short blocks. The *Hotel Utara* (☎ *401 2299*) at No 35 has doubles for RM25 with fan, or RM30 with air-con and bathroom. Across the tiny lane is the *NH Hotel* (☎ *401 7288*) at No 24, where air-con doubles with bathroom and TV are good value at RM50.

There's a good *Chinese coffee shop* at the Hotel Utara, though the whole town is just about bursting with them, as well as simple *Indian restaurants* dishing up *roti canai* (roti dipped in dhal or curry) and chicken biryani.

**Getting There & Away** The bus station on Jalan Raja is only 200m from the main road. Local buses make the winding journey to Tanah Rata in the Cameron Highlands every 1½ hours from 8 am to 6 pm (two hours,

RM3.70). Taxis to Tanah Rata (RM40) leave from the taxi station 100m farther down Jalan Raja away from the main road.

From the bus station there are a few departures to KL and Penang, but most express long-distance buses leave from the Restoran Caspian (☎ 401 1193), 9 Main Rd. Turn right as you come out of the bus station, then left at Main Rd, and the Restoran Caspian is four shops down from KFC. It also has a sub-agent, the Kah Mee Agency, directly opposite the bus station.

From various whistle-stops around the Restoran Caspian, passing air-con buses pick up passengers for: Hat Yai (11 pm, seven hours, RM36); Ipoh (hourly, 1½ hours, RM3.8); KL (hourly until 8.15 pm, two hours, RM7 to RM10); Kuantan (9 am and 10 pm, seven hours, RM24); Lumut (10.30 am, 1.45 and 5 pm, three hours, RM10); Melaka (10 am, noon and 3.30 pm, 4½ hours, RM18); Butterworth (12.30, 2.30 and 3.30 pm, four hours, RM15); and Johor Bahru/Singapore (10 am and 8.30 pm, seven hours, RM46). Some of these buses can also be booked for the same price or slightly more at CS Travel & Tours in Tanah Rata (see Organised Tours in the Cameron Highlands section later).

The nearest train station, known as Tapah Rd, is 9km west of town. Trains leave for Butterworth at 10.11 am and 5.37 pm; for KL at 7.55 am; and for Singapore via KL at 12.07 pm. Other south-bound services leave in the middle of the night. Buses to Tapah Rd station run from Tapah's bus station every 45 minutes between 7 am and 7 pm.

## CAMERON HIGHLANDS

Malaysia's most extensive hill station, about 60km off the main KL-Ipoh-Butterworth road at Tapah, is at an altitude of 1300m to 1829m. The Cameron Highlands encompasses a large area stretching along the road from the town of Ringlet, then through the main towns of Tanah Rata, Brinchang and beyond.

The Cameron Highlands takes its name from William Cameron, the surveyor who mapped the area in 1885. He was soon followed by tea planters, Chinese vegetable-farmers and wealthy colonialists seeking a cool escape from the heat of the lowlands.

The temperature rarely drops below 10°C or climbs above 21°C, and in this fertile area vegetables grow in profusion, flowers are cultivated for sale nation-wide and wild flowers bloom everywhere. It's also the centre of Malaysian tea production.

The cool weather tempts visitors to exertions normally forgotten at sea level. There's a network of jungle trails, waterfalls and mountains, an excellent golf course and less-taxing points of interest such as colourful temples, rose gardens and tea plantations where visitors are welcome.

Until recently, development of the Cameron Highlands was fairly limited, but construction of hulking apartment blocks has somewhat changed the old-fashioned, English atmosphere, and expanding farms and plantations have demolished some of the venerable old hiking trails. A new road is being pushed through Brinchang to link up with Simpang Pulai on the Lebuhraya (East-West Highway) tollway, which will make the Highlands much more accessible from Ipoh; but, mercifully, this isn't due for completion for a year or so yet.

Despite all the changes, the regular rain, dampness and hordes of other visitors, the Cameron Highlands is still a relaxing destination and one of Malaysia's most rewarding stopovers. If you bypass it, you'll really miss out.

### Orientation

Though the Cameron Highlands lies just over the Perak state border in Pahang, it can be accessed only from Perak. From the turn-off at Tapah it's 47km up to Ringlet, the first village of the Highlands and a primarily Malay town. On the way you'll pass the eye-catching waterfall **Lata Iskandar** at the Km 20 marker (20km from Tapah).

Soon after Ringlet you skirt the lake created by Sultan Abu Bakar Dam. About 13km past Ringlet, Tanah Rata is the main town of the Highlands. As you enter, new apartment blocks towering above give way to the busy Jalan Besar (Main Rd), lined with restaurants and old-fashioned shops.

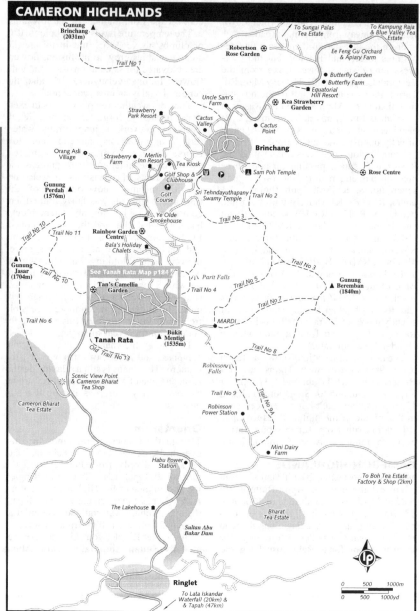

**CAMERON HIGHLANDS**

Gunung Brinchang (2031m)

To Sungai Palas Tea Estate

To Kampung Raja & Blue Valley Tea Estate

Robertson Rose Garden

Ee Feng Gu Orchard & Apiary Farm

Trail No 1

Butterfly Garden
Butterfly Farm
Equatorial Hill Resort

Uncle Sam's Farm

Kea Strawberry Garden

Strawberry Park Resort

Cactus Valley

Cactus Point

Brinchang

Orang Asli Village

Strawberry Farm

Merlin Inn Resort

Tea Kiosk

Golf Shop & Clubhouse

Sam Poh Temple

Rose Centre

Gunung Perdah (1576m)

Golf Course

Sri Tehndayuthapany Swamy Temple

Trail No 2

Ye Olde Smokehouse

Trail No 3

Trail No 10

Trail No 11

Rainbow Garden Centre

Bala's Holiday Chalets

See Tanah Rata Map p184

Parit Falls

Trail No 3

Gunung Jasar (1704m)

Trail No 10

Tan's Camellia Garden

Trail No 4

Trail No 5

Gunung Beremban (1840m)

Trail No 7

Trail No 6

MARDI

Tanah Rata

Bukit Mentigi (1535m)

Trail No 8

Old Trail No 13

Robinson Falls

Scenic View Point & Cameron Bharat Tea Shop

Trail No 9

Trail No 9A

Cameron Bharat Tea Estate

Robinson Power Station

Mini Dairy Farm

Habu Power Station

To Boh Tea Estate Factory & Shop (2km)

The Lakehouse

Bharat Tea Estate

Sultan Abu Bakar Dam

Ringlet

To Lata Iskandar Waterfall (20km) & & Tapah (47km)

PENINSULAR MALAYSIA

0    500    1000m
0    500    1000yd

Tanah Rata has a large Indian population, descendants of the Indian workers originally brought here to pick tea. Most visitors stay in Tanah Rata for its lively atmosphere.

A few kilometres past Tanah Rata is the golf course, clustered around which you'll find many of the Highlands' more expensive hotels. Beyond the golf course at around Km 65 you reach Brinchang, a more modern, Chinese town. Though Brinchang has a good range of facilities and is closer to many of the attractions, it has less character than Tanah Rata.

The road continues up beyond Brinchang to grungy Kampung Raja, a tea estate village, and the Blue Valley Tea Estate at Km 90. Flower gardens, strawberry stalls and butterfly farms are found along this stretch of road, as is the turn-off to Sungai Palas Tea Estate and Gunung (Mt) Brinchang (2031m).

## Information

At the time of writing, the Tanah Rata tourist office at the western end of Jalan Besar was closed indefinitely. Souvenir shops in Tanah Rata sell useful colour maps of the Cameron Highlands, but hikers should not assume that detail shown on these maps is completely accurate, or up to date. Budget guesthouses and family-run hotels are usually very reliable sources of information on the latest trail conditions, outlying sights and transport in the Highlands.

The post office, hospital, HSBC bank, police and bus station are all on Jalan Besar in Tanah Rata. Maybank and the Highlands Laundry are found in the lanes of Persiaran Camellia near the hotel construction site.

Most of the budget backpacker places in Tanah Rata offer Internet access (RM5 per hour). Internet cafes on the upper storeys of buildings in Persiaran Camellia (Mix House Net, HackerZ Cafe, and Pusat Komputer CL, for example) charge only RM3, though they are crammed with local students and noisy.

At Cameron Highland Online (www .cameronhighlands.com) you'll find an overview and short history of the Highlands, as well as limited hiking information and worthwhile links to guesthouse and hotel Web sites.

## Tea Plantations

A visit to a tea plantation is a popular Highlands outing. The first tea was planted here in 1926. The main company is the Boh Tea Estate, and its brands dominate the market for Cameron Highlands tea.

**Boh's Sungai Palas Tea Estate** is up in the hills north of Brinchang, off the road to Gunung Brinchang. The approach road leads past functional worker-housing and a Hindu temple to the attractive visitors centre. You can buy tea and tea sets in the gift shop, or sample the brew of your choice along with scrumptious baked goodies in tea rooms offering grand vistas out back.

The tea is still cured with wood fires, which imparts flavour to the finished product. The process is almost all mechanised now, including the picking and sifting into grades from dust to choice leaf. Free 15-minute tours showing the process are conducted from 8.30 am to 4.30 pm (closed Monday). Wait for a staff member to collect you from the video presentation room.

Public buses running between Tanah Rata and Kampung Raja pass the turn-off to

### Tea Processing

Tea bushes are plucked every seven to eight days, and though once done by hand, the process is now almost entirely mechanised in Malaysia. It takes 5kg of leaves to make 1kg of tea. The collected leaves are weighed and 'withered' – a drying process in which fans blow air across troughs to reduce the moisture content by about 50%. The dried leaves are then rolled to twist and rupture the leaf cells and release the juices for fermentation. The finer leaves are separated out and the larger ones are rolled again.

Fermentation, which is the oxidisation of the leaf enzymes, has to be strictly controlled to develop the characteristic flavour and aroma of the tea. The fermented leaves are 'fired', a process in which excess moisture is driven off in a drying machine. At this time the leaves become black. Finally, the tea is sorted into grades, and stalks and fibres are removed before it is stored in bins to mature.

Gunung Brinchang. From there it's 4km along the winding road past Robertson Rose Garden (worth a detour for its hilltop views) to the plantation entrance, after which it's another 15 minutes downhill to the visitors centre.

You can also visit other tea estates, but guided tours are usually given only for organised groups. One exception is **Boh Tea Estate**, south-east of Tanah Rata and 8km off the main road up to the Highlands. From the end of jungle trail 9A (see Hiking later in this section), it's only a 45-minute walk to the plantation and tours are given approximately hourly from 10 am to 3.30 pm.

### Other Attractions
The **Sam Poh Temple**, just below Brinchang about 1km off the main road, is a typically Chinese kaleidoscope of colours, with Buddha statues, stone lions and incense burners. It is signposted as the 'Tokong Temple' from the intersection at the main road in front of the Iris House Hotel. The nearby **Sri Tehndayuthapany Swamy Temple** is an equally colourful Hindu place of worship – the bright sculptures were created by artists brought from India.

**MARDI** is an agricultural research station east of Tanah Rata – tours must be arranged in advance. CS Travel & Tours may be able to make arrangements for you (see Organised Tours later in this section).

There are a number of **apiaries, flower and cactus nurseries, vegetable farms** and **strawberry farms** in the Highlands. The main season for strawberries is January.

There is an Orang Asli (aboriginal Malay) settlement near Brinchang, but it's a real village and not a tourist site. If you want to visit, hire a local Malay guide to accompany you and to act as an interpreter.

About 10km beyond Brinchang is the **Butterfly Garden**, where more than 300 varieties supposedly flutter around, but we dare you to count more than a handful; the collection of enormous rhinoceros beetles and scorpions is more satisfying. Next door, the **Butterfly Farm** is a virtually identical competing attraction, though travellers rate

Many species of butterflies wing their way around the Cameron Highlands.

it more highly. Both are open from 9 am to 6 pm daily; entry costs RM3.

**Gunung Brinchang** (2031m) is the highest point accessible by surfaced road on the peninsula. It's a long slog on foot, but if you are driving it's a must. The 7km road is narrow and incredibly steep in places, but the summit views are superb.

### Hiking
There are a variety of walks around the Highlands, many leading to waterfalls and mountain peaks. The start of the trails are marked with large, yellow-and-black signboards that are sometimes obscured. Unfortunately there are no high-quality, up-to-date contour maps available.

The popular tracks are reasonably well maintained and periodically cleared with brush cutters, but it doesn't take long for tracks to become overgrown, especially the less popular ones. There is little or no signposting of side trails, and you occasionally come across false trails that go nowhere. Guesthouses in Tanah Rata often employ informal guides who lead daily hikes, and they are a good source of information on the latest track conditions.

The trails generally pass through relatively unspoiled jungle, and the cool weather makes walking a pleasure. You should take care not to get lost and always carry water, some food and rain gear for the unpredictable weather. Trails 4 and 9A (as far as Robinson Falls) are easy walks taking an hour or less, while a combination of

## Jim Thompson

The Cameron Highlands' most famous jungle trekker was a man who never came back from his walk. American Jim Thompson is credited with having founded the Thai silk industry after WWII. He subsequently made a fortune, and his beautiful, antique-packed house beside a *khlong* (canal) in Bangkok is a major tourist attraction today. On 26 March 1967, while holidaying in the Highlands, Jim Thompson left his villa for a pre-dinner stroll – never to be seen again. Despite extensive searches, the mystery of his disappearance has never been explained. Kidnapped? Taken by a tiger? Or simply a planned disappearance or suicide? Nobody knows.

Trails 10 and 11 is more challenging. The rest may be tough-going, depending on your level of fitness.

Note that Trail 14 has been taken over and closed by farm expansion. Trail 13 starts from behind the Cameronian Inn, but it stops short at the concrete construction pylons.

Although walks around the Highlands are all relatively short, there is obviously the potential for longer hikes. A glance at the Perak map will indicate what a short, steep distance it is from the Highlands down to Ipoh or the main road. For any walk outside the immediate area, however, the local authorities have to be notified and a guide is necessary.

**Trail 1** This trail leads from around the side of the transmitter station on top of Gunung Brinchang down to the army camp just north of Brinchang. It is a steep, muddy, overgrown trail (often closed for repairs) and should only be tackled from the top down by experienced hikers. Take the 7km paved road to Gunung Brinchang through the tea plantations – a pleasant enough walk for a while, but dull eventually so try hitching. The trail down takes about 1½ hours, unless you get lost and wander through the jungle for a couple of days, as two foreigners did some time ago.

**Trail 2** Starting just before Sam Poh Temple outside Brinchang, this steep, strenuous hike follows a thin, slippery track for 1½ hours before it eventually joins Trail 3.

**Trail 3** This starts at Arcadia Cottage south-east of the golf course and climbs towards Gunung

Beremban (1840m), getting steeper near the summit. It is a strenuous three-hour walk all the way to the mountain, or an easier walk if you only go as far as Trail 5 and take that back to MARDI.

**Trail 4** Trail 4 starts next to the river just past the New Garden Inn in Tanah Rata. It leads to the Parit Falls, but unfortunately these are more like 'sewage falls' as all the garbage from the nearby village finds its way here. The falls can also be reached from the road around the southern end of the golf course. Both walks are about half a kilometre.

**Trail 5** Trail 5 starts at MARDI. Take the road inside the complex and follow the sign around to the left. It's a 1½-hour walk though open country and forest, and an easy walk if done downhill from Trail 3.

**Trail 6** One of the least popular and most overgrown routes, Trail 6 goes (once you find it, that is) from the end of the road at Bharat Tea Estate and merges with Trail 10 at the summit of Gunung Jasar (1704m). It's a 2½-hour uphill walk – take a guide.

**Trail 7** This one also starts inside MARDI. The beginning can be tough to find and you should allow all day – it's at least a steady three-hour uphill hike, with a very steep final climb to the summit of Gunung Beremban.

**Trail 8** This branches off Trail 9 just before Robinson Falls and is another steep three-hour approach to Gunung Beremban. Although a slightly easier walk, it's still a strenuous 2½ hours if done in reverse from the mountain.

**Trail 9 & 9A** Popular Trail 9 starts 1.5km from the main road in Tanah Rata. Take the road past MARDI and follow it all the way around to the right, where it ends at a footbridge. From here the trail leads downhill past Robinson Falls to a metal gate, about 15 minutes away. Trail 9, which is not recommended, goes through the gate and follows the water pipeline down a very steep, slippery incline through the jungle to the power station. We recommend taking Trail 9A, which branches off to the left before the metal gate and in about an hour empties out onto Boh Rd. Follow this to the main road, where you can either head east to Boh Tea Estate or west to Habu Power Station for buses back to Tanah Rata.

**Trails 10 & 11** Gunung Jasar is a fairly strenuous walk via Trail 10, starting behind the Oly Apartments in Tanah Rata. Go through Tan's Camellia Garden and uphill to the left. After reaching the summit, you can continue on towards Gunung Perdah, but you must bypass it and return by Trail 11, which joins up with Trail 10 halfway back to Tanah Rata.

## Other Activities

If you want a game of golf, you'll need to be suitably dressed (no singlets or 'revealing' shorts). Green fees are RM40 for a whole day (RM60 on weekends), or RM20 after 4 pm. Club, shoe and ball hire costs around RM40.

You can also swim, play a few sets of tennis or squash, and steam in the sauna at Strawberry Park Resort, up in the hills west of the golf course. You should phone ahead (☎ 491 1166) to check available times and rates.

## Organised Tours

CS Travel & Tours (☎ 491 1200), at 57 Jalan Besar in Tanah Rata; and Titiwangsa (☎ 491 1452) and Jade Holidays (☎ 491 2318) in Brinchang, sell tickets for popular half-day tours of the Highlands, leaving around 8.45 am and 1.45 pm (RM15). (They also organise various longer tours of the area.) This can be a good way of seeing all the various attractions, which are spread out and either difficult or impossible to reach by public transport. Places visited include a tea estate, a strawberry farm, the Sam Poh Temple, a butterfly farm and a rose garden (entry fees not included).

## Places to Stay

The Highlands can be very busy with Malaysian families during the school holidays, in April, August and December. During these times especially, you should book accommodation in advance. At the more expensive hotels, prices vary with demand; peak rates are on weekends and during holiday periods – prices are substantially lower during quiet periods.

Fortunately, Tanah Rata has a good selection of travellers' guesthouses to cheaply accommodate the scores of backpackers, as well as more-expensive hotels. In Brinchang, the secondary Highlands town 5km beyond Tanah Rata, hotel prices are lower; but there is almost no atmosphere here and little reason to stay, especially if you depend on public transport.

Many mid-range and top-end hotels are scattered around the Highlands, mostly between Tanah Rata and Brinchang.

## Places to Stay – Budget

**Guesthouses** In Tanah Rata your bus will probably be met by several guesthouse touts, perhaps the most laid-back of their kind in all of Malaysia. It's all pretty low pressure, which is an amazing feat and a credit to all the guesthouses, since the Cameron Highlands is one of the most heavily backpacked areas in all of South-East Asia. If you don't see the tout for the guesthouse you're headed to, ring them up and most will pick you up for free. If you choose to walk, it's no more than 20 minutes to any place in town.

A short way from the town centre (up a long flight of stone steps) is *Father's Guest House* (☎ 491 2484, fax 491 5484, @ fathersonline@hotmail.com). The old, bunker-style Nissen huts from the British occupation are surprisingly clean and comfortable inside. Still managed by the founder, this well-run guesthouse has a TV area with an extensive video collection and offers Internet access. Trekking guides lead hikes most days. Dorm beds cost RM8 to RM10, and doubles with shared shower start at RM20. In the greystone seminary house on the hill are a few rooms with French doors opening onto the garden and a small bathroom cubicle, costing from RM35.

Surrounded by rainforest, yet still very central is *Daniel's Lodge* (☎ 491 5823, 9 Lorong Perdah, @ danielslodge@hotmail .com). Be forewarned (or take heart) that it's jam-packed and an extremely social hostel. The trekking guides are reputedly good and loads of fun. Dorm beds are RM6 to RM8, and simple fan rooms start at RM16, rising to RM45 with bathroom and external window.

Another happening place is the very informal, reggae-style *Twin Pines Chalet* (☎ 491 2169), just a short walk from the town centre. The communal veranda is a good place for tuning into the travellers' grapevine. It is near a construction site, though, and the thin-walled rooms can be noisy. Rates are similar to Daniel's, and likewise it's often full.

On the same road as Twin Pines but in a quieter position, the *Cameronian Inn*

*(☎ 491 1327)* is another converted house with comparable facilities, including a small restaurant and TV/video room. Rooms from RM16 are internal-facing and dank, but those with bathroom, starting at RM30, are better value. Dorm beds are available for RM6, but this place is more popular with couples.

Just behind Twin Pines, the congenial *Papillon Guest House (☎ 274 3014, in KL ☎ 03-783 6745, fax 783 7485)* is in a spacious family house, with a kitchen, laundry and common living room. Simple singles go for RM25 and doubles with bathroom for RM35, including a light breakfast. Beds in roomy five- and 10-person dorms cost RM10.

**Hotels** Perched on a hill halfway between the Cameronian Inn and Twin Pines, the brand-new, family-run *Hillview Inn (☎ 491 5212, fax 491 2915, ☻ waterdivers@hot mail.com)* offers the best bang for your ringgit. It's impeccably clean, spacious and carpeted, and has hot water. Doubles cost from RM20 to RM60, depending on size and amenities. For now, it's a well-kept secret. Farther uphill, *Jurina Resort (☎ 491 5522)* is more expensive but the friendly, eccentric owner offers neat doubles for only RM40 in the low season.

The *Hotel BB Inn (☎ 491 4551, 79A Persiaran Camellia 4)*, in the newer section of Tanah Rata, has OK doubles for RM35, or from RM45 with balcony. Be sure to ask for one with a window.

Tanah Rata also has plenty of musty hotels along Jalan Besar. One good bet is the exceptionally friendly *Seah Meng Hotel (☎ 491 1618)* at No 39, where clean doubles with common bathroom cost RM25, or RM35 facing outside with bathroom. All of the other hotels are equally faded, and there's not much to choose between them. *Downtown Hotel (☎ 491 3159)* at No 41, and its sister establishment *The Orient Hotel (☎ 491 1633)* a few doors east at No 38, have carpeted singles/doubles for RM18/22, or RM25/38 with attached bath, all including a light breakfast.

The *Kavy Hotel (☎ 491 5652)*, at No 44A, has larger, more expensive doubles/

triples for RM39/RM49 and family rooms for RM80, all with bathroom. You may not want to stay, however, as Tanah Rata's only bar, the lively Ranch Pub, is downstairs.

Most of Brinchang's numerous hotels are situated on the central square, and are relatively uninviting and poor value, even though simple rooms with shared bath average RM25 to RM35. The basic *Hotel Sentosa (☎ 491 1907)* is just about the cheapest one. Next door, the friendlier *New Plastro Hotel (☎ 491 1009)* is somewhat dingy and loud, but good-sized doubles with bathroom cost only RM30. Farther along, *Highlands Hotel (☎ 491 1588)* is edging towards mid-range, and has more-tolerable (though overpriced) single/double rooms with bathroom from RM42/63.

## Places to Stay – Mid-Range
You don't get a lot of choice in the mid-range bracket, and prices are higher than elsewhere in Malaysia, though some negotiation is possible. Most are bland places that have seen better days.

Private apartments can be rented and are worth considering for longer stays. Check with the shops on Jalan Besar in Tanah Rata and on the eastern side of Brinchang's central square for 'apartment for rent' signs. *Shal's Curry House (☎/fax 491 2408)*, at 25 Jalan Besar in Brinchang, regularly advertises holiday apartment rentals.

**Tanah Rata** Just 1.5km along the road to Brinchang is the *Bala's Holiday Chalets (☎ 491 1660, fax 491 4500, ☻ balasch@ hotmail.com)*, a lovely refurbished colonial-era boarding school, set in a lovely hillside garden. Serene doubles without/with bathroom are RM45/66, larger family rooms cost RM80 and suites are RM100. There's a gourmet restaurant in the main house that serves tea and scones, as well as renowned curries once tasted by the sultan of Perak. A free shuttle pick-up is available from Tanah Rata, but the German-Malay management may be reluctant to welcome backpackers.

The *New Garden Inn (☎ 491 5170, fax 491 5169)* is next to the kids' playground in Tanah Rata. It has blocks of comfortable

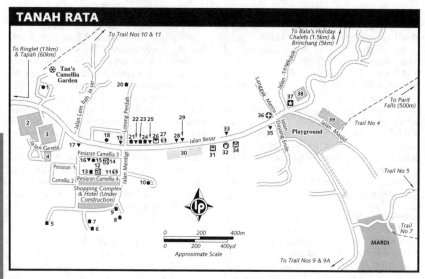

**TANAH RATA**

PENINSULAR MALAYSIA

modern rooms in the large grounds from RM120, but the low-season rate is only RM60. The place is nothing special and often empty, but rooms in the main building have more old-fashioned character.

**Brinchang** Brinchang has a few (mostly overpriced) mid-range hotels hogging the space around the central square. There are dozens of disappointing options here. Popular with KL residents on long weekend excursions, the *Hill Garden Lodge* (☎ 491 2988) on the square's western side has neat and tidy rooms with bathroom from RM98, though discounts are possible. The passable *Pines & Roses Hotel* (☎ 491 2203) has clean doubles with bathroom and TV for RM50/90 off-peak/peak. It's behind the Hotel Rosa Passadena on the downhill side of the square.

On the eastern side of the square, the more promising *Brinchang Hotel* (☎ 491 1755, fax 491 3452) has twins/triples/quads for RM57/68/78; all prices are RM21 higher during peak season. The *Parkland Hotel* (☎ 491 1299, fax 491 2366) has better doubles for RM123 (discounts offered in the low season) and apartments starting at RM300. The Parkland also manages the

*Kowloon Hotel* (☎ 491 1366) down the street, which has perkier rooms for marginally lower prices.

Downhill 1km past the square on the main road, the new *Iris House Hotel* (☎ 491 1818, fax 491 2828) isn't buzzing yet, but motel-like rooms are good value at RM88 for two people, including breakfast and dinner. It's at the turn-off to Sam Poh Temple.

**Places to Stay – Top End**
Charmingly 'olde worlde', *The Lakehouse* (☎ 495 6152, fax 495 6213), overlooking the lake 2km from Ringlet, is one of the most delightful hotels in the Highlands. Singles/doubles from RM275/310 are good value, but you really need your own transport to stay here.

**Tanah Rata** In Tanah Rata, the *Heritage Hotel* (☎ 491 3888, fax 491 5666) is part of a large, yet surprisingly empty apartment complex dominating the western edge of town. It's not worth writing home about, but worthwhile rooms start at RM300, and substantial discounts are often available.

Quite near the golf course, on the other side of Tanah Rata, *Ye Olde Smokehouse*

## TANAH RATA

**PLACES TO STAY**
3   Heritage Hotel
4   Father's Guest House
5   Cameronian Inn
6   Jurina Resort
7   Hillview Inn
8   Papillon Guest House
9   Twin Pines Chalet
13  Hotel BB Inn
20  Daniel's Lodge
21  Kavy Hotel; Ranch Pub
23  Downtown Hotel; Roselane Collectibles
24  Seah Meng Hotel
39  New Garden Inn

**PLACES TO EAT**
16  Restaurant Bunga Suria
17  Cameron Tandoori Restaurant;
    Old Tourist Office
19  Jasmine Restoran Cafe
22  Roselane Coffee Shop
25  The Orient Hotel & Restaurant
28  Restaurant Kumar
29  Restoran Thanam
30  Malay Food Stalls; Excellent Food Centre
33  Restoran No 14
35  Malay Food Stalls

**OTHER**
1   Oly Apartments
2   Convent
10  Town Council Offices (Majlis Daerah)
11  Maybank
12  Mix House Net & HackerZ Cafe
14  Pusat Komputer CL
15  Highlands Laundry
18  CS Travel & Tours
26  Post Office
27  HSBC Bank
31  Bus Station
32  Shell Petrol Station
34  Taxi Station
36  Hospital
37  Police Station
38  District Office

It's incomprehensibly popular with upscale Asian and European tourists, and, of course, golfers.

About 1km past the golf course towards Brinchang, at the top of a winding side road, the **Strawberry Park Resort** (☎ 491 1166, fax 491 1949) is a huge apartment-type setup popular with package tour groups, but it boasts a disco and good facilities, which are also available for day-use (see Other Activities earlier in this section). Studio/one/two/three-room apartments cost RM288/311/357/437, though promotional discounts knock off as much as 50%.

**Brinchang** The huge **Equatorial Hill Resort** (☎ 496 1777, fax 496 1333) is currently the Highlands' highest high-rise hotel. Several kilometres north of Brinchang, this luxury complex really is a case of over-the-top development and very remote. Doubles in the tower block cost from RM275, and one/two/three-bedroom apartments in the lower wing cost from RM429/514/594.

### Places to Eat
**Tanah Rata** The cheapest food in Tanah Rata is found at the rows of mainly Malay **food stalls** stretching down Jalan Besar towards the bus and taxi stations. One stall, the **Excellent Food Centre**, has an extensive menu of tasty cooking. Other places have Chinese fare and all the usual Malay dishes, including satay. If you've got a strong stomach and an early bus to catch, some are open for breakfast.

On the other side of the road is Tanah Rata's lively restaurant scene. A host of cheap and moderately priced restaurants line the wide footpath perched above the street. Many of them set up tables so customers can dine alfresco.

Two popular choices are **Restaurant Kumar** and the adjacent **Restoran Thanam** on Jalan Besar. Both serve Indian food, as well as Western breakfasts, juices, lassi and pancakes for the travellers' trade. For even cheaper Indian fare, **Restoran No 14** offers big *thali* (banana-leaf) meals and *masala dosa* (filled pancakes made from crushed lentils). It is so popular that it sometimes

(☎ 491 1215, fax 491 1214) is a cosy copy of an old English country pub, with exposed beams, low ceilings, open fireplaces and a suitably genteel atmosphere. Doubles with English breakfast start at RM440 and private suites cost RM748.

Overlooking the northern end of the golf course is the predictable **Merlin Inn Resort** (☎ 491 1211, fax 491 1178), where plain-looking doubles cost from RM299.

runs out of food, so don't leave your dining here too late.

In the new commercial block at 66A Persiaran Camellia 3, the **Restaurant Bunga Suria** is a serious contender for the title of best South Indian food in Peninsular Malaysia. Delicious samosas and banana-leaf set meals (vegetarian/non-vegetarian) start at just RM4. It's all so deliciously spicy that you may find yourself dining here every night of your stay.

Farther west, next to the old tourist office, the **Cameron Tandoori Restaurant** dishes up cheap north Indian fare to a local clientele.

Steamboat in the Highlands is a traditional treat. It's the Chinese equivalent of a Swiss fondue. You get plates of meat, prawns (shrimp), vegetables and eggs on skewers, and cook them yourself in a boiling stockpot over a burner on the table. You need at least two people, but the more the better. Try the set steamboat lunch or dinner at the **Orient Restaurant** on Jalan Besar; it's very good value at RM12 per person (minimum two people). Farther west is the **Jasmine Restoran Cafe**, with set four-course meals that are worthwhile for RM26.

Another Highlands tradition is (local) coffee or tea with scones and jam, served best at the tea estates themselves (see Tea Plantations earlier in this section). Two inexpensive cafes in Tanah Rata, the **Roselane Coffee Shop** and the **Downtown** (in the hotel of the same name), serve freshly baked pastries and do breakfasts from RM4. Out at **Bala's Holiday Chalets** you'll also find excellent scones with jam and cream.

All the mid-range and top-end hotels have their own expensive restaurants. **Ye Olde Smokehouse** is ideal for homesick Brits – you can get expensive tea and scones, sandwiches without crusts and fairly pricey meals.

**Brinchang**  Brinchang has a good night market, which sets up in the central square in the late afternoon. A permanent food-stall centre livens up the southern end of the square, and you can eat quite well for just a couple of ringgit.

Brinchang has excellent Chinese food, and steamboat features widely. For cheap, no-frills coffee-shop fare, **Restoran Kwan Kee** on the western side of the square is a good bet. The mid-range **Restoran Kowloon** across the way has a broad selection of Cantonese dishes from around RM15.

A few doors up is **Shal's Curry House** at No 25, which specialises in roti and *dosa* (pancakes) served on banana leaves (with imaginative strawberry, butter and coconut combinations), but also has clove and cardamom teas, fresh lassi and excellent apple strudel. The entertaining owner will regale you with anecdotes and show you his guest-book. Even if you're staying in Tanah Rata, this restaurant is worth a special trip, even if you have to walk the 5km uphill under your own steam.

## Getting There & Away
**Bus**  It's a long, gradual and often scenic climb from Tapah in Perak state to the Highlands, with plenty of corners on the way. From the golf course down to the main road junction, one visitor reported counting 653 bends. The road passes a number of Orang Asli villages and roadside huts where their produce is sold.

Be warned that the Highlands is where old Malaysian buses come to die. The bus drivers on this route seem to be frustrated racing drivers, especially on the stretch up from Ringlet, and almost everyone overtakes on blind corners. There are seven daily buses from Tapah to Tanah Rata between 8 am and 6 pm (two hours, RM3.70). Many of these rattle-trap buses stop to change vehicle and driver at Ringlet. From Tanah Rata, the first and last buses down to Tapah leave at 8 am and 5.30 pm.

A few direct long-distance services originate from the Tanah Rata bus station for KL (five hours, four daily, RM13) and Penang (8.30 am and 2.30 pm, six hours, RM18). These buses and other services leaving from Tapah can be booked at CS Travel & Tours (☎ 491 1200), 47 Jalan Besar, Tanah Rata. See also Getting There and Away in the Tapah section earlier in this chapter.

**Taxi** The taxi station in Tanah Rata is just east of the bus station on Jalan Besar. Things are much busier in the morning, so it's best to go then if you are looking for someone to share your ride. Full-taxi fares are RM40 to Tapah, RM70 to Ipoh and RM160 to KL.

## Getting Around

**Bus** Regal Transport Co keeps a throttle-hold on all public transport in the Highlands. Posted timetables don't often match reality, as drivers leave when they feel like it and, if buses break down, routes go out of service.

Getting between Tanah Rata and Brinchang is not a problem between 6.30 am and 6.30 pm, as buses run every hour or so. There are scheduled buses every hour from Tanah Rata to Kampung Raja, 23km away across the Highlands, but it's more like two or three hours until the next one happens by. It's quite a scenic trip, and you can hop off at various fruit and vegetable farms along the way. These buses also pass the turn-off to Gunung Brinchang and the Sungai Palas Tea Estate.

**Taxi** Taxi services from Tanah Rata include: Ringlet (RM12), Brinchang (RM4), Sungai Palas Estate (RM18) and Boh Tea Estates (RM16). For touring around, a taxi costs RM18 per hour, or you can go up to Gunung Brinchang and back for RM60. When you head back downhill to Tanah Rata you may be able to bargain down to a few ringgit, as drivers are glad to pick up at least a few passengers on the return trip.

**Bicycle** Mountain bikes are for rent at Roselane Collectibles shop just west of the Downtown Hotel on Jalan Besar in Tanah Rata. Rates are RM3 per hour, or RM15 for the 'day' (eight hours). But it's hilly around here, remember, and not easy cycling on used bikes.

## IPOH

The 'City of Millionaires' made its fortune from the rich tin mines of the Kinta Valley. Some of the mines around Ipoh are still producing today, and the city's elegant mansions testify to the success of many Chinese miners. With a population of 390,000 (over half a million if the surrounding districts are included) Ipoh is Malaysia's third-largest city, but development fever is less rabid in this Chinese-dominated city than in other parts of Malaysia. Although it replaced Taiping as Perak state's capital in 1937, Ipoh is not as bustling as its size might indicate, and has retained many of its historic buildings.

For the visitor, Ipoh is mainly a transit town, a place where you change buses if you're heading for Pulau Pangkor or Tapah, or where you pause to sample what is reputed to be some of the finest Chinese food in Malaysia. It may be worth a longer visit to explore outlying sights like the Buddhist temples cut into the limestone outcrops, the royal town of Kuala Kangsar or the eccentric Kellie's Castle. Ipoh itself, however, is a seedy, rough-and-tumble city and you're unlikely to want to linger longer than necessary.

'Old Town' Ipoh is west of the Sungai Kinta, between Jalan Sultan Idris Shah and Jalan Sultan Iskandar, and is worth a wander for the old Chinese and British architecture. The grand civic buildings close to, and including, the train station give some idea of just how prosperous this city once was. At the end of the 19th century the city expanded east over the river into 'New Town', which is another repository of colonial shophouses. While the city centre remains largely preserved and free from development, it is rather lifeless in the evenings.

## Information

The Perak Tourist Information Centre (☎ 241 2959, fax 241 2958) is in the old city council building at the corner of Jalan Bandaraya and Jalan Tun Sambanthan, opposite the Padang. It is open from 8 am to 4.30 pm on weekdays (closed for lunch from 1 to 2 pm), and in the morning on the second and fourth Saturday of every month. The staff hand out excellent city maps and brochures on other areas of Perak state, including Pulau Pangkor.

Banks include the HSBC and Standard Chartered Banks on Jalan Dato' Maharajah Lela near the clock tower, and Maybank on Jalan Bandar Timah.

PENINSULAR MALAYSIA

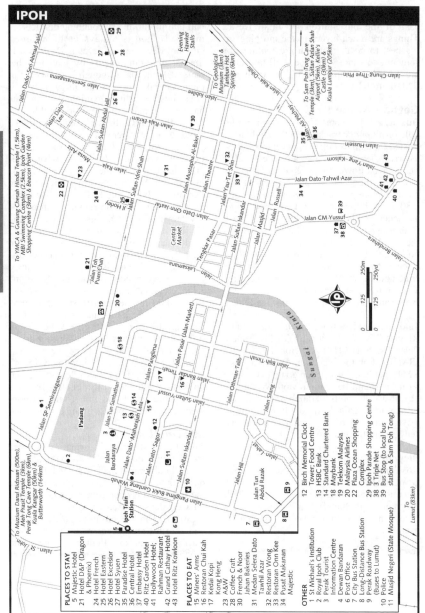

# IPOH

**PLACES TO STAY**
5   Majestic Hotel
21  Hotel D&P (Dragon
    & Phoenix)
24  Hotel French
25  Hotel Eastern
26  Hotel Excelsior
27  Hotel Syuen
35  Paradise Hotel
36  Central Hotel
37  Embassy Hotel
40  Ritz Garden Hotel
41  Hollywood Hotel;
    Rahman Restaurant
42  Grand Cathay Hotel
43  Hotel Ritz Kowloon

**PLACES TO EAT**
15  Miners' Arms
16  Restoran Chui Kah
17  Kedai Kopi
    Kong Heng
23  A&W
28  Coffee Craft
30  French & Noor
31  Medan Selera Dato
    Tahwil Azar
32  Restoran Wong
33  Restoran Onn Kee
34  Pusat Makanan
    Majestic

**OTHER**
1   St Michael's Institution
2   Royal Ipoh Club
3   Perak Tourist
    Information Centre
4   Dewan Bandaran
6   Post Office
7   City Bus Station
8   Long-Distance Bus Station
9   Perak Roadway
    (Buses to Lumut)
10  Police
11  Masjid Negeri (State Mosque)
12  Birch Memorial Clock
    Tower; Food Centre
13  HSBC Bank
14  Standard Chartered Bank
18  Maybank
19  Telekom Malaysia
20  Malaysia Airlines
22  Plaza Ocean Shopping
    Complex
29  Ipoh Parade Shopping Centre
38  3 Triple Net
39  Bus Stop (to local bus
    station & Sam Poh Tong)

Across the river on Jalan CM Yussuf, 3 Triple Net charges RM2 for an hour of Internet access.

The huge MBI Swimming Complex has an Olympic-size pool, a diving pool and Malaysia's first wave pool. It's open from 9 am to 9 pm daily, but is far north-east of town; take the No 113 Ipoh Garden bus.

Many of Ipoh's main streets have been renamed in recent years, and while the street signs give the new (and often overly lengthy) names, the streets may still be known by the old names. The main ones include Jalan Chamberlain (now Jalan CM Yussuf), Jalan Leech (Jalan Bandar Timah), Jalan Station (Jalan Dato' Maharajah Lela), Jalan Clarke (Jalan Sultan Idris Shah) and Jalan Kelab (Jalan Panglima Bukit Gantang Wahab!).

## Colonial Architecture

Ipoh's grand colonial architecture is found in the Old Town. Some structures look freshly white-washed, but other buildings have fallen into disrepair. Known locally as the 'Taj Mahal', the **train station** is a blend of Moorish and Victorian architecture, similar to KL's train station. It houses the wonderfully old-fashioned Majestic Hotel. Directly opposite, the **Dewan Bandaran** (Town Hall) is a dazzling white neoclassical building of grand proportions.

A short walk away on Jalan Dato' Sagor, the **Birch Memorial Clock Tower** was erected to the memory of JWW Birch, Perak's first British Resident, who was murdered at Pasir Salak. The friezes on the clock tower try to show more cultural sensitivity than Birch was reputed to have had, by depicting the growth of Asian as well as European civilisation.

The mock-Tudor **Royal Ipoh Club** overlooks the playing fields of the Padang and is still a centre of exclusivity. To the north of the Padang, **St Michael's Institution** is an imposing three-storey colonial building with arched verandas.

Old Town also features many rows of Chinese shophouses, though those in the New Town area east of the river are generally in better condition. After Georgetown, Ipoh has one of the most extensive areas of later shophouse architecture in Malaysia.

## Cave Temples

Ipoh is set among jungle-clad limestone hills that jut out spectacularly from the valley. The hills are riddled with caves that are a great source of spiritual power, and over the years favourite meditation grottoes have became large-scale temples. These colourful temples may have the flavour of being overcooked for tourism, but they still attract numbers of worshippers.

**Perak Tong** Founded in 1926 by a Buddhist priest, the main feature of this large and impressive complex of caverns and grottoes is the mystical murals on the interior walls, done by artists from across South-East Asia. There are several Buddha figures in the main chamber, as well as a huge bell that is rung every time someone makes a donation.

A winding series of 385 steps leads up through the cave and outside to the balconied areas above. There are good views of the surrounding countryside from here, but Ipoh's factories unfortunately clutter the immediate area.

The temple is open from 8 am to 6 pm daily; donations are requested. The cave is located 6km north of Ipoh. From the city bus station, Reliance bus No 141 stops at Perak Tong and continues to Kuala Kangsar (see that section later in this chapter).

**Sam Poh Tong** The Sam Poh Tong temple complex, a few kilometres to the south of Ipoh, is less popular than Perak Tong, the main attraction being the turtle pond in a small natural courtyard, created ages ago when the roof of a cave collapsed. Dozens of turtles swimming in the thick, green water are 'released' into the pond by locals, as it is considered good luck to do so.

Inside the temple there's a huge cavern with a small reclining Buddha, and various smaller caverns. There's a vegetarian restaurant to the right of the temple entrance. The ornamental garden in front of the temple is quite scenic, and pomelo stalls line the highway.

PENINSULAR MALAYSIA

The 128-year-old temple is open from 8 am to 4.30 pm daily. It can be reached by Kinta Bus No 66 (bound for Kampar) or No 73 from Ipoh's local bus station (50 sen). Both buses also pick up passengers at the bus stop on Jalan CM Yussuf.

**Kek Look Tong** To get off the beaten path, you can visit the smaller, more serene Kek Look Tong. From Sam Poh Tong (see that entry earlier) backtrack to the T-intersection and turn right, walk for 15 minutes, then turn right again before the first traffic light and follow the signs for Kek Look Tong. From the entrance to the cave temple you climb up to the Three Sages in the central cavern. At the back of the cave is a fat Chinese Buddha of Future Happiness sitting in the company of three other bodhisattvas, one teaching on a lotus and the others riding an elephant and a lion. Behind the cave is an ornamental garden with manicured ponds and pagodas, but the view is unfortunately scarred by fuming factories. Kek Look Tong is open from 7.30 am to 7.30 pm daily; donations are requested.

### Other Temples

**Meh Prasit** is a Thai Buddhist temple about 3km north of town on Jalan Kuala Kangsar, the main Taiping road, halfway to Perak Tong and reached by the same No 141 Kuala Kangsar bus. The temple's 24m-long reclining Buddha statue is one of the largest in Malaysia.

Less impressive, but closer to town, is **Gunung Cheroh Hindu Temple** on Jalan Raja Musa Aziz, just a short walk from the YMCA. It comes alive during the spectacularly masochistic-looking Thaipusam festival in February (see the boxed text in the 'Places of Worship' special section).

### Museums

Rock hounds might enjoy a visit to the **Geological Museum**, 5km east of the train station on Jalan Sultan Azlan Shah. Hundreds of mineral samples and fossils are on display. It is open from 8 am to 4.15 pm Monday to Friday and until 12.45 pm Saturday. Take a Tanjung Rambutan bus from the city

bus station, get off at the crossing of Jalan Sultan Azlan Shah, then walk south-east for 10 minutes.

A short distance north of the Padang, the **Muzium Darul Ridzuan** is housed in a 1926 tin miner's mansion that was used as an air-raid shelter during WWII. For real enthusiasts, the museum recounts the history of tin mining in Perak with photos, video documentaries and a model of an open-cast mine. It's open from 9 am to 5 pm Monday to Saturday; entry is free.

### Places to Stay – Budget

Most budget hotels are around Jalan CM Yussuf, south of the main drag in a run-down area. Rooms overlooking the street are plagued by traffic noise. Most of these places offer short-term 'day' rentals; with the First Sister Massage Saloon right around the corner, you be the judge.

Bottom of the barrel is the **Grand Cathay Hotel** (☎ 241 9685, 88 Jalan CM Yussuf), but what it lacks in ambience is more than made up for by the price and the charming day manager, who acts as a one-man tourist office. Large, scruffy doubles cost RM22 with shower only, and singles/doubles/triples with air-con cost RM23/28/35. Of a similar standard, but much less friendly, are the **Embassy Hotel** (☎ 254 9496), which has fan/air-con rooms with bathroom for RM28.50/41; and the equally discouraging **Hollywood Hotel**, which charges RM32.30 for air-con rooms with attached bath.

You're probably better off at the **Paradise Hotel** (☎ 254 2204, 29A Jalan Ali Pitchay), opposite the Central Hotel, where simple fan doubles cost RM28, or RM35 with bathroom, and better singles/doubles with air-con, TV, shower and toilet are RM35/45.

The mid-range **YMCA** also has dorm beds for RM15. (See its entry in the Places to Stay – Mid-Range section.)

### Places to Stay – Mid-Range

The **Ritz Garden Hotel** (☎ 254 7777, 79 Jalan CM Yussuf) is characterless, but fully-equipped rooms cost from RM70. Its sister hotel, **Hotel Ritz Kowloon** (☎ 254 7778, 92 Jalan Yang Kalsom), has smaller, virtually identical rooms for only RM57. Both hotels see a lot of day-use traffic (ahem).

The more desirable, renovated **Central Hotel** (☎ 242 4777, 20 Jalan Ali Pitchay) offers small standard doubles with all mod cons for RM90, while larger rooms with two/three beds cost RM100/113. Discounts of 30% are typical.

The **Hotel D&P (Dragon & Phoenix)** (☎ 253 4661, 23 Jalan Toh Puan Chah), near the Jalan Sultan Idris Shah bridge, is also well worthwhile, though removed from the action. Quiet air-con rooms with bathroom and TV are RM69.

The very run-down **Hotel French** (☎ 253 3111, 60 Jalan Dato Onn Jaafar) is in a livelier, but rougher, part of town near the central market. This top hotel has lost all of its shine, but standard air-con rooms from RM55 have plenty of retro 1960s character. Of a similar vintage and price range, though far better maintained, is the **Hotel Eastern** (☎ 254 3936, 118 Jalan Sultan Idris Shah), a few doors away.

The **YMCA** (☎ 254 0809, 211 Jalan Raja Musa Aziz) is very good value, but it's in a remote location 2km north of the central market. Air-con singles/doubles with private facilities in the old building cost RM30/40, or RM45/55 with TV and hot shower in the new building. The Y has large grounds, tennis courts, a pool table and a cafeteria. Take any Ipoh Garden or Hospital bus to the Jalan Hospital intersection, then walk five minutes along Jalan Raja Musa Aziz.

### Places to Stay – Top End
Ipoh's top hotels often offer major discounts (up to 50%) on the following quoted rates.

For style, but not service, the pick of Ipoh's hotels is undoubtedly the **Majestic Hotel** (☎ 255 5605, fax 255 3393) at the train station. Although not particularly well restored, this magnificent colonial edifice has at least maintained its character from the days when it was the preferred British hotel. Comfortable motel-like twins/triples costing RM132/143 on the 2nd floor face a courtyard, but go for the RM165 deluxe

rooms on the 3rd floor, which have parquetry floors, high ceilings and planters' chairs outside on the wide, arched veranda. Discounts of up to 45% may be available.

The older **Hotel Excelsior** (☎ 253 6666, 43 Jalan Clarke) has singles/doubles from RM200/210. Far more worthwhile, luxurious **Hotel Syuen** (☎ 253 8889, fax 253 3335, 88 Jalan Sultan Abdul Jalil) has singles and doubles from RM265, along with a swimming pool, disco, sports bar and bistro.

### Places to Eat
Ipoh is the home of the rice noodle dish known as *kway teow*, reputedly still the best in Malaysia. The city's most well-known place for kway teow is **Kedai Kopi Kong Heng** on Jalan Bandar Timah, a bustling restaurant serving a bit of everything. The kway teow soup has prawns (shrimp) and tender strips of chicken. The restaurant also has good roast chicken and *popiah* (similar to a spring roll, but not fried).

The Kong Heng is one of the oldest Chinese restaurants in the city, but there are several others like it, on and off Jalan Bandar Timah, which fill up quickly during the day. In the same area, the **Restoran Chui Kah** is an upmarket Chinese restaurant that specialises in steamboat.

At night, many of the restaurants in the Old Town are closed, so a good place to head for is Jalan Yau Tet Shin in New Town. On opposite corners, **Restoran Wong** and **Restoran Onn Kee** specialise in *tauge ayam* (chicken and bean sprouts) and kway teow. These popular coffee shops set up tables that spill out onto the footpath when diners flock here for dinner.

For Indian food, the welcoming **Rahman Restoran** (8 Jalan CM Yussuf), around the corner from the Hollywood Hotel, is very clean and has a range of vegetarian and nonvegetarian dishes.

Ipoh also has plenty of food-stall centres. On Jalan Raja Musa Aziz, the large **Medan Selera Dato Tawhil Azar**, better-known as the Children's Playground, has food stalls arranged around a small square. It's a popular place for Malay food in the evening, and is open late. The **Pusat Makanan Majestic** on Jalan Dato Tahwil Azar gets rowdy when market stalls are set up on the streets in the late afternoon. There's a row of more low-key evening *hawkers* east of Jalan Jubilee, and a small daytime *food centre* next to the Birch Memorial Clock Tower.

There's an *A&W* branch near the Plaza Ocean shopping complex. At 8 Jalan Dato Maharaja Lela, *The Miners' Arms* is a well-decorated English pub and is a good place to get meaty grills and bargain lunch sets (RM9).

The huge *central market* has a variety of fruit and vegies; it's a great place if you're putting your own meals together. The *French* and *Noor Jahan* bakeries on Jalan Raja Ekram sell Indian-style breads and pastries. There are supermarkets on the ground floor of the *Plaza Ocean shopping complex* and the larger, classier *Ipoh Parade shopping centre* on Jalan Abdul Adil. The latter also has a *Delifrance* and the quirky *Banana Paradise Cafe*, as well as a bowling alley, cineplex and bookshops.

Just west of Ipoh Parade, across from the Hotel Syuen, *Coffee Craft* is a noteworthy cafe for its hand-brewed coffees, mixed juices and light meals. It's a good place to hook up with local expats.

Far from the city centre, but worthy of mention nonetheless, is *Beacon Point* (☎ 546 9916, 41 Lintasan Perajurit 6). The brother-sister team that run this small cooking school and restaurant are delightful, and the brother was hired by Jodie Foster as her personal chef during the filming of *Anna & The King*. (See the boxed text 'The King & I, but not for Thais' in the Penang chapter.) The atmosphere is very casual, and the Western food is exquisitely done: filling lunch sets cost RM10, including delicious cake (walnut-carrot cake was Ms Foster's favourite). The restaurant is open from 11 am to 6 pm weekdays, and has a Saturday lunchtime buffet (RM14). From the local bus station, take a No 113 Ipoh Garden bus to Taman Perak (80 sen) or take a taxi (RM8). The restaurant is set back from the main road in a row of commercial shops, near the Taman Perak signboard.

## Getting There & Away

**Air** Pelangi Air (☎ 312 4770) flies several times a week to both KL (RM66) and Medan in Sumatra (RM228). Malaysia Airlines (☎ 241 4155, 253 0278), on Jalan Sultan Idris Shah, has a few daily departures to Johor Bahru (RM159) and KL (RM66). Car rental is available at the airport from Hertz (☎ 312 7109).

**Bus** Ipoh is on the main KL-Butterworth road; 205km north of the capital, 164km south of Butterworth. The long-distance bus station is south of the train station and the city centre, a taxi ride from the main hotel area. Numerous bus companies operate from this station, with services departing at varying times.

Destinations and standard fares include: Alor Setar (RM14); Butterworth (RM9); Hat Yai in Thailand; (RM28); Johor Bahru (RM33); Kota Bharu (RM18); Kuala Kangsar (RM3.05); KL (RM13, luxury express); Lumut (RM3.80); Melaka (RM17); and Tapah (RM3.80). Try to book your tickets in advance or turn up early, especially for the crowded, infrequent service to Tapah.

Perak Roadways has a separate terminus directly across Jalan Tun Abdul Razak, with regular buses to Lumut (1¾ hours, RM3.70).

The city bus station is north-west of the long-distance station on the other side of the roundabout. Local buses depart from here for outlying regions close to Ipoh, such as Batu Gajah and Gopeng (for Kellie's Castle), and Kuala Kangsar.

**Train** Ipoh's train station is on the main Singapore-Butterworth line and all trains stop here. Trains run to KL (RM22/40 2nd/1st class) at 1.40 and 10.05 am and 7 pm; the 10.05 am service continues to Singapore. Trains to Butterworth (RM21/36) leave at 1.29 and 11.08 am and 6.38 pm; the 1.29 am service continues to Hat Yai in Thailand.

**Taxi** Long-distance taxis depart from in front of the long-distance bus station, and there is another rank directly across the road. Whole-taxi fares include: Butterworth (RM100); Cameron Highlands (RM100); Ipoh airport (RM40); Kuala Kangsar (RM25); KL (RM120); Lumut (RM40); Taiping (RM40); and Tapah (RM40). Taxis from here cost a steep RM5 to RM6 anywhere around town, but in the city centre should only cost RM2 to RM3.

## AROUND IPOH
### Kellie's Castle
This amazing leftover from colonial times is set by a small river about 30km south of Ipoh. The castle referred to is, in fact, an old unfinished mansion, nicknamed 'Kellie's Folly'. It was cast in the mould of great colonial houses, complete with Moorish-style windows and a lift (elevator). Wealthy British rubber-plantation owner William Kellie Smith, who already lived in another splendid mansion in this area, commissioned the building of the 'castle', which was to be the home of his son. Seventy Hindu artisans were brought from Madras to work on the mansion. Smith died in Lisbon in 1926 on a trip home to England, and the house was never finished. The jungle has reclaimed some of the building, entwined with vines and massive trees, but it's now a well-tended tourist site. Kellie's Castle is open from 8.30 am to 6 pm daily, and admission is RM3.

About 500m from the castle is a **Hindu temple**, built for the artisans by Smith when a mysterious illness decimated the workforce and the remaining workers believed that the gods needed to be appeased. To show their gratitude to Smith, the workers placed a figure of him, complete with white suit and pith helmet, among the Hindu deities on the temple roof.

Kellie's Castle is inconvenient to reach without your own transport. From Ipoh's city bus station you can take either the frequent No 66 bus to Gopeng (RM1.30) or the less-frequent No 36 bus to Batu Gajah. The No 67 bus runs approximately every hour in either direction between Batu Gajah and Gopeng, passing in front of Kellie's Castle. You can also charter a taxi from Ipoh (RM35 return).

### Tambun Hot Springs
The Tambun Hot Springs are 8km northeast of Ipoh, beside a lake, at the base of forested limestone cliffs. These natural thermal springs have long been a popular getaway for locals, with various hot pools in which to 'take the waters' (RM5).

Regular buses from Ipoh's city bus station to Tanjung Rambutan pass the hot springs.

## LUMUT
Lumut is the departure point for Pulau Pangkor and – despite attempts to promote the town as a tourist destination in its own right – has little to offer apart from souvenir shops selling shells, and some reasonable beaches outside town. In Lumut the Visit Perak Year 2000 tourism campaign got off to a shaky start when an aerial sightseeing plane nose-dived into the waters off-shore; no passengers were aboard and both pilots were rescued by a passing fishing boat.

The Malaysian Navy has its principal base just outside town, and some 25,000 sailors make up the overwhelming majority of the town's inhabitants. You'll see the huge, Singapore-like apartment complexes of the naval quarters as you take the boat out to Pulau Pangkor.

The sailors frequent **Teluk Batik**, a good beach 7km from town. There's no bus service here, but a one-way taxi costs RM10.

### Information
The Tourism Malaysia office (☎ 683 4057) is midway between the jetty and the bus station on Jalan Sultan Idris Shah. Next door you'll find a moneychanger offering better rates than on Pulau Pangkor, and Maybank is farther down the street.

Motorists on their way to Pangkor can use the 24-hour, long-term car park behind the Shell petrol station, next to the bus station (RM6 per day).

### Places to Stay & Eat
If you get marooned on the way to Pangkor, Lumut has a few reasonable hotels and restaurants.

You'll find the ***Phin Lum Hooi Hotel*** (*☎ 683 5641, 93 Jalan Titi Panjang*) about half a kilometre out of town from the jetty, not far past the bus station. Fan/air-con rooms are RM18/26; the hotel is clean and friendly with a good, cheap restaurant downstairs. A few doors back is the ***Harbour View Hotel*** *(☎ 683 7888)*, offering comfortable standard/deluxe air-con rooms with attached bath for RM50/65.

On Jalan Iskandar Shah, near the jetty, ***Hotel Indah*** *(☎ 683 5064)* at No 208 is a good mid-range hotel with spotless air-con rooms for RM40, or RM45 facing the sea with a balcony.

About 1km farther out towards the navy base, the international-class hotel ***Orient Star*** *(☎ 683 4199)* is on the waterfront but has no beach. Doubles start at RM220, including breakfast.

## Getting There & Away

**Bus** Lumut is 170km south of Butterworth and 83km south-west of Ipoh, the main turn-off for Lumut on the KL-Butterworth road. The bus station is a 10-minute walk from the ferry jetty, and just east of the town centre. On Pulau Pangkor, the bus agent next to Pangkor town's Chuan Full Hotel handles bookings for the express buses.

Lumut is well connected to other destinations on the peninsula. The most-frequent buses take the new highway to/from Ipoh (hourly, RM3.80). Direct buses run hourly to/from KL (four hours, RM13.30) and a few times a day to/from: Butterworth (RM10); Johor Bahru/Singapore (RM40); Melaka (RM21); and Taiping (RM4.50). From Butterworth you can also take a bus to Taiping, then another bus to Lumut. There are no direct buses from Lumut to the Cameron Highlands; take a bus to Ipoh, then transfer to a bus to Tapah, then yet another local bus to Tanah Rata. Allow at least half a day.

**Taxi** Long-distance taxis from Lumut can be scarce late in the day. Typical fares are: Butterworth (RM120); Ipoh (RM40); and KL (RM150).

## PULAU PANGKOR

The island of Pangkor is not far from Lumut, and is easily accessible via Ipoh. It's a low-

key resort island noted for its fine beaches. These can be visited via the road running around the island; however, the jungle-clad hills of the interior are virtually untouched.

At 8 sq km, and with a population of 25,000, Pangkor is a relatively small island, but that hasn't stopped the state government from trying to promote it as one of Malaysia's main tourist destinations. Although development is relatively limited, Pangkor's laid-back, kampung feel is slowly disappearing. Before tourism took off, Pangkor's economy relied on fishing. Fishing and dried fish products are still a major industry for the island, particularly on the east coast.

Pangkor was a bit-player in the battle to control trade in the Strait of Melaka. In earlier times, the island was a favourite refuge of fishermen, sailors, merchants and pirates. In the 17th century, the Dutch built a fort here in their bid to monopolise the Perak tin trade, but were less than keen to defend Perak against Acehnese and Siamese incursions. The Dutch were driven out by a local ruler before returning briefly some 50 years later. In 1874 a contender to the Perak throne sought British backing, and the Pangkor Treaty was signed. As a result, British Resident JWW Birch was installed in Perak and the colonial era on the peninsula began.

Pangkor is a popular local resort, only a 30-minute ferry ride from Lumut on the mainland and close to large population centres, so crowds are inevitable. It's popular on weekends and holidays, but during the week the beaches are almost empty. A visit to the island is still principally a 'laze on the beach' operation, but there are also a few interesting things to do.

Many female travellers have reported serious harassment on Pangkor, especially when going off the beaten path into the jungle or cycling around the island. Following and molesting foreign women seems to be a local sport, even on the most populated beaches, and police do nothing to stop it.

## Orientation

Finding things on Pangkor is very simple. The east coast of the island, facing the mainland, is a continuous village strip

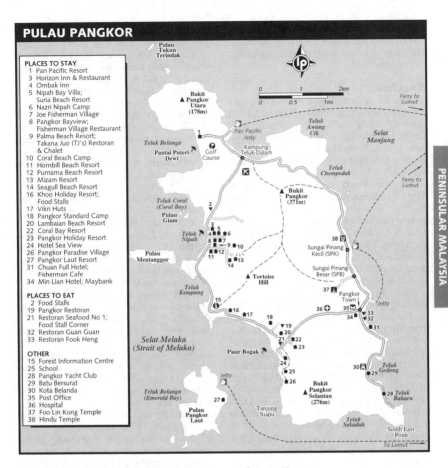

## PULAU PANGKOR

**PLACES TO STAY**
1 Pan Pacific Resort
3 Horizon Inn & Restaurant
4 Ombak Inn
5 Nipah Bay Villa;
   Suria Beach Resort
6 Nazri Nipah Camp
7 Joe Fisherman Village
8 Pangkor Bayview;
   Fisherman Village Restaurant
9 Palma Beach Resort;
   Takana Juo (TJ's) Restoran
   & Chalet
10 Coral Beach Camp
11 Hornbill Beach Resort
12 Purnama Beach Resort
13 Mizam Resort
14 Seagull Beach Resort
16 Khoo Holiday Resort;
   Food Stalls
17 Vikri Huts
18 Pangkor Standard Camp
20 Lambaian Beach Resort
22 Coral Bay Resort
23 Pangkor Holiday Resort
24 Hotel Sea View
26 Pangkor Paradise Village
27 Pangkor Laut Resort
31 Chuan Full Hotel;
   Fisherman Cafe
34 Min Lian Hotel; Maybank

**PLACES TO EAT**
2 Food Stalls
19 Pangkor Restoran
21 Restoran Seafood No 1;
   Food Stall Corner
32 Restoran Guan Guan
33 Restoran Fook Heng

**OTHER**
15 Forest Information Centre
25 School
28 Pangkor Yacht Club
29 Batu Bersurat
30 Kota Belanda
35 Post Office
36 Hospital
37 Foo Lin Kong Temple
38 Hindu Temple

PENINSULAR MALAYSIA

comprising Sungai Pinang Kecil (SPK), Sungai Pinang Besar (SPB) and Pangkor town, the main town.

The road that runs along the east coast turns west at Pangkor town and runs directly across the island, which is only 2km wide at this point, to Pasir Bogak. From there it runs north to the village of Teluk Nipah, where you'll find most of the budget accommodation. It then goes to the northern end of the island, past the new airport, to Pangkor's flash resorts. The road from there back to the eastern side of the island is winding and very steep in parts, but it's paved all the way.

## Information

The Maybank in Pangkor town, in the same building as Hotel Min Lian, is open the usual hours, and has an ATM. For travellers cheques and cash, the moneychanger back on the mainland in Lumut offers better rates (see Information in the Lumut section earlier).

There are Internet cafes in Pangkor town and at some of the budget accommodation at Teluk Nipah. Rates remain high (RM10 per hour), but the Seagull Beach Resort in Teluk Nipah charges RM7 and the Fisherman Cafe in Pangkor town only RM6.

The bus agent next to the Chuan Full Hotel in Pangkor town handles bookings for express buses originating from Lumut on the mainland.

## Beaches

The beach at **Pasir Bogak** is OK for swimming, but during holidays it's crowded – at least by Malaysia's 'empty beach' standards. It's a lovely, if rather narrow, white-sand beach. **Teluk Nipah**, a hilly 20-minute bicycle ride farther north, has a wider, better beach.

The best beach on this side is at **Coral Bay**, 10 minutes on foot north of Teluk Nipah. The water is a clear, emerald-green colour due to the presence of limestone, and usually the beach is quite clean and pretty.

In May, June and July turtles used to come in to lay their eggs at night on **Teluk Ketapang** beach, north of Pasir Bogak. Increasing numbers of gawking tourists have seriously affected the turtles, and sightings are increasingly rare. We strongly recommend that you refrain from contributing to this problem. For more information on sea turtles see the boxed text 'The Disappearing Turtles of the East Coast' in the Terengganu chapter.

At the northern end of the island at Teluk Belanga, **Pantai Puteri Dewi** (Golden Sands Beach) is pleasant enough, but access is restricted to Pan Pacific Resort guests. Day-trippers can visit for a ridiculous RM40 (including lunch). In between there are a number of virtually deserted beaches that you can reach by boat, motorcycle or on foot.

On nearby Pulau Pangkor Laut, **Emerald Bay** is a beautiful little horseshoe-shaped bay with clear water, fine coral and a gently sloping beach. The entire island of Pangkor Laut has been taken over by a hotel conglomerate, and even tour boats are prohibited from stopping at the beach.

## Exploring the Island

The island lends itself well to exploration by motorcycle, bicycle or on foot. Spend a day doing a loop of the island, following the paved road all the way around. By motorcycle it takes about two hours with stops,

around three or four hours by bicycle, or you could even walk it in a very long day.

Along the western side there are a few deserted beaches before the road heads inland past the airport to Kampung Teluk Dalam, a straggling fishing village. Unless you can talk your way in for nothing, there's not much point in forking out RM40 to visit the Pan Pacific Resort at Teluk Belanga, so keep heading east along the new road over the headland. This is a steep and twisting road through some superb **jungle**, though quite deserted, and women travellers have been attacked here.

On the eastern side, from SPK it's a nearly continuous village strip on to Pangkor town – messy but full of interest. There's lots to look at: boat building, fish being dried or frozen, and a colourful South Indian **Hindu temple**. This is principally the Chinese and Indian part of the island. In SPB the **Foo Lin Kong Temple**, on the side of the hill just west of the main road, is worth a quick look.

Pangkor's one bit of history is 3km south of Pangkor town at Teluk Gedong. The **Kota Belanda** (Dutch Fort) was built here in 1670, after the Dutch had been given the boot from Lower Perak by resentful local Malays. Despite frequent visits, the Dutch weren't able to reoccupy the site and rebuild the fort until 1743; only five years later they abandoned it for good after local warrior chiefs repeatedly attacked them. The old fort was totally swallowed by the jungle until 1973, when it was reconstructed as far as the remaining bricks would allow, which wasn't much.

On the waterfront 100m beyond the fort is **Batu Bersurat**, a mammoth stone carved with the symbol of the Dutch East India Company (Veerigde Oost-Indische Compagnie; VOC) and other ancient graffiti, including a faint depiction of a tiger stealing a child. This supposedly relates to an incident when the child of a local European dignitary disappeared while playing near the rock. The Dutch liked the idea of the tiger story; the more likely explanation is that the boy was abducted by disenchanted locals.

The road ends just past the fishing village of Teluk Gedong and the defunct Pangkor Yacht Club.

## Other Activities

Snorkelling gear, boats and even jet skis can be hired at hotels or on the beach at Pasir Bogak and Teluk Nipah. A small boat to take you **snorkelling** at small nearby islands or less-accessible beaches costs RM30 for three people, after negotiation. Boats can also be hired to go to Pulau Sembilan, a group of nine islands with deserted white-sand beaches that are popular for **sports fishing**, about 1½ hours south-west of Pangkor.

The island offers some interesting **walking** opportunities. A four-hour jungle trail crosses the island from Teluk Nipah and comes out near the Foo Lin Kong Temple, while another trail leads from Pasir Bogak to Bukit Pangkor before joining the east coast road. Walking trails are lightly used and often overgrown. Take a guide and *parang* (bush knife), and protect yourself against leeches and ticks. The Forest Information Centre at the northern end of Pasir Bogak, at the start of one of the trails, could advise you, but it's usually unstaffed. See the boxed text 'That Clinging Feeling' in the Sabah chapter for tips on dealing with leeches.

## Places to Stay

Pasir Bogak is the most developed beach, consisting of a string of mid-range hotels, a few restaurants and not much else, and while it's not the Costa Brava, it does get crowded. Teluk Nipah, probably the best beach on the island, is in transition from a small kampung to another Pasir Bogak as new mid-range hotels spring up around the local guesthouses. The only other developments on Pangkor are the mega-resorts on isolated beaches.

Rates at most places vary between peak (weekends and holidays) and off-peak seasons; the following prices quoted are 'off-peak', available from Monday to Friday and in the low season.

**Teluk Nipah** At the back end of the street farthest north on this beach, the longest-running travellers' place is *Joe Fisherman Village (☎ 685 2389)*. Accommodation consists of the usual, basic A-frame

'chalets', though these may be too rustic for some. The cost is RM20 for two, or RM30 for slightly more substantial cottages. Bicycle rental is available (RM15 per day).

Less cluttered than Joe's is *Nazri Nipah Camp (☎ 685 2014)* diagonally opposite. It's an extremely friendly place at the edge of the rainforest with simple A-frames for RM20, and bungalows and larger A-frames with bathroom from RM30. Some travellers report that the management won't fix anything that's broken, though the happy-go-lucky staff will sell you beer.

Towards the beach, accommodation is mostly mid-range. The *Nipah Bay Villa (☎ 685 2198)* has fairly luxurious air-con chalets for RM60/75 a single/double. In a newer blue-and-white building, *Suria Beach Resort (☎ 685 3922)* offers great rooms with air-con, hot shower and balcony for as little as RM50 in the low season. Another fairly new construction is the *Pangkor Bayview (☎ 685 3540)*, where comfortable rooms are pricey at RM95/120 in the low/high season.

Closest to the beach along this street in a garden setting is the low-key *Ombak Inn (☎ 685 3944)*. It has various options, from A-frame huts to spic-and-span fan/air-con bungalows with attached bathroom for RM30/35. Back on the main road, *Horizon Inn (☎ 685 3398)* has nice rooms facing the sea (and the motorbike drag races on the highway) for RM70 in the low season.

The street at the southern end of Teluk Nipah also has an increasing number of places to stay. The unbeatable *Hornbill Beach Resort (☎ 685 2005)* has charming hosts who offer high standards of accommodation and service. Attractive air-con rooms, the best in Teluk Nipah, face the beach or the jungle behind and cost RM100, including breakfast.

Heading back along this street are a number of good budget and overpriced mid-range places. *Palma Beach Resort (☎ 685 3693)* has quite nice wooden chalets with TV and air-con for RM95. *Takana Juo (TJ's) Chalet (☎ 685 4733)* has a few basic, but often full, bungalows with bathroom and hammock for RM25 beside its popular restaurant.

PENINSULAR MALAYSIA

Opposite TJ's, the new, backpacker-friendly **Purnama Beach Resort** (☎ 685 4585, **@** *amibas@maxis.ne.my*) offers Internet access, a book corner and a decent restaurant. Discounted weekday rates for fan rooms without/with bath are RM35/45, and RM65 with bath and air-con. All prices include breakfast. **Coral Beach Camp** (☎ 685 2711) is a long-running budget place with tiny A-frame huts for RM20 and doubles with bathroom for RM45.

Farther down and off to your right, the squeaky-clean **Seagull Beach Resort** (☎ 685 2878) has mini-huts with shared bathroom for RM20 and agreeable fan/air-con doubles in the main house for RM30/40. The courteous staff offer the cheapest Internet access on Teluk Nipah (RM7 per hour).

Almost at the end of the road, **Mizam Resort** (☎ 685 3359) is a hidden gem where discounted backpacker rates are RM30/40 for singles/doubles with air-con, TV and bathroom!

**Pasir Bogak** The rest of Pangkor's accommodation possibilities are grouped at each end of the beach at Pasir Bogak, where there is a mixture of top end and cheaper places to stay. The atmosphere is lacking compared to Teluk Nipah, however, and fewer overseas travellers stay here. It's geared more to Malaysians on holiday.

Starting at the western end, the main building of **Khoo Holiday Resort** (☎ 685 2190, fax 685 1164) is a rather ugly concrete conglomeration, but the simple wooden chalets with bathroom on the steep slope behind have great views across to Pulau Pangkor Laut. Backpacker rates of RM41/67 for fan/air-con rooms, including breakfast, offer good value for your ringgit.

The cheapest option is **Vikri Huts** (☎ 685 4258), a short distance south-east of Khoo's. Small, rustic A-frame huts with a mattress on the floor cost RM20 per person, but they're in a shady grove and remain fairly cool. Banana-leaf dinners are served straight from the family's kitchen.

If you continue east on the main road you'll reach the similarly styled **Pangkor**

**Standard Camp** (☎ 685 1878). Cramped three-person A-frame huts cost RM31.50/ 37.80 and two-person chalets go for RM42/52.50 in the low/high seasons. Bicycles are available for rent.

The other hotels are at the eastern end of the beach, where the road from Pangkor town crosses the island. North of the intersection, **Lambaian Beach Resort** (☎ 685 4020, fax 685 4022) is a solid mid-range place with twins/doubles for RM128/168. On the southern side, the **Hotel Sea View** (☎ 685 1605) has an inviting pool but very average air-con doubles with bathroom for RM115, and better family rooms or chalets for RM161, all including breakfast. Significant discounts may be available.

The **Pangkor Paradise Village** (☎ 691 3241, 685 1496) is a locals' retreat in a coconut grove at the southernmost end of Pasir Bogak, and is accessible only via a track leading around the side of a school. It has rather ordinary (and sometimes dirty) chalets for one or two people with fan/air-con for RM50/75, but the isolated little beach here and the serene location are the real attractions. There's a small restaurant right on the water.

On the road to Pangkor town, **Coral Bay Resort** (☎ 685 5111, fax 685 5666) is a bland complex with good-quality rooms from RM265 – rather overpriced since it's not even on the beach, though major discounts of more than 50% may be available.

**Pangkor Town** As the whole attraction of Pangkor is the beaches, there is little point in staying in Pangkor town, but if you get stuck, there are several cheap Chinese hotels.

**Min Lian Hotel** (☎ 685 1294), right above the Maybank, is tidy and welcoming. Air-con rooms start at RM40. **Chuan Full Hotel** (☎ 685 1123, 60 Jalan Besar) is a rickety old wooden hotel, but is immaculately kept and has a veranda at the back overlooking the waterfront. Singles/doubles cost RM15/20 with bathroom; air-con rooms cost RM35.

**Elsewhere on the Island** The lush, secluded grounds of the **Pan Pacific Resort**

(☎ 685 1091/1399, fax 685 1852) are at Teluk Belanga on the northern end of the island. Prices start at RM380 for standard rooms, RM580 for the 'House on the Rocks' and RM780 for a bungalow. Recreational facilities include a golf course, and the resort is on a very pleasant stretch of beach. Access is restricted to hotel guests, although day-trippers are admitted for RM40 (including lunch).

**Pangkor Laut** Pulau Pangkor Laut, dubbed 'Fantasy Island' and opposite Pasir Bogak, is totally in the grasp of the *Pangkor Laut Resort (☎ 699 1100, fax 699 1200)*. It is certainly exclusive and does its best to shun locals, day-trippers and other riff-raff. There are tennis courts, a small swimming pool, two restaurants, a disco and three or four private beaches around the island, including the picturesque Emerald Bay on the western side. Water sports equipment can be rented.

Rates for forest bungalows start at RM605, but you should really splurge on the picture-perfect villas built on stilts over the water for RM950 (you can sneak a peek at www.pangkorlautresort.com). There's a reservation office at Lumut on the mainland that arranges transport to the island by boat (or helicopter!).

### Places to Eat

**Teluk Nipah** Teluk Nipah has some basic *food stalls* at the beach and a couple of restaurants.

By far the most popular, and deservedly so, *Takana Juo (TJ's) Restoran* is a family-run Indonesian restaurant at the bungalows of the same name. TJ's cooks up delicious, cheap food – often with a teasingly long wait before it arrives. It's open for breakfast, lunch and dinner.

Downstairs from the Horizon Inn, *Restaurant Horizon* has sunset views, al fresco dining and some good seafood, though prices are high. Farther back from the beach along the same street, *Fisherman Village Restaurant* (not to be confused with Joe Fisherman Village) comes recommended by travellers, though it's usually only open for dinner.

**Pasir Bogak** All the hotels have restaurants, and there are a few other places to eat.

*Khoo Holiday Resort* has a good, inexpensive restaurant, and there are *food stalls* nearby.

At the opposite end of the beach, near the Lambaian Beach Resort, is a permanent *food-stall corner*. Here you'll also find the upmarket *Restoran Seafood No 1*, where an excellent meal of prawns, fish or crab costs around RM25 per person. The karaoke joint here constitutes Pangkor's only nightlife.

Tucked away along a small dirt road running alongside Pangkor Standard Camp, *Pangkor Restoran* is cheap for Chinese seafood and popular with locals.

The restaurant hidden away at *Pangkor Paradise Village* is outdoors, right by the beach. Although the food is only mediocre, it's an excellent place to watch the sunset.

**Pangkor Town** Pangkor town has a proliferation of cheap, Chinese *kedai kopi* (coffee shops), some of which serve excellent seafood. *Restoran Guan Guan* on Jalan Besar is an old favourite for seafood cooked any way you like; prices are posted on the wall-sized English menu. *Restoran Fook Heng* is also popular.

### Getting There & Away

**Air** Berjaya Air (☎ 685 5828) has flights almost every day between KL's Subang airport and Pangkor airport in the north (RM141).

**Boat** In the high season, the Pan Silver Ferry (☎ 685 1046) runs between Lumut and Pangkor town every 30 minutes from 6.30 am to 8 pm. Most ferries to Lumut stop at SPK before reaching Pangkor town, so don't hop off too soon. The one-way fare is RM2 for open-air boats or RM3 for air-con; just take whichever one departs first. On weekends and holidays, the last boat leaves Pangkor town at 8.40 pm and Lumut at 9 pm.

There are also ferries every 1½ to two hours in either direction between Lumut and the jetty at the northern end of the island, across the isthmus from the Pan Pacific Resort. The first ferry leaves Lumut at

8.30 am, and the last leaves at 6.30 pm (8 pm on Friday, Saturday and the eve of public holidays).

## Getting Around
There are no public buses available to tourists, so you will be forced to use Pangkor's shockingly pink minibus taxis. Set fares for up to three people from the jetty in Pangkor town include: Pasir Bogak (RM4); Teluk Nipah (RM10); Pan Pacific Resort (RM18); the airport (RM18); and around the island (RM35 to RM40).

An ideal way to see the island is by motorcycle or bicycle (see Exploring the Island earlier in this section). There are a number of places at Pangkor town, Pasir Bogak and Teluk Nipah that rent motorcycles for around RM30 per day and bicycles for RM15. Cars must be left on the mainland.

## KUALA KANGSAR
Beside the highway, north-west of Ipoh, Kuala Kangsar has been the royal town of Perak state since the sultan moved his capital here in the 18th century. It was also the first foothold for the British, who moved to control the peninsula by installing Residents at the royal courts in the 1870s. By the 1890s the rapid growth of the tin towns of Ipoh and Taiping overshadowed Kuala Kangsar, and the town remains a quiet backwater steeped in Malay tradition.

This small town has a split personality. The small central business area bustles, but to the south-east, overlooking the Sungai Perak, the royal district is spacious and quiet – this is the most attractive of all Malaysia's royal cities. Kuala Kangsar's main sights are few, but they're quite impressive and can easily be explored in a morning or afternoon, or as a day trip from Ipoh, including a detour en route to Perak Tong Temple (see that entry in the Ipoh section earlier in this chapter).

## Things to See
Heading out on Jalan Istana beside the wide Sungai Perak, the first striking example of the wealth of the sultanate is the small, but magnificent **Masjid Ubudiah**. The mosque appears as if viewed through a distorting mirror, since its minarets are squeezed up tightly against the superb golden onion-dome. It was completed in 1917, after delays due to WWI and rampant elephants that destroyed the Italian marble tiles.

Overlooking the river, **Istana Iskandariah** is a suitably opulent palace built in 1933. It is best viewed from the river side to appreciate the original palace, which mixes Art Deco with Islamic motifs. The 1984 annexe, on the southern side, is less striking. Unfortunately, the palace is not open to visitors.

Farther east is an earlier, wooden palace, **Istana Kenangan** (Palace of Memories), which served as the temporary royal quarters until the Istana Iskandariah was completed. This older palace was constructed in 1931, without the use of nails. It now houses the **Muzium Di Raja** (Royal Museum), with displays on the state's history and the Perak royal family. The museum is open from 9.30 am to 5 pm daily (closed 12.15 to 2.45 pm Friday); entry is free.

Closer to town on Jalan Istana near the Masjid Ubudiah, **Istana Hulu** is another substantial palace inspired by Victorian architecture. Built in 1903, it is now the Raja Perempuan Mazwin School.

Kuala Kangsar was the birthplace of Malaysia's great **rubber industry**. In the late 1870s, a number of rubber trees were planted by British Resident Hugh Low in his gardens in Kuala Kangsar, from seed stock allegedly either smuggled out of Brazil or taken from London's Kew Gardens. However, it was not until the invention of the pneumatic tyre in 1888, and then the popularity of the motor car at the start of the 20th century, that rubber suddenly came into demand and rubber plantations sprang up across the country. Almost all of the trees in the new plantations were descended from Low's original rubber trees, or from the Singapore Botanic Gardens. You can still see one of those first trees in the District Office compound.

The **Malay College** to the north of town is the most impressive colonial building in Kuala Kangsar. Established in 1905, it was the first and one of the only Malay schools

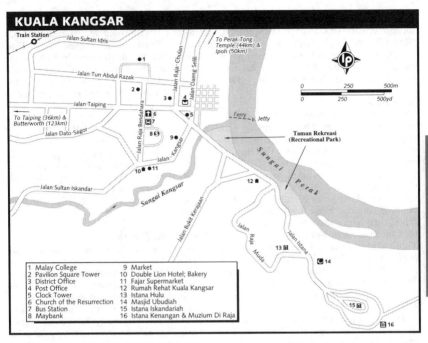

**KUALA KANGSAR**

1 Malay College
2 Pavilion Square Tower
3 District Office
4 Post Office
5 Clock Tower
6 Church of the Resurrection
7 Bus Station
8 Maybank
9 Market
10 Double Lion Hotel; Bakery
11 Fajar Supermarket
12 Rumah Rehat Kuala Kangsar
13 Istana Hulu
14 Masjid Ubudiah
15 Istana Iskandariah
16 Istana Kenangan & Muzium Di Raja

PENINSULAR MALAYSIA

to provide English education for the Malay elite destined for the civil service. It not only provided clerical workers for the British administration but also the nationalist leaders of the conservative 'Malaya for Malays' faction. In the 1950s Anthony Burgess wrote his first book while teaching here.

Opposite the Malay College, the **Pavilion Square Tower** is a delightful folly overlooking the surrounding parkland and playing fields. Built in 1930, this small, three-storey sports pavilion of Malay and colonial design allowed royalty and VIPs to view polo matches in comfort.

### Places to Stay & Eat

Kuala Kangsar has a couple of cheap hotels for an overnight stay. The most convenient is the recently renovated *Double Lion Hotel* (☎ 776 1010, 74 Jalan Kangsar), close to the bus station behind a tempting bakery. Large fan singles/doubles with

bathroom are good value at RM25/30. Newer air-con rooms at the rear with all mod cons cost RM70/80.

The best place in town is the modernised resthouse *Rumah Rehat Kuala Kangsar* (☎ 776 5872), just off Jalan Istana near a kris monument. Many of the spacious, air-con rooms overlook the river and range from RM70 to RM100. There's a reasonable Malay restaurant, also with a river view.

The *Fajar* supermarket and *KFC* are next to the Double Lion Hotel.

### Getting There & Away

Kuala Kangsar is 50km north-west of Ipoh, just off the main KL-Butterworth road. It's 123km south of Butterworth and 255km north of KL. Frequent bus connections include: Butterworth (RM8); Ipoh (RM3.05); KL (RM16); Lumut (RM6.50); and Taiping (RM2.05). There are occasional services to Kota Bharu (RM14.50).

PENINSULAR MALAYSIA

Taxis leave from next to the bus station for: Butterworth (RM54); Ipoh (RM26); KL (RM100); and Taiping (RM16).

The train station is less-conveniently located to the north-west of town. All KL-Butterworth trains stop in Kuala Kangsar.

## TAIPING

The 'Town of Everlasting Peace' hardly started out that way. Over a century ago, when it was known as Larut, the town was a raucous, rough-and-tumble tin-mining centre, the oldest one in Malaysia. Bitter feuds broke out three times between rival Chinese secret societies, with injury, torture and death taking place on all sides. When colonial administrators finally brought the bloody mayhem under control in 1874, they took the prudent step of renaming the town. Though it was then the largest and most important town in Perak, by 1890 Ipoh and the Kinta Valley had begun to overshadow Taiping as the centre of the tin industry, and the state capital was finally moved over in 1935.

Though Taiping has lost its former status, the tourist brochures still boast of the town's '31 Firsts' for Malaysia, including the first museum, the first railway, the first newspapers in English (and Tamil!) and the country's first zoo.

Taiping is now a low-key town, and any new developments are on the outskirts along the highway. The town centre is down-at-heel but lively, in contrast to the old colonial district centred on the town's famous green and tranquil Lake Gardens. Apart from misty, Chinese-looking views, Taiping also has quite a number of old, well-preserved Anglo-Malay buildings, good food in the night market, few other tourists and easy access to the hill station of Bukit Larut to the east.

## Information

There's a Tourist Police office at the taxi station on Jalan Iskandar, but it's unhelpfully unstaffed.

The centrally located Net Surfer Internet cafe on Jalan Lim Hee Tooi charges RM2 per hour.

## Taman Tasik Taiping

Taiping is renowned for its beautiful 62-hectare Taman Tasik Taiping (Lake Gardens), built beside the town in 1880 on the site of an abandoned tin mine. The well-kept gardens owe their lush greenery to the fact that Taiping's annual rainfall is one of the highest in Peninsular Malaysia. In the hills that rise above the gardens is Bukit Larut (formerly Maxwell Hill), the oldest hill station in Malaysia.

The Lake Gardens also contain the small, but pleasantly landscaped **Zoo Taiping**. It's open from 8.30 am to 6.30 pm daily, but you won't see many animals in the midday heat. Admission is RM2/4 for children/adults.

## Muzium Perak

North-west of the gardens, the Muzium Perak (State Museum) is housed in a fine colonial building. It's the oldest museum in Malaysia, operating since 1883, but not one of the best. Exhibits are mostly limited to detailed displays on the making of kris swords. The motley collection of stuffed Malaysian animals is slightly repugnant but very educational, and includes almost all native mammals and many birds. The museum is open from 9 am to 5 pm daily (closed from 12.15 to 2.45 pm on Friday); entry is free.

## Historic Buildings

A stroll around town will reveal reminders of Taiping's former glory. The neoclassical **District Office** on Jalan Alang Ahmad (it's set back from the street at the edge of Taiping's central Chinatown), and at the start of the colonial district around today's Lake Gardens. Around the corner is the **Perpustakaan Merdeka** (Independence Library), established in 1882. Closer to town on Jalan Kota, the 1890 **Jam Besar Lama** (Old Clock Tower) once functioned as Taiping's fire station. It's now, of all things, a travel agency.

Taiping was the starting point for Malaysia's first railway line, now defunct. Opened in 1885, it ran 13.5km to Port Weld. The original train station is a few steps west of gracious, colonial **King Edward VII**

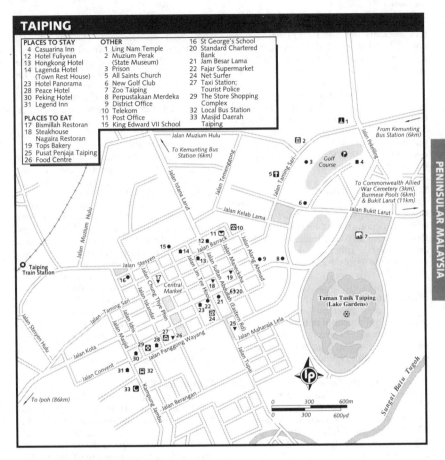

## TAIPING

**PLACES TO STAY**
4 Casuarina Inn
12 Hotel Fuliyean
13 Hongkong Hotel
14 Lagenda Hotel
(Town Rest House)
23 Hotel Panorama
28 Peace Hotel
30 Peking Hotel
31 Legend Inn

**PLACES TO EAT**
17 Bismillah Restoran
18 Steakhouse
Nagaira Restoran
19 Tops Bakery
25 Pusat Penjaja Taiping
26 Food Centre

**OTHER**
1 Ling Nam Temple
2 Muzium Perak
(State Museum)
3 Prison
5 All Saints Church
6 New Golf Club
7 Zoo Taiping
8 Perpustakaan Merdeka
9 District Office
10 Telekom
11 Post Office
15 King Edward VII School

16 St George's School
20 Standard Chartered
Bank
21 Jam Besar Lama
22 Fajar Supermarket
24 Net Surfer
27 Taxi Station;
Tourist Police
29 The Store Shopping
Complex
32 Local Bus Station
33 Masjid Daerah
Taiping

PENINSULAR MALAYSIA

**School**, the classrooms of which were used as torture chambers by the Japanese during WWII. Also on Jalan Stesyen are **St George's School** and the **Town Rest House** (1894), formerly the governor's residence and now the Lagenda Hotel. Another colonial-era landmark is the white-washed **New Golf Club** building on Jalan Bukit Larut, also dating from 1894.

Taiping has a number of fine old shophouses, such as the converted **Peace Hotel** on Jalan Iskandar. The Peranakan architecture has stucco tiles, stained glass, and beautifully carved bird and flower designs

on the upper wall dividers inside. Renovation would turn it into a real showpiece, but until then don't contemplate staying here – it's a seedy dive.

Opposite Muzium Perak, the **prison**, built in 1885 to house lawless miners, was used by the Japanese during WWII, later as a rehabilitation centre for captured Communists during the Emergency and then for housing political detainees under the Internal Security Act (ISA) ruling.

Just south-west of the museum and the prison, **All Saints' Church** (1887) is said to be the oldest Anglican church in Malaysia,

and it's looking its age. The church cemetery contains the historic graves of early
colonial settlers, most of whom were struck
down by tropical diseases or failed to
achieve the colonial pension needed to return home to Britain or Australia.

To the north of the museum, the colourful, gaudy **Ling Nam Temple** is the oldest
Chinese temple in Perak. The temple has
been recently renovated and there's not
much of the old temple left apart from a
boat figure dedicated to the emperor who
built China's first canal.

## Other Attractions

Taiping has a **Commonwealth Allied War
Cemetery** just east of the Lake Gardens,
with row upon row of headstones for the
British, Australian and Indian troops killed
during WWII. Farther on, down a side road,
the **Burmese Pools** are a popular bathing
spot by the river.

## Places to Stay

Taiping has an excellent selection of moderately priced accommodation. Most of the
cheap hotels are scattered around the central
market, the liveliest (but noisiest) part of
town. The better choices are a few streets
away.

The **Hongkong Hotel** (☎ 807 3824), at
79 Jalan Barrack (the entrance is on Jalan
Lim Tee Hooi), is close to everything, but in
a quiet side street. Its simplest fan rooms for
RM23 are small and rather grubby, but the
larger rooms with air-con for RM32 are a
better deal.

In the same area, the friendly **Peking
Hotel** (☎ 807 2975, 2 Jalan Idris) is a fine
old colonial building that served as the headquarters of the Kampeitei (Japanese military
police) during WWII. It's a cleaned-up version of the Peace Hotel (see Historic Buildings earlier), but the quiet, basic rooms for
RM27 are not very clean; better singles/
doubles with air-con cost RM35/RM40.

**Hotel Fuliyean** (☎ 806 8648, 14 Jalan
Barrack) is a newer mid-range hotel with
dazzling tilework everywhere. Immaculate
doubles/triples with bathroom, hot water,
TV and phone are great value at RM40/45.

The historic Town Rest House was once
the governor's residence. This old colonial
building's charm has survived a recent renovation, and it's now the pinkish **Lagenda
Hotel** (☎ 805 3333, fax 805 3355, 101 Jalan
Stesyen). Standard rooms (with TV, movies
and phone) start at RM70, including breakfast at the attractive coffee house downstairs.

Taiping's best hotel is the **Legend Inn**
(☎ 806 0000, fax 806 6666), a three-star
hotel opposite the local bus station, with
superior/deluxe rooms for RM76/96 after
discount, which is quite a bargain. Rooms
have all the trimmings, and the hotel has a
good coffee shop in the lobby.

Formerly the Rumah Rehat Baru resthouse, the chain **Casuarina Inn** (☎ 804
1339), near the Lake Gardens, is approached through the pillars of what was
once the British Resident's house – you can
drive through the remains of Hugh Low's
living room. This large, modern, concrete
resthouse was under renovation at time of
writing, but it looked to be only so-so value
at RM70 for doubles with bathroom, phone
and air-con, or RM103.50 for a family
room. It's close to Taiping's main attractions, but well out of the city centre, so
you'll need a taxi to get there.

## Places to Eat

Taiping has a good array of food centres.
The **Pusat Penjaja Taiping** takes up a whole
block on Jalan Tupai and serves mostly Chinese food, with a Malay section at one end.
The covered stalls next to the taxi station are
very clean and sell a variety of dishes. Taiping's large night market also has many
open-air eating stalls; *murtabak* (roti filled
with pieces of mutton, chicken or vegetables) and delicious *ayam percik* (marinated chicken on skewers) are specialities.

Taiping also has a host of coffee shops
serving economical food. One of the oldest
and most venerable is the **Bismillah
Restoran**, noted for its roti and biryani. It's
north of the central market at 138 Jalan
Taming Sari. More centrally, **Tops Bakery**
has good, cheap rolls and coffee. One block
west, **Steakhouse Nagaira Restoran** serves
Western set lunches for RM6, as well as

steaks. It attracts a mostly male lounge-clientele.

The relaxing *Lagenda Cafe* at the Lagenda Hotel and the Legend Inn's *lobby restaurant* both serve Western and Malaysian coffee-shop fare at slightly inflated prices.

The *Fajar supermarket* is on Jalan Lim Tee Hooi.

## Getting There & Away

Taiping is several kilometres off the main KL-Butterworth road. It's 99km south of Butterworth and 291km north of KL. The express-bus station is out in the sticks, at Kemunting near the highway, 7km north of the town centre. Frequent buses go to Butterworth (RM6), Ipoh (RM4) and KL (RM13.20), with less-frequent connections to other destinations like Kota Bharu (RM18), Johor Bahru (RM35) and Lumut (RM4.50).

There are no hotels nearby, nor any reason to stay in Kemunting – hop the next bus (80 sen) or taxi (RM5) to the town centre. If you just want to visit Taiping for the day, the left-luggage counter at the bus station is open from 9 am to 11 pm daily (RM2 per bag).

The local bus station is in the centre of Taiping, near the central market. Non-air-con buses depart for surrounding villages and Kuala Kangsar. You can get to Kemunting from the local bus station on the No 8 bus (80 sen).

All KL-Butterworth trains stop at Taiping's train station, 1km west of the town centre.

Regular long-distance taxis operate from the taxi station near the central market to Butterworth or Ipoh for RM50 and to Kuala Kangsar for RM22.

## BUKIT LARUT

The oldest hill station in Malaysia, Bukit Larut (Maxwell Hill) is 12km from Taiping, at an altitude of 1019m. It was formerly a tea estate named for the first assistant British Resident in Perak, who 'opened' the hill, and this quiet little station is simply a cool and peaceful place to visit. There are no golf courses, fancy restaurants or other hill-station trappings, let alone casinos. Few people visit Bukit Larut – in fact, bungalows here only accommodate around 70 visitors. During the school holidays, all are full.

Even if you don't stay, Bukit Larut can be an excellent day trip. Getting up to the hill station is half the fun, and once there, you've got fine views over Taiping and the Lake Gardens far below. On a clear day, from the road near the top you can see the coast all the way from Penang to Pulau Pangkor.

## Exploring the Hill

Most visitors go up and back by Land Rover, though the hill is also a favourite with locals who walk up in three to four hours. The walk along the road through the jungle is pleasant but taxing. You can also choose to take a Land Rover up and walk down.

The first stop is at the crumbling **Tea Gardens** checkpoint at the Batu 3.5 (Km 5.5) mark, where a ramshackle guesthouse and a few exotic trees are the only reminder of the former tea estate. Next up, at Batu 6 (Km 9.5), you'll find the Bukit Larut Guesthouse, Bungalow Beringin and a canteen for meals. The Land Rovers stop at the main administration office, where you book for the return journey if you haven't already – very advisable on weekends. There are some tame strolls through the nearby gardens from here.

The Land Rovers usually continue 2km up the hill to Gunung Hijau Rest House. Nearby are the Cendana, Tempinis and Sri Kanangan bungalows (see Places to Stay & Eat). From here it's a 30-minute walk along the road, noted for its profusion of **butterflies**, to the Telekom transmitter station at the top of the hill.

The jungle on the hill is superb, but the only real trail for exploring leads off the main road from between the two transmission towers. (It's best to do all your **walking** in the mornings, as afternoon rains cause dangerous, gigantic sparks – large enough to hit your head – along the transmission lines.) The trail follows a practically abandoned path to **Gunung Hijau** (1448m). You can usually only follow the leech-ridden path for about 15 minutes to an

PENINSULAR MALAYSIA

old pumping station (now, curiously, functioning as a small Shiva shrine) but even on this short walk there's a good chance of seeing monkeys and numerous birds. Beyond the shrine the trail is periodically cleared but quickly becomes overgrown; it's advisable to take a guide with you.

Walking back down the road, it takes half an hour from Gunung Hijau Rest House to the main post at Bukit Larut Guesthouse, another hour to the Tea Gardens checkpoint, then another 1½ hours to get to the Land Rover station at the bottom of the hill, near the Taiping Lake Gardens.

## Places to Stay & Eat

You can book space in one of the bungalows by ringing ☎ 807 7241, or by writing to the Officer in Charge, Bukit Larut Hill Resort, Taiping. If you haven't booked earlier, you can ring from the Land Rover station at the bottom of the hill.

*Bukit Larut Guesthouse* (1036m) *Gunung Hijau Rest House* (1113m) each have four doubles for RM15. The bungalows *Beringin* (1036m), *Cendana* (1139m) and *Tempinis* (1143m) are equipped with kitchens, so you need to bring provisions. Beringin and Cendana both accommodate up to eight people and cost RM150 and RM100 respectively. Tempinis can accommodate 10 people and costs RM100. You pay for the whole bungalow, regardless of how many people are in your party. Meals are available from the caretakers at the bungalows, but they need advance notice and they'll drive a hard bargain (as much as RM95 to start, just for dinner).

*Rumah Angkasa* and *Sri Kayangan* are more luxurious and normally available only for VIPs. The *Tea Gardens Guesthouse* has long been closed, but there are vague plans to renovate and reopen it.

There is a basic *camping ground* below the main resthouse near the Tempinis bungalow; it costs RM2 per person.

Next to the upper Land Rover office, the *Bukit Larut Guesthouse* is usually open for meals and has impressive views. Simple rice and noodle dishes are the main menu items.

## Getting There & Away

Prior to WWII, you had the choice of walking, riding a pony or being carried up in a sedan chair, as there was no road to the station. Japanese POWs were put to work building a road at the close of the war, and it was opened in 1948.

Private cars are not allowed on the road – it's only open to government Land Rovers, which run a regular service from the station at the foot of the hill, just above the Taiping Lake Gardens. They operate every hour on the hour from 8 am to 5 pm (until 4 pm in the low season), and the trip takes about 40 minutes.

The winding road negotiates 72 hairpin bends on the steep ascent, and there are superb views through the trees on the way up. The Land Rovers going up and those going down pass each other midway at the Tea Gardens. Fares are paid at the bottom of the hill – it's RM2 to the administration office and RM2.50 to Gunung Hijau Rest House. Alternatively, you can walk to the top in three or four hours.

To book a seat on a Land Rover (which is advisable), ring the station (☎ 807 7243) at the bottom of the hill. A taxi from central Taiping to this station, about 2km east of the Lake Gardens, should cost RM5.

# Penang

☎ 04

Penang state consists of Pulau Penang (Penang Island; also known as Pulau Pinang – Betelnut Island), and a narrow strip of mainland coast known as Seberang Prai (or Province Wellesley). While there's little to see on the coastal strip, the island itself and the state's capital, Georgetown, have been on the travellers' overland trail for many years.

## History

Penang has always attracted adventurers, dreamers, artists, intellectuals, scoundrels and dissidents. In 1786 Captain Francis Light, on behalf of the East India Company, acquired possession of Pulau Penang from the local sultan in return for protection against various enemies. He renamed it Prince of Wales Island, as the acquisition date fell on the Prince's birthday. It's said that Light fired silver dollars from his ship's cannons into the jungle to encourage his labourers to hack back the undergrowth for settlement.

Whatever the truth of the tale, he soon established the small town of Georgetown, also named after the Prince of Wales who later became King George IV, with Lebuh Light, Lebuh Chulia, Lebuh Pitt and Lebuh Bishop as its boundaries. Founding towns must have been a tradition for the Light family – Francis Light's son is credited with the founding of Adelaide in Australia, which is today a sister city to Georgetown. By 1800 Light had negotiated with the sultan for a strip of the mainland adjacent to the island; this became known as Province Wellesley, after the governor of India.

Light permitted new arrivals to claim as much land as they could clear, and this, together with a duty-free port and an atmosphere of liberal tolerance, quickly attracted settlers from all over Asia. Virtually uninhabited in 1786, by the turn of the 18th century Penang was home to over 10,000 people.

The local economy was slow to develop, as mostly European planters set up spice plantations – slow-growing crops requiring

## HIGHLIGHTS

- **Georgetown** – a melting pot of cultures with a wealth of preserved colonial, Chinese and Moorish architecture

- **Penang Hill** – superb views of the Selat Melaka (Strait of Melaka), an old-fashioned funicular railway and the colourful spectacle of nearby Kek Lok Si temple

- **Teluk Bahang** – forested headland hikes and a taste of *kampung* (village) life

- **Regional Food** – Nyonya cuisine, Chinese coffee-shops, spicy Indian and Thai cooking, fresh seafood and hawkers everywhere

a high initial outlay. Although the planters later turned to sugar and coconut, agriculture was hindered by a limited labour force.

In 1805 Penang became a presidency government, on a par with the cities of Chennai (Madras) and Mumbai (Bombay) in India, and so gained a much more sophisticated administrative structure. In 1816 the first English-language school in South-East Asia was opened in Georgetown.

PENINSULAR MALAYSIA

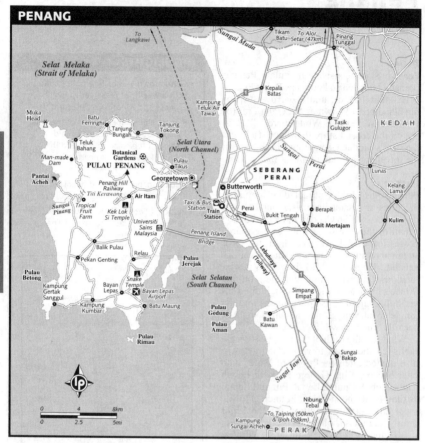

PENANG

# Seberang Prai

## BUTTERWORTH

You probably won't spend much time in the industrial town of Butterworth, as the main reason for coming here is to cross the channel to visit Pulau Penang. The town has a large ferry port and an airforce base.

The sole point of interest is the **Taman Burung Pulau Pinang** (Penang Bird Park), 12km east of the ferry terminal across the river. This landscaped park has more than 300 species of birds, mostly from South-East Asia, including 140 Malaysian varieties. It is open from

9 am to 7 pm daily; admission costs RM5/10 for children /adults. To get there, take the frequent No 515 TransitLink bus from stand No 16 at the Butterworth bus station (80 sen).

Most of the land transport (buses, trains, taxis) between Penang and other places in Peninsular Malaysia and Thailand leaves from Butterworth, not far from the train station and next to the terminal for ferries going to/from Georgetown.

## Places to Stay

Butterworth has a number of hotels, if for some reason you want to stop. Five minutes north of the bus station (take a left at the taxi-stand corner) is the dodgy, yet friendly **Beach Garden (Air-Cond.) Hotel (☎ 332 2845, 4835 Jalan Pantai).** Air-con rooms with private shower cost RM45.

Plenty of other hotels can be found a few kilometres north in the town centre proper; take a taxi. The **Ambassadress Hotel** **(☎ 332 7788, 4425 Jalan Bagan Luar)** has air-con rooms from RM52.50.

### Getting There & Away
See the Getting There & Away and Getting Around sections at the end of this chapter for information on transport to/from Butterworth.

# Pulau Penang

The 285 sq km Pulau Penang is the oldest of the British Straits settlements in Malaysia, predating both Singapore and Melaka. Penang's major city, Georgetown, is often referred to as Penang.

Central Georgetown is a sprawling, grotty Chinese city, steeped in history, with old-fashioned character that's fast disappearing. If you walk from the ferry to the main tourist centre around Lebuh Chulia in Chinatown, it would seem Penang missed the development boom that swept the rest of Malaysia in recent years. However, the repeal of rent control acts in January 2000 means that many tenants whose families have lived and run businesses in the old town for generations may soon be forced out, destroying Georgetown's historic neighbourhoods and much of its charm as well. High-rise apartments and industrial areas now crowd the outskirts of expanding Georgetown, especially south towards Penang Bridge and the airport, and west to the beaches.

Penang's beaches are touted as a big drawcard for visitors. Those along the north coast are the most visited and easily accessible. While the main resort of Batu Ferringhi has its appeal, the beaches are not nearly as spectacular as the tourist literature makes out. Beaches close to the city suffer from pollution, while those around the south of the island are undeveloped and

rather inaccessible. Most are not good for swimming, but are kept alive by hordes of package tour groups on holiday.

## GEORGETOWN
Georgetown is a real Chinatown, with more traditional Chinese flavour than Singapore or Hong Kong. Those larger cities have had their Chinese characteristics submerged, in part, under a gleaming concrete, glass and chrome confusion. In the older parts of Georgetown, however, the clock seems to have stopped 50 years ago, reminding one of Hong Kong's quieter, outlying rural islands. Georgetown is an easy-going, colourful city full of crumbling old shophouses, bicycle rickshaws and ancient trades.

The city has plenty of reminders of colonial rule, and its winding streets and old temples are always fascinating to wander around. Most visitors to Georgetown, which has countless hotels, restaurants and all the facilities of a major city. Those looking for the beach (such as it is) head to Batu Ferringhi, while more-intrepid folk are rewarded by the real *kampung* (village) atmosphere out at Teluk Bahang.

### Orientation
The old city of Georgetown has a population of 220,000 (400,000 if you count the greater urban area) out of a total of just over half a million for the whole island. Georgetown is on the north-eastern corner of the island, where the channel between island and mainland is narrowest.

A 24-hour vehicle- and passenger-ferry service operates across the 3km-wide channel between Georgetown and Butterworth on the mainland. South of the ferry crossing is the Penang Bridge, reputedly the longest in South-East Asia, which links the island with Malaysia's Lebuhraya (North-South Highway).

Georgetown is a compact city and most places can easily be reached on foot or by bicycle rickshaw. The old colonial district centres on Fort Cornwallis. Lebuh Pantai is the main street of the 'city', a financial district crammed with banks and stately buildings that once housed the colonial administration. After dark, exercise caution as this area becomes eerily deserted.

You'll find most of Georgetown's popular cheap hotels along Lebuh Chulia in Chinatown, a miniature version of Bangkok's Khao San Rd, packed with travel agencies, budget-priced restaurants and Internet cafes. At the northern end of Lebuh Chulia, Jalan Penang is a main thoroughfare and a popular shopping street. In this area are a number of upmarket hotels, including the venerable, crumbling Eastern & Oriental (E&O) Hotel at the waterfront end of the street. (See the boxed text in this chapter for this hotel's amazing story.)

If you follow Jalan Penang south, you'll pass the modern multistorey Kompleks Tun Abdul Razak (Komtar), where the Malaysia Airlines office is located, and eventually leave town and continue towards the Bayan Lepas International Airport. If you turn west at the waterfront end of Jalan Penang you'll follow the coastline and eventually come to the northern beaches, including Batu Ferringhi. This road runs right around the island back into town, via the airport.

Finding your way around Georgetown can be slightly complicated. Jalan Penang may also be referred to as Jalan Pinang or as Penang Rd – but there's also a Penang St, which may also be called Lebuh Pinang! Similarly, Chulia St is Lebuh Chulia; Pitt St is sometimes Lebuh Pitt, but is shown on some maps and signposts as Jalan Masjid Kapitan Keling. Some of the street signs still use the old spelling for Lebuh, which is Leboh. Maps are sold at bookshops (see Bookshops under Information later).

Bicycle rickshaws are the ideal way of getting around Georgetown, particularly at night when trishaw travel takes on an almost magical quality. For an excellent view over the whole sprawling scene of Georgetown, there's a viewing gallery on level 58 of Komtar. Buy your admission tickets (RM5) at the Penang Tourist Guides Association counter on the 3rd floor.

## Information
**Tourist Offices** The Penang Tourist Association (☎ 261 6663) is on Jalan Tun Syed Sheh Barakbah, near the intersection with Pesara King Edward, close to Fort Cornwallis. The central government tourist body, Tourism Malaysia (☎ 262 0066), has an office just a few doors away. Both offices are usually open from 8.30 am to 1 pm and 2 to 4.30 pm weekdays (closed from 12.30 to 2.30 pm on Friday) and from 8.30 am to 1 pm Saturday.

Although both organisations are somewhat useful, they'll probably point you in the direction of the Penang Tourist Guides Association office (☎ 261 4461) on the 3rd floor of Komtar on Jalan Penang. It is open from 10 am to 6 pm daily and staffed by helpful, patient volunteers who *really* know their stuff. Pick up a copy of the monthly *Penang Tourist Newspaper,* (around RM2) for background on Penang's multiethnic cuisine, comprehensive listings of current events and hotel promotions, as well as detailed pull-out maps. Other worthwhile book-length guides to Penang are sold here (see Bookshops later for recommended titles).

The tourism Web site at www.penang .net.my/ has general-interest information, background on island cuisine, events calendars, English-language yellow pages and even e-greeting cards.

**Consulates in Georgetown** Medan, the entry point from Penang to the Indonesian island of Sumatra, is counted as one of the 'usual' entry points where most travellers of nationalities are issued an entry permit for 60 days on arrival. The Indonesian consulate (☎ 227 4686) at 467 Jalan Burma, just west of the Adventist Hospital across from the Midlands 1-Stop shopping centre, can answer any inquiries.

For most nationalities, visas for Thailand are not required for visits of up to four weeks. For longer stays, apply for a visa at the Royal Thai Consulate (☎ 226 9484), 1 Jalan Tunku Abdul Rahman; take TransitLink bus No 7 or Sri Negara bus No 136 or 137. Visa applications are accepted from 9 am to noon Monday to Friday; pick-up is usually the following afternoon. The consulate has a reputation for being difficult with long stayers renewing their visas, but bona fide tourists shouldn't have problems. Tourist visas cost RM33 for two months; travel agencies along Lebuh Chulia will get you the visa for an additional RM10 or so – definitely worth the hassle saved. See Embassies & Consulates in Malaysia in the Facts for the Visitor chapter for addresses of other consulates in Georgetown.

**Immigration Offices** The immigration office (☎ 261 5122) is at 29A Lebuh Pantai, in the centre of town.

**Money** Branches of major banks are on Lebuh Pantai near the main post office. The Citibank on Jalan Sultan Ahmad Shah has 24-hour ATMs open 365 days a year.

At the north-western end of Lebuh Chulia there are numerous moneychangers open longer hours than the banks and with more-competitive rates. Moneychangers are also scattered around the banks on Lebuh Pantai and at the ferry terminal, although you'll probably get better rates on the mainland from the moneychangers at the Butterworth bus station.

Mayflower Tours (☎ 262 8198) at 274 Lebuh Victoria is the local American Express representative, though it only sells travellers cheques and handles cardholder mail. The office is open from 8.30 am to 5.30 pm weekdays, and until 1 pm on Saturday.

**Post** The main post office (GPO) is in the centre of town on Lebuh Downing, near the South Channel waterfront. It is open from 8 am to 5 pm Monday to Friday and until 1 pm on Saturday. There are also post offices on the ground floor of Komtar behind the KFC, and on Lebuh Buckingham near Lebuh Pitt (Jalan Masjid Kapitan Keling).

If you need a parcel wrapped for posting, Syarikat MS Ally shop on Lebuh Pantai, near the main post office, offers packing services from around RM4.

**Telephone** The Telekom Malaysia office next to the GPO is open from 8.30 am to 9 pm weekdays for Home Country Direct and collect calls. (See the table in the Malaysia Facts for the Visitor chapter for

Home Country Direct access codes.) If you use Telekom Malaysia's rates, you can save up to 33% by calling during non-peak hours (it varies by country).

**Email & Internet Access** There are plenty of Internet cafes around and prices hover at RM6 an hour. Most budget guesthouses have one or more computers, but you pay more for the convenience. In Chinatown, the Rainforest Cafe and the Green Planet restaurant charge RM5 an hour, while Eighteen (18) Internet Café has the cheapest rate at RM3.5 (minimum one hour). Outside Chinatown, there are a few upstart Internet cafes with speedy connections (RM4 per hour) on the 4th floor of Komtar.

**Travel Agencies** Penang has many travel agents, particularly at the northern end of Lebuh Chulia, that handle discounted airline tickets, though the prices are not as good as you'll find on Khao San Rd in Bangkok. Most, but not all, of the agencies in Georgetown are trustworthy. Silver-Econ Travel (☎ 262 9882) at 436 Lebuh Chulia and Happy Holidays (☎ 262 9222) at No 442 are reliable operators that many travellers use.

**Bookshops** The huge Popular Bookshop in Komtar stocks cheap novels, travel books, maps and a reasonable selection of books on Penang and Malaysia. Times is another English bookshop in Penang Plaza, with a smaller branch in the Lifestyle department store at Komtar.

Recommended titles include the *Penang Complete Visitor Guide* (around RM20) for background on popular (and obscure) sights across the island, along with colour maps and practical details. The Malaysian Nature Society's *Selected Nature Trails of Penang* (around RM15) gives directions for hikes on the island (with sketch maps), plus information on local flora and fauna. Reprints of *Streets of George Town, Penang: An Illustrated Guide* by Khoo Su Nin are sometimes available. This photographic guidebook takes on Georgetown's buildings and history street by street, perfect for do-it-yourself walking tours.

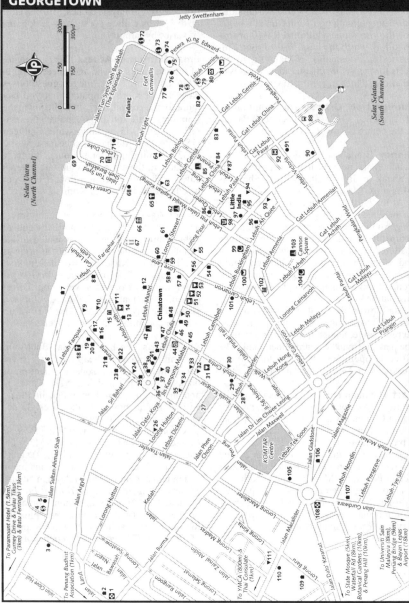

GEORGETOWN

# GEORGETOWN

**PLACES TO STAY**
- 2 Sheraton Penang
- 7 Eastern & Oriental (E&O) Hotel
- 8 City Bayview Hotel
- 12 SD Motel
- 13 Cathay Hotel; Waldorf Hotel
- 16 Malaysia Hotel
- 17 Hotel Continental
- 19 Polar Cafe
- 20 Peking Hotel; Soho Free House
- 21 Cititel Premier
- 22 Merchant Hotel
- 23 Towne House Hotel
- 25 Oriental Hotel; Kashmir Restaurant
- 37 Hang Chow Hotel; Eastern Hotel
- 38 Island City Hotel
- 43 Blue Diamond Hotel & Cafe
- 48 New Eng Aun Hotel
- 49 Swiss Hotel
- 54 Hong Ping Hotel; Coco Island Travellers Corner
- 57 Pin Seng Hotel
- 58 Love Lane Inn
- 59 Wan Hai Hotel
- 60 Oasis Hotel
- 83 D'Budget Hostel
- 86 Broadway Hostel
- 95 Coral Hostel
- 96 Golden Plaza Hostel
- 106 Shangri-La
- 107 Hotel Grand Continental
- 109 Sunway Hotel

**PLACES TO EAT**
- 9 Pintail Cafe & Bistro
- 10 MonSoon
- 11 Jaipur Court
- 24 Shin Miyako
- 26 Tandoori House

- 28 Kedai Kopi Kimberly
- 30 Green Planet
- 32 Diner's Bakery
- 33 Lovage Café
- 34 Hameediyah Restaurant
- 35 Taj Restaurant
- 36 Kedai Kopi Yasmeen
- 40 Café Tai Wah; Bamboo Village Hut
- 45 Hong Kong Restaurant
- 46 Sin Kuan Hwa Cafe
- 47 Secret Garden
- 50 Eng Thai Cafe
- 55 Hsiang Yang Fast Food
- 56 Rainforest Cafe
- 63 Dragon King
- 64 Shahabe Restoran
- 69 Esplanade Food Centre
- 84 Kaliamans Restaurant
- 87 Shusi Banana Leaf Restaurant
- 93 Restoran Tomyam
- 94 Meena Cafe
- 111 Oriental

**OTHER**
- 1 Penang Plaza
- 3 Eva Air; Sempati Air
- 4 Citibank
- 5 Singapore Airlines
- 6 Hertz Rent-a-Car
- 14 20 Leith Street
- 15 Cheong Fatt Tze Mansion
- 18 Protestant Cemetery
- 27 Chowrasta Bazaar
- 29 100 Cintra Street
- 31 Rock World
- 39 Happy Holidays
- 41 Silver-Econ Travel
- 42 Hainan Temple
- 44 Eighteen (18) Internet Cafe
- 51 Hong Kong Bar
- 52 Hard Life Cafe
- 53 Betelnut Café

- 61 Penang Heritage Trust
- 62 Kuan Yin Teng
- 65 St George's Church
- 66 Penang Museum
- 67 Cathedral of the Assumption
- 68 Supreme Court
- 70 Penang Library; State Art Gallery; Arts & Cultural Info Centre
- 71 City Hall
- 72 Tourism Malaysia
- 73 Penang Tourist Association; Langkawi Ferry Services
- 74 Kuala Perlis Langkawi Ferry Service Co; Ekspres Bahagia
- 75 Victoria Memorial Clocktower
- 76 Immigration Office
- 77 Dewan Undangan Negeri (State Assembly Building)
- 78 Standard Chartered Bank
- 79 HSBC Bank
- 80 Telekom Malaysia
- 81 Main Post Office
- 82 Syarikat MS Ally
- 85 Nin Yong Temple
- 88 Pengkalan Weld Bus Stop
- 89 Railway Booking Office
- 90 Newsia Tours & Travel
- 91 Mayflower Tours
- 92 TransitLink City Bus Station
- 97 HS Sam Book Store
- 98 Sri Mariamman Temple
- 99 Masjid Kapitan Keling
- 100 Post Office
- 101 Market
- 102 Syed Alatas Mansion
- 103 Khoo Kongsi
- 104 Acheen St Mosque
- 105 Malaysia Airlines
- 108 Gama Department Store & Supermarket
- 110 Thai Airways International (THAI)

**PENINSULAR MALAYSIA**

For second-hand books, check out the small shops along Lebuh Chulia, or browse through the huge selection at the back of the 2nd floor of Chowrasta Bazaar on Jalan Penang.

At the Little India end of Lebuh Chulia, between Lebuh Queen and Lebuh King, HS Sam Book Store is 'the most organized used book shop in town'. It's open from 9.30 am to 8.30 pm daily (except holidays). The amicable owner also sells reasonably priced souvenirs and textiles, organises tickets and transport rental, and offers Internet access and luggage storage.

**Libraries** The Penang Library (☎ 262 2255) is on the 1st floor of the Dewan Sri Pinang building on Lebuh Duke. It has a large collection of local-interest books and is open from 10.15 am to 6 pm Tuesday to Saturday, from 11 am to 4 pm on Sunday. On the ground level, the Arts & Cultural Info Centre (☎ 264 2273, ✉ artspen@tm.net.my) has a box office and listings of arts and cultural events in Penang.

The Alliance Française (☎ 226 6008) library, at 8 Jalan Yeoh Guan Seok, is open from 9.30 am to 1 pm and 2.30 to 7 pm daily except Sunday; it's only open from 2 pm on Monday and closes at 6 pm on Saturday. The Malaysian German Society Library (☎ 229 6853), at 250B Jalan Air Itam, is open from 9.30 am to 1 pm and 2.30 to 6 pm weekdays.

**Medical Services**  The *Penang Tourist Newspaper* (see Tourist Offices earlier in this section) has listings of medical services and community-based health organisations, such as the Women's Crisis Centre (☎ 228 0342) and Community AIDS Service Penang (☎ 229 9566).

The following hospitals are recommended for travellers:

**General Hospital** (☎ 229 3333) Jalan Residensi
**Penang Adventist Hospital** (☎ 226 1133) 465 Jalan Burma
**Loh Guan Lye Specialist Centre** (☎ 228 8501) 19 Jalan Logan

**Dangers & Annoyances**  Georgetown still bears traces of its seamier past, and though the opium dens have gone, heroin is a large problem. Beware of trishaw riders who offer drugs and remember that Malaysia's penalties for drug use are very severe (death for possession of more than 15g of any contraband). Prostitution is also big in Penang, and trishaw drivers will often try to push women, as much as drugs, onto solo male travellers.

At night the streets around the wharves and Little India can be deserted, and unaccompanied women will probably encounter hassles from passing motorists and pedestrians. There may be no-one around to help if serious trouble ensues; stay with a group or consider taking a taxi.

## Colonial District
As the oldest British settlement in Malaysia, many grand colonial buildings can still be found in Penang. Francis Light stepped ashore in 1786 on the site of Fort Cornwallis, which is the main attraction and a good place to start a tour of the colonial district around the waterfront. Many of the

buildings in the area are marked with signs explaining their history and significance. They're included in the *American Express Heritage Trails 1 & 2* numbered walking tours that also take in temples and mosques in old Chinatown farther inland. You can check out the route at the Web site at www .penang.insights.com.my/penang/html/trails .htm or pick up pamphlets delineating the routes at the tourist offices or the Penang Heritage Trust (☎ 264 2631) – see Chinatown this chapter.

Opposite the south-eastern corner of Fort Cornwallis is the **Victoria Memorial Clocktower**, a gleaming white tower topped by a Moorish dome. Donated by a local Chinese millionaire to honour Queen Victoria's Diamond Jubilee in 1897, it stands 18m (60 feet) tall – one foot for each year of her reign.

A typical feature of Malaysian colonial cities is the *padang,* an open playing field surrounded by public buildings. Georgetown's Padang stretches west from Fort Cornwallis to the **City Hall** (Dewan Bandaran), one of Penang's most imposing buildings, with fine porticos. The Penang Library behind it is not architecturally interesting, but houses the free **State Art Gallery**, which features rotating exhibits of contemporary art on the 3rd floor (open from 9 am to 5 pm, closed Friday).

On the southern side of the Padang is the neoclassical **State Assembly building** (Dewan Undangan Negeri), and north-west along Lebuh Light is the equally impressive **Supreme Court**.

Behind the Supreme Court, **St George's Church** on Lebuh Farquhar is the oldest Anglican church in South-East Asia. This gracefully proportioned building, with its marble floor and towering spire, was built in 1818 by convict labour. Also on Lebuh Farquhar is the double-spired **Cathedral of the Assumption**, named for the feast day on which its Catholic founders landed here from Kedah.

The **Protestant Cemetery** on Jalan Sultan Ahmad Shah contains the graves of Captain Francis Light (who was also Sir Thomas Stamford Raffles' brother-in-law) and Thomas Leonowens, the young officer who married Anna, the schoolmistress to the

King of Siam. The 1999 movie *Anna & The King* with Jodie Foster and Chow Yun-Fat was filmed in Malaysia, much of it in Penang (see the boxed text in this chapter).

**Fort Cornwallis** The timeworn walls of this fort in the centre of town are among Penang's oldest sights. It was here that Captain Light first set foot on the virtually uninhabited island in 1786 and established the free port where trade would, he hoped, be lured from Britain's Dutch rivals. At first a wooden fort was built, but between 1808 and 1810 convict labour replaced it with the present stone structure.

Today only the outer walls of the fort are standing. The area within is now a park, with souvenir shops and a couple of food outlets. There's not much to do except wander around the battlements, which are liberally studded with old cannons. Many of these were retrieved from local pirates, although they were originally cast by the Dutch.

**Seri Rambai**, the most-important and largest cannon, faces the north coast and dates back to 1603. It has a chequered history; the Dutch gave it to the sultan of Johor, after which it fell into the hands of the Acehnese. It was later given to the sultan of Selangor and then stolen by pirates before ending up at the fort. It is famed for its pro-creative powers, and childless women are advised to place flowers in the barrel of 'the big one' and offer special prayers.

Undergoing renovation at the time of research, the fort area was still open from 8.30 am to 7 pm daily; admission costs RM1.

**Penang Museum** From the town's foundation site it's only a short stroll to the Penang Museum on Lebuh Farquhar, recently renovated and now one of the best-presented museums in Malaysia. In front is a statue of Captain Light, which was removed by the Japanese during WWII but retrieved and re-erected, minus its sword, after the war. The excellent exhibits on the ground floor introduce Penang's immigration and ethnic history, with photos, documents, costumes, furniture and other well-labelled displays that are worth at least an hour of your time.

On the 2nd floor is the history gallery. An interesting section recounts the bloody nine days of rioting between Chinese secret societies in 1867, attributed by bewildered British authorities to a rambutan-throwing incident. Georgetown suffered a near civil war before the administrators took a firm hand. The societies were heavily fined and the proceeds used to build police stations that subsequently kept the peace.

Also upstairs are two smaller displays of early-19th-century oil paintings by Captain Robert Smith and prints showing landscape scenes of old Penang.

Outside, one of the original Penang Hill funicular railcars is now a kiosk selling souvenirs and drinks; all proceeds benefit the Penang Heritage Trust. The museum is open from 9 am to 5 pm daily (closed Friday) and admission costs RM1.

## Chinatown

Inland from the former British colonial district lie the twisting streets of the old city, dotted with temples, mosques and traditional businesses. The large Chinatown stretches from Lebuh Pantai to Jalan Penang. It's centred on Lebuh Chulia, which is still the lively heart of Georgetown, but pockets of Indian and Malay areas remain within and around it.

Georgetown is a delight to wander around any time of day. Set off in any direction and you're certain to find plenty of interest, whether it's the beautiful old Chinese shophouses, an early-morning vegetable market, a temple ceremony, the crowded antique shops or a late *pasar malam* (night market).

All the usual Chinese events are likely to be taking place at any time: a funeral procession with what looks like a run-down Dixieland jazz band leading the mourners, colourful parades at festival times or elderly women setting up their stalls for a day's business. All around you'll hear those distinctively Chinese noises – the clatter of mah-jongg tiles from inside houses, the trilling of caged songbirds, as well as the

## The King and I, but not for Thais

It was a long and very bitter debate between the Thai National Film Board and 20th Century Fox that finally brought the filming of *Anna and the King* to Malaysia in 1999. Anna Leonowens, the woman whose diaries are the basis of movies and the Broadway musical *The King and I*, was quite a controversial character in real life. Throughout her life – from her arrival in Singapore, to her time in the Siamese court to her death in Montreal in 1915 – she continuously falsified her own name and history, as well as that of her husband, Thomas Leon Owens, who lies buried in Penang's Protestant Cemetery.

Anna's diaries, published once she left Siam, contain dramatic, but unsubstantiated assertions that throw further doubt on her credibility. She was misinformed about Buddhism and spoke considerably less Thai than she claimed. Although Anna wrote that the king threw wives who were out of favour into dungeons, dungeons are impossible to build in water-logged Bangkok. She supposedly witnessed the public torture of a royal consort who had fallen in love with a monk, but no other Europeans in Bangkok at that time mentioned this event in later memoirs.

The Thai film board objects to *Anna and the King* for the same reasons it has never lifted the ban on the movie musical *The King and I*. The official Thai position is that the highly ethical and self-disciplined King Rama IV never came under the spell, romantic or otherwise, of the imperialistic, and by all accounts prudish, Anna Leonowens. The king's far-sighted reforms, which included abolishing slavery and applying Western science, sprang more from his 27 years as a Buddhist monk than from any chance meetings with Anna, his children's obstinate English teacher. The Hollywood versions of history offend Thai laws forbidding lese-majesty, or attacks and slurs upon the royal family. Remember that Thailand is a country where common citizens still treat royalty with utter respect, as anyone who has had to pay homage to His Majesty after the previews at a movie theatre in Thailand can attest.

However, the Thai government seems to have handled negotiations over *Anna and the King* with more than a little anti-*farang* (foreigner) feeling and national prejudice. Official, and rather hypocritical, statements by the government cast aspersions on Anna's 'doubtful racial origin' even as they objected to the movie's revisionist history on the grounds of racist imperialism. In good faith, Fox allowed Thai historians to collaborate on rewrites of the script, but all subsequent drafts were rejected by the film board. A Fox representative was quoted as saying, 'It was like we were a dirty thing that they (the Thais) did not want to touch'.

What Thailand refused, Malaysia welcomed with open arms and pockets. A model of Bangkok's Temple of the Emerald Buddha was rapidly built outside Ipoh, requiring 5 million nails and over 67,500L of water for the workers (for photos, see www.annaandtheking.com). On Pulau Langkawi, the set of King Rama IV's seaside summer palace and the jetty for royal barges still stretches out over the water at Pantai Kok. Many other locations in and around Penang were used, most notably at Khoo Kongsi clan house; there are photos of the dapper clan elders taking tea with Jodie Foster, at www.penang.net.my/khookongsi. The Penang Heritage Trust supports its preservation efforts by maintaining a virtual Film Location Heritage Trail of *Anna and the King*, at www.pht.org.my/AnnaKing.

Meanwhile, Thais owning, selling or screening copies of the movie risk up to one year in jail and a 10,000B fine, though this certainly hasn't stopped travellers' cafes on Khao San Rd in Bangkok from showing bootleg copies for all to see.

**Sara (Sam) Benson**

sound of loud arguments and conversations everywhere.

In January 2000, drastic rent de-control acts and evictions began to threaten this way of life, and most of Penang's historic buildings as well. The Penang Heritage Trust (☎ 264 2631), 26A Lorong Stewart, has campaigned with local citizens to fight against this. Its office is in the well-preserved Hainanese Mariner's Lodge, an eye-catching showpiece for its renovation efforts about town, which include the Carpenter's

Guild, 70 Love Lane and a clean-up of the Protestant Cemetery. Visit its Web site at www.pht.org.my to read about these projects and about the campaign to have Georgetown declared a Unesco World Heritage Site. You can support the trust by purchasing souvenirs and locally produced guidebooks at its office.

**Kuan Yin Teng** On Lebuh Pitt (Jalan Masjid Kapitan Keling), around the corner from the Penang Museum, is the temple of Kuan Yin, the goddess of mercy, good fortune, peace and fertility. Built in the early 19th century by the first Hokkien and Cantonese settlers in Penang, the temple is not impressive, but it's very central and popular among the Chinese community. There's often something going on: worshippers burning paper money at the furnaces in front of the temple; devotees offering joss sticks (incense) inside; or night-time puppetry or Chinese theatre on the goddess' birthday, celebrated at least three times yearly (lucky woman!) on the 19th day of the second, sixth and ninth lunar months.

**Hainan Temple** On Lebuh Muntri, this small gem demands a closer look. Dedicated to Mar Chor, the patron saint of seafarers, it was founded in 1866 but not completed until 1895. A thorough remodelling for its centenary in 1995 has refreshed its distinctive swirling dragon pillars and brightened up the ornate carvings. The small compound is usually buzzing with activity, but quiet benches out the front are ideal for people-watching.

**Khoo Kongsi** The Khoo Kongsi is in Cannon Square near the end of Lebuh Pitt (Jalan Masjid Kapitan Keling). A *kongsi* is a clan house, a building that's partly a temple and partly a meeting hall for Chinese of the same clan or surname.

Penang has many kongsi, but the clan house of the Khoo is by far the finest and is not to be missed. Its construction was first considered around 1835, but the permanent structure wasn't built until 1894. The building was so magnificent and elaborate that nobody was surprised when the roof caught fire on the night it was completed in 1901! That misfortune was interpreted as a message from above that they had really overdone it and the ancestors were jealous, so the Khoo rebuilt it in a marginally less extravagant style.

The present kongsi, which dates from 1906 but was recently extensively renovated, is also known as the 'Dragon Mountain Hall'. It's a colourful mix of dragons, statues, paintings, lamps, coloured tiles and carvings, all of which are shown in a virtual tour at the Web site www.penang.net.my/khookongsi.

In 1999, the Khoo Kongsi was a location set for the film *Anna & the King*. See the boxed text in this chapter.

**Acheen St Mosque** A short walk from the Khoo Kongsi, this Malay mosque on Lebuh Acheh is unusual for its Egyptian-style minaret (most Malay mosques have Moorish minarets). Built in 1808 by a wealthy Arab trader, the mosque was the focal point for the Malay and Arab traders in this quarter, the oldest Malay kampung in Georgetown.

**Syed Alatas Mansion** This mansion, just north of the Acheen St Mosque, on the corner of Lebuh Acheh and Lebuh Armenia, was the residence of Syed Mohd Alatas, a powerful Acehnese merchant of Arab descent. Syed Alatas led the local Acehnese community during the Penang riots of 1867 and organised resistance to the Dutch siege of Aceh (Sumatra) in the 1870s. The mansion was restored in 1994 and is open from 9 am to 5 pm weekdays and until 1 pm on Saturday; admission is free.

**Cheong Fatt Tze Mansion** Cheong Fatt Tze Mansion, on Lebuh Leith (formerly Water Lily Road), was built in 1870 by Cheong Fatt Tze, a local Hakka merchant-trader who established a vast financial empire throughout East Asia.

The magnificent 38-room mansion blends Eastern and Western influences to conform to feng shui (Chinese geomancy) by sitting on a 'dragon's throne' – a mountain (Penang Hill) behind and water (the Channel) in front.

It's one of only two surviving examples of the grandiose architectural style of wealthy overseas Chinese who tried to imitate the opulence of the Ching dynasty. Its features include ingeniously crafted louvred windows, Art Nouveau stained-glass windows, elaborate wrought ironwork and a superb glazed-tile roof adorned with ceramic motifs.

Although the building was undergoing renovation at the time of writing, regular tours were given at 11 am sharp on Monday, Wednesday, Friday and Saturday (RM10). Turn up on time, as reservations aren't accepted and enormous tour groups may squeeze you out. If you can't get in, it's still worth a walk over here to peek through the gate or to enjoy the vista from the pub directly opposite.

## Little India
Little India, with its spice and sari shops, Indian temples and restaurants, is centred on Lebuh Pasar. Here, Tamils from the south of India cool boiled milk by nonchalantly hurling it through the air from one cup to another. Money changing is almost exclusively an Indian enterprise here, and stocky Sikhs holding antique-looking guns can be seen guarding many banks and jewellery shops.

**Sri Mariamman Temple** About midway between Kuan Yin Teng and the Kapitan Keling Mosque you'll find this Hindu temple, another example of Penang's religious diversity. The Sri Mariamman Temple is typically South Indian; above its shrine rises an elaborately sculpted and painted superstructure representing Mt Meru, the cosmic mountain that supports the heavens. Built in 1883, it's Georgetown's oldest Hindu temple and a testimony to the strong Indian influence you'll find in this most Chinese of towns.

Penang's Thaipusam procession begins here (see Special Events later in this chapter, and the boxed text in the 'Places of Worship' special section), and in October a wooden chariot takes the temple's deity for a spin around the neighbourhood during Vijayadasami festivities.

**Masjid Kapitan Keling** Penang's first Indian Muslim settlers (East India Company troops) built this mosque at the junction of Lebuh Buckingham and Lebuh Pitt (Jalan Masjid Kapitan Keling). The mosque is yellow, in a typically Indian-influenced Islamic style, and has a single minaret. It looks sublime at sunset.

## Wat Chayamangkalaram
At Lorong Burma just off Jalan Burma, the main road to Batu Ferringhi, is the Temple of the Reclining Buddha. This brightly painted Thai temple claims its 33m-long reclining Buddha is the third-longest in the world – a dubious assertion since there's one other in Malaysia that is larger and at least half a dozen more scattered around Thailand, Myanmar (Burma), China and other countries. Nevertheless, it's a colourful temple and worth a visit.

The **Dhammikarama Burmese Buddhist Temple** stands opposite, with two large stone elephants flanking the gates. Penang's first Buddhist temple, built in 1805, it has been significantly added to over the years.

You can get to both temples on TransitLink bus No 202; Minibus No 26, 31 or 88; or Hin Bus No 93 from Komtar or along Lebuh Chulia.

## Penang Buddhist Association
Completed in 1931, this unusual Buddhist temple is on Jalan Anson. Instead of the typical colourful design of most Chinese temples, this one shows Art Deco influences and looks like a frosted cake, all white and pastel. Interior Buddha figures are carved from Italian marble, and glass chandeliers, made in Penang, hang from above. Penang's Buddhist community gathers here on Wesak Day to celebrate the triple holy-day of the Buddha's birthday, attainment of enlightenment and death.

## Other Mosques & Temples
The glossy, modern **Masjid Negeri** (State Mosque) at Air Itam offers good views from its 50m-high minaret.

**Nattukotai Chettiar Temple** on Waterfall Rd, near the Botanic Gardens (see that

PENINSULAR MALAYSIA

SARA J BENSON

The Penang Buddhist Association building (1931) in Georgetown shows Art Deco influences.

entry under Around Georgetown later in this chapter), is the largest Hindu temple in Penang and is dedicated to Bala Subramaniam. Farther along on the left side is a gate leading up to the **Waterfall Hilltop Temple**, the destination of the Thaipusam procession from Little India's Sri Mariamman Temple.

North-west of Georgetown, past Gurney Drive out at Tanjung Tokong, **Tua Pek Kong** is dedicated to the God of Prosperity and dates from 1837.

## Activities

Weekend **mountain-bike trips** are regularly organised by Penang's Knights of the Round Table (Kort), usually including a get-together at a local restaurant afterwards (check out the group's Web site at www.geocities.com/Yosemite/Campground/1907/index.html).

Malaysia is becoming a popular **golfing** destination and Penang has some exceptionally affordable international-standard golf courses – Japanese businessmen fly in for just a day or two to take advantage of them. The island's premier course is located at Bukit Jambul Country Club, near Bayan Lepas airport. Golf Malaysia rated it the second-most-beautiful course in Malaysia and the stunning and very challenging 18

holes were carved straight out of the rocky jungle terrain.

At the Penang Turf Club in Batu Gantong, horse-racing events take place on two consecutive weekends every two months. Seats are cheap, but gambling is illegal. **Horse riding** is sometimes offered on weekdays.

For **indoor pursuits**, there's Penang Bowl on Lebuh Farquhar in Georgetown. In the ritzy Pulau Tikus area west of Georgetown, Midlands 1-Stop has bowling alleys and a roller-skating rink. Near Bayan Lepas airport, Bukit Jambul Country Club has billiards facilities, as do several public pool halls in the city. At Bukit Jambul shopping complex, also near the airport, you'll find an indoor ice-skating rink for cooling off.

## Special Events

All the usual festivals are celebrated in Penang, but with this island's extraordinary enthusiasm. Current events, including workshops, cultural talks and art exhibitions, are listed in the *Penang Tourist Newspaper* (around RM2), available at tourist offices and bookshops.

The masochistic-looking **Thaipusam** festival is celebrated as fervently as in Singapore and KL, but without quite the same crowds. The Sri Mariamman, Nattukotai

Chettiar and Waterfall Hilltop temples (see those entries earlier) are the main centres of activity in Penang. (For more information on Thaipusam see the 'Places of Worship' special section).

**Chinese New Year** is celebrated with particular gusto in Penang. The Khoo Kongsi gets done up for the event, and dance troupes perform all over the city. On the night before the 15th day of the new year, a fire ceremony takes place at Tua Pek Kong temple. The next day is **Chap Goh Meh**, during which local girls throw oranges into the sea from the Esplanade. Traditionally, the girls would chant 'throw a good orange, get a good husband' while local boys watched and later contacted their dream girl through matchmakers.

New Years is also one of the only times to see Baba-Nyonya performances of *dondang sayang,* spontaneous and traditional love ballads bandied about between singers using Bahasa Malaysia and Hokkien dialects, all from atop a gaily decorated bus. Traditional *asli* musical accompaniment consists of violins, accordions, tambourines and skin drums played slowly enough to give singers time to compose their replies.

Other festivals include the **Penang International Dragon Boat Festival** held in June and the **Penang Food & Cultural Festivals** in August, highlighting the best of Penang's multiethnic heritage.

The mid-September **Lantern Festival** is celebrated by eating moon cakes, Chinese sweets once used to carry secret messages for underground rebellions in ancient China. In November and December the annual **Pesta Pulau Penang** (Penang Islands Festival) features various cultural events, parades and carnivals.

## Organised Tours

The big hotels and travel agents all book tours, but independent travellers can buy tickets from the Penang Tourist Association (☎ 261 6663) near Fort Cornwallis. Various tours include the half-day City Tour (RM22), full-day Round-Island Tour (RM35), Penang Hill & Kek Lok Si Temple Tour (RM35) and Georgetown By Night

Tour (RM30). On most of these tours, you're simply paying for transportation and not much else, though the Round Island Tour is more convenient than relying on the public buses to reach remote sights.

## Places to Stay – Budget

**Hostels** Hostels in Georgetown are relatively clean and well set-up for travellers, but rooms are thinly partitioned and spartan – you usually get a bed, a fan and that's about it.

One reliable choice is **D'Budget Hostel** *(☎ 263 4794, 9 Lebuh Gereja),* close to the ferry terminal and buses. A dorm bed costs RM7, small singles/doubles from RM22 to RM28, and larger rooms with air-con and shower are RM38. This hostel is big on security (curfew is at 1 am) and the rooftop sitting area is a winner, but some travellers lament the impersonal staff. Still, it's good value and quiet.

If you want to stay in the thick of little India, the blindingly bright white **Coral Hostel** *(☎ 264 4909/4961, 99–101 Lebuh King)* offers crowded dorms for RM7, but roomier, clean rooms for RM18/25 with fan, or RM35 with air-con. Staff are courteous and helpful, and there's no lock-out. However, the hostel's ultra-thin walls mean sleep is not assured.

**Golden Plaza Hostel** *(☎ 263 2388, 32 Lebuh Ah Quee)* is popular and has Internet access and non-stop Hindu epic movies in its common lounge. Staff are welcoming, but the rooms are nothing special. Beds in the large/small dorm cost RM8/10. Room prices start at RM16/25 and rise to RM45 for a 'suite' with air-con and balcony, all with shared bathroom. There's an excellent cheap restaurant downstairs.

**Broadway Hostel** *(☎ 262 8550),* at 35F Lebuh Pitt (which is also known as Jalan Masjid Kapitan Keling) is less popular with travellers but has good singles/doubles/triples, many with windows, for RM20/25/30. Rooms with air-con cost up to RM40, and dorm beds cost RM7.

The **YMCA** *(☎ 228 8211, ✉ ymcapg@po.jaring.my, 211 Jalan Macalister)* is at the top of this range. Rooms cost RM37 with

fan, or RM47 with air-con and TV, while
carpeted rooms with hot water cost RM62.
All rooms have showers and YMCA members receive a RM2 discount. It also has an
activities room, gym, squash courts and
cafeteria. Take a TransitLink No 7 bus, or a
Sri Negara No 136 or 137 bus from the jetty
or Komtar and get off at Jalan Perak.

**Hotels** Georgetown has several cheap hotels with character, but some are long over-
due for an overhaul. Stroll down Lebuh
Chulia or Love Lane and you'll come
across most of them. In most of the places
listed here, two people can share a bed in a
single room, while 'double' often means
two double beds.

Two extremely popular travellers' places,
though neither of them deserves to be, are
*Swiss Hotel* (☎ 262 0133, 431F Lebuh Chulia) and *New Eng Aun* (☎ 261 2333, 380
Lebuh Chulia) opposite. Both have travellers' cafes and are positioned far enough
back from Lebuh Chulia to insulate them
from street noise. The over-run Swiss Hotel
has tidy singles/doubles with fan and shared
bathroom for RM18.70/23.10. However,
you must be back by the 1 am lock-out, and
the staff tend to growl at guests any time of
day. The New Eng Aun has simple rooms
for RM20/25, or RM21/27 with shower and
shared toilet. Some of the rooms have had a
quick paint job recently, but most are still
rather decrepit. Female travellers have complained of harassment here, and the scruffy
atmosphere doesn't contradict these reports.

In the streets just off Lebuh Chulia there
are a number of other inviting places offering better-value lodgings.

*SD Motel* (☎ 264 3743, ✉ sd_motel@
hotmail.com, 24 Lebuh Muntri) is a definite
notch up in quality, with beds in spotless
six-person dorms for RM13 and doubles
with fan/air-con and hot-water shower for
RM22/28. The staff are accommodating and
provide lockers, book-exchange and travel
information. Being in a quiet location, this
place hasn't been discovered – yet, that is.

Under the same management as the Rainforest Cafe and Green Planet restaurants,
*Oasis Hotel* (☎ 261 6778, 23 Love Lane) is a

typical older-style Chinese house in a very
quiet area. A dorm bed costs RM8, and rooms
cost RM20 to RM35 with shower (but common toilet). It sees a lot of repeat business
from the kinder, gentler backpacker crowd.

The new *Love Lane Inn* (☎ 6013-431
7177, ✉ Ocean008@hotmail.com, 54 Love
Lane) comes recommended for its small,
roomy dorms (RM10) and cheerful singles/
doubles with fan for RM20/25. The interior
of the building is airy, squeaky-clean and
filled with sunshine. Almost opposite, *Wan
Hai Hotel* (☎ 261 6853) at No 35 has congested dorms costing RM8 for per bed and
basic rooms with shared bath from RM20.
It's a friendly, well-run classic Chinese
hotel, but it can be noisy.

Back closer to Lebuh Chulia, *Pin Seng
Hotel* (☎ 261 9004, 82 Love Lane) is tucked
down a little alley and is well insulated
from any street noise. Exceptionally clean
rooms vary from the crumbling to the pre-
sentable, so it pays to check a few. Simple
rooms start at RM18, or from RM25 with
shower (but no toilet).

Back on Lebuh Chulia, near the junction
with Jalan Penang, there are a few more
places if none of the previous appeal. *Hang
Chow Hotel* (☎ 261 0810, 511 Lebuh Chulia)
is a rickety old wooden hotel with simple
rooms from RM22. It has an excellent coffee
shop downstairs. The adjacent *Eastern Hotel*
(☎ 261 4597, 509 Lebuh Chulia) has slightly
better fan rooms for RM20 and doubles with
air-con and bath for RM33, but the loud calls
to prayer at the mosque next door may be a
deterrent.

*Blue Diamond Hotel and Café* (☎ 261
1089, 422 Lebuh Chulia) looks unpromising
with its modern facade and motley crowd of
hangers-on, but the cafe out the front pulls
in a steady stream of travellers. The management couldn't be less welcoming and some
guests report bed bugs. Small dorms cost
RM8 per person, simple singles/doubles are
RM20/25 with shower and fan, or RM25/30
with shower and toilet, rising to RM45 with
air-con.

*Polar Cafe* (☎ 262 2054, 48A Jalan
Penang) has fairly average rooms, but a very
social pub downstairs. Rooms with air-con,

PENINSULAR MALAYSIA

PENINSULAR MALAYSIA

bathroom and hot water are a bargain at RM40, including breakfast.

## Places to Stay – Mid-Range

The graceful old *Cathay Hotel (☎ 262 6271/6272, fax 263 9300, 15 Lebuh Leith)* is one of Penang's few well-maintained grand colonial hotels. The cavernous lobby nearly equals the exterior, though both are starting to look worn. Huge spotless rooms cost RM57 with fan and bathroom, or RM69 with air-con. The hotel is well located, within spitting distance of a few pubs and the beautiful Cheong Fatt Tze Mansion, but it does have a 'health club' (ahem).

If the Cathay is full, you could try next door at the *Waldorf Hotel (☎ 262 6140, 13 Lebuh Leith)*, which caters to Chinese tourists. It's a characterless, concrete box but has reasonable singles/doubles (all air-con) for RM49/55 with bathroom.

*Hong Ping Hotel (☎ 262 5243, 273B Lebuh Chulia)* is another, more-modern place right in the thick of things. It has reasonable rooms from RM60 with air-con, TV, phone and bathroom. The Coco Island Travellers Corner outside attracts huge crowds nightly for drinks and live music.

*Island City Hotel (☎ 263 7107, fax 264 3107)* is at the opposite end of Lebuh Chulia, next to the traffic roundabout. Clean, comfortable and tastefully decorated fan rooms are great value at RM32/27 with/without bath; rooms with air-con and shower cost RM37. Dorm beds are RM10.

While Lebuh Chulia is the main street for cheap hotels, busy Jalan Penang around the corner has a string of mid-range places, from three-star giants that have seen better days to smaller, fully air-con hotels. As most are used to serving a wealthier Chinese clientele, they may not welcome backpackers.

The cheaper options are on the western side of the street. The eerily dark *Peking Hotel (☎ 263 6191, 50A Jalan Penang)* has singles/doubles for RM46/57.50 with air-con, bathroom and TV. *Towne House Hotel (☎ 263 8621, 70 Jalan Penang)* is less shabby, but more expensive at RM60.

The bigger high-rises on the eastern side of Jalan Penang hold to a slightly higher standard, with coffee shops, car parking and room service. Well-appointed rooms with air-con, bathroom, TV and phone are often a bit tired-looking, but competition is stiff and discounts are readily offered. The newest high-rise is the *Cititel Premier (☎ 370 1188)*, a good if unsurprising place at No 66. Singles/doubles, all with excellent views, cost from RM125 after discount, including breakfast. *Oriental Hotel (☎ 263 4211)*, on the corner of Jalan Penang and Lebuh Chulia, has good-sized rooms from RM69 before discount, and an excellent Indian restaurant downstairs. On the next block, the *Merchant Hotel (☎ 263 2828)* has unexpectedly comfortable rooms from RM60.

Farther down, the relatively unwelcoming *Malaysia Hotel (☎ 263 3311, 7 Jalan Penang)* has rooms from RM136 including buffet breakfast, dropping to RM68 after discount. The adjacent *Hotel Continental (☎ 263 6388)* at No 5 has recently had a facelift, and now boasts a pool. Standard singles/doubles cost RM80.50/98, including breakfast.

If its distant location doesn't bother you, try the *Paramount Hotel (☎ 227 3649, 48F Jalan Sultan Ahmed Shah)*, about 1.5km north of Jalan Penang. This old seaside hotel is set back from the busy road, and although the old-style rooms with air-con and bathroom have seen better days, they're a bargain at RM57. There's a breezy seafood restaurant above the tiny private beach.

## Places to Stay – Top End

Penang's biggest hotels, of the resort variety, are out along the beaches and the road heading to Batu Ferringhi, but Georgetown has an increasing number of luxury hotels with swimming pools.

Opposite the crumbling Eastern & Oriental Hotel (see the boxed text in this chapter) at the top of Jalan Penang is the glaring multistorey *City Bayview Hotel (☎ 263 3161, 25A Farquhar St)*, topped by a revolving restaurant with great views over Georgetown (though the rotunda itself is a blight on the city skyline). Rates for fully equipped singles/doubles start at RM280/

## The Eastern & Oriental Hotel

The Eastern & Oriental Hotel, or at least what crumbling remains are left, stands at 10 Lebuh Farquhar at the seafront end of Jalan Penang. Built in 1885, the stylish E&O was the archetypal 19th-century colonial grand hotel – indeed, it was built by the four Sarkies brothers, the most famous hoteliers in the East, who were in fact Armenian immigrants from Turkey.

The Sarkies promoted the E&O as 'The Premier Hotel East of Suez' (a catchy phrase the brothers later used to advertise *all* their hotels), which supposedly had the 'Longest Sea Front of any Hotel' in the world. Beautiful gardens led down to the water and famous guests, including European literati, graced its grand lobby. It became the social centre for elite society in Penang, though European guests secretly favoured the hotel for its hot running water, a 'rare luxury in the East' (still today, as budget travellers will attest).

The E&O was the oldest and most stately of all the brothers' establishments, which quickly expanded to include the Crag Hotel on nearby Penang Hill (now a Public Works building), the Strand in Yangon (Rangoon) and the celebrated Raffles in Singapore. The Sarkies brothers achieved such fame in their lifetimes that a popular joke asked, 'Who are the Orang Sakai (the aboriginal inhabitants of Malaysia)?' Answer: 'A race of hotel proprietors inhabiting the jungles of Penang and Singapore'.

The E&O is now an inglorious shadow of its former self, the broken framework of the building and rubble poignantly crouching at the water's edge. In the last edition of this guidebook, we were so eager for total renovations of the historic hotel wing to be completed that we mistakenly reported the hotel (with its new condominium annexe) had reopened in 1998. Sadly, this isn't the case, as all renovations were halted by the Malaysian economic crash of the late 1990s, and today the landmark's future does not look promising. The same Raffles International group from Singapore that magnificently restored Raffles and other colonial masterpieces like the Grand Hotel d'Angkor in Cambodia to their former glory hasn't staked any interest in the E&O. Moreover, the Penang Heritage Trust reports that much of the historic building and its fixtures have already been thrown away.

It's not the first time, however, that the E&O's fortunes have gone bust. It didn't come into its prime until the 1920s, when the youngest of the Sarkies brothers, Arshak, made the place his home. Although the Sarkies almost closed the E&O when the rent was raised from $200 to $350 a month, Arshak (a gambler by nature) convinced the family to open the Raffles Hotel instead. Arshak's generosity was legendary; he often payed the £50 to £60 passage back to England for broken-hearted (and empty-pocketed) rubber planters and tin miners himself. Some observers said that Arshak ran the E&O not to make money, but to entertain: he seemed more keen to waltz around the ballroom with a whisky and soda balanced on his head than to add up a balance sheet. Shortly before his death, Arshak began lavish renovations to the E&O; this expense, coupled with loans to friends that were conveniently 'forgotten', finally bankrupted the family business in 1931. Still, Arshak's funeral was one of the grandest Penang has ever seen.

The E&O features in several stories by Somerset Maugham, who was a regular (and often difficult) guest. For more on dashing Arshak Sarkies, read George Bilainikin's entertaining *Hail Penang! Being the Narrative of Comedies and Tragedies in a Tropical Outpost Among Europeans, Chinese, Malays and Indians.*

**Sara (Sam) Benson**

300, or RM125/138 after seasonal discount. Although comfortable, rooms are looking worn.

Most other top-end hotels are scattered around Komtar in the business district, hardly an exciting place to stay, but luxury is surprisingly affordable here. *Hotel Grand Continental* (☎ 263 6688, 68 Jalan Gurdwara) has good-value rooms from RM115, including breakfast and dinner for two. The *Shangri-La* (☎ 262 2622), a block from Komtar on Jalan Magazine, boasts a host of bars and restaurants, with rooms starting at RM437/460. Discounts of 35% are common.

**Sunway Hotel** (☎ 229 9988, 33 Lorong Baru), off Jalan Macalister, offers well-appointed singles/doubles for RM200/280 – one of the best for the money in this range, though the location is removed from the action. Just as remote is the **Sheraton Penang** (☎ 226 7888, 3 Jalan Larut), another top-class place, though not quite as good as the best in its range. Rooms start at RM400, but are normally heavily discounted.

There are plenty of apartment hotels, mostly in Georgetown's suburbs, starting at RM120 per day for a studio. Weekly or monthly rentals attract significant discounts. **Stallions Apartments** (☎ 656 0118, fax 656 0063, 3A Jalan Bukit Dunbar), a few kilometres south of town, is one good option. Many others advertise in the *Penang Tourist Newspaper* (see Tourist Offices earlier).

## Places to Eat

Penang offers an enthralling food experience, with a wide range of restaurants and local specialities to tempt you. The Star news agency's on-line guide to Penang, at www.penang.thestar.com.my, has very up-to-date but selective recommendations for eating and entertainment in Georgetown and along the northern coast.

*Laksa assam,* or Penang laksa, is a fish soup with a sour taste from tamarind, or assam, paste; it's served with special white laksa noodles. Originally a Thai dish, *laksa lemak* has been adopted by Penang. It's similar to the Thai dish, except tamarind is substituted for coconut milk.

Apart from Melaka, Penang is one of the best places to try Nyonya (Straits Chinese) cuisine. Seafood is also very popular in Penang and there are many restaurants that specialise in fresh fish, crabs and prawns – particularly along the northern beach.

Despite its Chinese character, Penang also has a strong Indian presence and there are some popular specialities to savour. Curry Kapitan is a chicken curry that is supposed to have been named when a Dutch

sea captain asked his Indonesian mess boy what was to eat that night. The answer was 'curry, Kapitan', and it's been on the menu ever since.

**Hawker Food & Seafood** Georgetown has a big selection of street stalls, with nightly gatherings at places like the seafront **Esplanade Food Centre** behind the Penang Library. This is one of the best hawker centres, as much for the delightful sea breezes as the Malay stalls serving delicious Penang specialities. The more restaurant-like Chinese section features seafood and icy-cold beer.

Lorong Baru, just off Jalan Macalister, is another lively location where *food stalls* set up in the evenings. Two other hawker areas can be found north-west of Komtar, just off Jalan Burma on Lorong Selamat and Lorong Swatow. Lorong Swatow is good for laksa, *rojak* (green fruit salad in a spicy sauce) and *ais kacang,* a shaved-ice dessert.

In Chinatown another good **Malay food market** springs up every night along Lebuh Kimberley on the corner of Lebuh Cintra. Lebuh Chulia is always a great place for noodles at night. After 9 pm, small **Chinese stalls** set up tables on the footpath and the street is always a lively procession. Most stalls are found clustered around the Hong Ping Hotel at No 273.

Gurney Drive, 3km west along the coast on the way to Batu Ferringhi, is another popular seafront venue. Evening hawker-style restaurants here are noted for their seafood, including those in the lively **New Golden Phoenix** outdoor food-court and at the north-western end of the street. Many upmarket restaurants in old villas facing the foreshore have outdoor tables. **Kedai Makanan Song River** is popular and does great seafood; **Carnation,** which also has live music, and **Restoran Zeeland** are two other excellent spots.

**Oriental** (☎ 890 4500, 42 Tanjong Tokong), on the water at the north-western end of Gurney Drive, is another upmarket restaurant with excellent seafood. The Georgetown branch, at 62 Jalan Macalister, is favoured by locals for its reasonably priced seafood.

Other hawker venues and specialties are described in the *Penang Tourist Newspaper* (see Tourist Offices earlier in this chapter).

**Chinese** There are so many Chinese restaurants in Penang that it's hard to make recommendations.

Chinese fare of every imaginable type is sold from food carts and at small coffee shops around the old town. One of Georgetown's 'excellent Hainanese chicken-rice' purveyors is *Sin Kuan Hwa Cafe*, on the corner of Lebuh Chulia and Lebuh Cintra. Also very cheap is *Kedai Kopi Kimberly*, on Jalan Kimberly. Many other places serve classic dim sum in the mornings.

One of Chinatown's most popular outdoor fast-food places, just off Lebuh Chulia, is *Hsiang Yang Fast Food*. It's really a hawker centre, with an inexpensive Chinese buffet, noodles, satay and *popiah* (similar to an unfried spring roll) vendors.

*Hong Kong Restaurant* (29 Lebuh Cintra) serves savoury Cantonese food and also has an English menu. A few blocks down, *100 Cintra Street bazaar* has a simple outdoor coffee shop and the *Apricot Tea Corner* serves simple snacks and over 20 varieties of hot and iced tea (RM2 or less).

**Nyonya** Penang, like Melaka and Singapore, was the home of the Straits-born Chinese, or Baba-Nyonya, who combined Chinese and Malay traditions, especially in their kitchens. Penang's Nyonya cuisine is a tad more fiery due to the island's proximity to Thailand.

*Dragon King*, on the corner of Lebuh Bishop and Lebuh Pitt (Jalan Masjid Kapitan Keling), specialises in traditional Nyonya food and although it's a bit overpriced and the quality uneven, it's worth a try for deep-fried fish or *hong bak* (pork in thick gravy). Set-lunch menus of three dishes plus dessert cost only RM6. It's closed on Wednesday.

The small, air-con *77 Restaurant* (77D Gurney Drive), north-east of town, also has Nyonya food, including curried fish heads.

**Malay** *Shahabe Restoran* (10 Lebuh King) is good for very cheap Malay set-menu lunches. The menu pictures all the *nasi* (rice) dishes available, and roti canai is a steal at 60 sen.

You can also try regional Malaysian specialities at *Bamboo Village Hut* restaurant on Lebuh Chulia (see its entry under Indian later in this section), where the totally delicious menu can only be improved upon by the upstairs juice bar and Internet cafe, currently being built.

**Indian** The eateries in Penang's Little India are along Lebuh Pasar, between Lebuh Penang and Lebuh Pitt (Jalan Masjid Kapitan Keling), an on the side streets in between. Several small restaurants and stalls in this area offer cheap North Indian and South Indian food.

A number of unpretentious South Indian restaurants serving vegetarian and meat dishes can be found along Lebuh Penang. These include the popular *Shusi Banana Leaf Restaurant*, with cheap meals served on the traditional banana-leaf base; and the small *Meena Cafe* at No 118, dishing up good mutton or fish curries for around RM5. The air-con *Kaliamans Restaurant* at No 43 is a bit more upmarket and offers a broader range of subcontinental dishes, but it's often empty. *Kedai Kopi Yasmeen* (177 Jalan Penang), near the corner of Lebuh Chulia, is another place for *murtabak* (roti filled with pieces of mutton, chicken or vegetables), biryani or a quick snack of roti canai with dhal dip.

On Lebuh Campbell, *Taj Restaurant* at No 166 and *Hameediyah Restaurant* at No 164A are two Indian halal coffee shops with pre-war decor, good curries, *idli* (steamed rice-flour cakes) and murtabak at cheap prices. The Taj also has an upstairs, air-con section, which is amazingly dowdy.

For good North Indian curries and tandoori food in modern, air-con surroundings, head for *Kashmir Restaurant*, in the basement of the Oriental Hotel; travellers rave about it. In Chinatown on Lebuh Chulia, *Bamboo Village Hut* has amazing North Indian naan and tandoori in the evenings, accompanied by creamy lassi poured into real bamboo stems. At *Tandoori House* on Lorong Hutton you can eat well for around RM20 per person. The much classier *Jaipur Court (11 Lebuh Leith)*, in the renovated servants' quarters opposite Cheong Fatt Tze Mansion, serves truly fine cuisine at more-upmarket prices.

**Thai & Japanese** The lavish *MonSoon* restaurant, near the Cheong Fatt Tze Mansion, serves elegant Thai food for less than you'd expect (around RM15 per dish) and pipes out soothing jazz. The simple *Restoran Tomyam (21 Lebuh Chulia)* serves interesting spicy combinations from Islamic southern Thailand, like steamed fish with garlic and sour plum.

Next to the Oriental Hotel on Jalan Penang, *Shin Miyako* is an upstairs retreat that serves reasonable Japanese food.

**Breakfast & International** Lebuh Chulia has some delightfully old-fashioned coffee shops where you can take a leisurely, cheap breakfast at marble-topped tables while you peruse the *New Straits Times*. As well as coffee, tea and toast, those on Lebuh Chulia have much more extensive Western breakfast menus of muesli, porridge and other favourites. The excellent coffee shop at *Hang Chow Hotel* at No 511, and the very popular *Tai Wah Cafe (487 Lebuh Chulia)* buzz with activity. The quieter *Eng Thai Cafe* has been there for years, serving breakfast all day long, including super-fresh yoghurt.

Off the main drag of Lebuh Chulia, on Lebuh Campbell, the eclectic fusion menu at *Lovage Cafe* never disappoints. Its superior fare seems like a dream at prices like these – around RM10 for the boldly spiced 'Amazing Thailand' (prawns in curry) spaghetti or marinated Bombay Sapphire steak. With a selection of vegetarian dishes and fabulous desserts, this family-run restaurant deserves a far greater following. It's closed on Wednesday. The equally charming *Pintail Cafe & Bistro* is set among the art shops at the northern end of Jalan Penang. Deliciously creative juice drinks take up an entire menu themselves,

and the intriguing selection of East-West main dishes measures up to Lovage Cafe, though prices are higher in accordance with the swank, stylish interior.

*Green Planet (63 Lebuh Cintra)* and *Rainforest Café (294 Lebuh Cintra)* are two popular travellers' cafes. Virtual clones of each other, they offer the standard menu of pizza, lasagne, felafel and nachos for under RM15, as well as a few Nyonya dishes like cinnamon meat with pickled vegetables (RM12). Both offer Internet access (RM5 per hour). At Rainforest you can read (and add to) extensive travel-tips logbooks on India, Thailand, Africa and elsewhere.

Another travellers' hang-out is *Secret Garden* (☎ 262 9996, ✉ secretgdn@hotmail .com, 414 Lebuh Chulia). It's run by a German expat who serves a range of wholesome breakfasts and better-than-average Western food starting at RM4.50; nightly movies are shown in a separate room. The owner can also arrange tickets, rentals, visas and so forth for travellers.

Komtar has a *supermarket* and is a good hunting ground for fast food. On the 5th floor there's a lively, crowded *hawker centre* serving all the usual Chinese and Malay dishes, plus some Indian food. On the 1st floor you'll find the inexpensive chain restaurant *Satay Hut*, or for a meal with a view, there's *Tower Restaurant* on level 59, which has an upmarket Chinese a la carte menu.

Back in Chinatown, *Diner's Bakery* on Lebuh Campbell has take-away goodies ranging from Black Forest cake to Chinese peanut tarts, though there are cheaper bakeries around. *Soho Free House*, a bistro next to the Peking Hotel, serves hearty Anglo-Saxon grub like fish and chips and shepherd's pie.

North-west of Georgetown in the suburbs of Pulau Tikus, the *Midlands 1-Stop* shopping centre has a few fast-food outlets and there are plenty of upscale restaurants nearby for expats and the nouveau riche. *Sommeliers Restaurant & Wine Bistro (Havana Club)* (☎ 227 2133, 2 Brown Rd) is almost directly across the street from the shopping complex. The Italian chain *Modesto's* is a few blocks east, at the intersection on Jalan Burma.

## Entertainment

Lebuh Chulia is a good place to find a beer, as there are plenty of street-side cafes and bars popular with travellers.

*Coco Island Travellers Corner*, under the Hong Ping Hotel at No 273, has outdoor tables that are great for taking in the street life, plus some live cover bands performing until late. An unexciting food menu is available, if you're really hungry.

A couple of doors down, the colourful *Betelnut Cafe* attracts drinkers until the early hours. The *Hard Life Cafe* (☎ 262 1740) at No 363 grooves to a reggae beat and is usually full enough to spill out onto the footpath. If you're too happy here to go home, it has a few make-shift dorm beds available. Last, and least, *Hong Kong Bar* at No 371 is an air-con place popular with expat armed-forces personnel.

Around the corner on Lebuh Leith, opposite the Cheong Fatt Tze Mansion, is *20 Leith Street*, housed in the mansion's former servants' quarters. It's a favourite haunt for the more-moneyed class, and has a variety of bar areas, with tables out the front.

Georgetown used to have more discos that stayed open until around 3 am, but *Rock World*, set back from Lebuh Campbell, is the lone survivor. It still gets lively on weekends and features local Chinese bands. You can't miss the gargantuan neon spider web hanging over the front.

Most of Georgetown's real nightlife has moved out to the suburbs at Pulau Tikus near the Midlands 1-Stop shopping centre and nearby Gottlieb Rd, all several kilometres north-west of Georgetown proper. Popular spots include *Modesto's* (see Breakfast & International under Places to Eat earlier), on Jalan Burma in a line-up of copy-cat clubs. The trend-setting *Brix* and *Royal Bistro* are on Gottlieb Rd, which intersects Jalan Burma a few blocks west of Midlands 1-Stop.

## Shopping

Even though Penang lost its duty-free status to Langkawi back in the 1980s, it's still a good place to shop. Penang has plenty of outlets for cameras, electronics, clothes and shoes at competitive prices (though Kuala Lumpur has a wider range). Copies of brand-name goods are cheap. Bargaining is usually required, except in department stores.

Jalan Penang is the best shopping street in Georgetown. Start at Komtar, where dozens of small and large shops sell everything from clothes, shoes and electronics to everyday goods. Directly opposite Komtar is a collection of small shops selling pewter, jewellery, basketwork and other handicrafts. There are also camera specialists here. One recommended repair shop is Soon Camera Clinic, around the corner at 2–04 Wisma Central, 41 Jalan Macalister. Farther south on Jalan Gurdwara, Gama Departmental Store & Supermarket is good for cheap clothes and household goods.

A number of interesting shops in Chinatown sell art, antiques and curios. Prices range from the reasonable to the ridiculous, so bargain hard. At the top end of Jalan Penang near the crumbling E&O Hotel is a string of half a dozen art and craft shops. A wander along Lebuh Chulia will also turn up a selection, such as Oriental Arts & Antiques at No 440A. The no-name shop at No 369, next to the Hong Kong Bar, sells jade pendants and bracelets etched with Chinese characters and poetry from RM10 (translation included). Along the more old-fashioned streets like Rope Walk (Jalan Pintal Tali) you'll find unusual bargains – like a 'Beware of the Dog' sign that adds the warning in Malay ('Awas – Ada Anjing') and in Chinese characters. Local merchants have turned the 118-year-old building at 100 Cintra Street into an antiques bazaar, complete with a tiny Baba-Nyonya cultural exhibition on the top floor.

Also check out the second-hand shops on Pitt St (Jalan Masjid Kapitan Keling) near Lebuh Chulia, which specialise in old coins, banknotes and stamps. Lebuh Campbell is another good shopping street, and stalls at the intersection with Jalan Penang have a broad range of leather and rattan goods.

Penang Plaza on Jalan Burma near the Sheraton is a mid-sized shopping mall with a large supermarket and a few bookshops. Out at Pulau Tikus you'll find the typical suburban

PENINSULAR MALAYSIA

malls, including the Midlands 1-Stop shopping centre and Island Plaza shopping complex (with a cineplex and game centre).

Shopping possibilities in Batu Ferringhi range from the night market selling all sorts of souvenirs, copy watches and so on; to the large and expensive Yahong Gallery at 58-D Batu Ferringhi Rd, which sells Asian antiques and art. Cheap beachwear and light cotton clothes can be found at souvenir centres along the highway and on the beach near the guesthouse strip.

The Thieves' Market (now a morning flea market, said to be liveliest on Sunday) has moved to a car park behind the City Stadium on Lorong Kulit. It has all sorts of unsorted bric-a-brac (much of which is useless junk) but there are also antique pieces for sale – even the odd genuinely stolen item. Buses to Air Itam pass the flea market, but check the *Penang Tourist Newspaper* (see Tourist Offices earlier) to be sure it hasn't moved.

### Getting There & Away
See the Getting There & Away and Getting Around sections at the end of this chapter for information on transport to and from Georgetown.

## AROUND GEORGETOWN
### Penang Hill
Rising 830m above Georgetown, the top of Penang Hill provides a cool retreat from the sticky heat below, being generally about 5°C cooler than at sea level. From the summit there's a spectacular view over the island and across to the mainland. There are pleasant **gardens**, an old-fashioned kiosk, a restaurant and a hotel, as well as a **Hindu temple** and a **mosque** at the top. Penang Hill is particularly wonderful at dusk as Georgetown, far below, starts to light up.

Penang Hill was first cleared by Captain Light soon after British settlement in order to grow strawberries (it was originally known as Strawberry Hill). A trail to the top was opened from the Botanical Gardens waterfall and access was by foot or packhorse, or sedan chair for the wealthy. The official name of the hill was Flagstaff Hill

(now translated as Bukit Bendera), but it is universally known as Penang Hill.

Efforts to make it a popular hill resort were thwarted by difficult access, and the first attempt at a mountain railway proved to be a dismal failure. In 1923 a Swiss-built **funicular railway system** was completed, and the tiny, cable-pulled Penang Hill Railway cars have trundled up and down ever since. A few years ago the original funicular cars were replaced by more-modern ones, but the queues on weekends and public holidays can still be as long as ever. The trip takes a crawling 30 minutes, with a change of trains at the halfway point. On the way, you pass the bungalows originally built for British officials and other wealthy citizens.

A number of roads and **walking trails** traverse the hill. You can walk all the way to the Botanical Gardens in about three hours, from the trail near the upper funicular station or via the jeep track from the top. Take water and food on longer walks. The Bellevue Hotel (see Places to Stay later for details) has a good map in the lobby that shows trails. The hotel also has a small aviary garden featuring exotic birds, which is open from 9 am to 6 pm; entry costs RM2.

**Places to Stay** On top of Penang Hill, the small ***Bellevue Hotel*** (☎ 829 9500, fax 829 2052) is quiet with a delightful garden, a good restaurant and the best views in town. Buckminster Fuller was a regular guest here and photos and commentaries in the lobby commemorate him. Though an historic building, renovations have destroyed most of the hotel's architectural features. The rooms retain some character and are large and comfortable; a retreat here costs RM120/160 for singles/doubles. Access is via the funicular railway and a five-minute walk. Alternatively, ring to arrange a 4WD pick-up (RM40) from the Botanical Gardens.

**Getting There & Away** From Komtar, or along Lebuh Chulia, you can catch one of the frequent TransitLink buses (No 1, 101, 351 or 361), Yellow Bus No 85 or minibus No 21 to Air Itam. From Air Itam, walk five minutes to the funicular railway station or take the half-hourly TransitLink shuttle bus No 8. A taxi from the ferry terminal in Georgetown to the funicular station is RM12.

The funicular costs RM3/4 one way/ return. Departures are every 15 to 30 minutes from 6.30 am to 9.30 pm (to 11.15 pm on weekends). The queues at the bottom are often horrendous – waits of half an hour and more are not uncommon on weekends.

The energetic can get to the top by an interesting 5.5km hike, starting from the Moon Gate at the Botanical Gardens. The hike takes nearly three hours, so bring a water bottle and hat. The easier jeep trail to the top starts beyond the Moon Gate and is closed to private vehicles. Both routes meet near a small tea kiosk.

## Kek Lok Si Temple

The largest Buddhist temple in Malaysia stands on a hilltop at Air Itam, near Penang Hill. Founded by an immigrant Chinese Buddhist, construction started in 1890, took more than 20 years to complete and was largely funded by donations from Penang's Straits Chinese elite.

To reach the entrance, walk through arcades of souvenir stalls, past a tightly packed turtle pond and murky fish ponds, until you reach **Ban Po Thar** (Ten Thousand Buddhas Pagoda). A 'voluntary' contribution lets you climb to the top of the seven-tier, 30m-high tower. The design is said to be Burmese at the top, Chinese at the bottom and Thai in between. In another three-storey shrine, there's a large Thai Buddha image that was donated by King Bhumibol of Thailand. Standing high above all the temple structures is a striking white figure of Kuan Yin, goddess of mercy.

It's an impressive temple, though crowded with tourists as much as worshippers. You must take off your shoes to enter the temple, but beware of the 'one-shoe bandits', local pranksters who steal just one shoe. The temple is a short 10-minute walk from Penang Hill station (see the Penang Hill entry earlier), or you can hop on the half-hourly TransitLink shuttle bus No 8.

## Botanical Gardens

The 30-hectare Botanical Gardens off Waterfall Rd are also known as the Waterfall Gardens, after the stream that cascades through from Penang Hill. They've also been dubbed the Monkey Gardens for the many long-tailed macaques that appear on the lawn for a feed by the staff early each morning and late each afternoon. (Monkeys do bite, so it's probably best to leave the feeding to the staff.) Within the grounds are an orchid house, palm house, herbal garden, cactus garden and sun rookery. A path leads to the top of Penang Hill. The gardens are open from 5 am to 8 pm daily.

The half-hourly Sri Negara bus No 137 stops at the nearby Waterfall Hotel, a 1km walk from the gardens. TransitLink bus No 7 runs hourly from Komtar along Lebuh Chulia to the entrance.

## AROUND THE ISLAND

You can make a circuit of the island by car, motorcycle, bicycle (if you're keen), public transport or on a tour. If travelling by motorcycle or car, plan to spend about five hours, with plenty of sightseeing and refreshment stops. If you're on a bicycle, allow all day.

It's 70km all the way round, but only the north-coast road runs beside the beaches. The route takes you from Georgetown around the island clockwise. The road to Bayan Lepas and the airport is congested and built up, but it gets much quieter farther around on the island's western side.

## Museum and Art Gallery

Six kilometres south of Georgetown, on the sprawling campus of Universiti Sains Malaysia, the Museum and Art Gallery has a fine collection of traditional Malaysian and Indonesian musical instruments (including several full gamelan orchestras), aboriginal and Baba-Nyonya pieces, and fascinating contemporary Malaysian art and photography.

It's open from 10 am to 5 pm weekdays (closed from 12.15 to 2.45 pm on Friday and after 1 pm on Saturday). Take any Yellow Bus (except No 82 or 85) from Georgetown, but be sure to get off at the university stop before the bus turns onto the Penang Bridge and carries you away to the mainland.

## Snake Temple

Three kilometres before the airport, you'll see Penang's Snake Temple (Temple of the Azure Cloud) on the western side of the road. The temple is dedicated to Chor Soo Kong, a Buddhist priest and healer, and was built in 1850 by a grateful patient. The several resident (venomous) Wagler's pit vipers and green tree snakes are said to be fixed and slightly doped by the incense smoke drifting around the temple during the day, but at night slither down to eat the offerings. Admission is technically free, although 'donations' are demanded by the snake handlers.

Yellow Bus No 80 and Minibus No 32 run every 30 minutes from Komtar past the temple, or take Yellow Bus No 66 from Lebuh Chulia.

## Fishing Villages

About 3km after the snake temple, you reach the turn-off to the Chinese fishing village of **Batu Maung**. The renovated seaside temple here has a shrine dedicated to the legendary Admiral Cheng Ho (see the Melaka chapter for more information on this historic figure). The temple sanctifies a huge 'footprint' on the rock that's reputed to belong to the famous eunuch. Yellow Bus No 69, TransitLink 303 and Minibus 27 from Komtar all pass Batu Maung.

Back on the highway, the road climbs up, then drops down to Teluk Kumbar, from where you can detour to the fishing village of **Gertak Sanggul**, which has stalls on the seaside selling fresh fish. You'll pass some pint-sized scenic beaches on the way, although none are particularly good for swimming.

## Balik Pulau

A little farther north, Balik Pulau is the main town on the island circuit. There are a number of restaurants and food stalls here, but no accommodation – circuiting the island must be a one-day operation, unless you bring camping gear. Balik Pulau is a good place for lunch and the local speciality, *laksa balik pulau,* is a must. It's a tasty rice-noodle concoction with a thick fish-broth, mint leaves, pineapple slivers, onions and fresh chillies.

**Balik's Holy Name of Jesus Church** was built in 1854 and its twin spires stand out impressively against the jungle behind.

Balik Pulau is the terminus of Yellow Bus No 66 from Georgetown. You can also take Yellow Bus No 85, which takes the inland route.

## Sungai Pinang & Pantai Acheh

After Balik Pulau you pass through an area of Malay kampung and clove, nutmeg, rubber, even durian plantations. Sungai Pinang, a busy Chinese village built along a stagnant river, is worth a peek. Farther on is the turn-off to Pantai Acheh, another small, isolated fishing village.

About 2km farther north along the road to Teluk Bahang, the **Tropical Fruit Farm** (☎ 866 5168) raises over 140 types of tropical and sub-tropical fruit trees, native and hybrid. Interested visitors can stay in return for helping on the farm (though you need to phone ahead to organise this). The two-hour tours (RM20) are very educational and include a fruit sampler tasting. Tours are given every 30 minutes daily between 9 am and 5 pm.

The infrequent Yellow Bus No 76 runs between Balik Pulau and Teluk Bahang four times a day, passing Sungai Pinang and the fruit farm.

## Titi Kerawang

After the turn-off to Pantai Acheh, the road starts to climb and twist, offering glimpses of the coast and the sea far below. During durian season, stalls are set up along the road selling the spiky orbs, and you can see nets strung below the trees themselves to protect the precious fruits when they fall.

The jungle becomes denser here and soon you reach Titi Kerawang. Until recently, a waterfall flowed into a natural swimming pool just off the road, but the nearby dam has left the stream gully a trickle.

As you descend towards the north coast you'll pass the new dam and come upon the

**Forest Recreation Park**. Several kilometres south of Teluk Bahang, it has a forestry museum (closed Sunday), gentle trails through the jungle, a few small waterfall pools and a campsite.

A little nearer the coast is **Penang Butterfly Farm**, with a few thousand live butterflies representing over 50 species. It's open from 9 am to 5 pm weekdays and until 6 pm on weekends; admission costs RM5/10 for children/adults.

From here it's 1km north to the bus stop in Teluk Bahang, passing an **Orchid Farm** and the **Craft Batik** factory and shop along the way.

## Teluk Bahang

Finally, back at the coast, the village of Teluk Bahang marks the western end of the island's northern beach strip. The huge Penang Mutiara Resort at the eastern end of the bay and ugly multistorey housing may point to Teluk Bahang's future, but, for now, it's a laid-back, overgrown fishing village and relatively untouristed (give or take the odd day-tripper or tour bus hurtling round the central traffic roundabout). The effluvia from the many fishing boats and the refuse

washed down the river make this a dirty beach, but the stretch in front of the resort is good. The main reasons to visit Teluk Bahang are excellent seafood, tastes of kampung life and walks around the headland.

From Teluk Bahang you can trek down the beach to **Muka Head**, the isolated rocky promontory at the extreme north-western corner of the island marked by a lighthouse, which is off-limits (note the barbed wire and the sign depicting a guard shooting a flailing civilian). The trail passes the University of Malaysia marine research station and the privately owned Teluk Duyong beach. South of Muka Head is **Pantai Keracut**, also called Monkey Beach, where there are shelters, pit toilets and lots of bird- and monkey-life; camping is permitted.

The **Pinang Cultural Centre** (☎ 885 1175), down the road from the Penang Mutiara Resort, has a traditionally styled *balai* (meeting house) and Borneo longhouse. Local handicraft exhibitions and cultural shows, including music, dancing and a Malay wedding ceremony, are aimed mostly at large tour groups. The nightly buffet and dinner show costs an outrageous RM120, or RM130 if you come for the 'cultural tour' at

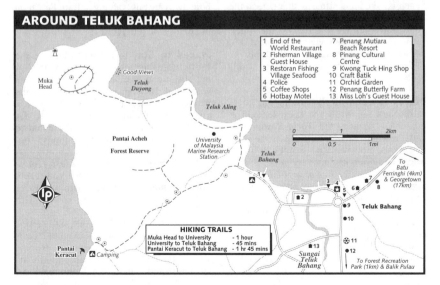

**AROUND TELUK BAHANG**

| | |
|---|---|
| 1 End of the World Restaurant | 7 Penang Mutiara Beach Resort |
| 2 Fisherman Village Guest House | 8 Pinang Cultural Centre |
| 3 Restoran Fishing Village Seafood | 9 Kwong Tuck Hing Shop |
| 4 Police | 10 Craft Batik |
| 5 Coffee Shops | 11 Orchid Garden |
| 6 Hotbay Motel | 12 Penang Butterfly Farm |
| | 13 Miss Loh's Guest House |

**HIKING TRAILS**

Muka Head to University - 1 hour
University to Teluk Bahang - 45 mins
Pantai Keracut to Teluk Bahang - 1 hr 45 mins

Muka Head

Teluk Duyong

*Good Views*

Teluk Aling

Pantai Acheh

Forest Reserve

University of Malaysia Marine Research Station

Teluk Bahang

To Batu Ferringhi (4km) & Georgetown (17km)

Teluk Bahang

Pantai Keracut

Camping

Sungai Teluk Bahang

To Forest Recreation Park (1km) & Balik Pulau

PENINSULAR MALAYSIA

6 pm. A shuttle service from all beach hotels is included in the price.

**Places to Stay** Although few travellers stay in Teluk Bahang, it has relaxed and inexpensive family homestays. The endearing *Miss Loh's Guest House* is set in a large garden and is so comfortable that some travellers end up staying a long, long time. Miss Loh can be contacted at the Kwong Tuck Hing shop, near the roundabout on the main road. Dorm beds cost RM8, singles/doubles from RM15/20.

*Fisherman Village Guest House (☎ 885 2936)* is in Kampong Nelayan, the Malay fishing kampung, and offers simple, tidy rooms in a family home for around RM20. Heading west from the roundabout, cross the water and take the first right after the T-intersection, then turn right again down a small lane and follow the signs.

The new *Hotbay Motel (☎ 885 1323)*, in the main shopping area east of the roundabout, offers good motel-style rooms for RM55 with fan, or RM65 with air-con.

*Penang Mutiara Beach Resort (☎ 885 2828, fax 885 2829)* is a top-class hotel, one of the best on the island. The sand on the beach is raked and sifted with a net, so the beach is spotlessly clean. A range of water sport activities are offered by the hotel. Rooms with garden views cost RM580, while rooms facing the sea are RM660.

*Camping* near the beach is also a possibility.

**Places to Eat** With all those fishing boats in the harbour, fresh and tasty seafood is guaranteed. *End of the World Restaurant*, at the western end of the village by the jetty, is famous; however, the seafood is overpriced and often just not very good. Expats in the know prefer *Restoran Fishing Village Seafood*, hidden away just east of the End of the World.

The main shopping area along the road heading east to Batu Ferringhi also has a few *coffee shops* offering Chinese dishes and seafood, and a couple of good *South Indian* places for murtabak and *dosa* (savoury Indian pancakes).

**Getting There & Away** Hin Bus No 93 runs from Georgetown every half-hour all the way along the north coast of the island as far as the roundabout in Teluk Bahang, as does hourly TransitLink bus No 202.

## Batu Ferringhi

The road from Teluk Bahang along the coast to Batu Ferringhi is a picturesque stretch of small coves and more beaches. Batu Ferringhi (Foreigner's Rock) is a resort strip stretching along Jalan Batu Ferringhi, the main drag, which is lined with big hotels, tourist shops and restaurants, as well as a good night market.

The beach is OK, but doesn't even compare to Malaysia's best, the water being not as clear as you might expect. The beach itself can be dirty, especially on weekends when hordes of day-trippers visit, and you may not feel like taking a dip. Though it can get crowded with holiday package groups and much of the greenery has been replaced by concrete, the luxury hotels offer great deals and cheaper accommodation is available if you just want a few days by the beach.

Although Georgetown is only half an hour away by bus, staying at Batu Ferringhi is inconvenient for exploring the city and old town in any depth.

**Places to Stay – Budget** Back in the 1970s when the grass was green and the living cheap and easy, Batu Ferringhi, along with Teluk Bahang, was a favourite on the budget travellers' trail. Batu Ferringhi is much more upmarket these days, so far fewer backpackers come here; those that do all crowd into the cheaper guesthouses opposite the beach.

The long-running *Baba Guest House (☎ 881 1686)* is the first place you reach. This tidy family home has plain rooms for RM25 and average air-con rooms with bathroom for RM60.

*Shalini's Guest House (☎ 881 1859, @ ahlooi@pc.jaring.my)* is in an old, two-storey wooden house next door. Rooms are spartan, but the comfortable family atmosphere and 2nd-floor balcony make it a

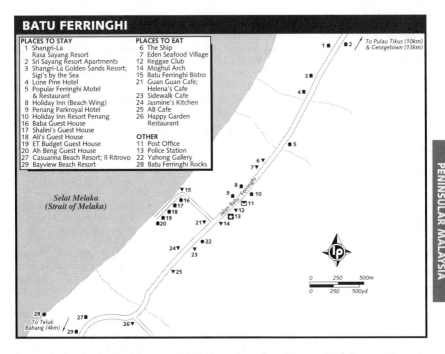

## BATU FERRINGHI

**PLACES TO STAY**
1 Shangri-La
  Rasa Sayang Resort
2 Sri Sayang Resort Apartments
3 Shangri-La Golden Sands Resort;
  Sigi's by the Sea
4 Lone Pine Hotel
5 Popular Ferringhi Motel
  & Restaurant
8 Holiday Inn (Beach Wing)
9 Penang Parkroyal Hotel
10 Holiday Inn Resort Penang
16 Baba Guest House
17 Shalini's Guest House
18 Ali's Guest House
19 ET Budget Guest House
20 Ah Beng Guest House
27 Casuarina Beach Resort; Il Ritrovo
29 Bayview Beach Resort

**PLACES TO EAT**
6 The Ship
7 Eden Seafood Village
12 Reggae Club
14 Moghul Arch
15 Batu Ferringhi Bistro
21 Guan Guan Cafe;
  Helena's Cafe
23 Sidewalk Cafe
24 Jasmine's Kitchen
25 AB Cafe
26 Happy Garden
  Restaurant

**OTHER**
11 Post Office
13 Police Station
22 Yahong Gallery
28 Batu Ferringhi Rocks

To Pulau Tikus (10km)
& Georgetown (13km)

*Selat Melaka
(Strait of Melaka)*

Jalan Batu Ferringhi

0    250    500m
0    250    500yd

To Teluk
Bahang (4km)

PENINSULAR MALAYSIA

---

better deal. Singles/doubles cost RM25/35, or RM45 with air-con, and meals are available.

Next along is *Ali's Guest House* (☎ 881 1316, @ alisguesthouse@hotmail.com), which may look inviting with its shady jungle of a garden, but the staff sure aren't polite. Rooms in the front with balcony cost RM30/35, and rooms at the back with bathroom cost RM40/45 (RM60/65 with air-con). The open-air bar and restaurant at the front is a popular gathering place for travellers.

Descending in popularity, *ET Budget Guest House* (☎ 881 1553) and *Ah Beng Guest House* (☎ 881 1036) are last in this line-up. Both places are double-storey houses with upstairs balconies and good views out to sea; the ET may be the only place around with working hot water. Both charge around RM30 for simple fan rooms and RM45 to RM55 for rooms with air-con, bathroom and (possibly) a TV.

**Places to Stay – Mid-Range** The only option in this price range (and it's a poor one) is *Popular Ferringhi Motel* (☎ 881 3333), which is, ironically, almost deserted. Compact air-con doubles with bathroom and TV start at RM80.50, which is no bargain considering there's no direct access to the beach.

**Places to Stay – Top End** Established in 1948, Batu Ferringhi's original hotel is the *Lone Pine Hotel* (☎ 881 1511), north-east of the budget strip. After a complete renovation in 1999, it has reopened as an 'exclusive yet informal' resort. Cosy rooms in the garden wing cost RM350, or from RM400 poolside. Promotional discounts of up to 40% may be available. You won't find the amenities of the bigger resorts here, but it does have refined, quiet appeal.

Batu Ferringhi's other 'international-standard' hotels, almost all of which are right on the beach, are strung out along several kilometres of coastline. Prices vary, depending on whether rooms face the beach, with major discounts offered outside the high season (roughly December through February). Privately owned and hotel facilities along the beach offer horse riding and water sports activities, including boat tours, jet skis, windsurfing and parasailing.

At the north-eastern end of the main beach area, *Sri Sayang Resort Apartments* (☎ *881 1113)* is a multistorey complex of suites with kitchenettes and balconies. There are laundry facilities, a pool, gymnasium and so on. One/two/three-bedroom apartments cost from RM88/138/198, plus an extra RM50 on Saturday.

Opposite is Shangri-La's *Rasa Sayang Resort* (☎ *881 1966, fax 881 1984),* the largest and most expensive of them all. Its design is an exotic interpretation of traditional Malay styles – it's the one place at Batu Ferringhi with real style and character. Singles/twins start at RM520/580, including breakfast and dinner. The adjoining *Golden Sands Resort* (☎ *881 1911, fax 881 1880)* is under the same management and guests at either place can use the facilities of both. Slightly less impressive rooms here cost RM320/340, again including breakfast and dinner.

Farther along is the bland *Holiday Inn Resort Penang* (☎ *881 1601),* charging RM395 for standard rooms in the renovated beach wing (jumping to RM525 if you actually want to see the sea).

Farther west is a string of tacky, aging resorts kept in business by short-term package tour groups from abroad. *Penang Parkroyal Hotel* (☎ *881 1133)* has a disco and charges the same rates as the older *Casuarina Beach Hotel* (☎ *881 1711, fax 881 2155),* which has singles/doubles for RM260/280. *Bayview Beach Resort* (☎ *881 2123, fax 881 2140)* has more-expensive standard rooms from RM357. As the beach slopes into the water more gradually here, the swimming is better.

**Places to Eat & Drink** The big hotels are full of passable-to-excellent, but always expensive, restaurants, including *Sigi's by the Sea* bistro in the Golden Sands Resort and the Casuarina Beach Hotel's Italian *Il Ritrovo*. The Rasa Sayang Resort is well-stocked with restaurants, including a Japanese restaurant and a 'British grill room'.

On Jalan Batu Ferringhi the upmarket *Eden Seafood Village* serves fresh seafood (plucked straight from the aquariums at the entrance). The galleon-styled monstrosity next door, *The Ship*, has a steak restaurant on the top deck and Captain's Cabin bar below.

The lively *Reggae Club* (☎ *881 1743)* is a popular place to chat with other travellers over a cold beer and hot nachos, and has a few makeshift hostel beds if you stay late. Diagonally opposite, the *Guan Guan Cafe* has mostly Chinese food but you can also get everything from steak and chips to seafood for around RM10.

At *Batu Ferringhi Bistro*, on the beachfront near the guesthouses, you can sit at tables by the sand while fresh fish is fried on a large open hotplate and wood-oven pizzas bake.

South-west on Jalan Batu Ferringhi, the fancy *Sidewalk Cafe* has terraced dining areas and Chinese food for around RM15 per main course. The *AB Cafe* nearby does filling breakfasts of French toast, banana pancakes or oatmeal porridge. Travellers recommend *Jasmine's Kitchen* for its clean kitchen and good Indian, Chinese, Malay and Western food.

Farther towards Teluk Bahang, the very pleasant *Happy Garden Restaurant* serves Western and Chinese meals at outdoor tables among flowering bougainvillea.

**Getting There & Away** Hin Bus No 93 (half-hourly), TransitLink 202 (hourly) and Minibuses 31A and 88A from Komtar take around 30 minutes to reach Batu Ferringhi.

### Pulau Tikus

Heading back into Georgetown from Batu Ferringhi, you'll pass **Tanjung Bungah** (Cape of Flowers), the first real beach close to the city, but it's not good for swimming. Inexplicably, big hotels and apartment blocks are cropping up everywhere, but Batu Ferringhi is still a better option.

After Tanjung Bungah, you'll enter the posh Pulau Tikus (Midlands) suburbs, full of discos, wining-and-dining venues, cinemas, and megamalls like Midlands 1-Stop and Island Plaza. Here is where you'll find all of Penang's expats and most of its beautiful people (see the Places to Eat and Entertainment sections under Georgetown earlier). A taxi from Lebuh Chulia to Midlands costs RM8.

Pulau Tikus is the beginning of scenic Gurney Drive, with its morning t'ai chi practitioners, great views of the approaching city, and hawker food. Eventually it intersects with Jalan Sultan Ahmad Shah, formerly 'Millionaire's Row', where nouveau riche Chinese in the early 20th century competed to see who could build the most impressive mansion. Many have now been demolished and abandoned, taken over by squatters, fronted by office space or even converted into fast-food outlets.

## GETTING THERE & AWAY
### Air
**Airline Offices** The Malaysia Airlines office (☎ 262 0011) at Komtar is open from 8.30 am to 6 pm Monday to Saturday and from 8.30 am to 1 pm on Sunday, but queues are often painfully long.

Other airlines with offices or agents in Penang include:

**Air Asia** (☎ 262 9882) 463 Lebuh Chulia
**Cathay Pacific** (☎ 226 0411) Menara PSCI, Jalan Sultan Ahmad Shah
**Pelangi Air** (☎ 227 7311) Penang Plaza, Jalan Burma
**Singapore Airlines** (☎ 226 3201) Wisma Penang Gardens, Jalan Sultan Ahmad Shah
**Thai Airways International** (☎ 226 6000) Wisma Central, 41 Jalan Macalister

**Malaysia** Penang is well served on the Malaysia Airlines/Pelangi domestic network, with several daily connections to Johor Bahru (RM178), Kota Bharu (RM87), KL (RM104) and Langkawi (RM51). Quoted fares exclude airport tax.

**Other Destinations** Penang is a major centre for cheap airline tickets, although international air fares are less competitive

than they used to be and not nearly as good as in Bangkok. There are fewer cut-and-run merchants at work nowadays, but it still pays to be cautious. Long-running, reliable agents are listed under Information earlier in this chapter.

Malaysia Airlines has at least one flight daily to Medan in Sumatra (RM231) and with Singapore Airlines (SIA) to Singapore (RM255). Thai Airways International flies between Penang and Hat Yai and to Phuket (RM262) and Bangkok (RM460) with Malaysia Airlines.

Other international connections include: Mumbai (SIA, RM1060); Los Angeles (Eva Air, RM1250); Hong Kong (Malaysia Airlines/SIA, RM710); London (Aeroflot, RM1380); and Sydney (Malaysia Airlines, RM1200). Return tickets on most routes offer substantial savings. One-way flights to Jakarta on SIA cost RM560, not such a bargain considering you could go overland to Singapore and fly from there for only RM255.

### Bus
Several long-distance bus services leave from Komtar in central Georgetown. Most depart from its basement, where the bus companies have ticket offices. While it may be more convenient to buy your tickets from travel agents on Lebuh Chulia (there are several near the Eng Aun and Swiss hotels) or some guesthouses and hotels, it's a safer bet to buy your ticket in person.

From Komtar there are several daily buses to KL, as well as one bus each to Kota Bharu and Kuala Terengganu – book well in advance. There are only two daily buses leaving Georgetown for the Cameron Highlands (8 am and 3 pm, RM15). Another option is to take a bus to Tapah, then change to a local bus up to Tanah Rata, the main Highlands town.

Many more buses leave from across the channel in Butterworth next to the mainland ferry terminal, and a few long-distance buses also leave from other parts of Georgetown. Newsia Tours & Travel (☎ 261 7933/1960), 35–36 Pengkalan Weld, is a major agent. Buses for other operators in the immediate vicinity stop along the side street next to the Newsia office.

Many long-distance buses depart in the evening. Typical fares include:

| destination | fare (RM) |
| --- | --- |
| Alor Setar | 5 |
| Cameron Highlands | 14 |
| Ipoh | 10 |
| Johor Bahru | 40 |
| Kota Bharu | 28 |
| KL | 18–20 |
| Kuala Perlis | 6.80 |
| Kuala Terengganu | 24 |
| Kuantan | 33 |
| Lumut | 10.30 |
| Melaka | 24–26 |
| Singapore | 36–42 |
| Taiping | 6 |
| Tapah | 14 |

There are also bus and minibus services out of Malaysia to: Hat Yai (RM18 to RM20); Krabi (RM28 to RM30); Phuket (RM38 to RM43); Surat Thani (RM28); and even Bangkok (RM80), though it's a long haul. The minibuses usually don't go directly to some destinations; you'll probably be dumped for a change of vehicle in Hat Yai or Surat Thani, sometimes with significant waiting times. It's best to buy your ticket from a guesthouse that contracts directly with a minibus agency, instead of from bucket shops on Lebuh Chulia. Then, if your minibus shows up two hours late, or not at all, you have someone to hold responsible.

## Train

The train station is across the channel from Georgetown, next to the ferry terminal and bus-and taxi-station in Butterworth.

The Malaysia Getting There & Away and Getting Around chapters have details on fares and schedules for the Butterworth, KL and Singapore line and international train services to Hat Yai and Bangkok in Thailand.

Make reservations at least a few days in advance at Butterworth train station (☎ 323 7962) or the train booking office (☎ 261 0290) located inside the ferry terminal on Pengkalan Weld in Georgetown.

## Car

Penang Bridge, completed in 1985, is one of the longest bridges in Asia at 13.5km. If you drive across to the island there's a RM7 toll payable at the toll plaza on the mainland, but no charge to return.

**Rental** Penang's a good place to rent a car, but you'll probably have to reserve in advance, especially for weekends and holidays or if you need an automatic car. Rates start at around RM95 per day plus RM15 insurance (for a manual transmission 1.3L Proton Iswara), but drop for longer rentals. Good deals can be found at smaller agents, though the main companies are also worth trying for special deals, especially Orix Rent-A-Car, which has impeccable service and great rates. Two cheaper agents are Hawk (☎ 881 3886), opposite the Shangri-La resorts in Batu Ferringhi; and New Bob Rent-A-Car (☎ 226 6111) at 11 Gottlieb Rd in Pulau Tikus and at Bayan Lepas airport (☎ 642 1111). The major companies in Georgetown are:

**Avis** (☎ 643 9633) Bayan Lepas airport
**Budget** (☎ 643 6025) Bayan Lepas airport
**Hertz** (☎ 263 5914) 38 Lebuh Farquhar
**Mayflower** (☎ 262 8196, at airport ☎ 641 1191) 274 Lebuh Victoria
**National** (☎ 262 9404, at airport ☎ 643 4205) 1 Weld Quay
**Orix** (☎ 261 8608, at airport ☎ 644 4772) 10th floor, MWE Plaza, 8 Lebuh Farquhar

## Taxi

The long-distance taxi mafia operates from a depot beside the Butterworth ferry terminal on the mainland. Typical whole-taxi fares are higher than from anywhere else in Peninsular Malaysia, and include such rip-offs as Alor Setar: (RM80); Ipoh (RM150); KL (RM280); Kuala Perlis (RM150); Kota Bharu (RM220); Lumut (RM180) and Taiping (RM150).

## Boat

Three companies currently operate boat services to Medan in Sumatra. These land in Belawan, and the journey to Medan is completed by bus (included in the price), usually taking about 4½ hours (but sometimes as long as five or six).

Both Kuala Perlis Langkawi Ferry Service Co (☎ 262 5630) and Ekspres Bahagia (☎ 263 1943) have offices near the Penang Tourist Association in Georgetown. Their shared ferries leave Georgetown at 9 am every day except Sunday; departures from Belawan are at 10 am daily except Monday (RM96/166 one way/return).

In the same office as the Penang Tourist Association, Langkawi Ferry Services (LFS; ☎ 264 2088) offers slightly faster boats to Medan and cheaper fares (3½ hours, RM90/160). LFS Ferries depart from Penang at 8 am on Monday, Wednesday and Friday; coming back, boats leave Medan at 10 am on Tuesday, Thursday and Saturday.

The same three companies also run daily ferries from Georgetown to Kuah on Langkawi (1¾ to 2½ hours, RM35/60). All boats leave at 8 am, returning from Langkawi at 5.30 pm.

## GETTING AROUND

Getting around the island by road is easiest with your own transport, particularly since the road does not run along the coast except on the northern side, and you have to leave the main road to get to the small fishing villages and isolated beaches.

## To/From the Airport

Penang's Bayan Lepas International Airport, with its Minangkabau-style terminal, is 18km south of Georgetown. There's a coupon system for taxis from the airport. The fare to Georgetown is RM20.

Taxis take about 45 minutes from the centre of town, while the bus takes at least an hour. Yellow Bus No 83 runs to/from the airport (RM1.45) hourly from 6 am to 9 pm, with stops along Pengkalan Weld, Komtar and Lebuh Chulia. Minibus No 32 shuttles from Komtar to the airport every 30 minutes (70 sen).

## Bus

There are several main bus-departure points in Georgetown, and half a dozen bus companies. The main city bus terminal is in the Komtar basement and almost all buses (including minibuses) stop here. Another main stand is at Pengkalan Weld, next to the ferry terminal jetty. TransitLink city buses all run via Pengkalan Weld, originating from the company's own terminal nearby on Lebuh Victoria, and Yellow Bus, Hin Bus and Sri

PENINSULAR MALAYSIA

### Bus Routes Around Penang

| destination | operator & route No | pick-up |
| --- | --- | --- |
| Air Itam | TL 1, 101, 351 or 361; YB 85; Minibus 21 | Pengkalan Weld, Lebuh Chulia, Komtar |
| Bayan Lepas airport | YB 83 | Pengkalan Weld, Lebuh Chulia, Komtar |
| Batu Ferringhi | HB 93 | Pengkalan Weld, Komtar |
| Botanical Gardens | TL 7 | Lebuh Chulia, Komtar |
| Gurney Drive | HB 93; TL 202; Minibus 26, 31 or 88 | Pengkalan Weld, Komtar |
| Penang Hill Railway | TL 8 | Air Itam |
| Pulau Tikus (Midlands) | HC 93; TL 202; Minibus 26, 31 or 88 | Pengkalan Weld, Komtar |
| Snake Temple | YB 66 | Pengkalan Weld, Lebuh Chulia, Komtar |
| Teluk Bahang | HB 93 | Pengkalan Weld, Komtar |
| Thai Consulate | SN 136 or 137; TL 7 | Pengkalan Weld, Lebuh Chulia, Komtar |

HB: Hin Bus; SN: Sri Negara; TL: TransitLink; YB: Yellow Bus

Negara buses all swing by the Pengkalan Weld stand. Most TransitLink buses also have stops along Lebuh Chulia.

Fares around town vary, but are typically under RM1. Some handy routes, as well as the operators, route numbers and pick-up points, are set out in the boxed table in this section. Minibuses all cost a standard 70 sen (exact change required) and you can only be sure of catching one at the Komtar centre, as wherever else they happen to stop along their route is at the mercy of the driver's whims.

For around RM5 you can circuit the island by public transport. Start with a Yellow Bus No 66 and hop off at the Snake Temple. This Yellow Bus No 66 will take you all the way to Balik Pulau, where you have to transfer to Yellow Bus No 76 for Teluk Bahang. There are only a few per day, roughly every 2¼ hours between 7.30 am and 7.15 pm, so it's wise to leave Georgetown early and check the departure times when you reach Balik Pulau. From Teluk Bahang, on the northern beach strip, take a TransitLink bus No 202 or a blue Hin Bus No 93 back to Georgetown via Batu Ferringhi.

See the table 'Bus Routes Around Penang' for information on some of the main services.

### Taxi

Penang's taxis all have meters, which drivers flatly refuse to use, so negotiate the fare before you set off. Typical fares around town are RM3 to RM6. Fares to outlying sights include: Pulau Tikus (RM8); Batu Ferringhi (RM20); Botanical Gardens (RM10); Penang Hill/Kek Lok Si Temple (RM10); Snake Temple (RM15); and Bayan Lepas airport (RM20).

## Motorcycle & Bicycle

You can hire bicycles from many places, including travellers guesthouses and shops along Lebuh Chulia or out at Batu Ferringhi. Bicycles cost RM10, and motorcycles start at RM30 per day. Just remember that if you don't have a motorcycle licence, your travel insurance probably won't cover you in the case of an accident.

## Trishaw

Bicycle rickshaws are an ideal way to negotiate Georgetown's backstreets and cost around RM1 per kilometre – but, as with taxis, agree on the fare before departure. From the ferry terminal, a trishaw to the cheap hotel area around Lebuh Chulia should cost RM6 (or you can walk there in 15 minutes). For touring around, the rate is about RM15 an hour.

## Boat

There's a 24-hour ferry service between Georgetown and Butterworth on the mainland. Ferries take passengers and cars every eight minutes from 6.20 am to 9.30 pm, every 20 minutes until 11.15 pm, and hourly after that until 6.20 am. Fares are charged only for the journey from Butterworth to Penang; returning to the mainland is free. The adult fare is 60 sen; cars cost RM7 (depending on the size) and motorcycles RM1.40.

# Kedah & Perlis

At the far north-western corner of Peninsular Malaysia, the picturesque states of Kedah and Perlis are the rice bowls of Malaysia, producing over half of the country's domestic supplies. Much of this agricultural region is covered by a panoramic sea of rice paddies towered over by limestone outcroppings that burst from the terrain. Perlis, once part of Kedah, is also the smallest state in Malaysia (approximately 800 sq km), and both states are important gateways into Thailand. This northern area is also strongly Islamic, and recent demonstrations by Muslim residents have urged the government to adopt a more orthodox interpretation of *syariah* (Islamic) law.

Apart from the main island resort of Langkawi, this corner of Peninsular Malaysia sees very few tourists. Women travellers can expect more hassle here than elsewhere on the west coast, as social attitudes are more conservative.

## Kedah

Kedah is very much a Malay state. It was controlled or influenced by the Thais for much of the 19th century, and the British did not gain a foothold until well after they had established themselves in most other parts of Malaysia. With miles of flat rice-paddy plains, it still has a largely rural feel.

For travellers, the most important towns in the state are Alor Setar and the small fishing ports of Kuala Kedah and Kuala Perlis, from where ferries operate to Langkawi. The small hill station of Gunung Jerai (Mt Jerai) and the archaeological remains of Lembah Bujang (Bujang Valley) are side trips of minor interest for those with time to spare.

Kedah state's business hours differ from most of the peninsula. Banks and government offices are usually closed Friday, but sometimes open a half-day on Saturday.

### HIGHLIGHTS

- **Pulau Langkawi** – a rugged, scenic island of white-sand beaches and jungle-clad hills
- **Alor Setar** – the grand Masjid Zahir and a unique mixture of British-colonial and Malay architecture

**PENINSULAR MALAYSIA**

## History

Settlement in Kedah goes back to the Stone Age; some of the earliest excavated archaeological sites in the country are found near Gunung Jerai. More recent finds in Lembah Bujang date back to the Hindu-Buddhist period in the 4th century AD, and the current royal family can trace its line back directly to this time. Discoveries in Lembah Bujang show that it was the cradle of Hindu-Buddhist civilisation on the peninsula and one of the first places to come into contact with Indian traders.

During the 7th and 8th centuries, Kedah paid tribute to the Srivijaya Empire of Sumatra, but later fell under the influence of the Thais until the 15th century, when the rise of

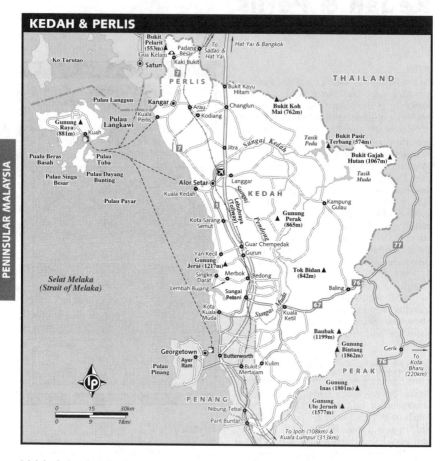

KEDAH & PERLIS

Melaka led to the Islamisation of the area. In the 17th century Kedah was attacked by the Portuguese, after their conquest of Melaka, and by the Acehnese, who saw Kedah as a threat to their own spice production.

In the hopes that the British would help protect what remained of Kedah from Thailand, the sultan handed over Penang to the British in the late 18th century. Nevertheless in the early 19th century Kedah once again came under Siamese control, where it remained, either directly or as a vassal, until early in the 20th century when Siam passed control to the British.

After WWII, during which Kedah (along with Kelantan) was the first part of Malaya to be invaded by the Japanese, Kedah became part of the Federation of Malaya in 1948, albeit reluctantly.

## SUNGAI PETANI

Known locally as SP, the acronym gives Sungai Petani an air of importance it doesn't deserve. The only reason to stop at this unremarkable town, on the highway between Butterworth and Alor Setar, is for transport connections to Gunung Jerai or the archaeology museum at Lembah Bujang.

If you get stuck, cheap hotels are within walking distance of the local bus station next to the central market. The *Hotel Duta* (☎ *421 2040, 7 Jalan Putri), with fan/aircon doubles for RM27.20/RM52.50, is the best of a bad bunch. *Seri Malaysia Hotel* (☎ *423 4060, fax 423 4106, Seksyen 21 Jalan Pasar)* has more-restful rooms from RM80, including breakfast. This mid-range hotel, set back 200m from the express bus station down a side street, is removed from the hubbub of the central market.

There are excellent Chinese and Malay *food stalls* in the lanes behind the HSBC Bank, just south-west of the clock tower. On the eastern side, *Eden Bakery* sells oven-fresh goodies and takeaway snacks. Inside *The Store* shopping centre (that glaring landmark to the north) you can dine in air-con luxury at *A&W* and other fast-food joints.

Sungai Petani is on Malaysia's main train line. The local bus station and taxi stand are on Jalan Putri, a few hundred metres south of the clock tower and one block west of the main street. The long-distance bus station is also south of the clock tower, but a few blocks east across a small bridge. From there, express buses run to Alor Setar (RM3.70, hourly).

## LEMBAH BUJANG

The area west of Sungai Petani was home to the most important Hindu-Buddhist kingdom on the Malay peninsula, dating from the 4th century AD. By the 7th century AD it was part of the large Srivijaya Empire of Sumatra, and it reached its architectural peak in the 9th and 10th centuries. Hindu and Buddhist temples were scattered from Gunung Jerai south to Kota Kuala Muda, and in Lembah Bujang alone some 50 archaeological sites have been already excavated.

The kingdom traded with India and the Khmer and Srivijaya kingdoms, and was visited by the well-travelled Chinese monk I-Tsing in AD 671. In 1025 Srivijaya and Bujang were attacked by the Cholas of India, but the Lembah Bujang kingdom later forged an alliance with the Cholas against the waning Srivijaya Empire. The region continued to trade, but by the 14th century its significance had faded and the temples were deserted with the coming of Islam. They remained buried in the jungle until first excavated by British archaeologist Quatrich-Wales in 1936.

Along the banks of the Sungai Bujang, the **Muzium Arkeologi** (Archaeological Museum) chronicles the excavations, and displays stone carvings, pottery shards and other finds from the digs. Most of the carvings have been lost, though the temples were not noted for extravagant carvings like those of contemporaneous Borobudur in Java. Only a handful of items are on display, such as a fragment of a wall frieze and a statue of the elephant god Ganesh. Most numerous are the Shivaite *yoni* fertility stones.

Though of enormous archaeological significance, the exhibits are neither breathtaking nor well labelled. The main interest is the partially restored *candi* (temples) behind the museum, but even these are unadorned and mostly only the bases remain. The largest and most significant temple is 1000-year-old **Candi Bukit Batu Pahat**. The entire complex is scheduled to become a National Historic Park when excavations are complete, but this is a long way off.

The museum is open from 9 am to 4 pm daily but closed from 12.15 to 2.45 pm on Friday; admission is free. It is off the Tanjung Dawai road, 2km north of the village of Merbok. From Sungai Petani, take a taxi (RM50) or one of the roughly hourly buses to Tanjung Dawai, get off at Merbok (RM1.40) and walk the 2km to the museum.

## GUNUNG JERAI

At 1217m, forest-clad Gunung Jerai dominates the surrounding flat plains. It was a sacred mountain in the ancient Hindu period and a landmark for ships from India and Indonesia.

From the base of the mountain, a steep and narrow road snakes its way 13km through a forest recreation park to a sleepy hill resort. From here there are expansive views north across the rice paddies of Kedah and over to Langkawi. As hill resorts go, this is definitely a minor one, well off the tourist route. Bring a friend, or lots of books.

PENINSULAR MALAYSIA

There are few opportunities for hiking or exploring away from the paved road. The road itself continues 3km past the resort to the peak and the remains of Candi Telaga Sembilan, a 6th-century Hindu bathing shrine, but the area is controlled by the army and is off limits.

A few kilometres downhill from the resort is a tiny forestry museum with exhibits on native trees and their uses, but little on the mountain's flora and fauna. The highlight is the enormous fossilised elephant dung. From the museum a paved trail leads through the forest to a waterfall and bathing pools.

## Places to Stay & Eat

*Perangian Gunung Jerai* (☎ 423 4345) is a low-key resort with accommodation in modern but worn chalets. Standard doubles with private balconies, hot water and towering ceilings cost RM65; deluxe family chalets are RM120, but in the low season the rate drops to RM60. Camping costs RM3 per site, plus RM2 per person (but tents cannot be hired).

An old, converted villa houses the moderately priced *Kayangan Cafe*, serving breakfast as well as Malaysian and Western dishes for around RM10.

## Getting There & Away

Gunung Jerai is about 30km north of Sungai Petani, and the turn-off is 3km north of Gurun just before Guar Chempedak. From the car park at the bottom of the mountain, 10-seat minibuses run up to the resort approximately every 45 minutes from 8.30 am to 5 pm (RM4). Private vehicles can also use the road.

Although the local No 2 bus between Sungai Petani and Alor Setar passes right by the car park on Hwy 1, the express services use the Lebuhraya (North-South Tollway) instead. From Sungai Petani you could also take a taxi or a local Guar Chempedak bus to the car park.

## ALOR SETAR

The capital of Kedah state is 93km north of Butterworth, on the main road to the Thai border. Few visitors stop in Alor Setar, the turn-off point to Kuala Kedah for ferries to Pulau Langkawi, but it does have a few points of interest. Don't loiter overnight if you can avoid it, as the town definitely has a rough edge; women travellers should be especially wary and expect plenty of hassle.

Alor Setar's long association with Thailand is evident in the Thai temples scattered around the city, but the main points of interest lie around the Padang, the old colonial town square, where some grand reminders of the sultanate are worth seeing, especially the Masjid Zahir (Zahir Mosque) and the Balai Besar hall.

Since Alor Setar was under Thai suzerainty until the 1909 Anglo-Siamese Treaty transferred rights to the British, the city shows fewer signs of Western colonial influence, and it is very much a Malay town, with fewer Chinese and Indians than other west-coast cities. The Indian community, centred north-west of the Padang, stays lively with hawker stalls and Hindi epic movies blaring from video shops. Alor Setar's self-effacing Chinatown, situated where the Sungai Anak Butik flows into the Sungai Kedah, is crammed with crumbling Chinese shophouses and hawker stalls – there are even Chinese ferrymen who will row you across the river for a few sen.

Alor Setar has the feel of a large village being dragged towards development, as wide paved roads and shopping plazas proliferate and the futuristic Menara Alor Setar (Telekom Tower) dominates the skyline, supposedly resembling a sheaf of rice plants. Visitors can zoom up all 165.5m and take a look at the countryside for RM3. The tallest building in town is still the UMNO Centre, not surprisingly as Alor Setar is a stronghold of this ruling Malay party, having provided the country's two longest-serving prime ministers, Tunku Abdul Rahman and Mahathir Mohamad.

## Information

The state tourist office (☎ 730 1957) is upstairs in the State Secretariat Building on Jalan Sultan Badlishah. It has a few brochures and staff can answer queries by

# ALOR SETAR

Sungai Anak Butik

Kampung Kanchut

To Muzium Negeri (1.5km);
Shahab Perdana
Express Bus Station (3.5km)
& Airport (10.5km)

Kampung Telok Sena

Jalan Menanti

Jalan Lumpur

Jalan Pintu Sepuluh

Jalan Telok Wanjah

Kampung Tuan Pah Merah

Lebuhraya Darul Aman (Jalan Kanchut)

To Kuala Kedah (17km) &
Kangar (45km)

Jalan Putra

Jalan Kampung Perak

Sungai Anak Butik

Kotar Star

Jalan Sultan Muhamad Jiwa

Jalan Tunku Yaakub

Jalan Sultan Badlishah

Jalan Kolam Air

Lorong Petani

The Padang

Jalan Mahsuri

City Point Plaza

Jalan Raja

Jalan Tunku Ibrahim

Jalan Langgar

Jalan Selamat

Jalan Limbong Kapal

Jalan Sungai Korok

Sungai Kedah

Jalan Pegawai

Jalan Seberang Perak

Lorong Puteh

Train Station

To Sungai Petani (58km) &
Butterworth (93km)

To Tokai

0   200   400m
0   200   400yd

**PLACES TO STAY**
4  Hotel Samila
6  Jollyfrog Hostel
8  Hotel Grand Crystal
15 Hotel Regent
18 Hotel Holiday Villa
21 Hotel Grand Continental
31 Hotel Lim Kung

**PLACES TO EAT**
5  Indian Food Stalls
19 Restoran Hajijah
20 Restoran Rose
25 Hai Choo
27 Hameem Kedai Makanan
28 Pekan Rabu
35 Hawker Food Stalls

**OTHER**
1  Wat Siam Nikrodharam
2  Plaza Internet
3  Telekom Tower
7  Sentosa Departmental Store;
   Sentosa Bowl; Plaza Putra
   Shopping Complex
9  Clock Tower
10 Balai Nobat
11 Masjid Zahir
12 Balai Besar
13 Muzium Di Raja
14 State Tourist Office;
   State Secretariat Building
16 Maybank
17 Telekom Malaysia
22 Bus Stop for Kuala Kedah &
   Sungai Petani & Shahab Perdana
   Express Bus Station
23 Wisma UMNO (UMNO Centre)
24 Balai Seni Negeri
   (State Art Gallery)
26 Post Office
29 Central Bus Station;
   Sing Tak Sing Hotel
30 Taxi Station
32 Overseas Union Bank
33 Standard Chartered Bank
34 Police Station
36 Rumah Kelahiran
   Mahathir Mohamad

PENINSULAR MALAYSIA

phone if you're stuck out in the boondocks of Kedah state.

At Plaza Internet on Jalan Sultan Badlishah, Internet access is cheap at RM2 an hour. For RM3 you can while away an hour until the next bus departure at Yuni Computer Cafe, just east of the Shahab Perdana express bus station on Jalan Mergong.

## The Padang

The large, open town square has a number of distinctive buildings around its perimeter. Currently under renovation, the open-sided **Balai Besar** (Royal Audience Hall)

was built in 1898 and is still used by the sultan of Kedah for royal and state ceremonial functions. Supported on tall pillars topped with Victorian iron lacework, it also shows Thai influences in its decoration.

Around the side of the Balai Besar is the **Muzium Di Raja** (Royal Museum), which served as the royal palace for the sultan and other members of the family from 1856. It displays the usual royal regalia along with musty dioramas and photographs from the 1904 gala wedding of five of the sultan's children. Tunku Abdul Rahman, a prince of the Kedah royal family, is honoured with his own displays. One tells the story of how the prince prophetically dreamed of Mahatma Ghandi and Jawaharlal Nehru just three days before Malaysia declared its own independence (and he became the nation's first prime minister). The museum is open from 10 am to 6 pm daily and closed noon to 2.30 pm on Friday; admission is free.

Housed in a fine colonial building at the southern edge of the square is the **Balai Seni Negeri**, the state art gallery, with a small but fascinating collection of contemporary Malaysian art, including Malaysian landscape watercolours by AB Ibrahim, and a *wayang kulit* puppet theatre. The gallery is open the same hours as the Muzium Di Raja and has an attached gallery shop.

On the western side of the square is the **Masjid Zahir**, the state mosque that opened in 1912. It is one of the largest and grandest mosques in Malaysia. Topped with Moorish domes and medieval and Mogul spires, it looks more like an eastern potentate's castle.

Farther north **Balai Nobat** (Hall of Drums), an octagonal building topped by an onion-shaped dome, houses the *nobat* (royal orchestra). Nobat is principally composed of percussion instruments, and the drums in this orchestra are said to have been a gift from the sultan of Melaka in the 15th century. It isn't open to the public and the instruments are only brought out on special occasions.

Looking like a twin to the Balai Nobat, the **clock tower** is another precious architectural whimsy of a type found all over Malaysia.

### Wat Siam Nikrodharam

This Thai Buddhist temple was built mostly by donations from the local Chinese community. An elaborate sculpture garden is in progress and a golden Garuda hovers over the entry to the main hall, inside of which sits a recognisably Thai image of the Buddha in the 'subduing Mara' posture. Along the outer walls of the temple grounds are inscriptions of the Buddha's teaching in three languages.

### Muzium Negeri

The Muzium Negeri (State Museum) is outside town, 2km north of the Padang. This small, dusty collection includes early Chinese porcelain pieces, artefacts from archaeological excavations at Lembah Bujang, and dioramas of royal and rural Malaysian life. A fabulous 'gold and silver tree', produced as a yearly tribute when Siam ruled Kedah, stands near the entrance.

The museum is open from 10 am to 6 pm daily, closed noon to 2.30 pm on Friday. Most local buses from town to the express bus station pass by the museum on Lebuhraya Darul Aman. A taxi from the town centre costs RM5.

### Rumah Kelahiran Mahathir Mohamad

This *kampung* (village) house at 18 Lorong Kilang, off Jalan Pegawai, is the family home and birthplace of the current prime minister. It has been turned into a museum, the only point of interest of which is its history of Dr Mahathir, the son of a teacher who became a doctor in Alor Setar before venturing into politics. Most educational are his articles on Malay themes, published in the *Straits Times* in the late 1940s under a pseudonym, providing some insight into Dr Mahathir's thinking and political development.

The museum is open from 10 am to 5pm daily, closed noon to 3 pm on Friday; admission is free.

### Places to Stay

Cheap hotels can be found along Jalan Langgar; they are noisy but OK for one night.

The *Hotel Lim Kung* (☎ 732 8353, 36 Jalan Langgar) in an old wooden building is not without charm, but has only very basic singles/doubles for RM14/18. A touch better is the *Sing Tak Sing Hotel* (☎ 732 5482) at No 74, right above the old central bus station, which offers simple fan rooms for RM17/21 or with attached bath for RM30.

Catering mostly to local men, the *Jollyfrog Hostel* offers extremely basic plywood-walled rooms, though air-con digs cost only RM25.

Mid-range hotels abound, and are preferable if your budget allows. The *Hotel Samila* (☎ 731 8888, 27 Lebuhraya Darul Aman) is a funky 1970s hotel. Doubles with all the trimmings cost RM62, including breakfast. The hotel also shows nightly movies in English or Chinese. The **Hotel Regent** (☎ 731 1900, 1536G Jalan Sultan Badlishah) is more central, but it has zero personality and the streetside rooms can be noisy. Air-con doubles cost RM66, including breakfast.

Just opposite the Regent, **Hotel Grand Continental** (☎ 733 5917) has singles/doubles from RM115/145, including taxes, but substantial discounts may be offered. Its smaller sister **Hotel Grand Crystal** (☎ 731 3333, 40 Jalan Kampung Perak) has doubles from RM160, including breakfast and taxes. It's in a more remote location, but it has a swimming pool and sometimes offers discounts of up to 50%.

Alor Setar's luxury hotel is the high-rise **Hotel Holiday Villa** (☎ 734 9999, 163 Jalan Tunku Ibrahim). Promotional rates for standard rooms are RM125/135, including breakfast.

### Places to Eat

Opposite the City Point Plaza shopping centre is **Restoran Hajijah**, a popular Thai Muslim place. The busy **Restoran Rose** around the corner on Jalan Sultan Badlishah is popular for Indian food, as is **Hameem Kedai Makanan** near the post office. The **Pekan Rabu** (Wednesday Market) goes on all day, every day, until late at night. Food, produce, household goods and handicrafts are all for sale; look for the dodol durian, a local sweet made from sticky rice, coconut and, yes, durian fruit.

In Alor Setar's little Chinatown, **Hai Choo** has been in business since 1862. It's so Chinese that it doesn't even have an English menu, but the food (specialities are seafood and steamboat) is very good and moderately priced. **Food stalls** at the nearby river confluence serve typical Malaysian hawker fare until late. Other **Indian food stalls** near the Telekom Tower sell takeaway snacks and mountains of Indian sweets.

### Getting There & Away

Alor Setar is 48km from the Thai border at Bukit Kayu Hitam. Frequent buses go from Alor Setar up to the border, from where minibus taxis go to Hat Yai (see Bukit Kayu Hitam later in this chapter for this border crossing). A direct train via the Padang Besar border farther west may be quicker and is certainly more convenient.

**Air** Sultan Abdul Halim Airport is 11km north of town just off the Lebuhraya. Malaysia Airlines (☎ 731 1106) flies twice daily to Kuala Lumpur (KL; RM113), and Pelangi has flights most days to Kota Bharu (RM71). There are a few car-rental agencies at the airport, including Hertz (☎ 714 4959).

**Bus** The central bus station on Jalan Langgar only handles some local buses, including to Sungai Petani (one hour, RM3.70), Kangar (one hour, RM3) and Kuala Kedah (30 minutes, 80 sen), from where ferries run to Langkawi. These buses also stop for passengers on Jalan Tunku Ibrahim opposite the Pekan Rabu market.

Long-distance buses leave from the modern Shahab Perdana express bus station on Jalan Mergong, 4km north of the town centre. For day-trippers, luggage storage is available (RM2 per bag). Frequent buses depart throughout the day for Bukit Kayu Hitam (RM3). There are also regular coaches to KL (RM21), Melaka (RM29), Butterworth (RM5) and Johor Bahru (RM45), as well as to east-coast destinations including Kuantan, Kuala Terengganu and Kota Bharu.

Local buses shuttle regularly between Shahab Perdana and the central bus station (60 sen), as do taxis (RM6).

**Train** The railway from Butterworth to Bangkok runs through Alor Setar and the border town of Padang Besar in Perlis. The International Ekspres via Hat Yai to Bangkok comes through at 4.15 pm, arriving in Bangkok at 11 am. Tickets cost RM52.80 for a seat and up to RM87.30 for an air-conditioned lower berth, but book well in advance. Alternatively, take the 8.27 am train to Hat Yai (1½ hours, RM8), a more scenic option than the bus – seats are usually available on the morning of departure. In the opposite direction, the train departs from Hat Yai at 3.10 pm and reaches Alor Setar just after 7 pm.

**Taxi** Rates for a four-passenger taxi from the taxi station include: RM24 to Bukit Kayu Hitam, RM48 to Butterworth, RM20 to Kangar, RM10 to Kuala Kedah and RM30 to Padang Besar.

## KUALA KEDAH

This busy fishing village 11km from Alor Setar is the southern gateway to Langkawi. The **Kota Kuala Kedah** is a fort built opposite the town on the farther bank of the Sungai Kedah. Constructed around 1770 to protect this main port of the sultanate from Siam, it fell to the Thais in 1821. The walls, cannons and gateway of this partially restored fort can be inspected.

There is little else to detain you from catching a ferry straight to Langkawi. Ferries leave approximately every half-hour to 1½ hours from 7 am to 6 pm (RM15), depending on the season.

## PULAU LANGKAWI

The 104 islands of the Langkawi group are 30km off the coast from Kuala Perlis, at the northern end of Peninsular Malaysia bordering Thailand. They're accessible by boat from Penang, Kuala Perlis, Kuala Kedah and Satun, Thailand, or by air from Penang, KL and Johor Bahru.

The islands, strategically situated where the Indian Ocean narrows down into the Straits of Melaka, were once a haven for pirates, and could easily have become the site for the first British foothold in Malaya instead of Penang. They were charted by Admiral Cheng Ho, ambassador of China's Ming Emperor, on his visit to Melaka in 1405, and for centuries they fell under Thai suzerainty.

The only island with any real settlement is 478.5 sq km Pulau Langkawi, with interior jungle-clad hills and fairly good beaches scattered around the coast. It is almost as big as Singapore Island, and like Singapore it is growing through land reclamation.

The name Langkawi combines the old Malay words 'helang' (meaning eagle) and 'kawi' (strong). Classical Malay literature claims the island as one of the resting places of Garuda, the mythological bird that became Vishnu's vehicle. The whole island is steeped in legends, and the favourite story is of Mahsuri, a maiden who was wrongly accused of infidelity and, before finally allowing herself to be executed, put a curse on the island for seven generations.

The curse seems to have expired and the island's 50,000 inhabitants are enjoying growing prosperity. Langkawi is a go-ahead area, targeted by the government for development as the country's premier tourist resort. The island is a symbol of the new Malaysia and a showcase for advancement of the *bumiputra* (indigenous Malays). Its development is backed enthusiastically by Prime Minister Dr Mahathir, who worked as a doctor on Pulau Langkawi in the 1950s before entering parliament.

Tourism took off in 1986 when Chinese-dominated Penang lost its duty-free status to the then Malay backwater of Langkawi. Billions of ringgit have since poured in to develop the island, which has excellent roads, gargantuan resort hotels, burgeoning shopping centres and an international airport. Most of the development is in the main town, Kuah, and at top-end beach resorts sprouting around the coast. But many grandiose hotels have already started to crumble and others were abandoned, half-finished, during the Asian economic downturn of the late 1990s.

Recent efforts have been made to broaden Langkawi's appeal beyond simple beach holidays, with a host of artificial tourist attractions, along with major annual events including the Langkawi International Maritime and Aerospace (LIMA) exhibition around November.

Away from the built-up areas, Langkawi is still a rural Malay island of small villages, rice paddies, water buffalo and natural beauty. As the beaches of Peninsular Malaysia's east coast attract more Western travellers, Langkawi still caters primarily to Malaysians, Singaporeans and the east Asian tourism market. Those coming from

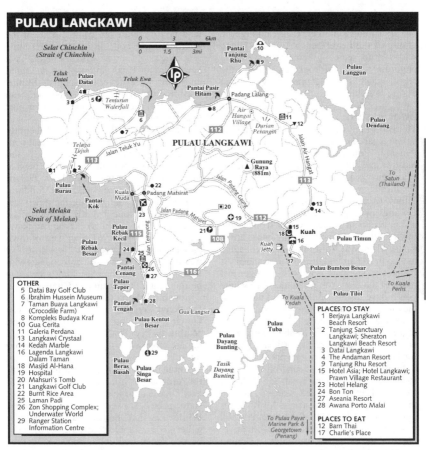

# PULAU LANGKAWI

**PENINSULAR MALAYSIA**

**OTHER**
5 Datai Bay Golf Club
6 Ibrahim Hussein Museum
7 Taman Buaya Langkawi
(Crocodile Farm)
8 Kompleks Budaya Kraf
10 Gua Cerita
11 Galeria Perdana
13 Langkawi Crystaal
14 Kedah Marble
16 Lagenda Langkawi
Dalam Taman
18 Masjid Al-Hana
19 Hospital
20 Mahsuri's Tomb
21 Langkawi Golf Club
22 Burnt Rice Area
25 Laman Padi
26 Zon Shopping Complex;
Underwater World
29 Ranger Station
Information Centre

**PLACES TO STAY**
1 Berjaya Langkawi
Beach Resort
2 Tanjung Sanctuary
Langkawi; Sheraton
Langkawi Beach Resort
3 Datai Langkawi
4 The Andaman Resort
9 Tanjung Rhu Resort
15 Hotel Asia; Hotel Langkawi;
Prawn Village Restaurant
23 Hotel Helang
24 Bon Ton
27 Aseania Resort
28 Awana Porto Malai

**PLACES TO EAT**
12 Barn Thai
17 Charlie's Place

Thailand may feel let down by Langkawi's high prices, cloudy waters, and less than spectacular diving and snorkelling.

The wet season in Langkawi is around April to October, and the dry is much drier than most of the peninsula.

## Orientation
Kuah, in the south-east corner of the island, is the main town and the arrival point for the ferries, but the beaches are elsewhere on the island.

On Langkawi's west coast, the most happening beach is Pantai Cenang, which is crammed with budget to mid-range hotels and restaurants. The water there can be fairly murky and jellyfish are occasionally seen. Pantai Tengah is almost a southerly continuation of Pantai Cenang. Nowadays the beach at Pantai Kok is deserted and much worse off, plus the only accommodation is in scattered luxury resorts.

The airport is on the island's central-west coast near Kota Kuala Muda. There are a few isolated resorts here, but the beach is one of the worst on Langkawi.

Along the north coast of the island virtually the only accommodation is at upmarket resorts, two at Teluk Datai in the west and one at Tanjung Rhu in the east. Tanjung Rhu is one of the better beaches on the island with white sand, green waters and a panoramic view of rock islands off the coast, which you can practically walk to during low tide.

## Information

Tourism Malaysia (☎ 966 7789) has an office in Kuah, 1km from the jetty along Jalan Persiaran Putra, a short distance past the mosque and across from the police station. It's open from 9 am to 5 pm Saturday to Wednesday, and closed after 1 pm on Thursday and all day Friday.

Langkawi is part of Kedah state, so banks and government offices are closed on Friday, often for the weekend. The only banks are at Kuah, where you'll also find moneychangers tucked in and around the duty-free shops. At Pantai Cenang there is a moneychanger just north of the Hot Wok restaurant. Elsewhere you'll have to rely on the resort hotels, and they may not change money for nonguests.

International telephone calls can be made at the Telekom office in Kuah on Jalan Pandak Mayah, and all larger resorts have phones for international calls using a phone card.

Internet cafes can be found on the upper storeys of shops around Kuah and at Pantai Cenang. The Store outlets scattered around the island also provided access for RM5 per hour. Connections can be agonisingly slow.

A few private companies run informative, but slightly outdated, Web sites, including www.delangkawi.com and www.tm.net.my/travel_station/langkawi, which introduce the island's history, recreational pursuits and current events with practical links to hotel and resort homepages.

Outside the jetty terminal in Kuah is a line-up of travel agencies for arranging car rental, boat trips and island tours. Accommodation booked here will almost certainly cost more than if you proceed directly to one of the beaches and look around.

## Kuah

The once small fishing village of Kuah is the island's main town. Though still not very large, it is a hive of activity, and the island taxi drivers even complain about the afternoon rush hour. In recent years, large shopping malls and new luxury hotels have been built in Kuah, although many stand empty or were never completed. Banks, duty-free shops and small emporiums can be found in the main centre of town, just over a kilometre from the jetty.

Out of town on the way toward the jetty is Kuah's picturesque **Masjid Al-Hana**, with its golden dome, Moorish arches and minarets rising above the palm trees. Next to the jetty, the **Lagenda Langkawi Dalam Taman** is a 20-hectare landscaped 'folklore' theme park stretching along the newly reclaimed waterfront, but it's entirely missable (RM2/5 kids/adults). At the **Langkawi Golf Club** (☎ 966 7195), 5km west of town past the hospital, green fees are RM60/80 weekdays/weekends. Lush golf courses with better upkeep and breath-taking views can be found at Teluk Datai and Gunung Raya.

Several kilometres north of Kuah is **Langkawi Crystaal**, Malaysia's only glass-blowing works, and, next door, the **Kedah Marble** quarry. Both are open to visitors, but are mostly aimed at stop-and-shop tour buses.

About 10km north of Kuah town, **Galeria Perdana** was established by Prime Minister Dr Mahathir to display hundreds of the state gifts bestowed by foreign nations. While this may not sound enticing, the gallery is a valuable showcase for the very best of Asian traditional crafts, as well as those of places as far flung as Africa and the South Pacific. Cambodian silver, Indonesian wayang kulit puppets, woodcarvings from Easter Island and velvet robes from Uzbekistan are just a sampling of the collection. The gallery is open from 10 am to 5 pm daily; admission is RM3.

## Mahsuri's Tomb & Padang Matsirat

These 'sites' are west of Kuah, a few kilometres off the road leading to the west-coast beaches and to the airport. Mahsuri was a legendary Malay princess, unjustly accused of adultery and sentenced to death. Her magical powers were so great that all attempts to execute her failed until the indignant Mahsuri *agreed* to die, but not before issuing the curse that 'there shall be no peace or prosperity on this island for seven generations'. As proof of her innocence white blood flowed from her veins, turning the sands of Langkawi's beaches white. The site is a complete rip-off, as there's nothing to see but a fenced-in slab of white stone (RM2).

A result of Mahsuri's curse can still sometimes be seen in the 'field of burnt rice' at nearby Padang Matsirat. There, villagers once burnt their rice fields rather than allow them to fall into the hands of Siamese invaders. It is said that heavy rain still sometimes brings traces of burnt rice to the surface.

## Pantai Cenang
This 2km-long strip of good beach lies at the south-western corner of Langkawi, 25km from Kuah. Pantai Cenang is where almost all of Langkawi's beach chalets are concentrated, and with its good assortment of restaurants and bars things get lively.

A sandbar appears at low tide, allowing you to inspect the local sea life. Between November and January you can walk across this sandbar to the nearby island of **Pulau Rebak Kecil**, but only for two hours around low tide. Another nearby island is **Pulau Tepor**, which can be reached by hired boat from Pantai Cenang.

At the southern end of Pantai Cenang, near Pantai Tengah, is the Zon duty-free shopping complex. **Underwater World** is a large aquarium with a walk-through tunnel for peering at the many varieties of fish up close. It recently launched 'Eat and Drink with Fishes', a thematic sea-bed dining experience. Five-course dinners are served, though one hopes not straight out of the tank. The aquarium is open from 10 am to 6 pm daily; admission is RM10/15 for children/adults.

At the northern end past the Pelangi Beach Resort is the new **Laman Padi** (Rice Garden) museum, with eye-catching rice fields and landscaped gardens on the grounds. The museum exhibits inside tell you everything (in English) you could possibly want to know about rice agriculture. If there's enough demand, visitors can participate in rice paddy activities – don't bump into the scarecrows. The complex is open from 10 am to 6 pm daily; entry costs RM2 for adults, and is free for children.

## Pantai Tengah
Pantai Tengah is a smaller, quieter beach just south of Pantai Cenang after the road skirts around a small rocky point. There have been major new resorts built here in recent years, as well as a few low-key places with chalet accommodation.

## Pantai Kok
On the western part of the island, 12km north of Pantai Cenang, Pantai Kok fronts a beautiful bay surrounded by limestone mountains and jungle. The water here isn't necessarily clearer than at any of the other beaches, though. The vermilion building stretching out into the water is the seaside summer palace set made for the 1999 movie *Anna & the King;* plans are in the works for converting the structure into a cultural museum.

## Telaga Tujuh
Telaga Tujuh is only a 2.5km walk inland from Pantai Kok. Water cascades nearly 100m down a hillside through a series of seven *(tujuh)* wells *(telaga)*. You can slide down from one of these shallow pools to another near the top of the falls – the stone channels are very smooth.

The only way to get there is by rented car, motorbike or taxi; drive to the end of the road, about 1km past Pantai Kok, then turn along with the road to the right until you reach the car park. From here it's a steady 10-minute climb through the rainforest (stay to the right) to the wells at the top of the falls.

## Teluk Datai
The beaches and jungle around Teluk Datai are some distance off the main road around the island. Here you'll find Langkawi's two exclusive resorts and the upmarket Datai Bay Golf Club (☎ 959 2620). The resorts'

PENINSULAR MALAYSIA

beautiful beaches are only for guests and day-trippers will be unfailingly driven away. The road continues past the resort to a headland where a short trail takes you through the jungle and down to the sea – a pleasant spot, but there is no beach to speak of.

On the way to Teluk Datai is the **Crocodile Farm**, where you can view saltwater crocodiles *(Crocodilus porosus)* at various stages of their development, with daily shows at 11.15 am and 2.45 pm, and hourly feedings. Though the farm is often deserted, the popular gift shop for crocodile skin products is, ironically, quite busy. The complex is open from 9 am to 6 pm daily; admission is RM5/7 for children/adults.

Farther along where the road turns west to follow the coast to Teluk Datai is the **Ibrahim Hussein Museum**. Completed in 1998, it makes for a quiet retreat into the forest. Currently the museum only displays the abstract and multi-media works of its founder, Ibrahim Hussein, some of whose work comments on the political situations in Myanmar (Burma), Hong Kong etc. The museum is open from 9 am to 6 pm daily. Admission is expensive (RM12), though it's worthwhile if you're a contemporary art fan or would like a chance to meet the artist himself, who can often be found at work on the grounds.

**Temurun Waterfall** is halfway between the museum and the resorts. The high falls are worth a look and the turn-off is just east of a huge concrete archway spanning the road.

## Pantai Pasir Hitam

Farther eastwards along the north coast, this beach is noted for its black sand, although it's not a real black-sand beach – it only has streaks of black caused by a spring that deposits mineral oxides. It's really a very contrived attraction, as the beach is only a couple of metres wide and is at the foot of a 5m drop, so you can't even walk along it. The waters off Pasir Hitam are dotted with huge boulders and the only notable sight is the unique Y-shaped jetty.

Before reaching the beach, you'll pass the **Kompleks Budaya Kraf**, an enormous handicrafts centre built in an extravagant neo-Islamic style. A wide range of regional and Malaysian-made goods are on sale from 10 am to 6 pm daily, from batik and *ikat* ('warp tie-dyeing' – fabric dyed on the loom) to pottery and woodcarvings, though there's nothing here than can't be found in KL or Penang for less.

## Tanjung Rhu

Just beyond Pasir Hitam at the village of Padang Lalang there's a roundabout with a turn-off to the north to Tanjung Rhu, while the main road continues back to Kuah.

Tanjung Rhu has one of Langkawi's wider, better beaches. The water is shallow and at low tide you can walk across the sandbank to the neighbouring islands, except during monsoon season. The water swirls across the bank as the tide comes in. There are mangrove cruises and kayaks can be hired.

Around the promontory, accessible by hired boat, is the **Gua Cerita** (Cave of Legends). Along the coast for a couple of kilometres before the beach, the tiny fish known as *ikan bilis* (anchovies) are spread out on mats to dry in the sun.

## Gunung Raya

The tallest mountain on the island (881m) can be reached by a snaking, paved road through the jungle. It is a spectacular drive to the top with views across the island and over to Thailand. At the top there's a lookout point and a small tea house with spectacular views, when it's not fogged over. Access to the mountain may occasionally be restricted by the government; the gate at the foot of the mountain will be lowered.

## Air Hangat Village

This 'hot-springs village' is towards the north of the island, not far from the turn-off to Tanjung Rhu. Like so many places on Langkawi, the springs are associated with an intriguing legend:

Pulau Langkawi's two most powerful families became involved in a bitter argument over a marriage proposal. A fight broke out and all the kitchen utensils were used as missiles. The gravy *(kuah)* was spilt at Kuah and seeped into the ground at Kisap ('to seep'). A pot landed at Belanga Perak (Broken Pot) and finally the saucepan of hot water *(air panas)* came to land here. The fathers of these two families got their come-uppance for causing all this mayhem – they are now the island's two major mountain peaks.

The hot springs today are nothing but a tourist trap for hotel buses that roll in every evening for the dinner and cultural show (RM50). Music and craft demonstrations are scheduled throughout the day, though finding staff willing to perform these can be challenging. The 'village' is open from 10 am to 6 pm daily (RM4).

### Durian Perangin
Roughly 15km north of Kuah is the turn-off to these waterfalls, which are 3km off the main road. In the dry season it's not very spectacular, though the swimming pools, 10 minutes' walk up through the forest, are always refreshingly cool. The falls are best seen at the end of the monsoon season – late September, early October.

### Organised Tours
The travel agents at the Kuah jetty organise tours, as do many shops along Pantai Cenang and most upmarket resorts. If you don't want to hire your own car or motorbike, there are cheap sightseeing (read: shopping) half-day tours that include Telaga Tujuh falls and Tanjung Rhu (RM20). Night market and village tours also happen a few days a week (two hours, RM10).

The islands off Langkawi's southern shore can be easily visited as a day trip. You can either charter a boat yourself, or join one of the organised 'island hopping' tours from Pantai Cenang or Kuah jetty, costing around RM30 per person. The organised trips almost always go to Pulau Dayang Bunting and Pulau Singa Besar, which has a 'wildlife reserve' (nothing but a petting zoo with peacocks, tame horses and the occasional water buffalo wallowing in the shallow waters off the beach). Some add a stop at the undeveloped beach on Pulau Beras Basah. During the monsoon season

from July to mid-September, the seas are usually too rough and unpredictable for boat trips.

### Nearby Islands
**Pulau Dayang Bunting** Tasik Dayang Bunting (Lake of the Pregnant Maiden), is located on the island of the same name. It is a freshwater lake surrounded by craggy limestone cliffs and dense jungle, and is good for swimming.

A legend states that a childless couple, after 19 years of unsuccessful efforts, had a baby girl after drinking from this lake. Since then it has been a popular pilgrimage destination for those hoping for children. Legend also says that the lake is inhabited by a large white crocodile.

Also on Pulau Dayang Bunting north of the lake is **Gua Langsir** (Cave of the Banshee), which is inhabited by thousands of bats. Most of the island-hopping tours give it a miss.

**Pulau Payar Marine Park** This marine park, 30km south of Langkawi and around 45 nautical miles from Penang, incorporates a number of islands, the largest being Pulau Payar. A large floating platform is moored off the island and includes an underwater observation chamber to view the reef. From here you can go snorkelling and diving, or rent glass-bottom boats. Inquire about the water conditions before you go, as it can be murky and you're unlikely to see as much as you would in eastern Malaysia or Thailand.

This upmarket marine tourism venture is visited on day tours from the Kuah jetty or by direct transfer from your hotel and costs RM280 including diving, or RM130 for snorkelling. Hotels and travel agents take bookings, or you can buy cheaper tickets from shops and accommodation around Pantai Cenang. Information is available from one of the main operators at www.sri wani.com.my/langkawicoral. You can also book tickets to the park from Penang.

### Places to Stay
Budget accommodation on Langkawi is now only available in Kuah and on the island's

PENINSULAR MALAYSIA

south-west coast at Pantai Cenang and Pantai Tengah. Even then it starts at around RM35 a night for the simplest room or beach chalet. Mid-range options are expensive compared with elsewhere in Malaysia, and the resorts range from small air-con chalets to five-star luxury. Package deals through travel agents or promotional discount rates in the low season are usually the cheapest ways to luxuriate on Langkawi's beaches.

During school holidays and the peak tourist season from November to February, Pulau Langkawi gets very crowded, though something can usually still be found. At other times of the year supply far outstrips demand.

**Kuah** Kuah has seen the greatest tourist development, which is hard to understand given its lack of beaches. A short ride by taxi will take you from the pier to any of Kuah's cheaper accommodation, which is strung out along the waterfront, and will do for a late arrival or catching an early ferry.

Past the mosque, roughly 1km from the pier, you'll come to two vaguely budget hotels. *Hotel Asia* (☎ 966 6216, 18 Jalan Taman Sentosa) has reasonable air-con doubles with bathroom from RM60. A few doors down at the gloomy *Hotel Langkawi* (☎ 966 6248), doubles cost RM25 for a small windowless box with fan and shared bathroom; RM50 with air-con, TV and private bath.

The central *City Bayview Hotel* (☎ 966 1818, fax 966 3888), another high-rise set back from the waterfront, has a rooftop pool. The promotional rate for singles/doubles is RM120/140, including breakfast. Nearer the mosque on the road from the jetty, the *Hotel Central* (☎ 966 858, fax 966 7385, 33 Persiaran Putra) has standard-issue rooms from RM79 for two people.

In case you're wondering, the medieval castle-looking hotel complete with moat at the northern end of town is the defunct Tiara Hotel, another testament to Pulau Langkawi's over-aggressive and over-ambitious development.

**Pantai Cenang** Pantai Cenang is the liveliest beach strip with accommodation from

budget to international standard, though most places are mid-range. They all straggle the 2km of beach between the turn-off to Kuah at the northern end and Pantai Tengah to the south. Unfortunately, because the blocks of land are long and narrow, the beach frontage is minimal so from some of the chalets the only view is of another chalet.

At the southern end of the beach, near the Zon shopping complex, the *Langkapuri Beach Resort* (☎ 955 1202) has small, comfortable cottages for RM95.

Directly opposite and across the road from the beach is the *Lagenda Permai Chalet* (☎ 955 2806, ✉ lagendapermai@ hotmail.com), formerly 2020 Chalets, a welcoming budget place with simple chalets for RM50 and larger ones for RM90 with air-con. Simple dorm beds cost RM20.

Moving along, the *AB Motel* (☎ 955 1300) is an older laid-back place facing the beach. Big chalets among palms and casuarina trees cost RM40, or RM60 with air-con, but you could do better.

Across the road from the beach, *Beachview Chalets* (☎ 955 8513, ✉ beach vu@hotmail.com) awaits you with hand-painted murals inside the chalets and super-friendly, helpful owners. It's a great place to meet other travellers around the breakfast table while sipping lassis and devouring pancakes. It may have no beach or view, but the spontaneous art classes and informal outings, plus the discount card valid at local restaurants and shops along the beach, more than make up for it. Dorm beds cost RM18, and chalets RM40 to RM68, depending on size and bathroom facilities. If it's full, you can sleep in the treehouse.

A short way along is the popular *Sandy Beach Resort* (☎ 955 1308/1662), where two-person A-frame chalets with fan and shower cost RM45; the ones near the beach are quite good, but towards the road they are packed a bit too tightly together. In the resort's hotel section directly across the road, air-con doubles with bathroom and TV go for RM70, and more deluxe carpeted bungalows for RM80.

Beside the Sandy Beach is a good mid-range place, the *Semarak Langkawi Beach*

Resort (☎ 955 1377), which has pleasant, roomy fan/air-con chalets with bathrooms on lawns facing the beach for RM70/95.

A few paces farther north you'll find the *Melati Tanjung Motel* (☎ 955 1099), where very basic free-standing beachfront chalets cost RM35, or RM65 with air-con.

The next place along is the *Chenang Beach Motel* (☎ 955 1395), also offering fair value for your money, with clean air-con doubles for RM55. For low-budget travellers, the *Grand Beach Hotel* (☎ 955 1457) has simple beachfront chalets with bathroom for RM35 – an especially good deal. Larger chalets with air-con, TV and hot water cost RM70.

Near the northern end of the built-up strip is the very pleasant *Beach Garden Resort* (☎ 955 1363), run by a German couple. It has a small swimming pool, a German library and just a dozen singles/doubles, which cost RM140/160 with air-con and bathroom, including breakfast. Its restaurant is excellent.

The most northerly place on this beach, out towards the airport, is the family-oriented *Pelangi Beach Resort* (☎ 955 1001, fax 955 1122), with a swimming pool, sports facilities, buffet restaurants and every imaginable cheesy luxury – even electric buggies to take you to your room. No expense has been spared, and the overpriced rates reflect this – the cheapest rooms are RM483/513, including breakfast and evening cocktails.

Though not many people stay there, *Bon Ton* (☎ 955 3643, ✉ bon_ton@hotmail .com) has enormous but basic chalets costing RM160 with fan and bath, set in the middle of rice fields. The restaurant and arts and crafts gallery are worth a stop, too. Bon Ton is on your left heading north out of Pantai Cenang, 500m past the Laman Padi complex and the Pelangi Beach Resort.

**Pantai Tengah** Several new hotels have been built at Pantai Tengah, though it's still less built up than Pantai Cenang.

Just after the headland that separates the two beaches is a cluster of three scruffy budget places all charging RM35 for basic

chalets and RM50 to RM75 for air-con bungalows: *Green Hill Beach Motel* (☎ 955 1935); *Sugary Sands* (☎ 955 3473); and *Tanjung Malie* (☎ 955 1895). All are pretty basic and little thought has gone into the location of the chalets.

Next along is the mid-range *Sunset Beach Resort* (☎ 955 1751). The brick chalets, all with bathroom and air-con, run in a line back from the beach, so they have no sea views. Rates start at RM68/80 for one/two people, including breakfast.

After a gap of undeveloped land you'll find the best value on this beach, the *Charlie Motel* (☎ 955 1200), which has been around for some years. Basic fan/air-con longhouse rooms with shower and (squat) toilet cost RM65/75; nicer chalets facing the beach go for RM85.

Finally, there are the luxury resorts. Inland from Charlie Motel at the large intersection at the southern end of Pantai Cenang is the startlingly pastel-pink *Aseania Resort* (☎ 955 2020, fax 955 2136), with luxurious superior/deluxe rooms from RM221/308, but promotional discounts may get you as much as 35% off. You can't miss the grandiose fountain in the driveway or the Hollywood-like ASEANIA sign glaring from the hilltop behind.

At the end of the road leading south from that intersection to the defunct Teluk Baru jetty is the *Awana Porto Malai* (☎ 955 5111, fax 955 5222), a luxury complex built in California-bungalow style. Discounted walk-in rates for singles/doubles are solid value starting at RM135, including breakfast. The location, opposite several tiny rock islands, is rather scenic and there's an adjacent bowling alley and cinema complex, as well as water-sports offices at the old jetty.

**Pantai Kok** Since all of the budget accommodation here was demolished in order to get rid of budget travellers, the only places to stay are the expensive, exclusive resorts scattered around the bay.

Past the headland at the north-western end of the beach is the *Berjaya Langkawi Beach Resort* (☎ 959 1888), one of the

PENINSULAR MALAYSIA

PENINSULAR MALAYSIA

largest on the island. Luxury chalets cost RM300 to RM380 and suites are available. It has an excellent range of sports facilities and a Japanese-style spa.

Several kilometres back towards Pantai Cenang is the charming *Tanjung Sanctuary Langkawi* (☎ *955 2977, fax 955 3978, ✉ sanctuar@tm.net.my)*, offering stylish luxury in harmony with nature. It's built on a forested, rocky headland with its own lovely beachlet, a beautiful swimming pool and a restaurant built on stilts over the water. Spacious chalets cost from RM200 with sea view or RM250 near the water, including breakfast.

Farther south-east is the sparkling *Sheraton Langkawi Beach Resort* (☎ *955 1901, fax 955 1968)*, with over 200 rooms arranged around a shady headland and a small beach. Rooms start at RM424 in the low season.

**Teluk Datai** Just past the Datai Bay Golf Club in a grandiose wooden Malay-style building within the rainforest, *The Andaman* (☎ *959 1088, fax 959 1168)* has its own private beach, gourmet Japanese restaurant and an on-staff naturalist who leads jungle walks. Doubles start at RM950, rising to RM4500 for the 'presidential suite'. It has a Web site at www.theandaman.com.

Farther on is *The Datai Langkawi* (☎ *959 2500, fax 959 2602)*, the island's most exclusive and isolated beach resort. Attractive low-lying chalets, many built on stilts over the water, are rustically set in the large grounds. They cost from RM1175 in the low season. Check out its Web site at www.ghmhotels.com/h-datai/index.htm.

**Tanjung Rhu** The best place to escape to on the island is *Tanjung Rhu Resort* (☎ *959 1033, fax 959 1899)*, tucked into a secluded cove with a glorious golden beach opposite several tiny islands. Its tasteful buildings are arranged around a central courtyard, with poolside doubles starting at RM770 to RM1650 for a luxury suite. This serene, eco-conscious resort is within walking distance of the public beach, with its food stalls and boat hire for day trips. Its Web site is at www.tanjungrhu.com.my.

**Kota Kuala Muda** Due to Kota Kuala Muda's relative isolation and poor beach, rates here are lower than elsewhere on the island, but the location is dull.

Catering largely to business travellers, the classy *Hotel Helang* (☎ *962 2020)*, between the airport terminal and the international exhibition and convention centre, has sound-proofed doubles from RM330, but offers generous low-season discounts.

## Places to Eat
**Kuah** You'll find *food stalls* in front of the City Bayview Hotel and on the nearby laneways of Lencongan Putra 1, 2 and 3, serving steaming hot hawker fare day and night. In the streets behind the Sime Langkawi Duty Free complex are some inexpensive *Chinese coffee shops*.

Kuah has some good seafood restaurants. For Chinese-style seafood try the cavernous *Prawn Village* restaurant near the Hotel Asia. Deliciously cooked dishes are generously portioned and not too expensive – take a group for sharing.

Nearer to the jetty, the new Langkawi Fair shopping complex has some fast food and a large *supermarket*. In the park opposite is *Rahim Cafe*, a simple open-air Malay restaurant.

About 500m uphill from the jetty at the yacht club is the breezy *Charlie's Place*, which has a great harbour view to complement its Western and Asian menu, including steaks (RM30) and elaborate desserts (RM10).

Nine kilometres north of Kuah on the island's east coast is *Barn Thai* (☎ *966 6699)*, an upmarket Thai restaurant with live jazz some nights (reservations advisable). It's accessible via an interesting 450m-long, raised walkway through a mangrove forest reserve, which is worth experiencing even if you don't eat there.

**Pantai Cenang** Many of the hotels at Pantai Cenang have OK restaurants, and they're all pretty much the same. For a splurge try the **Beach Garden Resort Bistro**, which serves excellent Western meals in a lovely restaurant and beer garden right on the beach. Lunch sets are a bargain at around RM13 to RM18, and the gourmet desserts are irresistible. You could also try a sumptuous buffet meal at the **Pelangi Beach Resort**.

Opposite the Semarak Beach Resort, **The Sailor** has bratwurst and other German fare. It's fairly popular, has a happy hour and a kids menu, and steak sets cost RM35. A hundred metres farther north is **Champor-Champor**, a tranquil garden restaurant offering imaginative Western-Asian fusion cuisine, including tasty vegetarian options. It has a good little bar for a drink, and the food (especially the soup) is fantastic, but prices are high, with mains at around RM20.

Another few hundred metres north, and only open from 7 am to 2.30 pm, is the **Breakfast Bar**, relied upon by locals and travellers alike. The entertaining staff will regale you with jokes, while cheerily (and quickly) serving up your choice of budget Western- or Asian-style breakfasts.

About 1km farther, past the new Laman Padi museum, is **Bon Ton**, a restaurant, art gallery and resort set in the middle of rice fields. It's open for lunch and dinner, and hosts nightly dance performances at 8.30 pm. It is set back from the road behind **Warung Kopi**, a bargain Malaysian food stall with some Japanese dishes on the dinner menu.

**Pantai Tengah** Pantai Tengah also has quite a few decent places to eat. The **Charlie Motel** is good for a cheap meal. The restaurant overlooks the beach and does a good job with Thai and Malaysian food. The **Oasis Beach Pub** next door is a congenial bar for drinking and also serves yummy North Indian tandoori fare. At the time of writing, the bar's lease was up and the owner planned to re-open in a new location, so ask around.

Back on the main road heading north towards Pantai Cenang is the **Eagle's Nest**, a small garden steakhouse with an intimate atmosphere, but it's only open for dinner and is usually packed.

A few kilometres south of Pantai Tengah proper, on the road leading to Teluk Baru, **Fat Mum's** comes highly recommended by travellers for spicy Chinese-style seafood and the house speciality, 'Noodles on Fire'.

**Other Beaches** The only restaurants on other beaches are found at the resorts, which are invariably atmospheric and up-market. The **Tanjung Sanctuary Langkawi** has a charming restaurant built on stilts right over the water.

At Tanjung Rhu there are several **food stalls** serving hawker fare at lunchtime to day-trippers.

## Shopping

Kuah is the main place to shop on Langkawi, but despite all the promotion as a duty-free shopping paradise, the range of goods is disappointing and the prices much the same as elsewhere in Malaysia. Duty-free shops can also be found at the ferry terminal, the airport and the Zon shopping complex at Pantai Cenang. Some resorts also have small shopping plazas.

Apart from cheap cigarettes and liquor, including Malaysian beer, shopping is geared to domestic visitors, offering oddities like kitchen utensils; or the Japanese market for imported designer T-shirts and fashion accessories at inflated prices. Electronics are no bargain and the variety is poor. You'll find a much bigger range of goods at the same or lower prices in KL and Penang. Langkawi Crystal glassware and marble souvenirs are the only significant locally made goods, and are best bought at the production sites on the road north from Kuah.

Legally, visitors must stay on the island for 48 hours before they are entitled to purchase duty-free items, though in practice the customs check upon departure may be lax.

## Getting There & Away

**Air** Malaysia Airlines (☎ 966 8611), at the Langkawi Fair shopping mall, and Air Asia (☎ 955 5688) have several flights daily between Langkawi and KL (RM135). Silk Air flies daily to Singapore (RM345), and

Malaysia Airlines also flies to Johor Bahru (RM194) and Penang (twice daily, RM51).

The island's international terminal is an impressive structure with a number of shops. A few hundred metres from the terminal is the international exhibition and convention centre.

**Boat** All passenger ferries to/from Langkawi operate out of Kuah.

From about 7.30 am to 6.30 pm, regular ferries operate roughly every hour in either direction between Kuah and the mainland ports of Kuala Perlis (45 minutes, RM12) and Kuala Kedah (one hour, RM15).

Three companies, Langkawi Ferry Services (LFS; ☎ 966 6316), Nautica Ferries (☎ 966 6950) and Ekspres Bahagia (☎ 966 5784), operate daily ferries between Kuah and Georgetown on Penang (RM35/60 one way/return, 2½ hours). Boats depart from Georgetown at 8 am and leave Kuah at 5.30 pm.

**Thailand** From the Kuah jetty, Langkawi Ferry Services makes three daily runs between 9.30 am and 4 pm to Satun on the Thai coast (approximately one hour, RM18). From the port a few *songthaews* (about RM20) and taxis go to Satun town, where you can make connections to Hat Yai or Phuket.

### Getting Around
**To/From the Airport** Taxi destinations from the airport include: Kuah jetty or Pantai Cenang (RM16), Pantai Kok (RM15), Tanjung Rhu (RM20) and Teluk Datai (RM40). Buy a coupon at the desk before leaving the airport terminal and use it to pay the driver.

**Taxi** As there are no public buses available to visitors, taxis are the main way of getting around, but fares are high. From the Kuah jetty, sample fares include: RM4 to Kuah town, RM14 to Pantai Cenang/Pantai Tengah and RM15 to Pantai Kok.

**Car** Cars can be rented cheaply, and touts from the travel agencies at the Kuah jetty will assail you upon arrival. The going rate starts at RM80 per day, but drops with bargaining. Cars and jeeps can also be rented more expensively at the upmarket beach resorts.

**Motorcycle & Bicycle** The easiest way to get around is to hire a motorbike (usually Honda 70cc step-thrus) for around RM35 per day, or RM60 for a real motorcycle. You can do a leisurely circuit of the island (70km) in a day. The roads are excellent and outside Kuah it's very pleasant and easy riding. Motorbikes can be hired at stands all over the island, and no-one seems to fuss about whether you have a licence or not. A few places also rent mountain bikes for RM15 per day.

### BUKIT KAYU HITAM
This is the main border crossing between Malaysia and Thailand, 48km north of Alor Setar. The Lebuhraya Tollway handles the vast majority of road traffic between the two countries, and all the buses to Hat Yai, Thailand, come this way so immigration processing on both sides of the border can become jammed. Taking the train via Padang Besar is almost always a quicker and more convenient alternative.

At the border post there are a few restaurants, private car-parking facilities and a Tourism Malaysia office. The easiest way to cross the border is to take a through bus all the way to Hat Yai (though when the border opens in the morning, the lines can be horrendous). Buses and taxis from Alor Setar run right up to the Malaysian customs post. From here walk a few kilometres past the big Zon duty-free shopping complex to the Thai checkpoint. Taxis on the other side run to Sadao (100B), from where there are buses on to Hat Yai.

If arriving from Thailand, ensure that your passport is stamped by the Malaysian border police – otherwise you may be fined for 'illegal entry' when you leave Malaysia.

There is no accommodation on the Malaysian side and the few questionable hotels on the Thai side are extremely overpriced. Even if you shell out for a taxi,

Fiddling away in a traditional house, Penang.

Downtown Chinatown, Georgetown

Guard lion, Penang

Fishing boats at Pulau Pangkor.

A traditional Malay house.

CLEM LINDENMAYER

Fishing boats, blue sea and blissful calm, Pulau Langkawi.

JEFF YATES

Morning market, Georgetown.

RICHARD I'ANSON

Lanterns at Kek Lok Si Temple, Georgetown.

you'll end up saving money (and headaches) by proceeding immediately to your next destination.

Once in Malaysia, you'll find taxis (RM30) and regular buses (RM3) to Alor Setar, from where frequent buses go to Kuala Kedah (for Langkawi), Butterworth, KL and destinations across the peninsula. Kuala Perlis, the other departure point for Langkawi, is more difficult to reach – first take a bus to Changlun, another to Kangar and then another to Kuala Perlis.

# Perlis

The tiny state of Perlis, tucked away in far north-west Malaysia on the Thai border, tends to be the forgotten state of Malaysia. Apart from a sugar refinery and cement factory, its economy is still dominated by agriculture. With few tourist attractions, Perlis is primarily a state to transit through. Kuala Perlis is one of the access ports for Langkawi, and Padang Besar is the main border town if arriving by train from Thailand.

Being a predominantly Muslim state, Perlis observes the same business hours as neighbouring Kedah.

## History

Perlis was originally part of Kedah, though it variously fell under Thai and Acehnese sovereignty. After the Siamese conquered Kedah in 1821, the sultan of Kedah made unsuccessful attempts to regain his territory by force until, in 1842, he agreed to accept Siamese terms. The Siamese reinstalled the sultan, but made Perlis into a separate vassal principality with its own raja.

As was the case in Kedah, power was transferred from the Thais to the British under the 1909 Anglo-Siamese Treaty, and the British installed a Resident at Arau. During the Japanese occupation in WWII, Perlis was 'returned' to Thailand, and then after the war it again returned to British 'protection' until it became part of the Malayan Union, and then the Federation of Malaya in 1957.

## KANGAR

Kangar, 45km north-west of Alor Setar, is the state capital of Perlis. It's a low-lying, modern town surrounded by rice paddies with little of interest for travellers. There are a few banks, a hospital, and countless restaurants and shops in the vicinity of the bus station. On the south side of the station you'll find hole-in-the-wall cybercafes all charging RM3 per hour for reasonably fast connections. If you're stuck for something to do, you can go see the town's mosque, **Masjid Alwi**, a 15-minute walk from the centre on Jalan Kangar.

## Places to Stay

The cheapest place in town is the *Hotel Ban Cheong (☎ 976 1184, 79 Jalan Kangar)*, a typical old Chinese hotel with basic doubles from RM24. It's on the corner of Jalan Kangar and the street running along the eastern side of the bus station.

The *Hotel Federal (☎ 976 6288, 104 Jalan Kangar)* is almost a mid-range place, with fan-cooled doubles with attached bath for RM48, and air-con doubles with bath and TV from RM69. The hotel also has very basic doubles above a nearby cafe for RM25. Coming from the bus station, head left for one block after reaching the Hotel Ban Cheong, from where you can see the Federal's 'Hotel' sign on the rooftop.

Top of the pile is the *Putra Palace (☎ 976 7755, fax 976 1049, 135 Persiaran Jubli Emas)*, a 1km walk from the bus station and 500m past the mosque. This international hotel is about the biggest thing in Kangar, and has a swimming pool, bar and restaurant with an affordable buffet. Doubles start at RM200 before discount.

There are numerous restaurants and cafes sprinkled around the bus station. Beside the Hotel Federal, *Restoran Soo Guan* has an English menu of sizeable Western and Malay dishes at reasonable prices.

## Getting There & Away

The bus station is central and has a few departures to KL (RM23), Butterworth (RM6.30), Alor Setar (RM3) and Kaki Bukit (every two hours, RM2.20). Regular

PENINSULAR MALAYSIA

buses run to Kuala Perlis (RM1) and Padang Besar (RM2.15).

If you're impatient to get to Langkawi, a taxi to Kuala Perlis from the bus station costs RM8.

## KUALA PERLIS

This small port town in the extreme north-west of the peninsula is visited mainly as a departure point for Langkawi. It is the closest access port to the island if coming from Thailand. The landing jetty for ferries is only 700m from the town centre.

The main part of Kuala Perlis consists of a couple of streets with a bank, several restaurants and shops, an Internet cafe and a couple of grotty places to stay. Kangar is only 11km away if you want access to more facilities. The older part of town has interesting houses and mosques built on stilts over the mangrove swamps.

### Places to Stay & Eat

On Jalan Kuala Perlis, *Pens Hotel* (☎/*fax 985 4122/4131*) is a passable mid-range hotel with singles/doubles from RM64/75. Along the same main street are a few uninviting, iffy hostels for dirt-cheap prices.

The basic *Asia Hotel* (☎ 985 5392) is on the outskirts of town, 1.5km along the road leading directly out from the jetty. Basic doubles cost RM35.

Near the jetty are several *Malay food stalls* serving Kuala Perlis' famous special laksa, as well as a few *Chinese restaurants*.

### Getting There & Away

The new bus and taxi station is a short walk from the jetty towards town. The frequent No 56 bus to Kangar (RM1) swings by the jetty before terminating at the station. Less frequent direct buses depart for Butterworth, Alor Setar, KL and Padang Besar. From the bus station or the jetty, taxis go to Kangar (RM8) and Padang Besar (RM20).

Ferries to Kuah, on Pulau Langkawi, leave at least hourly between 8 am and 6 pm (RM12). Massage chairs in the jetty waiting room will soothe your travel-weary bones for only RM2, and private car parks between the jetty and the new bus station will look after your vehicle for RM6 per day.

## PADANG BESAR

This border town to Thailand is 35km northeast of Kangar. The town itself is nothing special but it's a popular destination for Malaysians because of the duty-free market that operates in the neutral territory between the two countries. Near the large roundabout are a few banks that will change travellers cheques or handle Visa cash. Money-changers will give you even better rates for bank notes (foreign, or Thai baht) and have the added advantage of being open longer hours every day.

If arriving from Thailand ensure that your passport is stamped by the Malaysian border police – otherwise you may be fined for 'illegal entry' when you leave Malaysia.

There's some accommodation on the Malaysian and Thai sides of the border, but you're better off avoiding these mostly disreputable budget hotels and hiring a taxi or catching a bus to your next destination.

Malaysian buses stop near the large roundabout around a kilometre from the large border crossing complex on the Malaysian side. There are regular buses to/from Kangar (RM2.15) and infrequently to Kaki Bukit. The taxi stand is on the left before you reach the bus stop and fares are posted for all destinations, including Kaki Bukit (RM10) and Kangar (RM12), as well as Kuala Perlis and Penang.

Very few, if any people walk the more than 2km of no-man's land between the Thai and Malaysian sides of the border. Motorcyclists shuttle pedestrian travellers back and forth for RM3 (30B) each way, though bargaining is possible.

On the Thai side you can flag down buses to Sadao and Hat Yai from the main road. If you're coming from Hat Yai, travel agencies on Thanon Niphat Uthit 2, a five-minute walk from Hat Yai's train station, run share taxis to the Thai side of the border (35B), as well as through-bus tickets to popular Malaysian destinations and Singapore.

All in all, the train is a better bet, with connections from Padang Besar to Hat Yai at 9.35 am and 5.25 pm. Southbound trains stop at Hat Yai at 6.55 am and 3.10 pm. All passengers must disembark to clear customs and immigration (both Thai and Malaysian) before re-boarding.

## GUA KELAM

Near Kaki Bukit in the extreme north-west corner of the state, this limestone cave is the state's premier tourist attraction, which says little for tourism in Perlis. The cave is interesting enough, but difficult to reach.

The 'Cave of Darkness' is the only access to Wang Kelian State Park, an area of high quality tin ore, and in 1970 a suspension boardwalk was installed right through the 370m-long cavern. A river runs through the cave and emerges in a cascade at a popular swimming spot and a landscaped park. The old tin mine is a short walk from the far end of the cavern. Keep an ear open for motorcycles that may also use the boardwalk, and watch out for exploding guano (the build-up of phosphates is highly flammable).

Gua Kelam is open from 9 am to 6 pm daily; admission is RM0.50/1 for children/adults. The cave is a 1km walk from the small village of Kaki Bukit, 26km from Kangar and 14km from Padang Besar, but bus connections are only once every couple of hours. It's easier to take a taxi and visit the cave as a stopover between Padang Besar and Kangar (RM20, including driver's waiting time).

PENINSULAR MALAYSIA

# Negeri Sembilan

☎ 06

The small state of Negeri Sembilan (Nine States) is one of Malaysia's most unique, and it's a centre for the Minangkabau people, who originally came from Sumatra. To some extent, these people still follow *adat perpatih*, a matrilineal system of inheritance and communal village administration that is unique to Negeri Sembilan, though these customs are weakening.

Few foreign visitors include Negeri Sembilan in their itinerary, but the area around the capital, Seremban, has a few sights for those interested in the Minangkabau and their distinctive architecture. Negeri Sembilan's main tourist destination is the beach at Port Dickson, popular with Kuala Lumpur city dwellers, but keep in mind that Malaysia has far better beaches elsewhere on the peninsula.

## History

During the Melaka sultanate of the 15th century, many Minangkabau people from Sumatra settled here. They initially lived under the protection of the rulers of Melaka, but with the fall of Melaka to the Portuguese, the Minangkabau sought protection from the sultans of neighbouring Johor.

With the rising power of the Bugis in Selangor, the Minangkabau felt increasingly insecure, so they turned back to the royal house of Sumatra for protection. Raja Melewar, a Minangkabau prince from Sumatra, was appointed the first *yang dipertuan besar* (head of state) of Negeri Sembilan in 1773 by the *undang* (territorial chiefs). Out of this initial union emerged a loose confederation of nine *luak* (fiefdoms), although there is some debate about its exact make-up. The royal capital of Negeri Sembilan was established at Sri Menanti, and Raja Melewar, though essentially powerless, indulged himself here.

Like Selangor to the north, Negeri Sembilan was rich in tin, and so suffered the unrest and political instability that greed created for much of the 19th century. After

### HIGHLIGHTS

- **Seremban Region** – traditional Minangkabau culture and architecture
- **Port Dickson** – seaside resorts and the romantic old lighthouse at Tanjung Tuan (Cape Rachado)

Raja Melewar's death, the title of yang dipertuan was taken on by a succession of Sumatran chiefs, until a series of protracted tin-related wars from 1824 to 1832 led to the severance of political ties with Sumatra.

In the second half of the 19th century the civil disturbances and interstate rivalry continued, particularly in the northern state of Sungai Ujong. In the 1880s the British gradually intervened by increasing their influence in the area, and the territories of Sri Menanti, Tampin, Rembau and Jelebu were consolidated into a new confederacy controlled by a British Resident. In 1895 Sungai Ujong was added to the union, and these five districts now make up the bulk of the modern state of Negeri Sembilan, with an area of 6643 sq km.

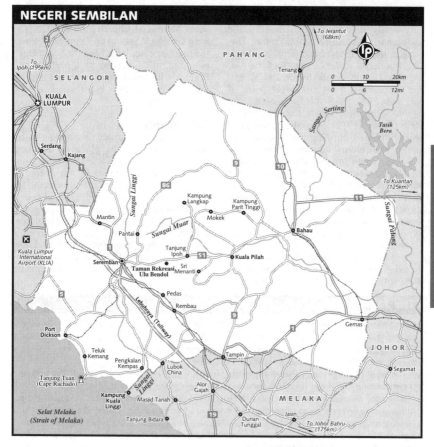

NEGERI SEMBILAN

## SEREMBAN

South of KL, the modern city of Seremban dates back to the tin boom of the late 19th century. The noisy central area is a grid of constant traffic, a few colonial shophouses and modern shopping centres. Though not brimming over with tourist interest, Seremban is a centre for Minangkabau culture. Buffalo horn roofs adorn many of the new buildings, such as the city hall, but the only real access to Minangkabau culture is at the Muzium Negeri on the outskirts of town.

Heading east to the hills bordering the city centre, Seremban takes on a different personality. The Lake Gardens are a low-key respite from the traffic, and farther into the hills is the old colonial district, with scattered bungalows, colonial buildings and parks favoured by t'ai chi practitioners.

In the town centre, ATMs can be found in Terminal 1 and Seremban Parade shopping centres. There is a moneychanger near the Catholic church on Jalan Tam Yuan. If you've got time between bus or train connections, Cyberpack Internet Cafe is a short walk north-east of the bus station (RM2.5 an hour).

## Architecture

No new building in Seremban is complete without a Minangkabau curved roof, but the

PENINSULAR MALAYSIA

only really fine melding of modern and traditional architecture is the **Dewan Undangan Negeri** (State Secretariat building). The wonderful multiple points of the roof are a striking landmark for central Seremban. Opposite is the **Istana Besar**, home of the sultan of Negeri Sembilan (closed to the public). Directly south is the neoclassical **State Library** (1912), Seremban's most imposing colonial building and once the offices of the colonial administration.

Farther south towards the city centre is the **Masjid Negeri** (State Mosque), with its nine pillars symbolising the nine original states of Negeri Sembilan. This monochrome, futuristic mosque is relatively restrained compared with some other mosques erected to the glory of Islam in Malaysia.

In the central area, colonial architecture includes the Catholic **Church of the Visitation**, with its Gothic spires, and the more

sober **Methodist Church** built in 1920. The **King George V School** on Jalan Za'aba was the premier colonial school for Seremban's elite and still functions as a high school. Formerly it must have been a most impressive colonial building, but it's now in a sad state of disrepair.

## Lake Gardens

The quaint Lake Gardens are a tame recreation reserve and the place for courting couples to commit *khalwat* ('close proximity' or public affection) in the evenings. There's a small aviary on the western side and an open pavilion where cultural events are sometimes staged. The gardens are at the edge of the green and tranquil colonial district that now mostly houses government quarters. There are many other parkland areas to the east of the Lake Gardens, including the **Hutan Rekreasi**, a small jungle park.

## The Minangkabau House

The Minangkabau house is probably the most distinctive Malay *kampung* (village) house. Its most striking feature is the upswept curve of the roofline, which resembles buffalo horns. The design was imported from Sumatra by the Minangkabau settlers, and may be partly responsible for their name, though some attribute it to their people's bull-like nature.

The word Minangkabau comes from *minang* (to win) and *kerbau* (water buffalo). The buffalo plays a leading role in Minangkabau tradition and the legend surrounding their origins.

When the Javanese came to the Minangkabau homelands in Sumatra to assume suzerainty, the Minangkabau were prepared to go to war, but to avoid bloodshed they proposed a bullfight. The Minangkabau sent a calf to fight the enormous Javanese bull – a ruse that stunned the bull and onlookers. The calf had been separated from its mother for several days before the fight and, with

sharp metal spears attached to its horns, went straight for the bull's belly in search of milk. The gored and bleeding bull took to its heels and the crowd shouted 'Minangkabau! Minangkabau!'.

The houses are made of wood and were traditionally built without the use of nails. In palaces and houses of important community members, the doorways were built so low that visitors were forced to bow their heads in respect on entering, like it or not.

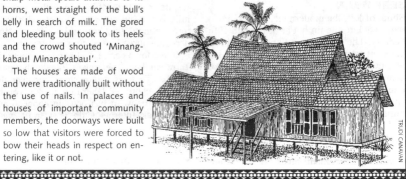

TRUDI CANAVAN

# SEREMBAN

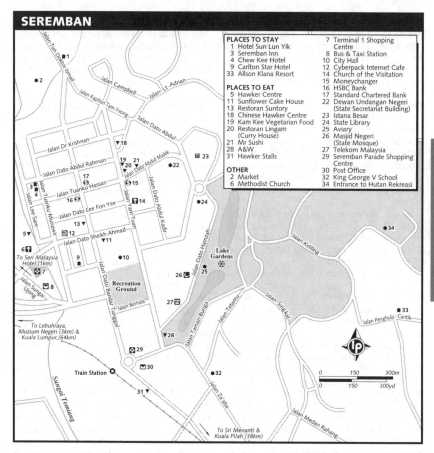

**PLACES TO STAY**
1 Hotel Sun Lun Yik
3 Seremban Inn
4 Chew Kee Hotel
9 Carlton Star Hotel
33 Allson Klana Resort

**PLACES TO EAT**
5 Hawker Centre
11 Sunflower Cake House
13 Restoran Suntory
18 Chinese Hawker Centre
19 Kam Kee Vegetarian Food
20 Restoran Lingam
   (Curry House)
21 Mr Sushi
28 A&W
31 Hawker Stalls

**OTHER**
2 Market
6 Methodist Church
7 Terminal 1 Shopping
   Centre
8 Bus & Taxi Station
10 City Hall
12 Cyberpack Internet Cafe
14 Church of the Visitation
15 Moneychanger
16 HSBC Bank
17 Standard Chartered Bank
22 Dewan Undangan Negeri
   (State Secretariat Building)
23 Istana Besar
24 State Library
25 Aviary
26 Masjid Negeri
   (State Mosque)
27 Telekom Malaysia
29 Seremban Parade Shopping
   Centre
30 Post Office
32 King George V School
34 Entrance to Hutan Rekreasi

PENINSULAR MALAYSIA

## Muzium Negeri

The Muzium Negeri (State Museum) is built in the style of a Minangkabau palace, and has some worn craft and historical exhibits. It covers the Emergency (see History in the Facts for the Visitor chapter), complete with gruesome post-capture portraits of the Communist leaders, reminiscent of those of the bullet-ridden Che Guevara.

Outside are two traditional Minangkabau houses on the museum grounds. The **Istana Ampang Tinggi** (Ampang Tinggi Palace) was originally constructed in the 1860s near Sri Menanti, a gift from the sultan to his daughter. Though small, it shows the intricate carving of palace architecture and traditional thatch roof. Minangkabau houses were built entirely without nails, though apparently this is now a lost art, as nails were used when the palace was reconstructed here. Next to the palace, the **Rumah Negeri Sembilan** is a less ornate traditional house with a shingle roof, but it shows the hallmark curved-roof style based on the buffalo horn.

The museum is inside the **Taman Seni Budaya** (Arts & Cultural Park), which also includes a *gasing* (top spinning) pavilion and a small tourist information office. The museum is open from 10 am to 6 pm daily, closed 12.15 to 2.45 pm on Friday; admission is free. It's 3km west of the bus station on the road to KL. From the town centre, several local buses will drop you here (40 sen) or you can take a taxi (RM5).

## Places to Stay

Seremban has a truly seedy collection of overpriced hotels in the central area, several of which are also boarding houses or bordellos. Even if it's late in the day, you shouldn't need to overnight in Seremban as KL, the beach at Port Dickson and even Melaka are only about an hour away by bus or train.

In the budget category, the *Chew Kee Hotel (☎ 762 2095, 41 Jalan Tuanku Munawir)* has rather simple doubles for RM30, but the air-con rooms with bathroom for RM50 are reasonable.

The mid-range hotels are preferable, but there are few bargains. The family-run *Hotel Sun Lun Yik (☎ 763 5735, 19 Jalan Tun Dr Ismail)* looks like new and offers clean singles/doubles for RM50/60. Its location opposite the market is a bit removed, but it does get you away from the worst parts of town. The well-run *Seremban Inn (☎ 761 7777, fax 763 7777, 39 Jalan Tuanku Munawir)*, a modern six-storey block in a central location, has hotel-quality twins/doubles from RM80, and family rooms for RM100. Closer to the train and bus stations, the *Carlton Star Hotel (☎ 762 5336)* has a lounge where the karaoke goes on until the wee hours. and the air-con rooms are nothing special at RM58/78 for singles/doubles.

Top-end hotels are more reasonably priced for the facilities on offer. The *Seri Malaysia Hotel (☎ 764 4181, fax 764 4179)* on Jalan Sungai Ujong has dependably well-appointed rooms for RM115, but is inconveniently located 1km west of the bus station, on the road to Muzium Negeri. The top hotel by far is the *Allson Klana Resort (☎ 762 9600, Jalan Penghulu Cantik)*, on a hill to the east of the Lake Gardens. Set in large grounds, it has all the luxuries of an international-class hotel. Singles/doubles start at RM300/320 before discount.

## Places to Eat

Minangkabau-style cooking is red-hot, due in part to generous additions of *chili padi,* a tiny firebomb of a thing. You should certainly dare to taste either *masak lemak* (fish, meat or vegetables cooked in coconut milk) or *rendang,* a thick, dry, meat curry usually served with rice cooked in coconut milk, all in a bamboo stem.

Seremban has a good selection of hawker centres for cheap eats. Food stalls, serving mostly Malay dishes and some spicy Minangkabau fare, can be found south of the train station and at the upstairs *hawker centre* on Jalan Lee Sam. Jalan Lee Sam also hosts the lively Saturday *pasar malam* (night market), which has plenty of food stalls. The best place for Chinese favourites is on the corner of Jalan Yam Tuan and Jalan Dr Krishnan, where hawkers set up alfresco tables in the car park on fine evenings.

The *Restoran Suntory* on Jalan Dato Bandar Tunggal has an extensive Chinese, Western and Malay menu at budget prices, plus friendly service, lots of loyal local clientele and air-con. A short distance south-east at *Sunflower Cake House* you can stock up on baked goods for only a few ringgit.

Heading east uphill toward the government buildings, you'll find a few other options. On Jalan Dato Abdul Malek, *Mr Sushi* has passable sushi for RM3 to RM6 (plates are colour-coded by price). Japanese set meals start at RM12 and all food is discounted between 2 and 3 pm and again later from 8 to 9.45 pm. Around the corner on Jalan Yam Tuan, the daringly named *Restoran Lingam* is a popular, cheap curry house, and almost next door is *Kam Kee Vegetarian Food,* a Chinese coffee shop.

Western chain restaurants can be found in the shopping centres across from the train station and next to the bus terminal, as well as at the *A&W* in the Lake Gardens.

## Getting There & Away

Seremban is 64km south-east of KL, about an hour on the Lebuhraya tollway. The city is a major suburban travel hub, and from the bus terminal on Jalan Sungai Ujong there are frequent departures to KL (one to 1½ hours, RM3.10), Melaka (1½ hours, RM3.90), Port Dickson (one hour, RM1.80) and other peninsular destinations. At the terminal there are relatively expensive left-luggage facilities on the ground floor, open from 7.30 am to 10 pm. Long-distance taxis operate from upstairs to destinations including Port Dickson (RM60), Sri Menanti (RM60) and Ulu Bendol (RM20).

Seremban is on the main north-south rail line from KL to Singapore. KTM Komuter trains, part of KL's city rail network, also run between Seremban and the historic main train station in KL every 20 minutes (last train 10 pm, 65 minutes, RM5.70).

## SEREMBAN TO KUALA PILAH

Heading east from Seremban the road meanders through the hills to the town of Kuala Pilah, passing through the heartland of Minangkabau culture surrounding the old royal town of Sri Menanti. Along the main road are a number of **Minangkabau houses**, though the traditional thatch of buffalo-horn roofs has been replaced by more utilitarian corrugated iron. The village of Terachi, 27km from Seremban at the turn-off to Sri Menanti, has some particularly fine traditional houses, as do the villages farther north including Pantai, and Sri Menanti itself.

### Taman Rekreasi Ulu Bendol

This dense forest park makes a good half-day trip from Seremban, only 19km away, and the primary dipterocarp rainforest has some excellent short walks. It's a popular spot with families on weekends, but during the week things are much quieter.

The well-maintained main trail from the unstaffed park headquarters (500m back along the paved road behind the restaurant and food stalls on the main road, where the Seremban–Kuala Pilah bus drops you off) follows Sungai Batang Terachi (Batang Terachi River). The route passes small cascading waterfalls before rising more sharply to the summit of Gunung Angsi (825m), with fine views across Seremban and out to the Selat Melaka (Strait of Melaka). The steeper sections can be taxing, but this is a

relatively easy 4.5km walk, taking around four hours return. Shorter self-guided trails, with plaques identifying the trees, branch out around the park headquarters.

Though usually done as a day trip, the park also has camping grounds and attractive but unfurnished cabins and chalets costing RM10 to RM30 per night. Bookings must be made in advance through the Pejabat Hutan Daerah (District Forest Office; ☎ 481 1036), located about 1km out of Kuala Pilah, towards Bahau.

Buses travelling between Seremban and Kuala Pilah drop passengers on the main highway in front of the park entrance (45 minutes, RM1.20).

### Sri Menanti

Sri Menanti, 6km off the Seremban–Kuala Pilah road, is the old royal capital, first settled over 400 years ago by Minangkabau immigrants from Sumatra. This sleepy hamlet is nestled in a highland valley surrounded by jungle hills, and the manicured lawns are as much a product of the sheep that wander around the town as the royal gardeners.

Just past Sri Menanti's own tiny Lake Gardens is **Istana Besar**, the impressive palace of the sultan of Negeri Sembilan, but it's not open to the public. Originally built in the 1930s, the later addition features a blue tiled Minangkabau roof.

Just beyond Istana Besar is **Istana Lama** (Old Palace), now a museum. The three-storey palace was constructed in 1908 as a temporary replacement for an even older palace that was razed to the ground by British soldiers during the Sungai Ujong wars. The palace is raised off the ground on 99 pillars, many of them carved, one for each of the legendary 99 *luak* (clan) warriors. It is topped by a tower that once served as the royal treasury. Though not particularly Minangkabau in style, it exemplifies early 20th-century Malaysian court architecture.

Dedicated to Negeri Sembilan's royalty, the **Muzium Di Raja** (Royal Museum) inside is filled with the usual assortment of royal regalia: costumes, weapons and preserved royal bedrooms. Memorabilia of the sultans features prominently, especially that of Tunku Abdul Rahman, the first *yang diper-tuan agong* (king of Malaysia), at the time of independence in 1957. Outside the museum on the palace grounds is a legendary stone, allegedly stabbed through by a magical *kris* (traditional sword) during an argument in olden times over *adat*, the Minangkabau matrilineal system. The museum is open from 10 am to 6 pm daily (closed from 12.15 to 2.45 pm on Friday).

Back towards the main road in the compound next to the mosque is the **Makam Di Raja** (Royal Cemetery), which has a distinctive Victorian/Moorish pavilion. The prominent grave of Tuanku Abdul Rahman is immediately inside the gates.

To get there from Seremban, first take a bus to Kuala Pilah (RM2.20), from where you'll have to charter your own taxi to Sri Menanti (around RM20 return).

## Kuala Pilah

Kuala Pilah, 40km east of Seremban, is one of the main towns in this strongly Minangkabau region. It is mostly a place for making transport connections, though it's a pleasant valley town. The interesting old **Sim Tong** Chinese temple, on the main street towards Bahau, is worth a look. Opposite is an elaborate Chinese-style arch dedicated to Martin Lister, the first British Resident of Negeri Sembilan. Kuala Pilah is also a good place to try Minangkabau cuisine like rendang, a fiery meat curry.

There's no reason for you to get stranded here, but if you do, Kuala Pilah has several cheap Chinese hotels in the immediate vicinity of the bus station. The *Hotel Hinyi* (☎ 481 8335, 227 Jalan Tung Yen) has good air-con rooms with bathroom for RM38. It's a couple of blocks south-west of the bus station.

From Seremban, a few companies run buses to Kuala Pilah, with departures roughly every half-hour (one hour, RM3.90). From Kuala Pilah it is possible to get connections east all the way to Kuantan and Kuala Terengganu, but unless you catch one of the two daily direct buses, you will first have to take a local bus to Bahau, on the highway 20km to the east.

## PORT DICKSON

Port Dickson is just a small port town of little interest, but it's the gateway to the stretch of beach extending 16km south to Tanjung Tuan (Cape Rachado). This beach is very popular with KL residents on weekends, and a string of mostly upmarket hotels is spread out all the way to Tanjung Tuan.

Despite their popularity, the beaches are disappointing. The sand varies from red to grey-white. The water, like elsewhere along the Selat Melaka, is murky and very shallow for swimming. Occasional oil spills from passing tankers don't help. If you are desperate for a quick seaside escape from KL, or just want to live it up at a resort, Port Dickson is OK for a couple of days, but Malaysia has better beaches.

Originally built by the Portuguese in the 16th century, the **Tanjung Tuan lighthouse** offers fine views. On a clear day you can see Sumatra, 38km away across the Selat Melaka. The turn-off to the lighthouse is near the Km 16 marker. Head down the road for 2km and then through the forest reserve for another kilometre to the lighthouse. Nearby you'll find the small **Blue Lagoon**, with its pretty little beach and assorted marine life.

### Places to Stay & Eat

The attraction is the beach, so don't bother with the hotels in Port Dickson town. The best beaches start from around the Km 8 peg. Most hotels are upmarket, and new resorts and condominiums keep springing up. On weekends many hotels of all price ranges are fully booked (except for the hostels), but on weekdays hefty discounts drop luxury room rates practically in your lap.

Just 3.5km south of town is Port Dickson's loveliest high-class resort, the *Paradise Lagoon Hotel* (☎ 647 7600, fax 647 7630, ✉ delta1@po.jaring.my). It charges RM115/220 on weekdays/weekends for standard rooms (a steal for what you get). The hotel has its own clean, artificial beach and a breathtaking inlet lagoon ringed by coconut palms.

*Rotary Sunshine Camp Holiday Hostel* (☎ 647 4090/3798), two kilometres farther south, has the cheapest, though barrack-like,

PENINSULAR MALAYSIA

dorm beds for RM7. The management is friendly and on weekdays you may have the place to yourself.

At Km 6 you'll soon come upon the self-proclaimed 'amazingly affordable' *Seri Malaysia Hotel* (☎ *647 6070, fax 647 6028), part of a popular chain of hotels. Quality rooms cost RM110/130 weekdays/ weekends. A few hundred metres farther, *Port Dickson Youth Hostel* (☎ *647 2188)* is set back from the road in spacious grounds, but attracts few visitors. A bed in a dorm costs RM10 with fan, or RM15 with air-con. There are many food stalls, local shops and restaurants along the main road directly in front of the hostel.

At Km 7.5, the *Bayu Beach Resort* (☎ *647 3703)* is a big hotel with a pool, bar and restaurants. Rooms and apartments are not especially good value for RM200 to RM480 on weekdays, but 30% discounts are sometimes available.

Past Km 8 is another collection of big hotels, the best being the Minangkabau-style *The Regency* (☎ *647 4090)*, with a pool, and tennis and squash courts. Superior/ deluxe rooms cost from RM160/220 on weekdays. You may want to just drop in at the 24-hour coffee shop, its bakery or *Sri Rama* Thai restaurant.

A selection of budget places can be found at Km 13, but they are extremely basic and usually only rented for the day by Malaysian families. The friendly but quite dilapidated *Hotel Kong Ming* (☎ *662 5683)* is right by the beach and single/doubles cost only RM20/30 (plus RM5 on weekends) for rooms with attached bath. Rooms without a bathroom cost the same, but face the sea.

In Teluk Kemang at Km 16 is the more upmarket *Guoman Resort* (☎ *662 7878)*, a sprawling new resort with a nine-hole golf course and deluxe rooms from RM260 on weekends, or RM180 on weekdays.

### Getting There & Away
Port Dickson is 90km south of KL, 32km south-west of Seremban and 94km north-west of Melaka. To Port Dickson by bus costs RM4.50 from Melaka, RM1.80 from Seremban and RM4.90 from KL's Puduraya bus station. From Port Dickson the taxi fare to KL or Melaka is RM80. The bus and taxi stations are next to each other in the centre of town.

From Port Dickson town, local buses (and buses to Melaka) will drop you off wherever you like along the beach. Share taxis that run up and down the coastal highway should cost RM1 for any ride along the beach or RM2 from the beach to town. If you charter a whole taxi, expect to bargain – the cheapest fares start around RM4.

## PENGKALAN KEMPAS
About 50km north-west of Melaka and 23km east of Cape Rachado is the small town of Pengkalan Kempas. Outside town a short distance in the direction of Lubok China and Melaka, a 'Kompleks Sejarah Pengkalan Kempas' sign indicates the **grave of Sheikh Ahmad Majnun**, about 100m off the road. This local hero died in 1467 and beside his grave, which is sheltered by a structure in the final stages of complete collapse, are three 2m-high stones standing upright in the ground.

These mysterious stones, known as the sword, the spoon and the rudder, are thought to be older than the grave. No one is quite sure why they are here, although similar pairs (not trios) of monoliths have been found elsewhere. Scholars think they were originally used as grave-markers, but many monoliths evolved into village shrines, worshipped by residents who thought the stones had the power to spontaneously grow taller.

Immediately in front of the grave is the locals' lie detector, at first glance just another stone but with a hole through it. The circular opening is said to tighten up on the arm of any liar foolish enough to thrust his or her hand through.

The buses that run along the coast every hour or so between Port Dickson and Melaka travel via Pengkalan Kempas.

# Melaka

The small city-state of Melaka (formerly Malacca) is one of the most intriguing areas on the peninsula. In the 15th century Melaka became the greatest trading port in South-East Asia and attracted waves of conquering Europeans. Though Melaka's importance has long since declined, it retains reminders of its rich history and a fascinating mixture of Chinese, Islamic and European culture.

## History

Under the Melaka sultanates, the city was a wealthy centre for trade with China, India, Siam (Thailand) and Indonesia, due to its strategic position on the Selat Melaka (Strait of Melaka). The Melaka sultanates were the beginning of what is today Malaysia, and some say this city is where you'll find the soul of Malaysia.

Back in the 14th century, Melaka was just another fishing village – until it attracted the attention of Parameswara, a Hindu prince from Sumatra. Parameswara had thrown off allegiance to the Majapahit Empire and fled to Temasek (modern-day Singapore), where his piracy and other exploits brought on a Siamese attack in 1398, forcing him to flee again to Melaka – there he set up his new headquarters.

Under Parameswara, Melaka soon became a favoured port for waiting out monsoons and resupplying trading ships plying the strategic Selat Melaka. Halfway between China and India, and with easy access to the spice islands of Indonesia, Melaka attracted merchants from all over the East.

In 1405 Admiral Cheng Ho, the 'three-jewelled eunuch prince', arrived in Melaka bearing gifts from the Ming emperor and the promise of protection from Siamese enemies. Based on these early contacts with China, Chinese settlers followed and came to be known as the Baba and Nyonya, or Straits Chinese. They are the longest-settled

## HIGHLIGHTS

- **Melaka's historic town centre** – fascinating examples of Portuguese, Dutch, Islamic and Chinese architectural styles
- **Nyonya cuisine** – exquisite Straits Chinese cooking in the city's restored Peranakan shophouses
- **Beaches** – the white sands of Pulau Besar or the rocky headlands of Tanjung Bidara

Chinese people in Malaysia and have added many Malay customs to their own heritage. Despite internal squabbles and intrigues, by the time of Parameswara's death in 1414, Melaka was already a powerful trading state.

The cosmopolitan centre also came in contact with Islam via traders from India. The third ruler of Melaka, Maharaja Mohammed Shah (1424–44), converted to Islam, and his son, Mudzaffar Shah, took the title of sultan and made Islam the state religion.

Under the banner of Islam, Melaka became the major entrepôt in South-East Asia, attracting Muslim Indian merchants from competing Sumatran ports. Melaka became a centre for Islam, disseminating the religion throughout the Indonesian archipelago. The Melaka sultans ruled over the greatest empire in Malaysia's history, and successfully repelled Siamese attacks. The Malay language became the lingua franca of trade in the region, and Melaka produced the first major piece of Malay literature, the *Sejarah Melayu* (or *Malay Annals*), a history of the sultanate.

In 1509 the Portuguese arrived at Melaka seeking the wealth of the spice and china trades, but after an initially friendly reception, the Melakans attacked the Portuguese fleet and took a number of prisoners.

This action was the pretext for an outright assault by the Portuguese, and in 1511 Alfonso de Albuquerque took the city, forcing the sultan to flee to Johor, where he reestablished his kingdom. Under the Portuguese, the fortress of A'Famosa was constructed, and missionaries like St Francis Xavier strove to implant Catholicism. While Portuguese cannons could easily conquer Melaka, they could not force Muslim merchants from Arabia and India to continue trading there and other ports in the area, such as Islamic Demak on Java, grew to overshadow Melaka.

The period of Portuguese strength in the east was short-lived, as Melaka suffered harrying attacks from the rulers of neighbouring Johor and Negeri Sembilan, as well as from the Islamic power of Aceh in Sumatra. Melaka declined further as Dutch influence in Indonesia grew and Batavia (modern-day Jakarta) developed as the key European port of the region. The Dutch eventually launched an attack on Melaka and in 1641, after an eight-month long siege, it passed into their hands.

Like their Portuguese predecessors, the Dutch ruled Melaka for only about 150 years. Melaka again became the centre for

PENINSULAR MALAYSIA

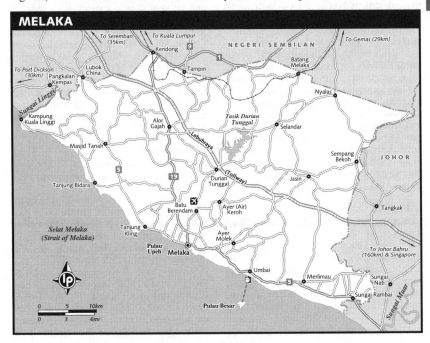

PENINSULAR MALAYSIA

peninsular trade, but only as a minor part of a greater empire; the Dutch directed more energy into their possessions in Indonesia. In Melaka they built fine public buildings and churches, which today are the most solid reminders of European presence in the city.

When the French occupied Holland in 1795, the British, allies of the Dutch, temporarily took over administration of the Dutch colonies. The British administrators, essentially traders, were opposed to the Dutch policy of trade monopoly and clearly saw the potential for intense rivalry in Malaysia between the Dutch and themselves. Accordingly, in 1807 they started to demolish A'Famosa fortress and forcibly remove Melaka's population to Penang. This would ensure that if Melaka was restored to the Dutch it would be no rival to the British Malayan centres. Fortunately Sir Thomas Stamford Raffles, the far-sighted founder of Singapore, stepped in before these destructive policies went too far, and in 1824 Melaka was permanently ceded to the British in exchange for the Sumatran port of Bencoolen (Bengkulu today).

Melaka, together with Penang and Singapore, formed the Straits Settlements, the three British territories that were the centres for later expansion into the peninsula. However, under British rule Melaka was always the lesser light of the Straits Settlements, and it was soon superseded by the rapidly growing commercial importance of Singapore. Apart from a brief revival of its fortunes in the early 20th century when rubber was an important crop, Melaka once again became a quiet backwater.

## MELAKA

Centuries ago the Portuguese writer Barbarosa wrote 'Whoever is Lord in Malacca has his hand on the throat of Venice,' and this historically important port city still bears testament to each of the three European incursions in Malaysia – Portuguese, Dutch and English. In the centre of town, much of the old Dutch city remains, and Medan Portugis is still home to Portuguese Eurasians, many of whom are practising

Catholics and speak Cristao, a medieval Portuguese dialect. Of all Melaka's mixed traditions, perhaps the most unique is that of the Baba and Nyonya, offspring of the original Straits Chinese settlers who intermarried and adopted many Malay customs.

Modern Melaka, long a sleepy town living on memories of past glories, experienced the sudden economic boom that swept Malaysia in the 1990s, starting with massive land reclamation projects that were halted by the Asian economic downturn later that decade. The historic waterfront has already retreated so far inland, however, that it has endangered the traditional livelihood of the Portuguese fishing community. A huge shopping complex and apartment blocks now enjoy Melaka's sea views.

Nevertheless Melaka rightfully remains one of Malaysia's premier tourist destinations. Delightfully old-fashioned Chinatown is still a place of intriguing streets lined with Chinese Peranakan shophouses and antique shops, atmospheric Buddhist temples and ancient mosques. The Dutch town square and Bukit St Paul offer nostalgic reminders of the now departed European colonial powers, while the Melakan version of the traditional Malay *kampung* (village) house, with its distinctive colourful tiled entrance steps, can still be seen along the river in east Melaka or the Tanjung Kling district north of the city (see the boxed text 'The Melaka House' later in this chapter).

## Orientation

Melaka is a small town, easy to find your way around and compact enough to explore on foot, bicycle or trishaw.

The interesting, older parts of Melaka are mainly on the eastern side of the river, particularly around Town Square, also known as Dutch Square, where the old Stadthuys (Town Hall) and Christ Church are solid reminders of the Dutch presence.

Rising above Town Square is Bukit St Paul (St Paul's Hill), site of the original Portuguese fort of A'Famosa. The ruins of St Paul's Church and the Porta de Santiago are the only remains of the Portuguese presence. Nearby are the Muzium Budaya (Cultural

Museum) and Proclamation of Independence Memorial, while the Maritime Museum is back on the river. Farther north is Melaka's tiny Little India, with its nighttime hawker stalls and sari shops.

All the historical points of interest are signposted on the 'American Express Heritage Trail', an excellent self-guided walking tour that also takes in parts of Chinatown. The trail brochures were out of print at the time of writing, but a signboard in front of the tourist office sketches out the route.

South of Melaka's old historical quarter are Mahkota Melaka and Taman Melaka Raya, two completely new areas built on reclaimed land. Most guesthouses, restaurants and cafes are strung along the main thoroughfare of Jalan Taman Melaka Raya (Jalan TMR) and its numerous side streets, most of which are confusingly named Jalan Melaka Raya and identified only by an individual number.

## Information

Day-trippers should not visit Melaka on Tuesday, when most museums (except for the Baba-Nyonya Heritage Museum) and even restaurants are closed.

The tourist office (☎ 283 6538) is in the heart of the city almost opposite Christ Church. Helpful staff hand out maps of Melaka with brief details on sights and outlying attractions. The office is open from 8.45 am to 5 pm daily (closed from 12.15 to 2.45 pm Friday). The Malacca Tourist Police (☎ 282 2222) is on the opposite corner.

The main post office is 3km north of central Melaka on Jalan Bukit Baru, on the corner of Jalan Panglima Awang. To get there, take bus No 19 from the local bus station. A more convenient post office is located in the centre of town on the ground floor of the Youth Museum.

For visa extensions, the immigration office (☎ 282 4958) is at Wisma Persekutuan on Jalan Hang Tuah. There is another post at the ferry dock on the river to handle departure and entry to/from Dumai (Indonesia).

Convenient banks for changing money include the Overseas Bank across the bridge from the tourist office, and Maybank and Bumiputra Bank in the Jalan TMR area. Bank Bumiputra has an exchange counter on the ground floor of the Mahkota Parade shopping complex, where you'll also find ATMs and moneychangers. Other moneychangers are scattered about town, especially Chinatown and near the bus stations.

The Telekom Malaysia office east of Bukit St Paul doesn't offer many calling services, but the payphones outside are some of the only ones in town that allow you to connect to toll-free numbers. The most convenient places for Internet access are cybercafes in Chinatown and the budget guesthouses, although they charge the highest rates (RM6 per hour). Cempaka Technology near Mei Chang cafe on Jalan TMR charges RM3 per hour; you can also scan, fax and make international calls here. It's open from 10 am to 10.30 pm daily.

The colourful Melaka State tourism Web site (www.melaka.gov.my) gives you a taste of Melaka's historical sights, ethnic communities, and arts and cultural events. For up-to-the-minute news on happenings about town and hotel promotions, plus a directory of links to cybercafes, 'in' restaurants and arts and antiques shopping, check out Melaka Net at www.melaka.net.

## Stadthuys

The most imposing relic of the Dutch period in Melaka is the massive red town hall and governors' residence, built between 1641 and 1660 and believed to be the oldest Dutch building in the East. It displays all the typical features of Dutch colonial architecture, including substantial solid doors and louvred windows. The other buildings around the Town Square and the old clock tower follow the same red theme.

Today the Stadthuys houses the musty but informative **History & Ethnography Museum**. Unlike most museums in Malaysia which give little or no explanation, here it would take a couple of hours to read your way through the detailed explanations of Melaka's past. On the ground floor are old maps, lithographs, oil paintings, stamps and ancient money, plus exhibits on the making of *kris* (traditional swords). Upstairs are displays on the culture and traditions of Melaka's various ethnic communities. The mildly interesting **Literature Museum** is in a separate building out the back.

The Stadthuys is open from 10 am to 6 pm. It is closed on Tuesday and from 12.15 to 2.45 pm on Friday; admission is RM2.

## Christ Church

Nearby, facing one end of the main square, is the bright red Christ Church. The pink bricks were brought from Zeeland in Holland and faced with local red laterite when the church was constructed in 1753. Under the British this Dutch Reformed church was converted for Anglican use, and the weathercock and bell tower were added, but it still has old Dutch and Armenian tombstones laid in the floor. Its massive 15m-long ceiling beams were each cut from a single tree.

## St Paul's Church

From the Stadthuys, steps lead to the top of Bukit St Paul, topped by the ruins of St Paul's Church. Originally built by a Portuguese captain in 1521 as the small 'Our Lady of the Hill' chapel, it was regularly visited by St Francis Xavier. Following his death in China, the saint's body was brought here and buried for nine months before being transferred to Goa in India, where it remains today. A marble statue of St Francis Xavier commemorates his interment here over 400 years ago.

In 1556 the church was enlarged to two storeys and a tower was added to the front in 1590. The church was renamed following the Dutch takeover, but when the Dutch completed their own Christ Church at the base of the hill, it fell into disuse. Under the British it lost the tower, although a lighthouse was built at the front, and the church eventually ended up as a storehouse for gunpowder. The church has been in ruins now for more than 150 years, but the setting is beautiful, the walls are imposing and fine old tombstones stand around the interior.

## Porta de Santiago

There are steps from St Paul's Church down the hill to Porta de Santiago, once the main gate – and all that remains – of the Portuguese fortress A'Famosa, originally constructed by Alfonso de Albuquerque in 1512. Stamford Raffles may have stepped in before the complete destruction of the old fortress, but it was a near thing. Curiously, this sole surviving relic of the fort bears the Dutch East India Company's coat of arms as this was part of the fort used by the Dutch after their takeover in 1670.

## Museums

All the museums in the vicinity of Bukit St Paul are open the same hours as the Stadthuys (see the earlier entry). Jalan Kota, the road encircling the base of Bukit St Paul, is closed off heading east from the Muzium Budaya, forcing you to either walk over the top of the hill or detour west through town back to the Stadthuys.

**Muzium Rakyat** The unique Muzium Rakyat (People's Museum) is just west of the Porta de Santiago. On the ground floor are dull displays explaining the local economy and society, however the upstairs sections are much more intriguing. On the 2nd floor, the 'Museum of Enduring Beauty' documents a variety of bizarre 'beautification' practices from around the world, ranging from tattooing, piercing and scarring to body stretching, foot binding, head shaping and modern cosmetic surgery. It's fascinating, but not for the faint-hearted. On the 3rd floor is a collection of beautiful Malaysian kites. Combined entry to all exhibits costs RM2.

**Muzium Budaya** At the eastern base of Bukit St Paul, the Muzium Budaya (Cultural Museum) is inside a wooden replica of a Melaka sultan's palace. This new building is based on descriptions from the *Malay Annals* of the original 15th-century palace, built entirely without nails. The exhibits here concentrate on traditional Melakan culture, including textiles, games, weaponry, musical instruments and even a diorama of the sultan's court. The museum also holds the Terengganu Stone with its early 14th-century Arabic and

Malay inscriptions, the first evidence of Islam on the peninsula. Admission costs RM1.50 (children 50 sen).

**Proclamation of Independence Memorial** Housed in a British villa dating from 1911, this historical museum is dedicated to events leading up to the announcement of Malaysia's imminent independence on 20 February 1956 at the 'warriors' field' across the road. Ironically, this grand building topped by Mogul-inspired domes was once the Melaka Club, a bastion of colonialism. Under renovation at the time of research, the museum should be open by the time you read this book.

**Maritime Museum** Next to the river near the tourist office, this museum is housed in a huge re-creation of the *Flora de la Mar,* a Portuguese ship that sank off the coast of Melaka while trying to transport Malaysian treasures back to Europe. The exhibits have detailed descriptions of Melaka's history, as well as ship models, dioramas and an interesting map room featuring charts dating back to Portuguese times. Guided tours (included in the RM2 entry price) are given twice daily in English.

Your ticket stub also entitles you to enter the **Royal Malaysian Navy Museum** across the street, which has navy memorabilia and salvaged remnants from the *Diana*, sunk off Melaka in 1817 while voyaging from Guangzhou (Canton) to Madras. A major salvage operation in 1993 recovered the ship and its cargo of tea, sugar and over 18 tons of chinaware. As new technology has made salvage expeditions in the Selat Melaka a viable business, there is concern that Melaka's land reclamation is permanently burying a potential treasure trove of historical artefacts.

## Chinatown
Melaka's Chinatown, west of the river, is a fascinating area to wander around. With twisting streets, Peranakan (Straits Chinese) shophouses, ancient temples and mosques, its history of settlement and trade is as fascinating as the reminders of colonial rule.

Although Melaka has lost its importance as a port, ancient-looking Sumatran schooners still sail up the river and moor at the banks. Today, however, their cargo is not the varied treasures of the East, but charcoal or lumber from Indonesia. There's a good view of the river and boats from the bridge beside the tourist office, and you can take a river boat tour (see Organised Tours later in this chapter).

Crossing over the bridge you enter **Jalan Hang Jebat**, formerly known as Jonkers St (or Junk St Melaka), famed for its interesting assortment of antique and craft shops, with the occasional Chinese or Hindu temples squeezed in between (see the following Cheng Hoon Teng entry). You can easily spend an hour or more browsing and, although you may still find some of the treasures of the East, don't expect any bargains.

Parallel to Jalan Hang Jebat, **Jalan Tun Tan Cheng Lock** is also worth a stroll. This narrow street, now a one-way thoroughfare with disturbingly fast-moving traffic, was the preferred address for wealthy Baba traders who were most active during the short-lived rubber boom of the early 20th century. These typical Peranakan houses, with their intricate tiles and plasterwork, exhibit Chinese, Dutch and British influences. The Baba-Nyonya Heritage Museum is the main highlight, but also stop to gaze at the fine Chee Mansion, set back from the street at No 117 (near Baba House).

Other points of interest in Chinatown are the **Sri Poyatha Venayagar Moorthi Temple**, dating from 1781 and dedicated to the elephant-headed Hindu deity Ganesh, and the **Kampung Kling Mosque**. This hoary mosque has a multitiered *meru* roof, which owes its inspiration to Hindu temples, and a Moorish watch-tower minaret typical of early mosques in Sumatra. Farther north, the similarly styled **Masjid Kampung Hulu** dates from 1728 and is the oldest mosque in Malaysia.

**Cheng Hoon Teng** This fascinating temple is the oldest Chinese temple in Malaysia and has an inscription commemorating Admiral Cheng Ho's epochal visit to Melaka.

PENINSULAR MALAYSIA

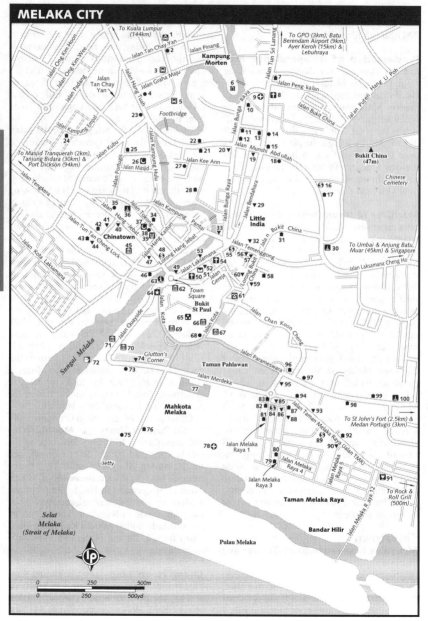

# MELAKA CITY

## MELAKA CITY

**PLACES TO STAY**
7 Hotel Grand Continental
10 Majestic Hotel
11 Ng Fook Hotel
12 Hong Kong Hotel
13 Renaissance Melaka Hotel
15 Accordian Hotel;
   Pizza Hut
17 Palace Hotel
21 Regal Hotel
22 May Chiang Hotel
24 Malacca Town Holiday
   Lodge 2
25 Belmount Hotel
28 Gold Leaf Hotel
31 Eastern Heritage Guest
   House
34 Chong Hoe Hotel
42 Hotel Puri
43 Baba House
46 Heeren House
58 Tony's Guest House
76 Century Mahkota Hotel
79 Samudra Inn
80 Melaka Arasma Belia Youth
   Hostel
81 Travellers' Lodge
82 Shirah's Guest House
83 Robin's Nest 1 & 2
87 Sunny's Inn
92 Malacca Town Holiday
   Lodge 1
94 Heritage Hotel
96 Hotel Equatorial
98 Hinly Hotel
99 Kancil Guest House

**PLACES TO EAT**
19 Centrepoint Food Court
20 Bunga Raya Cafe
29 Night Indian Hawker Stalls
32 Restoran Daun Pisang

33 Discovery Cafe
40 Geographér Café
41 Nancy's Restoran (Old China
   Cafe)
44 Restoran Peranakan
47 Jonkers Melaka Restoran
49 Manis Cafe
52 Kafe Loony Planet; Restaurant Kim Swee Huat
53 Iguana Riverfront Restaurant
56 Restoran Veni
57 Madras Cafe
59 UE Tea House
60 Capitol Satay
74 Bunga Raya Restaurant
85 Mei Chong; Cempaka
   Technology
86 Restoran Lim (Mee Yoke)
88 Tandoori House; Restoran
   Sari Rasa
90 Restoran Ole Sayang
93 Nyonya Makko
95 Malay Food Stalls

**OTHER**
1 Taxi Station
2 Market
3 Local Bus Station
4 Plaza Hang Tuah
5 Express Bus Station
6 Villa Sentosa
8 St Peter's Church
9 The Southern Hospital
14 Hawk Rent-a-Car
16 Maybank
18 Avis
23 Immigration
26 Masjid Kampung Hulu
27 Ekspo Melaka
30 Sam Po Kong Temple &
   Hang Li Poh Well
35 Lonely Creature

36 Cheng Hoon Teng
37 Kampung Kling Mosque
38 Harmony Street
39 Sri Poyatha Venayagar
   Moorthi Temple
45 Baba-Nyonya Heritage
   Museum
48 Overseas Bank
50 Christ Church
51 Post Office;
   Youth Museum
54 Church of St Francis Xavier
55 Public Bank
61 Telekom Malaysia
62 Stadthuys; History &
   Ethnography Museum;
   Literature Museum
63 Tourist Office
64 Tourist Police
65 St Paul's Church
66 Muzium Budaya
   (Cultural Museum)
67 Proclamation of
   Independence Memorial
68 Porta de Santiago
69 Muzium Rakyat (People's
   Museum)
70 Royal Malaysian Navy
   Museum
71 Maritime Museum
72 Ferries to Dumai
73 Dumai Ferry Ticket Agents
75 Mahkota Seaworld (Under
   Construction)
77 Mahkota Parade Shopping
   Complex
78 Mahkota Medical Centre
84 Maybank
89 Bumiputra Bank
91 Jim's Cottage Pub
97 Jin Trading (Bicycle Hire)
100 Chinese Temple

PENINSULAR MALAYSIA

The brightly coloured roof bears the usual assortment of mythical Chinese creatures. Entered through massive hardwood doors, the temple is equally colourful and ornate inside. The temple's ceremonial mast rises above the old houses in this part of Melaka.

Cheng Hoon Teng (literally, Temple of the Evergreen Clouds) was founded in 1646 by Kapitan China Lee Wei King, a native of Amoy in China. All materials used in building the original temple were imported from China, as were the artisans who designed and built it. The temple was constructed in southern Chinese style to pay respect to the San Y Chiao, or Three Teachings, of Buddhism, Taoism and Confucianism (note the three respective altars inside). At the time of research, this temple was undergoing major renovations and was completely covered up, except for the entryway.

**Baba-Nyonya Heritage Museum** At 48–50 Jalan Tun Tan Cheng Lock is a traditional Peranakan townhouse that has been made into a small museum. The architecture of this type of house, many examples of which survive in Melaka today, has been described as Chinese Palladian and Chinese Baroque. The interiors of these houses contain open courtyards that admit sun and rain.

The museum is arranged so that it looks like a typical 19th-century Baba-Nyonya residence. Furniture consists of Chinese hardwoods fashioned in a mixture of Chinese, Victorian and Dutch designs with mother-of-pearl inlay. There are also displays of 'Nyonya ware', multicoloured ceramic designs from the Jiangxi and Guangdong provinces in China, made specifically for Straits Chinese. Nyonya ceramics and tilework are usually a blend of pink, yellow, dark blue and green colours.

The museum (☎ 283 1273) is open from 10 am to 12.30 pm and 2 to 4.30 pm daily. Admission is RM8 (children RM4) and includes a 35-minute tour conducted (when there's sufficient demand) by the Baba family who own the house – well worth it if you are interested in Peranakan culture.

### Bukit China

In the middle of the 15th century the sultan of Melaka's ambassador to China returned with the Ming emperor's daughter to wed the sultan and thus seal relations between the two countries. She brought with her a vast retinue, including 500 handmaidens, and Bukit China (China Hill) was established as their residence. It has been a Chinese area ever since and, together with two adjoining hills, forms what is said to be the largest Chinese cemetery in the world outside China; comprised of more than 12,000 graves and covering 25 hectares. Some ornate graves date back to the Ming Dynasty, but most are now in a sorry state.

Chinese graveyards are often built on hillsides because the bulk of the hill shields the graves from evil winds, while the spirits get a good view of what their descendants are up to down below. In our more space-conscious modern world, Chinese graves are gradually losing their expansive traditional design.

### Sam Po Kong Temple & Hang Li Poh Well

Apart from his real-life role as an admiral and ambassador, Cheng Ho is also religiously venerated, and Sam Po Kong Temple is dedicated to him. Built in 1795, it's at the foot of Bukit China. The name comes from the legendary fish who once saved the Cheng Ho's life by sacrificing its body to plug a leak in the hull of the admiral's ship.

Next to the temple is a 15th-century well built by Sultan Mansor Shah for his Chinese wife, Princess Hang Li Poh. It was an important source of water for Melaka and a prime target for opposition forces wanting to take the city. Johor forces poisoned it in 1551, killing 200 Portuguese. The Dutch in 1606 and the Acehnese in 1628 subsequently employed the same tactic. The Dutch eventually built the fortifications that surround the well, but it has long since fallen into ruin. Taking a drink from the well was said to ensure a visitor's return to the city. Today the trickle of water is visibly impure, and tossing a coin is the recommended way of ensuring a return trip.

### St Peter's Church

This is the oldest functioning Catholic church in Malaysia – built in 1710 by descendants of early Portuguese settlers. Located on Jalan Bendahara, the church has a few old tombstones, stained-glass windows and a bell cast in Goa (India) in 1608. The church comes alive on Good Friday when Melakans flock here, many of them making it the occasion for a trip home from far-flung parts of the country.

### Villa Sentosa

While not an official museum, this 1920s Malay kampung house, beside the river in Kampung Morten, is open to the public. The family still lives here and one of the family members will show you around. Though not exactly full of collectibles and history, it provides a good opportunity to poke around a kampung house. Women (even in groups or with male companions) are strongly advised against visiting as many female travellers have reported being harassed and groped.

Villa Sentosa is open from 9 am to 5 pm daily (closed from 12.15 to 2.45 pm on

Friday). A donation is expected after the tour, after which you can wander around Kampung Morten, where there are a number of more traditional kampung houses.

## Medan Portugis

About 3km east of the city centre on the coast is the area known as Medan Portugis (Portuguese Square). The small kampung centred on the square is the heart of Melaka's Eurasian community, descended from marriages that took place between the colonial Portuguese and Malays 400 years ago. The settlement was first proposed to the British colonial government by a French missionary in the 1920s, but the square, styled after a typical Portuguese *mercado* and meant to give the settlement a cultural focus, wasn't completed until the late 1980s.

In the open square area, the Portuguese community office bulletin board displays advertisements for cultural events and news articles, including some concerning the damage Melaka's land reclamation has done to local family-run fisheries.

The kampung is unexceptional, however, and the square often empty, except on weekends. But the sea breeze is lovely while enjoying a relaxing beer or meal at the many restaurants in and around the square (see Places to Eat later in this chapter). Town Bus No 17 from the local bus station will get you here – see Getting Around later.

## Fort St John

Although the British demolished most of Porta de Santiago, they left the small Dutch fort of St John untouched. The fort was originally a Portuguese chapel dedicated to St John the Baptist until it was rebuilt by the Dutch in the 18th century. It stands on a hilltop to the east of town just before the turn-off to Medan Portugis – head east along Jalan Parameswara, then turn left into Jalan Bukit Senjuang. Only a few walls and cannon emplacements of the fort remain, but there are fine views from the hilltop.

## Masjid Tranquerah

This 150-year-old mosque, 2km towards Port Dickson, is of typical Sumatran design, featuring a square, multitiered roof. In its graveyard is the tomb of Sultan Hussein of Johor, who in 1819 signed over the island of

PENINSULAR MALAYSIA

## The Melaka House

The Melaka *kampung* (village) house follows the standard pattern of a wooden structure on short stilts, but is easily identifiable by its unique tiled front stairway that leads up to the front veranda. This colourful formal entrance to the house is used by guests, and the front veranda itself is used for entertaining.

The *tengah* (middle) section is the living area, and the steps at the side of the house here are only used by the family and friends. It would be inappropriate for guests to enter here. The *dapur* (kitchen and eating area) is at the rear of the house – the steps here are used only by women.

There are several Melaka houses at Kampung Morten.

Singapore to Stamford Raffles. The sultan later retired to Melaka, where he died in 1853. Take bus No 18 from Melaka's local bus station.

## Pulau Melaka

The construction of a new RM2 billion offshore island called Pulau Melaka is the culmination of a major land reclamation project that has dramatically altered Melaka's historic old town. This 2km-long artificial island will be separated from the mainland by a narrow, sheltered lagoon. Shops, condominiums, a five-star hotel, a theme park and public gardens are all being constructed, though work had recently come to a halt because of financial setbacks.

Pulau Melaka is only the first of a whole 'archipelago' of artificial islands planned – ostensibly to combat erosion – for Melaka state's coastline between Kuala Linggi and Sungai Rambai. Critics argue this will cause significant environmental damage to local fishing grounds and the natural formation of mangrove swamps.

## Organised Tours

From Singapore various tour companies offer 12- to 14-hour day tours of Melaka for around S$75 per person. Contact the Singapore Tourism Board (STB) in Singapore on ☎ 1-800 736 2000 for more information.

**Boat Trips** Parameswara Tours (☎ 286 5468) offers daily river boat tours of Melaka from the quay behind the tourist office. The trip takes 45 minutes, costs RM8 and passes old godowns, riverside fish markets and travels on to Kampung Morten, where the Villa Sentosa is located. On the way back it takes in the wharves farther downriver. Departures depend on both demand (minimum six passengers) and the tides, but scheduled times are usually posted the day before.

Boats can also be hired here for trips to offshore islands like Pulau Besar, and cost around RM20 per person (minimum 12 people) for a one-day trip. For regularly scheduled ferries to Pulau Besar, see Around Melaka later in this chapter.

## Special Events

Melaka celebrates all the major Malaysian holidays, including Chinese New Year, Thaipusam and National Day. You can see kite-flying exhibitions in late February and mid-May or Chinese dragon boat races in early June.

Good Friday and Easter Sunday processions are held outside at St Peter's Church, which is also the venue for the Festa San Pedro in late June, honouring this patron saint of the Portuguese fishing community. Celebrations normally include a float procession from the Porta de Santiago to Medan Portugis for cooking, fishing, handicraft and carnival festivities. Just before the Festa San Pedro, Melaka's Eurasian community hosts the Festa San Juan at the chapel on top of St John's hill. The Festa Santa Cruz in mid-September finishes with a candlelight procession of Melakan and Singaporean Catholics to Malim chapel.

## Places to Stay – Budget

**Guesthouses** Melaka has some excellent, and some so-so, travellers' guesthouses. Many are located in Taman Melaka Raya, the area of reclaimed land south of Jalan TMR. They are virtually all on the 2nd and 3rd floors of rather new and characterless blocks of buildings, but offer good atmosphere and facilities: common rooms with books, TVs and notice boards; small kitchens; and a variety of rooms. Though the interior walls are often only plywood and few rooms have windows, some have skylights. Plenty of competition keeps prices down. Dorm beds average RM9, though some places still charge the 'old' RM7 price. Basic singles/doubles start at RM15/20 and rise to RM35 or more for larger rooms with air-con. A light breakfast is often included in the price. The very cheapest rooms are in short supply and are usually full, although there's quite a turnover.

**Taman Melaka Raya** On Jalan Melaka Raya 1 (the street running south off the roundabout), you'll find a slew of popular guesthouses. **Robin's Nest 1** (☎ 282 9142) at No 205B is very clean and well run with a welcoming atmosphere. Dorm beds are RM9, and singles/doubles start at RM15/20. If they're full, you can hop next door into *Robin's Nest 2*. A few paces along at Nos 207–209, *Shirah's Guest House (☎ 286 1041)* has a cosy common room and informative bulletin boards; many Japanese backpackers stay here. Dorm beds cost RM8, fan singles/doubles start at RM15/20 and air-con doubles are RM35/45 with/without bathroom. Farther down the road, the long-running *Travellers' Lodge (☎ 281 4793)* at No 214B has similar rates and a large, welcoming common room and rooftop garden. It's raucously popular and often full.

At 48B Jalan Taman Melaka Raya (Jalan TMR), this area's main thoroughfare, the *Malacca Town Holiday Lodge 1 (☎ 284 8830)* may not have dorms or a decorated common room like most other hostels, but this place is kept squeaky clean and is well run. Simple singles/doubles cost from RM15/18. Some of the rooms look onto a balcony with lots of greenery.

On Jalan Melaka Raya 3, the *Melaka Arasma Belia Youth Hostel (☎ 282 7915)* is spotless, but strict and no one stays there given other options. Large, quiet dormitory rooms cost RM10 for a fan-cooled bed, or RM15 for air-con. *Sunny's Inn (☎ 227 5446)* at No 270A–B is looking worn but the happy-go-lucky staff show movies every night. Dorm beds cost RM9, a tiny single is RM15, but most rooms cost RM20 to RM35 for air-con with hot showers (but external toilet). At the southern end of this street, *Samudra Inn (☎ 282 7441)* at No 348B has family-run lodgings that get high marks for friendliness from travellers. Singles/doubles start from RM18/20 with fan and common bath, or RM35 and up for air-con with attached bath.

**Other Areas** Away from Taman Melaka Raya, there are a number of other guesthouses widely dispersed around town that often offer better value and a bit more peace. One of the best is the atmospheric *Eastern Heritage Guest House (☎ 283 3026, 8 Jalan Bukit China)*, well-located just a short walk from the town centre. It's housed in a superb old Melaka building dating from 1918, which has Peranakan tiling and impressive carved panelling. It has loads of character but the rooms are just typical guesthouse rooms, costing from RM18/26 a single/double or RM7 for a dorm bed. Downstairs is a common room, a dipping pool and a kitchen that serves meals.

*Tony's Guest House (☎ 012-688 0119, ✉ cobia43@hotmail.com)* at 24-G Lorong Bukit China is in a newer greenish-yellow building with outdoor balconies. Reception is in the copy shop next door and rooms seem reasonably priced at RM15/20 for singles/doubles (no dormitory).

At 177 Jalan Parameswara, near the Chinese temple, *Kancil Guest House (☎ 281 4044)* makes up for its marginally inconvenient location by offering spacious, secure lodgings. Open-plan dorm beds in the front entryway of the house are overpriced at RM12, considering they afford zero privacy, but clean, fan-cooled rooms with shared bath upstairs start at RM26. There's a pleasant garden out the back.

North of the river is *Malacca Town Holiday Lodge 2 (☎ 284 6905, 52 Kampung Empat)*. The location is slightly inconvenient – it's a bit of a walk to the historical sites – but it is close to the bus stations and, like its sister guesthouse on Jalan TMR, is impeccably clean. There is a good variety of rooms (no dorms) starting at RM15; quite palatial air-con rooms with bathroom range from RM36 to RM50.

**Hotels** The rambling old *Majestic Hotel (☎ 282 2367, 188 Jalan Bunga Raya)* is a classic place. High ceilings and swishing fans add to the cool lazy atmosphere and the staff may look vaguely surprised to see customers. Rates start at RM27 for a small room with fan up to RM63 for a large room with air-con and bathroom, but some can be pretty dirty.

Many cheap hotels are found along or just off of Jalan Munshi Abdullah running east of the bus terminal. The friendly *Ng Fook Hotel (☎ 282 8055, 154 Jalan Bunga Raya)*, just north of Jalan Munshi Abdullah, is basic but OK. Simple rooms without/with bath cost RM23/RM32, or from RM39 with air-con. A few doors away is the somewhat cheaper *Hong Kong Hotel (☎ 282 3392)*.

Hidden away in a backstreet of China-town (opposite the Kampung Kling Mosque) is the small *Chong Hoe Hotel (☎ 282 6102, 26 Jalan Tokang Emas)*. It offers good value, with simple fan rooms for RM20 and air-con singles/doubles with TV and bathroom for RM36/46.

The lovely petite *Hinly Hotel (☎ 283 6554, 150 Jalan Parameswara)* is an older-style converted house set back from the street and is very peaceful despite the busy road. Air-con singles/doubles with TV, phone and bathroom are a steal at just RM35/40.

The *Heritage Hotel (☎ 282 7515, 116A Jalan TMR)* has small, clean singles/doubles from RM25/40, but not all have windows. They also rent rooms by the day and are quite determined to attract travellers – look for the crowded information signs out front.

## Places to Stay – Mid-Range

Most of the mid-range hotels are in the northern part of town but the central China-town area has a couple of fabulous options.

The bright yellow *Hotel Puri (☎ 282 5588, fax 281 5588, 118 Jalan Tun Tan Cheng Lock)* is a superb old renovated Per-anakan manor house that once belonged to a rubber plantation owner. The elaborate lobby is decked out with beautiful old cane and inlaid furniture, and opens into a glassed-over inner courtyard. Very comfortable standard rooms with all mod cons start at RM130. Diagonally opposite in the same row of restored Peranakan shophouses at Nos 125–127 is *Baba House (☎ 281 1216, fax 281 1217)*. With its tilework, carved panels and cool, interior courtyard, this place has almost as much style as the Hotel Puri. Standard/deluxe rooms with bathroom cost RM85/110, though some don't have windows.

It's hard to beat *Heeren House (☎ 281 4241, fax 281 4239)*, right in the heart of town on the waterfront. Immaculate rooms in this former godown (warehouse) all overlook the river and have polished floorboards, a few pieces of antique furniture and all mod cons for RM139/149 on weekdays/weekends.

At the budget end of this category, the *Regal Hotel (☎ 283 5959, 66 Jalan Munshi Abdullah)* is just a few minutes' walk from the express bus station. Spacious, if rather dim, singles or doubles with air-con, TV and bathroom cost RM45. Opposite at No 52 is the friendly *May Chiang Hotel (☎ 283 9535)*, where somewhat nicer rooms cost RM40.

Better value is the quiet and friendly *Gold Leaf Hotel (☎ 283 6555, 31 Jalan Kee Ann)*, where clean, comfortable air-con rooms with bathroom, TV and phone cost just RM45. Quite a step up in price, but also in quality, the *Belmount Hotel (☎ 281 2888, 68 Jalan Portugis)* across the river has well-appointed doubles for RM108 (promotional discounts sometimes available).

Farther east is the small *Accordian Hotel (☎ 282 1911, 114 Jalan Munshi Abdullah)*. Air-con singles/doubles with bath are comfortable, if a bit faded, and start at RM58/69, including breakfast. On the same road, *Palace Hotel (☎ 282 5355, fax 284 1993)* at No 201 has similar rooms for RM92/115 and larger deluxe rooms for RM138/161 – discounts may be available.

## Places to Stay – Top End

Melaka has a couple of older high-rise hotels that are no longer up with the best, but most offer good facilities and substantial discounts. At the northern end of town, well away from the action, is the *Hotel Grand Continental (☎ 284 0088, fax 284 8125, 20 Jalan Tun Sri Lanang)*. It's quite popular with older European tourists and standard/deluxe rooms start at RM70/100.

Just off Jalan Merdeka on the reclaimed seafront behind the Mahkota Parade shopping complex is the new *Century Mahkota Hotel (☎ 281 2828, fax 281 2323)*. It has two large swimming pools, a few restaurants and bars, and tennis and squash courts. Rooms/one-bedroom suites start at RM300/350 before any promotional discount.

On Jalan Bandar Hilir, just north of the Jalan TAR roundabout, the sumptuous high-rise *Hotel Equatorial (☎ 282 8333, fax 282 9333)* charges from RM437/473 for singles/twins, but promotional rates dip as low as RM160.

The *Renaissance Melaka Hotel (☎ 284 8888, fax 284 9269)* on Jalan Bendahara used to be the most luxurious in town. Rooms start at RM437, and it still has good facilities, including tennis and squash courts, a swimming pool, lounge and a disco.

## Places to Eat

Melaka's food reflects its history, and fantastic coffee abounds. It is the home of Portuguese Eurasian food and Chinese Nyonya cuisine (done in Melaka with a salty Indonesian influence). Medan Portugis is the place to try Portuguese-influenced dishes, mostly seafood, though the fiery 'devil curry' is also worth a try. The classic Nyonya dish, laksa soup, is the best in Malaysia – the rich coconut base makes it tastier than the sour Penang variety.

Good, if slightly expensive, daytime cafes for Nyonya dishes can be found in restored Peranakan houses in Chinatown. *Nancy's Restoran (Old China Cafe) (15 Jalan Hang Lekir)* serves basic Nyonya set lunches for RM7.50 (closed Tuesday). Also good is the *Restoran Peranakan (107 Jalan Tun Tan Cheng Lock).*

*Jonkers Melaka Restoran (17 Jalan Hang Jebat),* a cafe in a craft shop, is highly recommended for its great home-made food served in a cool, central courtyard. Splurge on the gourmet Nyonya set lunches (RM20) and try its green-tea ice cream with ginger and lime or the truly exquisite cheesecakes (RM7).

In the evenings, excellent Nyonya fare can be had along Jalan TMR at the famed *Restoran Ole Sayang* at No 198 (closed Wednesday) or *Nyonya Makko* at No 123 (closed Tuesday). Both of these air-con restaurants serve a variety of Nyonya specialities from around RM8 per dish.

The cafe downstairs in *Heeren House* guesthouse has a delightful atmosphere and is a good place to buy cakes and Peranakan and Portuguese food. You can also get Western breakfasts here.

Along Jalan Merdeka, previously the waterfront, the permanent food stalls at *Glutton's Corner* serve all the usual hawker specialities. Look for the *o-chien* (oyster omelettes) or try the *Bunga Raya Restaurant* at Nos 39–40 for excellent steamed crabs (RM35).

The *Mahkota Parade shopping complex* down the road is mostly a centre for Western fast food, though the food court on the 1st floor has the usual Malaysian hawker favourites. You'll find a supermarket in the basement for self-catering. Outdoor hawker venues include the daytime *Centerpoint food court;* and in the evenings the *Indian vendors* on Jalan Bendahara in Little India, and the busy *Malay stalls* near the Jalan TMR roundabout.

At Nos 40–42 Jalan Laksamana, right in the centre of town, *Kafe Loony Planet* (yes, that's right, they've swiped our logo) is a universal favourite. It's in a converted old medicine shop, where old photos and newspapers cover the walls. Locals, expats and travellers alike favour knocking back a few imported beers in the expansive interior. The restaurant is open daily until midnight, even later on weekends/holidays, and you can even check your email for a fee.

Down the street at No 38 the long-running *Restaurant Kim Swee Huat* also caters to Western tastes; breakfasts are particularly good, with muesli, porridge, yoghurt, fruit salad and pancakes. If it's a view you're looking for, the *Iguana Riverfront Restaurant* opposite will provide one, though it may take quite a while to flag down the staff. We didn't brave the 'Viagra' chicken wings, but you certainly could.

Back in front of the Stadthuys, the peaceful *Manis Cafe (1 Jalan Laksamana)* serves up spicy laksa and other local favourites, plus a range of fabulous coffees. Courteous staff make this a pleasant retreat.

In Chinatown, the travellers cafe of choice (it's the only one) is *Geographér Café*. You can groove to the alternative music while you sink your teeth into Manis Melaka (coconut sugar and nuts over ice cream, RM5.50). The service may be much too laid-back, but there's nowhere else in Chinatown open late.

PENINSULAR MALAYSIA

The *UE Tea House (20 Lorong Bukit China)* is a simple Chinese coffee shop specialising in steamed dumplings. Directly opposite is *Capitol Satay*, where you cook the skewers yourself at tables – it's incredibly cheap.

Around the corner on Jalan Temenggong are two Indian places, *Madras Cafe* and *Restoran Veni*, which do cheap vegetarian and non-vegetarian set meals and *roti canai* (roti dipped in dhal or curry) breakfasts. Also on the edge of Little India, *Restoran Daun Pisang* serves exactly what its name says: good banana-leaf meals. There are several other night hawkers dishing up Indian fare farther north on Jalan Bendahara.

Farther west on Jalan Temenggong, on the riverside, *Discovery Cafe* is good for an outdoor drink if you happen to be passing by. Much farther north and quite out of the way, the *Bunga Raya Cafe* is noteworthy only for being Melaka's 'House of Wine', offering several foreign vintages by the bottle.

The lively Jalan TMR area, where many of the travellers' guesthouses are located, has a good range of cheap Chinese and Malay eateries. For duck-rice, noodles and other Chinese hawker fare, the *Restoran Lim (Mee Yoke)* is a good coffee shop. The *Mei Chong (158 Jalan TMR)*, an air-con bakery and cafe, serves a wide range of cakes and pastries with real coffee, and is surprisingly cheap.

A few doors down from Sunny's Inn, *Tandoori House* unsuccessfully attempts to be upmarket, but thankfully the North Indian food is superior and compensates for the appalling service and atmosphere. Next door the more justifiably popular *Restoran Sari Rasa* is a friendly Indonesian restaurant with dirt-cheap set meals. It's open very late.

On weekend evenings, it's worth making the trip out to Medan Portugis, where you can sample Malay-Portuguese dishes at outdoor tables facing the sea. Excellent seafood is served, and for around RM25 per person you can eat very well. Inside the square, *Restoran de Lisbon* has superb seafood – chilli crabs cost RM20, or the devil curry is RM10. You could also try *San Pedro (4 Jalan D'Aranjo)*, on the street immediately behind the square, with a more cosy, local atmosphere for Malay-Portuguese meals.

## Entertainment

The *Sound & Light Show*, held near the Porta de Santiago, is Melaka's most popular form of evening entertainment. It was closed at the time of research for system upgrades. When operational, the sound system booms and the ruins are lit up to present Melaka's history from a strongly nationalistic angle. It's nevertheless quite good theatre. Ask at the tourist information office if it's back on yet.

Melaka's nightlife is otherwise pretty unexciting. If you're a karaoke fiend, there are innumerable bars (girly and otherwise) in the alleyways off Jalan TMR. The small, homey *Jim's Cottage Pub (577 Jalan TMR)* is definitely an all-male enclave.

The *Rock & Roll Grill (☎ 284 9652, 34 Jalan Taman Melaka Raya 23)* is out of the way, but it advertises a free pick-up service, which makes it worth a look. Lots of red meat (steaks, burgers etc) is on the menu and its motto proudly proclaims 'No techno, no dangdut, no disco – classic rock, country, reggae and R&B only, please'. It's open daily until 1 am, but closed on Monday.

## Shopping

You could easily spend a couple of hours strolling through the many antique shops along Jalan Hang Jebat (Jonkers St) and Jalan Tun Tan Cheng Lock in Chinatown. Here you'll find Malaysia's best range of antiques, but not all of them are old and not all are from Malaysia. Prices are very high and haggling is essential. Shops are stocked with an impressive range of antique furniture, porcelain, old lamps, coins, *songket* (silk woven with gold threads), assorted bric-a-brac and crafts.

Squeezed between the Kampung Kling mosque and the Indian temple, Harmony Street is a pleasant shop to wander through, though prices are definitely inflated. For something different, Wah Aik at 92 Jalan Hang Jebat crafts doll-like shoes for bound feet, once the height of gruesome fashion for well-to-do Chinese women in Melaka. The shoes for bound feet cost RM75; or, if you can wait a few weeks, you can order some magnificent, custom-made Peranakan slippers.

The co-op artists at Lonely Creature at No 112 sell hand-made pottery and crafts, some traditional and some contemporary, at very reasonable prices. The Orangutan House, a shop at 59 Lorong Hang Jebat, sells work by young local artist Charles Cham, including printed T-shirts.

A few galleries, souvenir stalls and more upmarket shops selling trinkets (mostly from Indonesia) can be found across from Christ Church on Jalan Laksamana near the Stadthuys.

For cheap clothing and everyday goods, try Ekspo Melaka near the river on Jalan Kee Ann.

## Getting There & Away

Melaka is 144km from Kuala Lumpur (KL), 224km from Johor Bahru and just 94km from Port Dickson. Melaka's local bus station, express bus terminal and taxi station are all set back from Jalan Hang Tuah in the Kampung Morten area.

**Air** Pelangi Air (☎ 317 4175), based at the airport, flies several times per week to/from Pekanbaru (RM150) in Sumatra. There are currently no other scheduled flights to/from Melaka, although Malaysia Airlines (☎ 283 0654, 283 5722) has an office on the 1st floor of the City Bayview Hotel.

**Bus** Most of the bus company ticket offices are clustered around the express bus station. Half a dozen companies have air-con buses to KL throughout the day from 6 am to 7 pm (2½ hours, RM6.80). There are so many buses to KL that you can usually just turn up and get on the next one, but it pays to book tickets for any other destination at least the day before.

To Singapore, express buses leave approximately hourly from 8 am to 6 pm (4½ hours, RM11.50). On the weekends these buses can be fully booked, so purchase your ticket well in advance or, alternatively, take one of the frequent buses to Johor Bahru, which leave roughly every

hour between 8 am and 8 pm (three hours, RM10). Buses from Singapore to Melaka can be booked at the Lavender St bus station or from an agent operating out of the Lavender MRT station.

There are a few day and evening buses to Butterworth and Georgetown on Penang (seven hours, RM26), Ipoh (six hours, RM17) and Lumut (seven hours, RM20). To the east coast there are direct buses to Kuantan (8.30 am and 2 pm, five hours, RM14), Kuala Terengganu (9.30 am and 8.30 pm, nine to 10 hours, RM22.5) and Kota Bharu (approximately every second day, eight hours, RM32).

From the local bus station, the No 2 bus south to Muar leaves every half-hour throughout the day (one hour, RM2). Regular buses also go from here north along the coast to Port Dickson (RM4.50).

To Kuala Lumpur International Airport (KLIA), take a local bus to Sepang (1½ hours, RM5) and then another bus between 6.30 am and 8 pm to the airport (RM6).

**Train** The nearest train station is 38km north of Melaka at Tampin on the main north-south line from KL to Singapore. Local bus No 26 from Melaka runs to the Tampin bus station, but it's a few kilometres from there to the train station, so it's more convenient to take a direct taxi from Melaka instead (RM30).

**Taxi** Taxis leave across the road from the local bus station, just north of the market. Whole-taxi rates include: Port Dickson (RM80), Johor Bahru (RM160), Seremban (RM60), Mersing (RM150), KL (RM100) and KLIA (RM120).

**Car** If you're driving, Melaka's one-way traffic system will probably frustrate you at every turn.

If you want to rent a vehicle, the following companies have offices in Melaka:

**Avis** (☎ 282 4991) 124 Jalan Munshi Abdullah
**Hawk** (☎ 283 7878) 126 Jalan Bendahara

**Boat** High-speed ferries make the trip from Melaka to Dumai in Sumatra twice daily at around 9 or 10 am and again at 3 pm (1¾ hours, RM80/150 one way/return). Two companies, Madai Shipping (☎ 284 0671) and Tunas Rupat (☎ 286 1811), have ticket offices near the wharf and close to the express bus station. Same-day tickets are on sale after 8.30 am, but it's best to book the day before. Dumai is a visa-free entry port into Indonesia for citizens of most countries.

## Getting Around

Melaka's airport is at Batu Berendam, 9km north of the town centre. Take bus No 65 from the local bus station, or a taxi for RM10.

Melaka is easily explored on foot, but one useful service is Town Bus No 17, which runs every 15 minutes from the local bus station, past the huge Mahkota Parade shopping complex, to Taman Melaka Raya (40 sen) and on to Medan Portugis (80 sen).

Bicycles can be hired at some guesthouses or from Jin Trading at 53 Jalan Parameswara, where well-maintained racers and mountain bikes cost RM6 per day.

A trishaw (bicycle rickshaw) is an ideal way of getting around compact and slow-moving Melaka. You'll find only a handful of these left anywhere else in Malaysia and some of the drivers are real characters, tarting up their already colourful vehicles with strings of lights and jangling bells. By the hour they should cost about RM25, or RM6 to RM8 for any one-way trip within the town, but you'll have to bargain. Taxis are unmetered, and similarly charge a steep RM6 for a trip anywhere around town with an RM2 surcharge after dark.

## AROUND MELAKA
## Ayer Keroh

About 15km north-east of Melaka at the Melaka turn-off on the Lebuhraya, Ayer Keroh (also spelled Air Keroh) is home to a number of contrived tourist attractions popular with Malaysian and Singaporean families on weekends. Ayer Keroh can be reached on Town Bus No 19 from the local bus station in Melaka (30 minutes, RM1), or a taxi will cost around RM10. These attractions are deserted on weekdays and not worth much

more than a passing glance, with the exception of the Orang Asli Museum.

**Things to See & Do** Heading north from Melaka, the first point of interest is the lushly landscaped **Melaka Zoo**, where the small but well-fed collection includes Sumatran rhinos, Malayan sun bears and native guar oxen. It's open from 9 am to 6 pm daily; admission is RM1/3 for children/adults.

On the other side of the highway is the rather tacky **Taman Buaya Melaka** (Melaka Crocodile Farm), where you can inspect sluggish sauries in a series of soupy tanks; entry costs RM3/5 for children/adults. Just north is the small **Orang Asli Museum** (Muzium Orang Asli), with worthwhile exhibits on local indigenous tribes. The museum is open from 9 am to 6 pm daily (closed from 12.15 to 2.45 pm Friday); admission is RM1.

Farther north along the main road is **Hutan Rekreasi Air Keroh** (Air Keroh Recreational Forest), part secondary jungle and part landscaped park with paved trails, a 250m canopy walk, picnic areas and a forestry museum. It's a pleasant place for a stroll and entry is free, but it certainly ain't Taman Negara.

Just a few hundred metres on, **Taman Mini Malaysia/Asean** is the so-called 'main attraction' at Ayer Keroh. This large, but surprisingly empty theme park is dotted with examples of traditional houses from all 13 Malaysian states as well as neighbouring Asean countries. Each house contains a few handicrafts and wax dummies in trad-itional dress representing the region, but a lot of them look the same and you'll be stretching your Bahasa Malaysia skills because nothing is labelled in English. Guides inside each house are usually found dozing. Cultural dance and musical shows are held at 10.30 am on Wednesday and Saturday. The complex is open from 9 am to 5 pm daily; admission costs RM2/5 for children/adults.

About 2km farther north is the **Butterfly & Reptile Sanctuary**, which has a landscaped enclosure with only a sampling of butterfly species. Slightly more impressive is the collection of snakes, scorpions and enormous spiders. Entry is RM3/5 for children/adults.

**Places to Stay** Few visitors bother staying this far out. The *Air Keroh Recreational Forest* (☎ *232 8401*) has camp sites for 50 sen per person, small log cabins at RM20/25 for singles/doubles and more comfortable two-person chalets for RM50. It has been primarily set up for school groups. Reservations are strongly advised, although the rangers may let you stay if there's room when you turn up.

## Pulau Besar

The small island of Pulau Besar, south-east of Melaka and 5km off the coast, is a popular weekend getaway. The island has a few historic graves and reminders of the Japanese occupation during WWII, but the main reason to come here is for the clean white-sand beaches. The water is a little clearer than on the mainland and the hilly island is cloaked in greenery. There is also a golf course.

The only place to stay on Pulau Besar is the *Pandanusa Resort* (☎ *281 5939*), where luxury accommodation is not such a bad deal at RM99/129 per person on weekdays/weekends, including three meals.

Pulau Besar is most easily reached by boat from the new jetty at Anjung Batu, which is several kilometres past the old pier at Umbai, both south-east of Melaka. Regular boats depart from Anjung Batu every one to two hours (RM15), but from Umbai you'll need to charter a boat (RM80). You can reach either jetty in less than an hour by the No 2 local bus from Melaka.

## Tanjung Bidara

About 30km north-west of Melaka on the way to Port Dickson is Tanjung Bidara, one of the better beach areas along this stretch of coast. It is quiet and well away from the main highway, requiring you to take meandering back roads through rice paddies and farms to get to the shore. Although the water here is murky like everywhere else along the Selat Melaka, the sandy beaches are good for long, scenic walks and the greenery is reasonably prolific. The beach fills up on weekends and holidays, but otherwise you'll have it all to yourself.

The main stretch of beach is at Tanjung Bidara Beach Resort, where there is also a public beach area with food stalls. The *Tanjung Bidara Beach Resort* (☎ *384 2990*) is quiet and relaxing with a small swimming pool and a restaurant. Comfortable rooms facing the sea cost RM75/120 on weekdays/weekends, while more luxurious chalets are RM125/200.

Good budget accommodation is strung out along the beach for several kilometres, especially at Kampung Pasir Gembur. *Bidara Beach Lodge* (☎ *384 3340, 78 Lorong Haji Abdullah*) is a bit faded, but the friendly family who owns it offers double rooms with air-con, TV and bathroom for RM68, including breakfast. There are a few other newer places along the beach within walking distance.

Bus Nos 42 and 47 from Melaka go to Masjid Tanah, from where a taxi to Tanjung Bidara Beach Resort or Kampung Pasir Gembur costs RM6.

## Merlimau

Fifteen kilometres south of Melaka on the way to Muar is Merlimau, a small town that's worth a brief stop to see the exquisite chieftain's house, **Rumah Merlimau Penghulu**, 2km south of town. Built in 1894, it showcases traditional Melakan woodcarving among the eaves and ornate hand-painted tiles throughout. If the family agrees to show you around, a donation is expected.

# Johor

The state of Johor occupies the southern-most tip of the Malay Peninsula, and is connected to the island of Singapore by a causeway. Economically it is one of the most important states in the country, with huge rubber, palm oil and pineapple plantations, and a growing industrial base. It is also the most populated, and Johor Bahru, with over 812,000 people, is the second-largest city in Malaysia.

Most visitors pass through Johor on the way to or from Singapore or Pulau Tioman (Tioman Island, which is in Pahang state). However, Johor does have some attractions of its own, including the beautiful islands of the Seribuat Archipelago off the east coast; and Endau-Rompin National Park, one of the last undisturbed stands of lowland rainforest in Peninsular Malaysia.

## History

Johor's history is really a continuation of Melaka's. When the latter fell to the Portuguese in the 16th century, Johor became the pre-eminent Malay state, and its rulers (the first of whom was the son of the last sultan of Melaka) were seen as the protectors of the western Malay states. Early on the Portuguese attacked Johor, but eventually were more or less content to let the leaders rule from their capital on Sungai (River) Johor, even though they were something of an impediment to trade in the area.

The kingdom of Aceh on the northern tip of Sumatra also had ambitions in the area. The second half of the 16th century saw a three-way struggle between the Portuguese, Johor and Aceh for control of the peninsula and the Selat Melaka (Strait of Melaka). The Acehnese attacks on Johor continued well into the 17th century, and for a period from 1623 the kingdom's rulers had no fixed address, as their capital on the island of Lingga in Sungai Johor had been razed.

Johor's fortunes took a decided turn for the better with the coming of the Dutch, who allied themselves with Johor for a

## HIGHLIGHTS

- **The Seribuat Archipelago** – beautiful islands great for snorkelling, diving or lazing around on the beach
- **Johor Bahru** – a bustling city with a lively night market and historic colonial district
- **Endau-Rompin National Park** – pristine jungle and thundering waterfalls in a remote setting

combined (and ultimately successful) attack against the Portuguese at Melaka in 1641. Johor was freed from virtually all the tariffs and trade restrictions imposed on other states by the Dutch, in return for cooperation in helping to defeat the Portuguese. Johor also overcame threats from the Minangkabau and managed to ride out some domestic squabbling from within. By the end of the 17th century it was among the strongest Asian powers in the region.

A war with the Bugis in 1716 left Johor weakened, and further political instability followed when a Minangkabau, Raja Kecil of Siak, claimed the throne and overthrew

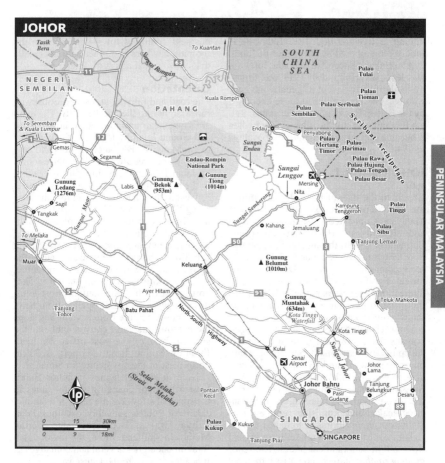

**JOHOR**

PENINSULAR MALAYSIA

the weak sultan in 1719. His control lasted for just two years, when Sulaiman, the son of the former sultan Abdul Jalil, was installed on the throne by the Buginese. His descendants ruled the state until it eventually disappeared in the early years of the 20th century. Throughout the 18th century the Bugis influence in the state increased. However, when the Dutch East India Company wrested control of Riau-Johor in 1784, the era of Bugis domination of western Malaya came to an end.

In 1819, with the court of the Johor sultan split by Malay and Bugis factions, Sir Thomas Stamford Raffles was able to bring about the cession of Singapore to the British and the pensioning-off of the sultans, while actual power went to the *temenggong* (Malay minister in charge of defence and justice). The temenggong continued to rule the state very ably, the most notable among them being the flamboyant Abu Bakar, who elevated himself to the position of sultan of Johor in 1886. Through his contacts with people in high places in London and Singapore, he was able to resist the British desire to bring Johor closer under its control. Abu Bakar also undertook an ambitious program of modernisation for the state, while continuing to live the high life. Today he is fondly remembered as the Father of Johor.

Abu Bakar's successor and son, Ibrahim, was less powerful and in 1914 was forced by the British to accept a 'general adviser' who had powers similar to those exercised by the British Residents in other states. Sultan Ibrahim was still the ruler of Johor when it became part of the Federation of Malaya in 1948.

## JOHOR BAHRU

☎ 07

Capital of the state of Johor, Johor Bahru is the southern gateway to Peninsular Malaysia. Connected to Singapore by road and rail across the 1038m-long Causeway, JB (as it is known throughout the country) inevitably suffers as a poor relation to its more glamorous neighbour. Despite its historical significance and various points of interest, few travellers pause in JB; it's just the place to get your passport stamped on the way in or out of Malaysia.

On weekends and public holidays, Singaporeans flock across the Causeway for sex, shopping and excitement, and Johor Bahru puts on a show. Central JB exudes a real border-town feel, with crowds, mostly male Singaporeans, cruising the streets. Street theatre is provided by medicine vendors dangling snakes and promising penis enlargement with their elixirs, or turbaned *bomoh* (Islamic spiritual healers) selling magical 'love oil' at astronomical prices. The *kedai gunting rambut* (barber shops) are a frequent sight, offering not haircuts, but women.

Despite its reputation as a sin centre, JB has closed its bawdier nightclubs in an effort to improve its image. A major part of the Singapore-Johor-Riau (Sijori) growth triangle, JB is a burgeoning centre of investment and construction. New roads, industrial estates, shopping centres and hotels are changing the face of the city. Yet JB is still chaotic and fairly tatty. It is both a breath of fresh air and a bad aroma as you arrive from squeaky-clean and sterile Singapore.

It's possible to spend an enjoyable day or two in JB; it has an excellent museum to

visit and a thriving night market. In the business centre of town you still see the footpath hawkers and other colourful stalls that are so much a part of Asia.

## Orientation

The road and railway across the Causeway run straight into the middle of JB. The main area for cheap and mid-range hotels is on and around Jalan Meldrum, in the centre of town. Many of JB's fancier hotels and new shopping centres are a few kilometres north on Jalan Tebrau, the main highway leading to the north and to the east coast.

West of the Causeway, Jalan Ibrahim runs along JB's waterfront. Here is the city's colonial district, with its parkland, colonial buildings and museum. In front of the colonial district, the modern Johor Bahru Waterfront City/Lot 1 shopping complex obscures the view across the Strait of Johor to Singapore.

The Larkin bus and taxi station is 5km north-west of the train station. Most long-distance buses and taxis operate from here. Local buses operate from several bus stops around town, the most convenient being the stop in front of the post office on Jalan Ibrahim. Sultan Ismail Airport is 32km north-west of the city centre, in Senai.

Note that street names in Johor Bahru have a habit of changing several times in the space of a few kilometres. For example, Jalan Air Molek suddenly becomes Jalan Yahya Awai as it crosses Jalan Gertak Merah. In similar fashion, the major Jalan Ibrahim undergoes several name-changes as it heads away from the Causeway.

## Information

The Tourism Malaysia office (☎ 222 3590) is on the 5th floor of the JOTIC building, on Jalan Air Molek, about 750m west of the Causeway. It's open from 9 am to 5 pm weekdays, and to 1 pm Saturday (closed second and third Saturdays). Also on the 5th floor of the JOTIC building, the slightly less informative Johor State Tourism office (☎ 223 4935) has similar hours to Tourism Malaysia.

The immigration office (☎ 224 4255) is on the 1st floor, Blok B, Wisma Persekutuan, Jalan Air Molek.

Decorated windows on Jalan Hang Jebat (formerly known as Jonkers St), Melaka.

Rainforest canopy, Taman Negara National Park.

Meeting up outside the mosque, Melaka.

Harvesting sap from a rubber tree, Johor.

JOHN BORTHWICK

Strolling the streets of Kuantan, Pahang.

RICHARD I'ANSON

Boats on the Melaka River, Melaka.

JOHN BORTHWICK

Smiling faces and a spot of fishing on the Sungai Kuantan, Pahang.

With so many people crossing to and from Singapore every day (many Malaysians commute to work there), there are dozens of moneychangers in the central area and the rates are competitive (but be sure to shop around for the best rates).

For international calls, go to the Telekom building opposite Puteri Pan Pacific Hotel in the city centre, where it's possible to make calls with a phone card at any time, or calls through the operator during business hours.

There are Internet cafes in most of the shopping malls around town, including Parallel Multimedia (10 am to 9.30 pm daily, RM3 per hour), on the 4th floor of the Johor Bahru City Square shopping complex. There's also the IRC Internet Centre on the ground floor of the JOTIC building.

### Royal Abu Bakar Museum
Overlooking the Strait of Johor, the Istana Besar was once the main palace of the Johor royal family. It was built in Victorian style by Anglophile sultan Abu Bakar in 1866, and is now open to the public as the Muzium Diraja Abu Bakar.

This is undoubtedly the finest museum of its kind in Malaysia, conveying the wealth and privilege of the sultans. It contains the sultan's possessions, including furniture and hunting trophies, and is set out much as it was when in use as the palace. The superb exhibits include Chinese, Japanese, Indian and Malay carved wooden pieces; an amazing full-size crystal-glass table and chairs from France. The hunting room has some bizarre exhibits from pukka days when wildlife was there to be shot, including elephant's-foot umbrella stands and antelope-leg ashtrays.

The palace is open from 9 am to 6 pm daily except Friday (no entry after 5 pm). Entrance for foreigners is a hefty US$7 (children US$3), payable in ringgit at lousy exchange rates. Still, it's well worth a visit.

The 53-hectare palace grounds (free entry) are beautifully manicured and provide a great breathing space in this fairly cramped city. There are good views across the strait, although Singapore's industrial backside is not terribly picturesque.

### Other Attractions
West of the museum is the most attractive part of Johor Bahru, the old colonial/royal district of greenery and fine buildings.

Behind the museum and approached through the palace gardens is a small **zoo**, once the private zoo of the sultan. It's open from 8 am to 6 pm daily (RM2/RM1 for adults/children).

Built from 1892 to 1900, the magnificent **Sultan Abu Bakar Mosque** is a mixture of architectural styles, but principally Victorian. The minarets look like British clock towers, and this mosque is difficult to distinguish from a colonial administrative building. It can accommodate up to 2000 people.

With a 32m stone tower, **Istana Bukit Serene** is the residence of the sultan of Johor. The palace was built in 1932 and features Art Deco influences. Though not open to the public, you can glimpse it along Jalan Skudai. It is on the waterfront, 5km west of the Abu Bakar museum.

One building that is hard to miss is the imposing 1940s **Bangunan Sultan Ibrahim** (State Secretariat Building) on Bukit Timbalan, overlooking the city centre. This city landmark has a 64m-high square tower, and looks like a medieval fortress transported from Mogul India.

### Places to Stay – Budget
Few visitors stay in JB; it's too close to the greater attractions of Singapore. On the other hand, Johor is an important business centre, so there are plenty of hotels, although prices are generally high for Peninsular Malaysia. Those on a tight budget may want to head to onward destinations rather than spend a night in JB.

The only real budget accommodation is the basic *Footloose Homestay* (☎ 224 2881, *4H Jalan Ismail),* in a quiet suburban neighbourhood just off Jalan Yahya Awai, with six dorm-beds for RM14 per person. It's a 15-minute walk from the train station, and

PENINSULAR MALAYSIA

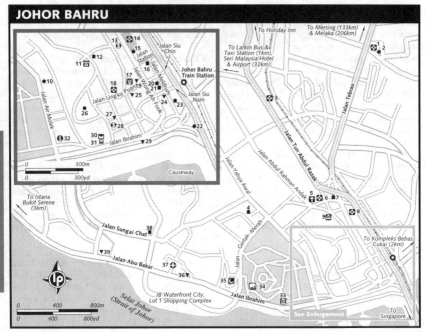

is best approached via Jalan Air Molek from the seafront. After crossing Jalan Gertak Merah, take the second turn on the left after passing a Shell petrol station, and look for the small sign about 150m up the hill.

## Places to Stay – Mid-Range

JB's mid-range hotels are clustered in the Jalan Meldrum neighbourhood, just west of the train station. Note that all hotels in this section raise their prices at the weekend by about 10%.

A good choice in terms of comfort is the *Causeway Inn* (☎ 224 8811), with clean, well-appointed rooms with air-con, TV and bathroom. Rooms with windows cost RM78; those without windows are RM66.

The other hotels in this range are less appealing. *Hawaii Hotel* (☎ 224 0633) has ageing but acceptable rooms with bathroom for RM40 with fan and RM50 with air-con. *Fortuna Hotel* (☎ 223 3210) has simple, reasonably clean rooms with air-con and

bathroom for RM60. Nearby, *Triumph Star Hotel* (☎ 224 9291) looks quite smart, but is a step down from the Causeway Inn. Air-con rooms with shower start at RM80.

If you don't mind being outside the city centre, *Seri Malaysia Hotel* (☎ 221 1002) is the best hotel in this price bracket, with clean, spacious air-con rooms with bath for RM80. It's very close to Larkin bus station; walk out the back (market end) of the station, take a left, walk past the petrol station and turn right; look for the large pink building.

## Places to Stay – Top End

*Tropical Inn* (☎ 224 7888) is conveniently located but its rooms are a little on the tatty side. Rates start at RM100 and include breakfast.

The nearby *Puteri Pan Pacific Hotel* (☎ 223 3333) is a much smarter affair with a swimming pool, fitness centre, business centre and four restaurants. Rooms start at RM168/188 for standard/deluxe. Competing

## JOHOR BAHRU

**PLACES TO STAY**
4   Footloose Homestay
7   Tropical Inn
12  Puteri Pan Pacific Hotel
16  Triumph Star Hotel
20  Fortuna Hotel
21  Hawaii Hotel
23  Causeway Inn
38  Hyatt Regency

**PLACES TO EAT**
19  Pasar Malam (Night Market)
24  Restoran Medina
25  Restoran Nilla
27  It Roo Café
29  Restoran High Street Café
36  Tepian Tebrau Food Centre
39  Selera Sungai Chat Food Centre

**OTHER**
1   Plaza Pelangi
2   Menara Pelangi; Malaysia
    Airlines
3   Best World
5   Church of the Immaculate
    Conception
6   Wisma Landmark Tower &
    Shopping Mall
8   Komtar Building
9   Taxi Stand – Taxis to Singapore
10  Immigration Office
11  Telekom
13  Public Bank
14  Johor Bahru City Square
    Shopping Complex; Times
    Bookshop; Parallel Multimedia;
    Medena Sclera Food Court

15  Johor Bahru City Square
    Tower;
    Maybank
17  Sri Mariamman Temple
18  Plaza Kota Raya
22  Immigration Checkpoint
26  Bangunan Sultan Ibrahim
28  Bank Islam
30  Post Office
31  Local Bus Stop
32  JOTIC;
    Tourism Malaysia Office;
    Food Court;
    IRC Internet Centre
33  Royal Abu Bakar Museum
34  Zoo
35  Sultan Abu Bakar Mosque
37  General Hospital

to be JB's best is the **Hyatt Regency** (☎ 222 1234) on Jalan Sungai Chat, 2.5km west of the city centre. Rooms start at RM150/180.

The **Holiday Inn** (☎ 332 3800), 2km north of the centre in Century Gardens on Jalan Dato Sulaiman, is another good choice, with rooms from RM180. There is a swimming pool, health club and restaurant.

### Places to Eat

Johor Bahru is a good place for food, especially seafood. It also has good hawker venues, the best being the very active **pasar malam** (night market) outside the Hindu temple on Jalan Wong Ah Fook. Local specialities include *laksa johor,* a noodle dish relying heavily on coconut; and *mee rebus,* noodles in a thick sauce that show the Javanese influence in Johor. Also try the excellent grilled fish cooked on banana leaves, and the filling claypot rice. A full meal here will cost less than RM10.

All the shopping malls around town have food courts. The best of these is **Medena Sclera** in the Johor Bahru City Square shopping complex. You'll find lots of other Western and Asian restaurants here. There's another good food court on the upper level of the **Plaza Kota Raya** shopping centre.

Down on street level, JB has some good Indian restaurants, including the ever-busy **Restoran Medina** on the corner of Jalan Meldrum and Jalan Siu Niam. It serves excellent *murtabak* (roti filled with mutton, chicken or vegetables), biryani and curries. Opposite the Sri Mariamman Temple, **Restoran Nilla** specialises in South Indian banana-leaf set meals. Most meals are vegetarian, but fish-head curry is also featured.

Two places with a somewhat Western slant are **Restoran High Street Café**, which does set dinners from RM15, and the attractive **It Roo Café**, which serves a varied menu of local and Western favourites (including fish and chips). The latter spot is also a good place to sit outside and have a beer, but keep in mind that it closes around 9 pm.

Singaporeans come across the Causeway in the evenings just to eat cheap seafood. The main venues are along the waterfront to the west of the city centre. The food is great, but the sea aspect is spoiled by the very busy road. The **Tepian Tebrau** food centre on Jalan Abu Bakar is famous for its excellent seafood. One kilometre farther west is **Selera Sungai Chat**, another well-patronised seafood centre specialising in *ikan bakar* (grilled fish).

For those who wish to self-cater, there is a good **supermarket** on the ground floor of Kompleks Tun Abdul Razal, the shopping centre beneath the Komtar building about 500m north of the train station.

PENINSULAR MALAYSIA

## Shopping

JB promotes itself as a major shopping destination, and shopping centres are being built at a frantic pace. Singaporeans do come across to do their shopping – petrol and groceries – but for most goods Singapore has better prices and a far better range. Major shopping centres in central JB are Plaza Kota Raya and the much flashier Johor Bahru City Square. Other large new malls to the north of the city centre include the Plaza Pelangi on Jalan Tebrau and Best World on Jalan Tun Abdul Razak.

Another shopping complex, designed specifically to cater to Singaporeans, is the newly finished Kompleks Bebas Cukai duty-free shopping centre, about 2km east of the Causeway (locals commonly refer to it by its English name, 'Free Zone Complex'). The complex also incorporates a ferry terminal that handles a lot of ferry traffic to/from Singapore and a few destinations in Indonesia (see the following Getting There & Away section).

## Getting There & Away

**Air** The Malaysia Airlines office (☎ 334 1001) is on the 1st floor of the Menara Pelangi building, on Jalan Kuning at Taman Pelangi, 2.5km north of the city centre. JB is well served by Malaysia Airlines flights and, as an incentive to fly from JB rather than Singapore, fares to other places in Malaysia are much lower than from Singapore. There are direct flights from JB to Kota Kinabalu (daily, RM347), Kuala Lumpur (daily, RM93), Kuching (daily, RM169) and Penang (daily, RM178). Malaysia Airlines also has direct international flights to Denpasar, Surabaya and Jakarta in Indonesia, as well as a host of more-distant Asian and Pacific destinations.

Pelangi Air (contact Malaysia Airlines) has flights to Padang Besar (three times weekly, RM260) and Palembang in Sumatra (four times weekly, RM280). International tickets are cheaper if purchased through a travel agent.

**Bus** Due to the hassles of crossing the Causeway – customs, immigration and so on – there's a wider selection of buses and long-distance taxis to other towns in Peninsular Malaysia from JB than from Singapore.

Frequent buses run between Singapore's Queen St bus terminal and JB's Larkin bus station, inconveniently 5km north of the city (a taxi to/from central JB should cost RM6). The most convenient service is the air-con Singapore–Johor Bahru Express, which runs roughly every 15 minutes from 6.30 am until 11 pm (RM2.40). At Larkin, buy your ticket at counter No 37; if you're in central JB you can buy tickets at the southernmost travel agent in the building block across the street from the train station and board the bus after clearing Malaysian immigration just before the Causeway.

The regular SBS (city bus) No 170 also runs between Larkin and Ban San terminal. Tickets cost RM1.20 and can be purchased on the bus. The bus departs from stand No 13 at Larkin. You can also board just before the Causeway (after clearing immigration).

For either bus, it is important to keep your ticket and carry all your luggage with you when you get off to clear immigration, as there's no guarantee that you'll board the same bus on the other side.

At Larkin bus station there are at least a dozen bus companies with departures throughout the day for major towns in Peninsular Malaysia. Destinations include: Melaka (three hours, RM10), Kuala Lumpur (four hours, RM16.50/20 regular/'business class'), Ipoh (eight hours, RM30) and Butterworth (11 hours, RM40). Most buses to Melaka come from Singapore, so it pays to book in advance. To the east coast, departures are to Kota Tinggi (one hour, RM3.30), Mersing (three hours, RM5.50), Kuantan (five hours, RM15.4), Kuala Terengganu (nine hours, RM24.10) and Kota Bharu (10 hours, RM29).

**Train** There are daily trains from JB to Kuala Lumpur and Butterworth, and these can be used to get to most places on the west coast. The line passes through Tampin (for Melaka), Seremban, Kuala Lumpur, Tapah Road (for Cameron Highlands), Ipoh and Taiping. It is also possible to change at

Gemas and board the 'jungle train' for connections to Taman Negara National Park and Kota Bharu.

The train station booking office is open from 9 am to 6 pm daily. There are also trains to Singapore, but it's more convenient to take a bus or taxi. See the Malaysia Getting Around chapter for timetable and fare information.

**Taxi** The long-distance taxi station is at the Larkin bus station (see Bus earlier). Regular taxi destinations and costs (per car) include Kota Tinggi (RM20), Kuala Lumpur (RM180), Kuantan (RM180), Melaka (RM124) and Mersing (RM64). There is a counter near the taxi stand with a board listing prices to most destinations.

Registered taxis to Singapore leave from a stand near Puteri Pan Pacific Hotel. A taxi across the Causeway to the Queen St terminal should cost RM28 for the whole vehicle. From Singapore to JB the fare is S$28. Local city taxis cannot make the run across the Causeway.

**Walking** It is possible to walk across the Causeway in both directions. In addition to being free of charge, this is the fastest way across when traffic clogs the roadway. The one-way journey on foot takes about 25 minutes (if you don't succumb to the heat and fumes mid-crossing).

**Boat** Ferries leave from the Kompleks Bebas Cukai, about 2km east of the Causeway. Sriwani Tours & Travel (☎ 221 1677), in the complex, handles tickets to most destinations.

There are daily departures to Batu Ampar (RM50) and Tanjung Pinang (RM55), both on Sumatra in Indonesia, and two daily departures to Tanah Merah (RM38) in Singapore.

Additional boats depart from Kukup, west of JB, to Tanjung Balai, also in Sumatra (see Kukup later).

## Getting Around
**To/From the Airport** JB's Sultan Ismail Airport is 32km north-west of town at Senai, on the road to Melaka and Kuala Lumpur. Local bus No 207 (RM2) runs to the airport from the Larkin bus station, but departures are infrequent. A taxi between the airport and JB is RM25 per car and takes 30 to 45 minutes, depending on the traffic.

**Taxi** Taxis in JB have meters and drivers are legally required to use them (most will do so without any fuss). You can go almost anywhere around JB for RM5, and taxis can be hired at around RM25 per hour for sightseeing.

**Car** The main car rental companies include:

**Budget** (☎ 598 1625) Lapang Terbang Sultan Ismail, Senai
**Mayflower** (☎ 224 1357) 2nd floor, Wisma Tan Chong, Jalan Tun Abdul Razak
**Orix** (☎ 224 1215) Level 1, JOTIC building, Jalan Air Molek

## AROUND JOHOR BAHRU
### Kukup
☎ 07
About 40km south-west of JB, on the Strait of Melaka and across from Sumatra, is the fishing village of Kukup. It's famous throughout Malaysia and Singapore for its seafood, especially prawns (shrimp), and for the open-air restaurants built on stilts over the water. Singaporeans, who are obsessed with the loss of their own *kampung* (village) life, flock to this village on weekends, mostly for the seafood. While there's no denying the quality of the seafood, the availability of similar fare in JB and the tattiness of the village make Kukup a low-priority destination for many travellers.

Next to Kukup is **Kampung Air Masin** (Salt Water Village), renowned for its top-quality *belacan* (prawn paste). Both villages are inhabited largely by Hokkien Chinese.

**Places to Eat** *Makanan Laut*, just up the street from the pier, is a good spot for lunch or dinner. It serves prawn dishes from RM16 and squid dishes from RM8 (try the crunchy fried baby squid) and an English menu is available.

**Getting There & Away** There is no bus service to Kukup; you'll have to take a share taxi (RM10 per car) to/from Pontian Kecil, 18km north of Kukup. There are regular buses (2½ hours, RM5) between JB and Pontian Kecil. A chartered taxi all the way to/from JB costs RM60.

Ferries run between Kukup's ferry terminal and Tanjung Balai in Indonesia. In either direction, ferries sail up to five times a day and cost RM35/50 one way/return. Call PT Marina at ☎ 696 1888 for more details.

## JOHOR BAHRU TO MELAKA

The main road north from JB runs to Melaka and Kuala Lumpur. It's a productive region of palm oil, rubber and pineapple plantations. Although there is little to detain the casual visitor, the coast road is fairly scenic and passes through some quaint kampung.

### Ayer Hitam
☎ 07

Ayer Hitam, 80km north-west of JB, is an important crossroads. Here you can turn left to go to Batu Pahat, Muar and Melaka, continue straight on for Seremban and Kuala Lumpur, or turn right for Keluang and Mersing on the east coast. Ayer Hitam is a popular rest stop for buses, taxis and motorists, so there are lots of small restaurants. **Kampung Macap**, south of Ayer Hitam, is well known for its Aw Pottery works.

### Batu Pahat
☎ 07

The riverine town of Batu Pahat is famed for its Chinese cuisine, although it also has a minor reputation as a 'sin city' for jaded Singaporeans. It has a few buildings of note, such as the town's **Art Deco mosque** and the **Chinese Chamber of Commerce building**. However, if you fancy a night in this region, it's probably better to head north to Muar.

**Places to Stay** The best choice is ***Rumah Persinggahan*** (*Batu Pahat Rest House;*

## Palm Oil

The oil palm (*Elaeis guineensis*) is probably the most common tree in Peninsular Malaysia today. When travelling along rural roads, particularly in Johor, Pahang and Sabah, you'll come across seas of oil-palm trees that stretch on to the horizon.

The oil palm was first introduced in the 1860s; seeds were brought from Sri Lanka (although the tree itself is a native of West Africa), but it was not until 1917 that the first oil-palm plantation was established. Since WWII Malaysia has been the world's top producer of palm oil, and current annual output is around 7.2 million tonnes.

The oil is extracted from the orange-coloured fruit, which grows in bunches just below the fronds. It is used primarily for cooking, although research is under way to find other uses, such as for engine fuel. Malaysia has invested heavily in palm oil, and it is one of the country's major primary industry exports. Unfavourable assessments of palm oil as an edible oil by the US Food & Drug Administration have caused an uproar in Malaysia, which blames the negative assessments on the US sunflower oil industry lobby.

MARTIN HARRIS

☎ 434 1181, 870 Jalan Tasek), which has large air-con standard/deluxe doubles for RM52/63. It's just by the roundabout in the south of town, where the roads from Ayer Hitam and Kukup meet; without your own transport, a RM5 taxi from the centre of town is a good idea.

The more basic *Fairyland Hotel* (☎ 434 1777, 91 Jalan Rahmat) has simple but clean rooms with fan for RM25, or RM35 with air-con. The slightly fancier *Hotel Carnival* (☎ 431 5122, 2 Jalan Fatimah) has air-con doubles from RM55. Both of these places are a fair distance from the bus station; a RM3 taxi ride is your best bet on a hot day.

**Getting There & Away** A local bus to/from Muar costs RM2.40 and takes 1½ hours. A local bus to/from JB costs RM5.70 and takes two hours.

## Muar
☎ 06

This riverside town, also known as Bandar Maharani, was once an important commercial centre. It is noted for its traditional Malay culture, including *ghazal* (female singers with an orchestra) music and the *kuda kepang* (horse trance) dance, originally from Java.

Muar is a typical Malaysian town with a bustling Chinatown of restaurants and hotels. Along the river you'll find the graceful colonial district, with its government offices, courthouse, customs house, school and Masjid Jamek, a Victorian fantasy of a mosque, in much the same style as JB's Sultan Abu Bakar Mosque.

At the mouth of the river, just past the mosque, Tanjung Riverside Park is a pleasant place for a picnic lunch, with creeper-festooned trees and the occasional timid monitor lizard hanging about.

There's an Internet cafe in the Wetex Parade shopping mall in the centre of town.

**Places to Stay & Eat** The very good *Rumah Persinggahan Tanjong Emas* (Muar Rest House; ☎ 952 7755, 2222 Jalan Sultanah) has huge air-con doubles for RM60. To get there, walk along the river

past the mosque, then turn left on Jalan Sultanah, following the signs for 'Rumah Persinggahan'. It's quite a way on a hot day, so you may want to spend RM5 on a taxi.

Muar also has plenty of cheaper hotels, many in the central Chinatown area. *Kingdom Hotel* (☎ 952 1921, 158 Jalan Meriam) charges RM28 for clean rooms with fan and bathroom, RM35 with air-con. *Classic Hotel Muar* (☎ 953 3888, 69 Jalan Ali) is the town's upscale option, with spacious, clean air-con rooms with hot water from RM120. To get to these two hotels from the local bus station, walk away from the river on Jalan Sisi, one street east of the larger Jalan Sulaiman.

For food, there are plenty of *kedai kopi* (coffee shops) scattered about Chinatown. Otherwise, there is a good *food court* and a *supermarket* in the Wetex Parade shopping mall near Classic Hotel Muar.

**Getting There & Away** There are two bus stations in Muar; the local bus station is west (downriver) of the bridge leading into town, and the long-distance bus station is east (upriver) of the bridge. Buses to/from JB (two hours, RM8) and Kuala Lumpur (2½ hours, RM9) operate from the long-distance bus station. Buses to/from Melaka (one hour, RM2.50), Batu Pahat (1½ hours, RM2.40) and Gunung Ledang/Segamat (one hour, RM2.40) operate from the local bus station.

## Gunung Ledang

The highest mountain in Johor, Gunung Ledang (formerly Mt Ophir; 1276m) is noted for the series of waterfalls that cascade down its jungle-clad slopes. Although most visitors only climb partway up the mountain to admire the falls, it's possible to climb all the way to the summit on a very demanding two-day round trip (there are several camp sites along the way). This climb makes a good introduction to tropical mountaineering and is recommended for those who don't have time for longer treks in Taman Negara National Park.

A simple hiking map is available at Gunung Ledang Resort (☎ 06-977 2888) at the

PENINSULAR MALAYSIA

base of the mountain. Those intending to climb to the summit must pay a RM3 camping fee and RM50 deposit (to ensure you take out your garbage). Day-trippers pay an entry fee of RM1 per person. Try to avoid the mountain on weekends, when it gets packed with local youths who come to swim in the pools at the base of the falls.

To get there, take a Segamat-bound bus (No 65, 30 minutes, RM2.40) from Muar and ask to be let off at Gunung Ledang (there's a large sign reading 'Gunung Ledang' near the bus stop). It's a 1km walk in from the main road to the start of the falls. On your return to Muar, wait at the bus stop on the opposite side of the main road.

## JOHOR BAHRU TO MERSING
### Kota Tinggi
☎ 07

The small town of Kota Tinggi is 42km north-east of JB on the road to Mersing. The town is of little interest, but the waterfalls at **Lumbong**, 15km north-west of the town, are a popular weekend retreat.

The falls, at the base of 634m **Gunung Muntahak**, leap down 36m and then flow through a series of pools that are ideal for a cooling dip. The smaller pools are shallow enough for children. Unfortunately, the natural beauty of the falls has been somewhat spoiled by the construction of Wet World Resort next to them. Those in search of a more pristine experience should try the falls at Gunung Ledang (see that entry earlier). Entry to the falls is RM2 per person, plus RM2.50 per car.

**Places to Stay & Eat** At the falls you can stay at *Wet World Resort* (☎ 883 6222), where overpriced air-con chalets cost RM150 on weekends and RM127 weekdays.

It is cheaper to stay in Kota Tinggi. The best option is *Sin May Chun Hotel* (☎ 833 3573, 26 Jalan Tambatan), where clean, spacious fan/air-con rooms cost RM20/32 with bathroom. The decent *Nasha Hotel* (☎ 833 8000, 40 Jalan Tambatan) has air-con singles/doubles with bathroom for RM33/46. Both hotels are just west of the bus station.

For meals, you will find several decent *Indian and Chinese restaurants* in the same area as the hotels. Otherwise, try the *food stalls* near the bus station.

**Getting There & Away** There are regular buses (No 41, one hour, RM3.30) between JB's Larkin bus station and Kota Tinggi. A local bus to/from Mersing takes two hours and costs RM4.90. From Kota Tinggi to the waterfalls, take the hourly bus No 43 (one hour, RM1) or a taxi (RM12 per car). If you have your own transport, take the road heading north out of the city just east of the bridge; follow the signs marked 'Air Terjun' (Waterfalls).

### Teluk Mahkota
A turn-off 13km north of Kota Tinggi leads down 24km of rough road to the sheltered waters of Teluk Mahkota (Jason's Bay). There are 10km of shallow, sandy beach at this isolated spot. Although secluded, the beach is not particularly good, and those in search of white sand and turquoise water would be better advised to try the islands and beaches farther up the east coast.

If you do find yourself in the region, it's worth travelling a little farther to the better beach just beyond the point at the southern end of the bay. To get to this beach, continue 10km south from Jason's Bay Beach Resort; after crossing a bridge, the road becomes dirt, after which it's a further 2km to a smaller dirt track on the left, which leads down to the beach. This is a good camping spot for travellers with bicycles or cars.

*Jason's Bay Beach Resort* (☎ 07-891 8077) has four-person chalets with fan and bathroom for RM80, or RM100 with air-con. It's also possible to camp here. Be sure to bring plenty of food with you, as there are no restaurants or shops in the area.

There is no bus service to Teluk Mahkota; a share taxi will cost RM100 per car from JB or RM60 from Kota Tinggi.

### Desaru
☎ 07

On a 20km stretch of beach at Tanjung Penawar, 88km east of JB, this resort area is a popular weekend escape for Singaporeans. The beach is decent, but access is almost entirely controlled by the giant resorts crowding the seafront. Anyone with a backpack would look distinctly out of place here as Desaru is largely the preserve of wealthy golfers.

**Places to Stay & Eat** Accommodation at Desaru is provided by expensive resorts. ***Desaru Golden Beach Hotel*** (☎ 822 1101) does, however, have a camping ground, called ***Desaru Leisure Camp*** (☎ 822 1205), which has tent sites for an inflated RM10 per person. Unless you cook your own food, you will have to eat in the resort restaurants. The resort also has top-end accommodation with the full range of amenities from S$180. Prices rise significantly on weekends.

**Getting There & Away** Buses (1½ hours, RM3.30) and taxis (RM100 per car) run to/from Kota Tinggi. From JB, buses cost RM5 and taxis cost RM100 per car. A popular way for Singaporeans to reach Desaru is to take the ferry to Tanjung Belungkur from North Changi for S$18, and from there take a taxi to Desaru for RM40 per car. For more details, see the Singapore Getting There & Away chapter or contact Ferry Fantasy (Singapore ☎ 02-545 3600).

## MERSING
☎ 07

The small fishing village of Mersing is the departure point for boats travelling between the mainland and Pulau Tioman and the other islands of the Seribuat Archipelago. While most travellers rush through Mersing on their way to the islands, the town itself is pleasant and a relaxing stopover. The river bustles with fishing boats, there are some good restaurants and you can even knock back a few beers without feeling distinctly out of place.

### Orientation
From the north or south, you'll enter Mersing at the town's main roundabout on Route 3. Leading off this to the east is Jalan Abu Bakar, the main street down to the jetty.

### Warning
If your bus pulls up near Mersing's first roundabout and is boarded by people claiming to be from an official tourist information service, chances are you've encountered a rather dastardly scam. The 'officials' will probably announce that this is the correct stop for all travellers bound for the islands. Once you are off the bus, they'll try to herd you into their private travel agency and subject you to a predictable hard-sell routine. Don't be fooled: You can purchase ferry tickets all over town at the same price and, outside the high season, it is not necessary to make room reservations before heading out to Pulau Tioman.

Jalan Ismail also meets the roundabout and runs roughly parallel to Jalan Abu Bakar for 150m or so. Most of the town's hotels, restaurants and banks are clustered on or near these two streets. A few hotels can also be found across the bridge to the north and down Jalan Nong Yahya, to the south off Jalan Ismail.

### Information
Ferry tickets can be purchased at most travel agents and guesthouses around town. Two reliable spots for tickets and sailing times are the ticket counter near the main jetty, and Mersing Waterworld travel agency, also near the jetty. The Mersing Tourist Information Centre (Metic; ☎ 799 5212) has a few leaflets but is not particularly informative. The Plaza R&R centre houses the offices of most of the island resorts (you can book packages to some of the smaller islands here) as well as long-distance bus ticket offices.

Travellers cheques can be changed at Bank Bumiputra or Maybank on Jalan Ismail.

There are several Internet cafes around town, including Cyber World! (RM4 per hour) on Jalan Abu Bakar, Nasa Net Café (RM3 per hour) over the Sea View Restaurant, and Mersing IT Centre (RM5 per hour) in the Plaza R&R centre.

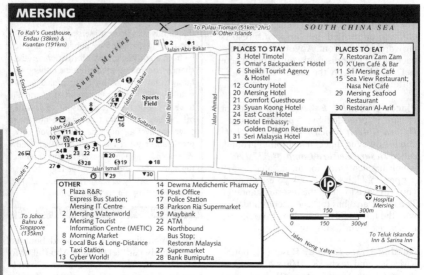

MERSING

| PLACES TO STAY | PLACES TO EAT |
|---|---|
| 3 Hotel Timotel | 7 Restoran Zam Zam |
| 5 Omar's Backpackers' Hostel & Hostel | 10 X'Uen Café & Bar |
| 6 Sheikh Tourist Agency & Hostel | 11 Sri Mersing Café |
| 12 Country Hotel | 15 Sea View Restaurant; Nasa Net Café |
| 20 Mersing Hotel | 29 Mersing Seafood Restaurant |
| 21 Comfort Guesthouse | 30 Restoran Al-Arif |
| 23 Syuan Koong Hotel | |
| 24 East Coast Hotel | |
| 25 Hotel Embassy; Golden Dragon Restaurant | |
| 31 Seri Malaysia Hotel | |

OTHER
1 Plaza R&R; Express Bus Station; Mersing IT Centre
2 Mersing Waterworld
4 Mersing Tourist Information Centre (METIC)
8 Morning Market
9 Local Bus & Long-Distance Taxi Station
13 Cyber World!
14 Dewma Medichemic Pharmacy
16 Post Office
17 Police Station
18 Parkson Ria Supermarket
19 Maybank
22 ATM
26 Northbound Bus Stop; Restoran Malaysia
27 Supermarket
28 Bank Bumiputra

## Activities

The best way to sample several of the islands of the Seribuat Archipelago without spending lots of cash is to join Omar's Island Hopping tour (☎ 799 5096, 019-774 4268). Run by the operators of Omar's Backpackers' Hostel (see Places to Stay – Budget), this tour stops for snorkelling and swimming at up to five of the islands near Mersing on a day trip aboard a converted fishing boat. The cost is RM70 per person, including snorkelling equipment, lunch and the marine park entrance fee. Also available is Omar's Overland Tour, which includes a jungle walk and stops at palm-oil and rubber plantations, a batik studio, orchid farm, traditional Malay kampung, and a latex processing facility. The one-day tour costs RM60, including lunch.

## Places to Stay – Budget

*Omar's Backpackers' Hostel (☎ 799 5096, 019-774 4268),* on Jalan Abu Bakar, is travellers' place with clean dorm beds for RM8 and good-value doubles for RM20. The owners are good sources of information about the islands and the Mersing area. A few doors down, *Sheikh Tourist Agency &*

*Hostel (☎ 799 3767)* has decent dorm beds for RM8 each, and an in-house travel agency that provides details about accommodation on the islands and transport.

Near the second roundabout on Jalan Abu Bakar, *Comfort Guesthouse (☎ 013-901 2690)* is a decent choice, with clean, semi-partitioned dorm beds for RM10 and private twin rooms with fan for RM25. This is a good option for late-night arrivals, as check-in is possible at any time.

There are a couple of Chinese cheapies on Jalan Abu Bakar. *East Coast Hotel (☎ 799 1337)* has decent fan rooms from RM15. Next door, *Syuan Koong Hotel (☎ 799 1498)* is a less inspiring choice, with rooms with fan for RM18, or RM28 with air-con.

## Places to Stay – Mid-Range

The best-value hotel in town is the popular *Hotel Embassy (☎ 799 3545),* where clean, comfortable rooms with bathroom, hot water and fan cost RM28, or RM40 with air-con. Another decent choice in this range is *Mersing Hotel (☎ 799 1004),* with rooms for RM20 with fan, or RM35 with air-con, all with bathroom. If both are full, try *Country Hotel (☎ 799 1799)*, which has acceptable rooms for RM18 with fan and RM35 with air-con. If you're willing to pay a bit more, *Seri Malaysia Hotel (☎ 799 1876)* has good air-con rooms with bath for RM70. The real attraction here is the swimming pool.

Those looking for more-atmospheric lodgings might want to try some of the interesting alternatives on the outskirts of town. About 2km south is the excellent *Teluk Iskandar Inn (☎ 799 6037, 1456 Jalan Sekakap)*, where large and airy two-person rooms cost RM90, including breakfast. The owners can prepare Malay food by arrangement. Nearby, *Sarina Inn (☎ 799 6012)* is built high on a hill overlooking the sea and charges RM60 for pleasant doubles that share a wide veranda. A taxi to either place will cost about RM5 from central Mersing, but it is also possible to call and arrange a pick-up.

In the other direction, about 1km north of town, *Kali's Guest House (☎ 799 3613)* is a pleasant place with two-person cabins for RM35 to RM70.

### Places to Stay – Top End
*Hotel Timotel (☎ 799 5888)* is the most up-scale hotel in Mersing, with clean and spacious rooms for RM98, including breakfast. The double rooms here have showers while the twin rooms have bathtubs. It's across the bridge on Jalan Endau.

### Places to Eat
There are several places around town for a *roti canai* (roti served with dhal or curry) and coffee breakfast. The best of these is *Restoran Al-Arif*, which also serves good Indian food for lunch and dinner. Another place serving decent Indian food is *Restoran Zam Zam*. For something approximating a Western-style breakfast try *Sri Mersing Café*.

For inexpensive Chinese fare, including breakfast, there's *Sea View Restaurant* (formerly the Ee Lo). Try its wild boar curry (RM6) or tasty hot-plate dishes.

Mersing, being a fishing port, is a good place for seafood, and there are several

Chinese restaurants that specialise in seafood dishes. *Golden Dragon Restaurant* below the Hotel Embassy is good, and also serves Western-style breakfasts. Perhaps the best choice for seafood is the air-con *Mersing Seafood Restaurant*, which costs a little more than some but turns out consistently tasty fare. Try the prawns with coconut sauce.

For Malaysian fare, the Plaza R&R has a small *food court* with hawker stalls selling the usual favourites. For satay in the evenings, head to the *hawker stall* near the first roundabout.

Lastly, the *X'Uen Café* is a good spot for a beer or light meal in the evening. With a pool table, dart board and decent music, this is about the closest that Mersing comes to a nightspot.

### Getting There & Away
Most long-distance buses start and terminate at the Plaza R&R, near the jetty. Destinations include Johor Bahru (12.30 pm, RM11), Kuala Lumpur (noon and 10 pm, RM16.60), Kuantan (noon and 10 pm, RM10.40) and Kuala Terengganu/Cherating (noon and 10 pm, RM18.80). The ticket booths are in the middle of the complex.

Other services, which do not originate in Mersing, stop at the Restoran Malaysia on the roundabout. You can buy tickets at the restaurant, but in peak travel periods it is sometimes difficult to get a seat. Destinations include Kuala Terengganu (RM18), Kuantan (RM10.35), Johor Bahru (RM7.60) and Singapore (RM11.10). Ask at the restaurant as arrival and departure times vary.

The local bus and long-distance taxi station is on Jalan Sulaiman, near the river. Taxi destinations and costs (per car) include Johor Bahru (RM64), Kota Tinggi (RM60), Kuantan (RM80), Endau (RM20) and Pekan (RM70). Local buses run to/from Johor Bahru (RM5.50) and Kota Tinggi (RM4.90).

### SERIBUAT ARCHIPELAGO
The Seribuat Archipelago, off the east coast of Johor, contains some of Malaysia's most beautiful islands. The largest and most

PENINSULAR MALAYSIA

popular of these, Pulau Tioman, is actually in Pahang, but is usually reached from Mersing, as are the archipelago's other islands. The smaller islands of the archipelago may not have the stunning natural scenery of Tioman, but they do offer some peace and quiet, as well as some decent snorkelling and diving.

Unfortunately, only Tioman has a regularly scheduled ferry service; the other islands are the domain of private resorts. If you want to visit these islands, it is necessary to book a package with one of the resorts, and the resort will arrange private transport to the island from Mersing.

It is extremely difficult for the independent traveller to visit any of these islands. The best you can hope to do is to hitch a ride with a group of package tourists heading out to one of the islands (and then hope the resorts have vacancies and will accept walk-in guests). If you want to visit some of the smaller islands of the archipelago, it's probably best to arrange a package at one of the resorts listed here. If you'd like to shop around and compare prices, most of these resorts have offices in Mersing's R&R Plaza.

For information and details on safe and responsible diving, see the 'Diving & Snorkelling' special section.

## Pulau Tioman

The giant of the archipelago, Tioman boasts the widest variety of beaches, great diving and snorkelling, and lots of inexpensive accommodation. For details see Pulau Tioman in the Pahang chapter.

## Pulau Besar

Also known as Pulau Babi Besar (Big Pig Island), this is one of the closest islands to the peninsula. It has a good white-sand beach on its western side and one or two secluded beaches on its isolated eastern side.

*D'Coconut* (☎ *019-271 4531*) is the best of the resorts on the island, with clean air-con double cabins with bathroom for RM165, including breakfast. The other places are overpriced and not geared towards independent travellers.

## Pulau Sibu

Pulau Sibu is quite close to the mainland and has a wide range of accommodation, much of it in the form of large holiday camps popular with Singaporean families.

Typical of the resorts on this island, *Sibu Island Cabanas* (☎ *07-331 7216*) offers full-board packages in its chalets starting at RM345 per person for two days.

Most travellers will probably prefer the secluded and atmospheric *Rimba Resort* (☎ *011-711 528*), which has its own private beach at the northern end of the island. The resort has an African theme and is conducive to serious relaxation. Full-board packages start at RM165 per person double occupancy (RM22 is charged each way for boat transfer).

## Pulau Rawa

The tiny island of Rawa, 16km from Mersing, has a fine white-sand beach, and the waters around the island are good for snorkelling.

*Rawa Safaris Island Resort* (☎ *07-799 1204*) has a variety of accommodation ranging from RM103 to RM230. With a wide range of facilities and activities, this is a good spot for families. *Le Club* (☎ *012-727 9559*) is a newer place costing from RM105 on weekdays and RM150 on weekends.

## Pulau Tinggi

Tinggi is probably the most impressive island when seen from a distance – it's an extinct volcano (*tinggi* means 'tall').

Accommodation is in resorts, although some locals may supply budget accommodation. The top spot is *Nadias Inn* (☎ *011-333 656*), where the air-con rooms cost from RM140 to RM200.

## Pulau Pemanggil & Pulau Aur

Far from the mainland, these two islands were not developed until fairly recently. With crystal-clear water and excellent coral, they are popular with divers, but all accommodation is resort-style and there are no facilities for independent travellers.

At the time of writing, Pulau Aur was wholly owned by *Aur Samudera Resort*, which sells only group diving packages in conjunction with Dive Atlantis (☎ 02-295 0377 in Singapore). Once on the island, chalets for up to three people cost RM60, and food is available at an extra charge.

Pemanggil is also controlled by large resorts and is basically off limits to independent travellers.

## Other Islands

There are several more small islands within about 20km of Mersing. These uninhabited islands include (from north to south) Harimau, Mensirip, Gual, Hujung and Tengah. The most famous of these is Pulau Tengah, which was once a Vietnamese refugee camp but is now home only to the sea turtles who come in July to lay their eggs. The island has some superb coral on its northern side. The other islands also have good coral and some isolated white-sand beaches.

There are no regularly scheduled ferries out to these islands. About the only way to visit them without spending hundreds of ringgit to charter a boat, is to join Omar's Island Hopping tour (see Activities in the Mersing section). See also Penyabong later for information on the northernmost islands of the archipelago.

## NORTH OF MERSING

There are some pleasant but shallow beaches along the coast north of Mersing. These see few visitors and some of them are good for camping, but they're hard to reach without your own transport. Off the coast, the uninhabited northern islands of the Seribuat Archipelago make for some interesting, off-the-beaten-track excursions.

## Penyabong

Fifty kilometres north of Mersing, Penyabong is the best mainland beach in the area. Several small islands of the Seribuat Archipelago lie just offshore and reward the adventurous traveller with a real desert-island experience. Among the most beautiful of these are Pulau Seribuat, with its lovely shallow lagoon and mangrove forest; nearby Pulau Sembilan and tiny Pulau Mertang Timor, with its fine white-sand beach.

**Places to Stay & Eat** About the only place to stay in Penyabong is *Zul's Guesthouse (☎ 07-794 2922)*, a funky little place with only four rooms, each of which can hold up to three people for a total of RM25. Breakfast is available for RM4.50 and dinner for RM8.

Zul and his partner run trips to the offshore islands in his boat. Day trips cost RM60 per person for a minimum of three people. In addition to day trips, he will drop campers off on an uninhabited island and pick them up again at a prearranged time for around RM250.

**Getting There & Away** The best way to get to Penyabong is to take a bus from Mersing to Endau (RM2), then take a taxi for RM15 per car. A taxi direct from Mersing costs RM25 per car. If you call ahead early enough, Zul's Guesthouse may be able to provide a pick-up in Mersing.

## ENDAU-ROMPIN NATIONAL PARK

Straddling the Johor-Pahang border, 870 sq km Endau-Rompin is the second-largest park on the peninsula after Taman Negara. The park's lowland forests are among the last remaining in Peninsular Malaysia and have been identified as harbouring unique varieties of plant life. Of these, the visitor is likely to encounter enormous umbrella palms, with their characteristic fan-shaped leaves, and *Livinstona endanensis,* a species of palm with serrated circular leaves. The park is also Malaysia's last refuge of the Sumatran rhinoceros, though they roam only remote areas of the park. Likewise, tigers are present, but are almost never spotted by visitors. See Fauna in the Facts about Malaysia chapter earlier in this book for more information.

Unfortunately, high permit fees and its isolated location make Endau-Rompin a difficult and expensive park to visit. Many travellers opt for organised tours (see Getting There & Away later) but it is possible to visit the park on your own, provided you have your own camping gear and are willing to make transport arrangements yourself.

PENINSULAR MALAYSIA

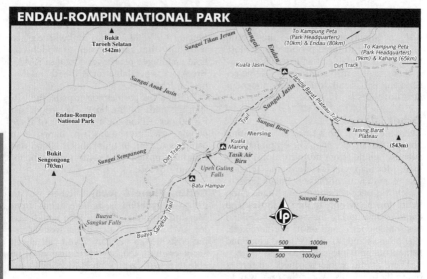

**ENDAU-ROMPIN NATIONAL PARK**

The accessible region of the park is confined to a small area along the banks of Sungai Endau and one of its tributaries, Sungai Jasin. A trip to the park usually involves a trek along the banks of these rivers, stopping to admire two impressive waterfalls along the way. The only other easily accessible trek in the park is the four-hour return trip up to the Janing Barat plateau, near the Kuala Jasin base camp.

Officials here generally require that you hire a guide to explore the park, but you may be able to get around this if you have experience with jungle trekking. Guides can be hired for RM35 to RM40 per day at the park headquarters at Kampung Peta. Other fees that you must pay at the park headquarters include: park entry permit of RM20 per person per visit; zone A permit (necessary to visit Kuala Jasin, Kuala Marong, Upeh Guling and Batu Hampar) of RM20 per person per visit; zone B permit (covers entry to all sites including Buaya Sangkut) of RM20 per person per visit; insurance of RM2 per person per visit; camp permit of RM10 per site per night; camera permit of RM10 per camera per visit; and fishing rod permit of RM10 per rod per day.

See the 'Considerations for Jungle Trekking' boxed text in the Malaysia Facts for the Visitor chapter for useful tips on preparing yourself for a trek.

**The Janing Barat Plateau** The Janing Barat plateau is a 500m-high sandstone plateau south-east of the Kuala Jasin base camp. The four-hour climb to the plateau and back is worth doing if you arrive at the base camp with time to spare on your first day. The trail starts from the dirt track behind the base camp; look for it heading into the woods opposite the path down to the camp.

The trail climbs gently for the first 100m or so, then steepens into a challenging uphill slog. Soon after starting the climb, the first *Livinstona endanensis* are visible on either side of the trail. Once on the plateau, the terrain levels out and becomes marshy; keep an eye out for pitcher plants, many of which sprout from the forest floor. There is nothing to mark the high point of the trail; simply walk across the plateau for a few hundred metres and then turn around. The return to base camp from the plateau is a quick one-hour downhill hike.

**Walking the Trail to Buaya Sangkut Falls** The main walk in the park is the trip along Sungai Jasin from the base camp at Kuala Jasin. Those with time for three nights in the park can usually reach the highest waterfall on the river, Buaya Sangkut; those with time for only two nights must usually turn around at Batu Hampar rocks or the falls at Upeh Guling.

After a night at the base camp at Kuala Jasin, the first day's hike involves crossing Sungai Jasin and following the level terrain along the river bank through the jungle for two hours to reach Kuala Marong (also known as Lembah Marong), a camp site at the confluence of Sungai Jasin and the much smaller Sungai Marong. On the far side of Sungai Marong, a narrow 300m-long track leads to Tasik Air Biru (which guides sometimes translate as 'Blue Lagoon'), a fine swimming hole with translucent emerald-green water that makes a good lunch stop.

After returning to Kuala Marong, a further 10-minute hike up Sungai Jasin brings you to the impressive falls at Upeh Guling. About 8m in height, these wide falls are notable for the water-sculpted pools in the rocks just above the falls. From Upeh Guling, it's a gentle 40-minute hike to the flat rocks and camp site of Batu Hampar. Along the way you'll see some huge umbrella palms and dipterocarp trees. If you reach Batu Hampar before noon and are in excellent shape, it's possible to continue on to the Buaya Sangkut and return all the way to Kuala Jasin in one day. Otherwise, camp at Batu Hampar or at Buaya Sangkut. Note that the sign at Batu Hampar reads 'Buaya Sangkut 2.2km'; this is a dangerous error – it's at least 4km to the falls. Because the path is quite faint, you should only attempt this hike with a guide.

The hike from Batu Hampar to Buaya Sangkut is a challenging three-hour slog over several ridges before coming out above the spectacular 40m drop of the main falls. It's possible to work your way down the side of the falls for a better view, but use extreme caution as the rocks can be treacherous. There is room to camp in the clearing above the falls. Your guide may know a way to the bottom of the falls other than to the route described here. From the falls, you must retrace your steps to return to the base camp at Kuala Jasin.

**Places to Stay** There are *A-frames* at Kuala Jasin and a *kampung hut* at Batu Hampar, but these are in a state of advanced decay and cannot be recommended (makes you wonder where all those entry fees go). *Camping* is the only real option for independent travellers or, if you're with a guide, you may be able to use the staff hut at Kuala Jasin. You can camp at Kuala Jasin, Kuala Marong, Batu Hampar and above the falls at Buaya Sangkut. Of these, Buaya Sangkut is the nicest and most remote location. A lightweight tent is the preferred option, but you can spread a ground sheet under the covered picnic platforms at Kuala Jasin and Kuala Marong – just be sure to bring some mosquito coils if you're going to sleep al fresco.

**Getting There & Away** There are two main routes into the park. The first involves taking the Keluang-Jemaluang road (Route 50) in Johor to a turn-off 5km east of the small town of Kahang (the turn-off is at mile marker 26 – 'Batu 26' in Bahasa Malaysia). From there it's a 56km drive over rough 4WD roads to Kampung Peta, the park's visitor centre. Unfortunately for those without their own 4WD vehicles, there is nowhere to rent one in the area. You might be able to convince a taxi driver in Mersing to attempt the route in the dry season; otherwise you'll have to find a local willing to drive you. At Kampung Peta, you can hire a boat (RM80) to take you the final 10km upriver to the base camp at Kuala Jasin.

Alternatively, boats can be hired in Endau to take you up Sungai Endau as far as Kampung Peta; the journey takes the better part of a day and costs about RM380 return *if* you can find a boatman willing to take you – try asking around the town jetty. Some boatmen also operate from the jetty at Nita, on a plantation road south-west of Mersing. Either way, the boat trip into and out of the park is one of the real highlights of a visit.

Because of the difficulties in arranging your own transport into the park, most travellers go on an organised tour. Mersing is the best place to arrange this; both Omar's Backpackers' Hostel (☎ 07-799 5096, 019-774 4268) and Sheikh Tourist Agency (☎ 07-799 3767) can arrange tours (see the Mersing section earlier in this chapter for more information). Per-person prices for all-inclusive two-night/three-day trips are around RM400; three-night/four-day trips cost around RM500.

Hotel Seri Malaysia (☎ 776 8690) in Tanjung Gemok in Pahang can also arrange tours – see the Endau section of the Pahang chapter. However, its tours don't hit the major sites in the park and are aimed more at Singaporean holiday-makers (with a free evening of karaoke thrown in after leaving the park).

# Pahang

By far the largest state in Peninsular Malaysia, Pahang has plenty to offer visitors. In addition to the tropical splendour of Pulau Tioman (Tioman Island), Pahang is home to some of Peninsular Malaysia's largest tracts of virgin jungle. While Taman Negara National Park is the state's most popular jungle park, nearby Kenong Rimba State Park is gaining in popularity. A different sort of jungle experience can be had on Tasik (Lake) Chini, a series of dark, swampy lakes surrounded by thick forest.

## History

Important archaeological finds dating to Neolithic times have been made along Pahang's Sungai (River) Tembeling. By the 8th century the Sumatran Srivijaya Empire held sway along the coast, until its collapse in the 14th century, after which Pahang became a Siamese dependency.

Pahang only really emerged as a separate political entity when the Melaka sultanate launched an attack against the Siamese in the middle of the 15th century and installed Muhammad, the eldest son of the Melaka sultan, as ruler.

In the 16th century the state became a pawn in the four-way struggle for ascendancy between Johor, Aceh (in what is now Indonesia), the Dutch and the Portuguese. In a period of 30 years it was sacked many times, its rich, mineral-based economy ruined, its rulers killed or abducted and much of its population murdered or enslaved. After the decline of the Acehnese empire in the mid-17th century, Pahang was ruled by Johor for 200 years.

From 1858 until 1863 Pahang suffered a protracted civil war brought about by a leadership struggle between two brothers, Wan Ahmad and Mutahir. On the death of their father, the sultan, Wan Ahmad finally won, and in 1887 he became sultan. His role from then on was reduced to a largely

## HIGHLIGHTS

- **Taman Negara National Park** – one of the oldest rainforests in the world, home to several endangered species and a profusion of exotic plants

- **Pulau Tioman** – an island made famous in the film *South Pacific*, offering excellent snorkelling, diving and mountainous jungle trekking

- **Cherating** – laid-back backpackers' pit stop, with a pleasant beach, good food and the best nightlife on the east coast

symbolic position as the British, who were interested in the state's commercial potential, had forced him to sign a treaty bringing Pahang under the control of a British Resident.

In 1896 Pahang was one of the four states that became the Federated Malay States (the others were Perak, Selangor and Negeri Sembilan). These in turn formed the Federation of Malaya in February 1948 and finally the Federation of Malaysia, as it is today, in 1963.

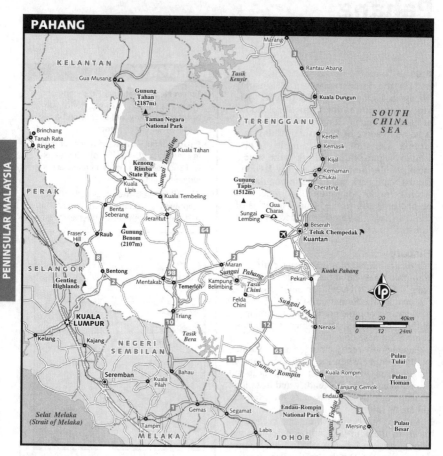

PAHANG

# Pulau Tioman

Turtle-shaped Pulau Tioman is the largest and most impressive of the east coast islands. Its sheer size (39km long and 12km wide) affords a variety of activities not found on most of the east coast's other islands. Visitors can snorkel and dive in the clear waters, laze around on white-sand beaches and explore the rugged trails of the interior.

Back in the late 1950s Hollywood got wind of Tioman and famously made it the setting for the mythical Bali Hai in the film *South Pacific*. Later, in the 1970s, *Time*

magazine proclaimed it one of the world's most beautiful islands. The crowds have been pouring in ever since for a taste of paradise; an airport has materialised, sandwiched between vertiginous mountains and the sea, and express boat services to the mainland have multiplied.

It comes as no surprise then, that Tioman today is geared almost entirely to tourism. The permanent population is small, with just a handful of small *kampung* (villages) dotted around the coast; the mountainous jungle of the interior is home only to monkeys and other wildlife. Visitors usually outnumber villagers, and at certain times of the year (usually July and August) Tioman can get quite crowded, especially in Salang and Air Batang (usually known as ABC).

Unfortunately, many parts of the island are decidedly run-down and some common areas are strewn with litter. Worse still, sandflies are endemic to many of the island's beaches and some tourists suffer badly from their bites. Check the Health section of the Malaysia Facts for the Visitor chapter for details on how to cope with bites and stings.

All in all, visitors heading to Tioman in search of an unspoiled tropical paradise are likely to be disappointed. Those who go with an idea of what to expect, however, and the energy to get off the beaten track, will still find some spectacular vistas. Furthermore, the underwater world around Tioman is largely intact and it still offers some of the best diving and snorkelling in Malaysia.

### Orientation & Information
The wide southern end of the island is wilder and more mountainous than the narrow northern end. Most of the places to stay can be found on the west coast of the island, with the expensive places clustered to the south and the budget places to the north, primarily in ABC and Salang. On the east coast, there is one very quiet beach, Juara, which has a few cheap places to stay for those who really want to get away from it all. With only one short stretch of road (on the western side of the island, running from Berjaya Tioman Beach Resort to the northern end of Tekek), transport around the island is still by creaky fishing boats or on foot, via rugged mountain trails.

You can cash travellers cheques at the Berjaya Tioman Beach Resort and some of the 'resorts' at Salang, although rates are poor – cash your cheques in Mersing in Johor before coming over.

There are numerous public phones at Tekek, ABC and Salang, but many are in disrepair. Only Telekom cards can be used for calls and these are on sale at shops around the island – though they frequently sell out. Most guesthouse owners will let you make calls on their portable phones, usually at prohibitive rates.

Bear in mind that everything stocked in shops on Tioman is shipped over from the mainland and tends to be expensive, so stock up on essentials before you arrive.

### Wildlife
Tioman is of great interest to biologists because of its relative isolation from the peninsula's forested terrain. The flora and fauna of the island is markedly different from that of the mainland. You have a good chance of seeing monitor lizards, long-tailed macaques and sea eagles. If you're really lucky, you may even spot some of the island's reclusive mouse deer.

The waters around Tioman shelter the usual technicolour schools of exotic fish and a surprising number of turtles. At Nipah, Juara and Pulau Tulai (Coral Island) you have a good chance of seeing turtles come ashore to lay their eggs.

### Activities
**Diving & Snorkelling** Virtually all the travellers centres have snorkelling equipment for hire, and there are a number of places offering scuba diving and PADI courses. Two of the more popular are DiveAsia (☎ 419 5017) and B&J Diving Centre (☎ 419 5555), both at Salang (DiveAsia also has a shop in Tekek and B&J has one in ABC). At DiveAsia, PADI open-water courses cost RM750, and two dives cost RM150/120 with/without equipment rental. At B&J, PADI open-water courses cost RM750, and two dives cost RM160/130 with/without equipment rental.

There is good snorkelling off the rocky points on the west coast of the island, particularly those just north of ABC, but the best snorkelling is around nearby Pulau Tulai, better known as Coral Island. Most chalet operators can arrange day trips to the island for about RM45, including equipment rental.

See the 'Diving & Snorkelling' special section for information about other dive sites and advice for safe and responsible diving.

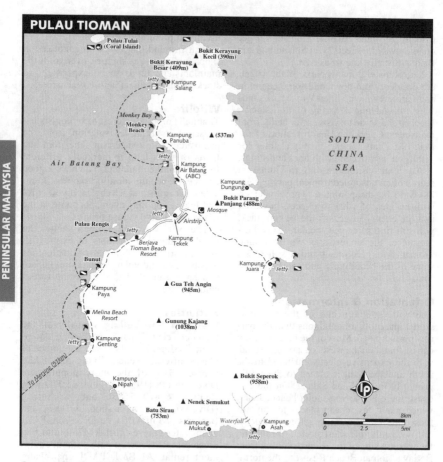

**PULAU TIOMAN**

- Pulau Tulai (Coral Island)
- Bukit Kerayung Kecil (390m) ▲
- Bukit Kerayung Besar (409m) ▲
- Jetty – Kampung Salang
- Monkey Bay
- Monkey Beach
- Kampung Panuba
- ▲ (537m)
- *Air Batang Bay*
- Jetty
- Kampung Air Batang (ABC)
- Kampung Dungung
- Bukit Parang ▲ Panjang (488m)
- Mosque
- Jetty
- Airstrip
- Pulau Rengis
- Jetty
- Berjaya Tioman Beach Resort
- Kampung Tekek
- Bunut
- Kampung Juara – Jetty
- Kampung Paya
- ▲ Gua Teh Angin (945m)
- Melina Beach Resort
- ▲ Gunung Kajang (1038m)
- Jetty – Kampung Genting
- *To Mersing (31km)*
- Kampung Nipah
- ▲ Bukit Seperok (958m)
- ▲ Batu Sirau (753m)
- ▲ Nenek Semukut
- Kampung Mukut
- *Waterfall*
- Kampung Asah
- Jetty

SOUTH CHINA SEA

0   4   8km
0   2.5   5mi

**Cross-Island Walk** The most popular walk is the cross-island trek from Tekek to Juara. While not too strenuous, parts of the walk are quite steep and hiking in tropical heat can be taxing – be sure to bring plenty of water. The walk starts about 1km north of the jetty in Tekek, near the convenience store. There is a sign at the start of the trail saying '4km' but the actual distance is closer to 7km.

The trail starts just after you pass the mosque on your left. At this point, it's a narrow track and a little tricky to follow; the best advice is to follow the power lines overhead. Soon after the mosque, you come to a set of concrete steps, which continue intermittently for most of the way to the top. Near the top of the hill, you pass a small waterfall, in which swimming is prohibited (not everyone obeys the sign).

Once over the top of the range, the trail slopes down more gradually and soon leaves the damp, dark jungle for the hotter and brighter open area of a rubber plantation and then coconut palms as you reach the coast. The walk to Juara takes 1½ to three hours. If you don't want to walk back, a ferry leaves Juara for Salang, ABC and

Tekek (RM20) at 3 pm. If you'd like to do the journey in reverse, a boat leaves Tekek for Juara every day around 5 pm (RM20), stopping at ABC and Salang along the way. Keep in mind that there probably won't be enough daylight left to hike back to Tekek the same day.

**Other Walks** You can walk along much of the west coast, but the trails are often difficult to follow, and you should take water.

From Tekek you can walk south to Berjaya Tioman Beach Resort in about 30 minutes, either by the road or by rock-hopping around the headland at low tide. From there you can walk through the golf course. Just before the telecommunications tower there is a trail to the beautiful, deserted beach of Bunut. From the end of the beach, the sometimes faint trail continues over the headland to a couple of rickety bridges across the mangroves just before Paya. From Paya you can walk south to Genting – the trail is easy to follow and there are houses along the way where you can ask directions.

Heading north from Tekek, you cross the small headland to ABC, and from Bamboo Hill Chalets, at the northern end of the bay, it's a 10-minute climb over the headland to Panuba Bay. From there it's another 40 minutes through the rainforest to a deserted yellow-sand beach known as Monkey Beach, where it continues at the other end over the next headland to the white-sand beach of Monkey Bay. At the end of this beach the trail starts the long, steep climb over the headland to Salang. The trail is not well marked here, but the undergrowth is not too thick if you lose it.

The walk from ABC to Salang takes about three hours and is a pretty strenuous undertaking. Those who don't fancy the long hot walk to the isolated beaches can arrange for one-way boat transport at most of the guesthouses in ABC or Salang.

## Places to Stay & Eat

Most foreign travellers gravitate to one of three beaches: ABC, Salang or Juara.

ABC is a long stretch of beach and, while there is a range of chalet operations to choose from, they tend to keep their distance from each other, giving the beach a less 'developed' feel. Salang, on the other hand, is somewhat cluttered, though the beach is quite good, and it is also the place to be if you want a good selection of restaurants and a couple of places to enjoy late-night drinks. Juara is a get-away-from-it-all destination. It has a great beach and just a few chalet outfits with restaurants, and everything winds down early. It's also the cheapest place to be based.

From June to August, when the island is swarming with people, accommodation becomes tight, but either side of these months it's a buyer's market. During the November-to-February monsoon the island is almost deserted.

Apart from the international-standard Berjaya Tioman Beach Resort, accommodation is mostly small and cramped wooden chalets and longhouse rooms. Chalets generally cost from RM20 to RM50, depending on facilities. For RM20 you'll get a small chalet with a double bed and bathroom. Once you start paying over RM25 you should also get a mosquito net and fan. For air-conditioning, you'll pay at least RM50 per night, but these rooms are usually much nicer than fan-only rooms. Most operations have a few larger family-cabins for those with children. Wherever you stay, it's worth bargaining, especially for longer visits.

**Resort** *Berjaya Tioman Beach Resort* (☎ 419 1000) is a sprawling place and the only international-class hotel on the island. It has 400 rooms priced from RM260, with discounts of up to 25% from November to February. Most rooms are chalet style with air-con. The hotel has an impressive range of facilities – a beautiful 18-hole golf course, tennis, horse riding, jet-skis, scuba diving and so on.

The resort can be heavily booked, particularly in the school holidays. The four restaurants are all good but, as you might expect, they're by no means low-budget options.

**Kampung Tekek** Tekek is the island's largest village, and its administrative centre.

The airport is here, and a few well-stocked shops. Tekek's beach is not among the best on the island. There is accommodation on the south side of the jetty, but most of it is in a state of advanced disrepair and we cannot recommend staying here.

**ABC (Air Batang)** ABC is a popular beach just over the headland, an easy walk to the north of Tekek. Along with Salang, it's the main travellers centre, with a string of chalet operations connected by a concrete path that runs the length of the beach. The northern end of the beach is somewhat rocky and poor for swimming; the southern end, near Nazri's Place, has the best white-sand beach.

Stepping off the jetty and heading north, the first place you come to is the *Chinese Restaurant*, one of the more competent restaurants on the beach, with good seafood and freshly squeezed juices – count on around RM15 for dinner. Next door is *South Pacific* (☎ 419 1176), a basic place offering chalets with fan for RM15, or RM25 with beachfront views. Next along is *Johan's House* (☎ 419 1359), a slightly more attractive place with chalets with fan for RM15 to RM45, or with air-con for RM60 to RM95. After Johan's is *Tioman Guest House* (☎ 419 1196), where decent standard/deluxe chalets cost RM20/35 with fan.

After Tioman Guest House, *Rinda Resort* (☎ 419 1157) has simple but clean chalets with fan for RM15. Considering the price, this is one of the better deals in ABC. After Rinda is *Nazri's Beach Cabanas* (☎ 419 1375). More commonly known as Nazri's II, bungalows are large and fairly clean, ranging in price from RM20 to RM70. The RM50 air-con chalets here are probably your best bet as the cheaper fan rooms are a little grim.

Just past Nazri's Beach Cabanas is the popular *ABC Bungalows* (☎ 419 1154), with a variety of chalets spread over pleasant, well-tended grounds. The simplest huts with fan cost RM12, while standard huts with fan and bathroom cost RM30. There's a decent restaurant out the front. The owners of this place offer some of the cheapest boat fares around the island.

Finally, at the far northern end of the beach is the lovely *Bamboo Hill Chalets* (☎ 419 1339, ✉ bamboosu@tm.net.my); its Web site is at www.pipkins.demon.co.uk/Bamboo/bamboo.htm. Perched on the rocks overlooking the water, the clean, well-kept chalets are by far the most pleasant place to stay on the island. With only six chalets, ranging from RM50 to RM100, the place is almost always full and calling or emailing ahead is a good idea. In an effort to cut down on litter, the owners will refill water bottles with filtered water for RM1 per 1.5L bottle (nonguests are welcome to bring their empties). A phone service is available as well.

Walking south from the ABC jetty, you soon come to *Mawar Resort* (☎ 419 1153), a decent place with standard cabins with fan and shower for RM25. Next along is *Mohktar's Place* (☎ 419 1148), a simple establishment with fan cabins for RM25.

The last accommodation option before the headland, *Nazri's Place* (☎ 419 1329) is popular with travellers and lays claim to the best stretch of beach in ABC. There are some dilapidated A-frames right on the beach for RM10, simple rooms with fan and shower set back from the beach for RM40, and beachfront rooms with air-con and shower for RM80. There is also a restaurant and Internet service (RM5 per 15 minutes) here.

**Kampung Panuba** Over the headland from ABC, *Panuba Inn Resort* (☎ 013-772 0454) has 30 chalets with fan and bathroom for RM35, or with air-con for RM58 to RM98. The chalets are built on a hill overlooking the bay and are quite attractive. It's certainly peaceful, but accommodation is limited and often taken by large dive-groups, so it's worth checking to see if there's room before lugging your gear over the headland (although it's not a long walk). You might also be able to convince the ferry operator to drop you right at the Panuba jetty, or you can get dropped at ABC and hire a boat for RM10.

**Salang** If you stopped at Tekek or ABC on the way, the small bay at Salang is likely to come as a surprise. The beach is beautiful, but the waterfront area is the most congested on the island. However, in terms of swimming and easy access to a variety of restaurants and nightlife, Salang is probably the best location on Tioman. It's popular with divers – two of Tioman's better dive centres are also located here (see the Diving & Snorkelling entry earlier in this chapter). The beach is about 700m long, and the jetty is towards the southern end.

There are places to stay on both sides of the jetty. On the southern side, *Khalid's Place* (☎ 419 5317) is a popular option. It's set back from the beach and has a nice garden, although there is some litter scattered about. Standard chalets cost RM55, and there are larger chalets for RM100 with air-con.

Next to Khalid's Place, *Pak Long* has newish fan rooms for RM35. Across the small creek is another cluster of chalet outfits. Most of these are cheap but grim.

North of the jetty, you'll find *Salang Dreams* restaurant and bar, which is popular in the evening as a spot to drink. Next door, *Salang Indah Resort* (☎ 419 5015) sprawls along the beach for some distance. It has a big restaurant, bar, shop and a wide variety of accommodation. Basic bungalows with fan and shower are RM35 and nicer cabins with air-con are RM90. Ask to see a few rooms as they vary in quality.

*Salang Beach Resort* (☎ 07-799 3607 in Mersing) is another resort-style operation with pricey chalets – RM40 with fan, or RM110 and up with air-con. There is also a large restaurant with lots of Chinese dishes (around RM10 per dish).

Near the northern end of the beach are two small, cheap, bungalow operations. *Ella's Place* (☎ 419 5004) has simple cabins with fan for RM25; next door, *Salang Huts* has similar cabins for RM25 and RM40.

**Juara** The only place to stay on the east coast of the island, Juara is less developed and quieter than most beaches on the west coast. The beach is excellent, though the sea is very rough in the monsoon season (November to February). This is a place for serious relaxation, since there is little to do except swim and laze away the day under the coconut trees. The best snorkelling is around the rocks at the northern end of the beach, where reef sharks sometimes make an appearance. Juara is also one of the cheapest beaches on the island, with bungalows ranging from RM15 to RM30.

About 150m north of the jetty, *Paradise Point* has small chalets with fan for RM15 and a decent restaurant. A few minutes' walk farther north brings you to the friendly *River View Place*, with clean chalets with fan and shower for RM15.

Just south of the jetty, *Kejora* is right on the beach and has clean chalets with RM25 with fan. There are two or three bungalow operations south of Kejora on this beach, but they operate only during the high season, if at all. Give them a try if the other places listed in this section are full.

The beach south of the jetty is bisected by a headland. On the far side of the headland, *Mizani* has a good beachside location and pleasant, simple cabins for RM20. At the far end of the beach, *Juara Saujana* (☎ 414 5349) has simple chalets with fan and shower for RM25.

If you'd like to come directly to Juara from Mersing, take a ferry to Tekek and wait on the pier for the 5 pm ferry to Juara. Once in Juara, it's possible to hitch a ride on the back of a motorcycle for RM5 to the more distant spots south of the jetty.

**Paya** Paya is a few kilometres south of the Berjaya Tioman Beach Resort. The beach is OK but nothing special. Most of the people coming to this beach are on package holidays, and costs are higher than elsewhere. This is a poor choice for independent travellers.

**Melina Beach Resort** Midway between Paya and Genting beaches, *Melina Beach Resort* (☎ 013-432 9066) has a lovely little bay all to itself and is a good spot for those with children or those who simply want to get away from it all. There are six semi-detached chalets here with air-con and bath for RM149 for two (the chalets hold up to four people; each additional person is RM25). The restaurant serves a variety of German food (the place is run by a family of German expats) and local food, with dinners averaging RM15 per person. Call in advance to make a booking and to arrange a pick-up from Genting.

**Genting**  Very few travellers stop at Genting, and with good reason: The beach is poor and tourist developments are aimed at free-spending Singaporeans. There is some reasonably cheap accommodation about, but most of it is resort-style, complete with karaoke. As with Paya, this is a poor choice for independent travellers.

**Nipah**  This is the place to stay if you really want to get away from it all. The beach is superb, with good snorkelling. Apart from a couple of longhouse blocks that are open only during the holiday periods, there's only one place to stay.

Prices at *Nipah Beach Resort* start at around RM30, but you may be able to bargain for something cheaper. To get here, take the ferry to Genting and bargain for a taxi-boat to Nipah (count on around RM25).

## Getting There & Away
**Air**  Berjaya Air (☎ 419 1303) has two daily flights to/from Kuala Lumpur (KL) for RM146. The airline has an office at Berjaya Tioman Beach Resort and at the airstrip.

**Boat**  Mersing in Johor is the main access port for Tioman. Several companies run ferry services to the island, all of which charge RM25 one way and RM45 return (unless you ask, you won't be given the RM5 discount on the return ticket). In theory, you must buy your tickets in advance from one of the agents near the jetty, but in practice you can buy one as you board if there is space.

Departure times vary with the tide, but are usually around noon from Mersing. For the return trip from Tioman, ask at the place you're staying for the next day's sailing times. From Mersing, ferries leave from the main jetty and stop at Genting, Paya, Berjaya Tioman Beach Resort, Tekek, ABC and Salang, in that order, picking up from those jetties in the reverse order on the return trip. Sailing time is about two hours. Regardless of which ferry company you use on the outbound trip, you can take any company's ferry on the return (tickets are transferable).

There are also several speedboat companies that do the trip between Mersing and Tioman in 1½ hours for RM30 one way (no discount for return trips). These operate from the same jetties as the big ferries and depart several times a day, making them a good option if you've missed the ferry. Tickets are sold by agents in Mersing or as you board in Tioman. Keep in mind that a ride on these boats can be very bumpy; take one of the larger ferries if you want a smoother ride.

**Singapore**  There's a daily high-speed catamaran service between Singapore and Pulau Tioman. It departs from Singapore's Tanah Merah Ferry Terminal daily at 8.30 am, and from Berjaya Tioman Beach Resort jetty at 2.30 pm. The trip takes four hours and costs S$90/114 one way/return. Bookings can be made at the desk in the lobby of Berjaya Tioman Beach Resort (☎ 419 1000), and in Singapore at Auto Batam (☎ 02-271 4866), 02-20 World Trade Centre. There are usually no sailings in the monsoon season, from October 31 to 1 March.

## Getting Around
The only regular boat service around the island is the Juara ferry, which leaves Tekek for Juara around 5 pm, stopping at ABC and Salang on the way (1½ hours, RM20). In the reverse direction, it departs from Juara daily at 3 pm, stopping at Salang and ABC on the way to Tekek.

For other journeys around the island, travellers are at the mercy of independent boat operators who generally charge outlandish prices for even the shortest of trips. A boat from Salang to ABC, for example, will cost about RM20. Most chalet operations can arrange these boats. ABC Bungalows, in ABC, offers the cheapest boat fares on the island.

Boat charter is expensive, costing between RM300 and RM400 per day.

You'll find information on exploring the island on foot in the Activities section earlier in this chapter.

# The Coast

## ENDAU TO KUANTAN
### Endau
There's little of interest in Endau, but you can hire boats to make trips up the remote Sungai Endau to Endau-Rompin National Park (see Endau-Rompin National Park in the Johor chapter). Farther north, the sleepy town of Pekan has a few attractions that just might merit a stop on the way to or from Kuantan.

**Places to Stay** There aren't any good places to stay in Endau; either spend the night in Johor (38km to the south) or try *Hotel Seri Malaysia (☎ 776 8690),* just across Sungai Endau in Tanjung Gemok, where clean air-con rooms with shower are RM75 including breakfast. The hotel is 300m east of Tanjung Gemok bus station.

### Pekan
The royal town of Pahang state has a couple of well-built white-marble mosques and the sultan's palace, the modern and downright ugly **Istana Abu Bakar**, on the Kuantan edge of town.

Much more interesting is the state **Museum Sultan Abu Bakar**, housed in a building constructed by the British for the local Resident. It has a wide variety of exhibits, although much of the labelling is in Bahasa Malaysia only. The museum is dedicated to the lives of the Pahang royal family, but there are also some natural history, ceramics and tin-mining displays. Across the street, there's an interesting display of traditional Malaysian watercraft in **Galeri Pengangkutan Air**. The museum and watercraft gallery are open daily from 9.30 am to 5 pm, except Monday (closed) and Friday (9.30 am to 12.15 pm). Entry to the museum is RM1 and includes admission to the gallery.

Sungai **Pahang**, crossed at this town by a lengthy bridge, is the longest river in Malaysia and was the last east-coast river to be bridged.

**Places to Stay** There's not much in the way of accommodation in Pekan, and most travellers visit as a day trip from Kuantan. *Hotel Pekan (☎ 422 1378)* is a typical Chinese hotel with clean but spartan rooms for RM18 with fan, or RM28 with air-con. *Deyza Hotel (☎ 422 3690)* next door is similar. Both of these places are in the shopping area about 10 minutes west of the bus station. *Pekan Rest House (☎ 013-931 0845)* has giant but slightly tatty rooms for RM30. It's 15 minutes' walk west of the bus station on Jalan Sultan Abu Bakar.

**Getting There & Away** The bus station is in the centre of town and bus No 31 runs regularly to/from Kuantan (one hour, RM2.70). In Kuantan, these buses operate from the local bus station. Local buses also run between Pekan and Kuala Rompin (one hour, RM2).

The taxi station is across the road on the bank of the river. A taxi to/from Kuantan costs RM25 per car.

## KUANTAN
About midway up the east coast from Singapore to Kota Bharu, Kuantan is the capital of the state of Pahang, and the start of the east-coast beach strip that extends all the way to Kota Bharu.

Kuantan is a well-organised, bustling city and a major stopover point when you are travelling north, south or across the peninsula. There's little of interest in Kuantan itself, but it's one of the more pleasant east-coast cities and there are a number of places of interest nearby.

### Information
The tourist office (☎ 516 1007), near the local taxi stand, has a few leaflets but is hardly worth a visit. It's open from 9 am to 4.40 pm Sunday to Friday (to 12.45 pm Saturday). The immigration office (☎ 514 2155) is in the Wisma Persekutuan, on Jalan Gambut.

Hamid Bros Books, on Jalan Mahkota, is a licensed moneychanger and also has some English-language books. The post office, Telekom office and most banks are on Jalan Haji Abdul Aziz (the continuation of Jalan Mahkota), near the soaring Masjid Negeri (Negeri Mosque).

The Network 21 Internet Café (RM4 per hour) is in Berjaya Megamall. Internet World (RM3 per hour) is in the long-distance bus station.

Mr Dobi, a laundry service near the Hotel New Meriah, charges RM6 for a full load of washing.

## Things to See

Kuantan's star attraction is **Masjid Negeri**, the east coast's most impressive mosque, which presides regally over the *padang* (city square). It's worth taking a stroll by at night, when the mosque is illuminated and takes on the appearance of a fantasy castle.

In the daytime, take a stroll along the river bank and watch the activity on the wide **Sungai Kuantan**. From the jetty near the local bus station you can get a ferry across the river (about 90 sen) to the small fishing village of **Kampung Tanjung Lumpur**.

The Kuantan area produces some good **handicrafts**, and there is a batik factory a few kilometres from the town centre, on the road to the airport. On Jalan Besar, near the Hotel Classic, there are a number of shops selling local trinkets and craftwork.

Kuantan's major attraction is the beach, **Teluk Chempedak**, about 6km from town. See the Around Kuantan section later for details.

## Places to Stay – Budget

The cheapest place in town is the grim *Tong Nam Ah Hotel* (☎ 514 4204) on Jalan Besar, where fan rooms start at RM16. *Hotel Baru Raya* (☎ 513 9746) is only slightly better, with fan rooms for RM25 and air-con rooms for RM35. It's open 24 hours, which is convenient if you arrive on a night bus.

*New Capital Hotel* (☎ 513 7276) is a better choice, with rooms for RM18 with fan and bathroom, or RM26 with air-con and bathroom. The rooms are aging but the

bedding is clean. A decent budget choice near the river is *Degaya Inn* (☎ 552 6708), which has small but reasonably clean air-con rooms for RM39.50.

*Hotel New Meriah* (☎ 525 433) has large, but slightly dingy, carpeted fan rooms with bathroom for RM28. Rooms with air-con cost RM30. The nearby *Hotel Embassy* (☎ 552 7486) is a less appealing place with fan rooms for RM25.

Near the central market are a few good hotels, including *Hotel Makmur* (☎ 514 1363), which has rooms with shared/private bathroom for RM22/35; all have air-con. Most of the rooms have no windows, but the place is fairly new and it's open 24 hours.

## Places to Stay – Mid-Range

There are some decent mid-range hotels in Kuantan, the best of which is the very good *Hotel Classic* (☎ 555 4599), with clean, spacious air-con rooms for RM55 including breakfast. *Suraya Hotel* (☎ 555 4266) is another good choice with clean standard/deluxe rooms for RM55/58. It's worth parting with the extra RM3 for a deluxe room here. *Hotel Pacific* (☎ 514 1980) is a similar but older place, with standard rooms for RM79 – overpriced in comparison to the mid-range places listed earlier. *Seri Malaysia Hotel* (☎ 555 3688) is an excellent mid-range choice, with clean air-con rooms from RM70. The only drawback is its somewhat inconvenient location northeast of the city centre.

## Places to Stay – Top End

Within Kuantan, the only international-class hotel is *MS Garden Hotel* (☎ 555 5899), near the Berjaya Megamall. The hotel has all the standard amenities, including a swimming pool. Spacious rooms here start at RM138. A better top-end choice in this area is the Hyatt Kuantan out in Teluk Chempedak (see Around Kuantan later for details).

## Places to Eat & Drink

Kuantan has a good selection of eating places. The small *food stalls* dotted along the river bank, across from Degaya Inn, are a great place to sit and watch the boats pass

# KUANTAN

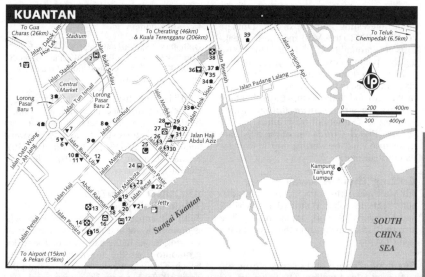

To Gua
Charas (26km)
Stadium
To Cherating (46km)
& Kuala Terengganu (206km)
To Teluk
Chempedak (6.5km)

SOUTH
CHINA
SEA

To Airport (15km)
& Pekan (35km)

Sungai Kuantan

Jetty

Kampung
Tanjung
Lumpur

PENINSULAR MALAYSIA

# KUANTAN

**PLACES TO STAY**
3 Hotel Makmur
4 Hotel Pacific
10 New Capital Hotel; Nasi
   Ayam New Capital
18 Hotel Baru Raya
19 Tong Nam Ah Hotel
20 Degaya Inn
22 Hotel Classic
29 Suraya Hotel
32 Hotel Embassy
34 Hotel New Meriah
37 MS Garden Hotel
39 Seri Malaysia Hotel

**PLACES TO EAT**
5 Food Stalls
6 Restoran Paruvathy

7 Restoran Biryani
11 Food Stalls
12 Swan Bakery
21 Outdoor Food Stalls
31 New Yee Mee Restaurant
35 Lot 66 Food
   Hawker Centre

**OTHER**
1 Hindu Temple
2 Long-Distance Bus Station;
   Internet World
8 Immigration
9 Malaysia Airlines
13 Kuantan Parade Mall;
   The Store Supermarket
14 Kompleks Teruntum
15 Tourist Office

16 Local Taxi Stand
17 Local Bus Station;
   Food Stalls
23 Moneychanger;
   Hamid Bros Books
24 Local Bus Stop for Northbound Buses
25 Masjid Negeri
26 Maybank
27 Telekom
28 Post Office
30 Standard Chartered Bank;
   ATM
33 Mr Dobi Laundry Service
36 Cave Pub & Grill
38 Berjaya Megamall;
   Network 21 Internet Café

by. Others can be found in the central market, on Jalan Bukit Ubi and inside the long-distance bus station.

There are indoor *food courts* in all of Kuantan's shopping malls, the best of which is inside Berjaya Megamall. Nearby, *Lot 66* hawker centre is popular with the locals in the evening, with stalls selling everything from satay to noodles.

There are some good Indian restaurants on Jalan Bukit Ubi, including *Restoran Biryani* and *Restoran Paruvathy*. In the same neighbourhood, *Nasi Ayam New Capital* is a good place for Chinese chicken-and-rice dishes.

The best Chinese food in town is at *New Yee Mee Restaurant*, near the mosque. In addition to the standard Chinese favourites, it serves the usual Chinese favourites and some interesting hotplate dishes. Dinners cost from RM10 to RM20 and noodle breakfasts cost around RM5 with tea. This is also a good spot to enjoy an evening beer or two.

For something resembling a Western-style breakfast in the morning, and a variety of Western and Malay dishes throughout the day, try the air-con *Swan Bakery*, which also serves a variety of fresh juices.

*Cave Pub & Grill* is one of the only bars in town and may be worth a stop, at least for its unusual interior.

## Getting There & Away

**Air** Malaysia Airlines (☎ 515 7055) has direct flights to Johor Bahru (daily, RM93) and KL (daily, RM74), among others. The airport is 15km away from the city – take a taxi (RM15).

**Bus** Long-distance buses operate from the station on Jalan Stadium. The ticket offices and information counter, as well as a food court, are on the 2nd floor of the building. Many companies operate the same routes, so it's simply a question of choosing your departure time.

There are services to/from the following cities (times listed here indicate departure from Kuantan): KL (hourly from 8.30 am to 1 am, five hours, RM12.20); Mersing (5 pm, 3½ hours, RM10.35); Johor Bahru (four daily, five hours, RM15.40); Singapore (four daily, six hours, RM16.50); Kuala Terengganu (10.30 am and 3 pm, four hours, RM9.60); Kota Bharu (hourly from 8 am to 11 pm, seven hours, RM17.20); Jerantut (10 am and 1 and 3 pm, 3½ hours, RM8.50); Melaka (1 am, six hours, RM14); and Penang (8.30 pm, 11 hours, RM26).

The local bus station for northbound buses is on Jalan Mahkota. There are services to and from Cherating/Kemaman (RM2.30), Teluk Chempedak (No 39, 60 sen), Marang (RM7) and Sungai Lembing (No 48, RM2.95). Most local buses are identified by their final destination rather than a number. You may have to wait around for a while before a bus to your intended destination arrives.

**Car** Several car-rental companies have offices in Kuantan.

**Budget** (☎ 552 7303) 49 Jalan Telok Sisek
**Mayflower** (☎ 538 3490) A7348 Jalan Beserah
**Orix** (☎ 515 7488) Ground floor, Grand Continental Hotel, Jalan Gambut

**Taxi** The long-distance taxi stand is in front of the long-distance bus station on Jalan Stadium. Destinations and costs (per car) include: Pekan (RM25); Mersing (RM80); Johor Bahru (RM180); Cherating (RM30); Kuala Terengganu (RM70); Jerantut (RM80); and KL (RM120).

## AROUND KUANTAN
## Teluk Chempedak

Teluk Chempedak, Kuantan's main beach, is quite pleasant and there are a number of walking tracks in the park area on the rocky promontory at the northern end of the beach. This was a quiet little place until the early 1970s, but now has an international-class hotel and a row of bars, clubs and restaurants. It's a popular promenade and meeting place in the evening and approaches the feeling of a European seaside resort. All in all, it makes a pleasant day-trip out of Kuantan, but if you're headed to the islands or to Cherating, there's little reason to stop for the night.

**Places to Stay & Eat** The top place in town is the *Hyatt Kuantan* (☎ 566 1234), which takes up most of the beachfront. It's got all the amenities you'd expect and a pleasant airy feel to the common areas. Room prices range from RM243 to RM301. If this is a little beyond your budget, the only other place to stay is the drab *Hotel Kuantan* (☎ 568 0026), with good fan rooms for RM44 and air-con rooms for RM55.

For a bite to eat, there are several restaurants and food stalls just back from the beach. The best of these is *Pataya*, a pleasant open-air restaurant specialising in seafood. For a drink in the evening, try the pubs on the road that heads back towards Kuantan – if you're lucky, you may even find one without karaoke.

**Getting There & Away** The No 39 bus from Kuantan takes you to Teluk Chempedak for 60 sen. You can catch it at the local bus station, or from the more convenient stop for northbound buses on Jalan Mahkota near the mosque. A taxi out to Teluk costs RM5.

## Beserah

Just 10km north of Kuantan, the small fishing village of Beserah is a Cherating that never really happened. While the beach itself is pleasant, if a little shallow, the run-down surroundings and lack of decent accommodation are usually enough to discourage the kind of long stays for which Cherating is famous.

**Getting There & Away** Buses that run from the local bus station in Kuantan to Kemaman, Balok and Sungai Karang all pass through Beserah. The fare from Kuantan is 60 sen. A taxi from Kuantan costs RM6.

Coming from the south, Beserah is poorly signposted – there is a small sign marked 'Beserah Beach' but you're better off looking out for the Mobil petrol station, from which it's a 20-minute walk to the beach. From the north, look for the large 'Pantai Beserah' sign.

## Gua Charas

Twenty-six kilometres north of Kuantan at Panching, the limestone karst containing Gua Charas (Charas Caves; also spelt Charah) towers high above the surrounding palm plantations. The caves owe their fame to a Thai Buddhist monk who came to meditate here about 50 years ago. There's a monk in residence, and the caretaker's wife can tell you about the caves.

It's a steep climb up a stairway to the caves' entrance – be very careful. The main cave is off to the right of the stairway. Watch your footing as you enter because it can be very slippery. After penetrating a surprising distance into the karst you come upon a 9m-long reclining concrete Buddha of little artistic merit. After leaving this cave, you can climb up to another cave that yields views over the

surrounding countryside – again, it's slippery so take care.

Admission is RM1. The caves are lit, but bring a torch (flashlight) to explore the side caverns, or hire one for RM2.

**Getting There & Away** Take a Sungai Lembing–bound bus (No 48) from the local bus station in Kuantan and get off at the small village of Panching, just past the sign reading 'Gua Charas 4km'. The ride takes a little under an hour and costs RM1.60. From the bus stop in town it's a hot 4km walk each way, but there's usually someone visiting the caves who will offer you a lift. Traffic is heaviest on Sunday. The alternative is to pay someone in Panching to give you a lift on the back of a motorcycle for around RM2. A taxi from Kuantan to the caves costs RM25.

## Tasik Chini

Tasik (Lake) Chini is actually a series of 12 lakes linked by vegetation-clogged channels. Around their shores live the Jakun people, an Orang Asli tribe of Melayu Asli origin. The Jakun believe the lake is home to a serpent known as Naga Seri Gumum, which is sometimes translated in tourist literature as 'Loch Ness Monster'. The best time to visit the lakes is from June to September when the lotus are in bloom.

Although getting to Tasik Chini is not that easy, it's worth the effort; it's a beautiful area, and you can walk for kilometres in jungle territory. However, you really have to make an effort to get off the beaten track. Although most visitors to the lakes travel around on high-speed motorboats, it's possible to rent a canoe and paddle yourself around the lakes (see Activities later in this section).

There is a low-key resort at the lakes, but you'll get a better feel for the area by staying at the nearby Orang Asli village of Kampung Gumum, from which you can make jungle treks and take boat trips. Boats cross the lake between the kampung and the resort on demand (RM5) but you can walk from one to the other in around 30 minutes.

**Activities** All the places listed under Places to Stay & Eat, later in this section, can arrange boat trips around the lakes. A six-lake tour costs RM20 per boat and takes around 20 minutes; a nine-lake tour costs RM30 per boat and takes around 45 minutes; and a 12-lake tour costs RM40 and takes around 1½ hours. These tours are rapid and noisy and may not appeal to some. Hiring your own canoe is a much more peaceful way to see the lakes, especially in the early morning, and dugout canoes are available for around RM5 per hour in the kampung. Other activities include **fishing, trekking** in the jungle around the lakes (ask at your lodgings for advice on trails) and **bird-watching**.

**Places to Stay & Eat** On the southern shore of the main lake, *Aseania Rimba Resort Lake Chini* (☎ 477 8037) has acceptable cabins with fan and bathroom for RM60. Deluxe fan cabins are better value at RM80 and pleasant air-con cabins are RM100. Some cabins are set aside for dormitory accommodation – a bed in a 10-bed cabin costs RM15. Outside school holidays you may have a dormitory to yourself. There's also a camp site where you can pitch a tent for RM3 per person. The restaurant at the resort serves simple food for RM4 to RM10 per dish. Accommodation, food and equipment rental are subject to a 10% service charge.

Across the lake at Kampung Gumum, there are several cheaper options. The most pleasant spot is *Kijang Mas Gumum Chalet* (☎ 422 1448, 011-950 700), which has clean chalets for RM30 and a decent dorm for RM10 per bed. It's the first place you reach as you walk up the hill from the dock. Up the hill, *Chini Gumum* (☎ 011-951 435) is slightly less inviting, with simple chalets for RM25.

The cheapest option in town is *Rajan Jones Guest House*, about 10 minutes' walk up the main road into the kampung. Rajan speaks excellent English and is knowledgeable about the Orang Asli. Accommodation is extremely basic but you can't argue about the price: RM18 per person, including breakfast and dinner.

**Getting There & Away** The best way to reach Tasik Chini is to take a bus to Felda Chini, south of the lake, from Kuantan or Pekan. Buses marked 'Cini' leave Kuantan's local bus station, near the river, six times daily (two hours, RM4.70). From there, you must hire a private car (someone will usually offer their services) to the resort or to Kampung Gumum, a journey of 12km (around RM5). When leaving the lakes, someone at the resort or Kampung Gumum will be able to arrange transport back to Felda Chini.

For a group of three or four, a taxi direct from Kuantan is another option. The cost is RM60 to the resort or Kampung Gumum. You can also visit the lake as part of a group tour from Cherating for around RM60 per person (ask at the Travelpost travel agency, among other places, in Cherating).

Another way to reach the lake is to catch a bus from Kuantan or Temerloh to Maran (RM7 or RM5, respectively), then take a taxi for the 12km ride to Kampung Belimbing; there are no buses and traffic on the road is unreliable for hitching. From Belimbing you must first pay RM10 for a boat across Sungai Pahang and then switch to another boat for the trip to Tasik Chini. The cost is RM60 per boat for a two-hour trip, including a tour of the lakes and a visit to an Orang Asli village. The price is the same if you just want to be dropped at the resort or Kampung Gumum. A boat carries four people. Needless to say, due to the expense involved, most travellers come via Felda Chini.

## BESERAH TO CHERATING
There are small resorts along this stretch of coast offering good mid-range to top-end accommodation. The sheltered beaches are quite good, but the water is very shallow when the tide is out.

*Gloria Maris Resort* (☎ 544 7788) is 11km from Kuantan, 1km past Beserah. The chalets are large, fairly clean and close to the beach. Chalets on the beach cost from RM69.

## CHERATING
Along with Pulau Tioman and the Perhentian Islands, Cherating is one of the most popular

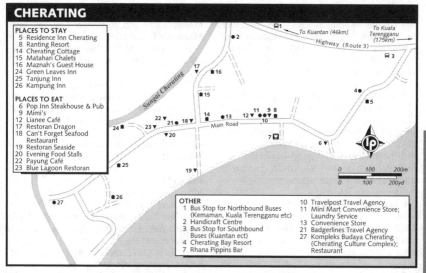

**CHERATING**

PLACES TO STAY
5 Residence Inn Cherating
8 Ranting Resort
14 Cherating Cottage
15 Matahari Chalets
16 Maznah's Guest House
24 Green Leaves Inn
25 Tanjung Inn
26 Kampung Inn

PLACES TO EAT
6 Pop Inn Steakhouse & Pub
9 Mimi's
12 Lianee Café
17 Restoran Dragon
18 Can't Forget Seafood Restaurant
19 Restoran Seaside
20 Evening Food Stalls
22 Payung Café
23 Blue Lagoon Restoran

OTHER
1 Bus Stop for Northbound Buses (Kemaman, Kuala Terengganu etc)
2 Handicraft Centre
3 Bus Stop for Southbound Buses (Kuantan ect)
4 Cherating Bay Resort
7 Rhana Pippins Bar
10 Travelpost Travel Agency
11 Mini Mart Convenience Store; Laundry Service
13 Convenience Store
21 Badgerlines Travel Agency
27 Kompleks Budaya Cherating (Cherating Culture Complex); Restaurant

To Kuantan (46km)
To Kuala Terengganu (175km)
Highway (Route 3)
Sungai Cherating
Main Road

PENINSULAR MALAYSIA

stops on the east coast. A travellers' kampung, complete with budget shacks by the sea; a handful of bars; some good restaurants and a decent beach, make Cherating the closest the east coast gets to southern Thailand.

Some people visiting Cherating settle down and stay for weeks. While the beach can't compare with the white-sand beaches of the Perhentians, the mellow atmosphere of the town keeps people around. Indeed, this is one of the few places on the east coast where you can party the night away without feeling distinctly guilty. When you do finally wake up, there are several places where you can make your own batik.

Cherating is also a good base from which to explore the surrounding area. Most of the guesthouses and the two travel agents on the main road can arrange tours to Gua Charas and Pandan Falls (RM50); Tasik Chini (RM60); and two-hour river cruises on Sungai Cherating (RM15).

### Information

There are no banks in Cherating; the two travel agents on the main road, Travelpost and Badgerlines, will change travellers cheques and cash, but the rates are poor.

Both places also rent bicycles, kayaks and windsurfers, have books available to rent, and offer Internet access (at exorbitant rates). For domestic and international phone calls, there are a few Telekom pay phones on the main road.

### Places to Stay

Accommodation ranges from basic A-frame huts, each with a double mattress and light (but no fan), to more comfortable 'chalets' with fan and shower. Most places have their own restaurants.

One of the best places for an extended stay is *Matahari Chalets* (☎ 581 9835), on the road between the beachfront and the highway. Chalets with balcony, fridge (yes, fridge), mosquito net and fan are a bargain at RM20. There's a common room with TV and a kitchen for guests' use. It's a very relaxed place and you can do batik courses here.

Between Matahari and the highway, *Maznah's Guest House* (☎ 581 9072) is a good choice for those on a tight budget. Simple A-frames cost RM16, including breakfast. It's a little run-down but quite friendly.

At the western end of the main road are two similar-looking places. The attractive *Tanjung Inn* (☎ *581 9081)* has chalets with bathroom and fan for RM45 and family chalets for RM65. Closer to the beach, *Kampung Inn* (☎ *581 9344*) has more-basic chalets for RM21.

One of the most interesting places in Cherating is *Green Leaves Inn* (☎ *010-337 8242)*. Set among low trees on the banks of Sungai Cherating, this place invites lengthy stays. The few A-frames here are very small and the facilities are quite basic, but the cool atmosphere and friendly owner more than make up for any shortcomings. Most A-frames cost RM25.

*Cherating Cottage* (☎ *581 9273)* has basic rooms with fan and bathroom for RM20, and nicer air-con rooms with TV and hot water for RM50. It's a little cluttered and chaotic.

Towards the eastern end of the main road is *Ranting Resort* (☎ *581 9068),* one of the better mid-range choices, with clean cottages with fan and bathroom for RM40, or with air-con for RM60. Room rates here include breakfast.

Continuing up the road towards the highway, you come to the giant *Residence Inn Cherating* (☎ *581 9333),* which has clean, resort-style rooms starting at RM79 from Sunday to Thursday, and at RM129 on Friday and Saturday. It's probably too sterile for most travellers' taste.

## Places to Eat

Most guesthouses have their own restaurants, but you'll find a few other restaurants in Cherating to choose from. *Mimi's* is a good spot to have breakfast and gets good reviews for lunch and dinner as well.

There are several establishments offering Chinese and Malay food. The *Can't Forget Seafood Restaurant* is a reliable place where dinners cost around RM10. *Restoran Seaside* has a good location right on the beach and serves similar fare at slightly higher prices. *Blue Lagoon Restoran* is a good choice for budget-conscious travellers; it has a large selection of dishes for around RM7 each. Other spots in Cherating

that serve Chinese and Malay fare include *Lianee Café* and *Restoran Dragon,* near Maznah's Guest House:

For strictly Malay fare at rock-bottom prices, try the *evening food stalls* along the main road.

If you don't mind paying higher-than-average prices, *Pop Inn Steakhouse & Pub* serves up good steaks, as well as other Western favourites, for around RM25.

*Payung Café* specialises in Italian cuisine and serves a variety of dishes for around RM10 each.

## Entertainment

Most of the Chinese-run restaurants in town serve beer. There are also two bars in town, *Pop Inn Steakhouse & Pub* and *Rhana Pippins Bar*. The Pop Inn has live bands on weekend evenings and, as it also serves food, is a good spot to start your night. Rhana Pippins, pleasantly located right on the beach, is a good place to rage until the wee hours of the morning. It starts to get crowded around midnight, and peaks at around 2 am. Since both these places are within easy walking distance of each other, it's possible to wander back and forth as the mood strikes you.

## Getting There & Away

Cherating is most easily reached from Kuantan. From the station for northbound buses on Jalan Mahkota, catch a bus marked 'Kemaman' and ask to be dropped at Cherating (look for a sign by the road that reads 'Pantai Cherating'). These buses leave every 30 minutes; the fare is RM1.50 and the journey takes one hour. When coming from the north, any bus heading for Kuantan will drop you on the main road. A taxi from Kuantan should cost about RM30 per car.

From Cherating to Kuantan, wave down a Kuantan-bound bus from the bus stop on the highway (Route No 3).

The two travel agents on the main road can arrange long-distance bus tickets and pick-ups (convenient for those heading north to places like Kuala Terengganu or Kota Bharu).

# Central Pahang

## JERANTUT
The small town of Jerantut is the gateway to
Taman Negara National Park. Most visitors
to the park spend at least one night here, but
the town has no real attractions.

### Information
Nusa Camp (☎ 266 1832) has an office at
the bus station that handles bookings for its
Taman Negara camp. The travel agent at the
train station has general information and can
take bookings for Taman Negara Resort.

There are several banks in town where
you can change cash and travellers cheques
(be sure to change money before heading
into Taman Negara).

You can stock up on supplies at the Jaya
Emporium or the market near the bus station. There is a good Chinese laundry on the
main road near Hotel Jelai. It provides
quick service for the inevitably stinking
trekkers coming out of Taman Negara.

AZM Internet Café near the train station
offers Internet access for RM4 per hour.

### Places to Stay
Jerantut has plenty of hotels, but the popular
places can get very busy during Taman Negara's peak period (usually April to August).

Perhaps the friendliest and most atmospheric in town is the small *Chong Heng
Hotel (Travellers Inn)* (☎ 266 3693) on
Jalan Besar. There are doubles for RM12
with fan, wash basin and a shared bathroom, and similar triples for RM18. The
owner is very knowledgeable about the
town and the park.

The small, friendly *Green Park Guest
House* (☎ 266 3884) on Jalan Besar has four-
bed dorms for RM8 per bed, and singles/
doubles/triples for RM12/20/27. Accommodation is simple, but snacks are served
and the owner (a former guide in Taman
Negara) is an excellent source of information, and arranges transport to the park as
well as tours within the park and around
Jerantut.

The cheapest hotels can be found on
Jalan Besar, south of the train station. The

### Warning
Competition is stiff between the various
guesthouses and hotels in Jerantut. This drives
some operators to use extreme measures to
'recruit' guests. When you arrive at the bus or
train station, be prepared for a hard sell.
Whatever you're told, keep in mind that there
are several places to stay in town – don't believe anyone who tells you they have the only
rooms in town!

best of the bunch is the clean, friendly *Hotel
Jelai* (☎ 266 7412), with air-con rooms with
bathroom for RM30, and similar triples for
RM40. If you have a big group, its RM60
quad rooms can sleep up to eight people.

Opposite the market, *Hotel Chett Fatt*
(☎ 266 5805) is a reasonable place if you
can't be bothered walking farther. It costs
RM15 for a fan room, and RM20 to RM28
for standard to deluxe rooms with air-con.
Right next door, *Hotel Sri Kim Yen* (☎ 266
2168) has decent air-con rooms with
shower for RM25.

### Places to Eat
The *food stalls* between the market and
train station are surprisingly good, offering
Thai dishes and seafood as well as the usual
Malay favourites. Cheap *kedai kopi* (coffee
shops) can be found along Jalan Besar and
in the buildings across from the bus station.

Head to *Nasi Ayamui* on Jalan Besar for
a tasty plate of Chinese-style chicken-rice
for less than RM5, including a drink.

The closest thing you will find to a
Western-style breakfast is the selection of
breads and pastries at *Good Point Confectionary* near the post office. This is more of
a takeaway place, but there are two small
tables and a cooler filled with a variety of
drinks.

For more-upmarket fare, particularly
good Chinese food, you'll have to hike or
take a taxi to the Chinatown area on Jalan
Besar (in the direction of Temerloh). Here,
you'll find several large *Chinese restaurants* where good meals can be had for
around RM15 per head.

PENINSULAR MALAYSIA

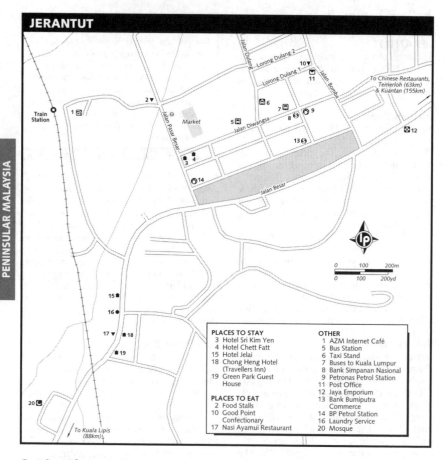

**JERANTUT**

To Chinese Restaurants, Temerloh (63km) & Kuantan (155km)

Train Station

Market

Jalan Pasar Besar

Jalan Dulang

Lorong Dulang 2

Lorong Dulang 1

Jalan Bomba

Jalan Diwangsa

Jalan Besar

To Kuala Lipis (88km)

0    100    200m
0    100    200yd

**PLACES TO STAY**
3 Hotel Sri Kim Yen
4 Hotel Chett Fatt
15 Hotel Jelai
18 Chong Heng Hotel (Travellers Inn)
19 Green Park Guest House

**PLACES TO EAT**
2 Food Stalls
10 Good Point Confectionary
17 Nasi Ayamui Restaurant

**OTHER**
1 AZM Internet Café
5 Bus Station
6 Taxi Stand
7 Buses to Kuala Lumpur
8 Bank Simpanan Nasional
9 Petronas Petrol Station
11 Post Office
12 Jaya Emporium
13 Bank Bumiputra Commerce
14 BP Petrol Station
16 Laundry Service
20 Mosque

## Getting There & Away

**Train** Jerantut is on the Tumpat-Gemas railway line (also known as the east-coast, or jungle, railway). A daily express to Singapore leaves at 1.28 am and arrives at 8.40 am. A daily express to KL leaves at 12.22 am and arrives at 6.50 am. A daily local train leaves for Singapore at 8.51 am and arrives at 5.55 pm. Another daily local train leaves at 3.25 pm for Gemas, from where you can catch another train to Singapore (nine hours in total). The express/regular fare to Singapore is RM19/15. Fares to KL are RM17/15.

Express trains to Wakaf Baharu (the nearest station to Kota Bharu on the Tumpat line) take six hours and leave at 1.28 or 2.45 am; otherwise, a local train leaves at 11.39 am and takes about 11 hours. All northbound trains go via Kuala Lipis and Gua Musang, and a Gua Musang–only train leaves at 4.43 pm. The express/regular fare to Wakaf Baharu is RM17/12.60.

Note that the National Rail Service (KTM) schedule changes every six months, so it's a good idea to double-check departure times with the owner of your guesthouse, or visit the KTM Web site at www.ktmb.com.my.

**Bus & Taxi** The bus stations and taxi stand are in the centre of town. Long-distance buses leave from the ticket offices near the taxi stand; local buses depart from the station across the street.

There are buses to/from KL's Pekeliling bus station (3½ hours, RM9.40) via Temerloh. The last bus leaves around 4 pm. If you miss the bus to KL, buses go every hour to Temerloh (one hour, RM3.50), from where there are more connections to KL and other destinations. There are also four daily buses to/from Kuantan (3½ hours, RM8.50).

The buses coming through from KL continue to Kuala Lipis; otherwise, take a bus to Benta Seberang (hourly from 7 am to 6 pm, RM3.30) and then another to Kuala Lipis.

Per car, taxis cost RM18 to Kuala Tembeling, RM24 to Temerloh, RM120 to Cherating, RM120 to KL and RM100 to Kuantan.

***Kuala Tembeling & Taman Negara*** Buses to Kuala Tembeling (45 minutes, RM1.20), for the boat to Taman Negara, leave at 8.15 and 11.15 am, and 1.45 and 5.15 pm. Be warned that bus schedules are unreliable and are not designed to arrive in time for boat departures to the park. From the jetty, buses to Jerantut come by at around 12.30 and 4 pm, but again, don't count on it.

The best bet is to take a taxi from Jerantut and Kuala Tembeling. A whole taxi costs RM18, but chances are you'll find other passengers to share. Per person, a taxi doesn't cost much more than the bus, and you don't have to worry about missing the boat.

Green Park Guest House arranges minibuses to Kuala Tembeling for RM5 per person, and can arrange transport by road all the way to Kuala Tahan for RM25 per person. Most visitors prefer to take the scenic river trip to the park from Tembeling, but if you're pressed for time, you can go one way by boat and one way by minibus (be warned, though, that the land route is a bumpy, pothole-ridden affair).

Lastly, beware of touts at the train and bus stations who tell you there are no boats running from Tembeling to the park; they're only trying to get you to take their very expensive alternatives.

## TAMAN NEGARA NATIONAL PARK

Peninsular Malaysia's greatest national park covers 4343 sq km and sprawls across the states of Pahang, Kelantan and Terengganu. The part of the park most visited is in Pahang.

Taman Negara is billed, perhaps wrongly, as a wildlife park. Certainly this magnificent wilderness area is a haven for endangered species such as elephants, tigers, leopards and rhinos, but numbers are low and sightings of anything more exotic than snakes, lizards, monkeys, small deer, and perhaps tapir, are rare. The birdlife is prolific, however, and chances are you'll see more insects – many at extremely close quarters – than you've ever seen in your life.

Taman Negara is not wide open savanna as in African game parks, and the jungle is so dense that you could pass within metres of an animal and never know it. Chances of spotting wildlife are greatest if you do an extended trek away from the heavily trafficked park headquarters, but sightings are never guaranteed.

For this reason, many travellers come away disappointed, but the greatest reward of a visit to Taman Negara is simply the chance to get out into one of the most pristine primary rainforests still standing. The jungle here is claimed to be the oldest in the world, having existed largely as it is for the past 130 million years. None of the ice ages affected this part of the world, and it has also been free of volcanic activity and other geological upheavals.

The 60km boat trip from Kuala Tembeling to Kuala Tahan (park headquarters) takes two to three hours, depending on the

TRUDI CANAVAN

**Tapir: round, shy and very big.**

PENINSULAR MALAYSIA

PENINSULAR MALAYSIA

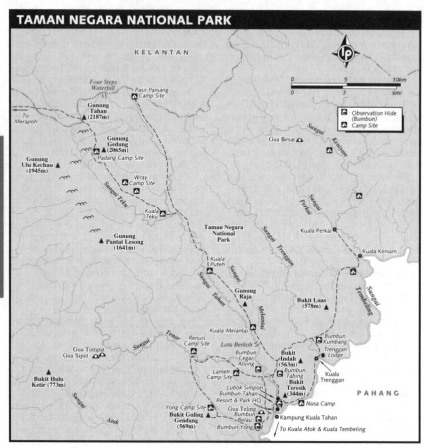

level of the river. You'll reach the park boundary near Kuala Atok, 35km from Kuala Tembeling.

Along the river, you'll see several Orang Asli kampung, local fishing people and domestic animals such as water-buffalo. You might also see monkeys, otters, kingfishers and hornbills from the boat. It's a beautiful journey.

The best time to visit the park is in the dry season between February and September, though the park is open during the rainy season, when it doesn't always rain, and the number of visitors drops dramatically at this time. The peak tourist season is from April to August.

Entrance to the park is RM1, a camera permit is RM5 and a fishing licence costs RM10. You get these at the office at the Kuala Tembeling jetty. If you're driving, there's a car park at the jetty that charges RM5 per day.

## Orientation & Information
The park headquarters and the privately run Taman Negara Resort are at Kuala Tahan. There is an information counter at the resort's reception area capable of dealing with

most queries regarding the park. The Wildlife Department (open from 8 am to 10 pm Saturday to Thursday, 8 am to 12.15 pm and 3 to 10 pm on Friday) is right around the corner from the reception area, and you must register with it before heading off into the park, or to other park accommodation outside the resort. Both the Wildlife Department and the resort have copies of the *Tourism Area in Taman Negara* map, which is OK for casual rambling but inadequate for any serious exploration. Unfortunately, outside the National Survey Department in KL, you won't find anything better. See Planning, later, for recommendations about useful books.

Facilities at Kuala Tahan include chalets, a hostel, camping ground, restaurant, cafeteria, and a shop selling a range of tinned foods, toiletries, batteries and snacks – all at inflated prices (stock up in Jerantut before heading to the park, or try the shops in the village). Camping, hiking and fishing gear can be hired from the camping ground office past the shop.

Every night at 8.45 pm a free video presentation is held in the Interpretive Centre near the cafeteria. Boats or guides for trekking can be arranged at the Wildlife Department office or at the resort, which also offers activities such as a night jungle walk (9.30 pm, RM15), cave trip (10 am and 3 pm, RM35), rapids-shooting on Sungai Tembeling (10 am and 2.30 pm, RM25) and a picnic trip to Lata Berkoh rapids (9.30 am and 2.30 pm, RM45); meet at the resort activities desk for these. Guides cost RM120 per day, whether hired at the resort or through the Wildlife Department (one guide can lead up to 12 people), plus a RM50 fee for each night spent out on the trail.

For those who don't want to pay resort prices, staying in the village of Kuala Tahan, directly across Sungai Tembeling from park headquarters, is a good option. In the village there are a couple of cheaper shops, restaurants moored on the river and a selection of budget accommodation. Access to the park is no problem; just hail a boat at any one of the floating cafes to take you across the river for RM1.

The only other places with organised accommodation (other than the hides – see Hides & Salt Licks later) are Nusa Camp, about 15 minutes by boat up Sungai Tembeling from the park headquarters; and the lodge at Kuala Trenggan, 9km by river or trail from Kuala Tahan. At the time of writing, the lodges at Kuala Keniam and Kuala Perkai were closed (see Places to Stay & Eat later).

**Planning** Although everyday clothes are quite suitable around Kuala Tahan, be well prepared if heading farther afield. Lightweight cotton clothing is ideal. Loose-fitting, long trousers are better than shorts and protect legs against scratches and insect bites. Whatever you wear, you'll soon be drenched in sweat and covered in mud. Take a water bottle, even on short walks, and on longer walks take water purifying tablets to sterilise stream water. See Basic Rules under Health in the Malaysia Facts for the Visitor chapter for information on water purification.

Good boots are essential. Lightweight, canvas jungle boots cost RM2.50 per day from the camping ground office and lace up high to help keep out leeches. Sleeping bags, tents, cooking gear and torches (flashlights) can also be hired for trekking or overnighting in a hide.

River travel in the early morning hours can be surprisingly cold – bring a light jacket or a fleece. Mosquitoes can be annoying, but you can buy repellent at the park shop.

Leeches are generally not a major problem, although they can be a nuisance after heavy rain. There are many ways to keep these little blood-suckers at bay – mosquito repellent, tobacco, salt, toothpaste and soap can all be used, with varying degrees of success. A liberal coating of insect spray over shoes and socks works best. Leech-proof socks are also an option. See the boxed text 'That Clinging Feeling' in the Sabah chapter for more insights.

The best book on Taman Negara is *Taman Negara: Malaysia's Premier National Park* by David Bowden. This book has detailed route maps and descriptions, as well as lots of valuable background information on the park.

**PENINSULAR MALAYSIA**

## The Future of Taman Negara

First established as a preservation area in 1937, Taman Negara is Malaysia's oldest and most prestigious national park. However, the largest protected area of primary rainforest on the peninsula is coming under increasing scrutiny. Promoted internationally as a wildlife haven and *the* place to experience the jungle in Malaysia, many doubt that the park can withstand the onslaught.

Since the park accommodation was privatised in 1991 and the facilities upgraded, visitor numbers have more than doubled to over 40,000 per year. The effects are very noticeable. Where large animals once roamed right up to park headquarters, sightings are now rare and the effective animal habitat area of the park has decreased. Trails around park headquarters are up to 4m wide and suffer from erosion due to the number of walkers.

The boom in visitors is not all bad news though, as the resort also provides necessary local employment, and the increased wealth from tourism, along with stiff government penalties, has helped eliminate poaching by villagers.

Poachers, attracted by the illicit trade in rare species and the high price of ivory and tiger bones, enter the park from the north. Poaching is largely blamed on Thais, but policing is difficult and few poachers are caught. The Orang Asli who live within the park are allowed to hunt and continue their traditional nomadic lifestyle, but their impact is relatively low.

Lack of government funding and understaffing means that the more remote parts of the park are largely beyond the control of the Wildlife Department. Taman Negara is home to perhaps 600 elephants and a high percentage of Malaysia's estimated 300 tigers, which are increasingly being pushed towards the Kelantan and Terengganu borders. However, these numbers are little more than guesswork as there have been no systematic studies of wildlife populations in the park in recent years.

Problems not only exist within the park but also outside it. Once animals would roam beyond the park boundaries into neighbouring districts, but increasing settlement along the park boundaries is eliminating this buffer zone, driving the animals farther into the interior.

With all the increased traffic putting strains on the park, there has been much talk of how to best preserve Taman Negara and cater to increasing visitor interest.

Solutions to the park's problems are hard to find, and even harder to implement. Though probably put forward to highlight the problems facing the Wildlife Department and spur the government to allocate more resources, one suggestion at a recent conference was to completely privatise the park. Restricting access, by introducing quotas or raising prices, also seems unpalatable as Taman Negara is one of Malaysia's major tourist attractions. Not only does it provide foreign income but it is an important educational resource for Malaysians, increasingly aware of the ecology and natural beauty of their own wilderness areas.

It should be available in the bigger bookshops of KL or through a search on the Web. Another book to try is John Briggs' *Parks of Malaysia*. You just may come across a copy of this in one of KL's bigger bookshops.

See the 'Considerations for Jungle Trekking' boxed text in the Malaysia Facts for the Visitor chapter for more information on preparing yourself for trekking.

### Hides & Salt Licks

Taman Negara has several readily accessible *bumbun* (hides), many close to Kuala Tahan and Kuala Trenggan. All hides are built overlooking salt licks and grassy clearings, which attract feeding nocturnal animals. There's a chance of spotting tapir, wild boar or deer, but sightings of elephant and other large game are extremely rare. Your chances of seeing wildlife will increase if you head for the hides furthest away from the park headquarters.

If you're staying overnight, you need to take your food and a sleeping bag. Hides are very rustic and have pit toilets. They cost RM5 per person per night and sleep six to eight people. It pays to book at the Wildlife Department the day before. Tabing and Kumbang are the most popular hides, and are easily accessible from Kuala Tahan.

Even if you're not lucky enough to see any wildlife, the fantastic sounds of the jungle are well worth the time and effort taken to reach the hides. The 'symphony' is best at dusk and dawn.

You'll need a powerful torch to see any animals that wander into the salt-lick area. It's best to arrange shifts where one person stays awake, searching the clearing with a torch every 10 to 15 minutes, while everyone else sleeps until it's their turn to take over.

Rats can be a problem at some of the hides. They search for food during the night and have been known to move whole bottles of cooking oil (one of their favourite treats) from hides to their nests. Either hang food high out of reach or, as one traveller suggested, leave some in the centre of the floor so you can see them – some of the rats are gigantic.

**Bumbun Tahan** This is an artificial salt lick less than five minutes' walk from the reception building. It's a clearing that has been planted with pasture grass and there's a waterhole nearby. This close to the resort, there's little chance of seeing any animals apart from monkeys.

**Bumbun Belau & Bumbun Yong** These hides on Sungai Yong sleep eight people and have water nearby. It takes about 1½ hours to walk to Bumbun Belau from the park headquarters, and you can visit Gua Telinga along the way (see Short Walks from Kuala Tahan under Mountains & Walks later). From Belau it's less than half an hour to Bumbun Yong. Both can also be reached by the riverboat service (RM30 per four-person boat) – see Getting Around later.

**Bumbun Tabing** The hide at this natural salt lick is about a one-hour walk from Kuala Tahan, and is equipped with a toilet, *tempat mandi* (bathing area) and bunks for eight people. Nearby, there's a river with

fairly clean water (though it should be boiled before drinking). A four-person boat to Tabing costs RM30.

**Bumbun Kumbang** You can either walk to Bumbun Kumbang (about five hours from Kuala Tahan) or take the riverboat service up Sungai Tembeling to Kuala Trenggan. The boat journey from Kuala Tahan takes about 35 minutes and costs RM80 per four-person boat, and then it's a 45-minute walk to the hide. The animals most commonly seen here are tapir, rats, monkeys and gibbons, but the odd elephant has also been spotted. There are bunks for six people here.

**Bumbun Cegar Anjing** Once an airstrip, this is now an artificial salt lick, established to attract wild cattle and deer. A clear river runs a few metres from the hide. Bumbun Cegar Anjing is 1½ hours' walk from Kuala Tahan, but after rain it may only be accessible by boat. Going by boat costs RM30 per four-person boat. There are bunks for eight people at the hide.

## Mountains & Walks
The major activity at Taman Negara is walking through the magnificent jungle. There's a wide variety of walking and trekking possibilities – from an hour's stroll to nine arduous days of up and down 2187m-high Gunung (Mt) Tahan.

The trails around the park headquarters allow for quick access to the jungle but are heavily trafficked. However, relatively few visitors venture far beyond the headquarters, and the longer walks are far less trammelled. A long day-walk will take you away from the madding crowd. Getting well away from it all requires a few days trekking and/or expensive trips upriver by boat.

**Short Walks from Kuala Tahan** Trails around park headquarters are easy to follow. They are signposted and have approximate walking times marked clearly along the way. If you're interested in birdlife, it's best to start walking before 8 am.

Heading out past the chalets and cafeteria, the Bukit Indah (Indah Hill) trail leads along

## Making the Most of Taman Negara

The vast majority of visitors to Taman Negara National Park never venture more than a few kilometres from the park headquarters at Kuala Tahan. Not surprisingly, they usually come away quite disappointed with the park. This is only natural – the park trails near the headquarters are well-travelled thoroughfares almost totally devoid of large wildlife (with the notable exception of lizards and monkeys). If you really want to experience all that Taman Negara has to offer, you'll have to venture deeper into the park. Indeed, more than any other destination in Malaysia, the more you put into a visit the more you'll get out of it.

This doesn't necessarily mean shouldering your pack and heading off on the nine-day slog up Gunung (Mt) Tahan (2187m), but it does mean you ought to consider an overnight trek or at least a long boat-trip up one of the park's rivers. If you aren't comfortable doing these things on your own, don't hesitate to join one of the multiday tours of the park that can be arranged at guesthouses and restaurants in Kampung Kuala Tahan. If you do plan on making some longer treks, you should consider bringing food and the proper equipment with you from outside the park, even outside the country, as very little is available in Malaysia.

Remember, it's a long trip into the park – it makes sense to go the extra few kilometres to enjoy the beauty of the park away from the crowds!

**Chris Rowthorn**

Sungai Tembeling to the **Canopy Walkway**. Suspended 25m above the ground between massive trees, it allows closer inspection of the higher reaches of the forest. It's open from 11 am to 2.45 pm every day, except Friday when hours are 9 am to noon. Entry is RM3/5 for children/adults.

From behind the canopy walkway a trail leads to **Bukit Teresik**, from the top of which are fine views across the forest. The trail is steep and slippery in parts but quite easily negotiated and takes about an hour up and back. You can descend back along this trail to the resort or, near the Canopy Walkway, take the branch trail that leads across to **Lubok Simpon**, a swimming area on Sungai Tahan. From here it is an easy stroll back to park headquarters. The entire loop can easily be done in three hours.

Past the Canopy Walkway, a branch off the main trail leads to **Bukit Indah**, another steep but rewarding hill-climb offering fine views across the forest and the rapids in Sungai Tembeling.

The well-marked main trail along the bank of Sungai Tembeling leads 9km to **Kuala Trenggan**. This is a popular trail for those heading to the Bumbun Kumbang hide (see that entry under Hides & Salt Licks

earlier in this section). You need to set out early and allow five hours. Though generally flat, it traverses a few small hills before reaching Sungai Trenggan, where Trenggan Lodge lies on the other side. From the lodge, boats go back to Nusa Camp and Kuala Tahan, or it's a further 2km walk to Bumbun Kumbang. An alternative, longer trail leads inland, back across Sungai Trenggan from Bumbun Kumbang to the camp site at Lubok Lesong on Sungai Tahan, and then back to park headquarters. This trail is flat most of the way and crosses many small streams. Count on six hours from Bumbun Kumbang. Check with park headquarters for river levels – Sungai Trenggan can only be forded when levels are low.

**Gua Telinga** This cave is south-west of the park headquarters, and it takes about 1½ hours to walk there, after first crossing Sungai Tahan by sampan (small boat). There is a stream through the cave and a rope to guide you for the 80m (bring a torch). It's a strenuous half-hour walk – and crawl – through the cave, and there are plenty of bat droppings that can't be avoided. You can either return to the main path through the cave, or take the path around the rocky outcrop at the far end of the cave. Once back at the main path, it's 15 minutes' walk to the Bumbun Belau hide, where you can spend the night or walk directly back to Kuala Tahan.

Heading north through the camping ground at Kuala Tahan, the trail leads all the way to Gunung Tahan, but you can do an easy day-walk to **Lata Berkoh**, the cascading rapids on Sungai Tahan. The trail passes Lubok Simpon swimming hole and Bumbun Tabing, 1¼ hours from Kuala Tahan. About 15 minutes farther is the turn-off to Lata Berkoh. There is one river crossing before you reach the falls, which can be treacherous if the water is high; don't attempt it in high water – hail one of the boatmen waiting on the opposite side to ferry you across. You may be able to hitch a ride back on one of the boats that stop just below the falls, but don't count on it.

**Short Walks from Nusa Camp** If you are staying at Nusa Camp there are a couple of interesting walks in the vicinity, outside the park. **Abai Falls** is only an hour's walk along a clear trail, and it's a great spot for a swim. **Gunung Warisan** is a small peak devoid of trees a couple of hours' walk from the camp. It's an excellent walk in the very early morning, but it gets hot in the afternoon as there is no shade.

**Longer Treks** The shortest of the longer treks is **Rentis Tenor** (Tenor Trail), which takes three days from Kuala Tahan. It's quite popular, but the trail is not always clear and a guide is needed. The first day involves getting a boat across Sungai Tahan at park headquarters, and then taking the trail to Gua Telinga and beyond for about seven hours, to Yong camp site. The second day is a six-hour walk to the Renuis camp site. On the third day you have to cross Sungai Tahan (up to waist-deep) to get back to Kuala Tahan. It's about a six-hour walk, or you can stop for another night at the Lameh camp site, about halfway.

Another popular walk is the trail from Kuala Trenggan to **Kuala Keniam**. It is normally done by chartering a boat to Kuala Keniam and then walking back to Kuala Trenggan. Taking at least six hours, the trail is quite taxing and hilly in parts, and passes a series of limestone caves. This walk can be combined with one of the Kuala Tahan–Kuala Trenggan trails to form a two-day trip, overnighting in the Trenggan Lodge or at Bumbun Kumbang (see Hides & Salt licks earlier). It is also possible to walk from Kuala Keniam to the lodge at Kuala Perkai, an easy two-hour walk.

The trek for the really adventurous is the ascent of **Gunung Tahan** (2187m), the highest peak in Peninsular Malaysia, 55km from park headquarters. It takes nine days at a steady pace, although it can be done in seven. This trek is certainly no picnic, but those who do it say it is well worth the effort. A guide is compulsory and can be arranged at Taman Negara Resort for RM500 for seven days plus RM50 for each day thereafter. Bring your own equipment or rent it from the resort. It's a good idea to organise this trek in advance, so you don't have to hang around park headquarters for a couple of days, which is often necessary. There are no shelters along the way, so you have to be fully equipped. For camping near the summit of Tahan you'll need a lightweight sleeping bag, blanket or tracksuit to sleep in.

## Fishing
Anglers will find the park a real paradise. Fish found in the park rivers include the superb fighting fish known in India as the *mahseer*, but here as the *kelasa*.

Popular fishing rivers include Sungai Tahan, Sungai Keniam (above Kuala Trenggan) and the remote Sungai Sepia. The best fishing months are February, March, July and August. A fishing permit costs RM10, and hiring a rod costs RM5 per day.

## Boat Trips
The easiest and least expensive way to get around the park by river is the riverbus service. There are scheduled departures to Nusa Camp, Bumbun Belau, Bumbun Yong, Kuala Trenggan and Kuala Keniam (see Getting Around later for details). Otherwise, boats can be chartered from park headquarters or Kampung Kuala Tahan.

PENINSULAR MALAYSIA

Boat charter can be very expensive unless you organise a group. Book a boat at park headquarters at least the day before and the staff may be able to combine individuals. You might also try asking at the restaurants on the river, which may be able to offer a cheaper rate. Boat trips to Lata Berkoh rapids, Kuala Trenggan and Kuala Keniam are all popular and can be combined with short or long walks. Prices for boats seating four/12 people include:

| | |
|---|---|
| Kuala Keniam | RM180/200 |
| Kuala Trenggan | RM80/120 |
| Lata Berkoh | RM90 (small boats only) |
| Kuala Perkai | RM200 (small boats only) |

## Organised Tours
Most of the guesthouses and restaurants in Kampung Kuala Tahan can organise guided tours through the park. You might also see what's scheduled at the Travel Post travel agency in Kampung Kuala Tahan (☎ 266 9442, ✉ the_guides@yahoo.com). It's near the police station, not far from Teresek View Motel. Its three-day/two-night tours through the park cost RM250 per person. The Green Park Guest House (☎ 266 3884) in Jerantut can also arrange tours in conjunction with the people at Travel Post.

## Places to Stay & Eat
**Kuala Tahan** All accommodation at park headquarters is operated by the privately run *Taman Negara Resort (☎ 266 3500, fax 266 1500)*. Bookings can also be made through its KL Sales Office (☎ 03-245 5585, 245 5430) at Lot G.01A, Ground floor, Kompleks Antarabangsa, Jalan Sultan Ismail, 50250 Kuala Lumpur.

You can camp at park headquarters for RM3 per person per night. Tents for two/four/six people can be hired for RM14/20/30 but be warned that tents may be entirely rented out during busy periods. Other camp sites with minimal facilities are scattered throughout Taman Negara.

The resort's hostel has nine fairly clean and comfortable rooms, each with four bunk-beds, overhead fans and personal lockers. Men and women share the dormitory rooms, but there are separate toilets

**Tour Warning**

We've received a number of letters and emails, especially from women, complaining about UBAT Adventure Tours. We suggest you check the details of its tours very carefully. Other operators mentioned in this book have been personally checked by the authors and should be reliable. However, you should always check terms and conditions carefully.

and showers. The hostel is overpriced at RM40 per person, including breakfast. At these rates you'd do much better across the river in the village.

Large rooms in the brick guesthouse (the old park accommodation centre) cost RM165 with air-con, hot water and slightly grotty bathrooms. More-attractive and luxurious wooden chalets, 85 in all, cost RM216, or RM300 for larger chalet suites. Top of the range are the two-bedroom VIP bungalows for RM600.

*Teresek Cafeteria* at the resort serves fried rice, noodles, spaghetti and the like for around RM5. Also at the resort, *Tahan Restaurant* is shockingly overpriced, even when taking into account its jungle location. Count on RM20 for breakfast and RM40 for dinner.

A final note about staying at the resort: many guests come away very disappointed with the service and facilities here. This, together with the high prices, makes staying at Kampung Kuala Tahan an attractive option.

**Kampung Kuala Tahan** The village of Kuala Tahan, directly across the river from park headquarters, is much cheaper than the resort in terms of accommodation and food. Although it's a rather unprepossessing spot, scruffy and strewn with litter, it's perfectly acceptable as a place to spend the night. Crossing the river is easy; sampans go on demand throughout the day and evening and cost RM1.

First on the right as you climb the steps away from the river is *Tembeling River Hostel & Chalets (☎ 266 6766)*, where a bed in the hostel costs RM10, two-person chalets cost RM45 with a fan and bathroom, and three-person chalets cost RM60 with fan and bathroom. All beds have nets and are fairly clean, and there's a good view over the river.

First on the left as you climb the steps is *Liana Hostel (☎ 266 9322),* which has a barracks-like but clean hostel with beds for RM10 each. There are fans in the rooms but no insect nets.

Fifty metres to the right from the top of the steps, *Ekoton Chalets (☎ 266 9897)* is a good mid-range choice, with clean air-con chalets for RM90 (unfortunately there are no nets on the windows – bring your own mosquito coils). It also has a rather unappealing 17-bed dorm with beds for RM13, and a five-bed dorm with beds for RM20. If you're after hostel accommodation, we recommend the other places in town.

In the middle of the village, *Agoh Chalets (☎ 296 7006)* is a poor choice, with small chalets with fan and bathroom for RM35. It also has a fan dorm with beds for RM12 each and an air-con dorm for RM20 per bed.

Beyond Agoh Chalets, *Teresek View Motel (☎ 266 9177)* has a large dorm with beds for RM10, small A-frame huts for RM40, and newish, good-value chalets with fan and bathroom for RM60. It also has some large semidetached triples with air-con and bath for RM80. This is one of the better places to stay. It also has a mini-mart with some of the lowest prices in the village.

Not far from Teresek View Motel, *Durian Chalet* is a rustic, woody place with double rooms with fan and shower for RM30. To get there, take the paved road uphill from the restaurants, turn left before Teresek View Motel, walk past the police station and the mosque and you'll see it on the right.

Floating barge *restaurants* line the rocky beach opposite park headquarters, all selling basic noodle and rice meals for as little as RM3. Some of these restaurants will prepare a dinner of fresh river fish if you order early in the day. All of them can arrange the same activities as the resort, usually for about 10% less than the resort charges.

**Nusa Camp** Quieter and away from park headquarters, *Nusa Camp (☎ 266 3034)* is

15 minutes up Sungai Tembeling from Kuala Tahan. It's much more of a 'jungle camp' than anything at park headquarters. Dorm beds cost RM15 (with a grotty bathroom and no insect nets) and slightly run-down A-frames are RM55. The clean, spacious double cottages with fan and bathroom are better value at RM90/100 (semi-detached/detached). The restaurant serves good but unexciting food for RM6 for breakfast, RM8 for lunch and RM8.50 for dinner.

Bookings can also be made in KL at the Nusa Camp desk at the Malaysia Tourist Information Complex (☎ 03-2164 3929, ext 112) on Jalan Ampang, or at its Jerantut office (☎ 266 2369) at the bus station. It runs its own boat from Kuala Tembeling, and a riverbus service between Nusa Camp and Kuala Tahan (see Getting Around later).

**Kuala Trenggan** About 35 minutes upstream from Kuala Tahan at Kuala Trenggan, *Trenggan Lodge* is a good spot to escape from the crowds. It has a restaurant and 10 rooms with bathroom. Rooms cost RM100 and can be booked through the resort.

**Kuala Perkai & Kuala Keniam** About an hour upstream from Kuala Trenggan, Keniam Lodge was being renovated at the time of writing and it was unclear when or if it was going to reopen. Likewise, the Wildlife Department's lodge at Kuala Perkai, two hours' walk past Kuala Keniam, was closed for repairs. Check with the resort to see if these are operational when you arrive in the park.

## Getting There & Away

The main way to get to Taman Negara is to take a bus or train to Jerantut, the gateway town to the park, then a bus or taxi to Kuala Tembeling. At least three boats per day leave Kuala Tembeling for park headquarters at Kuala Tahan. It is also now possible to go by road all the way to Kampung Kuala Tahan, just across the river from the resort and the park headquarters. But to do so is to miss the river trip, which is a big part of the Taman Negara experience.

**Bus & Taxi** See the Jerantut section earlier in this chapter for details on buses and taxis from Jerantut to Kuala Tembeling. Alternatively, from KL, a direct minibus (RM25) to the Kuala Tembeling jetty leaves daily at 8 am from the Hotel Istana in the Golden Triangle. The ticket office (☎ 03-245 5585, fax 245 5430) is across the street in the Kompleks Antarabangsa, next to the Hilton. The minibus leaves Kuala Tembeling for KL at 1.30 pm (tickets can be purchased at the Travel Post travel agency in Kampung Kuala Tahan).

**Car** A rough road now goes all the way from Jerantut to Kampung Kuala Tahan. The road is unsealed much of the way and, though negotiable by car when dry, it is recommended only for 4WD vehicles. The Green Park Guest House (see Jerantut earlier in this chapter) can organise transport to the park this way. Places to stay in Kuala Tahan can arrange a trip out on a local minibus that goes to Jerantut most mornings. In either direction, the ride costs RM25 per person, though you may be able to find cheaper rides from Kuala Tahan to Jerantut if you're willing to share the ride with school children. Though slightly quicker than the boat, the road is less interesting and much bumpier.

**Walking** You can walk into or out of the park via Merapoh, at the Pahang-Kelantan border. The trail from Merapoh joins the Gunung Tahan trail, adding another two days to the Gunung Tahan trek (see Longer Walks under Mountains & Walks earlier). Guides are compulsory and can be hired in Kuala Lipis to take you in (contact Mr Tuah in Kuala Lipis at ☎ 312 3277), but it is easier to arrange a guide at the park for the walk out (contact the Wildlife Department at the resort). It is also possible to enter or exit the park by walking over the mountains on the Pahang-Terengganu border and navigating the upper reaches of Sungai Tembeling by riverboat. Contact the Ping Anchorage in Kuala Terengganu (☎ 09-626 2020) for details and guides.

**Boat** The main entry point into the park is by riverboat from Kuala Tembeling, 18km north of Jerantut. Boats leave from the jetty, 500m west of the turn-off to the small village of Kuala Tembeling. Both regular boats and speedboats make the journey upriver. Be warned that services may be irregular during the November-to-February rainy season.

Regular boats depart each day at 9 am and 2 pm (2.30 pm on Friday) and speedboats depart at 1 pm. Boats are operated by the resort and Nusa Camp, whose boats also stop at park headquarters before continuing to Nusa Camp, so you can take either service regardless of where you stay. At Tembeling, the resort has an office up the steps above the jetty, and Nusa Camp has one near the parking area.

Regular boats take between two and three hours to make the journey upstream from Kuala Tembeling to park headquarters at Kuala Tahan, depending on how swiftly the river is flowing. Speedboats do the trip in one hour.

On the return journey, regular boats leave Kuala Tahan at 9 am and 2 pm (2.30 pm on Friday) and take two to 2½ hours; speedboats leave at 10 am and do the trip in about an hour. Regular boats cost RM19 each way and speedboats RM30; there is no discount for return tickets.

## Getting Around

The resort has daily boats that go upriver to Kuala Trenggan at 10 am and 2.30 pm for RM12 per person. In the reverse direction, boats leave Kuala Trenggan at 11.15 am and 3.15 pm. These services are intended for resort guests only and cost RM12 each way.

Nusa Camp also runs riverboat services upriver to Kuala Trenggan and downriver to Bumbun Belau and Bumbun Yong. Check with Nusa Camp or the resort for times and prices, as they vary considerably by season.

Keep in mind that these regularly scheduled riverboat services run pretty much on time during the peak season, but may be dropped entirely during the rainy season. Again, it's best to ask at Nusa Camp or the resort for up-to-the-minute information.

In addition to these boat trips, you can arrange private boat trips at the Wildlife Department, at the resort or at the restaurants

PENINSULAR MALAYSIA

in Kampung Kuala Tahan (the latter are usually 10% cheaper).

## KUALA LIPIS
At the confluence of the Lipis and Jelai rivers, Kuala Lipis is a small town with a strong colonial past. The centre of town, with fine rows of shophouses down the main street, is the busy Chinese commercial district. Farther south on the hilly outskirts, Kuala Lipis has a few reminders from the days when it was the most important town in Pahang.

Kuala Lipis was a gold-mining centre long before the British arrived in 1887, but its heyday began in 1898 when it became the capital of Pahang. Grand colonial buildings date from this period, and trade increased when the railway came through in 1924.

In 1955 the capital shifted to Kuantan, and Kuala Lipis went into decline. It is a sleepy town, but new construction and the delights of a shopping mall are signs of new wealth. The long-closed gold mines have been re-opened with the help of new technology.

Kuala Lipis makes a pleasant enough overnight stop, but the main reason to visit is to make a jungle trek in the nearby Kenong Rimba State Park (see Kenong Rimba State Park later in this chapter).

## Information
The so-called Tourist Information Centre at the train station is a private travel agent that sells its own trips to Kenong Rimba, but you can get a map of the town and have basic queries answered. The post office and a branch of Maybank are conveniently near the train station.

## Things to See & Do
Colonial-architecture buffs will appreciate the imposing **District Offices**, on a hill 1km south of the centre of town. The offices overlook the exclusive **Clifford School**, a grand public building that began life as the Anglo-Chinese School in 1913 and was later renamed after Sir Hugh Clifford, the second British Resident of Pahang.

The road next to the school leads up the hill to the **Pahang Club**, a sprawling wooden bungalow with wide, open verandas. With its planters chairs and hunting trophies, it clings to its colonial club traditions in the face of decay.

The **Rest House**, on another hill facing the District Offices, is a large, gracious building, once home to the British Resident. It houses a small museum in the foyer chronicling the town's history.

If you're in town on Friday evening, be sure to visit the excellent **night market** held in the parking lot next to the bus station.

## Places to Stay
Most of the hotels in town are on Jalan Besar (the main street) and Jalan Jelai (the street by the river), both of which are a short walk from the bus and train stations.

On Jalan Besar, on the right as you leave the train station, *Hotel Tong Kok* (☎ 312 1027) has single/double rooms for RM12/15 with fan and common bathroom. The reception is in the restaurant downstairs. Just two doors down, *Hotel London* (☎ 312 1618) is a similar place with basic fan rooms with common bathroom for RM15. Of the two, Hotel Tong Kok is probably a better choice.

Also on Jalan Besar, *Appu's Guesthouse* (☎ 312 3142) is a popular spot with travellers. Dorm beds cost RM7, fan rooms from RM15 and air-con rooms from RM30. To get there from the station, take a left on Jalan Besar and walk about 50m; it's on the right.

Down by the river, *Hotel Jelai* (☎ 312 1192, 44 Jalan Jelai) is a clean hotel with a variety of rooms costing from RM18 with fan to RM45 with air-con. This is probably the best value in town.

The fanciest hotel is *Lipis Inn* (☎ 312 5888) on Jalan Lipis Benta. Standard rooms here cost RM88, including breakfast, but you'd do almost as well at Hotel Jelai for half the price. It is near the Rest House, at the bottom of the hill.

## Places to Eat
For such a small town, Kuala Lipis has surprisingly good food, most of which is Chinese, reflecting the area's largely Chinese population. If you head straight out of the

PENINSULAR MALAYSIA

PENINSULAR MALAYSIA

station, you'll soon come to a covered alley heading down to the river. This is the culinary centre of Kuala Lipis and is filled with *small restaurants*. Many of these open only for breakfast and lunch, but some stay open for dinner as well. The best place is the *no-name joint* in the small alley that intersects the covered alley about halfway up. This place is only open for dinner and it serves some remarkably delicious stir-fries at bargain prices. Otherwise, there are plenty of *coffee shops* on Jalan Besar.

## Getting There & Away

Six buses per day run between Kuala Lipis and KL's Pekeliling bus station from 8 am to 6 pm (RM8). There are two departures daily to Kuantan (RM14), at 8 am and 3 pm. Two local buses go daily to Gua Musang (RM6.30), at 8 am and 1 pm, from where you can catch onward buses to Kota Bharu.

There is an express train to Singapore (eight hours, RM21) at 12.32 am, and a local train at 7.31 am. There is also an 11.26 pm express to KL (eight hours, RM18). Any Singapore-, KL- or Gemas-bound train will stop at Jerantut, the closest station for travellers on their way to Taman Negara National Park.

Express trains to Tumpat (five hours) leave at 2.31 and 3.38 am (RM16). A slow but interesting local ('jungle') train departs at 1.10 pm and takes eight hours to Wakaf Baharu, the closest station to Kota Bharu (RM16).

Taxis leave from the bus station for KL (RM100), Jerantut (RM40), Gua Musang (RM48), Temerloh (RM100), Kota Bharu (RM200) and Kuantan (RM150); these prices are per car.

## KENONG RIMBA STATE PARK

This 120 sq km forest park is a sprawling area of lowland forest rising to the limestone foothills bordering Taman Negara. The park can be explored on good three- or four-day jungle treks organised out of Kuala Lipis. The loop trail through the park provides an excellent opportunity to experience the jungle at close hand, and at affordable prices. Kenong Rimba is attracting an increasing number of visitors, but the

trail is still relatively untrammelled. See the 'Considerations for Jungle Trekking' boxed text in the Malaysia Facts for Visitor chapter for information on preparing for jaunts through the jungle.

Despite fanciful local claims that the park is a haven for elephants, tigers and rhinos escaping from over-touristed Taman Negara, big mammals are rare. Monkeys, wild pigs, squirrels, civets and possibly nocturnal tapir are all you should expect to see.

A permit from the District Forest Office is not required, contrary to what you may be told in Kuala Lipis, but you must be accompanied by a registered guide (see Organised Tours later).

## Walking the Trail

Access to Kenong Rimba is from a jetty on Sungai Pahang called Jeti Tanjung Kiara (see Getting There & Away later). From the jetty it is a 30-minute walk to the park entrance along the road through Kampung Dusun, which is just a scattering of a few houses and one small shop. Farther on from the shop, past the house with the 'souvenirs' sign, a side trail to the right leads to three **caves** – Gua Batu Tangga, Gua Batu Tangkup and Gua Batu Telahup. A number of confusing trails go through the swampy forest here. The guided trips include an exploration of the caves. The main trail eventually rejoins the road right at the entrance to the park, where there is a gate and a footbridge over a stream.

If you walk for another 30 minutes the trail brings you to **Gunung Kesong**, a large limestone outcrop. The forest department has a hut here. Sheltered by the hill, some of the trees here are enormous. Gunung Kesong contains a number of caves, the most impressive being **Gua Hijau**, the 'Bat Cave', on a side trail around to the right (east) across two bridges. It is a large cavern with hundreds of small bats hanging from the ceiling.

The trail leads north from Gunung Kesong through lowland forest to the waterfall of **Lata Kenong**, better known as the 'Seven Steps'. It is a three- to four-hour walk following Sungai Kenong and crosses small streams. About an hour before the falls is the first of two log bridges across the river that require something of a balancing act to negotiate. The less sure-footed can straddle their way across. The trail then crosses the foothills to the huts at the Kenong camp site just before the falls, a series of cascades.

From Lata Kenong, the trail continues up and down more hills with other river crossings to **Gunung Putih**. Though no mountain climbing is involved, this is the most strenuous part of the trek, taking about five hours and passing through some impressive forest. Gunung Putih is another rocky, cave-ridden outcrop that can be climbed via a side trail.

The main trail continues past Gunung Putih through the foothills, back to the lowland forest. Another side trail leads to a nearby **Orang Asli village**, home of the Batek people. The main trail leads back to Gunung Kesong, about four hours all up from Gunung Putih.

There are other side-trips to make in the park, including a visit to the Lata Babi waterfall, and to Gua Batu Tinggi, across the river from Kampung Dusun.

## Organised Tours

Guides are compulsory for entry to the park and can be arranged in Kuala Lipis.

The cheapest organised tours are offered by Appu of Appu's Guesthouse (see Places to Stay under Kuala Lipis earlier). Appu charges RM50 per person per day plus RM140 for the boat to and from Kuala Lipis and a RM4.50 per-person per-night camping fee.

Another popular operator is Persona Rimba Camp (☎ 312 5032) in the Stesyen building opposite the Kuala Lipis train station. Its camping tours of the park cost RM140 per person for three-day/two-night tours and RM185 per person for four-day/three-night tours. Mr Tuah (☎ 312 3277) at the Tourist Information Centre in the Kuala Lipis train station runs similar trips for RM200 and RM250 per person.

Prices for these tours include food, guide and all expenses in the park. These are no-frills jungle experiences – you camp in the park but all equipment and cooking is provided. Trips go when enough people are interested, usually every two or three days, or you can ring ahead to make a booking.

Considering the difficulties in locating a guide not affiliated with the organisations mentioned here, and all the costs involved, you won't save much money by organising the trip yourself. If, however, you would like to do so, these tour operators can put you in contact with guides and you can negotiate your own prices, itineraries and arrangements.

## Getting There & Away

Access to Kenong Rimba is from Kuala Lipis on southbound local trains to Batu Sembilan (Mile 9), a 30-minute trip. These depart Kuala Lipis daily at 7.31 am and 1.43 pm. From Batu Sembilan, hire a boat (RM20 per person) to Jeti Tanjung Kiara, just across the river from Kampung Kuala Kenong. Alternatively, on Saturday at noon there's a direct boat from Kuala Lipis to Jeti Tanjung Kiara for RM5 per person. In the reverse direction, this boat departs from Jeti Tanjung Kiara on Saturday mornings at around 7 am. For directions from Jeti Tanjung Kiara into the park, see Walking the Trail earlier.

## RAUB

You may find yourself in this large crossroads town getting transport connections to Bukit Fraser (Fraser's Hill) in Selangor, or to Kuala Lipis. From Raub (pronounced 'Rob'), frequent buses also go to KL's Pekeliling bus station.

Raub has a few cheap hotels on the main road, including the very basic *Hotel Raub (57 Jalan Kuala Lipis),* where singles/doubles cost RM15/22. The more gracious *Rumah Persinggahan (Rest House; 355 5230)* has large rooms for RM65.

## TEMERLOH

Temerloh is an old town on the banks of the enormous Sungai Pahang. It has a hint of colonial style and a colourful Sunday market. New industrial estates on the outskirts point to the future, and Temerloh is pressing to supersede Kuantan as the state capital. As the main city of central Pahang, it is a transport hub, the only real reason to visit.

The train station is 12km away at **Mentakab**, a thriving satellite of Temerloh that has a bustling nightly market.

## Places to Stay

To get to the first two hotels listed here, start with your back to the bus station, walk left, past the taxi stand, and continue up to the main street where you take a right and continue up to the second street on the right, Jalan Tengku Bakar. Fifty metres down this street you'll find *Hotel Isis (☎ 296 3136)*, which has rooms with fans and a common bath for RM20, or RM28 with air-con and bath. Farther along, *New Ban Hin Hotel (☎ 296 2331)* has similar rooms for RM16/28. Of these, Hotel Isis is the better choice.

One kilometre from the bus station, past the mosque, the old *Rumah Rehat Temerloh (Temerloh Rest House; ☎ 296 3218)* on Jalan Datok Hamzah has large and well-appointed rooms with air-con, hot water and TV for RM59.50. Next door, *Seri Malaysia Hotel (☎ 296 5776)* is a new and more luxurious hotel with rooms from RM79, including breakfast.

## Getting There & Away

Temerloh's bus station is central, about 400m from the budget hotel area. Buses go to all parts of the peninsula, including: Kota Bharu (eight hours, RM23) at 10 am and 10 pm; Melaka (four hours, RM8.50) at 9 and 10.15 am and 5 pm; and Penang (RM30) at 10.30 pm. Buses to Jerantut (RM3.50) leave every half-hour between 6 am and 6.45 pm. Buses to KL's Pekeliling bus station (RM6.10) leave almost every hour between 8 am and 8 pm, and there are hourly buses to Kuantan (two hours, RM5.70).

Taxis at the bus station go to Mentakab (RM6), Jerantut (RM24), Kuantan (RM48) and KL (RM60); these prices are per car.

Checking out a sea whip and a sea fan.

Seascape off Pulau Tioman.

Pulau Sipadan: awe-inspiring deep diving.

Why, hello, bicolour blenny.

Soft coral trees, Pulau Layang Layang.

# DIVING & SNORKELLING

 Surrounded by the waters of the Celebes Sea and the South China Sea to the east and the Strait of Melaka to the west, Malaysia has some of the best diving in South-East Asia. While not as cheap as Thailand nor as spectacular as Indonesia, reasonable prices, good variety and easy access make diving in Malaysia a good choice for first-timers and old hands.

Located in a series of marine parks established in the 1970s and 1980s, most of Malaysia's dive sites are now protected from the destructive activities that wreaked havoc on coral reefs in the past, such as dynamite fishing, collection of rare species and pollution from motorboat engines. Reefs are regenerating and the diving industry is booming.

Island-based boat dives are the most common, but a few areas, like Sabah's Pulau Sipadan (Sipadan Island), have some great sites right off the beach. Also increasing is the number of live-aboards that take divers to previously inaccessible spots. Most sites are over fairly shallow reefs, but there are also a couple of islands with deep drop-offs and even a few wreck dives in Malaysian Borneo.

The standards of diving facilities in Malaysia are generally quite high and equipment rental is widely available. Most places offer instruction leading to Professional Association of Diving Instructors (PADI) certification (which will then allow you to dive) and this certification is almost universally recognised. While it is possible simply to show up and dive at some of the larger dive centres like Pulau Tioman, it is usually a good idea to make some arrangements in advance, if only to avoid waiting a day or two before starting.

## EQUIPMENT

Although you can hire equipment through dive operators, many divers prefer to bring their own mask, snorkel and fins. They may also carry their own regulator, depth gauge and buoyancy control device (BCD). You don't really need a wetsuit in tropical waters to keep you at a comfortable temperature, but it will protect you from cuts, grazes and stings. Coral cuts are particularly prone to infection, so it's best to prevent them. A 4mm wetsuit is considered ideal for the tropics and a Lycra skin is also suitable in the right water conditions. Check what equipment you'll need with the boat operator when you book your dive.

Serious snorkellers are advised to bring their own equipment, at least mask and snorkel. Rental fees average around RM10 per day.

## PRICES

Most dive centres charge around RM160 for two dives, including equipment rental (RM130 without rental). PADI open-water courses average around RM800. Many resorts and dive operators also offer all-inclusive dive packages, which vary widely in price.

**Title page:** Diving on the wreck MV *Tung Hwang* (Photograph by Michael Aw).

## BOOKS

Jack Jackson's *The Dive Sites of Malaysia and Singapore* has detailed information on preparation for diving and snorkelling, and the individual sites in this region.

## DIVE SEASONS

The north-east monsoon brings strong winds and rain to the east coast of Peninsular Malaysia from early November to late February, during which time most dive centres simply shut down. Visibility improves after the monsoon, peaking in August and September. On the west coast conditions are reversed, and the best diving is from September to March.

In Malaysian Borneo the monsoons are less pronounced and rain falls more evenly throughout the year. However, the same general seasons apply, with the best diving on the east coast from May to November and on the west from October to March.

## CONSIDERATIONS FOR RESPONSIBLE DIVING

The popularity of diving is placing immense pressure on many sites in Malaysia. Please consider the following tips when diving or snorkelling and help preserve the ecology and beauty of the reefs:

- Do not use anchors on the reef, and take care not to ground boats on coral. Encourage dive operators and regulatory bodies to establish permanent moorings at popular dive sites.
- Avoid touching living marine organisms with your body or dragging equipment across the reef. Polyps can be damaged by even the gentlest contact. Never stand on coral, even if it looks solid and robust. If you must hold onto the reef, only touch exposed rock or dead coral.
- Be conscious of your fins. Even without contact the surge from heavy fin strokes near the reef can damage delicate organisms. When treading water in shallow reef areas, take care not to kick up clouds of sand. Settling sand can easily smother the delicate organisms of the reef.
- Practise and maintain proper buoyancy control. Major damage can be done by divers descending too fast and colliding with the reef. Make sure you are correctly weighted and that your weight belt is positioned so that you stay horizontal. If you have not dived for a while, have a practice dive in a pool before taking to the reef. Be aware that buoyancy can change over the period of an extended trip: initially you may breathe harder and need more weight; a few days later you may breathe more easily and need less weight.
- Take great care in underwater caves. Spend as little time within them as possible as your air bubbles may be caught within the roof and thereby leave previously submerged organisms high and dry. Taking turns to inspect the interior of a small cave will lessen the chances of damaging contact.
- Resist the temptation to collect or buy coral or shells. Apart from the ecological damage, taking home marine souvenirs depletes the beauty of a site and spoils the enjoyment of others. The same goes for marine archaeological sites (mainly shipwrecks). Respect their integrity; some sites are even protected from looting by law.
- Ensure that you take home all your rubbish and any litter you may find. Plastics in particular are a serious threat to marine life. Turtles can mistake plastic for jellyfish and eat it.

- Resist the temptation to feed fish. You may disturb their normal eating habits, encourage aggressive behaviour or feed them food that is detrimental to their health.
- Minimise your disturbance of marine animals. In particular, do not ride on the backs of turtles as this causes them great anxiety.

## DIVE SITES

Most of Peninsular Malaysia's dive sites are on the east coast. These include, working north to south, Pulau Perhentian, Pulau Redang, Pulau Kapas, Pulau Tioman and the many smaller islands of the Seribuat Archipelago. On the west coast of the peninsula, Pulau Payar, 30km south of Langkawi, offers decent diving for those who can't make it to the east coast.

In Malaysian Borneo, off Sabah, you'll find the islands of Tunku Abdul Rahman National Park, Pulau Labuan and the famous Pulau Sipadan. Those with more money and time can also try Pulau Layang Layang, 300km north of Kota Kinabalu, in the disputed Spratly chain. In Sarawak, diving is limited to a few shallow sites off Miri.

Snorkelling is possible at all the places listed in this section. However, some places are more snorkel-friendly than others – the Perhentians, Kapas and Tioman are inexpensive and popular options. Others, like

### Pre-Dive Safety Guidelines

Before embarking on a scuba diving, skin diving or snorkelling trip, give careful consideration to the following guidelines to ensure a safe, as well as enjoyable, experience. You should:

- Possess a current diving certification card from a recognised scuba diving instructional agency (if you are scuba diving).
- Be sure you are healthy and feel comfortable diving.
- Obtain reliable information about physical and environmental conditions at the dive site, for example from a reputable local dive operation.
- Be aware of local laws, regulations, and etiquette about marine life and environment.
- Dive at sites within your experience level; if available, engage the services of a competent, professionally trained dive instructor or dive master.

Underwater conditions vary significantly from one region, or even site, to another. Seasonal changes can significantly alter any site and dive conditions. These differences influence the way divers dress for a dive and what diving techniques they use.

Regardless of location, there are special requirements for diving in each particular area. Before your dive, ask about the environmental characteristics that can affect your diving and how local, trained divers deal with these considerations.

Redang and Sipadan, are more dive-oriented. Indeed, it makes little sense to pay the high prices involved in getting to these dive meccas if you are not going to dive.

There's a RM5 entry fee to dive in any of Malaysia's marine parks, but there's often no-one around to collect the money.

## Peninsular Malaysia

**East Coast** Dive sites off the east coast of Peninsular Malaysia include the following:

***Pulau Perhentian*** Twenty-one kilometres off the coast of northern Terengganu, the two islands of the Perhentian group (Besar and Kecil) offer some of the most accessible diving in Malaysia. Shallow coral gardens in clear water typify the diving, with some of the best sites around the Susu Dara group a few kilometres north-west of the main islands. With several dive centres and very competitive prices, this is a good place to get certified or take a few casual dives. You're likely to see schools of colourful reef fish, sea turtles, the occasional manta and perhaps a blacktip reef shark or two. For more information, see the Pulau Perhentian Diving & Snorkelling section in the Terengganu chapter.

***Pulau Redang*** One of Malaysia's most spectacular dive sites, Terengganu's Pulau Redang is actually a group of nine islands surrounded by fine coral reefs and very clear water. In addition to small reef fish, you may also see gropers, manta rays, sea turtles, some reef sharks, and perhaps even a whale or tiger shark. Most of the resorts on the island have their own dive centres and sell all-inclusive packages (see Places to Stay under Pulau Redang in the Terengganu chapter), but you can also arrange independent dive trips (again, see the Pulau Redang section).

***Pulau Kapas*** Pulau Kapas is a small, sandy island 6km off the coast of Marang in Terengganu. There are some decent coral gardens in the shallow waters around the island. While it is not particularly interesting for the experienced diver, the convenient location and shallow waters make Kapas a good place to learn. Most of the resorts on Kapas have their own dive centres; the best is at Kapas Garden Resort (see Pulau Kapas in the Terengganu chapter).

***Pulau Tioman*** The largest east-coast island, Pahang's Pulau Tioman has something for diver and non-diver alike. With lots of dive centres and low prices, Tioman is a great place to get your certification. Off Tioman and some of the smaller islands nearby, you'll find lots of shallow coral gardens, rocky points and deeper coral gardens. There is an excellent variety of fish, from colourful reef fish to large mantas and sharks. See Diving & Snorkelling under Pulau Tioman in the Pahang chapter for more details.

*The Seribuat Archipelago* While not as famous as Tioman, the other islands of Johor's Seribuat Archipelago offer some of the same conditions without the crowds. Diving is typically over shallow coral gardens and water clarity ranges from good to excellent. The most accessible islands include Besar, Sibu and Rawa; some of the best diving is around Pemangill and Aur (both of which are unfortunately expensive and hard to get to). Most of the resorts on the islands have their own dive centres (see the Seribuat Archipelago section in the Johor chapter) or you can visit their offices in Mersing, Johor, near the jetty.

**West Coast** Kedah's **Pulau Payar**, 30km south of Pulau Langkawi, has a good variety of coral, lots of reef fish and decent visibility. The construction of an artificial reef at the southern tip of the island has increased the number of fish species visible. Prices are higher here than on the east coast and access is a little inconvenient, with most boats leaving from Kuah on Langkawi. See Other Islands under Pulau Langkawi in the Kedah section of the Kedah & Perlis chapter.

## Malaysian Borneo

**Sabah** Sabah has some of the best dive sites in Malaysia, including the spectacular Pulau Sipadan.

*Tunku Abdul Rahman National Park* The five islands that make up this national park just off Kota Kinabalu's coast offer decent diving in a convenient location. The coral gardens in the shallow waters surrounding the islands are home to several varieties of reef fish, with the occasional reef shark swimming by to keep things lively. This is a good place to learn, but will probably bore more-experienced divers. For more details, contact Borneo Divers & Sea Sports (☎ 088-222226), Wisma Sabah, in Kota Kinabalu, or one of the operators listed under Organised Tours in the Kota Kinabalu section in the Sabah chapter.

*Pulau Labuan* Pulau Labuan offers some of the only wreck diving in Malaysia with two WWII and two more-modern wrecks lying off the coast. There are also some coral reefs around, but much of the coral has been destroyed by dynamite fishing. Soon to be gazetted as a marine park, the situation around Pulau Labuan will hopefully improve in the near future. Contact some of the agents listed in the Kota Kinabalu section in the Sabah chapter for more details.

*Pulau Sipadan* Malaysia's only world-class dive site, Pulau Sipadan is a five-hectare island sitting atop a 600m limestone pinnacle, 36km off the east coast of Sabah. With beautiful coral gardens ending in abrupt drop-offs, the diving around Sipadan is likely to thrill even the experienced diver. Highlights include sea turtles, leopard sharks, huge varieties of reef fish and the occasional school of hammerhead sharks. Due to the island's small size, the number of visitors is strictly limited, and all guests must stay in resorts owned by five dive companies. Needless to say, this drives prices up, and Sipadan is one of Malaysia's most expensive dive destinations. For more details contact Borneo Divers & Sea Sports or consult Organised Tours under Kota Kinabalu in the Sabah chapter.

***Pulau Layang Layang*** Three hundred kilometres north-west of Kota Kinabalu, Layang Layang, part of the famous Borneo Banks, is a six-hectare island surrounded by a large coral atoll. The diving here is excellent, with both shallow reef dives and impressive drop-offs. Count on seeing large pelagics, tuna, barracuda and the usual schools of reef fish. There is only one resort on the island but you can also dive the area from live-aboards operating from Sabah. See Organised Tours in the Kota Kinabalu section of the Sabah chapter.

**Sarawak** Diving in Sarawak is basically limited to a few shallow spots off the coast of Miri, including one decent wreck dive. With better spots to the north around Labuan and on Sipadan, it is unlikely that experienced divers will want to make this a high-priority destination. For more details on diving around Miri, contact Scuba Sarawak (☎ 085-423975, fax 413988), ground floor, RIHGA Royal Hotel, Miri.

---

## Beyond Sipadan

Pulau Sipadan may be the most famous island off Semporna, but other lesser-known spots are making a name for themselves, especially as Sipadan becomes saturated with tourists. Most of the islands now have at least one resort, but live-aboards are an increasingly attractive alternative to staying on the small, fragile islands. Live-aboard operators come and go; some dive outfits running trips in the area should be able to hook you up with one.

After Sipadan, Pulau Mabul, about 30 minutes by speedboat from Semporna, is perhaps the best-known of the area's islands, but there are others well worth a visit. Pulau Mantanani is a favourite of day-trippers and, like Mabul, has a resort. Pulau Pandanan is another small island about 50 minutes away from Semporna. The coral here has reportedly suffered above-average damage, but there are plenty of green and hawksbill turtles around. There is also accommodation on the island at Pasir Resort.

Once a proper island, Pulau Kapalai is now an eroded sandbar 15 minutes by speedboat from Sipadan. The Bajau-style Sipadan-Kapalai Dive Resort is here, and the macro life on the surrounding Ligatan Reefs is quite different from that found around Sipadan – seamoths, fire gobies, dragonets and giant frogfish are among the species encountered.

Pulau Lankayan is a near-paradise of pelagics and hard-to-spot coral dwellers. The tiny island features more than 20 dive sites, including two wrecks. Lankayan Island Dive Resort occupies a swath of the casuarina-cloaked island.

# Terengganu

☎ 09

The small east-coast state of Terengganu is, along with Kelantan to its north and west, one of the states richest in Malay culture. Until the completion of the roads to Kuala Lumpur (KL) and the west coast, this part of Malaysia was fairly isolated from the rest of the country and didn't receive many Indian and Chinese migrants. Consequently, cultural influences came more from the north. Traditional activities such as kite flying, top spinning, weaving of *songket* (fabric with gold threads) and batik printing are all alive and well here.

If you're seeking a beach to laze on for a few days, Terengganu has some of the best in the country, including those of Pulau Perhentian (the Perhentian Islands), Pulau Redang and Pulau Kapas. All of these islands are less developed than the more famous Pulau Tioman in Pahang and offer great opportunities for diving and snorkelling. On the mainland, Terengganu boasts fine beaches along most of its coastline.

Terengganu has always been a conservative Muslim state. Like Kelantan, it is governed by the conservative Islamic Party of Malaysia (PAS), which triumphed in recent state elections. One of the party's first acts was to remove statues from the city of Kuala Terengganu, in keeping with the Quranic injunction against the worship of idols. Needless to say, alcohol is hard to obtain in Terengganu – you won't find much beyond the occasional beer in a Chinese restaurant.

## History

When the Melaka sultanate was established in the 14th century, Terengganu was already paying tribute to the Siamese in the north, although a 1303 inscription at Kuala Berang establishes that an Islamic state existed here at that time. It wasn't long before Terengganu became a vassal of Melaka, but it managed to retain a large degree of independence during the Riau-Johor ascen-

PENINSULAR MALAYSIA

## HIGHLIGHTS

- **Pulau Perhentian** – perhaps the most beautiful in Malaysia, these islands have white-sand beaches and clear, aquamarine water
- **Pulau Redang** – some of the best diving in Peninsular Malaysia, and great beaches and walks for the non-diver
- **Pulau Kapas** – a pleasant little island that can be visited as a day trip
- **Tasik Kenyir** – an inland lake surrounded by thick jungle and high waterfalls

dancy, and was trading with Siam (now Thailand) and China.

Terengganu was formally established as a state in 1724. The first sultan was Tun Zainal Abidin, a younger brother of one of the former sultans of Johor. The close association with Johor was to continue for some years, and in fact, in the mid-18th century the sultan Mansur spent 15 years in Johor trying to rally anti-Bugis sentiment. After failing there, Mansur turned his attention to Kelantan and after some fighting and

343

PENINSULAR MALAYSIA

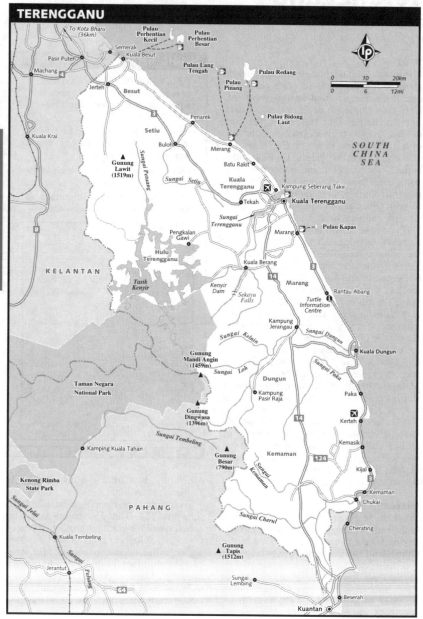

TERENGGANU

To Kota Bharu (36km)
Pasir Puteh
Machang
Semerak
Kuala Besut
Pulau Perhentian Kecil
Pulau Perhentian Besar
Pulau Lang Tengah
Pulau Pinang
Pulau Redang
Kuala Krai
Jerteh
Besut
Setiu
Penarek
Buloh
Merang
Batu Rakit
Pulau Bidong Laut
SOUTH CHINA SEA
Gunung Lawit (1519m)
Sungai Petuang
Sungai Setiu
Kuala Terengganu
Kampung Seberang Takir
Tekah
Kuala Terengganu
Pengkalan Gawi
Sungai Terengganu
Marang
Pulau Kapas
Hulu Terengganu
KELANTAN
Tasik Kenyir
Kuala Berang
Kenyir Dam
Sekayu Falls
Marang
Rantau Abang
Turtle Information Centre
Kampung Jerangau
Sungai Dungun
Gunung Mandi Angin (1459m)
Sungai Kelnin
Sungai Loh
Kuala Dungun
Sungai Paka
Taman Negara National Park
Dungun
Kampung Pasir Raja
Paka
Gunung Dingwasa (1396m)
Kerteh
Sungai Tembeling
Kemasik
Kamping Kuala Tahan
Gunung Besar (790m)
Kemaman
Sungai Kemaman
Kijal
Kenong Rimba State Park
Kemaman
Chukai
Sungai Jelai
PAHANG
Sungai Cherul
Cherating
Kuala Tembeling
Sungai
Jerantut
Sungai Pahang
Gunung Tapis (1512m)
Sungai Lembing
Beserah
Kuantan

0    10    20km
0    6    12mi

shrewd manoeuvring had his son installed as the ruler of Kelantan. The main legacy of Mansur's reign was that Terengganu became a vassal of the Siamese.

Terengganu was controlled by the Siamese for the duration of the 19th century. However, the Terengganu sultan, Baginda Omar, a man renowned for his intelligence and energy, kept the Siamese at arm's length and the state flourished under his rule.

In 1909 an Anglo-Siamese treaty saw power pass to the British. It was an unpopular move locally, and in 1928 a peasant uprising erupted. It was quickly put down and the British went about consolidating their power in the state until the Japanese arrived in WWII. During the Japanese occupation, control of the state was passed back to Thailand, but this was short-lived and Terengganu became a member of the Federation of Malaya in 1948.

# South of Kuala Terengganu

## KEMAMAN/CHUKAI
About 25km north of Cherating, Kemaman and Chukai are the first towns of any size north of Kuantan and also the first towns you reach in Terengganu state when travelling up the coast. The two towns have merged into one long, developed strip with little of interest to hold passing travellers. About the only reason to visit is to stock up on supplies for a stay in Cherating. If you do find yourself in town, you can check your email at the Internet centre (RM2.50 per hour) behind the bus station.

### Places to Stay
Given that cheap accommodation is available close by in Cherating, it is unlikely you will need to stay overnight in Kemaman or Chukai.

If you do need to stay, a reasonable Chinese cheapie is *Wawasan Hotel* (☎ 859 4628, 156 Jalan Sulaiman), with rooms from RM25. The hotel is a 10-minute walk north of the bus station (follow the river). Decent mid-range

rooms are available at *Hotel Tiara* (☎ 859 1802, K353–355 Jalan Kg Tengah), where prices start at RM45 for clean rooms with aircon and hot shower. The hotel is down the street that is roughly opposite the bus station (turn at the sign for Masjid Jamek).

### Getting There & Away
Buses cost RM1 to/from Cherating and RM2.30 to/from Kuantan. To Marang it's RM7.50 by express bus, or you can catch a local bus to Kuala Dungun and then another bus from there. Taxis (per car) cost RM15 to/from Cherating, RM24 to/from Kuantan, RM30 to/from Kuala Dungun, and RM60 to/from Kuala Terengganu.

## KEMASIK
Kemasik's palm-fringed beach has some of the clearest water on the east coast. Unfortunately, there is no accommodation in town. Without your own transportation, the best way to visit the beach is to take a local bus running between Kemaman/Chukai and Kuala Dungun. If you're driving, turn off Route 3 at the sign reading 'Pantai Kemasik'.

## KERTEH
Kerteh is a modern blot on the landscape that owes its existence to offshore oil. Esso and Petronas have their oil refineries here. The town has an airport, but public transport connections are not good.

## PAKA
The beach here is almost as good as the one at Kemasik, but the view is somewhat marred by the refinery a few kilometres down the coast. The village here is a little run-down but quite picturesque. Like Kemasik, there is no accommodation. The best way to visit Paka is to take a local bus running between Kerteh and Kuala Dungun. If you're driving, turn off at the sign for 'Pantai Paka'.

## KUALA DUNGUN
Kuala Dungun is the largest town on the coast between Kemaman/Chukai and Kuala Terengganu. The main reason to come here is to catch a bus or taxi out again, but there are plenty of hotels if you need to spend the

night. Most of the hotels are in the old town, a few kilometres off Route 3. The main bus station is also here.

*Hotel Kasanya (☎ 848 1704, 225 Jalan Tambu)* has decent, clean rooms with fan/air-con for RM18.90/3150. It's a five-minute walk from the bus station; cross the sports field and take a left on the main road.

## Getting There & Away

There are buses to/from Kuala Terengganu (RM4) and Kemaman/Chukai (RM4). To get to Rantau Abang (RM2), take a Kuala Terengganu–bound bus and ask to be dropped at Rantau Abang.

## RANTAU ABANG

Rantau Abang was once a popular destination for tourists who came to see the giant leatherback turtles come ashore to lay their eggs. Now that the turtles have all but disappeared (see the boxed text in this section), the tourists have also disappeared, and the village feels like a ghost town. However, the beach is still lovely and is perfect for long, solitary walks. Swimming is possible, but the undertow can be savage (parents should keep a close eye on their children).

Note that the nearest bank is at Kuala Dungun, 22km south.

**The Turtle Information Centre** (Pusat Penerangan Penyu Rantau Abang) is run by the Department of Fisheries, and is close to the town's budget accommodation. It has a few decent displays but is missable for all but the most ardent turtle-lover. The centre is open every day during the turtle-watching season (May to August), but is otherwise closed on Friday and public holidays.

---

## The Disappearing Turtles of the East Coast

Four species of turtle visit the east coast, along a strip of beach stretching from 35km to 150km north of Kuantan: the leatherback *(Dermochelys coriacea)*, the hawksbill *(Eretmochelys imbricata)*, the green turtle *(Chelonia mydas)* and the olive ridley *(Lepidochelys oliveacea)*.

Villagers believe that the giant leatherback turtles are attracted to Rantau Abang every year because of a large black stone resembling a turtle in the river. A more mundane explanation is that the beach has several features that make it a suitable incubation ground, including a sharp drop-off that makes the turtles' laborious climb onto land considerably easier. At other times of the year the leatherbacks wander as far as several thousand kilometres away, but between June and September they return to the Malaysian coast to lay their eggs.

Or at least they used to: Sightings of the turtles at Rantau Abang numbered almost 1000 back in the 1984 season; only four were spotted in the 1999 season. It would be nice to think that Rantau Abang's turtles had found themselves a lovely beach somewhere else, but turtles are guided by magnetic orientation and will always nest close to the place they were born – so unfortunately this is not a case of them having gone in search of greener pastures. Leatherbacks are facing extinction in many places in the world and Terengganu is no exception.

Researchers believe that what we are now seeing is the result of decades of incidental capture and turtle-egg harvesting. Biologists estimate that around one turtle hatchling in every thousand survives the 35 to 50 years it takes to reach maturity – turtle populations simply can't survive years of near-complete egg harvest.

While leatherback eggs are protected, in coastal markets it's common to see hundreds of eggs of the smaller green, hawksbill and olive ridley turtles. It may seem like an uphill battle, but there are some things you can do to help protect these magnificent creatures:

• Don't buy turtle eggs, turtle meat or anything made from turtle shell.
• Cross turtles and their eggs off your list of things to eat.
• Make sure your litter doesn't end up on beaches or in oceans.

August is peak egg-laying season for the leatherbacks, but they've also been known to come ashore in June and July. With so few turtles appearing, however, you'd have to stay for all of August to be sure of a sighting. For this reason, we don't recommend coming to Rantau Abang to see the turtles – it's better to think of it as a quiet beach resort.

## Places to Stay & Eat

Right on the beach, just south of the Turtle Information Centre, are two travellers' places. *Awang's (☎ 844 3500)* is the more popular of the two, with a wide range of accommodation from RM10 to RM120. Ask to see a few rooms as they vary in quality.

*Rantau Abang Beach Resort (☎ 845 4202)* next door has decent rooms for RM20 with bathroom and fan, or RM50 with air-con. Both Awang's and Rantau Abang offer discount rates in the off season.

*Dahimah's Guest House (☎ 845 2843)* is about 1km south towards Kuala Dungun and is a good option. Room prices range from RM35 to RM140, with discounts available outside the peak season. Some of the best rooms are over the lagoon that separates the hotel from the beach. It's a pretty spot and makes a quiet getaway for beach lovers.

Apart from the *restaurants* in the various hotels, there are a few *food stalls* next to the Turtle Information Centre.

## Getting There & Away

Kuala Dungun–Kuala Terengganu buses run in both directions every hour from 7 am to 6 pm and there's a bus stop near the Turtle Information Centre. To/from Kuala Dungun costs RM2; to/from Kuala Tereng-

---

## The Disappearing Turtles of the East Coast

- Make a donation to sea turtle conservation; check out the Web sites at www.uct.edu.my/seatru and www.wwfmalaysia.org, or leave a little something in a donation box at a turtle information centre.

If you do get to see a turtle, the egg-laying process is awesome. The female leatherback can weigh up to 750kg and reach up to 2m in length. After crawling up the beach, well above the high-tide line, each female digs a deep hole in the sand for her eggs (she usually digs and scratches several times before finding the best spot for them).

Into this cavity the turtle, with much huffing and puffing, lays between 50 and 140 eggs. Having covered them, she heads back towards the water. It all takes an enormous effort, and the turtle will pause to catch her breath several times. When the giant turtle reaches the water an amazing transformation takes place. The heavy, ungainly, cumbersome creature is suddenly back in its element and glides off silently into the night.

You can take steps to ensure that the turtle is disturbed as little as possible. If no beach rangers are around:

- Stay at least 10m away from any turtle crawling up the beach.
- Don't use torches (flashlights) or camera flashes.
- If you see a turtle crawling ashore, sit and wait patiently for her to crawl to the top of the dunes – do not impede her emergence. It be many hours before she is ready to lay eggs.

MARTIN HARRIS

**Leatherback turtles are facing extinction.**

- Resist the temptation to take photos of hatchlings making their way to the ocean.

If beach rangers are with you (or the turtle) they may allow you to get a little closer and take some flash photographs, but only once she has laid eggs (hopefully in time flash photography will be phased out).

ganu costs RM4. A taxi to/from Kuala Terengganu costs RM28.

## MARANG

Marang, a fishing village on the mouth of the Sungai (River) Marang, has long been a favourite stopover for travellers making their way along the east coast. Unfortunately, much of the town's traditional charm has fallen victim to an ill-planned modernisation program. Now, much of the once-picturesque waterfront area is occupied by characterless concrete structures.

Nonetheless, Marang is still worth a visit. The harbour is packed with colourful fishing boats, there are a few good beaches north and south of town and traditional Malay culture is still alive on the outskirts.

### Things to Do

If you'd like to get a glimpse of what Marang used to be like, you can travel up the Sungai Marang to Kampung Jenang to observe traditional Malay activities like *atap* (roof thatching) weaving, coconut-sugar making and the gathering of coconuts by trained monkeys. It's possible to visit the village as an easy day trip from Marang or Kuala Terengganu. Ping Anchorage (☎ 626 2020), in Kuala Terengganu, runs four-person trips up the river to Kampung Jenang for RM55 per person, including lunch (costs are higher for smaller groups).

If you are in town on Sunday, be sure to check out the excellent **Sunday market**, which starts at 3 pm near the town's jetties.

### Places to Stay & Eat

The spot most popular with travellers is the pleasant *Green Mango Inn*, on a hill near the jetty. Single rooms with fan go for RM10, doubles for RM15, and A-frames with fan for RM20. There are laundry facilities, a kitchen and a small library.

*Island View Resort* (☎ 618 2006) charges RM25 for rooms with fan and bathroom and

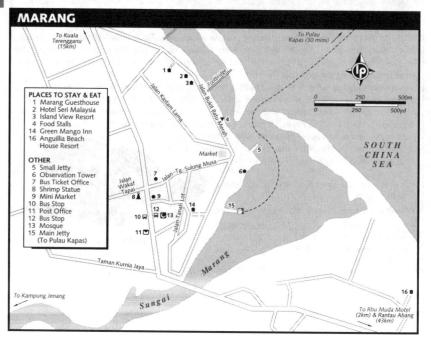

### MARANG

To Kuala
Terengganu
(15km)

To Pulau
Kapas (30 mins)

**PLACES TO STAY & EAT**
1 Marang Guesthouse
2 Hotel Seri Malaysia
3 Island View Resort
4 Food Stalls
14 Green Mango Inn
16 Anguillia Beach
House Resort

**OTHER**
5 Small Jetty
6 Observation Tower
7 Bus Ticket Office
8 Shrimp Statue
9 Mini Market
10 Bus Stop
11 Post Office
12 Bus Stop
13 Mosque
15 Main Jetty
(To Pulau Kapas)

Jalan Kastam Lama

Jalan Bukit Batu Merah

Footbridge

Market

Jalan-Tg. Sulong Musa

Jalan
Wakaf
Tapai

Jalan Tanah Lot

SOUTH
CHINA
SEA

Taman Kurnia Jaya

Marang

To Kampung Jenang

Sungai

To Rhu Muda Motel
(2km) & Rantau Abang
(43km)

RM40 upwards for air-con rooms. The rooms are a little run-down; definitely have a look before making up your mind.

*Marang Guesthouse* (☎ *618 1976)* is on a hill overlooking the town. It's a notch up from the other guesthouses and has its own restaurant. Rooms with fan are RM25 and nicer, air-con rooms are available from RM50.

Near Island View Resort, *Hotel Seri Malaysia* (☎ *618 2889)* has excellent air-con doubles from RM65, including breakfast. This is the best mid-range choice in town.

Across the bridge to the south-east, *Anguillia Beach House Resort* (☎ *618 1322)* is another good mid-range place. It's right on a nice stretch of beach in a lovely garden setting, but is slightly overpriced at RM50 for rooms with fan and RM70 upwards with air-con.

Farther south are more places to stay, but they are a long way from anywhere and see very few foreign guests. *Rhu Muda Motel* (☎ *618 2328),* between the main road and the beach, is well kept and has rooms for RM40 with fan, and chalets from RM60 with air-con.

Most of these places have their own *restaurant*, but you can also find some eats at the *food stalls* near the jetties.

### Getting There & Away

There are regular local buses to/from Kuala Terengganu (RM1) and Kuala Dungun/ Rantau Abang (RM3/2). For long-distance buses, there's a ticket office on Jalan Tanjung Sulong Musa, near the town's main intersection. There are three daily buses to/from KL (RM21.50), four to/from Johor Bahru (RM24.10) and five to and from Kuantan/Cherating (RM9.50/8).

There are four bus-stops on the main road. Southbound express buses usually stop in front of the mosque and northbound services will pick you up just north of the post office. This is not a hard and fast rule, however, and it's best to ask the owner of your guesthouse or someone at the ticket office first.

### PULAU KAPAS

Six kilometres offshore from Marang is the beautiful small island of Kapas, with clear

water and beaches of powdery white sand. All the accommodation is clustered together on two small beaches in the centre of the island, but you can walk around the headlands to quieter beaches. There is also a rough track across the middle of the island to the rocky eastern shore, which is good for sightseeing but dangerous for swimming.

Pulau Kapas is best avoided during holidays and on long weekends, when it is overrun with day-trippers. Outside of these times, the island is likely to be very quiet. It shuts down during the east coast's monsoon season (November to March).

It's possible to visit Pulau Kapas as a day trip from nearby Kuala Terengganu.

### Diving & Snorkelling

Kapas is billed as a snorkellers' paradise, though coral is scarce on the most accessible beaches facing the coast. Some of the best snorkelling is found around the northern end of the island.

All of the resorts listed here have dive centres. Kapas Garden Resort has scuba gear and a boat, and charges RM90/150 for one/two dives, including equipment.

Any of the budget places in town can organise snorkelling, and the cost is around RM30 for the day, including the return boat ride to Kapas. You can also arrange snorkelling trips for similar prices at any of the island resorts.

### Places to Stay & Eat

Many people visit Kapas on a day trip, but there are a number of places to stay on the island and each has its own restaurant. *Kapas Garden Resort* (☎ *010-984 1686, 04-899 4325),* run by a hospitable Dutch-Malay couple, is good value with rooms for RM75 with bathroom and fan. There are chalets for RM50. It's at the northern end of the island, around the corner from an excellent secluded beach.

Next door is *Mak Cik Gemuk Beach Resort* (☎ *618 1221),* which has lots of rooms from RM25 to RM45. The rooms are all set well back from the beach and are somewhat cramped; have a look before deciding.

PENINSULAR MALAYSIA

On the same beach, *Zaki Beach Chalet* (☎ 019-956 0513) is an inexpensive option, with rooms from RM20 to RM50. Again, have a good look before making up your mind.

A short walk around a headland brings you to a longer beach with a few more possibilities. The first is the upmarket *Kapas Island Resort* (☎ 622 0714), complete with swimming pool, where basic but clean rooms with fan and bathroom start at RM80 and chalets with air-con and bathroom start at RM120. The restaurant here is pretty good.

Nearby, *Tuty Puri Resort* (☎ 624 6090) is another large resort-style place, which charges RM80 for basic chalets with fan and bathroom and RM120 for deluxe chalets with air-con and bathroom. There are no nets on the windows here, so you may need to get some mosquito coils. Although it's overpriced, this is one of the nicer spots on the island.

The last place, at the southern end of the beach, is *Lighthouse* (☎ 626 5541), a budget-priced spot popular with backpackers. All the rooms are in one elevated longhouse. Dorm beds go for RM10 each and private rooms for RM25. This is about as close as Kapas gets to southern Thailand.

It is also possible to *camp* on some of the isolated beaches at the northern and southern ends of the island, but bring your own food and water.

Finally, those in search of something more exclusive can try *Gem Island Resort* (☎ 669 5910), the sole occupant of the small island immediately to the north of Pulau Kapas. Superior/deluxe/villa rooms cost RM170/185/200 per night. All-inclusive packages are also available and may represent significant savings for stays of more than two nights (contact Ping Anchorage on ☎ 626 2020 in Kuala Terengganu for details). The best rooms are the superior rooms in blocks 4 and 5, a good distance from the noisy generator. Call to make a reservation before heading out.

### Getting There & Away
Boats to Pulau Kapas leave from the larger of Marang's two jetties and tickets can be purchased from any of the agents nearby. Boats leave when four or more people show up, and charge RM25 return. Be sure to arrange a pick-up time when you purchase your ticket. You can usually count on morning departures at around 8 and 9 am. Some guesthouse operators also sell tickets, but will also charge a RM5 commission. Don't believe those who claim that their boat is the only sailing that day – they're just after an extra RM5.

# Kuala Terengganu

Standing on a promontory formed by the South China Sea on one side and the wide Sungai Terengganu on the other, Kuala Terengganu is the capital of Terengganu state and the seat of the sultan. Oil revenue has transformed Kuala Terengganu from a sprawling, oversized fishing village of stilt houses into a medium-sized modern city.

At first glance Kuala Terengganu appears much like any other Malaysian city, but give it a chance – the city and its surrounding areas are quite rich in Malay culture. It's also a good place to sample authentic Malay cuisine as well as some excellent Chinese seafood. Keep in mind though that it remains a fairly conservative place and has a strong Islamic presence – there's not much in the way of nightlife.

Kuala Terengganu is also convenient as a staging post to nearby attractions such as Tasik Kenyir, Marang/Pulau Kapas and Pulau Redang.

### Information
Jalan Sultan Ismail is the commercial hub of the town and home to most of the banks and office blocks. The state tourist office (☎ 622 1553) is near the post office and is a good source of information (closed on Friday). The Tourism Malaysia office (☎ 622 1433) can give you a full range of brochures for other parts of Malaysia and can also answer questions about local attractions and accommodation.

The immigration office (☎ 622 1424) is in the Wisma Persekutuan, on Jalan Sultan

Ismail. Golden Wood Internet Café (RM3 per hour) is conveniently in the centre of town. Mr Dobi, next to the Seaview Hotel, is a good laundry service.

## Things to See

Kuala Terengganu's compact **Chinatown** can be found on Jalan Bandar. It comprises the usual array of hole-in-the-wall Chinese shops, hairdressing salons and restaurants, as well as a sleepy Chinese temple and some narrow alleys leading to jetties on the waterfront. This is a good spot to sit outside and enjoy some good food in the evening (see Places to Eat later).

The **central market** is a lively, colourful spot, with fruit and foods of all types. When they say the fish is fresh, they really mean it – the fishing boats dock right outside. The floor above the fish section has a good collection of batik and songket.

Across the road from the market and next door to the state tourist office, look for the flight of stairs leading up to **Bukit Puteri**, a 200m hill with good views of the city. The hill is also home to the remains of a 19th-century fort (the legacy of inter-sultanate warfare), some cannons and a bell.

Continuing past the market, you come to **Istana Maziah**, the sultan's palace, on your right. The palace is closed to the public, except for some ceremonial occasions. Nearby is the gleaming **Zainal Abidin Mosque**.

On the ocean side of town, **Pantai Batu Buruk** is the city beach and a popular place to stroll in the evening when the food stalls open. It is a pleasant stretch of sand, but swimming can be dangerous here. Across the road, the **Cultural Centre** sometimes stages *pencak silat* (a martial-arts dance form) and *wayang kulit* (shadow puppet) shows on Friday between 5 and 7 pm, from 1 April to 31 October. Check with the state tourist office.

The excellent **Kompleks Muzim Negeri Terengganu** (Terengganu State Museum Complex) is a few kilometres south-west of town in Losong. The museum consists of several buildings spread out over rolling, manicured grounds on the banks of the wide Sungai Terengganu. In the main building, a vast concrete reproduction of a traditional Malay house, you'll find displays of textiles, crafts, Islamic articles and items related to the state's petroleum industry. Nearby, you'll find a full-size traditional Malay sailing vessel and an adjacent maritime gallery with displays on shipbuilding and fishing. However, the real highlight of the museum is Istana Tengku Long, a wooden palace that dates from 1888 and contains displays of royal artefacts. The entire complex is open from 9 am to 5 pm (closed Friday), and admission is RM5. Take minibus No 10, marked 'Muzim/Losong', from the main bus station (60 sen).

From the jetty near the Seri Malaysia Hotel you can take a 50-sen ferry ride to **Pulau Duyung Besar**, the largest island in the estuary. Fishing boats are built here using age-old techniques and tools; it's worth a wander.

## Places to Stay – Budget

*Ping Anchorage (☎ 626 5020, 77A Jalan Dato Isaac, upstairs),* is the number-one travellers place. It has a rooftop terrace, a detailed board describing local attractions and an affiliated cafe down the street. Beds in four-person dorm rooms are RM6 each and private rooms are RM12 to RM18, or RM20 with bathroom. The rooms are good and the owners friendly; its Web site is at www.pinganchorage.com.my. The attached travel agency organises economical tours to Pulau Kapas, Pulau Redang, Pulau Perhentian, Sekayu Falls and Tasik Kenyir.

*Awi's Yellow House (☎ 013-901 1756)* is a unique guesthouse built on stilts over the Sungai Terengganu. It's in the boat-building village on Pulau Duyung Besar, a 15-minute ferry ride across the river. A bed with mosquito net costs RM6 per night in the open dorm, and the small thatched rooms are RM15. The rooms are better value than the dorm, which is in bad condition. This is a beautiful, relaxed place and highly recommended. The catch is getting over here – boats can be infrequent during the day (outside peak hours). Take the ferry from the jetty near the Seri Malaysia Hotel,

**KUALA TERENGGANU**

SOUTH CHINA SEA

Pulau Wan Embong

Pulau Duyung Kecil

Pulau Duyung Besar

Chinatown

Stadium

Pantai Batu Buruk

To Airport (5km), Merang (38km) & Kota Bharu (159km)

Sports Ground

To Tasik Kenyir (55km) & Sekayu Falls (56km)

To Suterasemai Centre (5km) & Marang (15km)

then ask for directions upon arrival (everyone knows the way).

## Places to Stay – Mid-Range

Most mid-range accommodation is on Jalan Sultan Ismail. *Terengganu Hotel (☎ 622 2900)* is one of the cheaper options, with rooms at RM33 with fan or RM55 with air-con and bathroom. The rooms are clean enough, but not particularly inspiring.

*Hotel KT Mutiara (☎ 622 2655)* is a decent choice with air-con rooms for RM55 to RM85. A couple of doors along, *Kenangan Hotel (☎ 622 2688)* is a slightly shabby establishment with air-con rooms with bath for RM40. Down the street, the *Seri Hoover (☎ 623 3833)* offers ageing air-con standard/deluxe rooms for RM58/79.

Better mid-range value, *Seaview Hotel (☎ 622 1911),* close to Istana Maziah, has clean rooms with fan and bathroom cost RM45. Rooms with air-con and bathroom cost RM60.

*Motel Desa (☎ 622 3033)* is in a beautiful garden setting on the top of Bukit Pak Api, but unless you have your own transport it's a very inconvenient place to stay. Rooms with air-con and hot water go for RM65.

The best mid-range value in town is *Seri Malaysia Hotel (☎ 623 6454)*. Clean air-con rooms here, some with good views over the Sungai Terengganu, cost RM65 including breakfast. Another good choice is *Yen Tin Midtown Hotel (☎ 623 5288),* where clean, new rooms with air-con and hot water go for RM69/135 (standard/deluxe), including breakfast.

## Places to Stay – Top End

Working hard to capture the luxury market, the new *Hotel Grand Continental (☎ 625 1888)* has all the amenities you'd expect, including a swimming pool and a good restaurant. Spacious standard rooms with air-con, hot water, bath tub, TV and fridge go for RM115, including breakfast for two.

## KUALA TERENGGANU

**PLACES TO STAY**
1 Awi's Yellow House
2 Seri Malaysia Hotel
4 Terengganu Hotel
13 Seaview Hotel
21 Hotel Grand Continental
23 Yen Tin Midtown Hotel
24 Ping Anchorage
31 Seri Hoover
35 Kenangan Hotel
36 Hotel KT Mutiara
43 Park Royal Hotel
47 Motel Desa

**PLACES TO EAT**
3 Seri Binjai Restaurant
6 Outdoor Hawker Centre
7 Restoran Golden Dragon
19 Food Stalls

22 Tian Kee;
   Restoran Ocean
25 Ping Anchorage Travellers
   Café
32 Good Luck Restoran
33 Restoran Kari Asha
34 Sahara Tandori
46 Batu Buruk Food Centre

**OTHER**
5 Batik Gallery
8 Chinese Temple
9 Central Market
10 Bukit Puteri
   (Princess Hill)
11 Istana Maziah
12 Mr Dobi Laundry Service
14 Post Office
15 State Tourist Office

16 Jetty for Local Ferries
17 Jetty for Ferries to Pulau
   Redang
18 Express Bus Station
20 Astaka Shopping Centre
26 Golden Wood Internet Café
27 Zainal Abidin Mosque
28 Main Bus Station
29 Long-Distance Taxi Stand
30 Telekom Office
37 Convenience Store;
   Bookshop
38 Maybank
39 Immigration Office
40 Tourism Malaysia
41 Malaysia Airlines
42 Mosque
44 Hospital Terengganu
45 Cultural Centre

**PENINSULAR MALAYSIA**

***Park Royal Hotel*** (☎ 622 2100) has rates starting at RM220 (big discounts are often available). It has all the facilities of a top hotel, including a swimming pool, but standards aren't up to the level of the Grand Continental.

### Places to Eat
Kuala Terengganu is a good place to explore the wonders of Malay cuisine. Local specialities include *nasi dagang* (rice served over a banana leaf with curry, usually eaten for breakfast), and *kerepok* (a concoction of deep-fried fish paste and sago, usually moulded into rolls). You can sample these at most of the food centres listed here.

The two best food centres in town are ***Batu Buruk Food Centre***, with a pleasant outdoor location near the beach; and Chinatown's ***outdoor hawker centre***, which is divided into Chinese and Malay sections. Other food centres include the ***food court*** on the 2nd floor of Kompleks Taman Selera Tanjung and the *food stalls* on the 2nd floor of the central market.

For a Western-style breakfast, a variety of meals throughout the day and a cold beer in the evening, go to ***Ping Anchorage Travellers Café***. If you only need a little pick-me-up, try one of its excellent iced cappuccinos.

Chinatown is a good place for lunch or dinner. The area's best restaurant is ***Restoran Golden Dragon***, where you can get good seafood and pork dishes. It has outdoor tables and some of the staff speak English. Another place for good Chinese fare is ***Good Luck Restoran*** on Jalan Kota Lama, which has an extensive menu and outside tables.

For a serious splurge on Chinese seafood in a pleasant setting, try ***Tian Kee*** or ***Restoran Ocean***, on the beach near the Hotel Grand Continental. At Tian Kee, don't miss the tangy asparagus cooked with *belacan* (fermented prawn paste) and the buttered prawns (shrimp).

There are two decent Indian places on Jalan Air Jernih, ***Sahara Tandori*** and ***Restoran Kari Asha***; both serve filling meals for around RM5.

***Seri Binjai Restaurant*** near the waterfront is quite run-down, but is a good place to go for satay.

### Shopping
Kuala Terengganu is a good place to buy wicker goods, batik and songket. The Suterasemai Centre is a handicraft centre 10km from town in Rhusila, just before Marang; but the best place to buy handicrafts is upstairs at the central market. Prices at the market average RM80 to

RM250 for a 1 sq m piece of songket and RM20 to RM100 for locally made wicker baskets. Bargaining is possible here – and necessary to get fair prices. Try the Batik Gallery on Jalan Bandar in Chinatown, which has a wide variety of innovative batik designs.

## Getting There & Away
**Air** Malaysia Airlines (☎ 622 1415), 13 Jalan Sultan Omar, has direct flights daily to/from KL (RM104).

**Bus** The main bus station on Jalan Masjid Abidin serves as a terminus for all local buses. Some long-distance buses depart from here as well, but most use the express bus station in the north of town (ask at your lodgings or when buying your ticket if you're unsure).

At the local bus station, there are services to/from Marang (RM1), Rantau Abang (RM3), Kuala Dungun (RM4) and Merang (RM2).

From the express bus station, there are services running to and from the following places: Kuantan (RM9.60); Johor Bahru (RM24.10/35.10 regular/first class); Singapore (RM26.70/39); Melaka (RM23); KL (RM21.50/34.70); Ipoh (RM29); Kuala Besut (RM5.70); and Kota Bharu (RM7.50).

**Taxi** The main taxi stand is near the bus station. Regular taxi destinations include Marang (RM10), Merang (RM20), Kuala Besut (for Pulau Perhentian, RM40), Rantau Abang (RM28), Tasik Kenyir (RM45) and Kota Bharu (RM56). These prices are per car (non air-con).

## Getting Around
A taxi to the airport costs RM15. Local buses leave from main bus station in the centre of town. Taxis around town cost a minimum of RM5, but there are not many about; try at the long-distance taxi stand.

Kuala Terengganu was once the trishaw capital of Malaysia, and although numbers have dropped, they are still the main form of inner-city transport. Cost is roughly RM3 per kilometre.

## AROUND KUALA TERENGGANU
### Sekayu Falls
These waterfalls, 56km south-west of Kuala Terengganu, are part of a large rural park popular with locals on Fridays and public holidays. The falls extend quite a way up a mountainside; the main falls are 15 minutes in from the entrance. A further 20 minutes' walk brings you to the more attractive upper falls. Swimming is possible at both of the falls. Also in the park you'll find an **orchard** with a huge variety of tropical fruit.

To get there, catch a bus from Kuala Terengganu to Kuala Berang (RM4), and switch to a taxi (RM15 each way). You can ask the taxi to wait for you (free for up to one hour, RM12 per hour thereafter) or take your chances on finding another for the ride back. Ping Anchorage (☎ 626 2020) in Kuala Terengganu does day trips to the falls for RM40 per person including lunch.

### Tasik Kenyir
Tasik (Lake) Kenyir, formed by the construction of Kenyir Dam in 1985, covers over 38,000 hectares and contains 340 islands. The lake has been developed as an 'ecotourist' destination and there are now some 13 resorts dotted around the lake.

**Waterfalls** and **caves** are high on the list of Kenyir's attractions. These are reached by boat, either as day trips from the lake's main access point, Pengkalan Gawi, or from the resorts themselves. Perhaps more interesting are trips up the rivers that empty into the lake. Among these, a journey up the **Sungai Petuang**, at the extreme northern end of the lake, is a real highlight of a visit to Kenyir. When the water is high, it's possible to travel several kilometres up the river into beautiful virgin jungle.

Fishing is a popular activity and the lake is surprisingly rich in species, including *toman* (snake head), *buang* (catfish), *kelah* (a kind of carp), *sebarau* (another kind of carp) and *belida* (featherback).

Because the lake is a reservoir, the water level varies considerably, peaking at the end of the rainy season in March or April and gradually descending until the start of the next rainy season in November. When the water is high, the lake takes on an almost spooky air, with the tops of drowned trees poking through the surface; when the water is low, the lake is reduced to a series of canals through partially denuded jungle hills. Needless to say, the lake is at its most beautiful when the water is high, in late spring and early summer.

**Places to Stay** Most of the accommodation in the area is in resort chalets or floating longhouse structures built over the lake. There are no budget options. The resorts generally offer packages including meals and boat transport from the lake's main access point, Pengkalan Gawi. *Musang Kenyir Resort* (☎ 622 9917) is one of the better resorts on the lake, with a combination of floating-longhouse rooms and land-based chalets. Another decent choice is *Kenyir Remis Rakit* (☎ 681 2125).

Another option is to explore by houseboat, which allows you to reach remote regions of the lake. The only drawback is that you generally need a large group to make a trip on a houseboat economical (it may be possible to latch onto a big group leaving from Kuala Terengganu).

It's best to organise a trip to Kenyir at a travel agency in Kuala Terengganu. Ping Anchorage (☎ 626 2020) offers two-night/three-day packages at Musang Kenyir Resort for RM240 or RM260 (depending upon the type of room you choose), or at Kenyir Remis Rakit for RM296. It can also arrange two-night/three-day houseboat tours for RM210 per person (this is the price for a 10-person tour; smaller groups cost more).

**Getting There & Away** Tasik Kenyir is 15km west of Kuala Berang and 55km from Kuala Terengganu. The main access point is the jetty at Pengkalan Gawi, on the northern shore of the lake. To get there, take a taxi from Kuala Terengganu (RM60 per car each way). There are no buses to the lake from Kuala Terengganu.

**Getting Around** Travel around the lake is expensive as it is necessary to hire a boat (if you're staying at a resort, it will provide all

transport). Boat hire costs around RM100 per hour and an all-day fishing trip costs RM400. Rather than trying to organise things on your own, try joining a day tour from Kuala Terengganu; these cost RM60 to RM120 per day for four-person groups.

# North of Kuala Terengganu

North of Kuala Terengganu the main road (Route 3) leaves the coast and runs inland to Kota Bharu, 165km north, via Jerteh. The quiet coastal back road from Kuala Terengganu to Kuala Besut runs along a beautiful stretch of coast and is quite popular with cycling travellers.

## MERANG

Gateway to Pulau Redang, the sleepy little fishing village of Merang (not to be confused with Marang) is one of the few remaining villages of its kind where development hasn't gone ahead in leaps and bounds. There is little of interest in the village, but the beach is pleasant if you have to spend some time waiting for ferry connections to Redang.

### Places to Stay & Eat

The best place to stay is *Kembara Resort* (☎ 653 1770), about 500m south of the village (follow the signs from the main road). Dorm beds go for RM10 and pleasant chalets with fan and bathroom cost RM30. There are larger family chalets for RM40. A common kitchen is available for those who bring their own food.

In the centre of the village, *Merang Inn* (☎ 653 1435) is the only other place in town, with semidetached chalets for RM40 with fan and bathroom, or RM60 with air-con. It also has the village's only restaurant.

Wherever you plan to stay, it's wise to stock up on food supplies before arriving.

### Getting There & Away

There are daily buses from the main bus station in Kuala Terengganu to Merang

(RM2). Taxis from Kuala Terengganu cost RM20 per car. Coming from the north is more difficult and it is easiest to go south as far as Kuala Terengganu and then backtrack. Otherwise, taxis from Kota Bharu cost RM48 per car.

## PULAU REDANG

One of the largest and most inaccessible of the east-coast islands, Redang is also one of the most beautiful. Unfortunately, the island has been targeted by big developers and there are few options for the independent traveller. Considering the island's beauty, it may be worth paying the money for a package at one of the resorts.

Redang is one of nine islands that form a protected marine park, and it offers **excellent diving and snorkelling**. Silt from resort construction is said to have caused some coral damage, but concerted efforts are being made to prevent further damage – even snorkelling is restricted to certain areas.

Of most interest to travellers are the beautiful **bays** on the eastern side of the island, including Teluk Dalam, Teluk Kalong and Pasir Panjang. The huge Berjaya Island Resort and golf course are hidden on the north shore and the island's main village is in the interior. There's also a small camp site near the park headquarters on nearby Pulau Pinang.

Note that the island basically shuts down from 1 November to 1 March; the best time to visit is from mid-March to late September.

### Places to Stay

Accommodation on Pulau Redang is best organised as a package in Kuala Terengganu. Ping Anchorage (☎ 626 2020) in Kuala Terengganu has the cheapest deal at RM240 for two nights/three days, with camping equipment and meals provided. It also sells packages for all the resorts listed here at competitive prices.

Most of the small resorts are built on a beautiful stretch of white-sand beach known as Pasir Panjang, on the east coast of the island. At the northern end of the beach, *Redang Holiday Villa (☎ 622 3932)* is well situated and has clean rooms contained in one large building. Two-night/three-day packages including boat transfer and meals start at RM280.

Next along is *Coral Redang Island Resort (☎ 623 6200)*, a full-blown resort affair with overpriced but pleasant double rooms for RM276 per night, including meals.

Next door is *Redang Pelangi Resort (☎ 623 5202)*, which is a slightly more casual resort-style affair that offers two-night/three-day packages in air-con rooms for RM320 per person.

At the southern end of the beach, *Redang Bay Resort (☎ 620 3200)* has a commanding location, clean rooms and a good dive centre. Its two-night/three-day packages start at RM450.

In the bay directly south of Pasir Panjang you will find several more places to stay strung out along an excellent white-sand beach. The cheapest of these is *Redang Lagoon Chalet (☎ 827 2116)*, where two-night/three-day packages start at RM280. This is one of the few places that will accept walk-in guests, at a rate of RM80 per night, if there is space.

### Getting There & Away

Most visitors to Redang purchase packages that include boat transfer to the island. If you choose to go independently, you must hitch a ride on one of the resorts' boats. These usually operate from Merang, but at the time of writing, the silt in Merang's harbour had forced boats to operate from Kuala Terengganu.

Berjaya Island Resort ferries leave Kuala Terengganu daily at 10.30 am and 2.30 pm and cost RM40. In the opposite direction, boats leave Redang for Kuala Terengganu daily at 7.30 am and 12.30 pm (7 and 11.30 am on Friday). Note that priority is given to guests of Berjaya Island Resort and if its boat is full you will have to try to squeeze onto one of the other resorts' boats. Alternatively, you can charter your own speedboat at Merang Inn (☎ 653 1435) in Merang for RM240.

If you go over on the ferry, you'll be dropped at the island's main jetty. In order

PENINSULAR MALAYSIA

to get to the beaches of the east coast you will have to hire a taxi-boat for RM50 to RM60 (note that these can't land in rough weather).

It's also possible to visit Redang on a dive trip from Pulau Perhentian (see Diving & Snorkelling under Pulau Perhentian for details).

## KUALA BESUT

Kuala Besut, on the coast south of Kota Bharu, has a reasonably pleasant beach and is an interesting, though grubby, fishing village. A visit to this town is usually just a preliminary to a trip to the Pulau Perhentian.

### Orientation & Information

Taxis and local buses run to and from the taxi stand in the centre of town, very near the seafront. Around the square formed by the taxi stand you will find a few simple shops and restaurants. On the eastern side of the square, Perhentian Ferry Travel & Tours (☎ 691 9679) is a reliable travel agent that can arrange transport to and accommodation on the Perhentians. Its Web site is at www.perhentianferry.com.my. If you've got your own transport, there's a car park (RM5 per day) near the taxi stand.

### Places to Stay & Eat

There aren't many places to choose from. The cheapest option is *Yaudin Guesthouse* (☎ 691 0887), which has basic singles/doubles with fan for RM10/20 and air-con rooms for RM30. It's above Yaodin Holidays & Tours travel agency, a minute's walk from the taxi stand. At the time of writing, there were plans to relocate the guesthouse; you may have to ask around for the new location.

If you want a little more comfort, *Nan Hotel* (☎ 010-985 3414) is just down the road from the ferry pier and has rooms with bathroom and ceiling fan for RM40 and air-con doubles for RM55. All rooms are clean and can accommodate three people. The only drawback is the hotel's proximity to the mosque – you won't have to worry about oversleeping and missing the ferry!

There are a few *kedai kopi* (coffee shops) near the taxi stand as well as a *small store* where you can buy basic provisions.

### Getting There & Away

Kuala Besut is best reached from Kota Bharu to the north. By bus from Kota Bharu you can go via Jerteh (RM3.50) or via Pasir Puteh (RM2.50). From Jerteh to Kuala Besut it costs RM1 by bus and RM8 by taxi. From Pasir Puteh it's RM1 by bus and RM10 by taxi. However, since a taxi to/from Kota Bharu costs only RM24 per car, most people opt to go the whole way by taxi. From the south, you can go to/from Kuala Terengganu by bus (RM5.70) or taxi (RM40 per car).

## PULAU PERHENTIAN

A short boat trip from Kuala Besut will take you to the beautiful islands of Pulau Perhentian Besar and Pulau Perhentian Kecil, just 20km off the coast. These are arguably the most beautiful islands in Malaysia, with crystal-clear aquamarine water and white-sand beaches.

Activities on the islands include snorkelling and diving, jungle walks and just hanging around on the beach waiting for the coconuts to drop. Be warned that there is very little alcohol available on these relatively conservative islands – a Perhentian evening generally involves nothing more decadent than a decent meal and a good book.

Note that these islands basically shut down during the monsoon (usually from mid-November to early March).

### Orientation

A narrow strait separates Perhentian Besar, the big island, from Perhentian Kecil, the small island. While both islands have their strong points, most young budget travellers gravitate to Kecil, where there is an abundance of cheap accommodation. Some avoid the island precisely for this reason and head to Besar, where budget chalets can still be found. For the undecided, you can cross the strait from island to island for around RM10 (about 20 minutes).

PENINSULAR MALAYSIA

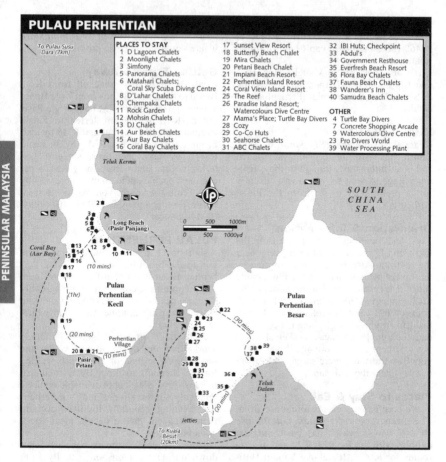

## PULAU PERHENTIAN

To Pulau Susu
Dara (7km)

**PLACES TO STAY**
1 D Lagoon Chalets
2 Moonlight Chalets
3 Simfony
5 Panorama Chalets
6 Matahari Chalets;
 Coral Sky Scuba Diving Centre
8 D'Lahar Chalets
10 Chempaka Chalets
11 Rock Garden
12 Mohsin Chalets
13 DJ Chalet
14 Aur Beach Chalets
15 Aur Bay Chalets
16 Coral Bay Chalets

17 Sunset View Resort
18 Butterfly Beach Chalet
19 Mira Chalets
20 Petani Beach Chalet
21 Impiani Beach Resort
22 Perhentian Island Resort
24 Coral View Island Resort
25 The Reef
26 Paradise Island Resort;
 Watercolours Dive Centre
27 Mama's Place; Turtle Bay Divers
28 Cozy
29 Co-Co Huts
30 Seahorse Chalets
31 ABC Chalets

32 IBI Huts; Checkpoint
33 Abdul's
34 Government Resthouse
35 Everfresh Beach Resort
36 Flora Bay Chalets
37 Fauna Beach Chalets
38 Wanderer's Inn
40 Samudra Beach Chalets

**OTHER**
4 Turtle Bay Divers
7 Concrete Shopping Arcade
9 Watercolours Dive Centre
23 Pro Divers World
39 Water Processing Plant

Teluk Kerma

*SOUTH CHINA SEA*

Long Beach
(Pasir Panjang)

Coral Bay
(Aur Bay)

(10 mins)

0    500    1000m
0    500    1000yd

Pulau
Perhentian
Kecil

Pulau
Perhentian
Besar

(1hr)

(30 mins)

(20 mins)

Perhentian
Village

Pasir
Petani

(10 mins)

Teluk
Dalam

(20 mins)

Jetties

To Kuala
Besut
(20km)

On Perhentian Kecil, the most popular spot is Long Beach (Pasir Panjang), an excellent white sandy beach with a string of economical bungalow operations. Perhentian Kecil is also the administrative centre and has a fair-sized village with a few kedai kopi and shops. Across the narrow waist of the island, Coral Bay is another popular spot with a decent stretch of beach and the best sunsets on the islands. The island also has several isolated bays with private beaches for those in search of solitude.

Over on Besar, most of the accommodation is clustered on the western side of the island along a series of beaches divided by rocky headlands. For those looking to get away from it all, a brief walk through the jungle leads to the isolated bay of Teluk Dalam, which has a wide beach and decent snorkelling.

## Information

It's very difficult to change money on the Perhentians. At present, only Perhentian Island Resort and Coral View Island Resort (on Besar) will cash travellers cheques, both at poor rates; bring plenty of cash over from the mainland.

PENINSULAR MALAYSIA

Most places will allow you to make telephone calls on their portable phones, but you'll pay dearly for the pleasure. If you can't stand a few days away from cyberspace, you can log on at Checkpoint on Besar for RM12 per 30 minutes. By the time this book goes to press, there will undoubtedly be more places offering Internet access – ask around.

## Diving & Snorkelling

There are good coral reefs off both islands and around nearby uninhabited islands, Pulau Susu Dara in particular. The best bets for land-based snorkelling are the northern end of Long Beach on Kecil, and the point in front of Coral View Island Resort on Besar. Most of the chalets organise boating trips for snorkelling, and these are well worth the RM15 or so per person. All places also rent out mask, snorkel and flippers for RM10 per day.

For scuba divers there are several operations on Perhentian Besar. Pro Divers World (☎ 019-363 3695), beside Coral View Island Resort, offers two dives with rental for RM140 and PADI open-water courses for RM750. Nearby, Watercolours (☎ 019-981 1852) is a competent outfit in front of Paradise Resort on the main beach. It offers two dives for RM140 and PADI courses for RM750. Farther down the same beach, Turtle Bay Divers (☎ 010-333 6647) offers two dives for RM140 and PADI courses for RM750. Turtle Bay Divers also offers two-dive trips to nearby Pulau Redang for RM210, a good way to see Redang without staying at one of the island's expensive resorts.

Over on Kecil, the diving scene is dominated by Coral Sky Scuba Diving Centre (☎ 010-910 1963), where two dives costs RM120 and PADI open-water courses go for RM650. It's a popular place and will try to help with accommodation when possible. You'll also find branches of Turtle Bay Divers and Watercolours at Long Beach on Kecil.

## Places to Stay & Eat

Accommodation on Besar is generally more upscale than on Kecil and usually includes a fan and attached bathroom. For an idea of what's available on the islands, visit Perhentian Ferry Travel & Tours' excellent Web site at www.perhentianferry.com.my. Also, be warned that some places, particularly on Kecil, have started to charge 'high-season' prices, usually from late May to early September. This practice is spreading so be ready for some surprises if you visit during this time.

No-one would call the Perhentians a gourmet paradise – you'll most likely have to put up with lots of *mee* (noodle) and *nasi* (rice) dishes, with the occasional fish dinner thrown in. Almost all chalet operations have their own restaurant, and there are one or two separate restaurants on the main beach on Besar and on Long Beach on Kecil. Those with special dietary requirements should consider bringing supplies over on the ferry.

**Pulau Perhentian Besar** There are three main beaches on Besar: the northern beach on the western side, which is dominated by Perhentian Island Resort; the main beach on the western side of the island; and Teluk Dalam, on the island's south-east coast.

*Perhentian Island Resort (☎ 691 0946)* overlooks perhaps the best beach on the islands – a beautiful half-moon bay with good coral around the points on either side. The resort is comfortable and attractive but not of international standard. Chalets range from RM200 to RM350, which is overpriced compared to the island's other offerings. Both rooms and meals are subject to a 10% service charge and 5% government tax. Keep in mind that you *don't* have to stay at the resort to enjoy its beach – anyone can walk over from the island's other beaches.

Besar's main beach is a quick clamber over a headland from the resort. This beach stretches all the way to the southern tip of the island, interrupted by several rocky headlands – at low tide you can walk around them on the sand, otherwise you'll have to go up and over along wooded trails. As a rule, the farther south you go, the cheaper the accommodation gets.

At the northern end of the beach, *Coral View Island Resort (☎ 010-903 0943)* is one

PENINSULAR MALAYSIA

PENINSULAR MALAYSIA

## Perhentian Accommodation Warning

In recent years, the Perhentians have exploded in popularity. In peak season, which is usually from late May to late September, it can be difficult to find a place to stay on some of the island's most popular beaches, Long Beach on Kecil in particular.

The peak-season scenario goes something like this: boat after boat pulls up on Long Beach to disgorge another group of hopeful travellers. Staggering under heavy packs in the hot sun, the new arrivals make their way desperately up and down the beach in search of a vacant room, only to find that even the most wretched accommodation is full. In frustration, they either camp out on the beach and wait for a room to open up, or make the 10-minute journey across the island to Coral Bay to repeat the process all over again.

The real tragedy here is that, while these folks go through hell to secure some pretty grim rooms, there are usually plenty of openings over on Besar or at some of Kecil's lovely isolated bays. So resist the temptation to join the lemmings!

of the island's smartest places, with a good restaurant and a great location. There are several kinds of rooms, chalets and A-frames ranging in price from RM100 to RM250.

Next door, *The Reef* is a reasonable choice with 11 simple chalets for RM60, the only drawback being the nearby generator. Next along, *Paradise Island Resort (☎ 010-911 3852)* is a fine place with clean chalets with fan and bathroom for RM40 to RM80. The restaurant here is quite good.

The last place on this section of beach is *Mama's Place (☎ 010-984 0232)*, a good option with standard rooms with fan and bathroom for RM55 and nicer chalets with fan and bathroom for RM75. It also has family rooms for RM85. The restaurant here does a good Malay-style fish dinner with all the trimmings for RM15 to RM20 if you ask early in the day.

Over the headland there is a crowded stretch of beach with some less appealing places to stay. The first is *Cozy (☎ 019-959 5646)*, a group of chalets built on the rocks overlooking the water and ranging from RM25 to RM80. The location is good but the chalets are a mixed bag. Down on the beach, *Co-Co Huts (☎ 019-910 5019)* has tightly packed A-frames set back from the beach for RM25. A-frames on the beach cost RM60. Behind Co-Co Huts, you'll find *Seahorse Chalets*, an inexpensive choice where standard/deluxe A-frames go for RM10/15. Next along, *ABC Chalets (☎ 697 7568)* has

scruffy rooms in an aging longhouse for RM25 and RM30. The next spot on the beach, *IBI Huts (☎ 010-910 6294)*, has huts with fan and bathroom for RM35/40. The location is pretty good but the huts aren't very special.

Clambering over the next headland brings you to a nice stretch of beach where you'll find the popular *Abdul's (☎ 010-983 7303)*. Options range from longhouse rooms for RM20 to chalets with fan and bathroom for RM40/50 and family rooms for RM80. This is about the best value on Besar. Down the beach from Abdul's, you'll find the *Government Resthouse*, the last place on the main beach, which is reserved for Malaysian politicos and their friends.

It is possible to *camp* on the beach beyond the Government Resthouse, although this area is far from quiet on long weekends.

An easily missed track leads from behind the second jetty over the hill to Teluk Dalam, a secluded bay with a long stretch of shallow beach. The first spot you come to is *Everfresh Beach Resort (☎ 697 7620)*, a rather ramshackle operation with A-frames for RM30 and bungalows for RM50. Next door, *Flora Bay Chalets (☎ 697 7266)* is a big place with a variety of slightly run-down accommodation for RM42 to RM150. Next along, *Fauna Beach Chalets (☎ 697 7607)* is a decent choice offering chalets with fan and bathroom for RM30 to RM45 and family chalets for RM60.

One of the most interesting places in Teluk Dalam is the intimate *Wanderer's Inn* (☎ 010-913 5460). Run by two independent Malay women, there are chalets for RM15 to RM25 and tent sites for RM5 to RM10. This is a very hip, laid-back place.

Last on the beach, *Samudra Beach Chalets* (☎ 010-983 4929) is a pleasantly isolated operation. Bungalows with fan and bathroom cost RM50, A-frames with fan and bathroom are RM30 and family chalets cost RM50 (all include breakfast and you get one night free if you stay five nights).

A trail leads from Fauna Beach Chalets around a water-processing plant over the middle of the island to Perhentian Island Resort. It may be marked 'no trespassing' but this doesn't deter most travellers.

**Pulau Perhentian Kecil** Accommodation over on Kecil is more basic and prices are generally lower – many hover at around RM20 for a chalet with two beds, a mosquito net and a well or common shower.

With a great strip of white sand out the front and good swimming and snorkelling, Long Beach is the most popular place on Kecil. Unfortunately, it's becoming overdeveloped and can be quite noisy. On the rocks at the southern end of the beach, *Rock Garden* has an interesting location and some of the cheapest standard/deluxe bungalows around at RM15/20 for rugged barebones huts; the best ones are high up on the rocks with a good view of the sea.

Down the hill, *Chempaka Chalets* (☎ 019-959 8659), run by the ever-helpful Musky, has good chalets for RM30 to RM50 and tent sites for RM12. Next door, *D'Lahar Chalets* is a poor choice with overpriced chalets (RM119/149) and noisy staff-parties. Set back from the beach, *Mohsin Chalets* (☎ 010-333 8897) is a slightly upscale option with fan chalets for RM60. Unfortunately, the generator is quite noisy.

In the middle of the beach, set back a bit, *Matahari Chalets* (☎ 019-956 5756) is a popular place with a range of accommodation. Simple chalets with fan are RM30 and A-frames with fan and bathroom are RM45

to RM70. This is one of the better choices on Long Beach and the restaurant here gets good reviews. Nearby, *Panorama Chalets* (☎ 010-912 2518) has basic chalets for RM25 to RM80. Next along, *Simfony* (☎ 019-959 1429) has basic A-frames with shared bathroom for RM15 to RM40, which aren't bad for the price.

At the northern end of the beach, *Moonlight Chalets* (☎ 019-985 8222) is another popular spot, with a range of accommodation from RM20 to RM50. It also has one of the better restaurants on the island, with a pleasant veranda.

A trail over the narrow waist of the island leads from Long Beach to Coral Bay (sometimes known as Aur Bay) on the western side of the island. The beach is decent and gets good sunsets but, like Long Beach, its popularity has caught up with it and it's a little crowded and noisy. The southernmost place to stay is *Butterfly Beach Chalet*, which has an interesting location on the rocks but some seriously tatty chalets. However, new ones are under construction and might be worth a look. Next door, *Sunset View Resort* (☎ 012-938 8083) has a good location but its slightly run-down chalets cost RM90 (at this price you'd do much better on Besar).

Central *Coral Bay Chalets* has some of the nicest A-frames on the beach, which rent for RM50. Since there are only four of them, they're usually full. Next door, set back a little from the water, *Aur Bay Chalets* (☎ 010-985 8584) has rooms without/with shower for RM20/40. Back on the beach, *Aur Beach Chalets* has chalets for RM30 to RM50. Nearby, *DJ Chalet* (☎ 010-985 2546) is set back from the beach and has rooms for RM20 and RM30 with bathroom. This is a friendly place, but the rooms are getting pretty run-down.

There are a number of small bays around the island, each with one set of chalets, and often only accessed by boat. *D Lagoon Chalets* (☎ 010-985 7089) is on Teluk Kerma, a small bay on the north-eastern side of the island. This is one of the better places on Kecil, with good coral and a tranquil, isolated location. There are longhouse rooms

PENINSULAR MALAYSIA

and chalets ranging from RM25 to RM50. For those of you with a Tarzan-and-Jane fantasy, there's also a super-cool tree house for RM20. There's a small restaurant, and tracks lead to a couple of very remote beaches in the north-western corner of the island.

On the south-west coast, *Mira Chalets* is another interesting choice on a secluded beach. The chalets, which cost RM20 to RM50, are run-down but very funky. The elevated restaurant has great views over the water and walking tracks lead through the rainforest to Pasir Petani (20 minutes) and north to Coral Bay (one hour).

On the south coast at the lovely isolated beach of Pasir Petani, there are a couple of places. The cheaper of the two is *Petani Beach Chalet* (☎ 019-313 3887), which has just a few simple chalets by the beach for RM70. Next door is the upmarket *Impiani Beach Resort* (☎ 010-903 0500), where nice chalets with air-con and bathroom cost a healthy RM170. While you can get here on foot from Mira Chalets or Perhentian village, it's much easier to get dropped off by boat, especially when you first arrive with all your luggage.

## Getting There & Away

Speedboats and regular boats run between Kuala Besut and the Perhentians. Speedboats depart from Kuala Besut at around 9.30 and 10.30 am, and 1 and 3 pm daily (30 minutes, RM30 one way). Slowboats leave approximately every hour from 9.30 am to 4.30 pm daily (about 1½ hours, RM20 one way). The boats will drop you off at any of the beaches. In the other direction, speedboats depart from the islands daily at around 8.30 am, noon and 4 pm; slowboats hourly from 8 am to 2 pm. It's a good idea to let the owner of your guesthouse know a day before you leave so they can arrange a pick-up. Tickets are sold by several travel agents around town, the best of which is Perhentian Ferry Travel & Tours (☎ 691 9679) – see the Orientation & Information entry under Kuala Besut earlier.

Note that you can board a speedboat in either direction with a slowboat ticket if you pay the RM10 fare difference.

A couple of things to keep in mind: The waves on Long Beach can be hazardous – when the waves are high get dropped off or picked up on the other side of the island at Coral Bay. Also, guesthouse operators on Kecil now charge RM2 for ferry pick-ups and drop-offs.

## Getting Around

While there are some trails around the island, the easiest way to go from beach to beach or island to island is by boat. Most resort and chalet owners can arrange for a boat and driver. From island to island, the trip costs RM10 per boat, and a jaunt from one beach to another on the same island usually costs about RM8.

# Kelantan

☎ 09

Kelantan is Malaysia at its most Malayan – a centre for Malay culture, crafts and religion. It's the place to watch batik being made, see kite-flying contests, admire traditional woodcarving techniques, photograph colourful marketplaces and marvel at the skills of *songket* (fabric woven with gold thread) weavers and silversmiths.

The capital, Kota Bharu, is a good place to sample this traditional culture, and makes a good base from which to explore the surrounding countryside; but the true Malay spirit is found in the villages of Kelantan.

The most conservative state in Peninsular Malaysia and a last bastion of opposition rule, Kelantan's government is an alliance of the dominant Islamic Party of Malaysia (PAS) and the National Front (BN). The government has tried for years without success to impose *syariah,* or Islamic law, on its citizens. It's still a poor state and is a world apart from the go-go western states of Peninsular Malaysia.

The Kelantan state economy is driven by the production of rice, based mainly on the fertile plain of the Sungai (River) Kelantan, which flows due north, reaching the sea just north of Kota Bharu. Fishing and tobacco growing are other important activities.

## History

Archaeological finds at Gua Musang and Gua Cha have turned up evidence of human settlements dating back to prehistoric times.

In later times (early Christian era), Kelantan was influenced by the Indianised Funan kingdom on the Mekong River. Farming methods used in Kelantan are based on Funan practices; the *wayang kulit* (shadow play) and weaving methods are also thought to have come from Funan.

After being a vassal of first the Sumatran Srivijaya Empire, and then the Siamese, Kelantan came under the sway of the new Melaka sultanate in the 15th

PENINSULAR MALAYSIA

## HIGHLIGHTS

- **Kota Bharu** – a bastion of traditional Malay culture, with the best night market in the country

- **The 'jungle railway'** – from Tumpat down into Pahang state; it's a great way to see Malaysia's mountainous interior without breaking into a sweat

- **The Tumpat region** – an area of strong Thai influence, with several unusual wats scattered between pleasant farming *kampung* (villages)

century. With the demise of that sultanate in the 17th century, Kelantan was ruled by Johor and then, the following century, by Terengganu.

By the 1820s Kelantan was the most populous and one of the most prosperous states on the Malay Peninsula. As was the case in Terengganu, it managed to escape the ravages of the disputes that plagued the west-coast states, and so experienced largely unimpeded development. Also like Terengganu, Kelantan had strong ties with Siam (now Thailand) throughout the 19th century, before control was passed to the British following the signing of an Anglo-Siamese treaty in 1909. The biggest upheaval came in the late 18th century, when the state was plagued by a spate of natural disasters – hurricanes, famine and cattle plagues – and many of its residents migrated to Kedah.

Kelantan was the first place in Malaya to be invaded by Japanese troops in WWII. During the Japanese occupation, control of the state was passed to Thailand, but in 1948 Kelantan became a member of the Federation of Malaya.

## KOTA BHARU

In the north-eastern corner of the peninsula, Kota Bharu is the termination of the east-coast road, and a gateway to Thailand.

At first glance, Kota Bharu is much like other east-coast cities – a modern, architecturally uninspired town, set on the banks of a wide river. But if you scratch the surface, Kota Bharu has a number of attractions and is a good base for exploring the surrounding region. Many travellers plan an overnight stop here en route to or from Thailand or Pulau Perhentian (Perhentian Islands).

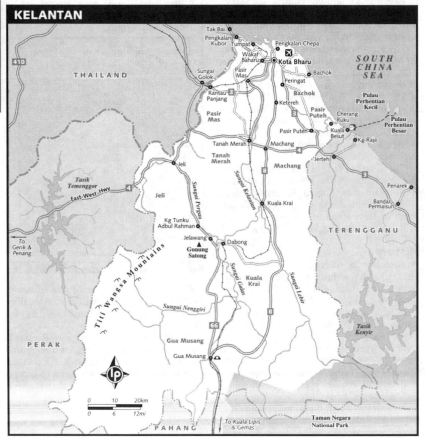

## Orientation & Information

The centre of town is a busy area north of the clock tower, bounded by Jalan Pintu Pong, Jalan Kebun Sultan/Jalan Sultan Mahmud, Jalan Hospital and Jalan Temenggong.

The Kota Bharu tourist information centre (☎ 748 5534) is open Sunday to Thursday from 8 am to 1 pm and 2 to 4.45 pm, and is closed on Friday and Saturday. It's on Jalan Sultan Ibrahim, just south of the clock tower.

The immigration office (☎ 748 2120) is at Wisma Persekutuan on Jalan Bayam.

The Thai consulate (☎ 744 0867) is on Jalan Pengkalan Chepa, and is open from 9 am to noon and 2 to 3.30 pm Sunday to Thursday.

Banks are open from 10 am to 3 pm Saturday to Wednesday, 9.30 to 11.30 am Thursday, and are closed on Friday. If you need to change money after banking hours, the Maybank moneychanger near the central market is usually open to 7 pm.

If you need to log on, try McCyber Internet Café (RM3 per hour) in the McDonald's near the central market, or the AF Cyber Café (RM2.50 to RM5 per hour, depending on the speed of the machine) around the corner.

In Kelantan, state offices are closed Thursday afternoon and Friday, but open on Saturday and Sunday.

## Padang Merdeka

Padang Merdeka (Independence Square) is a strip of grass that was established as a memorial following WWI. It is best-known as the place where the British exhibited the body of Tok Janggut, 'Father Beard', a respected elder who was killed at Pasir Puteh in 1915 after leading a 2000-strong uprising against British imperialism (more specifically, British land taxes).

**Museums** The real attraction of the Padang Merdeka area is the cluster of museums close by. They are all open from 8.30 am to 4.45 pm daily except Friday.

Starting closest to the river, the first museum you come to is **Bank Kerapu** (WWII Memorial Museum; RM2). It's basically a collection of photographic memorabilia illustrating the perfidy of the Japanese, but there is also some hardware (Japanese swords) on display. It's housed in Kota Bharu's first stone building, built in 1912 by the Mercantile Bank and later occupied by the Hongkong & Shanghai Bank.

The mosque-like building across the road from Bank Kerapu is **Muzium Islam** (Islamic Museum). The building was once known as Serambi Mekah, or the 'Veranda to Mecca' – a reference to its days as Kelantan's first school of Islamic instruction. Nowadays it celebrates the percolation of Islam into the everyday life of the state. The collection is quite small; entry is free.

Farther along again is **Istana Jahar** (Royal Customs Museum; RM2). This beautiful old wooden structure dates to 1887 and is worth a look. There are excellent displays of songket and other textiles, silver craft and royal artefacts. Inside, take note of the wrought-iron staircases that lead upstairs to a glorious wooden veranda. Outside, you'll find the Weapons Gallery with a small collection of spears and *kris* (daggers).

From Istana Jahar, turn left (north) and look for the sky-blue building that houses **Istana Batu** (Royal Museum; RM2). The building was constructed in 1939 and served as the palace of the crown prince from 1969 until it was donated to the state. It now houses a royal dining room, an opulent living room, replicas of the crown jewels and other royal bric-a-brac.

Across the road is **Kampung Kraftangan** (Handicraft Village; RM1). This is a touristy affair, featuring a museum with displays of silversmithing, batik making and other cultural activities.

Opposite Istana Batu, surrounded by walls and closed to the public, is the **Istana Balai Besar** (Palace of the Large Audience Hall).

## Muzim Negeri Kelantan

The Muzim Negeri Kelantan (State Museum) is opposite the clock tower, next to the tourist information centre. It brings together an eclectic array of artefacts, crafts, paintings and photographic displays, all

# KOTA BHARU

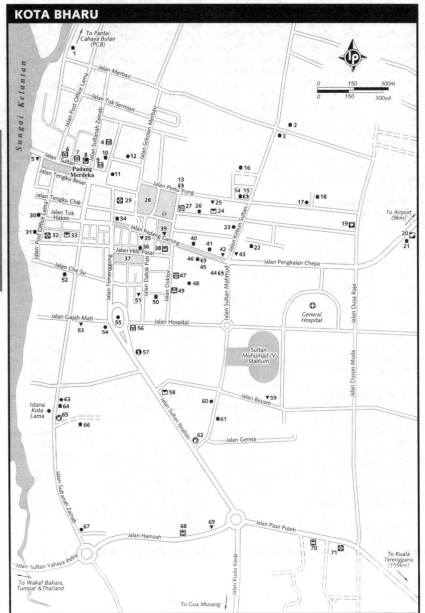

## KOTA BHARU

**PLACES TO STAY**
1 Eastana Guesthouse
2 KB Garden Hostel
3 Star Hostel
10 Safar Inn
14 Juita Inn
16 Ideal Travellers' Guest House
18 Zeck Traveller's Inn
21 Rainbow Inn
22 Friendly Guest House
30 Hotel New North Malaysia;
   Anata no Restaurant & Café
31 Diamond Puteri Hotel
34 Temenggong Hotel
36 Thye Ann Hotel
40 KB Backpackers Lodge
41 Kencana Inn
46 KB Backpackers Lodge Two
50 Hotel Ansar
52 Crystal Lodge
61 Hotel Perdana; Avis
64 Menora Guest House
66 Rebana House

**PLACES TO EAT**
5 Food Stalls
25 Muhibah Vegetarian
   Restaurant
35 Restoran Razak
39 Night Market

42 Restoran Golden City; The
   Fame Kopitiam N' Café
43 Seri Dewi
51 Muhibah Vegetarian
   Restaurant
53 Meena Curry House
59 Food Stalls
69 Food Stalls; Outdoor Market

**OTHER**
4 Istana Batu
   (Royal Museum)
6 Bank Kerapu (WWII
   Memorial Museum)
7 Muzium Islam
8 State Mosque
9 Istana Jahar
   (Royal Customs Museum)
11 Istana Balai Besar
12 Kampung Kraftagan
   (Handicraft Village)
13 Maybank Moneychanger
15 Mayban Finance
17 Bird-Singing Venue
19 Sun Café
20 Thai Consulate
23 Bicycle Rental
24 Post Office
26 Rosli Abdullah Foto;
   AF Cyber Café

27 McCyber Internet Café
28 Central Market
29 Bazaar Buluh Kubu
32 Hankyu Jaya Department
   Store
33 Post Office
37 Old Central Market
38 Central Bus & Taxi Station
44 Maybank
45 Hongkong Bank
47 Telekom
48 Microwave Relay Tower
49 Taxi Station
54 Malaysia Airlines
55 Clock Tower
56 Muzim Negeri Kelantan
57 Tourist Information Centre
58 Post Office
60 Gelanggang Seni
   (Cultural Centre)
62 Petrol Station
63 Silver Shops
65 Caltex Petrol Station
67 Silversmith
68 External (Jalan Hamzah) Bus
   Station
70 Langgar Bus Station
71 Kota Seri Mutiara Mall;
   Billion Supermarket

connected in some way or another with Kelantan state. There's some excellent Ming- and Qing-dynasty porcelain downstairs and kites upstairs. The downstairs local art exhibit is given over to a nostalgic celebration of kampung life. It is open from 8.30 am to 4.45 pm daily except Friday; entry is RM2.

### Markets
Kota Bharu's **central market** is one of the most colourful and active in Malaysia. It is in a modern, octagonal building with traders selling fresh produce on the ground floor; and spices, basketware and other goods on the floors above. Near the market is the **Bazaar Buluh Kubu**, a good place to buy handicrafts.

The **old central market** consists of a complete block of food stalls on the ground floor, and a good selection of batik, songket and clothes on the 1st floor.

### Gelanggang Seni
Kota Bharu provides an opportunity to see top-spinning, traditional dance-dramas, wayang kulit and other traditional activities. The place to go is Gelanggang Seni (Cultural Centre), across the road from Hotel Perdana on Jalan Sultan Mahmud. Free afternoon and evening sessions are held on Monday, Wednesday and Saturday from 1 March to 30 October, except during Ramadan. Check with the tourist information centre (☎ 748 5534) for more details, as times vary.

### Organised Tours
Some of the guesthouses around town run tours around Kota Bharu and the surrounding areas. KB Backpackers Lodge (☎ 743 2125) can arrange four-hour cultural tours of Kota Bharu (RM40), two-night/three-day trips to the Jelawang area (RM200) and one-day waterfall tours (RM20, including

PENINSULAR MALAYSIA

lunch). Zeck Traveller's Inn (☎ 743 1613) can arrange similar tours.

## Special Events

Each year around August, Kota Bharu has a **bird-singing contest**, when you can see Malay songbirds perform. Every Friday morning there's also a bird-singing contest out near Zeck Traveller's Inn. Here the locals hang their decorative bird cages up on long poles, then sit back and listen. It happens to a lesser extent on other days of the week as well. Ask at the tourist information centre for more details.

The spectacular **kite festival** is usually held in May, the **drum festival** in July and the **top-spinning contest** in September. The Sultan's Birthday celebration involves a week of cultural events. The dates vary, so check with the tourist information centre or get hold of Tourism Malaysia's *Calendar of Events* brochure.

Stay on your perch for the annual bird-singing contest.

## Places to Stay – Budget

Locals count upwards of 60 guesthouses in Kota Bharu. Many have bicycles and cooking facilities. For anyone spending more than a couple of days in Kota Bharu, the best places to be based are the 'homestays' on the outskirts of town. The guesthouses in the centre of town are generally noisy and slightly claustrophobic, though few of them lack smiles or useful travelling tips.

***Zeck Traveller's Inn*** *(☎ 743 1613)* is a popular spot with a friendly, informative owner. It's your standard-issue guesthouse and the rooms are clean, if a little cramped. It's around 15 minutes' walk from the centre of town. Out by the Thai consulate, ***Rainbow Inn*** *(☎ 743 4936)* is a small place with rooms for RM10 and RM15. It's got a nice garden but gets a bit of noise from the main road.

If you want to be more centrally located yet insulated from the traffic noise, a decent choice is the ***Ideal Travellers' Guest House*** *(☎ 744 2246),* in a private house down an alley off Jalan Pintu Pong. Dorm beds here cost RM6 and private rooms range from RM12 to RM35. It also runs ***Friendly Guest House*** *(☎ 744 4832),* a few hundred metres away. It's not as attractive, but is quiet and has rooms for RM15.

One of the best places in the centre of town, ***KB Backpackers Lodge*** *(☎ 743 2125)* is a friendly and popular place. It has dorm beds (RM8) and private rooms (RM15 to RM22), a pleasant common area and cooking facilities. The owners can help with local and ongoing travel arrangements, and have Internet and fax facilities. If the main building is full, try ***KB Backpackers Lodge Two*** across the street.

***Menora Guest House*** *(☎ 748 1669)* has a variety of accommodation, from dorm beds for RM5 to large air-con doubles for RM30. This place is cleaner than many other guesthouses in town. Although on a busy road, it's fairly quiet, and the rooftop terrace is popular.

Not far south of the Menora is ***Rebana House*** – look for the faded sign pointing up an alley next to the Caltex petrol station. It's a lovely house, decorated Malay-style with

PENINSULAR MALAYSIA

Top spinning competition, Kelantan. (My top's bigger than your top.)

CHRIS MELLOR

JEAN-BERNARD CARILLET

Traditional dancer, Kelantan.

Kite maker, Kota Bharu, Kelantan.

RICHARD I'ANSON

Reclining Buddha, Tumpat, Kelantan.

CHRIS ROWTHORN

RICHARD I'ANSON

Boats on the beach, Marang, Terengganu.

RICHARD I'ANSON

Central market, Kota Bharu, Kelantan

ANDERS BLOMQVIST

Lazing on idyllic Long Beach, Pulau Perhentian Kecil, Terengganu.

lots of artwork around. There's a variety of rooms available, from the RM9 dorm and poky RM13 singles to some beautiful larger rooms for RM19. The place is well decorated, but the owners seem rather indifferent.

In the north of town, *Eastana Guesthouse* (☎ 747 9380) is a clean but drab place with beds in the dorm for RM10 and private rooms for RM25 to RM30.

Another option is one of the old Chinese hotels – they are usually noisy and seedy, but relatively inexpensive, with rooms for RM15 to RM20. Possibilities include *Thye Ann Hotel* (☎ 748 5907), near the bus station, and *Hotel New North Malaysia* (☎ 748 2553), by the river.

If you're willing to pay slightly more, there are two good-value, but characterless, places out on Jalan Merbau. *Star Hostel* (☎ 748 6115) has clean air-con rooms for RM35. Across the street, *KB Garden Hostel* (☎ 748 5696) is really a hotel masquerading as a guesthouse, with air-con rooms for RM35.

## Places to Stay – Mid-Range
Mid-range accommodation in Kota Bharu tends to be overpriced and run-down. Hopefully, by the time this book goes to press there'll be some new places in this price bracket.

*Kencana Inn* (☎ 744 7944) is fully air-conditioned and conveniently located and has rooms for RM46 and upwards. The rooms are getting a little worn but the price is reasonable.

*Safar Inn* (☎ 747 8000), in a quiet part of town between Istana Jahar and Istana Batu, has decent rooms from RM75. *Hotel Ansar* (☎ 747 4000) has standard rooms for RM80, which is slightly overpriced considering the condition of the rooms.

*Temenggong Hotel* (☎ 748 3481) is a decent mid-range choice with rooms in the new wing for RM73. This is perhaps the best of a bad lot here in Kota Bharu.

*Crystal Lodge* (☎ 747 0888) rivals the Temenggong as the best-value mid-range place in town, with newish rooms for RM78.20. The draw here is the rooftop restaurant and the convenient location.

*Juita Inn* (☎ 744 6888) is priced higher than most in this range, at RM95/110 for singles/doubles. The rooms are, in fact, something of a step down in quality.

## Places to Stay – Top End
The top hotel is undoubtedly the new *Diamond Puteri Hotel* (☎ 743 9988). Near the waterfront, this sprawling international-class hotel has all the amenities you'd expect. Standard rooms start at RM255, and deluxe rooms and suites are also available.

The 136-room *Hotel Perdana* (☎ 748 5000) on Jalan Sultan Mahmud is the other contender in the luxury market. Standard rooms are listed at RM170 but promotional rates are often available.

## Places to Eat & Drink
The best and cheapest Malay food in Kota Bharu is found at the *night market*, opposite the central bus station. The food stalls are set up in the evening and there's a wide variety of delicious, cheap Malay food. Just bear in mind that the whole thing closes down for evening prayers between 7 and 7.45 pm, and Muslims and non-Muslims alike are forced to vacate the premises.

The night market is a good place to snack-track and then buy rice wrapped in a banana leaf from one of the rice stalls. You can then sit at any of the tables, eat your meal and order a drink (nothing alcoholic). Traditionally you eat with the right hand – each table has a jug of water and a roll of tissue paper to clean your fingers – but forks and spoons are readily available. Local specialities include *ayam percik* (marinated chicken on bamboo skewers) and *nasi kerabu* (rice with coconut, fish and spices). More-unusual options include blue rice, hard-boiled quail eggs and that old favourite, barbecued stingray.

It's easy to write off the rest of Kota Bharu after the night market, but there's a surprising amount of good food around town. More *food stalls* can be found next to the river opposite the Padang Merdeka, by the Jalan Hamzah bus station and at the Sultan Muhamad IV stadium.

*Restoran Razak*, on the corner of Jalan Datok Pati and Jalan Padang Garong, is cheap and has good Indian halal food. For an excellent and cheap lunch of Indian curry on a banana leaf, try *Meena Curry House* on Jalan Gajah Mati. More Indian curries can be had at the *Seri Dewi* restaurant on Jalan Kebun Sultan.

There are also plenty of Chinese restaurants around town, including good chicken-rice places on Jalan Padang Garong near Kencana Inn. The oddly named *Anata no Restaurant & Café*, on the ground floor of Hotel New North Malaysia, cooks up a very good Cantonese-style duck and rice, and serves ice-cold beer. For more-upscale Chinese fare, try *Restoran Golden City*, which serves good stir-fries, seafood and a selection of Thai favourites.

Vegetarians will love *Muhibah Vegetarian Restaurant* on Jalan Pintu Pong, which serves meatless Malay, Western and Chinese dishes, as well as fresh fruit juices and soy milk. There's another branch on Jalan Datok Pati, but it's not quite as good.

Surprisingly for conservative Kelantan, there are actually a few bars in Kota Bharu. For a beer and a blast of Western pop music, try *The Fame Kopitiam N' Café* above Restoran Golden City. Another place for an evening beer is *Sun Café*, out on Jalan Dusa Raja.

## Shopping
Kota Bharu is a centre for Malay crafts. Batik, songket, silverware, woodcarving and kite-making factories and shops are dotted around town.

One of the best places to see handicrafts is on the road north to Pantai Cahaya Bulan (PCB). There are a number of workshops, representing most crafts, stretched out along the road all the way to the beach. Unfortunately, it's hard to visit these without your own transport; an alternative is to join an organised tour (see Organised Tours earlier).

The markets are as good a place as any to buy handicrafts, if you know the prices and bargain hard. Figure on RM5 to RM100 for decorative kites and RM30 to RM200 for real flying kites, RM7 to RM50 for batik pieces and at least RM100 for 1 sq m of batik.

## Getting There & Away
For information on travelling between Kota Bharu and Thailand, see the Thailand entry at the end of this section.

**Air** The Malaysia Airlines office (☎ 744 7000) is opposite the clock tower on Jalan Gajah Mati. There are direct flights to/from Johor Bahru (RM194) and Kuala Lumpur (KL; RM104).

**Bus** The state-run SKMK is the largest bus company, and runs all the city and regional buses as well as most of the long-distance buses. It operates from the central bus station (city and regional buses) and the Langgar bus station (long-distance buses), in the south of the city. All the other long-distance bus companies operate from the Jalan Hamzah external bus station. On arrival in Kota Bharu some of the buses will drop you at the central bus station, but they don't depart from there.

SKMK is the easiest to deal with, as it has ticket offices at all the bus stations. While long-distance departures are from the Langgar bus station, a few evening long-distance buses also go from the central bus station. Ask which station your bus departs from when you buy your ticket, and book as far ahead as possible, especially for the Butterworth and Penang buses.

SKMK has regular buses from the central bus station to Kuala Terengganu (three hours, RM7.50) and Kuantan (seven hours, RM17.20). Other SKMK buses leave from Langgar bus station. Buses to Johor Bahru (10 hours, RM29 air-con), Singapore (12 hours, RM30) and KL (nine hours, RM28) leave at 8 pm (also 9 pm to KL). 'Business class' buses (with fewer seats) are available for these routes as well. The buses to Butterworth (eight hours, RM19) and Penang (RM19.50) leave at 9 pm. There is a bus to Jerantut (RM20) at 6 am. Other destinations are Alor Setar, Gerik, Kuala Dungun, Mersing and Temerloh.

The other companies cover many of the same routes and are worth trying if the SKMK buses are full. Buy your tickets at the Jalan Hamzah external bus station; or at the Bazaar Buluh Kubu, where some of the companies have agents. Your guesthouse operator can tell you where to go.

All regional buses leave from the central bus station. Destinations include: Wakaf Baharu (Nos 19 and 27, 60 sen), Rantau Panjang (No 29, RM2.70), Tumpat (No 19, RM1.30), Bachok (Nos 2B, 23 and 29, RM1.70), Pasir Puteh (No 3, RM2.50), Jerteh (No 3, RM3.50), Kuala Krai (Nos 5 and 57, RM4), and Gua Musang (No 57, RM6). Note that some of these may be identified by destination rather than number.

**Train** The so-called 'jungle railway' starts at Tumpat and goes through Kuala Krai, Gua Musang, Kuala Lipis and Jerantut (for Taman Negara National Park), and eventually meets the Singapore–Kuala Lumpur line at Gemas. There are express and local trains on this line. The nearest station to Kota Bharu is Wakaf Baharu, a 60-sen trip on bus No 19 or 27. Times listed here are for Wakaf Baharu.

There is a daily express train all the way to KL at 6.56 pm. It stops at Kuala Lipis, Jerantut and Gemas before arriving in KL at 6.50 am the following day. There is also a daily express to Singapore at 8.01 pm making the same stops en route before arriving at 8.40 am the following day. Note that as both of these trains leave in the evening, you'll miss out on most of the jungle scenery.

A local train leaves daily at 6.06 am and stops at almost every station before arriving at Gemas at 7.35 pm. There are also two local trains daily that only go as far as Gua Musang, one at 3.47 am and one at 1.46 pm. From there, you can catch an ongoing express train the same day to KL or Singapore, or wait until the following morning and continue south on a local train.

Note that the National Rail Service (KTM) schedule changes every six months, so it's a good idea to double-check departure times with the owner of your guesthouse or visit the KTM Web site at www.ktmb.com.my. KTM has a ticket office (counter 5) at the Jalan Hamzah bus station in Kota Bharu. See the introductory Getting Around chapter for train timetable and fare details.

Finally, for those who plan to catch an early morning 'jungle train' should arrange for the taxi to Wakaf Baharu the *night before* you plan to leave, as it's extremely difficult to find a taxi on the street in the early morning. Alternatively, you might consider spending the night in Pasir Mas and catching the train from there.

**Taxi** The taxi station is on the southern side of the central bus station, and there is an overflow station during the day at the site of the night market. Although private cars will also offer their services, it's best to take an official taxi as these are cheaper and safer.

Taxi destinations and costs per car include Butterworth (RM180), KL (RM200), Kuala Terengganu (RM56), Kuala Lipis (RM140) and Kuantan (RM120).

**Car** Avis has an office (☎ 748 4457) in Hotel Perdana on Jalan Sultan Mahmud.

**Thailand** The Thai border is at Rantau Panjang (Sungai Golok on the Thai side), 1½ hours by bus from Kota Bharu. Bus No 29 departs on the hour from the central bus station, and costs RM2.70. From Rantau Panjang walk across the border; it's about 1km to the station (a trishaw costs RM5). Malaysian currency is accepted in Sungai Golok. Share taxis from Kota Bharu to Rantau Panjang cost RM16 per car and take 45 minutes.

From Sungai Golok there is a train to Surathani at 6 am, to Bangkok at 10.05 am and an express train to Bangkok at 11 am. All stop at Hat Yai and Surathani. Buses to Hat Yai leave from the Valentine Hotel in Sungai Golok until 3 pm, and there are taxis to Yala and Narathiwat town.

An alternative route into Thailand is via Pengkalan Kubor, on the coast. It's more time-consuming and very few travellers go this way. See the Around Kota Bharu section later for more details.

## Getting Around
**To/From the Airport** The airport is 9km from town. You can take bus No 9 from the old central market; a taxi costs RM12.

**Bus** Most of the city buses leave from the middle of the old central market, on the Jalan Hilir Pasar side; or from opposite the Bazaar Buluh Kubu.

**Trishaw** Trishaws still linger on, though most people nowadays get around on motorbikes. A short journey of up to 1km costs RM3.

**Bicycle** There's a bicycle rental shop on Jalan Kebun Sultan where you can rent old creakers for RM5 per day.

## AROUND KOTA BHARU
### Masjid Kampung Laut
Reputed to be the oldest mosque in Peninsular Malaysia, Masjid Kampung Laut was built about 300 years ago by Javanese Muslims as thanks for a narrow escape from pirates. Built entirely of wood, without the use of nails, the mosque contains some impressive woodcarvings.

It originally stood at Kampung Laut, just across the river from Kota Bharu, but each year the monsoon floods caused considerable damage to the mosque, and in 1968 it was moved to a safer location. It now stands about 10km inland at Kampung Nilam Puri, a local centre for religious study. Note that entry is forbidden to non-Muslims.

To get there, take bus No 4 (RM1.20) from Kota Bharu's central bus station and get off at Nilam Puri. Try to go in the morning, when the mosque is least crowded.

### Pantai Cahaya Bulan (PCB)
PCB is a Malay abbreviation that sounds far more appealing translated into English – the

---

**The East Coast House**

The *kampung* (village) houses of Kelantan and Terengganu differ quite markedly from those found in the western peninsular states. The most obvious difference is that the roofs are tiled and show a Thai or Cambodian influence.

As in Thai houses, the walls and columns of the east-coast houses are well carved, and there are far fewer windows.

---

'Beach of Passionate Love'. At least that is what it was once called. Pantai Cinta Berahi is now known as Pantai Cahaya Bulan – 'Moonlight Beach' – in keeping with Islamic sensitivities. Fortunately the same acronym applies and everyone refers to it as PCB.

PCB is 10km north of Kota Bharu, only 30 minutes by bus. It's a good day trip on a sunny day, but hardly the kind of place you'd want to retire to. Accommodation is provided by shabby resorts, and even the beach looks a little tired.

**Getting There & Away** Take bus No 10 (80 sen) from Kota Bharu. A taxi costs RM12.

### Pantai Irama
Pantai Irama (Beach of Melody) at Bachok has landscaped gardens along the foreshore and is popular with day-trippers. Like most of the beaches around Kota Bharu, it's pleasant but nothing special. *Motel Bachok* (☎ *778 8462*) offers mid-range accommodation.

Bus Nos 23 and 39 (RM1.70) run out to the beach.

### Other Beaches
Thirteen kilometres from Kota Bharu and 3km beyond the airport, **Pantai Dasar Sabak** is a beach with a history. On 7 December 1941, the Pacific theatre of WWII commenced on this beach when Japanese troops stormed ashore, a full hour and a half before the rising sun rose over Pearl Harbor.

Other beaches close to Kota Bharu include **Pantai Dalam Rhu**, near the fishing village of Semerak, not too far from the Terengganu state border. It's sometimes known as Pantai Bisikan Bayu, the 'Beach of Whispering Breeze'. North of Kota Bharu there's **Pantai Seri Tujuh** (see that entry in the Tumpat District section later).

### Tumpat District
Tumpat district is a major agricultural area bordering Thailand, and the Thai influence is very noticeable. Small villages are scattered among the picturesque rice fields, and there are a number of interesting Thai

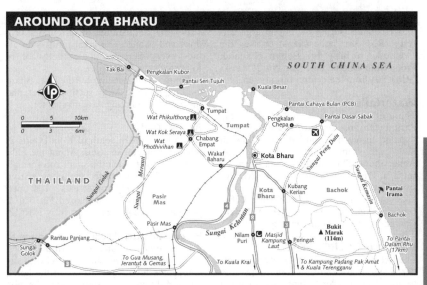

**AROUND KOTA BHARU**

Buddhist temples, such as Wat Phothivi-han. Other places of interest include the beach resort at Pantai Seri Tujuh, and Pengkalan Kubor is an exit point for Thailand. Tumpat town is at the end of the railway line, but it has no hotels.

**Temples** Claimed to be one of the largest temples in South-East Asia, **Wat Phothivi-han** is a Buddhist temple with a 40m-long reclining Buddha statue. It was built in 1973. The Buddha statue itself is unremark-able, but the novelty of finding a wat in strongly Muslim Kelantan is enough to add some interest. There is a resthouse available for use by sincere devotees, for a donation.

To get to Wat Phothivihan, take bus No 19 or 27 from Kota Bharu to Chabang Empat. Get off at the crossroads and turn left (south-west). Walk 3.5km along this road, through interesting villages and paddy fields, until you reach Kampung Jambu and the reclining Buddha (about one hour). A taxi to the wat from Chabang Empat, if you can find one, costs RM4.

The region is dotted with Thai-influenced temples, and the Wesak Festival (usually held in April or May) is a particularly good time to visit them. At Chabang Empat, if you take the turn to the right (north) at the light in front of the police station, you will come to **Wat Kok Seraya** after about 1km. This wat houses a modest standing Buddha. Continuing north about 4km in the direction of Tumpat, you will come to **Wat Phikulthong**, housing an impressive gold, standing Buddha. There are pleasant grounds for strolling. You can get to these wats on bus No 19; continue past Chabang Empat and ask the driver to let you off in front of these temples.

**Pantai Seri Tujuh Resort** This down-market beach resort is on a long spit of land, with a sweeping stretch of beach facing the sea and a quiet bay behind. It is popular during holidays, but otherwise very quiet. The surrounding villages are still very traditional and you can see Malay fishing boats being built at a few shipyards. The government-run *Chalet Pantai Seri Tujah* (☎ 721 1753) has air-con chalets from RM65, but they're nothing special.

**Pengkalan Kubor** Right on the Thai border, Pengkalan Kubor is the immigration checkpoint for this little-used back route into Thailand. During the day a large car-ferry (RM1 for pedestrians) crosses the river over to busy Tak Bai in Thailand. From Kota Bharu, take bus No 27 or 43 (RM1.80) from the central bus station.

## Waterfalls

There are a number of waterfalls in the Pasir Puteh area. **Jeram Pasu** is the most popular; to reach it you have to follow an 8km path from Kampung Padang Pak Amat, about 35km south of Kota Bharu en route to Pasir Puteh. Bus No 3 (RM2.90) from Kota Bharu's central bus station will take you as far as Padang Pak Amat. Other falls in this area include **Jeram Tapeh**, **Cherang Tuli** and **Jeram Lenang**.

## EAST-WEST HIGHWAY

The Lebuhraya (East-West Highway) starts near Kota Bharu and runs roughly parallel to the Thai border, eventually meeting Route 76 at the town of Gerik. It's something of an engineering masterpiece, and the views from the highway are often superb, including the vast expanse of Tasik (Lake) Temenggor, a reservoir similar in appearance to Terengganu's Tasik Kenyir. The best way to travel this route, without your own car, is to take any bus between Kota Bharu and Gerik (or between Tanah Merah and Gerik). From Kota Bharu, buses to Ipoh and Butterworth/Penang use this route.

## JUNGLE RAILWAY

Known as the 'jungle railway' or the 'east coast railway', this line traverses Peninsular Malaysia's mountainous, jungle-clad interior. The line is an engineering marvel and the views are often superb – it's well worth the trip if you have the time.

Commencing in Tumpat, near Kota Bharu, the line runs through Kuala Krai, Gua Musang, Kuala Lipis and Jerantut (the access point for Taman Negara National Park), and eventually meets the Singapore–Kuala Lumpur railway line at Gemas. While express trains make the journey by night, those who want to see the jungle are advised to take a daytime local train. If you

do you'll probably find yourself sharing a seat with vast quantities of agricultural produce and babies. The local trains stop almost everywhere and don't strictly adhere to posted schedules.

For more information see the Kota Bharu Getting There & Away section earlier, and the Malaysia Getting Around chapter.

## Kuala Krai

Kuala Krai, 65km south of Kota Bharu, is not an attraction in itself. About the only thing to do is to visit the small zoo specialising in local wildlife, including native bears and musang (civet cats). It's open from 9 am to 6.30 pm (closed 12.30 to 2 pm) daily except Friday, and entry is RM2.

**Places to Stay** About the only place to stay in town is *Hotel Seri Maju* (☎ 966 6000), an overpriced Chinese hotel with air-con rooms for RM50. To get to the hotel, take a right out of the station, then the next left; it's above the Wang Fu Emporium one street north of the main road.

**Getting There & Away** Bus No 5 to/from Kota Bharu is RM4. A taxi to/from Kota Bharu costs RM26 per car. Kuala Krai is on the jungle railway; northbound locals depart at 9.27 am and 3.42 pm; northbound expresses depart at 5.54 and 7.10 am and 6.42 pm; southbound locals depart at 5.03 and 8.28 am and 3.24 pm; and southbound expresses depart at 8.04 and 9.10 pm. Local trains are usually around 30 minutes late.

## Jelawang/Dabong Area

There are several minor attractions in the Jelawang/Dabong Area (sometimes known as the 'Jelawang Jungle Park'). The area is usually visited as part of a tour organised in Kota Bharu (see Getting There & Away later). Although the gateway to the area, the small kampung of Dabong, is accessible by logging roads, it's easier and much more scenic to take a riverboat from Kuala Krai to Dabong.

There are several caves in the limestone outcrops a few kilometres south-east of town. Of these, the most impressive is

**Stepping Stone Cave**, a narrow 30m corridor through a limestone wall that leads to a hidden grotto and then on to **Kris Cave**, named for a stalactite that resembles a kris. These two caves *should not* be attempted by those with claustrophobia. **Gua Ikan** (Fish Cave) is the most accessible of the caves and is consequently covered with graffiti by local youths. You may be able to find a local guide in Dabong to take you out to the caves (there is no public transport), but it's better to visit them as part of a tour from Kota Bharu.

From Dabong, you can cross the Sungai Galas for 60 sen and take a minivan (RM2) out to the falls on 1421m-high Gunung Satong. The main falls are a 20-minute climb past the forgettable Perdana Satong Resort. A further 45 minutes' climb brings you to the top of the falls and a camp site. From here you can make longer excursions to the summit of Gunung Satong and the **upper falls**.

**Places to Stay & Eat** *Rumah Rehat Dabong* (Dabong Resthouse; ☎ 744 0725) has fan rooms for RM20 and air-con rooms for RM40; ask at the district office opposite the resthouse. *Baha's Camp* (☎ 019-959 1020), above the falls on Gunung Satong, charges RM3 per night for tent sites and RM10 for simple huts. The only restaurant in the area is the *no name joint* at Dabong station, which serves simple noodle and rice dishes. You can also shower here for 50 sen.

**Getting There & Away** A boat leaves Kuala Krai for Dabong every day (except Friday) at 10.30 am. The three-hour ride through the jungle is quite scenic and costs RM5. In the opposite direction, the boat leaves Dabong every day (except Friday) at 6 am. Alternatively, Dabong is on the jungle railway; there are five northbound trains a day (to Kuala Krai and Wakaf Baharu) and five southbound trains (all stop in Gua Musang and some continue south to Gemas, Singapore or KL).

Getting to Dabong on your own is quite simple, but seeing the sites in the area is very difficult to do independently. For this reason, most travellers come as part of an organised tour. KB Backpackers Lodge (☎ 743 2125), in Kota Bharu, offers two-night/three-day tours to the area for RM200 per person. It can also organise longer excursions and day trips to the area.

## Gua Musang

Gua Musang is a small frontier town that forms the centre of the region's booming lumber business. The town is named after the caves in the limestone outcrop towering above the train station. The musang is a native civet cat that looks like a cross between a large cat and a possum, with long fur and a long curling tail. Unfortunately, hunters have killed most of these cave dwellers.

It is possible to explore the caves, but it is a very steep, hazardous climb to the entrance, which is above the kampung next to the railway line, 150m from the train station (walk south along the train tracks). Don't attempt the climb in wet conditions and be sure to take a torch (flashlight) or at least some candles. A guide is recommended and local children will usually offer their services for RM5 to RM10.

Once you complete the dangerous climb to the caves, you'll have to shimmy through a narrow opening and do some scrambling to reach the main chamber, which extends some 150m before opening onto the opposite side of the mountain. There are no views, but the chamber is impressive and a good guide can point out rocks that resemble various animals.

**Places to Stay** There are several hotels on the main road that leads away from the train station. The best of these is *Evergreen Hotel* (☎ 912 2273), on the left just before the bend in the road, where clean rooms with air-con cost RM35. On the right side of the same road, closer to the station, *Hotel Gunung Emas* is a standard Chinese cheapie with rooms from RM15. Farther down this road, around the bend on the right, *Hotel Usaha* (☎ 912 4003) is a newish place with decent rooms from RM50 with air-con.

**Getting There & Away** Bus No 57 to/from Kota Bharu costs RM6. Bus No 52 to/from Kuala Lipis costs RM6.30. Gua Musang is also on the jungle railway; northbound locals depart at 5.42 am and 12.50 pm; northbound expresses depart at 4.01 and 5.10 am and 8.05 pm; southbound locals depart at 5.25 and 11.32 am; and southbound expresses depart at 9.58 and 11.03 pm. Local trains are usually around 30 minutes late.

PENINSULAR MALAYSIA

# Sarawak

The name 'Borneo' has long meant magic to travellers, and if you skip Sarawak you'll miss something special. The state boasts excellent national parks, one of the most pleasant cities in Asia and a diverse, thriving tribal culture whose hospitality to strangers is unmatched. Independent travel is easy in Sarawak and the local tourist information service is very good.

Sarawak isn't a lost paradise, however. Towns and surrounding areas are modernised, and 'development' – mainly rapacious logging, palm plantations and diabolical dam projects such as Bakun – continues to take a toll on the environment and the local cultures that sustain it. At the same time, local people are quite adept at living in the present tense, and you can safely leave images of wide-eyed natives in loincloths to the anthropologists. Many tribal folks are as comfortable and successful in the big city as anyone else – some of those dancers in tourist performances also hold PhDs. The state tourism minister, Dr James Masing, is pretty fly for an Iban guy, and his ministry maintains that Sarawak welcomes tourism but has no desire to remake itself in the image of mass-tourism brochures.

The heart of Sarawak is still the rainforest, whose major arteries are mighty rivers snaking to the South China Sea. These rivers and their tributaries are the lifeline for the tribal longhouses, and despite the mass-transit express boats churning along huge rivers such as the Batang Rejang, traditional-style longboats (now motorised) remain the essential means of getting around upriver. Kapit and Belaga, upriver from Sibu on the Rejang, are the towns to head for if longhouses and river adventures are in your plans.

Aside from the wildlife and jungle at Bako and Kubah in the west, caves are a highlight of Sarawak's system of national parks, and visitors can choose between the Dante-like depths of the Great Cave at Niah

## HIGHLIGHTS

- **Kuching** – an elegant city dotted with historic buildings, fine museums and great dining and drinking options

- **Kelabit Highlands** – superb trekking in clear mountain air and wonderful longhouse hospitality

- **Bako National Park** – one of the state's finest parks, with an enjoyable coastal aspect

- **Gunung Mulu National Park** – pristine rainforest with limestone pinnacles, massive caves and the Headhunters' Trail

- **Gunung Gading National Park** – a chance to see rafflesia, the world's largest flower

- **Batang Rejang** – the biggest of Sarawak's serpentine rivers, leading to isolated longhouse communities

- **Longhouses** – extraordinary structures that give shape to a thriving tribal life

**MALAYSIAN BORNEO**

or the cavernous curiosities of Gunung Mulu, both in the north-east.

Beyond the Headhunters' Trail at Gunung Mulu National Park, if you've got an interest in jungle trekking and local culture, the Kelabit Highlands are not to be missed.

## History

From the 15th until the early 19th century Sarawak was under the loose control of the sultanate of Brunei. It was only with the

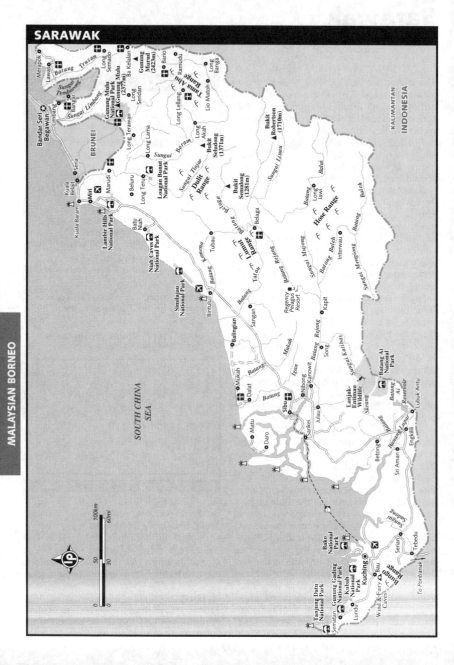

MALAYSIAN BORNEO

arrival of Sir James Brooke, the first of the three 'white raja', that it became a separate political region.

James Brooke, invalided from the British East India Company, set off on a journey of discovery armed with a sizeable inheritance and a well-armed ship. He arrived in Sarawak in 1839 only to find the local viceroy, Prince Makota, under siege by rebellious Bidayuh and Malays of the Sungai (river) Sarawak. Brooke's fortuitous arrival put him in the perfect position to ingratiate himself with the local leaders. He put down the rebellion, and by way of reward the sultan of Brunei installed him as Raja of Sarawak on 18 September 1842.

When James Brooke died in 1868 he was succeeded by his nephew, Charles Brooke. Through a policy of divide-and-rule among the local tribes, and the sometimes ruthless punishment of those who challenged his authority, Brooke extended his control and the borders of his kingdom during his long reign, which lasted until his death in 1917.

The third white raja was Charles Vyner Brooke, second son of Charles Brooke, who was to be last in this Boys' Own dynasty of white potentates.

Sarawak's period as the personal kingdom of the Brooke family ended with the arrival of the Japanese in WWII. When the Japanese forces capitulated in August 1945, Sarawak was placed under Australian military administration until April 1946, when Charles Vyner Brooke, who had fled to Sydney during the war, made it known that he wanted to cede Sarawak to the British. The Bill of Cession was debated in the State Council (Council Negeri) and was finally passed in May 1946. On 1 July Sarawak officially became a British crown colony, thus putting Britain in the curious position of acquiring a new colonial possession at a time when it was shedding others.

Cession was followed by a brief but bloody anticessionist movement supported chiefly by Anthony Brooke, Charles Vyner Brooke's nephew and heir apparent to the white-raja title, and about 300 government officers who had resigned in protest at being excluded from the political process.

The conflict climaxed in late 1949 when the governor of Sarawak, Duncan Stewart, was murdered by a Malay student. By 1951 the movement had lost its momentum and Anthony Brooke urged its supporters to give it up.

Along with Sabah (then North Borneo) and Brunei, Sarawak remained under British control when Malaya gained its independence in 1957. In 1962 the British proposed inclusion of the Borneo territories into the Federation of Malaya. At the last minute Brunei pulled out, as it (that is, Shell Oil) didn't want to see the revenue from its vast oil reserves channelled to the peninsula. At the same time, Malaya also had to convince the United Nations that Filipino claims to North Borneo were unfounded, as were Indonesia's claims that the formation of Malaysia was a British neocolonialist plot. The agreement was finally hammered out in July 1963, and in September of the same year the Federation of Malaysia was born.

This was also when the Indonesian Konfrontasi (Confrontation) with Malaysia seriously got going. The Konfrontasi was proclaimed by then-Indonesian-President Achmed Soekarno, and aimed to violently destabilise the fledgling state. Indonesian paramilitary raids and regular-army attacks across Kalimantan's border with Sarawak and Sabah continued until 1966. At its height 50,000 British, Australian and New Zealand forces were deployed in the border area, where some horrific confrontations occurred.

Internally, Sarawak also faced conflict during the early 1960s. The state had a large population of impoverished Chinese peasant farmers and labourers, and it was these people who found appeal in the North Kalimantan Communist Party, which supported guerrilla activity. Communist aspirations in Borneo were killed off, however, after the collapse of the Indonesian Communist Party in 1965, after which time Indonesians and Malaysians combined forces to drive communists out of their bases in Sarawak.

Today, Sarawak is doing better than its neighbour, Sabah. Kuching has weathered the Asian financial flu of the late 1990s, a situation that has given state leaders some

**MALAYSIAN BORNEO**

pause in their grandiose development plans. Nonetheless, and somewhat curiously, development is heading simultaneously in opposite directions: Palm plantations are starting to spread Sabah-like along the coast, while towns clamour for high-tech wafer-chip plants (like the massive new factory outside Kuching) to replace dependence on plantations.

## Visas & Permits

Even though Sarawak is part of Malaysia, it has its own immigration controls. You will have to clear immigration every time you cross a border – from the peninsula or Sabah, and of course from Brunei or Indonesia.

The separate controls are designed to protect indigenous people from being swamped by migrants from the peninsula and elsewhere. They have also served to restrict foreigners' access to many of those same local people, especially where devastating logging practices have ignited political protest in the past.

A major new reason for the controls is smuggling – the state government has begun to aggressively protect selected species of plants and animals from poachers. State paranoia is not without reason: Often poachers pose as disinterested researchers. In fact, with the power to patent individual genes, as well as to patent profitable herbal remedies and the like, multinational corporations now have the ability to stop local people from growing, let alone using, the plants and herbs they've lived with since time immemorial – a frightening prospect.

On arrival, travellers of most nationalities will be granted a one-month stay. Since you could easily spend a month exploring Sarawak, you may have to extend your visa. Extensions can be granted at the immigration offices in Kuching and in Miri (see those sections later for contact details) – just say how much you love the place and want to see the national parks. The Sarawak state government is touchy about researchers, journalists, photographers and the like arriving unannounced, so remember to make it clear that you're a tourist, and nothing more.

If you plan to visit any of the longhouses above Kapit on the Rejang or Baleh rivers, you will need a permit, which can be obtained in Kapit without fuss or fee. Permits are also required from the district office in Miri or Marudi for travel to Bario and the Sungai Baram beyond Marudi.

## National Parks

The Malaysian jungles contain some of the world's oldest undisturbed areas of rainforest. It's estimated that they've existed for about 100 million years, since they remained largely unaffected by the far-reaching climatic changes brought on elsewhere by the Ice Ages.

Fortunately, quite large areas of some of the best and most spectacular of these rainforests have been made into national parks, in which all commercial activities are banned. A lot of effort goes into maintaining them and making them accessible to visitors, and you cannot help but be captivated by the astonishing variety of plant and animal life.

The parks closest to Kuching are probably the best value overall: Bako for wildlife, Kubah for unspoiled nature and Gunung Gading for a chance viewing of the rarely blooming rafflesia flower. Always take along your passport for registering at the park.

At the time of writing several new areas had just been gazetted as protected, including a scaled-down tract in the Kelabit Highlands and the potential diving destination of Talang-Talang near Kuching. There are currently 10 national parks in Sarawak:

**Bako National Park (27 sq km)** North of Kuching
**Batang Ai National Park (240 sq km)** Some 250km east of Kuching
**Gunung Gading National Park (54 sq km)** On Sarawak's extreme western tip near Sematan
**Gunung Mulu National Park (529 sq km)** East of Marudi near the Brunei border
**Kubah National Park (22 sq km)** Just 20km west of Kuching
**Lambir Hills National Park (69 sq km)** Some 32km south of Miri
**Loagan Bunut National Park (10.7 sq km)** Protects Sarawak's largest freshwater lake, in the Miri hinterland

MALAYSIAN BORNEO

**Niah Caves National Park (31 sq km)** Massive caves, and source of the raw ingredient for bird's nest soup; about halfway between Bintulu and Miri

**Similajau National Park (75 sq km)** On the coast, north-east of Bintulu

**Tanjung Datu National Park (13 sq km)** Near Gunung Gading National Park

Currently, Batang Ai, Loagan Bunut and Tanjung Datu do not have accommodation or visitors' facilities.

**Permits & Costs** National park permits are required, but these are largely a formality. They are generally issued as a matter of course when you check in at the park headquarters, so there's little point in trying to get one in advance. The penalty for visiting national parks without a permit is a fine of RM1000 *and* six months in prison (at least it's not death), so always check in at the park headquarters before going any further.

Charges and accommodation for national parks have been standardised across Sarawak. Most of the incidental charges are small, and go towards upkeep of the park, but they can add up. There is a 10% non-refundable reservation charge for accommodation bookings, or the full amount if the total is less than RM10. In other words, if you book a room in a chalet for one night at RM120, you will end up spending RM132. All national parks have a park entrance fee of RM3, RM1 if you are under 18. There are also fees for cameras brought into the parks: RM5 per camera and RM10 per video camera. Professional filming in the parks costs RM200.

## Accommodation
Top-end accommodation and restaurants in Sarawak add a total of 15% government tax onto their basic charges; the total you pay is the 'net' price. Published rates are mostly '++', meaning the 5% and 10% taxes have to be added. Many hotels routinely quote net rates, however, and promotions often include the tax as well. In this chapter we've given the (net) rate you'd actually pay at the time of writing.

## Getting There & Away
For information on getting to Sarawak, see the individual Getting There & Away sections throughout this chapter, especially the entry under Kuching.

## Getting Around
**Air** Malaysia Airlines has a comprehensive network of domestic flights, including its rural air service, which consists of 18-seater Twin Otter aircraft. The Malaysian government subsidises domestic flights, which can be a real bargain. This is just as well, because flying is sometimes the only practical means of reaching a remote area. If you plan to visit places such as Bario and Long Lellang in the highlands, chances are you'll be going at least one way by plane. Kuching and Miri are connected to each other and to Sabah by regular flights on 120-seater Boeing 737s, while Sibu and Bintulu are served by 50-seater Fokker F50s.

Places in Sarawak served by Malaysia Airlines flights are Ba Kelalan, Bario, Belaga, Bintulu, Kuching, Lawas, Limbang, Long Lellang, Long Seridan, Marudi, Miri, Mukah, Mulu and Sibu.

The main hassle with taking Twin Otter flights into the interior is that they are subject to the vagaries of the weather, and some routes – Mulu is the most infamous – are absurdly overbooked and under-resourced. In the dry season (April to September) weather is usually not a problem, but in the wet season it can rain continuously for a few days. If you are relying on these flights make sure you have some time up your sleeve to allow for delays.

During school holidays (mid-May to mid-June and late October to early December) it is virtually impossible to get a seat on *any* Twin Otter flight into the interior at short notice. You could turn up at the airport in the hope of a cancellation.

Flights to Mulu and Bario suffer from overbooking year-round: People book flights they have little intention of taking that day just to be on the safe side. So far, cancellation penalties (25% of the ticket cost) on the Mulu route haven't been a deterrent. Stay tuned. A Sarawak state airline

MALAYSIAN BORNEO

may soon be getting off the ground in an effort to solve the problem.

The free baggage allowance on the Twin Otters is only 10kg per person, but *if* the plane can take the extra weight, excess baggage only costs from 40 sen to RM1.30 per kilogram, depending on the distance flown.

With the cost of accommodation in Brunei so high, many people fly straight over, although it is possible to transit overland in a day without having to stay overnight. One option is to fly from Miri to Labuan (RM66), a duty-free island off the coast of Sabah from where there are plane and boat connections to the mainland and to Kota Kinabalu (KK). You can also fly direct to KK (RM82 on Twin Otters, RM95 on larger aircraft) or via KK to other towns in Sabah.

**Land** Travel by road in Sarawak is generally good, and the trunk road from Kuching to the Brunei border is surfaced all the way. Travellers arriving from elsewhere in Malaysia will be pleasantly surprised by the sanity Sarawakian drivers generally display.

Between Sibu, Bintulu and Miri there are plenty of buses daily travelling in each direction – an estimated 70 companies operate on these routes. At the moment Sibu to Bintulu takes three hours, Bintulu to Niah Caves takes two hours, Niah Caves to Miri is two hours and Miri to Kuala Baram (on the Brunei border) is one hour. For locals, the road between Kuching and Sibu has all but replaced express boats as the preferred route between the two cities.

There are also buses heading west from Kuching to Bau, Lundu and Sematan, and north to Bako Bazaar (for Bako National Park).

Hitchhiking is possible in Sarawak, although traffic is usually light. In this chapter we've indicated where hitching is feasible. However, hitching is never entirely safe and travellers who decide to hitch should understand that they are taking a small but potentially serious risk. People who do choose to hitch will be safer if they travel in pairs and let someone know where they are planning to go.

Note that just before this book went to press, Malaysian transport officials announced a nation-wide bus-fare hike of up to 30%. Fare increases affect all buses in Peninsular Malaysia and Malaysian Borneo, including local, minibus, minivan and intercity services. It's always a good idea to check prices before planning your route from A to B, but we suggest you be especially diligent in checking current bus fares with local operators.

**Boat** War parties and traders used to rely on oars to get them up and down Sarawak's rivers; these days travel on larger rivers, such as the Rejang and Baram, is accomplished in fast passenger launches known by the generic term *ekspres*. These long, narrow boats carry around 100 people, and look a bit like ex-Soviet jumbo jets with the wings removed. Powered by turbo-charged V12 diesel engines, they can travel up to 60km/h and create a powerful wake that has motorised canoes scattering for calmer waters.

Express boats boast air-con powerful enough to preserve a mammoth. Take a blanket or warm clothing for the trip, or park yourself topside (but watch you don't burn in the sun). A highlight of these floating meat lockers is the in-transit entertainment. River travel used to be measured in bends; that is, a certain longhouse would be so many bends up a river. Today it is measured in violent videos – the launches usually screen very loud World Wresting Foundation videos or kung fu movies.

Where and when the express boats can't go, river travel is still mainly by longboat, though these are now motorised. Longboats are a great way to get around, but note that they aren't called 'wideboats' – watch your balance getting in and out, especially with heavy gear.

Hiring a longboat is often your only option for reaching many spots. Be prepared to pay a fair bit for the experience, as fuel isn't cheap in remote areas (ie, most of Sarawak) and boatmen expect to be rewarded for their time and trouble. Getting a group together to share costs can be worth the time and effort it may take to organise.

# West Sarawak

## KUCHING
☎ 082

Kuching means 'cat' in Malay, and Sarawak's capital lives by its name. The spotless city combines feline grace and charm with a certain capriciousness – whatever your expectations, Kuching is sure to toy with them. Many travellers consider Kuching one of the most refined, attractive cities in South-East Asia. Others find it a tad sterile, and the mini version of Kuala Lumpur's Golden Triangle gripping the waterfront around the Holiday Inn is an uninspiring model for the rest of the city's development.

Whatever your impressions, Kuching is certainly unique, a city unlike any other you'll see in Borneo. Residents clearly love their home and are fairly fond of each other too – a long custom of intermarriage, among other reasons, has encouraged a laudable level of racial and religious tolerance. Once the city's got its claws into you it's easy to spend more time here than planned – don't forget to get out and explore the rest of Sarawak.

Kuching is the best base from which to start exploring the state, and there's plenty in and around Kuching to keep you busy for at least several days. Nearby are longhouses, caves and a number of excellent national parks, including Bako (especially good for proboscis monkeys) and Gunung Gading (where you have a good chance of seeing the rafflesia, the world's largest flower).

Built principally on the south bank of the Sungai Sarawak, Kuching was known as Sarawak in the 19th century. Before James Brooke settled here, the capital had been variously at Lidah Tanah and Santubong. Kuching was given its name in 1872 by Charles Brooke.

Although Kuching is quite a large city, the centre is very compact and seems isolated from the suburbs by the river and its landscaped parks and gardens, which make it as green a city as you'll find in South-East Asia. The usual frenetic commerce is conducted in busy streets lined with historic buildings, but within a short walk is one of Asia's best museums (Sarawak Museum), a collection of Chinese temples and the striking Masjid Negeri (State Mosque). The south bank of the river has been paved and landscaped and a peaceful promenade links the main attractions.

## Orientation

The main sights – and most of the city – are on the south bank of the Sungai Sarawak. Almost all attractions and places of importance to travellers are within easy walking distance of each other. Although parts of town are obscured by low hills, everything is deceptively close. The western end is overlooked by the green-and-white Masjid Negeri, and is home to markets, local bus stations and museums. All hotels, places to eat, banks, airline offices and the main post office are between the mosque and the Great Cat of Kuching, 2km east. The waterfront is a quiet thoroughfare between the eastern and western parts of town.

Looking north across the river from the open-air market is the *istana* (palace); nearby, Fort Margherita occupies a low hill and is visible from most points along the waterfront; the Ministerial Complex is the ugly multistorey building in the background.

You should only need to use public buses or taxis to reach the Cat Museum and Timber Museum in Petra Jaya (north of the river), the airport (about 12km away), the long-distance bus station (5km) and the wharf for the boat to Sibu (6km).

**Maps** Periplus produces *Sarawak & Kuching* as part of its Malaysia Regional Maps series. This excellent folding, colour production has detailed maps of Kuching, Bintulu, Miri, Sibu, Kapit and Gunung Mulu National Park. It is readily available in bookshops in Kuching (see Bookshops under Information later in this section).

For good topographic maps, try the Lands & Survey Department (Jabatan Tanah dan Ukar), on the 7th floor of the state government offices, near the end of Jalan Simpang Tiga. Large-scale maps (1:1000,000 and 1:500,000) of Sarawak are readily available,

# KUCHING

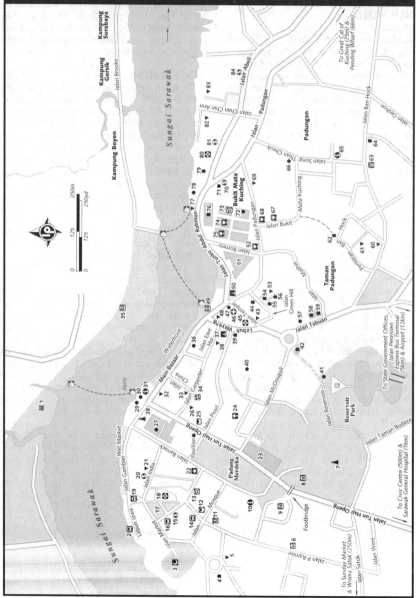

MALAYSIAN BORNEO

## KUCHING

**PLACES TO STAY**
4 Arif Hotel; Arif Internet Café
23 Merdeka Palace Hotel;
   Restorante Beccari;
   Victoria Arms
39 St Thomas Diocesan Rest
   House
42 Fata Hotel
44 River View Inn
51 Hilton Hotel
54 Goodwood Inn
55 Mandarin Hotel
56 Orchid Inn
58 Borneo Hotel
59 B&B Inn
62 Telang Usan Hotel
64 Hotel Grand Continental
76 Crowne Plaza Riverside
   Kuching; Riverside Shopping
   Complex
79 Kuching Holiday Inn;
   Mohamed Yahia & Sons

**PLACES TO EAT**
5 Medan P Ramlee
17 Open Air Market
21 Jubilee; MJ Abdul Rashid
   Café; Malaya Restaurant
26 National Islamic Cafe
32 Biryani Cafe
33 Chinese Food Centre
38 Life Cafe
43 Green Hill Corner
48 Denis' Place
53 Ah Ka Su Seafood

60 Hornbill's Corner Cafe
61 See Good Food Centre
69 Top Spot Food Court
77 Khatulistiwa Cafe; Disco
82 New Kuching Food Centre
83 Benson's Seafood Centre

**OTHER**
1 Istana
2 STC Buses
3 Masjid Negeri
6 Islamic Museum
7 Heroes' Monument
8 Sarawak Museum
   (Old Wing)
9 Sarawak Museum
   (New Wing)
10 Visitors' Information Centre
11 Sikh Temple
12 Borneo Highway Express; PB
   Ekspres
13 Star Internet
14 CLL Buses
15 Bank of Commerce
16 Petra Jaya Bus Station
18 Electra House
19 Taxi Stand
20 Majid & Sons
22 Central Police Station
24 Anglican Cathedral
25 Main Post Office
27 Court House
28 Brooke Memorial
29 Square Tower
30 Sarawak Steamship Building

31 Sarawak Tourist Association
34 Sang Ti Miao Temple
35 Fort Margherita
36 Borneo Adventure
37 Hong San Temple
40 Bishop's House
41 Red Crescent Building
45 Medan Pelita Mall
46 Chan Clinic
47 Sarawak Batik Art Shop
49 Chinese History Museum
50 Tua Pek Kong Temple
52 De Tavern; The Royalist
57 Ting & Ting Supermarket
63 Hindu Temple
65 Tourism Malaysia;
   Royal Brunei Airlines
66 Malaysia Airlines;
   American Express
67 Eagle's Nest
68 Amigos Cafe & Bistro
70 Standard Chartered Bank
71 Singapore Airlines
72 City Laundry &
   Dry Cleaning
73 Cyber City
74 Vampire
75 Cat City
78 Riverbank Suites ;
   Sushi Tei; Club II;
   Phenomenon
80 Sarawak Plaza; Belle's
   Bookshop; Cactus Flower
81 Pacific Bank
84 Maybank

but to obtain the more-detailed 1:50,000 maps of various parts of the state you need security clearance from the police headquarters in the centre of town.

## Information

**Tourist Offices** Kuching has two excellent tourist information offices. The Visitors' Information Centre (☎ 410944, fax 256301, ❸ sarawak@po.jaring.my) is on Jalan Barrack, near the new wing of the Sarawak Museum. The centre's staff are knowledgeable about local culture and can tell you when special events are scheduled. The National Parks & Wildlife desk (☎/fax 248088) in the office can arrange permits and accommodation for Bako, Gunung Gading and Kubah National Parks, and for Matang and Semenggoh Wildlife Centres. The Visitors' Centre is open weekdays from 8 am to 6 pm, Saturday to 4 pm, and Sunday and holidays from 9 am to 3 pm.

The privately run Sarawak Tourist Association (STA; ☎ 240620, fax 427151) is in an octagonal building on Main Bazaar, on the waterfront. It distributes leaflets on accommodation, sights and transport, and its staff can help you book longhouse tours. STA hands out a decent map of Kuching with useful bus schedules on the back. It is open Monday to Thursday from 8 am to 12.45 pm and 2 to 4.15 pm; Friday from 8 to 11.30 am and 2.30 to 4.45 pm; and Saturday from 8 am to 12.45 pm.

For general information on Sabah and Peninsular Malaysia, Tourism Malaysia

MALAYSIAN BORNEO

(☎ 246775) has an office in the Rugayah building, on Jalan Song Thian Cheok. The ground-floor office is often unattended, but you can help yourself to leaflets; staff can be found upstairs. Tourism Malaysia is open the same hours as the STA office.

The free *Official Kuching Guide* is an excellent locally produced publication with a wealth of information on Kuching and surrounding sights. It should be available in the arrivals hall at the airport, at tourist offices and at some hotel desks, but you may have to ask for it. Travelcom Asia, the fine company behind the guide, is planning to post an expanded and updated online version with video clips and more. The site, at www.borneotravel.com, should be operational by the time you read this.

**Consulates & Immigration Offices** The immigration office for visa extensions (☎ 245661) is on the 2nd floor of the state government offices on Jalan Simpang Tiga, about 3km south of the centre, towards the airport.

The Indonesian Consulate (☎ 241734) is at 5A Jalan Pisang. It is open weekdays from 8 am to noon and from 2 to 4 pm. At the time of writing people of most nationalities did not require visas to enter Indonesia by air at Pontianak, or by land at Entikong, where two-month entry permits are issued. A visa is required if entering Indonesia through a nonrecognised crossing. Stick to the visa-free crossings; two-month Indonesian visas currently cost a whopping RM160. Four colour photos are required, and if you drop off your passport before 9.30 am you can collect it that afternoon.

To get to either office, catch a CLL (blue-and-white) bus No 6, 11, 14A or 14B from near the Masjid Negeri; the fare is 60 sen.

**Money** There's an exchange counter and a Maybank ATM at the airport.

The Pacific Bank near the Sarawak Plaza is a good bet for changing travellers cheques and cash. Branches of the Public Bank are also reliable. The Hongkong Bank (HSBC) is another option, though service can be quite slow. The Standard & Charted Bank is fickle about the travellers cheques it accepts, and it charges a steep commission on transactions. Banking hours are weekdays from 9.30 am to 3.30 pm and Saturday from 9.30 am to 11.30 am.

American Express (☎ 252600) has an office on the 3rd floor of the Malaysia Airlines building, on Jalan Song Thian Cheok.

Majid & Sons is a licensed money-changer at 51 Jalan India; it doesn't charge a commission, but only exchanges cash.

Even in Kuching it can be hard to get change for large-denomination bills (RM50 or RM100 notes). Stock up on small notes.

**Post & Communications** The main post office is in the centre of town on Jalan Tun Haji Openg. It is open weekdays from 8 am to 4 pm, Saturday from 8 am to 6.30 pm and on Sunday from 9 am to 4 pm; it gets very crowded on weekends. Next door there's a POS2020 office, which sells stationery, sticky tape, packaging and so on. It's open weekdays from 9 am to 4 pm and Saturday from 8 am to 3 pm.

The post office and many mid-range and top-end hotels have fax facilities.

*Email & Internet Access* Kuching has Sarawak's quickest Internet connections and it has plenty of cybercafes, including:

**Arif Internet Café** In the front of the Arif Hotel (RM4 per hour). There's no minimum charge here and there are more terminals in the back.

**Cyber Borneo** In the Medan Pelita mall; open from 10 am to around 10 pm (RM4/6 per 30 minutes/one hour). Oddly, it asks for payment in advance.

**Cyber City** Behind the Riverside Crowne Plaza; open from 9 am to 10 pm (RM6 per hour or RM2 for up to 20 minutes).

**Waterfront Cyber Café** Next to the STA office on the waterfront; open from 9 am to midnight (RM3.50/7 for 30 minutes/one hour).

**Bookshops** Kuching bookshops offer a huge range of books on every topic to do with Sarawak and Sabah, including history, culture, headhunting, wildlife, horticulture, arts and crafts. Most also stock good maps of Sarawak.

The best range of books on Borneo and Malaysia is at Mohamed Yahia & Sons, in the lobby of the Holiday Inn. On the 2nd floor of the Sarawak Plaza, Belle's Bookshop has a good range of titles on every topic. The bookshop at the Sarawak Museum has good books on Borneo, and Times Books, on the 1st floor of the Crowne Plaza shopping complex, has a good but expensive range of novels and general titles.

**Laundry** City Laundry & Dry Cleaning, behind the Crowne Plaza, is central, cheap and efficient. A 2kg load costs around RM14.

**Medical Services** Sarawak General Hospital (☎ 257555) is at 1½ Mile, off Jalan Rock. The privately run Timberland Medical Centre (☎ 234991) is at Mile 3, Jalan Rock. Both are fine, inexpensive facilities with English-speaking doctors.

For basic bumps and travel ailments, Chan Clinic, at 98 Main Bazaar on the waterfront is excellent.

Pharmacies are abundant and well-stocked. One of the best in town is Apex Pharmacy, on the 1st floor of Sarawak Plaza; it's open until 9 pm.

## Waterfront

The south bank of the Sungai Sarawak between the Beijing Riverbank restaurant and the markets at the western end has been tastefully developed with a paved walkway, lawns and flowerbeds, a children's playground, cafes and food stalls. It's a quiet, pleasant place to walk or sit and watch the *tambang* (river ferries) with their lanterns glide past. In the evening couples and families promenade past lone souls dangling fishing rods over the railing. There's a relief map of historic Kuching and fountains are lit up at night.

A tambang is a traditional double-oared boat, and these days motorised versions ferry passengers back and forth across the river all day until late; the jetty near the istana services Fort Margherita; downstream past the fort, the jetties service a series of Malay *kampung* (villages) on the northern side of the river. The north bank of the river is earmarked for development along the lines of the south bank's promenade, and may look quite different (not necessarily better) than it does today.

The river crossing costs 30 sen for locals; tourists are usually asked to pay RM1. You can leave the exact change on the prow as you leave, or pay the boatman directly. If you want to hire a tambang for a river cruise, the charge is RM25 to RM30 for up to an hour – agree on the fare before you take the ride.

## Istana

This shingle-roofed, white palace, set amid rolling lawns on the north bank of the river, was built by Charles Brooke in 1870. During the Japanese occupation prisoners were detained in the basement. It's now the governor of Sarawak's residence and not open to the public, but it looks very grand, especially when lit up at night. It's in plain view from the western end of the waterfront.

## Fort Margherita

Built by Charles Brooke in 1879 and named after his wife, the Rani Margaret, Fort Margherita guarded the approach to Kuching against pirates. Sitting on a knoll opposite the waterfront, this little white fort, complete with battlements, offers fine views along the river. The fort now houses the Police Museum (Muzium Polis), which looks a like a dungeon designed by the Keystone Kops. The museum was under renovation at the time of writing, which might make it more interesting – it might also give the fort a much-needed facelift.

Fort Margherita is open every day, except Monday and public holidays, from 10 am to 6 pm. There's no entry charge but you have to show your passport at the guard's room at the entrance.

To get there, take a tambang from the landing behind the Square Tower to the bus stop below the fort.

## Sarawak Museum

This is one of the best museums in Asia and consists of two main sections, connected by a footbridge over Jalan Tun Haji Openg. Both are highly recommended.

MALAYSIAN BORNEO

At the time of writing the museum was undergoing major renovations, with a new library being constructed next to the museum's new wing, and some exhibits being moved between buildings. There were also plans for an 'interactive' display for kids.

Built in the style of a Normandy townhouse, the old wing was opened in 1891 under the direction of noted anthropologist Alfred Wallace, a contemporary of Darwin who spent two years in Kuching at the invitation of Charles Brooke. The new, aircon wing features displays on the culture and way of life of Sarawak's many tribal peoples.

In the various buildings you'll find stuffed and mounted animals (that look like they've been there since 1891); displays on longhouse life, with artefacts including skull trophies; and photographs of tribal people from the early 20th century. Arts on display include ceramics, brassware, Chinese jars and furniture, and there's a replica cave and a description of harvesting birds' nests for soup. There is a program of temporary exhibitions and the museum presents slide shows and videos daily on a range of topics. There's also a souvenir and gift shop, which has a good range of postcards.

The museum is open daily from 9 am to 6 pm; entry is free, though a small fee may be introduced in the near future.

On the museum grounds past the old wing are pleasant gardens, pavilions and the **Heroes' Monument**, dedicated to fallen heroes of past military conflicts.

## Islamic Museum

Islam has far less hold on Sarawak than on the rest of Malaysia, but the excellent Muzium Islam Sarawak is one of Kuching's surprises. Housed in a beautifully restored building are seven galleries exhibiting aspects of the Malay Islamic heritage. Among the various exhibits are ceramics, costumes and jewellery, weaponry, science and technology displays and Islamic art.

The museum is on Jalan P Ramlee, near the new wing of the Sarawak Museum. It is open daily from 9 am to 5 pm and entry is free.

## Chinese History Museum

This small museum is lodged in one of the few original waterfront buildings to survive the redevelopment of Kuching. It began as the Chinese courthouse in 1912. Inside, historical notes and photos document the Chinese migration to Sarawak and the formation of trading associations. Examples of traditional furniture, musical instruments and costumes are also on display.

The Chinese History Museum is on the waterfront opposite the Tua Pek Kong Temple. The museum is open daily from 9 am to 5.30 pm; entry is free.

## Cat Museum

Kuching's one-of-a-kind Cat Museum pays homage to the origins of the city's name. It's all pretty lighthearted and kitsch, with plenty of trivia, photos, children's art and movie posters featuring cats. While many visitors find it as fascinating as a furball, real cat-lovers (you know who you are) will adore it!

The Cat Museum is in the UFO-shaped DBKU building, north of the river. It is open Tuesday to Sunday from 9 am to 5 pm; entry is free, although there is a camera/video charge of RM3/5. It's too far to walk, so take Petra Jaya bus No 2B; the fare is 60 sen.

## Timber Museum

This is the timber industry's answer to all the criticism about logging. The presentations are professional but tinder-dry, and only industry insiders are likely to be captivated.

Opening hours are Monday to Thursday from 8.30 am to 4 pm, Friday from 8.30 to 11.30 am and 2.30 to 4.30 pm, and Saturday from 8.30 am to 12.30 pm. Entry is free.

The Timber Museum is across the river in Wisma Sumber Alam, Petra Jaya. Take Kuching Matang Transport (yellow-and-orange striped) bus No 8 from near the market; the fare is 90 sen.

## Courthouse & Brooke Memorial

The courthouse was opened in 1874 and is still in use today. It was the third to be built on this site, and was previously the centre of

MALAYSIAN BORNEO

government operations. The clock tower at the front was added in 1883, and there's a small granite memorial to Charles Brooke facing the river. State magistrate councils were held in the courthouse until 1973, when the government complex on Jalan Tun Haji Openg opened.

The courthouse is at the northern end of Jalan Tun Haji Openg, opposite the Square Tower. It's a quiet corner of town, with shady benches under massive fig trees; it also affords a pleasant passageway between Jalan India and Jalan Carpenter.

## Temples, Mosques & Churches

Kuching's Chinese temples are modest affairs, although there are a few colourful examples around town. Historically, the most significant is the **Tua Pek Kong Temple**, across the road from the Chinese History Museum. The temple is dedicated to the patron saint of overseas Chinese. Officially, it is dated to 1876, but written sources mention it as long ago as 1846, which would make it the oldest building in Kuching.

The **Hong San Temple**, at the junction of Jalan Carpenter and Jalan Wayang, dates back to 1897 and is also worth a look; it is dedicated to a young boy who distinguished himself in the Great Fire of Kuching. A large **Chinese gate** over the eastern end of Jalan Padungan frames views of the Great Cat of Kuching.

Other colourful, religious buildings include a **Hindu temple** on Jalan Ban Hock near the Grand Continental Hotel (you're welcome to wander inside the temple compound, but take your shoes off before stepping on the tiles). There's a **Sikh temple** off Jalan Mosque, and an **Indian mosque** dating back to the 1850s can be found down a passageway between Nos 37 and 39 Jalan India.

Completed in 1968, the **Masjid Negeri** looks impressive, particularly from across the river, but is otherwise uninteresting. There's no admission for non-Muslims from Thursday 3 pm to Friday 3 pm, Saturday from 4 to 6 pm and Sunday from 2 to 5 pm.

Kuching's **Roman Catholic cathedral** is 500m south of the Sarawak Museum on Jalan Tun Haji Openg.

## Civic Centre

About 1km south of the city centre, along Jalan Tun Haji Openg, a white tower looking like an upside-down, half-furled umbrella on stilts dominates the skyline. This is Kuching's Civic Centre, and on a clear day it offers a panoramic view.

To get to the Civic Centre, walk down Jalan Tun Haji Openg and turn left at Jalan Budaya; most buses going past the main post office will get you here. Entry to the viewing platform is RM2.

## Reservoir Park

A peaceful oasis, not many travellers get down to this small, landscaped park south of the centre, but it's a pleasant place for a picnic, stroll or a jog. After a few days of museums and handicraft shops, parents with young children will be grateful it exists.

To get to the park, follow the road just past the Fata Hotel (there's a small sign for the park) and take the second lane to your left (it's just past the Red Crescent building) to the car park.

## Kuching Architecture

There are many historic **godowns** (river warehouses), dwellings and other buildings of note in the blocks around the waterfront and markets. Their often-decaying facades are part of Kuching's distinctive character.

The small **Square Tower**, on the waterfront opposite the istana, was built in 1879 as a prison. On Jalan Tun Haji Openg, opposite the main post office, there is a curious three-storey building known as **the Pavilion**. Built in 1907, it has been home to various government bodies. The **main post office** itself is a grandiose structure fronted by Corinthian columns.

Near the Anglican cathedral, the **bishop's house** is the oldest dwelling in the state. It was built in 1849 and was occupied by the first Anglican bishop of Borneo. You can wander around the cathedral grounds but the bishop's house is not open to the public.

## Cat Statues

The large white, blue-eyed pussycat perched at the eastern end of Jalan Padungan is

Hello, Kitty – Kuching style.

MARK DAFFEY

MALAYSIAN BORNEO

known as the **Great Cat of Kuching**. Other kitsch cat statues can be seen opposite the Holiday Inn Kuching and on the waterfront. Just in case you forgot, Kuching means 'cat' in Malay.

## Markets
Kuching's best market – and one of the best in Sarawak – is the **Sunday-morning market** along Jalan Satok. It is sometimes very busy and can be well worth the walk. The market actually begins late on Saturday afternoon, when villagers bring in their produce and livestock and start trading. They sleep at their stalls and resume trading at around 5 am on Sunday.

The air is heady with the smell of fresh coriander, ginger and herbs you've never seen before, stacked among piles of bananas, mangoes, custard apples and obscure jungle fruits. Fresh fish and other seafood takes up one section, while elsewhere wild boars and goats are butchered to hang with turtles and other free-range meat. (See the boxed text 'The Disappearing Turtles of the East Coast' in the Terengganu chapter, and resolve not to let turtle pass your lips.) Other stalls sell beautiful orchids, live fish hanging in plastic bags of water, birds in cages, pets – you name it, it's for sale. There are also plastic toys, clothes and other odds and ends that are usually reserved for Woolworth's. Food stalls set up near the pedestrian overpass.

To reach the Sunday market from the museum, walk along Jalan Tun Haji Openg and turn right at Jalan Satok; the market is on your left about 500m along.

The **open-air market** at the western end of the waterfront, on Jalan Market, is small and not particularly interesting unless you hit a day when some villagers are in town. At the waterfront there is an outdoor area, and a clothes and hawker centre in a large white building. Along Jalan Gambier there are open-air food stalls, where fresh vegetables and foodstuffs can also be bought.

## Jalan Carpenter
This narrow street, lined with old Chinese shops, is signposted as Jalan Ewe Hai at its eastern end. Jalan Carpenter exists on two levels: On the street there are busy little shops and coffee shops, and above, the families who run them live cheek-by-jowl behind whitewashed walls and painted shutters.

Jalan Carpenter burned down in the Great Fire of Kuching in 1884, and rows of brick terraces replaced the original thatched buildings. It is picturesque and interesting to wander along and photograph, particularly on Sunday morning when it's a bit quieter.

## Riverside Kampung
Across the river from the waterfront you'll see traditional Malay houses and mosques stretching away to the east. There are four main kampung here, and all are under some threat from development plans for the riverbank. As long as they last, the kampung are a world away from the commerce and tourism of central Kuching, and you're welcome to hop a tambang across the river and wander around.

## Organised Tours
There is an incredible array of travel agents and tour operators in town, and most of the hotels listed in Places to Stay offer tours or have links with an operator. The STA office can help narrow your choices. All the agents offer city tours, longhouse tours, and tours to national parks and other points of interest around Sarawak. Some can cater for special interests, such as photography, natural history and textiles or crafts.

Most tours are priced for a minimum of at least two people (and often five or six);

if you're on your own, you could pay an awful lot (from RM350 to more than RM1000) for a couple of days upriver. If you pay for a trip based on three people and six turn up, expect to have some money returned to you. Trips are often cancelled because of insufficient numbers, particularly with the cheapie tour operators – refunds should be immediate if a trip is cancelled.

If you're looking for a group to join, you can leave a contact number with tour operators; the STA office in Kuching will also take your details and try to help.

Besides day trips in and around Kuching town, many travel agents offer longer trips to national parks or to longhouses along the Skrang, Lemanak and Rejang rivers. However, the Skrang has been heavily exploited by tourism since the 1970s, and you're much better off opting for a trip up the Lemanak. If you're interested in the Rejang and its tributaries, you may find better deals from Sibu or Kapit operators (see also the Belaga section later in this chapter).

Half-day city tours are around RM40; day trips to longhouses at Annah Rais are around RM120 per person; and expect to pay at least RM350 each for a two-day (one-night) longhouse trip for a minimum of two people on the Lemanak. Longer trips to more remote-longhouses around Batang Ai will cost much more, but you're guaranteed a far less touristy experience.

The MV *Equatorial* cruises up and down the Sungai Sarawak in the evening if there is sufficient demand. A two-hour sunset cruise costs RM30. Departures are at 5.30 pm from the wharf behind Sarawak Plaza, but contact Leisure Holidays (☎ 240566), 37 Jalan Padungan, to see if the boat is going.

Following are a few of the well-established operators:

**Borneo Adventure** (☎ 245175, fax 422626, @ bakch@po.jaring.my) 55 Main Bazaar. This award-winning company sets the standard in projects involving Sarawak's indigenous people. Ecotourism here is more than electric motors and slick marketing, but Borneo Adventure isn't a budget operation. It's best to contact the busy office before dropping by. Web site: www.borneoadventure.com

**Borneo Interland Travel** (☎ 413595, fax 411619) 1st floor, between Nos 62 and 63 Main Bazaar. This is a general agency offering a wide variety of tours, including a boat tour of the Sungai Sarawak.

**Borneo Explorations** (☎ 257784, fax 421419, @ btt@po.jaring.my) 15 Jalan Green Hill. This place books trips throughout Sarawak and Sabah.

If you have problems with a tour outfit, the tourist offices can do little; the Licensing Office in KK, Sabah, is the place to direct your complaint: Pejabat Pendaftaran (Licensing Office; ☎ 088-269711, fax 269713), Lot B, 6.5B, Tingkat 6, Bangunan KWSP, Block D, 88100 Kota Kinabalu.

## Places To Stay – Budget

Decent budget accommodation in Kuching is thinning faster than Bruce Willis' hair. Many of the cheapest places are now home to long-term migrant workers with little money and no options. If you get stuck for a place, try the eastern part of town around Jalan Padungan, but be prepared for some sleazy or slack lodging standards.

Kuching's only backpacker hostel is *B&B Inn* (☎ 237366, 30 Jalan Tabuan), next to the Borneo Hotel. It's close to all attractions, clean and friendly, has left-luggage facilities and a kitchen, and can help with travel information and longhouse tours. A bed in a six-bed dorm costs RM15. Fan-cooled and air-con singles/doubles are also available, starting at RM23/31. It has a payphone and Internet access (RM5 per hour).

*St Thomas Diocesan Rest House* (☎ 414027), at the back of the Anglican cathedral, is sometimes full of folks on church business, but if not, you're welcome to stay – just ask for the friendly caretaker, Puli Kanto. Rooms with fan and shared bathroom cost RM18 to RM25, while larger, fan-cooled flats with bathroom cost RM30 to RM35. This is a quiet place, but security is a bit loose. To get here, walk around to the main driveway off Jalan McDougall.

In general, hotel prices start at around RM25 to RM30 for a single – there are a couple of cheaper options around town, but

MALAYSIAN BORNEO

these tend to be seedy or long-term rental joints where sleep is not guaranteed.

The friendly *Arif Hotel (☎ 241211)*, near Masjid Negeri, has reasonable fan-cooled rooms for RM25 with shared toilet and cold shower, or RM35 with attached bathroom. Larger air-con doubles with bathroom cost RM50, and family-sized rooms are RM60.

## Places To Stay – Mid-Range

Kuching has dozens of mid-range hotels that compete keenly for business, so most are reasonably priced. Discounts are usually available out of tourist season, and it's worth asking for one at any time. Except for the lodging houses, these places all have IDD (International direct dial) phones, and payment by credit card is accepted.

On Jalan Green Hill there's a cluster of older 'lodging houses' that mostly cater to long-term residents. There's little difference between them – they are all acceptable, if a bit stark, and cost roughly the same. *Mandarin Hotel (☎ 418269, 6 Jalan Green Hill)* has rooms for RM40 with double bed, or for RM45 with twin beds. *Orchid Inn (☎ 411417, 2 Jalan Green Hill)* has singles starting at RM28 and bigger rooms for RM35 to RM45. The *Goodwood Inn (☎ 244862)*, at No 16, has dark, bare singles/doubles/twins starting at RM35/40/45.

Also on Jalan Green Hill is the *River View Inn (☎ 412551)* at No 22. This is a larger hotel with a lift (elevator), and it's probably the best of the Green Hill bunch. Basic but airy rooms cost RM45 to RM65. At the eastern end of Jalan McDougall, the *Fata Hotel (☎ 248111)* has an old and a new wing. Small singles/twins in the old wing (it has a 1st-floor lobby) cost RM47/51; some rooms at the back of the building are quiet and look out over parkland. Rooms in the new wing have slightly better beds and cost RM55 and up.

Some of the good upper mid range places provide reasonably priced alternatives to the top-end hotels. Top of the list is the popular *Telang Usan Hotel (☎ 415588, fax 425316, ✉ tusan@po.jaring.my)*, on Jalan Ban Hock. It is Sarawak's only Orang Ulu (Upriver People) owned and managed hotel, and the Kenyah decor inside is just

one of the touches that make it stand out. Promotional rates range from RM70/80 for a standard room to RM100 for a deluxe.

*Borneo Hotel (☎ 244122, fax 254848, 30 Jalan Tabuan)* is a few notches below Telang Usan. It is Kuching's longest-running hotel, and while some rooms are fine (notably those on the 1st floor), others are dark and cramped. Standard singles/doubles/triples are RM76/85/95.

At the time of writing, a three-star hotel was being built on Jalan Temple near Tua Pek Kong Temple.

## Places To Stay – Top End

*Hotel Grand Continental (☎ 230399, fax 255099, ✉ mag@asiatravel.com)*, on Jalan Ban Hock, is a reasonable option, and close enough to the city centre to walk. Rooms range from somewhat musty to quite cosy; discount rates start at RM130, including breakfast.

*Kuching Hilton Hotel (☎ 248200, fax 428984)* has the finest rooms in its class and the full complement of services, plus the best handicrafts shop in town (see Shopping later this section). Published rates for standard singles/doubles start at RM350/380, and suites start at RM720. Substantial discounts are often available but it's a popular hotel and bookings are advised.

On Jalan Tunku Abdul Rahman, the state-run *Holiday Inn Kuching (☎ 240277, fax 426169, ✉ hikrsv@po.jaring.my)* is central and right next to the river. It's popular with families, though the service is ordinary and rooms are pretty average for the price. Rooms facing town cost RM167/195; a river-view double costs RM218.

*Crowne Plaza Riverside Kuching (☎ 247078, fax 231354, ✉ cprk@po.jaring.my)* is across from the Holiday Inn and has a similar standard of service, but its rooms are better than its older competitor's. Discounts can bring the outlandish room rates down to a bearable RM230. The Riverside complex also houses a pricey, Parkson-led shopping centre.

The five-star *Merdeka Palace Hotel (☎ 258000, fax 425400, ✉ mpalace@po.jaring.my)* is on Jalan Tun Haji Openg, next to the *padang* (town square). It is taste-fully fitted out and, as well as the manda-tory business centre, pool and gymnasium, there's an excellent coffee shop, cigar bar, pub and a very good restaurant. Published rates for standard rooms start at RM290/310; suites start at RM640. Dis-counts of 40% are often available, and busi-ness rates can be up to 60% lower than published.

## Places to Eat

Kuching has the best selection of food in Borneo, and the choice ranges from hawker-stall fare through good seafood to 1st-class Italian. At the cheaper end expect to pay RM3 to RM4.50 for standard rice and noodle dishes, beef, roti or *murtabak* (roti filled with pieces of mutton, chicken or vegetables). Seafood prices vary according to demand and availability – check prices before ordering. For good and even excel-lent Western fare look into the upmarket hotels, where prices are reasonable by Western standards.

**Breakfast** This is indeed the most impor-tant meal of the day in Kuching, where breakfast is almost an art form. It seems nearly everyone converges on their favourite hang-out in the morning to savour a bowl of cheap Chinese porridge or laksa. Try the *Chinese Food Centre* opposite Sang Ti Miao Temple on Jalan Carpenter. There are also plenty of places serving Western-style breakfasts – at RM4.50 to RM5.50, the *Khatulistiwa Cafe* (see Malay, Chinese & Western later in this section) is probably the best-value in town. Any *kedai kopi* (coffee shop) can cook an egg upon re-quest to go with your coffee or tea, and an order of toast is very cheap.

The *Cactus Flower*, at the main entrance to the Sarawak Plaza, is a good spot for a strong cup of coffee (RM1.85) and a morn-ing snack.

**Food Centres** The so-called *open-air market* (it's covered) on Jalan Market near the taxi stand is one of the largest and most popular food centres. One section mostly

serves halal food and the other section has mostly Chinese.

The *Top Spot Food Court*, off Jalan Padungan behind the Malaysia Airlines building, is a popular food-stall centre on top of a car park. It is clean and salubrious and specialises in fresh seafood.

Across from the Arif Hotel is *Medan P Ramlee*, where you'll find good, inexpen-sive outdoor Malay food stalls.

The *Chinese Food Centre*, on Jalan Car-penter, is an excellent spot for an afternoon feast of fish balls, prawn soup or satay (30 sen per stick).

**Malay, Chinese & Western** *Khatulis-tiwa Cafe* is in the thatched, round structure resembling Beijing's Temple of Heaven (it's actually modelled on a Bidayuh skull house) on the waterfront, next to the River-side Suites. Kalu, as it's known to regulars, is a 24-hour open-air restaurant serving good Malay, Chinese and Western food for around RM7. It's a pleasant place for break-fast or dinner, catching the breeze and watching the lantern lights of tambang drift by. It's often busiest around 2 am when the clubbers surface for some carbohydrates and fresh air. Upstairs is a lively dance club popular with a younger crowd.

For something cheaper, *Green Hill Cor-ner*, opposite the Medan Pelita mall, has a good selection of Malaysian Chinese dishes.

*Hornbill's Corner Cafe*, on Jalan Ban Hock, is a popular steamboat restaurant where you select your own seafood and meats, then cook them at the table. The all-you-can-eat rate is RM8/16 for kids/adults; only take what you're going to eat, though – as elsewhere in Sarawak, you'll be charged for leftovers. It's a lively place with good draught beer and it's great for a group of people.

Jalan India has three tempting options: the *Jubilee*, at No 49; *MJ Abdul Rashid Cafe*, next door at No 47; and the *Malaya Restaurant* at No 53. All serve inexpensive Malay curries. Not far away, on Jalan Car-penter, is the *National Islamic Cafe*, which serves tasty, cheap Malay food and has ex-cellent roti and murtabak.

*Biryani Cafe (16 Main Bazaar)* has a nice variety of cheap Indian curries and good *roti canai* (roti served with a curry sauce).

**Seafood** Kuching restaurants offer a good variety of seafood. Local specialities include steamed pomfret fish and sambal prawns. *See Good Food Centre* is a great Chinese seafood restaurant near Telang Usan Hotel. Here you can try local Sarawak specialities such as lobster in pepper sauce, *midin* (crispy jungle fern) or *ambol* (finger clam). The latter looks like a fleshy worm; it's delicious steamed with ginger and lemongrass, but is also known locally as *monyet punya* – literally 'monkey's got one' – and you'll never look at a monkey the same way again. The friendly staff will help you choose.

Good, cheap seafood can be enjoyed at *Ah Ka Su Seafood*, near the Greenwood Inn off Jalan Green Hill. The *New Kuching Food Centre* is a reasonably priced open-air restaurant that sets up tables and chairs on the waterfront in the evening. *Benson's Seafood Centre*, around the corner, is a bit more expensive but has some of the best seafood in town.

The best Western cuisine is served at the international hotels, although it's expensive by local standards and alcohol will probably double your bill. Setting the pace is the Merdeka Palace Hotel, where the outstanding *Ristorante Beccari* has superb pasta dishes and pizza costing RM18 to RM28; a glass of house wine is RM16. The Beccari also has an excellent all-you-eat buffet on Wednesday and Sunday.

The Hilton houses several restaurants, the best of which is the *Steakhouse*. It offers a fixed-price three-course dinner for RM39 plus drinks, and is good value for a special night out.

Many travellers homesick for a real Western-style restaurant rave about *Denis' Place (80 Main Bazaar)*, near the Chinese History Museum. The coffee and sweets are excellent, and there's a great range of salads (around RM7), burgers (RM12) and the like.

In the Riverside Suites, *Sushi Tei* is a small, corner cafe offering great sushi (RM3.80 to RM6.80) – it's a handy source of protein before sliding into a nearby bar.

**Vegetarian** *Life Cafe (108 Jalan Ewe Hai)*, next to the Hong San Temple, is a classy, tastefully decorated tea shop serving delicious Chinese vegetable dumplings and rice dishes for RM3 to RM4. There's also an excellent range of Chinese teas and the best coffee in Kuching. It's closed on Sunday.

The food court downstairs in the *Medan Pelita mall* has one or two inexpensive stalls specialising in vegetarian food.

**Self-Catering** *Ting & Ting Supermarket* is just a few doors down from the Borneo Hotel; there's another well-stocked supermarket in the basement of the *Sarawak Plaza*, and a smaller one in the *Medan Pelita mall*.

## Entertainment

Sarawakian hospitality is best appreciated over a drink (or several), and locals are only too happy to oblige. It's worth getting out in the evening at least once – you are much more likely to meet people (and possibly get some useful upriver contacts) in a bar than you are at a cheap hawker stall or a restaurant.

Outside the top-end hotel bars, prices are very reasonable, with beer averaging about RM5 to RM8 a bottle. Asking for a discount in bars is very bad form, but canned beer is often much cheaper than bottled beer.

Along with best of most everything else, Kuching has the liveliest and most varied nightlife in Borneo. Aside from the ubiquitous karaoke lounges, there are lots of bars and nightclubs to choose from. Large raves (perfectly legal) take over a covered car park or similar venue every few months – check with the guys at Club II (see later in this section) to see if there are any on while you're in town.

It's busy somewhere in town every night, and Wednesday and Friday are ladies' nights in several spots. As with elsewhere in Borneo, things don't get started until quite late – a bar may be deserted at 11 pm and pumping at 1 am. Established bars are packed on weekends with everyone from logging barons to transvestites. There's usually a convivial atmosphere, so be prepared for a late night.

Opposite the Hilton car park are two very friendly pubs. *De Tavern* is Kayan-run and though it has lost a step over time, first-time visitors are still treated to a free tipple of *tuak,* the potent Iban rice wine. Above De Tavern is *The Royalist* – it's named after James Brooke's sloop, honoured for first bringing beer to Sarawak. As at De Tavern, simply front up to the long central bar – the rest will take care of itself.

*Amigos Cafe & Bistro* is on Jalan Bukit Mata Kuching, at the crossroads of the nightlife zone. Food is pricey and less than authentic (but would you trust the tuak in Tijuana?); still, it's a decent spot for a beer in the afternoon or early evening.

Along from Amigos is the *Eagle's Nest,* nocturnal home to a large brood of expats and local regulars. There's nearly always a good crowd as the evening wears on and Kuching's best DJ warms up. The Eagle's Nest is open from 11.30 am until way past your bedtime. Next door, some of the best noodles in town are served till midnight.

In the blocks of buildings behind the Crowne Plaza you'll find several nightspots, as well as some handy late-night food stalls. *Vampire* is a serious trance bar that's plenty of fun. For live music, *Cat City* features Filipino and occasionally Kuala Lumpur (KL) cover bands; this place is either dead or throbbing. The bands also turn up at the yuppie-friendly *Victoria Arms* pub in the Merdeka Palace Hotel, though drinks here are expensive and dance music dominates during the long breaks.

The Riverside Suites has some pleasant terraced places overlooking the water. *Club II* is a small, friendly bar run by Dayak dudes, and *Phenomenon,* with its trippy decor, is a good bar when the crowd turns up.

In addition to the disco above the Khatulistiwa Cafe (see Malay, Western & Chinese under Places to Eat earlier), *Peppers* dance club in the Hilton is popular, particularly on ladies' nights.

*Hornbill's Corner Cafe* (see Places to Eat) is a great open-air pub/restaurant that gets packed on Saturday nights with football-mad Sarawakians watching telecasts on the TV.

## Shopping

Kuching is the handicraft centre of Borneo. There are dozens of shops selling arts and crafts scattered around the city. Don't expect many bargains, but don't be afraid to negotiate, either – there's plenty to choose from, and the quality varies as much as the prices. It's best to spend some time browsing to familiarise yourself with prices and range before committing yourself to a purchase – see the 'Crafty Shopping' boxed text in this chapter for more information.

The best area to start browsing is along Main Bazaar, where every second shop seems to be a gallery-style craft centre. Even if you are not thinking of buying, it is well worth ducking into some of these places. Some are piled with all manner of bric-a-brac, others are presented like studios – most make for fascinating browsing and the shopkeepers are mostly very laid-back.

Some of the better choices in town include Fabrito, at 56 Main Bazaar, which has beautiful textiles such as hangings and clothing. It also stocks cheap-but-good Indonesian imitations. Galeri M, at 26 Main Bazaar (also in the lobby of the Kuching Hilton), guarantees authenticity. It has an outstanding range of quality new and antique pieces, from beads and baskets to textiles and spears. Galeri M is known for its fair dealings with local artists and craftspeople.

Nelsons Gallery, at 84 Main Bazaar, is also good and has a large range of items at reasonable prices. Sarakraf, at 14 Main Bazaar, was set up by the Sarawak Economic Development Corporation, and is a good place for smaller and cheaper items. Sarawak House, at 67 Main Bazaar, has a small range of superb pieces, and Unika Sarawak, 5 Lebuh Wayang, also has some quality pieces.

Pang Ling is a noted batik artist who draws his inspiration from many years of upriver visits to longhouses. His prices are very reasonable, and his studio, Sarawak

MALAYSIAN BORNEO

MALAYSIAN BORNEO

## Crafty Shopping

If you're looking for authentic tribal artefacts in Malaysian Borneo, it's just as well to save your money for Kuching. Sabah's selection is poor and much of the stock in Sarawak towns started out in Kuching.

You can, of course, go directly to the source. Women in well-touristed longhouses often set up craft markets for visitors, and buying a basket or weaving is a good alternative to 'paying' for your visit with a T-shirt or similar gift. Farther afield, ask around for items of interest – trekking guides should be able to help. However, there's not necessarily a lot out there: The Kuching art market has already absorbed a great number of tribal artefacts from longhouses as far away as the Rejang.

The most-visible crafts tradition is maintained by the Iban, whose intricate paintings and carvings decorate everything from tourist leaflets to buildings. Genuine pieces may be very old, venerated or functional, and will command hundreds, if not thousands, of ringgit. The Iban are also famous for *pua kumba*, a masterful weaving style incorporating traditional motifs. Another popular craft worth a long look is beadwork. Beads originating from as far away as Venice have been traded by many Borneo tribes for centuries.

As with art markets everywhere, the onus is on the buyer to be aware. The bulk of what's on offer is churned out for tourists, and although a piece may actually come from a longhouse, it will probably have no traditional significance. Many of the more garish and polished pieces are actually mass produced outside Sarawak and even beyond Borneo.

Artificially 'aged' items are also commonplace, and many galleries have a back room where the 'real items' are kept. Sometimes these are authentic pieces, but often they aren't. Items are often composites as well: Old handles and clasps may be fixed to a medicine chest made last Wednesday in Pontianak. One way to tell the difference is by the speed the price falls. If the price quickly drops dramatically, you're almost certainly dealing with a purely tourist-trade item.

### Restrictions

Most outlets can organise the necessary fumigation of wooden artefacts, as well as shipping. Some antiquities – cannon and jars in particular – are difficult to export. You'll need permission from the Sarawak Museum, and you should have this *before* you purchase the item.

The hornbill is a totally protected bird, so even though hornbill parts are sometimes sold under the counter, if you're caught trying to take them out of the state you're in a whole lot of trouble. Forget about bear and leopard teeth, too – sale of any parts of these animals is prohibited. Deer are protected but not restricted, so it is possible to apply for a licence to export deer horn.

Some countries restrict the importation of weapons as souvenirs. For example, Australian customs officials seem worried about the safety of suburban stray cats if blowpipes get in (they may have a point). The legendary *parang*, once the head-hunting tool of choice, is another trinket you may have trouble explaining to the postman or baggage inspector back home.

---

Batik Art Shop, at 1 Jalan Temple, houses some fine weavings as well.

Look out for *Borneo: A Photographic Journey* by photographer Dennis Lau; a rare touch for a coffee-table book, the accompanying text is informative without trying to compete with the beautiful photos.

There are numerous shops around town selling gold jewellery. Outlets for dried Chinese delicacies, such as birds' nests and shark fins, are also common – there's an interesting example next to McDonald's in the eastern end of town.

Everyday items such as baby supplies are readily available at the Nguikee branch in the Sarawak Plaza.

### Getting There & Away

**Air** The Malaysia Airlines office (☎ 244144) is on Jalan Song Thian Cheok;

it is open weekdays from 8 am to 5 pm, and Saturday to 1 pm. The office is usually horribly crowded, and you're better off dealing with a travel agent if you can. Singapore Airlines (☎ 240266) is in the Ang Chang building on Jalan Tunku Abdul Rahman. Royal Brunei Airlines (☎ 243344) has an office on Jalan Song Thian Cheok.

**Peninsular Malaysia & Singapore** The regular Malaysia Airlines fare between KL and Kuching (1¾ hours) is RM262. There are early-morning flights for RM187. Malaysia Airlines has at least eight daily flights between KL international airport and Kuching, and two daily flights to KL's Subang Airport.

Malaysia Airlines has at least four flights per day to Johor Bahru (RM169) and two daily flights to Singapore (RM286).

**Malaysian Borneo** Although Malaysia Airlines has an extensive provincial network, none of the flights to the interior operates from Kuching – they exit Sibu and Miri. From Kuching there are flights to Sibu (10 daily, RM72), Bintulu (at least six daily, RM117), Miri (at least five daily, RM164), KK (at least seven daily, RM228) and Labuan (one daily, RM199). There's also a daily Twin Otter service to Mukah (RM76).

**Brunei & Indonesia** Malaysia Airlines has three flights a week between Kuching and Bandar Seri Begawan (RM309) in Brunei.

It also operates four flights per week between Kuching and Pontianak, in Kalimantan. The fare is RM276, plus RM20 departure tax. Pontianak is a visa-free entry point to Indonesia, and travellers of most nationalities do not require a visa – but check with the Indonesian consulate first.

**Other Destinations** Malaysia Airlines flies between Kuching and Perth (Australia) on Saturday; the airline also flies twice a week between Kuching and Manila (Philippines).

Malaysia Airlines has a joint service with Dragonair flying three times a week to Hong Kong.

**Bus** Long-distance buses leave from the regional express-bus terminal on Jalan Penrissen at 3rd Mile, about 5km south-east of the city centre. Buses for Sri Aman, Sarikei, Sibu, Bintulu and Miri leave from here and several bus companies have daily services to all these places; some also have a regular service to Pontianak in Kalimantan.

Around 18 city buses pass by the express-bus terminal; these buses run regularly from 6 am to 6 pm, and there are few buses till around 9.30 pm. It's easiest to catch buses in front of the general post office (50 sen); allow at least 20 minutes for the trip.

Except on weekends and public holidays, there's usually no need to book – just roll up, buy a ticket and hop on. Most of the long-distance bus companies have ticket offices at or near the Petra Jaya bus station. Check the daily papers for times and fares, or ask at the tourist office to see if there are changes to the schedules. Long-distance buses are modern, with air-con and with kung fu movies.

The main long-distance companies are: Biaramas Express (☎ 452139, 429418), on Jalan Khoo Hun Yeang; and Borneo Highway Express (☎ 619689) and PB Ekspres (☎ 461277, 456261), both of which are on Jalan P Ramlee near the corner of Jalan Mosque. Dalat-Miri Bas Ekspres (☎ 578213) has a couple of buses a day between Kuching and virtually every destination in the state.

**Sarikei** Several bus companies make the trip to Sarikei (four hours, RM28); most departures are between 6.30 am and 12.30 pm, but buses continue until around 10 pm.

**Sibu, Bintulu & Miri** Overnight buses to Sibu are a popular option. Buses leave Kuching for Sibu (seven hours, RM32) from morning until around 11 pm.

Buses to Bintulu run daily between around 6.30 am and 10 pm (11 hours, RM52). If you're crazy about bus rides, you can take an express bus all the way to Miri (15 to 16 hours, RM70).

**South-West Sarawak** Companies servicing Kuching and nearby towns are: Chin

Lian Long (CLL; ☎ 422767); Matang Transport Company (☎ 422814); Petra Jaya Transport (☎ 429418); Regas Transport (☎ 242966); and Sarawak Transport Company (STC; ☎ 242967).

Borneo Highway Express and PB Ekspres have booths near the corner of Jalan Mosque and Jalan P Ramlee, at the bottom of the Saujana car park. Services depart from the bus stands near the market at the western end of the Kuching waterfront; many buses then stop along Jalan P Ramlee near the corner of Jalan Mosque, or in front of the post office.

Generally there is no need to book, but you can buy tickets at the Biaramas Express booking office (☎ 452139, 429418), on Jalan Khoo Hun Yeang.

See individual Getting There & Away entries for information on south-west Sarawak bus travel.

**Indonesia** Several companies have a daily service to Pontianak (around nine hours, RM34.50) in Kalimantan. Biaramas Express has departures from Kuching at 7, 8, 9 and 10.30 am and 12.30 pm; it currently does the return trip at 8 am (30,000Rp).

Buses cross at the Tebeduen-Entikong border. This is a visa-free entry point into Indonesia for citizens of most nationalities, but check with the Indonesian Consulate in Kuching before leaving. (See Consulates & Immigration Offices earlier in this section.) It is a slow haul from Serian to Tebedu on the Sarawak side, but there's a good highway from Entikong to Pontianak.

**Boat** One boat per day leaves Kuching for Sibu (about 4 hours). At the time of writing this was at 8.30 am – but highly likely to change – and advance booking was not possible. Check with the STA office (see Tourist Offices earlier) for the latest on booking and for schedule changes; get to the dock an hour before sailing to be on the safe side. Economy/1st-class tickets cost RM35/39 each way.

Boats leave from the Bintawa Express wharf in the suburb of Pending, about 6km east of the city centre. Catch CLL bus No

17 or 19 (70 sen) from in front of the main post office, or Regas bus No 1C (90 sen) from the bus stop near the Chinese History Museum; the trip takes about 20 minutes.

## Getting Around

**To/From the Airport** The green-and-cream STC bus No 12A does a loop that takes in the airport (90 sen). It runs approximately every 50 minutes between 6.30 am and 7.10 pm – ask whether it's headed back to town before you board. The blue-and-white CCL bus No 8A does a direct run between the city and airport (90 sen).

In town, catch one of the buses on the waterfront at the western end of the Main Bazaar, or outside the main post office. The airport bus shelter is about 100m to the right of the terminal as you exit.

Airport taxis run on a coupon system. A taxi between Kuching airport and the city centre costs RM17.50; the coupon booth is to the right as you leave the terminal.

**Bus** Most points of interest around the city and nearby towns are serviced by a good local bus network. At first the system may seem chaotic because there's no central terminal, but the five local companies congregate near the market at the western end of the waterfront.

The *Kuching City Map*, available free at the STA office, has the latest information on local buses, times and fares.

**Taxi** Kuching's taxis are unmetered, so agree on the fare before getting in. Taxis can be found waiting at the market, at the express-bus station and outside major hotels. There is usually no problem flagging down a taxi on main streets, even late at night. A taxi radio call service can be reached on ☎ 348898 (☎ 367898 after hours). Most short trips around town cost RM5.

**Car** Car rental costs in Sarawak start at around RM150 per day. Mayflower Car Hire (☎ 575 233) has a counter at the airport; the STA office and upmarket hotels can also help arrange car hire. At around

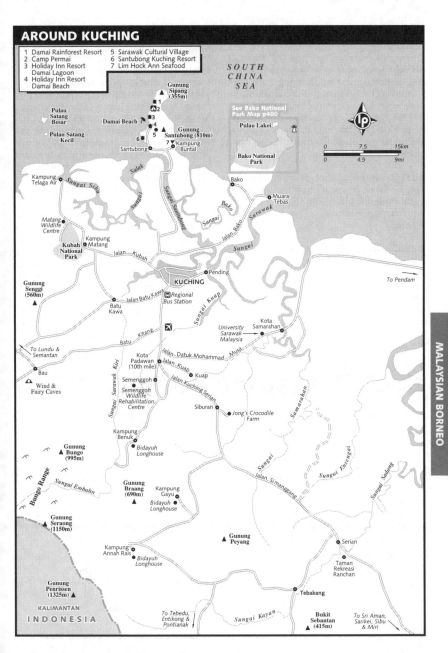

# AROUND KUCHING

1 Damai Rainforest Resort
2 Camp Permai
3 Holiday Inn Resort
  Damai Lagoon
4 Holiday Inn Resort
  Damai Beach
5 Sarawak Cultural Village
6 Santubong Kuching Resort
7 Lim Hock Ann Seafood

SOUTH
CHINA
SEA

See Bako National
Park Map p400

Pulau Lakei

Bako National
Park

Gunung
Sipang
(355m)

Damai Beach

Gunung
Santubong (810m)

Kampung
Buntal

Pulau
Satang
Besar

Pulau Satang
Kecil

Santubong

0        7.5        15km
0      4.5        9mi

Kampung
Telaga Air

Sungai Sibu

Salak

Sungai

Sungai Santubong

Sungai

Bako

Sarawak

Bako

Muara
Tebas

Matang
Wildlife
Centre

Kampung
Matang

Kubah
National
Park

Jalan — Kubah

Jalan Bako

Sungai

Pending

Gunung
Senggi
(560m)

KUCHING

To Pendam

Jalan Batu Kawa

Regional
Bus Station

Sungai Kuap

Batu
Kawa

Kitang

Kota
Samarahan

Batu

Sungai Sarawak Kiri

Jalan Datuk Mohammad

University
Sarawak
Malaysia

Musa

To Lundu &
Semantan

Kota
Padawan
(10th mile)

Jalan Kuap

Kuap

Bau

Wind &
Fairy Caves

Semenggoh
Semenggoh
Wildlife
Rehabilitation
Centre

Jalan Kuching Serian

Siburan

Jong's Crocodile
Farm

Sungai Samarahan

Kampung
Benuk

Bidayuh
Longhouse

Gunung
Bungo
(995m)

Sungai Embahn

Gunung
Braang
(690m)

Kampung
Gayu

Bidayuh
Longhouse

Sungai

Jalan Simanggang

Sungai Engsagai

Sungai Sadong

Bungo Range

Gunung
Seraong
(1150m)

Gunung
Peyang

Serian

Kampung
Annah Rais

Bidayuh
Longhouse

Taman
Rekreasi
Ranchan

Gunung
Penrissen
(1325m)

KALIMANTAN

INDONESIA

To Tebedu,
Entikong &
Pontianak

Sungai Kayan

Tebakang

Bukit
Sebantan
(415m)

To Sri Aman,
Sarikei, Sibu
& Miri

MALAYSIAN BORNEO

RM1 per litre, petrol is cheap by Western standards.

**Bicycle** Kuching is a bicycle-friendly city and there are some good riding trails outside town. Unfortunately, no one officially rents out bikes. If you're determined, ask around at the bike shops on Jalan Ewe Hai. Ghee Hoe Hin Trading, at No 88, may be able to help; it also sells quality bikes from around RM300.

**Boat** Small boats and express boats ply the Sungai Sarawak, connecting the small villages around Kuching. For river crossings, see the Waterfront entry earlier in this section.

## BAKO NATIONAL PARK

Bako is Sarawak's oldest national park, protecting 2728 hectares of an unspoilt promontory between the mouths of the Sarawak and Bako rivers. It's a beautiful spot, where mangroves fringe the coasts and the rocky headlands are indented with clean beaches. The park features seven of the state's main vegetation types. These include rainforest and *kerangas,* a distinctive plant community that grows on the sandstone plateau that forms the backbone of the national park. Botanically, Bako is a fascinating place where you can easily see four species of pitcher plant within an hour's walk of park headquarters (see Flora & Fauna in the Facts about Malaysia chapter for more on these and other plants).

Bako is most famous for its wildlife and it is the best place in Sarawak to see the rare proboscis monkey. Macaque monkeys are common, and they're fun to watch as they forage along the beach in the evening.

A permit is needed if you intend to stay at Bako, but is not necessary for a day trip. Permits and accommodation can be organised at the Visitors' Information Centre (☎ 088-410944) in Kuching. Telephone bookings are accepted, but must be confirmed and paid for at least three days before your intended departure. If you get caught short of time on a day trip, it is possible to stay overnight at the park, *if* a bed is available (unlikely on weekends). Staff at the park headquarters can arrange your permit and accommodation by phoning Kuching.

Register for the park upon arrival at the boat dock in Bako Bazaar. (See the National

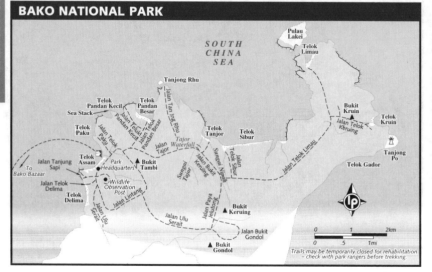

BAKO NATIONAL PARK

Parks section earlier in this chapter for fees.) Bako National Park is well worth a visit, but being only 37km north of Kuching it is popular with day-trippers.

## Park Headquarters
From Bako Bazaar it's a 30-minute boat ride to park headquarters (☎ 011-225049) at Telok Assam, where you'll find accommodation, a cafeteria and the park office. The office is about 100m along the shore from the landing dock. Staff will show you to your quarters and can answer any questions about trails. There's a large trail map hanging outside the office; ask for a free copy. Storage lockers are available for RM3.

There's a good information centre here, with photos and displays on various aspects of the park's ecology. An entertaining video on the proboscis monkey is shown at regular times and on request – ask at the office.

## Walking
Bako has more than 30km of well-marked trails, ranging from short walks around park headquarters to strenuous day walks to the end of the peninsula. Guides are available (RM5 per hour), but it's easy to find your way around because all trails are colour-coded with paint on trees or rocks next to the path. You don't have to go far to see wildlife, and there are walks to suit all levels of fitness and motivation. Plan your route before starting out on longer walks, and aim to be back at Telok Assam before dark, at about 6.45 pm. Some trails may be closed for maintenance after the wet season – check at the park office before setting out.

If you have only one day in Bako, try to get here early and attempt the **Jalan Lintang**: It traverses a range of vegetation and climbs the sandstone escarpment up to the kerangas, where you'll find many pitcher plants.

The longest trail is **Jalan Telok Limau**, a 10km walk that's impossible to do as a return trip in one day. You will need to carry camping equipment or else be collected by boat. Arrange a pick-up with the park warden, but expect to be charged about RM100. The park's main trails are listed in the 'Walking Trails' table in this section; the

Proboscis monkeys inhabit the forests of Borneo.

times given are those recommended by the national park (fast walkers will complete trails in half the time).

Take adequate water on all hikes; it gets particularly hot in the kerangas and there's no shade for long stretches.

## Wildlife
Walking trails pass through peat swamp, rainforest and, on the low sandstone plateau behind Telok Assam, kerangas. The latter is a fascinating ecosystem where pitcher plants are common, especially near the intersection of the Jalan Lintang and Jalan Ulu Serait trails. This kerangas is the spitting image of some parts of the Australian east coast, although it is botanically very different.

Common animals include the long-tailed macaque and silver leaf monkey, large monitor lizards, palm squirrels and, at night, bearded pigs, mouse deer, civets and the culago, or flying lemur. The best places to look for the proboscis monkey are along the Telok Paku and Telok Delima walking trails, a short distance from the park headquarters: Walk very quietly and listen for them crashing through the trees – they will see you long before you see them.

Bird-watching is best near the park headquarters, especially in and around the mangroves at Telok Assam. Although there are

MALAYSIAN BORNEO

## Walking Trails – Bako National Park

| trail name | destination | walking time |
|---|---|---|
| Jalan Bukit Keruing/Jalan Bukit Gondol | mountain path | 7 hours |
| Jalan Lintang | circular path | 3–4 hours |
| Jalan Serait | park boundary | 1½ hours |
| Jalan Tanjor | waterfalls | 2 hours |
| Jalan Tanjung Rhu | cliffs/viewpoint | 2½ hours |
| Jalan Tanjung Sapi | cliffs/viewpoint | ½ hour |
| Jalan Telok Delima | mangroves | ¾ hour |
| Jalan Telok Paku | Cove Beach | ¾ hour |
| Jalan Telok Pandan | Cove Beach | 1½ hours |
| Jalan Ulu Serait/Jalan Telok Limau | Pulau Lakei (Island) | 8 hours |

about 150 species on the park list, many of these are migrants that are only present during the wet season.

**Warning** The long-tailed macaques that hang about park headquarters are great to watch but they are cunning and mischievous, an attitude fostered by tourists who persist in offering them food. Do not leave valuables, food or drink unattended, especially on the beaches, at the canteen or on verandas. Lock all doors and close all bags – they (both macaques and some tourists) are quick opportunists and will make running leaps at anything they think they can carry off, including drink bottles, food, laundry, sunglasses and hats. It's wise to leave the monkeys in peace – the males can be aggressive and put up some impressive threatening displays. If you get bailed up, yell for the park staff. Monkeys are not a problem after dark.

### Beaches
The beach at Telok Pandan Besar is only accessible by boat from park headquarters. If you're thinking of hitching a boat ride to or from a beach, it's probably only cost effective for a group. Boats to beaches near park headquarters will cost around RM25 (one way or return), but to beaches farther away it is quite expensive (eg, RM80 to Telok Sibur). Pulau Lakei, on the park's northeastern tip, is accessible by boat (RM120) and accommodation may be completed by the time you read this.

### Places to Stay & Eat
There is plenty of accommodation at Bako National Park, including recently spruced-up two- and three-room chalets, as well as hostels and a muddy campground. You can book accommodation through the Visitors' Information Centre (☎ 088-410944) in Kuching.

*Hostel* rooms with shared kitchen and bathroom sleep four and cost RM10.50 per person. Fan-cooled *chalets*, with various sized rooms, are also available; a double room costs RM42. Bookings are essential for the chalets and advisable for the hostel rooms, though you should be able to get a bed if you just front up during the week.

*Camping* costs RM4 per site, but the camp site is a swamp for much of the year. There's a shower block and lockers can be hired for RM3 per day. Bring your own utensils, sheets and sleeping bags. The monkeys are a particular nuisance near the campground and will steal anything that is not firmly secured.

The park *cafeteria* is open from 8 am to 9 pm. It sells cheap noodle and rice meals. The adjoining shop sells a good variety of reasonably priced tinned and dried food, chocolate, biscuits, film and toiletries, although fresh bread and vegetables are not always available.

### Getting There & Away
To get to Bako from Kuching, first take a bus to Bako Bazaar in Kampung Bako, then charter a boat to the park. Petra Jaya bus No 6 leaves from near the market in Kuching every

40 minutes (approximately) from 6.40 am to 4 pm (45 minutes, RM2.10/3.80 one way/ return – valid for a week). The last bus back to Kuching leaves Kampung Bako at 5 pm.

A boat from Bako Bazaar to the park headquarters costs RM30 each way for up to 10 people (RM3 for each additional person). The chances are that someone on the bus will be looking to share a boat, especially on a weekend; tourists sometimes wait at the boat dock for the same reason.

Take note of the boat's number, and be sincere when you agree to a pick-up time – boatmen have been burned by tourists who renege on a deal and return on another boat. As a result, boatmen are often reluctant to return later the same day (tides and rough seas can also be a factor). If you do want to share another boat back, tell park headquarters your boat number – staff are happy to call and cancel your original boat.

It's a pleasant 30-minute boat trip past coastal scenery, fishing boats and people duck-diving for finger clams in the bay. From November to February the sea is often rough, and at times it may not be possible for boats to approach or leave Telok Assam. Take a waterproof jacket to protect against spray in the open boats.

## SANTUBONG & DAMAI
☎ 082

The Santubong Peninsula is an exclusive tourist area 32km north of Kuching near the mouth of the Sungai Santubong. It's a picturesque place with jungle trekking on nearby Gunung Santubong and good seafood at two small fishing villages, Santubong and Buntal. The peninsula has the nearest beach to Kuching, other than those in Bako National Park (see earlier in this chapter), and is very popular with local people on weekends. You can see primitive rock carvings at Sungai Jaong, about 1.5km upriver from the coast, and the peninsula also has the Sarawak Cultural Village – a photogenic ethnic theme park well worth a stop.

### Sarawak Cultural Village
Surrounding an artificial lake at the foot of Gunung Santubong, the Sarawak Cultural Village is an excellent living museum. It has examples of **traditional dwellings** built by different peoples of Sarawak – in this case Orang Ulu, Bidayuh, Iban and Melanau – as well as Malay and Chinese houses. There are six buildings in all, plus a shelter of the type the nomadic Penan periodically live in. The dwellings are inhabited by tribespeople who demonstrate **local arts and crafts**, including basketry and weaving, top spinning, blowpipe shooting and sago processing. Even travellers who have ventured to the Borneo interior are generally impressed by this unique opportunity to see the original styles of the now-modernised longhouses.

All the tribespeople are paid to take part in the daily activities, and they sell their products and handicrafts. Great pains are taken to make the village authentic – just to prove the point, the nomadic Penan occasionally go AWOL.

The village has a restaurant and souvenir shop and is open from 9 am to 5.15 pm daily; entry is a hefty RM45 (RM22.50 for children aged six to 12). A visit is capped by a cultural show at 11.30 am and 4.30 pm. It is all quite touristy, of course, but tastefully done and sincere in intent. For more information and bookings, phone ☎ 082-846411. The Holiday Inn Kuching offers a good package for RM60, which includes the shuttle bus from Kuching, admission to the village and lunch.

There's no public transport to the village, but a shuttle bus leaves the Holiday Inn Kuching at 9 am and 12.30 pm, returning at 1.45 and 5.30 pm (RM10 each way).

### Jungle Walks
The Santubong Peninsula offers good jungle trekking within easy reach of Kuching, and the more adventurous can attempt the ascent of **Gunung Santubong** (810m).

An easy to moderate circular walk starts near the Holiday Inn Resort and ends near the cultural village, passing a pretty **waterfall** on the way. There's a cafe at the beginning where you can pick up a map, but the trail is marked with splashes of paint so it's very hard to get lost.

## Places to Stay & Eat

Accommodation in Santubong and Damai is mainly resort style, and not cheap. However, mid-range travellers will now have an option, as a new *B&B* was about to open at the time of writing. Rates will be around RM70 per person; for more details, ring Polycarp Teo Sebom on ☎ 010-887 1017.

The Holiday Inn chain has stamped its name on two places here: *Holiday Inn Resort Damai Beach (☎ 846999, fax 846777, ✉ hirdb02@po.jaring.my)*, which has a small beach created from imported sand; and *Holiday Inn Resort Damai Lagoon (☎ 846900, fax 846901)*. Both resorts were offering identical promotional rates at the time of writing: standard rooms at RM160, larger rooms at RM170 and suites starting at RM370. Both resorts are five minutes' walk from the Sarawak Cultural Village.

*Santubong Kuching Resort (☎ 846888, fax 846666)* provides a wide range of services and offers activities such as tennis, basketball, water sports, golf and mountain biking. Published room rates start at RM138, rising to RM253 for suites and RM379.50 for chalets. Discounts are usually available.

*Damai Rainforest Resort (☎ 846487, fax 846486)* also offers decent promo rates on its eco-friendly 'concept' accommodation: A six-person room in its 'longhouse' costs RM75 per person (it's regularly RM120); beds in an air-con 'tree house' are RM120 and in a 'log cabin' RM140. Camping facilities are available and tents can be hired.

Damai Rainforest Resort also runs *Camp Permai*. It caters mostly for school groups, but independent travellers are welcome. There's a variety of accommodation, from camping to air-con tree houses and log cabins; substantially discounted rates may be available for tree-top cabins on weekdays. Tree-top accommodation starts at RM80 per night and campers can stay for RM6.

There are seafood restaurants at Santubong and Buntal. *Lim Hock Ann Seafood*, in Kampung Buntal, has a wooden deck on stilts overlooking the South China Sea; it's a perfect place to sink a few beers and watch the moon rise over Bako Peninsula. The food is fresh but prices are subject to seasonal variation – expect to pay around RM10 for some dishes.

There are sterile *restaurants* at the resorts where you can enjoy international cuisine at international prices.

## Getting There & Away

To reach Buntal and Santubong, take Petra Jaya bus No 2B from near Kuching's open-air market (RM2.30). The last return bus leaves for Kuching at 6 pm; if you want to stay for a meal the only option is to fork out for a taxi back to Kuching (45 minutes).

There's no bus to the resorts, but the shuttle bus from Holiday Inn Kuching goes to both Damai resorts (RM10 one way); departures from Kuching are at 9 am and 12.30, 3.15, 6.30 and 8.45 pm. The shuttle returns to Kuching at 1.45, 5.30 and 7.15 pm.

A taxi to the resorts costs RM25 to RM30; if you want to be picked up after dinner expect to pay RM60 for the return trip. Taxis can also be hired from the resorts out to Buntal and Santubong.

## KUBAH NATIONAL PARK

Just 20km west of Kuching, Kubah National Park is the nearest national park to the city and it makes an easy and rewarding day trip. Its 2230 hectares protect a range of forested sandstone hills that rise dramatically from the surrounding plain to a height of 450m. There are waterfalls, rainforest walking trails and lookouts. Kubah's beautiful rainforest is home to a wide variety of palms and orchids, but there is less chance of encountering animals here than in Bako National Park.

Walking trails include the paved entrance road, which runs right up to the summit of Kubah's highest peak, **Gunung Serapi**; it's a two- to three-hour walk and the peak is often shrouded in mist but there are lookouts along the way. You can probably cadge a lift up then walk down. Most of the other trails run off the entrance road: **Rayu Trail** links Kubah with the Matang Wildlife Centre, 5km from the turn-off, and takes about three hours to walk; **Waterfall Trail** takes about 45 minutes from the turn-off and ends at a natural swimming pool.

There's a RM3 park entrance fee plus a RM5/10 camera/video fee payable at the gate. A hand-drawn map that shows the trails is available at the park office.

## Places to Stay

Kubah park headquarters offers hostel, resthouses and double-storey chalet accommodation. In the comfortable, clean *hostel*, fan-cooled rooms sleeping two/four/six people cost RM20/40/60, with pillows and linen supplied. There's a kitchen with all facilities, including a fridge.

Air-con *chalets* with all facilities sleep six people and cost RM180; less-swanky *resthouses* sleeping 12 cost RM120. Kubah is entirely self-catering; if you have transport you can get supplies in the local kampung or even dine back in Kuching; otherwise you'll have to bring all you require. Accommodation booking (☎ 088-410944) is essential for weekend stays; at other times you can just turn up.

## Getting There & Away

Matang Transport Co bus No 11 leaves Kuching for Kubah roughly every 50 minutes between 7 am and 4.30 pm (30 minutes, RM1.65). The bus will drop you at Sungai Cina, from where it's a 300m uphill walk to the park entrance.

A taxi from town will cost at least RM50 return; arrange with the driver a time to be picked up. Another option is to drive, but the park is not well signposted: Follow the signs to Matang then turn left at the crossroads 200m past the Red Bridge; the park entrance is about 3.5km farther on.

## MATANG WILDLIFE CENTRE

Adjacent to Kubah National Park, the Matang Wildlife Centre was once scheduled to replace Semenggoh Wildlife Rehabilitation Centre, but at the last minute Semenggoh was given a reprieve.

The Matang centre is open to visitors and is popular with locals, who come to swim in the nearby river on weekends. There's accommodation, a cafeteria and a very good information centre here. Park entry costs RM3 plus a RM5/10 camera/video fee.

At the time of writing, the rehabilitation program had not started, but a twice-daily feeding program for orang-utans, hornbills, sambar deer and crocodiles may be underway by the time you read this. There are rainforest walking trails – including the **Sungai Rayu Trail**, which links up with Kubah National Park (three to four hours) – and other developments planned include a butterfly farm. Check with the Visitors' Information Centre in Kuching for the current program.

A four-person room in Matang's *hostel* costs RM40 (RM10 per bed); a *chalet* sleeping four costs RM120; a *camp site* costs RM4. Book accommodation at Kuching Visitors' Information Centre (☎ 088-410944).

## Getting There & Away

At present, the only practical options for getting to Matang Wildlife Centre from Kuching are by taxi (about RM35 one way) or with a tour.

You can take a bus part of the way to the Kubah National Park turn-off, but it's a farther 12km to Matang.

## SEMENGGOH WILDLIFE REHABILITATION CENTRE

Semenggoh (sometimes spelled Semenggok) is Sarawak's equivalent to the orang-utan sanctuary at Sepilok in Sabah. In some ways it's better than Sabah's more famous tourist attraction, as it is a low-key place that has so far avoided Sepilok's circus-like atmosphere.

The centre attempts to rehabilitate orang-utans, monkeys, honey bears and other unfortunate creatures that have been orphaned or illegally caged. You're not guaranteed to see wild orang-utans, because they're set free and only return when they're hungry (usually outside the fruiting season in the forest).

The semiwild orang-utans are fed at 8.30 to 9 am and again at 3 to 3.15 pm, so it's best to time your visit to coincide with one of these sessions. The centre is open every day from 8 am to 12.45 pm and from 2 to 4.15 pm.

A (free) permit is required to visit the centre and can be arranged at the Visitors' Information Centre in Kuching. There is no accommodation or cafeteria at Semenggoh.

## Longhouse Visits

Many of the tribes living upstream on Sarawak's rivers reside in longhouses – gigantic wooden structures on stilts, where the entire population lives under one roof, with separate rooms leading on to one long communal veranda.

Tourism has had a big impact on the way longhouses operate, and communities along rivers easily accessible from cities have often seen their legendary hospitality turned into a business. Traditionally, the longhouse has always been open to passing travellers and traders. But with many tour companies simply depositing customers on longhouse verandas, this legendary hospitality is changing. At worst – mainly along the Skrang south-east of Kuching – you may be handed a welcoming glass of *tuak* (rice wine) with one hand while the other is held out for 10 ringgit.

Some of the more-conscientious tour operators have made provisions for a limited number of guests with certain longhouses, and cultural shows, craft markets and other activities are laid on. In these cases, the longhouse communities have accepted tourism, but on their own terms; other communities have chosen to stay out of the tourism economy altogether.

You can of course head upriver on your own, but you'll still need to find someone to take you to a longhouse. Without an introduction local people are not going to invite you into their homes. An invitation is essential, and turning up unannounced is not just bad manners; in some circumstances it can be a minor catastrophe, particularly if there has been a recent death or if certain rituals are under way.

When you arrive at a longhouse, you may be surprised to find that it's quite modernised, with satellite TV, electric lighting, corrugated iron and other upgrades – the Iban are, after all, living in the 21st century. For a taste of the past, fine examples of traditional longhouses are on display at the Sarawak Cultural Village.

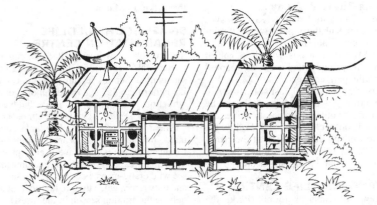

MARTIN HARRIS

A longhouse is a way of life, not just a building. It embodies a communal lifestyle, and you may find the place all but deserted when you visit, as the younger people are often off working the fields, hunting or out on other business. Travellers often find the elders don't speak English and given the cultural differences there is little to talk about anyway – a frustration for everyone, especially the host. To avoid this, ask who will be around before you go, then try to organise some shared activities that will give you and your hosts some common ground. For example, a jungle walk or a river trip to a longhouse can be a real education if you've got a good guide – a longhouse visit and river trip aren't two separate journeys: A longhouse *is* part of the jungle. Many travellers have had unforgettable

MALAYSIAN BORNEO

## Longhouse Visits

experiences participating in longhouse life by sharing in the cooking, helping out in the fields or gathering fruit and herbs.

If you're taking a tour, ask what you're in for – plenty of operators offer pretty minimal itineraries. Also be clear on the lodging arrangements if you're staying overnight. Often you'll stay at purpose-built guesthouses nearby rather than in the longhouse itself; some travellers prefer this, as there's more privacy and the facilities (eg, toilet and shower) may be cleaner and more modern.

Gifts are another area where misunderstandings can occur. You can often judge a tour company's relations with a longhouse community by the attitude they have towards giving gifts. Many outfits will get you to buy some T-shirts, coffee mugs or sweets for the kids (tooth decay is already rampant in many communities). A gift is more than an object of exchange, however, and longhouse communities do not traditionally require gifts of guests. Some communities are in need of schoolbooks, others could use fishing line and hooks, and cosmetics and tobacco are appreciated at many. Your tour company or guide should be able to tell you what to bring to a specific longhouse community. If you're visiting independently, it's polite to bring a small gift for the family of the person who invites you. Some enterprising travellers have found that buying a pig (about 450 ringgit) at a market and loading it onto an upriver-bound longboat got them invitations to stay for as long as they wished! If gifts aren't your thing – and some people find the concept of handing out treats demeaning to locals – by taking a local longboat and buying a handicraft from the longhouse you are already contributing to the longhouse economy.

There's no getting around it: A longhouse visit is going to cost money. Tours are not cheap and if you go on your own you'll still need to pay for transport – a boat plus boatman and/or Land Cruiser and driver, and maybe a guide fee along the way. But if you want a unique, once-in-a-lifetime experience, make room in your budget for a trip; the Kelabit Highlands and the Belaga area on the Batang Rejang are two good places to combine jungle/river trips with a longhouse visit.

### Longhouse Etiquette

Most importantly, never enter a longhouse without permission; always wait to be invited in. If there is a *pemali* (ritual prohibition) in force (usually after a death or some misfortune), which is indicated by a bunch of branches tied to the rail at the bottom of the ladder or by a white flag near the entrance, you won't be invited in.

On arrival at the longhouse, your guide will take you to see the *tuai rumah* (chief). You'll then usually be offered a place to stay for the night and be invited to join them for a meal. Always remove your shoes. Chances are you'll be given a welcome drink of tuak; drink it, or at least some of it. Accept food and drinks with both hands rather than with just one.

Meals are usually taken with the tuai rumah; they are eaten while seated on the floor, and using both hands. Don't point your feet at anyone when sitting on the mat, and don't spit or blow your nose during a meal. The food may be very simple but eat some of it, or at the very least touch the food and then touch your mouth. Food is plentiful and vegetarians are well catered-for, but note that the Iban in particular honour their guests by serving meat for special occasions. You can always take along some food of your own to throw into the communal pot.

When washing or bathing in the river, men are expected to wear at least underpants, and women should stay covered with a sarung. Nudity is definitely not on.

In the evenings there'll probably be a lot of tuak drinking, and you may well be expected to sing and dance. Join in and don't be afraid to make an idiot of yourself – the locals will love it! Tuak may taste mild but it is pretty potent stuff, and you can expect an impressive hangover the next day. The accepted way to drink it is from the glass in a single shot.

MALAYSIAN BORNEO

## Getting There & Away
Semenggoh is 32km south of Kuching. To get there, take STC bus No 6, 6A, 6B or 6C from Kuching (40 minutes, RM1.50). There are eight buses running daily between 7 am and 2 pm. Tell the driver you wish to get off at the Forest Department Nursery, then follow a boardwalk through the forest to the centre (about 30 minutes). The last bus back to Kuching passes Semenggoh at 4 pm.

## BIDAYUH LONGHOUSES
The most interesting and unspoilt longhouses in Sarawak are those farthest from large settlements, particularly along the upper reaches of the Rejang, Baleh, Belaga, Balui and Baram rivers. If you're not planning on going that far, or if you would like a preview, the Bidayuh longhouses are the closest to Kuching. All have been on the tour operators' circuit for years and the communities are used to tourists. You'll experience none of the hospitality Sarawak's longhouses are famed for – polite indifference will be about the extent of it.

**Kampung Benuk** is a 35km bus ride south of Kuching, followed by a short walk. **Kampung Annah Rais** is one of the best-known 'tourist' longhouses. It's an impressive structure, with more than 100 doors; it has preserved its traditional look, largely because the deal with the tour agencies doesn't allow the use of nontraditional materials. (Corrugated iron is good for roofs but bad for tourism.) The villagers also keep the tour operators informed of any special festivities taking place in the village. **Kampung Gayu** is another village visited by tour groups, and there are many others in this area.

## Getting There & Away
To get to the longhouses from Kuching, STC bus No 9A goes to Annah Rais at 9, 10.20 and 11.30 am (one hour, RM5.10). For Kampung Benuk take STC bus No 6 (RM1.50) and ask the driver to let you off. Departure times are at 7.15, 8.10, 10.20, 11.20 and 11.50 am, and 1.20 pm; buses return at 7.55, 8.50 and 11 am, and at noon, 12.30 and 2 pm. To reach the other longhouses you'll have to walk, hitch or hire a car.

## GUNUNG PENRISSEN
Gunung Penrissen is a 1325m-high mountain just over the border in Kalimantan, Indonesia. Experienced, well-equipped climbers can climb the mountain, but it's a strenuous two- to three-day trek. There are no regular treks up the mountain, although an adventure tour company in Kuching may be able to put together a package for you – the new resort near the mountain may also have something. It's cheaper for a group to attempt the climb because, apart from transport costs, guides need to be hired in Kampung Annah Rais or in nearby Kampung Padawan.

The **Borneo Highlands Resort** is purported to be South-East Asia's largest hill resort, or it will be by the time it's completed. The massive development – consisting of a golf course, hotel, chalets, gardens and whole new support town – sits on Gunung Penrissen Plateau, an hour's drive from Kuching. Check with the Visitors' Information Centre (☎ 082-410944, fax 256301, ℮ sarawak@po.jaring.my) in Kuching for the latest information.

## JONG'S CROCODILE FARM
As these places go, Jong's (☎ 082-863570) is relatively inoffensive. There are impressive specimens kept safely behind bars, cute baby crocs and gruesome photos of a famous man-eater and its final victim. But when crocodiles aren't eating they don't do much, and the other animals, including monkeys, hornbills and beautiful leopard cats, are probably more interesting.

Jong's is open from 9 am to 5 pm daily; entry is RM5/3 for adults on weekdays/weekends and RM1 for children at any time. Ring the farm or its Kuching office (☎ 082-242790) for a current schedule of feeding times.

The croc farm is 29km south-east of Kuching, at Siburan. From Kuching, STC bus No 3, 3A, 9A or 9B will drop you at the turn-off on the highway (40 minutes, RM2.50), from where it is a short walk.

## WIND CAVE & FAIRY CAVE
Bau is an old gold-mining town, south-west of Kuching. There's nothing to see here.

MALAYSIAN BORNEO

However, a few kilometres south in a range of steep limestone hills are two very different cave systems that make an interesting day trip. Take a picnic lunch, drinks and a good torch (flashlight) for exploring the caves (torches can also be hired at the entrance to each cave).

About 3km south-west of Bau, the Wind Cave is a network of underground streams on the banks of the Batang Kayan. It's easy to walk through the caves on elevated boardwalks (though it isn't lit), or else you can walk around the jungle-clad perimeter of the park. You can walk right through the caves to the river, where there are barbecues, *food and drink stalls* and changing facilities. The river is usually quite shallow and safe to swim in; it's a popular spot with locals on weekends.

About 5km farther south, Fairy Cave is an extraordinary elevated cave: A massive concrete walkway leads up to the entrance, 30m above the ground in the side of a cliff. After a steep, slippery climb, you enter a grotto formed by the collapse of the cave roof. For generations this area has been used as a shrine by Chinese, who offer incense and other goods to various anthropomorphic cave formations. It's quite large and you could easily spend an hour exploring it.

### Getting There & Away
From Kuching take STC bus No 2 to Bau (one hour, RM3). Buses leave every 40 minutes between 6 am and 6 pm.

To get to the caves, take a bus from Bau bazaar and ask the driver to let you off at the turn-off, from where it is about 700m to Wind Cave and 1.3km to Fairy Cave. The walk to Wind Cave from Bau takes about an hour; Fairy Cave is much farther and you may have to hitch.

### LUNDU
☎ 082
This quiet little town sits between the forested bulk of Gunung Gading National Park and the Sungai Kayan. To most travellers it's simply the transport node for the national park, but there are far worse places to get stranded. Lundu was established by

Datuk Sulaiman and his followers, who arrived from Kuching and settled the area. Some time later, they were attacked by 2100 pirates arriving in 70 vessels. Story has it that Datuk Sulaiman killed 2070 of them before he was beheaded, after which the pirates fled, leaving Lundu in peace. That's the word on the street, anyway.

Lundu has a fish market along the riverfront and a hawker centre at the western end of town. The town centre is a square bounded by old godown (warehouses), and brightly painted houses line the quiet country lanes. Worth checking out is the garish **rafflesia monument** near the bus station.

The road north out of town leads to **Pandan** (10km) and **Siar** (8.5km) beaches. They're both OK, but are strewn with flotsam and hardly worth a special trip.

### Places to Stay & Eat
Lundu has a couple of hotels that are OK if the national-park accommodation is full. *Cheng Hak Boarding House (☎ 735018, 51 Lundu Bazaar)* has simple rooms with shared bathroom for RM25 with fan, or RM35 with air-con. The office is at the Goh Joo Hok shop, a few doors down from the *Lundu Gading Hotel (☎ 735199),* which has air-con rooms with/without bathroom for RM58/48.

There are Chinese *kedai kopi* around the square and the *hawker centre* cranks up in the evening.

### Getting There & Away
STC bus No 2B leaves Kuching for Lundu at 8 and 11 am, and 2 and 4 pm (two hours, RM7.80). The last bus returns to Kuching at 4 pm.

STC bus No17C makes the trip from Lundu to Gunung Gading National Park (50 sen) in the morning and afternoon.

### GUNUNG GADING NATIONAL PARK
The chief attraction at Gunung Gading is the **rafflesia**, and this is one of the best places in Borneo to see this rarity. The rafflesia blooms year-round but at unpredictable times and places, and a measure of luck is

MALAYSIAN BORNEO

necessary to see it. Check whether any are in bloom before heading to the park by ringing the park headquarters (☎ 082-735714) or the parks desk at the Visitors' Information Centre (☎ 082-248088) in Kuching. Because rafflesia bloom for only a few days, get to Gunung Gading as soon as you can if one is in bloom. If it's off the trail you may need a guide to find it, which should cost only RM5 per hour, but quiz the park staff first and don't just automatically hire a guide. After all, the world's largest flower is hard to miss at nearly 1m in diameter!

This is a pleasant and often deserted national park with well-marked **walking trails**, a swimming hole and good accommodation. A large colour-coded map outside the park office indicates the walking trails and times. One of the easiest is to a lookout point near the park headquarters (1½ hours), and there's a **natural swimming pool** a few minutes from the office that's popular with locals. The energetic can climb to the summit of 906m-high **Gunung Gading** (six hours return). Wildlife is not easy to see because much of the walking is under the canopy.

There's a good information centre at the park, with photos and displays on rafflesia, wildlife and the local culture.

Remember to get a permit from the Visitors' Information Centre in Kuching before heading out to Gunung Gading; the usual park entry and camera fees can be paid at the gate.

### Places to Stay & Eat

There's good, clean accommodation at the park headquarters, but no shop or canteen so you'll have to bring your own supplies or trudge the 2km to Lundu for an evening meal.

The *hostel* has fan-cooled rooms with pillows and blankets for RM10 per person, or RM40 for a four-bunk room. There's a shared bathroom and fully equipped kitchen with a fridge and gas stove. Air-con *chalets* with cooking facilities, fridge and TV sleep six people and cost RM120. Book ahead on weekends and school holidays through the Visitors' Information Centre (☎ 082-410944) in Kuching.

The park accommodation is better value than the lodging in Lundu but if it's full, hotels in Lundu do have the advantage of being close to cafes. (See the Lundu section earlier for details.)

### Getting There & Away

For the first part of the journey from Kuching, see the Lundu Getting There & Away entry earlier. From Lundu, take bus No 17C (50 sen) and ask to be dropped off at the park; the entrance is 2km north of Lundu on the road to Pantai Pandan. If you miss a bus, it's probably as quick to walk from Lundu as the park entrance is another 500m from where the bus drops you.

## SEMATAN
☎ 082

Sematan is a small coastal village near the western border of Sarawak. The **beach** is clean, deserted and lined with coconut palms, but the water is very shallow and only good for paddling. All things considered, it is a long way to go for a so-so beach. But it is popular with well-to-do Kuching residents, many of whom have beach bungalows here.

Sematan's importance may grow when visitors' facilities at Tanjung Datu National Park are improved. At present, Lundu is a more pleasant kampung and its beaches are more accessible.

### Places to Stay & Eat

A few hundred metres out of town on the road to Lundu, the *Sematan Hotel* (☎ 711162) has reasonable fan-cooled rooms with shared bathroom costing RM22 to RM30; better air-con rooms start at RM50 with bathroom.

For an interesting *homestay* option in the area, see the Tanjung Datu National Park entry later.

Sematan has a couple of Chinese *kedai kopi* and *food stalls* at the small market.

### Getting There & Away

To get to Sematan from Kuching, first take a bus to Lundu (see that section earlier), where you can catch STC bus No 17 which leaves regularly for Sematan (about one hour, RM2).

The beach is about 1km west of town.

## TANJUNG DATU NATIONAL PARK

This is the smallest of Sarawak's national parks. It is in the far west of the state, abutting the border with Kalimantan. Its 1379 hectares protect rainforest, unpolluted rivers and near-pristine beaches.

There are currently no facilities for visitors. Access is only possible by boat from Sematan; ask around in the kampung, but negotiate a price before you set out. If you visit Gunung Gading on the way, someone at the park office may be able to organise a boat for you, otherwise try the District Office in Sematan.

Another option is a homestay program at Telok Serabang and Telok Melano, two kampung at the north-western tip of Sarawak. These fishing villages are an hour or two from Sematan, depending on the boat used. Plenty of activities can be arranged through the program, including visits to the national park. For more details, contact Abang Zulkifli (☎ 082-245481, fax 256871, ✉ gazul@tm.net.my) at Projek Perintis Homestay, Fisheries Department, Kuching.

## SERIAN
☎ 082

Serian is a very small Bidayuh town 65km south-east of Kuching. Tour groups often stop here to pick up gifts on the way to longhouses along nearby rivers such as the Lemanak. Serian boasts a bustling **market**, where people from nearby longhouses come to sell jungle fruits and herbs, snake meat, sago worms and other unusual produce.

### Getting There & Away

STC express bus Nos 3 and 3A run between Kuching and Serian (one hour, RM5) from 6.30 am and 5.30 pm. The bus station is in the centre of Serian, near the market.

If you are going to Sri Aman, you could also try hitching; Taman Rekreasi Ranchan is a park up a side road off the road to Sri Aman, and there's lots of traffic on weekends. The other option is to take a taxi.

## SRI AMAN
☎ 083

Originally known as Simangangg, Sri Aman is a quiet town on the muddy Batang Lupar, halfway between Kuching and Sarikei. Sri Aman's main claim to fame is a tidal bore that periodically sweeps up the river, scattering all craft in its path; it nearly took the life of Somerset Maugham, an event he recorded in a short story called *The Yellow Streak*. Raja Brooke's **Fort Alice**, a little downstream, was inexplicably earmarked for demolition at the time of writing.

There is decent budget lodging in Sri Aman. However, since longhouses in the area are visited on tours, independent travellers tend to let this sleepy town lie.

The Skrang, Lemanak and Ai rivers flow into the Lupar, and many of the tours organised out of Kuching bring groups to the longhouses along these tributaries. See the 'Longhouse Visits' boxed text earlier in this chapter.

There isn't a lot of river traffic at Sri Aman itself, and most boats to the Lemanak and Ai rivers leave from Engkilili, or outside town where the highway crosses the Batang Lupar.

## BATANG AI NATIONAL PARK

Batang Ai covers 24 sq km and protects the catchment of the Batang Ai reservoir, formed by a hydro-electric scheme 250km east of Kuching. The park's rainforest features wildlife such as orang-utans, gibbons and hornbills. There is no visitors' centre here and no accommodation. Access is possible by chartering a boat from Batang Ai, but it is difficult and expensive. Until facilities are developed, the park is best visited as part of a longhouse tour. Some travel agencies in Kuching can arrange nearby longhouse accommodation and treks into the park (see Organised Tours in the Kuching section earlier for agent details).

One excellent option is the *Hilton Batang Ai Longhouse Resort (☎ 083-584338)*. It isn't cheap, but the standard of

MALAYSIAN BORNEO

## Iban Words & Phrases

As with other local peoples in Sarawak, the Iban use Malay for some common phrases and words:

| | |
|---|---|
| Good morning. | *Salamat pagi.* |
| Good afternoon. | *Salamat tengah-hari.* |
| Good night. | *Salamat malam.* |
| Goodbye. | *Salamat tinggal.* |
| Thank you. | *Terima kasih.* |

Iban words and phrases include:

| | |
|---|---|
| How are you? | *Gerai nuan?* |
| Pleased to meet you. | *Rindu amat betemu enggau nuan.* |
| See you again. | *Arap ke betemu baru.* |
| What's your name? | *Sapa nama nuan?* |
| Where do we bathe/ wash? | *Dini endor kitai mandi?* |
| Can I take a photograph of you? | *Tau aku ngambi gam bar nuan?* |
| I'm sorry. | *Aku minta ampun.* |
| Where? | *Dini?* |
| What? | *Nama?* |
| I | *aku* |
| you | *nuan* |
| today | *saharitu* |
| tomorrow | *pegilah* |
| day | *hari* |
| night | *malam* |
| good | *manah* |
| not good | *jai also enda manah* |
| eat | *makai* |
| drink | *ngirup* |
| go | *bejalai* |

accommodation, guides and cultural and nature excursions make it well worth the splurge. Quality longhouse tours and jungle treks can be arranged from here. All rooms have air-con, and the hotel has a swimming pool, bar and restaurant. Standard rooms cost RM185 and suites are RM255, including breakfast. A transfer from Kuching (RM95) takes four to five hours, followed by a short boat ride to the resort. For more details, contact Borneo Adventure (☎ 438741, fax 438740, @ endaya@pd.jaring .my) – see Organised Tours in the Kuching section earlier.

# The Batang Rejang

The mighty Batang Rejang is the main artery of trade with the interior for all of central and southern Sarawak. Scattered along its banks, and those of its tributaries, particularly in the upper reaches, are longhouses of the Iban and other tribes. Staying at a longhouse is one of the highlights of a trip to Sarawak. However, as with everything in Borneo, you have to pick your spot and know what to look for.

For example, if you only go as far as Kapit, the Rejang will appear to be little more than a wide, muddy conveyor belt for the rapacious logging industry. The Rejang and its tributaries – the Baleh, Belaga and Balui rivers – have been carrying topsoil and old-growth forest wasted by logging for years, and it's not a pretty sight.

Then there's the bungled Bakun Dam project, about an hour upriver from Belaga. After many delays – mainly due to mismanagement, financial problems and the sheer audacity of the project's original scale – the dam is finally near completion. The government is less paranoid about travel in the area than it once was, no doubt because there's little left about which to protest. The area south of the dam has already been emptied of an estimated 11,000 tribal people to make room for the reservoir; communities have been resettled to the north.

The best time for a trip up the Rejang is in late May and early June. This is the time of Gawai, the Dayak harvest festival, when there is plenty of movement on the rivers and the longhouses welcome visitors. There are also plenty of celebrations, which usually involve the consumption of copious quantities of *arak* (local liquor) and tuak.

Along the river, the only hotel accommodation available is in Song, Kanowit, Kapit and Belaga.

MALAYSIAN BORNEO

## Rejang Longhouses

There are longhouses all the way along the Rejang. While most visitors head for Kapit and Belaga, there are plenty of longhouses around Kanowit and Song. Those farther upriver will not necessarily be more traditional; most are made from modern building materials. In fact, many longhouse communities are moving towards individual houses, which fare much better in the event of a fire (fire can destroy a longhouse in as little as 30 minutes).

To arrange a visit, the most important factor is time. If you are short of it, take a tour. Most travellers head for Kapit, a small administrative town upriver. Kapit is the last big settlement on the river, and it's to here that the longhouse people come for supplies. Farther upriver, Belaga is smaller and more laid-back; it's a regular meeting place for friends and relatives from far-flung communities. In either town, the best strategy for finding someone to take you to a longhouse is to make yourself known around town – sit in the cafes and get talking to people.

Apart from a trip to the Pelagus Resort, travel beyond Kapit requires a permit (see Permits under Kapit later for details). The permit is merely a formality, and you'll probably never be asked for it.

## SIBU
☎ 084

Sibu and Kuching are the Yin and Yang of urban Borneo. A rough, river town plagued by failed public campaigns to urge residents to smile, Sibu was once known as New Foochow. It was so-named after Chinese migrants who came from Foochow province in the early years of the 20th century. In fact, New Foochow resembles nothing so much as 'old Foochow'. Beyond the strip of crowded restaurants along the waterfront, Sibu is largely an uninviting place.

Sibu is the gateway to the Batang Rejang, and you may find yourself staying overnight here. If you do, take care along the dark, deserted streets in the centre of town. Sarawak's second-largest city may be the centre for trade between the coast and the vast upriver hinterland, but it's also the

KELLI HAMBLET

**A traditional Iban longhouse, rarely seen nowadays.**

main training ground for organised-gang members, some of whom may get in your face when they're bored.

The gangs go with the territory, as the Brookes were happy to let Sibu's capitalists manage the extraction of upriver wealth. This alone should have put a smile on local faces, as Sibu reputedly boasts more millionaires than any other city in Borneo. Situated 60km upstream from the sea, it's here that the interior's raw materials – logs, gravel, minerals and agricultural produce – are brought for transhipment and export. The wide, muddy river hosts a motley procession of fishing and cargo boats, tugs, brooding barges laden with timber, hyperactive express boats and speedboats skipping over their wash.

## Orientation

Sibu lies on the north bank of the Rejang near its confluence with Batang Igan. The town's frantic commerce belies the fact that all places to stay and eat, express-boat wharves and banks, are within an easy walk of the waterfront. A graceful seven-storey Chinese pagoda marks the western edge of the waterfront and a small clocktower marks the eastern; between the two, an enormous, concrete market-building broods over Jalan Channel.

The wharf for express boats to Kuching is in the centre of town, near the pagoda; boats to Kapit and other interior centres leave from 200m farther upstream. Also on the waterfront is the local bus station; the long-distance bus terminal is at Sungai Antu, 3km west of town. The airport is 20km east of the town centre.

MALAYSIAN BORNEO

The helpful Visitors' Information Centre (☎ 340980, fax 341280, @ stbsibu@tm.net.my), at 32 Jalan Cross in the centre of town, can help with travel inquiries. It's open weekdays from 8 am to 5 pm, and Saturday to 12.50 pm. Note that Jalan Cross is marked 'Jalan Lintang' on many maps.

### Information
The post office, on Jalan Kampung Nyabor, is open Monday to Saturday from 8 am to 5 pm. There are a couple of cybercafes on the 4th floor of Wisma Sanyan, on Jalan Causeway at the end of Jalan Morshidi Sidek; they charge RM4 per hour and stay open until about 10 pm.

### Things to See & Do
Most people use Sibu as a transit point at which to catch boats travelling upriver – few would find another reason to stay. The grotty, uninspiring markets can be skipped without regret, but it's hard to miss the pagoda dominating the waterfront. The 100-year-old **Tua Pek Kong Temple** is beside the Kuching wharf, and its seven-tiered **Kuan Yin pagoda** (completed in 1989) adds a touch of class to Sibu. This colourful temple is guarded by two gilt lions and a host of writhing dragons, and by a caretaker who'll probably want to give you a crash course in Taoism. Climb to the top of the pagoda for a great view over the river, particularly good at sunset when hundreds of swifts wheel around the tower at eye level.

The **Dewan Suarah Sibu** (Civic Centre Museum) is worth a visit. It presents the story of settlement on the Rejang through displays about the Chinese settlers and the indigenous Iban and Melanau cultures; displays include antiques, artefacts and photos. The museum guide will be glad to tell you lots about the Mukah area if you're headed that way.

The museum is open Tuesday to Sunday from 10.30 am to 5.30 pm; admission is free. To get here, take Sungei Merah bus No 1, 1A or 4 (40 sen) from the local bus station on the waterfront; the museum is down the side street by a petrol station.

### Organised Tours
Sazhong Trading & Travel Services (☎ 336017, fax 338031, @ sazhong@tm.net.my), beneath the Villa Hotel in the centre of town, is run by the amiable Frankie Ting. An ardent promoter of all things Sibuan, Frankie is the guy to see if you're stuck for a hotel, or looking for a longhouse tour in the area or farther afield. Sazhong Trading is also a Malaysia Airlines agent.

### Places to Stay – Budget
Sibu has dozens of budget hotels, although many are dark and seedy, and are dodgy for women travellers especially.

By far the best place to stay is the Methodist guesthouse, **Hoover House** (☎ 332491), next to the church on Jalan Pulau. It's excellent value: a bed in a fancooled/air-con dorm is RM12/15. Clean, well-kept air-con singles/doubles with attached bathroom are RM20/30. Guests can also safely store their gear while they're travelling upriver. Book ahead if you can; the guesthouse is often full.

There are a few budget hotels around the local bus station that don't operate as brothels. The **Holiday Hotel** (☎ 317440, 16 Jalan Tan Sri) is a clean boarding house where simple fan-cooled rooms cost RM15/26, and air-con rooms with shower and toilet go for RM32.

**To-Day Hotel** (☎ 336499, 40 Jalan Kampung Nyabor) is a friendly, well-run place that welcomes travellers. Clean, air-con rooms with bathroom and TV cost RM28/30. Similar rates and reasonable rooms are available at **Hotel Emas** (☎ 319887), on Jalan Foochow, across the main road from the Premier Hotel.

### Places to Stay – Mid-Range
Sibu has many centrally located mid-range hotels that are good value. All have air-con rooms (usually carpeted) with phone, TV and attached bathroom.

**Sarawak Hotel** (☎ 333455, 34 Jalan Cross), on the corner of Jalan Wong Nai Siong, is recommended, provided you get a room away from the noisy 1st-floor pub. Bright, clean rooms with a double bed are

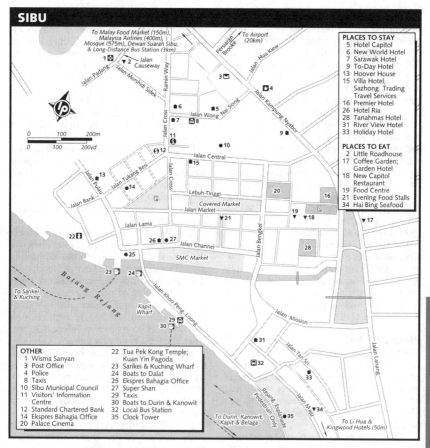

**SIBU**

To Malay Food Market (150m),
Malaysia Airlines (400m),
Mosque (575m), Dewan Suarah Sibu,
& Long-Distance Bus Station (3km)

To Airport
(20km)

**PLACES TO STAY**
5 Hotel Capitol
6 New World Hotel
7 Sarawak Hotel
9 To-Day Hotel
13 Hoover House
15 Villa Hotel;
   Sazhong Trading
   Travel Services
16 Premier Hotel
26 Hotel Ria
28 Tanahmas Hotel
31 River View Hotel
33 Holiday Hotel

**PLACES TO EAT**
2 Little Roadhouse
17 Coffee Garden;
   Garden Hotel
18 New Capitol
   Restaurant
19 Food Centre
21 Evening Food Stalls
34 Hai Bing Seafood

**OTHER**
1 Wisma Sanyan
3 Post Office
4 Police
8 Taxis
10 Sibu Municipal Council
11 Visitors' Information Centre
12 Standard Chartered Bank
14 Ekspres Bahagia Office
20 Palace Cinema
22 Tua Pek Kong Temple; Kuan Yin Pagoda
23 Sarikei & Kuching Wharf
24 Boats to Dalat
25 Ekspres Bahagia Office
27 Super Shan
29 Taxis
30 Boats to Durin & Kanowit
32 Local Bus Station
35 Clock Tower

**MALAYSIAN BORNEO**

RM40, twins are RM45 and a room with a double and single bed is RM60. Next to the Visitors' Information Centre is the *Green View Hotel*, which is actually an extension of the Sarawak Hotel.

Opposite Sarawak Hotel is *New World Hotel* (☎ 310311, 1 Jalan Wong Nai Siong), which has rooms from RM33/35. *Hotel Capitol* (☎ 336444, 19 Jalan Wong Nai Siong) has good rooms with IDD phones for RM40/48, but the 1st-floor Hideaway Pub can make this place a bit noisy.

The friendly *Hotel Ria* (☎ 326622, 21 Jalan Channel) has very basic but clean fan-cooled rooms for RM33. It is also handy to the markets and wharves. If the Ria is full, its staff will try to squeeze you into the *Villa Hotel* (☎ 337833, 2 Jalan Central), which is of a similar standard and price.

*Li Hua Hotel* (☎ 324000), about 300m south-east along the river from the bus station, is conveniently located and good value, with decent rooms starting at RM45.50. Swirling clouds of swiflets nesting on window sills make rooms on upper floors seem like a night in the Niah Caves.

## Places to Stay – Top End

Two of the pricier hotels are very close to the centre of town on Jalan Kampung Nyabor. The *Premier Hotel* (☎ 323222, fax 323399) is popular with tour groups and charges RM126/149 for standard singles/doubles and RM184 for twins. Suites cost between RM270 and RM570. If you get a discount, it's not a bad deal because these rates include a good buffet breakfast. All rooms have a minibar, IDD phone, cable TV and in-house movies. The Premier also has a lounge where Filipino cover bands have regular gigs. Nearby, *Tanahmas Hotel* (☎ 333188, ✉ tanahmas@po.jaring.my) struggles to compete with its better-value neighbour. Smaller rooms start at RM152/170; rooms facing the river cost RM175/193. Suites are also available.

Just south of Li Hua Hotel is the four-star *Kingwood Hotel* (☎ 335888, fax 334559), on the waterfront on Jalan Lanang. It is very popular and is excellent value, with a rooftop swimming pool overlooking the river. Large, well-appointed rooms start at RM156/179.

## Places to Eat

The best cheap food in Sibu is found at the various hawker centres and food stalls. There's a small two-storey *food centre* at the eastern end of Jalan Market, at the rear of the Palace Cinema, where stalls sell Malay curries, roti and laksa as well as Chinese food.

In the late afternoon, a host of *food stalls* set up near the massive, concrete SMC Market, selling delicious snacks such as *pau* (steamed dumplings), barbecued chicken wings and all manner of sweets. This is a fun way to sample local fare for a pittance and the food is usually very fresh.

There's a good nightly *Malay food market* at the northern end of town. To get there, follow Jalan Kampung Nyabor through the roundabout past the intersection with Ramin Way – you can't miss the neon palm trees.

The riverfront area near the Mehung Hotel has a number of Chinese restaurants. *Hai Bing Seafood* (also signposted as 'Hai Bing Coffee Shop'), at 31 Jalan Maju, serves excellent local dishes in both its indoor and outdoor sections. Depending on the number of dishes you order, expect to pay about RM8 to RM15 for a large meal. The Chinese *kedai kopi* along the waterfront are open for breakfast well before dawn – great if you're taking an early boat. There's also a small *supermarket* where you can get snacks, drinks and a paper for the trip upriver.

For a sit-down Chinese meal at an upmarket, air-con restaurant, try *New Capitol Restaurant*, diagonally opposite the Premier Hotel. There are some expensive dishes on the menu, but if you choose carefully you'll only need to spend a few ringgit on a pretty good feed.

The *Premier Hotel* has one of the best restaurants in town, though it's not cheap by the time you add on tax. *Coffee Garden* is a good restaurant in the Garden Hotel, over the main road from the Premier Hotel. It has a large selection of very reasonably priced Chinese, Malay and Western dishes – *kampua*, a local mixed-noodle dish, is just RM3.50. Get your order in before 8.30 pm, when the loud band gets going.

*Little Roadhouse*, upstairs at No 4 Jalan Causeway, is a pleasant surprise. This tasteful, terraced cafe/pub serves good burgers (RM5.50) and pasta for RM5 to RM9; beers are RM5. It is closed on Monday. This is as friendly a place as you'll find in Sibu.

For self-catering and munchies for the boat, head up to the *Super Shan* supermarket near the Hotel Ria.

## Getting There & Away

**Air** The Malaysia Airlines office (☎ 326166) is at 61 Jalan Tunku Osman, a few minutes' walk north of the town centre. It is open weekdays from 8 am to 5 pm, and Saturday from 8 am to 12.30 pm.

Malaysia Airlines flights go to main centres around Sarawak and in the interior, including Kuching (10 daily, RM72) and Bintulu (six daily, RM64). Two of the Bintulu flights go on to Miri (RM112), and one daily flight goes direct. There are four daily flights from Miri to Sibu. The smaller

MALAYSIAN BORNEO

Twin Otters run between Sibu and Miri five days a week (RM30), and six days a week between Sibu and Mukah (RM30).

There are direct flights twice daily to KK (RM180) in Sabah and at least once a day to KL international airport (RM320).

**Bus** The main bus lines have ticket stalls at the long-distance bus station, north-west of town at Sungai Antu, as well as around the local bus station on the waterfront. Schedules change often – check with the ticket agents (some are actually small shops) by the local bus station for the most recent schedule. The Visitors' Information Centre has a city map with a detailed schedule of local and long-distance buses on the reverse side. There should be no problem getting a seat if you arrive 15 minutes before departure, but it may pay to book ahead for weekends and school holidays.

There are express buses to Kuching running regularly from 6.30 am to 11.30 pm (about seven hours, RM32). The trip to Kuching is fairly uneventful, and many people take a night bus to save time and a hotel bill.

Buses run regularly to Sarikei (RM6) between 6 am and 4 pm.

Lanang Road buses make the trip to Mukah at 6.30 and 11.30 am, and 12.30 and 2.30 pm daily (3½ hours, RM13.85). Note that the non-air-con buses leave from the local bus station (RM12.80).

There are services to Bintulu, 220km away, virtually every hour between 6 am and 6 pm (three hours, RM16.50); the last bus leaves Sibu at 11.30 pm.

Buses regularly depart from Sibu for the 418km trip to Miri from around 5.30 am to 11.30 pm (7½ hours, RM34). Ideally, purchase your ticket half a day or more in advance, although it's safe to turn up an hour or so before departure.

**Boat** Passenger express boats travel between Sibu and Kuching, and up the Rejang to Kanowit, Song and Kapit. Services to Kuching leave from the wharf near the Chinese pagoda; all upriver services leave from the wharf near the market.

The service between Sibu and Kuching has suffered due to the popularity of the night buses: There is only one boat to Kuching per day (four hours, RM35/38 economy/ 1st class), which currently leaves Sibu at 11.30 am, although this will almost certainly change – check at the wharf or with the Visitors' Information Centre.

Getting to Kapit is the first leg of the journey up the Batang Rejang. Boats cover the 130km or so from Sibu to Kapit in just 2½ hours (that's one-and-a-bit kung fu movies). The first boat leaves Sibu at around 6 am. The fare is RM15. Other boats leave Kapit approximately hourly until about 2.30 pm. Just go down to the Kapit wharf and ask which boat is next to leave. People are very helpful and the boats usually have a 'clock' showing intended departure time.

All boats to Kapit pass Kanowit and Song, and may stop at smaller settlements and logging camps en route. There are also a few scheduled services to Song between around 7.30 am and 1 pm (two hours, RM10). Some services also call at Kanowit (about one hour, RM6). If you want to get off at Kanowit, tell the driver or ticket seller before you board.

Boats from Sibu go beyond Kapit only during the rainy season, when there is sufficient water – if there's enough water they go all the way to Belaga. If there's insufficient water, you'll have to switch to a speedboat in Kapit. Getting to Belaga from Sibu, you should expect an overnight stay in Kapit, as the first express boat from Sibu doesn't always connect with the last regular service to Belaga.

Speedboats make the trip to Dalat (three or four hours, RM18), which is handy for connections to Mukah. Boats leave when full, from the dock opposite the Kuan Yin pagoda; the first boat leaves at around 7.30 am and the last at either 12.30 or 2 pm.

## Getting Around

Sibu's airport is 20km east of town. Bus No 3A leaves from the blue bus shelter about 250m around to the left of the airport terminal as you exit. It runs into town every 1½ hours from 6.30 am to 6 pm (about 30

MALAYSIAN BORNEO

minutes, RM2). You could also try flagging down any rural bus that passes by. The taxi fare into town is RM22.

The local bus station is on the waterfront. To get to the long-distance bus station, take Lanang Road bus No 7 from the local bus station. It leaves every 15 minutes between 6 am and 9 pm (60 sen). A taxi costs RM7.

If you arrive in Sibu by boat, the wharves are only a few minutes' walk from all the main hotels and restaurants.

## KANOWIT

This small riverside settlement is the last stop on the Rejang that's connected to the coast by road – it's boat only from here on upstream. A few intrepid travellers use Kanowit as a jumping-off point for long-house stays along the Sungai Kanowit. This can work wonderfully, but not without an invitation (see the boxed text 'Longhouse Visits' earlier in this chapter).

A white-raja fortification, **Fort Emma** sits to the right of the wharf, but it's not open to the public. There's also a colourful **clock-tower** decorated in Iban 'tree-of-life' style and a brightly painted **Chinese temple**.

### Getting There & Away

Several buses leave Sibu daily for Kanowit, from 6 am to around 4.30 pm (one hour, RM5.70); there are five or six buses back to Sibu, leaving Kanowit between 6 am and 5pm.

If travelling by boat, check at the Sibu wharf for an express boat that will drop you at Kanowit (one hour, RM6). Some have a scheduled stop at Kanowit, but they are few and far between.

Iban 'Tree of Life' design

## KAPIT
☎ 084

Kapit is another Rejang river town dating to the days of the white raja – historic Fort Sylvia still stands on the riverbank. The biggest settlement for 100km in any direction, Kapit is where upriver people come to buy, sell and exchange goods, and to sample the diversions of urban life.

The river bank at Kapit is steep and in the dry season, when the water level falls, it's quite a drop to the river. Kapit is a small place and everything is within an easy stroll. There's nothing much to do here, but the town offers some good accommodation.

There are two thoroughly urbanised longhouses about 7km from town along Jalan Selerik.

### Information

If you need to change cash or travellers cheques, there are plenty of banks in town. The MBF is near the roundabout at the western end of town; there's a Maybank and ATM next to the Hotel Meligai and the Hock Hua Bank is on Jalan Wharf. There's also a licensed moneychanger a few doors up from the Ark Hill Inn.

Email access can be very slow upriver, and a bit pricey. De Cybershop, on the 1st floor of the building next to the Jade Corner Restaurant & Pub, has terminals for RM8 per hour. It is open Monday to Saturday from 9 am to midnight, and Sunday from noon.

**Permits** A permit is not required to reach Kapit, or to reach the Pelagus Resort, farther up the Batang Rejang. If you want to travel beyond the Pelagus Rapids to Belaga, or anywhere up the Baleh, you must get a permit in Kapit.

Go to the Pejabat Am office on the 1st floor of the State Government Complex; it's the first building as you enter the gate. Fill in the necessary form and sit tight for 10 minutes. It's a painless procedure – the form asks for your cholera vaccination expiry date, but this is not checked. Don't be surprised if one of the enterprising officials in the office gives you the hard sell on a longhouse tour while you're waiting!

A permit is currently valid for six days, and is good for travel up the Rejang as far as the Bakun Dam area (officially, the Bakun HEP Protected Area), an hour beyond Belaga. It's also valid up the Batang Baleh for an unspecified distance.

The government offices in Kapit keep regular office hours, so if you arrive after lunch on a Saturday you'll have to wait until Monday morning to get a permit for the rest of trip.

## Things to See & Do

For a bit of outdoor action combined with a visit to a longhouse, the **Baleh-Kapit Raft Safari** is an annual two-day event that's open to all. Participants in teams of six to eight race traditional wooden rafts down the Sungai Sut, a river near Kapit, stopping overnight at a longhouse. Categories of competition include men's and women's; the cost of hiring a raft is US$100 and there's an entry fee of US$50 per team. The safari is usually held in April but dates change, so check with the Visitors' Information Centre in Kuching or Sibu for details.

During the day, Kapit's **waterfront** is always packed with ferries, barges and people coming and going. It's fascinating to watch the activity on the water and to watch the people shouldering incredible loads of every description up from the wharf.

Some evenings you'll hear a frantic thrumming on big drums coming from the bright yellow-and-red **Hock Leong Tieng temple**. With its whitewashed walls and sturdy new roof, **Fort Sylvia** (1880) is probably the prettiest of the raja fortifications. It's just along to the left as you climb the jetty steps; currently it's closed to the public.

Also worth a look is the small **museum** in the lavish civic centre (RM2.5 million was spent on this). It's open Monday to Thursday and on Saturday, from 9 am to noon and 2 to 4 pm. It has a couple of cultural displays and there's a relief map showing all the longhouses in the area.

## Organised Tours

The venerable Tan Teck Chuan runs Kapit Adventure Tours (☎ 796352, fax 796655, ℮ Chuan_7d@tm.net.my). Mr Chuan is an experienced guide and can arrange longhouse visits and tours upriver, varying from the mildly exotic to the wildly adventurous. You'll find his office upstairs (next to the

**MALAYSIAN BORNEO**

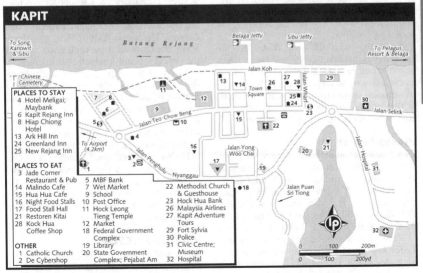

**KAPIT**

PLACES TO STAY
4 Hotel Meligai; Maybank
6 Kapit Rejang Inn
8 Hiap Chiong Hotel
13 Ark Hill Inn
24 Greenland Inn
25 New Rejang Inn

PLACES TO EAT
3 Jade Corner Restaurant & Pub
14 Malindo Cafe
15 Hua Hua Cafe
16 Night Food Stalls
17 Food Stall Hall
21 Restoren Kitai
28 Kock Hua Coffee Shop

OTHER
1 Catholic Church
2 De Cybershop
5 MBF Bank
7 Wet Market
9 School
10 Post Office
11 Hock Leong Tieng Temple
12 Market
18 Federal Government Complex
19 Library
20 State Government Complex; Pejabat Am
22 Methodist Church & Guesthouse
23 Hock Hua Bank
26 Malaysia Airlines
27 Kapit Adventure Tours
29 Fort Sylvia
30 Police
31 Civic Centre; Museum
32 Hospital

Konica sign) at 11 Jalan Tan Sit Leong on the eastern side of the town square.

## Places to Stay

If you're on a tight budget, head for the **Kapit Rejang Inn** (☎ 796709), on Jalan Temenggong Jugah. Rooms with a single bed are RM15/20 for one/two persons, while rooms with a double bed are RM18/24. The management here is helpful and welcomes travellers.

Kapit has a glut of mid-range hotels. All have clean rooms with air-con, TV and attached bathroom. The friendly **Hiap Chiong Hotel** (☎ 796314) has large, well-appointed singles/doubles for RM40/45. There's no lift, but if you're willing to climb, cheap twin rooms for three people cost RM58 (2nd floor) and RM40 (3rd floor).

The pleasant **Ark Hill Inn** (☎ 796168, Lot 451 Jalan Penghulu Geridang) has airy, tiled single/double rooms for RM30/50, and three-person rooms for RM60.

The **New Rejang Inn** (☎ 796600, 104 Jalan Teo Chow Beng) has comfortable rooms with phone and fridge for RM40/45, and a deluxe room with two double beds for RM55; this is probably the best-value hotel in town. If you can manage the stairs, **Greenland Inn** (☎ 796388) has immaculate rooms for RM65/75 – even the cockroaches look spit-polished.

At the top end of the scale, **Hotel Meligai** (☎ 798103), on Jalan Teo Chow Beng, has a grand entrance and uniformed staff, but it doesn't live up to its pretensions. Rather ordinary, air-con rooms are listed at RM50/60; better rooms on the upper floors cost RM70/80. A discount may be available.

## Places to Eat

**Food stalls** set up in the evening at the night market, by the wet market at the western end of town, as well as near the triangular, covered hall off Jalan Penghulu Nyanggau. The hall itself is composed of food stalls. For Malay, food including roti, head to the **Malindo Cafe** near the Well Inn.

Kapit has a number of good Chinese **kedai kopi**, particularly around the square and along the riverfront. You can grab breakfast before your boat leaves at **Kock Hua Coffee Shop** on Jalan Wharf. **Hua Hua Café**, on Jalan Teo Chow Beng, is a reasonably priced Chinese cafe. The **Jade Corner Restaurant & Pub**, above the cafe of the same name, is reputed to be Kapit's best Chinese restaurant. The most interesting eatery in town is the upmarket, outdoor **Restoren Kitai**, which is composed of tables joined by wooden boardwalks over the pond near the permit office.

There's also an expensive, air-con restaurant/bar at the **Hotel Meligai** that does Western-style breakfasts.

## Getting There & Away

The airstrip in Kapit is now closed to commercial traffic. There are plenty of boats, although the only sure way to find out when they leave is to ask at the wharves.

Boats leave for Sibu half-hourly from about 7.30 am to noon, and less frequently until around 2.30 pm (2½ to three hours, RM15).

Express launches leave for Belaga at around 8 and 9 am daily (six hours, RM25). When the river is low, express boats can't get past the Pelagus Rapids, about 45 minutes upstream, and smaller speedboats are used instead. The speedboats aren't cheap, but they are quicker than the bigger express boats (around 4½ hours, RM60). The speedboats leave from around 8 am until noon from either wharf – just ask which boat to take.

Many of these boats go on towards the Bakun Dam area. The speedboats make a number of stops, depending on demand, and will drop you off at the Pelagus Resort for RM20. There may also be a late-morning boat from Kapit to various points upriver, including the resort, for RM10.

If you want to charter a longboat to take you upriver, you're looking at around RM200 per day, excluding fuel. All up, the trip will be around RM250, including the operator and someone to keep an eye out for obstructions when the river is low.

## PELAGUS RESORT

Right next to the powerful Pelagus Rapids, **Regency Pelagus Resort** (☎ 084-779050) offers an upmarket opportunity to visit nearby Iban and other Orang Ulu **long-houses**, as well as the rainforest in a part of Sarawak that would otherwise be inaccessible. There is a 4km **walking trail** that follows the rapids for part of the way.

The resort (recently incorporated into the Regency hotel chain) is modelled on an Iban longhouse. Rooms overlook the river at this tasteful, unique set-up, and the roar of the rapids is a memorable lullaby at night. There's a restaurant and swimming pool, and tours to nearby longhouses can be organised. Air-con/fan-cooled rooms are RM180/160 for two; this should include the boat transfer from Kapit (a 45-minute trip that is regularly RM55 on the resort's launch). Twin-share packages that include accommodation, meals and boat transfer from Kapit start at RM165 per person.

## BELAGA
☎ 084

Belaga is a small but pleasant bazaar town and administration centre on the upper reaches of the Rejang where it divides into the Belaga and Balui rivers. Its close, friendly population makes it an excellent base from which to explore the interior of Sarawak; there are many Kayan and Kenyah **longhouses** along the rivers. If you speak with a local on the way upriver, you may end up being invited to stay at their longhouse – it's polite to bring a small gift for the family of the person who invited you. Otherwise, chances are you will find someone in Belaga (or they will find you) with a suggestion of a longhouse to visit or an offer to guide you. If you have the time, it's worth developing some real contacts – if it's only a matter of business, local boatmen will charge RM50 just to take you across the river.

A few part-time operators offer **jungle treks** at reasonable rates, about RM150 for three days/two nights; longer treks are also available. The nearest longhouse to Belaga is a 45-minute walk, and a pretty **waterfall** is a short boat ride away.

Boats will drop you at the bottom of a steep set of concrete steps leading up to the three-street town centre; the hotels and cafe are all here, across from the small park.

The helpful Malaysia Airlines office (☎ 461240) is on the main street. It is open daily from 9 am to 5 pm, and has several terminals for email and Internet access (RM9 per hour).

### Places to Stay & Eat
Belaga's accommodation is cheap and caters to local people dropping into town for extended stays. The *Belaga Hotel* *(☎ 461244)* has seen better days and you're better off staying elsewhere; grotty rooms with *mandi* (South-East Asian washbasins) cost RM30. In the same block, the *Bee Lian Inn (☎ 461439)* has decent rooms with warm-water showers for RM25; larger rooms are RM40. The *Sing Soon Hing Hotel (☎ 461257)* has basic fan-cooled rooms for RM20 and air-con rooms for RM30. *The Hock Chiang Inn (☎ 461258)* is closest to the dock and offers reasonable singles/doubles for RM35/40.

There's a simple *kedai kopi* downstairs at the Belaga Hotel and a much better *cafe* beneath the Hock Chiang Inn.

A good place for a meal and a chance to meet Kayan and Kenyah people is the *Lai Bin Ong Cafe,* two streets back from the main drag. This is about the only place in town open after 7 pm.

### Getting There & Away
**Air** The Malaysia Airlines office (☎ 461240) is on the main street. It is open daily from 9 am to 5 pm.

There are no longer any flights between Sibu and Belaga; Twin Otter flights between Belaga and Bintulu run once a week (at the time of writing, on Wednesday); the fare is RM40.

Flights are sometimes cancelled due to the weather, so you may end up taking a boat the following day. If you're in a hurry to leave Belaga, another option is to arrange a Land Cruiser direct to Tubau (from where you can catch a boat to Bintulu). This will cost around RM250 (see the Upriver from Belaga section for a cheaper but more circuitous option).

MALAYSIAN BORNEO

## Nightlife, Orang Ulu Style

If you don't fancy the idea of having your face smeared with greasy soot and being dumped unceremoniously in the river, then perhaps you should steer well clear of the Kayan and Kenyah tribes. But if you do give them a wide berth, be warned that you'll miss out on one of the best travel experiences in Borneo.

The two tribes are numbered among the Orang Ulu (a general term, literally meaning 'upriver people', which covers a host of different inland tribes). The Kayan and Kenyah tribes are the people you're most likely to meet when travelling on the upper Rejang or upper Baram rivers.

Both tribes are originally from central Kalimantan (Indonesia), and have been moving downriver into Sarawak for centuries, fighting fierce territorial wars with the Iban that ended as recently as 1923. They have different languages but similar cultures, based on settled dry rice-farming. Sarawak's most artistic peoples, the Kayan and Kenyah build imposing longhouses, with exquisite woodcarvings and 'tree of life' paintings, and like all Sarawakians, they take hospitality very seriously.

If you visit a longhouse around Belaga or the upper Baram, you won't encounter a boisterous Iban-style welcome, but appearances can be deceptive. The Kayan and Kenyah are more reserved and refined than the Iban, but if you spend a day or two with them they will start to let their hair down. At sunset, huge glasses of *borak* (sour, very potent rice wine) are handed out and downed to a chorus of *'duiiiii ...'*, the local drinking song. Cigarettes made from fierce local tobacco are passed around. *Sape* players weave complex and haunting melodies on their mandolin-like instruments, and long-eared, tattooed women sing songs of praise to the guests, all the while chewing on betel nut.

You may be treated to warrior dances from the men and fan dances from the young women, and even a display of traditional wrestling. And if you're lucky, the festivities will last to sunup, when the soot-smearing and dunking take place. It's the traditional Orang Ulu sense-of-humour test, given only to true friends. After such a memorable night you probably need a bath anyway.

Mike Reed

Belaga's tiny airstrip is 20 minutes downriver by longboat (RM5), followed by a short jungle walk after clambering up a set of precarious riverbank steps! Check in at the Malaysia Airlines offices the day before your flight to arrange transport to the airport. You'll meet the Malaysia Airlines clerk – who is also your boatman – at the Belaga dock about two hours before the flight. He'll get you to the quaint hut that functions as the airport terminal, where you and your gear are carefully weighed like boxers before a title bout.

**Boat** See the Kapit section for details of boat departures from Kapit to Belaga (six hours, RM25). Returning to Kapit, express boats leave Belaga early (between 6 and 6.30 am) to hook up with the boats from Kapit to Sibu. The fare is the same but the trip downstream can be faster. A boat

schedule may be posted outside the Hock Chiang Inn.

Boats go upriver from Belaga as far as the Bakun Dam area near Rumah Apan (about one hour, RM10), from where you can explore the resettled river country north of the Rejang. It's possible to do a loop back to Bintulu this way (see Upriver from Belaga, following, for details).

### UPRIVER FROM BELAGA

With the Bakun Dam more-or-less completed, the forest beyond Belaga has changed forever. The forest around the dam site was long ago clear-cut for quick profit, and a massive reservoir will soon inundate all that remains. Longhouses along the lower Sungai Balui have been emptied of their communities, and families 'resettled' in the Sungai Asap area north of the Rejang.

When the Asian financial crisis of 1997–98 began to bite, the Bakun Dam, like other grandiose development schemes, was scaled down. It is, however, still a massive project that has uprooted an estimated 11,000 people from their small river communities. People are given financial compensation for the loss of ancestral homelands, but it is often less than the amount asked for a house in Asap. The situation is similar to that experienced by Iban around Batang Ai when a reservoir was created there. And sure enough, a Bakun Resort is in the works to put a positive spin on the sordid history of the Bakun Dam development.

Bakun is an awful lot bigger than Batang Ai. However, it remains unclear what purpose the dam serves – Sarawak doesn't need the electrical power (not that it's been offered much) and nor does the Peninsular Malaysia. Mrs Mahathir didn't raise a dummy, but many experts are still scratching their heads over this one (Anwar Ibrahim, incidentally, was loudly opposed to the dam).

With a permit from Kapit, you can travel to near the dam – boatmen will refuse to take you farther than you're permitted to travel. The nearest longhouses to Belaga – such as Uma Aging and Uma Kahei – are mostly Kayan, but Uma Neh is a Kejaman longhouse and Long Semiang is a Lahanan longhouse within a 30-minute boat ride of Belaga. Boats will not turn up unannounced, so you'll need an invitation to a longhouse from someone in town.

You can take a boat as far as it's allowed to go (RM10), from where you can travel by road to Asap and then on to Tubau. Drivers ask around RM30 for the two-hour trip to Asap and another RM25 for the 1½-hour journey to Tubau.

From Tubau there are express boats to Bintulu (three hours, RM18). In the dry season it's also possible to travel overland between Belaga and Bintulu via Tubau, but the cost of a Land Cruiser (at least RM250) and the condition of the logging roads make it a considerably less appealing option than the boat.

# North-East Sarawak

## MUKAH
☎ 084

This small town on the coast north of Sibu is seldom visited by travellers, but it is a delightful spot to chill out for a day or two, especially after the rigours of travel up the Rejang.

Most of the local people are Melanau (as is Sarawak's chief minister), and the area's major attraction is the **Kaul Festival**, currently held on the second Sunday in April. Pesta Kaul, as it's locally called, is a lively surf-side celebration that includes enchanting enactments of Melanau rituals and games to honour the spirits of the sea.

Kampung Tellian is a pleasant water village just beyond the centre of town; here you'll find **Lamin Dana**, a Melanau cultural centre and guesthouse built from traditional materials on the grounds of a Melanau highhouse. The only remaining example of the distinctive high-house is at the Sarawak Cultural Village at Damai (see Santubong & Damai earlier in this chapter). The folks who run this museum also live in it – the house features exhibits including heirlooms and handicrafts. Among things offered are traditional massage by the village midwife (RM30 for one hour), river tours that visit a sago farm and old-style sago bakehouse, and Melanau delicacies such as *umai* (raw fish marinated and served with onions), smoked fish and sago shoots (RM10). Cultural shows can also be arranged.

Lamin Dana is usually open daily from 9 am to 5 pm. Because the family who runs it lives here, you can safely drop by between 8 am and 7 pm. Entry is RM3/1 for adults/children under 13 years, and there is a camera/video fee.

To reach Lamin Dana from town, take a Tellian bus (40 sen) and tell the conductor where you want to go. Lamin Dana can also arrange longboat transport (RM2 per person) to or from the town centre – an enjoyable way to reach the water village. A taxi will cost RM5.

MALAYSIAN BORNEO

## Places to Stay & Eat

*Lamin Dana* (☎ *873871, 010 260 6931, 013 353 1932, fax 687886,* ✆ *drose102@hotmail .com, dlaga@tm.net.my*) charges RM50 for an upstairs room with twin beds, and RM100 for a four-person room (discounts are available for stays of three nights or longer). Rooms are simply furnished, toilets and showers are clean and Melanau-style breakfast is free. The house has only nine rooms, so advance booking is a good idea.

If the cultural centre is full, there are several reasonable hotel options around town. *Sarina Hotel* (☎ *872659*) is on Jalan Orang Kaya Setia Raja, and has rooms for RM35 to RM85. *Pantai Beach Harmony Resort* (☎ *872566*) is on Jalan Mukah Oya, 4km from town; rooms in its six chalets range from RM35 to RM50.

## Getting There & Away

Mukah's airstrip is just outside town; a Malaysia Airlines van will drop you at your lodging for RM5. Malaysia Airlines Twin Otters fly between Mukah and the following centres: Bintulu (weekly, RM44); Kuching (daily, RM76); Miri (daily, RM55); and Sibu (six days a week, RM30).

From Sibu, buses make the trip to Mukah at 6.30 and 11.30 am, and 12.30 and 2.30 pm daily (3½ hours, RM13.85/12.80 air-con/non-air-con). From Bintulu, Dalat-Miri Bas Ekspres leaves for Mukah at 7 am and 1 pm daily (RM17.10). You can also take a bus between Mukah and Dalat.

See the Sibu Getting There & Away section for details of boat travel to Dalat.

## BINTULU

☎ 086

At the mouth of the Batang Kemena, Bintulu is a minor commercial centre servicing offshore oil and gas installations and upriver logging. Bintulu came under James Brooke's sway in 1861, and a forgettable **memorial** near the town centre commemorates Sarawak's first Council Negeri (National Council), formed in 1867. There's a colourful **Chinese temple** near the waterfront and a bathing beach north of town, but Bintulu is really only a transit stop for most travellers.

Travellers heading north to Niah Caves and Miri, and south to Sibu, the Rejang and Kuching, may need to use Bintulu's bus station as a staging post. If you're going to nearby Similajau National Park, you might also end up overnighting in Bintulu.

Similajau National Park, a 45-minute drive north-east of Bintulu, is mainly worth visiting if you're not going to any of the parks around Kuching, especially Bako. (See the Similajau National Park section later in this chapter.) If you are self-catering at Niah Caves, Bintulu is a good place to stock up with provisions, although Niah has a good, cheap cafeteria.

## Orientation & Information

Bintulu lies along the east bank of the Batang Kemena, within walking distance of the river mouth. The airport bisects the town and marks the northern edge of the centre. (Bintulu's claim to fame is that it's listed in the *Guinness Book of Records* as the town closest to an airport in the world.) All the places to stay and eat, banks and other services are squashed between the airport and the riverbank. The waterfront just north of the shopping area along Jalan Masjid has several clean, bustling markets. The long-distance bus station is 5km north of town at Medan Jaya; take a local bus or taxi between here and the town centre.

The Hong Leong Bank, opposite the local bus station, is a good place to change cash or travellers cheques.

Star Internet is in the block of buildings just beyond KFC. It charges RM5 per hour and is open daily from 8 am to 9 pm.

## Places to Stay – Budget

Bintulu's budget lodging is nothing to write home about. Of the hotels that aren't brothels, *Capital Hotel* (☎ *331167*) on Jalan Keppel is the bottom of the barrel. It has a few scruffy fan-cooled rooms with stained sheets, shared toilet and mandi for RM15. Air-con rooms with shared toilet cost RM20, and you'll pay RM30 for the luxury of a phone and private toilet and mandi.

*Dragon Inn* (☎ *315150, 1 New Commercial Centre*) is opposite the Plaza Hotel. It's brighter and more pleasant than the Capital but it can be noisy; basic singles/doubles cost RM25/35.

## Places to Stay – Mid-Range

Most of the hotels in Bintulu are fairly new, air-con, mid-range places whose rooms have TV, IDD phone and attached bathroom. They are all of a similar standard and there is little difference between them.

*Sea View Inn (☎ 339228, Taman Sri Dagang)* has the best location – on the waterfront – and is basic but good value. Rooms overlooking the river cost RM40. *Queen's Inn (☎ 338922)*, at No 238 along the waterfront has singles/doubles for RM40/45.

Among the cluster of hotels at this end of Jalan Masjid is *My House Inn (☎ 336399)* at No 161, where rooms are reasonable at RM40/45. This place is quieter than its neighbours, which are sandwiched between karaoke bars and discos.

*Fata Inn (☎ 332998, 113 Jalan Masjid)* is very clean and friendly; rooms cost RM42/48. *Welcome Inn (☎ 315266)*, on the corner of Jalan Masjid and Jalan Pedada, has decent rooms for RM45/47, and larger doubles for RM55.

*Kintown Inn (☎ 333666, 93 Jalan Keppel)* is good value. Refurbished, quiet and clean rooms with double beds go for RM60/69; twins are RM55/63.

For more-upmarket mid-range accommodation, try *Royal Inn (☎ 332166, 10 Jalan Pedada)*. Hefty discounts (up to 40%) can make the Royal reasonable value, but the published rate of RM97.75 net for a standard single is absurd. *Sunlight Inn (☎ 332577)*, on the corner of Jalan Abang Galau and Jalan Pedada, is a step down in quality from the Royal, but rooms are cheaper at RM50/55 a single/double.

Rooms are a bit stuffy but otherwise OK at the friendly *Hoover Hotel (☎ 337166, 92*

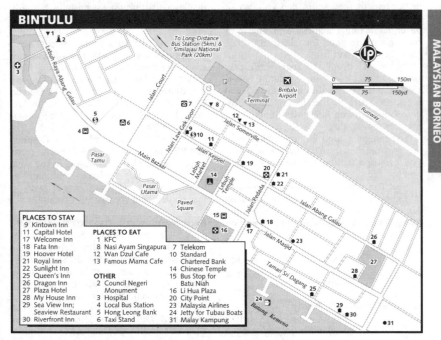

**BINTULU**

To Long-Distance Bus Station (5km) & Similajau National Park (20km)

Bintulu Airport

Terminal

Runway

Pasar Tamu

Pasar Utama

Main Bazaar

Paved Square

Jalan Court

Jalan Law Gek Soon

Jalan Somerville

Jalan Keppel

Lebuh Market

Lebuh Temple

Jalan Pedada

Jalan Abang Galau

Jalan Masjid

Taman Sri Dagang

Batang Kemena

Lebuh Raya Abang Galau

| PLACES TO STAY |
| --- |
| 9  Kintown Inn |
| 11  Capital Hotel |
| 17  Welcome Inn |
| 18  Fata Inn |
| 19  Hoover Hotel |
| 21  Royal Inn |
| 22  Sunlight Inn |
| 25  Queen's Inn |
| 26  Dragon Inn |
| 27  Plaza Hotel |
| 28  My House Inn |
| 29  Sea View Inn; Seaview Restaurant |
| 30  Riverfront Inn |

| PLACES TO EAT |
| --- |
| 1  KFC |
| 8  Nasi Ayam Singapura |
| 12  Wan Dzul Cafe |
| 13  Famous Mama Cafe |

| OTHER |
| --- |
| 2  Council Negeri Monument |
| 3  Hospital |
| 4  Local Bus Station |
| 5  Hong Leong Bank |
| 6  Taxi Stand |
| 7  Telekom |
| 10  Standard Chartered Bank |
| 14  Chinese Temple |
| 15  Bus Stop for Batu Niah |
| 16  Li Hua Plaza |
| 20  City Point |
| 23  Malaysia Airlines |
| 24  Jetty for Tubau Boats |
| 31  Malay Kampung |

MALAYSIAN BORNEO

*Jalan Keppel).* Standard singles are RM65 and larger singles/doubles cost RM69/75.

**Riverfront Inn** *(☎ 333111),* at No 256 on the waterfront, is probably the best value in town. It's a pleasant hotel and popular with expat oil workers, so it may be full. Large windowless rooms start at RM63; rooms with a river view start at RM80.

### Places to Stay – Top End

The **Plaza Hotel** *(☎ 335111, 116 Jalan Abang Galau)* was once the swankiest hotel in town, but it has all the charm of a suburban shopping mall. Rooms are good value, however, if you get a discount (quite likely); there's also a rooftop swimming pool here. Promotional rates on standard rooms are RM80, including breakfast. Deluxe rooms cost RM103 and suites are RM167.

### Places to Eat

The top floor of the **pasar utama** (new market) is the place to go for hawker food. It has dozens of food stalls, and you can sit and look out over the river. The stalls at the **pasar tamu** (night market), near the local bus station, are good for take-away satay, grilled chicken and fish.

By the waterfront, the **Seaview Restaurant** is a kedai kopi with standard Chinese food, and toasted sandwiches and coffee at breakfast. There are literally dozens of Chinese **kedai kopi** on Jalan Masjid, all offering very similar fare.

You can get a good Western-style breakfast downstairs at the **Riverfront Inn**, where you can also try the Melanau speciality, umai.

Near the airport, **Nasi Ayam Singapura** is a good, air-con stop for lunch. **Famous Mama Cafe**, farther along Jalan Somerville, does cheap and tasty halal Indian food; on the same street is the **Wan Dzul Cafe**, also good value.

There are kedai kopi and other shops opposite the long-distance bus station that stay open well into the night.

### Getting There & Away

**Air**  The Malaysia Airlines office (☎ 331554) is on Jalan Masjid and is open weekdays from 8.30 am to 4.30 pm and on Saturday from 8.30 am to 12.30 pm.

Malaysia Airlines has regular flights to Sibu (six daily, RM64), Kuching (at least six daily, RM117), Miri (at least three daily, RM69) and KK (two or three daily, RM127). Twin Otters fly once a week (currently on Wednesday) to Mukah (RM40) and Belaga (RM40).

With the runway bisecting the town, the terminal is about 100m from the main street. Taxis meet the flights and a ride to any hotel shouldn't cost more than RM5.

**Bus**  Bus services to Miri, Batu Niah, Sibu, Sarikei and Kuching and other destinations leave from Bintulu's long-distance bus station, about 5km from town at Medan Jaya; take a local bus from the station near the covered markets, departing hourly from 7.15 am to 9.15 pm (50 sen). A taxi costs RM8.

Various bus companies occupy the ticket booths at the long-distance bus station, and display departure times and fares. Usually you can just buy a ticket and get on the next bus.

Note that the posted bus services aren't always running, so it's best to ask ahead of time. The main companies servicing Miri, Batu Niah, Sibu, Dalat, Sarikei and Kuching are: Biaramas Express (☎ 339821); Borneo Highway Express (☎ 339855); Freesia Express; Lanang Express (☎ 338518); Syarikat Bas Suria (☎ 335489); Dalat-Miri Bas Ekspres (☎ 331007); Hornbill Bas Ekspres; and PB Ekspres (☎ 314355). Several other companies service small towns in the area.

There is no bus service to Similajau National Park – see Getting There & Away in that section later for transport details.

**Batu Niah**  Hornbill Bas Ekspres has eight daily buses from the long-distance bus station to Batu Niah, departing between 6 am and 4.30 pm (2 hours, RM12). Syarikat Bas Suria coaches leave from in front of the Li Hua Plaza – the posted departure times are roughly the same as Hornbill's.

**Mukah & Dalat**  Dalat-Miri Bas Ekspres does the Mukah-Oya-Dalat run from Bintulu at 7 am and 1 pm daily. The fare to Mukah is RM17.10 and to Dalat RM21.

**Miri** There are numerous departures for Miri between 6 am and 11.30 pm daily (4½ hours, RM18); bookings shouldn't be necessary. Express buses to Miri pass the turn-off to Batu Niah, but they don't go there (see Getting There & Away in the Niah Caves National Park entry later in this chapter for more information).

**Sibu, Sarikei & Kuching** There are dozens of departures for Sibu every day between 6 am and 11.30 pm (3 hours, RM16.50). All major companies ply this route, although departures are more frequent in the morning.

Many of the services to Sibu continue via Sarikei to Kuching. It's a long haul that can be speeded up by taking the bus to Sibu, then the fast passenger ferry to Kuching – *if* you can get to Sibu in time for the morning sailing (see the Sibu section earlier for details). The fare to Sarikei is RM24 and to Kuching it's RM52.

**Boat** Express launches go up the Batang Kemena as far as Tubau (three hours, RM18), from where you can arrange a ride to Belaga (see the Upriver from Belaga section earlier for details). Boats leave from the jetty every hour between 7 am and 3 pm.

## Getting Around
Everything in the town centre is a short walk south of the airport terminal. Taxis meet all flights.

Taxis congregate at the Chinese temple, the airport and at the big taxi stand near the markets. Most taxi fares around town are RM5. The trip to the long-distance bus station costs RM10, and the fare to Similajau is RM35.

For car hire, call Wendy on ☎ 019-885 1158.

## SIMILAJAU NATIONAL PARK
A 45-minute drive north-east of Bintulu, this park's deserted, sandy beaches are among the best in Sarawak. The park isn't the best managed in the state, and a visit

won't add much to the experience of Bako National Park. Still, Similajau is a quiet spot and if you're looking to break your journey for a day, the walks can be rewarding. Access to the park is by car or taxi only.

Similajau occupies a narrow coastal strip 30km long but only a few kilometres wide. Green turtles sometimes come ashore to lay their eggs on the park's more-remote beaches. Because Similajau is flanked by logged forest it's a haven for **wildlife**: A recent survey recorded 230 bird species, making it one of the most diversely inhabited areas in Sarawak. The forest is also home to 24 species of mammals; there are a few shy macaques around the park headquarters.

There are pavilions along the casuarina-lined beach as well as decent accommodation and an information centre at the park headquarters. It's easy to spend a day or two walking in the coastal rainforest or lazing on the beach.

Permits and accommodation for the park can be booked through the National Parks & Wildlife office in Miri (☎ 085-434184, fax 434179) – see Tourist Offices in the Miri section later. There is currently no booking office in Bintulu. A permit for the park can also be arranged on arrival, and the standard RM3 entrance fee and RM5/10 camera/video fee are charged. The park headquarters office (☎ 086-391284) is open daily until 5 pm. It occupies the south bank of the mouth of the Sungai Likau, although most of the park lies north of the river, and is accessed by a suspension bridge. The river crossing is a bit Tarzanesque – crocodiles occasionally lurk around the mouth of the river, especially in the early morning and evening.

## Walking Trails
Similajau has a limited trail network, the backbone of which is a long trail (9.8km from park headquarters) to Golden Beach. In other words, to get much out of the park, you'll be spending the better part of the day on a long, hot walk. Take lots of water.

Trails are well marked and a guide isn't necessary. After crossing the river from headquarters, head left off the boardwalk

MALAYSIAN BORNEO

towards the headland. It's about half an hour's walk to a pavilion from where you can enjoy the view back along the coast towards Bintulu.

Farther along the coast, the main trail leads to **Turtle Beach** (2½ to three hours) and **Golden Beach** (3½ to four hours), two beautiful, deserted spots where turtles come ashore to lay their eggs. Other trails forge into the low hills behind the coast to **Selunsur Rapid** (two to 2½ hours) and **Kolam Sebubong**, which can be reached only by boat (about a 30-minute ride) then a 15-minute walk.

To get to Kolam Sebubong you'll have to organise a boat at the park headquarters. The boat should cost RM75 (based on a rate of RM15 per person for a minimum of five people for one hour); you could also be dropped off at the beaches along the way, and walk back.

You might be able to arrange a boat up the mangrove-lined Sungai Likau for RM50 per hour (one hour should be enough). If you go in the early morning, you'll see a range of birds, including hornbills, and maybe mammals or even crocodiles.

### Places to Stay & Eat
Similajau can be visited as a day trip from Bintulu, but if you're going to tackle the trails, you'll want to stay here overnight. Accommodation is comfortable, at least in the newest building, called Hostel 3. A bed in the four-room, fan-cooled *hostels* costs RM10. The air-con *chalets* have two rooms, each sleeping four people and costing RM60. There is also a *campground* (RM4 per person) that has pretty grotty toilets.

When we visited, the park's *cafeteria* had been all but devoid of food for some time; bottled water (RM3) was available, but that was about it. Hopefully, the situation will have improved by the time you read this. To be safe, bring along your own provisions, but take note that the accommodation has no cooking facilities.

### Getting There & Away
Access to Similajau is via a rough, deserted logging road that turns off the highway

some 20km north of Bintulu. There's no public transport; a taxi will cost RM35 each way (RM30 if you drive a hard bargain), so negotiate with the driver and arrange a time to be picked up. You may be able to talk a boat operator into taking you from Bintulu, but expect to pay hundreds of ringgit – this would only be economical for a group.

## NIAH CAVES NATIONAL PARK
☎ 085
This small national park near the coast between Miri and Bintulu protects one of Sarawak's most famous attractions, the Niah Caves. Niah Caves National Park is about 115km south of Miri and its centrepiece is the Great Cave, one of the largest caves in the world. The park is dominated by a 394m-high limestone massif, Gunung Subis, that is usually visible from quite a distance.

In 1958, archaeologists discovered evidence of human occupation of the caves area dating back some 40,000 years. Rock paintings were found in what has become known as the Painted Cave, and the discovery of several small canoe-like coffins indicate that this site was once used as a burial ground. A reconstruction of the cave and some of the artefacts found here can be seen in the Sarawak Museum in Kuching. To protect the site, entry to the Painted Cave is prohibited, but you can peer in from the entrance.

The Niah Caves are home to a whole lot of bats. They are also an important nesting site for swiftlets, which supply the vital ingredient for the famous bird's-nest soup. Traditionally, the Penan have been custodians and collectors of the nests, while the Iban have had the rights to the caves' other commodity, bat guano. During the harvesting season nest collectors live in the caves, and the tools of their trade can be seen inside: massive bamboo poles lashed together and wedged against the cave roof above.

A lot of money has been spent promoting the Niah Caves as a tourist site, including a sultan's ransom for the flashy visitors'-centre-cum-museum, over the river from the park headquarters. It's a lovely Malay-style building that has some interesting displays on the geology, archaeology and ecology of the caves.

The other side of tourism promotion, however, is local inflation. Outside suppliers to Batu Niah businesses have been cashing in by regularly increasing prices, and some prices in town may have risen by the time you visit.

## Permits & Costs

A permit is needed to visit Niah Caves; it is issued without fuss at the park headquarters (☎ 737450) at Pangkalan Lubang. You can book accommodation at the visitors' information centres in Miri or Kuching, but make sure you get a receipt to present if requested at the park office at Niah. Upon arrival you must register at the office and pay the RM3 park entrance fee and RM5/10 camera/video fee.

Bookings are advisable for accommodation at Pangkalan Lubang. If you're staying at the hostel you can usually turn up without a booking, especially during the week. If it's busy and there's no accommodation, the worst you'll have to do is head the 4km back to Batu Niah, where there are three hotels.

## Batu Niah

The bus from Bintulu or Miri will drop you in the centre of Batu Niah town. It's a 4km walk along the river to the park headquarters (follow the path past the red Chinese temple); you can also go by taxi or by longboat if a boatman is available – someone in town may also offer to drive you for a small fee. The road and river trail to the headquarters are behind the town centre to the left from where the bus stops, and the boat dock is directly to the right. Batu Niah has some decent food and lodging – see Places to Stay & Eat later in this section.

## Niah Caves

To get to the caves from park headquarters you must first take a boat across the Sungai Niah; the jetty is down the path between the office building and the cafeteria. It's not very far to the opposite bank, but crocodiles are sometimes seen in the river, so fork out for the ferry. During the day the ferry costs 50 sen; from 5.30 pm until the last crossing at 7.30 pm it costs RM1.

Once across the river, follow the 3km-long raised boardwalk to the caves (note that it can get very slippery when it's raining).

MALAYSIAN BORNEO

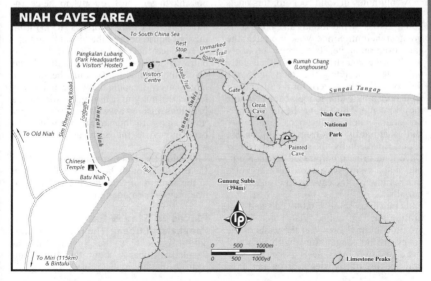

**NIAH CAVES AREA**

To South China Sea

Pangkalan Lubang
(Park Headquarters
& Visitors' Hostel)

Rest Stop

Unmarked Trail

Boardwalk

Visitors' Centre

Madu Trail

Sungai Subis

Gate

Great Cave

Painted Cave

Rumah Chang
(Longhouses)

Sungai Tangap

Niah Caves
National
Park

Sim Kheng Hong Road

Footpath

Sungai Niah

To Old Niah

Chinese Temple

Batu Niah

Trail

Gunung Subis
(394m)

To Miri (115km)
& Bintulu

0    500    1000m
0    500    1000yd

Limestone Peaks

The boardwalk passes through primary rainforest, but most visitors are so intent on reaching the caves that they miss the wildlife along the way. The boards are loose in places and make a lot of noise, but if you stop for a while you'll hear lots of birds and may also see macaques. As well as the hundreds of beautiful butterflies, wildlife in the area includes squirrels, flying lizards and a striking emerald green lizard that sometimes sits on the boardwalk.

Shortly after the rest stop about 500m along, you'll pass an unmarked boardwalk branching off to the left – keep going straight. As you approach the caves, the trail skirts jagged limestone outcrops that appear like ancient ramparts festooned with giant vines and creepers. Shortly before the cave entrance the boardwalk forks; head to the right for the caves – the left fork goes to the village of Rumah Chang, where there are a couple of longhouses. Villagers usually sit at the junction selling cold beer and soft drinks. The trail goes under a large overhang with stout stalactites, called the **Trader Cave** – but wait for it; you ain't seen nothing yet. The trail then rounds a corner to enter the vast **Great Cave**.

As big holes in solid rock go, this one's impressive – the Great Cave measures 250m across at the mouth and 60m at its greatest height. Since you approach the cave from an angle, its enormity probably won't strike you straight away. It's usually only after descending the steep stairs into the bowels of the cavern for a half-hour or so that visitors pause to look back at where they've come. This (or maybe the treacherous stairs) explains the occasional 'holy shit!' that briefly rises from the improbable depths. Incidentally, the spirits of the Great Cave tend to be unimpressed by such outbursts and visitors are asked to keep noise to a minimum – the cave itself is an ancient burial site.

At one time, some 470,000 bats and four million swiftlets called Niah home. There are no current figures, but the walls of the caves are no longer thick with bats and there are fewer birds' nests to harvest. Several species of swiftlet nest on the cave walls; the most common by far is the glossy swiftlet, whose nest contains vegetation and is not harvested. For obvious reasons, the species whose nests are edible are far less abundant and can only be seen in the remotest corners of the cavern. Several species of bat also roost in the cave, but they are not in dense colonies and must be picked out in the gloom among the birds' nests – take a powerful torch (flashlight).

The best time to see the cave wildlife is at dusk, during the 'changeover', when the swiftlets return to their nests for the night and the bats come hurtling out for the night's feeding. You will have to hurry back to the river, though, as the last ferry crossing is at 7.30 pm.

Inside the cave, the boardwalk continues down to the right, but you'll need a torch to explore any distance. In the harvesting season you'll probably see nest collectors going about their business. The stairs and handrails leading down into Gunung Subis are usually covered with dirt or guano, and can get very slippery in places. Allow a good hour to explore the Great Cave; the trail branches around a massive central pillar but both branches finish at the same point and it's impossible to get lost if you stick to the boardwalk. There's no need to hire a guide, although you can hire torches (RM5) from the first house beyond the visitors' centre.

To reach the **Painted Cave**, follow the pathway all the way through the Great Cave; the Painted Cave is just beyond the larger cavern's gaping maw. The entrance is fenced off but you can glimpse some cave paintings inside, as well as some empty 'death ships', the human cargo of which has been moved to the Sarawak Museum in Kuching.

Outside the main entrance to the Great Cave, trails through the jungle will take you to the summit of **Gunung Subis**. The park headquarters provides a trail map.

## Places to Stay & Eat

**Pangkalan Lubang** The park accommodation is next to the Sungai Niah at Pangkalan Lubang, about 4km from Batu Niah.

The *hostel* has comfortable four-bed dorms with fan costing RM10.50 per bed, or RM42 for the room. Also available are four-bed rooms in *chalets* for RM63, and air-con, two-bed *VIP chalets* at RM210. On checking in you are issued with a sheet and a blanket, and utensils are provided if you want to cook. You can also camp for RM4 per night and hire a fly for RM8.

The park has a *canteen* with quite a good range of noodle and rice meals, and you can buy a limited range of provisions here. In the dry season the rainwater tanks may dry out, so the water is drawn from the river and must be boiled before drinking.

**Batu Niah** If you arrive outside the park office hours, or don't want to stay at the park, there are three hotels in Batu Niah.

*Niah Cave Hotel (☎ 737726),* back from the town square along the river, is a friendly place. Simple, clean, air-con singles/doubles cost RM22/26 with shared toilet. There's a *bar* downstairs that may serve food, but there are plenty of cheap eateries around the small town.

*Park View Hotel (☎ 737021),* on the town square, offers fine fan-cooled rooms for RM25 and air-con singles/doubles for RM35/45 with bathroom and TV. You may not get much sleep though, as there's a late-night disco next door. *Niah Cave Inn (☎ 737333)* is the big hotel on the corner as you arrive in Batu Niah. It's the best hotel (and the best pun) in town, with air-con, TV, fridge and IDD phones. Rooms are RM52/57.

The *Seng Kee Seafood Restaurant,* next door to the Cave Inn, serves excellent Chinese food and has plenty of vegetarian options. All dishes are reasonably priced.

### Getting There & Away
Access to Batu Niah, the town nearest the caves, is by road only. Batu Niah is 13km west of the highway between Miri and Bintulu; the turn-off is 102km south of Miri. Express buses make a brief stop at the junction, which has a small market and a few shops, but if you take one of these buses you'll have to make your own way to Batu Niah.

There are services to Batu Niah from both Miri and Bintulu; check departure times with the Visitors' Information Centres in Miri or Bintulu.

The last bus leaves Batu Niah at 3.30 pm, so if you're visiting the caves as a day trip, arrive early. If you do miss the last bus, private cars will offer lifts from Batu Niah to the highway turn-off (you shouldn't pay more than RM15) to catch the Miri or the Bintulu bus. Express buses stop at the junction, and the fare may be a bit a bit higher than normal (eg, RM10 to Miri instead of the regular RM8.50).

**Bintulu** Hornbill Bas Ekspres has eight daily buses from the express-bus station to Batu Niah (two hours, RM12) between 6 am and 4.30 pm. Syarikat Bas Suria coaches leave from in the front of the Li Hua Plaza.

From Batu Niah to Bintulu, buses leave at 6, 7, 10 and 11 am, noon, and at 1.30 and 3 pm. Buses leave from the open area in the centre of town. There is no ticket agency – pay as you board.

**Miri** Syarikat Bas Suria has buses to Batu Niah (two hours, RM8.50) leaving hourly from around 6.30 am to 4 pm. From Batu Niah to Miri, there are departures roughly hourly from 6 am to 3 pm. Catch these same buses for Lambir Hills National Park, 32km from Miri (RM2).

### Getting Around
Transport to the park headquarters from Batu Niah is usually by taxi or boat. The boat trip costs RM10, plus RM2 per person for more than five people. Taxis also cost RM10. Boats do most of their business in the morning; after noon it is usually quicker to get a taxi, a few of which are always waiting next to the bus stand. The boat trip is an exhilarating few minutes' journey past jungle-clad limestone cliffs.

You can also walk along the 4km track that runs alongside the river past the red Chinese temple. Whichever way you decide to do it, make sure you check in at the park office on arrival.

MALAYSIAN BORNEO

MALAYSIAN BORNEO

## LAMBIR HILLS NATIONAL PARK

A regional attraction and a popular weekend retreat for Miri residents, Lambir Hills National Park has pleasant rainforest walking trails, a picturesque natural swimming pool and riverside picnic shelters. At its closest point, the park is only 20km from Miri and city residents come by the car load to do the 15-minute walk to the pretty waterfalls, one of which cascades into a good swimming hole.

Lambir Hills makes an easy and enjoyable day trip from Miri, though you can always stay longer. While it doesn't have the spectacular scenery of Niah Caves and Gunung Mulu National Parks or the diversity of Bako National Park, Lambir Hills is excellent for short jungle walks.

The national park covers 6952 hectares and protects a range of low sandstone hills that reach a height of 465m at Bukit Lambir. Much of the forest was logged before the park was declared, but the secondary forest is beautiful in its own right and Lambir Hills boasts a good range of wildlife.

Officially, the trails are open from 8 am to 4 pm weekdays, and from 8 am to 5 pm on weekends and public holidays, but if you are seriously interested in wildlife-watching you will have to get an earlier start. Wildlife here includes gibbons, tarsiers, pangolins and barking deer, though you are unlikely to see any of these close to the park headquarters. Lambir Hills is also home to many species of birds.

Located next to the highway, the park headquarters is 32km from Miri. Here you'll find the park office and information centre, a canteen and accommodation. Permits and accommodation bookings can be arranged at the Visitors' Information Centre (☎ 085-434181) in Miri. Park entrance and camera fees are payable at the office.

### Walks

Walking times given here are those posted at park headquarters; halve them if you are fit. The most popular walk is to **Latak Waterfall** – an easy 15-minute stroll from the headquarters. The trail passes two minor falls before reaching the main waterfall, where there are picnic shelters, a changing shed and a large, clear pool, ideal for swimming. This walk is much quieter on weekdays.

From Latak Waterfall the main trail heads off to **Bukit Pantu** (about 1½ hours), the nearest peak to the headquarters, and Bukit Lambir. Just above the falls, at the start of the trail, is a 40m-high tree tower. If you have a head for heights the view of the forest canopy is magnificent, although the tower sways a bit in the breeze.

The main trail goes all the way to **Bukit Lambir** (3½ hours), from where there are fine views. Off the main trail there are many worthwhile waterfall detours: Nibong (about two hours); Pantu (just over one hour); Pancur (2½ hours); Dinding (about 2½ hours); and Tengkorong (two hours). The trail is steep and slippery in places, but the walks are not overly strenuous. Bukit Pantu is a straightforward climb, but the stretch to Bukit Lambir can be tiring.

It is possible to arrive at the park in the morning, walk to Bukit Lambir and back, then be on your way to Miri or Niah Caves National Park, but this doesn't leave much time to appreciate the forest or its wildlife. Register your name at the booth at the start of the trail before you head off.

### Places to Stay & Eat

Accommodation at the park is comfortable, but it's only a few hundred metres from the main highway so you won't feel like you're in the middle of the jungle. You should book at the Visitors' Information Centre in Miri in advance, particularly on weekends, though you are unlikely to be turned away if you don't have a reservation.

Accommodation at the park is limited. Rooms in the *resthouses* sleeping two and three people cost RM40; if they're not full you could probably talk them into letting you have a bed for less.

There are no cooking facilities at the lodgings, but the park has a *canteen* that sells rice and noodle dishes, drinks and basic provisions. Opening hours depend on demand, but are generally from 8 am to about 7 pm.

A stilt village perched on the riverbank, Sarawak.

An Iban baby taking a dip.

Sungai Sarawak, Kuching

Penan woman, Marudi

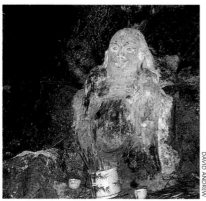
Fairy Cave, Sarawak

Pristine beach at Bako National Park, Sarawak.

Sunset over Kota Kinabalu, Sabah.

Longhouse on the Sungai Skrang, Sarawak.

Boardwalk, Niah Caves National Park, Sarawak

Not-so-traditional sampan, Kuching, Sarawak.

## Getting There & Away

Lambir Hills National Park is on the main highway and is easily accessible by bus from Miri. Take any Batu Niah bus for RM2.40 (see Getting There & Away in the Niah Caves National Park section earlier), or any nonexpress bus going to Bintulu. Returning to Miri, buses from Batu Niah pass Lambir Hills and cost RM6.

From the park you must stand out the front and hail a bus; park staff can tell you when they pass. Heading south, the last buses to Batu Niah and Bintulu pass at around 3 pm. Heading north to Miri, the last buses leave at around 4.30 pm. The express buses might stop for you, but don't count on it.

## MIRI
☎ 085

Miri is Sarawak's most northerly city, a major commercial centre and the life-support system for local oil workers. It's not an unpleasant place, but there is little to hold travellers for long; most simply overnight in Miri en route to Niah Caves, Gunung Mulu, Bario, or farther afield.

Miri is something of a transition town between Sarawak and Sabah – there's a strong Muslim presence here and there are plenty of palm plantations surrounding the town. As a long-time service centre for the river towns and the crude oil industry, Miri can be unrefined compared to many places in Sarawak. But if you're yearning for the bright lights, Miri has plenty of good restaurants and several good nightspots.

Since the Asian financial crisis a few years back, Miri has slowed down. Many of the expat oil workers are gone, land speculators have made their mint and moved on, and border-hopping Bruneians now prefer to stay home and watch TV. As a result, those once-trendy shopping malls are looking a little bit lonely.

## Orientation & Information

Miri lies on a narrow plain between the east bank of the Sungai Miri and low hills that were once covered in oil wells and the source of the city's wealth. Most places to stay and eat are within walking distance of other places you're likely to visit, but you'll need a bus or taxi to get to the long-distance bus station or airport. A few blocks north of the town centre are a couple of modern shopping malls, the main post office and the immigration office.

The local bus station and the stop for Lambir Hills and Niah Caves are close to the Visitors' Information Centre.

**Tourist Offices** The Visitors' Information Centre (☎ 434181, fax 434179, ✆ stb@ po.jaring.my) is on Jalan Melayu, at the southern end of the town centre. The helpful staff can provide bus times, and information on places to stay and tours. The centre is open Monday to Thursday from 8 am to 4.30 pm, Friday to 4.45 pm, and Saturday to 12.45 pm.

The National Parks & Wildlife office (☎ 434184, fax 434179) is housed in the Visitors' Information Centre. This is where you organise permits and accommodation for Gunung Mulu, Niah Caves, Lambir Hills and Similajau National Parks.

Travelcom Asia, which produces the excellent *Official Kuching Guide,* has an on-line version of its Miri guide in the works. It should be up and running by the time you read this – visit the Web site at www.borneo travel.com.

**Permits** In this area the only travel permits you'll need are to reach Bario for trekking in the Kelabit Highlands and for visiting longhouses upriver from Marudi.

Present your passport at the Pejabat Residen on Jalan Kingsway. You'll have to fill in a form with details of your intended visit, including your expected length of stay – there's currently no time limit. Your passport will be photocopied, then the Resident will sign the permit. Although it appears a formality, when you fill in the form keep the details simple – you're a tourist, right? Permits are free of charge and worth getting, as you may well be asked to produce one, especially in Bario.

**Money** The Standard Chartered Bank on Jalan Calliandra is best equipped for changing travellers cheques, but it charges

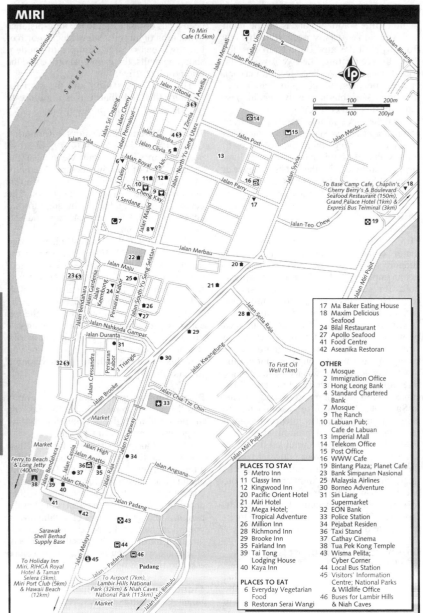

**MIRI**

To Miri
Cafe (1.5km)

To Base Camp Cafe, Chaplin's,
Cherry Berry's & Boulevard
Seafood Restaurant (150m),
Grand Palace Hotel (1km) &
Express Bus Terminal (3km)

To First Oil
Well (1km)

Market

Market

Ferry to Beach
& Long Jetty
(400m)

Sarawak
Shell Berhad
Supply Base

To Holiday Inn
Miri, RIHGA Royal
Hotel & Taman
Selera (3km),
Miri Port Club (5km)
& Hawaii Beach
(12km)

To Airport (7km),
Lambir Hills National
Park (32km) & Niah Caves
National Park (113km)

Padang

Market

**PLACES TO STAY**
5  Metro Inn
11 Classy Inn
12 Kingwood Inn
20 Pacific Orient Hotel
21 Miri Hotel
22 Mega Hotel;
   Tropical Adventure
26 Million Inn
28 Richmond Inn
29 Brooke Inn
35 Fairland Inn
39 Tai Tong
   Lodging House
40 Kaya Inn

**PLACES TO EAT**
6  Everyday Vegetarian
   Food
8  Restoran Serai Wangi

17 Ma Baker Eating House
18 Maxim Delicious
   Seafood
24 Bilal Restaurant
27 Apollo Seafood
41 Food Centre
42 Aseanika Restoran

**OTHER**
1  Mosque
2  Immigration Office
3  Hong Leong Bank
4  Standard Chartered
   Bank
7  Mosque
9  The Ranch
10 Labuan Pub;
   Cafe de Labuan
13 Imperial Mall
14 Telekom Office
15 Post Office
16 WWW Cafe
19 Bintang Plaza; Planet Cafe
23 Bank Simpanan Nasional
25 Malaysia Airlines
30 Borneo Adventure
31 Sin Liang
   Supermarket
32 EON Bank
33 Police Station
34 Pejabat Residen
36 Taxi Stand
37 Cathay Cinema
38 Tua Pek Kong Temple
43 Wisma Pelita;
   Cyber Corner
44 Local Bus Station
45 Visitors' Information
   Centre; National Parks
   & Wildlife Office
46 Buses for Lambir Hills
   & Niah Caves

a hefty RM20 per transaction and 15 sen per cheque: Change as much as possible in one go. Other major banks are clustered near the Imperial Mall. There are money-changers on and around Jalan China that are open longer than banks, but they only change cash.

**Post & Communications** The post office is about 10 minutes' walk north of the centre along Jalan Sylvia.

There are several cybercafes in town, and doubtless will be more by the time you read this.

**Cyber Corner** 1st floor, Wisma Pelita; open to 8 pm daily (RM1 for 10 minutes' email access, RM3/5 for 30 minutes/one hour)
**Planet Cafe** 1st floor, Bintang Plaza (RM6 per hour)
**WWW Cafe** Near Imperial Mall; open from 10 am to 1 am daily (RM6 per hour)

**Bookshops** The Pelita Book Centre, on level 3 of the Imperial Mall, has a small range of Borneo-related books. There is a popular, huge bookshop on the 2nd floor of Bintang Plaza that has a more general selection.

## Things to See & Do
The atmospheric old part of town begins around the southern end of Jalan Brooke; this is the area most worth a wander. The markets here are lively, especially in the morning, and there's plenty of commerce along the five-foot ways (covered walkways) in the shophouse blocks. The **Central Market** offers stupendous discounts on sinful items such as cigarettes and alcohol; **Tamu Muhibbah** is a newer market complex where local Dayaks come to Miri to sell their vegetables. The wide courtyard of **Tua Pek Kong temple** near the fish market is a good spot to watch the river traffic float by.

On the low ridge behind the town centre is Malaysia's first **oil well**, a wooden structure dating from 1910, from where you can get good views across Miri to the South China Sea.

Miri has a passable beach at **Taman Selera**, 3km south of town. There are closer beaches on the spit next to the long jetty, where the oil-rig boats pull in, but they are strewn with logs and rusting industrial debris – take the free ferry across the river.

**Hawaii Beach** is a clean, palm-lined beach about 15 minutes south of town by bus. To get there, take Bakam bus No 5 (RM1.50); it runs between 6.30 am and 6.30 pm from the local bus station.

**Diving** Aside from the islands of Talang-Talang near Kuching, Miri is about the only area in Sarawak where it's possible to dive. Within a short boat trip from Miri are several small shoals (45 minutes away) and a reef (two hours). A Japanese WWII wreck, the *Atago-maru,* lies off the long jetty south of town. Outside the rainy season, visibility is good at the reef (up to 20m), though there's less to see here than there is at Sabah's better dive spots. Seridan Mulu (see Organised Tours later in this section) can organise trips, equipment and training.

## Organised Tours
Miri has plenty of travel agents with whom to book flights and confirm tickets. Numerous tour operators organise trips to Gunung Mulu and Niah Caves National Parks as well as to other places – the Visitors' Information Centre has plenty of brochures. Visiting the caves in Mulu is easy and cheaper as an independent traveller, but if you want to trek to the Pinnacles or along the Headhunters' Trail, you should compare tour companies' prices.

A full-day tour to Niah Caves costs about RM180. Published prices for Mulu trekking are hundreds of ringgit, but often include accommodation at Royal Mulu Resort; you don't have to stay at the resort but you'll have to negotiate another price with the tour company. Some of the more-established tour operators are:

**Borneo Adventure** (☎ 438741, fax 438740, ✆ endaya@pd.jaring.my) 2nd floor, Lot 171A, Jalan Brooke. A long-established and reliable operator.
**KKM Travel** (☎ 417899, 011-205284, 011-295676, ✆ kkm@kc.com.my) A couple of nice guys running tours to Mulu through the Mulu Rainforest Lodge.

**Seridan Mulu** (☎ 414300, fax 416066, ✉ info@ seridanmulu.com) Lobby arcade of the Rihga Hotel. This outfit does trips to Mulu as well as scuba diving off Miri.

**Tropical Adventure** (☎ 419337, fax 414553) Ground floor, Mega Hotel. Adventure caving tours to Mulu.

## Places to Stay – Budget

Miri has little in the way of budget accommodation. The cheaper places to stay are all near the markets at the southern end of town. They are handy if you are heading on to Niah Caves the next day, but most are noisy and seedy. If you can afford one, the mid-range hotels offer much better value for money.

The cheapest option is the dorm in the *Tai Tong Lodging House* (☎ 411498, 26 Jalan China), where bunk beds in the lobby cost RM10. Basic but clean singles/doubles are RM28/30 with fan and shared bathroom, or RM36/42 with air-con and attached toilet and shower. This place seems to have recently been cleaned up, though women travellers might still prefer a room to a dorm bed.

*Fairland Inn* (☎ 413898), on the square near Jalan Anatto, is quieter than the Tai Tong and probably a better choice. Small, clean air-con rooms with windows, bathroom and TV cost RM35. If you're stuck, the friendly *Kaya Inn* (☎ 438858) on Jalan China has bed-sized rooms for RM25/30.

## Places to Stay – Mid-Range

As is the case elsewhere in Sarawak, there's plenty of choice in mid-range hotels. All have attached bathrooms, air-con and carpet, and most provide a TV and IDD phone.

The best value in this range is probably the *Richmond Inn* (☎ 413289), on Jalan Setia Raja. Large, pleasant rooms in this friendly hotel are RM50, and larger rooms go for RM60 and RM70.

Across Jalan Brooke, the *Miri Hotel* (☎ 421212), at No 47, has clean, spacious single/doubles starting at RM57/69. For the extra ringgit this hotel is very good value and prices include cable TV. *Pacific Orient Hotel* (☎ 413333, 49 Jalan Brooke) is a step up in price at RM76/79, though rooms and

service are not as good as at the Miri. *Kingwood Inn* (☎ 415888, fax 415009, 826 Jalan Yu Seng Utara) is quiet and of a similar standard to the Miri Hotel. Rooms with twin beds and fridge are RM75; rooms with a double bed are RM90.

Two decent places are in the side streets off Jalan North Yu Seng Utara. Rooms at the *Classy Inn* (☎ 412533) are good value for RM50. *Metro Inn* (☎ 411663) has bright, airy rooms starting at RM55/58.

Farther down Jalan Yu Seng Selatan, *Million Inn* (☎ 415077, 6 Jalan Yu Seng Selatan) is nothing special, but the upstairs rooms are all right for RM48/55, and a lot quieter than the rooms downstairs.

## Places to Stay – Top End

During Miri's high times, big, modern hotels went up all over town. Some of these places are now looking decidedly shabby and neglected, and big discounts are a matter of course.

Miri's best hotel is the five-star *Rihga Royal Hotel* (☎ 421121, fax 421099 ✉ info@rihgamiri.com), on the beach about 4km south of the town centre. There's a beautiful swimming pool, gym, business centre, restaurants and coffee shops. Published rates range from RM270/305 for singles/doubles to RM414/448 for chalets, but discounts of up to 40% are likely.

Next door, *Holiday Inn Miri* (☎ 418888, fax 419999, ✉ himiri@po.jaring.my) looks tired, but it has an international-standard fitness centre and a Jacuzzi with swim-up bar. Promotional rates can make this hotel a good-value option: Weekday promo rates start at RM90++ or RM115++ with a sea view. The Holiday Inn has a free shuttle service into town.

In the northern part of town, the poshest and pinkest place is the four-star *Grand Palace Hotel* (☎ 428888, fax 427777, ✉ jrobson@pc.jaring.my, Km 2 Jalan Miri Pujut). Singles/doubles cost RM195/218 to RM253/276; suites are available, as are healthy discounts.

*Mega Hotel* (☎ 432432, fax 433433) dominates Miri's skyline and is right in the centre of town. In addition to its attached shopping mall and restaurant, the hotel has the standard swimming pool, Jacuzzi and business centre. Published rates start at RM240/280 for standard rooms and suites start at RM460.

## Places to Eat

There are plenty of good places to eat in Miri, especially in the blocks between Jalan Brooke and the waterfront, and there's something to suit every budget.

One of the best places in town is also one of the cheapest. *Ma Baker Eating House*, near the Imperial Mall, is a friendly place serving great Malay, Chinese and Western-style dishes in air-con comfort. The 'Western breakfast' here is excellent and only RM2.80, and there's a good hot-bread shop next door. The *Base Camp Cafe*, near Bintang Plaza, also serves Western-style breakfasts, plus steaks (RM12), salads and the usual noodle and rice dishes, all at very reasonable prices. Ma Bakers and the Base Camp are both closed on Monday.

Other cheap choices include a small *food centre* near the Tua Pek Kong temple, where you'll find the usual Malay and Chinese hawker stalls. There's also a small fruit and vegetable market. Inside this market, *Aseanika Restoran* does excellent roti and serves Indonesian food. Farther south-east, the *Tamu Muhibbah* has food stalls open during the day. Near the Mega Hotel, the friendly *Restoran Serai Wangi* serves delicious Malay meals.

*Cafe de Labuan* is a covered bar and food-stall zone, which is fine for lunch or a cheap evening meal and a beer.

*Bilal Restaurant* is one of the better Indian restaurants you'll find and it is very good value. It is on Jalan Persiaran Kabor, a pedestrian mall, and in the evenings tables are set up on the pavement. The curries, tandoori dishes and excellent roti are all recommended. The Chinese *kedai kopi* outside the Miri Hotel is a popular evening spot.

On Jalan Yu Seng Selatan there are quite a few more upmarket and fast food places. One of the best restaurants in Miri is the open-air *Apollo Seafood*, which serves superb Chinese food, steamboat and, of course, seafood. Prices are reasonable, but it can get packed.

The best seafood in Miri is probably at *Maxim Delicious Seafood*, 100m north of Bintang Plaza, though it's not cheap. Fresh fish in banana leaves is one of the specialities. In the same part of town near the Grand Palace Hotel, *Boulevard Seafood Restaurant* is also recommended.

*Everyday Vegetarian Food* on Jalan Royal looks after vegetarian tastes.

About 1.5km north of the centre is the *Miri Cafe*. In the evening this friendly open-air bar/restaurant serves a wide range of good, affordable Western-style meals, plus Chinese and Malay food. The beach-side *Taman Selera* food centre is 3km south of town (take bus No 11; 50 sen). It cranks up in the evening and is popular with locals.

For self-catering, the *Sin Liang Supermarket* serves the southern end of town, while the Bintang Plaza has a large *Tops* supermarket on the ground floor.

## Entertainment

During the oil industry's boom years, Miri had an extremely well lubricated nightlife. A scuzzy residue coats some of the remaining scene, but there are still places worth dropping into for a drink or a dance, or to catch a live band. As is the case elsewhere in Sarawak, things don't get going until around 11 pm. Most places charge no cover and beers usually cost around RM9.

Across from the Base Camp Cafe is *Chaplin's*. They don't make pubs like this any more – it's a classic expat bar. It's also a very friendly spot for a beer while you watch the footy on TV. Nearby *Cheery Berry's* is a pricier place featuring Filipino cover bands.

*The Ranch* is the best place for live bands, which start around 10.30 pm; it gets packed by midnight some nights. Beers here are a hurtful RM11.20, but worth it if a band like the Headliners is playing. Down the lane from The Ranch is the sometimes-rowdy *Labuan Pub*, which also has a popular disco upstairs.

*Clippers* is an English-style pub out at the Holiday Inn where techno music is played; it attracts many Miri locals on the weekends. *Rigs*, next door at the Rihga Royal, is a trendy spot, but drinks are very expensive. Also at the Rihga, *Flags Bar* has a happy hour between 5 and 9 pm, when drinks are two for the price of one.

The *Miri Port Club*, near the Rihga, looks a bit toffee-nosed, but beers are a working-class RM6. It's a great spot for dinner or a drink at sunset.

## Shopping

Miri has a few arts-and-crafts stores, but the range is pretty junky and nowhere near as good as in Kuching. The Imperial and Bintang shopping plazas have the best selection of handicraft shops.

The new shopping malls have stores selling every imaginable type of consumer good. Of interest to many travellers, PC software and computer games are incredibly cheap, and the most recent stuff is readily available. Music CDs and cassettes are also good value, but you'll have to wade through a lot of Chinese pop.

## Getting There & Away

**Air** The Malaysia Airlines office (☎ 411444) is behind the Mega Hotel on Jalan Yu Seng Selatan; the office is hopelessly crowded and you can probably get what you need at the efficient Harrisons travel agent (☎ 410339) next door. For flights in and out of Bario and Mulu, book as far in advance as possible – but note that there is a cancellation penalty on Mulu flights (at the time of writing, 25% of ticket price).

Malaysia Airlines has Twin Otter services to: Bario (daily except Wednesday and an extra flight Monday, RM70); Lawas (at least three daily, RM59); Limbang (at least two daily, RM45); Long Banga (three weekly, RM67); Long Lellang (weekly, RM66); Long Seridan (weekly, RM57); Marudi (two to six flights daily, RM29); Mukah (daily, RM55); and Mulu (twice daily, RM69).

Bigger aircraft fly to Bintulu (at least three daily, RM69), Kuching (at least five daily, RM164), Labuan (twice daily, RM66) and Sibu (four daily, RM112); there are also

cheaper Twin Otter services to Sibu twice a week (RM75).

There are Twin Otter flights to KK in Sabah (three weekly, RM82) and flights on larger aircraft (at least five daily, RM95).

**Bus** For the latest bus information, check the English-language newspapers or ask the Miri Visitors' Information Centre. The long-distance bus station is about 4km north of the centre along Jalan Miri Pujut; note that local buses also go to Lambir Hills and Niah Caves National Parks.

As well as the destinations listed here, there are a few services available on less-travelled routes, such as the long haul to Pontianak in Kalimantan.

Buses to Kuala Baram and the crossing to Brunei depart from the local bus station at the southern end of the town centre.

Major bus companies serving Miri include Syarikat Bas Suria (☎ 430416, 434317), PB Ekspres (☎ 435816) and Dalat-Miri Bas Ekspres (☎ 424101).

***Bintulu, Batu Niah & Lambir Hills*** There are express-bus services daily to Bintulu, roughly every hour between 6 am and 8.30 pm (about 4½ hours, RM16.80/18 non-air-con/air-con).

Syarikat Bas Suria has buses to Lambir Hills (45 minutes, RM2.40) and Batu Niah (two hours, RM8.50), leaving hourly from around 6.30 am to 4 pm from the bus shelter on Jalan Padang (over the road from the local bus station).

***Mukah*** Syarikat Bas Suria has a bus from Miri to Mukah at 7.30 am; it returns from Mukah at 8.30 am.

***Sibu*** Among other bus companies, Syarikat Bas Suria travels to Sibu six times daily between 7 am and 9 pm, and on Sunday at 5.30 pm (about eight hours, RM34).

***Kuching*** The trip to Kuching is a long haul that can be done direct (15 to 16 hours, RM70). The major companies each have a couple of daily buses from Miri; at the time of writing departures were at 7, 8.30 and 11.30 am, and 3 and 9 pm.

**Marudi** The Belait Transport Company has buses to Kuala Baram every half-hour between 5.30 am and 9.30 pm (about one hour, RM2.50). From Kuala Baram, express boats to Marudi (three hours, RM18) leave from about 7 am to 3 pm; services are frequent until around 10 am.

**Brunei** It's a convoluted bus journey from Miri to Bandar Seri Begawan, Brunei's capital.

Belait Transport Company plies the route between Miri and Kuala Belait, the first leg of the trip, and has its office at the local bus station. Five services daily run to Kuala Belait between 7 am and 3.30 pm (2½ hours, RM12.20).

There's a river crossing at Kuala Baram, where vehicles often have to queue for the ferry; passengers can wait by the edge of the river, leaving their bags on the bus. The Malaysian immigration checkpoint is just across the river. After clearing immigration you reboard the bus for the two-minute ride to the Brunei immigration checkpoint. Here you must take all your belongings with you through passport control and customs.

A Brunei bus will then take you to the Sungai Belait for another ferry crossing. The queues here are often horrendous and can last for hours; the driver and passengers leave the bus on one side, cross on the ferry (free), then board a bus on the other side of the river for Kuala Belait.

At Kuala Belait bus station you can change to a connecting bus to Seria. Start your journey early to avoid having to spend the night in Kuala Belait, where accommodation is expensive. If you need to change money, there's a branch of the HSBC (Hongkong Bank) opposite the Kuala Belait bus station.

From Seria, you must take another bus to Bandar Seri Begawan. See the Seria section in the Brunei chapter for details.

### Getting Around
The Miri Visitors' Information Centre hands out a handy schedule of local buses, printed on the back of the town map.

For the long-distance bus station, bus No A1 leaves regularly from the local bus station next to the Visitors' Information Centre (50 sen).

Bus No 28 runs between the local bus station and the airport every 70 minutes from 6.10 am to 7 pm (20 minutes, RM1). Heading into town, the airport bus stop is to the left of the terminal as you exit.

Taxis from the airport run on a coupon system; a cab to a central hotel costs RM14. Other destinations are by negotiation – a taxi from the city centre to the long-distance bus station should be RM10. A taxi between Miri and Kuala Baram costs RM20.

## LOAGAN BUNUT NATIONAL PARK
This little-visited park in the Miri hinterland covers 10.7 sq km and protects the largest natural freshwater lake in Sarawak – although at 650 hectares it's not exactly huge. The surrounding forest hosts breeding colonies of **water birds** such as darters, herons and egrets. Local Berawans practise a unique form of fishing that has enabled them to keep the lake stocked with fish even during times of drought.

For keen wildlife-watchers, or those trying to get off the tourist trail, Loagan Bunut is an interesting trip. Access is difficult and there are no visitors' facilities in the park, but there is a nearby hostel with basic fan-cooled rooms. The hostel has cooking facilities and fresh water, but you must bring your own supplies.

### Getting There & Away
Most travellers visit the park as a day trip with a tour. If you want to visit independently, you'll be better off in a group since expensive river travel is involved. From the local bus station in Miri, take a bus to Tinjar or Lapok (2½ hours, RM8.50), from where you'll have to charter a car or Land Cruiser to Logan Pengkalan, and from there a boat to the park. Contact the Parks & Wildlife office (☎ 085-434184) in Miri for the current prospects of getting there this way.

## MARUDI
☎ 085
Marudi is upriver from Miri. Its main attraction is yet another of the Brooke outposts,

MALAYSIAN BORNEO

**Fort Hose**, which doubles as a fine local museum. Fort Hose is on a low hill at the eastern end of town. A small, colourful **Chinese temple** is conveniently located next to the main brothel (!) in front of the wharf.

Marudi sits on the north bank of the Batang Baram, and the main street, Jalan Cinema, is aligned roughly east–west. It's a small town and most places to stay and eat are within a block or two of the main street. A square runs from Jalan Cinema down to the river and all boats moor at the adjacent jetty.

If you've come into contact with leeches in Bario or Mulu, the interest you arouse in Marudi's idle street youth will seem quite familiar. The area around the Zolo Hotel is known for its evening rowdiness, but Marudi is basically a friendly town where people will go out of their way to help travellers.

Although the forest between Marudi and Kuala Baram on the South China Sea has long since been demolished, travel beyond Marudi to upriver longhouses is still quite pleasant and rewarding – at least once you get to Long Lama. Locals in Marudi can help arrange a visit – the longhouses are welcoming if you're expected.

There is a road network around Marudi and you can visit **longhouses** at Long Selaban and Long Moh. You can travel much farther afield, though you'll have to arrange a lift locally.

### Places to Stay & Eat

Marudi's cheap hotels are pretty grotty and sleep tends to be low on the list of guests' priorities, but there are a number of inexpensive options on the main street. *Mayland (☎ 755106)*, at the western end of the main street, has fairly shabby, air-con rooms with bathroom starting at RM30. *Hotel Zola (☎ 755311)*, on Jalan Cinema, has better air-con rooms with TV for RM30 to RM50. Be warned: The area out the front of the hotel can get a bit rowdy at night.

At the popular one-star *Mount Mulu Hotel (☎ 756671)*, one block north of the main street, clean air-con rooms are RM45; this is probably the best value in town. *Grand Hotel (☎ 755711)*, at Marudi Bazaar, is two blocks north of Jalan Cinema and was once Marudi's grandest accommodation. Spacious air-con rooms have TV and video; cheaper rooms start at RM42 and bigger rooms with bathroom are RM65.

There are plenty of *kedai kopi* around the square and along the main street at the western end of town. There's more-expensive fare to be had at the *Grand Hotel* restaurant.

### Getting There & Away

**Air** The Malaysia Airlines agent is Tan Yong Sing (☎ 755480), next to the Grand Hotel. The airline operates Twin Otter flights to Bario (daily, RM55); Long Banga (twice weekly, RM59); Long Lellang (weekly, RM46); Long Seridan (weekly, RM42); and Miri (two to six daily, RM29).

Flights are often full – especially to Bario – and it's advisable to book ahead. However, space often becomes available at the last minute, so it's worth rolling up to the airport just in case. The airport is a 10-minute walk (1km) from the centre of town.

**Boat** The express boats from Marudi to Kuala Baram operate roughly every hour between 8.30 am and 3 pm (2½ hours, RM18).

Heading upriver from Marudi, express boats to Kuala Apoh and Long Terawan (depending on the water level) leave when they have enough passengers (3½ hours, RM20). Daily express boats to Long Lama cost RM18; check at the wharf for departure times.

Time and frequency of travel beyond Long Lama depends on the river's water level.

### BATANG BARAM

The Batang Baram is north-east Sarawak's main artery. From Marudi this massive river runs deep into the interior through Kayan and Kenyah territory, and via its Dapur tributary continues right up into the Kelabit Highlands around Bario. Its upper reaches are home to the Penan, the seminomadic hunter-gatherers who have become symbolic of a disappearing way of life for the indigenous Dayak tribespeople of Sarawak.

The Baram region is one of the major remaining areas of primary forest in Borneo, and one of the most heavily logged. The north-east has long been the centre of dispute between the government, logging companies and local tribes.

Logging roads in the Baram catchment have been blockaded many times in the past, and activists, including tribespeople, have been arrested. These days barricades are less common than briefs brought to the courts; in fact, the main problem for travellers – and locals – is the illegal logging operators, who are not always happy to see strangers. You may be turned back from certain routes, especially where fresh logging roads are being cut.

A permit is required to travel upriver of Marudi. You can get one at the Pejabat Residen in Miri (see Orientation & Information in the Miri section earlier). If you have plenty of time and money, and want to experience a remote longhouse, exploring this region can be worthwhile. Travel agents in Miri can arrange tours along the Baram. Be warned, though, that much of the forest has been devastated and it's not a pleasant sight.

### Getting There & Away

Doing it alone is not particularly easy or cheap. Express boats go from Marudi as far as Long Lama, and from there it is possible to go by regular boat to Long Miri. From Long Miri travel is by smaller longboat, which must be chartered (at least RM150 per day, plus fuel). It's a full day's travel by boat to Long Akah, and then a day or more to Long Matoh.

The alternative is by road, which involves expensive 4WD hire. From the main highway south of Miri it is possible to go by a good logging road to Long Miri and all the way to Long Akah. This road is being pushed farther into the jungle towards Long Lellang and beyond.

## GUNUNG MULU NATIONAL PARK

☎ 085

Gunung Mulu is the most heavily promoted of Sarawak's national parks and it is one of the most popular destinations in the state. The park is an unspoilt wilderness offering caving, trekking and wildlife. It can be enjoyed simply for its beauty or as a challenge that even experienced outdoors enthusiasts will relish.

At 529 sq km, Gunung Mulu is also Sarawak's largest national park. Among its remarkable features is the fact that two mountain ranges, one of sandstone and one of limestone, abut within its boundaries. The sandstone peaks rise to 2377m-high Gunung Mulu, and limestone Gunung Api reaches 1750m. In between are more rugged mountains, deep gorges with clear rivers, and a unique mosaic of habitats supporting fascinating and diverse wildlife. Beneath the ground is a network of underground passages, stretching some 51km. A few years ago cave explorers here discovered the largest chamber in the world, the Sarawak Chamber.

Keen cavers will get their money's worth at Mulu, but many travellers will want more reasons for making the trip to the park. Mulu's most famous attractions are the Pinnacles – a forest of razor-sharp limestone peaks towering 45m above the rainforest – and the so-called Headhunters' Trail, which follows an old tribal war path. See the Trekking in Sarawak special section for details on treks in the park.

Access to the park is, in principle, simple. In reality, you're at the mercy of Malaysia Airlines' woeful service to this major tourist destination. Expect to wait several days to a week to be confirmed on one of the 18-seater Twin Otter flights. Even though the plane may be half-empty when you board, flights are heavily booked. However, cancellations are common despite the penalty charged. You can probably get to Mulu easily enough on standby, but getting back out this way might mean a few extra days at the park.

Transport hassles are one reason many travellers resort to tours, even though Mulu is easily explored without a prearranged package. The other reason is cost: Trekking independently can be prohibitively expensive unless you're with a group, and if you

MALAYSIAN BORNEO

aren't on a tour, boat fees around the park amount to longboat robbery. Reportedly, some trekkers have also been charged high fees to use facilities (such as stoves) on trails that are supposed to be free of charge.

## Permits & Bookings

When you get to the park office, a park permit will be issued and you'll be allocated a room or bed; see Places to Stay & Eat later in this section for more information. Here you must also pay the RM3 park entry fee, plus the standard camera and video fee.

Accommodation bookings can be made at the Visitors' Information Centre (☎ 085-434184) in Miri. You can simply turn up at the park office and book, but it's a popular spot and you run the risk of finding all accommodation booked out. There is accommodation outside the park, but it's expensive or else run by tour companies, and also may be full.

## Hiring Guides

A visit to Mulu can be expensive if you go trekking or visit some of the more-remote parts by boat, but the only compulsory fees are for the Show Caves. Although in reality an 'entry charge', these are called 'guide fees' – the chances of actually spotting a park guide in the wild are remote (the guides at the caves are usually from private tour companies). In any case, a guide is unnecessary, as the caves are well lit and you can't get lost.

The park office handles all bookings and fees for guides, and can also arrange transport. On arrival, some boat operators will offer to arrange a cave tour for you on the spot. Avoid them if you are looking for a group to join – transport and a guide can be arranged at any time at the park office.

The cost for trekking guides depends on the distance covered and the number of people trekking – the park office has a schedule of fees. For example, for a group of five trekking to the Pinnacles over three days and two nights a guide will cost RM110; and to the summit of Gunung Mulu RM264. There's an additional fee of RM8 per night at Camps 3, 4 and 5. Bigger

groups bring down the cost for each individual, but if a group is too large you'll see less wildlife along the way.

Boat hire is by negotiation, but costs are extremely high: from RM85 for Clearwater Cave to RM250 for the Pinnacles trek (see the 'Trekking in Sarawak' special section). If you want to visit all the caves and do a lot of trekking, an organised tour starts to look cost effective. Most travel agents charge around RM350 for four days and three nights and RM500 for six days and five nights. This includes a visit to all the caves, a trek, all transfers and accommodation. Packages that include accommodation at Royal Mulu Resort cost a whole lot more.

The reason given for the high boat costs is that propellers get broken when the water is low, and besides this, fuel has to be flown in. True, but on every short trip to Clearwater Cave boatmen are nearly covering the cost of a new propeller (RM175). Boatmen have reportedly been stiffed by some tour companies for fees, so perhaps independent travellers are paying part of the price. Whatever the case, the prohibitive fees are unfortunate because by the time you've made the trek to the caves and looked around, you'd probably rather not have to do the slippery boardwalk one more time. It's also a pleasant ride down the river.

## Show Caves

The Deer, Lang, Clearwater and Wind Caves are all known as the Show Caves, and are easily accessible to visitors. Other caves are closed to the public because they are inaccessible or considered dangerous, while others contain fragile formations that park authorities want to protect from further deterioration.

Due to the availability of power for lighting, the Clearwater and Wind Caves are officially open only in the morning and the Deer and Lang Caves only in the afternoon. Power failures are not uncommon, but natural light to some extent illuminates much of the Clearwater and Wind Caves in particular.

A 'guide fee' of RM18 gives access to the Deer and Lang Caves or to the Clearwater and Wind Caves.

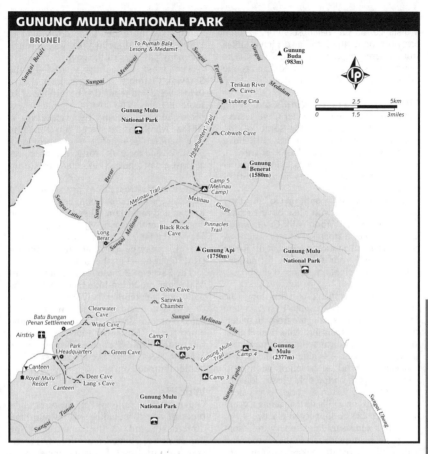

## GUNUNG MULU NATIONAL PARK

BRUNEI

To Rumah Bala
Lesong & Medamit

Sungai Belait

Sungai Mentawai

Sungai

Sungai Terikan

Sungai

Gunung
Buda
(983m)

Medalam

Terikan River
Caves

Lubang Cina

Gunung Mulu
National Park

Headhunters' Trail

Cobweb Cave

Gunung
Benerat
(1580m)

Sungai Berat

Sungai

Melinau Trail

Camp 5
(Melinau
Camp)

Melinau

Gorge

Sungai Lutut

Sungai Melinau

Black Rock
Cave

Pinnacles
Trail

Long Berar

Gunung Api
(1750m)

Gunung Mulu
National Park

Cobra Cave

Sarawak
Chamber

Clearwater
Cave

Sungai

Melinau

Paku

Batu Bungan
(Penan Settlement)

Wind Cave

Airstrip

Camp 1

Park
Headquarters

Green Cave

Camp 2

Gunung Mulu Trail

Camp 4

Gunung
Mulu
(2377m)

Canteen

Royal Mulu
Resort

Canteen

Deer Cave
Lang's Cave

Camp 3

Sungai Tapin

Gunung Mulu
National Park

Sungai Tanoil

Sungai

Sungai Ubong

0    2.5    5km
0    1.5    3miles

MALAYSIAN BORNEO

**Deer Cave & Lang's Cave** Deer Cave and adjoining Lang's Cave are the closest caves to the park headquarters, an easy 3km walk along a boardwalk. At 2160m long and 220m deep, they have the world's largest cave passage. Both are very safe, with walkways and wooden steps where necessary.

Lang's Cave is lit each afternoon until 4 pm, though a strong torch is still useful for the darker areas. There are pretty **stalagmites and stalactites** and some other strange formations. Water cascades from openings in the roof after heavy rain. You enter the cave on one side of the mountain

and exit from the other; it takes about 30 minutes to walk the entire length.

Deer Cave is a gaping cavern in the mountainside, huge beyond comprehension. It doesn't have the attractive formations of Lang's Cave, but you will wander through with mouth agape until you're assaulted by the stink of ammonia from the piles of guano on the floor. Look up and you'll see the cause – some two million **free-tailed bats** clinging to a roof so distant that they appear as a seething black mass. The bats emerge from the cave entrance between 5 and 6 pm each night in a vast chittering stream that can last for half an hour. They can be seen from quite a distance, and a 'bat observatory' station has been built; there are also picnic tables from where you can get a great view. The swarm is a sight not to be missed and is one of the wildlife highlights of Mulu.

**Clearwater Cave & Wind Cave** Wind Cave is part of the Clearwater Cave system and the starting point for some of the longest tunnels. It opens out in a cliff above the Sungai Melinau and has a boardwalk and stair system that does a loop around some impressive caverns and beautiful limestone formations.

It's not marked on park maps, but to get to the Wind Cave you first have to pass through the small **Moon Milk Cave**, which is at the top of a steep set of stone steps. A good torch and caution are essential: Roots snake around your feet, rock formations hang at head height and parts of the boardwalk are rotten.

The Clearwater Cave is 51km long (the longest cave passage in South-East Asia) and 355m deep. It takes its name from an underground river that spills through a natural grate to form a crystal-clear **swimming pool** near the cave entrance. A bridge over the river is reached by the path on the left of the cave entrance. The path on the right passes some of the cave's finer features. Access is via steep concrete steps up a hillside then along a walkway, which can be slippery in places.

There's a pleasant but slippery trail from the park headquarters to the Wind and Clearwater Caves that takes about an hour to walk, and which follows the Sungai Melinau for part of the way. The walk from the Wind Cave to Clearwater Cave takes about 15 minutes.

**Adventure Caving** There are plenty of other caves in the park, and new caves are regularly discovered. It is estimated that the number already explored represents only about 40% of the total number of caves in Gunung Mulu National Park.

It is possible to explore the nooks and crannies of the Show Caves away from the pedestrian boardwalks, and a few other caves are open to experienced cavers. Adventure caving expeditions allow you to crawl, climb and swim your way through the many passages of the caves.

The most frequently visited is the **Sarawak Chamber**, the largest known cave in the world and reputed to be the size of 16 football fields. The cost of a guide to explore the chamber and two side caves is RM88, which can be shared between up to five people. Equipment is not provided, however, and the park headquarters requires at least a day's notice before any trip.

**Other Activities** Prices are what you'd expect at a resort, but nonguests can hire **kayaks** and **mountain bikes** (RM25 for the first hour) at the Royal Mulu (see Places to Stay & Eat later). There are some good biking trails near the resort, and **rock climbing** (RM36 per hour) on the premises.

The **Battle of Borneo** is the mother of all Malaysian mountain-bike races, held in the park each September. Anyone is welcome to join, and events include raft races and runs. For the Battle of Borneo race, the entry fee is RM200 per four-person team. For more details, contact organisers in Miri (☎ 085-419337, fax 414503, @ info@ battleofborneo.com).

### Wildlife

Gunung Mulu National Park features eight types of forest, including peat swamp, tall dipterocarp and, at the summits of the higher peaks, stunted moss forest. Thousands of species of plants have been recorded here, and each new scientific expedition finds new species. Among the finds are over 170 species of orchid and 10 species of pitcher plant.

A staggering 275 species of birds have been recorded at Mulu (the highest number so far in Sarawak), as well as 75 species of mammals, 74 of frogs, 281 species of butterflies and – while we're counting – 458 species of ants. Mulu is part of traditional Penan hunting grounds and the tribe is still allowed to hunt in the park. Fear not: You won't encounter the business end of a blowpipe on your travels – tourism has made larger birds and mammals scarce near trails.

Around the park headquarters you'll see a few common species of birds, such as bulbuls and sunbirds, but look out for the white-fronted falconet – the world's smallest bird of prey and only slightly larger than a sparrow. The walks to the Show Caves can be very good for spotting birds, particularly in the early morning. At the caves themselves you'll see plenty of swiftlets nesting on the cave walls, as well as a selection of birds of prey that pick off the bats as they come pouring out in the evenings. Along the rivers you can see the stork-billed kingfisher, with its massive red bill; and the amazing black-and-red broadbill – a clownish-looking bird with a fat blue bill.

With the exception of bats, most of Mulu's mammals are shy and difficult to see, although you'll probably encounter squirrels along the trails. Look out for the pygmy squirrel along the boardwalks, and the striking Prevost's squirrel in the trees.

So long as it's not raining you'll see an incredible variety of butterflies along the trails. When it is raining you can expect lots of leeches (but not many different species), and they'll be very glad to see you. See the boxed text 'That Clinging Feeling' in the Sabah chapter for hints on letting them know their affections are not welcome.

## Batu Bungan Penan Settlement

The Gunung Mulu region is mainly home to the Berawan people, but the government has settled a Penan group on the banks of the Sungai Melinau as part of its campaign to 'civilise' these nomads.

There are actually two Penan settlements at Mulu: Long Iman is well south of the park headquarters along the Sungai Tutoh and is not open to tourists without an invitation; Batu Bungan is a stark reminder of the consequences of 'modernisation' for people who never asked for its blessings in the first place.

In fact, Batu Bungan has never been blessed. A fire a few years ago destroyed the original ramshackle longhouse. The government dumped lumber on the site, but the Penan aren't carpenters and have since been left by their benefactors – public and private – to 'show some initiative' and take a keen interest in properly rebuilding their alien home.

The patchwork housing at Batu Bungan can be seen through the trees across the river as you walk to the Clearwater Cave. Boats carrying tour groups drop by the small market where women set up on the riverbank at around 9 am. You're welcome to stop and look at the fine **rattan weaving** on sale (the plain, dark-coloured bracelets are worn by the Penan in the jungle; the more colourful, patterned bracelets are for tourist trade), but the rest of the village is private housing.

The Penan are highly regarded by Borneo tribes as 'the true people of the forest'. They are a shy people, even when dealing with other tribes, so if you visit the market, folks will be more at ease if you speak softly, move slowly and avoid large, sudden gestures. Hardly any English is spoken here, but there will probably be a tour guide around in the mornings to help with translations.

A large primary school serving the two Penan settlements has been built nearby, and you'll probably hear the children before you see them. The settlement can also be reached by a path leading towards the river from the airport – take a left on the boardwalk and then the first right to reach the river.

## Places to Stay & Eat

Given Mulu's popularity and the preference for tour groups, it can sometimes be difficult to book a place to stay, but private accommodation is available outside the park. Note that there are no cooking facilities at the park, though you can boil water and make toast at the hostel.

The standard of accommodation at the park is very good. There's a roomy 15-bed *hostel* and an 18-bed *annexe* for RM10. A three-person room in the *resthouse* is RM75. *Chalets* start at RM60 per four-person room, rising to RM90 for three people in the *VIP chalet*.

There are two places to eat near the park headquarters: a *cafeteria* with a pool table, inside the park just along from the hostel;

MALAYSIAN BORNEO

and a *canteen* across the river from the park headquarters, at the end of the suspension bridge. Each is open from 8 am to around 9 pm (though the cafeteria inside the park often closes earlier); cheap and simple meals, soft drinks and beer are available at both. The canteen sells bottled water (RM3/6 for small/large bottles). It has a deck over the river and is a pleasant place for a meal. Western-style breakfasts cost RM10, and while service can be slow, portions are usually large when they arrive.

The ***Royal Mulu Resort*** (☎ 790100, fax 790101, ✉ rihgas1@po.jaring.my) is a luxury hotel complex about 3km from the park entrance. It is tastefully built around limestone bluffs overlooking the river, with nicely appointed rooms and a garden full of flowers, butterflies and birds. It has a swimming pool, and the friendly Berawan staff will help arrange outdoor activities. Published room rates for travellers not on tours are RM241 to RM287, and suites cost RM575 to RM2300. These prices usually include breakfast, and discounts are often available. The resort has a useful Web site at www.rihgamulu.com.

The resort's *coffee shop/restaurant* is expensive and has a Club Med air about it on busy nights; the food is all right, but it's not worth a special trip from the park unless you're dying for fish and chips.

The *canteen* just across the river from the Royal Mulu Resort is a good place to buy basic noodle and rice dishes as well as soft drinks. It's also a good spot for an evening beer; if you're staying at the resort, the short walk will save you lots of money.

## Getting There & Away
The only practical way in and out of this popular park is currently via Miri, and the vast majority of travellers make the trip on one of the overbooked 18-seater planes. Book as far in advance as possible.

**Air** Malaysia Airlines has Twin Otter flights between Mulu and Miri twice a day (RM69), though cancellations due to weather are not uncommon. Upon request the pilot will fly in low between the peaks before circling back to land – a breathtaking experience.

**Bus & Boat** It is possible – but difficult, time consuming and no cheaper – to get to Mulu by a combination of bus and boat. From Miri take a local bus to Kuala Baram (RM2.20). Buses leave regularly, but if you want to get to the park in one day, take the 6 am bus; alternatively, stay in Marudi overnight.

From Kuala Baram there are express boats to Marudi (8.30 am to 3 pm, three hours, RM18). Launches go from Marudi to Long Terawan when there are enough passengers (RM20). If the water is high enough they go all the way through; if not, change boats at Long Apoh.

Travel from Long Terawan to the national park is by charter boat. Long Terawan does not welcome drop-in overnight guests, so pre-arrange a boat to Mulu. Ask around in Marudi before you set off; the park headquarters at Mulu has set the boat fee at RM150 for up to five people, or RM35 each for six or more passengers, but you may have to pay more, especially on short notice. The journey takes around two hours.

It's easier to arrange a Long Terawan boat from Mulu (ask at park headquarters or at the canteens) and it's easier to fly into Mulu than back out, so it makes sense to do the river trip on the way out of the park. You need to be up at 4 am to get the boat to Long Terawan in time to connect with the express boat to Marudi. The Mulu-Miri run will take eight to 10 hours.

If you're up for the time and effort (as well as the ringgit), the river ride is a unique experience, and a great alternative to flying both ways.

## Getting Around
The park headquarters is a 3km walk from the airport along the road to Royal Mulu Resort; the park turn-off is on the left, about 10 minutes' walk from the airport. Minivans run between the airport and headquarters, but there's no regular service. You can cadge a lift with one of the resort vans (about RM2).

*(Continued on page 453)*

# TREKKING IN SARAWAK

Sarawak offers a range of jungle trekking options for the fit and adventurous, as well as more-gentle ambles for those who don't aspire to superhuman status. Remember, this is hiking through rainforest in hot, humid and sometimes wet conditions, so it's exhausting and you'll probably have leeches for company. But the rewards are valuable if you persist – you'll see superb rainforest and alpine plateaus in the Kelabit Highlands, stone forests and jagged peaks in Gunung (Mt) Mulu National Park, and have the opportunity to visit fascinating longhouses.

## PLANNING
### When to Go

Although the wettest months in Sarawak are from October to March, the timing of monsoon seasons has been less consistent in recent years. Sarawak has high rainfall year-round and you should be prepared for heavy rain on one or more days of your stay. Flights in and out of Gunung Mulu and Bario will be cancelled if the weather is poor, so be prepared to be stranded for a couple of days on the return trip.

### What to Bring

There are no special equipment requirements to enjoy walking in the region, but it can get cold at night and rain for days on end – take a waterproof jacket. Good running shoes are preferable to stiff, heavy walking boots, and a pair of thongs (flip-flops) is useful for going in and out of longhouses. Wear light cotton clothing and carry a light pullover and trousers for the evenings. If camping or staying in a longhouse, you will need a sleeping bag or blankets.

Leeches will keep you company on many walks – see the boxed text 'That Clinging Feeling' in the Sabah chapter for advice on what to bring and how to deal with them.

If you're sleeping in the jungle, a camping poncho is a definite asset. This is a light-weight sheet of tough material that is large enough for you cocoon yourself in at night yet still breathe. It's perfect for keeping the creepy-crawlies (especially leeches) out. A good poncho costs about RM50 and should be available at camping supply shops in Miri and Kuching.

Most of your load's weight will be water. Take a good canteen – plastic bottles are a nuisance to carry. Remember to drink a lot to replace the fluids you lose sweating. It's also generally safe to drink water from streams (upstream from the longhouse, of course); ask your guide for advice. A good torch (flashlight) is a must at night; insect repellent and sunscreen will also be useful. For other tips on getting prepared, see the 'Considerations for Jungle Trekking' boxed text in the Malaysia Facts for the Visitor chapter.

## Tips for Walks & Treks

Longhouse visits are one of the main experiences travellers look for in Sarawak. Guides in Bario will often take tourists on a walk to a long-house, which is interesting but often not very satisfying. There is usually a language barrier to overcome, and no-one but a few old folks may be around, as the younger crew are off in the fields. But the basic issue is establishing some common ground with whomever you encounter. If you've been on a jungle walk, your guide has pointed out some features of the forest and you've picked off a few leeches, you'll find even hand-gesture conversations can go well beyond 'Where are you from?'.

The jungle has a lot to teach, and even a day or two with an experienced guide yields lots of useful local knowledge. Don't be afraid to ask your guide to point out plants and other features along your way. You may learn that those nasty-looking red ants are really good for septic wounds, or learn to find a fern that is a valuable diarrhoea-stopper; there's even a tree sap that is an unfailing, waterproof fire-starter.

A good guide should have the ability to gauge your abilities and the confidence to push you a little, rather than taking the easiest way as a matter of course. The elevation in the Kelabit Highlands means it's a pleasant temperature, and whether you're on a half-day walk or a five-day hike, you'll probably find you can always go a little further than you thought.

In fact many people find that they get stronger the longer they stay in the jungle, and if you've done a night walk in the rain-forest (highly recommended!), trails that previously seemed treacherous will be that much easier. When crossing those slippery log bridges, trying taking off your shoes and doing it in socks – you'll get a much better grip (bare feet are as slippery as shoes).

## Responsible Trekking

Remember the golden rule of garbage: if you carried it in, you can – and should – carry it out. Don't overlook those easily forgotten or in-convenient items, such as silver paper, plastic wrapping, water bottles, sanitary napkins and so forth. Never bury your rubbish – it may be out of sight, but it won't be out of reach of animals.

Where there is a toilet, please use it. Where there is none, bury your waste. Dig a small hole 15cm deep and at least 100m from any watercourse. Consider carrying a lightweight trowel for this purpose. Cover the waste with soil and a rock. Use toilet paper sparingly and bury it as well. If the area is inhabited, ask locals if they have any concerns about your chosen toilet site.

The indigenous Penan people are allowed to hunt in Gunung Mulu; otherwise, hunting is illegal for everyone in national parks and reserves.

Clearwater Cave, Gunung Mulu National Park, Sarawak

Deer Cave, Gunung Mulu National Park

The Pinnacles, Gunung Mulu National Park

Climbing to the Pinnacles, jungle style.

Splendor beneath the surface, Gunung Mulu National Park, Sarawak.

Deer Cave, Gunung Mulu National Park

Guide on the river, Gunung Mulu National Park.

# GUNUNG MULU NATIONAL PARK

Gunung Mulu National Park offers excellent jungle trekking for the fit and determined. There are three main treks in Mulu – the Gunung Mulu Trail, the Pinnacles Trail and the Headhunters' Trail. An attempt at any of them will involve some expense and it's best to go with a group to reduce the cost of transport and guide. Ask around when you get to park headquarters to see if anyone's interested in sharing costs.

You should not attempt any of the following trails without a guide – and you won't be permitted to anyway. Expect rain, leeches, slippery and treacherous conditions, and a very hot workout – carry lots of water. Your guide should let you go at your own pace. Many who attempt the Pinnacles or Gunung Mulu don't make it to the top. Guides can be arranged at the park headquarters.

## TREKS
### The Pinnacles
The Pinnacles is an incredible stone forest towering 45m high, halfway up the side of Gunung Api. Getting to the Pinnacles involves travel by boat and a tough three-day trek.

The trek to the Pinnacles starts with a two- or three-hour boat trip (depending on the level of the river) from park headquarters to Long Berar. From here it is an 8km trek to Camp 5 by the Sungai (River) Melinau. Camp 5 is hostel-style accommodation with running water, cold showers, a cooking area, 'American' toilet and covered sleeping quarters. Sleep overnight at this picturesque spot before climbing Gunung Api.

You'll have to climb virtually the whole distance to see the Pinnacles – there's no easy way out. The three- to four-hour ascent is very steep and slippery in parts. It's best to start early in the morning, when it's a lot cooler and you're more likely to see wildlife. The ultimate destination is a small viewing point looking out over the Pinnacles. It is possible to camp here, but the Pinnacles trip is usually done in one day and most trekkers return to Camp 5. If you start at sunrise it's possible to continue back to park headquarters.

From Camp 5 you can walk north to Lubang Cina on the Sungai Terikan. From this river it is possible to continue right down to Limbang on the coast via the Sungai Medalam, though this journey is usually done in reverse.

Guides' fees are RM110 for a three-day/two-night trek; each extra day costs RM20 plus RM10 allowance per night. The rate for boat hire to Long Berar from park headquarters is RM350 return for one to four people, or RM85 per person for five or more. One way costs RM200 for up to four people, or RM45 per person for five or more.

### Gunung Mulu Trail
The climb to the summit is normally done as a four-day trek and is the highlight of many a traveller's visit to Mulu. You must carry enough

food for the entire trip, as well as your own cooking utensils and a sleeping bag (it gets quite cold at night). It's not unusual for it to rain every day, so you could find yourself wallowing in mud along the way. Good walking shoes are a must.

**Camps** There are several camps (basic wooden huts) along the trail; Camps 1, 3 and 4 are the ones usually used for overnight stops. The most common schedule involves an easy first day (about three or four hours' walking) and overnight at Camp 1 beside a beautiful river. On day two you're faced with a long (four or five hours), hard and extremely steep climb to Camp 4. If it hasn't rained, there won't be any water at Camp 4, so carry some up from Camp 3.

On day three leave your pack at Camp 4 and climb to the summit of Gunung Mulu. You can either sleep at Camp 3 another night and return to park headquarters on day four, or descend the mountain in one day. The latter is quite tough on the legs, but you can cool down in the river along the way.

If you are reasonably fit and healthy, the return trip to Gunung Mulu can be done in three days, which evens out the exertion. If you leave park headquarters at dawn or earlier, you can reach Camp 3 in one long day and sleep there. See the Gunung Mulu National Park section in the Sarawak chapter for details on how to arrange accommodation.

## Headhunters' Trail

The Headhunters' Trail is a backdoor route from Gunung Mulu to Limbang and can be done in either direction, although most organised trips start in the national park. This trail is named after the Kayan war parties that used to make their way up the Sungai Melinau from the Baram area to the Melinau Gorge, then drag their canoes overland to the Sungai Terikan to raid the peoples of the Limbang region. A 3m-wide road lined with poles was used to move the canoes, and a canal was dug around Batu Rikan.

To do the Headhunters' Trail independently you should gather a group together to share costs, and ask around for a guide at park headquarters. The usual procedure is to take a boat to Long Berar (RM250), walk to Camp 5 (about four hours) and overnight there (RM8 per person) on the first day. Day two involves an 11km walk to the Sungai Terikan (four or five hours), where you can spend the night at the rangers' station (Mentawai) or proceed to Rumah Bala Lesong, an Iban longhouse another three or four hours away. After overnighting in the longhouse, it's a boat trip farther downriver to Medamit, from where it is possible to travel by minibus to Limbang.

The boat from the Sungai Terikan to Medamit should cost about RM500; the guide's fee will come to about RM230; a suitable payment for food and lodging at the longhouse will be about RM20; and the minibus from Medamit to Limbang costs RM5. Extra costs include food for the stay at Camp 5, gifts for the longhouse and a tip for your guide if you feel it is warranted.

You could do the Pinnacles trek, return to Camp 5 then set off on the Headhunters' Trail the following day. This trip is equally possible in the opposite direction – take a bus to Medamit, where a boat can be arranged to the longhouse or the ranger's station at Mentawai.

# BARIO & THE KELABIT HIGHLANDS

Bario is ringed by forested hills, and a network of basic roads and tracks offer some great trekking options. There are plenty of possibilities for easy walks to nearby longhouses, longer hikes into Kalimantan and tough treks to the spectacular peaks guarding the Kelabit Highlands.

Of the longhouses close to town, you can walk south-east to Pa Umor (about one hour) and nearby Pa Ukat. The trail then continues to Pa Lungan. There's a Kelabit burial ground close to the centre of town on the way to Pa Ramapuh, a village in Bario about a 1½-hour walk away. There is a waterfall about an hour beyond Pa Ramapuh. Another day-walk is to Pa Berang, a Penan settlement three hours from Bario. Keep an eye out for the *dolmen* (stone burial markers) dotted throughout the Highlands; new ones are sometimes found when a new trail is blazed through the forest.

Longer, more strenuous walks can take you through superb rainforest and on to alpine plateaus, staying overnight at longhouses en route; or across the Indonesian border and back. For certain sectors you are strongly advised to hire a guide – trails are sometimes indistinct, terrain can be rugged, and it may be wet and slippery. Visitors occasionally get lost up here and you should seek local information before setting out.

One option is the two-day walk to Ba Kelalan and then a flight out. It's also possible to walk to Long Lellang and catch a flight – timing is important, as flights to Marudi (RM46) and Miri (RM66) only leave on Wednesday. The trip to Long Lellang is a four- to six-day trek. Expect rain, mud, leeches and some regrets, because jungle walking is no Sunday stroll. But if you're prepared, the experience is unforgettable. Guides are recommended, and essential for longer walks away from inhabited areas.

The guestbooks in the lodges and longhouses are full of good information. Many Kelabit are Christians and don't smoke, so bring sugar, vegetable seeds, tea or something imaginative for the chief, rather than cigarettes. Note that longhouses in the area normally charge for an overnight stay – RM15 is the usual charge, and meals are extra.

Whatever you do, don't bring shotgun shells as a gift (or for any other purpose). It may have worked many years ago for bartering travellers like Eric Hansen (author of the brilliant and occasionally mimicked *Stranger in the Forest*), but things have changed and nowadays hunting is strictly controlled. Locals get a monthly ration of shells; if the authorities catch a foreigner (ie, you) carrying them, you'll be in a world of hurt.

# TREKS

Gem's Lodge (☎ 085-657083 in Miri; ask for Gerewat Gala) and Tarawe's do a wide variety of tailor-made shorter walks and longer treks – see Places to Stay & Eat in the Bario section for information on these places. A five-day wildlife-spotting trip involves trekking to undisturbed jungle patches and *leeks* (watering holes) tracking wildlife (here's your chance to add a few bird and animal calls to your repertoire) and staying in jungle camps and a longhouse along the way. Proboscis monkeys and bucking deer, as well as the endangered black monkey *(wawa)* and hornbill are among the wildlife on your viewing menu.

A day trip to the **salt lick** *(main tudtuh)*, an hour's walk from the lodge is fascinating, as you'll learn the local method of salt processing, done in giant vats over a roaring fire.

Because of encroaching logging in Sarawak, much of the wildlife has moved south, and the Kalimantan loop from Pa Umor can offer the best chance to see birds and animals.

Long Bawan is the main border town and one of two entry points to Kalimantan in the area.

## Pa Umor–Lembudud–Long Bawan–Pa Umor
This is a three-day trip; Lembudud is the first settlement across the Indonesian border south of Pa Umor.

## Pa Umor–Tang Paya–Long Bawan–Jungle Camp–Pa Umor
This is either a four- or five-day trip; the longer hike involves staying in a jungle camp an extra night and walking via Long Medang.

## Bario–Pa Lungan–Gunung Murud
If you are poking around Bario without a guide, a four-hour walk on a wide trail takes you to Pa Lungan, a friendly longhouse with a pleasant river to swim in. The chief has a room for visitors with mats, blankets, pillows and mosquito net.

If anyone is available (this may take a few days), you can hire guides here to climb Gunung Murud (2423m), Sarawak's highest peak.

With Gem's Lodge, Batu Lawi or Gunung Murud is a five-day trip staying in hunters' camps or setting up a jungle camp.

## Bario–Ba Kelalan
Another possibility is to walk to Ba Kelalan, a day's walk beyond Pa Lungan, and then fly to Lawas (daily flights in the morning only, RM46). Walks in this area are not a picnic – you need to have your own food and shelter and be prepared for some hard slogging. It's a good idea to hire a local guide. You'll also need a Border Permit from the immigration office in Bario, as the route takes you into Kalimantan via Pa Rupai. Tarawe's or Gem's Lodge can help arrange this.

Gem's Lodge will also arrange a five-day trip to Ba Kelalan via Gunung Murud.

*(Continued from page 446)*

## BARIO

Bario is a small settlement in a beautiful valley 1500m up in the Kelabit Highlands, close to the Indonesian border. A trip to the Kelabit Highlands is a highlight of any visit to Borneo, and though it doesn't look the part, Bario is the centre of it all.

Sleepy Bario played a pivotal role in Borneo's modern history: It was to here that Major Tom Harrisson and a British commando unit parachuted during WWII to organise resistance against the Japanese occupation. During the Konfrontasi with Indonesia in the early 1960s, the area was again the scene of aerial bombings and nasty guerilla fighting. Some of the tribespeople involved in both conflicts still live in nearby longhouses.

Part of Bario's appeal lies in the hospitality of the Kelabit people, but it also lies in its clear mountain air and splendid isolation. The region features Kenyah and Kelabit **longhouses**, and it has great **highland treks** to suit all levels of fitness and motivation. The nearby hills are covered in largely untouched forest and have **abundant wildlife**, and in the kerangas are pitcher plants, rhododendrons and orchids. The hills around Bario are now officially protected, although illegal logging has already encroached on some of the longer trails.

Tour companies visit the area, but it is easy to organise your own trekking with one of the lodges (see Places to Stay & Eat later in this section). Trekking on your own is not recommended – it's very easy to get lost in the maze of overgrown, new and washed-out trails that crisscross the area.

You need a permit to visit Bario, and it's not unusual for it to be checked at some point – with many Indonesians making their way through Bario to logging camps, the immigration officer has to be seen to be doing his job. A permit can be obtained from the Pejabat Residen in Miri (see Orientation & Information in the Miri section earlier in this chapter for details).

You can walk to Kalimantan (Indonesia) from Bario – the first settlement you'll

MARTIN HARRIS

**The process of ear-extending started at an early age for this Kelabit woman.**

reach is about a two-day trek away. You'll need to get a permit from the immigration officer in Bario before setting out.

Bario is indeed isolated. Aside from hiking in, the only access to the highlands is by air. There is no regular phone service (communication is by radiotelephone) and the Malaysia Airlines desk doesn't have a computer to confirm bookings. Travellers should bring enough cash for accommodation, food and guides; small denominations, such as RM10, RM5 and RM1, will be useful – and take extra in case you are stranded. There are no credit-card facilities in the Kelabit Highlands. Bario and Ba Kelalan have shops where you can stock up on basic supplies and purchase gifts to take to the longhouses.

Bario is a Christian community and drinking in public is decidedly uncool (though this doesn't seem to bother the Malaysian army boys sipping Sibu-made ginseng whisky in the cafes); however, beer can be bought in the shops and consumed sin-free at the lodges.

Considering the rates charged elsewhere in Sarawak for simple longhouse visits, guide fees in the Kelabit Highlands are very

MALAYSIAN BORNEO

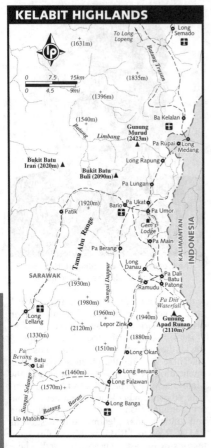

KELABIT HIGHLANDS

roads. There is a long row of tiny shops selling a few necessities (expensive, as they have to be flown in), which might be considered the centre of town. This is also where you'll find Tarawe's, the Malaysia Airlines desk and the police office. The immigration office is near the junction of the airport road and the rutted road to the shophouses (turn left from the airport) and Gem's Lodge (turn right).

The airport is about a 30-minute walk south of the blue-roofed shophouses. To reach the centre of town from the airport, head up the road (bear right at first), then take a left at the junction where a massive, incongruous building sits (this is supposed to one day be a lodge; construction was halted at the time of writing). You probably won't have to walk anyway – everyone here is welcoming, and you are bound to be offered a lift.

### Places to Stay & Eat

There are two excellent backpacker/trekker lodges in the area. *Tarawe's* is a long-running lodge, just past the row of shophouses in Bario. You can't book ahead, but half the town turns up to meet the plane, so someone will point you in the right direction or perhaps give you a lift.

Lodging at Tarawe's is RM15 per person in a three-bed room. Tarawe's welcomes travellers and is a fund of information on local trekking, history and customs, and John Tarawe and his brother Liam are very good guides. The only knock on Tarawe's is the occasional inconsistency of its meals. The food can be excellent, but if no one's around to cook, travellers have been left to fend for themselves in the very basic cafes nearby (there are no restaurants as such in Bario).

The brand new *Gem's Lodge* (☎ 085-657083 in Miri; ask for Gerewat Gala) is brilliant. Situated by a river some 6km south-east of Bario near the longhouse village of Pa Umor, this simple and comfortable lodge is run by James Jaman Riboh (Jaman) and his wife. Clean, spacious rooms are RM15 per person; separate chalets may also be available by the time you read this.

Here you'll eat a vast array of local produce (plus a few jungle delicacies) cooked

reasonable. Tarawe's (see Places to Stay & Eat) generally charges about RM80 per day. You'll pay about RM65 per day at Gem's Lodge for the longer, tougher treks; shorter walks are RM50 per day.

See the 'Trekking in Sarawak' special section for information on short ambles and long treks in the area.

### Orientation

Bario is not actually a town in the usual sense; rather, it's a lush valley settlement dotted with longhouses, wet-rice fields, a church or two and a couple of rough dirt

Kelabit-style; portions are huge and delicious. Homemade bread accompanies many meals. Breakfast at the lodge costs RM5, lunch is RM8 and dinner is RM12.

Jaman is hands-down the best guide in Bario, if not all of Sarawak, and a trek with him is a treat.

### Getting There & Away
The Malaysia Airlines agent is in the long shophouse row near Tarawe's in the centre of Bario. The only way into Bario (other than by walking) is on a Malaysia Airlines Twin Otter flight from Miri (RM70), usually via Marudi (RM55). There are currently two flights to Miri on Monday – one via Marudi, the other direct – and one daily on Tuesday, Thursday and Friday. Planes fly in and out in the morning only.

Flights are dependent on the weather and cancellations are not uncommon, so make sure your schedule isn't too tight. These flights are often booked out in advance, especially during the school holidays, but it's possible that a seat will become available at the last minute. If you do fly to Bario on standby, get your flight out confirmed straight away if possible – you don't want to cut short a trek just to come back to the airport in the hope of a seat.

## LIMBANG
☎ 085
This small, prosperous town on the Batang Limbang is sandwiched between the two parts of Brunei. There's not much to do here except have a few beers in the evening by the river. Then again, if you've just come from Brunei or the Headhunters' Trail, this may be all you need.

### Orientation & Information
The main part of Limbang sits along the east bank of the Sungai Limbang, which throws its loops across a forested plain before emptying into Brunei Bay. A range of low hills farther east marks the border with Brunei's Temburong district.

The older part of town is only a couple of hundred metres square and is bordered on the riverbank by a two-storey, blue-roofed

## Kelabit Words & Phrases

The Kelabit use Malay for some common phrases:

| | |
|---|---|
| Good morning/ afternoon. | Salamat pagi. |
| Good night. | Salamat malam. |
| Goodbye. | Salamat tinggal. |
| Thank you. | Terima kasih. |

Kelabit phrases and words include:

| | |
|---|---|
| How are you? | Kan doo tah iko? |
| Pleased to meet you. | Mawang niat petulu nganuih. |
| See you again. | Petulu baruh. |
| What's your name? | Anun ngadan nuidih? |
| Where do we bathe/ wash? | Ngapah inan diu? |
| I'm sorry. | Mutuh doo iuh. |
| Where? | Ngapah? |
| What? | Anun? |
| I | u-ih |
| you | iko |
| today | adto kinih |
| tomorrow | adto riak |
| day | adto |
| night | dadtan |
| good | doo |
| not good | da'at |
| eat | kuman |
| drink | mirup |
| go | ame |
| go for a walk | ame nalan-nalan |
| sleep | rudap |
| lodge | rumah tumpang |
| longhouse | rumah kadang |
| jungle | pulung |
| leech | lamatak |
| wild boar | baka |
| bucking deer | tela'o |

Kelabit forms of address include:

| | |
|---|---|
| grandmother/ grandfather | tapu |
| older man | tamah |
| older woman | sinah |
| chief | tua kampung |

MALAYSIAN BORNEO

market. The massive peach-and-green complex looming over the wharf area is the Purnama Hotel and its attendant shopping mall, the largely empty Limbang Plaza. Beyond this, and downstream about 200m from the old town, are concrete blocks of shophouses with cafes, karaoke bars and snooker halls; here you'll find accommodation and some good riverside eateries. On the opposite bank of the river stretches a pleasant stilt village punctuated by the domes of makeshift mosques.

Boats to Brunei and Labuan leave from the wharf below the blue-roofed new market, and taxis park just outside. Boats to Lawas tie up at the jetty a few hundred metres downstream. Buses leave from a stand a couple of blocks east of the river, behind the old part of town. The airport is about 4km south of town.

There are several moneychangers across the road from the Brunei–Labuan wharf, and there is a Maybank near the Muhibbah Inn. A tourist office and a cybercafe or two may be up and running in Limbang Plaza by the time you read this.

## Things to See & Do

A **tamu** (weekly market) is held on Friday in the car park in front of the new market. It is attended by villagers from the surrounding district, who are mainly Bisayah and speak the Brunei Malay dialect, which is still strong here.

Limbang's small but excellent **Muzium Wilayah** is upstairs in another of Charles Brooke's forts, and is definitely worth the five-minute walk along the river. The collection is well presented and features exhibits of archaeology, culture and crafts of the region. The museum is open daily (except Monday and public holidays) from 9 am to 6 pm; entry is free. To get here, follow the riverbank upstream (south) past the police station; there's a well-carved replica of the totemic Pagul pole at Batang Pirak (near Medamit) out the front.

Down the road from the museum and up a steep drive is a pretty **park** with an artificial lake backed by forest. It's a pleasant place to kill time if you're waiting for a flight.

## Places to Stay

Some of the cheap-looking places on and around the main street opposite the wharf are decidedly sleazy. The decent places are mostly mid-range, air-con hotels, some at which you can pay by credit card.

**Muhibbah Inn** (☎ 212488) is a maze of corridors where air-con singles/doubles with toilet are RM35/50. Windowless rooms at the **Metro** (☎ 211133), near the market, start at RM50/52 with air-con, shower, TV and minibar; those with a window are RM63. This is a popular hotel and is often full.

There are three mid-range hotels on the riverfront in the northern part of town. The rather tatty **Centre Point Hotel** (☎ 213699) is the cheapest; windowless, air-con rooms with toilet go for RM35, while rooms with a view are RM40/45. You'll have to pay in cash here. Better rooms at the **Royal Park Hotel** (☎ 212155) start at RM48/50; **National Inn** (☎ 212922) has the best rooms of the bunch, starting at RM44/48 (cash only).

The best place in town is the peachy new four-star **Purnama Hotel** (☎ 216700, fax 216711). It's something of a rarity – a very friendly luxury hotel. Published rates start at RM184, but promotional rates on large double rooms may be as low as RM88.

## Places to Eat

There are **food stalls** on the 1st floor of the waterfront market and at the bus station. Cheap Malaysian food, roti and murtabak can be had in the **halal cafes** in the same building as the Muhibbah Inn.

Two good spots for dinner are near the National Inn and Royal Park Hotel on the riverside. **Maggie Cafe** serves excellent grilled fish and cold beer at tables overlooking the river. Next door, **MC Corner BBQ Cafe** is a good place for a bit to eat and offers a range of meat and vegetable dishes.

**Kuali Cafeteria**, in the Purnama Hotel, is a very good, affordable restaurant with a range of Western-style dishes – sirloin steak is RM15 and beer is RM6.50 (plus tax) – and a breakfast buffet.

## Entertainment
Weekend refugees from Brunei can be found gazing in wonder at Filipino bands in the *Purnama Hotel* lounge. In the newer blocks a few hundred metres north of the Purnama is the late-night *Hollywood Disco*. A cover charge of RM5 gets you in – getting out again is your problem. The locals take partying seriously here.

## Getting There & Away
**Air** Malaysia Airlines has Twin Otter flights to Miri (two to six daily, RM45), Lawas (five weekly, RM25) and KK (two weekly, RM60). The airport is 4km south of the town centre. A taxi to the airport costs RM5 per person if there's a full load; it's hard to get a taxi to take you on your own for less than RM10.

**Bus** It is possible to travel by road between the two halves of Brunei via Limbang. For connections to Bandar Seri Begawan, Brunei's capital, there is a scheduled bus from Limbang to Kuala Lurah on the Brunei border (12 buses daily between 5.30 am and 5.30 pm).

There's no bus service to the nearby eastern Brunei border, but taxis regularly make the trip for about RM20, and all the way to Bangar by negotiation. Make sure you call at the Brunei immigration checkpoint on the road into Bangar; it is open daily from 6 am to 10 pm. From Bangar it is possible to go overland to Lawas and on to Sabah, but it involves an expensive taxi ride (see the Lawas section later for details).

Regular buses to other parts of the Limbang district leave from the bus station at the north-eastern corner of the old town. There are services to Pandaruan, Buagsiol, Batu Danau, Kubong, Ukong, and Tedungan. If you are planning to do the Headhunters' Trail (see the 'Trekking in Sarawak' special section) into Gunung Mulu National Park, the bus for Medamit leaves roughly every hour between 5.30 am and 4.30 pm and costs RM5.

**Boat** Speedboats make mostly morning runs between Limbang and Bandar Seri Begawan (about 30 minutes, RM15 or B$10). The boats go when they have a full load of 12 passengers, so you may have a bit of a wait after 9 am or so. The last boat in each direction leaves at around 4.30 pm.

An express boat goes to Lawas every morning at 7.30 am (30 minutes, RM20). The express boat to Labuan in Sabah leaves at 7.30 and 8 am (two hours, RM10). From Labuan to Limbang the boat leaves at 12.30 and 2.30 pm. Buy your ticket at the wharf.

## LAWAS
☎ 085

Lawas is a busy little town on the banks of the Batang Lawas. Like Limbang, it is a transit place where you may find yourself en route to or from Brunei and Sabah, or to take the short flight to Miri. Logging is a big industry in this part of Sarawak and a logging road runs from Lawas to Long Semado. It is impossible to get lost here: The bus station is in the middle of town and places to stay and eat are in the shophouses surrounding it.

The airport is about 2km from town.

## Places to Stay & Eat
There are several budget hotels in town; rooms are basic but OK and cost around RM35. There are a couple of overpriced top-end options near the airport as well.

An interesting alternative to staying in town is the *Southern Comfort Lodge* (☎/fax 493523, ✆ ctx@tm.net.my), in a peaceful riverside jungle setting. B&B rates are RM25 per person, and additional meals are available. There's a large waterfall a half-hour trek from the lodge. The lodge is 30 minutes from town, at the end of the Lawas-Damit road past the last village of Long Ugui; you can get there by bus (RM1.60), taxi (RM25) or private vehicle.

Lawas has *food stalls* on the top floor of the riverside market and clustered around the tiny town padang. There are numerous good *kedai kopi* around town.

## Getting There & Away
**Air** Ngan Travel Services (☎ 285368) in town is the Malaysia Airlines agent.

MALAYSIAN BORNEO

Twin Otters fly to KK (weekly, RM47), Miri (at least three daily, RM59), Limbang (three per week, RM25) and Ba Kelalan (daily, RM46). To Lawas, there are flights four days a week (two on Monday) from Limbang.

**Bus & Taxi** There are daily buses to KK (RM24) and the towns en route. It's a long trip over a road that's nightmarish in places.

If you miss the express service to KK, there's a direct minibus to Beaufort (RM15).

If you miss the boat to Brunei, you could travel by taxi to Bangar, in Temburong, then take a boat to Bandar Seri Begawan. You'll first need to clear Malaysian immigration at the Lawas ferry wharf, then get the taxi to take you to the Brunei immigration office (a few kilometres the other side of Bangar) before bringing you back to the Bangar wharf. All up, this should take about 40 minutes and the taxi should cost RM100. Boats for Bandar Seri Begawan leave regularly from Bangar, until about 4.30 pm (B$7).

**Boat** All boats leave from the riverside wharf east of the town centre.

An express boat to Limbang (30 minutes, RM20) leaves between 8 and 9 am – check the current schedule at the wharf. If you're heading to Brunei, the only boat leaves at 7 am daily (RM20); it returns at 12.30 pm.

## MERAPOK

Merapok is a one-street hamlet in the middle of nowhere, but it does have a pool hall where you can pot a few balls while you wait for a bus. The Sabah–Sarawak border and the police checkpoint are a few hundred metres out of town. There is an immigration post on each side of the border and you must report to both. They are open until 6 pm; the police checkpoint handles immigration formalities outside office hours.

### Getting There & Away

Minibuses go to Lawas and Sipitang, though you may be in for a wait. You can also catch the Kota Kinabalu–Lawas bus on the highway. If you want to try hitching, traffic is regular but light.

MALAYSIAN BORNEO

# Sabah

Sabah is Malaysia's northernmost state, and together with Sarawak makes up Malaysian Borneo. Though they share the same island, Sabah and Sarawak are very different entities; indeed, travellers venturing from Sarawak will discover another side of Borneo here. Sabah's local people – the Kadazan, Dusun, Murut, Bajau, Bugis and Rungus are among the main groups – are low-key compared to Sarawak's, yet very hospitable in their own right.

The state is known abroad mainly for its incredible natural features. There are gorgeous beaches to lie on and coral reefs to explore, though most visitors head straight up the craggy slope of Mt Kinabalu (4101m), one of the highest yet most accessible mountains in South-East Asia, and the most tempting to climb.

Sabah remains something of a frontier state, whose natural riches have drawn traders and raiders for centuries. Among its past masters have been Sulu sultans and foreign invaders, and it has seen its share of bloody conflict; its present masters are plantation owners, real estate barons and those with the power to grant logging concessions in irreplaceable rainforests.

Malaysia's hold on parts of the territory is tenuous: Sabah's proximity to Indonesia and the Philippines ensures both nations claim areas of the state as their own. Sabah and the southern Philippines have many cultural similarities – not least of which is a strong Islamic tradition – and visitors will encounter plenty of Filipino migrants who eke out a living while living in massive stilt villages on the outskirts of southern cities like Sandakan and Tawau.

Independent travel in Sabah is limited compared to neighbouring Sarawak. Many travellers will be dealing with tour outfits at some point, whether it's for diving, watching turtles lay eggs or roaming along the Sungai (River) Kinabatangan. At the same time, the state's highlights are concentrated in a few spots and some (like Mt Kinabalu)

## HIGHLIGHTS

- **Mt Kinabalu** – an improbably high granite peak and unbeatable summit-view sunrises
- **Sungai Kinabatangan** – perhaps the best wildlife-watching in South-East Asia
- **Sepilok Orang-Utan Rehabilitation Centre** – a rare chance to see these marvellous apes up close and personal
- **Tunku Abdul Rahman National Park** – white-sand beaches to laze on, just a short boat ride from Sabah's capital
- **Poring Hot Springs** – natural thermal pools to take the chill off Mt Kinabalu
- **Kota Belud Market** – a huge and colourful local market popular with Sunday tourists
- **Islands off Semporna** – gorgeous islands, superb diving conditions

are easy to reach on your own. In truth, given the prominence of palm plantations, illegal logging roads and abandoned upriver longhouses, there's probably less reason to wander far off the beaten trail in Sabah than in Sarawak.

Budget travellers will find Sabah more expensive than Sarawak and Peninsular Malaysia, and pricey tours are virtually obligatory for some sights and activities. However, regardless of your bottom line, if you pick your spots (and your tour operators) wisely, you'll get your money's worth

MALAYSIAN BORNEO

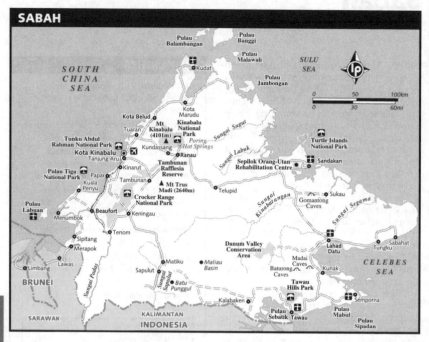

SABAH

and maybe more. Most of the major attractions do have inexpensive accommodation and cheap eats, and mid-range travellers will generally find Sabah offers good value for money.

## History

Before Malaysia's independence Sabah was known as North Borneo and administered by the British North Borneo Company. After WWII both Sabah and Sarawak were handed over to the British government, and both decided to merge with the peninsular states to form the new nation of Malaysia in 1963.

But Sabah's natural wealth attracted other prospectors and its existence as a state was disputed by two powerful neighbours – Indonesia and the Philippines. There are close cultural ties between the people of Sabah and the Filipinos of the nearby Sulu Archipelago and Mindanao. Several small islands to the north of Sabah are disputed by the Philippines, and a busy smuggling trade

operates from Sabah into Mindanao. Mindanao's Muslim rebels often retreat down towards Sabah when pursued by government forces and pirates based in the Sulu Sea continue to raid parts of Sabah's coast.

After independence, Sabah was governed for a time by Tun Mustapha, who ran the state almost as a private fiefdom and was often at odds with the central government in Kuala Lumpur (KL). In 1967 he even threatened secession. He disappeared from the political scene in 1975. In 1985 the Kadazan-controlled Sabah United Party (Parti Bersatu Sabah; PBS) came into power and joined the National Front Alliance.

However, tensions with the federal government were rife. In 1990 the PBS pulled out of the alliance with the National Front just days before general elections. The PBS claimed that the federal government was not equitably returning the wealth that the state generated and, in 1993, it banned the export of logs from Sabah, largely to reinforce this point. The federal government used its powers to overturn the state decision. Though there is always talk of handing back more of the profits that Sabah's natural resources deliver to KL, to date nothing has changed – the crumbs KL leaves on the table for each state amounts to only 5% of the pie.

Partly as a result of its bad relations with the federal government, Sabah is currently the poorest of Malaysia's states. Although it is rich in natural resources, one-third of the population lives below the poverty line. Part of the problem is a bizarre rotation system that forces a change of political administration in Sabah every two years. This serves the federal government well, since politicians aren't in power long enough to implement anything autonomous; in fact, they aren't around long enough to do much of anything – beyond perhaps setting themselves up for a comfortable life after office.

## Visas & Permits

Sabah is semi-autonomous, and like Sarawak it has its own immigration controls. On arrival most nationalities are likely to be given a visa for two months' stay and it is rare to be asked to show money or onward tickets. Most visitors arrive at the state capital, Kota Kinabalu (KK), but it is possible to travel into Sabah overland from Sarawak via Brunei; by boat from Kalimantan (Indonesia) to Tawau (this is now a visa-free route); or from the Philippine city of Zamboanga to Sandakan. See the relevant destination sections for more details of these routes.

Visas can be renewed at immigration offices at or near most points of arrival, even at small places like Merapok near Beaufort. If you miss them it's not a problem – just report to another immigration office, even if it's several days later, and explain your situation to the officials.

Apart from entry to national parks and other reserves (see individual park entries for conditions), permits are required to visit Pulau Sipadan (Sipadan Island), the Danum Valley Conservation Area, the Maliau Basin and the Gomantong Caves.

## National Parks & Other Reserves

Sabah's national parks and their inhabitants are among the main reasons tourists visit the state. Many of the best reserves are privately owned. The experience offered at these places is 1st class, but everywhere in Sabah you'll feel the grasping tentacles of private enterprise – a visit can be costly and prices always seem to be rising. With a couple of exceptions it is possible to travel independently, so travellers can reduce costs.

Sabah's national parks preserve some outstanding scenery, wildlife and habitats. Accommodation and facilities are usually very good and if you are prepared to spend the money, they can be excellent. Budget accommodation is available in or near the major reserves and, if the weather is kind, camping is possible in some.

A lot of effort goes into park maintenance and access, and you will be captivated by the astonishing variety of plant and animal life that is generally easy to see. Sabah's major parks include:

**Crocker Range National Park (139 sq km)** Preserving a huge swathe of forested escarpment overlooking the coast, this park has no facilities yet.

**Kinabalu National Park (754 sq km)** Easily accessible from KK, this is the state's largest and most popular national park. It offers straightforward climbing at Mt Kinabalu and there's a thermal-pool system at Poring Hot Springs. The park has very good facilities and accommodation.

**Pulau Tiga National Park (15 sq km)** This park comprises three islands 50km south-west of KK: one was formed by volcanic mud eruptions, one is famous for breeding sea snakes and the third has been virtually washed away by wave action. The islands are difficult to reach, but accommodation is available.

**Tawau Hills Park (29 sq km)** Near Tawau in the state's south-east, this park has forested volcanic hills, waterfalls and hot springs. There's basic accommodation and facilities, but the park is seldom visited and access is difficult.

**Tunku Abdul Rahman National Park (49 sq km)** This park is a group of five islands, one quite large, a few kilometres west of the capital. Features of TAR National Park include beaches, snorkelling and hiking. There's good accommodation on several islands.

MALAYSIAN BORNEO

**Turtle Islands National Park (17 sq km)** This national park comprises three tiny islands 40km north of Sandakan that protect the nesting ground of green and hawksbill sea turtles. There's accommodation on one of the islands.

Two cave systems – Gomantong and Madai – are administered by the Wildlife Department and can be visited; reserves run by the Sabah Foundation include the Danum Valley Conservation Area and the Maliau Basin; the Sepilok Orang-Utan Rehabilitation Centre is a non-government reserve.

## Costs

Compared to most of the region, Sabah is an expensive place to travel around. Only at a few places, such as KK, Sepilok, Mt Kinabalu and Poring Hot Springs, will you find accommodation that could be classed as 'budget'. Be prepared to fork out at least RM20 per night – and often much more – for a place to sleep.

Many of the cheaper places to stay are used for prostitution. This doesn't mean you can't stay, but they tend to be seedy, noisy and probably aren't secure – a bang on the door at 3 am is not uncommon. This inevitably pushes the budget traveller up the price scale to mid-range accommodation. At some places, such as Danum Valley, Turtle Islands and Pulau Sipadan, you'll have no choice but to pay through the nose for accommodation. At others, for example along the Sungai Kinabatangan, tours are pretty much the only way to get around. KRK 'Mai Aman is a fledgling network of mid-range B&Bs and resorts around Sabah that may offer some good deals and interesting trips; its Web site is at www.skynary .com/maiaman.

Top-end accommodation and restaurants in Sabah add a total of 15% government tax onto their basic charges; the total you pay is the 'nett' price. Published rates are mostly '++', meaning that 5% and 10% taxes have to be added. Many hotels routinely quote nett rates, however, and promotions often include the tax as well. In this chapter we've given nett prices. In federally administered Labuan, the total tax is 10%.

## Getting Around

**Road** Sabah has a good road system and most major roads are sealed, including the highway from KK to Sandakan and Tawau. Notable exceptions are the 47km stretch between Beaufort and Sipitang in the south – a real kidney-bruiser – and between Kota Belud and Ranau in the north. Probably the worst stretch is between Ranau and Keningau, where minivans sometimes have to turn back because the perilous cliffside gravel road is impassable after heavy rain.

Subsidence and washouts frequently put stretches of highway under repair and can slow down a trip considerably – the route between Ranau and Sandakan can be unreliable in wet weather. Although it's sometimes marked on maps, the route from Tawau to Keningau is an unsealed logging road and little-used by travellers.

Express buses, minibuses and minivans run between KK and most major centres, including Mt Kinabalu. The big state-of-the-art express buses are all air-con; the smaller, often older, minibuses may or may not be. Minivans are small, eight-seater vans (usually white), which can be stuffed with as many passengers and gear as the laws of physics permit. Express buses are relatively punctual and usually cost only a few ringgit more than minivans. Minivans only leave when full but, once under way, they are quick and efficient. They don't have air-con and can get crowded; on the other hand, if you want to share an experience with the locals and don't mind a toddler or two on your lap, minivans are a good option.

There are frequent departures of buses and minivans from most centres until around noon; afternoon departures can be scarce. See individual destination entries for more information.

Hitchhiking is possible in Sabah, although traffic is usually light. In this chapter we've indicated where hitching is feasible. However, hitching is never entirely safe and people who decide to hitch should understand that they are taking a small but potentially serious risk. People who choose to hitch will be safer if they travel in pairs and let someone know where they are planning to go.

**Train** Sabah's only railway runs between KK and Tenom via Papar and Beaufort. For details, see Getting There & Away in the Papar and Beaufort sections.

# Kota Kinabalu

☎ 088

Sabah's capital, Kota Kinabalu, sits on the edge of the South China Sea overlooking a cluster of coral-fringed islands. With the towering Crocker Range as a backdrop and the cloud-shrouded peaks of mighty Mt Kinabalu in the far distance, the modern suburbs of KK – as everyone calls it – sprawl aimlessly for many kilometres along the coast and inland.

KK is not without appeal, but it's a functional place built mainly for state functionaries and their business partners. Part of the reason for KK's undistinguished character goes back to WWII when Jesselton, as it was then known, was razed by the retreating British in order to prevent the Japanese using it as a base for operations. Just three years later Jesselton was again flattened, this time by Allied bombing as the Japanese were pushed out of Borneo. The city was rebuilt from scratch and renamed Kota Kinabalu in 1963.

When the usual precautions are taken, KK is a reasonably safe city. Late at night, streets and alleys near the waterfront, such as in Kompleks Sinsuran, are probably best avoided. In the heart of town around the Hotel Kinabalu, male travellers may have to break the hearts of a few transvestites if trying to get home after 1 am or so; female travellers will be distinctly more comfortable if they aren't out alone at this hour.

While Sandakan to the south-east is also a good base from which to explore Sabah, it's worth spending a couple of days in KK to get your feet wet in the state, organise your itinerary, hit an offshore island and sample the city's excellent food (enjoy it while you can, because food is very basic elsewhere in Sabah). And, of course, there is the ascent of mighty Mt Kinabalu to prepare yourself for.

## Orientation

The international airport at Tanjung Aru is 7km south of the city centre, which is bounded on the north by the upmarket bayside suburb of Likas. The city centre is compact and walkable – this is where most places to stay and eat, banks, tourist offices, tour operators, the main post office and transport centres are located. The booking office for Mt Kinabalu, major airline offices and a few other administrative offices are just south of the city centre.

The city centre itself is a compact, concrete grid between the waterfront and a range of low, forested hills to the east. The area can be a bit disorienting – unlike snowflakes, it seems no two streets in KK are unalike. There are few landmarks to take bearings by, especially at night. The wide avenues running parallel to the sea are crossed by numerous short streets, so the trick is to figure out which of the (more or less) north-south avenues you're on, then orient yourself to a hotel, shopping centre or other landmark (an enormous sign advertising cigarettes is the main sight in the middle of the grid).

The main road changes name four times between the southern end of town and the north: at the southern end it's called Jalan Lebuh Raya Pantai Baru, then Jalan Pasar Baru, Jalan Tun Razak and Jalan Haji Saman.

KK's main shopping complexes line the main drag. On the western side of Jalan Tun Razak are two sprawling, grid-like blocks of dilapidated two- or three-storey shophouses: Kompleks Segama and Kompleks Sinsuran. Between Jalan Haji Saman and the waterfront there's the newer Wisma Merdeka and at the opposite end, on the way to the airport, you'll find the huge Centre Point and Api-Api centres. Opposite the Api-Api Centre there's Asia City, a concrete maze with some fine restaurants. There's an undeveloped landfill on the northern edge of the city, and between town and the airport a massive reclamation project, Sutera Harbour, has become a luxury resort development.

There is no single bus station; rather, there are three areas in central KK where you can find the bus you want – see Getting There &

Away and Getting Around later in this section. Taxis can be found all over town, but seem to congregate in the area between the main post office and the council offices. Ferries leave for the islands of TAR National Park, as well as for Pulau Labuan, from the waterfront behind the Hyatt Regency.

## Information

**Tourist Offices** There are two tourist offices in town. Tourism Malaysia (☎ 248698, Ⓔ mtpbbki@tourism.gov.my) is on the ground floor of the EONCMG Life building on the corner of Jalan Gaya and Jalan Dua, at the northern end of the city centre. This office is useful for general queries about travel in Sabah and the rest of Malaysia, and has plenty of free brochures. It is open weekdays from 8 am to 12.45 pm and 2 to 4.15 pm, and on Saturday until 12.45 pm.

For specific questions about independent travel in Sabah, head across the road to the Sabah Tourism Promotion Corporation (STPC; ☎ 218620) at 51 Jalan Gaya, in the historic post office building. It's open weekdays from 8 am to 5 pm, and on Saturday to noon. Staff can answer most queries and hand out informative brochures on Sabah's tourist attractions. There's also a shop selling a few touristy handicrafts, maps and books.

You'll find a useful Sabah tourism Web site at www.jaring.my/sabah.

**National Park & Conservation Area Bookings** Accommodation in Kinabalu National Park (including Poring Hot Springs and the mountain huts) and on Manukan in Tunku Abdul Rahman National Park is privately run. Bookings are handled by Kinabalu Gold Resorts (☎ 257941, fax 242861, Ⓔ nature@kinabalu.net), 3rd floor, Block C, Kompleks Karamunsing. The office is open daily from 8.30 am to 5 pm. Kompleks Karamunsing is south of the city centre, about five minutes' walk along Jalan Tunku Abdul Rahman past the Hotel Shangri-La then off to the left.

Mt Kinabalu is very popular with both overseas visitors and locals, and accommodation at the park headquarters is often booked up a week in advance. You might

get a dorm bed in the off-season if you just roll up to the park, but the further ahead you make reservations, the better.

The Sabah Parks office (☎ 211881) is at Block K, Kompleks Sinsuran, Jalan Tun Fuad Stephens. This office handles reservations for accommodation at Pulau Tiga National Park. Opening hours are Monday to Thursday from 8.30 am to 4 pm, Friday from 8.30 to 11.30 am and 2 to 4 pm and Saturday from 8.30 am to noon.

Bookings and permits for the Danum Valley Conservation Area and Maliau Basin can be arranged through Innoprise Jungle Lodge (☎ 243245, fax 262050, Ⓔ ijl@ po.jaring.my), 3rd floor, Block D, Sadong Jaya Kompleks, KK; or through Borneo Nature Tours (☎ 089-880206, fax 885051), 1st floor, Block 1, Lot 6, Fajar Centre, PO Box 61174, 91120, Lahad Datu.

**Consulates in Kota Kinabalu** The Indonesian consulate (☎ 219110) is south of the city centre off Jalan Kemajuan. Visas can be issued here without fuss on the day of application. There is an Australian consulate (☎ 236569) on the 10th floor of the Wisma Yakim building.

**Visas** The immigration office (☎ 280772) is on the 4th floor of Wisma Dana Bandang, the tall building near Jalan Tunku Abdul Rahman. It's open weekdays from 8 am to 1 pm and 2 to 4.30 pm (closing at 11.30 for lunch on Friday) and Saturday from 8 am to 1 pm.

**Money** Most major banks have branches at the northern end of town, where you'll find the Standard Chartered and Hongkong Bank (HSBC). Standard Chartered offers the best exchange rates, but takes a hefty commission of RM20 per transaction. Sabah Bank is next to the Sabah Parks office, and there are plenty of other banks around the city centre. You'll find moneychangers on the ground floor of Centre Point and Wisma Merdeka.

**Post & Communications** The main post office, in the city centre, has an efficient poste restante counter. Opening hours are 8 am to 5 pm Monday to Saturday. Parcels are weighed and sent from the open-air offices to the left of the main entrance.

For international telephone calls, most public phone booths are Uniphone but if you have a Telekom card, you can use the blue Telekom booths around town. There are some near the post office and at the Telekom office on Jalan Tunku Abdul Rahman, a 10-minute walk south of the city centre, where there are also international telephone booths.

Among KK's many cybercafes are:

**AB Cyber.net** 1st floor, above the KFC on Jalan Haji Saman; open from 10 am to 6 pm; RM4 per hour
**Cyber Land** Above Burger King near the Hyatt Regency Hotel; open from 9.30 am to 2 am; RM4 per hour
**KK Internet** On Jalan Haji Saman near Ang's Hotel; promotional rates at the time of writing were RM3 per hour
**www.cyclone.net** 1st floor, near SEDCO; open from 10 am to 3 am; RM4 per hour

**Bookshops & Libraries** Borneo Books, on the ground floor of Wisma Merdeka, has a good selection of Borneo-related titles, including some less-common books.

The State Library, on Jalan Tunku Abdul Rahman, is open to the public from 9 am daily, closing at 9 pm on weekdays, 5 pm on Saturday and at 1 pm on Sunday. The British Council Library (☎ 248055) is on the 1st floor of the EONCMG Life building at the northern end of the city, above the Tourism Malaysia office.

**Film & Photography** There are photo processing labs throughout the city centre and in the shopping malls. Fuji is the most popular brand of film on sale, followed by Konica, but only print film is widely available – if you have particular film requirements, you should buy them before you get to KK.

Scubazoo Images (☎ 232068, fax 237068, ✉ scubazoo@yahoo.com), on the 4th floor of Wisma Sabah, does high-quality underwater photography and films.

**Laundry** There are branches of Laundry Mart on the ground floor of Block A, Kompleks Segama and in Centre Point.

**Medical Services** The Queen Elizabeth Hospital (☎ 218166) is on Jalan Penampang, past the Sabah Museum. Dial ☎ 999 in emergency.

Klinik Dr Suzain (☎ 223185), ground floor, Wisma Yakim, is a women's clinic open 24 hours a day.

## Sabah Museum & Science Centre

The Sabah Museum is a modern four-storey structure inspired by the longhouses of the Rungus and Murut tribes. It's a little south of the city centre, on a hill on the corner of Jalan Tunku Abdul Rahman and Jalan Penampang. The museum and gardens are definitely worth a visit, the adjoining science centre and art gallery less so.

Inside are good collections of tribal and historical artefacts, including ceramics; nicely presented exhibits of flora and fauna, with a display of Sabah's spectacular butterflies and other insects; and the 'time tunnel', an absorbing walk that traces the history of KK with artefacts, old photos, costumes and weaponry. The top floor is devoted to Muslim culture and history, but it's pretty dull stuff compared to the excellent Muslim displays in Kuching and Brunei. From here you can get onto the roof for good views across to the state mosque.

The Science Centre & Art Gallery is next to the main building. Displays change periodically, but include demonstrations and exhibitions of the latest in computer technology and telecommunications. On the 1st floor there's an art gallery where the work of local artists is displayed. It's not terribly well organised and there's next to no biographical information, but some of the paintings and sculptures are quite good.

The museum, science centre and art gallery are open daily, except Friday (and 1 May), from 9 am to 5 pm. Entry is free.

To get there, catch a bus along Jalan Tunku Abdul Rahman for 50 sen and get off just before the mosque.

MALAYSIAN BORNEO

## State Mosque

This is a fine example of contemporary Islamic architecture, set some distance from the heat and noise of central KK. It's south of the city centre past the Kampung Air stilt village, not far from the Sabah Museum; you'll see it on your way to or from the airport.

The majesty of this mosque has been upstaged by the glittering newer mosque at Likas Bay; nonetheless, the state mosque is impressive from a distance, and can accommodate 5000 male worshippers and has a balcony where there's room for 500 women to pray. Non-Muslim visitors are allowed inside, but must remove their shoes before entering and dress appropriately. See the 'Places of Worship' special section for information on mosque etiquette.

To reach the mosque, take a bus along Jalan Tunku Abdul Rahman.

## Atkinson Clock Tower

This very minor attraction has the dubious distinction of being one of the only structures to survive the Allied bombing of Jesselton in 1945. It's a square, 15.7m-high wooden clock tower that was completed in 1905 and named after the first district officer of the town, FG Atkinson, a high achiever who died of malaria aged 28.

The clock tower stands on a low hill near the main police station on Jalan Balai Polis, close to the city centre.

## Markets

The market is in two sections – the waterfront area for fish and an area in front of the harbour for fruit and vegetables. The area next to the main market on the waterfront is known as the Filipino Market; all the stalls are owned by Filipinos and they sell a variety of handicrafts made in the Philippines.

A night market fills Jalan Sentosa and adjoining streets on some nights; it's geared mainly to locals and most stalls sell clothing. On Sunday morning a street market sets up along Jalan Gaya and spills onto side streets.

## Other Attractions

While neither are exactly tourist highlights, in addition to the squatters' stilt village offshore at Pulau Gaya, KK has its own stilt village, **Kampung Air**, just south of the city centre off the main drag, Jalan Lebuh Raya Pantai Baru. Once an extensive settlement stretching south along the shore, all that remains is a small collection of rickety dwellings cut off from the sea by a massive land reclamation scheme.

You can wander up to the observation pavilion on **Signal Hill**, at the eastern edge of the city centre, to escape the traffic and to get another take on the stilt village at Pulau Gaya. The view is best as the sun sets over the islands. To get there, take the path behind the Backpacker Lodge to the steps leading up to Jalan Bukit Bendera.

## Organised Tours

There's a host of tour operators offering expensive trips to Mt Kinabalu, Kota Belud, Sepilok and other places that are easy to get to. You might need to get in touch with an operator, however, if you're planning to do any diving. Budget places to stay can often put you onto a cheap operator, though as with more-expensive outfits, be sceptical about promises and ask lots of questions – there are plenty of unscrupulous or just plain poor-quality operators out there.

Some of the more established operators are:

**Abdillah Sipadan Paradise/Adventure Journey World Travel** (☎ 221586, fax 248331, ✉ jworld@po.jaring.my) Ground floor, Block A, Taman Fortuna Shoplots, Jalan Penampang, KK; has lodging on Pulau Sipadan

**Borneo Action** (☎ 267190, fax 267194, ✉ info@borneoaction.com) Ground floor, Block 3, Api-Api Centre; dive shop (☎ 246701) on the ground floor of Wisma Sabah; next door in the Api-Api Centre is the affiliated travel-agent Tarie Travel & Tours (☎ 267196, fax 267195). Borneo Action has a good reputation for looking after its clients; diving is its speciality but the company offers a range of tours and has good live-aboard connections.

**Borneo Adventure** (☎ 238731, fax 238730, ✉ babki@po.jaring.my) 5th floor, 509–512 Gaya Centre. This award-winning company is the cream of the crop, with very professional staff, imaginative itineraries, and a genuine interest in local people and the environment.

**Borneo Divers** (☎ 222226, fax 221550, ✉ bdivers@po.jaring.my) 9th floor, Stamford College Bldg, 53 Jalan Gaya; the dive shop (☎ 222227) is on the ground floor of Wisma Sabah. The longest-established Borneo dive outfit, it can arrange courses and dives just about anywhere, and has accommodation on Pulau Sipadan.

**Borneo Eco Tours** (☎ 234009, fax 233688, ✉ betsb1@po.jaring.my) 2nd floor, Shop Lot 12A, Lorong Bernam 3, Taman Soon Kiong. Offers upmarket 'adventure' tours to the Kinabatangan area, based at the spiffy Sukau Rainforest Lodge. Trips to Batu Punggul can also be arranged.

**Borneo Sea Adventures** (☎ 230000, fax 221106, ✉ bornsea@pop1.jaring.my) 1st floor, 8A Karamunsing Warehouse. Another dive company that has accommodation on Sipadan, it also offers dive tours to the Mantanani islands, off Kota Belud.

**Borneo Wildlife Adventure** (☎ 213668, 233866, fax 219089, ✉ bwa@tm.net.my) 1st floor, Lot F, General Post Office bldg. Arranges affordable tailor-made adventure and educational tours.

**Discovery Tours** (☎ 221244, fax 221600, ✉ distour@po.jaring.my) 3rd floor, Wisma Sabah. Offers rafting trips on the Kiulu and Padas Rivers, and day tours around KK.

**Sutima Express** (☎ 016-836 2412, fax 242519, ✉ abidinajak@hotmail.com); has an office at the jetties behind Wisma Merdeka. In addition to TAR National Park trips, Sutima can arrange day trips for fishing (RM480 per boat plus bait and gear), and white-water rafting on the Kutima and Padas Rivers west of KK.

**Wildlife Expeditions** (☎ 246000, fax 231758, ✉ leegn@pc.jaring.my) Ground floor, Tanjung Aru Resort; also has an office in Sandakan (see Organised Tours in the Sandakan section for tour details).

If you have a bad trip with an operator in Sabah or Sarawak, the place to take your complaint is the Pejabat Pendaftaran (Licensing Office; ☎ 269711, fax 269713), Lot B, 6.5B, Tingkat 6, Bangunan KWSP, Block D, 88100 KK

## Places to Stay – Budget
KK has the best range of backpackers' accommodation in Sabah. The hostels in particular are excellent places to gather travel information, hook up with fellow travellers and chill out after the inevitable ascent of Mt Kinabalu.

There are two cheap options in Kompleks Sinsuran, near the Filipino Market. Affiliated with the Trekkers Lodge Pantai on Jalan Pantai, the popular *Trekkers Lodge* (☎ 252263, ✉ trekkerslodge@hotmail.com), on the 3rd floor in Block L, is a long-standing hang-out for budget travellers, though it has seen better days. Still, at RM13, including breakfast, the dorm beds are good value. Also available are singles/doubles for RM20/25 with fan, RM36/40 with air-con (RM45 with bathroom). The hostel also has laundry facilities and can arrange tours.

Next door on the 2nd floor, *Borneo Wildlife Youth Hostel* (☎ 213668, ✉ bwa@tm.net.my) has basic but clean dorm rooms at RM10 per bed for HI or ISIC card holders, and RM12 for others; rooms are available for RM24. At the time of writing it was the cheapest place in town and guests were well looked-after by Cecilia, the manager. However, the hostel was scheduled for renovations and new management.

The super-clean and friendly *Backpacker Lodge* (☎ 261495, ✉ backpackerkk@yahoo.com) at Australia Place has beds in segregated dorms for RM18, including breakfast. There's also a double room if you want privacy, though at RM40 it's way overpriced. There are laundry facilities, a small fridge, books to borrow and tour information, and it's well positioned for places to eat and transport.

*Trekkers Lodge Pantai* (☎ 213888, 4th floor, 46 Jalan Pantai), with an entrance from the lane at the back, is another central option. Beds in the small fan/air-con dorms are RM17/20 and basic double rooms are RM37/43; the fan dorm gets a lot of traffic noise. Internet access is available for RM5 per hour. The place closes at midnight and guests don't get a key.

*Farida's Bed & Breakfast* (☎ 428733, ✉ faridabb@hotmail.com, 413 Jalan Saga), at Likas Bay, is a delightful place set in quiet suburbia 6km north of town. Although it's a long way from the city centre, it knows just what backpackers want and can arrange transport and tours to sights around KK. Dorm beds are RM18 per person, and rooms

# KOTA KINABALU

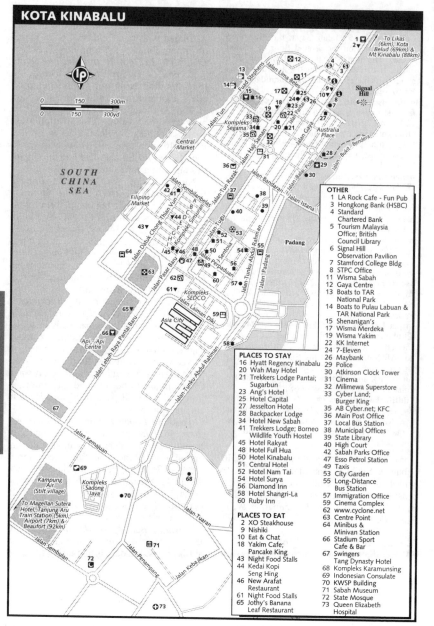

**OTHER**
1 LA Rock Cafe - Fun Pub
3 Hongkong Bank (HSBC)
4 Standard
  Chartered Bank
5 Tourism Malaysia
  Office; British
  Council Library
6 Signal Hill
  Observation Pavilion
7 Stamford College Bldg
8 STPC Office
11 Wisma Sabah
12 Gaya Centre
13 Boats to TAR
  National Park
14 Boats to Pulau Labuan &
  TAR National Park
15 Shenanigan's
17 Wisma Merdeka
19 Wisma Yakim
22 KK Internet
24 7-Eleven
26 Maybank
29 Police
30 Atkinson Clock Tower
31 Cinema
32 Milimewa Superstore
33 Cyber Land;
  Burger King
35 AB Cyber.net; KFC
36 Main Post Office
37 Local Bus Station
38 Municipal Offices
39 State Library
40 High Court
42 Sabah Parks Office
47 Esso Petrol Station
49 Taxis
53 City Garden
55 Long-Distance
  Bus Station
57 Immigration Office
59 Cinema Complex
62 www.cyclone.net
63 Centre Point
64 Minibus &
  Minivan Station
66 Stadium Sport
  Cafe & Bar
67 Swingers
  Tang Dynasty Hotel
68 Kompleks Karamunsing
69 Indonesian Consulate
70 KWSP Building
71 Sabah Museum
72 State Mosque
73 Queen Elizabeth
  Hospital

**PLACES TO STAY**
16 Hyatt Regency Kinabalu
20 Wah May Hotel
21 Trekkers Lodge Pantai;
  Sugarbun
23 Ang's Hotel
25 Hotel Capital
27 Jesselton Hotel
28 Backpacker Lodge
34 Hotel New Sabah
41 Trekkers Lodge; Borneo
  Wildlife Youth Hostel
45 Hotel Rakyat
48 Hotel Full Hua
50 Hotel Kinabalu
51 Central Hotel
52 Hotel Nam Tai
54 Hotel Surya
56 Diamond Inn
58 Hotel Shangri-La
60 Ruby Inn

**PLACES TO EAT**
2 XO Steakhouse
9 Nishiki
10 Eat & Chat
18 Yakim Cafe;
  Pancake King
43 Night Food Stalls
44 Kedai Kopi
  Seng Hing
46 New Arafat
  Restaurant
61 Night Food Stalls
65 Jothy's Banana
  Leaf Restaurant

SOUTH
CHINA
SEA

Central
Market

Filipino
Market

Api-Api
Centre

Kompleks
SEDCO

Asia City

Kompleks
Sadong
Jaya

Kampung
Air.
(Stilt village)

To Magellan Sutera
Hotel, Tanjung Aru
Train Station (5km),
Airport (7km) &
Beaufort (92km)

Signal
Hill

Australia
Place

Padang

To Likas
(6km), Kota
Belud (69km) &
Mt Kinabalu (88km)

MALAYSIAN BORNEO

are RM22/25 per person single/double. To get there, take any minibus that goes along Jalan Tuaran and get off at the Likas Baptist church. Walk 100m down Jalan Likas and then turn right into Jalan Saga – Farida's is 200m on the left.

The travellers' hostels provide better value for money than KK's budget hotels, many of which tend to be noisy and a bit seedy. Some mid-range hotels have cheaper fan-cooled rooms on the higher floors – it's worth asking.

*Hotel Surya* (☎ *246001),* on Jalan Merdeka near the long-distance bus station, is clean and good value. Air-con rooms with toilet are RM35, and twins/triples are RM40/45. Entrance is from the alley around the back, or you can walk through the restaurant on the ground floor.

For a little more money, *Hotel Rakyat* (☎ *222715),* in Block I of Kompleks Sinsuran, is very good. Rooms in this clean, friendly, Muslim-run hotel cost RM37 with fan and bathroom, and RM40 to RM55 with air-con and bathroom. It's central and handy for cheap eating.

If the above are full, the *Central Hotel* (☎ *513522, 5 Jalan Tugu)* has air-con rooms with attached bathroom for RM40/45. Nearby on Jalan Merdeka, you'll find the *Hotel Nam Tai* (☎ *514803).* It's fairly clean and has double rooms for RM35 to RM45.

## Places to Stay – Mid-Range
KK has dozens of mid-range hotels, though a room that would cost RM40 elsewhere in Malaysia costs RM60 and upwards in KK. All are carpeted with air-con, IDD phones and TV; extras may include a minibar and a bath.

*Hotel New Sabah* (☎ *224590)* is in Block A of Kompleks Segama. Rooms are acceptable, if a bit dull, at RM47/57 for singles/doubles; go for the quieter ones at the southern end, away from the neighbouring billiards hall.

The well-organised *Hotel Kinabalu* (☎ *245599, 21 Jalan Tugu)* has pleasant rooms for RM50/60. *Hotel Full Hua* (☎ *234950, 14 Jalan Tugu)* is a friendly place with big rooms that cost RM60 and up

to RM88 for a king-sized room. These two places offer some of the best mid-range value in this part of town.

*Diamond Inn* (☎ *261222),* Jalan Haji Yakub, has big but worn rooms for RM45/55 and twins for RM65. *Ruby Inn* (☎ *213222),* Jalan Laiman Diki, is part of the same chain and has spacious rooms with a fridge for RM50 a single and RM60 for doubles or twins.

There are a couple of good mid-range places at the top end of Jalan Haji Saman. *Wah May Hotel* (☎ *266118),* at No 36, is a well-run and popular hotel with small singles for RM55 and larger singles/ doubles from RM60/65. Nearby, *Ang's Hotel* (☎ *234999),* on the corner of Lorong Bakau and Jalan Pantai, is one of the city's older places (check out the charming lift); it's a bit faded but rooms are still comfortable and clean. Windowless air-con rooms are RM48, and rooms with a double bed and natural light cost RM56.

*Hotel Capital* (☎ *231999, fax 237222, 23 Jalan Haji Saman)* is an upmarket option at the northern end of town. With a discount, rooms are very good value: standard rooms are RM70/80, and suites are RM196 and RM220. For an extra RM7 you'll get a good breakfast.

## Places to Stay – Top End
Among the seemingly endless redevelopment of KK are some massive new luxury hotels offering all the trappings of the leading hotels in Singapore and KL. Competition is fierce, and promotional discounts are often there for the asking.

The three-star *Hotel Shangri-La* (☎ *212800, fax 212078,* ✉ *kkshang@po .jaring.my, 75 Bandaran Berjaya)* is a brass-and-marble slab south of the long-distance bus station, and is popular with local businesspeople; published room rates start at RM185/215.

The four-star *Jesselton Hotel* (☎ *223333, fax 240401,* ✉ *jesshtl@po.jaring.my, 69 Jalan Gaya)* is the oldest of KK's many hotels and the best place to stay in town. Its 33 rooms are tastefully decorated in mock-colonial wood and marble. Published rates start at RM280/340, and RM750 gets you a night in a gorgeous suite with a rock pool and alcove. Discounts of 40% are available on standard rooms, 30% on the suite. There's also a very good restaurant, coffee shop, business centre and a red hansom cab to shuttle you to the airport.

The *Hyatt Regency Kinabalu* (☎ *221234, fax 218909,* @ *mciid633584@mcimail .com), Jalan Datuk Salleh Sulong, is in a perfect location opposite the waterfront and has a swimming pool, restaurants and business facilities. It lacks the class and charm of the Jesselton, but is more expensive; standard rooms are RM356, although discounts are likely, especially on rooms without a sea view.

If you have no reason to stay in the city centre, it's worth considering the five-star *Shangri-La Tanjung Aru Resort* (☎ *225800, fax 244871,* @ *star@po.jaring.my),* on the beach at Tanjung Aru near the airport. The resort is the flagship of upmarket travel in Sabah and hosts plenty of dignitaries. It has an impressive array of facilities, tasteful rooms and published rates from RM370 to RM1800.

Another five-star option is *Magellan Sutera Hotel* (☎ *312222, fax 312020,* @ *sutera@suterah.po.my)* at the sprawling Sutera Harbour complex just south of the city centre. Rooms rates vary with the tides, as plenty of significant specials are offered to attract business; published rates are RM565 to RM3500. The Magellan is one of two hotels on this tourism reclamation site, which features the obligatory golf course, luxury condos and the like.

## Places to Eat

For variety of restaurants and quality of food, Kota Kinabalu ranks up there with Kuching as the best city in Malaysian Borneo. There are Chinese *kedai kopi* (coffee shops) and Malaysian halal restaurants scattered everywhere but particularly in the Segama and Sinsuran complexes, Asia City and opposite the long-distance bus station. Other choices include fine seafood, Indian, Japanese and Western restaurants in the city centre.

**Food Stalls** The best night market in town is at the *SEDCO Complex* (although this is the old name, everyone still calls it this). The speciality is seafood, but other dishes are also available. The stall owners have an uncanny instinct for the arrival of rain and can have the whole area covered in minutes. Hawkers set up around the *Filipino Market* at night and in the vacant lot near Asia City on Jalan Pasar Baru. The top floor of the *central market* also has good food stalls.

KK's shopping malls are good foraging-grounds for cheap fare. During the day, the food court on the 6th floor of *Wisma Merdeka* is the place to go for good cheap eats – including vegetarian food – and views over the islands.

**Chinese** The *kedai kopi* under Ang's Hotel is a great spot but gets very crowded – get a seat early. *Kedai Kopi Seng Hing*, in Block E of Kompleks Sinsuran, is an unremarkable Chinese cafe that serves remarkable prawn *mee* (noodle) soup at lunchtime – recommended. Dim-sum breakfasts can be enjoyed on weekends at the air-con restaurant downstairs at the *Hotel Nan Xing*.

**Indian** For cheap Indian food, try *New Arafat Restaurant* in Block I of Kompleks Sinsuran. This 24-hour place is run by very friendly Indians and serves good curries, roti and *murtabak* (flat, pancake-like bread filled with pieces of mutton, chicken or vegetables). This and other Indian places in Sinsuran get crowded with people watching loud videos in the evenings.

For fine Indian cooking, look no further than *Restoran Ranasahib*, in Block G of Asia City. There is a large range of vindaloo, masala and tandoori, and if you have a favourite that's not on the menu, just ask and they might be able to whip it up. The mango lassi is a classic – leave room for one or two.

*Jothy's Banana Leaf Restaurant*, in the Api-Api Centre, is very good and quite cheap; fine curries and roti are served on banana leaves in quiet, air-con comfort.

**Malay** Cheap 24-hour *halal restaurants* opposite the long-distance bus station on

Jalan Tunku Abdul Rahman serve roti and murtabak, which make ideal snacks before you hop on a bus. Tell the bus touts where you are and they'll come and get you when it's time to leave.

*Eat & Chat*, across from the SPTC office on Jalan Gaya, has cheap and delicious Malay, Western and Chinese food; the tasty RM4 lunch buffet makes it popular with students and office workers.

Air-con restaurants in upmarket hotels serve more-expensive (but good), Malay fare as well as Western favourites. The *Tivoli Restaurant* in the Hotel Shangri-La has a good evening Malay buffet.

**Western** For something a little upmarket, the *XO Steakhouse (54 Jalan Gaya)* serves 'air-chilled' steaks flown in from Australia and the USA, and the three-course set lunch is good value at RM16.

The best – and probably the most expensive – Western food in town is at the *Gardenia* in the Jesselton Hotel. The diverse menu includes good beef cuts and fresh fish.

*Bistretto* is a clean, bright place with an Italian theme, on the ground floor of Kompleks Karamunsing. The selection includes delicious toasted sandwiches, soups, pastas and savoury pancakes, which can be followed by excellent milk shakes, ice cream and sundaes.

Among the good hotel restaurants that serve fish and chips, burgers and other favourites are the *Wishbone Cafe & Restaurant* in the Jesselton Hotel (don't go past the durian ice cream), and *Sri Kapitol Coffee House* in the Hotel Capital.

**Other Food** The restaurants and coffee shops at the *Jesselton*, *Capital* and *Hyatt* hotels do decent Western-style breakfasts, but they aren't cheap. The Hyatt starts at 6 am but is overpriced at RM28 for an ordinary buffet.

For expensive but good Japanese food, try *Nishiki*, opposite the Tourism Malaysia office.

*Season Cake House* has a branch in the Milimewa Superstore and one in Wisma Merdeka that does delicious waffles – turn

right as you go in the main entrance on Jalan Haji Saman then follow your nose.

If you're in the neighbourhood, breakfast is good value at the *Hotel Shangri-La Hotel* restaurant – a hearty 'American breakfast' is RM11.90. For a cheap alternative to the pricey Western hotel breakfasts, try the *Pancake King* or *Yakim Cafe*, at the same spot on Jalan Haji Saman; the King is famed for his peanut pancakes (70 sen each).

## Entertainment

Unless you're up for a trip to the suburbs or love karaoke, KK's nightlife is mostly limited to hotel bars and discos. Nothing much happens until very late; don't arrange any activities for the morning after if you are planning a night out.

By default, the evening often starts at *Shenanigan's*, a squeaky-clean yuppie bar around the side at the Hyatt. Live bands perform most nights from 9 pm and the place gets packed on weekends. Entry is free and drinks are reasonably priced (beer is RM7.50) during happy hour (till 9.30 pm); the dress code – no singlets or flip flops (thongs) – is usually enforced.

The name changes, but there's always a bar upstairs at 49 Jalan Gaya; presently it's the *LA Rock Cafe – Fun Pub*. It's cheap and friendly, though it's very much a local scene – this is where Filipinos and their friends unwind. *Stadium Sport Cafe & Bar*, on the 1st floor of Block 3 in the Api-Api Centre, is open from 4.30 pm, though it's usually deserted till much later. It's popular with expats for a cheap beer (RM5.50) and not a bad place to wait it out till the dance clubs get rolling.

*Swingers* is the best dance club in town, and often features live bands. It's on the 1st floor of the Tang Dynasty hotel, a location that guarantees drinks will be overpriced; a jug (pitcher) of beer is RM47. There's another large dance club in the Pan Pacific hotel south of the city centre, but it's very hard to get a cab back to town late at night.

One entertainment option that you'll see advertised in lights along the streets of KK is *MTV parlours*, one of Taiwan's gifts to modern culture. Here you can rent and

MALAYSIAN BORNEO

## And the Bands Play On

Wander into a hotel bar in Sabah or Sarawak and chances are a microphone will occupy centre stage. The odds are about even that the mike will be firmly gripped by a besotted businessman croaking his favourite karaoke tune, or by a smooth Filipina songstress (or two or three) dressed in go-go boots and backed by an organ-grinder with a bad perm.

Welcome to the world of live entertainment, Borneo style. Because of its proximity to the southern Philippines, most of the live bands making the rounds of bigger hotels and nightclubs are from Mindanao. These are often family affairs, someone's cousin filling in on guitar while the elder brother makes a visit back home.

The quality of the music is as variable as the line-up – while most singers have Mariah Carey and Britney Spears down pat, attempts at a Santana guitar solo may be hit and miss. Still, as cover bands go, they can be very entertaining, and often note-perfect. The Piccolo Band, most of whom are from the Philippine island of Palawan, bring the house down with an uncanny version of George Michael doing Queen. And you'd swear Matchbox 20 had turned up for a gig until you saw the six-piece Indonesian band on stage.

The same goes for the increasing number of bands from KL on the scene. The talent is sometimes stretched thin, but there are some outstanding musicians that play a wide range of music, from country and western to hip-hop. One of the best bar bands around is the Headliners – big Bob and the band know what you want, and can deliver on everything from classic Bread to Pink Floyd and the Beastie Boys. There isn't a cooler bass player in Borneo, and the lead female vocalist may be tiny but she hardly needs a microphone to out-sing Whitney Houston.

Unfortunately, outside the big hotels there aren't many venues for live bands – and most of the hotel lounges are set aside for the questionable tastes of local businessmen (which run to the aforementioned go-go boots and lots of Chinese pop songs). In what may prove to be test of will between government and business, Dr Mahathir would like to replace those Filipino bands with Malays – musicians are among the 160-odd occupations recently declared suitable only for Malaysians. While Filipino and Indonesian migrant workers are being squeezed on all sides, two factors favour the continued good fortunes of the Filipino bands – the comparatively cheap cost, and those go-go boots...

watch laser-disc movies or grainy pirated tapes of new Hollywood releases in private rooms. There's no limit to how many can share the fun, and you can drink, smoke and eat in the rooms. Costs are RM20 to RM30 per movie and many places stay open till 11 pm or later.

## Shopping

Although a major centre, KK isn't a great place for handicrafts. Nearly everything on offer is mass-produced for the tourist trade – from factory-made batik to scorpions mounted as paperweights, fridge magnets and key rings. Wisma Merdeka has plenty of outlets for these souvenirs on its ground floor. If you're travelling on to Kuching in Sarawak, save your money till you get there.

You can buy Filipino crafts in the market on the waterfront; folk medicines, cheap clothes, watches, sunglasses and virtually anything else can be found in the markets around town.

## Getting There & Away

**Air**  The Malaysia Airlines office (☎ 213555) is on the 11th floor of the Gaya Centre.

The KWSP building, over the other side of town on Jalan Tunku Abdul Rahman, has offices for a number of other airlines, including Dragonair (also Cathay Pacific Airways; ☎ 254733), Royal Brunei Airlines (☎ 242193), Singapore Airlines (☎ 255444) and Thai Airways International (☎ 232896).

Travel agents closer to town all book Malaysia Airlines flights for the same price.

***Sabah & Sarawak*** KK is the hub of the Malaysia Airlines network in Sabah and there are regular flights to Bintulu (one or two daily, RM127), Kuching (up to seven daily, RM228), Pulau Labuan (seven daily, RM52), Lahad Datu (at least three daily, RM106), Miri (at least five daily, RM96; Twin Otters fly four times weekly for RM82), Sandakan (usually seven daily, RM83), Sibu (usually three daily, RM180) and Tawau (usually nine daily, RM104). There are five weekly flights to KK from Sandakan (RM69).

***Peninsular Malaysia & Singapore*** The cheapest way of getting from Peninsular Malaysia to KK is by purchasing a 14-day advance-purchase ticket from Johor Bahru (daily flights, RM295); the regular fare is RM347. There are also economy night flights from KL for RM306, advance-purchase fares for RM372 or the regular fare of RM437.

The KK-Singapore fare is RM584, so it is cheaper to take the flights to/from Johor Bahru and cross the Causeway on the Malaysia Airlines bus, which takes you right into Singapore.

***Other Destinations*** Malaysia Airlines has at least one flight daily, except Saturday, to Bandar Seri Begawan (BSB) in Brunei (RM103). The airline also flies daily direct between Hong Kong and KK, as well as to Manila in the Philippines three times a week and to Cebu City twice a week.

**Bus** There is no main bus station in KK; long-distance air-con express buses, long-distance minibuses and minivans depart from two places around the city centre. Note that transport may leave for some destinations from both spots, and the asking price may not be quite the same.

***Long-Distance Bus Station*** Air-con express buses are the best way to reach Mt Kinabalu and major towns on the east coast. Buses leave from the area south-east of the municipal offices on Jalan Tunku Abdul Rahman; long-distance buses leave in the morning from about 6.30 am. Some minibuses and minivans also operate from here.

Touts will accost you well before you reach the bus park; they're a bit in-your-face but don't get flustered – most are helpful and will guide you to the right bus. A myriad of companies service the main routes; many (but not all) have wooden shacks where you can check current schedules and make advance bookings. It's probably better to book ahead on weekends for Sandakan, but generally you can just turn up before the scheduled departure time and hop on. In any case, the bus may wait for an hour or so for more passengers to turn up. Main destinations and fares from here are as follows; current schedules for express buses on the longer routes should be checked in advance, and note that prices will have risen by up to 30% by the time you read this.

**Beaufort** Minivans leave throughout the day (morning is most reliable) for the trip to Beaufort (RM7); they will drop you in Papar for RM4. Minibuses (RM8) do the run at 8 am and 1.30 pm.

**Keningau** Buses leave at 7 and 10 am, and 1 and 4 pm (RM15).

**Kota Belud** There are departures until 5 pm, but most are in the morning (two hours, RM5).

**Kota Marudu & Kudat** Services leave at 7.30, 9.30 and 11 am; minivans stop at Kota Marudu (RM10) on the way to Kudat (three hours, RM15).

**Lahad Datu (for connections to Semporna)** There's an express bus at 7.30 am (RM35).

**Lawas (Sarawak)** A bus leaves at 1.30 pm; buses pass through Papar, Beaufort and Sipitang. The trip to Lawas takes about four hours (RM25).

**Mt Kinabalu** Buses leave for the national park around 7 am daily (RM15, three hours) – check the schedule in advance, and book on weekends. You could also take any bus going to Ranau or Sandakan and ask to be dropped off at the entrance road, from where the park headquarters is 100m uphill. Minivans do the trip for RM10.

**Ranau (for Poring Hot Springs)** There are morning departures from around 8.30 am (3½ hours, RM15). All Ranau buses and minivans pass the entrance to Mt Kinabalu National Park (RM10); ask to be dropped off.

**Sandakan** Services depart daily between 7 and 9 am (six hours, RM25); it's advisable to book ahead on weekends.

**MALAYSIAN BORNEO**

**Semporna** There's an express bus at 7 am (RM50); buy your ticket a day in advance at the green Pengang Kutan booth.

**Tawau** Express buses leave at 7, 7.20, 7.30 and 8.30 am, and 8 pm daily (nine hours, RM45).

Land Cruisers may be running to Sandakan and Tawau in the morning; ask around at the bus station the day before you plan to depart. These cost more than buses, but are often faster and more comfortable.

You can take buses via Sipitang all the way to Lawas and on to Brunei from here as well.

***Centre Point Lot*** The large vacant lot behind Centre Point is a busy minibus and minivan depot. Most transport from here is local, but there are plenty of departures for centres around KK, such as Penampang, Papar and Tuaran, and farther north to Kota Belud and Kudat.

Minivans have rough schedules, but leave when they're full. You'll be pressured by touts to take a certain van, but don't commit yourself until you see how many people are on board. There'll often be more than one minivan leaving and if yours is empty, there could be a long wait until it fills up. If you get to the bus stand and there isn't a minivan with even one passenger going your way, hang back for a few minutes; chances are there's one that's nearly full doing a lap of the town trying to fill the last couple of seats.

Departures are frequent in the early morning; there are often far fewer later in the day. The general rule is make sure you travel early, and the farther you travel the earlier you should leave.

Some examples of services from here are:

**Beaufort** Regular departures until about 5 pm (two hours, RM7).

**Kampung Likas (Likas Bay)** Frequent departures between 6.30 am and 5 pm (70 sen).

**Keningau** Regular departures until about 5 pm (about 2½ hours, RM10).

**Kudat** Departures until about 5 pm (three to four hours, RM15).

**Papar** Departures until 5 pm (one hour, RM3).

**Ranau** Mainly early-morning departures, but may leave as late as 6 pm; all buses and vans

pass Kinabalu National Park (3½ hours, RM10 or RM15).

**Tambunan** Departures to about 5 pm (about 2½ hours, RM10).

**Tamparuli** Regular morning departures, some minivans until 5 pm (RM3).

**Tuaran** Departures throughout the day (30 minutes, RM2).

As with express buses, if you're heading for Kinabalu National Park from KK, you can take a minivan for Ranau or Sandakan and get off at the park entrance; ask the driver to drop you off.

**Train** Sabah's only railway runs between Tanjung Aru train station, Papar, Beaufort and Tenom. See the Papar and Beaufort Getting There & Away sections for more details.

Tanjung Aru train station (☎ 254611 for schedules and bookings) is 5km south of the city centre, close to the airport.

**Taxi** There are share-taxis to many minivan destinations. They also leave when full, but the fares are much higher than the minivans. Their big advantage is that they are much quicker and more comfortable.

A couple of share-taxis do a daily run between KK and Ranau (RM15 per person or RM60 for the whole taxi), and can get you to/from the turn-off to park headquarters at Mt Kinabalu (also RM15).

**Boat** Passenger boats leave daily for Pulau Labuan (about 1½ hours, RM28/33 for economy/1st class) from the jetties behind the Hyatt Regency; from Labuan there are connecting services to Brunei. Like their cousins in Sarawak, these are long, narrow and fast ferries, on which you'll be assaulted by Chinese pop videos en route. The ride is generally smooth, however, as long as the sea is not too rough.

Two companies have offices at the jetties. Among the fast ferries, the *Labuan Express* leaves KK at 8 and 10 am, and 1.30 and 3 pm; it makes the return trip at 8.30 and 10.30 am, and 1 and 3 pm. The *Express Ming Hai* leaves KK at 8 and 10 am, returning at 1 and 3 pm.

Boarding time is 15 minutes before departure, and because Labuan is a Federal Territory you will need to take your passport with you.

There's usually no need to book in advance but if you want to, you can contact Rezeki Murni (☎ 236834), 1st floor, Lot 3, Block D, Kompleks Segama.

The South China Sea is generally calmest in the early morning, but can get quite rough later in the day. Services may be disrupted and even cancelled when smoke haze is bad. See the Labuan Getting There & Away section for return times.

For boats to KK's offshore islands, see Getting There & Away in the Tunku Abdul Rahman National Park section.

## Getting Around

**To/From the Airport** KK's modern international airport is at Tanjung Aru, 7km south-west of the city centre. Minivans run to the airport till 10 pm from behind Centre Point; the fare is RM2. Air-con minibuses are less frequent but cheaper at RM1.

Buses marked 'Putatan' from the local bus station also pass the airport turn-off. Departures are irregular, but there is usually at least one an hour during the day; the fare is RM1. This bus stops opposite the access road, from where it's a 10-minute walk to the terminal. Heading into town, there's a bus stop to the right as you leave the airport, 10 minutes' walk from the terminal.

The airport is new and modern, with a post office, hotel and car-rental booking kiosks (often unattended), a Telekom office, exchange bureaux (open only for international flights), a good but expensive bookshop, a fish shop and junk-food outlets.

The 15-minute taxi ride to the airport normally costs RM13 or RM14, but you may be charged more late at night. Leaving the terminal, there's a taxi desk on the ground floor where you can buy a fixed-price coupon for RM12.50 into town.

**Bus** Local buses leave from the stand between the municipal offices and Jalan Tun Razak. The only time you'll probably need one is to get to the airport (RM1) or to

Tanjung Aru train stati
vans that pass the airport a
station. If you don't feel li
Kompleks Karamunsing south
centre, jump on a bus going al
Tunku Abdul Rahman (50 sen).

**Taxi** KK's taxis are plentiful, and there a
several hubs in the city centre where they
congregate – try outside the Hotel Kinabalu
or near the Milimewa Superstore. They are
not metered, so negotiate the fare before
you set off. Theoretically, taxis operate on a
zone system (RM4 in town); in practice,
most trips around town cost RM4 to RM6.

Taxi stands are all over town, but most
can be found in the area between the municipal offices and the main post office.
There is often a surcharge (around RM5) on
night rides, especially for trips out of the
city centre; it can also be difficult to get a
taxi to come out to pick you up at night.

**Car** There are a couple of car-rental booths
near the taxi stand at the airport, though they
are often unstaffed. The bigger hotels and the
Tourism Malaysia office can also help
arrange car rental; it's expensive but competition is brisk and you should be able to get
a better deal for longer rental. The going rate
for a Proton Iswara is RM180 per day, while
a Toyota Land Cruiser costs around RM480
per day. Read the fine print: a surcharge of
RM100 per day is sometimes levied for
travel outside a 50km radius of KK.

## AROUND KOTA KINABALU
## Tunku Abdul Rahman National Park

Five lovely islands a short distance west of
KK – Pulau Manukan, Gaya, Sapi, Mamutik and Sulug – and the reefs in between
make up TAR National Park, which covers
a total area of just over 49 sq km. Only a
short boat ride from the city centre, they
offer crystal-clear water and some excellent
beaches.

Unfortunately, much of the coral around
the islands has been destroyed by dynamite
fishing, and experienced divers and
snorkellers will likely be disappointed.

...on (50 sen). Mini-
...lso pass the train
...e walking to
... of the city
...ng Jalan

...l fish, how-
...pportunities
...offers easy

...on Gaya,
...possible to
...sy enough
...oy a day
...peach – or

...transport is provided by Kotkas Sabah, as well as by Sutima Express, which has an office at its jetty on the KK side. Sutima also rents snorkelling gear for RM15 per day and tents for RM10 per night. For more details, contact the Sutima Express main office (☎ 016-832 3144), 1st floor, Lot 5, Block A, Kompleks Sinsuran.

There's a park entrance fee of RM2 per person, which is valid for all the islands.

**Pulau Manukan** Manukan is the most popular destination for KK residents and has well-developed facilities. It is the second-largest island in the group and its 0.2 sq km are largely covered in dense vegetation. There's a good beach with coral reefs off the southern and eastern shores, and a walking trail around the perimeter. There's quite a good range of tropical fish – and many can be seen simply by looking down from the jetty.

Other wildlife includes the Tabon scrub-fowl, a primitive bird that lays its eggs in piles of rotting vegetation. The birds are shy, but can be seen by walking quietly along the island's jogging path early or late in the day. In the gardens around the chalets you may see sunbirds and fruit-pigeons.

Equipment for hire includes mask, fins and snorkel (RM15), surf mats (RM5) and rubber tubes (RM5); a security deposit is payable. There's a shop selling post-cards, T-shirts, sun hats, ice creams and souvenirs.

**Pulau Gaya** With an area of about 15 sq km and rising in places to an elevation of 300m, Pulau Gaya is by far the largest island in the park. It's also the closest to KK and is virtually covered in undisturbed tropical forest. There are about 20km of marked hiking trails and a good stretch of white sand – Police Beach – at Bulijong Bay. The trails may be rather overgrown, and the shallow water at Police Beach washes a fair bit of garbage ashore. If you're lucky, you may see monkeys, pangolins or even a bearded pig.

**Pulau Sapi** Pulau Sapi (Cow Island) lies just off the south-western tip of Pulau Gaya and is the most-visited island in the park. With an area of only 0.1 sq km, the island has good beaches, a nature trail and some of the best snorkelling in the park. Macaques live in the forest and sometimes go down to the beach to look for crabs – they also come looking for foolish tourists handing out food and can be quite aggressive; mind your bags and other gear if macaques are about.

There is no accommodation on Sapi, but there are shelters, changing rooms, toilets and barbecue pits. Snorkelling equipment can be hired at RM15 for a snorkel and mask.

**Pulau Mamutik** This is the smallest island in the park and is less-visited by tourists than its nearby neighbours. There are good beaches right around the island and some good coral reefs, particularly on the eastern side.

**Pulau Sulug** This island, covering less than 1 sq km, is the least visited of the group, probably because it's the farthest away from KK. It has only one beach, on the eastern shore, but the snorkelling is quite good and it makes a quiet day trip.

**Stilt Villages** Some of the islands are home to small stilt villages, but an impressive and illicit version of Brunei's famous Kampung Ayer has grown in front of Pulau Gaya – it can easily be seen from the city waterfront. Unlike Brunei's water villages, however, this floating suburb is not a tourist attraction. It is mainly inhabited by Filipino refugees, who you'll see hopping into speedboats to be ferried back home.

The village is generally considered a no-go area, and it wouldn't be wise to hop in a

MALAYSIAN BORNEO

boat and go exploring through the maze of rickety plankwalks – someone may be poor and desperate enough to relieve you of your valuables. Also, tourists have reportedly been told on occasion to pay double the agreed-upon price when they landed at the village.

**Places to Stay & Eat** Kinabalu Gold Resorts (☎ 088-257941, fax 242861, ✆ nature@kinabalu.net – see Information in the KK section) manages *Manukan Island Resort*, which has chalets, a restaurant, swimming pool and squash courts. The chalets sleep up to four people and have air-con; all are fully furnished with a desalinated shower and kitchen/dining facilities. A chalet unit costs RM161 per night during the week, and RM230 per night on weekends and holidays.

There is dorm-style accommodation on *Mamutik*, though it was closed for renovations at the time of writing. As with other accommodation in TAR National Park, bookings are through Kinabalu Gold Resorts.

A study in contrast to Pulau Gaya's other stilt village, *Gayana Resort Bay* is a luxury development similar to the Dragon Inn at Semporna, where thatched bungalows sit on stilts over the water. There's a restaurant and water-sports centre; around the point is the Reef Project building, where research is conducted and public awareness of coral-reef destruction is raised. Published rates for accommodation are astronomical (RM330 to RM350), but sizeable discounts should be available. Contact the main office (☎ 0188-264461, fax 264460, ✆ gayana@tm.net.my), ground floor, Wisma Sabah, KK, for more details.

It is possible to *camp* on Gaya, Sulug, Mamutik and Sapi for RM5 per person, if you bring your own tent and apply for permission in writing from the Sabah Parks office (☎ 088-211881), Block K, Kompleks Sinsuran, Jalan Tun Fuad Stephens (see Information in the Kota Kinabalu section earlier). Officially, you must do this 'well in advance'.

*Coral Garden Seafood Restaurant* on Manukan is open from 7 am to 9 pm, and serves a wide range of Western and Malay dishes, and good seafood, though price depends on availability.

**Getting There & Away** Boats to the islands leave from jetties behind Wisma Merdeka, near the Hyatt Regency. There are plenty of aggressive touts who will try to get you to charter a boat to the islands for RM25 each way (they'll take RM20). Ignore them and head for the Kotkas Sabah jetty – Kotkas is a legitimate operation that runs boats regularly every day, despite what the touts from other boat operators may tell you. Scheduled departures to Manukan are at 8, 9, 10 and 11 am, and noon, 2 and 4.30 pm. The fare is RM5/10 return for children/adults, and the trip to Manukan takes about 40 minutes. Boats leave Manukan at 7.30, 9.30, 10.30 and 11.30 am, and 1, 3 and 4 pm. Depending on demand, most call at Pulau Sapi as well. The only disadvantage to the Kotkas boats is that a minimum of three passengers are required to depart – after 9 am, you may have a wait on your hands if you're on your own.

Another good option is Sutima Express, which has boats to all the islands (RM6/10 for children/adults return) plus Police Beach (RM10/15). A minimum of six passengers is needed, however. Sutima also arranges island-hopping charters in a glass-bottom boat.

Apart from the charter costs, you'll also have to pay the RM2 park fee, which covers all the islands.

### Beaches

There are a few shallow paddling beaches near the highway south of KK. The nearest is at the plush Shangri-La Tanjung Aru Resort (see Places to Stay – Top End in the KK section), but other accommodation is available along the coast between the airport and Papar. The beaches won't win any awards, but you could pleasantly laze away a day or two before catching a plane. Women travellers who aren't covered from head to toe while sunbathing can expect to be gawked at by local men on any beach.

**Places to Stay** *Seaside Travellers Inn* (☎ 088-750555, ✆ stinnjo@tm.net.my,

*House 30, Gaya Park),* off Jalan Penampang, is 20km south of KK; it is a reasonable alternative to the resorts. A bed in a fan-cooled dorm with shared bathroom costs RM25; economy rooms with shared facilities are RM33 to RM55. More-expensive rooms and bungalows cost RM66 to RM99 with hot water, air-con and TV. All prices include a continental breakfast.

Nearby is the better but pricier **Langkah Syabas Beach Resort** (☎ *088-752000, fax 752111,* @ *lsr@po.jaring.my),* with 14 chalets just off the beach. Published rates are RM154 for a semi-detached chalet to RM209 for a deluxe detached unit. The resort also sports a pool, restaurant and bar; airport transfers are free.

**Getting There & Away** To get to the beaches south of KK, take a Papar minivan (RM3) from behind Centre Point. For the Seaside Travellers Inn, get off near the Km 20 mark; the inn is a short walk past the school.

### PULAU LAYANG LAYANG

Some 300km north-west of KK, Layang Layang is a tiny island surrounded by a coral atoll. It's an exclusive dive location and part of the famous (among divers, at least) Borneo Banks. Wall diving is excellent here; some serious macro diving is also possible, as the area is visited by hammerhead sharks and manta rays.

Layang Layang has a growing reputation among divers as a good alternative to the wasted coral found in many other spots around Sabah. Another part of the appeal is the chance to splash around in a geopolitical hot-spot, as Layang Layang is one of the disputed Spratlys, a collection of about 600 islands, reefs and atolls strategically located in the South China Sea. With the prospect of undersea oil reserves and rich fishing, parts of the Spratlys are claimed by China, Vietnam, Taiwan, the Philippines, Malaysia and even plucky Brunei. China and Vietnam have already clashed over Chinese occupation of several islands, and Malaysia has a small naval base on Layang Layang.

Layang Layang covers less than 1 sq km, but is surrounded by an atoll more than 7km long and 2km wide. The diving is excellent, particularly down the wall, where pelagic species such as tuna and barracuda are encountered, and reef sharks and hammerheads are seen regularly. Soft corals are a feature and manta rays are visible in shallower water. The island is also a breeding ground for sea birds such as boobies and terns.

### Getting There & Away

Layang Layang can only be visited as part of an expensive tour. There is only one resort on the island and live-aboard vessels depart from KK between April and September. See Organised Tours in the KK section for outfits offering dive charters; live-aboards are an increasingly popular option.

# South of Kota Kinabalu

The Crocker Range is the backbone of western Sabah, rising from near Tenom in the south and culminating in the north at massive Mt Kinabalu and its outlier, Mt Trus Madi. Nearly 1500m below the range is the fertile coastal plain, where KK and other large settlements sit. Logging has taken a devastating toll on most of Sabah, but the Crocker still has some good stands of intact forest, and much of it is now preserved as the Crocker Range National Park. Unfortunately, the park has no facilities, trails or accommodation.

A highway climbs steeply from KK over Gunung Alab to Tambunan then veers south to the central valley towns of Keningau and Tenom. From here you can travel by road to Batu Punggul.

Heading south from KK, another road follows a coastal plain past Papar before reaching Beaufort, Sipitang and the Sarawak border. A popular and scenic way of closing the loop is to take the railway from Beaufort to Tenom, and there's a rough overland route between the coast road and Keningau.

## TAMBUNAN RAFFLESIA RESERVE
☎ 088

Near the top of the range next to the highway is the Tambunan Rafflesia Reserve, devoted to the world's largest flower. The rafflesia is a parasitic plant that grows hidden within the stems of jungle vines until it bursts into bloom. The large bulbous flowers can be up to 1m in diameter. The 12 or so species of rafflesia are found only in Borneo and Sumatra; several species are unique to Sabah, but their blooming is unpredictable.

The Rafflesia Information Centre (☎ 774691), on the highway 59km from KK, has interesting displays and information on the rafflesia. It is open weekdays from 8 am to 12.45 pm and 2 to 5 pm, and on weekends from 8 am to 5 pm. From the centre, trails lead into the forest where the rafflesias can be found. Whether you will find one in bloom is very much a matter of luck, though the staff at the centre can tell you of the latest sightings. The flowers may be close to the information centre or involve a walk deep into the forest. In theory, guides are available to take you to the flowers at fixed times, but staff are actually rarely available.

Even if there are no rafflesias, there are pleasant walks at the reserve. There is also a good walk to **Sensuron Waterfall**, just off the highway about 4km from the information centre towards KK. It is a 45-minute walk down to the falls from the highway, and near the starting point on the other side of the road is a lookout point and picnic tables.

### Places to Stay & Eat

There is no accommodation at the reserve. The *Gunung Emas Highlands Resort* (☎ 215499, 256955, fax 238158, Km 52, Jalan KK-Tambunan) is perched on the side of the mountain 7km back towards KK from the Rafflesia Information Centre. The views are superb and the climate is refreshing, if not downright cold.

The resort has rooms ranging from dorm beds for RM15 to a 'tree-top cabin' for RM38. Simple but comfortable rooms in the main building annexe start at RM68 and climb to RM99. The cabins are on the other side of the highway and a steep climb up the mountain; they are built around tree trunks. They're a great novelty, but small and very rustic; it is an almost vertical walk up to the shower blocks near the cabins and down to the restaurant on the highway.

The *restaurant* at the resort serves good Chinese dishes. On weekends it is overrun with day-trippers, and cars and noise from video games destroy the tranquil atmosphere.

Farther on towards Tambunan, the *Gunung Alab Resort (☎/fax 302279, Mile 33, Jalan Penampang)* is a smaller and newer hotel with a *halal restaurant* and superb views over the Crocker Range. Spotless but characterless rooms cost RM60 with shared bathroom or RM80 with attached bathroom.

### Getting There & Away

Take a Tambunan or Keningau minivan from KK to the reserve or the resort for RM10. From Tambunan the cost is RM4 and the journey takes 30 minutes.

### TAMBUNAN

Tambunan, a small agricultural service town about 81km from KK, is the first settlement across the Crocker Range. The region was the last stronghold of Mat Salleh, who became a folk hero for rebelling against the British late in the 19th century. He eventually negotiated a truce with the British, which so outraged his own people that he fled to the Tambunan plain where he was eventually besieged and killed. His gravestone is in a cemetery just off the main road, 750m out of town towards Ranau.

There's nothing of interest in the town, but if you have your own 4WD, or are well equipped for trekking, there are some interesting side trips. **Mawar Waterfall** is a pretty waterfall in the Crocker Range, though getting to it is an expedition. From Tambunan head towards Ranau; 7.5km past the turn-off to KK there is a small shop and a very difficult-to-see sign to 'Air Terjun Mawar'. Turn left and keep going past rural areas and new Murut settlements, high up into the mountains. It is beautiful countryside, though the road is long and tortuous and fords a small river.

## Getting There & Away

Regular minivans ply the roads between Tambunan and KK (RM10), Ranau (RM6), Keningau (RM7) and Tenom (RM8).

## MT TRUS MADI

On the opposite side of the highway from Tambunan's shopping area, a road leads to Sabah's second-highest peak – 2642m-high Mt Trus Madi. Though Trus Madi is surrounded by logging concessions, the upper slopes and peak are wild and jungle-clad, and there is talk about turning the mountain into an eco-tourism wilderness reserve before the loggers reach the summit.

There are a couple of muddy trails to the summit that are treacherous in parts – just the thing for those who find Mt Kinabalu a bit pedestrian. Independent trekkers must be well equipped and take all food and water up the mountain.

Before setting off you are strongly advised to hire a guide, or at least get maps and assistance from the Forestry Department (Jabatan Perhutanan; ☎ 087-774691) at the District Office in Tambunan. It might also be able to arrange transport for the 1½-hour trip up to the trails. Some tour operators from KK have treks to Trus Madi – including a combined ascent of Trus Madi and Kinabalu if you're feeling restless – see Organised Tours in the KK section for suggested operators.

To get to the mountain from Tambunan, take the road towards Kaingaran. Past Kampung Batu Lapan take the road to the right, which leads to a network of logging roads. With good maps or a guide, it is possible to go by 4WD up to about 1500m, from where it is a five- to seven-hour climb to the top of Trus Madi. From Tambunan it's a 28km walk to the peak along the pleasant valley road then up through logging roads.

## KENINGAU

Keningau is a haphazard timber and agricultural boomtown, and you are only likely to stop here to change buses. Attracted by the prospect of well-paid employment, people have flocked here from neighbouring districts, as well as from Indonesia and the Philippines, and the town's population has more than doubled since the 1960s. There is a large **tamu** (weekly market) every Thursday; though the town is deep in the heart of Murut country, it's most unlikely you'll see anyone dressed in traditional tribal wear.

In the unlikely event you are forced to overnight in Keningau, there are plenty of hotels. The cheaper places are very seedy, but Keningau has been feeling hard times for a while and top-end accommodation can be a bargain.

## Getting There & Away

Share-taxis and minivans are the only transport available; these leave for Tenom from around the central square by the market, while for Ranau and KK, flocks of lazing minivans loiter about 300m to the north, across from the BP petrol station and the KFC.

The cheapest way to travel from Keningau to KK is by minivan (2½ hours, RM15) – the trip in the opposite direction is cheaper, but that's Sabah for you. Share-taxis do the Keningau-KK journey for about RM30.

The journey from Keningau to Tenom costs RM5 by taxi or minivan, and takes about one hour along a good road with lovely views of the mountains. There are also taxis and minivans to Tambunan (RM7) and Kuala Penyu (morning only, RM6).

The last minivan to Ranau (RM15) leaves at noon, so don't be late arriving in Keningau. The road to Ranau is a shocker. The hairpin gravel road follows a deep river-chasm much of the way – it's so bad that drivers actually resort to seatbelts, a real novelty in Sabah. After heavy rain the bank is often washed away in places. The trip is decidedly dicey, and vehicles may have to turn back. If you make it to Ranau from here, you can go on to either Sandakan or Kinabalu National Park.

A logging road also runs down the rugged and spectacular Crocker Range from Keningau towards the coast, then links up with the Papar-Beaufort road. It is only recommended for 4WD vehicles – and

MALAYSIAN BORNEO

remember that logging trucks always have right of way.

## TENOM
☎ 087

Nestled in a lovely cool, cloud-shrouded valley, Tenom is the home of the friendly Murut people, most of whom are farmers. Soya beans, maize and vegetables are grown in this fertile area, and there are several cocoa plantations. The area is also populated by Dusun, Indians and Chinese. Tenom is the end of the railway line from Tanjung Aru in KK.

Despite the peaceful setting, there's nothing to do in the town. The Agricultural Park Sabah has an Orchid Centre outside town (see the following Around Tenom section), which makes an interesting diversion. About 10 minutes out of town on the road towards Beaufort is a recently built replica of a **Murut longhouse**, which houses the fledgling Murut Cultural Centre. The centre was built to record something of the area's local traditions, as longhouses as far away as Tomani have either been burnt or abandoned in the last few years.

Tenom is a compact little place and it's very easy to find your way around. Minivans

park near the *padang* (town square) and cruise up and down the main street, while taxis wait near the Hotel Sri Perdana.

### Places to Stay
The best-value place in town is the popular *Hotel Sri Perdana (☎ 734001),* Jalan Tun Mustapha. Promotional rates for clean, comfortable air-con singles/doubles are just RM30/40; twins are RM35.

*Hotel Sri Jaya (☎ 735669),* Jalan Padas, is also good value. Rooms with air-con, TV and bathroom cost from RM30/35. Opposite, the upmarket *Orchid Hotel (☎ 737600)* is newer and has singles/doubles for RM42/60, twins for RM72 and triples for RM83; suites go for RM110.

*Hotel Perkasa Tenom (☎ 735811)* perches high on a hill above the town like a Transylvanian castle. Its 70-odd fully air-con rooms, restaurant and minibars seem totally over the top for sleepy Tenom, and in fact it has a very low occupancy rate – at the time of writing, rooms were going for just RM50. It's a very steep walk, so if you want to check in, phone from the town and someone will come down to collect you; otherwise, take a taxi.

MALAYSIAN BORNEO

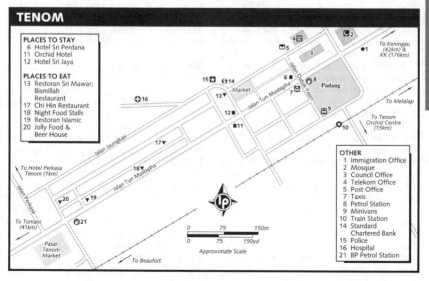

**TENOM**

PLACES TO STAY
6  Hotel Sri Perdana
11 Orchid Hotel
12 Hotel Sri Jaya

PLACES TO EAT
13 Restoran Sri Mawar;
   Bismillah
   Restaurant
17 Chi Hin Restaurant
18 Night Food Stalls
19 Restoran Islamic
20 Jolly Food &
   Beer House

To Keningau
(42km) &
KK (176km)

Padang

To Melalap

To Tenom
Orchid Centre
(15km)

Jalan Datuk Yassin

Jalan Tun Mustapha

Market

To Hotel Perkasa
Tenom (1km)

Jalan Jaungkan

Jalan Tun Mustapha

Jalan Perkasa

To Tomani
(41km)

Pasar
Tenom
Market

To Beaufort

0    75    150m
0    75    150yd
Approximate Scale

OTHER
1  Immigration Office
2  Mosque
3  Council Office
4  Telekom Office
5  Post Office
7  Taxis
8  Petrol Station
9  Minivans
10 Train Station
14 Standard
   Chartered Bank
15 Police
16 Hospital
21 BP Petrol Station

## Places to Eat

*Food stalls* set up in the evening in the car park down the main road from the padang. There are plenty of *kedai kopi* in town selling basic Chinese food. *Chi Hin Restaurant*, not far from the Hotel Kim San, stays open fairly late.

For good Indian food, roti and murtabak, try the restaurant beneath the *Hotel Sri Perdana*; it's friendly and stays open late. Other good options are the *Bismillah Restaurant* and neighbouring *Restoran Sri Mawar*; *Restoran Islamic* is also recommended.

The more upmarket *Jolly Food & Beer House* offers alfresco dining in the evenings, or you can try the air-con bar section inside. The *OK Corner* restaurant in the Hotel Perkasa serves moderately priced Chinese, Malay and Western food.

## Getting There & Away

Because of the state of the railway to Beaufort (and the burnt-out forest around it) and the road between Keningau and Ranau, it might be best to travel direct between KK and Tenom. However, the drive from Tenom to Keningau is beautiful, as this part of the Crocker Range was spared from fire.

**Bus** Lots of minivans park around the padang along Jalan Datuk Yasin; when they're ready to go, they cruise up and down the street drumming up business. Most are going to Keningau (one hour, RM5), but some go to KK (three to four hours, RM25). There are also regular services to Tambunan (RM8).

**Train** Although the railway line goes as far as Melalap, farther up the valley, Tenom is the railhead as far as passenger trains are concerned. The 46km journey to Beaufort was once a popular tourist attraction, but a massive fire has destroyed the forest along the way. Even if there were something to see, the safety record on this stretch of track is not inspiring – see Getting There & Away under Beaufort for more details.

**Taxi** Taxis congregate opposite the petrol station near the Hotel Sri Perdana. Share-taxis also make the run to Keningau (RM5),

Ranau (RM20) and KK (RM25). Early morning is the best time to catch one.

## AROUND TENOM
### Tenom Orchid Centre

This expanded tourism and research facility is part of Taman Pertanian Sabah (Agricultural Park Sabah), and is run by the Department of Agriculture; facilities were being built at the time of writing. The Orchid Centre has been established over a period of years by a British man Anthony Lamb, who has spent many years in Borneo. Expanded gardens, displays and facilities – including camping grounds and bike hire – should be fully operational by the time you read this.

Entrance to the Orchid Centre (☎ 087-737952) is RM3/5 for students/adults. It's open Tuesday to Friday from 8.30 am to 4.30 pm, and on weekends from 9 am; it is closed Monday.

The Orchid Centre is at Lagud Seberang, about 15km south-east of Tenom. Agricultural Park Sabah also sponsors research programs into cocoa, food crops, coffee, fruit trees and apiculture (bee-keeping).

To get there, take a minivan from beside the padang in Tenom. They run about every hour or so throughout the morning (RM2), but services dry up in the late afternoon. Taxis do the return trip for RM20; negotiate how long you want the driver to wait.

## BATU PUNGGUL

Not far from the Kalimantan border, Batu Punggul is a jungle-topped limestone outcrop towering nearly 200m above Sungai Sapulut. This is deep in Murut country and Batu Punggul was one of several sites sacred to these people. It is difficult and expensive to get here, but this is a beautiful part of Sabah that few tourists visit, and it offers a chance to rub shoulders with the Murut. The trip involves a long ride over rough logging roads via Keningau to the village of Sapulut, from where it is about three to five hours (depending on the water level) by motorised longboat along the jungle-lined Sungai Sapulut.

The only place to stay is the *Batu Punggul Lodge*. Accommodation is on floor mats and must be pre-arranged by the Rural

MALAYSIAN BORNEO

Development Corporation (☎ 088-440158 in KK; contact Sansi Mansir). There are forest trails and it's possible to climb the outcrop and explore caves. The resort centres on a traditionally styled Murut longhouse, and offers jungle walks, canoeing and visits to nearby caves. It's a popular place with youth groups and can get crowded, but mostly it's nearly empty. Tours are done by Borneo Eco (☎ 088-234009, fax 233688 in KK; ☻ betsb1@po.jaring.my) – see Organised Tours in the KK section earlier.

### Getting There & Away
It's possible to do a trip independently, although it's expensive and arranging transport farther than Keningau or Tenom is tough. It is probably as well to consider a package with a tour company. These aren't cheap either – a three-day/two-night trip costs around RM2200. Guests at the lodge usually go by road from Keningau to Sapulut and then take a longboat up the river to the lodge.

### BEAUFORT
☎ 087
Beaufort is a quiet provincial town on the Sungai Padas, about 90km south of KK. Its blue-painted, two-storey wooden shophouses have a certain dilapidated charm, and the people make you feel welcome, but the only reason to stop is to change buses or catch the train.

There's a branch of the HSBC that will change travellers cheques. There is no bank at Sipitang, farther south-west.

White-water rafting is popular through the Padas Gorge south of Beaufort, and is at its best between April and July, when the water level of the Sungai Padas creates Level II to III conditions. Rafting day trips out of KK cost RM150 to RM180 per person, and normally require 24 hours advance notice to arrange. For rafting contacts, see Organised Tours in the KK section earlier.

### Places to Stay & Eat
If you miss your connections, you'll have to spend a night in Beaufort. The two hotels in town are of the same standard, and both charge around RM35/40 for air-con singles/doubles. The *Beaufort Hotel* (☎ 211911) is near the mosque and the *Mandarin Inn* (☎ 212800) is across the river. The Beaufort Hotel wins by a nose for position.

MALAYSIAN BORNEO

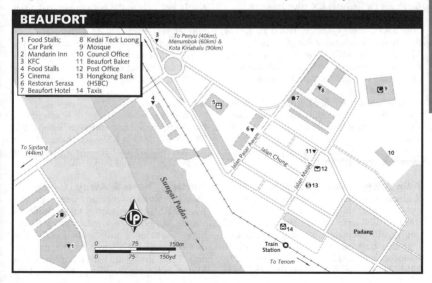

BEAUFORT

| 1 | Food Stalls; Car Park | 8 | Kedai Teck Loong |
| 2 | Mandarin Inn | 9 | Mosque |
| 3 | KFC | 10 | Council Office |
| 4 | Food Stalls | 11 | Beaufort Baker |
| 5 | Cinema | 12 | Post Office |
| 6 | Restoran Serasa | 13 | Hongkong Bank (HSBC) |
| 7 | Beaufort Hotel | 14 | Taxis |

To Penyu (40km), Menumbok (60km) & Kota Kinabalu (90km)

To Sipitang (44km)

Jalan Pasar Awam
Jalan Chung
Jalan Masjid

Sungai Padas

Padang

Train Station

To Tenom

0    75    150m
0    75    150yd

*Restoran Serasa*, on Jalan Pasar Awam, is a friendly place for lunch – the *roti canai ayam* (roti filled with chicken) is very good. *Restoran Kim Wah*, underneath the Beaufort Hotel, does good Chinese food and has an air-con section around the corner. The nearby *Kedai Teck Loong* has a wide range of fresh fruit juices. *Beaufort Baker* near the market has a good selection of cakes, buns and other pastries – if you're just passing through, you'll have time to duck in when the bus stops. There are also food stalls near the Mandarin Inn and by the northern end of the bridge.

### Getting There & Away

**Bus** Buses and minivans gather in the centre of town along Jalan Pasar Awam and behind the Beaufort Hotel. A couple of express buses leave in the morning and afternoon for KK (1½ hours, RM14). The express bus from KK to Lawas passes through Beaufort at around 3 pm; the fare from Beaufort to Lawas is RM15. Minibuses to Kuala Penyu (RM6) leave in the morning only.

Minivans cruise around town honking hopefully at pedestrians when they're nearly full. There are frequent departures for Papar (RM6) and KK (two hours, RM7), and less-frequent departures for Sipitang (1½ hours, RM6), Lawas (RM15), Kuala Penyu (until around 2.30 pm, RM5) and Membakut (RM6). The road to Kuala Penyu is a disaster, so start out early to make sure you get back on the same day – there's nowhere to stay there.

To Menumbok (for Labuan) there are plenty of minivans until early afternoon. The trip, along a gravel road, takes one hour and costs RM6.

Express buses to Sipitang pass through from KK until 1.30 pm.

**Train** It is possible to take the Sabah State Railway from KK to Beaufort, but it's a slow, rather dull stretch (three hours, RM4.80) and a bus or minivan is quicker. If you're still interested, schedules and bookings can be made through the stations at Beaufort (☎ 211518), Tenom (☎ 087-735514) and Tanjung Aru (☎ 088-254611).

The stretch of track between Beaufort and Tenom was once a popular tourist attraction – it's still possible to do it, but you won't see much. The track follows the Sungai Padas, though a couple of years ago a huge fire wiped out the forest on both sides of the river; all that's left is stunted palms, some fledgling secondary growth and the blackened trunks of scraggly trees.

To top it off, the safety record on the narrow-gauge line from Beaufort up to Tenom is worrying – five derailments had occurred in the same month we took the train, one of which sent several tourists to hospital. Subsequent accidents – reportedly caused by poor track-maintenance and driver error – have killed at least one person.

Major delays are also common, and if you get stuck in the middle of nowhere you'll find the trains lack interior lights, drinking water and rudimentary safety equipment – considering a good proportion of the passengers are elderly women and small children, this makes for a rather unsatisfying experience. All in all, it's better to take the bus.

## KUALA PENYU

Kuala Penyu is at the northern end of a flat, swampy peninsula dotted with water buffalo. If you want to get to Pulau Tiga National Park, this is the place to come. The town is unremarkable, but there are some good beaches nearby. The best is around the headland from the estuary, 8km out of town; there are picnic tables and toilets but no other facilities.

There's nowhere to stay in Kuala Penyu, but if you book ahead through Sabah Parks (☎ 088-211881) in KK – see Information in the KK section earlier – you can stay in Pulau Tiga National Park.

### Getting There & Away

Take a minivan from behind Centre Point in KK for RM10; the journey takes about two hours. Minivans to Kuala Penyu (RM5) leave Beaufort until around 2.30 pm, minibuses (RM6) leave in the morning only. From the Kuala Penyu turn-off on the Menumbok road, it's a long, dusty road that

MALAYSIAN BORNEO

ends at a river on the other side of the town – a car ferry shuttles across between 6 am and 6 pm. A minivan from Kuala Penyu to Menumbok costs RM5; the journey to Tenom costs RM6.

## PULAU TIGA NATIONAL PARK

The name Pulau Tiga means simply 'Three Islands', but only two of the original three remain in this 15 sq km park north of Kuala Penyu. Pulau Tiga is the largest island; about 1km to the north-east lies tiny Pulau Kalampunian Damit; and in between are the remains of the third island, now only a sandbar eroded by wave action.

**Pulau Tiga** was formed by the eruption of mud volcanoes. It is covered by dense vegetation, but volcanic activity in the form of bubbling mud and escaping methane gas can still be seen at the summit of the island. There are walking trails, fine sandy beaches and good snorkelling around the island.

Tiny Pulau Kalampunian Damit is little more than a large rock covered in dense vegetation, but it is famous for the sea snakes that come ashore in their hundreds to mate. On any one day up to 150 snakes can be present, curled up under boulders, among roots and in tree hollows. It's a fascinating phenomenon made enigmatic by the fact that the snakes are never seen on nearby Pulau Tiga. Not surprisingly, the local name for this islet is Pulau Ular – **Snake Island**. Negotiate transport to this island with your boatman. Beware of the snakes – all sea snakes are poisonous.

At the time of writing, the fragile islands were closed to visitors for the filming of what turned out to be the remarkably popular TV show *Survivors*. In hindsight, the premise couldn't miss: pit 16 photogenic, middle-class Machiavellians against each other and see how low they'll sink to sustain their 15 minutes of fame. Part 'real time' soap opera and part *Lord of the Flies,* the show was so successful that other 'exotic' locales (including the Australian Outback) are slated to be reduced to TV-sized playgrounds for more outdoor parlour games.

Normally there is an inexpensive dorm and some room-style accommodation on the main island, but Pulau Tiga is very difficult and expensive to reach. Accommodation can be booked through the Sabah Parks office (☎ 088-211881) in KK (see Information in the KK section earlier), but staff cannot arrange transport to the islands. Take all supplies with you, including water.

To get to Pulau Tiga, take a minibus from KK to Kuala Penyu, then ask around for a boatman – a boat should cost around RM120 for the return trip. Arrange a time for the boat's return, but don't leave it too late so you can get a minivan from Kuala Penyu.

## PAPAR

This is a cosy little coastal Kadazan town 38km south of KK. Local produce includes coconut wine and there's a tamu (weekly market) on Sunday. There's a beach out of town where you can swim, and you can take a boat ride along the Sungai Papar.

### Getting There & Away

Minivans leave throughout the day from KK (one hour, RM3 or RM4). Express buses also pass by and can drop you in the town.

On Wednesday and Saturday, Sutera Harbour operates a renovated Vulcan steam engine for tourists, which does the run from Tanjung Aru train station in KK to Papar and back. The trip costs RM160, including lunch, and lasts about three hours. For times and bookings, ring ☎ 088-253131 in KK.

For considerably less you can pack a lunch and hop a Beaufort-bound diesel train with the locals, getting off at Papar (one hour, RM2.40) and returning to KK later. Tanjung Aru train station (☎ 088-254611) in KK will have the latest schedule. This stretch of track is reasonably safe.

## SIPITANG

Sipitang is 44km south of Beaufort, 144km from KK and the closest town in Sabah to the Sarawak border. Located on a wide, shallow bay, Sipitang is pleasant enough, though the only reason to stop here is to organise bus connections. If you are heading to Lawas for a boat to Brunei or Limbang, you should spend the night in Lawas or you'll miss the early-morning departures.

MALAYSIAN BORNEO

The Sarawak border is 18km south and buses stop at Merapok, where passports and visas are checked at both Sabah and Sarawak immigration offices. The offices are open every day from 6 am until 10 pm; see the Sarawak chapter for more details.

Sipitang has a number of *kedai kopi* and *food stalls* on the main street, and some reasonable, easy-to-find *hotels* (starting at around RM25) if you have to stay the night.

### Getting There & Away

Minivans ply between Beaufort and Sipitang throughout the day and cost RM6, and buses go to Merapok in Sarawak for RM3. From Beaufort there are buses and trains to KK and Tenom (see Getting There & Away in the Beaufort section earlier). The 47km road to Beaufort is a dusty bone-cruncher. In contrast, the good road south to Merapok and Lawas is sealed and scenic in parts, as it runs parallel to jungle-clad mountains.

# Pulau Labuan

☎ 087
Labuan is an island about 8km off the coast of Sabah at the mouth of Brunei Bay. It has an interesting history, but unless you are a keen wreck-diver the only reason to come here is to catch a ferry to Sarawak or Brunei.

Just to confuse regional politics, Labuan is a Federal Territory governed directly from KL. Before the Asian financial crisis a few years ago sank a whole lot of floating capital, the government poured money into the island and pushed it as a major offshore banking haven. Nowadays, Labuan is a lonely duty-free port whose potential patrons – Bruneians once desperate to part with excess petro-dollars – generally stay away in droves.

The Sultan of Brunei ceded Labuan to the British in 1846 and, apart from three years under Japanese occupation, it remained British for 115 years. Labuan's modern anonymity belies the fact that it was the cockpit of Borneo during WWII. The Japanese landed here and the Allies counter-invaded; the Japanese forces in North Borneo surrendered here at the end of the war; and the Japanese officers responsible for the 'death marches' from Sandakan (see the boxed text 'The Sandakan Death Marches' later) were tried by an Australian War Crimes Court on Labuan. There's a war cemetery and peace park to mark these horrific events, and WWII veterans sometimes make a pilgrimage to see the memorials.

Labuan was also once a coal-mining centre and now has major petroleum gas installations.

Bandar Labuan is the main town and the transit point for ferries. The population is a polite mix of orthodox-Muslim Malays, a large contingent of Indians, plus a sprinkling of Bugis and Bajau people.

### Information

Labuan has a helpful Tourism Malaysia information office (☎ 423445, fax 423446, ℮ mtpblbu@tourism.gov.my) on the corner of Jalan Dewan and Jalan Berjaya. It's open daily, except public holidays, from 9 am to 5 pm.

There are numerous banks around town – the HSBC bank is the best for changing travellers cheques. Moneychangers around town will change cash and travellers cheques at good rates; try Syarikat K Abdul Kader at 90 Jalan OKK Awang Besar. There's also a Maybank in the Financial Park shopping complex, as well as a post office.

Harrisons Travel (☎ 412557, fax 414588) is a handy travel agent on the roundabout just east of the boat docks.

There is a Super Wash laundry on Jalan Tun Mustapha, just behind the bus station.

Family Fun, probably the biggest cybercafe in Borneo, is on the 1st floor of Financial Park; rates are RM4 per hour. There's another cybercafe on the ground floor of the Milimewah Superstore building; it's open till midnight (to 4 pm on holidays) and also charges RM4 per hour.

### Things to See & Do

If you're arriving by boat, you can't miss the looming steel-and-glass shopping fortress called **Financial Park**; this is the town's No 1 'attraction', and the place where all that duty-free spending is meant to happen. Prices are generally no cheaper than elsewhere, however, though you can pick up a good German-made bidet for that special someone. Financial Park is open from 10 am to 10 pm daily, but most shops are closed by 8 pm on weekdays.

A much more interesting sight lies behind it: the **An'nur Jamek Mosque**. This is one distinctive house of worship – it looks a lot like Darth Vader's summer home. The mosque can be reached by a 15-minute walk up Jalan Tun Mustapha from the centre of town.

Bandar Labuan has a covered **market** at the western end of town. Water-taxis carry passengers to the two nearby **stilt villages** of Patau-Patau; a water-taxi (RM10) from near the market will take you on a tour of the kampung.

**Labuan War Cemetery** has row upon row of headstones dedicated to the nearly 4000 Commonwealth servicemen, mostly Australian and British, who lost their lives in Borneo during WWII. The cemetery is near the golf course, about 2km east of town along Jalan OKK Abdullah.

A **Peace Park** on the west of the island at Layang Layangan commemorates the place of Japanese surrender and has a Japanese war memorial.

The island has some good **beaches** at Pohon Batu and south from Layang Layangan along the west coast, but ask locals whether there are jellyfish or stingrays before swimming here. A **chimney** is all that remains of an old factory at the north of the island; it's a minor attraction from where there are good views along the coast.

Pulau Kuraman, Pulau Rusukan Kecil and Pulau Rusukan Besar are uninhabited islands lying south-west of Labuan that are now protected as a **marine park**. The beaches are pristine, but dynamite fishing has destroyed much of the coral. **Pulau Papan** is another island, 5km south-east of Bandar Labuan, that has been developed as a tourist attraction – it makes for a pleasant day trip.

Trips to the islands, cruises and other activities can be arranged (24 hours advance notice) through the Labuan Water Sports Centre (☎ 019-850 0526, 010-882 1475) at the front of the Waterfront Financial Hotel. Return fares to Pulau Papar are RM10/15 per child/adult.

**Wreck Diving** The wreck diving here is among the best in Asia. Four shipwrecks have been discovered off Labuan. Two were sunk during WWII and two were commercial vessels that sank in the 1980s.

The **American Wreck** is the USS *Salute,* a minesweeper built in late 1943 and sunk – by a mine – in 1945. This wreck sits on the sandy bottom at 33m.

The identity of the **Australian Wreck** is still uncertain. It was a freighter built in Rotterdam in 1900, captured by the Japanese in 1942 and sunk by the Royal Australian Air Force (hence the name) in 1945.

The **Cement Wreck** is the MV *Tung Hwang,* a freighter that hit a sandbank in 1980 while carrying cement for the sultan of Brunei's new palace. It sits upright in 30m of water and its masts are 8m below the surface.

The **Blue Water Wreck** is the MV *Mabini Padre,* a Philippine trawler that sank in November 1981. Being farther offshore, this wreck usually has the best visibility.

Of all the wrecks, the Cement Wreck is the easiest to dive and is used for wreck-dive training. The American Wreck and the Blue Water Wreck are for experienced wreck-divers only.

Borneo Divers (☎ 415867, fax 413454) has an office in the Milimewah building and a dive shop at the Waterfront Financial Hotel. Two dives at a wreck cost RM250 to RM300 if you're on your own; two or more divers pay RM125/185 to RM150/200 for one/two dives.

If you want to warm up for the wrecks, Borneo Divers also has introductory dives off Pulau Papar for RM160; a snorkelling trip costs RM100. The tourist office can also provide a list of dive operators.

## Places to Stay – Budget
Budget accommodation in Bandar Labuan is limited and pretty poor, though you may scam a discount if business is slow.

MALAYSIAN BORNEO

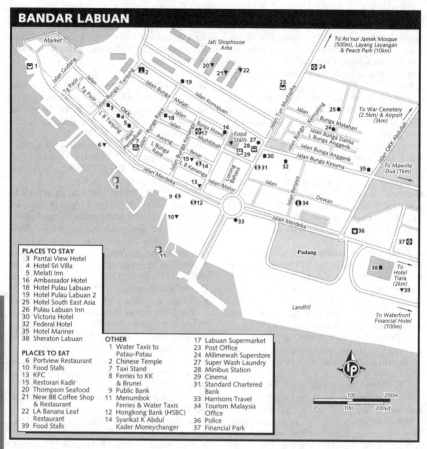

**BANDAR LABUAN**

PLACES TO STAY
3 Pantai View Hotel
4 Hotel Sri Villa
5 Melati Inn
16 Ambassador Hotel
18 Hotel Pulau Labuan
19 Hotel Pulau Labuan 2
25 Hotel South East Asia
26 Pulau Labuan Inn
30 Victoria Hotel
32 Federal Hotel
35 Hotel Mariner
38 Sheraton Labuan

PLACES TO EAT
6 Portview Restaurant
10 Food Stalls
13 KFC
15 Restoran Kadir
20 Thompson Seafood
21 New 88 Coffee Shop
   & Restaurant
22 LA Banana Leaf
   Restaurant
39 Food Stalls

OTHER
1 Water Taxis to
   Patau-Patau
2 Chinese Temple
7 Taxi Stand
8 Ferries to KK
   & Brunei
9 Public Bank
11 Menumbok
   Ferries & Water Taxis
12 Hongkong Bank (HSBC)
14 Syarikat K Abdul
   Kader Moneychanger
17 Labuan Supermarket
23 Post Office
24 Milimewah Superstore
27 Super Wash Laundry
28 Minibus Station
29 Cinema
31 Standard Chartered
   Bank
33 Harrisons Travel
34 Tourism Malaysia
36 Police
37 Financial Park

**MALAYSIAN BORNEO**

*Pantai View Hotel (☎ 411339),* on Jalan Bunga Tanjung, has fan-cooled rooms with shared bathroom for RM28; air-con singles/doubles with bathroom and TV are RM38/48. This is a lodging house for long-term types; if you can afford it, you're better off elsewhere.

Around the corner on Jalan OKK Awang Besar, *Hotel Sri Villa (☎ 413605)* is another low-rent option, with fan rooms for RM35 and air-con rooms for RM40; toilets are shared.

The best option by far in this price range is *Melati Inn (☎ 416307),* where air-con

rooms with shared bathroom go for RM35 and singles/doubles with attached bathroom cost RM35/40.

## Places to Stay – Mid-Range
*Hotel South East Asia (☎ 414112)* is at the edge of the night-life/red-light district on Jalan Bunga Seroja; it has air-con rooms for RM40 and twins for RM50.

The other mid-range hotels are a noticeable jump up in quality and price. On Jalan Bunga Kesuma, the *Federal Hotel (☎ 411711)* has small, faded but clean rooms for RM66/88, but offers substantial discounts, the total depending on whether you pay by cash or credit card. *Victoria Hotel (☎ 412411)*, on Jalan Tun Mustapha, has older standard rooms for RM58/78.

*Hotel Pulau Labuan (☎ 416288)*, on Jalan Bunga Raya, is staffed by an exceptionally sour bunch but the rooms are big and clean; standard (windowless) rooms start at RM78. The same people run the smaller and newer *Pulau Labuan Inn (☎ 416833)*, which is in the lap of the red-light zone and offers smaller rooms starting at RM59.

Whatever else Labuan has, it could use a few more names for its hotels – the new *Hotel Pulau Labuan 2 (☎ 422388)* has very good rooms with double bed for RM82, or RM98 for twins; family rooms are RM118 and suites fetch RM138. The *Ambassador Hotel (☎ 423233)*, behind the Labuan Supermarket, is a small, new hotel. Plain but clean and comfortable rooms go for RM77/88.

The two-star *Hotel Mariner (☎ 418822)*, on the corner of Jalan Bunga Kesuma and Jalan OKK Abdullah, has small, so-so rooms starting at RM82.50/92.50.

## Places to Stay – Top End

Labuan's best hotels are east of the town centre. The *Sheraton Labuan (☎ 422000, fax 422222, 462 Jalan Merdeka)* has rooms starting at RM181.50 (with 30 days advance notice) and RM214.50 (7 days advance); luxurious suites can be had for RM385 to RM825, and the Royal Suite is listed at RM2750. This fine hotel has a pool, a good restaurant, a pub with live bands (and a reasonable happy hour till 9.30 pm) and wall safes in the rooms.

Nearby, the four-star *Waterfront Financial Hotel (☎ 418111, fax 413468)*, Jalan Wawasan, is a rambling complex with large gates and a small marina. The outdoor swimming pool is great, and the restaurant isn't bad. Published room rates are RM360 to RM580, and suites cost a whole lot more; discounts of 50% are often available.

The five-star *Hotel Tiara (☎ 414300, fax 410195)* is a little out of town on Jalan Tanjung Batu, towards the Labuan War Cemetery, but it's nicely positioned near a quiet beach. The hotel has seen more-prosperous days and staff are over-trained and under-employed. Published rates for a large suite start at an ambitious RM308, though a promotional rate of RM120, including breakfast, makes it quite worthwhile.

## Places to Eat

Bandar Labuan has plenty of cafes and restaurants. In duty-free Labuan alcohol is cheap and a big bottle of beer can cost as little as RM3.

You'll find *food stalls* on Jalan Muhibbah between the Labuan Supermarket and the cinema. There's an excellent and affordable *food-stall centre* next to the park between the Sheraton Labuan and the Waterfront Financial Hotel; it's open all day but evenings are when it's all happening – there's plenty of variety to choose from and it's hard to go wrong here.

*Restoran Kadir*, on Awang Besar near the moneychanger, is a friendly Indian restaurant with good, cheap fare from breakfast to dinner.

The rapidly developing area of concrete shophouses north of Hotel Pulau Labuan 2 is a good area for restaurants; among the popular choices for dinner and a beer are *Thompson Seafood*, *LA Banana Leaf Restaurant* and *New 88 Coffee Shop & Restaurant*.

Good seafood can be enjoyed at the *Portview Restaurant*, right next to the jetty where you catch the boat for KK or Brunei.

## Getting There & Away

**Air** Malaysia Airlines has a desk at the airport, and Labuan is well served by the Malaysia Airlines domestic network. There are regular flights to KK (four to six daily, RM52), KL (two nonstop daily, RM437), Kuching (daily, RM199) and Miri (twice daily, RM66). There are also two flights a week (Saturday and Sunday) to BSB in Brunei (RM63). Twin Otter services to Labuan were cancelled at the time of writing.

**Boat** Passenger boats are plentiful and some morning boats can fill up quickly; tickets can be bought in advance or just before departure at the small kiosk at the ferry terminal building. You pay a 50 sen departure tax at the gate before boarding. Boat services from Bandar Labuan include the following:

**Sabah** Speedy passenger ferries connect Labuan to KK. The trip takes about 1½ hours and costs RM28/33 for economy/1st class. Tickets can be bought at the dock. There are a number of boats making the run, but schedules can be erratic – check at the dock. Among the more regular services, the *Labuan Express* leaves Labuan at 8.30 and 10.30 am, and 1 and 3 pm; it leaves KK at 8 and 10 am, and 1.30 and 3 pm. The *Express Ming Hai* leaves for KK at 1 and 3 pm, and does the run to Labuan at 8 and 10 am.

For Menumbok (around 1½ hours, RM10) there are several daily departures; the last boat leaves at 3 pm. A slow car-ferry also chugs across to Menumbok from the dock next to the customs wharf; there are normally two departures a day (most are currently at 8 am and 1 pm); foot passengers pay RM5 for the trip.

Small launches also connect Bandar Labuan and Sipitang. They operate from 10 am to noon and go when full (about one hour, RM20) from the main (KK/Brunei) ferry terminal.

**Sarawak** Express boats to Limbang (two hours, RM10) leave at 12.30 and 2.30 pm; from Limbang departures are at 7.30 and 8 am.

**Brunei** Six or seven passenger boats depart for Muara port in Brunei daily. Normal departure times are between 8.30 am and 4.30 pm, but the schedule changes and extra services may be available on weekends and public holidays. The journey to Muara takes 1½ to two hours and costs RM12/24 for children/adults, or B$8/15 if coming from Brunei.

### Getting Around
**To/From the Airport** The airport is serviced by bus Nos 2, 3, 4, 5 and 6 (RM1.50); a taxi should cost around RM8 from town.

**Bus** Labuan has a good minibus network. Buses leave regularly from the parking lot off Jalan Mustapha. Their numbers are clearly painted on the front, and fares range from 50 sen for a short trip to RM2 for a trip to the top of the island. Other destinations and fares are as follows:

**No 1** war cemetery (RM1)
**No 2** mosque and Patau-Patau (RM1.20)
**No 3** Bebuloh (RM1.50)
**No 4** mosque, Peace Park and Layang Layangan (RM1.20)
**No 6** mosque and chimney (RM1.50)

**Car** Padas Jaya Rent-A-Car (☎ 425220, fax 421028), on the ground floor of Financial Park, has Proton Sagas for RM80 a day plus RM20 per day for insurance; car options and rates rise to RM850 a day for a Jaguar Sovereign (plus RM50 a day insurance).

**Taxi** Taxis – often unmetered private cars – are plentiful. There's a taxi rank in the town centre. The standard fare for a journey of up to a few kilometres is RM5.

# North of Kota Kinabalu

The road north from the capital leads to small coastal towns and stilt villages, then over low hills to the small market town of Kota Belud. The route to Kota Belud is well travelled and almost *de rigueur* on the itineraries of tour groups – although many travellers may find the crowded Sunday market at Kota Belud a bit underwhelming.

Beyond Kota Belud the highway traverses fertile plains planted with rice, coconut, oil palm and bananas. A scenic peninsula with some nice beaches leads into the country of the Rungus people and on to the isolated town of Kudat.

Kudat doesn't see many tourists and is the end of the line for all but the boldest: ownership of the islands to the north and east is disputed by the Philippines and out of bounds to most foreigners.

## TUARAN
☎ 088

Tuaran, 33km from KK, is a bustling little town with tree-lined streets. Tamu (market) day is Sunday, and on the road into town you'll spot a newish, nine-storey **Chinese pagoda**.

There's a turn-off 2km before Tuaran that leads to two luxury resorts and **Mengkabong Water Village**, a Bajau stilt village built over an estuary. It was once a very picturesque spot, though it's hardly the 'Venice of the East' claimed in tourist brochures. Unfortunately, it has become modernised and incredibly garbage-strewn in recent years, and is now of little interest to travellers.

There's a much better stilt village at **Penimbawan**. To get there, take a minivan to Susarup (RM2); these leave a block back from the main street behind the Orchid Hotel. You then charter a motorboat at the Susarup jetty for RM40. The trip up the clear, clean river takes about 15 minutes, and the boat will wait while you wander the plankwalks of this very friendly and authentic village. The boatman may charge less if you just want to float by and take photos.

For another RM10 you can get him to take you out to the mouth of the South China Sea – the approach to the big waves is worth the extra ringgit, and there are some sandy stretches that are popular for picnics and swimming. Coming back, take a minivan to Tuaran and change there for KK – drivers ask absurd prices for the trip from Susarup to KK.

### Places to Stay

Tuaran is best done as a day trip, but if you get stuck here, *Orchid Hotel (☎ 793789),* on the main street just past the clock tower, has very basic but clean rooms without toilet for RM40; singles/doubles with toilet are RM60/80.

There are a couple of luxury resorts on the road to Mengkabong Water Village; both are set on nice beaches. *Sabandar Bay Resort (☎ 088-787722, fax 787575; KK sales office),* off Jalan Pantai Dalit, is a four-star splash-out with hotel-style rooms and semidetached and detached chalets.

Published room rates are RM260 to RM480; discounts are usually available.

Going up a star, *Shangri-La's Rasa Ria Resort (☎ 792888, fax 792777, @ rrr@po.jaring.my)* is a humungous development adjoining the Dalit Bay Golf & Country Club; rooms are the last word in luxury and there are a couple of good restaurants. Published room rates are RM325 to RM850, but special packages are often offered.

### Getting There & Away

Minivans go regularly between KK and Tuaran (30 minutes, RM2). Minivans from Tuaran to Tamparuli are RM1; to Mengkabong they are less frequent and cost 60 sen. Regular minivans go from Tuaran to Kota Belud (30 minutes, RM5).

The resorts have regular shuttle services to KK – phone for times. Hitching from Tuaran is a good bet on weekends, but you be careful now, hear?

## KOTA BELUD
☎ 088

Every Sunday a huge **tamu** takes place on the outskirts of this small, sleepy town. This market is a congested, colourful and dusty melee of vendors, hagglers and innumerable goods piled under one roof and spilling out into the car park – everything your average family could want is here, from polyester pants and plastic toys to fresh fish and fruit.

A tamu is not simply a market where villagers gather to sell their farm produce and to buy manufactured goods from traders; it's also a social occasion where news and stories are exchanged. Farmers haggle all morning over the price of a buffalo calf and the Bajau sell their horses, although tourists now outnumber cattle and the horsemen have mostly moved to a quieter spot away from the car park.

A tamu is not in itself a tourist attraction, either; Kota Belud hosts a market supplying everyday needs, but this one happens to be a lot bigger than most. Tourists looking for tribal handicrafts and traditional clothing are likely to be disappointed, but the market *is* fun and you can enjoy a very good breakfast

**MALAYSIAN BORNEO**

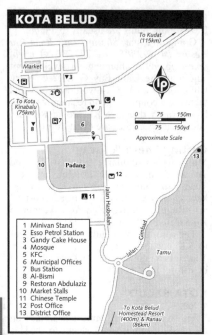

## KOTA BELUD

To Kudat
(115km)

Market

To Kota
Kinabalu
(75km)

Padang

Jalan Hasbollah

Jalan Gimbad

Tamu

0      75      150m
0      75      150yd
Approximate Scale

1  Minivan Stand
2  Esso Petrol Station
3  Gandy Cake House
4  Mosque
5  KFC
6  Municipal Offices
7  Bus Station
8  Al-Bismi
9  Restoran Abdulaziz
10 Market Stalls
11 Chinese Temple
12 Post Office
13 District Office

To Kota Belud
Homestead Resort
(400m) & Ranau
(86km)

**MALAYSIAN BORNEO**

here after looking around. If you're looking for tribal handicrafts, you may have more luck at the Sunday tamu at **Sikuati**, 23km from Kudat, which is attended by the Rungus people who live in nearby longhouses.

You may be told that the best time to arrive at the market is 6 am – this is true if the sight of yawning Bajau women laying out fruit in semi-darkness fascinates you; if not, just try to be there before the tour buses take over (which happens by 9 or 9.30 am).

### Places to Stay & Eat
Most people visit Kota Belud as a day trip from KK. Since you can make it from KK in plenty of time for the market, the only imaginable reason to overnight here is the stunning view of Mt Kinabalu at first light – try not to gloat while the clouds roll in on the climbers shivering on the summit.

The only accommodation around is at the over-priced *Kota Belud Homestead Resort* (☎ 977062), about 1km south of the padang.

Tiny boxes in an ersatz Bajau-style dorm are RM40/80 for singles/doubles, or RM100 if you want your own toilet and shower. The main building is occupied by Shell Oil workers, and no meals are available to tourists.

Kota Belud is not a gastronome's delight, but plenty of tasty snacks can be picked up at the Sunday market. There are a few Chinese and halal *coffee shops* in the northern part of town around Pasar Besar – these are close to transport, so they're handy if you're not on a tour. *Gandy Cake House* is a good bakery for cakes and pastries. *Restoran Abdulaziz*, in the centre of town, is about the only place open in the evening; the food is uninspiring but cheap – this place is also the centre of Kota Belud's nightlife, and you can watch TV with the locals if you're staying overnight.

### Getting There & Away
The main area for minivans and share-taxis is at the bus station in front of Pasar Besar, the old market. Most of these serve the Kota Belud–KK route, which costs RM5 and takes about two hours. A freeway covers most of the route from KK to Kota Belud. On Sunday, tamu day, the number of minivans and taxis has to be seen to be believed. On other days it's much quieter.

Minivans north to Kudat cost RM10 and take up to two hours; the road can be rough in places.

To get to Kinabalu National Park, take any minibus going to KK and get off at Tamparuli, about halfway there. The trip takes about half an hour and costs RM5. There are several minivans from Tamparuli to Ranau every day until about 2 pm. All of them pass the park entrance – tell the driver to drop you off there. The ride to the park is RM5 and to go all the way to Ranau costs RM10. The journey to the park headquarters, along a good sealed road, takes about an hour from Tamparuli; the direct road from Kota Belud to Ranau is very rough and not used by minivans. A minivan to KK from Tamparuli is RM3.

*(Continued on page 507)*

# CLIMBING KINABALU

Towering above the coastal plain and what's left of the lush tropical forests of northern Borneo, Mt Kinabalu is the biggest tourist attraction in Sabah and the centrepiece of the vast 754 sq km Kinabalu National Park. At 4101m, it is the highest mountain between the mighty Himalayas and New Guinea. And it's still growing: researchers have found it increases in height by about 5mm a year. It is 50km inland, but on a clear day you can see the Philippines from the summit; clear days are rare, however, as the mountain is usually socked-in with cloud by mid-morning.

Mt Kinabalu is one of the easiest mountains in the world to climb, and thousands of people of all ages and fitness levels scale the summit every year. No special skills or equipment are required; all you need is some stamina, determination and weatherproof clothing – it can get very cold and wet up there.

Those who persevere will be rewarded with a memorable experience. The views are magnificent, even before you get to the top, and the sunsets are incredible.

While the climb is the main reason most foreigners come to the park, only about 10% of the 170,000 people who visit the park each year actually climb the peak. The park itself is a beautiful spot, and many visitors come just to escape the heat and humidity of the coast. There are walking trails in the rainforest at the base of the mountain, the climate is agreeably cool – even cold at night – and the accommodation is very good. Other facilities are also good, though as a privately run and very popular park, price rises and extra fees where possible seem to be a fact of life.

## HISTORY

The first recorded ascent of the mountain was made in 1851 by Sir Hugh Low, the British colonial secretary on Pulau Labuan (Labuan Island). Kinabalu's highest peak is named after him, as is the mile-deep 'gully' on the other side of the mountain.

In those days the difficulty of climbing Mt Kinabalu lay not in the ascent itself, but in getting to the mountain's base through the trackless jungles – and finding local porters willing to go there. The tribesmen who accompanied Low believed the mountain was inhabited by the spirits of their dead. Low was therefore obliged to protect the party, and a guide carried a large basket of quartz crystals and teeth, as was the custom. The ceremonies performed by the guides to appease the spirits upon reaching the summit became more elaborate as time went on, so that by the 1920s they had come to include loud prayers, gunshots, and the sacrifice of seven eggs and seven white chickens; however, in recent times the custom appears to have died out.

These days there's a sealed road all the way from Kota Kinabalu (KK) to the foot of the mountain, but Low's Gully – the abyss on the other

## The Legend of Mt Kinabalu

A local Kadazan legend tells how Mt Kinabalu got its name. Many years ago, the emperor of China heard that on this mountain there was a fabulous pearl guarded by a dragon. He told his three sons that whichever of them could bring him the pearl would be the next emperor.

Two sons tried and failed; the third son managed to snatch the pearl, but just as he was sneaking away the dragon woke and gave chase. The prince hid in the jungle with the pearl while the rest of his party went on, with the dragon in hot pursuit. They jumped back into their boat and hightailed it for China, but still the dragon followed. In desperation they fired their cannons at it. Thinking the cannonballs were the pearl, the dragon devoured them and eventually drowned.

Meanwhile, back in the jungle, the prince took a local wife and raised a family, but after some years decided it was time to return to China to claim the throne. He promised his wife he would come back to fetch her, but of course he never showed up. In despair she climbed to the top of the mountain to pray for his return and died in the process. Hence *Kina*, meaning China, and *balu*, widow.

side of the summit – didn't give up its secrets as easily as Low's Peak. The first expedition to abseil into the gully got lost for several days, and it was only as recently as February 1998 that a joint British-Malaysian expedition explored the bottom, returning with several newly discovered species of plants and insects.

## GEOLOGY

From its immense size you might think Mt Kinabalu is the ancient core of Borneo, but the mountain was actually formed relatively recently. Its origins go back a mere nine million years, to when a solidified core of volcanic rock began swelling up from the depths below and pushed its way through the overlying rock. This upward movement is apparently still continuing.

In geological terms Mt Kinabalu is still very young. Little erosion has occurred on the exposed granite rock-faces around the summit, though the effects of glaciers that used to cover much of the mountain can be detected by the trained eye. The glaciers have disappeared, but at times ice forms in the rock pools near the summit.

## FLORA

Exhilarating though it is, the climb to the top isn't the only rewarding experience that awaits you. Mt Kinabalu is a botanical paradise in which over half the species growing above 900m are unique to the area; many more are no doubt blooming, unnamed, in unexplored gullies and ridges. Among the more-spectacular flowers are over 1000 species of orchids and many rhododendrons; numerous species grow in profusion along the summit trail.

The park's most famous plant inhabitants are the insectivorous *Nepenthes* (pitcher plants). The only place where they rival Mt Kinabalu for profusion is Bako National Park in Sarawak. Pitcher plants come in many shapes, sizes and colours, although you probably won't be as lucky as the 19th-century botanist Spencer St John, who reported finding a specimen of *Nepenthes rajah* with a pitcher 30cm in diameter – it contained 2.5L of watery fluid and a drowned rat!

Most pitcher plants are only large enough to trap unwary insects attracted to the nectar that the plants secrete. On your way to the summit, try exploring a few metres into the undergrowth on either side of the trail – you're bound to come across one sooner or later.

Park headquarters is surrounded by tall dipterocarp forest, better known as rainforest, characterised by huge trees with buttress roots. The canopy is dense and festooned with creepers, ferns and orchids. Some spectacular fungi grow on the forest floor.

Between 900m and 1800m the forest is composed chiefly of oaks, laurels and chestnuts, and this type of forest occupies half the park's area. In this vegetation zone trees are smaller and more light passes through the canopy, allowing the growth of a dense ground-cover and an abundance of orchids and mosses.

Above 1800m, where annual rainfall can reach more than 450cm, there is a distinct transition to dense, stunted rhododendron forest, the trunks and branches of which are often covered with mosses and orchids.

On the windswept slopes above Laban Rata the vegetation is stunted and clings to niches in the granite; sayat-sayat is a common woody shrub at this height. The uppermost slopes of the mountain are bare of plant life.

## FAUNA

Nearly all of Borneo's mammal species have been recorded in Mt Kinabalu National Park, though more are seen in the lowland rainforest surrounding Poring Hot Springs than at higher altitudes around park headquarters. The park is surrounded by cultivation and villages, and poaching is common along the borders; edible species such as deer and monkey are not as common as they once were.

Still, the overall variety is staggering, and among the park's more commonly seen mammals are many species of squirrel. Prevost's squirrel, with grey, orange and black fur, is a particularly handsome species, and the mountain ground squirrel is frequently seen along the summit trail. Around park headquarters, tree-shrews can sometimes be seen raiding rubbish bins.

Bird-watchers will be that bit closer to heaven, as more than 280 species of birds have been recorded, including nearly all of Borneo's endemic species. The action starts around park headquarters, where common birds among the noisy, feeding, flocks include the Bornean treepie (a noisy relative of the magpie), fantails, bulbuls, sunbirds and laughing-thrushes. The veranda at Restoran Kinabalu Balsam is a good place to sit and watch the birds, and there are excellent bird-watching opportunities on the walking trails in the early morning – especially the Liwagu and Silau-Silau trails.

If you're climbing to the summit, look out for a number of birds seen only at higher altitudes. These include the Kinabalu friendly warbler, which is found only on these slopes, the dainty mountain black-eye and the mountain blackbird.

Other wildlife includes colourful butterflies and the moon moth – a huge green moth with long, trailing wing-streamers.

## ORIENTATION & INFORMATION

Kinabalu park headquarters is 88km from Kota Kinabalu (KK) and set in beautiful gardens with a magnificent view of the mountain. At 1588m it is an agreeably cool climate – the average temperature ranges from 20°C during the day to 13°C at night.

Accommodation at park headquarters can be tight and even tighter on the mountain. Reservations are the preserve of Kinabalu Gold Resorts (☎ 088-257941, fax 242861, @ nature@kinabalu.net); see Information in the KK section. In theory only advance reservations are accepted; in practice, you *can* roll up to the park office and pray for a pillow for the night – you might get lucky and find a space in a dorm, but don't count on it.

On arrival, once you've paid your entry fee at the park gate – RM1.50/3 per child (under 18)/adult – you check in at the park office. If you are staying overnight, present your reservation slip from KK and you'll be allocated your bed or room. Valuables can be deposited in safety boxes at the office and excess baggage can be stored here (RM1 per item) until you return from the mountain.

All the hostels and resthouses are within walking distance of the park office. In the visitors' centre down the road past the hostels is the Liwagu Restaurant and an exhibit centre; a slide show (RM1/2) presented here (weekdays at 2 pm and weekends at 7.30 pm) gives an excellent introduction to the mountain.

Next to the park office is a souvenir shop selling T-shirts (RM20), film, ice creams and souvenirs. If you don't have a raincoat, you can buy one here for RM15. There's also a reasonable range of books on the park and other places in Sabah, and a 30-minute photo-processing service. The shop is open from 7 am to 7 pm.

By the way, people engage in endless debate over the mountain's true height, and the 'I climbed Kinabalu'–type apparel at the shop doesn't help, since it sports three different heights (but then, T-shirts generally make unreliable altimeters). Never mind. At the rate the mountain is growing, in a couple of hundred years your shirt will be wrong anyway.

Victoria & St Andrew's Peaks, Kinabalu National Park, Sabah

MARK DAFFEY

Scaling Mt Kinabalu, Sabah.

JEAN-BERNARD CARILLET

Lamban Rata resthouse, Kinabalu National Park, Sabah

DAVID ANDREW

K8 on the summit trail – conquering Mt Kinabalu, Sabah.

MARK DAFFEY

Tropical rainforest and jungle steams en route to the summit of Mt Kinabalu, Sabah.

Poring Hot Springs: a soothing soak for summit-weary bones, Sabah.

## Permits & Guides

A climbing permit and Climber's Personal Accident Insurance are compulsory for any ascent of Mt Kinabalu. The permit fee for foreigners is RM50 for adults and RM25 for anyone under 18; insurance costs RM3.50 per person per journey. All this is payable at park headquarters before you climb.

A guide is only compulsory if you intend to venture beyond Laban Rata, ie, to the summit. Guide fees are RM60 per trip for one to three persons, RM65 per day for four to six people, and RM70 per trip for seven to eight climbers (the maximum per guide).

There are conflicting opinions about the use of guides, and it's expensive if you can't share the cost with other people. Sabah Parks says guides are compulsory because climbers can 'easily lose their way on the rock surface when the fog and mist start covering the upper part of the mountain'. Another theory is that compulsory guides greatly reduce the chances of people stealing pitcher plants and smuggling them out of the country.

On arrival at the park headquarters, you will be told to come to the park office on the morning of your climb and a guide will be assigned to you. On most mornings there is a throng of people waiting for a guide – the earlier you start the better. The park staff will try to attach individual travellers to a group so that guide fees can be shared – but ask, just in case. Couples can expect to be given their own guide.

The guides and porters are usually Kadazan from local villages, and not employees of the national park. Some of these professional guides are amazing: one is 55 years old and has climbed Mt Kinabalu more than 700 times in 16 years as a guide! On the other hand, some travellers have complained that their guide was useless and sloped off at the first opportunity. A good guide should be able to point out pitcher plants and other interesting sights; if you have a special interest ask the park office if it can find you a knowledgeable guide.

Porters are optional and expensive. A porter's fee is RM70 per trip for a maximum load of 10kg up to the Panar Laban huts. For the second segment, up to the Sayat-Sayat hut, it's RM80 per trip; from there to the summit costs RM90.

## Equipment

As long as it's not raining you can walk as far as Laban Rata in normal hiking gear. Dress in layers so you can take off and put on clothes as necessary. It's only at the summit that you'll need warm clothes – and then you'll really need them. You'll appreciate gloves and a woollen hat, and a raincoat should be carried at all times. Wear strong, comfortable shoes with good grip – gym shoes are probably best, but make sure they can be easily dried or frostbite may be a problem.

A torch (flashlight) is required if you're getting up before dawn – these can be hired for RM5. Bring snacks for the climb and food if you intend to do your own cooking. Water bottles can be filled along the trail, except between Laban Rata and the summit. Don't be fooled by the clouds –

the sun is fierce at that altitude and to avoid sunburn it is very important to carry sunblock. Bedding is provided in the huts en route, but if you're staying beyond Laban Rata, pick it up from there on the way through.

## WALKING TRAILS

It's well worth spending a day exploring the marked trails around park headquarters; if you have time, it may be better to do it before you climb the mountain as you may not feel like it afterwards. All the trails and lookouts are shown on the Kinabalu Park Headquarters & Trails map.

All the trails link up with others at some stage, so you can spend the whole day, or indeed days, walking at a leisurely pace through the beautiful forest. Some interesting plants, plenty of birds and, if you're

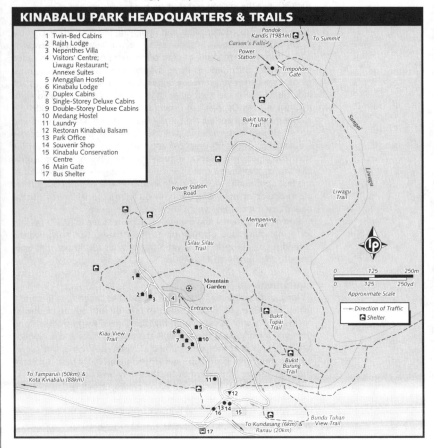

**KINABALU PARK HEADQUARTERS & TRAILS**

1 Twin-Bed Cabins
2 Rajah Lodge
3 Nepenthes Villa
4 Visitors' Centre;
  Liwagu Restaurant;
  Annexe Suites
5 Menggilan Hostel
6 Kinabalu Lodge
7 Duplex Cabins
8 Single-Storey Deluxe Cabins
9 Double-Storey Deluxe Cabins
10 Medang Hostel
11 Laundry
12 Restoran Kinabalu Balsam
13 Park Office
14 Souvenir Shop
15 Kinabalu Conservation
   Centre
16 Main Gate
17 Bus Shelter

lucky, the occasional mammal can be seen along the Liwagu Trail, which follows the river of the same name. When it rains, watch out for slippery paths and armies of leeches.

At 11 am each day a guided walk (RM1.50/3) starts from the park office and lasts for one to two hours. It's well worth taking and follows an easy path. The knowledgeable guide points out flowers, plants, birds and insects along the way. If you set out from KK early, it's possible to arrive at the park in time for the guided walk.

Many of the plants found on the mountain are cultivated in the Mountain Garden behind the visitors' centre; it's open at 9 am, noon and 3 pm, and is also well worth a look (entry RM2.50/5).

## THE CLIMB

Climbing Mt Kinabalu is normally a two-day excercise. Most people climb as far as Laban Rata or the nearby huts the first day, then climb to the summit at dawn and return to park headquarters that day. The park headquarters reckons you should be underway by 10 am to make Laban Rata in good time, but this is probably conservative – leaving by 11 am should be fine if you're reasonably fit, though most people set off between 8 and 9 am.

Dawn on the summit is often an all-too-brief glimpse across Borneo at 6 am before the clouds roll in along the mountainous spine stretching towards the morning light. Sometimes the summit is socked-in already, at other times the sun shines through till 10 am or later. You won't know until you get there, but that's part of the adventure. Many people climb as far as Laban Rata, stay overnight and descend the next morning – the views are still special, there are no guide fees to pay and the really hard yards at the summit approach can be left to others.

Either way, it is wise to stay overnight at the park headquarters at least the night before the climb. This will allow you to make an early start and to acclimatise a bit – Mt Kinabalu is high enough for altitude sickness to occur.

The climb is uphill 99% of the way; it is unrelenting, steep in places and there are seemingly endless steps – actually there are 2500 – as far as Laban Rata. Then it gets a whole lot tougher. The trail becomes even steeper as you approach the summit, then disappears altogether on vast, near-vertical fields of slippery granite. Every step can be a struggle as you gasp for breath in the thin air. Still keen?

The secret to climbing Mt Kinabalu is stamina. Take it slowly – very slowly if you are tired and out of breath. Many people start off briskly then have to take frequent and increasingly longer rest-breaks, while the old hands just keep trudging along. Take it easy and walk at a comfortable pace.

Signboards showing your progress are spaced along the trail and there's a marker every 500m. There are rest shelters (pondok) at regular intervals, with clean squat-style toilets and tanks of cool, fresh

drinking water. The walking times that follow are conservative esti-
mates published by the Sabah Parks office.

## Park Headquarters–Power Station
The trail officially starts at the Timpohon Gate (1866m), from where
it's an 8.72km walk to the summit. Unfortunately it's nearly an hour's
uphill walk from park headquarters to the gate – or power station, as
it's commonly called. A minivan shuttles back and forth from the park
office area to the power station between 7 am and about 5 pm; it takes
only 15 minutes, costs RM2 and will considerably shorten your day's
walking. An earlier start can be negotiated with the park office.

It is not much fun walking along the road, though the Liwagu Trail
to the power station is a scenic alternative for those who can afford to
add an extra three hours or so to the climb.

## Power Station–Layang Layang
After a short, deceptive *descent*, the trail leads up steep stairs through
magnificent tall forest. There's a small waterfall – Carson's Falls –
beside the track shortly after the start, and the forest can be alive with
birds and squirrels in the morning. Five pondok are spaced at intervals
of 15 to 35 minutes and it's about three hours to Layang Layang
(2621m), where there's a small staff-quarters. At Pondok Kandis
(1981m) the tall forest gives way to dense, stunted rhododendron
forest. Near Pondok Lowii (2286m) the trail follows an open ridge
giving great views over the valleys and up to the peaks.

## Layang Layang–Pondok Paka
It's about 1¾ hours on to Pondok Paka (3053m), the seventh shelter
on the trail and 5.5km from the start. The trail passes through increasingly stunted rhododendron forest, leaving walkers more open to
the elements. Occasional flat sections come as a relief after the endless
steps. Cloud often closes in by late morning, refreshing the beard moss
and orchids growing on the trees. This stretch is good for pitcher
plants, although you probably won't see any growing by the side of
the track – look among the dense vegetation.

A half-hour detour can be made to Paka Cave – a rock overhang
with a bamboo platform where the early explorers spent the night
before tackling the summit. It is not that interesting and can be left for
the descent, when the lungs are less taxed.

## Pondok Paka–Laban Rata
Laban Rata (3272m) marks the treeline and is the night's resting spot
for most people attempting the summit. This leg takes about 45
minutes to walk. The hut has heating, hot water, comfortable beds and
a restaurant with fine views. This is the place to rest, commiserate with
or boast to your fellow climbers and settle in for the night, though
some people press on to the spartan Sayat-Sayat hut after a meal.

## Laban Rata–Sayat-Sayat

The one-hour climb to Sayat-Sayat hut (3668m) involves crossing the sheer Panar Laban rock-face. Vegetation is no more than waist high, except where overhangs provide some respite from the wind. It is one of the toughest parts of the climb and doesn't get any easier in the dark and cold at 4 am, when the early risers from Laban Rata are urged onwards to see the dawn.

Thick ropes are used to haul yourself up the granite sheets; it's hard work, hauling and juggling a torch, but in a way it's good to be using arm muscles instead of legs! Narrow wooden steps and hand rails help in places, but often you'll use the smooth, gnarled branches of bushes for support as you gasp for breath.

## Sayat-Sayat–Summit

The steepest and hardest part of the climb is saved till last. Past Sayat-Sayat, more desolate rock-faces and hoisting await the string of climbers stretched out in the dark, trying to keep warm while holding ropes and torches. In the daylight, thick veins of quartz can be seen stretching as straight as painted lines on the rock-face.

The summit looks deceptively close and, although it's just over 1km, the last burst can take up to two hours from Sayat-Sayat. Many people are reduced to crawling on hands and knees up the last few boulders to the small area that is the top of Borneo. Climbers crowd together and huddle against the cold, priming their cameras for a shot of the sunrise, the nearby Donkey Ears and St John's Peaks, and the mysterious abyss of Low's Gully. When the sun has risen and the photos are taken, there is a quick exodus down the mountain to Laban Rata, while the late risers, perhaps the wisest of all, make their way to the less crowded summit.

The climb down to the Power Station takes about five hours – don't underestimate the descent and leave plenty of time to get back before nightfall. Allow another hour to walk from the power station to your accommodation. While it is easier than the climb up, it can be a lot more damaging on under-used muscles. Aim to leave the summit by about noon and to be well underway by 1 pm. The weather can close in very quickly and, although you probably won't get lost, the granite is slippery even when it's dry – and it can get very wet at the top.

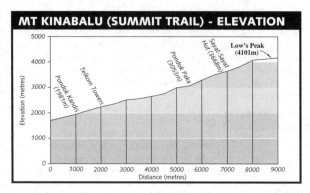

MT KINABALU (SUMMIT TRAIL) - ELEVATION

First-class certificates are issued for RM2 to those who complete the climb, but certificates are also issued for making it to Laban Rata – no mean feat in itself. They can be collected at the park office.

## PLACES TO STAY

Overnight accommodation is available around park headquarters, on the Ranau road between the park turn-off and Kundassang, at Poring Hot Springs, in the resthouse on the mountain and in mountain huts on the summit trail.

Accommodation in the park is booked at Kinabalu Gold Resorts (☎ 088-257941, fax 242861, ✉ nature@kinabalu.net); see Information in the KK section for details. Book as far in advance as possible (at least several days to a week), and note that on weekends, school holidays and public holidays all the accommodation may be taken. Mountain huts also need to be booked.

Reservations can be made by email, fax or phone, but they will not be confirmed until fully paid for. Deposits are theoretically required for accommodation in the park (eg, RM20 for a dorm bed and RM100 for an annexe suite), payable when you check in at park headquarters. In fact you may not be asked to leave a deposit, but bring some extra cash for the purpose.

### Park Headquarters

There's a variety of very good accommodation at the park headquarters to suit all budgets. The cheapest places are the 46-bed *Medang Hostel* and the 54-bed *Menggilan Hostel*, which cost RM12 per person, or RM6 for anyone younger than 18. Both hostels are clean and comfortable, have cooking facilities and a dining area with an open fireplace; hot water for showers is sporadic.

The rest of the accommodation at park headquarters is good but expensive; rates jump considerably on weekends and public holidays – and prices at the park are always on the rise. The rates listed in this section are for the whole room or chalet.

Twin-bed cabins are RM58/92 on weekdays/weekends. The annexe suites are in the visitors' centre and sleep up to four people for RM115/184. Two-bedroom duplex cabins, which can sleep up to six people, cost RM173/230 per night; it's the same rate for five-person single-storey deluxe cabins. Double-storey deluxe cabins sleeping seven cost RM207/288.

Going up in quality and price, the two-bedroom *Nepenthes Villa*, which sleeps four people, is RM207/288; at the four-bedroom *Kinabalu Lodge*, eight people can share the cost – RM311/414 per night. At the top of the range, *Rajah Lodge* sleeps 10 people and costs RM929/1150.

There are two restaurants at park headquarters. The cheaper and more popular of the two is the canteen-style *Restoran Kinabalu Balsam*, directly below the park office, which offers basic but decent Malaysian, Chinese and Western dishes at reasonable prices; RM5 should get you full.

There is also a small but well-stocked *shop* in the canteen selling tinned and dried foods, chocolate, beer, spirits, cigarettes, T-shirts, bread, eggs and margarine. A packed lunch (chicken, sandwiches, fruit and soft drink) for your climb costs RM12. You can sit and admire the mountain from a covered balcony.

The *Liwagu Restaurant* in the visitors' centre is more expensive than the Balsam, but there's a huge range of dishes, including Malaysian and Chinese noodles, rice and seafood standards. An 'American breakfast' is pretty ordinary here for RM12; the cheaper breakfast at the Balsam canteen is better value.

Both restaurants are open every day at 6 am, closing at 10 pm on weekdays and 11 pm on weekends and public holidays.

## On the Mountain

On your way up to the **summit** you will have to stay overnight at one of the mountain huts at around 3300m, or at the 54-bed *Laban Rata Resthouse*, which costs RM29 per person in four-bed rooms. It has heating, hot water (showers can be scalding) and a restaurant, and is by far the most comfortable overnight stop on the mountain. It also has one double room with bathroom for RM115 and a four-bed suite with bathroom for RM230.

At Laban Rata there's a *restaurant* selling hot noodle- and rice-meals for about RM6.50 to RM7.50; the restaurant is open for regular meals, and also from 2 to 3 am so you can grab some breakfast before attempting the summit climb.

There's also a *shop* selling film, cold drinks, headache tablets and other basic medicines, chocolates and – don't laugh – walking sticks; you may find this a shrewd purchase for the descent.

It's only RM12 to stay in the mountain huts (RM6 for those under 18) near Laban Rata. There are the 12-bed *Waras* and *Panar Laban* huts and the 44-bed *Gunting Lagadan* hut, which has a basic kitchen.

These places are more spartan and aren't heated, but a sleeping bag is provided and they're close to the restaurant.

If you're one of those people who likes a cold shower and a 10km hike before breakfast, you'll love the **Sayat-Sayat** hut. This 10-bunk tin shed is about 1.5km from the summit and is the most primitive of the lot. There's no electricity, and water has to be carried up (or you can boil muddy water from a nearby stream). It also costs RM12, or RM6 for those under 18.

For most climbers the huts around Laban Rata are far enough to walk in one day, but if you stay overnight in the Sayat-Sayat hut, you don't have to get up in the middle of the night in order to reach the summit by dawn. Collect sleeping bags (RM5) at Laban Rata on the way through if you intend staying there.

It may not matter where you overnight because the air is rather thin and you may sleep quite fitfully. It's *very* cold in the early morning (around 0°C!), so take warm clothing with you.

## Outside the Park
It is preferable to stay in the park, mainly because the lodging is reasonable value and access to the park and mountain is simple – reportedly, some travellers have been charged an entry fee every time they entered the park gates (keep your receipt just in case).

If the park accommodation is full, there are a number of places to stay along the road between park headquarters and Kundassang. Some have great mountain views, though most look out over the cultivated valley south of the park. Published rates are listed here but discounts should be available, especially when things aren't so busy. The Kundassang area has plenty more lodging, but it is inconvenient for the park.

A few hundred metres towards Ranau from the park turn-off, *Rina Ria Lodge (☎ 088-889291)* has two dorms with beds for RM15 per person and rooms from RM60/100 to RM150/200 on weekdays/weekends. All rooms have balconies overlooking the valley, and there's a shop with a good range of tinned and dried goods.

About 1.5km farther, *Fairy Garden (☎ 088-889688)* looks like a Tibetan lamasery dangling over the drop. Rooms cost RM50 to RM120, and there's a cavernous air-con restaurant. The **Kinabalu Rose Cabin** *(☎ 088-889233, fax 889800)* is 2km from the park entrance and has modern, air-con rooms for RM70 to RM100, and suites sleeping four for RM126.

Kundassang is at the bottom of the mountain, halfway to Ranau, and has a grotty market that straggles the roadside. Perched high on a hill above town is the three-star **Hotel Perkasa Mt Kinabalu** *(☎ 088-889511 for reservations)*, the most luxurious accommodation near the park. Singles/doubles cost RM135/165 and suites start at RM250. It has restaurants, a tennis court and 360° views, but it's a soulless place. The hotel shuttle bus charges RM15 for the 7km trip to park headquarters and RM25 to Poring Hot Springs.

On the other side of town towards Ranau, *Kinabalu Pine Resort* (☎ 088-889388; ☎ 889288 sales office) is a tasteful and comfortable upmarket hotel with great views of the mountain. The midweek rates are RM121, including 'American breakfast', rising to RM145 on weekends.

Kinabalu Gold Resorts (☎ 088-257941, fax 242861, @ nature@ kinabalu.net) manages the *Mesilau Nature Resort,* along a road past Kampung Mesilau on the Karamunsing side of the mountain; this large complex sports several hostels and a range of chalets; rates are RM40 to RM740. From the resort, an alternative approach to the summit trail links with Layang-Layang hut.

## GETTING THERE & AWAY

All buses and minivans between KK and Ranau or Sandakan pass the park turn-off, from where it's 100m uphill to park headquarters. From Kota Belud, north of KK, change at Tamparuli for Ranau and the park.

### Kota Kinabalu

Air-con express buses leave from the long-distance bus station in KK for the national park (three hours, RM15) at around 7 am every day; minivans make the trip from the same station for RM10. For Sandakan, most buses leave between 7 and 9 am; there are departures to Ranau (RM10) as late as 12.30 pm from the long-distance bus station, but in the afternoon you'd be safer taking a bus or minivan (RM10 or RM15) from behind Centre Point. The trip to the turn-off takes about 3½ hours.

If you're heading back towards KK, minivans pass the park entrance until mid-afternoon, but the best time to catch one is between 8 am and noon. Stand by the side of the main road to wave one down. If you can't be bothered waiting, hitching is possible. A couple of share-taxis do the run from Ranau to KK (RM15 per person) in the morning.

### Kota Belud & Tamparuli

Tamparuli is where the road up the coast to Kudat branches for Kota Belud and Ranau. If you've been visiting Kota Belud and plan to head for Kinabalu National Park, first go to Tamparuli.

There are several minivans and share-taxis daily from Tamparuli to Ranau (until about 2 pm); these will drop you at the park entrance (two hours, RM5). A taxi will cost at least double the price. It's about 2½ hours' travelling time to the park from Kota Belud.

### Poring Hot Springs

Minivans leave from in front of park headquarters at Mt Kinabalu to Poring for RM10; these currently leave at 9 am, and 1 and 4 pm. Otherwise, make your way to Ranau in the morning and catch a minivan for the hot springs from there.

## Ranau & Sandakan

To travel east from the park headquarters wait at the side of the main road for a minivan going to Ranau or Sandakan, or hitch. Air-con express buses to Sandakan pass park headquarters until about noon. There may be no free seats on the weekend. The trip to Sandakan takes at least four hours and costs RM20.

Minivans pass the park entrance en route to Ranau until about 5.30 pm, but they are much less frequent in the afternoon. The 22km journey to Ranau takes about half an hour (RM5).

MARK DAFFEY

**Left:** Hiker on the route to Low's Peak (4101m) on Mt Kinabalu, with South Peak in the background.

(Continued from page 492)

# KUDAT
☎ 088

Kudat is a quiet port town in the very north of Sabah, 190km from KK. Kudat has a noticeable Filipino influence, as much of the trade here is with the Philippines, and the surrounding countryside is the home of the friendly Rungus people, tribal cousins of the Kadazan.

Kudat has little of interest and few travellers make it this far north. There are fine beaches west of town and it is possible to visit Rungus longhouses near the highway, but you'll need a car or taxi to reach them.

## Places to Stay & Eat
*Hotel Sunrise* (☎ 611517), in the old part of town near the minivan station, is a friendly place and the best value in town; fan-cooled/air-con rooms with shared bathroom cost RM20/28; air-con single/doubles with bathroom and TV are RM40/48. *Hotel Kinabalu* (☎ 613888) is one of several similar hotels on Jalan Melor in the new section of town; decent air-con rooms with TV and bathroom cost RM42/56.

*Restoran Saijana* is off Jalan Lintas, a block north-east of the Hotel Sunrise, diagonally opposite a new Hokkien temple. It's a very welcoming halal place that serves tasty and cheap dishes.

## Getting There & Away
There are Malaysia Airlines Twin Otter flights from Kudat to KK (three weekly, RM50) and Sandakan (five weekly, RM54).

Several minivans a day make the three- to four-hour trip from KK for RM15. The two-hour journey from Kota Belud costs RM10.

There is an express boat leaving from the old part of town for nearby Pulau Panggi (RM10); there are no tourist facilities on the island, however, and foreigners don't seem to be encouraged to visit.

## AROUND KUDAT
You'll find some of the best beaches in Sabah around Kudat, where the water is shallow and

safe for paddling. **Bak Bak**, about 11km from Kudat, is the town beach. It has clear water, picnic and toilet facilities and food stalls on weekends, though the beach itself is only a narrow strip of sand against a retaining wall. The fishing villages farther north of Bak Bak have some even better white-sand beaches, but there is no accommodation and they are difficult to get to.

Many Rungus people build their own houses in preference to living in the highly flammable traditional longhouses, but there are still some interesting longhouses around Kudat. If you visit one, it's polite to take a few small gifts of food or cigarettes. The best known of these longhouses is **Matunggung**, on the highway south of Kudat. It is well frequented by tour groups, but there are other longhouses found farther inland from the highway. Matunggung is a traditional thatched-roof longhouse with enclosed bamboo-slatted sides. Inside, each family's living quarters, called *valai*, is composed of sleeping, dining and living areas, and an attic.

The traditional dress for Rungus women is a black sarong and colourful, beaded necklaces. On festive occasions, heavy brass bracelets are worn as well. The Rungus tribes produce some elaborate beadwork and you can sometimes buy their handicrafts at the Sunday tamu held at **Sikuati**, 23km south of Kudat. Sikuati is on the highway, 1km from the coast, where there is a good beach. Teluk Sikuati has a long, sweeping white-sand beach, though the water can be choppy and it is not as clear as that around Bak Bak.

## Getting There & Away
Bak Bak is difficult to get to from Kudat without your own transport – count on at least RM20 for a taxi there and back; arrange a time for pick-up. Sikuati and Matunggung are both on the highway and minibuses can drop you off.

# RANAU
☎ 088

Ranau is a curious collection of concrete shopblocks on the route between KK and

Sandakan – a bit like a Mexican border-town without Antonio Banderas. There's a busy **tamu** on Saturday at the bridge a few hundred metres south of town, but few travellers stay overnight since the big attraction is Poring Hot Springs (see the following section), about 19km to the north. Ranau is primarily a place to get a bus connection to/from Poring or Mt Kinabalu.

Ranau measures only a few hundred metres square. Express buses park at the top end of town behind the Esso petrol station. In the blocks of shophouses across the road there are cafes and hotels, and minibuses line up in droves down the main street to the west of the bus stand.

### Places to Stay & Eat

If you get stuck, Ranau has a couple of pricey mid-range hotels to choose from. *Hotel Ranau (☎ 875661)* is the first place you see when entering the town and is opposite the Shell petrol station. The choice ranges from simple, fan-cooled singles/doubles for RM30/45 to rooms with air-con, TV and toilet for RM70. *Hotel Kinabalu (☎ 876028)*, west of the main street, has similar rooms and even similar decor – all garish plastic and frills – for about the same price. Both are of a good standard, but the Hotel Kinabalu is a tad better. Discounts are likely to be available at both.

Ranau has plenty of *coffee shops*; most are Chinese but simple Malay meals are also available.

### Getting There & Away

Morning bus and minivan services operate regularly from Ranau. Minivans to Tambunan cost RM6. The minivan trip to Keningau (RM15) can be hazardous to your lunch – see the earlier Keningau Getting There & Away section for details.

**Kota Kinabalu** Express buses leave Ranau for KK (about 3½ hours, RM15) from 7 am to about 1.30 pm. Minivans (RM10 or RM15) and share-taxis (RM15) leave Ranau daily until about 3 pm. It is best to catch them in the morning because afternoon runs are less frequent.

All bus services to KK pass the entrance to Mt Kinabalu National Park (RM5). If you get stuck, you can charter a minivan to park headquarters for RM20.

**Sandakan** All buses to Sandakan pass the Sepilok Orang-Utan Rehabilitation Centre (see that section later in this chapter); ask to be dropped off. Air-con express buses are the best way to travel, and these leave Ranau for Sandakan between 7.30 am and noon; the fare is RM25 and the journey takes about four hours. Minivans go throughout the day but can take a while to fill up, especially in the afternoon.

**Poring Hot Springs** On weekends it's easy and cheap to get to the hot springs from Ranau. Drivers cruise around the blocks, shouting 'Poring, Poring!'. The price is RM4 per person and the transport leaves when it's full (which usually doesn't take long because many locals go there for afternoon trips).

On weekdays it isn't quite so easy, especially if you arrive in Ranau during the afternoon. If this happens you'll have to ask around the cafes and shops to see if anyone wants to share the cost.

Share-taxis are available, but drivers will probably try to convince you to charter the whole taxi. Charter costs RM20 to Poring, which is fine between three or four people, but painful if you're on your own. Bargain hard, though paying RM20 is better than staying in Ranau.

## PORING HOT SPRINGS

The Poring Hot Springs were developed by the Japanese during WWII and since the war have become a popular weekend retreat for locals. The complex is actually part of the Kinabalu National Park, but the park headquarters is 43km away via Ranau.

Steaming, sulphurous water is channelled into pools and tubs in which visitors can relax their tired muscles after the trek to the summit of Mt Kinabalu. The pools are in a pretty garden setting with hibiscus and other flowers, which attract hordes of butterflies. Poring is also famous among bird-watchers, and a good selection of birds can be seen around the gardens and along walking trails.

You may want to choose your attractions carefully, as management has decided to soak guests with separate fees for each part of the hot springs – in total this currently adds up to RM30 for non-Malaysian adults. Entrance to the hot springs costs RM1.50/3 per child/adult (a child is considered anyone under 18).

In addition to the attractions described in this section, there is a Tropical Garden (from 1.30 pm, RM1/3), a Butterfly Farm (9 am to 4 pm, RM2/4), an Orchid Garden (from 2.30 pm, RM5/10) and a slide show (from noon, RM2).

### Baths

The outdoor tubs are of varying sizes and can easily fit a couple of people. They have hot- and cold-water taps, so you can regulate the temperature to your liking. The water from the springs is very hot – you can boil eggs for breakfast in it (but, as the sign indicates, only inside a plastic bag). The baths are open from 7 am to 6 pm daily, although locals flaunt this rule.

Folks wear swimming costumes in the baths, but Western women will probably be ogled in the tubs.

Private spa cabins are also available. A standard cabin has a tub and shower, and costs RM15 per hour. Larger spa cabins can accommodate up to eight people. The deluxe cabins have a lounge area, Jacuzzis, shower and toilet, and cost RM20 an hour.

After a hot bath you can take a cooling dip in the rock pool.

### Canopy Walkway

This unusual attraction consists of a series of walkways suspended from trees up to 30m above the jungle floor. It offers a monkey's-eye view of the surrounding forest, but the springy walkways are not for the faint-hearted. It's quite safe and great fun, but get there early if you want to see birds or other wildlife.

The canopy walkway is open between 9 am and 4 pm. Admission is RM1.50/3 for children/adults and there's a camera/video

There's a good *restaurant* ov... the swimming pool between the ... and the river. There are also ... sive *eating places* right o... entrance. If you're se... buy food for cooking ... is cheaper if you b...

### Getting Th...
Poring is ... sealed r... taxi o... Ra...

see but the surrounding forest is very pretty.

**Langanan Waterfall** is a steep walk and a farther 1¼ hours away on the same trail via Kipungit and the bat caves. It's best to set out early and take plenty of water. This walk is legendary among bird-watchers as a haunt of the rarely seen blue-banded pitta.

### Places to Stay & Eat

If you intend to stay overnight, you are supposed to reserve and pay for accommodation at the Kinabalu Gold Resorts office (☎ 088-257941, fax 242861, @ nature@ kinabalu.net) in KK– see Information in the KK section–you could take pot luck and just show up, but Poring is a popular place, especially on weekends.

The older *Kelicap Hostel* has 24 beds and *Serindit Hostel* is a newer, 44-bed dorm. There are clean, spacious kitchens with gas cookers. Both hostels cost RM12 per person (RM6 if under 18 years of age), and blankets and pillows are provided free of charge.

Cabins with cooking facilities and chalets with air-con and all facilities are also available. A cabin sleeping six people costs RM87/115 on weekdays/weekends; a cabin sleeping four costs RM69/92; and a chalet sleeping six costs RM207/288.

The mosquitoes at Poring can be vicious, so take coils and insect repellent.

A campground is also available for RM6 per tent. Tents can be hired through the park office at the springs. Pillows and blankets can be hired for 50 sen each.

rlooking
public baths
three inexpen-
pposite the park
-catering, you can
here as well, though it
ring your own from KK.

**re & Away**

9km north of Ranau along a
ad and can be reached by minivan,
hitching. Access is generally from
au (see the Ranau Getting There &
way section earlier for details), but a few
minivans run from the park headquarters at
Mt Kinabalu to Poring for RM10; these currently leave at 9 am, and 1 and 4 pm.

Leaving Poring can be tricky. Minivans
leave for Ranau from outside the park office
at the springs at around 6.30 am, and then
at roughly 10 am and 2 pm, depending on
demand; the fare is RM5. On weekends
there are nearly always share-taxis parked
near the office; the fare is by negotiation but
if it's a full load it should only cost RM5 per
person.

The park staff can probably help arrange
a lift. Otherwise, wait for a minivan that is
dropping off passengers from Ranau.

# East Sabah

After enjoying Sabah's main tourist attraction, Mt Kinabalu, many travellers head for
the Sepilok Orang-Utan Rehabilitation
Centre near Sandakan. Sepilok's orang-
utans are a major draw, but this part of
Sabah offers plenty more, especially if it's
wildlife you're after.

One or two sights are pretty well the exclusive preserve of tour groups – but an en-
thusiast's route could take in Sepilok, a
half-day at the Gomantong Caves, a trip to
the fabulous Sungai Kinabatangan and
some world-class diving or snorkelling at
the islands off Semporna. And if your budget allows it, you could indulge in a few
days at the magnificent Danum Valley for
an upmarket rainforest experience, or even
explore the Lost World of the Maliau Basin.

## SANDAKAN
☎ 089

Sandakan is a busy, chaotic commercial
centre at the entrance to a beautiful, island-
studded bay. Most activity centres on the
docks and wharves that sprawl along the
waterfront for many kilometres. Barges,
ferries and motorboats of every description
buzz around, unloading fish and other produce, and taking away rattan, timber, rubber, copra, palm oil and even birds' nests.
West of town, passenger ferries shuttle back
and forth to Zamboanga in the Philippines.
In the bay, container vessels ride at anchor
awaiting their turn to unload.

Compared to Sabah's relatively anonym-
ous state capital, Sandakan has character
and even a certain downmarket charm. The
real attractions lie outside town, but there
are some good beaches nearby, excellent
seafood to enjoy and mesmerising views
from the hills at sunset.

Forty kilometres offshore is Turtle Islands National Park, one of the world's few
turtle sanctuaries, and farther afield there's
the Gomantong Caves and superb wildlife-
watching along the Sungai Kinabatangan.

As for annoyances, Sandakan seems to
have a higher-than-average number of kids
demanding 'one ringgit' from tourists, apparently on the grounds that they are…short.
Women travellers might be more comfortable in pairs at night around the waterfront.

### History

At the height of the timber boom Sandakan
was said to have the world's greatest concentration of millionaires. It was perhaps
an extravagant claim, but the area has always been renowned for luxury goods such
as pearls, sea cucumbers and birds' nests,
and so attracted trade from the nearby
Philippines and as far away as China.

In the 18th century Sandakan came under
the suzerainty of the Sultan of Sulu, who
ruled the southern islands of what is now
the Philippines. British traders came to the
region in the 19th century, but the first foreign settlement was mainly by Germans
who settled on Pulau Timbang, in Teluk
Sandakan, in the 1870s.

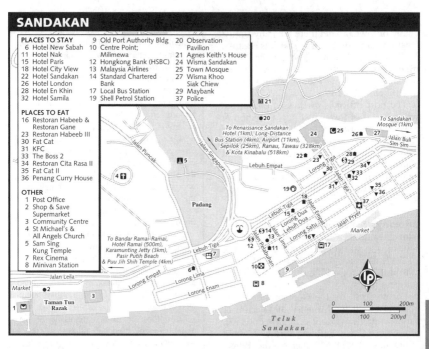

**SANDAKAN**

PLACES TO STAY
6  Hotel New Sabah
11  Hotel Nak
15  Hotel Paris
18  Hotel City View
22  Hotel Sandakan
26  Hotel London
28  Hotel En Khin
32  Hotel Samila

PLACES TO EAT
16  Restoran Habeeb &
    Restoran Gane
23  Restoran Habeeb III
30  Fat Cat
31  KFC
33  The Boss 2
34  Restoran Cita Rasa II
35  Fat Cat II
36  Penang Curry House

OTHER
1  Post Office
2  Shop & Save
   Supermarket
3  Community Centre
4  St Michael's &
   All Angels Church
5  Sam Sing
   Kung Temple
7  Rex Cinema
8  Minivan Station

9  Old Port Authority Bldg
10  Centre Point;
    Milimewa
12  Hongkong Bank (HSBC)
13  Malaysia Airlines
14  Standard Chartered
    Bank
17  Local Bus Station
19  Shell Petrol Station

20  Observation
    Pavilion
21  Agnes Keith's House
24  Wisma Sandakan
25  Town Mosque
27  Wisma Khoo
    Siak Chiew
29  Maybank
37  Police

To Sandakan
Mosque (1km)

To Renaissance Sandakan
Hotel (1km); Long-Distance
Bus Station (4km), Airport (11km),
Sepilok (25km), Ranau, Tawau (328km)
& Kota Kinabalu (518km)

Jalan Buli
Sim Sim

Jalan Puncak

Jalan Singapura

Lebuh Empat

Padang

Lorong Tiga

Lorong Dua

Lebuh Tiga

Lorong Satu

Jalan Tiga

Jalan Empat

Jalan Pryer

Market

To Bandar Ramai-Ramai,
Hotel Ramai (500m),
Karamunting Jetty (3km),
Pasir Putih Beach
& Puu Jih Shih Temple (4km)

Lebuh Tiga

Jalan Pelabuhan

Jalan Leila

Lorong Empat

Lorong Lima

Lorong Enam

Market

Taman Tun
Razak

Teluk
Sandakan

0    100    200m
0    100    200yd

MALAYSIAN BORNEO

In 1878 Baron von Overbeck, an Austrian, acquired a lease from the Sultan of Sulu for much of eastern Sabah, and this was later sold to Alfred Dent, a Hong Kong–based publisher. Sandakan was established by the British Resident William Pryer, and it boomed. In 1884 Sandakan became the capital of British North Borneo, and it remained the capital until the Japanese invasion; subsequent Allied bombing in 1945 virtually destroyed the town. In 1946 the capital was moved to Jesselton, now called Kota Kinabalu.

## Orientation

The centre of Sandakan consists of only a few blocks squashed between the waterfront and a steep escarpment from where you can look out over the bay. In the centre you'll find most of the hotels and restaurants, banks, the Malaysia Airlines office, and the local and long-distance bus stations. The main road west along the bay, Jalan Leila, passes the commercial centres of Bandar Ramai-Ramai and Bandar Leila, where there are more hotels, places to eat and backpackers' accommodation.

Streets in the town centre are numbered Jalan Dua, Jalan Tiga (1st St, 2nd St) etc, and 'Jalan' and 'Lebuh' seem to be used interchangeably. Fortunately, the town centre is very small and it's hard to get lost.

The local bus station is right by the markets along the waterfront. Local buses and minivans also leave from the open area just past the old Port Authority building. Express buses to KK and other destinations leave from the long-distance bus station, 4km north of the town centre.

## Information

At the time of writing a tourist office was planned for the waterfront area in the vicinity of the post office, and should be open by the time you read this.

The immigration office is in the Secretariat building, just past the roundabout at

Batu 7 on the Ranau road, 11km from the centre of town. To get there take any Batu 7 ('batu' means 'mile') or higher bus (Batu 8, 12, 19, 30 etc). If you're going to the Philippines, you can clear immigration at the Karamunting Jetty (about 4km west of town) before boarding.

The post office is on Jalan Leila at the western end of town, just past the Shop & Save Supermarket.

There is a cybercafe on the 1st floor of Centre Point; it's open till 9.30 pm and charges RM4 per hour. Sandakan Cybercafe is on the 3rd floor of Wisma Sandakan; it's open until about 9 pm and also charges RM4 per hour.

**Bookings & Permits** Bookings for Turtle Islands National Park are now the monopoly of Crystal Quest (☎ 212711, fax 212712, ❸ cquest@tm.net.my), 12th floor, Wisma Khoo Siak Chiew; it is open usual business hours.

For a permit for the Gomantong Caves, you must visit the Ministry of Tourism & Environment's Wildlife office (☎ 666550), housed in a flashy building at Batu 7, about 500m past the 11 Km peg on the Ranau road.

## Things to See & Do

The town doesn't have any 'must see' attractions, but it's pleasant enough to walk around the busy **waterfront** and watch the fishing boats, barges and ferries around the wharves.

The **market** is always a hive of activity, though it can get a bit fetid in the heat of the day. Locals will warn you about pickpockets; we have had no complaints from travellers, but guard your valuables just in case.

The **Puu Jih Shih Temple**, 4km west of the town centre, is a large Buddhist temple perched on a steep hill overlooking Teluk Sandakan. Take a bus to Tanah Merah and ask for the temple. Near the temple on the coast road is **Pasir Putih Beach**, a dull patch of grey sand overlooked by a good seafood restaurant. Closer to the centre of town, the **Sam Sing Kung Temple** dates from 1887 and fronts the padang.

## The Sandakan Death Marches

Sandakan was the site of a Japanese prisoner-of-war camp during WWII, and in September 1944 there were 1800 Australian and 600 British troops interned here. What is probably not widely known is that more Australians died here than during the building of the infamous Burma Railway.

Early in the war, food and conditions were bearable, and the death rate was around three per month. But as the Allies closed in towards the end of the war, it became clear to the officers in command that they didn't have enough staff to guard against a rebellion in the camps. They decided to cut the prisoners' rations to weaken them; disease spread and the death rate began to rise.

It was also decided to move the prisoners inland – 250km through the jungle to Ranau. On 28 January 1945, 470 prisoners set off; 313 made it to Ranau. On the second march, 570 started from Sandakan; just 118 reached Ranau. The 537 prisoners on the third march were the last men in the camp.

Conditions on the marches were deplorable: many men had no boots, rations were less than minimal and many men fell by the wayside; the Japanese disposed of any prisoners who couldn't walk. Once in Ranau, the surviving prisoners were put to work carrying 20kg sacks of rice over hilly country to Paginatan, 40km away. Disease and starvation took a horrendous toll, and by the end of July 1945 there were no prisoners left in Ranau. The only survivors from the 2400 at Sandakan were six Australians who escaped, either from Ranau or during the marches.

For some religious extravagance and fine views over the stilt villages that line Sandakan Bay, visit **Sandakan Mosque**, 1km east of town. Another building of note is **St Michael's & All Angels Church**, built in the 19th century and one of the few stone buildings in Malaysian Borneo.

For a fine view over the town and bay, head up the hill towards the Renaissance Sandakan Hotel and turn right at Jalan Istana near the roundabout. An **observation** pavilion a few hundred metres along offers panoramic views. Just behind is **Agnes Keith's House**, an old two-storey wooden villa; at the time of writing the house was being renovated as a memorial. Keith was an American who came to Sandakan in the 1930s with her husband, who was the Conservator of Forests. She wrote about her experiences in three books, the most famous being *Land Below the Wind*. She was imprisoned by the Japanese during WWII – just one of her many adventures in Sabah.

The **Australian War Memorial** is in a quiet, wooded park just past the government buildings at Batu 8 (Km 12) on the road to Ranau. Despite its tranquil appearance, this was the site of the Japanese POW camp and the starting point for the infamous 'death marches' to Ranau (see the boxed text 'The Sandakan Death Marches' in this section). Large, rusting machines under the trees have plaques telling how many men died during their construction and how prisoners tried to sabotage them. It's fascinating but grim reading, and despite the tropical heat the place has a melancholy if not eerie air. It is not surprising that local ghost stories abound.

To get there, take any Batu 8 or higher bus and get off at the Esso petrol station about 1km on the right past the government buildings at the airport roundabout. Walk along Jalan Rimba for about 10 minutes; the camp is on the right, about 100m after the road turns to gravel. It is well signposted on the main road.

## Organised Tours

It's easy to visit the Sepilok Orang-Utan Rehabilitation Centre independently and you can also get to Gomantong Caves if you are determined, but the Sungai Kinabatangan is virtually impossible to reach without taking a tour – and a guide is recommended for upriver exploration in any case, as travellers get lost there from time to time.

Sandakan has plenty of tour operators offering trips to these places and farther afield. Among the more established ones are:

**Discovery Tours** (☎ 274106, fax 274107) 9th floor, Wisma Khoo Siak Chiew
**Seagull Sea Transport** (☎ 213503, fax 217807) 1st floor, Wisma Khoo Siak Chiew. Seagull is SI Tours' affiliate in town.
**SI Tours** (☎ 673503, fax 673788, ℮ sitours@ po.jaring.my) 1st floor, Sandakan airport terminal bldg. SI can arrange trips to Pulau Seligan and organise Sukau lodging for the Kinabatangan.
**Uncle Tan's** (☎ 089-531917, fax 531639, ℮ tan sulim@tm.net.my) The first and still the best for the Kinabatangan; see the Sepilok Places to Stay section later, and the Sungai Kinabatangan section later for information on river trips. Uncle Tan can also take you turtle-watching – a four-island trip costs RM180, including meals.
**Wildlife Expeditions** (☎ 219616, fax 214570, ℮ sliew@po.jaring.my) Room 903, 9th floor, Wisma Khoo Siak Chiew; also has a desk at the Renaissance Sandakan Hotel and an office in KK (☎ 088-246000, fax 231758, ℮ leegn@ pc.jaring.my). The company runs upmarket tours to Sepilok and the Kinabatangan, and takes snorkelling trips off Pulau Libaran.

## Places to Stay – Budget & Mid-Range

If you are only visiting Sandakan to see the Orang-Utan Rehabilitation Centre at Sepilok, it's better to stay out there, since it's about 25km from the town centre (see Places to Stay in the Sepilok section later). Besides, there is hardly any budget lodging in Sandakan, and the few really cheap places that exist are usually establishments of short-time ill-repute or serve as housing for long-term immigrants.

*Hotel Paris* (☎ 218488), on Lorong Dua, has clean singles/doubles from RM25/35 with fan and bathroom, and air-con doubles with bathroom for RM48. *Hotel London* (☎ 216371), on Lebuh Empat, is basic but clean and well run, and staff can help with local information and maps. Air-con rooms with bathroom cost RM40/50.

*Hotel En Khin* (☎ 217377, 50 Lebuh Tiga) is a friendly Chinese place with no-frills air-con rooms for RM40/50.

*Hotel New Sabah* (☎ 218711), off Jalan Singapura, has good rooms with air-con, TV and bathroom for RM50/58. *Hotel Samila* (☎ 271555), opposite KFC on Jalan Tiga, is a welcoming establishment with good air-con rooms with double bed advertised at RM58 (but RM50 is more likely); twins are RM68 and family rooms are listed at RM98.

*Hotel City View (☎ 271122),* on Lebuh Tiga, has well-appointed standard rooms for RM60/75 and larger ones for RM85/95. The street noise can be very loud. *Hotel Nak (☎ 272988),* on Jalan Pelabuhan, was once Sandakan's best but it's looking the worse for wear and prices have dropped; dim rooms cost RM65/75. Ask for a room facing the harbour.

*Hotel Ramai (☎ 273222),* on Jalan Leila about 1km west of the post office, has spacious rooms starting at RM65/75 and suites for RM120/140. The rooms overlooking the main road are a bit noisy.

### Places to Stay – Top End

The well-scrubbed but cheerless *Hotel Sandakan (☎ 221122, fax 221100, ✉ tengis@tm.net.my),* next to Wisma Sandakan, is a centrally located two-star hotel with a restaurant, lounge and business centre. Published rates start at RM173/196 for singles/doubles and RM219 for twins. Discounts may be available.

The only international-standard hotel in town, and a favourite of the Sepilok tour groups, is the five-star *Renaissance Sandakan Hotel (☎ 246149, fax 266149),* about 1.5km up the hill from the main roundabout in town. It's pretty spiffy, with a swimming pool, sporting facilities, lounge and restaurants set in quiet gardens. Room prices are RM310 to RM340, and suites cost RM500 to RM1700.

### Places to Eat

Despite its size, Sandakan has nowhere near KK's variety of restaurants. Sandakan has many cheap *Chinese restaurants* and *kedai kopi,* particularly near the waterfront, serving standard rice or noodle dishes.

For no-frills food, some of it fine Filipino fare, try one of the stalls in the waterfront *market* next to the local bus station. A couple of ringgit will get you a decent meal but choose carefully, as hygiene might not be 1st class. The food-court-style restaurants on the 1st floor of *Centre Point* are a

bit more expensive, but the quality is generally reliable. There's more market food at the *night market* that sets up outside the post office each evening.

For good Malay food, try the *Restoran Habeeb* on Jalan Pryer near the market; it does excellent murtabak, and also has an air-con room upstairs. There are a couple of similar places close by, including the *Restoran Gane. Restoran Habeeb III,* opposite Wisma Sandakan, is a friendly spot popular with young people; the food is cheap and very good value.

*Restoran Cita Rasa II* is a cheap and relaxing refuelling stop on Lebuh Tiga. *The Boss 2* nearby serves good, cheap Malay dishes; it's air-conditioned and has freshly squeezed vegetable- and fruit-juices for RM2 to RM3.50. *Fat Cat II* is a fast-food-style restaurant opposite the *Penang Curry House* on Lorong Satu; there's another *Fat Cat* on Lebuh Tiga. The Penang serves a mean murtabak and has a great selection of other affordable Indian food.

Upmarket places offer more-expensive Western and Asian dining possibilities. The pick of the bunch is probably *Ming Restaurant* in the Renaissance Sandakan Hotel, which offers excellent Cantonese and Sichuan food, and a dim sum breakfast and lunch. The best value is probably *Hawaii Restaurant* in the City View Hotel; decent Western food is reasonably priced (a large chef's salad is RM7) and beer is available.

### Getting There & Away

**Air**  The Malaysia Airlines office (☎ 273966) is at Wisma Sabah, opposite the Hotel Nak; office hours are weekdays from 8.30 am to 5 pm, and Saturday until 1 pm.

Sandakan is well served by the Malaysia Airlines' domestic network, and there are direct flights to KK (six or seven daily, RM83) and Tawau (two daily, RM74). There are also a couple of Twin Otter flights most days to Kudat (RM54), as well as five weekly flights to KK (RM69) and a Thursday flight to Tawau (RM61).

**Bus**  The long-distance bus station is inconveniently located in a large parking lot at

MALAYSIAN BORNEO

Batu 2½, 4km north of town. Air-con express buses to KK, Semporna and Tawau congregate here. Most buses – and all minivans – go in the morning. Local buses for central Sandakan pass by the bus station; a taxi to the centre of town is RM5. Coming from town, catch a bus here from the local bus station at the waterfront.

Schedules change and, though the bus companies have booths at the station, it's hardly worth coming all the way out here to find out when the next day's buses run. Tung Ma Express (☎ 210054) is one of the larger companies; SIDA (☎ 019-853 8445) is another. If it's open, the tourist office at the waterfront should also be able to help.

Most express buses to KK (six hours, RM25) leave at 7 or 8 am (the last one is currently at noon). The same buses pass the turn-off to Kinabalu National Park headquarters (RM25). Minibuses to Ranau cost RM25 and the journey takes about four hours.

Buses depart daily for Lahad Datu (about three hours, RM15) and Tawau between 6 and 9 am (about 5½ hours, RM25).

There's also a bus to Semporna (about 5½ hours, RM20) at 8 am. If you miss the bus to Semporna, you can take one to Lahad Datu, from where there are more-frequent minivans to Semporna.

Minivans depart frequently throughout the morning for Lahad Datu, some going on to Tawau. There are also frequent minibuses for Sukau (RM10), but these leave from the local bus station in town.

**Boat** Passenger ferries run between Sandakan and Zamboanga (18 hours, RM60) in the Philippines; it is a popular route with overseas Filipinos returning to visit their families. Schedules are uncertain, as ships often break down. Tickets can be bought in advance from the Karamunting Jetty, about 4km west of town, where you also clear immigration when boarding. Take a Pasir Putih bus (90 sen).

## Getting Around

**To/From the Airport** The airport is about 11km from the town centre. The Batu 7

Airport bus (70 sen) runs by the airport but stops on the main road about 500m from the terminal. Airport-bound buses leave from behind Centre Point in town. A coupon taxi from the airport to the town centre costs RM16.50; going the other way, you can get a cab for RM15.

**Car** Inno Travel & Tour Services (☎ 671718, fax 672001, @ myen@pop .jaring.my) runs Sandakan's only car-rental business. Its office is at the airport terminal.

A Proton Iswara costs RM180 per day, including insurance and unlimited kilometres; a 4WD Nissan Safari costs about RM425.

**Taxi** Taxis are plentiful. They cluster near the markets and main hotels and are easy to hail along main roads. Trips around the town centre should cost RM4, and a trip to Puu Jih Shih Temple should be RM6.

## SEPILOK ORANG-UTAN REHABILITATION CENTRE
☎ 089

One of only four orang-utan sanctuaries in the world, Sepilok is about 25km north of Sandakan. The centre was established in 1964; it now covers 40 sq km and has become one of Sabah's top tourist attractions.

The centre has doubtless suffered from its own success – so many camera-clicking tourists are turned loose on the viewing platforms that the atmosphere can be a bit like a circus or a zoo. More seriously, constant contact with humans has exposed the orang-utans to diseases, which can make rehabilitation to the wild all but impossible.

The balance between its roles as research centre and tourist attraction is difficult to sustain – staff used to guide small groups of tourists through after giving them an educational briefing. Even with these limitations, however, visitors usually remember the sight of semi-wild orang-utans looping through the trees as a highlight of their trip to Borneo.

Orang-utans are the only species of great ape found outside Africa. A mature male is an impressive, not to mention hairy, creature with an armspan of 2.25m, and can weigh up

MALAYSIAN BORNEO

to 144kg. It was once said that an orang-utan could swing from tree to tree from one side of Borneo to the other without touching the ground. Sadly this is no longer the case, and hunting and habitat destruction continue to take their toll.

Orphaned and injured orang-utans are brought to Sepilok to be rehabilitated to return to forest life, and so far the centre has handled about 100, although only about 20 still return regularly to be fed. It's unlikely you'll see anywhere near this number at feeding time – three or four is more likely. Females that have returned to the wild often come back to the feeding platforms when they're pregnant and stay near the sanctuary centre until they've given birth, after which they go back to the forest.

The orang-utans are fed fruit, such as bananas, twice daily from a platform in the forest, about 10 minutes' walk from the centre. This feeding is just to supplement what they can find for themselves in the jungle – if trees are fruiting, few apes will turn up.

Young orang-utans in particular are endlessly appealing, with ginger fur and intelligent eyes. Macaques may also join the feeding and photo frenzy – it's quite dim under the forest canopy and if you're snapping pics, you'll need ASA 400 film.

## Orientation & Information

The feeding schedule can change, and the morning and afternoon programs are posted at the visitor reception centre (☎ 531180), where there is a souvenir shop and a cafeteria. There's also a Nature Education Centre with interesting displays about the wildlife in the reserve.

Admission to the centre is RM10, and visiting hours are from 9 am to 12.30 pm and 2 to 4.30 pm daily except Friday, when lunch closure is at 11.30 am. A 25-minute video, *Orphans of Borneo*, is shown at the park office at 8.40 and 10.40 am, and 3.30 pm. To see the whole program you should arrive early because it can get crowded. Feeding time is at 10 am and 3 pm; get there early to enjoy the show.

There are lockers for your valuables – orang-utans have been known to relieve

tourists of hats, sunglasses, cameras and even clothing.

## Walking Trails

Walking trails lead farther into the forest, but they are only open at specified times and you have to get permission at the visitor reception centre to use them. Trails range in length from 250m to 5km, and different trails are open during the year; a mangrove forest walk may be available (you may need to arrange in advance – check with the reception centre first).

Note that you wander through the forest at your own risk. Although orang-utans are not usually aggressive, on no account should you provoke or pester any wild animal. If you are carrying any food, the macaques will scent it and try to relieve you of it – don't argue with them because they'll probably win.

Make sure you wear hiking boots and take water; expect to find leeches and plenty of mosquitoes.

## Places to Stay & Eat

After KK, Sepilok has the best selection of backpackers' accommodation in Sabah, and there's no need to stay in more expensive Sandakan unless everything in Sepilok is full. Places to stay can be found along Jalan Sepilok, the 2.5km-long road to the rehabilitation centre.

**Sepilok** *Sepilok B&B* (☎ 532288, @ splbb@Sabah.com.my) is set in peaceful gardens about 250m off Jalan Sepilok (don't be fooled by the sign on the road that says '100m'), about 1km short of the rehabilitation centre entrance. There are four dorms sleeping 10 for RM20 each; these are OK, but the fan-cooled twin-share rooms are over-priced at RM45. All rates include breakfast and free tea and coffee. We've had mixed reports about this place – many are satisfied but some travellers find staff rude.

*Sepilok Jungle Resort* (☎ 533031, fax 533029, @ sepilokjr@yahoo.com) is much closer to the rehabilitation centre, and well back off Jalan Sepilok to the left as you

MALAYSIAN BORNEO

approach. Tour companies are fond of this place, though the concrete bamboo style is rather tacky and management gives guests the hard-sell on additional tours – a real turn-off. It has a range of accommodation, including fan-cooled dorms for RM20 a bed; fan-cooled doubles/twins for RMRM50/60; and air-con rooms for RM75 to RM120, including TV and minibar.

*Sepilok Resthouse* (☎ 534900, ℮ sephse@ tm.net.my) is close to the visitor reception centre. Single rooms with shared/attached toilet are RM45/65; fan and air-con rooms for one or two persons are RM50.

The *cafeteria* at the rehabilitation centre is open from 7 am to 4 pm, and serves breakfast, sandwiches, noodle and rice dishes, and drinks. At busy times it may run out of all but the basics. There's a small *supermarket* about 1.5km back towards the highway, not far from the Sepilok B&B turn-off.

**North of Sepilok** *Labuk B&B* (☎ 533190, Mile 15, Jalan Labuk) is a couple of kilometres back along the KK road. This delightful family-run concern sleeps 14 guests in fan-cooled bunk or double rooms with shared facilities for RM20 per person. Dinner is also available. Labuk often acts as an informal host to visiting wildlife researchers and you'll probably find yourself in stimulating company here.

*Uncle Tan's* (☎ 531917, fax 531639, ℮ tansulim@tm.net.my, Block B, SEDCO Complex, Mile 16, Jalan Labuk) is the home of the near-legendary Uncle Tan, about 3.5km from the Sepilok turn-off towards KK. Accommodation is very basic and it's a busy household – some travellers find it more convenient to stay closer to town but still do all their Kinabatangan travel through Tan (see Organised Tours in the Sandakan section earlier and the Sungai Kinabatangan section later for details). A bed in simple dorms costs RM20, including all meals; the food can be excellent.

### Getting There & Away
To get directly to the rehabilitation centre from Sandakan, take the blue Labuk bus marked 'Sepilok Batu 14' from the local bus stand next to the central market on the waterfront. The fare is RM2 and the journey takes about 30 minutes. Minivans also make the trip every hour or so.

Regular buses marked 'Batu 14' or higher can drop you at the turn-off to Jalan Sepilok, 1.5km from the orang-utan centre. Buses passing the Sepilok turn-off can also drop you back at Labuk B&B (Batu 15 bus and higher) or Uncle Tan's (Batu 16 and up). Just ask the driver and remind him as you get closer; the fare is 40 sen, or RM1.5 from the centre of town.

Returning from Sepilok, the last bus leaves the centre for Sandakan at 4.30 pm.

Most of the backpackers' hostels can organise transport to/from the bus station and the airport for a nominal fee.

## TURTLE ISLANDS NATIONAL PARK
Also known as the Pulau Penyu National Park, this park comprises three small islands – Pulau Selingan, Pulau Bakungan Kecil and Pulau Gulisan – that lie 40km north of Sandakan, within swimming distance of nearby islands of the Philippines.

Though their numbers have fallen off (some travellers have complained that you'll see more rats on the islands than turtles), two species of marine turtles – the green and hawksbill – come ashore here to lay their eggs at certain times of the year. Since their laying seasons are virtually complementary, it's possible to see either species at almost any time of year.

Sea turtles are harmless vegetarians that spend most of their lives at sea. They are strong, graceful swimmers that grow to a great age and size. The green turtle commonly lays on Pulau Selingan and Pulau Bakungan Kecil between July and October; and the smaller hawksbill turtle lays its eggs on Pulau Gulisan from February to April. The eggs are collected by permanent staff based on Pulau Selingan and transferred to fenced hatcheries, where they are safe from illegal collection by fishermen who eat or sell them.

For more information on sea turtles (and how you can make sure you do them no harm), see the boxed text 'The Disappearing

MALAYSIAN BORNEO

MARK DAFFEY

**Turtle hatcheries safeguard precious eggs**

Turtles of the East Coast' in the Terengganu chapter.

Other nearby islands with turtles can also be visited – see Organised Tours in the Sandakan section for more details.

### Places to Stay & Eat

It is no longer possible to visit Turtle Islands on a day trip, and any excursion must be arranged through Crystal Quest (☎ 089-212711, fax 212712, ℮ cquest@tm.net .my), 12th floor, Wisma Khoo Siak Chiew, Sandakan. Crystal Quest is expensive, and guards its monopoly zealously. Ask about tour packages for the separate accommodation and transport prices listed here.

The only accommodation is in pricey *chalets* on Pulau Selingan. For chalets with shared toilets, rates are RM125 to RM145 per person on a twin-share basis, or RM215 to RM235 for a single occupant; meals are included. Chalets with toilet are RM150 to RM170 per person (twin share) or RM265 to RM285 if you are on your own. For RM230 a night, you can buy your own

meals from the restaurant (about RM25 a meal).

Try to book ahead because facilities are limited and tour companies often take bulk bookings.

### Getting There & Away

Transport to the islands with Crystal Quest is RM50/100 for children/adults (a child is under 10 years of age). It might pay to shop around: you can book accommodation with Crystal Quest and arrange transport through another tour company.

## GOMANTONG CAVES

These limestone caves are Sabah's most famous source of the swiftlets' nests used for that Chinese panacea, bird's-nest soup. The caves are on the opposite side of the bay from Sandakan, about 20km inland, and are difficult for independent travellers to reach. In theory, a permit is required and should be obtained in advance from the Ministry of Tourism & Environment's Wildlife office (☎ 089-666550) in Sandakan (see Information in the Sandakan section earlier), but if you just front up you should be able to talk your way in.

The most accessible of the caves is a 10-minute walk along the trail near the information centre and office. A boardwalk leading off to the right doubles back to the entrance road – it's a pleasant walk but it won't get you to the caves. Continue past the living quarters of the nest collectors to get to the main cave, **Simud Hitam** (Black Cave). You can venture in, though it involves wading through ankle-deep guano alive with insects. In the nesting season, you can watch the nests being collected from the cave's roof, as they are at Niah Caves in Sarawak, by men climbing long, precarious bamboo poles.

The left-hand trail from the office leads to the top of the mountain. After a few metres the trail forks again. To the right, a 15-minute walk brings you to a top entrance to the cave, while the left-hand trail continues for 30 minutes and leads high up the mountain to **Simud Putih** (White Cave). This cave contains the more-valuable white

MALAYSIAN BORNEO

nests. Both trails are steep and involve some sweaty rock-climbing.

The area around the caves is covered in forest and dense vegetation. There's plenty of wildlife, especially birds, and the walks are worthwhile, but the caves are difficult to reach. The great caves of Gunung Mulu and Niah national parks in Sarawak are more spectacular and easier to visit, and the Madai Caves (see that section later in this chapter) near Lahad Datu are quite interesting and more accessible.

## Getting There & Away
It is possible to visit the caves on public transport, but it takes at least two hours from Sandakan and may involve a lot of walking. First, take any Lahad Datu minivan and ask to be dropped at the Sukau turn-off. The turn-off is in the middle of nowhere, but there's a small shop from where infrequent buses pass the turn-off to the caves, 20km along the road to Sukau. The chances of a lift are quite good because there's an almost constant stream of traffic to the oil-palm plantations. From the turn-off it is 4.5km to the park headquarters. Be prepared to walk. There's a security gate 4km from the caves. If you don't have a booking, tell security that the Wildlife office was shut; you'll have to sign a visitors' book and give your passport number.

All things considered, if you're desperate to see the caves it's probably better to take a tour; most operators include it as part of a package to the Sungai Kinabatangan (see Organised Tours in the Sandakan section earlier for a list of tour operators).

## SUNGAI KINABATANGAN
Sungai Kinabatangan is Sabah's longest river and measures 560km from its headwaters in the south-west state to the point where it empties into the Sulu Sea, east of Sandakan. Logging and clearing for plantations have devastated the upper reaches of the river, but by a strange irony the riverine forest near the coast is so hemmed in by oil-palm plantations that an astonishing variety of **wildlife** is common and easy to see.

This is one of the best places in Borneo – indeed, in all of South-East Asia – to observe wildlife, and the Kinabatangan is a highlight of any nature-lover's trip to Sabah. The river is interesting at any time of year. Most bird activity happens in the wet season (October to March), but conditions are uncomfortable – and mammals can be seen at any time of year. However, during the dry season, the river's oxbow lakes may not have water in them.

A narrow corridor of rainforest clings to the northern riverbank from the San-dakan–Lahad Datu road downstream to the mangrove-fringed estuary. Sightings of the unique proboscis monkeys are common among the mangroves in the late afternoon; two macaque species – long-tailed and pig-tailed – are common; and orang-utans are also seen, particularly downstream.

There's a chance of seeing marbled cats in the forest, and flat-headed cats are seen regularly at night along the Menungal (a tributary of the Kinabatangan); other mammals include elephant (very shy), deer and giant squirrel.

Bird-watchers will find the **bird-spotting** incredible: all eight of Borneo's hornbill species are seen regularly; two species of the gorgeous pittas are reasonably common; and rarities include Storm's stork and the bizarre Oriental darter, or snake-bird.

There are trails around Uncle Tan's Wildlife camp (see Places to Stay later in this section), and the occasional rhino has dropped by, but the best way to see animals is to cruise up and down the river or its tributaries in a small boat. You can ask to be landed at certain spots, such as oxbow lakes, and walk through the forest, but the best viewing is from boats. Spotlighting trips can also be arranged – you'll almost certainly see the large buffy fish-owl.

The success rate of animal-spotting largely depends on the local knowledge of your guide – don't be afraid to ask hard questions about the specifics of your trip before you sign up. Elephants and other larger animals come and go – herds often break up to get through the palm plantations encroaching in many areas. For more on the future of wildlife and the wetlands of the Lower Kinabatangan, see the boxed text 'Banking on the Kinabatangan' in this section.

## Banking on the Kinabatangan

The lower Sungai (River) Kinabatangan floodplain is one of those rare places on the planet. The wetlands are home to an astonishing variety and richness of wildlife, of the sort otherwise-sober people get understandably misty-eyed over.

There are other reasons for tears, however; the area is seriously threatened by Sabah's plantation and logging obsession. Larger animals, like the Asian elephant and Sumatran rhino, as well as proboscis monkeys and orang-utans, are being squeezed out of their habitat for the sake of palm oil, and the river is slowly choking on silt from upriver logging. Hunting parties from the logging camps and their city friends are known to cruise the river, and the bodies of bullet-riddled proboscis monkeys have been found along the banks.

In 1999 some 27,000 hectares in the lower Kinabatangan were declared a protected area, and the World Wide Fund for Nature (WWF) has been actively working on its Partners for Wetlands project in the area. The WWF conservation project involves trying to convince logging companies and plantation owners that they can make their pile while still preserving the essentials of the environment. The project's co-ordinator, Cede Prudente, is a deeply committed and capable local administrator who has managed to get plantation owners to agree in principle to establishing corridors for animals to pass through – an essential concession. It seems the foreign banks funding these plantations would like to see a few environmentally friendly gestures before renewing loans, so the landowners are inclined to oblige.

Despite some successes and the clout given to the project by the government, the WWF has its critics. The organisation relies heavily on foreign advisors who make the rounds of global hotspots in style – as much as 78% of the WWF budget reportedly goes to administration. Critics say more local experts would cost much less, encourage domestic awareness and provide more-intimate knowledge of the ecosystems involved. Also, the WWF brief is quite limited: It is a curiously IMF–style approach to the environment, where upriver communities are, so far, simply slated to fit in to the new tourism economy generated by conservation and more-upmarket lodges.

There is also concern that unless the upriver logging stops, the Kinabatangan has a short future, regardless of what happens in the floodplain downstream – the damage from silting and deforestation is simply too great to bear. Nonetheless, in Sabah money does all the talking (and listening), and the WWF 'partnership' with big business recognises the reality that the loggers and palm-oil barons are not going away any time soon. At least the Wetlands project is a start, and a chance for the unique Kinabatangan, where virtually none existed a few years ago.

You can contact the Partners for Wetlands Sandakan office (☎ 089-225101, fax 225103, ✉ wetlandp@tm.net.my), visit its Web site at www.borneo-online.com.my/wwf or write to:

WWF Malaysia
Partners for Wetlands Project
WDT 49, PPJU, 90309 Sandakan, Sabah

If you wish to bring gifts for local people in the river villages, No 12 fishing hooks, sewing needles and paperclips are prized commodities. In exchange, you could find yourself consuming large quantities of *tapai*, the local firewater – if you've abused *tuak* in Sarawak, the hangover will be familiar.

Warning: one gift item *not* to bring along is shotgun shells. Hunting is a serious threat to much wildlife in the area, and is illegal in protected areas (and illegal for foreigners anywhere). If you are caught with shotgun shells in your possession, you are going to be in serious trouble.

### Places to Stay & Eat

Independent travel to the Kinabatangan is virtually impossible – and good guides are a must off the beaten track – but if wildlife is your passion, make room in your budget to visit this incredible place. Backpackers and budget travellers are catered for in jungle camps, and there's a cluster of more expensive lodges near the riverside village of Sukau.

***Uncle Tan's Wildlife Camp*** is a long-standing budget option. It's ultra-basic accommodation, but among diehards it's a legend; the food is very good and many return for a second visit. Uncle Tan is a busy man these days, but his trips go well beyond the electric-motor 'eco-tourism' some of the big, expensive operators are content to provide.

Although basic, Tan's camp is well equipped for contingencies and his guides are among the best around – an important consideration if you want to see the best of the wildlife, upriver villages and generally have an adventure in reliable hands. A two-night/three-day trip costs RM130, plus RM15 per day at the camp; this includes transport between the camp and Sandakan, plus all meals. Excursions include a homestay at an upriver Rungus longhouse. Contact Uncle Tan at Uncle Tan's (☎ 089-531917, fax 531639, ✉ tansulim@tm.net.my, Block B, SEDCO Complex, Mile 16, Jalan Labuk), about 3.5km from the Sepilok turn-off towards KK.

Sukau is the main village on the lower Kinabatangan, 25km along the road past the Gomantong Caves. ***Lodges*** operated by tour companies near Sukau offer wildlife experiences and more, in upmarket comfort. There's not much difference between them; all have comfortable, mosquito-proof rooms with fan and bathroom, fully catered meals and bar, and trained guides.

On a twin-share basis, expect to pay about RM250 per night at a lodge, including transfers; most tours include Gomantong Caves as a part of the package, but you can opt out of this if you wish. See the Sandakan and KK Organised Tours sections earlier for companies that use the lodges.

### Getting There & Away
Transport to Uncle Tan's is by minivan from Sandakan to where the highway crosses the river, and then by boat for the hour-long trip to the camp. All camp and lodge operators will arrange transport to/from the river, and can help with forward transport farther south if you need it.

If you're heading farther south ask to be dropped at the highway, from where you can catch a minivan to Lahad Datu or possibly a bus to Semporna – it'll save you repeating the long drive from Sandakan.

## LAHAD DATU
Lahad Datu is a dusty, isolated and xenophobic plantation-and-timber boomtown bordering a lovely bay. This area of eastern Sabah around the Celebes Sea is known for its pirates, who are equipped with the essentials of modern piracy – machine guns and speedboats. Don't even think about trying to catch a boat from here. Pirate raids on ships and coastal villages are not uncommon, and raids on buses have also been reported on the back roads.

There is no good reason to stop here – and a couple of good reasons not to – but you may find yourself changing buses in town on the route between Sandakan and Semporna.

### Getting There & Away
Lahad Datu has an airport, with at least three daily flights to KK (RM106).

Express buses, minibuses and minivans leave from a vacant lot near the waterfront. There are frequent minivan departures for Sandakan (three hours, RM15), Semporna (two hours, RM10) and Tawau (2½ hours, RM10). Air-con minibuses to Sandakan are RM12.

There are plenty of departures to all places until around 3 pm; buses and vans to Semporna and Tawau pass the Kunak turn-off for Madai Caves; the fare is RM7. The road north to Sandakan and south to Semporna and Tawau is a relentless monotony of palm plantations – if you go all the way to Tawau, you'll be seeing tidy rows of squat palm trees in your sleep.

## DANUM VALLEY CONSERVATION AREA
Danum Valley is part of a vast logging concession owned by the Sabah Foundation,

which set aside the conservation area to preserve 43 sq km of pristine wilderness on the Sungai Segama, about 85km west of Lahad Datu. For some years research into rainforest ecology was carried out at a field studies centre, and the area has been well patronised by foreign politicians and Hollywood starlets. In recent years ordinary travellers have been selling their house pets into slavery to afford a glimpse of the magnificent rainforest here.

All is not rosy in the valley, however. To the west of the conservation area is a massive new pulp-wood project (mainland Chinese are said to be the beneficiaries). Although this has caused outrage among conservation groups around the world, such practices are quite consistent with Sabah's rather desperate resource-management strategy. So far it looks like the logging will simply continue and the conservation area may one day be as large as a tall tourist can see on a carefully guided walk.

Despite the logging, the conservation area still manages to support an incredible diversity of wildlife. At present, botanical riches include 200 species of trees per hectare; 275 bird species have been recorded, including many endemic to Borneo; and 110 species of mammals have been seen, including great rarities such as the Sumatran rhino and the beautiful clouded leopard.

Borneo Rainforest Lodge (BRL; see Places to Stay & Eat later) will try to give you a rainforest experience with an emphasis on education. On arrival you will be given an introductory slide show on Danum Valley and assigned a guide who will try to arrange activities to suit you. If you have a particular interest insist on a specialist – some travellers have complained that their guides didn't seem to know much.

## Jungle Walks

A number of trails have been cleared around the BRL, although you won't be allowed on most without your guide. To be fair, there is a chance of running into potentially dangerous animals, such as elephants or sun bears, but it would be hard to get lost on the trails.

There's a short nature trail near the lodge that points out interesting facts about the surrounding forest, but you'll probably be so overwhelmed by the colours and sounds that you'll just want to absorb it as you walk along.

Longer trails follow the Sungai Segama, but one of the best climbs is up a bluff where there's an ancient hardwood coffin and the remains of bodies buried in a cliff face. On the return you can swim at refreshing waterholes – natural Jacuzzis.

Night walks are organised most nights and led by guides. There's a chance of seeing snakes, frogs and mammals, such as flying squirrels and bearded pigs.

Comfortable, durable footwear is a must. Leeches are common when it's wet – see the boxed text 'That Clinging Feeling' later in this chapter for tips on dealing with leeches.

## Canopy Walk

One of the highlights of Borneo Rainforest Lodge is a walkway suspended 25m above the rainforest floor. It's an ideal spot to look for birdlife and saves you craning your neck to look into the treetops. At the time of writing the canopy walkway had been damaged by a storm – check that it's open before booking so you don't miss out.

## Night Drives

Not to be missed! This is the best way to see some of the valley's mammals. Successful wildlife-viewing depends on many factors, but on a good night this is as close as you'll get to an African safari in South-East Asia. Expect to see one or two species of giant flying squirrels, sambar deer, civets, porcupines and possibly even leopard cats; lucky sightings could include elephants, slow loris and clouded leopards.

Night drives leave the Borneo Rainforest Lodge most evenings; the best trips are the extended night drives, which depart at about 8.30 pm and return at 1 or 2 am. The cost is about RM50 per person. Things you'll be glad you brought include a light waterproof jacket, camera with flash, binoculars and powerful torch.

## Bird-Watching

Although there is a high diversity of bird species, rainforest birding can oscillate between spectacular and niggardly; you have to put in the hours. The best vantage points are along the access road to the BRL – ask the staff to drive you up to the entrance in the late afternoon, and then walk the 4km back to the lodge. You'll hear much more than you see, but hornbills are relatively common and argus pheasants are often heard.

## Field Studies Centre

The field centre was set up by the Sabah Foundation, the Royal Society and a number of private companies to provide facilities for research and education in the rainforest. Many of the sponsors are involved in logging and one of the main areas of study is forest regeneration. It is not possible to stay at the field centre, but if you want to see scientists in their natural habitat, it can be visited as a day trip.

## Places to Stay & Eat

Access to Danum Valley is tightly controlled and only possible as part of a tour or by booking direct.

Accommodation is in the *Borneo Rainforest Lodge*, a 1st-class resort with vast, comfortable rooms, good dining and a bar. The lodge can sleep up to 60 people. Costs, on a twin-share basis in standard chalets with full board, are RM350 per night per person, or RM551 if you're on your own. Activities such as day- and night-walks are included in the price, but extended night drives are extra. There's also an entry fee of RM30 per person and transport costs.

There's also a *tented camp*, 5km walk from the lodge, where you can stay for RM250 per person (twin share). Although it's a wilderness experience, staff will cook and attend to your whims so you won't be too uncomfortable.

Bookings and permits can be arranged through Innoprise Jungle Lodge (☎ 088-243245, fax 262050, @ ijl@po.jaring.my), 3rd floor, Block D, Sadong Jaya Kompleks, KK; or through Borneo Nature Tours

(☎ 089-880206, fax 885051), 1st floor, Block 1, Lot 6, Fajar Centre, PO Box 61174, 91120, Lahad Datu.

## Getting There & Away

Borneo Rainforest Lodge is 97km by road from Lahad Datu. Access to Danum Valley is only by the lodge's transport. There is a checkpoint at the start of the logging concession and you will not be allowed entry without a permit. There is a RM30 fee for entry into the conservation area.

Guests of BRL are met at Lahad Datu airport and shuttled out to Danum Valley in air-conditioned comfort. The fee for this is RM100 per person.

## MADAI CAVES

Like the better-known Gomantong Caves to the north, these limestone caves are famed for their birds' nests. At the entrance to the cave system is a sprawling *kampung* (village) of empty wooden shanties. When the swiftlets start nesting these become the temporary dwellings of the nest collectors. So highly prized are these little cups of bird saliva that the collectors risk life and limb by climbing to the roof of the caves on precarious bamboo poles to gather the nests. The most valuable – and rarest – nests are the white ones, which can fetch RM2000 or more for a kilogram.

Seeing the caves requires a bit of planning if you intend to do the right thing. The caves shelter ancestral tombs, and you must have permission from the local villagers to enter; an experienced local guide is needed to go any distance inside. Technically, you are also supposed to inform the local District Office (in Lahad Datu), as well as the Wildlife Department office, prior to your visit. The Wildlife Department office in Sandakan (☎ 089-666550) can get you started on the paper trail. For details, see the earlier Sandakan section.

The caves are near the Lahad Datu–Tawau Hwy. The turn-off (signposted 'Gua Madai') is 69km from Lahad Datu, and then it's 3.5km to the caves. Make yourself known at the village – since foreign visitors are unlikely to be poachers,

MALAYSIAN BORNEO

## That Clinging Feeling

Invariably on a rainforest walk, the subject of leeches comes up. Actually, you may not encounter any of the slimy little vampires while walking through much of Borneo's forest – the Danum Valley has its share, and Kubah National Park and the Kelabit Highlands are two likely leech havens in Sarawak – but if the trail is leafy and it's been raining, you'll probably have plenty to talk about.

The local leeches are maddeningly tiny – so small, in fact, they can squeeze through tight-knit socks. They don't stay very tiny for very long, however, since once a leech has become attached to you, it won't let go until it has sucked as much blood as it can hold. Only then will the bloated, sated little parasite release itself and make its way back to the forest floor. Your souvenir of the experience will be a telltale trickle of blood down your leg, or a red-stained sock.

Two species are common: the brown and the tiger leech. The tiger leech is recognisable by its cream and black stripes, but you'll probably feel one before you see it. Unlike the brown leech, whose suction is painless, tiger leeches sting a bit. Brown leeches hang around on or near the forest floor, straining to grab onto your boot or pants as you pass. Tiger leeches lurk on the leaves of small trees and tend to get you between the waist and neck.

Safe and effective ways to dislodge leeches include flicking them off sideways – any attempt to pull a leech off by the tail will only make it dig in harder – and burning them with a cigarette or match (cruel, but strangely satisfying).

Leeches are harmless, but bites can become infected. Prevention is better than cure, but once they sense blood, these clinging critters are persistent. Insect repellent is a limited deterrent; nonetheless, applied to your feet and ankles and then to your socks and shoes, it might slow down the old or infirm ones.

Even if you don't smoke, you'll want to invest in some tobacco – it's the best leech-prevention method going, and Kelabit hunters swear by it. Not unlike yuppies, leeches have a powerful aversion to tobacco, and a well-placed pinch keeps the parasites at bay (or at least to a minimum). Rolling tobacco is the easiest to apply: Spread some around the ankles (inside your socks) every few hours; moisture from sweat or rain will do the rest.

Soaking your socks in salt is not a good idea, despite what you may have heard. The salt won't be effective for long and will irritate your feet if you're walking for any length of time. Ash actually kills leeches faster than salt does; if it's not too wet, sprinkle a ring of ash around your sleeping area.

After a day or two in the jungle, you'll probably be seeing leeches in your sleep. Look at it this way: You'll have something to talk about when you visit a longhouse, and a leech bite is proof you made it to a primary rainforest, the only place leeches are found in Borneo.

it's doubtful you'll be challenged if you're just looking around.

### Getting There & Away

All buses between Lahad Datu and Semporna or Tawau pass the turn-off to the caves; you should be able to get a minivan to take you all the way to the caves, but you may have to walk back out to the highway. Buses run to the caves from the small town of Kunak for RM2, but you could be in for a long wait. Traffic on the road to the caves is light.

## SEMPORNA
☎ 089

Semporna is just about the end of the road in south-eastern Sabah. This mainly Bajau town really comes alive at the end of March when a colourful regatta takes place, but normally it's a quiet place. It's on a pretty bay sprouting sprawling stilt villages, and there are islands with good beaches not far offshore. Its proximity to Indonesia and the Philippines ensures a hefty police presence; the patrol boats are also there to deter dynamite fishing, which has done considerable damage to many of the reefs around the popular dive destinations lying off Semporna.

Semporna is usually only visited as a base for diving and snorkelling day trips or live-aboards to Pulau Mabul or Pulau Sipadan, the famous dive island 36km to the south-east of the town. The best dive seasons are between April and July/August – especially in April and June – and during November and December.

The Dragon Inn and Ocean Tourism Centre is a large development of fancy thatched huts on stilts over the harbour. It consists of a hotel, restaurant, souvenir shop and a pathetic aquarium at the end of the pier. The complex is connected to the shore by a causeway; along this road, just past the entrance to the Dragon Inn, is the Malaysia Airlines hut and the Sipadan dive shops.

Minivans will drop you in the centre of town; to reach the causeway from there, walk east past the small children's park and playing field, and follow the road around to the left. On the shore between the town centre and the causeway is a fish market and outdoor food stalls.

One thing you might want to bring along to Semporna is a large can of tout repellent (a baseball bat is a tempting suggestion) – you can't walk far, let alone sit down for a meal in the market, without a couple of tour-mongering misanthropes descending on you like flies on day-old murtabak. Some of these predators are very persistent, and some are Westerners.

Be warned: Apart from the legitimate dive operators – who are all happy to produce a licence and dive-master certification if asked – there are a lot of cheapo operators out there (the names change as soon as they get a bad rep) who are happy to take your money and leave you high and dry on an isolated island. A deal that sounds too good to be true almost certainly is – which is not to say the pricey big companies are always good value (just a whole lot safer).

## Dive Operators
See the Organised Tours entry in the KK section for details of dive outfits running trips in the area, many of which also run resorts.

The Sipadan Water Village Resort is somewhat confusingly located on Pulau Mabul; its office (☎ 089-752996, fax 752997, ✆ swvill@tm.net.my) is in Tawau, on the 1st floor of Wisma MAA in the Bandar Sabindo area near the waterfront. Also in Tawau is the head office of Pulau Sipadan Resort & Tours (☎ 089-765200, fax 763575, ✆ psrt@po.jaring.my), 1st floor, 484 Block P, Bandar Sabindo. This company can arrange lodging on Kapalai and Lankayan. It does have an office in Semporna, at the far end of the causeway.

Accommodation at island resorts is normally figured on a twin-share basis – add at least 50% to the price if you're on your own. Some examples of going rates follow; remember that the closer you are to the source, the more room you have for negotiation.

Standard rates at the Sipadan Water Village Resort on Mabul are US$680 for five days/four nights (twin share), plus US$90 per day of diving. An all-inclusive package, ex-Tawau, costs about RM2350, plus RM430 per extra day (subtract RM430 for four days/three nights).

A night on Sipadan, plus two days diving, costs around US$675 (twin share); extensions are around US$130 per day. Mabul is thus a much cheaper option (which isn't to say it's cheap).

Several dive operators put together interesting all-inclusive packages – Borneo Action (☎ 088-267190, fax 267194, ✆ info@borneoaction.com) has its office on the ground floor of Block 3 in the Api-Api Centre in KK, and its dive shop (☎ 088-246701) on the ground floor of Wisma Sabah (see Organised Tours in the KK section). It offers combined stays on Sipadan, Mabul and Pandanan, for example.

Operators offer a small discount for snorkellers; it's probably not worth all that money to snorkel off Sipadan, but several other islands make very good snorkelling destinations.

## Places to Stay & Eat
The main hotel in Semporna is the *Dragon Inn* (☎/fax 781088), built on stilts over the water. This is where tour companies will

usually book you if you stay in Semporna. Service has improved and prices had dropped at the time of writing; with the discounts offered, this is a good-value place to stay.

A bed in the roomy air-con long house costs RM15, with attached toilets and *mandi* (South-East Asian washbasin). This 18-bed dorm fills quickly, and it's a better choice than the more-expensive but poky four-bed dorm (RM20 a bed). The bamboo-and-thatch air-con rooms are RM82.50 (but likely will be discounted to RM60); these are quite tastefully designed, and include double bed, TV and wood-encased shower. The published rate for family rooms is RM110, up to RM330 for the VIP suite.

If you prefer solid ground under your accommodation, on the edge of the town centre is *Damai Travellers Lodge* (☎ *782011*), on the 3rd floor opposite the mosque, overlooking the harbour and the cheapest lodging around. Dorm beds in a 10-bed room are RM10 and a clean standard room with toilet is RM45; twins are RM55.

In the centre of town, somewhat run-down rooms at *Sin Hun Fah Hotel* (☎ *781993*) go for RM35 (fan) and RM40 to RM45 (air-con); entrance to the hotel is down the side-alley.

In the new blocks behind the Milimewa store to the north of the town is *Lee's Resthouse & Cafe* (☎/fax *784491*, ✉ *joejack@ tm.net.my*). This is a clean, new hotel, where rooms with double bed go for RM50 and twins are RM60; breakfast is included.

The *Pearl City Chinese Restoran* is a good but pricey seafood restaurant in the Dragon Inn complex: the small portions with rice are filling but affordable, and fresh fish and lobster can be bought by the gram or kilogram. It does a decent breakfast from 6.30 am and is open late if you want to sip a beer while the world floats by.

The *Floating Restoran & Bar* is a cheaper, but uninviting, seafood option halfway along the causeway to the Dragon Inn.

The *food stalls* next to the fish market are cheap and great for lunch or dinner – if you buy seafood at the market, a couple of these places can cook it for you. Unlike the Dragon Inn, however, the market is not a tout-free zone.

## Getting There & Away

Coming into Semporna, buses and minivans drop passengers around the Shell petrol station in the town centre. Tawau minivans (1½ hours, RM5) leave from here, but for Lahad Datu (2½ hours, RM10) and Sandakan (RM20) you have to head along Jalan Iman Jayani past the mosque. Minivans depart until about noon.

The Dragon Inn charges RM350 per boat for a trip to Mabul or Sipadan, but you'll probably have transport arranged with a tour company anyway. A two- or three-hour trip on a fishing boat around the nearby stilt villages can be arranged for about RM100 – ask in restaurants.

## PULAU SIPADAN

This small island 36km off the south-east coast of Sabah attracts experienced and novice divers from all over Asia and farther afield. Sipadan is the tip of a limestone pinnacle that rises 600m from the seabed. Within 25m of the eastern side of the island you can float over a near-vertical 'wall' and gaze into the inky depths. It's rather awe-inspiring; myriads of colourful tropical fish swim in the warm water near the surface, but deep down huge groupers and wrasse nose about, and the water gets so dark you don't know what may be lurking there.

The best way to find out is to scuba dive down the wall. The sea is teeming with marine life and the island is billed as one of the world's great diving destinations.

Sipadan is fringed by a beautiful white-sand beach, but it takes only half an hour to walk around the island and the real fun is under the water. To get the most out of a visit you should dive; it's an expensive place and if you're only snorkelling there's better value to be had on other islands around Semporna. See the 'Beyond Semporna' boxed text in the 'Diving & Snorkelling' special section for details.

In April 2000 the island made headlines around the world when gunmen landed on the island, over-powered the lone policeman and made off to the Philippines with 20 hostages, including a number of foreign tourists. The island was closed off for a couple of days, but soon got back to business as normal; security on the island and in nearby waters has been notably increased and visitors can expect more protection than they previously had in these troubled waters. Increased security may not be up to the daunting task, however. The Sipadan hostages were eventually released after nearly five tense months in captivity, but at least one other kidnapping (of Malaysians) has since occurred on the surrounding islands.

Note also that divers paying for a package to Sipadan may end up diving elsewhere – it's common to be offered Roach Reef as a substitute – due to problems getting access to the island.

## Diving

Dives are held from early morning until after dark by all operators, and qualified personnel accompany each trip. All visitors are briefed on local conditions when they arrive, and equipment can be hired on the island or is included in the price of a package.

Diving off the wall can be exhilarating and frightening. The deeper water offshore is home to schools of barracuda and tuna, occasional whale sharks and friendly hammerheads, which sometimes investigate a dive team. Sea turtles are common, and experienced divers can explore an undersea cavern in which turtles periodically lose their way and perish.

The best snorkelling is near the jetty, where you can float over the drop-off and watch a good variety of common wrasse, parrotfish, batfish and others. In the shallow water around the island you won't have to go far to see turtles and you can also snorkel around the dive boats in deeper water. The current over the reef can be quite strong.

Borneo Divers has installed a hyperbaric (decompression) chamber on the island. Make sure your travel insurance covers diving accidents, because at US$1000 an hour the decompression chamber is no tanning salon. Besides, a chamber is not a magic cure for the bends – casualties may need urgent evacuation to Sandakan – so it's worth taking diving-safety instructions to heart.

## Places to Stay & Eat

Sipadan has suffered considerably from uncontrolled resort construction and waste from the large number of tourists staying on the island. The number of visitors is now strictly limited to 80 people per night and permits are required to keep track of numbers. Plans also call for the six remaining dive operators with resorts on Sipadan to form a consortium to provide accommodation – a development that may squeeze out a few of the smaller players. The companies currently operating dive resorts on Sipadan have huts on the causeway by the Dragon Inn – see Organised Tours in the KK section for a list of contacts. At the time of writing, efforts were also underway to form a consortium of dive operators to manage the fragile island, and some of the players now running trips to Sipadan may eventually drop out of the picture.

The small number of people allowed on the fragile island, plus the fact that permits need to be arranged, makes booking at least 24 hours in advance necessary. However, such short notice only works if there's a cancellation – most of the time, the island is booked solid weeks in advance.

Accommodation is in comfortable, rather than luxurious, fan-cooled chalets with bathrooms and desalinated showers (some of which have been known to flood the bedroom floor). All meals are included in packages and the food is generally but not always good; alcoholic drinks are extra.

## Getting There & Away

The 45-minute boat ride from Semporna is usually included in the dive package. Getting to Sipadan under your own steam is expensive. Hiring a fishing boat for a day trip from Semporna costs around RM250, but a group could share the fee. Dive centres ask about RM400 for their speedboats.

## TAWAU
☎ 089

A mini-boomtown way down south near the Indonesian border, Tawau is a centre for the shipping of timber, rubber, Manila hemp, cocoa, copra and tobacco. It's a

**MALAYSIAN BORNEO**

tough-looking town with no identifiable attractions, but the seamier side of Tawau isn't generally a threat to travellers. Though Tawau is known as a Bugis city, a massive stilt village east of town houses many of the Filipino and Indonesian immigrants you'll encounter eking out a living on the waterfront. Much of the town is dark and deserted at night, save for knots of men hanging around street corners. Travellers, especially women, may feel much more comfortable in pairs after dark.

The nearby Tawau Hills Park has hot springs and waterfalls, though it is seldom visited and there's no public transport. For most travellers Tawau is a transit point for dive-trip packages to Sipadan or Mabul, and the embarkation point for Tarakan in Kalimantan.

## Orientation & Information

All places to stay and eat, banks and bus stations are in or near the town centre. The only time you're likely to need public transport is to get to the airport, which is 1km north-west of town.

There's no tourist office, although the reception desk at the Belmont Marco Polo Hotel may be able to help with inquiries.

The Malaysia Airlines office (☎ 765522) is in Wisma SASCO on the eastern edge of the town centre. It is open weekdays from 8.30 am to 5 pm, and on Saturday from 8 am to 1 pm.

Tawau is a visa-free port for travel to/from Tarakan and Nunakan in Kalimantan, Indonesia; if you have queries or difficulties, the Indonesian consulate (☎ 772052) is on Jalan Apas, 3km from the town centre on the main road coming into town.

Email and Internet access is available at Cyberland, upstairs off Jalan Musantara near the waterfront; it charges RM3 per hour and is open till midnight. In the eastern part of town is City Internet Zone on Jalan Perbandaran – it's open till midnight;

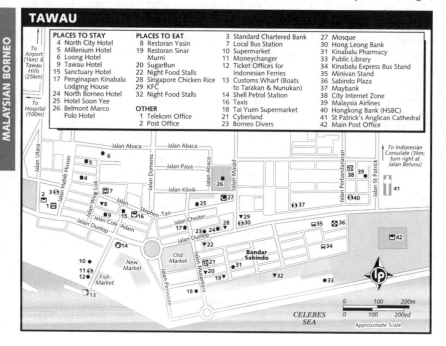

**TAWAU**

**MALAYSIAN BORNEO**

| PLACES TO STAY | PLACES TO EAT | 3 Standard Chartered Bank | 27 Mosque |
|---|---|---|---|
| 4 North City Hotel | 8 Restoran Yasin | 7 Local Bus Station | 30 Hong Leong Bank |
| 5 Millenium Hotel | 19 Restoran Sinar | 10 Supermarket | 31 Kinabalu Pharmacy |
| 6 Loong Hotel | Murni | 11 Moneychanger | 33 Public Library |
| 9 Tawau Hotel | 20 SugarBun | 12 Ticket Offices for | 34 Kinabalu Express Bus Stand |
| 15 Sanctuary Hotel | 22 Night Food Stalls | Indonesian Ferries | 35 Minivan Stand |
| 17 Penginapan Kinabalu | 28 Singapore Chicken Rice | 13 Customs Wharf (Boats | 36 Sabindo Plaza |
| Lodging House | 29 KFC | to Tarakan & Nunukan) | 37 Maybank |
| 24 North Borneo Hotel | 32 Night Food Stalls | 14 Shell Petrol Station | 38 City Internet Zone |
| 25 Hotel Soon Yee | | 16 Taxis | 39 Malaysia Airlines |
| 26 Belmont Marco | **OTHER** | 18 Tai Yuen Supermarket | 40 Hongkong Bank (HSBC) |
| Polo Hotel | 1 Telekom Office | 21 Cyberland | 41 St Patrick's Anglican Cathedral |
| | 2 Post Office | 23 Borneo Divers | 42 Main Post Office |

Old meets new in Singapore.

Eating out – Singapore's national obsession.

Shopping on Arab Street, Singapore.

Waterfront wining and dining, Singapore.

Singapore skyline

Jame'Asr Hassanil Bolkiah Mosque, Brunei

Omar Ali Saifuddien Mosque, Brunei

Brunei's rambling Kampung Ayer stilt village.

hourly rates from Monday to Thursday are RM3 per hour, and RM4 from Friday to Sunday.

## Diving

There is so-so diving off **Roach Reef**, about halfway between Tawau and Pulau Sipadan. The reef is mainly used for PADI training, though you're better off doing the course out of KK, since transport costs are lower there. If you are based in Semporna, you'll have to transfer to Roach Reef via Tawau.

Bookings for Pulau Sipadan, Mabul and other islands off Semporna can be made at the Borneo Divers office (☎ 761259, fax 761691), upstairs at 46 Jalan Dunlop. Borneo Divers also runs trips to Roach Reef, and has packages to the pristine islands off Tarakan in Kalimantan.

Recent government agreements have opened the door for dive trips from Sabah to this unexploited area of Indonesia. Borneo Divers has connections to a resort on **Pulau Sangalaki**, about 150km south-east of Tarakan; there are 11 dive sites around the island, which is noted for its varied and abundant macro life. Other nearby dive spots include Pulau Kakaban and Pulau Maratua.

## Places to Stay – Budget

The so-called budget hotels in Tawau are poor value for money. There are a couple of basic lodging houses that aren't brothels, but they are not recommended for women travellers.

The cheapest is the rather dodgy-looking **Penginapan Kinabalu Lodging House** on Jalan Chester, where very basic rooms without toilet are RM15. Much better is the **Hotel Soon Yee** (☎ 772447, 1362 Jalan Stephen Tan), where a simple fan-cooled room costs RM18, and air-con singles/ doubles with toilet are RM28/32. This is generally a well-run place, though rooms may be a bit musty.

## Places to Stay – Mid-Range

If you're desperate, **Tawau Hotel** (☎ 771100, 73 Jalan Chester) has primitive, very musty fan-cooled rooms for RM27.50

and air-con singles/doubles with bathroom for RM38.50/49.50.

**Loong Hotel** (☎ 765308), on Jalan Abaca, has clean air-con rooms with bathroom, TV and a decent double bed for RM40; a twin-bed room is RM50.

**The Sanctuary Hotel** (☎ 751155), on Jalan Chester, is a good option. Clean and spacious but spartan singles/doubles/ triples in this quiet hotel go for RM52/58/65; twins are RM65.

**North Borneo Hotel** (☎ 763060, 52–53 Jalan Dunlop) is good value at RM70/80 for comfortable singles/doubles; some dive outfits book travellers here. The related **North City Hotel** (☎ 773100) has smaller but perfectly adequate rooms for RM50/60.

**Millenium Hotel** (☎ 771155, 561 Jalan Bakau) is a friendly place with airy, bright rooms with double bed for RM58; twins are RM68.

## Places to Stay – Top End

Tawau's top hotel is the **Belmont Marco Polo** (☎ 777988, fax 763739, ✉ bmph@ tm.net.my), on the corner of Jalan Abaca and Jalan Klinik. Roomy singles/doubles start at RM165/178; suites start at RM470. There's a business centre and restaurants, and the front desk can arrange airport transfer and car hire.

## Places to Eat

There's plenty of choice in Tawau. **Hawkers' stalls** seem to spring up wherever there's a vacant lot and you won't have to go far for a cheap feed. Indonesian and Malay favourites can be picked up at the old and new markets, and along the waterfront. Tawau is also renowned in Sabah for its seafood, not least because it is comparatively cheap – wealthy fish-fanciers from as far away as Singapore and Taiwan come to Tawau just to pig out at the waterfront markets.

For good Malay food, try **Restoran Sinar Murni**, near the waterfront, and the central **Restoran Yasin**, which does good murtabak and curries. There's a good Chinese **kedai kopi** downstairs at the Loong Hotel, and a more basic **Singapore Chicken Rice** outlet near the North Borneo Hotel.

MALAYSIAN BORNEO

## Getting There & Away

**Air** Malaysia Airlines has flights between Tawau and KK (at least seven daily, RM104), and Sandakan (twice daily, RM74). There's also a Thursday Twin Otter flight from Sandakan (RM61).

**Bus** Express buses for KK depart from the vacant lots at the eastern end of the town centre. Minibuses and minivans for other destinations depart from the block next to Sabindo Plaza, off Jalan Dunlop.

Express buses to KK (nine hours, RM45 or RM50) leave daily between 6.30 am and 8 pm; there are frequent departures till 9.30 am. Book ahead if travelling on the weekend – ticket booths line the street where the buses park.

There are frequent minivans to Semporna (1½ hours, RM5) and Kunak (RM5), Lahad Datu (2½ hours, RM10) and Sandakan (5½ hours, RM25). These start leaving around 8 am. Air-con buses leave for Sandakan (RM20) between 6 and 9 am. The Sandakan air-con buses leave from the minivan station.

Land Cruisers leave from about 7.30 am until mid-morning for KK (RM60), Sandakan (RM25) and Lahad Datu (RM10).

**Boat** Boats for Indonesia leave from the customs wharf next to the fish market. Purchase tickets at either of the shipping booths near the customs wharf opposite the fish market. A sign displays the next sailing times. The trip to Tarakan takes three hours and costs RM75; Nunukan is 1½ hours away and the trip costs RM25.

The *CB88 Express* currently departs at 2 pm daily for Nunukan and Tarakan in Kalimantan. The *KM-Saturiah II* sails to Nunukan at 4 pm.

This route is now visa-free; all you need to bring is your passport. Ringgit can be exchanged for rupiah at the moneychanger near the ticket offices.

## Getting Around

Probably the only time you'll need to use local transport is if you're going to/from the airport, 1km north-west of the town centre. Heading to the airport, hitching is very easy, or you can take a taxi from the stand on Jalan Stephen Tan for RM6.50.

## TAWAU HILLS PARK

Hemmed in by agriculture and human habitation, Tawau Hills Park (Taman Bukit Tawau) is a small reserve that includes forested hills rising dramatically from the surrounding plain. The park was declared in 1979 to protect the water catchment for settlements in the area, but not before most of the accessible rainforest was logged. Much of the remaining forest clings to steep-sided ridges that rise to 1310m Gunung Magdalena.

On a clear day the park's peaks make a fine sight. A trail leads to hot springs and a waterfall three hours' walk north of the park headquarters, and there's a 30-minute walk to 530m **Bombalai Hill** to the south. Old forestry trails crisscross the forest north of the headquarters, but they aren't signposted and you could get lost.

Tawau Hills is about 25km north-west of Tawau. The park is seldom visited and there's no public transport; you'll have to take a taxi from town (one hour, about RM30).

RAFFLES HOTEL

Singapore

# Facts about Singapore

## HISTORY

Malay legend has it that long ago a Sumatran prince visiting the island of Temasek saw a strange animal, which was identified to him as a lion. The good omen prompted the prince to found a city on the spot of the sighting which he named Singapura ('Lion City' in Sanskrit).

This may be a legend, but it is no less plausible than much of Singapore's official history. From the arrival in 1819 of Sir Thomas Stamford Raffles – officially declared Singapore's founder in the 1970s in order to 'neutrally' settle rival claims by local Malays and Chinese – to the present, Singapore's past has been moulded to fit political and economic demands. Nonetheless, beneath the serene surface of gentrified colonial buildings lies an intriguing tale of the rise and fall of local empires, European colonial 'great games' and the enduring legacy of 19th-century British rule.

## Early Empires

Chinese traders en route to India plied the waters around what is now Singapore from at least the 5th century AD. Some sources claim that in 1292 Marco Polo visited a flourishing city where Singapore now stands.

It is certain, however, that Singapore was not the first of the great entrepôt cities in the region. By the 7th century Srivijaya, a seafaring Buddhist kingdom centred on Palembang in Sumatra, held sway over the Strait of Malacca (now Melaka); by the 10th century it dominated the Malay peninsula as well. At the height of Srivijaya's power, Singapore was at most a small trading outpost.

Raids by rival kingdoms and the arrival of Islam spelled the eclipse of Srivijaya by the 13th century. Based mainly on the thriving pirate trade, the sultanate of Melaka quickly acquired the commercial power once wielded by Srivijaya. It was a cosmopolitan, free port emporium at which traders were spared the complex procedures found elsewhere for dealing with 'polluting' foreigners – money spoke first in Melaka.

## Colonial Great Games

Armed with the cross and cannon, the Portuguese took Melaka in 1511, hoping to drive Islam and its trading hegemony out of the region. Once the city had fallen to the mercantile Christians, however, Melaka's Muslim traders moved on. The equally ardent Dutch founded Batavia (now Jakarta) to further undermine Melaka's position, finally wresting the city from their European competitors in 1641.

In the late 18th century the British began looking for a harbour in the Strait of Melaka to secure lines of trade between China, the Malay world and British interests in India. Renewed war in Europe led, in 1875, to the annexation of the Netherlands by France, prompting the British to seize Dutch possessions in South-East Asia, including Melaka.

When, after the end of the Napoleonic Wars, the British agreed to restore Dutch possessions in 1818, there were those who were bitterly disappointed at the failure of the dream of British imperial expansion in South-East Asia. One such figure was Stamford Raffles, lieutenant-governor of Java. Raffles soon procured permission to found a station to secure British trade routes in the region. The Dutch beat him to his choice of Riau, an island near what is now Singapore, and Raffles was instructed to negotiate with the sultan of nearby Johor for land.

## Raffles' City Emerges

When Raffles landed at Singapore in early 1819, the Empire of Johor was divided. When the old sultan had died in 1812, his younger son's accession to power had been engineered while an elder son, Hussein, was away. The Dutch had a treaty with the young sultan, but Raffles threw his support behind Hussein, proclaiming him sultan and

MARTIN HARRIS

**Sir Thomas Stamford Raffles
(1781–1826)**

installing him in residence in Singapore. In Raffles' plans the sultan wielded no actual power but he did serve to legitimise British claims on the island.

Raffles also signed a treaty with the more eminent *temenggong* (senior judge) of Johor and set him up with an estate on the Singapore River. Thus, Raffles had acquired the use of Singapore in exchange for modest annual allowances to Sultan Hussein and the temenggong; a cash buy-out of the pair in 1824 saw transfer of Singapore's ownership to Britain's East India Company. In 1826 Singapore, Penang and Melaka became part of the Straits Settlements, controlled by the East India Company in Calcutta but administered from Singapore.

Raffles' first and second visits to Singapore in 1819 were brief, and he left instructions and operational authority with British Resident Colonel William Farquhar, formerly the Resident (chief British representative) at Melaka. Three years later, Raffles returned to run the now-thriving colony for a year, with a vision to make Singapore the lasting successor to the great entrepôts of the Srivijaya Empire, but under the rule of British law and empire.

While Raffles was a firm believer in Britain's right to rule, he also preached the virtues of making Singapore a free port and opposed slavery. He also proclaimed limitations on indentured labour. Raffles was a keen and sympathetic student of the peoples of the region, though in typically colonial fashion he romanticised the distant Malay past while regarding Malays of the present as degraded and lacking in Protestant work ethic – a view that ironically still prevails.

Raffles initiated a town plan that included levelling one hill to form a new commercial district (now Raffles Place), and erecting government buildings around another, Forbidden Hill (now Fort Canning Hill). The plan also embraced the colonial practice, still operative in Singapore today, of administering the population according to neat racial categories, with the Europeans, Indians, Chinese and Malays each living and working in their own separate and distinct quarters.

## How the East was Won

Recognising the need for cooperation with Chinese communities, Raffles also sought registration of the *kongsi* (clan organisations for mutual assistance known variously as ritual brotherhoods, heaven-man-earth societies, triads and secret societies). Labour and dialect-based kongsi became increasingly important to Singapore's success in the 19th century as overseas demand for Chinese-harvested products grew enormously. Singapore's access to kongsi-based economies in the region, however, depended largely on revenues from an East India Company product from India sold into China – opium.

Farquhar had established Singapore's first opium farm for domestic consumption, and by the 1830s excise and sales revenues of opium accounted for nearly half the administration's income, a situation that continued for a century after Raffles' arrival. But the British Empire produced more than Chinese opium addicts; it also fostered the Western-oriented outlook of Straits-born Chinese.

SINGAPORE

## The Peranakan

The Peranakan are the descendants of early Chinese immigrants who settled in Melaka and married Malay women. With the formation of the Straits Settlements, many moved to Penang and Singapore. The Peranakan culture and language are fascinating hybrids of Chinese and Malay traditions: the Peranakan (the Malay word for half-caste) took the names and religion of their Chinese fathers, but the customs, language and dress of their Malay mothers. Nyonya cooking is perhaps the best metaphor for Peranakan culture – Chinese dishes with Malay ingredients and flavours.

Baba is the term for a Peranakan man and Nyonya is a woman, so the term Baba-Nyonya is used. However, Peranakan also used the terms 'Straits-born' or 'Straits Chinese' to distinguish themselves from later arrivals from China, whom they looked down upon.

Peranakan were often wealthy traders, allowing them to indulge their passions for sumptuous furnishings, jewellery and brocades. Peranakan terrace houses were gaily painted, with patterned tiles embedded in the walls for extra decoration; heavily carved and inlaid baroque-style furniture was favoured. Nyonya wore fabulously embroidered *kasot manek* (slippers) and *kebaya* (blouses over sarongs) tied with beautiful *kerasong* brooches, usually of fine filigree gold or silver. Babas assumed Western dress in the 19th century, reflecting their wealth and contacts with the British, and their finery was saved for important occasions such as the wedding ceremony, a highly stylised and intricate ritual exhibiting *adat* (Malay customary law).

The Peranakan patois is a Malay dialect but contains many Hokkien words, making it largely unintelligible to Malay speakers. It is a dying language – it is estimated that fewer than 5000 people speak it in Singapore. Western culture is supplanting Peranakan tradition among the young, and intermarriage with the broader Chinese community as well as the language policies of the government are helping in its decline. The Peranakan are ethnically Chinese, and Mandarin, which they are required to study at school, is increasingly used as the main language at home, along with English. *Mas Sepuloh* by William Gwee is a widely available book on the Peranakan language.

Peranakan societies such as the Peranakan Association and the Gunong Sayang Association report growing interest in Peranakan traditions as Singaporeans discover their roots, but when the older generation passes it is likely that Peranakan culture and language will be consigned to history books.

The Peranakan Place Museum offers visitors to Singapore a look inside a Baba-Nyonya house as it was in the early 20th century. The Katong district has a number of Peranakan restaurants and the Katong Antique House on East Coast Rd is a repository of Peranakan artefacts. See the Things to See & Do section in the Singapore chapter for information about these attractions.

You can also see Peranakan architecture and eat Peranakan food in the Malaysian states of Penang and Melaka, also home to the Baba-Nyonya people.

---

In the 19th century women were rarely permitted to leave China; thus, Chinese men who headed for the Straits Settlement of Singapore were likely to marry Malay women – see the boxed text 'The Peranakan' later in this section. These creole Baba Chinese (the more general term Peranakan is now preferred in Singapore) found an identity in loyalty to the Union Jack, and British law and citizenship. The British could count on those Baba with capital and a local family to stay put, while other traders were considered less reliable.

The authorities needed all the help they could get, for while revenues and Chinese labourers poured in until the early 1930s, Singapore was continually plagued by bad sanitation, water-supply problems and man-eating tigers, by piracy on the seas, and by the strain of imposing European ideals on an essentially Chinese city. Despite a massive fall in rubber prices in 1920, the ensuing decade saw more boom times. Immigration soared, and millionaires, including Chinese migrants such as Aw Boon Haw, the 'Tiger Balm King', were made overnight. In the 1930s and early 40s, politics dominated the intellectual scene. Indians looked to the sub-continent for signs of the end of colonial rule, while Kuomintang (Nationalist) and Communist Party struggles in the disintegrating Republic of China attracted fervent attention. Opposition to Japan's invasions of China in 1931 and 1937 was near universal in Singapore.

## Japanese Rule

Singaporean Chinese paid a heavy price for opposing Japanese imperialism when General Yamashita pushed his thinly stretched army into Singapore on 15 February 1942. For the British, who had established a vital naval base near the city in the 1920s, surrender was sudden and humiliating. The loss of Singapore has been blamed on everyone from British Prime Minister Winston Churchill to squabbling British commanders and the wholesale desertion of Australian troops under the divisive command.

The Japanese ruled harshly in the renamed city of Syonan (Light of the South). Yamashita had the Europeans herded onto the Padang; from there they were marched away for internment, many of them at the infamous Changi Prison. Chinese Communists and intellectuals, however, were targeted for execution, though there was little method or distinction in the ensuing slaughter. Thousands of Chinese were murdered in a single week. Malays and Indians were also subject to systematic abuse.

As the war progressed inflation sky-rocketed. Food, medicines and other essentials became short in supply, to the point where in the last phase of the war people were dying of malnutrition and disease. The war ended suddenly with Japan's surrender on 14 August 1945, and Singapore was spared the agony of recapture.

## Postwar Alienation

The British were welcomed back to Singapore although their right to rule was now in question. Plans for limited self-government and a Malayan Union were drawn up, uniting the peninsular states of British Malaya with Crown possessions on Borneo. Singapore was excluded, largely because of Malay fears of Chinese Singapore's dominance.

Singapore was run-down and its services neglected after the war. Poverty, unemployment and shortages provided a groundswell of support for the Malayan Communist Party, whose freedom fighters had emerged as heroes of the war. The Communist General Labour Union also had a huge following, and in 1946 and 1947 Singapore was crippled by strikes.

Singapore moved slowly towards self-government. The Malayan Democratic Union, a socialist group, was the first real political party, but it became increasingly radical and boycotted Singapore's first elections in 1947. After early successes, the Communists realised they were not going to gain power under the colonial government's political agenda and they began a campaign of armed struggle in Malaya. In 1948 British authorities declared the Emergency: the Communists were outlawed and a bitter guerrilla war was waged on the peninsula for 12 years. There was no fighting in Singapore, but left-wing politics languished under the repression of Emergency regulations.

## Lee Kuan Yew's Singapore

By the early 1950s, the Communist threat had waned and left-wing activity was again on the upswing, with student and union movements at the fore of political activity.

One of the rising stars of this era was Lee Kuan Yew, a third-generation Straits-born Chinese who had studied law at Cambridge University. The socialist People's Action Party (PAP) was founded in 1954 with Lee as secretary-general. A shrewd politician, Lee appealed for support to both the emerging British-educated elite and to radicalist passions – the party included a Communist faction and an ambitious post-Raffles plan of its own: strong state intervention to industrialise Singapore's emporium economy.

Under the arrangements for internal self-government, the PAP won a majority of seats

SINGAPORE

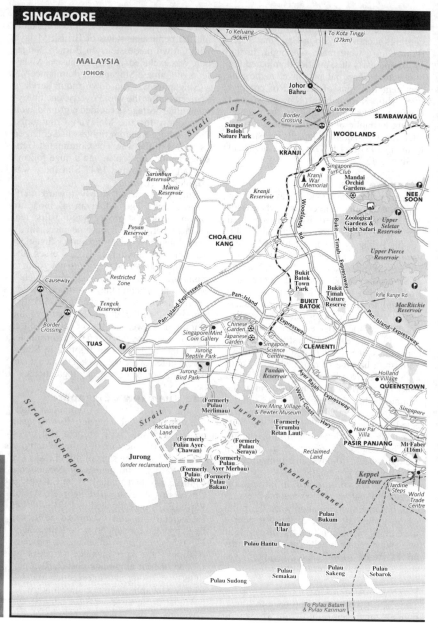

# SINGAPORE

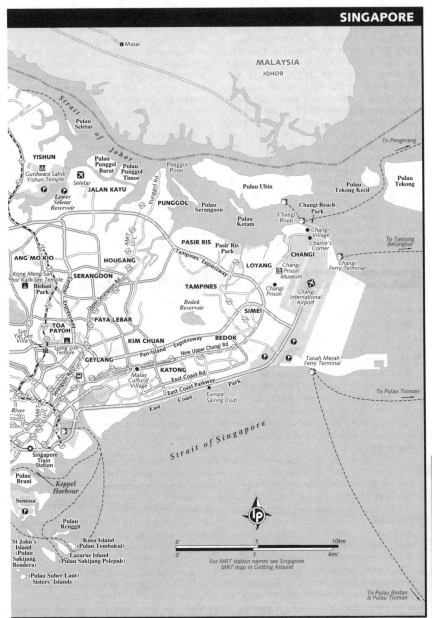

SINGAPORE

MALAYSIA
JOHOR

Masai

Strait of Johor

To Pengerang

Pulau
Seletar

YISHUN
Gurdwara Sahib
Yishun Temple
Lower
Seletar
Reservoir
Seletar
JALAN KAYU

Pulau
Punggol
Barat
Pulau
Punggol
Timor

Punggol
Point

Punggol Rd

PUNGGOL

Pulau Ubin

Pulau
Tekong Kecil

Pulau
Tekong

Pulau
Serangoon

Pulau
Ketam

Changi Beach
Park
Changi
Point

PASIR RIS
Pasir Ris
Park

Changi
Village
Charlie's
Corner

CHANGI

To Tanjung
Belungkur

ANG MO KIO
Kong Meng San
Phor Kark See Temple
Bishan
Park

HOUGANG

SERANGOON

Tampines Expressway

LOYANG
Changi
Prison
Museum

Changi
Ferry Terminal

TAMPINES

PAYA LEBAR

Upper Serangoon Rd

Bedok
Reservoir

SIMEI

Changi
Prison

Changi
International
Airport

TOA
PAYOH
Sun
Yat Sen
Villa
Siong Lim
Temple

Central Expressway

MRT
U/C

KIM CHUAN

Pan-Island Expressway

BEDOK

New Upper Changi Rd

GEYLANG

Serangoon Rd

KATONG
Malay
Cultural
Village
East Coast Rd
East Coast Parkway
East Coast Park

Europa
Sailing Club

Tanah Merah
Ferry Terminal

To Pulau Tioman

Strait of Singapore

River

MRT
U/C

Singapore
Train
Station

Pulau
Brani

Keppel
Harbour

Sentosa

Pulau
Renggit

St John's
Island
(Pulau
Sakijang
Bendera)

Kusu Island
(Pulau Tembakul)

Lazarus Island
(Pulau Sakijang Pelepah)

(Pulau Suber Laut)
Sisters' Islands

0        5        10km
0        3        6mi

For MRT station names see Singapore
MRT map in Getting Around

To Pulau Tioman

To Pulau Bintan
& Pulau Tioman

SINGAPORE

in the new Legislative Assembly in 1959, and Lee Kuan Yew became the first Singaporean to hold the title of prime minister.

By the early 1960s Britain had found a way to exit colonial rule in the region. A new state of Malaysia, uniting Malaya with Sabah, Sarawak and Singapore, would balance ethnic numbers and politically unify long-standing economic ties. The arrangement lasted only two years – in 1965 Singapore was booted out of the federation, mainly because Malay fears of Chinese control remained unassuaged. The island was left to fend for itself as the Republic of Singapore. Despite Lee Kuan Yew's public tears and real fears at the messy divorce, both Peninsular Malays and Singapore's Chinese were mostly relieved that the marriage of convenience was over.

Making the most of one-party rule in independent Singapore, under Lee's paternal control the PAP set to work moulding its multiracial citizens and fragile state into a viable entity. Industrialisation paid off, and ambitious infrastructure, defence, health, education, pension and housing schemes were rigorously pursued. Housing and urban renovation, in particular, despite their controversial impact on Singapore's physical environment, have been keys to the PAP's success.

Ostensibly following the basic tenets of Confucianism, Singapore's leaders sought order and progress in the strict regulation of social behaviour and identity: banning chewing gum and smoking in public, installing cameras and automatic locks in lifts to catch public urinators in the act, setting up state-sponsored matchmaking venues and offering financial incentives to well-educated Chinese women to have more children.

## Singapore-Malaysia Relations

Ever since the untidy divorce in 1965 when Singapore was unceremoniously kicked out of its short-lived union with Malaysia, relations between the two countries have been warm(ish) at best, pretty chilly at worst.

Senior minister and former Singaporean prime minister Lee Kuan Yew didn't improve matters when in early 1997 he suggested that the city of Johor Bahru (on the Malaysian side of the Causeway) was 'a place of gangsters and car-jackers'. It took a goodwill visit the following year by current prime minister Goh Chok Tong to smooth the ruffled feathers.

It's not hard to see why things haven't always been smooth between the two nations. Singapore, the upstart sibling, was dismissed by Malaysia at the time of the separation for refusing to afford the same rights to its own Malay citizens as were afforded by Malaysia. Singapore ultimately came out on top with a well-ordered society and a well-run economy, while Malaysia, the big brother, still wrestles with economic woes, unemployment and other social ills that little brother seems to have largely eliminated.

Then there are the niggling unresolved issues like dual territorial claims over a small island in the Singapore Strait, and Malaysian Railways land-holdings on Singapore. There are also petty restrictions on Malay citizens operating freely within Singapore's commercial sector, and vice versa, and there is an unspoken grudge held by the Chinese over positive discrimination in Malaysia in favour of the *bumiputra* (native Malays).

However, the two nations are more united by common interests than divided by dissimilarities. Talk of reunification does resurface regularly in the press on both sides of the Strait. There has even been a serious proposal by some keen advocates of union to fill in the Strait, using Singapore's technical expertise in landfilling operations to physically join the two nations.

The two will only survive and thrive through tolerance, trade and exchanges of technology and ideas. The prevailing thinking has it that Singapore and Malaysia have to engage in a mutually profitable symbiosis and buck the trend in a region that has had more than its fair share of recent discontent.

Under Lee, high economic growth rates supported political stability, which was further ensured by exiling or jailing dissidents, banning critical publications and controlling public speech. In Prime Minister Goh Chok Tong's more relaxed, liberalised regime of the 1990s, politicians who raise touchy issues tend to find themselves suddenly accused of defamation.

### Life after Lee

In 1990 Lee Kuan Yew resigned as prime minister (though he still holds the conspicuous position of Special Minister), the same year the Mass Rapid Transit (MRT) subway system – an impressive testament to Singapore's ultra-modernisation and technological capabilities – was completed.

Now Lee, the 'father of modern Singapore', and Goh's PAP face a situation all parents face. Having reared a population of mobile technophiles for a globalised economy, the children have grown up. Many, especially Indian and Chinese professionals, find better prospects elsewhere; those who remain, like Malay and Chinese youths, are chided for chafing at old expectations. The Lion City has plenty of courage and brains; many Singaporeans seem to feel what it needs now is a heart.

### GEOGRAPHY

Singapore consists of the main, low-lying Singapore Island and 58 much smaller islands within its territorial waters. It is situated just above 1°N in latitude, a mere 137km north of the equator. Singapore Island is 42km long and 23km wide, and with the other islands, the republic has a total landmass of 646 sq km (and growing through land reclamation). The other main islands are Pulau Tekong (24.4 sq km), which is gazetted as a military area but planned to be semi-residential eventually; Pulau Ubin (10.2 sq km), which is a rural haven from central Singapore; and Sentosa Island (3.3 sq km), Singapore's fun park. Built-up urban areas comprise around 50% of the land area, while parkland, reservoirs, plantations and open military-areas occupy 40%. Remaining forest accounts for only 4%.

Bukit Timah (Hill of Tin), in the central hills, is the highest point on Singapore Island, at an altitude of 162m. The central area of the island is an igneous outcrop, containing most of Singapore's remaining forest and open areas. The western part of the island is a sedimentary area of low-lying hills and valleys, while the south-east is mostly flat and sandy.

Singapore is connected to Peninsular Malaysia by a main 1km-long causeway and a newer bridge-cum-causeway on the west of the island.

### CLIMATE

Singapore has a typically tropical climate. It's hot and humid all year, and can be very uncomfortable initially. But once you're used to the tropics it never seems too uncomfortable. The temperature almost never drops below 20°C (68°F), even at night, and usually climbs to 30°C (86°F) or more during the day. Humidity hovers around 75%.

Rain, when it comes, tends to be short and sharp. You may be unlucky and be rained on every day of your visit, but don't believe local legend about it raining every day for months on end. Only about half the days of the year receive rain. Singapore is wettest from November to January and driest from May to July, but the difference between these two periods is not dramatic and the country gets an abundance of rainfall every month.

Because Singapore is almost on the equator, there are some 12 hours between sunrise and sunset. The sun shines for about half of the day on average (less from November to January). Much of the sunshine is filtered through thin cloud but can be intense.

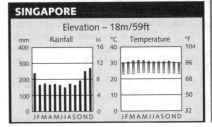

## ECOLOGY & ENVIRONMENT

Singapore stands out as an environmentally enlightened country in the region. Strict laws control littering and waste emissions, and though industry in the past may have developed with a relatively free hand, Singapore is now much more environmentally aware.

Though little is left of Singapore's wilderness, growing interest in ecology has seen new bird-sanctuaries and parkland areas gazetted by the government. In such a built-up urban environment, the government has always been aware of the need for sound planning, and ordinary Singaporeans, who perhaps crave wide-open spaces, are increasingly focusing on the environment.

The most significant contribution to a healthy environment has been the government's commitment to public transport and control of the motor car.

## FLORA & FAUNA

Singapore was once covered in tropical rainforest, with mangrove and beach forest in the coastal areas. Today only around 300 hectares of primary rainforest and 1800 hectares of secondary forest remain in the centre of the island, in and around the Bukit Timah Nature Reserve. The undeveloped northern coast and the offshore islands are still home to some mangrove forest.

Although they are now believed to be extinct from the island, tiger, clouded leopard, slow loris, Malayan porcupine and mouse deer all once inhabited Singapore. The animal that you are most likely to see is the long-tailed macaque, known locally as *kera* – the grey-brown monkeys that form troupes in forest areas. Squirrels are common; Singapore has several species of flying squirrel, and the tree shrew, which looks like a squirrel but is classified as a primate. The flying lemur is occasionally sighted, as are civet cats *(musang)* and the distinctive pangolin (also known as the scaly anteater), but these are all nocturnal.

Reptiles, frogs and toads are frequently encountered. The reticulated python, which grows up to 10m long, is one of Singapore's most common snakes, while other island species include the poisonous pit viper and black spitting cobra.

Singapore has over 300 bird species and migrant species are observed from September to May. In urban areas common birds include the myna, Eurasian tree sparrow, black-naped oriole, yellow-vented bulbul and spotted dove.

Abundant insect life includes numerous species of butterfly and moth, of which the atlas moth is one of the world's largest. Scorpions include the wood scorpion and the large scorpion. Bites are painful but not fatal.

You'll find indepth information on some of Singapore's fauna species under Flora and Fauna in the Facts about Malaysia chapter.

Visitors who want to sample some of Singapore's natural flora and fauna should visit Pulau Ubin (see the Northern Islands section under Things to See & Do in the Singapore chapter), an island off the north-eastern corner of Singapore. Alternatively, take a hike in the Bukit Timah Nature Reserve (see under Things to See & Do in the Singapore chapter for full details).

## GOVERNMENT & POLITICS

Singapore's government is based on the Westminster system. The unicameral parliament has 83 elected members representing 52 electoral divisions. Voting in elections is compulsory. Governments are elected for five-year terms, but a ruling government can dissolve parliament and call an election at any time.

As well as elected members the government has instituted a system that allows it to appoint an opposition. Nonconstituency Members of Parliament (NCMPs) are members who have failed to win enough votes, but are appointed to parliament as runners-up if fewer than four opposition members are elected. Nominated Members of Parliament (NMPs) are six prominent citizens that are appointed to give nonpartisan views. NCMPs and NMPs are not allowed to vote on financial and constitutional bills, although they can participate in parliamentary debate.

SINGAPORE

Singapore also has a president (currently Ong Teng Cheong), who is elected to the position by popular vote. The position is largely ceremonial and real power lies with the prime minister and his government.

The legal system is also based on the British system. The Supreme Court is the ultimate arbitrator and consists of the High Court, the Court of Appeal and the Court of Criminal Appeal. Most cases are heard by District Courts and Magistrates Courts, except for the most serious criminal and civil hearings.

The judiciary's independence is enshrined in the constitution, but many judges are appointed on short tenure and their reinstatement is subject to party approval. Rulings that have gone against the government have seen new laws quickly enacted by parliament to ensure government victory.

Singapore's Internal Security Department keeps detailed records of its citizens and there is widespread fear of losing jobs, promotion opportunities or contracts as a result of criticising the government. And there are some fairly dire consequences for those who cross the line where public debate is concerned. One opposition candidate, Tang Liang Hong, faced 11 defamation suits based on remarks he made during the campaign leading up to the 1997 election. He fled into exile. A worldwide injunction was taken out in January 1997 preventing him from disposing of his assets. Another opposition politician JB Jayaretnam was also sued for remarks made during the campaign.

## ECONOMY

Singapore has recorded a phenomenal economic growth-rate averaging some 9% over the past 30 years. The Asian financial crisis of the mid-1990s put a temporary damper on this, with growth slumping to 0.4% in 1998. But the economy bounced back in 1999, with growth in the 2000s expected by some to far exceed this.

Apart from its harbour and its people, Singapore has no natural resources. Yet despite this, and despite its small size, it has one of the highest living standards in Asia, with a per capita GDP of around US$30,000.

The *World Competitiveness Yearbook* in 1998 put Singapore second only to the USA.

Singapore guarantees its citizens decent housing, health care, high standards of education and superannuation, making it a welfare state in comparison with its Asian neighbours. There are no unemployment payments or programs, but the unemployment rate is negligible and the government insists that anyone who wants work can find it. In fact, Singapore has to import workers from neighbouring countries, particularly to do the hard, dirty work that Singaporeans no longer want any part of.

All workers and their employers make sizeable contributions to the Central Provident Fund (CPF), a form of superannuation that is returned on retirement. Some CPF savings, however, can be used to purchase government housing.

## POPULATION & PEOPLE

Singapore's polyglot population numbers 3.1 million. It's made up of 77.3% Chinese, 14.1% Malay, 7.3% Indian and 1.3% from a variety of other races.

Singapore's population density is high, but the government waged a particularly successful birth control campaign in the 1970s and early 1980s. In fact, it was so successful that the birth rate dropped off alarmingly, especially in the Chinese community. Later policies offered tax rebates of up to S$20,000 for couples who had a third and fourth child.

Government policy has always been to promote Singapore as a multicultural nation in which the three main racial groups (Chinese, Indians and Malays) can live in equality and harmony while still maintaining their own distinct cultural identities. See Society & Conduct in the Facts about Malaysia chapter for information on Chinese, Indian and Malay customs. The government strives hard to unite Singaporeans and promote equality, though there are imbalances in the distribution of wealth and power among the racial groups. For the most part, however, the government is successful in promoting racial harmony, a not-always-easy task.

**SINGAPORE**

## Chinese

The Chinese first settled in Nanyang, as South-East Asia is known in China, as far back as the 14th century. In the 19th and 20th centuries waves of Chinese migrants in search of a better life poured into Singapore and provided the labour that ran the colony.

The migrants came mostly from the southern provinces: Hokkien Chinese from the vicinity of Amoy in Fujian Province; the Teochew from Swatow in eastern Guangdong Province; Hakka from Guangdong and Fujian; and Cantonese from Canton. Hokkiens and Teochews enjoyed an affinity in dialect and customs, but the Cantonese and Hakka may as well have come from opposite ends of the earth. The Chinese settlers soon established their own areas in Singapore, and the divisions along dialect lines still exist to some extent in the older areas.

Settlement for the immigrants was made easier by Chinese organisations based on clan, dialect and occupation. Upon arrival, immigrants were taken in by the various communities and given work and housing. The secret societies were particularly prevalent in Singapore in the 19th century; they fulfilled many useful social functions and were more-powerful forces in the lives of Chinese residents than was the colonial government. However, they eventually declined and became nothing more than criminal gangs.

Nowadays, most Chinese in Singapore are born there. The campaign to speak Mandarin has given the Chinese a common dialect (see the boxed text 'Speak Mandarin – Please!') but English is also a unifying tongue. Increasing Westernisation and English-language education have for the most part not undermined traditional customs and beliefs.

## Malays

The Malays are the original inhabitants of Singapore. They are the main racial group throughout the region stretching from the Malay peninsula across Indonesia to the Philippines. Many Malays migrated to Singapore from the peninsula, and significant numbers of Javanese and Bugis (from Riau and Sulawesi) also settled in Singapore.

### Speak Mandarin – Please!

Singapore is a country with many languages and people, but it is the Chinese who ultimately predominate. When their forbears came from China they brought with them a number of Chinese languages and dialects – including Hokkien, Teochew, Hakka, Cantonese and Mandarin – most of which are as dissimilar as foreign languages. The British colonialists temporarily solved the problem by making English the *lingua franca* of the tropical colony and to a large degree that remains the case today.

However, the Singapore government, in an effort to unite its disparate Chinese peoples, has been encouraging minority-language speakers to use the language of administration used by Beijing – Mandarin. It is hoped this step will help eliminate disunity and differences, and the concept of a better Singaporean nation can be realised.

The campaign initially targeted monolingual Chinese speakers, but over the years it has spread to encompass English-educated Chinese who have begun to show an increasing willingness to use Mandarin as their main vehicle for communication in business and pleasure. The government is so intent on its Speak Mandarin Campaign that it has a Web site where would-be converts can be motivated. It's at www.gov.sg/spkmandarin.

Malays in Singapore are almost without exception Muslim. Islam is the major influence in everyday life and is the rallying point of Malay society. The month of Ramadan, when Muslims fast from sunrise to sunset, is the most important month of the Islamic year. Hari Raya Puasa, the end of the fast, is the major Malay celebration. See Festivals & Events under Public Holidays & Special Events in the Malaysia Facts for the Visitor chapter, earlier in this book.

## Indians

Indian migration dates mostly from the middle of the 19th century when the British recruited labour for the plantations of Malaya. While many Indians arrived in

Singapore, most passed through and eventually settled in Malaya.

In Singapore, approximately 60% of the Indian population is Tamil and 20% is Malayali, from the southern Indian state of Kerala. The rest come from all over India and include Bengalis, Punjabis and Kashmiris. The majority of Indians are Hindu, but a large number are Muslim and there are also Sikhs, Parsis, Christians and Buddhists.

## EDUCATION

Singaporean children start school at around six years of age and all undertake a minimum of 10 years formal education. The curriculum in schools is set by the Ministry of Education. All students are bilingual: English is the medium of instruction, and pupils also study their mother tongue.

## ARTS

Singapore has entered the 21st century with an ambitious goal: to become an artistic and cultural hub for the region and, indeed, to secure recognition in world terms as a leader in artistic and cultural endeavours. One of the most visible expressions of this is the S$500 million arts complex, Esplanade – Theatres on the Bay, scheduled to open in 2002. The first stage of the project will see the opening of two large theatres: an 1800-seat concert hall and a 2000-seat lyric theatre. Rehearsal rooms will double as smaller performance venues. More theatres will be incorporated in later developments.

## Music & Dance

The Singapore Symphony Orchestra (SSO), established in 1979, was Singapore's first professional orchestra. The orchestra has a busy schedule, giving some 100 (usually sold-out) performances annually at the Victoria Concert Hall. The Singapore Chinese Orchestra, which was set up in 1997, puts on about 20 performances of traditional Chinese music a year.

The most important dance company, Singapore Dance Theatre (established in 1988), stages about 28 performances a year, usually at the Kallang and Victoria Theatres. These performances range from classical

MARTIN HARRIS

**The lion dance is undergoing a huge revival and dozens of troupes perform year-round.**

ballet to contemporary dance. The Nrityalaya Aesthetics Society at 155 Waterloo St holds workshops and holds performances of South Indian dance and music.

**Lion Dance** This dance is accompanied by musicians who bash cymbals and drums to invoke the spirits. The intricate papier-mâché lion's head is worn by the lead performer while another dancer takes the part of the body.

The dance is usually performed during Chinese festivals to gain the blessings of the gods, and traditionally a dance troupe would be paid with *ang pow* (red packets of money), held up high to be retrieved with acrobatics. The dragon dance is a variation on the same theme.

## Chinese Opera

*Wayang* (Chinese opera) in Singapore and Malaysia is characteristic of the Cantonese

SINGAPORE

style. What it lacks in literary nuance is made up for by the glaring costumes and crashing music that follows the action. Performances can go for an entire evening. The acting is heavy and stylised, and the music can be searing to Western ears, but it is well worthwhile attending a performance if you should chance upon one. Street performances are held during important festivals such as Chinese New Year, Festival of the Hungry Ghosts and the Festival of the Nine Emperor Gods.

The band that accompanies the action is usually composed of fiddles, reed pipes and lutes, drums, bells and cymbals. There is little scenery and props rarely consist of more than a table and chairs – it is the action that is important.

### Literature

Singapore has recently experienced a literary boom and many young novelists are hard at work writing in English about Singapore. Of the old guard, Goh Sin Tub is a respected writer who has written many books. *Goh's 12 Best Singapore Stories* is widely available. *Juniper Loa* by Lin Yutang is set mostly in the 1920s and is typical of earlier literature looking back at the motherland and the immigrant experience. It is about a young man who leaves China for Singapore; Juniper Loa is the woman he leaves behind.

Of the recent novelists, Philip Jeyaretnem is one of the leading lights and his *Raffles Place Ragtime* is a Singaporean bestseller. *A Candle or the Sun* by Gopal Baratham was published in 1991, after years of rejection by skittish Singaporean publishers. It is about a Christian group that runs foul of the authorities by questioning the government's authoritarianism. Suchen Christine Lim's *Fistful of Colours*, a winner of the Singapore Literature Prize, contrasts the difference and tensions between the modern and traditional, and the old and the young in Singapore's ethnic communities. Catherine Lim is another highly regarded woman writer. Her books, such as *Little Ironies – Stories of Singapore*, are mostly about relationships, with Singapore as a backdrop.

### Film

Singapore's film industry has experienced a strong revival since its long period of dormancy between 1978 and 1991. The new era was marked with the release of *Medium Rare*, directed by Australian Arthur Smith and produced by Singaporean Errol Pang.

*Bugis Street* was released in 1995 under a new RA rating (Restricted Artistic; to be shown only in specially licensed inner-city theatres and only to people 21 years and over). It was criticised as being melodramatic and cliched. It did, however, manage to get past the censors with barely any cutting (something that probably wouldn't have happened if the RA rating, introduced in 1991, did not exist), and grossed some S$1 million at the box office.

Meanwhile, Eric Khoo, having won the inaugural short-film competition at the Singapore International Festival of Film, completed his first feature using the proceeds of that win. The film, *Mee Pok Man*, released in 1995, had a mainly amateur cast and was hailed as a true Singaporean film. It has been shown at more than 30 film festivals around the world.

The biggest commercial success to date has been *Money No Enough* directed by Tay Teck Lock, which grossed some S$6 million at the box office – second only to *Titanic* that year. Other successful productions include the 70s disco take *Forever Fever* directed by Glen Goei, which was bought by US distributor Miramax Film, and *Liang Po Po* directed by Teng Bee Lian, which became Singapore's third-highest grossing film in 1999. Some eight films were released in 1999.

## SOCIETY & CONDUCT

The government is keen to define the Singaporean identity, especially in its promotion of Asian Values. Its neo-Confucian ideals are based on subservience to family and society, hard work and the desire to succeed. This dovetails neatly with the government's authoritarian notions of 'Asian democracy', which argues that Western pluralism and democracy are luxuries that Singapore cannot afford. Traditional Chinese

## Kiasu or What?

One of the buzz words since the 1990s in Singapore has been *kiasu*. This Hokkien word meaning 'afraid to lose' is best summed up by Mr Kiasu, a Singaporean cartoon hero, whose philosophy includes: Always must win; Everything also must grab; Jump queue; Keep coming back for more; Look for discounts; Never mind what they think; Rushing and pushing wins the race; and Winner takes it all! all! all!

And are Singaporeans kiasu? At the risk of generalising, it's true that they are competitive and a bargain will never pass a Singaporean by, but would the country's economy be so dynamic if they were otherwise? It can be frustrating trying to get out of a lift or MRT train as fellow passengers push to get off while boarding passengers rush to get in, but it is better than trying to board the subway in New York or Tokyo. Singaporeans haven't inherited the British love of queues and, as in most Asian countries, don't have much time for the deferential excesses of continually saying 'please', 'thank you' and 'sorry', but in a world of plastic smiles and 'have a nice day' the no-nonsense Singaporean approach has something going for it.

So, when in Singapore, hunt out those bargains, don't pay unless you have to, overindulge at buffets and have a kiasu good time.

culture is emphasised, yet Singapore enjoys diverse and growing cultural expression, despite political restrictions.

See Society & Conduct in the Facts about Malaysia chapter for information on Chinese, Malay and Indian customs.

## RELIGION

The variety of religions found in Singapore is a direct reflection of the diversity of races living here. The Chinese are predominantly followers of Buddhism and Shenism (deity worship), though some are Christians. Malays are overwhelmingly Muslim, and most of Singapore's Indians are Hindus, though a sizeable proportion are Muslim and some are Sikhs.

Traditional religious beliefs remain important, and Singaporeans celebrate the major festivals associated with their religions. See Festivals & Events under Holidays & Special Events in Malaysia's Facts for the Visitor chapter for information on some of these.

The government is wary of religion and has abolished religious instruction in

schools with the stated aim of avoiding religious intolerance and hatred. The government's official philosophy is Confucianism, which is not a religion as such but a moral and social model. Its ideal society is based on the Confucian values of devotion to parents and family and loyalty to friends, and the emphasis is on education, justice and good government.

For information on the major religions of the region, see the Religion section in the Facts about Malaysia chapter.

## LANGUAGE

The four official languages of Singapore are Mandarin, Malay, Tamil and English. Malay is the national language. It was adopted when Singapore was part of Malaysia, but its use is mostly restricted to the Malay community. Tamil is the main Indian language; others include Malayalam and Hindi.

Chinese is still widely spoken, especially among the older Chinese. The most common dialects are Hokkien, Teochew, Cantonese,

SINGAPORE

Hainanese and Hakka. See the 'Speak Mandarin – Please!' boxed text earlier in this chapter.

Singapore has developed its own brand of English, humorously referred to as Singlish. It contains borrowed words from Hokkien and Malay, such as *shiok* (delicious) and *kasar* (rough), and is often a clipped form of English, dropping unnecessary prepositions and pronouns. The ever-present 'lah' is an all-purpose word that can be added to the end of sentences for emphasis.

Should you wish to try your hand at Malay, you'll find a guide to the language and a list of useful words and phrases in the Language chapter towards the end of this book.

# Facts for the Visitor

## PLANNING
### When to Go

Any time. Climate is not a major consideration; Singapore gets fairly steady year-round rainfall. Your visit may coincide with various festivals – Singapore has something happening every month (see Public Holidays & Special Events later in this chapter). Thaipusam, occurring in the Hindu month of Thai (January or February) is one of the most spectacular festivals. If shopping and eating are your major concerns, July is a good time to visit, because the Singapore Food Festival and the Great Singapore Sale are held then.

### Maps

Various maps, many in Japanese as well as English, are available free at tourist offices, the airport on arrival, and at some accommodation and shopping centres. The free *Map of Singapore,* available from the Singapore Tourism Board (STB) as well as hotels everywhere, is very good and very easy to follow. Of the commercial maps, *Nelles* and *Periplus* are also good. The *Singapore Street Directory* is essential if you plan to drive. Also check out Lonely Planet's *Singapore City Map,* a durable, full-colour, laminated fold-out map with a full index of streets and sights.

## TOURIST OFFICES
### Local Tourist Offices

The STB's head office is at Orchard Spring Rd, but the office at Suntec City is larger and provides a wide range of services, including tour bookings and event ticketing.

**STB Tourist Information Centre**
 (☎ 1-800 736 2000) 1 Orchard Spring Rd; open from 8.30 am to 5 pm weekdays, to 1 pm Saturday
**Singapore Visitors Centre**
 (☎ 1-800 332 5066) 3 Temasek Boulevard 01–35/37/39/41, Suntec City Mall; open from 8 am to 8 pm daily

### Tourist Offices Abroad

STB offices overseas include:

**Australia**
 (☎ 02-9290 2888, fax 9290 2555) Level 11, AWA Bldg, 47 York St, Sydney NSW 2000
**Canada**
 (☎ 416-363 8898, fax 363 5752) Suite 1000, Standard Life Centre, 121 King St West, Toronto ON M5H 3T9
 Web site: www.singapore-ca.com
**China**
 *Shanghai:* (☎ 021-6336 0607, fax 6336 8565) Room 1103, Shui On Plaza, 333 Huai Hai Zhong Rd, Shanghai
 *Hong Kong:* (☎ 852-2598 9290, fax 2598 1040) Room 2003, Central Plaza, 18 Harbor Rd, Wanchai, Hong Kong
**France**
 (☎ 01 4297 1616, fax 01 4297 1617) Centre d'Affairs Le Louvre, 2 Place du Palais-Royal, 75044 Paris Cedex 01
**Germany**
 (☎ 069-920 7700, fax 297 8922) Hochstrasse 35–37, 60313 Frankfurt-am-Main
**Japan**
 (☎ 03-3593 3388, fax 3591 1480) 1st floor, Yamato Seimei Bldg, 1-1-7 Uchisaiwai-cho, Chiyoda-ku, Tokyo 100
 Web site: www.int-acc.or.jp/singapore
**Republic of Korea**
 (☎ 02-399 5570, fax 399 5574) 9th floor, Young Poon Bldg, 33 Sorin-Dong, Chongro-ku, Seoul
**Switzerland**
 (☎ 01-211 7474, fax 211 7422) Löwenstrasse 51, CH-8001, Zurich
**Taiwan**
 (☎ 02-718 5280, fax 719 1049) Unit H, 6th floor, Hung Tai Centre, 168 Tun Hwa North Rd, Taipei
**UK**
 (☎ 020-7437 0033, fax 7734 2191) 1st floor, Carrington House, 126–130 Regent St, London W1R 5FE
**USA**
 *Chicago:* (☎ 312-938 1888, fax 938 0086) Suite 2615, 180 North Stetson Ave, Chicago Il 60601
 *Los Angeles:* (☎ 323-852 1901, 852 0129) Suite 510, 8484 Wilshire Blvd, Beverly Hills CA 90211

*New York City:* (☎ 212-302 4861, fax 302 4801) 12th floor, 590 Fifth Ave, New York, NY 10036
Web site: www.singapore-usa.com

## TRAVEL AGENCIES

There are many travel agencies in Singapore. The Yellow Pages telephone directory has listings.

STA Travel (☎ 737 7188, fax 737 2591, @ sales@statravel.com.sg) is at 33A Cuppage Rd, Cuppage Terrace (off Orchard Rd). It also has offices at the National University of Singapore (☎ 773 9188), Lower Kent Ridge Rd; and at Singapore Polytechnic (☎ 777 3688), 500 Dover Rd. It's Web site is at www.statravel.com.sg.

Other agents worth trying include Harharah Travel (☎ 337 2633, fax 337 4973, @ hartlv@pacific.net.sg), 171A Bencoolen St, and Airpower Travel (☎ 334 6571, fax 334 6826, @ pmtls@mbox2 .singnet.com.sg), 131A Bencoolen St.

## VISAS & DOCUMENTS

Citizens of British Commonwealth countries (except India) and citizens of the Republic of Ireland, Liechtenstein, Monaco, the Netherlands, San Marino, Switzerland and the USA do not require visas to visit Singapore. Citizens of Austria, Belgium, Denmark, Finland, France, Germany, Iceland, Italy, Japan, Korea, Luxembourg, Norway, Spain and Sweden do not require visas for stays of up to 90 days for social purposes.

Usually you will be given a 30-day visitor's visa if you arrive by air and a 14-day visa if you are arriving by land or sea. Extensions can be applied for at the Immigration Department head office (☎ 391 6100 – automated hotline), 10 Kallang Rd, one block south-west of Lavender Mass Rapid Transit (MRT) station.

### Driving Licence

If you plan to be driving in Singapore, bring your current home driver's licence and an International Driving Permit issued by a motoring association in your country.

## Student & Youth Cards

Students should bring their international student card – it's not of much use because student discounts are almost invariably for Singaporeans only, but you might be able to bluff a discount at some attractions. A Hostelling International (HI) card is not worth acquiring specifically for your trip to Singapore, as the country has no HI hostels – but, again, bring it if you have one because flashing it like a student card might bring discounts.

## EMBASSIES & CONSULATES

### Singaporean Embassies

Some Singaporean embassies and high commissions overseas include:

**Australia** (☎ 06-273 3944, fax 273 3260) 17 Forster Crescent, Yarralumla ACT 2600
**Brunei** (☎ 02-227583) 5th floor, RBA Plaza, Jalan Sultan, Bandar Seri Begawan
**China** (☎ 010-6532 3926, fax 532 2215) No 1 Xiu Shui Bei Jie, Jianguomenwai, Beijing 100600
**France** (☎ 01 450 03361, fax 01 450 05875) 12 Square de L'Avenue Foch, 75116 Paris
**Germany** (☎ 0228-951 0314, fax 310 527) Südstrasse 133, 53175 Bonn
**Indonesia** (☎ 021-520 1489, fax 520 2320) Jalan HR Rasuna Said, Block X/4, Kacling 2, Jakarta
**Japan** (☎ 03-3586 9111, fax 5561 9176) 5-12-3 Roppongi, Minato-ku, Tokyo 1060032
**Malaysia** (☎ 03-1261 6277) 209 Jalan Tun Razak, Kuala Lumpur 50400
**Netherlands** (☎ 04-404 211, fax 404 2460) Weena 607, 3012 CN Rotterdam
**New Zealand** (☎ 04-479 2076, fax 479 2315) 17 Kabul St, Khandallah, Wellington
**Thailand** (☎ 02-286 2111, fax 670 8001) 129 South Sathorn Rd, Bangkok 120
**UK** (☎ 020-7235 8315, fax 7245 6583) 9 Wilton Crescent, London SW1X 9RW
**USA** (☎ 202-537 3100, fax 537 0876) 3501 International Place NW, Washington DC 20008

### Embassies in Singapore

Diplomatic missions in Singapore include:

**Australia** (☎ 836 4100) 25 Napier Rd
**Brunei** (☎ 733 9055, fax 737 5275) 325 Tanglin Rd

**Canada** (☎ 325 3200, fax 325 3297) 15–00 IBM Towers, 80 Anson Rd
**China** (☎ 734 3273, fax 734 4737) 11–01 Tanglin shopping centre, 19 Tanglin Rd
**France** (☎ 466 4866, fax 466 1072) 5 Gallop Rd
**Germany** (☎ 737 1355, fax 737 2653) 14–01 Far East shopping centre, 545 Orchard Rd
**India** (☎ 737 6777, fax 732 6909) 31 Grange Rd
**Indonesia** (☎ 737 7422, fax 737 3819) 7 Chatsworth Rd
**Japan** (☎ 235 8855, fax 733 1039) 16 Nassin Rd
**Malaysia** (☎ 235 0111, fax 733 6135) 02–06, 268 Orchard Rd
**Myanmar** (☎ 735 0209, fax 735 6236) 15 St Martin's Drive
**Republic of Korea** (☎ 256 1188, 356 1805) 10–03 101 Thomson Rd
**Thailand** (☎ 737 2644, fax 835 4991) 370 Orchard Rd
**UK** (☎ 473 9333, 475 9706) 100 Tanglin Rd
**USA** (☎ 476 9100, fax 476 9340) 27 Napier Rd

## CUSTOMS

Visitors to Singapore are allowed to bring in 1L of wine, beer or spirits duty-free. Electronic goods, cosmetics, watches, cameras, jewellery (but not imitation jewellery), footwear, toys, arts and crafts are not dutiable; the usual duty-free concession for personal effects, such as clothes, applies. Singapore does not allow duty-free concessions for cigarettes and tobacco. Importing chewing gum is banned and possession of the stuff is considered an offence.

Duty-free concessions are not available if you are arriving from Malaysia or if you leave Singapore for less than 48 hours (so you cannot stock up on duty-free goods on a day trip to Batam in Indonesia).

Drugs, fire crackers, toy currency and coins, obscene or seditious material, gun-shaped cigarette lighters, endangered species and their by-products, and pirated recordings and publications are prohibited. The importation or exportation of illegal drugs carries the death penalty for more than 15g of heroin, 30g of morphine or cocaine, 1.2kg of opium, 500g of cannabis, 200g of cannabis resin, 1000g of cannabis mixture, 250g of methamphetamine and 250g of Ice. Trafficking in Ecstasy (more than 150 tablets) carries a penalty of 30 years' jail and 15 strokes of the *rotan* (a cane made of rattan).

Penalties for trafficking in lesser amounts range from a minimum of two years in jail and two strokes of the rotan to 30 years and 15 strokes of the rotan. If you bring in prescription drugs you should have a doctor's letter or a prescription confirming that they are necessary.

There is no restriction on the importation of currency.

## MONEY
### Currency
The unit of currency is the Singapore dollar. Singapore uses 1c, 5c, 10c, 20c, 50c and S$1 coins, while notes come in denominations of S$2, S$5, S$10, S$50, S$100, S$500 and S$1000; Singapore also has a S$10,000 note – not that you'll see many.

### Exchange Rates
The following were the rates at the time this book went to press:

| country | unit | | dollar |
|---|---|---|---|
| Australia | A$1 | = | S$0.95 |
| Brunei | B$1 | = | S$1.00 |
| Canada | C$1 | = | S$1.18 |
| euro | €1 | = | S$1.49 |
| France | 10FF | = | S$2.28 |
| Germany | DM1 | = | S$0.76 |
| Indonesia | 1000rp | = | S$0.20 |
| Japan | ¥100 | = | S$1.64 |
| Malaysia | RM1 | = | S$0.46 |
| New Zealand | NZ$1 | = | S$0.71 |
| Thailand | 100B | = | S$4.10 |
| UK | UK£ | = | S$2.51 |
| USA | US$1 | = | S$1.74 |

### Exchanging Money
Most of the major banks are in the CBD, although there are also a number of major banks along Orchard Rd and local banks all over the city. Exchange rates tend to vary from bank to bank and some even have a service charge on each exchange transaction – this is usually S$2 to S$3, but can be more, so ask first. Most banks are open

SINGAPORE

from 9.30 am to 3 pm on weekdays (to 11.30 am Saturday).

Moneychangers do not charge fees, so you will often get a better overall exchange rate for cash and travellers cheques with them than at the banks. You'll find money-changers in just about every shopping centre in Singapore. Make sure you use one that is licensed. Most shops accept foreign cash and travellers cheques at a slightly lower rate than you'd get from a moneychanger.

Apart from changing other currencies to Singapore dollars, moneychangers also sell a wide variety of other currencies and will do amazing multiple-currency transactions in the blink of an eye. You can even get good rates for some restricted currencies.

**Cash** Cash is always useful and usually necessary when buying small items such as meals in hawker centres, food courts and bars, and for buying items from street vendors. Many of the cheaper places to stay insist on cash payment.

**Travellers Cheques** This time-honoured method of safe money transport is still popular and is a fail-safe fall-back should the ATMs, credit card dial-up links and cashcard systems of Singapore fail. It is a good idea to always have some travellers cheques as they can often be used instead of direct cash payments in shops and restaurants. Travellers cheques can be bought at post offices in Singapore.

**ATMs** Most ATMs will accept Visa, MasterCard and cards connected to the Plus or Cirrus networks. ATMs can be found in most large shopping centres and MRT stations. It is a good idea to credit your account with cash before you go to avoid any unpleasant surprises when you get back. It also reduces the risk of running out of credit when you most need it. It is best to only use ATMs that are outside banks, for easier retrieval of your card should it be inadvertently swallowed up.

**Credit Cards** All major credit cards are widely accepted. The tourism authorities

suggest that if shops insist on adding a credit card surcharge (which they should not do), you contact the relevant credit company in Singapore. Most hotels and car-hire companies will insist on a credit card and will probably demand full payment up-front if you cannot produce one. Credit card companies in Singapore can be reached on:

| | |
|---|---|
| **American Express** | ☎ 299 8133 |
| **Diners Card** | ☎ 294 4222 |
| **JCB** | ☎ 734 0096 |
| **MasterCard & Visa** | ☎ 1-800-345 1345 |

## Costs

Singapore is much more expensive than other South-East Asian countries and the strength of the Singapore dollar against most currencies has seen a substantial rise in costs for most visitors.

If you are travelling on a shoestring budget, the prices will come as a shock but you can still stay in Singapore without spending too much money. The great temptation is to run amok in the shops and blow your budget on electrical goods or indulge in all the luxuries you may have craved while travelling in less-developed Asian countries.

Expect to pay S$10 to S$15 for a dorm bed, S$30 to S$36 for a single and S$35 to S$46 for a double in a cheap hotel or guesthouse. Public transport is cheap and you can eat well in Singapore for a reasonable price: A good meal at a food centre can cost less than S$5. So it is possible to stay in Singapore for less than S$25 a day, though S$50 is a more realistic minimum. You should be prepared to spend a lot more if you want to eat in restaurants (count on S$20 to S$30 for sit-down dining), check out the nightlife or visit a lot of the attractions.

If you have more to spend, most of your cash will be absorbed in hotel bills and restaurants. Mid-range, second-string hotels charge S$60 to S$100, though hotels at the top of this range are of a pretty good standard. International-standard hotels charge upwards of S$300. Depending on discounts available, top-end hotels may offer good value for the facilities on offer.

SINGAPORE

## Tipping & Bargaining

Tipping is not usual in Singapore. The most expensive hotels and restaurants have a 10% service charge, in which case tipping is discouraged. Don't tip at hawker stalls, though the more expensive coffee shops and restaurants that do not add a service charge may expect a tip. Taxi drivers don't expect a tip and may actually round a fare down if it is 10c or 20c above an even dollar – they may expect you, similarly, to round it up. Staff in the international hotels, such as room staff or the doorman who hails your taxi, may expect a tip if they have provided good service.

Bargaining is falling by the wayside in Singapore, but tourists should still expect to haggle for luxury items and souvenirs in some stores. It is unnecessary to bargain for everyday goods or transport, as happens in many Asian countries, though it doesn't hurt to ask about discounts at the more expensive hotels.

Many shops and department stores have fixed prices for clothes and luxury items. A fair number of small shops in the tourist areas, especially electronic shops, don't display prices. In this case bargaining is almost always required, and a request for prices is usually greeted with talk of special offers and the production of a calculator. For antiques, handicrafts and other tourist-oriented items, a price tag doesn't mean you can't bargain, and you usually should.

Some smaller traders put only a small mark-up on goods, while others are very greedy – you need to have some idea of the regular prices.

## Taxes & Refunds

Singapore has a 3% Goods and Services Tax (GST) applied to all goods and services. Visitors purchasing goods worth S$300 or more through a shop participating in the GST Tourist Refund Scheme can apply for a GST refund. These shops display a 'tax-free shopping' logo, and when you purchase an item you must fill in a claim form and show your passport. You will receive a global refund cheque. Present this cheque (or cheques) and your passport

and goods at customs at Changi Airport. Customs then stamps your cheque(s), which you can then cash at the cash refund counters at the airport. Refer to the STB brochure *Tax Free Shopping in Singapore*.

In addition to the 3% GST, a 10% service charge and 1% 'cess' (government entertainment tax) is added to the bill at the more expensive hotels and restaurants, as well as at most nightspots and bars. This is the 'plus-plus-plus' that follows some quoted prices (as in S$120+++). Some of the cheaper establishments don't add taxes but absorb them into the quoted price, which is 'net+', such as S$70 net+.

## POST & COMMUNICATIONS
## Post

Postal delivery in Singapore is very efficient and post offices provide a number of services other than selling stamps, including public telephones and the sale of packing material. Letters addressed to 'Poste Restante c/o GPO' are held at the Eunos Post Office at 10 Eunos Rd, next to the Eunos MRT. Poste restante (☎ 741 8857) is open from 8 am to 6 pm weekdays and until 2 pm Saturday.

The Comcentre, where you can also post letters, is at 31 Exeter Rd, very near Somerset MRT station. It's open from 8 am to 6 pm weekdays and until 2 pm Saturday. The Changi Airport branches in the Terminal 1 and Terminal 2 departure lounges are open from 8 am to 9 pm daily. Otherwise, there are some 96 post office branches scattered throughout the island. Normal business hours are from 8.30 am to 5 pm weekdays and from until 1 pm Saturday.

**Post Codes** There is now a six-digit postal code system that should be used when addressing mail to and within Singapore. Ask for the *Postal Code Directory* at any post office or call the Postal Code HelpLine (☎ 1-800-842 7678) to find a particular code. Alternatively, visit the Web site at www.singpost.com.sg, for full details.

The system is, not surprisingly, very efficient. The first two digits are the sector code, which defines a particular area in Singapore, and the last four digits are the delivery point – the house or particular building.

In theory, you could address a mail item to someone using the postal code only and it should get there.

The number to call for postal enquiries is ☎ 1605.

**Postal Rates** Local mail charges are 22c for letters and small packets under 20g, and 30c for those under 50g. Letters under 200g are 80c (small packets 50c) and S$1.50 under 500g (small packets 60c to 80c depending on weight – up to 500g).

Airmail letters cost 60c for the first 20g to most of Asia (to Malaysia costs 35c), 70c to Australia, Japan and New Zealand, and S$1 to the USA and Europe. Every additional 10g costs 25c, 30c and 35c respectively. Small packets under 20g cost 35c to airmail to most of Asia, 40c to Australia, Japan and New Zealand, and 50c to the USA and Europe. Every additional 10g costs 15c, 20c and 25c respectively. Airmail postcards cost 30c to Malaysia and 50c to everywhere else. Aerograms cost 50c to anywhere in the world.

Surface mail rates to anywhere except Malaysia start at 40c (under 20g). To Malaysia, letters under 20g are 35c and small packets are 30c.

## Telephone

You can make local and international calls from public phone booths. You can make international calls from booths at the Comcentre 24 hours a day. Most phone booths take phonecards, and some take credit cards, although there are still booths around that take coins. As well as public phones and hotels, you can make international phone calls at selected post offices.

There are no area codes for Singapore; telephone numbers are no more than seven digits unless you are calling toll-free (1-800). Mobile numbers are generally prefixed 001 or 010.

Useful numbers include:

| | |
|---|---|
| **Directory information** | ☎ 100 |
| **Flight information** | ☎ 1-800-542 4422 |
| **STB 24-hour Touristline** | ☎ 1-800-736 2000 |

**Phonecards** The easiest way to make a telephone call (international or local) is to dial it yourself from a public pay phone. Phonecards are available from 7-Eleven stores, post offices, Telecom centres, stationers and bookshops, and come in denominations of S$2, $5, S$10, S$20 and S$50.

Lonely Planet's eKno Communication Card provides low-cost international calls across many countries, a range of innovative messaging services, free email and travel information – for local calls, you're usually better off with a local card. You can join online at www.ekno.lonelyplanet.com, where you can also find the best numbers to join on the phone – from Singapore you can join by dialling 800-101-1217, or from anywhere else by dialling the international access number 1-213-927-0100 and pressing 0 to connect to the 24-hour customer service centre. Once you have joined, check the eKno Web site for the latest economy access numbers and updates on new features.

**Credit-Card Phones** Credit-card phones are also available (just swipe your AmEx, Diners Club, MasterCard or Visa through the slot). At the Telecom centres, there are also Home Country Direct phones – press a country button to contact the operator then reverse the charges or have the call charged to an international telephone card acceptable in your country. The Home Country Direct service is available from any phone by dialling the appropriate code; see the 'Home Country Direct Access Codes' in Malaysia's Facts for the Visitor chapter earlier in this book.

**Mobile Phones** You'll find that your mobile phone will automatically tune in to one of Singapore's two GSM digital providers, as long as you have requested the global roaming facility from your home provider.

## Fax

Faxes can be sent from all post offices, Telecom centres and hotels, but the service tends to be costly.

## Email & Internet Access

There are numerous outlets where you can access the net in Singapore, and many places to stay (even budget places) have Internet access. The rate is generally $3 for half an hour.

**Pacific Internet** (www.pacfusion.com.sg) has Internet facilities at the following places, all easily accessible from the MRT: Bugis Junction, B1-07, 200 Victoria St (9.30 am to 9.30 pm); Suntec City 02-066 (10 am to 10 pm); Wisma Atria, B1-47, 435 Orchard Rd (10 am to 10 pm)
**Cyber-Action** 01–06 Burlington Square, 17 Bencoolen St (9.30 am to 9.30 pm)
**CyberArena Internet Point** Capital Bldg 01-09, 11 Stamford Rd; $H_2O$ Mall, 39 Cuppage Terrace (10 am to midnight)
**The Singapore Visitors Centre** The centre at Suntec City (01-35, 3 Temasek Blvd) has several Internet machines – and you can get coffee and snacks here too. It's open from 8 am to 8 pm daily.

The National Library, on Stamford Rd next to the National Museum, has a wonderful multimedia centre on the 2nd level where you can access the Internet (Web only) for just S$2 per hour. There are also Internet centres at Changi International Airport.

## INTERNET RESOURCES

There's plenty of information about Singapore on the Internet. Look via the usual search engines, or check out Lonely Planet's Web site at www.lonelyplanet.com, which has lots of helpful links.

Most of the sites here also provide useful cross links.

**www.newasia-singapore.com**
Singapore Tourism's site, with plenty of links to things to see and do.
**www.happening.com.sg**
An offbeat, online listings magazine with articles, reviews and 'what's on' information (updated daily).
**www.asia1.com.sg**
The Web site of Asia One, the company that owns Singapore's newspapers, with links to the *Straits Times*, the *New Paper* and the *Business Times*.
**www.sintercom.org**
A great, general link to Singapore's burgeoning Internet community.

**www.changi.airport.com.sg**
A detailed guide to Singapore's world-leader of an airport.

## BOOKS

Singapore and Malaysia have long provided a fertile setting for novelists, and Joseph Conrad's *The Shadow Line* and *Lord Jim* both use the region as a backdrop. Somerset Maugham spent time in Singapore writing his classic short stories, many of which were set in Malaya – look for *Borneo Stories*.

See under Literature in the Arts section of the Facts about Singapore chapter for more information on home-grown literature.

Large, well-stocked bookshops in Singapore include Kinokuniya and Borders on Orchard Rd, and the MPH bookshop on Stamford Rd.

## Lonely Planet

Lonely Planet publishes the *Singapore city guide*, the *Malay phrasebook*, the *Mandarin phrasebook,* and the *South-East Asia phrasebook. South-East Asia on a shoestring* is LP's overall guidebook to the region. There are individual guidebooks to most South-East and North-East Asian countries.

## History & Politics

*A History of Singapore* by CM Turnball is the best choice for a detailed overview of the tropical city-state from prehistory to the present. It is an excellent scholarly work that is also very readable and is a mine of interesting information. The author has also written *A Short History of Malaysia, Singapore & Brunei*.

*Raffles* by Maurice Collis is the straightforward story of the man who founded Singapore.

*Lee Kuan Yew – The Struggle for Singapore* by Alex Josey covers all the twists and turns of the former prime minister's rise to power and the successful path along which his PAP has piloted Singapore.

For an insight into both sides of the PAP story, *No Man is an Island* by James Minchin is one of the best reads available. It's a warts-and-all portrait of Lee Kuan

SINGAPORE

Yew which, not surprisingly, is hard to find in Singapore.

Chee Soon Juan's book *Dare To Change: An Alternative Vision For Singapore* roundly criticises the government and offers social-democratic alternatives. It was such a local success that it has been followed by *Singapore: My Home Too.*

Another thorn in the side of the government, Christopher Lingle is a former National University of Singapore academic. His 1994 article in the *International Herald Tribune*, questioning the independence of the judiciary, resulted in yet another defamation suit in the government's favour. Dr Lingle fled the country and continues the battle in *Singapore's Authoritarian Capitalism*, a damning study of political repression and the 'Asian Values' professed by the government.

Written by the man who single-handedly brought down Barings Bank through a series of ill-conceived futures speculations, Nick Leeson's *Rogue Trader* makes fascinating reading. See the 'Rogue Trader – Nick Leeson' boxed text in the Singapore chapter later.

### People & Society

*Tales of Chinatown* by Sit Yin Fong is a readable and informative piece about Chinese life. Fong was a journalist in Singapore for many years and writes anecdotal short stories about Chinese customs and beliefs.

*Son of Singapore* by Tan Kok Seng is the fascinating autobiography of a labourer who grew up in Singapore in the 1950s.

*The Babas Revisited* by Felix Chia is a classic study of the history, culture and language of the Straits Chinese.

### Architecture

*Pastel Portraits – Singapore's Architectural Heritage* by Gretchen Liu was first published in 1984. Much has changed since then, but this beautiful book, with its wonderful photography, provides an excellent insight into how rich that heritage actually is.

Another beautiful book is Robert Powell's *Living Legacy – Singapore's Architectural Heritage Renewed*. First published in 1994 it investigates the issues surrounding the preservation and renovation of Singapore's architectural heritage.

### General

*Portraits of Places* by Brenda SA Yeoh & Luly Kong is an interesting sociological study of changing Singapore, examining selected areas from Orchard Rd to Kampong Wak Selat, the 'last village in Singapore', near Kranji.

Birdwatchers might want to get hold of *Birds – An Illustrated Field Guide to the Birds of Singapore* written by Lim Kim Seng, a local birdwatcher. Some 350 species of resident and migrant birds are covered in this excellent guide.

## NEWSPAPERS & MAGAZINES

English dailies in Singapore are the *Straits Times* (which includes the *Sunday Times*), the *Business Times* and the *New Paper,* an evening tabloid.

The *New Paper* is a long way behind the *Straits Times* in circulation and is seen as the fun alternative. It is similar to an English tabloid and comes up with some amazingly trite, attention-grabbing headlines. It contains very little news.

The press in Singapore (which is largely owned by the gigantic Singapore Press Holdings) knows its limits and holds off on criticism of the government. The foreign media sometimes doesn't know its limits and the government is not above restricting the circulation of foreign publications that do not report to its liking. Nevertheless, *Time, Newsweek* and many other foreign magazines are readily available. Pornographic publications are strictly prohibited under the Obscene Publications Act.

## RADIO & TV

The Radio Corporation of Singapore is the country's largest network, with 12 local and three international radio stations. It has five English-language stations: Gold 90.5FM, Symphony 92.4FM, NewsRadio 93.8FM, Class 95FM and Perfect 10 98.7FM. Private stations include Safra

Radio's English-language Power 98FM, a 24-hour station aimed at the 18- to 35-year-old audience, and Passion 99.5FM, which is an arts station. The BBC broadcasts on 88.9FM.

The Television Corporation of Singapore is the largest terrestrial broadcaster. It has two 24-hour channels, TC5 (English) and 8 (Mandarin). Singapore Television 12 operates two free-to-air channels: 12 and Arts Central. Channel 12 caters mainly to Malay and Hindi speakers. Arts Central focuses, as its name implies, on the cultural and arts scene in Singapore. Its programs are in English. Singaporeans can also pick up Malaysian television – TV1 and TV2 – although the reception is notoriously bad.

## VIDEO SYSTEMS

Singapore uses the PAL video format, which is used in Australia and most of Europe.

## PHOTOGRAPHY & VIDEO

Film is cheap and readily available. So is processing. There are numerous one-hour and same-day print processing places in Singapore, including in Lucky Plaza on Orchard Rd and the Little India Arcade, and the Mustafa Centre on Serangoon Rd. For a processing centre near you, refer to the *Yellow Pages*. Professional processing services are also advertised in the *Yellow Pages*.

Expect to pay around S$8.30 for a 36-exposure roll of transparency film to be developed and mounted (usually same-day service as long as you drop off in the morning). Print film costs around S$5 for a 36-exposure roll. Processing costs around S$2 plus 30 to 40 cents per print (the price varies depending on the size and the finish).You can buy PAL, NTSC and SECAM video tapes in Singapore.

While there are no specific restrictions relating to photography in Singapore, you should exercise common sense and common courtesy. Worshippers in temples and particularly in mosques may not want you to take photos; if in doubt, ask. Even if you are allowed to photograph in such a place, avoid using your flash.

If you're looking for technical tips, pick up a copy of *Travel Photography: A Guide to Taking Better Pictures,* written by renowned travel photographer, Richard I'Anson.

## TIME

Singapore is eight hours ahead of GMT/UTC (London), two hours behind Australian Eastern Standard Time (Sydney and Melbourne), 13 hours ahead of American Eastern Standard Time (New York) and 16 hours ahead of American Pacific Standard Time (San Francisco and Los Angeles). So, when it is noon in Singapore, it is 8 pm in Los Angeles and 11 pm in New York the previous day, 4 am in London and 2 pm in Sydney.

## ELECTRICITY

Electricity supplies are dependable and run at 220V to 240V and 50 cycles. Plugs are of the three-pronged, square-pin type used in the UK. Bring your own adaptors.

## WEIGHTS & MEASURES

Singapore uses the metric system, though you may occasionally come across references to odd measurements, such as the *thola,* an Indian weight, or *batu,* the Malay word for mile (literally meaning stone). There is a metric conversion table inside the back cover of this book.

## LAUNDRY

Singapore has plenty of laundries, although you will usually have to wait three to four days for your laundry to be returned. Laundries are listed in the buying guide of Singapore's *Yellow Pages*. Expect to pay around S$2.50 to have a small item such as a skirt, shirt or pants/trousers washed, and S$5 for dresses.

## HEALTH

In Singapore you can eat virtually anything and not worry, and the tap water is safe to drink. Vaccinations are required only if you come from a yellow fever area, and Singapore is not a malarial zone. The main health concern is the heat: it is important to avoid dehydration. If you do need medical attention during your visit, you'll find an excellent standard of health care available.

The first recorded case of sexually transmitted HIV in Singapore was in 1985. As of March 1998 a total of 775 cases of HIV infection had been recorded; of these 144 had developed full-blown AIDS and 261 had died. Around 96% of those who become infected with HIV do so via sexual transmission, and the great majority are heterosexual. Action for AIDS is a non-government organisation formed in 1989 to educate Singaporeans about HIV/AIDS and to provide support for those affected by it. Its web site is at www.afa.org.sg.

See the Health section in Malaysia's Facts for the Visitor chapter for general tips on healthy travelling, and for specific information on health issues relevant to travelling in this region.

## WOMEN TRAVELLERS

Singapore is probably the safest Asian country in which to travel, and sexual harassment is very rare. Women are not cloistered in Singaporean society and enjoy much more freedom and equality than in many other Asian countries. Government policy favours sexual equality, and abortion is available on request, although not for 'foreign' (non-Singaporean) citizens.

## GAY & LESBIAN TRAVELLERS

Homosexuality is illegal in Singapore and you can be sentenced to between 10 years and life for engaging in homosexual activities. Singapore isn't completely straight, however, and there is a local gay and lesbian scene. A good place to start looking for information is on the Utopia Web site at www.utopia-asia.com.

## DISABLED TRAVELLERS

Singapore is not an especially difficult place to get around if you have a sight or mobility impairment. Where there are stairs, lifts invariably provide an alternative, and shopping emporiums in and around Orchard Rd are spacious, well serviced and well organised. Most attractions,

such as the Night Safari, are wheelchair accessible. Medical facilities are excellent, and mobility aids and other items can be easily bought.

*Access Singapore* is a useful guidebook produced by the Singapore Council of Social Services. It provides details on the various facilities available in specific hotels, attractions and shopping centres. It's available from STB offices (see Tourist Offices earlier in this chapter for addresses) or contact the National Council of Social·Services (☎ 336 1544, fax 336 7732) at 11 Penang Rd.

## SENIOR TRAVELLERS

Singapore is an ideal destination for senior travellers who want a taste of Asia without the hassles of less-developed countries. The health-care system is on a par with any Western country, access facilities to hotels and restaurants are excellent and there is a wide range of ready-made tours to cater for all tastes.

Singapore is a remarkably safe city and it's very easy to get around on public transport. The humid weather, however, can prove tiring – although travellers on guided tours tend to spend most of their time in air-conditioned buses or buildings.

The STB publishes a booklet called *Mature Travellers*, though in practice the information it contains is also useful for younger travellers.

## TRAVEL WITH CHILDREN

Singapore is a safe and healthy country for children, and it is easy and cheap to get around. In addition, Singaporean society is very family orientated; eating out as a family is a perfectly ordinary thing to do, and hotels are usually able to provide family rooms, extra beds or cots. As far as things to see and do go, Singapore provides non-stop entertainment, with family attractions, the top of the list. Entry prices are reduced for children and family packages are also good value.

## DANGERS & ANNOYANCES

Singapore is a very safe country with low crime rates. Pickpockets are not unknown,

SINGAPORE

## The 'Fine' Country

'Singapore is a fine country', said the taxi driver. 'In Singapore we have fines for everything.'

Singapore has a number of frowned-upon activities, and the sometimes Draconian methods of dealing with minor transgressions has caused both mirth and dread among visitors. The famous anti-long-hair campaign is a thing of the past, but it wasn't that long ago that long-haired men were turned away on arrival in the country, or given a short-back-and-sides on the spot.

Singapore remains tough on a number of other minor issues, however, and the standard way of stamping out un-Singaporean activities is to slap a S$1000 fine on any offender. Actually, it is very rare that anybody gets fined that amount, but the severity of the fines is enough to ensure compliance.

Smoking in a public place – buses, lifts, cinemas, restaurants, air-conditioned shopping centres and government offices – earns a S$500 fine. You can smoke at food stalls and on the street (as long as you dispose of your butt, of course). The move to ban smoking in private cars was eventually quashed because of the difficulty of enforcing it. A few years ago it was the fashion among Singapore subversives to urinate in elevators but a successful campaign of heavy fines and security cameras has stamped that one out.

Jaywalking is a relatively minor crime – walk across the road within 50m of a designated crossing and it could cost you S$50. There is a successful anti-littering campaign (with a fine of up to S$1000 for dropping even a cigarette butt on the street) and, not surprisingly, Singapore is amazingly clean.

The Mass Rapid Transit (MRT), Singapore's pride and joy, attracts some particularly heavy fines. Eating, drinking and smoking on the system are forbidden and attract a S$500 fine.

Gum chewing is also a frowned-upon activity in Singapore. Antisocial elements used to leave their gum deposits on the doors of the MRT, causing disruptions to the underground rail services. The sale, importation and even possession of chewing gum is now banned and subject to heavy fines.

---

but in general, crime is not a problem. This is not surprising, given the harsh penalties meted out to offenders and the fact that hundreds of suspected criminals are held in jail without trial because the government does not have enough evidence to ensure conviction.

The importation of drugs (see Customs earlier in this chapter) carries the death penalty and, quite simply, drugs in Singapore should be avoided at all costs – not that you are likely to come across them. In case you think the government is bluffing, the tally of executions for drug convictions currently stands at over 40, an astonishing number given the size of Singapore's population.

### EMERGENCIES

Useful emergency numbers include:

| | |
|---|---|
| Fire/Ambulance | ☎ 995 |
| Police | ☎ 999 |

Raffles SurgiCentre (☎ 334 3337), at 01–00 182 Clemenceau Ave, is a 24-hour walk-in clinic; and the Singapore General Hospital Accident & Emergency Department (☎ 321 4311), also open 24 hours, is on Outram Rd.

### BUSINESS HOURS

In Singapore, government offices are usually open from Monday to Friday and on Saturday morning. Hours vary, starting at around 7.30 to 9.30 am and closing between 4 and 6 pm. On Saturday, closing time is between 11.30 am and 1 pm.

Shop hours are also variable. Small shops are generally open from 10 am to 6 pm weekdays, while department stores and large shopping centres are open from 10 am to 9 or 9.30 pm, seven days a week. Most small shops in Chinatown and Arab St close on Sunday, though Sunday is the busiest shopping day in Little India.

Banks are open from 9.30 am to 3 pm weekdays (to 11.30 am Saturday).

**SINGAPORE**

## PUBLIC HOLIDAYS & SPECIAL EVENTS

The following days are public holidays in Singapore:

| | |
|---|---|
| **New Year's Day** | 1 January |
| **Chinese New Year** | 12–13 February 2001 |
| **Hari Raya Haji** | 6 March 2001, 23 February 2002 |
| **Good Friday** | April |
| **Labour Day** | 1 May |
| **Wesak Day** | 7 May 2001 |
| **National Day** | 9 August |
| **Deepavali** | November |
| **Christmas Day** | 25 December |
| **Hari Raya Puasa** | 17 December 2001, 06 December 2002 |

There are an amazing number of celebrations in Singapore. Although some of them have fixed dates, the Hindus, Muslims and Chinese follow a lunar calendar, which varies annually. In particular, the Muslim festivals vary constantly, moving back about 11 days each year. The STB puts out a *Festivals & Events* brochure each year, and the *Singapore Official Guide* has more specific and detailed listings for each month.

### January–February

**Ponggal** This is a harvest festival and the time for thanksgiving. It is celebrated by South Indians, especially at the Sri Mariamman Temple on South Bridge Rd, where rice, vegetables, sugarcane and spices are offered to the gods.

**Chinese New Year** Dragon dances and pedestrian parades mark the start of the new year. Families hold open house, unmarried relatives (especially children) receive *ang pow* (gifts of money in red packets), businesses traditionally clear their debts and everybody wishes you a *'kong hee fatt choy'* (a happy and prosperous new year). Chinatown is lit up, especially Eu Tong Sen St and New Bridge Rd, and the 'Singapore River Hong Bao Special' features *pasar malam* (night market) stalls, variety shows and fireworks.

**Chingay** This occurs on the 22nd day after the Chinese New Year. Processions of Chinese flag bearers parade down Orchard Rd balancing 6m- to 12m-long bamboo flag poles. Lion dancers, floats and other cultural performers join in the celebrations.

**Thaipusam** This is one of the most dramatic Hindu festivals, in which devotees honour Lord Subramaniam. See 'Thaipusam' in the 'Places of Worship' special section earlier in this book for details on this spectacular event. In Singapore, Hindus march in a procession from the Sri Srinivasa Perumal Temple on Serangoon Rd to the Chettiar Hindu Temple on Tank Rd; in the evening, the procession continues with an image of Subramaniam in a temple car.

**Hari Raya Puasa** The major Muslim events are connected with Ramadan, the month during which Muslims do not eat or drink from sunrise to sunset. In the evenings food stalls are set up in the Arab St district near the Sultan Mosque. Hari Raya Puasa marks the end of Ramadan with three days of celebration; Geylang Serai, a Malay area, is draped in lights for the occasion. It is a short walk from Paya Lebar station, down Tanjong Katong Rd to Geylang Rd, the main shopping street.

### March–April

**Qing Ming Festival** On 'All Souls' Day', Chinese traditionally visit the tombs of their ancestors to clean and repair them and make offerings. The Kong Meng San Phor Kark See Temple, about 1.5km west of the Bishan MRT station, receives many visitors.

**Hari Raya Haji** This is a Muslim festival in honour of those who have made the pilgrimage to Mecca. Sacrifices of goats and other animals are offered to Allah and the meat is distributed among the poor. Prayers are said at mosques throughout the city.

### April–May

**Wesak Day** Buddha's birth, enlightenment and death are celebrated by various events, including the release of caged birds to symbolise the setting free of captive souls. Temples such as the Buddhist Lodge on Kim Yam Rd, just off River Valley Rd, and the Temple of 1000 Lights on Serangoon Rd throng with worshippers.

### May–June

**Birthday of the Third Prince** The child-god is honoured with processions, and devotees go into a trance and spear themselves with spikes and swords during this Chinese festival. Celebrations are held at various temples and on Queen St, near Bencoolen St.

**Dragon Boat Festival** Commemorating the death of a Chinese saint who drowned himself as a protest against government corruption, this festival is celebrated with boat races across Marina Bay.

**Singapore Festival of Arts** A biennial event held every even-numbered year, this festival has a world-class program of art, dance, drama and music. It's a great opportunity to view emerging and established local talent

**Festival of Asian Performing Arts** Held every odd-numbered year, this festival showcases dance, song and drama from all over South-East Asia.

## July–August

**Singapore Food Festival** Celebrating the national passion, this month-long festival throughout July has special offerings at everything from hawker centres to gourmet restaurants.

**Great Singapore Sale** Orchard Rd is decked with banners and merchants are encouraged by the government to drop prices in an effort to boost Singapore's image as a shopping destination. It is held for one month around July and usually overlaps in part with the food festival.

**Singapore National Day** On 9 August a series of military and civilian processions and an evening fireworks display celebrate Singapore's independence in 1965.

**Festival of the Hungry Ghosts** The souls of the dead are released for this one day of feasting and entertainment on earth. Chinese operas and other events are laid on for them and food is put out (the ghosts eat the food's spirit but leave the substance for mortal celebrants).

## September–October

**Birthday of the Monkey God** The birthday of T'se Tien Tai Seng Yeh is celebrated twice a year at the Monkey God Temple on the corner of Eng Hoon St and Tiong Poh Rd near the Tiong Bahru Market. Mediums pierce their cheeks and tongues with skewers and go into a trance, during which they write special charms in blood.

**Thimithi (Fire-Walking Ceremony)** Hindu devotees prove their faith by walking across glowing coals at the Sri Mariamman Temple.

**Moon-Cake Festival** The overthrow of the Mongol warlords in ancient China is celebrated by eating moon cakes and lighting colourful paper lanterns. Moon cakes are made with bean paste, lotus seeds and sometimes a duck egg.

**Navarathri** In the Tamil month of Purattasi, the Hindu festival of 'Nine Nights' is dedicated to the wives of Shiva, Vishnu and Brahma. Young girls are dressed as the goddess Kali; this is a good opportunity to see traditional Indian dancing and singing. The Chettiar, Sri Mariamman and Sri Srinivasa Perumal Temples are centres of activity.

SUSAN STORM

Chinese opera performances mark the Festival of the Hungry Ghosts.

## October–November

**Pilgrimage to Kusu Island** Tua Pek Kong, the god of prosperity, is honoured by Taoists in Singapore who make a pilgrimage to the shrine on Kusu.

**Deepavali** Rama's victory over the demon king Ravana is celebrated with the 'Festival of Lights', with tiny oil lamps outside Hindu homes and lights all over Hindu temples. Little India is ablaze with lights for a month to celebrate this most important Hindu festival.

**Festival of the Nine Emperor Gods** Nine days of Chinese operas, processions and other events honour the nine emperor gods. The centre of activities is the Kiu Ong Yiah Temple opposite the Singapore Crocodile Farm on Upper Serangoon Rd.

## FOOD & DRINKS

Eating is a national pastime in Singapore, and the variety of places to enjoy it is simply astonishing. Hawker centres and their more-sanitised counterparts, food courts, are everywhere and you can get a filling meal at either for S$5. If you can afford to eat at more expensive places, the range of cuisines is enormous. You can get pretty

SINGAPORE

## Sugar Cane Deliverance

If you are in Singapore around Chinese New Year (January/February) and chance upon people wandering around with large sugar canes in their hands, do not be surprised. You are witnessing a cultural manifestation of the Hokkien Chinese people.

The ninth day of the Chinese New Year has special significance for the Hokkiens, who each year celebrate the birthday of Tian Gong (Tee Kong in Hokkien), the God of Heaven. The main celebration takes place at midnight the day before, with offerings of food such as chicken, duck and fruit.

It is also customary to place two pieces of sugar cane at the altar or entrance of the home as a symbol of deliverance, because of an incident during the Song dynasty (960–1279). The Hokkiens provoked the emperor's wrath by pledging allegiance to a rebel group. They hid in sugar cane farms for eight days, until they were finally pardoned by the emperor because it was a festive season.

Today sellers of sugar cane make a quick dollar by selling around the streets of Singapore – and yet another Chinese tradition lives on.

much anything you want in the way of drinks: soft drinks (local and imported), mineral water, coconut water, fresh and canned fruit drinks, iced tea and herbal drinks. Alcohol is expensive; expect to pay around S$5 for a can of beer. The local beer is Tiger, although a large range of imported beers (and wines and spirits) is also available.

See the 'Tastes of Malaysia, Singapore & Brunei' special section earlier in this book for information on the region's cuisine.

# Getting There & Away

## AIR
### Airports & Airlines

Singapore is a major South-East Asian travel hub. Changi, Singapore's huge international airport, is consistently rated one of the world's best, and for good reason. It is ultra-efficient and boasts every conceivable amenity. There is plenty of information: There are information counters in Terminal 1 and Terminal 2, copies of the free glossy magazine *Changi International* placed at strategic spots, and free copies of the pocket guide *Singapore Changi Airport*, which has nifty fold-out pages listing all the services and amenities – with diagrams of both terminals.

Singapore does have another 'international' airport – forgotten Seletar in the north of the island, which handles a few services for the smaller regional airlines.

Following are some of the major airline offices in Singapore. Check the *Business Yellow Pages* for any that are not listed here.

**Aeroflot** (☎ 336 1757) 01-02/02-00 Tan Chong Tower, 15 Queen St
**Air Canada** (☎ 256 1198) 01–10 101 Thomson Rd
**Air India** (☎ 225 9411) 17-01 UIC Bldg S, Shenton Way
**Air New Zealand** (☎ 535 8266) 24-08 Ocean Bldg, 10 Collyer Quay
**American Airlines** (☎ 339 0001) 04–01 114 Middle Rd
**British Airways** (☎ 839 7788) 04-02 The Promenade, 300 Orchard Rd
**Cathay Pacific Airways** (☎ 533 1333) 16-01 Ocean Bldg, 10 Collyer Quay
**Garuda Indonesia** (☎ 250 5666) 13–03 United Square
**KLM-Royal Dutch Airlines** (☎ 737 7622) 12-06 Ngee Ann City Tower, 391A Orchard Rd
**Lufthansa Airlines** (☎ 245 5600) 05-01 Palais Renaissance, 390 Orchard Rd
**Malaysia Airlines** (☎ 336 6777) 02-09 Singapore Shopping Centre, 190 Clemenceau Ave
**Pelangi Airways** (☎ 481 6302) Bldg 24, 960 Seletar Airport West Camp
**Philippine Airlines** (☎ 336 1611) 01-10 Parklane Shopping Mall, 35 Selegie Rd
**Qantas Airways** (☎ 839 7788) 04-02 The Promenade, 300 Orchard Rd
**Royal Brunei Airlines** (☎ 235 4672) 04–08 25 Scotts Rd
**Royal Nepal Airlines Corporation** (☎ 339 5535) 03–07 3 Coleman St
**Silk Air** (☎ 225 4488) 30 Airline Rd
**Singapore Airlines** (☎ 223 8888) Level 2, The Paragon, Orchard Rd
**Thai Airways International** (☎ 1-800 224 9977) 02-00 The Globe, 100 Cecil St
**United Airlines** (☎ 873 3533) 01-03 Hong Leong Bldg, 16 Raffles Quay

If you are flying with Singapore Airlines you can check in downtown (The Paragon, Orchard Rd) up to 48 hours before departure. Bring your ticket and passport. You can't check in baggage here – you must do that at the airport upon departure, as usual. You can also check in by phone (☎ 540 3033), fax (543 0979) or email (check-in@ singaporeair.com.sg). Details can be found on its Web site at www.singaporeair .com.sg. Several other airlines offer facilities checking in early, so it's worth asking if your airline has this service.

### Departure Tax

The airport departure tax (Passenger Service Charge; PSC) from Changi is S$15 and is normally included in the cost of your air ticket.

### The USA

One-way tickets to Singapore in the low season start from as little US$615 from the US east or west coasts and from around US$1000 return. From Singapore to either the east or west coasts, one-way economy fares cost around S$900 at the time of writing.

Singapore Airlines and others have direct flights but it is usually cheaper to fly via another port, such as with China Airlines via Taipei or with Cathay Pacific Airways via Hong Kong. From the east or west coasts expect to pay US$615 to US$900 one way and US$1200 to US$1500 return.

It is also worth looking into Circle Pacific flights. There are numerous combinations of destinations you can include. Expect to pay around US$2000 to go from New York or Los Angeles to Singapore via Fiji, Auckland (New Zealand), Sydney (Australia) and Bali, then back home via New Delhi and Paris. For information on current options, try the following sites: www.airtreks.com; www.tiglion.com; and www.ticketplanet.com.

Discount travel agents in the USA are known as consolidators. San Francisco is the ticket consolidator capital of America, although some good deals can be found in Los Angeles, New York and other big cities. The *New York Times,* the *Los Angeles Times,* the *Chicago Tribune* and the *San Francisco Examiner* all produce weekly travel sections in which you'll find any number of travel agents' ads. Council Travel, America's largest student travel organisation, has around 60 offices in the USA; its head office (☎ 800-226 8624) is at 205 E 42 St, New York, NY 10017. Call it for the office nearest you or visit its Web site at www.ciee.org. STA Travel (☎ 800-777 0112) has offices in major cities; its Web site is at www.statravel.com.

## Canada
The fare from Vancouver to Singapore ranges from C$710 to C$1000 one way (C$1388 to C$1744 return). Prices are similar from Montreal.

Canadian discount air-ticket sellers are also known as consolidators and their air fares tend to be about 10% higher than those sold in the USA. The *Globe & Mail,* the *Toronto Star,* the *Montreal Gazette* and the *Vancouver Sun* carry travel agents' ads and are a good place to look for cheap fares.

Travel CUTS (☎ 800-667 2887) is Canada's national student travel agency and has offices in all major cities. Its Web address is www.travelcuts.com.

## Australia
Advance-purchase return fares from the Australian east or west coasts vary from around A$700 to A$1000 return, depending on the season and the length of stay. One-way economy fares from Singapore are about S$740 to Sydney, and S$640 to Perth.

Many of the airlines that fly from Australia to Asia, the Middle East and Europe stop over in Singapore. Two of the cheapest are Gulf Air and Lauda Air.

The travel sections of weekend newspapers, such as the *Age* in Melbourne and the *Sydney Morning Herald,* are good places to look for air-fare deals.

STA Travel (☎ 03-9349 2411) has offices in all major cities. Call ☎ 13 1776 Australia-wide for the location the branch nearest you, or visit its Web site at www.statravel.com.au. Flight Centre (☎ 13 1600 Australia-wide) has dozens of offices throughout Australia. Its Web address is www.flightcentre.com.au.

## New Zealand
Return fares from Auckland to Singapore range from NZ$1000 to NZ$1700 depending on when you fly, which airline you fly with and whether you are paying for a normal economy ticket or a special offer. Round-the-World (RTW) and Circle Pacific fares for travel to or from New Zealand are usually the best value – often cheaper than a return ticket. Depending on which airline you choose, you may fly across Asia, with a stopover in Singapore. Flights from Singapore to Auckland cost from around S$970 one way.

The *New Zealand Herald* has a travel section in which travel agents advertise fares. Flight Centre (☎ 09-309 6171) has a large central office in Auckland at National Bank Towers (corner of Queen and Darby Sts) and many branches throughout the country. STA Travel (☎ 09-309 0458) has offices in all major towns and cities.

## The UK
Fares from London are around £350 (some as low as £300) return and around £230 one way in the low season (mid-year). Over the peak Christmas/New Year period, return fares can top £600 (£300 one way), although by shopping around you can probably get a better price than this. Flights to London start at around S$1100 one way.

Airline-ticket discounters are known as bucket shops in the UK. The advertisements of many travel agents appear in the travel pages of the weekend broadsheets, such as the *Independent* on Saturday and the *Sunday Times*. Look out for free magazines, such as *TNT*, which are widely available in London.

For students or travellers under 26, popular travel agencies in the UK include STA Travel (☎ 020-7361 6161), which has an office at 86 Old Brompton Rd, London SW7 3LQ, and other offices in London and Manchester. Visit its Web site at www.statravel.co.uk. Usit Campus (☎ 0870-240 1010), 52 Grosvenor Gardens, London SW1WOAG, has branches throughout the UK. Its Web site is at www.usitcampus.com.

Both of these agencies sell tickets to all travellers but cater especially to young people and students. Charter flights can work out as a cheaper alternative to scheduled flights if you do not qualify for the under-26 and student discounts.

Other recommended travel agents include: Trailfinders (☎ 020-7938 3939), 194 Kensington High St, London W8 7RG; Bridge to the World (☎ 020-7734 7447), 4 Regent Place, London W1R 5FB; and Flightbookers (☎ 020-7757 2000), 177–178 Tottenham Court Rd, London W1P 9LF.

## Continental Europe

The cheapest flights to Paris and Frankfurt from Singapore start at around S$1500.

Though London is the travel discount capital of Europe, there are several other cities in which you will find a range of good deals. Generally, there is not much variation in air-fare prices for departures from the main European cities. All the major airlines are usually offering some sort of deal, and travel agents generally have a number of deals on offer, so shop around.

Across Europe many travel agencies have ties with STA Travel, where cheap tickets can be purchased, and STA-issued tickets can be altered (usually for a US$25 fee). Outlets in major cities include:

ISYTS (☎ 01-322 1267, fax 323 3767) 11 Nikis St, Upper Floor, Syntagma Square, Athens

Passaggi (☎ 06-474 0923, fax 482 7436)
Stazione Termini FS, Gelleria Di Tesla, Rome
STA Travel (☎ 030-311 0950, fax 313 0948)
Goethestrasse 73, 10625 Berlin
Voyages Wasteels (☎ 08 03 88 70 04 – this number can only be dialled from within France, fax 01 43 25 46 25) 11 rue Dupuytren, 756006 Paris

## Asia

Although most Asian countries now offer fairly competitive air deals, Bangkok, Singapore and Hong Kong are still the best places to shop around for discount fares. Hong Kong's travel market can be unpredictable, but some excellent bargains are available if you are lucky. From Singapore, return flights to Bangkok start at around S$320, and return flights to New Delhi, Chennai (Madras) and Mumbai (Bombay) in India at around S$715.

**Malaysia** The shuttle service operated by Malaysia Airlines and Singapore Airlines has frequent flights between Kuala Lumpur (KL) and Singapore for RM152 (S$115 from Singapore); seats are available on a first-come, first-served basis. Booked seats cost RM222 (S$182). Malaysia Airlines also connects Singapore to Kuantan (RM204, S$140), Langkawi (RM305, S$211) and Penang (RM255, S$176) in Peninsular Malaysia; and Kuching (RM286, S$199) and Kota Kinabalu (RM584, S$403) in Malaysian Borneo. First-class fares are around 40% extra.

Silk Air (☎ 1800-223 8888) has daily flights to/from Kuantan (RM204, S$158) and Langkawi (RM478, S$211).

Return fares are double the one-way fares quoted here. Fares from Singapore to Malaysia are always quoted in Singapore dollars and from Malaysia to Singapore in Malaysian ringgit. With the considerable difference in the exchange rate it is much cheaper to buy tickets in Malaysia, so rather than buying a return fare to KL from Singapore, buy a one-way ticket and purchase the return leg in KL.

Going to Malaysia, you can save quite a few dollars if you fly from Johor Bahru (JB) rather than Singapore. For example, to Kota

SINGAPORE

Kinabalu the fares are RM347 from JB but S\$403 from Singapore. To persuade travellers to take advantage of these lower fares, the SPS (☎ 250 3333) bus service operated by Malaysia Airlines runs directly from the Copthorne Orchid Hotel, 214 Dunearn Rd, to the JB airport. It costs S\$12 and takes about two hours. In Singapore, tickets for internal flights originating in Malaysia are only sold by Malaysia Airlines (☎ 336 6777), 02-09 Singapore Shopping Centre, 190 Clemenceau Ave, 200m south-west of Dhoby Ghaut MRT.

**Indonesia** A number of airlines fly from Singapore to Jakarta for as low as S\$120/200 one way/return. Flights to Bali start at S\$310/490 with Garuda Indonesia, the main carrier. Garuda Indonesia also has direct flights between Singapore and Medan, Padang, Palembang, Pekanbaru, Pontianak and Surabaya.

Indonesian domestic flights are cheaper if tickets are bought in Indonesia. For Pontianak in Kalimantan and some destinations in Sumatra, such as Pekanbaru, it is cheaper to take the ferry to Pulau Batam (Batam Island) and then a domestic flight from there. Garuda Indonesia offers an internal air pass costing US\$300 for three flights, but this is only economical for very long distances.

For international flights, the travel agencies on Jalan Jaksa, Jakarta's budget accommodation area, are good places to look. Indo Shangrila Travel (☎ 625 6080), Jalan Gajah Mada 219G, is a large ticketing agent and often has good deals.

## LAND
## Malaysia

**Bus** The Causeway is the main link between Singapore and the mainland. An impressive piece of engineering in its day, it has difficulty coping with the traffic on weekends, especially on long weekends and public holidays. If you're travelling by private vehicle or taxi, try to avoid these times. Take a bus – buses sail on past in the express lane while cars are stuck in the interminable queues.

A new bridge-cum-causeway on the western side of Singapore, linking the Singapore suburb of Tuas with Geylang Patah in Malaysia, alleviates some of the bottleneck problems at the main Causeway, but is not of immediate use to travellers without their own transport.

The air-con express bus operated by Singapore-Johor Express Ltd (☎ 292 8149) departs for JB every 15 minutes between 6.30 am and 11 pm from the Queen St bus terminal, on the corner of Queen and Arab Sts. It costs S\$2.40. Alternatively, the public SBS bus No 170 leaves from the Ban San terminal and costs S\$1.10; Bugis MRT subway station is within walking distance. Bus No 170 can be hailed anywhere along the way, such as on Rochor, Rochor Canal or Bukit Timah Rds.

The bus stops at the Singapore checkpoint, but don't worry if it leaves while you clear immigration – keep your ticket and you can just hop on the next bus that comes along. The bus then stops at Malaysian immigration and customs at the other end of the Causeway, 1km away. After clearing the Malaysian checkpoint, you can catch the bus (again – your ticket is still valid) to Larkin bus station on the outskirts of JB, or you can walk to town from the Causeway. Moneychangers, whose first offer will usually be less than the going rate, will approach you, and there are plenty of banks and official moneychangers in JB.

If you are travelling beyond JB, it is easier to catch a long-distance bus straight from Singapore, but there is a greater variety of bus services from JB and the fares are cheaper.

In Singapore, long-distance buses to Melaka and the east coast of Malaysia leave from and arrive at the bus terminal on the corner of Lavender St and Kallang Bahru, opposite the large Kallang Bahru complex. Take the MRT to Lavender, then bus No 5 or 61; otherwise it's a 500m walk from the MRT station.

Pan Malaysia Express (☎ 294 7034) has express buses to KL (S\$30) daily at 9 am and 4.30 pm and nonexpress buses (S\$25) at 11 am and 10 pm. It also has buses to Mersing (S\$11.10) at 9 and 10 am, and 10 pm; to Kuantan (S\$16.50) at 10 am and

10 pm; and to Kota Bharu (S$35.10) at 7.30 pm.

Also at the Lavender St bus terminal, Hasry (☎ 294 9306) has standard buses to KL (S$17) at 8, 9 and 10 am, and 2 and 9.30 pm; Super VIP coaches (S$25) at 8.30, 9.30, 10 and 10.30 am and at noon, 2.30 and 8.30 pm; and buses to Melaka (S$11) at 8.30 am and 2.30 pm. The journey to KL takes between five and six hours, depending on the bus.

Melaka-Singapore Express (☎ 293 5915) has buses to Melaka at 8, 9, 10 and 11 am and 2, 3 and 5 pm. The fare is S$11 for an air-con bus and the trip takes 4½ hours. It is preferable to buy your ticket the day before departure; many travel agents also sell bus tickets to Malaysia.

For destinations north of KL, most buses leave from the Golden Mile Complex at the north-eastern end of Beach Rd; Lavender MRT station is about 500m away. This terminal handles all the buses to Thailand and northern destinations on the way, such as Ipoh, Butterworth, Penang and Alor Setar. The trip to Penang costs around S$33 and most buses leave in the afternoon and evening. Bus agents line the outside of the building. Gunung Raya (☎ 294 7711) is one of the bigger agents for Malaysian west-coast destinations.

Morning Star Travel (☎ 292 9009) at Lavender MRT station has buses to KL (S$25) at 8 am and 10 pm, to Penang (S$38) at 9 pm and to Melaka (S$15) at 8 am (weekends only). All buses leave from next to the MRT station.

You can also catch buses to KL from the Queen St bus terminal. KL-Singapore Express (☎ 292 8254) has buses to KL at 9 am and at 5 and 10 pm for S$23.

**Train** Singapore is the southern terminus of the Malaysian railway system, Keretapi Tanah Malayu (KTM).

The Singapore train station (☎ 222 5165 for fare and schedule information) is on Keppel Rd, south-west of Chinatown, about 1km from Tanjong Pagar MRT station. The booking office is open from 8.30 am to 2 pm and 3 to 7 pm.

Daily departures from Singapore station include three trains to KL; three ordinary trains to Gemas, Kluang and Gua Musang (on the east-coast line to Tumpat); and an express train to Tumpat, in the very north-east of Malaysia. See 'Timetables for Main West-Coast Services' and 'Timetables for Main East-Coast Services' in the Malaysia Getting Around chapter, earlier in this book. Also have a look at the '*International Express*' table in the Malaysia Getting There & Away chapter.

All trains are efficient, well maintained and comfortable, but ordinary and mail trains stop at all stations and are slow. The express trains are well worth the extra money. For further details check out the KTM Web site at www.ktmb.com.my or email passenger@ktmb.com.my.

While there is a noticeable jump in comfort from 3rd to 2nd class, 1st class is not much better than 2nd class, and is considerably more expensive.

You can buy a 30-day rail pass allowing unlimited travel in Malaysia for US$120, or a 10-day pass for US$55. The pass entitles you to travel on any class of train, but does not include sleeping-berth charges. Rail passes are only available to foreign tourists and can be purchased at KL, JB, Butterworth, Pelabuhan (Port) Klang, Padang Besar, Wakaf Baharu and Penang train stations in Malaysia.

Customs and passport clearances take place at Woodlands station for all departures to and from Malaysia.

**Taxi** Malaysia has a cheap, well-developed, long-distance taxi system that makes travel a real breeze. A long-distance taxi plies between set destinations, and as soon as a full complement of four passengers turns up, off you go. From Singapore, the best bet is to go to JB and then take a taxi from there – it's cheaper and there are many more services – but Singapore also has such taxis to destinations in Malaysia.

Taxis for JB leave from the Queen St terminal. The trip costs S$6 per person, and an extra S$1 if there are long delays at the Causeway. Since travellers who are not

**SINGAPORE**

Singaporean or Malaysian take longer to clear the border, they are likely to have to pay more or to hire a whole taxi (S$28).

## Thailand

**Bus**  If you want to go direct from Singapore to Thailand overland, the quickest and cheapest way is by bus.

The main terminal for buses to and from Thailand is at the Golden Mile Complex on Beach Rd. A number of travel agents specialising in buses and tours to Thailand operate from there. Among these, Grassland Express (☎ 292 1166) has buses to Hat Yai at 7 pm. Phya Travel (☎ 293 6692) has buses to Hat Yai and Bangkok at 6.30 pm, with connections to Phuket and Suratthani from Hat Yai. Kwang Chow Travel (☎ 293 8977) has a bus to Hat Yai and Bangkok at 6.30 pm. Most buses leave in the afternoon and travel overnight.

Fares cost from around S$35 to S$45, depending on the quality of service, though all buses are air-con. The S$45 VIP coaches have videos.

**Train**  The rail route into Thailand is on the Butterworth-Alor Setar-Hat Yai route, which crosses into Thailand at Padang Besar. Train connections to/from Singapore are at Butterworth. You can take the *International Express* from Butterworth in Malaysia all the way to Bangkok with connections from Singapore. See the *'International Express'* table in the Malaysia Getting There & Away chapter for fare and schedule information.

A variation on the *International Express* is the *Eastern & Oriental Express*, which departs on alternate Wednesdays, Fridays and Sundays. The train is done out in antique opulence and caters to the well heeled – it's South-East Asia's answer to the *Orient Express*. It takes 42 hours to do the 1943km journey from Singapore to Bangkok. Don your linen suit, sip a gin and tonic and dig deep for the fare: from S$2350 per person in a double compartment, up to S$6000 in the presidential suite. You can also take the train just to KL or Butterworth for less. For further details call

☎ 392 3500, fax 392 3600, or check out the Web site at www.orient-express.com.

## SEA

Singapore has a number of ferry connections to Malaysia and the Indonesian islands of the Riau Archipelago. Cruise trips in the region are also very popular with Singaporeans.

The big cruise centre at the World Trade Centre (WTC), south-west of the Singapore train station, is the main departure point for ferries and cruises. The WTC is a mini Changi airport, with duty-free and other shops. A host of agents handle bookings for the ferries, cruises and resorts. To get to the WTC, take the MRT to Tanjong Pagar station, then bus No 10, 97, 100 or 131. Bus Nos 65 and 143 go from Serangoon Rd via Orchard Rd to the WTC. From the colonial district, bus Nos 97 and 167 go from Bencoolen St, and bus No 100 goes from Beach Rd.

The Tanah Merah ferry terminal, to the east near Changi airport, also handles ferries to the Indonesian island of Pulau Bintan, and may handle other services in the future. To get to there, take the MRT to Bedok and then bus No 35. The Bus-Plus service departs from the terminal for Tampines and City Hall MRT stations for S$45 per person on Saturday, Sunday and public holiday evenings (☎ 481 8566 for enquiries). The taxi fare from the city is around S$16 to S$17.

Changi Village, at the far eastern tip of Singapore, also has ferries to Malaysia. Take bus No 2 to Changi Village and then a taxi; the ferry terminal is behind Changi airport, just off Changi Coast Rd.

## Malaysia

**Tanjung Belungkur**  There's a ferry from Changi ferry terminal (☎ 545 3600) to Tanjung Belungkur, east of JB. It is primarily a service for Singaporeans going to Desaru in Malaysia. The 11km journey takes 45 minutes and costs S$18/28 one way/return. Ferries leave Singapore at 7.30 and 11.30 am and 4 and 8 pm; from Tanjung Belungkur departures are at 9.30 am and 1.30, 5.30 and 9.30 pm. There are buses from the Tanjung Belungkur jetty to Desaru and Kota Tinggi.

**Pengerang** Ferries go from Changi Village to Pengerang, across the strait in Johor, Malaysia. This is an interesting back-door route into Malaysia. Ferries don't have a fixed schedule, which is most unlike Singapore, and leave throughout the day when a full quota of 12 people is reached. The cost is S$10 per person or S$60 for the whole boat. The best time to catch one is early in the morning, before 8 am. Clear Singapore immigration at the small post on the Changi River dock.

**Pulau Tioman** Auto Batam (☎ 271 4866), 02-20 World Trade Centre, is the agent for a high-speed catamaran that does the trip from the WTC to Pulau Tioman in four hours. Departures are at 8.30 am from the Tanah Merah ferry terminal, and the fare is S$90/148 one way/return. There are no services during the monsoon season from 31 October to 1 March.

### Indonesia

Curiously, no direct shipping services run between the main ports of Indonesia and near-neighbour Singapore, but it is possible to travel between the two countries via the islands of the Riau Archipelago, the cluster of Indonesian islands immediately south of Singapore.

The two most visited islands are Pulau Batam and Pulau Bintan, both of which can be reached by ferry from Singapore. Travellers of most nationalities are issued a tourist pass for Indonesia, valid for 60 days, upon arrival and do not require a visa. The ferries are modern, fast and air-conditioned, and show movies. From Batam boats go to Sumatra, a popular way to enter this Indonesian state.

**Pulau Batam** Pulau Batam is a resort and industrial park. From Singapore it only takes half an hour to reach Sekupang or 45 minutes to Batu Ampar, both on Pulau Batam.

Departures are from the WTC. The main agents for boats to Pulau Batam are Auto Batam (☎ 271 4866) and Dino Shipping

(☎ 270 2228), both with offices at the WTC. Between them they have dozens of departures every day, at least every half-hour from 7.30 am to 8 pm. Tickets cost S$17 one way. Ferries dock at Sekupang, from where you can take a boat to Tanjung Buton on the Sumatran mainland. From there it is a three-hour bus ride to Palembang. This is a popular travellers' route to Sumatra.

Ferries to Batu Ampar, close to Pulau Batam's main town, Nagoya, depart roughly every hour from 7.50 am to 8.15 pm. Dino Shipping also has several ferries a day from the Tanah Merah ferry terminal to Nongsa, in the north of the island.

**Pulau Bintan** The same companies that operate ferries to Pulau Batam also have ferries to Pulau Bintan. From here ferries go from the Tanah Merah ferry terminal (☎ 542 7102) to Tanjung Pinang, the main city on the island, at 9.10 am and 1.10 and 5.25 pm on weekdays; 11.10 am, 1.10, 3.25 and 5.25 pm on weekends and public holidays. On Saturday there are additional services at 9.10 and 9.56 am. The journey takes about 1½ hours and costs S$39/42 one way/return. Ferries leave Tanjung Pinang at 10.10 am and 2.10 and 6.20 pm on weekdays; and at 10.10 and 11 am and 12.20, 2.10, 4.20 and 6.20 pm on weekends and public holidays.

There are boats to Lobam (45 minutes, S$35/47), on the western side of Bintan, at 8.10 am and 1.25 pm on weekdays; and at 8.10 am on Saturday. There's no Sunday service. Lobam is connected to Pulau Batam by regularly departing local ferries.

**Pulau Karimun** Dino Shipping has three ferries daily from the WTC to Tanjung Balai, the main port on Karimun, another Riau resort-island of minor note. The cost is S$26/40 one way/return.

## CRUISES

There is no shortage of cruises that operate from Singapore or include the city in their itineraries. International companies such as P&O, Seven Seas, CTC and Winstar call in at Singapore, but the best deals are with the local operators that offer popular cheap cruises from the WTC.

Cruises to Phuket, Langkawi, KL, Port Dickson and Melaka leave weekly. Expect to pay from S$199 for a two-night cruise to Port Dickson and Pelabuhan Klang, and from S$299 for a three-night cruise to Phuket and Langkawi. The best deals are advertised in newspaper travel sections, but check for 'administration fees' and 'holiday surcharges'. A S$30 seaport tax is usually payable as well. You could also try Star Cruises (☎ 226 1168, fax 220 6805), at 11 Shenton Way, which has a range of cruises throughout Asia and the Pacific.

# Getting Around

## AIR
### To/From The Airport

Changi International Airport is at the eastern end of Singapore, about 20km from the city centre. Airport buses and public buses (which you catch in the basement), taxis and the more expensive limousine services run along the expressway into the city centre.

The most convenient bus is the airport shuttle service – six-seater maxicabs that will take you to your hotel (except to Le Meridien Changi, which has its own shuttle, and to hotels on Sentosa Island) or to anywhere in the CBD. The shuttle operates daily from the arrivals halls of both terminals from 7 am to 11 pm, departing every 15 minutes between 6 pm and 11 pm and every 30 minutes outside these times. It costs S$7 per person (S$5 for children), and you pay the driver. Bookings can be made at the airport-shuttle counters at the arrivals halls in both terminals.

Public bus No 36 leaves Changi airport for the city approximately every 10 minutes between 6 am and midnight. You should carry the right change (S$1.50) when you board.

As the bus approaches the city, it comes off the flyover into Raffles Blvd and then Stamford Rd. For Beach Rd, get off when you see the round towers of the Raffles City skyscraper on your right, just past the open playing fields of the Padang on your left. A half-kilometre farther along is the National Museum and the stop for Bencoolen St. The bus then continues up Penang Rd, Somerset Rd and Orchard Blvd (which all run parallel to Orchard Rd). When heading out to the airport, catch this bus on Orchard or Bras Basah Rds.

Taxis from the airport are subject to a S$3 supplementary charge on top of the metered fare, which is around S$12 to most places in the city centre. This supplementary charge only applies to taxis departing from the airport.

There's also a limousine taxi service available between 6 am and 2 am: It costs S$35 to any destination in Singapore. You can choose between a Mercedes and a London cab. There are counters in the airport arrivals area where you can book.

The easiest way to get to Singapore's second 'international' airport, Seletar airport in the north, is by taxi (around S$14).

## BUS

While the Mass Rapid Transit (MRT) system is easy and convenient to use, for door-to-door public transport it is hard to beat the buses. You rarely have to wait more than a few minutes for a bus and they will take you almost anywhere you want to go.

Bus fares are 60c (70c for air-con buses) for the first 3.2km and go up in 10c increments for every 2.4km to a maximum of S$1.20 (S$1.50 air-con). When you board the bus drop the exact money into the fare box. No change is given. Bus stops usually have fare and route information displayed, and the tourist office has brochures available. If you're confused, ask the driver!

Farecards (see Fares & Farecards under Mass Rapid Transit later in this chapter) can also be used on buses that have validator ticket machines. Put the card in the validator, select the correct fare and then retrieve your Farecard and bus ticket from the slot below.

### Tourist Buses

The 'SIA Hop-On', run by Singapore Airlines, passes Orchard Rd, Bugis Junction, Suntec City, the Colonial District, Clarke Quay, Boat Quay, Chinatown and the Botanic Gardens. It operates daily (every 30 minutes) between 8.30 am and 7 pm and runs on a continual loop. It's free if you can show a boarding pass or ticket for either Singapore Airlines or Silk Air. Other passengers pay S$5 (children S$3) for an all-day pass. Tickets can be bought either from the bus driver or from hotels, and pamphlets *(SIA Hop-On)* with bus routes and times are available from hotels and STB offices.

SINGAPORE

The Singapore Trolley is a grotesque bus made up to look like an old-fashioned tram. Its route takes in the Botanic Gardens, the Orchard Rd area, the Colonial District, CBD, Chinatown and the World Trade Centre (WTC), with the trolley stopping at all the major hotels and points of interest. It's a handy route and the bus is certainly distinctive and easy to find. All-day (from 9.40 am to 4.55 pm) tickets cost S$14.90 for adults and S$9.90 for children (the price includes a riverboat ride from Clarke Quay). You can buy tickets from the driver or from hotels.

## MASS RAPID TRANSIT

The ultramodern MRT subway system is the easiest, quickest and most comfortable way to get around Singapore. It can transport you across town in air-conditioned comfort in minutes.

The MRT was primarily designed to provide a cheap, reliable rail service from the housing estates to the city centre and industrial estates. Most of the 44km of underground track is in the inner-city area, but out towards the housing estates the MRT runs above ground. Extensions are currently under way that will create new MRT stations at Chinatown, the WTC, Clarke Quay and Little India.

The trains run from around 6 am to midnight. At peak times, trains run every three to four minutes, and off-peak every six to eight minutes.

## Fares & Farecards

You can buy a single-trip ticket or a stored-value card (called a Farecard). Single-trip tickets cost from 70c to S$1.60. Ticket machines take 10c, 20c, 50c and S$1 coins; they also give change. There are also machines that give change for S$2 notes.

Farecards cost from S$12 (plus a S$2 deposit) up to S$50 and can be purchased from the TransitLink sales offices at MRT stations, the main bus interchanges and at

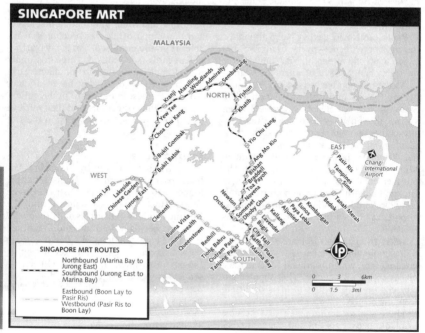

**SINGAPORE MRT**

SINGAPORE MRT ROUTES

Northbound (Marina Bay to Jurong East)
Southbound (Jurong East to Marina Bay)
Eastbound (Boon Lay to Pasir Ris)
Westbound (Pasir Ris to Boon Lay)

7-Eleven stores. Farecards can be used on buses as well as the MRT.

Another option is a tourist day-ticket, which gives you 12 rides on buses and trains for S$10 (valid for one day's travel). The tickets can be bought from MRT stations and bus interchanges.

You can also purchase special-edition souvenir tourist tickets that give you all the benefits of the Farecard for only S$7 (with a stored value of S$6), but they are only valid for the MRT and cannot be topped up. You keep the ticket as a souvenir when you return home.

## CAR

Singaporeans drive on the left-hand side of the road and it is compulsory to wear seat belts. Unlike in most Asian countries, traffic is orderly, but the profusion of one-way streets and the fact that streets change names (sometimes several times) can make driving difficult for the uninitiated. The *Singapore Street Directory* is essential for negotiating the city.

### Rental

If you want a car for local driving only, many of the smaller rental operators quote rates that are slightly cheaper than the major companies. Rental rates are more expensive here than in Malaysia, and there are expensive surcharges to take a Singaporean rental car onto the mainland. If you intend renting a car to drive in Malaysia for any length of time, it is much better to rent in Johor Bahru.

Rates start at S$150 a day, while collision damage waiver will cost about S$20 per day for a small car such as a Toyota Corolla or Mitsubishi Lancer. Special deals may be available, especially for longer-term rental. There are car-hire booths at Changi airport and in the city. Addresses of some of the main operators are:

**Avis** (☎ 737 1668) 01-01 Concorde Hotel, 317 Outram Rd
**Budget Rent a Car** (☎ 532 4442) 26-01A Clifford Centre, 24 Raffles Place
**Hertz Rent-a-Car** (☎ 734 4646) 125 Tanglin Rd
**Thrifty** (☎ 338 7900) 80 Middle Rd

## Restricted Zone & Car Parking

From 7.30 am to 6.30 pm weekdays, and from 10.15 am to 2 pm Saturdays, the area encompassing the CBD, Chinatown and Orchard Rd is a restricted zone. Cars may enter as long as they pay a surcharge. Vehicles are automatically tracked by sensors on overhanging gantries that prompt drivers to insert a cashcard into their in-vehicle unit, which then extracts the appropriate toll. The same system is also in operation on certain major highways. Rental cars are subject to the same rules.

Anyone who doesn't pay the entry toll is automatically photographed by cameras on the gantries and a fine will soon arrive at the car owner's address.

Parking in many places in Singapore works on a coupon system. You can buy a booklet of coupons at parking kiosks and post offices. You must display a coupon in your car window with holes punched out to indicate the time, day and date your car was parked.

## TAXI

Singapore has plenty of taxis. They cost S$2.40 for the first kilometre, then 10c for each additional 240m.

From midnight to 6 am there is a 50% surcharge on top of the meter fare. As mentioned earlier in the airport section, there is a surcharge of S$3 for each journey originating *from* the airport. Telephone bookings attract an extra charge ranging from S$2.80 to S$3.20 depending on which taxi company you are dealing with. There is also a S$1.50 surcharge on all trips from the CBD between 4.30 and 7 pm on weekdays and from 11.30 to 2 pm on Saturday. You may also have to pay a surcharge (see Restricted Zone & Car Parking in the Car section earlier) if you take the taxi into the CBD during restricted hours. If you pay by credit card, you pay an extra 10% of the fare.

Singapore taxi drivers are often refreshingly courteous and efficient, and the cars themselves are super-clean because drivers can be fined for driving a dirty cab. You can flag down a taxi any time on most roads and outside major shopping centres and hotels.

SINGAPORE

Look for the special taxi stands (they have signs) where you can queue for the next available taxi. You can also order a taxi by phone, a process that is computerised and extremely efficient. Dial the number and you will be asked your location and name. You then get transferred to an automatic message that tells you the number (ie, number-plate) of the cab that has been designated to you. You then wait and watch for the cab with this numberplate.

Taxi companies include:

**CityCab**
| cash bookings | ☎ 552 2222 |
| credit card bookings | ☎ 553 8888 |
| **Comfort CabLink** | ☎ 552 1111 |

## BICYCLE

Singapore's fast-moving traffic and good public transport system do not make cycling such an attractive proposition, though an increasing number of enthusiasts are regularly seen pedalling the tarmac in the outer suburbs. Cycling up to Changi Village and then taking the bike over to Pulau Ubin (see Other Islands under Things to See & Do in the Singapore chapter) is a very popular activity among expat cyclophiles. There is a great mountain-bike track encircling the base of the Bukit Timah Nature Reserve for anyone wanting to burn off a few excess kilos. (See Northern & Central Singapore under Things to See & Do in the Singapore chapter for further details on Bukit Timah.)

Bicycles can be hired at a number of places on the East Coast Parkway, but they are intended mostly for weekend jaunts along the foreshore. Mountain bikes, racers and tandems are available for around S$5 per hour. See East Coast & Changi under Things to See & Do in the Singapore chapter for details.

Bikes can also be rented on Sentosa Island and Pulau Ubin.

## TRISHAW

Singapore's bicycle trishaws are fast disappearing, although you'll find a few still operating in Chinatown and off Serangoon Rd. Trishaws had their peak just after WWII, when motorised transport was almost nonexistent and trishaw riders could make a very healthy income. Today there are only around 300 trishaws left in Singapore, and they are mainly used for local shopping trips or to transport articles that are too heavy to carry. They rarely venture onto Singapore's heavily trafficked main streets.

The trishaws tend to congregate in large numbers in the pedestrian mall at the junction of Waterloo and Albert Sts, at the northern end of the colonial district. You can also usually find them outside major hotels such as Raffles. Always agree on the fare beforehand: Expect to pay around S$25 for half an hour. Trishaw tours of Chinatown and Little India are run from a number of the larger hotels.

## BOAT & FERRY

You can charter a *bumboat* (motorised sampan) to take a tour up the Singapore River or to go to the islands around Singapore. There are regular ferry services from the WTC to Sentosa and the other southern islands, and from Changi Village to Pulau Ubin. You can also take river cruises, or boat cruises around the harbour – see the Organised Tours section later for details.

## WALKING

Getting around the old areas of Singapore on foot has one small problem – apart from the heat and humidity that is. The problem is the 'five-foot-ways'. A five-foot-way, which takes its name from the fact that it is roughly five feet wide, is the walkway at the front of traditional Chinese shophouses that are usually enclosed, verandah-like.

The difficulty with them is that every shop's walkway is individual. It may well be higher or lower than the shop next door or closer to or farther from the street. Walking thus becomes a constant up-and-down and side-to-side business, further complicated by the fact that half the shops seem to overflow right across the walkways (forcing you to venture into the street) and bikes or motorcycles are parked across the walkways.

## ORGANISED TOURS

A wide variety of tours can be booked at the desks of big hotels or through individual operators such as those listed in the *Singapore Official Guide*. Any of Singapore's travel agents can book tours for you, and you can also arrange tours through the STB offices. There are tours to the zoo, the night safari and the Jurong Bird Park (expect to pay around S$33 for an adult and S$16 for a child for the basic tour – meals are extra). There are also round-the-island tours (S$69/35 for adults/children). Other tours include Painted Faces, in which you get a behind-the-scenes look at Chinese opera; In Harmony with feng shui; and Flavours of New Asia, which takes you around Singapore's main ethnic areas, and Singapore at night. The STB offices have full details and brochures, and can make bookings.

The Singapore Trolley (see under Tourist Buses in the earlier Bus section) allows you to put together your own tour of central Singapore. It plies a set route and you can get on and off where you like.

## Special Interest Tours
Singapore-born Geraldene Lowe-Ismail has been leading walking tours of Singapore for nigh on 40 years. She's a mine of information and her tours give a unique insight into Singapore's history and culture. Geraldene charges S$80 an hour – you may be able to join a group to reduce costs. You can do walking tours of Chinatown and Little India; tours that take you to the best places for buying and viewing collectibles and antiques; culinary tours; tours of WWII sites and tours that give you an insight into Singapore's architectural heritage. She will also tailor tours to suit your particular interests. In addition to English, she conducts tours in Italian. You can contact her on ☎/fax 737 5250.

Another guide recommended for walking tours is Mabel Long (☎ 448 6957, pager 9516 3710). She also charges S$80 an hour. If you wish to contact Mabel or Geraldene, your best chance of getting hold of them is in the morning or the evening.

Subaraj Rajathurai specialises in birdwatching and nature tours, and his enthusiastic and knowledgeable guidance is highly regarded. You can contact him on ☎/fax 787 7048 or ✉ serin@swistech.com.sg.

Sonja Navakas (☎ 466 1227) of Individual Pursuits takes a variety of trips ranging from easy to challenging (the latter option including the Seven Summits of Singapore, including Telok Blangah, Mt Faber and Kent Ridge). There are also tours through Chinatown and Little India, as well as nature-oriented trips through the MacRitchie and Seletar Reservoirs. Customised trips are also an option. The trips cost around S$75 per person. For more information see the company's Web site at www.individualpursuit.com.

## Cruises
**River Cruises** One of the best ways to get a feel for central Singapore and its history is to take a river cruise. You can join a half-hour bumboat tour of the river from Clarke Quay, Raffles Landing or Boat Quay. It costs S$10 for adults (S$5 for children). The tours operate regularly between 9 am and 9 pm; at night, illuminated red Chinese lanterns hang from the boats' canopies. The recorded commentary is a bit cheesy, but the trip itself is pleasant.

**Harbour Cruises** A whole host of operators have harbour cruises departing from Clifford Pier, just east of Raffles Place. Companies offer *towkang* (Chinese junk) cruises as well as a number of lunch and dinner cruises. Most of them do the rounds of the harbour, which involves a lot of time passing oil refineries, then a cruise past Sentosa and the southern islands of St John's, Lazarus and Kusu. The short stop at Kusu is worthwhile and you will get some good views of the city and harbour.

Fairwind (☎ 533 3432) has 2½-hour tours aboard a Chinese junk. They leave at 10.30 am and 3 pm and cost S$20.60 for adults and S$10.30 for children. Watertours (☎ 533 9811) operates tours on the *Cheng Ho,* a replica of a Ming dynasty junk. They leave at 10.30 am (S$24/12 for adults/children; includes a stopover at Kusu Island) and 3 pm (S$49/25 – includes high tea and a Kusu stopover). There are also dinner cruises.

It is also possible to charter boats – the STB can put you in touch with charter-boat operators.

SINGAPORE

# Singapore

## Orientation

Singapore is a city, an island and a country. While there are built-up, high-density areas all around the island, the main city area is in the south.

**The City** Sir Thomas Stamford Raffles (see the Facts about Singapore chapter) founded Singapore on the Singapore River, and this waterway is still very much at the heart of the city. Just south of the river mouth is the Central Business District (CBD), centred around Raffles Place. Along the river banks are the popular renovated districts of Boat Quay and Clarke Quay.

To the south-west, Chinatown adjoins the CBD, farther inland from Robinson Rd. South Bridge Rd runs through the centre of Chinatown, while New Bridge Rd farther west is the main shopping area.

To the north of the river is the colonial district, with many reminders of British rule, as well as a number of top-end hotels and shopping centres. The Raffles Hotel is on the corner of Bras Basah and Beach Rds. Between Rochor and Bras Basah Rds is the main budget accommodation area, centred on Beach Rd and Bencoolen St. Farther north are Little India, centred on Serangoon Rd, and Arab St. Both are interesting, more traditional areas.

From the colonial district, Bras Basah Rd heads north-west to become Orchard Rd, Singapore's main tourist area, with dozens of hotels, shopping complexes, restaurants and bars.

**Singapore Island** On the western side of the island, Jurong is an industrial area, but it also contains a number of tourist attractions. The east coast has some older suburbs and a major beach park, and at the far east of the island is Changi International Airport. The eastern and north-eastern parts of the island are home to some huge housing developments. The central north of the island has much of Singapore's undeveloped land and

## HIGHLIGHTS

- **Boat Quay & Clarke Quay** – an evening of alfresco dining at one (or more!) of Boat Quay's tempting restaurants and bars, or under the stars at the more family-oriented Clarke Quay

- **Zoological Gardens** – spacious, well-designed enclosures – an animal resort compared to most zoos

- **Jurong Bird Park** – beautifully landscaped gardens with a huge variety of birdlife, including some particularly talented feathered performers

- **Bukit Timah Nature Reserve** – a walk in the jungle, about as far away from the busy city as possible

- **Orchard Road** – a dazzling strip of modern delights, with shopping centres, luxury hotels, hundreds of restaurants and a profusion of nightspots

- **Botanical Gardens** – an enormous collection of diverse plant species (including thousands of orchids!) nurtured in manicured gardens, a herbarium and in primary jungle

most of the remaining forest. Points of interest include the zoo and a number of parks. The north-west is less developed, especially along the coast, which is a live firing area containing many reservoirs.

**Addresses** Unlike many cities in Asia, Singapore is well laid out, with signposted streets and logically numbered buildings. As many of the shops, businesses and residences are in high-rise buildings, addresses are often preceded by the number of the floor and then the shop or apartment number. Addresses do not quote the district or suburb. For example, 05-01 The Heeren, 260 Orchard Rd, is outlet No 01 on the 5th floor of The Heeren building.

# Things to See & Do

Singapore's greatest attraction is its ability to offer a taste of Asian culture in a small, accessible package, as well as the opportunity to pursue a range of activities.

## COLONIAL SINGAPORE

The mark of Stamford Raffles is indelibly stamped on central Singapore. His early city plans moved the business district south of the river and made the area north of the river the administrative area. This early framework remained the plan for central Singapore through generations of colonial rule and the republican years of independence. While Singapore is now a modern city, many reminders of old Singapore remain.

North of the river is colonial Singapore, where you'll still find the imposing monuments of British rule – the stone grey edifices of the City Hall, Parliament House and National Museum, the churches and Victorian architecture. Many of these buildings still serve their original purpose. The CBD is the commercial heart of Singapore, though its monuments are now the skyscrapers of modern finance. Dividing these two areas is the Singapore River, which has always been the centre of Singapore. It was the site of the first British arrivals and for a long time the main artery of Singapore's trade.

The colonial district is easily reached by Mass Rapid Transit (MRT); get off at either the City Hall or Raffles Place stations. The quickest option is to walk the short distance from the Raffles Place MRT station to Cavenagh Bridge and the Singapore River, a good starting point for a tour of the area.

### Singapore River

The river was once the thriving heart of Singapore but is now a quiet pedestrian precinct – an escape for lunchtime office workers, a weekend haunt for wedding photography sessions or the place to dine in one of the renovated terraces or *godown* (river warehouses) next to the river. The bustling activity of bumboats (small motorised boats), cranes and yelling, sweating labourers have

Half lion, half fish, the merlion is the symbol of Singapore.

all gone, and the new river front is a recreational stretch of photo opportunities and colonial restoration.

At the mouth of the river stands Singapore's symbol of tourism, the **Merlion**, a much photographed water-spouting, half-lion/half-fish statue. The small park around it is open from 7 am to 10 pm daily. Heading upstream, **Anderson Bridge** is the first of the old bridges spanning the river. The next along is **Cavenagh Bridge**, built in 1869, now for pedestrians only. It provides good access to **Empress Place**. Named in honour of Queen Victoria, Empress Place is the city's oldest pedestrian area, and is surrounded by many reminders of British rule. The **Empress Place building**, built in 1865, is an imposing Georgian structure that was once a court house and later housed a number of government offices. Most recently used as a museum, it was undergoing further refurbishment at the time of writing.

Nearby, next to the river at Raffles Landing Site, is **Raffles' Statue**, standing imperiously by the water. It's approximately in the place where Stamford Raffles first set foot on the island of Singapore.

CHRIS MELLOR

# CENTRAL SINGAPORE

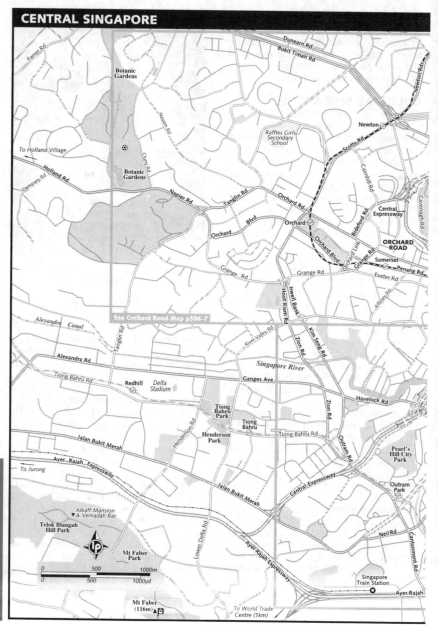

SINGAPORE

See Orchard Road Map p596-7

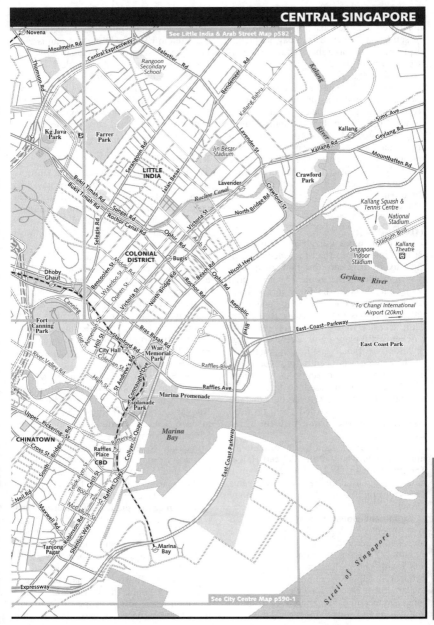

CENTRAL SINGAPORE

See Little India & Arab Street Map p582

See City Centre Map p590-1

SINGAPORE

Naturally, there are plenty of places to eat along the river, the most popular strip is on the south bank, where **Boat Quay** is a picturesque area of restored shops with soaring office buildings behind.

Crossing the river, North Boat Quay leads upriver to **Clarke Quay**. The old Clarke Quay godowns on this bend of the river have been completely rebuilt in the name of restoration. It is a popular dining spot, well stocked with eating possibilities from satay stalls to wine bars and floating restaurants on the river. The central square regularly has music and other diversions. On Sunday afternoon a market is held on Read Bridge, the pedestrian footbridge which crosses the river.

## The Padang

There is no more quizzical a symbol of British colonialism than the open field of the Padang. It is here that flannelled fools played cricket in the tropical heat, cheered on by members in the Singapore Cricket Club pavilion at one end of the Padang. At the other end is the Singapore Recreation Club, set aside for the Eurasian community. Cricket is still played at weekends, but segregation is, officially, no longer practised.

The Padang was a centre for colonial life and a place to promenade in the evenings. The Padang also witnessed the beginning of the end of colonial rule; it was here that the invading Japanese herded the European community, before marching them off to Changi Prison.

The Padang is ringed by imposing colonial buildings. The **Victoria Concert Hall & Theatre**, built in 1862, was once the town hall. It is now used for many cultural events and is the home of the Singapore Symphony Orchestra.

**Parliament House** is Singapore's oldest government building. Originally a private mansion, it became a court house, then the Assembly House of the colonial government and finally the parliament house for independent Singapore. High St, which runs next to Parliament House, was hacked from the jungle to become Singapore's first street, and was an Indian area in its early days.

The **Supreme Court** and **City Hall** are two other stoic colonial buildings on St Andrew's Rd. Built in 1939, the Supreme Court is a relatively new addition, and is notable for what it replaced – the Grand Hotel de L'Europe, which once outshone Raffles as Singapore's premier hotel. This fine building features Corinthian column murals by Italian artist Cavaliere Rodolfo Nolli. Next door, City Hall was where Lord Louis Mountbatten accepted the Japanese surrender in 1945.

## Raffles Hotel

The Raffles Hotel on Beach Rd is far more than just an expensive place to stay, and more than the best-known hotel in Singapore. It's a Singapore institution, an architectural landmark that has been classified by the government as a part of Singapore's 'cultural heritage'.

The Raffles was opened in 1887 by the Sarkies brothers, three Armenians who built a string of hotels that become famous throughout the east. They include the Strand in Yangon (Rangoon) and the E&O in Penang (see the boxed text 'The E&O Hotel' in the Penang chaptér), as well as the Raffles. It started as a 10-room bungalow, but its heyday began with the opening of the main building in 1899.

The Raffles soon became a byword for oriental luxury and featured in novels by Joseph Conrad and Somerset Maugham. Rudyard Kipling recommended it as the place to 'feed at' when in Singapore (but he advised against staying there), and in its Long Bar, Ngiam Tong Boon created the Singapore Sling cocktail in 1915 (see the boxed text 'Singapore Sling' in the 'Tastes of Malaysia, Singapore & Brunei' special section for the cocktail's recipe).

More recently, the Raffles underwent extensive renovations and extensions; it had fallen from grace and could not compete with Singapore's modern hotels. It reopened in 1991, once again a top hotel, though for some it wasn't the same old Raffles.

The **lobby** of the restored main building is open to the public (dress standards apply) and high tea is served in the Tiffin Room, though the Writers' Bar next door is little more than an alcove. In the other wings, the **Long Bar** or the **Bar & Billiard Room** are the places to sip Singapore Slings at S$18 a pop.

The Raffles Hotel Arcade is a collection of expensive shops, and hidden away on the 3rd floor is the **Raffles Hotel Museum**. It is well worth a look, especially the old postcards. Admission is free and it is open daily from 10 am to 9 pm. Raffles memorabilia, including the hotel crockery, are on sale at the museum shop. Next to the museum, **Jubilee Hall theatre** puts on various performances.

## Churches

The most imposing examples of colonial architecture between Coleman St and Bras Basah Rd are the churches.

**St Andrew's Cathedral** is Singapore's Anglican cathedral, built in Gothic style between 1856 and 1863. It's in the block surrounded by North Bridge Rd, Coleman St, Stamford Rd and St Andrew's Rd. The Catholic **Cathedral of the Good Shepherd** on Queen St is a stolid neoclassical edifice built between 1843 and 1846 and is a Singaporean historic monument.

The magnificent St Joseph's Institution, a former Catholic boy's school, is now the Singapore Art Museum (see the following entry). On the corner of Bras Basah Rd and Victoria St, the equally impressive **Convent of the Holy Infant Jesus** is now part of the Chijmes restaurant and bar complex.

The Armenian **Church of St Gregory the Illuminator** on Hill St is the oldest church in Singapore.

## Singapore Art Museum

One of Singapore's finest colonial buildings, St Joseph's Institution, near the corner of Bras Basah Rd and Queen St, has been restored and converted into this fine arts museum.

Rotating exhibits showcase modern art from Singapore and South-East Asia. Even if the art is not your cup of tea, the building is worth a look and the museum has a good cafe, Dôme, facing Queen St.

The museum is open from 9 am to 5.30 pm daily, closed Monday. Entry costs S$3 (children S$1.50).

## Fort Canning

If you continue north-west up Coleman St from the Padang, you pass the Armenian Church of St Gregory the Illuminator and come to Fort Canning Hill, a good viewpoint over Singapore. Once known as Forbidden Hill, it contains the shrine of Sultan Iskander Shah, the last ruler of the ancient kingdom of Singapura. Archaeological digs in the park have uncovered Javanese artefacts from the 14th-century Majapahit Empire.

When Stamford Raffles arrived, the only reminder of any greatness that the island may once have claimed was an earthen wall that stretched from the sea to the top of Fort Canning Hill. Raffles built his house on the top of the hill, and it became Government House until the military built Fort Canning in 1860. There is little left of the historic buildings that were once on the hill, but it is a pleasant park and you can wander around the old Christian cemetery and see the many gravestones with their poignant tales of hopeful settlers who died young.

## National Museum

North of Fort Canning on Stamford Rd, the National Museum traces its ancestry back to Raffles himself, who first suggested the idea of a museum for Singapore in 1823. The original museum opened in 1849, then moved to another location in 1862 before being re-housed in the present building in 1887.

The museum is not extensive but has substantial collections focusing on regional cultures, history and craft. It is open from 9 am to 5.30 pm and till 9 pm on Wednesday; closed Monday. Entry is S$3 for adults (S$1.50 children). The National Museum shop is nearby on Armenian St.

## Asian Civilisations Museum

Opened in 1997 this museum at 39 Armenian St features a permanent display of furniture, ceramics, jade and other arts, which trace the development of Chinese civilisation.

Opening hours and entry costs are the same as the National Museum. A museum shop is just inside the entrance.

SINGAPORE

## Singapore Philatelic Museum

Nearby, this philatelic museum has well presented rare and not-so-rare stamps from Singapore and elsewhere. It's open daily from 9 am to 4.30 pm; closed Monday and public holidays. Entry is S$2 (children S$1).

## New Bugis St

For years Bugis St was famous as Singapore's raucous transvestite playground. It was demolished during the building of the MRT, and a new, sanitised replica was constructed in its place. New Bugis St, as it's known, is just south-west of the MRT station. Although a pale shadow of its former self, it is nevertheless a pleasant place to hang out in the evening. Some of the open-air restaurants and bars stay open until 3 am, or until the last customers go home. There are fruit and food stalls, and you can pick up an imitation of an expensive watch or a T-shirt.

## Kuan Yin Temple

This temple on Waterloo St is one of the most popular Chinese temples – after all, Kuan Yin is one of the most popular goddesses. The flower sellers and fortune tellers out the front make it one of the liveliest temples in Singapore. A few doors away is **Sri Krishnan Temple**, which also attracts worshippers from the Kuan Yin Temple, who show a great deal of religious pragmatism by also burning joss sticks and offering prayers at this Hindu temple.

## Central Business District

Once the vibrant heart of Singapore, **Raffles Place** is now a rather barren patch of grass above the MRT station surrounded by the giant high-rise buildings of the CBD.

Farther south you'll find large office blocks, airline offices, shops and the **Lau Pa Sat** hawker centre. Singapore's disappearing Chinatown is inland from this modern city centre.

## ARAB ST

While Chinatown provides Singapore with a Chinese flavour and Serangoon Rd is where you head to for the tastes and smells of India, Arab St is the Muslim centre. Along this street, North Bridge Rd and side streets with Malay names like Pahang St, Aliwal St, Jalan Pisang and Jalan Sultan, you'll find batik from Indonesia and sarung, *hookahs* (water-pipes), rosaries, flower essences, *hajj* (pilgrim) caps, *songkok* hats, basketware and rattan goods.

## Walking Tour

The easiest way to begin a tour of the Arab St area is to take the MRT to the Bugis station and walk up Victoria St to Arab St.

Arab St is traditionally a textile district, and while the big merchants inhabit the textile centre on Jalan Sultan, Arab St is still alive with textile shops selling batiks, silks and more mundane cloth for a sarung or shirt. A number of craft shops sell leather bags and souvenirs, and up towards the end of Arab St near Beach Rd are the caneware shops.

**Sultan Mosque** (see the following entry), the focus for Singapore's Muslim community, is on the corner of Arab St and North Bridge Rd. It is the largest mosque in Singapore and the most lively. You'll also find good Indian Muslim food at restaurants across the street on North Bridge Rd. One street back towards the city is **Haji Lane**, a narrow picturesque lane lined with two-storey shophouses that contain a number of textile and other local businesses. Kazura, at No 51, is a traditional perfume business with rows of decanters containing perfumes such as 'Ramadan' and 'Aidal Fitri' for the faithful.

If you have time for a detour north-east along Beach Rd, the **Hajjah Fatimah Mosque** is interesting. It's a monument built around 1845 by Melakan-born Malay woman Hajjah Fatimah, on the site of her home. The architecture shows colonial influences.

Otherwise, turn back up Arab St. Heading north-east up Baghdad St from Arab St, you find more batik and craft shops. During the month of Ramadan, when Muslims fast from sunrise to sunset, the area is alive with food stalls, especially on **Bussorah St**, one block east of Arab St, where the faithful

SINGAPORE

come to buy food at dusk. Bussorah St has become the new yuppie Arab St. The old terraces have been renovated and palm trees have been planted to give that Middle Eastern 'oasis look'.

If you turn left into Sultan Gate you come to the historic gates that lead to the **Istana Kampong Glam**. The *istana* (palace) was the residence of Sultan Ali Iskander Shah and was built around 1840. The Kampong Glam area is the historic seat of the Malay royalty, resident here before the arrival of Stamford Raffles. In the early days of Singapore, it was allocated not only to the original Malays but also to Javanese, Bugis and Arab merchants and residents.

The palace is undergoing redevelopment and will re-open around 2002 as a museum. You can walk across a piece of vacant land on your left (as you are facing the palace) to Kandahar St, behind the Sultan Mosque. Muscat St winds behind the mosque back to Arab St, or you can continue up Kandahar St to North Bridge Rd. Cross over North Bridge Rd and you'll find a number of venerable Indian halal restaurants selling *roti prata* (a bread dish) and biryani.

Occupying the corner of Jalan Sultan and Victoria St, **Malabar Muslim Jama-Ath Mosque** is a beautiful little mosque covered in blue tiles, which is at its fairy-tale best when lit up in the evenings during Ramadan. Behind it is the old **Kampong Glam cemetery**, where it's said that the Malay royalty is buried among the frangipani trees and coconut palms. Many of the graves have fallen into ruin, but more recent graves are tended, evidenced by cloths placed over the headstones.

## Sultan Mosque

The Sultan Mosque on North Bridge Rd near Arab St is the biggest mosque in Singapore. It was originally built in 1825 with the aid of a grant from Stamford Raffles and the East India Company as a result of Raffles' treaty with the sultan of Johor. A hundred years later, the original mosque was replaced by a magnificent gold-domed building. The mosque is open to visitors from 5 am to 8.30 pm daily; if you can manage it, the best time to visit is during a religious ceremony.

## LITTLE INDIA

Although Singapore is a predominantly Chinese city, it does have its minority groups and the Indians are probably the most visible, particularly in the colourful streets of Little India along Serangoon Rd. This is an area, like Chinatown, in which you can simply wander around and take in the flavours. Indeed, around Serangoon Rd it can be very much a case of following your nose because the heady aroma of Indian spices and cooking seems to be everywhere.

If you want a new sari, a pair of Indian sandals, a recent issue of *India Today* or the *Indian Movie News,* a tape of Indian music or a framed portrait of your favourite Hindu god, then Little India is the place to go.

### Walking Tour

Little India is pretty compact – you can sample its sights, scents and sounds in an hour or two. Sunday is the big day in Little India, when the temples are buzzing and hundreds of Indian men and Bangladeshi immigrant workers come out to socialise, milling around the streets arm-in-arm or squatting by the side of the road to chat.

The **Zhujiao Centre** on Serangoon Rd near Buffalo Rd is Little India's market. It was known as the KK market (Kandang Kerbau, meaning 'cattle pens', as this was once a cattle-holding area) before it was rehoused in this modern building. Downstairs is a 'wet market', the Singaporean term for a produce market; this is one of the liveliest local markets in Singapore, selling all types of fruit and vegetables as well as meat and fish. The hawker centre here has plenty of Indian food stalls. Upstairs, stalls sell a variety of clothes and everyday goods, and you can also buy brassware and Indian textiles.

Across Serangoon Rd, the **Little India Arcade** has its fair share of tourist-oriented souvenir shops, but manages to maintain the traditional atmosphere of Little India, with Indian textile, grocery and flower shops. From here wander around the backstreets with the names of imperial India, such as

SINGAPORE

# LITTLE INDIA & ARAB STREET

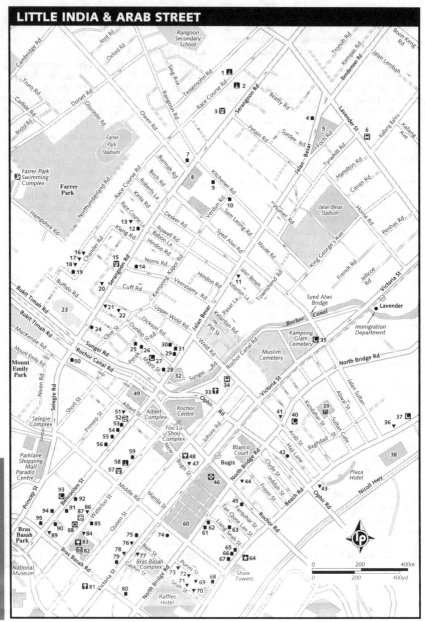

SINGAPORE

# LITTLE INDIA & ARAB STREET

## PLACES TO STAY

| | |
|---|---|
| 4 | Cactus Hotel |
| 7 | Fortuna Hotel |
| 9 | New Park Centra Singapore |
| 10 | Tai Hoe Hotel |
| 12 | Broadway Hotel; Delhi |
| 14 | Little India Guest House |
| 19 | Kerbau Hotel |
| 25 | Madras Hotel |
| 26 | Perak Lodge |
| 28 | Mayo Inn |
| 29 | Haising Hotel |
| 30 | Dickson Court Hotel |
| 31 | Boon Wah Hotel |
| 45 | New 7th Storey Hotel |
| 50 | Albert Court Hotel |
| 53 | Summer View Hotel; D'Lemon Tree Thai Kitchen & Cafe |
| 54 | Hawaii Hostel; Harharah Travel |
| 55 | Goh's Homestay; Airpower Travel |
| 59 | South East Asia Hotel |
| 60 | Hotel Inter-Continental |
| 61 | Waffle's Homestay |
| 62 | Ah Chew Hotel/Homestay |
| 63 | Season Homestay |
| 65 | Beach Hotel |
| 66 | Park View Hotel |
| 67 | Lee Travellers Club |
| 68 | Shang Onn Hotel |
| 75 | Allson Hotel |
| 79 | Victoria Hotel |
| 80 | Carlton Hotel |
| 85 | Waterloo Hostel |
| 90 | City Bayview Hotel |
| 91 | San Wah Hotel |
| 92 | Peony Mansions; Peony Latin House; Peony Mansion Travellers' Lodge; Lee Boarding House |

| | |
|---|---|
| 94 | Hotel Bencoolen |
| 95 | Hotel Rendezvous |

## PLACES TO EAT

| | |
|---|---|
| 5 | Lavender Food Centre |
| 11 | Berseh Food Centre |
| 13 | No Signboard Seafood |
| 16 | Delhi Restaurant |
| 17 | Banana Leaf Apolo |
| 18 | D'Deli Pubb & Restaurant |
| 20 | Madras Woodlands Ganga |
| 21 | Komala Vilas |
| 22 | Madras New Woodlands |
| 36 | Golden Mile Food Centre |
| 41 | Zam Zam; Victory Restaurant |
| 43 | Bangles |
| 44 | Food Centre; Bak Kut Teh Stall |
| 47 | New Bugis St |
| 51 | Wing Seong Fatty's (Albert) Restaurant |
| 69 | Yet Con |
| 70 | Imperial Herbal |
| 71 | Soup Restaurant |
| 72 | Kimchi |
| 73 | Yhingthai |
| 76 | Hawker Centre |
| 77 | Xiang Man Lou Food Court |
| 78 | Victoria St Food Court |
| 84 | Nan Tai Eating House |
| 86 | Indochine al Fresco Café |
| 89 | Kopitiam |

## OTHER

| | |
|---|---|
| 1 | Leong San See Temple |
| 2 | Temple of 1000 Lights |
| 3 | Sri Srinivasa Perumal Temple |
| 6 | Lavender St Bus Station |
| 8 | Mustafa Centre |
| 15 | Sri Veeramakaliamman Temple |

| | |
|---|---|
| 23 | Zhujiao Centre; Wet Market; Hawker Centre |
| 24 | Little India Arcade; Shops; Food Stalls; Taj Jazzaurant |
| 27 | Abdul Gaffor Mosque |
| 32 | Sim Lim Tower |
| 33 | Church of Our Lady of Lourdes |
| 34 | Queen St Bus Terminal |
| 35 | Malabar Muslim Jama-Ath Mosque |
| 37 | Hajjah Fatimah Mosque |
| 38 | Concourse Shopping Centre |
| 39 | Istana Kampong Glam |
| 40 | Sultan Mosque |
| 42 | Kazura |
| 46 | Bugis Junction; Food Junction; Seiyu; Cold Storage Supermarket; Sketches; Coffee Bean And Tea Leaf; DeliFrance; Kinokuniya; Pacific Internet |
| 48 | Boom Boom Room |
| 49 | Sim Lim Square; Tenco Food Centre; Computer Shops |
| 52 | Cyber-Action |
| 57 | Sri Krishnan Temple |
| 58 | Kuan Yin Temple |
| 64 | Central Police Station |
| 74 | Thrifty |
| 81 | Cathedral of the Good Shepherd |
| 82 | Singapore Art Museum; Dôme |
| 83 | Hu'u Bar |
| 87 | Action Theatre |
| 88 | Maghain Aboth Synagogue |
| 93 | Bencoolen Mosque |

Clive, Hastings and Campbell. This is the heart of Little India, with a variety of shops selling spices, Indian music tapes, saris, religious artefacts and everyday goods for the Indian household. Dunlop St in particular maintains much of its old-fashioned charm.

Apart from the ubiquitous gold shops, there are a couple of interesting **jewellers** on Serangoon and Buffalo Rds that make jewellery crafted with traditional designs.

At the southern end of Race Course Rd is the best collection of non-vegetarian eater-

ies in Singapore, from the tandoori food of North India to Singapore's famous fish-head curry, which sounds and looks terrible, but tastes delicious.

On the corner of Belilios and Serangoon Rds is the **Sri Veeramakaliamman Temple**, a Shivaite temple dedicated to Kali.

Farther north-east along Serangoon Rd is the **Mustafa Centre**, which is a good place to hunt for reasonably priced electrical and electronic items. Also in this area, in the alleyways behind Desker Rd, are the infamous brothels. Rows of blockhouse rooms line the alley with women standing in doorways while a constant stream of men wander past. Outside, hawkers sell condoms and potency pills, and makeshift tables are set up with card games to gamble on.

In complete contrast, the **Sri Srinivasa Perumal Temple** is a large temple dedicated to Vishnu. The temple dates from 1855 but the impressive *gopuram* (tower) is a relatively recent addition, built in 1966. Inside the temple, you will find a statue of Vishnu and his consorts, Lakshmi and Andal, as well as his bird-mount Garuda. This temple is the starting point for devotees who make the walk to the Chettiar Hindu Temple during the Thaipusam festival (see Chettiar Hindu Temple in the following Orchard Rd section).

Not far from the Sri Srinivasa Perumal Temple is the **Temple of 1000 Lights** (see the following entry). It's a glitzy, slightly tacky Thai-influenced temple, but one of Singapore's best known, and it welcomes visitors. A more beautiful temple is the **Leong San See Temple** over the road. This Buddhist and Taoist temple has some fine ceramic carvings inside.

From Little India, you can wander across to **Jalan Besar**. The Indian influence is not so noticeable here; the fine old pastel-coloured terraces with intricate stucco and tiles are Peranakan in style. Of particular note are the terraces on Petain Rd, and those on the corner of Plumer Rd and Jalan Besar.

A number of traditional businesses are on and around Jalan Besar, and the area around Kelantan and Pasar Lanes is a place to look for antiques. On Sunday there's a flea market selling everything from old shoes and computer chips to motorcycle parts, and if you rummage around you can find old coins, porcelain and brassware.

Just off Jalan Besar on Dunlop St, down towards Rochor Canal Rd, is the **Abdul Gaffoor Mosque**. It's an intriguing fairytale blend of Arab and Victorian architecture.

## Temple of 1000 Lights

Towards the north-eastern end of Race Course Rd at No 366, close to the corner of Serangoon and Beatty Rds, is the Sakaya Muni Buddha Gaya Temple, or the Temple of 1000 Lights. This Buddhist temple is dominated by a brightly painted 15m-tall seated figure of Buddha. The temple was inspired by a Thai monk named Vutthisasara. Although it is a Thai-style temple, it's actually very Chinese in its technicolour decoration.

Apart from the Buddha image, the temple has a huge mother-of-pearl footprint, complete with the 108 auspicious marks that distinguish a Buddha foot from any other 2m-long foot. It's said to be a replica of the footprint on top of Adam's Peak in Sri Lanka.

Inside the giant statue is a smaller image of the reclining Buddha in the act of entering nirvana. You can access the interior via a door in the back of the statue. Around the base, models tell the story of Buddha's life, and, of course, there are the 1000 electric lights that give the temple its name.

## ORCHARD RD

Singapore's international tourists and its wealthy residents also have whole areas of Singapore to themselves. Orchard Rd is where high-class hotels predominate, and north-west of this busy thoroughfare you enter the area of the Singapore elite. Prior to independence, the mansions of the colonial rulers were built here, and today the wealthy of Singapore, as well as many expatriates, live in these fine old houses.

Orchard Rd itself is mostly a place to shop, eat and stay. Its rows of modern shopping centres hold a variety of shops selling everything from the latest Japanese gadgets to the antiques of the East. Here you'll also find most of Singapore's international hotels, many nightspots, and a host of restaurants, bars and lounges. It's a showcase for modern Singapore and the delights of capitalism, but it also has a few points of cultural interest for which you don't need a credit card.

### Peranakan Place

Among the glass and chrome is Peranakan Place, a complex of old Baba-Nyonya shophouses on the corner of Orchard and Emerald Hill Rds. The **Peranakan Show-**

house Museum is a shophouse filled with artefacts, furniture and clothing which, if traditional Straits Chinese culture interests you, shouldn't be missed. The museum is in a terrace house a few doors north of Orchard Rd. Tours of the museum are available Monday to Friday from 10 am to 3 pm (S$10 adults, S$5 children).

From Peranakan Place wander north up Emerald Hill Rd, where some fine terrace houses remain. This whole area was once a nutmeg plantation owned by William Cuppage, an early Singapore settler. Around 1900, much of it was subdivided, and it became a fashionable residential area for Peranakan and Straits-born Chinese merchants. Today it is a fashionable drinking spot with some good bars.

Peranakan Place is just north of Somerset MRT station.

### Istana
The Istana is the home of Singapore's president and is also used by the prime minister for ceremonial occasions. Formerly Government House, the Istana is set about 750m back from the road in large grounds. The closest you are likely to get to it is the well-guarded gates on Orchard Rd, but the Istana is open to the public on selected public holidays, such as New Year's Day. If you are lucky enough to be in Singapore on one of these days, take your passport for identification and join the queues to get in.

### House of Tan Yeok Nee
On the corner of Clemenceau Ave and Penang Rd, just south of Orchard Rd, the House of Tan Yeok Nee was built in 1885 as a townhouse for a prosperous merchant in a style then common in the south of China. This national monument was the Salvation Army headquarters for many years. It is now awaiting renovation and is closed to the public.

### Chettiar Hindu Temple
On Tank Rd at the intersection of River Valley Rd, not far from Orchard Rd, this temple was completed in 1984 and replaces a much earlier temple built by Indian *chettiar*

(money lenders). It is a Shivaite temple dedicated to the six-headed Lord Subramaniam, and is at its most active during the Thaipusam festival, when the procession ends here. Worshippers make offerings of coconuts, which are smashed on the ground.

## CHINATOWN
Singapore's cultural heart is Chinatown, providing a glimpse of the old ways – the ways of the Chinese immigrants that shaped and built modern Singapore.

Many buildings in this area have been demolished and redeveloped over the last 30 years, though the greatest changes have occurred since around 1990.

Chinatown is still a good place to wander around. Though many of the traditional crafts and businesses have gone, it contains some of Singapore's most notable temples and there are plenty of eating and shopping possibilities.

### Walking Tour
You can start a Chinatown walking tour from the Raffles Place MRT station in the CBD. From the station, wander west along Chulia St and south down Philip St to the Wak Hai Cheng Bio Temple. This Teochew Taoist temple has some interesting scenes depicted under, and on top of, the roof of the main temple.

Continue down Philip St and over Church St to Telok Ayer St. Until relatively recently this area was a clamouring district of traditional business, but the blocks around Pekin and Cross Sts have been redeveloped and restored, and now house restaurants and shops.

At the junction with Boon Tat St, you'll find the Nagore Durgha Shrine, an old mosque built by Muslims from south India during 1829 and 1830. Just a little southwest down the street is the Chinese Thian Hock Keng Temple, or Temple of Heavenly Happiness, one of the most interesting temples in Singapore.

Continue walking along Telok Ayer St and you'll soon come to the Al-Abrar Mosque, which was originally built in 1827 and rebuilt in its present form from 1850 to 1855.

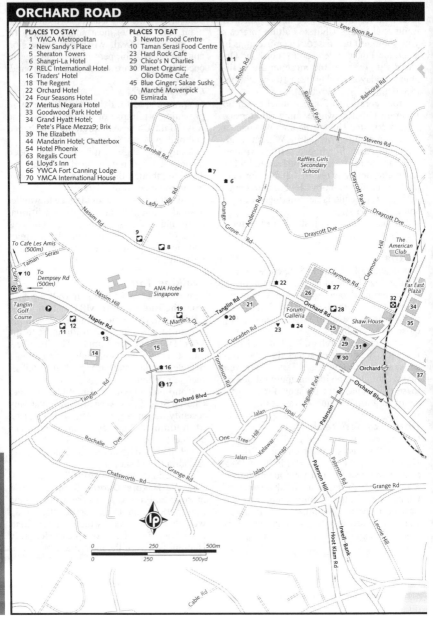

# ORCHARD ROAD

**PLACES TO STAY**
1 YMCA Metropolitan
2 New Sandy's Place
5 Sheraton Towers
6 Shangri-La Hotel
7 RELC International Hotel
16 Traders' Hotel
18 The Regent
22 Orchard Hotel
24 Four Seasons Hotel
27 Meritus Negara Hotel
33 Goodwood Park Hotel
34 Grand Hyatt Hotel;
  Pete's Place Mezza9; Brix
39 The Elizabeth
44 Mandarin Hotel; Chatterbox
54 Hotel Phoenix
63 Regalis Court
64 Lloyd's Inn
66 YWCA Fort Canning Lodge
70 YMCA International House

**PLACES TO EAT**
3 Newton Food Centre
10 Taman Serasi Food Centre
23 Hard Rock Cafe
29 Chico's N Charlies
30 Planet Organic;
  Olio Dôme Cafe
45 Blue Ginger; Sakae Sushi;
  Marché Movenpick
60 Esmirada

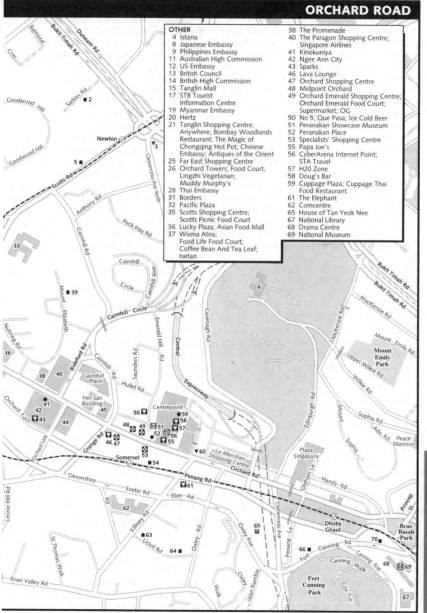

## ORCHARD ROAD

**OTHER**

4 Istana
8 Japanese Embassy
9 Philippines Embassy
11 Australian High Commission
12 US Embassy
13 British Council
14 British High Commission
15 Tanglin Mall
17 STB Tourist
Information Centre
19 Myanmar Embassy
20 Hertz
21 Tanglin Shopping Centre;
Anywhere; Bombay Woodlands
Restaurant; The Magic of
Chongqing Hot Pot; Chinese
Embassy; Antiques of the Orient
25 Far East Shopping Centre
26 Orchard Towers; Food Court;
Lingzhi Vegetarian;
Muddy Murphy's
28 Thai Embassy
31 Borders
32 Pacific Plaza
35 Scotts Shopping Centre;
Scotts Picnic Food Court
36 Lucky Plaza; Asian Food Mall
37 Wisma Atria;
Food Life Food Court;
Coffee Bean And Tea Leaf;
Isetan

38 The Promenade
40 The Paragon Shopping Centre;
Singapore Airlines
41 Kinokuniya
42 Ngee Ann City
43 Sparks
46 Lava Lounge
47 Orchard Shopping Centre
48 Midpoint Orchard
49 Orchard Emerald Shopping Centre;
Orchard Emerald Food Court;
Supermarket; OG
50 No 5; Que Pasa; Ice Cold Beer
51 Peranakan Showcase Museum
52 Peranakan Place
53 Specialists' Shopping Centre
55 Papa Joe's
56 CyberArena Internet Point;
STA Travel
57 H2O Zone
58 Doug's Bar
59 Cuppage Plaza; Cuppage Thai
Food Restaurant
61 The Elephant
62 Comcentre
65 House of Tan Yeok Nee
67 National Library
68 Drama Centre
69 National Museum

SINGAPORE

A right turn and then another right turn will bring you into **Amoy St**, a Hokkien area that once catered to sailors and the sea trade. This street has been almost totally modernised.

Continue north-east up Amoy St and turn left (north-west) up Cross St to Club St. The quiet area around Club St, Ann Siang Rd and Ann Siang Hill was a clove and nutmeg plantation until it became a prime residential area for Hokkien merchants. This area was noted for its highly decorated terraces, a number of which housed the old Chinese guilds, though only a few remain now. **Ann Siang Hill** in particular has some fine terrace houses, both restored and untouched.

Farther south, South Bridge Rd becomes Neil Rd. The region between Neil and Tanjong Pagar Rds is the **Tanjong Pagar** conservation area, the first major restoration project in Chinatown. In this area, beautifully restored terraces accommodate a variety of restaurants and bars. The old Jinrikisha station right on the corner of Neil and Tanjong Pagar Rds, now a restaurant, is an interesting triangular building that was once a depot for the hand-pulled rickshaws.

South-west of Tanjong Pagar, the **Bukit Pasoh area** is a traditional part of Chinatown. Bukit Pasoh Rd is known as the street of the clans because of the many clan association houses here. Keong Saik Rd is a curving street of old terraces with coffee shops, clan houses and clubs.

Heading back to the centre of Chinatown, north-east up to South Bridge Rd, you enter the **Kreta Ayer district**, the real heart of the area. The street hawkers and many of the traditional businesses have gone, but some of the old atmosphere of Chinatown remains. The Chinatown Complex, on the corner of Trengganu and Smith Sts, is a lively local shopping centre and a popular meeting place outside in the cool of the evening. Along with Smith St, Temple, Pagoda and Mosque Sts are traditionally the heart of old Chinatown, but new developments have destroyed a lot of the atmosphere and most of Pagoda St has been renovated. Smith St has gold, jade, souvenir and traditional medicine shops. The whole area has plenty of old and new souvenir and trinket shops selling masks, reproduction bronzes, bamboo ware, carvings and silk garments. Bargain hard.

Also in this area is the **Sri Mariamman Temple**, Singapore's oldest Hindu temple (see its entry in this section). The **Jamae (or Chulia) Mosque** on South Bridge Rd is only a short distance from the Sri Mariamman Temple. It was built by Indian Muslims from the Coromandel Coast of Tamil Nadu between 1830 and 1855.

Across New Bridge Rd from Pagoda St is the huge **People's Park Complex**, a modern shopping centre with much more local appeal than the Orchard Rd centres.

Farther north-east along Eu Tong Sen St is the former **Tong Chai Medical Institute**. The magnificent building, a national monument, now houses a nightclub. To finish off the walk, and perhaps quench your thirst with a beer (well deserved of course), head east along North Canal Rd until you hit Boat Quay's bars and restaurants, a 10-minute walk from here.

## Thian Hock Keng Temple

The Temple of Heavenly Happiness on Telok Ayer St in Chinatown is one of the most colourful temples in Singapore. The temple was originally built in 1840 and dedicated to Ma-Cho-Po, the queen of heaven and protector of sailors.

At that time it was on the waterfront and, since many Chinese settlers were arriving by sea, it was inevitable that a joss house be built where they could offer thanks for a safe voyage. As you wander through the courtyards of the temple, look for the rooftop dragons, the intricately decorated beams, the burning joss sticks, the gold-leafed panels and, best of all, the beautifully painted doors.

## Sri Mariamman Temple

The Sri Mariamman Temple on South Bridge Rd, right in the heart of Chinatown, is the oldest Hindu temple in Singapore. It was built in 1827 but rebuilt in 1862. With its colourful *gopuram* (tower) over the entrance gate, this is clearly a temple in the South Indian Dravidian style. A superb collection of colourfully painted Hindu figures decorate the gopuram.

Around October each year, the temple is the scene for the Thimithi festival, during which devotees walk barefoot over burning coals – supposedly feeling no pain (spectators report that quite a few hotfoot it over the final few steps).

## EAST COAST & CHANGI

East Coast Park is a popular recreational haunt for Singaporeans. It is the place to swim, windsurf, lie on the sand, rent a bike or, of course, eat. The stretch of beach along the south-east coast, south of the East Coast Parkway expressway, was born of reclaimed land and won't win any awards as a tropical paradise, but it is by far Singapore's most popular beach and has good recreational facilities.

Farther inland are the interesting areas of Geylang and Katong, largely Malay districts, which are rarely visited by foreign tourists. Geylang is as close to a 'Little Malaysia' as you'll find; and Katong, centred on East Coast Rd, has Peranakan influences and interesting dining possibilities.

Changi is known for its famous airport and infamous prison, both attractions in their own right, while farther out is Changi Village and its nearby beach.

### Geylang

If you want to experience Malaysia, the real thing is just across the Causeway. However, there are Malay areas in Singapore, though Malay culture is not so obvious nor easily marketed as a tourist attraction.

Geylang Serai is a Malay residential area, though you are not going to see traditional *atap* (thatch-roofed) houses and sarung-clad cottage industry workers. The area has plenty of newer high-rise buildings, though there are some older buildings around, especially in the *lorong* (alleys) that run off Geylang Rd. These lorong house one of Singapore's most active red-light districts.

Geylang Serai is easily reached by taking the MRT to the Paya Lebar station. From here it is a short walk south down Tanjong Katong Rd to Geylang Rd, the main shopping street.

A short walk east along Geylang Rd will bring you to the **Malay Cultural Village**. This complex of traditional Malay-style houses was built as a showpiece of native culture, though it hasn't really taken off as a tourist attraction. On weekends it does attract Singaporean families seeking *kampung* (village) nostalgia, but it is very quiet during the week. Admission is S$5 for adults (S$3 children), and it's open daily from 10 am to 10 pm. The Cultural Museum has a display on weaving, *kris* (traditional swords), kitchen items, and a display on traditional weddings, with a bridal chamber included. The Kampong Days display is in a separate building where waxwork figures and various artefacts are employed to create pictures of a typical kampung community in the 1950s and 1960s.

Just next door to the cultural village is the **Geylang Serai Market**. It's hidden behind some older-style housing blocks on Geylang Rd, and entrance is through a small laneway that leads to a crowded, traditional Asian market that hasn't yet been rebuilt as a concrete box. It's a good place to browse and much more interesting than most of Singapore's new markets. It reaches its peak of activity during Ramadan, when the whole area is alive with market stalls that set up in the evenings to cater for the faithful after their long day of fasting.

### Katong

From the Geylang Serai Market you can head down Joo Chiat Rd to the East Coast Rd and explore the Katong district. **Joo Chiat Rd** has a host of local businesses operating during the day, and at night the restaurants and music lounges are popular. Despite some restoration, the streetscape has largely escaped the developer; fine Peranakan-style terraces and some of old Singapore's atmosphere remains.

On Koon Seng Rd, just west around the corner from Joo Chiat Rd, are some of the finest **terrace houses** in Singapore. They exhibit the typical Peranakan love of ornate design and are decorated with plaster stucco dragons, birds, crabs and brilliantly glazed tiles. *Pintu pagar* (saloon doors) at the front

# CITY CENTRE

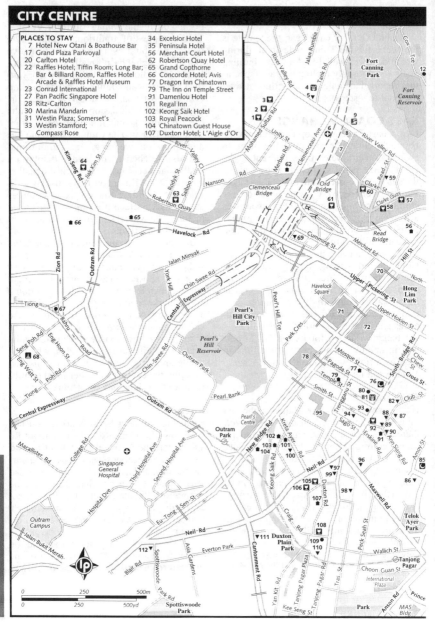

**PLACES TO STAY**
7 Hotel New Otani & Boathouse Bar
17 Grand Plaza Parkroyal
20 Carlton Hotel
22 Raffles Hotel; Tiffin Room; Long Bar;
Bar & Billiard Room, Raffles Hotel
Arcade & Raffles Hotel Museum
23 Conrad International
27 Pan Pacific Singapore Hotel
28 Ritz-Carlton
30 Marina Mandarin
31 Westin Plaza; Somerset's
33 Westin Stamford;
Compass Rose

34 Excelsior Hotel
35 Peninsula Hotel
56 Merchant Court Hotel
62 Robertson Quay Hotel
65 Grand Copthorne
66 Concorde Hotel; Avis
77 Dragon Inn Chinatown
79 The Inn on Temple Street
91 Damenlou Hotel
101 Regal Inn
102 Keong Saik Hotel
103 Royal Peacock
104 Chinatown Guest House
107 Duxton Hotel; L'Aigle d'Or

SINGAPORE

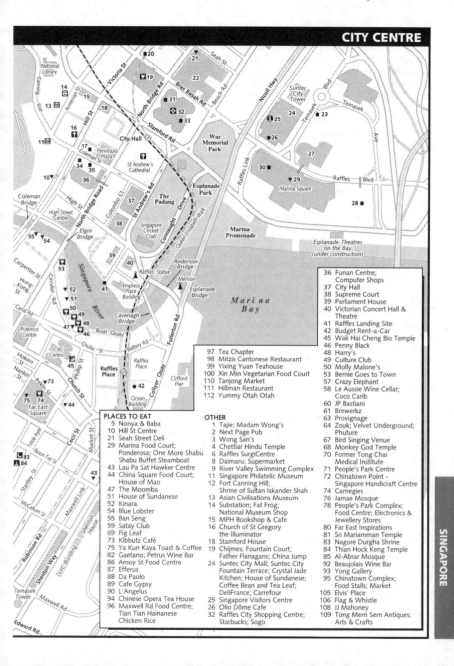

**CITY CENTRE**

**SINGAPORE**

**PLACES TO EAT**
5 Nonya & Baba
10 Hill St Centre
21 Seah Street Deli
29 Marina Food Court;
   Ponderosa; One More Shabu
   Shabu Buffet Steamboat
43 Lau Pa Sat Hawker Centre
44 China Square Food Court;
   House of Mao
47 The Moomba
51 House of Sundanese
52 Kinara
54 Blue Lobster
55 Ban Seng
59 Satay Club
69 Fig Leaf
73 Kibbutz Café
75 Ya Kun Kaya Toast & Coffee
82 Gaetano; Petrus Wine Bar
86 Amoy St Food Centre
87 Efferus
88 Da Paolo
89 Cafe Gypsy
90 L'Angelus
94 Chinese Opera Tea House
96 Maxwell Rd Food Centre;
   Tian Tian Hainanese
   Chicken Rice

97 Tea Chapter
98 Mitzis Cantonese Restaurant
99 Yixing Yuan Teahouse
100 Xin Min Vegetarian Food Court
110 Tanjong Market
111 Hillman Restaurant
112 Yummy Otah Otah

**OTHER**
1 Tajie; Madam Wong's
2 Next Page Pub
3 Wong San's
4 Chettiar Hindu Temple
6 Raffles SurgiCentre
8 Daimaru; Supermarket
9 River Valley Swimming Complex
11 Singapore Philatelic Museum
12 Fort Canning Hill;
   Shrine of Sultan Iskander Shah
13 Asian Civilisations Museum
14 Substation; Fat Frog;
   National Museum Shop
15 MPH Bookshop & Cafe
16 Church of St Gregory
   the Illuminator
18 Stamford House
19 Chimes; Fountain Court;
   Father Flanagans; China Jump
24 Suntec City Mall; Suntec City
   Fountain Terrace; Crystal Jade
   Kitchen; House of Sundanese;
   Coffee Bean and Tea Leaf;
   DeliFrance; Carrefour
25 Singapore Visitors Centre
26 Olio Dôme Cafe
32 Raffles City Shopping Centre;
   Starbucks; Sogo

36 Funan Centre;
   Computer Shops
37 City Hall
38 Supreme Court
39 Parliament House
40 Victorian Concert Hall &
   Theatre
41 Raffles Landing Site
42 Budget Rent-a-Car
45 Wak Hai Cheng Bio Temple
46 Penny Black
47 Harry's
49 Culture Club
50 Molly Malone's
53 Bernie Goes to Town
57 Crazy Elephant
58 Le Aussie Wine Cellar;
   Coco Carib
60 JP Bastiani
61 Brewerkz
63 Provignage
64 Zouk; Velvet Underground;
   Phuture
67 Bird Singing Venue
68 Monkey God Temple
70 Former Tong Chai
   Medical Institute
71 People's Park Centre
72 Chinatown Point -
   Singapore Handicraft Centre
74 Carnegies
76 Jamae Mosque
78 People's Park Complex;
   Food Centre; Electronics &
   Jewellery Stores
80 Far East Inspirations
81 Sri Mariamman Temple
83 Nagore Durgha Shrine
84 Thian Hock Keng Temple
85 Al-Abrar Mosque
92 Beaujolais Wine Bar
93 Yong Gallery
95 Chinatown Complex;
   Food Stalls; Market
105 Elvis' Place
106 Flag & Whistle
108 JJ Mahoney
109 Tong Mern Sern Antiques;
   Arts & Crafts

of the house are another typical feature – letting in the breeze while retaining privacy.

Farther south, Joo Chiat Rd runs into **East Coast Rd**, a well-to-do, 'village' shopping stretch that is the centre of Katong. Before land reclamation moved the beach, Katong was a quiet village by the sea. Now East Coast Rd bustles with city traffic and Singapore's modern developments have engulfed the east coast. Despite this, Katong retains its delightful village atmosphere.

It is worth wandering the back-streets of Katong around Joo Chiat and East Coast Rds, where you'll find more terraces, coffee shops and temples. Just off East Coast Rd on Ceylon Rd is the **Hindu Senpaga Vinayagar Temple**, and about 1km away on Wilkinson St is a Sikh temple, **Sri Guru Nanak Sat Sangh Sabha**.

East Coast Rd changes its name to Mountbatten Rd as it heads into the city and crosses Tanjong Katong Rd, which leads back to Geylang and the Paya Lebar MRT station. This area contains a number of grand old villas. Mountbatten Rd also has some fine old houses.

**Parkway Parade**, a huge shopping centre on Marine Parade, is near the end of Joo Chiat Rd. The East Coast Park and seaside is just behind it, but you have to cross the East Coast Parkway expressway – take a taxi.

From East Coast Rd, bus Nos 12 and 32 head into the city along North Bridge Rd in the colonial district, while bus No 14 goes down Stamford Rd and then Orchard Rd.

### East Coast Park

Stretching along Singapore's south-east coast on reclaimed land, East Coast Park comes alive on the weekends with Singaporeans relaxing by the beach, eating at seafood outlets or indulging in more strenuous sporting activities. The foreshore parkland has a track running right along the coast for bicycling, jogging or rollerblading, and you can hire bicycles, canoes and sailboards. The beach is reasonable, with a continuous sandy stretch and calm waters, though like all of Singapore's beaches the water is hardly crystal clear.

The **Singapore Crocodilarium** is at 730 East Coast Parkway and has a large number of crocodiles crammed into concrete tanks. It's open daily from 9 am to 5 pm, and admission costs S$2 for adults and S$1 for children.

The **Europa Sailing Club** (☎ 449 5118) is a private club that rents sailboards to the public for S$20.60 for the first two hours and S$10 for each subsequent hour. Bicycles and canoes can also be hired at the kiosk near the seafood centre.

The only bus is No 401, operating from Bedok MRT station along the service road in the park on Sunday and public holidays. All other buses whizz by on the East Coast Parkway expressway so you'll have to catch a taxi.

### Changi Prison Museum

On Upper Changi Rd is a museum dedicated to the memory of those who did time as POWs during WWII. Nearby is a poignant replica of the simple thatched prison chapel built and used by Allied prisoners of war during their horrific internment at the hands of the Japanese. Pinned to the chapel are notes from those who lost loved ones in Changi. The museum features drawings made by the prisoners depicting life in Changi, as well as photographs and other exhibits providing an overview of the war in Asia. The museum is open Monday to Saturday from 9.30 am to 4.30 pm, though you can visit the chapel outside these hours.

You can get here on bus No 2 from Victoria St in the colonial district.

### Changi Village

The village of Changi, on the east coast of Singapore, is an escape from the hubbub of central Singapore. Don't expect to find traditional kampung houses – the buildings are modern – but Changi does have a village atmosphere. Changi's beach is not exactly a tropical paradise, but it has a good stretch of sand and offers safe swimming. It's popular on weekends but almost deserted during the week. The food in Changi is an attraction, and there are some good seafood restaurants and food stalls near the beach.

SINGAPORE

From Changi, you can catch ferries to Pulau Ubin (see the Other Islands section later in this chapter). Ferries also go to Pengerang across the strait in Malaysia (see the Singapore Getting There & Away chapter).

You can reach Changi on bus No 2 from Victoria St in the colonial district; it also passes Changi Prison.

## NORTHERN & CENTRAL SINGAPORE

Singapore has been dubbed the 'Garden City' and with good reason; it's green and lush, with parks and gardens scattered everywhere. In part, this fertility is a factor of the climate. The government has backed up this natural advantage with a concentrated program that has even turned the dividing strip on highways into flourishing gardens – you'll notice it as you drive into Singapore from Malaysia on the Causeway.

Despite the never-ending construction, land reclamation and burgeoning Housing & Development Board (HDB) estates, Singapore has large areas of parkland and even natural forest. These areas are mostly found to the north of the city in the centre of Singapore Island.

### Botanic Gardens

Singapore's 127-year-old Botanic Gardens are on the corner of Cluny and Holland Rds, not far from Orchard Rd. They are a popular and peaceful retreat for Singaporeans.

The Botanic Gardens contain an enormous number of plant species, in both a manicured garden setting and in four hectares of primary jungle. The gardens also house the **herbarium**, where much work has been done on breeding the orchids for which Singapore is famous. The orchid enclosure contains over 12,000 orchids representing 2000 species and hybrids in total. In an earlier era, Henry Ridley, director of the gardens, successfully propagated rubber tree seeds sent from Kew Gardens (London) in 1877, after they were smuggled out of Brazil. Consequently, the Singapore Botanic Gardens pioneered the Malayan rubber boom.

The 54-hectare gardens are open daily from 5 am to midnight; admission is free. Early in the morning, you'll see hundreds of Singaporeans jogging here.

Within the Botanic Gardens is the **National Orchid Garden**, with the world's largest display of orchids featuring over 60,000 orchid plants. Admission is S$2, and it's open from 8.30 am to 7 pm.

The gardens can be reached on bus No 7 or 174, which run along Stamford Rd and Orchard Blvd, or bus No 106, which runs along Bencoolen St and Orchard Blvd.

### Bird Singing

One of the nicest things to do in Singapore is to go and hear the birds sing. The Chinese love caged birds, as their beautifully ornate birdcages indicate.

The main bird-concert venue is at the junction of Tiong Bahru and Zion Rds. It's generally busiest on Sunday morning from around 8 to 11 am, so this is a good time to visit. The coffee shop here is always well patronised.

To get there take the MRT to the Tiong Bahru station, then walk east 500m. By bus, take No 123 from Orchard Rd.

### Zoological Gardens

In the north of the island at 80 Mandai Lake Rd, Singapore's world class zoo has over 2000 animals, representing 240 species, on display in almost natural conditions. Wherever possible, moats replace bars, and the zoo is spread out over 90 hectares of lush greenery. Exhibits of particular interest are the pygmy hippos, Primate Kingdom, Wild Africa and Children's World. As well as providing a play area, Children's World includes a domesticated animals section where children can touch the animals, see Friesian-cow milking demonstrations and sheep dogs in action at the sheep roundup show.

There is a breakfast program at 9 am and high tea at 4 pm, where you are joined by one of the orang-utans. There are also animal shows and feedings at various times during the day; details are available at the entrance.

SINGAPORE

The zoo is open daily from 8.30 am to 6 pm. Entry is S$10.30 for adults (S$4.60 for children aged three to 12). A combined zoo and Night Safari ticket is S$21.60 (S$12.80), Breakfast with an Orang-utan (including zoo entry) costs S$15.45 (S$11.33) and high tea S$13 (S$10.30). To get to the zoo, take the MRT to Ang Mo Kio station, and then catch bus No 138.

**Night Safari** Not content with having an excellent zoo, Singapore also has the impressive Night Safari, on a 40-hectare site next to the zoo on secondary forest. It's open nightly from 7.30 pm to midnight, walking trails crisscross the park and allow a unique opportunity to view nocturnal animals. The park is divided into a number of habitats, focusing mostly on Asian wildlife, and special lighting picks out the animals. With 1000 animals representing 100 species, the Night Safari is not as diverse as the zoo, but wandering the trails at night is a recommended experience.

There is also a tram, with a running commentary, which loops through the park and stops near the East Lodge restaurant at the far side of the park. Noisy, camera-flashing passengers can spoil the ride, despite exhortations to keep quiet and avoid flash photography. The western side of the park is only accessible by tram. To explore all of the park, it is best to do a complete loop and then walk around the trails. The complete East Loop walking trail is 2.8km in length and will take you about an hour.

Entry costs S$15.45 for adults (S$10.30 for children). Including the tram ride, the cost is S$18.45 (S$12.30).

Transport details for the Night Safari are the same as for the zoo.

## Mandai Orchid Gardens

Singapore has a major business in cultivating orchids and the Mandai Orchid Gardens, beside the zoo on Mandai Lake Rd, is the best place to see them – four solid hectares of orchids! The gardens are open from 8.30 am to 5.30 pm daily; admission is S$2 for adults, S$0.50 for children. To get here take SBS bus No 138 from the Ang Mo Kio MRT station.

## Bukit Timah Nature Reserve

Singapore is not normally associated with nature walks and jungle treks, but they can be enjoyed at this 81-hectare nature reserve. It is the only large area of primary forest left in Singapore and is a haven for the island's wildlife. On Upper Bukit Timah Rd, 12km from the city, the reserve also boasts the highest point in Singapore, the 162m-high Bukit Timah itself .

The reserve is run by the National Parks Board, and at the entrance is an exhibition hall with interesting displays on Singapore's natural history. Adjoining the hall are changing rooms and showers. The other national parks run by the board are the much more urban Fort Canning Park and the Botanic Gardens.

Of the walks in the park, the most popular is the summit walk along a paved road to the top of Bukit Timah. Even during the week it attracts a number of walkers, though few venture off the footpath to explore the side trails. The road cuts a swathe through dense forest, and near the top there are panoramic views across Upper Pierce Reservoir.

The best trails to explore the forest and see the wildlife run off the summit road. Try the North View, South View or Fern Valley paths, where it is hard to believe that you are in Singapore. These paths involve some scrambling over rocks in parts, but are easily negotiated.

The park has over 800 species of native plants, including giant trees, ferns and native flowers. Wildlife is difficult to see, though long-tailed macaques and squirrels are in abundance. Flying lemurs, reticulated pythons and birds such as the racquet-tailed drongo and white-bellied sea eagle inhabit the reserve. Try to pick up either one of the two editions of *A Guide to the Bukit Timah Nature Reserve* explaining the reserve's flora and fauna (available at Mobil and BP petrol stations and some bookshops).

The exhibition hall is open from 8.30 am to 6 pm. Entry is free. It's a good idea to bring a water bottle if you intend to go on extended walks. A towel and even a change of clothes are also worth bringing, as the

SINGAPORE

walks are strenuous in parts and the conditions are hot and very humid.

To get to Bukit Timah, take bus No 171 or 182, which both run along Orchard and Stamford Rds in the colonial district and pass the Newton MRT station. Get off just past the 12km mark at the large, yellow Courts Mammoth Super Store on Upper Bukit Timah Rd. The entrance to the park is on the other side, about 1km along Hindhede Drive.

## Sungei Buloh Nature Park

This 87-hectare wetland nature reserve is home to 140 species of birds, most of them migratory. From the visitor centre with its well-presented displays, trails lead around ponds and mangrove swamps to hides for observing the birds. The birdlife, rather than the walks, is the main reason to visit as the area is mostly former orchard and fish ponds.

Sungei Buloh is open from 7.30 am to 7 pm weekdays and from 7 am on weekends and holidays. Admission is S$1 for adults (children 50c). Audiovisual shows on the park's flora and fauna are held at 9 and 11 am, and 1, 3 and 5 pm (on Sunday hourly between 9 am and 5 pm). Guided walks are available for groups given a month's notice (☎ 794 1401). Allow yourself three hours to do the park justice.

The park is in the north-west of the island, overlooking the Straits of Johor. Take the MRT to Kranji or Woodlands and then TIBS bus No 925.

## Other Parks

Despite Singapore's dense population, there are many small parks and gardens.

**MacRitchie Reservoir** has a 12-hectare park area with a jogging track, exercise area, playground and tea kiosk. It is a pleasant retreat from the city, and popular with joggers. A band often plays on Sunday (check the newspapers). To the north of MacRitchie Reservoir is **Upper Seletar Reservoir**, where paddle boating is possible, and farther east is **Lower Seletar Reservoir**, where you can go fishing. For MacRitchie Reservoir take the MRT to Toa Payoh and

then bus No 157. For Upper Seletar take bus No 138 from the Ang Mo Kio MRT station. For Lower Seletar, take the MRT to Yishun, then bus No 851, 852, 853, 854 or 855.

Off Kampong Bahru Rd, the 116m **Mt Faber** is a pleasant park with fine views over the harbour and the city. To get there, take the cable car up from the World Trade Centre (WTC). Mt Faber can be conveniently visited in conjunction with a trip to Sentosa Island.

**Pasir Ris Park** on the north-east coast is for the most part a manicured park with a narrow stretch of beach. The park also has a wooden walkway that goes through a mangrove swamp area that is good for birdwatching. The park is often empty during the week, but comes alive on holidays and weekends, when the nearby union-run NTUC Pasir Ris Resort fills up. To get here take the MRT to Pasir Ris station and then bus No 354 to the NTUC resort. Alternatively, take a taxi from the station.

**Bukit Batok Town Park**, also known as Little Guilin, was a quarry and is now a park. It's often compared to the spectacular limestone formations and lakes of Guilin in southern China, hence the name. This pleasant park is built around a hilly outcrop and lake, but it is a poor imitation of Guilin. It is near the Bukit Gombok MRT station, 14km north-west of the city.

## Holland Village

If you're wondering what the life of an expatriate is like, head for Holland Village. It's on Holland Rd, a westerly continuation of Orchard Rd, and services the garden belt suburbs of the well-to-do.

Holland Village is, in fact, just a suburban shopping centre where foreigners can shop, sip coffee and feel at home, but it has a definite village community atmosphere. It is best known for its host of fashionable restaurants and watering holes, concentrated on Lorong Mambong, just back from the main road. The modern Holland shopping centre complex is a good place to look for antiques, furnishings and crafts, including porcelain ware, batik, wood carvings and so on.

The nearest MRT station is Buona Vista, about a 15-minute walk along Buona Vista Rd from Holland Village. Or take bus No 7, 105 or 106 from Penang Rd/Orchard Blvd.

## Temples

The central city areas of Singapore provide plenty of opportunities to experience Singapore's colourful temples, but a couple of temples of note are found in the outer areas.

**Siong Lim Temple** This is one of the largest temples in Singapore and includes a Chinese rock garden. It was built in 1908 but includes more recent additions. It features Thai Buddha statues and 2000kg incense burners. There is a monastery next to the main temple, and next to the monastery is another temple featuring a gigantic Buddha statue. It's at 184E Jalan Toa Payoh, north of the city centre, about 1km east from the Toa Payoh MRT station.

**Kong Meng San Phor Kark See Temple** This is the largest temple in Singapore and covers 12 hectares. A modern temple, it is impressive in size and design, though its main function is as a crematorium: Funerals, complete with paper effigies, are frequent. The attached old people's home is reminiscent of the old 'death houses' that used to exist in Chinatown's Sago St. Old folk were once packed off to death houses towards the end of their lives, thus avoiding the possible bad luck of a death in the home. The temple is on Bright Hill Drive, about 1.5km west of the Bishan MRT station.

## Kranji War Memorial

Near the Causeway off Woodlands Rd, the Kranji War Memorial includes the graves of thousands of Allied troops who died in the region during WWII. The walls are inscribed with the names of those who died, and a register is available for inspection. It can be reached by SBS bus No 170 from Rochor Rd.

## Housing Estates

Still another side of Singapore is found in the modern HDB satellite cities like Toa Payoh, Pasir Ris, Tampines and Bukit Panjang.

Nearly 90% of Singaporeans live in these government housing blocks, and once again it's a program that Singapore manages to make work.

While high-rise housing has become a dirty word in many countries, in Singapore it's almost universally popular. Many of the residents own their own flats, with subsidised interest rates provided by the HDB.

The MRT makes it simple to visit HDB areas. Just jump on a train and pop up somewhere like Toa Payoh, or Tampines, where you'll find the big new Century Park shopping mall. True, you won't see stunning architecture and breathtaking landscapes, and you won't be spellbound by exotic ritual, but you will get a glimpse of what life is like for the overwhelming majority of Singapore's residents. The estates are often good places to shop – straightforward, cheap and without the inflated prices and haggling that often go with the more popular tourist areas – and, of course, there are plenty of places to eat. You may find the best *ah balling* (fishball soup) or the cheapest chicken-rice in Singapore.

## Sun Yat Sen Villa

This old villa (built in the 1880s) was the one-time residence of the Chinese revolutionary Republican leader Sun Yat Sen (who following the overthrow of the Qing dynasty became president of post-Imperial China in 1912). The house, a national monument, is a fine example of a colonial Victorian villa. Since 1966 it had been used as a library and museum. In 1999 it was closed for renovation and refurbishment. It will reopen as the Sun Yat Sen Nanyang Memorial Hall – check to see if it's opened when you visit. Items pertaining to Sun Yat Sen's life and work will be on display.

The villa is at 12 Tai Gin Rd, about 500m south of Toa Payoh MRT station. Bus No 145 from Balestier Rd passes this way.

## JURONG

Jurong town, west of the city centre, is more than just a new housing area. A huge industrial complex has been built on land that was still a swamp at the end of WWII.

Today, it is the powerhouse of Singapore's economic success story. The Jurong area also has a number of tourist attractions, in Jurong Town itself and on the way to Jurong from the city centre.

## Haw Par Villa

This theme park with its intriguingly grotesque statuary is about 10km west of the city centre, at 262 Pasir Panjang Rd. The park was built in 1937 using S$1 million of the fortune that the Aw brothers made from their miracle cure-all Tiger Balm. In 1990 the park went hi tech, but this didn't last and it is now pared back to its original concept. Favourite displays include the '10 courts of hell', where sinners get their gory comeuppance in the afterlife; and the 'moral lessons' aisle, where sloth, indulgence, gambling and even wine, women and song, lead to their inevitable unhappy endings. The gardens are a popular Singaporean family outing. Entry is S$5 for adults and S$2.50 for children. The gardens are open daily from 9 am to 5 pm. To get here take SBS No 200 from Buono Vista MRT, bus No 10, 30 or 188 from the WTC, or No 143 from Orchard Rd.

## Jurong Bird Park

This beautifully landscaped 20-hectare park has over 8000 birds representing 600 species and includes a two-hectare walk-in aviary with an artificial waterfall at one end. Exhibits include everything from cassowaries, birds of paradise, eagles and cockatoos, to parrots, macaws and even penguins in an air-con underwater viewing gallery. The nocturnal house includes owls, kiwis and frogmouths. The **South-East Asian Birds Aviary** is a major attraction and features a simulated rainforest thunderstorm every day at noon. A number of shows are held throughout the day; you'll find details at the entrance.

You can get around the park on foot or on the 1.7km air-con panorail (S$2.50, children S$1). The park is open from 9 am to 6 pm weekdays and from 8 am weekends and public holidays. Entry is S$10.30 for adults (S$4.12 for children). To get here

take SBS bus No 194 or 251 from Boon Lay MRT station.

## Jurong Reptile Park

Formerly known as the Jurong Crocodile Paradise, this theme park has recreated itself to encompass more than just crocs and now boasts a scaly collection of other reptiles and amphibians such as Komodo dragons and giant tortoises.

Although the emphasis is less on crocs than before, there are still plenty of these fierce creatures to be seen.

The park, across the road from the Jurong Bird Park, is open from 9 am to 6 pm daily. Entry is S$7 for adults (S$3.50 children). Transport details are the same as for Jurong Bird Park.

## Chinese & Japanese Gardens

Off Yuan Ching Rd, the Chinese and Japanese gardens adjoining Jurong Bird Park each cover 13.5 hectares. The Chinese Garden, occupying an island on Jurong Lake, is colourful and has a number of Chinese-style pavilions. The main attraction is the large *penjing* (Chinese bonsai) display. Linked by a bridge, the less-interesting Japanese Garden has large grassed areas and a few buildings. Garden lovers will find Singapore's Botanic Gardens of more interest, but the Chinese Garden is very pleasant and a must for bonsai enthusiasts.

The gardens are open from 9 am to 7 pm Monday to Saturday and from 8.30 am on Sunday and public holidays. Admission to both gardens is S$4.50 for adults and S$2 for children. The Chinese Garden MRT station is right by Jurong Lake and a five-minute walk away from the Chinese Garden.

## Singapore Science Centre

On Science Centre Rd, off Jurong Town Hall Rd, the Science Centre attempts to make science come alive. There are handles to crank, buttons to push, levers to pull, and microscopes to look through. Subjects range from tortoises to information technology. Primarily aimed at encouraging an interest in science among school children, adults also find the hands-on approach irresistible.

In the aviation section you can ride through a volcano in the Millennium Simulator (S\$3/2 for adults/children). At the time of writing construction was underway to expand the exhibit area. It's open Tuesday to Sunday (closed Monday) from 10 am to 6 pm. Entry costs S\$3/1.50. Next door is the **Omni-Theatre**, which features Imax 3D movies (S\$12/10; showtimes are 10.30 and 12.15 am, 2, 3.45, 5.30 and 7.15 pm, plus 9 pm on weekends and public holidays), and the **Virtual Voyages** simulation theatre (with showings every 20 minutes between 10 am and 8.30 pm; S\$6/4). The science centre's Web site is www.sci-ctr.edu.sg. The theatres operate on the same opening times as the science centre.

To get there, take the MRT to Jurong East. Take the left-hand exit and walk through the shopping centre and across the main road (Jurong Town Hall Rd). The centre, opposite, is well signboarded. A taxi from Orchard Rd takes around 20 minutes.

### New Ming Village & Pewter Museum

This pottery workshop at 32 Pandan Rd produces reproduction porcelain from the Ming and Qing Chinese dynasties. You can see the artisans create their pottery and, of course, you can buy their works. It is open daily from 8.30 am to 5.30 pm. Admission is free. The complete production process is done on the premises and guided tours are available on demand for groups.

Ming Village is owned by Royal Selangor Pewter. Consequently the village also has a small pewter museum with some interesting pieces, and the showroom sells an extensive selection of pewter as well as pottery. Although the pewter is made in Malaysia, the polishing and hand-beaten designs are demonstrated at the village.

To get there, take the MRT to Clementi and then bus No 78 to Pandan Rd.

### Singapore Mint Coin Gallery

This gallery, at Singapore's mint on Jalan Boon Lay just east of the Boon Lay MRT station, exhibits coins and medals from Singapore and a few coins from around the world. This place is essentially an outlet for the gold medallions that the mint sells, but a few mint sets of Singapore coins are also for sale. Only dedicated coin enthusiasts would want to make the trip out here. It is open Monday to Friday from 9 am to 4.30 pm. Admission is free.

## SENTOSA ISLAND

Sentosa, just off the south coast of Singapore, is the granddaddy of all Singapore's fun parks. It is Singapore's most visited attraction and it's packed at weekends.

Like its beaches of imported sand, Sentosa is a purely synthetic attraction, but it is a good place for children and there's enough to keep adults occupied. Sentosa has museums, aquariums, beaches, sporting facilities, walks, rides and food centres. There's easily enough to do to fill a day and if that isn't enough there's a camping ground, a hostel and three hotels.

Sentosa is open daily from 7.30 am until around 11 pm, or an hour or so later on weekends. Many of the attractions close at 7 pm but cultural shows, plays and music performances are sometimes held in the evenings – contact the tourism board office, ring the Sentosa information hotline on ☎ 1800-736 8672 or check out its Web site at www.sentosa.com.sg.

Basic admission to Sentosa is S\$5 (S\$3 for children under 12); after 6.30 pm it's S\$3 (children S\$1.80). Most of the attractions cost extra and the toll can really add up if you want to see them all.

A free bus service runs around the island, with departures every 10 minutes. There's also a free monorail loop service, which is scenic but slow. You can also get around Sentosa by bicycle; rentals are available from the hire kiosk by the ferry terminal.

### Underwater World

This spectacular aquarium is one of Sentosa's most popular attractions. Displays include a turtle pool, moray eel enclosure, reef enclosures with live coral, and a theatre. These exhibits are mere entrees to Underwater World's 'travellator', an acrylic tunnel that takes spectators through the main tanks as all manner of fish swim around in all their natural glory. There is nothing quite like the sight of a huge manta ray, 60kg grouper or shark swimming overhead. Divers feed the fish at 11.30 am, and 2 and 4.30 pm. Qualified divers can get an eyeful from the inside out in the 90-minute Dive with the Sharks experience (bookings required; ☎ 275 0030). The newest attraction at Underwater World is the Dolphinarium, which opened in March 2000. Underwater World is open from 9 am to 9 pm. Entry is S$13 for adults (S$7 children). Check out its Web site at www.underwaterworld.com.sg.

## Images of Singapore

Here you take a tour through Singapore's history and explore its various cultures. The exhibit starts with Singapore as a Malay sultanate and takes you through its establishment as a busy port and trading centre, its trials during WWII and the subsequent Japanese surrender. Scenes are recreated using life-like wax dummies, film footage, and dramatic light and sound effects. Festivals of Singapore, the newest section, is a *tour de force* of the rites and rituals important to Singapore's various ethnic communities. Again, they are evoked using wax dummies, dramatic lighting and sound. The exhibition is open from 9 am to 9 pm and costs S$5 for adults (S$3 children).

## Fort Siloso

Dating from the 19th century, this was built as a military base and series of gun emplacements linked by underground tunnels. But when it came to the test with the Japanese invasion in WWII, the guns were all pointing in the wrong direction. The island was used by the various Japanese as a prisoner-of-war (POW) camp.

From 1989 until 1993, Fort Siloso housed Sentosa's most unusual 'attraction', political prisoner Chia Thye Poh. Arrested in 1966 for allegedly being a Communist, Chia served 23 years in jail before being banished to complete his bizarre sentence among the holiday delights of Sentosa.

A guided walk leads around the gun emplacements, tunnels and buildings, with waxwork re-creations of life in a colonial barracks. A mini sound-and-light show relives the period immediately before the Japanese invasion, and a 'Behind Bars' exhibit focuses on prison life for the POWs. Though not wildly exciting, it is one of Sentosa's more interesting attractions.

Fort Siloso is open from 9 am to 7 pm. Entry is S$3 for adults and S$2 for children.

## Fantasy Island

This is a huge water theme park with swimming pools, 13 different water rides and 31 slides. Rides range from 'river rafting' to the more terrifying Gang of Four, Blackhole and Kyag slides. There is also an entertainment mall with electronic games. It's great for the kids, but bad for the wallet. It's open from 10.30 am to 6 pm (till 10 pm on Friday, Saturday and public holidays). Entry is S$16 for adults, S$10 for children.

## Volcano Land

Based on a Mayan city and dominated by a giant, concrete volcano, Volcano Land is Sentosa's tackiest attraction. Supposedly following in the footsteps of explorer Professor Hugo II, you descend inside the volcano where you are treated to a movie on the evolution of life. The eruption finale is a fizzer and when the exit doors open to reveal the gift shop it is almost a relief. Save your S$12 (children S$6). The volcano 'erupts' every half-hour with a bang and a puff of smoke – you can see it from the outside. It's open from 10 am to 7 pm.

## Butterfly Park & Insect Kingdom Museum

At the Butterfly Park, you can walk among more than 50 species of live butterflies. In the museum there are thousands of mounted butterflies, rhino beetles, *Dynasties hercules* (the world's largest beetles) and scorpions, among other insects. It's open from 9 am to 6.30 pm; entry is S$6 for adults and S$3 for children.

## Asian Village

This collection of craft shops and some food outlets reflects Asia's various cultures.

SINGAPORE

The theme park buildings are vaguely styled after traditional houses. Entry is free; it's open from 10 am to 9 pm.

The adjacent Adventure Asia funfair has roller coaster rides, bumper cars and a ride called the octopus that spins you around in little carriages. Adventure Asia is open from 9 am to 7 pm, and costs S$10 for unlimited rides.

## Other Attractions

The **Maritime Museum** (open from 10 am to 7 pm; entry free) charts the course of the history of Singapore's port, the world's busiest. On display are boats and artefacts illustrating the history of trade, and fishing equipment such as harpoons and traps. **Sentosa Orchid Gardens** (open from 9.30 am to 6.30 pm; entry costs S$3.50/2 for adults/children) has orchids from around the world and a grove of Tembusu trees and MacArthur pines, which are illuminated with fairy lights at night. The 3-D theatre, **Cinemania**, is open from 11 am to 8 pm; entry costs S$10/6.

Of the free attractions, there's a **Nature Walk**, though, in typical Sentosa fashion, it has been livened up in part with dragons and fossils. Long-tailed macaques are common, but hide your food from these aggressive monkeys. You can also wander around the impressive ferry terminal, Fountain Gardens and Flower Terrace.

The **Musical Fountain** spurts water to music and flashing coloured lights, while the 37m Merlion, which towers over it, is also illuminated by laser light.

The **pasar malam** (night market) stalls sell souvenirs. Nearby is the **Rasa Sentosa Food Centre** – naturally Sentosa has a hawker centre – and the ferry terminal also has some dining possibilities.

## Beaches & Recreational Facilities

Sentosa's southern coastline is devoted to beaches: Siloso Beach at the western end, Central Beach and Tanjong Beach at the eastern end. As a tropical paradise, Sentosa has a long way to go to match the islands of Malaysia or Indonesia, but in a case of 'if Mohammed won't come to the mountain' Singapore has imported its beaches from Indonesia and planted coconut palms to give it a tropical ambience. The imported sand does at least make for what are Singapore's best beaches. Pedal cats, aquabikes, fun bugs, canoes and surfboards are all available for hire.

Sentosa has a 5.7km-long bicycle track that loops the island and takes in most of the attractions. Bicycles can be hired at bicycle stations on the track, such as the kiosk at Siloso Beach or at the ferry terminal, and cost S$3 to S$10 an hour.

There are three golf courses: two 18-hole courses at the Sentosa Golf Club (Serapong, open to the public Monday, and Wednesday to Saturday; Tanjong open to the public on Sunday; both cost S$120 a round); and Sijori Wondergolf (open from 9 am to 9 pm; adults S$8 to S$10, children S$4 to S$6), which has 45 putting greens in three fun courses around hazards such as ravines, caves and waterfalls.

## Getting There & Away

Take SBS bus No 65 or 143 or Sentosa Bus Service E from Orchard Rd; No 61, 84, 143, 145 or 166 from Chinatown; or Sentosa Bus Service C from Tiong Bahru MRT to the WTC. Tourist buses such as the Singapore Trolley also run to the WTC. From the bus terminal across from the WTC take Sentosa Bus Service A. Services A and C run every 10 minutes between 7 am and 10.30 pm (S$6/4 for adults/children; S$4/2.40 after 6.30 pm). Bus service E runs every 20 to 30 minutes between 10 am and 10.45 pm daily (S$7/5; S$5/$3 after 6.30 pm). The Sentosa bus fares include the cost of admission.

Ferries run every 20 minutes to/from the WTC between 9.30 am and 9 pm on weekdays, and from 8.30 am to 10 pm weekends and public holidays. The one-way fare is S$2.30 (child or adult).

You can also go across by cable car from either the top of Mt Faber or from the Cable Car Towers adjacent to the WTC itself. It costs S$6.90 one way for adults and S$3.90 for children. The cable cars operate every 20 minutes between 9.30 am and 9 pm on weekdays, and 8.30 am and 10 pm on weekends and public holidays. The cable car ride, with its spectacular views, is one of the best parts of a visit to Sentosa. Take the ferry across and then the cable car back to Mt Faber – it is easier walking down Mt Faber than up.

## OTHER ISLANDS

Singapore's other islands include Kusu and St John's, Pulau Sakeng and the Sisters' Islands (all south of Singapore), and islands such as Pulau Bukum, which are used as refineries and for other commercial purposes. Farther south are many more islands, including the scattered Indonesian islands of the Riau Archipelago. There are also islands to the north-east between Singapore and Malaysia.

### St John's & Kusu Islands

Although Sentosa is Singapore's best known island, there are two others that are also popular with locals as city escapes: St John's Island (Pulau Sakijang Bendera) and Kusu Island (Pulau Tembakul). On weekends they can become crowded but during the week you'll find them fairly quiet and good places for a peaceful swim. Both islands have changing rooms, toilet facilities, grassy picnic spots and swimming areas.

St John's Island is the bigger of the two and has a few safe swimming lagoons, though the water can sometimes be a bit on the dodgy side – hardly surprising given all the passing shipping. There is not much to do here other than walk along its rather uninspiring concrete pathways and relax in its shady picnic areas. You're better off bringing your own picnic, as the culinary offerings are limited.

Kusu is more interesting, but it can be fully explored in no more than an hour. The island has a Chinese temple, Tua Pek Kong, near the ferry jetty, and a Malay shrine, Keramat Kusu, up a steep flight of steps to the top of a hill at the end of the island. Though Keramat worship is frowned upon by the Islamic clergy (it's too animistic for their liking), this is Singapore's most popular shrine, especially for childless couples; their prayers for children are marked by the

### Ferry Schedule to Kusu & St John's Islands

**Monday to Saturday**
*Depart from*

| WTC | Kusu | St John's | Kusu |
|-----|------|-----------|------|
| 10.00 | 10.45 | 11.15 | 11.45 |
| 13.30 | 14.15 | 12.45 | 15.15 |
|  | (last ferry) |  | (last ferry) |

**Sunday & Public Holidays**
*Depart from*

| WTC | Kusu | St John's |
|-----|------|-----------|
| 09.45 | 10.20 | 10.35 |
| 11.15 | 11.50 | 12.05 |
| 12.45 | 13.20 | 13.35 |
| 14.15 | 14.50 | 15.05 |
| 15.45 | 16.20 | 16.35 |
| 17.15 | 17.50 | 18.05 |
| (last ferry) | (last ferry) | (last ferry) |

pieces of cloth tied around trees on the way up to the shrine. Kusu is the site of an important annual pilgrimage in the ninth lunar month, honoured by Taoists. There's also a turtle sanctuary here.

You can get to St John's via Kusu by ferry from the WTC (round trip S$9 adults, S$6 children to both or either). Although there are ferries daily, the only way to see both islands conveniently is on Sunday, when you can hop off the ferry at Kusu, then get on again when it next passes through to St John's. From St John's you can take a ferry back at your leisure. That will give you about 1½ hours on each island, which is more than enough if you just want a taste of the places. On other days you are limited to a half-hour visit to Kusu and over two hours on St John's, as long as you take the 10 am ferry. There is accommodation only on St John's. A fully equipped holiday bungalow that sleeps up to 10 people (from S$50 a night to S$200 a night, depending on which days you want to stay) is available by booking in advance via the Sentosa Information Office (☎ 270 7888/9).

SINGAPORE

Most of the harbour tours pass St John's Island and stop at Kusu for 20 minutes or so (see Organised Tours in Singapore's Getting Around chapter).

## Other Southern Islands

Many of the islands on Singapore's southern shore accommodate the refineries that provide much of Singapore's export income. Others, such as **Salu**, **Senang**, **Rawai** and **Sudong**, are live firing ranges. **Pulau Sakeng** has a village and many inhabitants work at nearby **Pulau Bukum**, where the Shell oil refinery is located.

There are a couple of off-the-beaten-track islands where you can find a quiet beach. The **Sisters' Islands** are good for swimming and are a popular diving spot with coral reefs nearby. **Pulau Hantu** is a popular excursion for swimming.

To reach these islands, rent a motorised bumboat from Clifford Pier at Marina Bay. Expect to pay around S$50 per hour. The boats will take from six to 12 people. You can approach individual boat owners or contact the Singapore Motor Launch Owners' Association (☎ 532 5652) on the 1st level of Collyer Quay (Clifford Pier).

## Northern Islands

The easiest northern island to visit is Pulau Ubin, which makes a pleasant day trip and is reached by boat from Changi Village. Pulau Tekong, Singapore's largest island, is off-limits since the military took it over in the early 1990s.

**Pulau Ubin** From Changi Village, you can wander down to the ferry jetty and wait for a bumboat to take you across to Pulau Ubin. You can tell that this is a different side of Singapore by the fact that there's no timetable; you wait for the ferry to fill up and it goes when a quota of 12 people is reached. Pulau Ubin has quiet beaches and a kampung atmosphere. This rural island is as unlike modern Singapore as you will find. It is also a natural haven for many species of birds that inhabit the mangroves and forest areas. However, Pulau Ubin has been earmarked for development. Public pressure

has so far stopped this from happening, but if you want to see it the way it's always been, it may be prudent to visit soon.

There is an information centre (open daily) a minute's walk from the jetty where the bumboats dock. It provides a free brochure, *The Pulau Ubin Experience,* which has a map. The brochure details the hazards you should avoid: tidal rivers, abandoned wells and houses, granite quarries and so on.

The best way to explore the island is by bicycle; bikes can be hired from around S$3 per day. There are numerous bicycle-hire places near the jetty. En route you will see several temples, including a Thai Buddhist temple. It is a peaceful rural scene of fish farms, coconut palms and a few houses.

Accommodation is limited. Yet to open at the time of writing was the upmarket ***Ubin Lagoon Resort*** (☎ 887 4368) at Ponggol Marina. Accommodation costs S$215 for a duplex (maximum four people) during the week (S$240 on weekends); and S$150 for a chalet (S$170) – maximum two people. Entry for nonguests costs S$8 for adults and S$4 for children. Ferries will continue to Ponggol Marina from Changi Point (S$2 one way). Other than that, there is camping at Noordin Beach and nearby Mamam Beach. It's free, but pretty basic and there's no potable water, so bring your own.

The island's most popular seafood restaurant is ***Ubin Seafood*** (☎ 545 8202), open from 11.30 am to 9 pm, although near the jetty are several inexpensive, informal *eateries*.

Bumboat ferries to the island cost S$1.50 each way and run from 6 am to 10 pm.

## ACTIVITIES

Singapore's private clubs and country clubs have excellent sporting facilities but there are also fine public facilities, such as those at Farrer Park near Little India, and a host of commercial ventures.

**Archery** You can practice archery at an air-con, indoor venue at Universal Archery (☎ 332 0056), 236/243 Marina Square, 6 Raffles Blvd. It's open daily from 10 am to

3 am. It has four areas, including an 18m range for skilled archers. Instructors are on hand for novices. It costs S$5 (18 arrows per game) Monday to Friday (10 am to 5 pm), and S$7 after 5 pm weekdays, on weekends and public holidays. The Archery Club of Singapore (☎ 773 4824) is at 131 Portsdown Rd.

**Badminton** Badminton is popular in South-East Asia and the region has produced more than a few world champions in the sport. Courts at the Singapore Badminton Hall (☎ 344 1773), 102 Guillemard Rd, east of town in Geylang, are open from 8 am to 11 pm; bookings are essential.

**Bowling** Tenpin bowling is very popular in Singapore. The cost per game is around S$3.50; shoe hire is around S$1. Check the *Buying Guide Yellow Pages* for a full list. Some alleys include:

**Superbowl** (☎ 221 1010) 15 Marina Grove, Marina South
**Victor Superbowl** (☎ 223 7998) 7 Marina Grove, Marina South

**Cricket** The Singapore Cricket Club (☎ 338 9271), Connaught Drive, holds matches every weekend on the Padang from March to October. The club is for members only but spectators are welcome.

**Cycling** Recreational cycling ranges from a leisurely peddle along the foreshore of the east coast to mountain biking at Ulu Pandan.

The easiest riding possibilities are along the east coast and at Sentosa and Pulau Ubin. Bikes can also be hired at these places.

Bukit Timah has two mountain-bike trails, 7km in all, running around the edge of the nature reserve between Chestnut Ave and Rifle Range Rd. The trails cut though jungle and abandoned quarry sites and, though hilly in parts, are well surfaced.

Two Wheel Action (☎ 463 2143) organises Sunday rides in collaboration with the Singapore chapter of the Hash House Harriers. You bring your own bike and meet at a pre-ordained point for a casual ride to some location on the island. Cost is S$10 per session, or S$100 for an annual membership. Weekend excursions to the Riau Archipelago in Indonesia are also arranged for around S$140 all-inclusive.

Sonja Navakas of Individual Pursuits (☎ 466 1227) takes a variety of trips ranging from easy to challenging. There are tours through Chinatown and Little India, as well as nature-oriented trips to the MacRitchie and Seletar reservoirs. Customised trips are another option. The trips cost from around S$75 per person.

**Golf** Singapore has plenty of golf courses, though some are members only or don't allow visitors to play on weekends. A game of golf costs around S$90 on weekdays, and from S$100 to S$220 on weekends. Club hire is expensive. The following courses all have 18 holes except Changi, Seletar and Warren, which are nine-hole courses:

**Changi Golf Club** (☎ 545 5133) Netheravon Rd, Changi Village
**Jurong County Club** (☎ 560 5655) 9 Science Centre Rd, Jurong
**Keppel Club** (☎ 273 5522) Bukit Chermin, Pasir Panjang
**Marina Bay Golf & Country Club** (☎ 221 2811) 6 Marina Green, Marina Bay
**Raffles Country Club** (☎ 861 7655) 450 Jalan Ahmad Ibrahim, Tuas
**Seletar Country Club** (☎ 481 4745) Seletar Airbase, Jalan Kayu
**Sembawang Country Club** (☎ 257 0642) Sembawang Rd, Nee Soon
**Sentosa Golf Club** (☎ 275 0022) Sentosa Island
**Singapore Island Country Club** (☎ 459 2222) Upper Thomson Rd, Nee Soon
**Warren Golf Course** (☎ 777 6533) Folkestone Rd, Clementi

Singapore has driving ranges at the Parkland Golf Driving Range (☎ 440 6726), 920 East Coast Parkway. It costs S$6 for 85 balls. At Dixie's Minigolf Adventure (☎ 338 3373), 01-04/05 Marina Square, anyone can have a go at putting around 18 holes on the indoor, air-con course. It's open from noon to 1 am weekdays and 10 am to 1 am weekends. It costs up to S$12.50/10 for adults/children.

SINGAPORE

**Rock Climbing** There are two outdoor rock climbing places in Singapore: Dairy Farm Quarry and Hindhede Quarry (both near Bukit Timah) – the latter only open to members of the Singapore Mountaineering Federation. There are some 20 routes up Dairy Farm; most are bolted and most can be done with a 50m rope. You can join regular climbers who come here on weekends – contact an outdoor equipment shop such as Fall Factor (☎ 273 0141), Block 125, 01-170 Bukit Merah Lane 1. There's usually no charge, but you need your own gear.

**Squash** Most of the island's country clubs have squash courts. Fees are between S$7 and S$9 per hour (the more expensive fees apply to air-con courts). Some of the public courts include:

**Kallang Squash & Tennis Centre** (☎ 440 6839) Stadium Blvd, Geylang
**West Coast Recreation Centre** (☎ 778 8966) 12 West Coast Walk, Clementi

**Swimming** Singapore has a number of beaches for swimming – try East Coast Park, Changi Village, Sentosa or the other islands. Singapore also has plenty of public swimming pools; admission is S$1 (S$1.20 on weekends). Two public swimming pools are:

**Farrer Park Swimming Complex** (☎ 299 1002) Dorset Rd
**River Valley Swimming Complex** (☎ 337 6275) River Valley Rd

**Tennis** Tennis courts cost up to S$10 per hour to hire. Courts available include:

**Farrer Park Tennis Courts** (☎ 299 4166) Rutland Rd
**Singapore Tennis Centre** (☎ 442 5966) 1020 East Coast Parkway

**Water Sports** The Europa Club (☎ 449 5118), 1212 East Coast Parkway, is the place to go for windsurfing and sailing. Sailboards cost S$20 for two hours' hire; lessons are available. The centre also rents laser-class boats for S$20 per hour. Sailboards and aquabikes are available for hire on Sentosa.

The Changi Sailing Club (☎ 545 2876), 32 Netheravon Rd, rents j-24s (24-foot keel boats) on one-day charters for S$180 a day including petrol. You will need to show a sailing proficiency certificate.

You can water ski in Singapore – but the latest thing is wakeboarding (a wakeboard looks a bit like a snowboard). Cowabunga Ski Centre (☎ 344 8813), 10 Stadium Lane, Kallang, is the home of the Singapore Water Ski Federation and offers water-skiing/wakeboarding lessons and equipment (from S$80 per hour on weekdays and S$100 on weekends, including boat, driver and equipment; bookings required). MaxOut (☎ 581 3637) also has wakeboarding (instruction available) from S$60 an hour; trips leave daily, except Tuesday, from the Pasir Ris Beach Park, Carpark E, Elias Rd.

## COURSES
At the Raffles Culinary Academy you can learn how to make some of those dishes that are so enjoyed in Singapore, and delve into the secrets of the Raffles kitchens at the same time. Prices for same-day sessions range from S$60 to S$125. For information contact Raffles Hotel (☎ 337 1886, fax 339 7650, ✉ raffles@raffles.com) or check its Web site (www.raffleshotel.com).

If you want to learn calligraphy or brush painting, tuition is available from S$5 an hour at the Yong Gallery (☎ 226 1718) at 260 South Bridge Rd in Chinatown.

# Places to Stay

## PLACES TO STAY – BUDGET
### Bencoolen St Area
Bencoolen St is within walking distance of the city centre, Orchard Rd and Little India.

**Guesthouses** *Goh's Homestay (☎ 339 6561, fax 339 8606, ✉ minggoh@pacific .net.sg, 169-D Bencoolen St, 4th floor)* is a friendly place with a comfortable sitting area next to a small kitchen/canteen (which guests may use). The rooms, while small, are clean and there is air-con. Linen (and lockers for dorms) is included in the price of S$14/36/46/52 for a dorm bed/single/ double/triple. Breakfast and snacks are also available. There is Internet access and International Direct Dialing (IDD). Laundry costs S$10 per load.

The *Hawaii Hostel* (☎ *338 4187, 171-B Bencoolen St, 2nd floor)* has small, tidy aircon rooms (S$30 for two, S$25 for one), a kitchen area with a fridge (bring your own camping stove), and laundry (S$8 per load). Breakfast (tea/coffee, bread and jam) is included.

*Green Curtains* (☎ *334 8697, fax 334 7014, 131/A Bencoolen St)* has rooms on three floors for S$30 a single or double with air-con (S$25 with fan) and S$10 for a bed in an air-con dorm. The rooms are a reasonable size; bathrooms are shared. Renovations were underway at the time of writing. There is Internet access next to the travel agent downstairs.

Farther south on the other side of the road is *Peony Mansions*, a rabbit warren of budget accommodation at No 46–52. This is Singapore's original backpackers' centre. There is no street sign; go round the back of the building and take the lift or the stairs to one of three budget places here.

On the 3rd floor is *Peony Latin House* (☎ *339 6308)*, a basic place with fan dorms for S$7, singles/doubles from S$15/$20 and air-con doubles from S$35 (includes attached bath).

On the 4th floor is the reception for *Peony Mansion Travellers' Lodge* (☎ *338 5638)*, where fan/air-con doubles cost S$20/35 and singles S$18/35. The air-con rooms have a TV and a bathroom that two rooms share. There is an air-con dorm at S$9 a bed. Internet and laundry services are available.

On the 7th floor, *Lee Boarding House* (☎ *338 3149, fax 333 1997)* has a variety of options. An air-con double is S$42 to S$50 with attached bath, S$38 with common bath; a fan double costs S$28. A fan/air-con single costs S$22/30 and a bed in a dorm is S$9/10. These prices are somewhat negotiable. There is a laundry service. On the street level of Peony Mansions there's a communication centre where you can use email and make international phone calls.

## Airport Hotel Desk

If you arrive in Singapore without a hotel booking, don't despair. The efficient Singapore Hotel Association has four desks at Changi International Airport:

**Terminal 1**: east wing (open from 10 am to 11 pm daily); west wing (open from 7 am to 2 am daily – Saturday until 11.30 pm)
**Terminal 2**: north wing (open from 7 am to 11 pm daily); south wing (open from 7 am to 6 am daily – Monday until 11.30 pm)

There are dozens of hotels on its list ranging from S$45 a night right up to Raffles at S$600-plus. There is no charge for the service, and promotional/discounted rates are passed on to you when available. You can also book the hotels over the Internet via the Singapore Hotel Association's Web site at www.stayinginsingapore.com.sg.

*Waterloo Hostel* (☎ *336 6555, fax 336 2160,* ✉ *waterhtl@mbox4.singnet.com.sg, 55 Waterloo St, Catholic Centre Bldg, 4th floor)*, on the street parallel to Bencoolen St, is a tidy Catholic-run hostel with a variety of rooms. A single is S$59 with attached bath and S$49 with common bath. A double costs S$71 with attached bath, S$60 with shower only and S$55 with common shower. Dorm beds cost S$20. All rooms have air-con (except dorms), TV and telephone. Breakfast is included. Other facilities include safe deposit boxes, laundry services and Internet access.

**Hotels** The *San Wah Hotel* (☎ *336 2428, 36 Bencoolen St)* is an old-fashioned Chinese hotel (the only one of its kind on this street) set back from the road. Although rather shabby, it's got character. Rooms for one or two people cost S$50 with fan and S$55 with air-con.

## Beach Rd & Around

Beach Rd, a few blocks south-east from Bencoolen St toward the waterfront, is another centre for cheap hotels. If you aspire to the Raffles Hotel but can't afford it, at least you can stay nearby.

**Guesthouses** The *Lee Travellers Club* (☎ 339 5490, 75 Beach Rd), on the 6th floor of the Fu Yeun building, with more rooms on the other floors, is a large, popular place with clean rooms. A dorm with fan costs about S$9, with air con and attached bath S$10, a single with fan is S$20 and a double with fan is S$25 to S$32. An air-con double/triple costs S$35/40. There's a small kitchen for guests' use, a noticeboard and plenty of info for travellers.

The tidy *Season Homestay* (☎ 337 2400, 27-A Liang Seah St) is just off Beach Rd. Breakfast (plus tea and coffee) is included in the price of S$25/35 for a fan/air-con room (one or two people) and S$9 for a dorm (locker included).

On the corner of Liang Seah St and North Bridge Rd is the *Ah Chew Hotel/Homestay* (☎ 837 0356, 496 North Bridge Rd), with common bathrooms, laundry service, and free coffee and tea. There are five air-con dorm rooms in which a bed costs S$12. A no-frills single or double is S$25 with fan, or S$30 with air-con. You can climb up to the rooftop, dry your clothes up there or just sit and read.

Nearby (entry through the Naz 24-hour restaurant) is *Waffle's Homestay* (☎ 334 1608, 490 North Bridge Rd), which has basic rooms, common bathrooms, a sundeck and laundry service. Dorms cost S$8 to S$9, doubles with fan/air-con are S$26/30.

**Hotels** The quaint old-style Chinese *Shang Onn Hotel* (☎ 338 4153, 37 Beach Rd) is on the corner of Purvis St. The rooms (there are 10) are surprisingly sizeable, albeit no frills. The common bathrooms are clean. Singles/doubles/triples (with fan) are priced at S$30/34/45.

## Chinatown

Chinatown is an interesting area to stay and it has a few cheap hotels, most of which are within walking distance of the train station, and Outram Park and Tanjong Pagar MRT stations.

**Guesthouses** The *Chinatown Guest House* (☎ 220 0671, 325D New Bridge Rd, 5th floor), opposite Pearl's Centre, has a three-bed dorm with attached bathroom, balcony and window for S$10 a bed, and another three-bed dorm with no windows for the same price (S$5 extra for air-con). There's a small single room with common bathroom for S$25, a double with common bath for S$30, an air-con double with common bath for S$40 and an air-con double with attached bathroom for S$45. There's a decent-sized, clean, fully equipped kitchen for guests. It's about the cheapest option in Chinatown and handy for Outram Park MRT station.

**Hotels** The *Keong Saik Hotel* (☎ 223 0660, fax 225 0660, ✉ keongsaik@pacific .net.sg, 69 Keong Saik Rd) is in a restored shophouse with polished wooden floors. The standard rooms are small and window-less but tidy. Better are the larger (superior) rooms with windows. Single/double standard rooms cost S$55/65, and superior rooms cost S$65/75.

The *Regal Inn* (☎ 323 1551, fax 323 3122, ✉ regalinn@cyberway.com, 50 Keong Saik Rd) has reasonable, if small, rooms in a restored shophouse starting at S$60/70. Each has a window, TV, air-con and a small bathroom with a shower.

## Little India & Jalan Besar

**Hotels** The *Boon Wah Hotel* (☎ 299 1466, fax 294 2176, 43A Jalan Besar) on the corner of Upper Dickson Rd has reasonable singles/doubles with air-con, TV and bathroom for S$45/50.

At the *Haising Hotel* (☎ 298 1223, fax 298 6609, ✉ hs@haising.com.sg, 37 Jalan Besar), tidy if small air-con rooms with attached bath cost S$40 a single and S$50 to S$70 a double. Rooms all have TV and there is Internet access.

The *Little India Guest House* (☎ 294 2866, fax 298 4866, 3 Veerasamy Rd) is just off Serangoon Rd in the heart of Little India. It is more a small hotel than a guesthouse. The rooms are OK; the bathrooms are very clean. Single/double/family rooms with fan are S$35/40/60 (S$40/45/75 with air-con). The ladies' bathroom is on level three and the men's on level two.

The new *Madras Hotel* (☎ 392 7889, fax 392 6188, ✉ madrashotel@pacific.net.sg, 28–32 Madras St) has all the essential facilities (attached bath, air-con, TV) and rooms are tidy enough. There's an inexpensive vegetarian restaurant at street level. Singles are S$60, twins and doubles are S$70, and family rooms are S$100.

The former Palace Hotel (where Tony and Maureen Wheeler wrote the 1st edition of *South-East Asia on a Shoestring* in a back room) has been gutted, renovated and re-launched as the *Cactus Hotel* (☎ 391 3913, 407 Jalan Besar). The rooms are plain but tidy enough at S$50 for two (including air-con).

### Orchard Rd

There are three YMCAs in the Orchard Rd area; they take men, women and couples. Book at least six weeks in advance for the YMCA International and around three weeks in advance for the others. Non-YMCA members must pay a small charge for temporary membership.

The *YMCA International House* (☎ 336 6000, fax 337 3140, ✉ hostel@ymca .org.sg, 1 Orchard Rd) is opposite Bras Basah Park in the colonial district. It's a handy location and the facilities include a fitness centre, roof-top swimming pool, squash and badminton courts, and billiard room. There's also a restaurant, which offers a cheap daily set meal. All rooms have air-con, TV, telephone and attached bathroom, but are of a fairly average standard and becoming expensive at S$90/105/125 for a single/double/family room and S$135 for a superior room. All prices are nett and include breakfast. A bed in a dorm costs S$25.

Nearby, the *YWCA Fort Canning Lodge* (☎ 338 4222, fax 337 4222, ✉ ywcasin@ mbox3.singnet.com.sg, 6 Fort Canning Rd), close to the Dhoby Ghaut MRT station, offers good accommodation, a coffee house, cafe, a swimming pool and a tennis court. Singles/doubles are S$95/105 (breakfast included). Not all have attached bath, so it pays to ask for one. A dorm costs S$45.

The *YMCA Metropolitan* (☎ 737 7755, fax 235 5528, ✉ hostel@mymca.org.sg, 60 Stevens Rd) also has well-appointed rooms, a sizeable pool and cafe. It is a 15-minute walk north of Orchard Rd. Singles/doubles with bathroom, TV and air-con start at S$70 for a standard room to S$110 for a deluxe.

### Other Areas

*New Sandy's Place* (☎ 734 1431, fax 738 8580, ✉ sandygiam@hotmail.com, 3C Sarkies Rd) is just off Bukit Timah Rd and next to Alliance Français. This is a friendly, homey place. There is a variety of rooms ranging from bunk beds for S$15 to a room with attached bath for S$55 for two. You can walk here from the Newton MRT station.

### PLACES TO STAY – MID-RANGE
### Colonial District

The *City Bayview Hotel* (☎ 337 2882, fax 338 2880, 30 Bencoolen St) has a rooftop swimming pool and very good single/twin rooms with attached bath, TV and air-con from S$165/175.

*Hotel Bencoolen* (☎ 336 0822, fax 336 2250, ✉ bencoolen@pacific.net.sg, 47 Bencoolen St) is good value. The rooms are reasonably sized and well appointed, all have windows and there is rooftop spa. Prices start at S$88 for a queen-sized room and include breakfast.

The *Summer View Hotel* (☎ 338 1122, fax 336 6346, ✉ summerviewhtl@pacific .net.sg, 173 Bencoolen St) is a newish place with OK doubles, including attached bath, air-con and TV, from S$138. Adjacent is D'Lemon Tree Thai Kitchen & Cafe.

The *South East Asia Hotel* (☎ 338 2394, fax 338 480, ✉ seahotel@mbox2.singnet .com.sg, 190 Waterloo St) is quiet and offers good value for money. All rooms have air-con, bathroom, TV and phone. There's a busy eating place on the ground floor, and a couple of temples, flower sellers and markets virtually right outside. Singles/doubles cost S$69/86.

SINGAPORE

The **Beach Hotel** (☎ 336 7712, fax 336 7713, @ bhotel@singnet.com.sg, 95 Beach Rd) has 33 tidy, reasonably sized rooms with modern facilities. Singles or doubles are S$96, superior rooms are S$110 and deluxe rooms cost S$120.

The **Park View Hotel** (☎ 338 8558, fax 334 8558, 81 Beach Rd) has comfortable standard rooms with/without windows for S$150/140.

The **New 7th Storey Hotel** (☎ 337 0251, fax 334 3550, @ nsshmail@mbox2.singnet .com.sg, 229 Rochor Rd) sits in splendid isolation on a patch of land that until a few years ago was also occupied by shophouses and a wet market. It is a reliable budget hotel with reasonable rooms for S$48 with shared bath, S$68 with attached bath and S$72 for a deluxe room. There is air-con and TV in all rooms.

The **Victoria Hotel** (☎ 338 2381, fax 334 4853, 87 Victoria St) is an unpretentious budget hotel with clean (if a little spartan) good-sized rooms with air-con, TV and attached bathroom for S$60 for two people.

## Orchard Rd Area

The **RELC International Hotel** (☎ 737 9044, fax 733 9976, @ relcih@singnet .com.sg, 30 Orange Grove Rd) has large, well-appointed rooms, each with a balcony. RELC stands for Regional English Language Centre, and the bottom floors have conference rooms and teaching facilities. There's a free shuttle to the city centre every hour between 10 am and 4.15 pm. Rooms start at S$132 for a superior twin to S$165 for an alcove suite (rates inclusive of breakfast). Children under 12 are free.

**Lloyd's Inn** (☎ 737 7309, fax 737 7847, 2 Lloyd Rd) is less than 10 minutes' walk south of Orchard Rd along Oxley Rd. It's in a quiet street among old villas and the rooms are spread out, motel style, around the reception building. It's slightly dated but tidy and good value at S$65 for a standard and S$75 for a deluxe room (ie, larger and with fridge). Bookings are advisable.

**Regalis Court** (☎ 734 7117, fax 736 1651, @ regaliscourt@pacific.net.sg, 64 Lloyd Rd) is a boutique hotel in a large colonial-era

building. The floors are polished teak and the interior decoration has a Peranakan flavour. The rooms themselves are fairly ordinary, but all have air-con. Prices start at S$89 for a single or double; rooms with windows are more expensive but slightly smaller than those without.

## Chinatown

The cute **Damenlou Hotel** (☎ 221 1900, fax 225 8500, 12 Ann Siang Rd) has character and a good restaurant. Single/double rooms cost S$90/100 for a standard and S$120/130 for a deluxe.

**Dragon Inn Chinatown** (☎ 222 7227, fax 222 6116, 18 Mosque St) is in a row of renovated shophouses. The rooms have air-con, bath and TV, but the small singles for S$78 are dark and many are located around the noisy air-con shaft. The doubles are much better at S$98, or S$118 for the larger rooms.

The **Royal Peacock** (☎ 223 3522, fax 221 1770, @ rpeacock@cyberway.com.sg, 55 Keong Saik Rd) is next to the Keong Saik Hotel. Another restored shophouse hotel in this street of restored shophouse hotels, it has quite plush rooms for S$135/150 (no windows) and from S$170/185 with windows.

**The Inn on Temple Street** (☎ 221 5333, fax 225 5391, @ theinn@mbox4.singnet .com.sg, 36 Temple St) occupies five restored shophouses. There are 42 rooms, a cafe, lounge and bar. Rooms start at around S$100 for two, including breakfast. All rooms have attached bath, windows, TV, fridge and safe.

**Robertson Quay Hotel** (☎ 735 3333, fax 738 1515, @ rqhotel@mbox3.singnet.com.sg, 15 Merbau Rd) is a modern, distinctive round building right near Clarke Quay. There is even a round swimming pool on the roof. There are 150 rooms: singles/doubles are S$120/150; the 16 office-convertible rooms are S$120 each.

## Little India

The pick of the bunch is the tasteful **Perak Lodge** (☎ 299 7733, fax 392 0919, @ reservations@peraklodge.net, 12 Perak Rd), a small, private guesthouse in a renovated Peranakan-style building. Standard singles

SINGAPORE

are S$60 without TV and S$70 with TV (standard doubles are S$80). Superior singles/doubles are S$80/90 and deluxe rooms are S$90/100.

About 300m from the Perak Lodge is the *Mayo Inn* (☎ 295 6641, fax 296 8545, 9A Jalan Besar). Rooms are reasonably sized and clean, but those overlooking the main street are noisy. Rooms go for S$60/81.

The *Kerbau Hotel* (☎ 297 6668, 54/62 Kerbau Rd) has clean, tidy rooms, albeit very small. All have air-con, but those on the ground floor don't have windows. A single is S$50, a double/twin and deluxe S$60 (deluxe is bigger and invariably has windows). All rooms have TV and attached bath.

The multistorey *Broadway Hotel* (☎ 292 4661, fax 291 6414, ☺ bw030303@asian connect.com, 195 Serangoon Rd) is one of the oldest of the hotels in Little India, but well maintained. The rooms have air-con, TV and bathroom, and cost S$80 to S$90 for a single and S$90 to S$100 for a double. The good Delhi restaurant, a branch of the better-known one on Race Course Rd, is right next door.

The *Dickson Court Hotel* (☎ 297 7811, fax 297 7833, ☺ dicksonl@magix.com.sg, 3 Dickson Rd) is a boutique hotel with 51 well-appointed rooms from S$105 for two people (S$69 single). Designed around new shophouses, it has style but some rooms are small and dark. There's also a restaurant and bar.

The *Fortuna Hotel* (☎ 295 3577, fax 294 7738, 2 Owen Rd) is a good mid-range hotel in this area. Rooms start at S$38. there is a good Indian restaurant (Nirvana) on level two.

Close to Serangoon Rd, the *Tai Hoe Hotel* (☎ 293 9122, fax 298 4600, 163 Kitchener Rd) is a brisk, modern hotel offering tidy, good value rooms with bathroom, TV, phone and bar fridge. Standard doubles are S$60 and triples S$80.

## PLACES TO STAY – TOP END
## Orchard Rd

Orchard Rd is where everyone wants to stay, and consequently hotels tend to be a little more expensive here than elsewhere. This is very much the tourist centre of Singapore,

with a profusion of hotels, airline offices and shopping centres. The area is well serviced by the MRT, with Somerset and Orchard stations both on Orchard Rd.

*The Elizabeth* (☎ 738 1188, fax 732 3866, ☺ elizabpr@pacific.net.sg, 24 Mount Elizabeth Rd) is in a quiet spot just off Orchard Rd. There are 256 guestrooms, restaurants, a lobby lounge and a pool. Superior singles/doubles are S$260/300; a two-bedroom suite is S$950.

*Hotel Phoenix* (☎ 737 8666, fax 732 2024, ☺ rsvp@phoenix.hotelnet.com.sg, 277 Orchard Rd) is a four-star hotel with 392 rooms, most outfitted with multimedia computers and personal exercise equipment. All guests have free access to the nearby Ray Wilson Fitness Centre. Prices start at S$240/260 for single/double deluxe rooms.

*Meritus Negara Hotel* (☎ 737 0811, fax 737 9075, ☺ negara.mns@meritus-hotels .com, 10 Claymore Rd) was opened in 1996. It's quite central, situated as it is just off Orchard Rd. Superior rooms start at S$280 and there is no charge for children under 12 (maximum two).

The *Orchard Hotel* (☎ 734 7766, 733 5482, ☺ orchard@singnet.com.sg, 442 Orchard Rd) has 680 rooms, including 13 executive suites. There is a sizeable rooftop pool and a gym. Prices start at S$280.

The *Traders' Hotel* (☎ 738 2222, fax 831 4314, ☺ thsbc@pacific.net.sg, 1A Cuscaden Rd) has an impressive water wall running the length of its large lobby. Prices here are a little cheaper than at places closer to Orchard Rd, at S$235/265 for a standard single/double.

The *Four Seasons Hotel* (☎ 734 1110, fax 733 0682, ☺ bizcentre@pacific.net.sg, 190 Orchard Blvd) is in a quiet, tree-lined street just off Orchard Rd. It offers luxury accommodation from S$435/475 for a standard single/double room to S$580/620 for an entry-level suite. There's also air-con tennis courts.

*Goodwood Park Hotel* (☎ 737 7411, fax 732 8558, ☺ enquiries@goodwoodpark hotel.com.sg, 22 Scotts Rd) oozes history. Designed to resemble a Rhine castle, it was

SINGAPORE

built in 1900 and served as the base for the Teutonia Club until 1914, when it was taken over by the British. During WWII it accommodated Japanese officers, and was returned to the British after the war's end. It was bought by a local businessman in 1963. Deluxe rooms start at S$385/425.

The *Grand Hyatt Hotel* (☎ 738 1234, fax 732 1696, *e* sales@hyatt.com.sg, 10–12 Scotts Rd) has a vast lobby and excellent facilities, including a pool, gym and two tennis courts. Deluxe rooms are S$450.

The *Mandarin Hotel* (☎ 737 4411, fax 732 2361, *e* mandarin.tsm@mertus-hotels .com, 333 Orchard Rd) is in a handy location and has a 24-hour restaurant. Comfortable rooms start at S$400.

*The Regent* (☎ 733 8888, fax 732 8838, *e* regent@singnet.com.sg, 1 Cuscaden Rd) has guestrooms with marble bathrooms and teak furniture. There's a good gym and a rooftop pool. Prices start at S$350.

At *Shangri-La Hotel* (☎ 737 3644, fax 737 3257, *e* shangsin@singnet.com.sg, 22 Orange Grove Rd) prices start from S$375 for a deluxe room in the Tower Wing.

The *Sheraton Towers* (☎ 737 6888, fax 737 1072, *e* anssh2@po.pacific.net.sg, 39 Scotts Rd) is yet another place that oozes opulence. Deluxe rooms are S$370, deluxe rooms with terrace and towers rooms are S$430. Suites start at S$700.

## Colonial District

*Allson Hotel* (☎ 336 0811, fax 339 7019, *e* allson.sales@pacific.net.sg, 101 Victoria St) is handy to Bugis Junction and Suntec City Mall. Prices start at S$220/240 for a single/twin deluxe room.

The *Excelsior Hotel* (☎ 338 7733, fax 339 3847, *e* pen_exc@ytchotels.com.sg, 5 Coleman St) has 271 guestrooms. Prices start at S$230/250 for a superior room; suites start at S$420.

The *Carlton Hotel* (☎ 338 8333, fax 339 6866, *e* RoomReservations@Carlton.com .sg, 76 Bras Basah Rd) is an efficient, modern hotel in a handy location. Standard rooms are S$300/320, deluxe rooms S$320/340, Carlton Club rooms cost S$340/360 and suites start at S$450.

*Hotel Inter-Continental* (☎ 338 7600, fax 338 7366, *e* sinhb-resvn@interconti .com, 80 Middle Rd) has a very appealing Peranakan style integrated into its design. The shophouse-style rooms (S$420) and suites (S$720) have a lot of character.

The *Peninsula Hotel* (☎ 337 2200, fax 336 3120, *e* pen_exc@ytchotels.com.sg, 3 Coleman St) is an older hotel minutes from the City Hall MRT station. Rooms cost from S$220/240.

The *Grand Plaza Parkroyal* (☎ 336 3456, fax 339 9311, *e* gph01@pacific .net.sg, 10 Coleman St) opened in 1996. It has 338 guestrooms and suites from S$280/300 for superior rooms. The 9th- and 10th-floor 'Orchid Club' rooms are aimed at business travellers and come with a butler service. These rooms start at S$330/360.

*Hotel Rendezvous* (☎ 336 0220, fax 337 3773, 9 Bras Basah Rd) overlooks Bras Basah Park. Superior rooms start at S$300/330 to S$800 for the top-of-the-line Stamford Suite.

There is a cluster of luxury hotels in the Marina Square area, with dedicated facilities for business travellers and well-heeled travellers.

The *Conrad International* (☎ 334 888, fax 333 9166, *e* conradsg@singnet.com.sg, 2 Temasek Boulevard) opened in 1997 opposite Suntec City Mall. Superior rooms are S$360; executive rooms S$460.

The *Marina Mandarin* (☎ 338 3388, fax 339 4977, *e* mms888@singnet.com.sg, 6 Raffles Boulevard, Marina Square) is a luxury hotel with rooms for S$340, and suites at S$600.

*Pan Pacific Singapore Hotel* (☎ 336 8111, fax 339 1861, *e* panpac@pacific .net.sg, 7 Raffles Blvd, Marina Square) is a luxury hotel with deluxe rooms for S$320 and upwards.

The *Ritz-Carlton* (☎ 337 8888, fax 338 001, *e* reservations@ritz-carlton.com.sg, 7 Raffles Ave) has a striking entrance, with huge round windows that look out on landscaped gardens. Rooms start at S$430.

The *Westin Stamford* (☎ 338 8585, fax 338 2862, *e* westin1@singnet.com.sg, 2 Stamford Rd) and its twin, the *Westin Plaza*, soar above Raffles City shopping centre; the Stamford Rose restaurant on the Stamford's 70th floor has some of the best views in Singapore and is one of the world's highest restaurants. There is a pool, as well as a fitness room, not to mention about a dozen restaurants and lounges, and efficient business facilities. Rooms start at S$340/360 for singles/doubles (more for a harbour view).

*Raffles Hotel (☎ 337 1886, fax 339 7650, @ raffles@raffles.com, 1 Beach Rd)* is, well – Raffles. It's a name that is firmly associated with Singapore in travellers' minds, and just about everyone who comes to this city makes the pilgrimage here. There are 104 suites, with timber floors, 14-foot moulded ceilings and period furnishings. Facilities include fine dining (there's even a Braille version of the in-suite food and drink menu), upmarket shopping, swimming pool and health club, special facilities for children and more. Suites start at S$650, with the most expensive falling in the S$6000 to S$8000 bracket.

### Chinatown

The *Duxton Hotel (☎ 227 7678, fax 227 1232, @ duxton@singnet.com.sg, 83 Duxton Rd)* in the Tanjong Pagar area is a boutique hotel in a renovated terrace. Rooms are furnished in period style and the suites have an attractive mezzanine bedroom. A studio room is S$180 and a superior room is S$210.

The *Concorde Hotel (☎ 733 0188, fax 733 0989, @ singapore@concorde.net, 317 Outram Rd)* is a striking, smokey-coloured modern building with an atrium that soars 27 storeys. It has tidy, pleasant rooms, an outdoor pool and gym, and restaurants. Room prices start at S$210/230 for a superior single/double. Suites start at S$400.

At the *Hotel New Otani (☎ 338 3333, fax 339 2854, @ newotani@singnet.com.sg, 177A River Valley Rd)* you take the lift up to the reception on the 7th floor, from where you get great views of the river. Trader Vic's restaurant is on the 5th floor. The hotel is right on Clarke Quay. Rooms start at S$260/280 and suites at S$600.

Right on the river is a rather imposing hotel, the *Grand Copthorne (☎ 733 0880,*

*fax 737 8880, @ grandcopthorne@cdhotels .com.sg, 392 Havelock Rd)*. There is a very attractive conservatory-style cafe (Brio's) just off the lobby where a buffet breakfast is served. Superior rooms start at S$300/330. Executive club rooms start at S$360/420 and suites at S$550.

The *Merchant Court Hotel (☎ 337 9993, fax 336 9993, @ info@merchantcourt.com .sg, 20 Merchant Rd)*, also right on the river front, is directly opposite Clarke Quay. A superior room costs S$275/305, a merchant club room is S$335/365 and a studio is S$365/395. Suites start at S$810.

### Little India

The *Albert Court Hotel (☎ 339 3939, fax 339 3252, @ sales.mktg@albertcourt.com .sg, 180 Albert St)*, at the southern edge of Little India, is a boutique hotel in a shophouse redevelopment. There are 136 rooms with all mod-cons, including CNN and a choice of fan or air-con. Rooms start at S$190/210 single/double.

The relatively new *New Park Centra Singapore (☎ 291 5533, fax 297 2827, @ newpark@singnet.com.sg, 181 Kitchener Rd)* has a swimming pool and restaurants, plus a shuttle service to Orchard Rd. Rooms start at S$200/220.

# Places to Eat

## HAWKER CENTRES & FOOD COURTS

Hawker centres in Singapore are all under cover. Food courts are found mainly in shopping centres and have air-con. Both offer a tremendous variety of food and you can eat well for S$5.

### City Centre

Near the waterfront towards Chinatown is *Lau Pa Sat* on Raffles Quay. There has been a market here since 1822, although the iron lacework structure you see today was shipped out from Glasgow in 1894. A few souvenir stalls hug Lau Pa Sat's perimeter and there are occasional cultural exhibitions. But the main emphasis is on the

SINGAPORE

favourite Singaporean pastime, food. Many stalls are open 24 hours. Lau Pa Sat is more sanitised and expensive than the usual hawker centres, but quasi-mobile hawkers set up in the evening on Boon Tat St, where the dining is cheaper and cooler.

## Orchard Rd

*Newton Food Centre* is near the north-eastern end of Scotts Rd, near the Newton MRT station. It is very popular with tourists and therefore tends to be a little more expensive, but it is lively and open 24 hours. It has recently been renovated.

The *Scotts Picnic Food Court* in the Scotts shopping centre on Scotts Rd, just off Orchard Rd, is a glossy food court, with stalls offering a variety of international Asian cuisine, including Thai and Japanese.

Orchard Rd has a number of other food courts. *Orchard Emerald Food Court* in the basement of the Orchard Emerald shopping centre, on the corner of Emerald Hill Rd, has a range of Asian food. In the same vein are the food stalls downstairs in *Orchard Towers*, on the corner of Orchard and Claymore Rds (at the west end of Orchard Rd), and the *Food Life Food Court* on the 4th floor of the Wisma Atria. The latter is small but has a good selection of local dishes and 'moderne' decor from the 1950s.

The *Asian Food Mall* in the basement of Lucky Plaza has a good range of local hawker favourites and is as cheap as you'll find anywhere.

The *Taman Serasi Food Centre* has one of the best settings – it's next to the Botanical Gardens north-west of the city centre on Cluny Rd, just off Napier Rd. The stalls are predominantly Malay. Try the 'roti John', a type of fried sandwich with chilli, washed down with the fabulous soursop fruit juice.

## Colonial District

On the corner of Bencoolen and Albert Sts, in the basement of the Sim Lim Square complex, is the *Tenco Food Centre*, a very clean establishment.

On the corner of Bras Basah Rd and Bencoolen St is the clean, efficient *Kopitiam*.

It's open 24 hours, it's very handy if you are staying nearby and there's a good selection: Korean, Malay, Chinese and Western, as well as an outlet serving fresh fruit juices and more than 40 desserts.

The *Nan Tai Eating House* at Block 262 Waterloo St has several stalls, including some specialising in vegetarian food and chicken-rice. Sajis stall has good Indian *rojak* (spicy salad).

*Food Junction* in the basement of the Seiyu department store, Bugis Junction, 200 Victoria St, is busy and brisk. There is a good selection of Japanese food, including teppanyaki (sit around a hot plate while the chef whips up your meal), as well as Thai, Hong Kong, bubbling claypot concoctions, chicken-rice and more.

*New Bugis St*, right in the middle of the bustling open market on Victoria St, has Malay, Indonesian, Thai and Chinese food, and does a brisk trade in the evening when passersby are wooed by people brandishing illustrated menus.

Also on Victoria St you'll find the *Victoria St Food Court* next to the Victoria Hotel. There's an air-con section at the back and a bar with draught beer. Food includes fried chicken-wing rice, chicken-rice with noodles and Thai halal. Not far away, next to the Allson Hotel, is a *hawker centre* with a distinctive shrine outside – at night it's aglow with yellow light bulbs. The centre is usually full after dark and stays that way until it closes around midnight. Stalls offer everything from Western grills (lamb chops, steak), fish and chips, seafood, Malay (satay, nasi lemak), Teochew porridge, duck-rice and vegetarian. Across the road the *Xiang Man Lou Food Court* has Malay and Indian tandoor stalls, which also offer Chinese favourites. It's open 24 hours.

At 752 North Bridge Rd, across the road from Bugis Junction, is a little *food centre* underneath an HDB complex. At the *Bak Kut Teh* stall at the back you can get a bowl of delicious peppery pork rib soup for S$4. It's open daily from 4 to 11 pm.

The *Hill St Centre* at 64 Hill St, opposite the huge Funan complex, has a couple of floors with Chinese and Indian food stalls.

The **Marina Food Court** at Marina Square is a bright, modern place with a good selection. Noodle soups, fish soup, chicken-rice (Loy Kee; stall No 12), Malay food, Korean, Thai, halal, desserts (Swensen's) and Western grills are available.

At the **Suntec City Fountain Terrace** you can watch the fountain water plunge into the pool from the level above. There's a good selection, including Shanghainese, Thai, Malay, Indian and Korean. When we visited, the Economical Rice stand had people queuing for its 'three items for S$3.80' deal.

### Little India & Arab St

On Serangoon Rd at the start of Little India, the large **Zhujiao Centre** is a market with a number of food stalls. As you would expect, Indian food dominates. Opposite the market, the **Little India Arcade** has vegetarian and non-vegetarian food, Kerala specialities and North Indian tandoori dishes.

On Jalan Besar there are two food centres, the **Berseh Food Centre**, halfway down on the corner of Jalan Berseh, and the lively **Lavender Food Centre** at the end of Jalan Besar near Lavender St, which is good for seafood and stays open until early morning.

Right on the outskirts of Little India, near Arab St, is the **Golden Mile Food Centre** at 505 Beach Rd. This is the best place in Singapore to try soup *tulang;* beef bones stewed in blood-red, spicy tomato gravy. It costs S$4 a bowl. Head for stalls 13 and 15 in the basement.

### Chinatown

Chinatown has a number of excellent food centres. The **People's Park Complex** (not to be confused with the People's Park *Centre*) on Eu Tong Sen St has a good, large food centre, and the **Maxwell Rd Food Centre** is an old-fashioned centre on the corner of South Bridge and Maxwell Rds.

Some of the best Chinese food stalls in town are on the 2nd floor at the **Chinatown Complex** on the corner of Sago and Trengganu Sts, where there is also a market.

**China Square Food Court** on Telok Ayer St has three floors of food and is incredibly busy at lunchtime; ride up and

down the escalators to get a bird's eye view of what's on offer.

Other hawker centres include the **Amoy St Food Centre**, where Amoy St meets Telok Ayer St, and the **Tanjong Market** near the MRT station.

The **Satay Club**, which once held court near the Padang, can now be found in the evening at Clarke Quay, where over a dozen vendors fan their charcoal grills. At just 40c a stick, it's a tasty bargain.

## CHINESE

Many Chinese restaurants cater for family and work groups, offering banquets for eight or more people. For groups, they offer a wonderful opportunity to try a whole range of dishes at a reasonable price. Even at the a la carte restaurants, dishes are meant to be shared, and restaurants offer small, medium and large servings to cater for different sized groups.

### Cantonese

**Crystal Jade Kitchen** (☎ 338 3511, B1-013/014 Suntec City Mall, 3 Temasek Boulevard) is a busy place with a vast a la carte menu and several set menus to choose from. Mains are all under S$20, with many under S$10.

**Mitzis Cantonese Restaurant** (☎ 222 0929, 24/26 Murray Terrace), in Chinatown, has a large range available in small, medium and large servings. Small dishes start at around S$8. It's open from 11.30 am to 3 pm and 5.30 to 10 pm.

Farther south, **Hillman Restaurant** (☎ 221 5073, 01-159, Block 1 Cantonment Rd) is a favourite for its seafood and meat claypot in delicious sauces. You can eat well for S$10. It's open from 11.30 am to 2.30 pm and 5.30 to 10.30 pm.

**Lingzhi Vegetarian** (☎ 734 3788, B1-17/18 Orchard Towers, 400 Orchard Rd) has Western as well as traditional Chinese fare, including such imaginative dishes as wild Brazilian mushrooms with yellow fungus and braised wolfberry leaves. It's open from 11.30 am to 3.30 pm and 6 to 10 pm. At the entrance is an outlet selling vegetarian dumplings, cakes and spring rolls.

SINGAPORE

*Wing Seong Fatty's (Albert) Restaurant* (☎ 338 1087, 01-31 Burlington Square, 175 Bencoolen St) has been popular with Westerners ever since Fatty became a favourite with British troops stationed in Singapore during the Malayan Emergency. There is a wide selection and a choice of small, medium and large sizes. Small portions (still pretty generous) start at S\$5 for fried rice and noodle dishes to S\$50 for large portions of the most expensive item on the menu – shark's fin. It's a brisk, efficient place where you won't be kept waiting. It's open daily from noon to 11 pm.

## Hainanese

In Singapore this style of cuisine is virtually synonymous with chicken-rice. Almost every hawker centre and food court has a chicken-rice outlet.

The *Chatterbox* (☎ 831 6288, 333 Orchard Rd) at the Mandarin Hotel has good albeit pricey (S\$16) chicken-rice. It's open 24 hours.

*Tian Tian Hainanese Chicken Rice* at the Maxwell Rd Food Centre (stall 01-10) in Chinatown is brisk, efficient and very good. It costs around S\$3 per serve. It's open from 10 am to around 7.30 pm.

*Yet Con* (☎ 337 6819, 25 Purvis St), near Raffles Hotel, is a traditional, old-style place with consistently good chicken-rice, although the crispy pork is pretty moreish and the steamboat looks interesting. A plate of rice plus a dish of pork, chicken and pickled vegetables costs S\$3.50. It's open from 11 am to 9.30 pm.

## Hunanese

Subtle seasonings and spicy tastes sharpened by the liberal use of dark soy sauce characterise this type of cuisine.

At *House of Mao* (☎ 533 0660), in the China Square Food Court, Chinatown, you too can share the Chairman's love of spicy food. It's Hunanese with a dash of continental. The restaurant is crammed with all manner of Mao memorabilia and the staff wear Mao caps and uniforms. The all-you-can-eat dinner buffet (Monday to Friday dinner; Saturday and Sunday lunch) costs S\$19.80. The House of Mao is open from 11.30 am to 2.30 pm and 6.30 to 10 pm.

## Szechuan

Spicy Szechuan, or Sichuan, food is popular with Singaporeans and restaurants are fairly common, though usually expensive.

At *The Magic of Chongqing Hot Pot* (☎ 734 8135, 04–06/07 Tanglin shopping centre, 19 Tanglin Rd) you can cook your own food at your table in pots of boiling, spicy stock, then dip it in a sauce of your choice. Choose from an extensive MSG-free menu that includes seafood, meat, eggs and vegetables (including such intriguing items as hairy melon and abalone mushroom). It's open from noon to 3.30 pm and 5.30 to 11 pm. The hot pot a la carte buffet is S\$13.90.

The quaintly named *Yummy Otah Otah* (☎ 226 2501, 69 Spottiswoode Park Rd) is located in a shophouse in an enclave of beautifully restored shophouses south-west of Chinatown. The hot and sour soup, diced chicken with chilli, and prawns and tomato sauce are all redolent of Szechuan cuisine, although there are less traditional dishes as well. Prices are moderate. It's open from 11.30 am to 2 pm and 6.30 to 10 pm.

## Teochew

The Teochew from south-eastern China near Guangzhou (Canton) are famous for their food stalls, their fiery temperament and for inventing the steamboat – a kind of Chinese fondue cooking. Their delicious braised duck with soy sauce and fresh chillies is a well-known regional speciality.

*Ban Seng* (☎ 533 1471, 20 Upper Circular Rd) is right on the river and is a very pleasant spot of an evening. Try Teochew-style braised goose (from S\$18), prawn rolls (from S\$8), crayfish with chilli (seasonal) and Teochew steamed vegetables (from S\$18). Desserts include the traditional dish of yam paste with gingko nuts (from S\$10). It's open from noon to 2 pm and 6 to 10 pm.

## East-West/Fusion

The *Fig Leaf* (☎ 536 2677) is in the swish new Central Mall complex just south of the river. Items include braised sea bass with fried Japanese eggplant salad (S$22) and jasmine scented smoked duck (S$12/20 for entree/main). It's open from noon to 2 pm and 6.30 to 9.30 pm.

## INDIAN FOOD

The largest range of Indian cuisine can be found in Little India. It's also excellent value for money and, if you're on a budget, dining in Little India is a good way to stretch your food dollar.

At *Banana Leaf Apolo* (☎ 293 8682, 54 Race Course Rd) dine off the eponymous leaf in a modern, air-con setting. *Thali* (rice, vegetables, soup, curries and bread) starts at S$6 and most mains are around S$4. A speciality here is fish head curry (S$18 small, S$22 medium, S$26 large). It's open from 10 am to 10 pm.

The *Delhi Restaurant* (☎ 296 4585, 60 Race Course Rd) has a range of vegetarian and non-vegetarian food. Try tandoori chicken, *rogan josh* (lamb curry), fish masala or *Kashmiri pulau*. The *D'Deli Pubb & Restaurant* (☎ 294 5276) at No 48 has similar fare, as well as a bar.

*Komala Vilas* (☎ 293 6990, 76–78 Serangoon Rd) serves terrific, inexpensive vegetarian food. Snacks include *vadai* (spicy, fried lentil patty), *idli* (steamed rice cake), samosa, *bonda* (spicy, fried potato balls) and *dosa* (pancakes). The vegetable biryani is particularly tasty, and the daily specials are good value. There's an efficient takeaway service – place your order with the cashier, collect a number and wait for it to come up on the electronic display in the front window. It's open from 7 am to 11 pm.

Nearby, *Madras New Woodlands* (☎ 297 1594, 12–14 Upper Dickson Rd) serves good vegetarian food, including filling thali (S$5 for the set dinner) on banana leaves. The service is gracious and the portions immense.

Back from Serangoon Rd, *Madras Woodlands Ganga* (☎ 295 3750, 22 Belilos Lane) has a comfortable lounge with a bar separate from the main dining area. The all-you-can-eat buffets are good value at S$7.90 for lunch and S$9.90 for dinner. It's open from 11 am to 3 pm and 6 to 11 pm.

*Taj Jazzaurant* (☎ 291 4680, 02-01 Little India Arcade, 48 Serangoon Rd) has consistently good North and South Indian food. There is live music from 7.30 pm every evening, mostly Indian popular music (the band will play requests). As it's upstairs, you can sit near a window and watch the activity down on the street. It's open from 11 am to 3 pm and 6 to 10 pm. Lunch is a buffet (S$9) and dinner is a la carte.

*Bangles* (☎ 295 1755, 5 Jalan Kledek) specialises in North Indian and Mughlai cuisine, although dishes from other parts of India (eg, Goan fish curry) are also on the menu. There is a range of vegetarian meals for under S$10, seafood (eg, crayfish curry for S$9.90) and biryani. Desserts include a very delicious *falooda* (sweet, milky drink flavoured with rosewater and served cold). The restaurant is housed in a prewar shophouse that is decorated with Indian furniture, carpets and brassware to give it a cosy feeling. It's open from 6.30 to 10.30 pm.

At *Zam Zam* (☎ 298 7011, 699 North Bridge Rd) and at *Victory Restaurant* next door you can watch the skilful murtabak makers at work. Both restaurants have been turning out good, inexpensive food in this part of town since the early 20th century. It's open from 7 am to 11 pm.

There are numerous Indian restaurants elsewhere in Singapore, although those on and around Orchard Rd tend to be rather more expensive.

The *Bombay Woodlands Restaurant* (☎ 235 2712, B1-01/02 Tanglin shopping centre) specialises in vegetarian fare; a leaflet at the front door details the moral, spiritual and health benefits of vegetarianism. Starters include idli, *pakora* (vegetable fritter), *dahi vada* (spicy, fried lentil patties served with yoghurt) and *upma* (savoury, semolina-based South Indian dish, usually served with coconut chutney) – all from S$4. Mains include various thali, *uthappam* (thin, lentil-flour pancakes with spicy vegetable filling), dosa and rice dishes (many under S$10).

*Kinara* (☎ 533 0412, 57 Boat Quay) has a pleasant upstairs dining area in a renovated shophouse outfitted to look like a traditional *haveli*, a multistorey merchant house of the

**SINGAPORE**

type seen in Rajasthan. You can look over the river while feasting on moderately priced Punjabi food. It's open from 11.30 am to 2.30 pm and 6.30 to 10.30 pm.

## OTHER ASIAN FOOD
### Peranakan/Nyonya

The Peranakan, also known as Straits Chinese, were successful traders with a distinctive culture and architecture. Descendants of early Chinese immigrants who married Malay women, they also developed a unique cuisine that blends Chinese ingredients with Malay sauces and spices.

*Blue Ginger* (☎ 222 3928, 05-02C, The Heeren, 260 Orchard Rd) serves consistently good quality Peranakan cuisine. It's open from 11.30 am to 3 pm and 6 to 10 pm.

*Nonya & Baba* (☎ 734 1386, 262 River Valley Rd), with its Peranakan-style decor, is a pleasant spot to sample Peranakan delights such as *bakwan kepiting* soup, *nyonya mee* (Nyonya-style noodles) and deep-fried trebok fish. Just south of Forth Canning, the restaurant is open from 11 am to 3 pm and 6 to 10 pm.

### Indonesian

*Alkaff Mansion* (☎ 278 6979, 10 Telok Blangah Green, Telok Blangah Hill Park), south-west of the city, is set in an attractive historic house built in the 1920s for the wealthy Alkaff family. The service complements the grand colonial ambience; the *rijstaffel* (rice table; at least 10 dishes) is served by women wearing traditional Malay dress. The set Western dinner is available from 7 to 10.30 pm (S$65), the riijstaffel is the same (S$60), and the buffet starts at 7 pm in the Mansion Hall and costs S$30 (Sunday to Thursday) or S$35 (Friday and Saturday). All menus change regularly; the buffet features a different cuisine daily (eg, Italian on Tuesday, Indian on Wednesday).

At *House of Sundanese* (☎ 534 3775, 55–55A Boat Quay) you can sample the spicy cuisine of West Java. Try crisp fried prawns with *sambal* (chilli, onion and prawns) and *petai*, *cumi cumi baka* (charcoal grilled squid) or *ikan sunda* (fried dancing fish). It's open from 11.30 am to

3 pm and 6 to 10 pm weekdays (from noon to 3.30 pm and 5.30 to 10 pm on weekends). There is another outlet at Suntec City Mall (B1-063, ☎ 334 1012) and at 218 East Coast Rd (☎ 345 5020).

### Japanese

You can sample Japanese food cheaply at *Food Junction* in the basement of the Seiyu department store at Bugis Junction. The *Cold Storage supermarket* adjacent has a sushi and sashimi selection (you can buy sushi from 70c per piece). The *supermarket* in the basement of Daimaru at 177 River Valley Rd is also well stocked with all manner of Japanese foods.

A slightly more expensive alternative is *Sakae Sushi* (☎ 235 9083, 05-01 The Heeren, 260 Orchard Rd), where you can watch little containers of various sushi interspersed with pots of wasabi trundle past you at eye level on a conveyor. Pick out what you want and pay at the end. All colour plates are S$1.90; premium sushi plates are S$6.50.

Or you could try *One More Shabu Shabu Buffet Steamboat* (☎ 339 9496, 02-211/212 6 Raffles Boulevard), east of the Padang, which has 80 steamboat items on display. Cook your choice at your table and eat all you want. Lunch is from 11.30 am to 5 pm (costs S$11.80) and dinner from 5 to 10 pm (S$13.50).

### Korean

*Kimchi* (☎ 333 9282, 36 Purvis St) is one of several good restaurants in this street near Raffles Hotel. The setting is very pleasant and prices are moderate. Try the *dak han ma ree* (spicy herbal chicken hot pot) or *kori chim* (oxtail stew). It's open from noon to 2.30 pm and 6.30 to 10 pm.

### Thai

The Golden Mile Complex at 5001 Beach Rd, just north-east of Arab St, is a modern shopping centre catering to Singapore's Thai community. Here you'll find a number of small *coffee shops* serving Thai food and Singha beer. Prices are cheap – you can get a good meal for S$5.

In Cuppage Plaza just off Orchard Rd, *Cuppage Thai Food Restaurant* (☎ 734 1116, 49 Cuppage Terrace) has mains in small and medium sizes, starting from S$9. It's open from 6 to 11 pm.

*D'Lemon Tree Thai Kitchen & Cafe* (☎ 338 1122, 173 Bencoolen St) at the Summer View Hotel has Thai curries from S$8 and seafood from S$10 to S$20. Most mains are around S$10. There's also a Western menu. It's open from 11am to 11 pm.

*Yhingthai* (☎ 337 1161, 36 Purvis St) serves Thai and Thai-Chinese cuisine. Familiar favourites include green and red curries (S$10 for a small size) and tom yam soup (from S$10), as well as dishes such as claypot prawns with crystal noodles (from S$16). It's open from 11.30 am to 2 pm and 6 to 10 pm.

## Vietnamese

*Indochine al Fresco Café* (☎ 333 5003, 42 Waterloo St) has a lovely setting, back from the road in a colonial-style building that also houses Action Theatre. The food is Vietnamese and Laotian: entrees include *yum sen* glass noodle salad (S$8.50), and mains (from around S$14) include fragrant sticky rice, steamed fish in coconut curry, and minced chicken with lime and chilli. It's open from 11.30 am to 2 pm and 6 to 10 pm (till 12 am on Friday and Saturday).

## INTERNATIONAL FOOD
### American

*Hard Rock Cafe* (☎ 235 6256, 02-01 50 Cuscaden Rd), near Orchard Rd, has good burgers (S$12 to S$14), mud pie and pot roast. It's open from 11 am to 10.30 pm.

The *Ponderosa* (☎ 339 6495, 6 Raffles Boulevard) is a relatively informal place with sirloin for about S$20. There's also chicken and seafood, burgers, a salad buffet and a kid's menu (S$7.50). It's open from 11.30 am to 9.30 pm (till 10 pm Saturday).

*Seah Street Deli* (☎ 337 1886, 01-22 Raffles Hotel Arcade, 1 Beach Rd) has bagels, pastrami sandwiches, BBQ ribs and fish and chips (both S$10.95), pumpkin pie, pretzels and salads. It's open from 11.30 am to 9.30 pm (till 10.30 pm Friday and Saturday).

### Australian

At *The Moomba* (☎ 438 0141, 52 Circular Rd), behind Boat Quay, Aboriginal paintings and a good Aussie wine list (each dish comes with a recommended wine) complement the modern cuisine, which includes BBQ'd kangaroo loin and chargrilled Australian beef. Mains are upwards of S$25. It's open from 11 am to 3 pm and 6.30 to 11.30 pm (closed Sunday).

### French

*L'Aigle d'Or* (☎ 227 7678) in the Duxton Hotel, Chinatown, serves exquisite French food in elegant surroundings. Try the panfried foie gras with raspberry sauce and rhubarb ravioli. The set lunch is S$36. It's open from noon for lunch and from 7 pm for dinner.

Nearby, *L'Angelus* (☎ 225 6897, 85 Club St) is set in a restored shophouse and is popular with the French expat community. Mains range from S$18 to S$25. There's a set lunch for S$22 and a good wine list. It's open from noon to 2 pm and 7 pm to late, and is closed Saturday lunch and all day Sunday.

### Italian

*Da Paolo* (☎ 224 7081, 80 Club St) is set in a restored shophouse on a street filled with great little restaurants. Prices are moderate, and the food is fresh, innovative and appealing. It's open from 11.30 am to 2.30 pm and 6.30 to 11.30 pm Tuesday to Sunday (no lunch on Saturday).

Close by, *Gaetano* (☎ 325 3360, 21 Mohamed Ali Lane) serves authentic Italian cuisine with an innovative touch. Prices are reasonable; a set lunch is S$28. It's open from 12 to 2.30 pm and 7 to 10.30 pm.

*Pete's Place* (☎ 730 7113, Grand Hyatt Hotel, 10–12 Scotts Rd) is not signposted; go into the hotel lobby and look for the stairs that take you down below the lobby level. The buffet lunch (11.30 am to 2.30 pm) is good value at S$19.50 (Monday to Saturday). The Sunday brunch buffet (11.30 am to 2.30 pm; S$25) has free-flow juice, coffee and tea. The a la carte dinner is from 6 to 11.30 pm daily.

SINGAPORE

At *Sketches (☎ 339 8386, 01-85, 200 Victoria St)* at Bugis Junction pick up the form on your table and fill out the multiple choice options. Hand your form to the waiter and relax with a drink while the chef whips up your customised meal. The tiramasu dessert is very good. A beer and a main serve of pasta will cost around S$28.

## Mexican

*Cha Cha Cha (☎ 462 1650, 32 Lorong Mambong, Holland Village)* is a busy little place west of the city, where you can eat inside or out on the terrace. You can try burritos, tacos, enchiladas and other typically Mexican fare plus rich Kahlua chocolate mousse. Prices are very reasonable. It's open from 11.30 to 11 pm (till 12 am Friday and Saturday).

*Chico's N Charlies (☎ 734 1753, 05-01 Liat Towers, 541 Orchard Rd)* was one of the first Mexican restaurants in Singapore. Mexican standards plus Tex Mex are available. The buffet lunch is good value (S$10.50). It's open from 11 am to 11 pm (last order 10.30 pm).

## Middle Eastern & Mediterranean

*Cafe Gypsy (☎ 227 7769, 92 Club St)*, in Chinatown, is one of the newer places in this enclave of interesting restaurants. The food ranges from Lebanese to Greek, Moroccan, French and Spanish. Mains are around S$25 and include dishes like grilled sea bass with anchovies, capers and black olives. There's a tapas menu that changes every two to three weeks. It's open from 11.30 am to 3 pm and 6.30 pm to midnight (no lunch on Saturday; closed Sunday).

*Efferus (☎ 324 6768, 47 Club St)* serves Middle Eastern fare with an Australian influence. Generous mains cost S$20 to S$30. The menu changes every six weeks or so. It's open from 11.30 am to 10.30 pm Monday to Thursday and to 11 pm Friday and Saturday.

Farther north, the *Kibbutz Café (☎ 438 2221, 5 Pekin St)* is the place to try Israeli food: pitta served with pate (hummus, chicken liver, eggplant), felafel, stuffed cabbage, and *halva* ice-cream. It's open from 11.30 am to 3 pm and 6.30 to 10 pm.

*Esmirada (☎ 735 3476, Peranakan Place, 180 Orchard Rd)* has something from just about every part of the Mediterranean: couscous, paella, moussaka, lasagne and bouillabaisse. It's fairly pricey (S$29.50 for couscous and the same for bouillabaisse) but a popular spot, especially in the evening.

Out west, *Michelangelo's (☎ 475 9069, 01-60 Chip Bee Gardens, Holland Village)* has a good selection of pastas, soups and salads. Try the seafood pasta or the penne vodka. Prices are moderate. It's open from 11.30 am to 2.30 pm and 6.30 pm till late. *Original Sin (☎ 475 5605, 01-62 Chip Bee Gardens, Holland Village)* specialises in good, fresh vegetarian food with a Mediterranean slant. The menu includes salads and pizzas, and a daily frittata. Prices are moderate. It's open from 11.30 am to 2.30 pm and 6 to 11 pm.

## Other International Food

*Marché Movenpick (01-03 The Heeren, 260 Orchard Rd)* has various European-style outlets in a large, enclosed dining area that includes a children's playground: There's a grill, seafood, pizza, salads, roast potato, pasta, fresh juices, a wine cellar and a beer garden. You can also make your own sandwiches. Your various purchases are totted up for you automatically and you pay on departure. It's open from 11 am to 11 pm.

*Mezza9 (☎ 730 7188, Grand Hyatt Hotel, 10–12 Scotts Rd)* is a classy place at the head of a staircase that sweeps up from the Hyatt's expansive lobby. There are six display kitchens: a patisserie, deli, Western grill, steam basket, yakitori kitchen and sushi bar. You can watch the chefs at work and gaze upon the ingredients artfully displayed. There is a Sunday 'munch' from 11 am to 3 pm (S$69 including free flow of Moet et Chandon champagne). To book, call ☎ 730 7188 or email @ mezza9@hyatt .com.sg.

## SEAFOOD

At the *Blue Lobster (☎ 538 0766, Upper Circular Rd)* you can dine beside the river or inside the restaurant. Oysters are flown in, and there's barramundi (S$28) and a variety of other seafood. The seafood platter is S$59 per person. It's open Monday to Saturday from noon to 2.30 pm and 7 to 10 pm.

*No Signboard Seafood* (☎ 293 0355, 9 Race Course Lane) is handy if you are staying near Little India. It's a friendly, low-key place and a good spot to try chilli crab (expect to pay around S$32 per person). It's open from 2 pm to midnight.

## HERBAL & SOUP RESTAURANTS
Let food be your medicine at one of Singapore's herbal soup restaurants, or at the Imperial Herbal.

At the *Imperial Herbal* (☎ 337 0491, 41 Seah St), beside Raffles Hotel above the Metropole Hotel, you can have a Chinese physician check your pulse and tongue and prescribe something on the menu that will get your Yin and Yang back in balance. It's open from 11.30 am to 2.30 pm and 6.30 to 10.30 pm.

Nearby, the *Soup Restaurant* (☎ 333 9388, 39 Seah St) has a range of MSG-free, double-boiled herbal soups (all under S$12). Also worth trying is the Samsui ginger chicken (S$12 or S$24), a traditional festive dish enjoyed by the hardy south Chinese Samsui women construction workers. The setting is traditional-shophouse style.

## ORGANICS
*Planet Organic* at Wheelock Place near Orchard Rd provides MSG-free and pesticide-free food: fresh juices, teas, salads and snacks. It also stocks organic packaged and fresh foods and other health products.

## VEGETARIAN
Most food courts and hawker centres have vegetarian outlets – or at least some dishes that use no meat. Little India is also a good place to go for vegetarian food. Recommended are *Komala Vilas, Madras New Woodlands* and *Madras Woodlands Ganga*, all of which appear in the Indian entry earlier in this section. Another good place is *Original Sin* at Holland Park (see Middle Eastern & Mediterranean earlier).

Chinese restaurants that serve no meat or fish include *Lingzhi* (see Cantonese under Chinese). A less expensive option is the *Xin Min Vegetarian Food Court* (☎ 324 2481, 29 Kreta Ayer Rd), just a few doors down from the Chinese Buddhist Association in Chinatown.

## BREAKFAST
You can breakfast with an orang-utan (daily at 9 am) at the Zoological Gardens for S$15.45 (children S$11.33). The price includes admission to the zoo and a generous buffet breakfast. See Northern & Central Singapore earlier in this chapter for more details.

You can also have breakfast with the birds at the *Jurong Bird Park* (☎ 264 2055), which is served from the time the park opens. There is a choice of *kaya* (made from coconut and egg) and roti with a half-boiled egg (a traditional breakfast; S$5.50), nasi lemak (S$5.50), or a Western-style breakfast with eggs, sausage, toast and juice (S$6.30). (Breakfast is in addition to your entry ticket).

*Ya Kun Kaya Toast & Coffee* at Chinatown's Far East Square serves a traditional *kopitiam* breakfast of kaya toast and *kopi*. The bread is sliced thin, the crusts cut off and then toasted until dark and crispy. The kaya melts into the toast. It's open from 7.30 am to 10 pm weekdays and from 9 am to 5 pm weekends.

All hotels serve breakfast, usually a buffet. *Chatterbox* at the Mandarin Hotel off Orchard Rd is better known for chicken-rice, but serves an American buffet breakfast for S$23 (from 7.15 to 10 am). About 1km north-west, the plush *Four Seasons Hotel* has an express breakfast buffet on Monday to Saturday from 7 to 9.30 am. The Continental option is S$23 and cooked is S$31.

## HIGH TEA & TIFFIN
For high tea with a great view, head for the *Compass Rose* bar at Westin Stamford. A high-tea buffet is served from 11.30 am to 5.30 pm (S$28).

The *Tiffin Room* at Raffles Hotel is the classic location for a tiffin curry buffet. Lunch (S$35) is served from noon to 2 pm, and dinner (S$45) from 7 to 10 pm. You should book at least a day in advance (☎ 337 1886).

You can have high tea at the *Verandah Bar* at the classy, historic Alkaff Mansion *(☎ 278 6979, 10 Telok Blangah Green)* on weekends between 3 and 5.30 pm. The menu changes regularly and features Asian and Western fare.

## CAFES

Espresso (along with muffins, cake, bagels, croissants and all the usual cafe fare) is readily available. *Coffee Bean And Tea Leaf* has some 25 branches in Singapore including: 82 Boat Quay, Bugis Junction, Holland Village, Suntec City Mall (two outlets) and the Wisma Atria shopping centre on Orchard Rd.

*Starbucks* similarly has numerous outlets, including at the WTC, Raffles City shopping centre, Orchard Point, Marina Square and Changi International Airport.

The classy *Dôme*, with its Australian roasted beans, can be found at the Singapore Art Museum, and the equally classy *Olio Dôme Cafe* is at Suntec City Mall and Wheelock Place.

*DeliFrance* has numerous outlets around town, including at Bugis Junction and Suntec City Mall. Offerings include croissants, cakes and cooked breakfasts (S$5.40 for bacon, eggs and tomato).

*Cafe Les Amis* at the Botanic Gardens (Cluny Rd entry) enjoys a pleasant setting overlooking the gardens. Breakfast is served from 7.30 to 10.30 am (Western or Asian; S$8.50); from 11.30 am to 7.15 pm you can get coffee and cold drinks, snacks and sandwiches and light meals, such as Cantonese fried rice (S$5.50) and pasta (from S$11).

*Fat Frog (☎ 338 6201, 45 Armenian St)* is in the same building as the theatre/gallery space Substation. It's a good spot to take a break if you're visiting the nearby National Museum. It's open from 11.30 am to midnight Sunday to Thursday and until 1 am Friday and Saturday. Another option if you are in this area is the little *cafe* on the 1st level of the MPH bookstore across the road.

Outfitted with an old-style coffee house look, it even serves kaya.

## TEA HOUSES

Taking time out in a traditional tea house is a pleasant way to relax. Arguably the most well-known tea house in Chinatown is the *Tea Chapter (☎ 226 1175, 9A Neil Rd)*. As a newcomer you will be given a brief demonstration of the art of tea appreciation. Then, with your hot water bubbling away over a little spirit stove, your packet of tea at the ready and your tea drinking paraphernalia neatly laid out on a little cloth, you can relax and enjoy. It's open daily from 11 am to 11 pm.

Nearby is another place, the *Yixing Yuan Teahouse (☎ 224 6961, 30 Tanjong Pagar Rd)*. Here too you can sample a variety of teas, nibble on sweet tea cakes and just take your time. It's open daily from 11 am to 11 pm. Both places offer courses in English on the art of tea.

## SUPERMARKETS

*Cold Storage* has several branches, including one in the basement of the Seiyu department store at Bugis Junction and at 293 Holland Rd in Holland Village. *Diamaru* is at the Liang Court shopping centre and is open until midnight daily with a wide selection of Japanese food. *Sogo* is at Raffles City shopping centre *(252 North Bridge Rd)*, and the French hypermarket *Carrefour* is on the 1st level at Suntec City.

There are dozens of *7-Eleven stores* including 321 Orchard Rd, and 75 and 245 Victoria St.

# Entertainment

Singapore's nightlife is burgeoning, as the young middle class spends its increasing wealth on entertainment. It's not of the Bangkok 'sex and sin' variety, nor does a wild club scene exist, but the huge number of bars and discos are becoming increasingly sophisticated.

Boat Quay is packed nightly until the early hours of the morning, and Orchard Rd and Chinatown also have their fair share of good bars. Smoking is permitted in bars, though if food is served smoking is restricted until after meal times.

The live music scene in the bars is less healthy. It's limited to a few venues and only a small roster of bands and performers. For better bands, you have to go to the clubs and discos, where a cover charge normally applies. At such places dress is smart casual, drinks are expensive and the bands mostly play covers. Almost every four-star hotel has a Filipino band playing in the lobby, every five-star hotel has a jazz band and even many three-star hotels can muster up a piano.

Highbrow entertainment such as classical music, ballet and theatre can also be enjoyed in Singapore, as well as Chinese opera and tourist-oriented cultural shows. In addition, Singapore regularly hosts touring international shows. Tickets for most of these shows, which are widely advertised, can be bought at Sistic (bookings ☎ 348 5555) and TicketCharge (☎ 296 2929).

The *Straits Times* newspaper is good for cultural and special events, while *Eight Days,* the weekly TV and entertainment magazine, has listings. *This Week In Singapore* has full details on what's on. For nightlife look out for *I-S Magazine* and *Pop Out,* which are both free and come out twice a month. You can generally find copies at hotels, cafes and Singapore Tourism offices.

## PUBS & BARS

The time to drink is during happy hour, which is usually from around 5 to 8 or even 9 pm. At these times drinks are as cheap as half-price. Most of the bars also serve food and serious drinking is done outside meal times, but you can grab a stool at the bar anytime.

### Orchard Rd Area

*Brix,* in the Grand Hyatt Hotel on Scotts Rd, is a popular place that attracts a fashionable crowd. There are two sections: a wine and whisky bar and a piano bar. The decor is plush and the crowd is generally in their 20s or 30s.

If you fancy yet another Irish pub with expensive pints of Guinness or Kilkenny, **Muddy Murphy's** in the basement of the Orchard Towers is a handy hangout for Celtic expats. The top bar is narrow and smokey, and only opens in the evening.

*The Elephant (165 Penang Rd)* is housed in an historic colonial-era building, the former Oxley Plantation Mansion. It's furnished with antiques and art. There's veranda seating upstairs and down, with old-style wicker chairs to sink back in.

Emerald Hill Rd has a collection of bars in the renovated terraces just up from Orchard Rd. *No 5* at, you guessed it, 5 Emerald Hill Rd, is very popular with a largely tourist clientele and its chilli vodka has a mean reputation. The bar is crowded, though you can drink at the tables outside, and acoustic music plays upstairs. Next door at No 7, *Que Pasa* is a popular tapas bar with a Spanish theme. Smokers will enjoy the snazzy upstairs smoking room. It's a lot quieter than No 5.

Next along, *Ice Cold Beer* has the coldest beer in town and lots of different brands. You can even watch movies for free upstairs. Upstairs at Peranakan Place on the corner of Emerald Hill and Orchard Rds, **Papa Joe's** is another popular place with a covers band on the weekend and a first drink cover charge.

Nearby, the **H2O Zone** *(23 Cuppage Terrace),* near the corner of Orchard Rd, is a small place with a saxophone saloon, good blues and jazz from 9.30 pm till late and an alfresco dining area. *Doug's Bar* at No 41 also has R&B and jazz from 9 pm till around 1 am, and tables outside for diners.

### Colonial District

You can have a drink at *Raffles Hotel* at the Long Bar or in the Bar & Billiard Room, where that infamous tiger was supposedly shot. One of the favourite pastimes in the Long Bar is throwing peanut shells on the floor – swinging stuff. There's no dress code at the Long Bar. The Bar & Billiard room is relaxed, and you can recline in the wicker chairs. Both bars have light jazz in the evening from 7.30 pm and serve food.

SINGAPORE

Chijmes Complex on Bras Basah Rd, a former convent complex, now houses up-market bars and restaurants. The *Fountain Court*, with gurgling water, stone walls and greenery all dominated by a rather imposing Gothic chapel is a very atmospheric spot for a pre-dinner cocktail, while *Father Flanagans* – yet another Irish pub – serves a mean but pricey pint of Guinness stout. Next to Father Flanagans, *China Jump* is a hot bar where things really happen after 10 pm. Smart dress code applies.

The *Compass Rose (70th floor, Westin Stamford, 2 Stamford Rd)* has stunning views and prices to match. Smart casual is the dress standard (ie, no jeans, T-shirts, or sandals).

The *Hu'u Bar (71 Bras Basah Rd)* at the Singapore Art Museum is a fairly popular after-work spot for expats. Later on, the young and fashionable gather to listen to DJs spin acid jazz.

If you can't afford a fancy bar, go to *New Bugis St*, one block south of Bugis MRT station. You can have a beer at the food stalls under the stars until 3 am, or whenever everyone goes home. If you want to pay more, there are a couple of places that have karaoke and bad Filipino bands.

## The River

The renovated banks of the Singapore River in the centre of town, especially Boat Quay, are the happening place in Singapore. Farther along the river, Clarke Quay is less frenetic and a little more spread out, with several colourful streets all with their fair share of watering holes and restaurants.

**Boat Quay** This place has become so incredibly popular that the rest of Singapore seems dead in comparison. The crowds start coming around 6 pm for a quiet drink or a meal, and keep growing through the night. Weekends are busy until 2 or 3 am, while weekdays are marginally quieter and most bars close by 1 am. Boat Quay attracts everyone from the rich and famous to young Singaporean kids vomiting into the gutter after a night of over-indulgence.

Boat Quay has so many bars that you can just wander along until one takes your fancy. At the eastern end, *Harry's*, at No 28, gets going early in the evening as city workers flock for happy hour until 8 pm. Corporate high-fliers and wannabes, mostly expats, bullshit each other over beer and are joined later in the evening by a mixed, up-market crowd who come for the jazz bands. You can even order a Bank Breaker and reflect on the life and times of one of Harry's better-known former customers (see the boxed text 'Rogue Trader – Nick Leeson'). Things stay pretty busy until at least midnight. Harry's is also a good jazz venue.

*Penny Black (26/27 Boat Quay)* is in the spirit of a traditional English pub, with British ales and a popular bar menu. You can sit at tables outside if you wish. Nearby, *Molly Malone's (42 Circular Rd)* is an Irish pub with Guinness on tap and traditional Irish bands upstairs.

Back on Boat Quay, *Culture Club*, at No 38, has a pool table, a dart board and occasionally decent bands. Way down the end, *Bernie Goes to Town* is an American roadhouse-style place with a laid-back atmosphere, live music every night (and jamming on Sunday; jazz and R&B), and a generous selection of steaks and burgers.

***Clarke Quay & Robertson Quay*** Though the quieter cousin of Boat Quay, Clarke Quay has a good selection of places for a beer. The bars tend to be more convivial and don't get so overwhelmed by crowds.

The *Crazy Elephant*, beside the river at Trader's Market, has some decent rock bands (and a Sunday night blues jam) and plenty of room on the pavement outside for chatting. *Le Aussie Wine Cellar* nearby is the place to come for Australian wines, which you can take away or drink outside by the river. *Coco Carib* is the place for Caribbean rhythm; sometimes musicians set up outside where the diners are. *JP Bastiani (☎ 339 0392, 01-13 Clarke Quay)* is a wine merchant with a very chic wine bar where high fliers like to be seen. The *Boathouse Bar* at the Pacific-themed Trader Vic's in the Hotel New Otani serves an astonishing variety of cocktails, and the band plays requests.

## Rogue Trader – Nick Leeson

When the beer is flowing at Harry's bar on Boat Quay, the talk among the expat regulars occasionally turns to the subject of one of the bar's most infamous patrons. On 23 February 1995 Nicholas William Leeson, general manager at Barings Futures Singapore, a shade short of his 28th birthday, disappeared from his office having single-handedly wrought a disaster of catastrophic financial dimensions.

He had totally wiped out the 233-year-old Barings Investment Bank in a cumulative series of ill-conceived investment gambles on the derivatives market – a game that few in financial circles knew much about nor cared to master. He bet heavily on the future direction of the Nikkei index, which he hoped would rise at the beginning of 1995. With the Japanese economy on a gradual slide, and coupled with the Kobe earthquake, Leeson's financial gambles on the Nikkei went from bad to ruinous.

All this time Leeson had managed to persuade his superiors that he was making money for Barings when, in fact, he was losing money by the barrow-load. Since he acted as both front-office trader and back-office settlements manager he was able to disguise his manoeuvrings, while at the same time pulling in an enormous salary of his own. By December 1994, the cumulative debt in the optimistically numbered account, No 88888, had topped S$512 million. By the end of his gambling spree he had cost Barings US$1.4 billion.

CLINT CURÉ

Nick Leeson was a working-class Londoner with a thirst for the good life and a brash ability to persuade others that he was doing fine in what is generally viewed as a high-risk financial activity. When the chips were down he finally skipped Singapore. He was arrested in March 1995 while on a stopover in Germany and extradited back to Singapore, where he was tried and sentenced to 6½ years in prison (he was released early for good behaviour). The Dutch bank ING bought Barings for a nominal £1 stake.

The 1998 movie *Rogue Trader* glamorised the whole affair for the big screen, starring Ewen McGregor as Leeson.

*Brewerkz (30 Merchant Rd)* in the Riverside Point Centre, across the river from Clarke Quay, is a micro-brewery-cum-restaurant offering no fewer than five locally produced boutique beers, including the popular India Pale Ale. The menu includes pizza and pasta dishes from S$16, and mains such as steak, roast chicken, ribs and fish and chips from S$26.

Robertson Quay is just a short walk from Clarke Quay. At the time of writing this area was still so new that it was fairly quiet. At No 30, right on the river, is *Provignage* (The Wine Cave), a place where wine appreciation is taken pretty seriously. The emphasis is on French and Italian wines, although others do feature, including wines from Spain, Chile and Australia. There are regular tastings – phone ☎ 834 1490 for details.

### Chinatown

The Club St/Ann Siang Hill area is a good hunting ground for interesting, innovative restaurants and bars housed in attractive restored shophouses. *Beaujolais Wine Bar (1 Ann Siang Hill)* is a cosy, comfortable spot. Just off Club St, *Petrus Wine Bar (23 Mohamed Ali Lane)* is a classy companion to the excellent Gaetano Italian restaurant next door.

Farther south, Duxton Hill has a string of bars that are pleasant, if relatively quiet

SINGAPORE

places to have a drink. *Elvis' Place (1A Duxton Hill)* is lined with Elvis memorabilia, though it has foregone the 50s music and is much like any other bar. Farther along at No 10, the *Flag & Whistle* is a quiet English-style pub. *JJ Mahoney (58 Duxton Rd)* has Belgium and American beers. There's a band on the ground floor, a games room bar on the 2nd floor and karaoke on the 3rd.

The Far East Square has a couple of popular places. *Carnegies (44/45 Pekin St)* has a rock 'n' roll theme with plenty of memorabilia, and a hearty meaty menu.

## Holland Village

This is where the expat community gathers to eat, drink and socialise. *Wala Wala* is an American-style restaurant and bar. It's generally packed on Friday and Saturday evenings, with seating on two floors and al fresco dining. *Tango's* at No 35 is a sleek, minimalist place with beer, wine and a good selection of pasta. You can sit indoors or outside. At *Baden Baden* across the road you can get German and north European beers. The menu features German favourites such as meatballs and schnitzel.

## Other Areas

It's hard to beat the Verandah Bar at *Alkaff Mansion (10 Telok Blangah Green)* for atmosphere. It's on the 2nd level and looks out over extensive gardens towards the sea. It's open from mid-afternoon (when high tea is served). The dress code is smart casual.

## DISCOS & NIGHTCLUBS

Singapore has no shortage of discos. They tend to be big on decor and yuppie hang-outs with strict dress codes. A cover charge of S$15 to S$20 usually applies (S$25 to S$35 on weekends). Women often pay less.

Some venues don't have a cover charge, but drinks are expensive and you can expect to pay around S$10 for a glass of beer. Those that do have a cover charge usually include the first drink free. For most venues, 10% service charge and 4% government tax are added to the drinks and the cover charge.

## Orchard Rd

The Orchard Rd area is the main centre for nightlife, with a host of discos, clubs and bars mainly in the hotels and hidden away in the shopping centres.

*Sparks,* on level 7 of Ngee Ann City has one of the biggest dance floors in Singapore. The very young crowd jumps to the biggest music system in town, and everything stops for the dazzling laser show.

The *Lava Lounge* on the 3rd floor of the Orchard Building (above Ray Wilson's California Fitness Centre) is decked out in 70s retro complete with swirling red, orange and blue lighting. There's a small dance floor, pool tables, and karaoke rooms upstairs. The music is a mix of house and garage, and the crowd here mainly in their 20s and 30s.

*Anywhere (04-08 Tanglin shopping centre, 19 Tanglin Rd)* is a long-running rock 'n' roll venue. The band Tania has been playing here since 1981 and features a cross-dressing lead singer. The band has a regular following of mostly expats and can belt out a good song when they try. This place has a casual, convivial atmosphere and no cover charge.

*Hard Rock Cafe (50 Cuscaden Rd)* has the usual rock memorabilia and a good atmosphere. It has better bands than most venues and occasionally imports some big names from overseas. The music and cover charge starts, and the ash trays come out, after 10.30 pm when the dining stops. It stays open until around 2 or 3 am.

## Other Areas

*Zouk (17–21 Jiak Kim St),* near the Havelock Rd hotels, is a legendary dance club housed in an old *godown* (warehouse) by the Singapore River. A cover charge of S$20 (women) and S$25 (men) applies on Friday and Saturday, when the music features house, and, on Wednesday, retro. Adjacent are *Phuture* (S$23 men and women), which features drum and base, and *Velvet Underground* (S$25), which focuses on dance and garage. DJs from abroad, particularly New York, are usually featured on weekends. Check out what's on at its Web site (www.zoukclub.com.sg).

Just off River Valley Rd, about 800m west of Clarke Quay, is Mohamed Sultan Rd, home to a growing number of popular late-night bars and clubs housed in restored shophouses. One of the more popular among expats and tourists is *Next Page Pub* at No 17. Inside red lanterns give the dark wood panelling a warm glow, and the sound system pumps out 80s and 90s music (no techno). *Tajie* nearby always seems to have a long queue of eager young people who don't mind waiting to get inside. *Madam Wong's* next door at No 28–29 is another popular Chinese-themed place, and features 80s music. *Wong San's* at No 12 is in a similar vein, with intimate plush booths to sit in and the ubiquitous red lanterns casting their glow overhead.

The *Boom Boom Room* (☎ 339 8187, 3 New Bugis St) is a supper club affair with a cabaret and Singapore's only regular stand-up comic. On Tuesday to Thursday entry is S$17 (including two standard drinks); Friday and Saturday it's S$23. The show itself kicks off around 10.45 pm. The Boom Boom Room is open Tuesday to Thursday from 8.30 pm to 2 am, and Friday and Saturday to 3.30 am. It's closed Sunday and Monday.

## JAZZ & BLUES

Many bars feature bands. Live music imports dominate – mostly Filipino bands but occasionally Western musicians – playing jazz, pop covers, old favourites or, just occasionally, something more risqué like the blues.

For jazz, R&B and blues, try the *H₂O Zone* (see Pubs & Bars earlier), where a band plays on a small platform behind the bar from around 9 pm. *Harry's* bar on Boat Quay is an ever popular jazz venue. *Somerset's*, in the Westin Plaza, is probably *the* jazz venue in terms of playing proficiency. The Bar & Billiard Room and the Long Bar at *Raffles Hotel* have jazz after 7.30 pm. *Fat Frog* (45 Armenian St), at the Substation, is more cafe than bar, but you can have a drink here while listening to live music, including jazz, on Friday and Saturday evenings.

## CLASSICAL MUSIC

The Singapore Symphony Orchestra gives around 100 performances annually at the *Victoria Concert Hall & Theatre*.

## THEATRE

The nascent theatre scene is starting to come of age as Singaporeans become more interested in cementing their identity. More local plays are being produced, and alternative theatre venues are helping to foster an interest in theatre. The S$500-million plus Esplanade – Theatres on the Bay venue, to open in 2002, will provide an added boost.

*Action Theatre* (42 Waterloos St) has an ongoing program showcasing new and established talent (bookings and enquires ☎ 296 2929).

The *Substation* (☎ 337 7535, fax 337 2729, ❷ admin@substation.org.sg, 45 Armenian St) has a lively arts program that includes a theatre festival, performances of new and improvised music, art exhibitions, rock and blues performances, and film. The publication *Substance,* which has reviews and a rundown of activities, is available from the theatre. Its Web site is at www.substation.org.

The main venues for theatre are the *Drama Centre* (☎ 336 0005) on Canning Rise, just north-east of Fort Canning Park; the *Victoria Theatre* (☎ 345 8488), Empress Place, opposite Boat Quay; and the *Kallang Theatre* (☎ 345 8488), opposite the National Stadium on Stadium Rd, east of town. Performances range from local and overseas plays staged by a variety of local theatre companies, to international blockbusters.

*Raffles Jubilee Hall Theatre Playhouse,* in the shopping arcade behind Raffles Hotel, puts on various performances including dance, musicals and plays. For programs and ticket prices as well as bookings call the playhouse at ☎ 331 1719.

The Singapore Festival of Arts, which features many drama performances, is held every second year around June. Music, art and dance are also represented at the festival, which incudes a Fringe Festival featuring plenty of street performances.

## CHINESE OPERA

A low-key introduction to Chinese opera can be had at one of the tea house evenings organised by the nonprofit opera company the Chinese Theatre Circle (☎ 323 4862). Every Tuesday and Friday at 8 pm at the *Chinese Opera Tea House (5 Smith St, Chinatown)* there is a brief talk (in English) on Chinese opera followed by a short excerpt from a Cantonese opera classic, performed by professional actors in full costume. Delicious lychee tea and little tea cakes are included in the price of S$15. The whole thing lasts around 45 minutes and you can take photos. Bookings are recommended.

## CULTURAL SHOWS

At the *Marina Mandarin (☎ 338 3388, 6 Raffles Blvd)* there is an Association of South-East Asian Nations (Asean) program every evening. It features dancing and music from all over the region. The show with dinner costs S$38+++ (dinner served at 7.30 pm). The show only is S$23+++ (starts at 8.15 pm).

# Spectator Sports

## HORSE RACING

The horse-racing calendar is part of the Malaysian circuit and races are held once a month at the brand new Singapore Turf Club (☎ 879 1000), 1 Turf Club Ave, Woodlands, in the north of the city, near the Woodlands MRT station. There's a four-level grandstand with a seating capacity of up to 35,000. Admission to the non-air-con seating is S$5 (S$10 for air-con). For S$20 tourists can access the air-con gold card room (bring your passport). A dress code applies here: Men must wear a collar, shorts and jeans are out, and men and women must wear closed shoes (no sandals). Races are held for 32 weeks of the year; contact the information line in this entry or consult the *Straits Times* for details. All betting is government controlled, and the minimum win or placed bet is S$5. A lot of money passes through the windows on race days.

# Shopping

One of Singapore's major attractions is shopping. The sheer range is impressive and prices for many goods are still competitive with other discount centres, but these days, with tariffs dropping everywhere around the world, Singapore is not the bargain centre it once was. 'Duty free' and 'free port' are somewhat throwaway terms. Remember that not everything is loaded down with import duty in your own country and Singapore also has some local industries to protect.

Before you leap on any item as a great bargain, it pays to know prices at home. You should also shop around to compare prices. Even when prices are displayed it doesn't always mean that prices are fixed.

Guarantees are an important consideration if you're buying electronic gear, watches, cameras and the like. Make sure your guarantee is international and is filled out correctly with the shop's name and the serial number of the item.

As important as the guarantee is the item's compatibility back home. You don't want to buy a brand or model for which there are no spares or agents back home.

Check for the right voltage and cycle when you buy electrical goods. Singapore, Australia, New Zealand, Hong Kong and the UK operate at a voltage of 220V to 240V at a frequency of 50Hz, while the USA, Canada and Japan use 110V to 120V at 60Hz. Check the plug – most shops will fit the correct plug for your country.

If you have any problems take your purchases back to the shop, though many, particularly the small ones, are not noted for their after-sales service. If you fail to get satisfaction from your point of purchase, contact the Singapore Tourism Board (see details in Singapore's Facts for the Visitor chapter) or the Small Claims Tribunal (☎ 435 5946, fax 451 4207), or check out the Web site at www.gov.sg/judiciary/subct/courts/scat.html. The Small Claims Tribunal is at the Apollo Centre, 05-00, 2 Havelock Rd, and tourist complaints are usually heard within two or three days.

SINGAPORE

## GST

Almost all goods and services are levied with a 3% Goods and Services Tax (GST). A tax refund on goods worth S$300 or more can be applied for through shops participating in the GST Tourist Refund Scheme. These shops display a 'tax free shopping' logo, though often it's more hassle than it's worth. For more details see Money in Singapore's Facts for the Visitor chapter.

## WHERE TO SHOP

Singapore is wall-to-wall with shops and, while there are certain places worth heading to for certain items, shopping centres usually have a mixture of shops selling electronics, clothes, sporting goods and so on. Shopping centres are found all over town, but, of course, Orchard Rd is famous for its profusion of shopping possibilities.

### Orchard Rd

The major shopping complexes on and around Orchard Rd have a mind-boggling array of department stores and shops all manner of thingst. The prices aren't necessarily the best, but the range is superb and this is certainly a good place for high quality, brand-name items. The following is an overview and is by no means exhaustive.

Orchard Point, Orchard Plaza and Cuppage Plaza, clustered together near Somerset MRT station, have a variety of shops and food outlets. Next along is Centrepoint, one of the liveliest shopping centres, with good bookshops on the 4th floor and carpets on the 5th floor.

Past Peranakan Place, Orchard Emerald has watches and electronics, and the basement has a large supermarket, food stalls and restaurants. Next door, OG is a straightforward department store.

Across Orchard Rd next to Somerset MRT station, the Specialists' shopping centre is older and quieter. It has the John Little department store and a good range of sporting goods shops.

On the corner of Orchard Rd and Orchard Link is Ngee Ann City, which houses the large Takashimaya department store, which itself houses the giant Kinokuniya bookstore.

The basement is great for food, especially Japanese food, while the individual shops are dominated by exclusive outlets.

Opposite Ngee Ann City, The Paragon and The Promenade are two other upmarket shopping centres with many designer boutiques. A little farther west and much more downmarket is Lucky Plaza, a bustling, hustling place with dozens of shops crammed together. It's good for cheap clothes, bags and shoes, but bargain hard and shake off the touts and pesky tailors. Opposite Lucky Plaza is Wisma Atria, which has an Isetan department store and lots of boutiques.

On Scotts Rd, the Scotts shopping centre has plenty of boutiques and an excellent food court in the basement.

At the top of Orchard Rd, the Far East shopping centre has some sporting shops that cater for golfers and cyclists. The Forum Galleria is dominated by Toys 'R' Us, with other children's gear specialists in the same centre.

Tanglin Rd is quieter and has far fewer of the hard-sell commercial enterprises of the kind found on Orchard Rd. The Tanglin shopping centre has Singapore's best selection of expensive Asian arts and antiques. It's well worth a browse and some refined bargaining if you want to buy.

### Colonial District

Raffles City is architecturally one of the most impressive shopping centres in Singapore and has some interesting small shops, as well as the Sogo department store. East of Raffles City, Marina Square has a huge array of shops in a massive complex, which also includes three hotels and plenty of restaurants.

Raffles Hotel has a shopping area, which, as you would expect, is firmly upmarket with designer clothes, collectibles, antiques and art. Stamford House, on the corner of Stamford Rd and Victoria St, is a beautifully restored building with a host of shops selling furniture, paintings, home fittings and knick-knacks.

Farther north, Bugis Junction on Victoria St comprises shophouse recreations covered by an atrium, the large Seiyu department store, and numerous interesting boutiques, consumer electronics and a branch of the Kinokuniya bookstore.

On Bencoolen St, Sim Lim Square is known as the place to buy computers and electronic goods. Sim Lim Tower across Rochor Canal Rd is a big electronics centre with everything from capacitors to audio and video gear. These two centres are popular with tourists looking for bargains, so the first asking price is often higher than you'll find elsewhere.

## Chinatown

Chinatown is a popular shopping area with more local flavour. The People's Park Complex and People's Park Centre are good places to shop. They form a large complex with plenty of electronics, clothing and department stores. The electronics are only as cheap as you make them. The Chinatown Complex has an interesting market for everyday goods and cheap shops. Chinatown Point specialises in craft shops. A good place to hunt for antiques, collectibles and all sorts of interesting knick-knacks are the streets near the Sri Mariamman Temple: Pagoda, Trengganu, Temple and Smith Sts.

## Other Areas

In Little India the Mustafa Centre has electrical and everyday goods at honest prices. Arab St is good for textiles, basketware and South-East Asian crafts.

East of the city is Parkway Parade on Marine Parade Rd, a large, general shopping centre that is popular with beachgoers. It has some larger discount shops for electronics.

Housing estate areas have plenty of shopping strips for cheaper clothes and household items, and bargaining is the exception rather than the rule. Try Ang Mo Kio, Bedok, Clementi, Toa Payoh or Geylang – all easily reached by MRT. Tampines has the big Century Park shopping mall.

## WHAT TO BUY

From CDs to luggage and from oriental rugs to model aeroplanes, Singapore's shops have whatever you might want. This section, though only a sample of Singapore's shopping possibilities, suggests places to start looking.

## Arts, Crafts & Antiques

Singapore has no shortage of arts and antiques, mostly Chinese but also from all over Asia. When buying antiques, ask for a certificate of antiquity, which is required in many countries if you want to avoid paying customs duty. A good guide to the complexities of this sort of shopping is *Antiques, Arts & Crafts in Singapore* by Ann Jones.

Tanglin shopping centre on Tanglin Rd is one of the easiest places to find arts and antiques. Antiques of the Orient (02–40) is a good place to find antiquarian books, maps and prints. Raffles Hotel Shopping Arcade has several outlets.

Dempsey Rd, off Holland Rd past the Botanic Gardens, is another good place to look; there are several warehouses here offering a variety of items, including Kashmiri carpets, teak furniture, landscaping ornaments and more.

In Chinatown, try Far East Inspirations at 33/33A Pagoda St, where there is a good selection of quality Chinese antiques ranging from substantial pieces of furniture, such as beds, couches and painted wedding chests, to ceramics and embroidery.

Also in Chinatown, at 51 Craig Rd, is the fascinating Tong Mern Sern Antiques Arts & Crafts; Motto: 'Some fools buy some fools sell'. You can rummage around three floors packed with a huge assortment of stuff, including old suitcases, clocks, watches, architectural pieces such as carved lintels, apothecary bottles, traditional lamps, silverware, furniture, paintings, old tiles, religious statues, books and records.

Yong Gallery at 260 South Bridge Rd in Chinatown has calligraphy (you can get a piece made to order), Chinese seals (chops), antique fabrics, traditional Chinese knots made into tassels and other items, as well as 'naive' peasant paintings, traditional paper cutouts and wood carvings.

In the Holland Road shopping centre, in Holland Village, there are dozens of interesting shops that sell all sort of things, from cloisonné ware to Korean chests.

The Singapore Handicraft Centre, in Chinatown Point, has dozens of shops that deal in Chinese lacquerware, pottery and jewellery. The centre also sells some Indonesian and other Asian crafts.

Arab St is a good place to look for South-East Asian crafts, such as caneware, batik and leather goods. In Chinatown, around Smith St, there are shops selling goods that range from trinkets and souvenirs, basketware, fans and silk dressing gowns to more-expensive curios and antique pottery.

## Cameras & Film

Cameras are available throughout the city, though camera equipment is not such a bargain here these days – camera prices are often just as heavily discounted in many Western countries as in Singapore or Hong Kong.

For information on the costs of developing film in Singapore see the Photography & Video section in Singapore's Facts for the Visitor chapter.

## Computers

Computer systems and laptops are a good buy, though for US-made or Japanese-made name-brand hardware the prices are not always as low as you'll find in the countries of origin. Be wary of the cheap, no-name brands, mostly from Taiwan, that you won't be able to get support for back home. Computer components and accessories that are made in Singapore, such as hard disks, are very competitively priced, as are blank disks and accessories.

Singapore is enforcing international copyright laws, so cheap software and software manuals are not openly on display as in other Asian countries. The Funan Centre on North Bridge Rd is Singapore's main computer centre. There are dozens of shops on the top floors as well as a large Challenger Superstore. The top floors of Sim Lim Square, on the corner of Bencoolen St and Rochor Canal Rd, are good hunting grounds for cheap computers, software and accessories.

## Electronic Goods

TVs, CDs, VCRs, VCDs, DVDs – you name it, all the latest high-tech audiovisual equipment is available all over Singapore, much of it at very competitive prices. With such a range to choose from, it's difficult to know what to buy; it pays to do a little research into makes and models before you arrive. Make sure your guarantees are worldwide, your receipts are properly dated and stamped, and your goods are compatible with electricity supplies and systems in your country of origin.

There are two main types of TV system used: PAL in Australasia and much of Europe and NTSC in the USA and Japan – video recorders must be compatible with the system you use.

Sim Lim Square, on the corner of Bencoolen St and Rochor Canal Rd, has a concentrated area of electronics shops, and Sim Lim Tower, nearby on Jalan Besar, has a huge selection of goods, but be wary and be prepared to bargain hard.

Mustafa Centre in Little India has well-priced appliances and sound systems – but you should bargain.

## Jewellery

Gold jewellery is priced according to its weight and quite often the design and work is thrown in for next to nothing. The gold used is often 22 to 24 carat, and you should always retain a receipt showing weight and carat. There are gold merchants all over Singapore's city centre, but you'll find a concentration in Little India along Serangoon Rd, and in the People's Park Complex in Chinatown.

Singapore is a good place to buy pearls and gemstones, but you really need to know the market to determine whether or not you're getting a good deal.

Jade is a Chinese favourite – and it is expensive. In general, the lighter the colour the more expensive it is. Beware of imitation jade and make sure you don't pay too much for cheap jade, such as the dark Indian variety. It's important to examine solid jade pieces for flaws, as these may be potential crack lines.

SINGAPORE

## Music

CDs cost around S$16 to S$20 in department stores and discount bins, and around S$20 to S$25 for more obscure imports. Arguably the most extensive selection of music in Singapore is to be found at HMV, where there are separate floors dedicated to Western pop, Asian pop, and classical and jazz (the store has soundproof listening lounges for classical and jazz). In the Orchard Rd area, Tower Records on the 4th floor of the Pacific Plaza, and Borders at Wheelock Place (also in the Orchard Rd area), have good selections of music.

Brunei

# Brunei Darussalam

Wedged between the north-eastern corner of Sarawak and the South China Sea, Brunei is one of the smallest countries in the world – it's also one of the wealthiest. A curious reminder of the British colonial legacy and the power of companies (in this case Shell Oil) to shape countries, this tiny Islamic sultanate is all that remains of an empire that controlled all of Borneo in the 16th century.

The country's full name is Negara Brunei Darussalam, which is usually translated as 'Brunei – the Abode of Peace'. And with alcohol virtually unobtainable, no nightlife to speak of and a political culture of quiet acquiescence to the edicts of the sultan and Islamic laws, it certainly is peaceful.

Presiding over it all is His Majesty Sultan Haji Hassanal Bolkiah Mu'izzaddin Waddaulah, the 29th of his line and better known as the Sultan of Brunei. Though his fortunes have dipped in the last few years, the sultan remains among the most conspicuously wealthy men in the world.

The sultan's bottom line is also that of his country. Brunei's economy is almost wholly fuelled by oil, which comes mainly from offshore wells at Seria and Muara. As long as the oil lasts (2020 is tagged as the watershed year), Brunei's upriver forests are safe from the fate of neighbouring Sabah and Sarawak – clean, clear rivers still flow through towns like Tutong and the beautiful Temburong district in the country's east.

In the meantime, Brunei's citizens enjoy patronage that even the Beverley Hillbillies would envy. There are pensions for all, free medical care, free schooling, free sport and leisure centres, cheap loans, subsidies for many purchases (including cars), short working weeks, no taxes and the highest minimum wages in the region.

Visitors will be disappointed if they expect Brunei to be an Islamic alternative to Western-style modernity – Shell's oil lubricates a middle-class dreamworld more

## HIGHLIGHTS

- **Omar Ali Saifuddien Mosque** – a massive tribute to Brunei's wealth and devotion to Islam
- **Kampung Ayer** – mazes of plankwalks linking the capital's sprawling stilt villages
- **Brunei Museum & Malay Technology Museum** – excellent exhibits on Brunei, Islam and traditional Malay culture
- **Jerudong Park Playground** – wholesome evening entertainment on the rides at this enormous amusement park
- **Temburong** – your chance to knock on an Iban longhouse door on a jaunt through the jungle

familiar to viewers of *The Brady Bunch* than to readers of *Arabian Nights*. And with little to stress them out, citizens seem content to window-shop by day and watch TV at night. In Brunei, it might be said, the mass of Malays lead lives of sensory deprivation.

Bruneians are a friendly and welcoming people who are justly proud of their rich heritage. Most visitors are scratching around for something to do after a couple of days, but Brunei is a strangely fascinating anomaly in South-East Asia that draws its share of sightseers. The country's *Leave It to Beaver* lifestyle has its appeal, and many Western expats enjoy the simple living and good working conditions that Brunei offers.

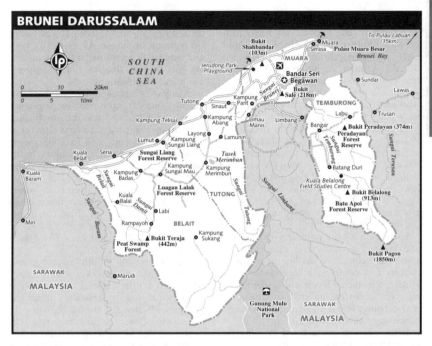

## BRUNEI DARUSSALAM

With 2001 declared Visit Brunei Year, new tourism facilities and special events may get off the ground.

The capital, Bandar Seri Begawan (or BSB), is a pleasant city with impressive mosques, some excellent museums and the sprawling stilt villages of Kampung Ayer. Brunei is expensive compared with other parts of Borneo, but with the reins pulled in on the local economy, some accommodation is more affordable than it once was.

# Facts about Brunei

## HISTORY

In the 15th and 16th centuries Brunei Darussalam, as the country is formally known, was a considerable power in the region with its rule extending throughout Borneo and into the Philippines.

The Spanish and Portuguese were the first European visitors, arriving in the 16th century. The Spanish actually made a bid to take over, but were soon ousted.

The arrival of the British in the guise of James Brooke, the first white raja of Sarawak, in the early 19th century, spelt the end of Brunei's power. A series of 'treaties' was forced onto the sultan as Brooke consolidated his hold over Kuching. He aimed to develop commercial relationships and suppress piracy, a favourite Bruneian and Dayak occupation (piracy was a common excuse for justifying European land grabs). Brunei became a British protectorate in 1888 and was gradually whittled away until, with a final dash of absurdity, Limbang was ceded to Sarawak in 1890, thus dividing Brunei into two parts.

In 1929, just as Brunei was about to be swallowed up entirely, oil was discovered. The present sultan's father, who abdicated in 1967, kept Brunei out of the Malayan confederacy, preferring that the country remain a British protectorate.

In 1962, in the lead up to amalgamation with the new state of Malaysia, the British pressured Sultan Omar Saifuddien to hold elections. The opposition Ra'ayat Party, led by AM Azahari, which wanted to keep Brunei independent and make the sultan a constitutional monarch within a democracy, won an overwhelming victory. As the sultan's plans to take Brunei into union with Malaysia became clear, Azahari fled to the Philippines, from where he directed an armed rebellion with the support of Indonesia. The rebellion was quickly crushed with British military backing and the sultan later opted for independence from Malaysia. The 'Abode of Peace' has been under emergency laws ever since, though you'll see little evidence of this.

Early in 1984 the popular young sultan and *yang di-pertuan* ('he who is lord') somewhat reluctantly led his tightly ruled country into complete independence from Britain. The then 37-year-old leader rather enjoyed the British umbrella and the colonial trappings that it entailed, and independence was almost unwanted.

Brunei has shown a trend towards Islamic fundamentalism since independence; Melayu Islam Beraja (MIB) is the name given to the national ideology. It stresses Malay culture, Islam and monarchy, and is promulgated through the ministries of education, religious affairs and information. In 1991 the sale of alcohol was banned and stricter dress codes were introduced; in 1992 the study of MIB became compulsory in schools.

The emergency laws are still in place and there's little evidence of a gathering tide of democratic reform, but that's not to say things aren't changing. In recent years the government has recognised a relatively small but growing unemployment problem, and disaffected youths have been blamed for isolated incidents of crime.

Symbolic of the country's economic and familial underbelly is surely the sultan's younger brother, Prince Jefri. The prince was never exactly a poster boy for common sense, let alone Islamic virtue. While indulging in (ahem) a 'flamboyant' lifestyle,

Prince Jefri played at being finance minister and running the Amedeo Development Corporation, a classic Asian family conglomerate with diversified interests, including golf courses, five-star hotels, fisheries and telecommunications.

Salacious scandals and rumours of impressive financial corruption/incompetence forced the sultan to sack Jefri as finance minister in 1997, but the worst was yet to come. Amedeo collapsed in 1998 owing some US$16 billion to its creditors. In the fall-out a few cabinet officials lost their posts and Prince Jefri's son, Hakim, was sacked as chairman of government-owned Datastream Technology, a lucrative telecom company. In a clear sign of his continuing displeasure, the following month the sultan formally named his eldest son, Al-Muhtadee Billah, as heir to the throne.

The government initially assured everyone that currency reserves would easily cover Jefri's little financial boo-boo, but it is now clear that the Amedeo disaster has seriously affected the Brunei economy. In fact, the sultan went so far as to pursue Jefri (who had fled to far-away Britain) in the courts for the return of up to US$35 billion that the prince was alleged to have siphoned off while finance minister.

Averting an embarrassing and revealing trial, in May 2000 the sultan reached an out-of-court settlement with Jefri that would see the return of all of the prince's assets to the state. (You have to feel for poor Jefri – he, his four wives and 35 children will have to make do on an allowance of US$300,000 a month.) The resulting cash infusion leaves the country in better shape financially, but the carefree days of free-spending Bruneians border-hopping to Borneo's bars and boutiques is all but over.

## GEOGRAPHY

Present-day Brunei is one of the smallest countries in the world: the entire sultanate covers an area of only 5765 sq km. It has no mountain ranges or great rivers, and at its widest the larger, western part measures only 120km from side to side. White sandy beaches along the coast give way to low hills rising to around 300m in the interior. BSB overlooks the estuary of the mangrove-fringed Sungai (River) Brunei, which opens onto Brunei Bay and the eastern part of the country, Temburong.

Temburong consists of a coastal plain drained by Sungai Temburong and rises to a height of 1850m at Bukit Pagon, the highest peak in the country. Two other main rivers drain the country – the Belait and Tutong.

Western Brunei is divided into the three administrative districts of Muara–Bandar Seri Begawan, Tutong and Belait. Apart from the capital city, the main settlements are Seria and Kuala Belait. Temburong makes up a fourth district, to the east, and is a sparsely populated area of largely unspoilt rainforest. Approximately 75% of Brunei retains its original forest cover.

## CLIMATE

Being a slice of Borneo, Brunei is subject to that great island's prevailing climatic conditions. Thus, it is out of the typhoon belt and enjoys high average temperatures, humidity and rainfall.

Temperatures are consistently around 24°C minimum and 31°C maximum, with an average humidity of 79%. Average annual rainfall is about 3295mm, though Brunei doesn't really have marked wet and dry seasons. The wettest months are from September to January, during the north-east monsoon, and the driest period is February to April.

Changes in climatic patterns, which have been popularly attributed to the El Niño effect, have contributed to a recurring smoke-haze problem in Brunei. During dry months, when there is no wind, open burning in Brunei can cause dense smoke to linger over parts of the country, reducing visibility, and endangering the health of old people and children.

## GOVERNMENT & POLITICS

Brunei is an Islamic sultanate, and His Majesty the sultan (the 29th in a line going back to the 14th century) appoints ministers to assist him in governing the country. The sultan himself holds the three key cabinet positions: He is the prime minister, defence minister and finance minister. He is also yang di-pertuan, head of the religion of the country. One of the sultan's brothers is minister of foreign affairs. Democracy is not on the government's agenda; the only democratic elections ever held were in 1962.

Judicial power is vested in the Supreme Court (comprising the Court of Appeal and the High Court) and the Magistrate's Court. *Syariah*, or Islamic, courts deal with offences against Islam committed by Muslims. The judicial system is loosely based on the British system, but the philosophy of MIB is being applied to the law.

Brunei is an active member of Asean and enjoys close relations with near neighbours Malaysia and Singapore.

## ECONOMY

Oil! The country is virtually dependent on the stuff and the pumps are not expected to run dry until at least 2020. In anticipation of that inevitable dark day, the government has instituted some economic diversification plans. These include more rice-farming, some forestry and eventual self-sufficiency in beef production. To this latter end, the government bought a cattle station in Australia's Northern Territory that is larger than Brunei itself! Fresh beef is flown into BSB daily, a large percentage of the country's rice comes from Thailand, and most of its fruit and vegetables are imported from Sarawak and Sabah.

Brunei exports a small amount of rubber; more importantly, it is one of the world's largest exporters of liquefied natural gas. Japan and Korea are its main oil and gas markets. The government, with Brunei

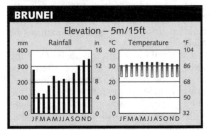

Shell Petroleum (the only oil company with a major stake in Brunei), is by far the nation's largest employer. All government workers get subsidised holidays and trips to Mecca.

Traditional agriculture in Brunei consists of shifting cultivation, which continues in remote areas. Farming is largely a part-time occupation, and there are no large estates in Brunei. About 80% of the country's food is imported.

The formation of a trading bloc with nearby countries has resulted in the cumbersome but potentially fruitful BIMP-EAGA, which stands for Brunei, Indonesia, Malaysia and Philippines – East Asian Growth Area.

## POPULATION & PEOPLE

Brunei's population is about 330,000 people, two-thirds of whom live in the BSB-Muara district (though only some 60,000 people live in BSB itself). The Belait district has around 67,000 people, and Tutong has 36,000. Only 9000 people are registered in Brunei's hinterland, the Temburong district.

Malays, including indigenes of the Kedayan, Tutong, Belait, Bisayah, Dusun and Murut peoples, constitute 67% of the population. Another 20,000 people (6% of the population) are Iban, Dayak and Kelabit; Chinese make up 15% of the total. The rest are migrant workers servicing the oil fields; Western expats (often teachers); and Filipinos and Indonesians working in shops, cafes and generally doing labour upwardly Bruneians refuse to do.

## ARTS

During the height of the Brunei sultanates, Kampung Ayer's brass and silver artisans produced work of fine design and great beauty. Brass gongs, cannon and household vessels, such as kettles and betel containers, were prized throughout Borneo and beyond. They were often embossed with designs of serpents and animals, or with verses from the Quran, and prized pieces were believed to have special powers. Cannon, in particular, were used not only for war, but for paying dowries and for ceremonial purposes. Today they are family heirlooms and can be found in Malay homes or remote Dayak villages, where they have been given spiritual significance. There's a good collection of cannon pieces in the Brunei Museum.

Artisans used the wax technique to cast brass, a method believed to have been introduced during the reign of Sultan Bolkiah at the end of the 15th century. The art declined with the fortunes of the Brunei sultanate, and the great brassware of Brunei is now a lost tradition.

Silverwork was probably introduced from Java about the same time as brass casting, and Portuguese explorer Antonio Pigafetta noted the silver and gold vessels he found in Brunei in 1521. Silversmithing, like brass casting, was an art passed down through families and guilds in Kampung Ayer. The exponents of silverwork these days are to be found at the Handicraft Centre, which was set up to preserve Brunei's dying crafts.

The weaving art of *jong sarat* has survived, and jong sarat sarung are still prized for ceremonial occasions. Jong sarat uses gold thread and coloured cotton, woven on a loom in stylised floral designs known as *sukma-indera*. Bright colours are used sparingly and the designs are restrained.

## SOCIETY & CONDUCT

Bruneians are mostly Malay, and their customs, beliefs and pastimes are very similar, if not identical, to those of the Malays of West Malaysia. *Adat* (customary law) governs many of the ceremonies in Brunei, particularly on royal and state occasions. There is even a government department of *adat istiadat*, which is responsible for preserving ceremony and advising on protocol, dress and heraldry. See Society & Conduct in the Facts about Malaysia chapter for more-detailed information and explanations of Malay customs.

The usual Asian customs apply: Only the right hand should be used for offering or passing something; pointing with the forefinger is rude (it should be done with the thumb); and beckoning someone is done with an open hand with the fingers waving downwards. Bruneians shake hands by only lightly touching then bringing the hands to the chest; and it is not customary to shake hands with the opposite sex.

Islam requires a certain attention to detail, and there are a few dos and don'ts to consider. Muslims fast between sunrise and sunset during Ramadan, so food and even coffee should not be offered to Muslims at these times – non-Muslims may eat without worry of offence, however. Casual touching in public is frowned upon, and forget about groping or snogging your loved one on the street – this is illegal. When entering a mosque or a house, remove your shoes first.

Men and women are expected to dress 'respectably'; men wearing singlets on the street, and women wearing dresses above the knee or sleeveless tops is considered rude (and they mean it – you won't be allowed on rides at Jerudong Park Playground and certainly won't be allowed inside a mosque).

## RELIGION

Brunei is a reasonably strict Muslim country, and a Ministry of Religious Affairs has been set up to foster and promote Islam. The ministry has special officers who investigate breaches of Islamic law by Muslims, and apparently government men prowl the streets after dark looking for unmarried couples standing or sitting too close to each other. This crime is known as *khalwat*, and getting caught can mean imprisonment and a fine. The sale of alcohol is banned and non-Islamic restaurants (such as Chinese places) display signs stating that they are not suitable for Muslims (don't get excited – it's because they serve pork, not alcohol).

The constitution permits other religions to be practised in peace and harmony, and non-Muslim visitors needn't worry about being spat upon and abused for being infidels. Bruneians are generally reserved in public and are polite and hospitable, and not all are as zealous as the government.

## LANGUAGE

The official language of Brunei is Malay but English is also widely spoken. Jawi (Malay written in Arabic script) is taught in schools, and most signs in the country are written in both Jawi and Roman script. See the Language chapter at the back of this book for a guide to Malay and a list of useful words and phrases. For a more comprehensive guide to the language get a copy of Lonely Planet's *Malay phrasebook*.

# Facts for the Visitor

## PLANNING
### Maps
If you're thinking of exploring the hinterland with a rental car, the *Road Map and Street Index of Brunei Darussalam*, published by Shell, is an excellent publication. Apart from detailed maps of all built-up areas, it has information on where to go and what to see. Shell also publishes a folding road map of Brunei, but it is not as useful. See Bookshops in the BSB section for a reliable place to pick up maps.

## TOURIST OFFICES
A new tourist information centre may have opened in BSB by the time you read this (see Information in the BSB section later in this chapter for more details). There is an information desk at the airport where you should pick up some useful leaflets and the informative *Explore Brunei* booklet. *Explore Brunei* has a map of BSB and useful information on sights and accommodation.

## VISAS & DOCUMENTS
For visits of up to 14 days, visas are not necessary for citizens of Belgium, Canada, France, Germany, Indonesia, Japan, Luxembourg, the Netherlands, New Zealand, Norway, the Philippines, South Korea, Sweden, Switzerland, Thailand and the Republic of the Maldives. British, Malaysian and Singaporean citizens do not require a visa for visits of 30 days or less. US citizens do not need a visa for visits of up to 90 days.

People of all other nationalities must have a visa to visit Brunei. Brunei embassies

BRUNEI

overseas have been known to give incorrect advice, so you should double-check if your nationality is not listed in this section and you are told that you do not require a visa to enter the country.

Note that if you need a visa for Brunei and don't already have one, you cannot enter the country by land or sea – there are no visa-granting facilities at the borders with Sabah and Sarawak. Australian citizens can fly in, however, as 72-hour transit visas are granted (free of charge) at Brunei International Airport. Upon arrival Australians can also get a 48-hour visa for B$1 and a two-week visa for B$15. These are single-entry visas, so it's not possible to hop back and forth between Brunei and Sarawak's Limbang district this way. Multiple-entry visas can be arranged in advance through Canberra (the cost is B$20 for a three-month visa).

Assuming your visa requirements are in order, entering from Sarawak or Sabah is pain-free – there's no money-showing, no requirement for an onward ticket and it's unlikely your bags will even be looked at. A one-week visa is more or less granted automatically and if you ask you can usually get two weeks – it might be useful, you never know.

Transit passengers are issued a 72-hour visa at the airport and if you intend to make a short trip to Brunei, it would be worth taking advantage of this visa. Three days is enough to see most of the sights, but this visa does tie you to travelling by air.

### Driving License

You'll need an International Driving Permit to motor around Brunei. See Car under Getting There & Away in the BSB section for more details.

## EMBASSIES & CONSULATES
### Brunei Embassies

Brunei has diplomatic offices in the following countries:

**Australia** (☎ 02-6290 1801, fax 6286 1554) 16 Bulwarra Close, O'Malley, ACT 2606
**Canada** (☎ 613-234 5656, fax 234 4397) 395 Laurier Ave East, Ottawa ON, K1N 6R4

**France** (☎ 01-53 64 67 60, fax 53 64 67 83) No 7, Rue de Prespargy, Paris 75017
**Germany** (☎ 030-206 07 06, fax 206 07 66 6) Kronenstrasse 55–58, 10117 Berlin
**Indonesia** (☎ 021-574 1437, fax 574 1463) Suite 1194, Wisma GKBI, 28 Jalan Sudirman, Jakarta 10210
**Japan** (☎ 03-3447 7997, fax 3447 9260) 5-2-6 Kita-Shinagawa, Shinagawa-ku, Tokyo 141
**Malaysia** (☎ 03-261 2828, fax 263 1302) 8th and 9th floors, Wisma Sin Heap Lee, Jalan Tun Razak, 50400 Kuala Lumpur
**Philippines** (☎ 02-816 2836) 11th floor, BPI Bldg, Ayala Ave, Makati, Manila
**Singapore** (☎ 065-733 9055, fax 737 5275) 325 Tanglin Rd, Singapore 247955
**Thailand** (☎ 02-391 6017, fax 381 5921) No 154, Soi Ekamai 14, 63 Sukhumvit Rd, Bangkok 10110
**UK** (☎ 020-72581 0521, fax 7235 9717) 19 Belgrave Square, London SW1X 8PG
**USA** (☎ 202-237 1838, fax 885 0560, @ info@bruneiembassy.org) 3520 International Court, Washington DC 2008

## Embassies & Consulates in Brunei

Countries with diplomatic representation in BSB (area code ☎ 02) include:

**Australia** (☎ 229435) 4th floor, Teck Guan Plaza, Jalan Sultan
**Canada** (☎ 220043) Suite 51–52, Britannia House, Jalan Cator
**France** (☎ 220960) 301–306, 3rd floor, Jalan Kompleks, Jalan Sultan; also 5th floor, Teck Guan Plaza
**Germany** (☎ 225547) 6th floor, Wisma Raya Bldg, Jalan Sultan
**Indonesia** (☎ 330180) Simpang 528, Lot 4498, Jalan Muara, Kampung Sungai Hanching
**Japan** (☎ 229265) 1 and 3 Jalan Jawatan Dalam, Kampong Mabohai
**Malaysia** (☎ 345652) Lot 27 and 29, Simpang 396–39, Jalan Kebangsaan Lama, Kampong Sungai Akar, Mukim Berakas B
**New Zealand** see Australian embassy; honourary consul (☎ 331612)
**Philippines** (☎ 241465) 4th and 5th floors, Badiah Bldg, Mile 1, Jalan Tutong
**Singapore** (☎ 227583) 5th floor, RBA Plaza, Jalan Sultan
**UK** (☎ 222231) 2nd floor, Unit 2.01, Block D, YSHHB Complex
**USA** (☎ 229670) 3rd floor, Teck Guan Plaza, Jalan Sultan

Austria, Bangladesh, Belgium, China, Denmark, Finland, India, Iran, Korea, Myanmar (Burma), the Netherlands, Norway, Oman, Pakistan, Saudi Arabia, Sweden, Thailand and Vietnam also have diplomatic representation in Brunei.

## CUSTOMS
Duty-free allowances for persons over 17 years of age are 200 cigarettes or 250g of tobacco, 60ml of perfume and 250ml of eau du toilette. Non-Muslims may import two bottles of liquor (about 2L) and 12 cans of beer, which must be declared upon arrival.

The importation of drugs carries the death penalty.

## MONEY
### Currency
The official currency is the Brunei dollar (B$), but Singapore dollars are equally exchanged and can be used. Banks give around 10% less for cash than they do for travellers cheques.

Brunei uses 1c, 5c, 20c and 50c coins, and B$1, B$5, B$10, B$50, B$100, B$500, B$1000 and B$10,000 notes.

### Exchange Rates
The following table shows the exchange rates at the time this book went to press:

| country | unit | Brunei dollars |
| --- | --- | --- |
| Australia | A$1 | B$0.95 |
| Canada | C$1 | B$1.18 |
| euro | €1 | B$1.49 |
| France | 10FF | B$2.28 |
| Germany | DM1 | B$0.76 |
| Indonesia | 10,000Rp | B$0.20 |
| Japan | ¥100 | B$1.64 |
| Malaysia | RM10 | B$0.46 |
| New Zealand | NZ$1 | B$0.71 |
| Philippines | P100 | B$3.80 |
| Singapore | S$1 | B$1.00 |
| Thailand | 100B | B$4.10 |
| UK | UK£1 | B$2.51 |
| USA | US$1 | B$1.74 |

### Exchanging Money
Travellers cheques can be exchanged readily at major banks in BSB and Kuala Belait, although a hefty commission is charged for

the privilege. American dollars and pounds sterling are the safest currencies to travel with, but you shouldn't encounter any problems with other Western currencies. If you're travelling to expensive Brunei from Malaysia, remember that nobody in hotels or shops will want your ringgit. If you haven't already purchased Brunei dollars in Labuan, there are moneychangers in Muara to tide you over till you get to BSB.

International credit cards such as Visa, Diners Club and American Express are readily accepted at most hotels; in fact it's usually the expected method of payment. Likewise, if you're dining at hotel restaurants, credit card payments are fine. There are ATMs outside major banks and in the YSHHB Complex in BSB. If you're flying to BSB you can change money at the airport (moneychangers are open for all flights), but if you take a free shuttle bus to one of the major hotels you'll probably get a better rate at the banks in the city centre.

### Costs
If you're travelling from Malaysia you'll find costs much higher in Brunei. Accommodation in particular is expensive by South-East Asian standards; there is only one budget option in the country and it cannot always be relied upon for a bed, though mid-range hotels are of a high standard and are cheaper than many comparable top-end places in Malaysia. Transport is comparable to prices in Sabah and Sarawak in Malaysia, and you won't have to use it much anyway. Food is reasonably priced unless you eat at Western restaurants, and with no alcohol available, you won't have that drinks bill to face.

## POST & COMMUNICATIONS
Post offices open from 7.45 am to 4.30 pm Monday to Thursday and Saturday (8 to 11 am and 2 to 4 pm Friday; closed Sunday).

Letters (to 10g) cost B$0.75 to Australia and New Zealand, B$0.90 to the UK, and B$1.20 to the USA and Canada. An airmail postcard to Malaysia and Singapore is B$0.20; to most other places in South-East Asia it's B$0.35; to the Pacific, Europe, Africa, and Australia it's B$0.50; and to the

BRUNEI

Americas it's B$0.60. Aerograms are B$.045 regardless of destination.

Phonecards – Hallo Kad and JTB are the most common – are available from Telecom offices and retail stores in denominations of B$10, B$20, B$50 and B$100. They can be used in public booths to make international calls. Most hotels have International Direct Dialling (IDD) phones, and faxes can be sent from the Telecom office or from major hotels.

To call Brunei from outside the country, the country code is 673; from Brunei, the international access code is 00.

See Post & Communications in the BSB section later in this chapter for details of email and Internet access. BruNet, at www.brunet.bn, is a Web site set up by the Ministry of Communications that offers a range of Internet services, including email access and bulletin boards. The daily *Borneo Bulletin* has a simple Web site at www.brunet.bn/news/bb/front.htm.

## BOOKS

Books on Brunei are few and far between, but there are a few useful titles for travellers and some glossy publications that make good permanent mementos.

*By God's Will – A Portrait of the Sultan of Brunei* by Lord Chalfont is a measured look at the sultan and Brunei. The recent *New World Hegemony in the Malay World* by Geoffrey C Gunn makes up much of the ground covered since Lord Chalfont's book.

For an exhaustive analysis of everything to do with Brunei, including statistics, the glossy government publication *Brunei Darussalam in Profile* is available on request from Brunei diplomatic missions. The more-independent *Brunei Country Review* edited by Robert C Kelly et al is more down-to-earth, especially for those entering Brunei on business or for employment. The *Brunei Yearbook,* published by the Borneo Bulletin, is also informative. *Brunei Darussalam in Brief* and *Selamat Datang* are other useful publications.

## NEWSPAPERS & MAGAZINES

The *Borneo Bulletin* is the country's English-language daily. Newspapers from Malaysia and Singapore are available, as are magazines including *Time, Newsweek* and *Asiaweek*. The government prints two newspapers in Malay: *Media Pertama* and the weekly *Pelita Brunei. Brunei Darussalam Newsletter* is a bimonthly English-language newsletter covering the sultan's official engagements or public utterances.

Prominent in most hotel lobbies is *Regal,* a glossy lifestyle magazine advising Bruneians how to emulate Singapore yuppies. Among reviews of the latest products from Rolex and real estate strategies for trendy overseas suburbs, there are occasionally interesting articles on Brunei's history, culture and wildlife.

## RADIO & TV

Brunei has two radio channels transmitting on both the medium wave and FM bands – one in Malay, called the National Network, and the other in English, Chinese and Gurkhali (for the Gurkha soldiers who guard Brunei's oilfields), the Pilihan Network. English transmission times are from 6.30 to 8.30 am, 11 am to 2 pm and 8 to 10 pm. A third network, Pelangi Network, is bilingual (Malay and English) and operates on the FM band. Five times a day, during Muslim prayer times, the radio and TV transmit the muezzin's call nationally. London's Capital Radio and Capital Gold can be picked up on the FM band.

Brunei is proud of the fact that it was the first country in the region to introduce colour TV in 1975, although you'll probably be underwhelmed by the quality of local content. Radio & Television Brunei (RTB) transmits local and overseas programs for about eight hours on weekdays, 12 hours on Friday and 15 hours on weekends. TV is broadcast on channel 5 for most of the country; Malaysian TV can also be received. Major hotels usually provide free access to cable networks, such as CNN, BBC or HBO.

## TIME

Brunei is in the same time zone as Malaysia and Singapore: 16 hours ahead of US Pacific Standard Time (PST; San Francisco and Los

Angeles), 13 hours ahead of US Eastern Standard Time (EST; New York), eight hours ahead of Greenwich Mean Time (GMT; London) and two hours behind Australian Eastern Standard Time (EST; Sydney and Melbourne). Thus, when it is noon in Brunei, it is 8 pm in Los Angeles and 11 pm in New York the previous day, 4 am in London, and 2 pm in Sydney and Melbourne.

## ELECTRICITY

Electricity supplies are reliable and run at 220–240V AC, 50 cycles. Plugs are of three square-pins, as in Malaysia and Singapore.

## WEIGHTS & MEASURES

Like almost everywhere in the world, Brunei uses the metric system.

## HEALTH

Generally speaking, Brunei has high standards of hygiene. Tap water is considered safe to drink and there is no risk of malaria. Smoke haze has caused serious health concerns in the past few years – check the situation first if you plan on visiting in March or April.

Remember that this is a tropical climate, so take the usual precautions against heat exhaustion and dehydration – see Environmental Hazards in the Health section in the Malaysia Facts for the Visitor chapter.

The Hart Medical Clinic (☎ 02- 225531), 1st floor, Wisma Setia, is a clinic in the centre of BSB. The RIPAS hospital just north of Jalan Tutong is a fully equipped, modern hospital.

Proof of yellow fever vaccination is required if you are travelling from an infected area.

## WOMEN TRAVELLERS

Brunei is a very safe country in which to travel. Orthodox Muslim women cover up from head to toe, with only the face and hands exposed, though quite a few young women do not cover their heads. Because of the British colonial heritage and large expat community, most Bruneians are used to Western ways – nonetheless, bare shoulders and short dresses are considered inappropriate.

To avoid offence, dress should be conservative and not revealing. There's no need to cover elbows and knees, or to wear a scarf, unless you really want to impress a pious host. There are strict dress and behaviour rules for visiting mosques (see the 'Places of Worship' special section earlier in this book). The usual Western swimwear is fine at hotel pools, and a one-piece bathing suit or T-shirt and shorts will attract less attention elsewhere. Needless to say, topless bathing is not accepted.

## EMERGENCIES

If you are in need of an ambulance when in Brunei, dial ☎ 991; dial ☎ 993 for police and ☎ 995 in case of fire.

## BUSINESS HOURS

Government offices are open from 7.45 am to 12.15 pm and 1.30 to 4.30 pm daily (closed Friday and Sunday). Private business offices are generally open from 9 am to 5 pm weekdays and from 9 am to noon on Saturday; banks are open from 9 am to 3 pm weekdays and from 9 to 11 am Saturday. Most shops in the central area open daily around 9 am and are closed by 6 pm. Shopping malls generally open an hour or so later and close at 9.30 or 10 pm (some may close earlier on Sunday). In major shopping precincts, such as Jalan Tutong and Gadong, shops stay open until 9 or 9.30 pm. Hours may be shorter during Ramadan.

## PUBLIC HOLIDAYS & SPECIAL EVENTS

Holidays and festivals in Brunei are mostly religious celebrations or festivities that mark the anniversaries of important events in the history of the country.

As in Malaysia and Singapore, the dates of most religious festivals are not fixed because they are based on the Islamic calendar.

Fixed holidays are:

**New Year's Day** 1 January
**National Day** 23 February
**Royal Brunei Armed Forces Day** 31 May
**Sultan's Birthday** 15 July
**Christmas Day** 25 December

Variable holidays include:

**Chinese New Year** 12–13 February 2002
**Hari Raya Aidiladha** (Feast of the Sacrifice) 6 March 2001, 23 February 2002
**Hizrah** (Islamic New Year) 26 March 2001, 15 March 2002
**Birth of the Prophet** 4 June 2001, 24 May 2002
**Ascension of the Prophet** 15 October 2001, 4 October 2002
**Hari Raya Aidifitri** (end of Ramadan) 17–18 December 2001, 6–7 December 2002

The most celebrated dates on Brunei's calendar are the two Hari Rayas: Hari Raya Aidilfitri is a festive day to mark the end of Ramadan, while Hari Raya Aidiladha celebrates the culmination of the Hajj, or holy pilgrimage.

# Getting There & Away

## AIR
Royal Brunei Airlines has pared back its services considerably, and now has few direct flights beyond Singapore, Kuala Lumpur and Hong Kong. Royal Brunei has healthy competition from Malaysia Airlines and Singapore Airlines, and prices are generally similar on shared routes. That said, good discounts can be found on Royal Brunei if you buy your ticket in the country of your departure; being a Muslim airline, Royal Brunei does not serve alcohol on its flights.

For airline offices in Brunei, see the Getting There & Away entry under BSB later in this chapter.

## Departure Tax
There is a departure tax of B$5 when flying to Malaysia and Singapore, and B$12 to all other destinations.

## Malaysia & Singapore
To Kuching the one-way economy fare is B$141 (RM309 from Kuching), Kota Kinabalu B$81 (RM103 from KK), Kuala

Lumpur B$347 (RM544 from KL) and Labuan B$37 (RM63 from Labuan). Because of the difference in exchange rates it is around 40% cheaper to fly to Brunei from Malaysia than vice versa. The standard economy fare to Singapore is B$347/412 one way/return. Discounts are not usually available on these flights.

## Other Asian Destinations
Asian destinations where Royal Brunei Airlines offers reasonable promotional prices include Bangkok (B$220/430 one way/return), Jakarta and Manila (both B$430 return), and Hong Kong and Taipei (both B$450 return). The cheapest fare to Tokyo is via Singapore on Singapore Airlines (B$970 plus taxes). It's also worth asking about Asean Circle Trip tickets, which permit stopovers in a loop between cities in Vietnam, Thailand, the Philippines, Malaysia, Indonesia and via Singapore. Tickets cost B$701 to B$1020, depending on the number of stopovers requested.

## Australia
From Sydney or Brisbane the cheapest flights are A$1049 return with Singapore Airlines (via Singapore, 35-day validity); a one-way ticket valid for 12 months is A$819. Going the other way, fares are B$900/1063 one way/return to Adelaide, Brisbane, Melbourne or Sydney. Fares to Perth are B$650/789.

## UK, Europe & North America
Fares to London are B$1122/1280 one way/return. At the time of writing, Singapore Airlines was offering a promotional fare of B$850 return. For flights to North America, including Los Angeles, San Francisco, Vancouver or across to New York, the fare is B$1199/1670.

## LAND
The main overland route is via bus to/from Miri in Sarawak. See the Seria Getting There & Away section under Around BSB later in this chapter for details. It is possible to travel overland between Limbang or Lawas in Sarawak and Bangar in the eastern

part of Brunei, although a boat to BSB is the usual and far more convenient option. Overland travel between Lawas and Bangar is expensive. See Bangar in the Temburong section later in this chapter and the Limbang and Lawas sections under North-East Sarawak in the Sarawak chapter for details on these border crossings.

## SEA
Boats connect Brunei to Lawas and Limbang in Sarawak, and to Pulau Labuan, from where boats go to Sabah. With the exception of boats destined for Limbang, all international boats now depart from Muara, 25km north-east of BSB, where Brunei immigration formalities are also handled.

Normally the South China Sea is glassy smooth, but during the wet season it can get choppy.

### Pulau Labuan
Labuan is a duty-free island between Brunei and Sabah from where you can take a ferry direct to Kota Kinabalu or Menumbok (for a bus to Kota Kinabalu or Lawas in Sarawak); and flights to Sabah, Sarawak or West Malaysia. For more details, see the Pulau Labuan Getting There & Away section in the Sabah chapter.

Buy your ticket at the dock the previous day if you are catching an early boat, especially on weekends and public holidays, and aim to check in 45 minutes before departure time to clear immigration. You'll need to catch the first express bus to Muara from BSB to get the first ferry.

From Muara, there are seven daily express boats to Labuan (taking 45 minutes to one hour). Departures are currently half-hourly between 7 and 9 am, and there are boats at 1, 1.30 and 3.30 pm. From Labuan, boats leave between 8.30 and 4.30 pm daily. The fare from Brunei is B$8/15 for children/adults (RM12/24 from Labuan).

### Sarawak
Boats to Limbang leave from the customs wharf at the end of Jalan Roberts in BSB, where there is also an immigration office. Private express boats do this run between 7 am and 4 pm, and depart when full. Buy your ticket at the customs wharf. The fare is B$10 (RM15 coming from Limbang) and the trip takes about 30 minutes.

From Limbang you can fly to Miri, Lawas or Kota Kinabalu. Limbang is an uneventful river town and is also one end of the famed Headhunters' Trail. See Limbang under North-East Sarawak in the Sarawak chapter for further details.

One express boat daily goes from Muara to Lawas (B$15, two hours). See Getting There & Away under Lawas in the Sarawak chapter for details of flights in Sarawak.

# Getting Around

Transport around Brunei is by bus, rental car or taxi. The public bus system is cheap and reliable, but only in and around BSB. Buses run between 6 am and 6 pm daily. Buses on the main highway between BSB and Kuala Belait are regular.

If you want to get off the main road to explore the hinterland, a rental car is the least-expensive option (see Car under Getting There & Away in the BSB section). Organised tours are pricey and metered taxis are prohibitively so (see Travel Agencies under Information in the BSB section for more information). Driving in Brunei is on the left.

Hitchhiking is another option. In Brunei, hitchhikers are such a novelty that the chances of getting a lift are fairly good, although cars hurtle along the main highway and are less inclined to stop on long stretches. While Brunei is generally a safe place to travel, hitching is never entirely safe anywhere, and we don't recommend it. Travellers who do decide to hitch should understand that they are taking a small, but potentially serious, risk. People who choose to hitch will be safer if they travel in pairs and let someone know where they are planning to go.

Regular boats connect Bangar in the Temburong district with BSB. Taxis are the only means of transport around Temburong.

BRUNEI

# Bandar Seri Begawan

☎ 02

Despite the sultan's large stable of polo ponies, Brunei is basically a one-horse country. The capital, Bandar Seri Begawan, is by far the largest town in Brunei and the location of nearly all the country's sights. It's a calm, clean, compact town of some 60,000 people, half of whom live in the terrific tangle of plankwalks and telephone wires comprising the stilt villages that fringe BSB's rivers.

Islam and oil money are BSB's defining characteristics. Arabic script graces the street signs, and domes, minarets and bank towers punctuate the skyline. The sprawling public buildings, mosques and stadiums, culminating conspicuously in the splendour of the sultan's palace, are testament to the twin pillars on which the capital rests.

The streets are quiet even when they're full of people and you won't see any bicycles, trishaws or even motorcycles on the wide streets – late-model Land Cruisers are about as exotic as street life gets. The real action is on the rivers, especially first thing in the morning and just before sunset – at these times an armada of water taxis storms the city centre to ferry residents to work or back home to Kampung Ayer.

The stilt villages collectively called Kampung Ayer (which simply means 'Water Village' – see the boxed text 'Kampung Ayer' in this section) are BSB's biggest draw, though the city has some fine museums and its mosques are spectacular, especially at night. It's a good thing the mosques are illuminated because aside from TV, there's virtually nothing to do after dinner. On the plus side, there is a good selection of restaurants. If you're prepared to pay, you can tuck into some fine Italian and Indian food.

## Orientation

Central BSB is a compact grid aligned roughly north-south and bounded on three sides by water: the Brunei and Kedayan rivers on the south and west, respectively, and a tidal canal on the east. In the city centre you'll find most hotels and places to eat, banks, the bus station, airline offices and shops. The Omar Ali Saifuddien Mosque on the western edge of the city centre dominates the ground; a new bank tower obscures the skyline in front of it. Most sights are within walking distance or a short bus ride of the city centre.

Between Omar Ali Saifuddien Mosque and the riverfront, pedestrians run the gauntlet of two massive twin Malay-style buildings. Together these form an ultra-chic shopping mall, the Yayasan Sultan Haji Hassanal Bolkiah Complex. Usually written as the YSHHB Complex and simply called Yayasan, the mall leads to Jalan MacArthur, across which are waterfront cafes and the customs wharf for boats to Sabah and Sarawak.

Stilt villages sprawl along the opposite bank of the Sungai Brunei, and along both banks of the Sungai Kedayan to the northwest. From Omar Ali Saifuddien Mosque you can navigate plankwalks through a stilt village to a new mosque farther up the Kedayan.

## Information

**Tourist Offices** There has been talk of opening the country's first tourist information centre near the Brunei Hotel, but at the time of writing nothing had yet come of the discussions.

*Explore Brunei* is the free government tourist guide and contains much useful information for visitors. It is well worth chasing up a copy; the guide should be available at major hotels, travel agents and at the airport information desk.

**Money** All banks in BSB charge a commission to cash travellers cheques. Least expensive is the Hongkong Bank (HSBC), which charges B$10.50; the Standard Chartered usually offers higher exchange rates but charges B$15 commission per transaction! Penukar Wang is a moneychanger on Jalan Sultan near the customs wharf; you can also change money at the airport.

**Post & Communications** The main post office is on the corner of Jalan Sultan and Jalan Elizabeth Dua. It is best avoided at lunchtime, when it is understaffed.

The LA Cybercafe is at the waterfront end of the Yayasan Complex on the 1st floor. It's open from 10 am to 9 pm Monday to Saturday (to 7 pm or earlier Sunday). Email and Internet rates work out to about B$7 per hour, and you may be asked for your passport number when you first sign in.

**Travel Agencies** In the city centre there's a host of travel agents where you can book flights and local tours. Prices for tours depend on the number of paying customers, and are far cheaper if there are two or more people. Half-day tours of BSB start at B$45 per person, and a range of expensive trips into the countryside start at B$55 (B$25 for children). Operators include:

**Eco Tours & Travel** (☎ 223420, fax 221967, ✉ Ecotvl@hotmail.com) Ground floor, Britannia House, Jalan Cator. Offers tours to the sights in and around BSB, as well as running trips to Temburong.
**Freme Travel Service** (☎ 234280, fax 234284) 4th floor, Wisma Jaya, Jalan Pemancha. Offers general tours including BSB sights.
**Jasra Harrisons** (☎ 243911, fax 243904, ✉ jasratvl@brunet.bn) On the corner of Jalan MacArthur and Jalan Kianggeh. A good general travel agent, and the sales agent for British Airways and Qantas; it also organises trips to Temburong, including stays at the Trandie Marina Resort.
**Sunshine Borneo Tours & Travel** (☎ 441791, fax 441790, ✉ sunshine@brunet.bn) 2nd floor, Block C, Abdul Razak Complex, 3½ Km Jalan Gadong. It runs tours of the city, and farther afield in Brunei and the rest of Borneo.
**Wildman Tours** (☎ 786987) Jalan Muara, outside town. Contact Mark Dandy for details of Temburong tours.

**Bookshops** The biggest and best range of books and magazines is at Paul & Elizabeth Book Services, on the 2nd floor of the YSHHB Complex; this is one of the few places that stocks maps of Brunei. Wordzone Bookshop, in the basement of the YSHHB Complex, has a small range of periodicals and newspapers. Magazines and a limited range of books are available at the airport. STP Distributors has a handy stationery store on Jalan Sultan.

**Cultural Centres** The British Council is a long way out of town at 45 Simpang 100, Jalan Tungku Link. It's open Monday to Thursday from 8 am to 12.15 pm and 1.45 to 4.30 pm, and from 8 am to 12.30 pm Friday and Saturday.

Alliance Française (☎ 343245) is at Simpang 465, Jalan Muara, on the way to the airport.

## Omar Ali Saifuddien Mosque
Named after the 28th sultan of Brunei, this golden-domed structure was built in 1958 and stands next to the Sungai Kedayan in its own artificial lagoon. It is one of the tallest buildings in BSB and one of the most impressive structures in South-East Asia.

This grand mosque makes an impressive sight at any time: lit up at night, or silhouetted as the sun sinks over the stilt village next door. You'll probably hear the call to prayer echo throughout the city centre, starting from before dawn.

The interior is simple but tasteful, although no match for the stunning exterior. The floor and walls are made from the finest Italian marble; the stained-glass windows were crafted in England; and the luxurious carpets were flown in from Saudi Arabia and Belgium. A Venetian mosaic of 3.5 million pieces decorates the inside of the main dome, and pools and quadrants surrounding the building throw beautiful reflections. The ceremonial stone boat sitting in the lagoon is a replica of a 16th-century *mahligai* barge.

You may be allowed to take the elevator to the top of the 44m minaret or walk up the winding staircase without charge. The view over the city and Kampung Ayer is excellent.

The mosque is open to non-Muslims between 8 am and noon, 1 and 3 pm and 4.30 and 5.30 pm (ie, outside prayer times) Saturday to Wednesday. It is closed to non-Muslims on Thursday, and on Friday it is open only from 4.30 to 5 pm. The compound is open between 8 am and 8.30 pm.

BRUNEI

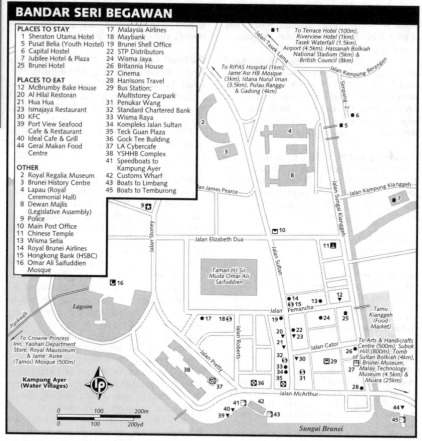

## BANDAR SERI BEGAWAN

**PLACES TO STAY**
1 Sheraton Utama Hotel
5 Pusat Belia (Youth Hostel)
6 Capital Hostel
7 Jubilee Hotel & Plaza
25 Brunei Hotel

**PLACES TO EAT**
12 McBrumby Bake House
20 Al Hilal Restoran
21 Hua Hua
23 Ismajaya Restaurant
30 KFC
39 Port View Seafood
Cafe & Restaurant
40 Ideal Cafe & Grill
44 Gerai Makan Food
Centre

**OTHER**
2 Royal Regalia Museum
3 Brunei History Centre
4 Lapau (Royal
Ceremonial Hall)
8 Dewan Majlis
(Legislative Assembly)
9 Police
10 Main Post Office
11 Chinese Temple
13 Wisma Setia
14 Royal Brunei Airlines
15 Hongkong Bank (HSBC)
16 Omar Ali Saifuddien
Mosque

17 Malaysia Airlines
18 Maybank
19 Brunei Shell Office
22 STP Distributors
24 Wisma Jaya
26 Britannia House
27 Cinema
28 Harrisons Travel
29 Bus Station;
Multistorey Carpark
31 Penukar Wang
32 Standard Chartered Bank
33 Wisma Raya
34 Kompleks Jalan Sultan
35 Teck Guan Plaza
36 Gock Tee Building
37 LA Cybercafe
38 YSHHB Complex
41 Speedboats to
Kampung Ayer
42 Customs Wharf
43 Boats to Limbang
45 Boats to Temburong

To Terrace Hotel (100m),
Riverview Hotel (1km),
Tasek Waterfall (1.5km),
Airport (4.5km), Hassanah Bolkiah
National Stadium (5km) &
British Council (8km)

To RIPAS Hospital (1km),
Jame'Asr HB Mosque
(3km), Istana Nurul Iman
(3.5km), Pulau Ranggu
& Gadong (4km)

Jalan Tasek Lama
Jalan Kampung Berangan
Simpang 2
Jalan James Pearce
Jalan Stoney
Jalan Sungai Kianggeh
Jalan Kampung Kianggeh
Jalan Elizabeth Dua
Jalan Sultan
Taman HJ Sir
Muda Omar Ali
Saifuddien
Lagoon
Plankwalk
To Crowne Princess
Inn, Yaohan Department
Store, Royal Mausoleum
& Jame' Asree
(Tamoi) Mosque (500m)
Kampung Ayer
(Water Villages)
Jalan Roberts
Jalan Pretty
Jalan Pemancha
Jalan Cator
Jalan McArthur
Tamu
Kianggeh
(Food
Market)
To Arts & Handicrafts
Centre (500m), Subok
Hill (800m), Tomb
of Sultan Bolkiah (4km),
Brunei Museum,
Malay Technology
Museum (4.5km) &
Muara (25km)
Sungai Brunei

0    100    200m
0    100    200yd

Remember to dress appropriately and to remove your shoes before entering. Muslim
travellers can enter the mosque to pray at
any time.

### Brunei Museum

This excellent museum is at Kota Batu,
4.5km east of the centre of BSB, and overlooks the Sungai Brunei. The Brunei Museum contains one of the finest galleries in
the world, and combined with a visit to the
Malay Technology Museum on the riverbank below, it is definitely worth the short
trip from town.

The Brunei Museum has displays of artefacts representing the cultural heritage of
Brunei, including musical instruments, baskets and brassware, and a large collection of
Chinese ceramics dating from 1000 AD. A
natural history section features exhibits of
mounted mammals, birds and insects. There
is also a gallery for temporary exhibits –
pottery from a 15th-century shipwreck was
on display at the time of writing.

These galleries are fine, but they give
little hint of what awaits in the breathtaking
Islamic gallery. Here you'll find an astonishing, brilliantly arranged collection of

beautiful ceramics, jewellery, silverwork and weaponry from across the Islamic world. The illuminated Quran alone are worth the trip out to the museum, but there are also jade sword handles inlaid with gems to admire, and begging bowls intricately carved from coconut husks – every trip to the gallery turns up a treasure you missed the last time.

The museum is open Tuesday to Thursday from 9.30 am to 5 pm; from 9.30 to 11.30 am and 2.30 to 5 pm Friday and from 9 am to 5 pm on weekends (closed Monday). Bags must be left at the door and can be stored in lockers. Admission is free.

Purple bus Nos 11 and 39 pass the museum (B$1). Otherwise, it's a bit of a walk from town but you may be able to catch a lift. After visiting the museum, you can walk down the steep bank to the Malay Technology Museum.

## Malay Technology Museum

This impressive museum, built on the edge of the river below the Brunei Museum, has three galleries devoted to traditional lifestyles and artisans.

Gallery 1 features water villages and has reconstructions of how kampung architecture has evolved over the last 150 years or so. Gallery 2 has exhibits of handicrafts and fishing techniques practised by the people of the water villages. These include silversmithing, brass casting and weaving, and there are some fine examples on display. Gallery 3 shows the tools and techniques used by the indigenous tribes of the interior for food gathering, agriculture and hunting, although the mannequins in striped pyjamas look more like convicts than indigenous Bruneians. Brunei's first gunboat is on display in front of the museum.

The museum is open the same hours as the Brunei Museum, and entry is free.

## Royal Regalia Museum

This museum was gutted by fire early in 1998 but the contents were saved and the building has been carefully reconstructed. It is devoted to the Sultan of Brunei – no surprises there – and displays photographs of HM and other members of the royal family. Among the priceless artefacts are his report from Sandhurst Royal Military Academy, and coronation hardware such as the throne, crowns, ceremonial sceptres, *kris* (traditional swords) and costumes.

Opening hours are Sunday to Saturday from 8.30 am to 5 pm, and from 9 to 11 am and 2.30 to 5 pm Friday. Entry is free.

## Brunei History Centre

The Brunei History Centre is devoted to researching Brunei's history and recording the sultan's family history. At the entrance to the centre is a small museum that details the lineage of the sultan. The museum has replicas of all the royal tombs and shows their locations around BSB. The centre and the museum are open Monday to Thursday and on Saturday from 7.45 am to 12.15 pm and 1.30 to 4.30 pm; it is closed on Friday. Admission is free.

## Arts & Handicrafts Centre

This grandiose handicraft centre was built to help develop local craftwork. It's on the waterfront towards the Brunei Museum, visible from town and within easy walking distance. However, if you're interested in traditional crafts it is disappointing; only new silverwork and weaving produced by the students are available, and some items are very expensive. A traditional umbrella costs about B$20; model water taxis start at B$200; a kris and scabbard will set you back about B$500; and silverwork starts at B$10 and goes up to thousands of Brunei bucks for intricate pieces. Workshops are open to visitors.

The centre is open Monday to Thursday and on Saturday from 8 am to 12.15 pm and 1.30 to 4.30 pm, and from 8.30 am to 2 pm Friday and Sunday. Entry is free.

## Taman Peranginan Tasek

This park is a pleasant retreat from the city. It has picnic areas and peaceful walks to a small waterfall and reservoir.

The park is a short distance from town. Walk along Jalan Tasek Lama north from the city centre past the Terrace Hotel, and

BRUNEI

## Kampung Ayer

This is the place that spawned all those 'Venice of the East' cliches throughout the region – except in this case, it was once an apt description. At least Antonio Pigafetta – who tagged along on one of Magellan's big overseas spice-hunts – thought so. He coined the phrase in honour of the great collection of wooden stilt villages he encountered at Kota Batu (just east of modern central BSB) in 1521.

Except for the *istana* (palace) and a few royal houses, the capital of the sultan's then-extensive empire was built entirely on poles and plankwalks over Sungai Brunei. By the 18th century, the *kampung* (villages) had become known abroad for their artisan guilds – a certain kampung might be famed for its brasswork, another for weaving.

The villages have long since spread along the banks of Sungai Brunei and Sungai Kedayan, and much of the capital's population still comes ashore from Kampung Ayer each morning to service the sultan's land-based city. There are now 28 kampung in all, housing about 30,000 people – when BSB was being modernised many elected to stay in these dwellings, although today quite a few houses are colourless pre-fab constructs that hardly evoke the glory days of Pigafetta's enthusiasm. Inside, houses have also moved on, and modern plumbing, electricity and colour TVs are the norm. The kampung are serviced by schools and clinics – of cement rather than wood – shops, mosques and a water-borne fire brigade (fires are not uncommon, and the average dwelling takes all of seven minutes to burn to the waterline).

A visit to one of the more traditional-style kampung is probably the most interesting experience you'll have in Brunei. These are a maze of wooden plankwalks connecting brightly painted shacks to shops, villages to schools, clinics to workshops. It's fascinating to wander at random – even if you do end up in someone's kitchen. Bougainvilleas festoon the eaves as they surely did in Pigafetta's time and, underneath it all, egrets poke about for mudskippers among the piles of garbage. BSB's people are at their least reserved and most friendly here at their close-knit riverside homes – you can expect to be mobbed along the plankwalks by children and heartily heralded from verandas.

The quickest – and best – way to get to Kampung Ayer is to select a plankwalk next to the YSHHB Complex or the Omar Ali Saifuddien Mosque and start wandering. You'll soon reach Kampung Tamoi, which sports a spiffy new mosque on shore. Don't be surprised to see new blocks of modern housing in this and other areas. At the rate houses burn down, the government has been keen to replace older-style dwellings with more durable mass housing.

To get to the kampung across Sungai Brunei, a water taxi can take you across for a negotiable fee – expect to pay B$1 or more. A boat trip right around Kampung Ayer takes at least 30 minutes, and the boat operators will probably ask B$30 for their efforts. Bargain hard – B$10 is more like the 'real' price. Water taxis shuttle people back and forth between early morning and late evening, and congregate at the area next to the customs wharf.

There are all sorts of shops and businesses among the houses in Kampung Ayer. You might stumble across a handicraft shop selling silverwork, brass, woven cloth and baskets. If not, ask a boat operator to take you to one.

after two sets of traffic lights turn right. From the entrance gates by the parking lot, it is about 1km to the falls – continue past the flowerbeds and picnic tables, then follow the stream to the falls. They are best in the wet season, when the water is deeper – you can swim here but women should remember that the usual rules of modesty apply; T-shirts and shorts are OK. Another road by the gate leads to a 15-minute walk uphill to a view over the reservoir.

The Sheraton Utama Hotel hands out a map for joggers that shows the walks.

### Jame'Asr Hassanil Bolkiah Mosque

This is the largest mosque in Brunei, constructed at great expense, and as the local tourist literature trumpets is 'a symbol of Islam's firm hold in the country'. It's a fabulous sight. Situated in Kampung Kiarong, a few kilometres from the city centre, it is known locally as the Kiarong Mosque. Take bus No 1 or 22 to get there.

## Tamoi Mosque

The newest mosque in town is the Jame' Asree mosque, usually called the Tamoi mosque, after the stilt village in which it resides. Strikingly illuminated, the mosque is a prominent addition to the evening skyline, especially at sunset as you look along the Sungai Kedayan. By day the modern-style mosque is far less interesting, but it's a fascinating and enjoyable walk to the mosque via the village plankwalks leading off from the YSHHB Complex and Omar Ali Saifuddien Mosque.

## Istana Nurul Iman

The sultan's palace, Istana Nurul Iman, is an impressive sight, especially when lit up at night. It is larger than the Vatican Palace and no expense was spared: It cost US$350 million and, among other features, has 1788 rooms, 200 toilets and a banquet hall with seating for 4000. Unfortunately, the istana is only open to the public during Hari Raya Aidilfitri, the end of the fasting month of Ramadan, when the sultan often deigns to meet his people.

The istana is 4km out of town on the Tutong road, and the grounds look on to the Sungai Brunei. You could spend a leisurely hour walking there, or charter a water taxi then walk to the front of the palace. Tutong and Seria buses pass the istana, but they are infrequent. On the hill opposite the istana are homes belonging to other members of the royal family.

## Other Attractions

Overlooking the river about 500m from the Yaohan department store is the **Makam Di-Raja** (Royal Mausoleum), the burial place of the last four sultans; other members of the royal family are buried in the grounds.

On the other side of town on the way to the Brunei Museum is the **Tomb of Sultan**

**Bolkiah** and mausoleum of the fifth sultan of Brunei, who lived from 1473 to 1521, during a period when Brunei was the dominant power in the region. The small tomb and garden is in the historic setting of Kota Batu and the view across the river is fine; otherwise, it's a very minor attraction.

All over town you'll notice uniquely designed, oversized state buildings that seem to serve no other purpose than to attest to Brunei's wealth and to glorify the reign of HM. The **Lapau** (Royal Ceremonial Hall) and **Dewan Majlis** (Legislative Assembly) complex are opposite the youth centre in the city centre. The Lapau was the coronation hall for the sultan in 1968. Royal ceremonies are occasionally held here, but it lies empty most of the time. None of these buildings can be visited.

There is a brightly painted, newish **Chinese temple** on the corner of Jalan Elizabeth Dua and Jalan Sungai Kianggeh. It's probably not worth going far out of your way for, but it's a busy place on Saturday evening, and Chinese opera is sometimes staged here.

Fine views of Kampung Ayer and the approach to BSB can be had from **Subok Hill** (Bukit Subok). After the Handicraft Centre on Jalan Kota Batu, turn left and follow the road up the hill. The Foreign Affairs ministry is also on Subok Hill.

In the middle of the river across from the Istana Nurul Iman, **Pulau Ranggu** is home to a large colony of proboscis monkeys – Brunei is one of the strongholds of these amazing primates. Macaques also inhabit the island. If you take a water taxi along the river around sunset you may glimpse a monkey; the bargaining price will probably start at B$60. Nearby on the riverbank, the Persiaran Damuan is a landscaped park from where you can get good views of the istana. Access is from Jalan Tutong.

## Activities

The **Hassanal Bolkiah National Stadium** is of Olympic proportions and includes a track-and-field complex, tennis centre, squash courts and swimming pool. It is open to the public daily from 8 am to noon and 1.30 to

4.30 pm, and the pool is often nearly deserted. The stadium is 5km north of the city; to get there, take purple bus No 01 or 34.

There's an international-standard golf course at **Mentiri Golf Club** near BSB, and there's a driving range at the Royal Brunei Sports Complex near the airport.

Some tour operators run **dive trips** to a few spots in the area, including the wrecks off Pulau Labuan, but you're probably better off dealing with Labuan operators or saving your money for the islands off Semporna in Sabah.

## Places to Stay – Budget

The only budget option in Brunei is *Pusat Belia* (☎ 222900, 08-765515), a youth hostel on Jalan Sungai Kianggeh, a short walk from the city centre. A bed in an air-con four-bed dorm costs B$10 (no bathroom). The hostel is often empty but can sometimes fill up with sports groups. Technically you should have a youth hostel or student card to stay, but it doesn't matter much – entry to this bizarrely officious establishment is at the discretion of the front desk, and if they don't mind the look of you *too* much, you'll get a bed. Some males with long hair have been turned away.

Regardless of your fashion sense, personal hygiene or star sign, the hostel does not accept guests after 9 pm. Office hours are from 7.45 am to noon only on Monday to Saturday; the desk should also be attended from 2.30 to 9 pm on Friday and Sunday.

The youth centre, which the hostel is part of, has a swimming pool (entry B$1) and a cafe with a very limited menu.

If you draw a blank here and can't afford the mid-range places, you're in trouble. Some travellers have resorted to sleeping out in the parks or on a beach when the youth centre has been full, but this is not appreciated by the authorities and you run the risk of having your slumber disturbed by the police. Showers are available in the changing rooms of the youth centre pool for B$1.

## Places to Stay – Mid-Range

If you are on a tight budget, the jump in price from budget to mid-range accommodation will probably give you hysterics. If it's any consolation, all rooms include air-con, TV, hot water and IDD phones.

Off Jalan Tasek Lama just behind the Pusat Belia, *Capital Hostel* (☎ 223561, No 7 Simpang 2) has faded rooms, but they are cheap by Brunei standards – singles/doubles are B$55/65. The restaurant downstairs serves reasonably priced meals and Western breakfasts.

*Terrace Hotel* (☎ 243554, fax 227302, ✉ terrahtl@brunet.com), just north of the Sheraton on Jalan Tasek Lama, has simple rooms for B$66. The hotel's restaurant is pretty good and there's a swimming pool.

*Jubilee Hotel* (☎ 228070, fax 228080, ✉ jubilee@brunet.bn) is on Jalan Kampung Kianggeh. Small but comfortable rooms with spacious bathrooms cost B$70, including breakfast; suites are B$121/125. A small supermarket and an excellent coffee shop, Max's Cafe, (see Places to Eat later in this chapter) are attached.

*Crowne Princess Inn* (☎ 241128, Km 2.5 Jalan Tutong) is near the Yaohan department store (see Shopping for directions to the area). It is inconveniently located but is popular and reasonably priced. Standard rates are B$110 for a room, but discount rates (B$70) are routinely offered.

## Places to Stay – Top End

BSB has a good selection of top-end hotels, although the mid-range accommodation is perfectly adequate. For the extra money you can take advantage of trappings such as a pool, business centre and minibar full of soft drinks.

Centrally located on the corner of Jalan Sungai Kianggeh and Jalan Pemancha, *Brunei Hotel* (☎ 242372, fax 226196, ✉ Bruhot@brunet.bn) is the city's oldest. It is heavily pushed by tour groups and travel agents, but it isn't really special. Reasonable rooms start at B$178/198 for singles/doubles, though a discount rate – B$110 on standard rooms – is a good deal if you get it.

*Sheraton Utama Hotel* (☎ 244272, fax 221579) is Brunei's top hotel and is close to the city centre on Jalan Tasek Lama. Rooms start at B$230 and rise to B$1620 for the classiest three-room suite. The Sheraton has a pool, restaurants and a business centre.

**Riverview Hotel** (☎ 238238, fax 237999, ✉ rivview@brunet.bn, Km 1 Jalan Gadong) is one of Brunei's best. It is north of town on the way to the airport. Published rates are B$175/195 and suites are B$230 to B$880; discounts should be available.

**The Centrepoint** (☎ 430430, fax 430200), in the Gadong shopping precinct, has serviced apartments starting from B$235, climbing to B$1650 for the Presidential Suite; discounts may be available. There's an impressive range of marble-clad facilities, including an expensive Chinese restaurant, business centre, swimming pool, sports centre and private dining rooms – what more could you want, besides a stiff drink? There's a branch of the Yaohan Megamart downstairs.

## Places to Eat

Most eateries in the capital are open daily, though the trendier places tend to open later in the morning, from around 9 or 9.30 am.

All the hotels and the youth centre have their own restaurants. The **canteen** in the youth centre is cheap but the choice is very limited. The meals at the **Capital Hostel** are pretty good and quite cheap; tasty Hokkien noodles and other dishes cost around B$5.

There are food stalls and street cafes in the centre of BSB, and cheap outdoor eating can be enjoyed at several spots around this area. The **Gerai Makan** food centre is on the riverfront just over the canal from the customs wharf, although not much happens in the evening.

The best – and cheapest – food stalls are at the local food market, **Tamu Kianggeh**, across the canal near the intersection of Jalan Sungai Kianggeh and Jalan Pemancha. It's not very extensive but has plenty of local colour and is a popular spot for lunch. Water taxis hurtle up and down the canal transporting passengers to and fro. You can get good food starting at B$1, including satay, barbecued fish, chicken wings and **kueh melayu** (sweet pancakes filled with peanuts, raisins and sugar).

There are clean, air-conditioned **food courts** on the 2nd floor of Wisma Setia, on Jalan Pemancha, and on the 1st floor of the YSHHB Complex.

The main street, Jalan Sultan, has the cheapest restaurants in the city centre. **Ismajaya Restaurant** has rice and curry meals for around B$3; across the road is the comparably priced **Al Hilal Restoran**. Next door to Al Hilal is **Hua Hua**, which is a bit more expensive – about B$6 to B$8 for most dishes – but very good. It has a wide range, including seafood, noodles and claypot dishes. The Hua Hua and the Ismajaya stay open until 9 pm. On Jalan MacArthur, the **Sri Indah Restoran** has decent roti and murtabak.

BSB has some good bakeries. Decent French pastries can be enjoyed at **Delifrance**, on the ground floor of the YSHHB Complex, and across from the Brunei Hotel is a branch of the Australian **McBrumby Bake House**. Excellent coffee and muffins can be found at **Deli-Bites**, on the 1st floor of the Jubilee Hotel.

For real pizza and gourmet pasta, go to **Fratini**, on the ground floor of the YSHHB Complex. An imaginative selection of pizzas and pasta dishes range from B$11 to B$15, and lots of specials are on offer.

The **Port View Seafood Cafe & Restaurant** and **Ideal Cafe & Grill** are two good spots to watch the water traffic as the sun sets. The Port View is the better of the two – the cafe has its own reasonably priced menu or you can order from the restaurant upstairs; you can also swig a Shirley Temple here for B$4.

The shopping area on Jalan Tutong around the Yaohan department store has a number of restaurants. Most are moderately priced Chinese **kedai kopi** (coffee shops), some of which stay open as late as 10 pm.

The restaurant at the **Crowne Princess Inn** offers a reasonably priced Sunday **dim sum** (Chinese sweet and savoury buns, dumplings and mini-dishes served at breakfast and lunch) from 7.30 to 11 am, but the main draw here is in the evening when – gasp – live music can be heard until midnight. Usually a couple of musicians are on offer; Thursday is an off night and a band often appears on Saturday.

If you're looking for a late-night meal, or just a place to go, the wonderfully retro *Max's Cafe* at the Jubilee Hotel is open from 10 am to 2 am daily. This place sports a jukebox, red vinyl booths and Edward Hopper posters – the burgers and shakes are OK too.

For self-catering, *Hua Ho* supermarket in the basement of the YSHHB Complex stocks every type of food product imaginable.

## Shopping

Most of the quality shopping is in the air-conditioned plazas. The gigantic YSHHB Complex has a dazzling selection of ritzy shops selling watches, sunglasses, Iranian chandeliers and other essentials. It also houses franchises like the Body Shop.

The huge Yaohan department store sells imported clothes, electrical goods and books; the supermarket in the basement is stocked with imported foodstuffs from around the world. Nearby are a number of shopping plazas, such as Plaza Athirah, Mohamad Yossof and Badiah. It's about 20 minutes' walk to the Yaohan department store from the city centre via the stilt villages, starting from the back of Omar Ali Saifuddien Mosque. By road, it's about 1.5km north along Jalan Sultan, then west on Jalan Tatong.

The other big shopping centre is at Gadong, about 5km north-west of the city centre. There's no reason to make a special trip here, but there are plenty of supermarkets and department stores, a couple of decent bookshops, a number of restaurants and the Yaohan Megamart all collected together in the massive air-con Centrepoint shopping centre.

There are numerous photo-processing, camera and film shops in the shopping malls in the city centre and at Gadong, although if you have any special film requirements you should get them before you come to Brunei. There is no advantage to buying duty-free in Brunei, since the exchange rate in Malaysia will get you far more for your money.

## Getting There & Away

**Air** Airlines flying into Brunei include Royal Brunei Airlines, Malaysia Airlines, Singapore Airlines and Thai Airways International. Tickets to Malaysia and Singapore are at a fixed rate, but other international tickets are up to 20% cheaper if bought through travel agents rather than the airlines. Royal Brunei Airlines' travel shop sells discounted fares; it's in the same building as its office.

Airline offices or general sales agents in BSB include:

**British Airways** (☎ 225871); see the earlier Travel Agents section for Jasra Harrisons

**Garuda Indonesia** (☎ 235870) 49–50, 3rd floor, Wisma Raya, Jalan Sultan

**Malaysia Airlines** (☎ 224141) 144 Jalan Pemancha

**Royal Brunei Airlines** (☎ 242222) RBA Plaza, Jalan Sultan

**Singapore Airlines** (☎ 244901) 49–50, 1st floor, Wisma Raya, Jalan Sultan

**Thai Airways International** (☎ 242991) 401–403, 4th floor, Kompleks Jalan Sultan, 51–55 Jalan Sultan

**Bus** The main highway in Brunei links BSB to Seria, Kuala Belait and the Sarawak border near Kuala Baram. For Miri in Sarawak, take a bus to Seria, where you change for Kuala Belait and then change again to get to Miri. Set out early from BSB if you want to reach Miri in one day. See the Seria Getting There & Away entry in the Around BSB section later in this chapter for details.

It is possible, though difficult, to reach Limbang by road through Bangar from BSB; from there you could travel overland to Lawas, although boat is a cheaper and quicker option. It has been said that the government deliberately keeps the roads out of Brunei in a miserable condition to make any invasion by land difficult...

The bus station for both local and long-distance buses in BSB is on Jalan Cator (beneath the multistorey car park).

There are many buses every day to Seria (1½ to two hours, B$6) between 7.30 am and about 3 pm. Buses leave from the rear section of the bus station in BSB – the buses have destination signs on the front, but unlike other routes, this one is not signposted.

**Car** Hiring a car is the only feasible way to explore the hinterland of Brunei, though you could comfortably see most sights in two days.

Rental rates start at about B$120 per day for a Toyota Soluna – if you want to blend in, rates for a Mercedes or Volvo start at B$298. Prices include free mileage and insurance, although surcharges apply if the car is taken into Sarawak. Discounts may be available, depending on demand and season – don't be afraid to ask. Most rental agencies will bring the car to your hotel and arrange to pick it up when you've finished with it. Petrol is cheap and the main roads are in good condition, but the back roads can be appalling. There are a dozen or so car-rental companies, including Avis Rent A Car (☎ 422284, ✉ ncsbsb@ brunet.bn), Budget U-Drive (☎ 445846) and National Car Systems (☎ 224921), all in the Jalan Gadong area.

**Boat** Apart from flying, the only way to get to Pulau Labuan for connections to Sabah, or to the Sarawak outposts of Limbang and Lawas, is to use a launch or launch-taxi combination. See the Bangar Getting There & Away section under Temburong later in this chapter for details.

Regular launches ply between BSB and Bangar in Temburong. The first departure is around 7 am and the last at 5 pm. Launches leave when full from the jetty near the Gerai Makan food centre; the trip costs B$7/14 one way/return.

## Getting Around
**To/From the Airport** BSB's big, modern airport is 8km north-west of the city. Purple bus Nos 11, 23, 24, 36, 38 and 57 will get you to/from the airport for B$1. As you leave the terminal, walk diagonally right across the car park to get to the bus stop.

Some major hotels have courtesy phones at the arrivals hall that you can use to request a free pick-up.

Purple PPP taxis will get you between the airport and city for B$6 or B$7 – these taxis

are supposed to operate on a fixed-price zone system, but don't bother trying to tell them that; agree on the fare before you step in. A regular metered taxi costs around B$20.

**Bus** The government bus network reaches most sights in and around the city, and also serves the international ferry terminal at Muara. The bus station is beneath the multistorey car park on Jalan Cator; route maps for local buses are clearly displayed at the station and route numbers are emblazoned on the front of each bus. A route map is reproduced in the *Explore Brunei* booklet. Apart from the Muara express service, all fares are B$1. Most buses run every 15 to 20 minutes, and the system operates daily between 6.30 am and 6 pm. Useful routes include:

**Airport** – Bus Nos 11, 23, 24, 36, 38 and 57
**Brunei Museum & Malay Technology Museum** – Bus Nos 11 and 39
**Gadong Shopping Precinct** – Bus No 1
**Hassanal Bolkiah National Stadium & Immigration Department** – Bus Nos 1 and 34
**Jame'Asr Hassanil Bolkiah Mosque** – Bus Nos 1 and 22
**Jerudong Park Playground** – Bus Nos 55 and 57
**Muara** – Bus Nos 37, 38 and 39

Buses leave for the ferry terminal at Muara every half hour between 6.50 am and 4.50 pm; the trip takes 40 minutes and the fare is B$2. The last bus back is at 5 pm.

**Taxi** There are two options for taxis around BSB. The PPP taxis (better known as purple taxis) theoretically operate on a zone system; in practice, you should always agree to the fare beforehand, and expect to pay B$4 (plus B$1 if you book by phone) for a trip in town (the zone rate is B$3). Purple taxis operate from 6 am to 10 pm; they aren't plentiful but they do cruise around, and tend to congregate at the bus station. They can also be booked until 7 pm on the PPP hotline (☎ 394949).

The other option – a metered taxi – is for the frantically needy or the fantastically rich. A metered taxi to the ferry terminal at Muara will cost about B$75! The flagfall is B$3, a surcharge of B$5 applies for trips to/from the airport and the meters tick over very quickly. Between 9 pm and 6 am a surcharge of 50% of the metered fare is effective. There is also a B$1 charge for each item of luggage put in the boot (trunk). The best places to look for a taxi are at the bus station on Jalan Cator and at the Sheraton Utama.

**Water Taxi** Water taxis are longboats with powerful outboard motors that hurtle up and down the Sungai Brunei, transporting passengers to/from Kampung Ayer's stilt villages. They are most easily caught near the customs wharf or the Tamu Kianggeh food market. Fares start at B$0.50 and reach up to B$2, although you'll have to bargain a bit. To charter a boat for a tour of Kampung Ayer and the river shouldn't cost more than B$20 per hour – it could be less if you bargain hard.

# Around Bandar Seri Begawan

None of Brunei's sights is more than a few hours from the capital, but a car is essential to reach most of them. There's not a great deal to see – some good beaches and forest reserves make pleasant day trips, and with some extra effort and expense you can take some river trips and visit a longhouse, a traditional-style communal tribal dwelling. For trekking and wildlife-viewing in pristine rainforest, head for Temburong. Other than camping, the only accommodation outside BSB is at Kuala Belait, which is just a transit point for travel to/from Miri in Sarawak; and at the Kuala Belalong Rainforest Field Studies Centre, in the Batang Apoi Forest Reserve.

## JERUDONG PARK PLAYGROUND
The sultan presented this sprawling amusement park to his adoring subjects to mark his 48th birthday in 1994. Jerudong Park Playground is near the coast north of BSB and is claimed to be the biggest amusement park in the world (although the Disney Corporation may dispute this). It certainly

is huge – even if the whole of Kampung Ayer turned up on a Sunday (unlikely), the place would probably still seem deserted.

All rides used to be free but some now cost B$2; you rarely have to queue for any. They lack the daredevil feel that some of their counterparts in other countries have, but it is a great place to take children. However, just to remind you that this is Brunei, women wearing sleeveless tops are not allowed on the rides.

The playground is open from 5 pm to midnight Wednesday, 5 pm to 2 am Thursday and Saturday; and 2 pm to midnight Friday, Sunday and public holidays. The park is closed Monday and Tuesday. There are food and drink stalls at the car park.

### Getting There & Away
It's easy to get to the playground – just take purple bus No 55 or 57 from the multistorey car park – but the last bus leaves at 5.30 pm and getting back to town can be a problem. Major hotels have shuttle services with prearranged pick-up times; for B$20 per person it's hardly cheap, but unless you cadge a ride from a friendly local or expat, it's that or take a metered taxi. Some companies run expensive tours to the playground.

### WASAI KANDAL
Wasai Kandal is a forested area 12km from central BSB. The path to Tinggi Waterfall, the most impressive falls, passes a small waterfall, ponds and pools on the way. Then a rough track proceeds to Rendah Waterfall, which has another picnic area. It is about a half-hour walk each way. The trail starts at Kampung Kilanas, which is just off Jalan Tutong before the turn-off to Limau Manis. You'll have to hire a taxi to get here.

### BEACHES
Muara is a small container port at the top of the peninsula north of BSB. Two kilometres from town, **Pantai Muara** (Muara Beach) is a popular weekend retreat. The white sand is clean, but like many beaches in Borneo it is littered with driftwood and the debris of logging. It is quiet during the week and has food stalls, picnic tables and a children's

playground. Other beaches around Muara include **Serasa** and **Meragang**.

Take bus No 37, 38 or 39 from BSB to Muara town (B$2); purple bus No 33 will take you from there to Pantai Muara or Pantai Serasa; the fare is B$1. You'll have to get to Meragang under your own steam or hitch a ride; the beach is about 4km west of Muara along the Muara-Tutong Hwy.

## PULAU SELIRONG

This small island off Brunei Bay, about 45 minutes by boat from Muara, is on the itinerary of some tour companies. It's reportedly a pleasant, mangrove-littered spot, and the source of much of the timber for Kampung Ayer. However, it is *also* reportedly home to many venomous snakes, and some tour companies refuse to take visitors there because of the risk involved.

## LIMAU MANIS

Limau Manis is a kampung 35km south-west of BSB, a few kilometres from the Sarawak border. Brunei has an immigration post here, but the Malaysian equivalent is at Limbang. It is possible to go by road from Limau Manis through Sarawak's Limbang district to Temburong, the eastern half of Brunei, but public transport stops at the border. To get to Limau Manis take bus No 42, 44 or 48.

## TUTONG

Tutong is the main town in Tutong district and is about halfway between Seria and BSB. Buses to Seria pass by on the main highway, but if you want to see the attractions around Tutong you really need a hire car – getting anywhere by taxi will cost a small fortune.

### Pantai Seri Kenangan

This popular beach (often simply referred to as Pantai Tutong) has picnic tables and a simple restaurant. It is on a spit of land with the ocean on one side and the Sungai Tutong on the other. The white-sand, casuarina-lined beach is probably the best in Brunei. The royal family has a surprisingly modest **istana** at Pantai Seri Kenangan, which is a couple of kilometres off the highway just outside Tutong town. The turn-off to the

beach is near the Tamu Tutong, where a **market** is held daily in the morning. The road to the beach continues for another 5km to Kuala Tutong; the beach at the end of the road is quiet and ideal for camping.

## TASIK MERIMBUN

Tasik Merimbun, 27km inland from Tutong, is Brunei's largest lake. It is a pretty, tranquil spot surrounded by forest where you might see monkeys and birdlife. Wooden walkways lead around the shore to picnic pavilions and this picturesque, swampy lake has an island in the middle. There's a restaurant overlooking the lake near the car park.

The only way to get here is by car. Access is via an appalling road; the lake is poorly signposted and you could easily get lost – ask for Tasik Merimbun.

## LABI

Before Seria, a road branches inland to Labi. About halfway to Labi is the **Luagan Lalak Forest Reserve**, where there are good views over a lake that fills up in the rainy season. From Labi several modern, relatively small **Iban longhouses** can be visited, including Rumah Panjang Mendaram Besar and Rumah Panjang Teraja.

There are fine views over the forest from the road, but there's very little traffic so you'll have to walk if you don't have transport. A trail leads to **Rampayoh Waterfall** where the sealed road ends, about two hours' walk away. At the end of the road, past Rumah Panjang Teraja, there's the Sungai Teraja and a trail to another waterfall and **Bukit Teraja**, which is the highest hill in the area and affords fine views across Brunei and Sarawak. The main trail to the summit is signposted and starts about 6km beyond Rampayoh. The walk through primary forest takes about two hours to the top.

It is also possible to visit Dusun and Penan villages, but this involves hiring a boat (expect to pay around B$300 per day) to take you deep into the interior along the Sungai Belait. The best place to hire a boat is at Kampung Sungai Mau, on the Labi road where it meets the Sungai Belait before Luagan Lalak.

## SERIA

Seria is a transit stop on the road to Sarawak, an unappealing company town sprawling along the coast between Tutong and Kuala Belait. It consists of some big Shell Brunei installations, the Ghurkha battalions that protect them and hundreds of prefab dwellings where expat workers live.

The coastal plain between here and Kuala Belait is the main centre for oil production in Brunei, and at a beach just outside of town the **Billionth Barrel Monument** commemorates the billionth barrel of oil produced at the Seria field. It's hardly worth stopping for.

There are a few modern blocks of shops and a market, but the nearest accommodation is in Kuala Belait. If you're travelling by bus to Miri, you must change at Seria.

### Getting There & Away

About 10 antiquated buses a day bounce along the road from BSB (B\$6, two hours). The first bus leaves the BSB bus station at 7.30 am and the last one leaves Seria at 3 pm. More-comfortable buses to Kuala Belait (B\$1) leave at 7, 9 and 10.30 am, and 1 and 3 pm only.

If you are headed for Sarawak, you can buy your tickets all the way through to Miri from the bus station in Seria. This comes to B\$11.20 and includes your ticket to Kuala Belait (B\$1), from Kuala Belait to the border (B\$5.50) and from the border to Miri (the fare is RM4.70, but you're charged B\$4.70). There are two problems with buying your ticket in Seria, though: First, if you do the maths, you'll notice that you are charged in Brunei dollars for the last leg, not ringgit (but the same thing happens in Kuala Belait). Worse, there are in fact *two* buses leaving for Kuala Belait at the times listed – only one of which will get you to Kuala Belait in time to make the bus connections for the border.

Buses from Kuala Belait to the border leave 30 minutes after the Seria departures, ie, at 7.30, 9.30 and 11 am, and at 1.30 and 3.30 pm; so if you miss your connection, you've got a couple of hours to kill in lovely downtown Kuala Belait. By all means ask the driver in Seria if the bus will make the Miri connections before you board.

## KUALA BELAIT
☎ 03

The last town before Malaysia, Kuala Belait is the main town in Belait district and the place to get buses to Miri. 'KB' (not to be confused with Kuala Baram on the Sarawak side of the border) has colonial shophouses in the town centre and a reasonable beach, though you won't miss much if you just pass through. The best place to change money is at the HSBC bank, diagonally opposite the bus station on Jalan McKerron.

You can hire a motor launch by the market for trips up the river to **Kuala Balai**, a small river village that was once the largest settlement in the district. It is now almost deserted because the residents have left to find work in the oil industry on the coast. The 45-minute trip (one way) goes by good jungle at the river's edge. Along the way ask the boatman to stop at the wooden case of skulls mounted on stilts. Price is by negotiation, but expect to pay about B\$150 each way for the river trip.

### Places to Stay & Eat

At the cheaper end of the scale is a *Government Rest House* (☎ 330780); at B\$50 per person it isn't all that cheap, however, and advance bookings must be made. It is on the beach, a 10-minute walk along Jalan McKerron from the bus station, then 200m to the right.

In town, *Hotel Sentosa* (☎ 334341, 92 Jalan McKerron) is near the bus station; comfortable but ordinary singles/doubles with air-con, TV and phone cost B\$80/90.

*Seaview Hotel* (☎ 332651) is on Jalan Maulana, 4km from town on the beach road to Seria. It's the best hotel outside BSB, and prices reflect this – rooms cost B\$100/120, including breakfast. There's a swimming pool and a well-stocked supermarket frequented by expats; the hotel can also arrange car rental.

Kuala Belait has plenty of *kedai kopi* within striking distance of the bus station.

## Getting There & Away

See the Seria section for details of buses to Kuala Belait and on to Miri. Buses for Malaysia leave Kuala Belait at 7.30, 9.30 and 11 am, and at 1.30 and 3.30 pm; the fare is B$10.20 for the 2½-hour trip to Miri.

From Kuala Belait it's a five-minute bus ride (20-minute walk) to the Sungai Belait, where a car ferry plies back and forth to the other side. Once across the river it's a short ride to the Brunei immigration checkpoint. After going through Brunei customs you'll board a Malaysian bus to get to the Malaysian immigration checkpoint. From here it's a short ride to the queue at the Sungai Baram, which usually takes 15 to 30 minutes to cross. From here the road to Miri is good.

If you miss the last bus from Kuala Belait, a share-taxi to the border will cost B$60 (B$15 per person for four people).

# Temburong

Temburong district is the eastern slice of Brunei, surrounded by Sarawak and cut off from the sultanate when Raja Brooke grabbed what is now the Limbang district. It is a quiet backwater reached by boat from BSB and rarely visited by travellers. The boat trip in itself is worthwhile: The boats go down the Sungai Brunei and into the open sea, then weave through the maze of dense mangroves fringing Brunei Bay into the mouth of the Sungai Temburong. Police boats wait in hiding, checking for illegal immigrants – take your passport just in case. Temburong has little industry or development and much of the district is unspoilt forest.

Bangar can be visited in a day trip from BSB if you catch an early boat. The Peradayan Forest Reserve is a good outing for a jungle walk, or you can visit the Iban longhouse at Batang Duri. For a longer jungle experience, the Kuala Belalong Rainforest Field Studies Centre in the Batu Apoi Forest Reserve receives visitors, but at the time of writing permits for the reserve were only being granted to those on tours. You may also need a permit to visit the Peradayan Reserve. For visits to either reserve, call the Forestry Department (☎ 02-381687) in BSB for information on the current protocol.

## BANGAR

Bangar is a sleepy, pleasant little town on the banks of the Sungai Temburong. It is the district centre and has a row of shops, a mosque and government offices, but there is no accommodation. There are a couple of coffee shops, which may also have information about arranging transport.

The immigration office is a few kilometres west of Bangar on the way to Limbang; it's open from 6 am to 10 pm daily.

## Getting There & Away

**Road** Temburong has two main roads; both are sealed but traffic is light. One leads south to Batang Duri and the other runs between the east and west borders with Sarawak.

Taxis are the only form of transport in the district and they congregate near the wharf. They are unmetered and prices must be negotiated.

Taxis go to Limbang in Sarawak for about B$15. There is no border post, so make sure you stop at the immigration office in Bangar before leaving Brunei. Report to immigration in Limbang.

It is possible, but expensive, to cross the eastern border to Lawas in Sarawak. A taxi to Lawas costs about B$80, including a trip to the immigration office near Bangar. In Lawas, clear immigration at the jetty where the Brunei ferries tie up. This is an alternative route into Sabah, but it's cheaper to take a boat from Muara.

Hitching is possible, though you may be in for a wait, especially on the way back from Batang Duri. The road to the Peradayan Forest Reserve – and Lawas – is across the bridge from Bangar wharf.

**Boat** From BSB, launches leave when full from the jetty near the Gerai Makan food centre (45 minutes, B$7/14 one way/return). For the return journey, buy your ticket at Bangar wharf. Boats leave BSB and Bangar approximately every 30 minutes between 7 am and 5 pm.

## BATANG DURI

Batang Duri is an Iban longhouse on the Sungai Temburong, 17km south of Bangar. Boats to the Kuala Belalong Rainforest Field Studies Centre leave from the village jetty. If you visit the longhouse, introduce yourself first, preferably to the *penghulu* (chief). Take your shoes off when you enter and don't wander up and down the veranda; this is like walking unannounced into someone's lounge room. Batang Duri can be visited as a day trip or as part of a tour, but overnight stays must be pre-arranged.

### Taman Batang Duri

This park and small zoo is about 2km north of Batang Duri. There are forlorn-looking civets, monkeys, otters and birds, and a stall selling snacks and drinks. It is open until 6 pm daily; admission is free.

There are boat tours down the Sungai Temburong to Batang Duri. A private taxi to Batang Duri from Bangar costs B$10 each way.

## BATU APOI FOREST RESERVE

This reserve protects a large area of primary rainforest that covers most of southern Temburong, and includes the small Ulu Temburong National Park. A permit is required to visit the reserve, and at the time of writing was only being issued through travel agencies, ie, you have to take a tour.

Tour companies in BSB (see Travel Agencies under Information in the BSB section) can also arrange accommodation at the Field Studies Centre. A visit to the park is not cheap: With a minimum of two people, prices start at B$198 per person for a two-day trip, which involves staying overnight at a Murut village on the way up the Sungai Temburong and a day trip to the national park.

### Kuala Belalong Rainforest Field Studies Centre

This scientific research centre is in Ulu Temburong National Park, and was developed by Brunei Shell and the Universiti Brunei Darussalam to provide facilities for research into tropical rainforest. It is primarily for

scientists and is visited by school groups, though interested overseas visitors can stay at the centre.

The forest is rich in flora and fauna, and the jungle can be explored along walking trails. The main trail is a rugged two-day walk to Bukit Belalong, and there's a canopy walkway that is among the largest in the world.

Access to the centre is by longboat from Batang Duri.

## PERADAYAN FOREST RESERVE

This forest reserve is about 15km from Bangar along the road to Labu. It protects the forested peaks of Bukit Patoi and Bukit Peradayan. Walking trails lead to the summits and this is the most accessible rainforest for visitors to Brunei. You'll have to start early to maximise chances of seeing the mainly nocturnal mammals, but the park also contains many bird species, including hornbills.

The most popular walk is to **Bukit Patoi**, and starts at the entrance to the park. The trail is steep in parts but is well marked, with rest huts along the way. It is about a half-hour walk to Batu Berdinding, a sandstone outcrop, and then another 15 minutes to the summit. All up, the walk shouldn't take more than an hour with plenty of rests on the way. At the summit there are fine views to the east across the South China Sea and the Lawas area of Sarawak – if there's no smoke haze.

Most walkers descend back along the trail, but it is possible to continue over the other side of the summit and around to Bukit Peradayan. This trail is harder and indistinct in parts, though trees are marked to show the way. The trail eventually rejoins the road, 12km from Bangar near the Labu Km 5 marker. Three hours should be allowed for the walk from Bukit Patoi to Bukit Peradayan and back to the road.

There are picnic tables and a toilet block at the start of the trail, but bring water and food for the walk. The return taxi trip from Bangar should cost around B$20. The driver will wait for you to do the summit walk, or if you want to spend more time in the reserve, arrange a time for him to return.

# Language

Bahasa Malaysia (known officially as Bahasa Melayu or simply Malay) and Bahasa Indonesia are virtually the same language – only a few differences in vocabulary distinguish the two. Many of these differences are in the loan words – English-based for Malay and Dutch-based for Indonesian. If you're coming from Indonesia and have developed some proficiency in the language, you may initially be confused by Malay pronunciation. Bahasa Indonesia is a second language for most Indonesians – pronunciation is learnt in schools and, as a result, tends to remain fairly standard. Bahasa Malaysia, however, is subject to greater regional variation in pronunciation and slang – so much so that a Malaysian from Negeri Sembilan may have difficulty understanding someone from Kelantan.

In its most basic form, Malay is very simple. Verbs aren't conjugated for tense; the notion of time is indicated by the use of adverbs such as 'yesterday' or 'tomorrow'. For example, you can change any sentence into the past tense by simply adding *sudah* (already). Many nouns are pluralised by simply saying them twice – thus *buku* is 'book', *buku-buku* is 'books', *anak* is 'child', *anak-anak* is 'children'. There are no articles (a, an, the). Thus 'a good book' or 'the good book' is simply *buku baik*. There is no verb 'to be', so again it would be *buku baik* rather than 'the book is good'. Malay is also a very poetic and evocative language – 'the sun', for example, is *matahari*, or 'the eye of the day'.

Many Malay terms have found their way into the everyday English of Malaysia. You'll often see the word *bumiputra* (literally 'sons of the soil') in English-language newspapers, usually in ads for positions vacant; it's a term used to indicate that the job is open only to 'native' Malays, not Indian Malaysians or Chinese Malaysians. Similarly, you may see English-language articles about *jaga keretas*, the people who operate car-parking rackets – pay them to 'protect' your car while it's parked or you'll wish you had. Another expression is *khalwat* (literally 'close proximity') – unmarried Muslim couples definitely do not wish to find themselves suspected of *khalwat*!

For a more comprehensive guide to Bahasa Malaysia, get hold of Lonely Planet's *Malay phrasebook*. It's a handy pocket-sized introduction to the language.

## New Spelling

The new spelling system of Bahasa Malaysia brings it into line with Indonesian. However, many of the old spellings are still in use for places and people's names. The main changes are that the letter **c** replaces the combination 'ch' (as in 'church'), and the letter **u** often replaces 'o' when it occurs in a word-final syllable, eg, *kampung* not 'kampong', *teluk* not 'telok'.

## Pronunciation

Most letters are pronounced the same as their English counterparts, although a few vowels and consonants differ.

### Vowels

| | |
|---|---|
| **a** | as the 'u' in 'hut' |
| **e** | a neutral vowel such as the 'e' in 'paper' when unstressed, eg, *besar* (big); sometimes hardly pronounced at all, eg, in the greeting *selamat*, (when said quickly, pronounced more like 'sla-mat'). When the stress falls on **e** it's more like the 'a' in 'may', eg, *meja* (table). There's no single rule which determines whether **e** is stressed or unstressed. |
| **i** | as in 'hit' |
| **o** | as in 'note' |
| **u** | as in 'flute' |
| **ai** | as in 'aisle' |
| **au** | a drawn out 'ow', as in 'cow' |
| **ua** | each vowel is pronounced, as 'oo-a' |

## Consonants

Consonants are pronounced much the same way as they are in English, with these few exceptions:

| | |
|---|---|
| c | as the 'ch' in 'chair' |
| g | always hard, as in 'go' |
| ng | as the 'ng' in 'singer' |
| ngg | as 'ng' + 'g' (as in 'anger') |
| j | as in 'join' |
| r | pronounced clearly and distinctly |
| h | as the English 'h' but slightly stronger (like a sigh); at the end of a word it's almost silent |
| k | as English 'k', except at the end of the word, when it's more like a silent closing of the throat |
| ny | as the 'ni' in 'onion' |

## Word Stress

In Malay words, most syllables carry equal emphasis; as a general rule stress falls on the second-last syllable. The main exception is the unstressed e in words such as *besar* (big), pronounced 'be-SAR'.

## Greetings & Civilities

| | |
|---|---|
| Good morning. | *Selamat pagi.* |
| Good day. (around midday) | *Selamat tengah hari.* |
| Good afternoon. | *Selamat petang.* |
| Good night. | *Selamat malam.* |
| Goodbye. (said by person staying) | *Selamat tinggal.* |
| Goodbye. (said by person leaving) | *Selamat jalan.* |
| Yes. | *Ya.* |
| No. | *Tidak.* |
| Please. | *Tolong/Silakan.* |
| Thank you (very much). | *Terima kasih (banyak).* |
| You're welcome. | *Sama-sama.* |
| Sorry/Pardon? | *Maaf.* |
| Excuse me. | *Maafkan saya.* |
| How are you? | *Apa khabar?* |
| Fine thanks. | *Khabar baik.* |
| What's your name? | *Siapa nama kamu?* |
| My name is ... | *Nama saya ...* |
| Where are you from? | *Dari mana asal saudara?* |
| I'm from ... | *Saya dari ...* |
| How old are you? | *Berapa umur saudara?* |

### Signs

| | |
|---|---|
| **Masuk** | **Entrance** |
| **Keluar** | **Exit** |
| **Panas/Sejuk** | **Hot/Cold** |
| **Di Larang Merokok** | **No Smoking** |
| **Buka** | **Open** |
| **Tutup** | **Closed** |
| **Telepon** | **Telephone** |
| **Tandas** | **Toilets** |
| **Lelaki** | **Men** |
| **Perempuan** | **Women** |

| | |
|---|---|
| I'm (20 years old). | *Umur saya (duapuluh tahun).* |
| Good/Very nice. | *Bagus.* |
| No good. | *Tidak baik.* |
| Good/Fine. | *Baik.* |

## Language Difficulties

| | |
|---|---|
| Do you speak English? | *Bolehkah anda berbicara bahasa Inggeris?* |
| I understand. | *Saya faham.* |
| I don't understand. | *Saya tidak faham.* |
| Please write that word down. | *Tolong tuliskan perkataan.* |
| Please repeat it. | *Tolong ulangi.* |

## Getting Around

| | |
|---|---|
| How can I get to ...? | *Bagaimana saya pergi ke ...?* |
| How many km? | *Berapa kilometre?* |
| Where is ...? | *Di mana ...?* |

| | |
|---|---|
| What time does the ... leave? | *Pukul berapakah ... berangkat?* |
| boat | *bot* |
| bus | *bas* |
| rickshaw/trishaw | *beca* |
| ship | *kapal* |
| train | *keretapi* |

| | |
|---|---|
| Where can I hire a bicycle? | *Di mana tempat sewa basikal?* |
| Where can I rent a car? | *Di manakah saya boleh menyewa kereta?* |
| Please give me two tickets. | *Tolong berikan saya dua tiket.* |
| ticket window | *tempat tikit, kaunter* |
| 1st/economy class | *kelas satu/ekonomi* |

## Directions

| | |
|---|---|
| Which way? | *Ke mana?* |
| Go straight ahead. | *Jalan terus.* |
| Turn left. | *Belok kiri.* |
| Turn right. | *Belok kanan.* |

| | |
|---|---|
| at the T-junction | *di pertigaan* |
| at the traffic lights | *di lampu lalu lintas* |
| in front of | *di hadapan* |
| next to | *di samping/di sebelah* |
| behind | *di belakang* |
| opposite | *berhadapan dengan* |
| here/there | *di sini/di sana* |
| north | *utara* |
| south | *selatan* |
| east | *timur* |
| west | *barat* |

## Around Town

| | |
|---|---|
| Where is a/the ...? | *Di mana ada ...?* |
| bank | *bank* |
| embassy | *kedutaan besar* |
| hospital | *hospital* |
| hotel | *hotel* |
| museum | *muzium* |
| police station | *stesen polis* |
| post office | *pejabat pos* |
| public telephone | *telepon umum* |
| public toilet | *tandas awam* |
| tourist office | *pejabat pelancong* |
| town square | *dewan perbandaran* |

| | |
|---|---|
| What time does it open/close? | *Pukul berapa buka/tutup?* |
| I want to call ... | *Saya mau menelefon ...* |
| I want to change a travellers cheque. | *Saya mau menukar cek pengembaraan.* |

## Accommodation

| | |
|---|---|
| hotel | *hotel* |
| cheap hotel | *hotel yang murah* |
| nice hotel | *hotel yang bagus* |
| inexpensive hotel | *hotel yang murah* |

| | |
|---|---|
| I'd like a room ... | *Saya perlu bilik ...* |
| for one person | *untuk satu orang* |
| for two people | *untuk dua orang* |
| with a bathroom | *dengan bilik mandi* |
| with air-con | *dengan alat penyejuk* |

| | |
|---|---|
| Is there a room available? | *Ada bilik kosong?* |
| How much per night/person? | *Berapa harga satu malam/orang?* |
| May I see the room? | *Boleh saya lihat biliknya?* |
| I don't like this room. | *Saya tidak suka bilik ini.* |

| | |
|---|---|
| bed | *tempat tidur* |
| dirty | *kotor* |
| expensive | *mahal* |
| room | *bilik* |
| sleep | *tidur* |
| soap | *sabun* |

## Food

| | |
|---|---|
| I don't want ... | *Saya tidak mau ...* |
| chicken | *ayam* |
| fish | *ikan* |
| meat | *daging* |

| | |
|---|---|
| beef | *daging lembu* |
| chicken | *ayam* |
| crab | *ketam* |
| egg | *telur* |
| fish | *ikan* |
| frog | *kodok* |
| pork | *babi* |
| potatoes | *kentang* |
| prawns | *udang* |
| vegetables | *sayur-sayuran* |

| | |
|---|---|
| fried rice | *nasi goreng* |
| boiled rice | *nasi putih* |
| rice with odds & ends | *nasi campur* |
| fried noodles | *mee goreng* |
| soup | *sup* |
| noodle soup | *mee kuah* |
| fried vegetables & crispy noodles | *cap cai tami* |
| sweet & sour omelette | *fu yung hai* |

| | |
|---|---|
| sweet | *manis* |
| steaming hot | *panas* |
| spicy hot | *pedas* |
| cold | *sejuk* |
| delicious | *enak* |
| special | *istimewa* |

## Drinks

| | |
|---|---|
| coconut milk | *air kelapa* |
| coffee | *kopi* |
| drinking water | *air minum* |
| drinks | *minum-minum* |
| milk | *susu* |
| orange juice | *air jeruk/air oren* |
| sugar | *gula* |
| tea (without sugar) | *teh (tanpa gula)* |

## Shopping

| | |
|---|---|
| How much? | *Berapa?* |
| Can you lower the price? | *Boleh kurang?* |
| | |
| barber | *tukang cukur* |
| bookshop | *kedai buku* |
| chemist/pharmacy | *farmasi* |
| grocery | *kedai makanan* |
| market | *pasar* |
| night market | *pasar malam* |
| shop | *kedai* |
| shopping centre | *pusat membeli-belah* |
| this | *ini* |
| that | *itu* |
| big | *besar* |
| small | *kecil* |

## Health

| | |
|---|---|
| Where is a ... | *Di mana ada ...* |
| dentist | *doktor gigi* |
| doctor | *doktor* |
| hospital | *hospital* |
| pharmacy | *apotik/farmasi* |
| | |
| I'm allergic to ... | *Saya alergik kepada ...* |
| penicillin | *penisilin* |
| antibiotics | *antibiotik* |
| | |
| I'm pregnant. | *Saya hamil.* |
| | |
| antibiotics | *antibiotik* |
| antiseptic | *antiseptik* |
| aspirin | *aspirin* |
| medicine | *ubat* |
| penicillin | *penisilin* |
| quinine | *kina* |
| sleeping pills | *pil tidur* |
| tablet/pill | *pil* |

## Emergencies

| | |
|---|---|
| Help! | *Tolong!* |
| There's been an accident! | *Ada kemalangan!* |
| Call a doctor! | *Panggil doktor!* |
| Call an ambulance! | *Panggil ambulans!* |
| Stop! | *Berhenti!* |
| Go away! | *Pergi!* |
| I've been robbed! | *Saya dirompak!* |
| I'm lost. | *Saya sesat.* |

## Time, Days & Numbers

| | |
|---|---|
| When? | *Bila?* |
| How long? | *Berapa lama?* |
| What time is it? | *Pukul berapa?* |
| 7 o'clock | *pukul tujuh* |
| hour | *jam* |
| week | *minggu* |
| year | *tahun* |
| tomorrow | *besok* |
| yesterday | *kelmarin* |
| | |
| Monday | *hari Isnin* |
| Tuesday | *hari Selasa* |
| Wednesday | *hari Rabu* |
| Thursday | *hari Kamis* |
| Friday | *hari Jumaat* |
| Saturday | *hari Sabtu* |
| Sunday | *hari Minggu* |

| | |
|---|---|
| ½ | *setengah* |
| 1 | *satu* |
| 2 | *dua* |
| 3 | *tiga* |
| 4 | *empat* |
| 5 | *lima* |
| 6 | *enam* |
| 7 | *tujuh* |
| 8 | *delapan/lapan* |
| 9 | *sembilan* |
| 10 | *sepuluh* |
| 11 | *sebelas* |
| 12 | *dua belas* |
| 20 | *dua puluh* |
| 21 | *dua puluh satu* |
| 22 | *dua puluh dua* |
| 30 | *tiga puluh* |
| 53 | *lima puluh tiga* |
| 100 | *seratus* |
| 1000 | *seribu* |

LANGUAGE

## Singlish

One of the most intriguing things the visitor to Singapore will notice is the strange patois spoken by the locals. Nominally English, it contains borrowed words from Hokkien and Malay, such as *shiok* (delicious) and *kasar* (rough). Unnecessary prepositions and pronouns are dropped, word order is flipped, phrases are clipped short, and stress and cadence are unconventional, to say the least. The result is known locally as Singlish. Singlish is frowned upon in official use, though you'll get a good idea of its pervasive pronunciation characteristics if you listen to the news bulletins on TV or the radio.

While there isn't such a thing as Singlish grammar, there are definite characteristics. First off, there's the reverse stress pattern of double-barrelled words. For example, in standard English the stress would be '*fire*-fighter' or '*theatre* company' but in Singlish it's 'fire-*fighter*' and 'theatre *company*'. Word-final consonants – particularly 'l' or 'k' – are often syncopated and vowels are often distorted; a Chinese-speaking taxi driver might not understand 'Perak Road' since they pronounce it 'Pera Roh'. The particle 'lah' is often tagged on to the end of sentences as in, 'No good, lah', which could mean (among other things) 'I don't think that's such a good idea'. Requests or questions will often be marked with a tag ending since direct questioning is considered rude. So, a question such as 'Would you like a beer?' might be rendered as 'You want beer or not?', which might come across to speakers of Western English as being extremely rude. Verb tenses tend to be nonexistent; future, present or past actions are all indicated by time phrases, so in Singlish it's 'I go tomorrow' or 'I go yesterday'.

The following are some of the most frequently heard Singlishisms:

*ah beng* – low class, uneducated person with no fashion sense or style; red neck
*Aiyah!* – 'Oh, dear!'
*Alamak!* – exclamation of disbelief or frustration, like 'Oh my God!'
*ayam* – Malay word for chicken; adjective for something inferior or weak
*blur* – a slow or uninformed person
*buaya* – womaniser, from the Malay for crocodile
*Can?* – 'Is that OK?'
*Can!* – 'Yes! That's fine.'
*char bor* – babe, woman
*cheena* – old-fashioned Chinese in dress or thinking (derogatory)
*go stun* – to reverse, as in *Go stun the car* (from the naval expression 'go astern')
*heng* – luck, good fortune (Hokkien)
*hiao* – vain
*inggrish* – English
*kambing* – foolish person, literally 'goat' (Malay)
*kenna ketok* – ripped off
*kiasee* – scared, literally 'afraid to die'; a coward
*kiasu* – literally 'afraid to lose'; selfish, pushy, always on the lookout for a bargain
*lah* – generally an ending for any phrase or sentence; can translate as 'OK', but has no real meaning; added for emphasis to just about everything
*looksee* – take a look
*malu* – embarrassed
*minah* – girlfriend
*Or not?* – general suffix for questions, as in *Can or not?* (Can you or can't you?)
*see first* – wait and see what happens
*shack* – tired
*shiok* – good, great, delicious
*steady lah* – well done, excellent; an expression of praise
*Wah!* – general exclamation of surprise or distress
*ya ya* – boastful, as in *He always ya ya*

# Glossary

**adat** – Malay customary law

**adat temenggong** – Malay law with Indian modifications, governing the customs and ceremonies of the sultans

**air** – water

**air terjun** – waterfall

**alor** – groove; furrow; main channel of a river

**ampang** – dam

**ang pow** – red packets of money used as offerings, payment or gifts

**arrack** – Malay local alcohol

**atap** – roof thatching

**Baba-Nyonya** – descendents of Chinese immigrants to the Straits Settlements (namely Melaka, Singapore and Penang) who intermarried with Malays and adopted many Malay customs; also known as Peranakan, or Straits Chinese; sometimes spelt *Nonya*

**Bahasa Malaysia** – or Bahasa Melayu; Malay language

**bandar** – port

**Bangsawan** – Malay opera

**batang** – stem; tree-trunk; the main branch of a river

**batik** – technique of imprinting cloth with dye to produce multicoloured patterns

**batu** – stone; rock; milepost

**belukar** – secondary forest

**bendahara** – chief minister

**bendang** – irrigated land

**bomoh** – Islamic spiritual healer

**British Resident** – chief British representative during the colonial era

**bukit** – hill

**bumboat** – motorised *sampan,* or small boat

**bumiputra** – literally, sons of the soil; indigenous Malaysians

**bunga raya** – hibiscus flower (national flower of Malaysia)

**dada** – drugs

**dato, datuk** – literally, grandfather; general male non-royal title of distinction

**dipterocarp** – family of trees, native to Malaysia, that have two-winged fruits

**dusun** – small town

**genting** – mountain pass

**godown** – river warehouse

**gua** – cave

**gunung** – mountain

**hilir** – lower reaches of a river

**hutan** – jungle; forest

**imam** – keeper of Islamic knowledge and leader of prayer

**istana** – palace

**jalan** – road

**kain songket** – traditional Malay hand-woven fabric with gold threads

**kali** – river

**kampung** – village; sometimes spelt *kampong*

**kangkar** – Chinese village

**karst** – characteristic scenery of a limestone region, including features such as underground streams and caverns

**kedai kopi** – coffee shop

**kerangas** – distinctive vegetation zone of Borneo, usually found on sandstone, containing pitcher plants and other unusual flora

**khalwat** – literally, close proximity; exhibition of public affection between the sexes

**kongsi** – Chinese clan organisations, also known as ritual brotherhoods, heaven-man-earth societies, triads or secret societies; meeting house for Chinese of the same clan

**kopi tiam** – coffee shop (Singapore)

**kota** – fort; city

**kramat** – Malay shrine

**kuala** – river mouth; place where a tributary joins a larger river

**labuan** – port

**laksamana** – admiral

**langur** – small, usually tree-dwelling monkey
**laut** – sea
**lebuh** – street
**Lebuhraya** – expressway or freeway; usually refers to the North-South Highway, which runs from Johor Bahru to Bukit Kaya Hitam at the Thai border
**lorong** – narrow street; alley
**lubuk** – deep pool

**macaque** – any of several small species of monkey
**mandi** – South-East Asian wash basin
**masjid** – mosque
**Melayu Islam Beraja** – MIB; Brunei's national ideology
**merdeka** – independence
**Merlion** – half-lion, half-fish animal; symbol of Singapore
**muara** – river mouth
**muezzin** – mosque official who calls the faithful to prayer

**negara** – country
**negeri** – state
**nyonya** – see *Baba-Nyonya*

**orang asing** – foreigner
**Orang Asli** – literally, Original People; Malaysian aborigines
**Orang Laut** – literally, Coastal People
**Orang Ulu** – literally, Upriver People

**padang** – grassy area, usually the city square
**pantai** – beach
**parang** – long jungle knife
**pasar** – market
**pasar malam** – night market
**Pejabat Residen** – Resident's Office
**pekan** – market place; town
**pencak silat** – martial-arts dance form
**penghulu** – chief or village head
**pengkalan** – quay
**Peranakan** – literally, half-caste; refers to the *Baba-Nyonya* or Straits Chinese
**pua kumbu** – traditional finely woven cloth
**pulau** – island
**puteri** – princess

**raja** – prince; ruler
**rakyat** – common people
**rantau** – straight coastline
**rattan** – stems from climbing palms used for wickerwork and canes
**rimba** – jungle
**rotan** – cane used to punish miscreants
**roti** – bread (as in *roti canai*, flaky Indian bread normally served with *dhal* or with curry)

**sampan** – small boat
**samsu** – Malay alcohol
**sarung** – all-purpose cloth, often sewn into a tube, and worn by women, men and children; also spelt *sarong*
**sebrang** – far bank of a river
**selat** – strait
**semenanjung** – peninsula
**simpang** – junction of more than two roads
**songkok** – traditional Malay headdress worn by males
**sungai** – river
**syariah** – Islamic system of law

**tambang** – river ferry
**tamu** – weekly market
**tanah** – land
**tanjung** – headland
**tasik** – lake
**teluk** – bay; *telok* in Singapore
**temenggong** – Malay administrator
**towkang** – Chinese junk
**tuai rumah** – longhouse chief (Sarawak)
**tuak** – local 'firewater' alcohol (Malaysian Borneo)
**tunku** – prince

**ujung** – cape

**warung** – small eating stalls
**wayang** – Chinese opera
**wayang kulit** – shadow-puppet theatre
**wisma** – office block or shopping centre

**yang di-pertuan agong** – Malaysia's head of state, or 'king'
**yang di-pertuan besar** – head of state in Negeri Sembilan
**yang di-pertuan muda** – under-king
**yang di-pertuan negeri** – governor

## ABBREVIATIONS AND ACRONYMS

**APEC** – Asia-Pacific Economic Cooperation

**Asean** – Association of South-East Asian Nations

**KTM** – Keretapi Tanah Malayu; Malaysian Railways System

**LRT** – Light Rail Transit (Kuala Lumpur)

**MCP** – Malayan Communist Party

**MIB** – Melayu Islam Beraja; Brunei's national ideology

**MRT** – Mass Rapid Transit (Singapore)

**PAP** – People's Action Party

**PAS** – Parti Islam se-Malaysia

**PIE** – Pan-Island Expressway, one of Singapore's main road arteries

**UMNO** – United Malays National Organisation

# Glossary of Asian Culinary Terms

**achar** – Indian vegetable pickle

**ais kacang** – similar to *cendol* but made with evaporated milk; also spelt *ice kacang* (Malay/Indonesian)

**aloo gobi** – potato and cauliflower dish (Indian)

**attap seeds** – sugar plam seeds used in *cendol* and *ais kacang*

**ayam goreng** – fried chicken (Malay)

**bak chang** – rice dumpling filled with savoury or sweet meat and wrapped in leaves (Chinese)

**bak choy** – variety of Chinese cabbage that grows like celery, with long white stalks and dark green leaves

**bak kutteh** – pork-rib soup with hints of garlic and Chinese five-spice (Chinese)

**banana-leaf meal** – see *thali*

**beef rendang** – beef stewed with spices and coconut milk (Malay/Indonesian)

**belacan** – fermented prawn paste used as a condiment in Chinese, Malay and Indonesian cuisine

**belacan kankung** – green vegetables stir-fried in prawn paste (Malay)

**bhindi** – okra or lady's finger (Indian)

**bird's nest** – edible nest of the swiftlet, made chiefly of glutinous secretions from their salivary glands (Chinese)

**biryani** – basmati rice and meat, seafood or vegetables (North Indian)

**brinjal** – aubergine or eggplant (Indian)

**buah keras** – see *candle-nut*

**candle-nut** – *kemiri* in Indonesian, *buah keras* in Malay; smallish white-fleshed nut, shaped like a hazelnut

**cardamom** – seed pods of a member of the ginger family; fragrant spice often used in North Indian and Mogul dishes

**carrot cake** – popular omelette-like dish made with radishes, egg, garlic and chilli (Nyonya)

**cendol** – dessert of ice shavings topped with coloured syrups, brown sugar syrup and coconut milk, filled with red beans, *attap* seeds and jelly (Malay/Indonesian)

**chapati** – griddle-fried wholewheat bread (Indian)

**char kway teow** – broad noodles, clams and eggs fried in chilli and black bean sauce (Chinese)

**char siew** – sweet roasted pork fillet (Chinese)

**cheng ting** – dessert of sugar syrup with pieces of herbal jelly, barley and dates (Chinese)

**chicken-rice** – steamed chicken, rice boiled or steamed in chicken stock, a clear soup and slices of cucumber

**chilli padi** – extremely hot small chilli

**choi sum** – popular Chinese green vegetable, served steamed with oyster sauce

**chye tow kway** – see *carrot cake*

**claypot rice** – rice cooked in a clay casserole with pieces of chicken, Chinese mushroom, Chinese sausage and soy sauce (Chinese)

**congee** – Chinese porridge

**coriander** – fragrant herb with pungent leaves and stems; also known as Chinese parsley

**daun kunyit** – turmeric leaf (Malay)

**daun pisang** – banana leaf, used as a plate in Malaysia

**dhal** – a dish of pureed lentils (Indian)
**dian xin** – see *dim sum*
**dim sum** – Chinese sweet and savoury buns, dumplings and mini-dishes served at breakfast and lunch; also known as *dian xin*
**dosa** – light, crispy pancake brimming with potatoes, onions and spices (Indian)
**dow see** – fermented, salted black beans (Chinese)

**es avocado** – chilled avocado vegetable shake (Malay/Indonesian)
**es delima** – dessert of water chestnut in sago and coconut milk (Malay/Indonesian)

**fish-head curry** – red snapper in curry sauce; a famous Singaporean Indian dish
**fish sauce** – liquid made from fermented anchovies and salt; used widely in South-East Asian cooking

**gado gado** – cold dish of bean sprouts, potatoes, long beans, tempeh, bean curd, rice cakes and prawn crackers, topped with a spicy peanut sauce (Malay/Indonesian)
**galangal** – ginger-like root used to flavour various dishes
**garam masala** – sweet, mild mixture of freshly ground spices, usually black peppercorns, *coriander* seeds, cumin seeds, cloves and black *cardamom* (Indian)
**garoupa** – white fish popular in South-East Asia
**gathat** – large pan (Indian)
**ghee** – clarified butter (Indian)
**gingko nut** – meaty nut used in soups and desserts or roasted and chopped for sauces, salads and meat dishes
**gulab jumun** – fried milk balls in sugar syrup (Indian)
**gula jawa** – brown palm sugar sold in thin blocks (Malay)

**Hainanese chicken-rice** – Singaporean speciality: chicken served with spring onions and ginger dressing, soup and rice boiled in chicken or coconut oil (Hainan)
**halal** – food that has been prepared according to Muslim dietary laws
**hoisin sauce** – thick sweet-spicy sauce made from soya beans, red beans, sugar, flour, vinegar, salt, garlic, sesame, chillies and spices (Chinese)
**Hokkien mee** – yellow noodles fried with sliced meat, boiled squid, prawns and strips of fried egg (Chinese)

**idli** – steamed rice cake (Indian)
**ikan asam** – fried fish in sour *tamarind* curry (Malay)
**ikan bilis** – small, deep-fried sardines or anchovies (Malay/Indonesian)

**kaen cud** – soup (Thai)
**kaen paad** – curry (Thai)
**kaen phet kai** – hot chicken curry (Thai)
**kai tom kha** – *lemon grass* chicken soup with coconut milk (Thai)
**kang kung** – water convolvulus; thick-stemmed type of spinach (Chinese)
**kari ayam** – curried chicken (Malay/Indonesian)
**kecap** – soy sauce (Malay/Indonesian)
**keema** – spicy minced meat (Indian)
**kemiri** – see *candle-nut*
**kepala ikan** – fish-head, usually in a curry or grilled (Malay/Indonesian)
**khao** – rice (Thai)
**kofta** – minced meat or vegetable ball (Indian)
**korma** – mild curry with yoghurt sauce (Indian)
**kueh melayu** – sweet pancakes filled with peanuts, raisins and sugar (Malaysian)
**kueh mueh** – Malay cakes
**kway teow** – broad rice-noodles (Chinese)

**laksa** – spicy coconut soup of thin white noodles garnished with bean sprouts, quail eggs, prawns, shredded chicken and dried bean curd; also called *nyonya laksa* to differentiate it from *penang laksa,* a version that has a prawn-paste-based gravy and does not have coconut milk added to it (Malay/Singaporean)
**laksa balik pulau** – rice-noodles with a thick fish broth, mint leaves, pineapple, onions and fresh chillies (Nyonya)
**laos** – see *galangal*
**larb** – minced chicken or pork flavoured with spices, herbs and lime (Thai)
**lassi** – yoghurt-based drink (Indian)

**lemon grass** – a stalk with a strong lemon-citrus taste and long, spear-shaped, grass-like leaves; *takari* in Thai, *sereh* in Indonesian

**lombok** – type of hot chilli (Malay)

**lontong** – rice cakes in spicy coconut-milk gravy topped with grated coconut and sometimes bean curd and egg (Malay/lndonesian)

**lor mee** – noodles with slices of meat, eggs and a dash of vinegar in a dark brown sauce (Chinese)

**masala** – spices (Indian)

**masala dosa** – thin pancake rolled around spicy vegetables with *rasam* on the side (Indian)

**mee** – noodles

**mee goreng** – fried noodles (Indonesian)

**mee pok** – flat noodles made with egg and wheat (Chinese)

**mee rebus** – yellow noodles served in a thick sweetish sauce made from sweet potatoes, garnished with sliced hard-boiled eggs and green chillies (Malay)

**mee siam** – white thin noodles in a sourish and sweet gravy made with *tamarind* (Malay)

**mee soto** – noodle soup with shredded chicken (Malay)

**mi krob** – crisp, thin noodles with shrimp, egg and sweet and sour sauce (Thai)

**morel** – mushroom of genus *Morcella*

**mulligatawny** – spicy beef soup (Indian)

**murgh** – chicken (Indian)

**murtabak** – *roti prata* filled with pieces of mutton, chicken or vegetables (Indian)

**naan** – tear-shaped leavened bread baked inside a clay oven (Indian)

**nasi biryani** – saffron rice flavoured with spices and garnished with cashew nuts, almonds and raisins (Malay/lndonesian)

**nasi goreng** – fried rice (Indonesian)

**nasi kampur** – buffet of curried meats, fish and vegetables, served with rice (Malay)

**nasi lemak** – rice boiled in coconut milk, served with fried *ikan bilis,* peanuts and a curry dish (Malay)

**nasi padang** – Malay rice and the accompanying meat and vegetable dishes (Malay)

**pak krasan** – leafy cabbage-like legume unique to Thailand

**pakora** – vegetable fritter (Indian)

**pappadam** – Indian cracker

**paratha** – bread made with *ghee* and cooked on a hotplate (Indian)

**phrik** – chillies (Thai)

**pilau** – rice fried in *ghee* and mixed with nuts, then cooked in stock (North Indian)

**pisang goreng** – banana fritters (Indian)

**pla thot sam rot** – fried *garoupa* with sweet-and-sour sauce (Thai)

**poo paad gari** – curried crab (Thai)

**popiah** – similar to a spring roll, but not fried (Chinese)

**pudina** – mint sauce (Indian)

**raita** – side dish of cucumber, yoghurt and mint (Indian)

**rasam** – spicy soup (Indian)

**rendang** – spicy coconut curry with beef or chicken (Indonesian)

**rijstaffel** – literally, rice table; a buffet of Indonesian dishes (Dutch)

**rogan gosh** – stewed mutton in a rich sauce (Indian)

**roti canai** – breakfast meal made from *roti prata* dough dipped in *dhal* or curry; *roti chanai* in Singapore (Indian)

**roti prata** – flat pancake-like bread (Indian)

**saag** – spicy chopped spinach dish (Indian)

**salam** – leaves used much like bay leaves in cooking (Malay)

**sambal** – sauce of chilli, onions and prawn paste which has been fried (Malay)

**sambal udang** – hot curried prawns (Malay)

**sambar** – fiery mixture of vegetables, lentils and split peas (Indian)

**samosa** – pastry filled with vegetables or meat (Indian)

**santen** – coconut milk (Malay)

**satay** – meat skewered onto wooden sticks and grilled (Malay/Indonesian)

**sereh** – see *lemon grass*

**shiitake** – firm, brown-black mushroom with pale cream gills that is fragrant and has intense flavour when cooked; sometimes known as black or winter mushrooms (Japanese/Chinese)

**som sa** – citrus fruit unique to Thailand
**soto ayam** – spicy chicken soup with vegetables and potatoes (Malay)
**steamboat** – style of cooking in which meats, seafood and vegetables are dipped into a pot of boiling clear stock and cooked at the table (Teochew)
**straw mushroom** – tall, thin, leafy mushroom; also called grass or paddy straw mushroom
**Szechuan** – region in south central China famous for its spicy cuisine; also spelt Sichuan

**tahu goreng** – fried soya bean curd and bean sprouts in peanut sauce (Malay)
**takari** – see *lemon grass*
**tamarind** – large bean from the tamarind tree with a brittle shell and a dark brown, sticky pulp; used for its sweet-sour taste
**tandoori** – Indian style of cooking in which marinated meat is baked in a clay oven
**taro** – vegetable with leaves like spinach, stalks like asparagus, and a starchy root similar in size and taste to the potato
**tau hui** – by-product of the soya bean served as a dessert with sugar syrup
**teh kosong** – tea without milk or sugar
**teh-o** – tea without milk
**teh tarek** – tea made with evaporated milk, which is literally 'pulled' or 'stretched' from one glass to another (Indian)
**tempeh** – preserved soybeans that have been deep-fried (Malay)
**thali** – rice, curried vegetables, soup, curries and bread; often served on a banana leaf (Indian)
**tikka** – small pieces of chicken, fish or other meat served off the bone and marinated in yoghurt before baking (Indian)
**tom yum kung** – hot-and-sour spicy seafood soup (Thai)

**umai** – dish of marinated raw fish served with onions (Melanau, Sarawak)

**vindaloo** – fiery curry with a vinegar base (Indian)

**won ton mee** – soup dish served with shredded chicken or pieces of braised beef (Chinese)

**yam** – Thai word for 'salad'; *yam nua* is popular Thai beef salad
**yong tau foo** – bean curd stuffed with minced meat (Hakka)
**yu char kway** – deep-fried Chinese bread sticks
**yu tiao** – deep-fried pastry eaten for breakfast or as a dessert (Chinese)

# Acknowledgments

## THANKS

Many thanks to the travellers who used the last edition of *Malaysia, Singapore & Brunei* and wrote to us helpful hints, useful advice and interesting anecdotes:

Shirley Abdullah, Raf Aerts, Maureen Aleman, Zahid Ali, James Alley, Richard Alvoid, Marius Andersen, Line Anderson, Mark Anderson, Sarah Anderson, Mr & Mrs I Andrews, Lee Ann Kosternik, Katrin Arendt, Zoe Arnautov, J Arthur Freed, Alice Aruthan, Keld Asnaes, Ida Astrid Lundell, F Audet, Friedrich August Bielerstein, Jorg Ausfelt, David Bachmann, Johor Bahru, Stuart Baker, S Bakke, Vivienne Bamford, Siew Bang Chang, Andre Barneveld Binkhuysen, Craig Barrack, D Barrington-Leach, Aram Barsoumian, Shibu Basheer, Jocelyn Bateman, Rod Bateman, S J Bater, Peter Beglin, Jussi Behrndt, John Beilinski, David Bell, Michele Bennett, Walter Berry, Christopher Betz, Deborah Beveridge, Micharl Biernik, Gavin Biggs, J P Bingham, Steve Black, Alastair Blois-Brooke, M Blyth, Oliver Boedeker, Andy Bolas, Janice Bomford, Cisca & Harry Bos, Dr W H Bos, Amanda Bowen, L Bowman, Jenny Brain, M J Branch, Lena Brate, Val Braun, John Brickwood, Paul Brinkhof, Tim Britten, Glyn Britton, Leslie & Ian Brodie, John Bromley-Barratt, Colin Brown, Doug Brown, Gretchen Brown, Naomi Brown, Peter Brown, Geoff Browne, Kevin Browning, Susan Bucciero, Tara Buckley, Rebecca Burdon, Lachlan Burnet, Andrew Burnett, Pierre Burny, Michelle Butt, Joshua Button, Chris Cadman, Claire & Ross Campbell, Lea Campbell, Fernando Campos, Mike Canavan, Alberto Fontanillo Carrascal, Jackie Carver, Guglielmo Cascioli, Xavier Cazauran, Danny Chang, Kym Channell, Peter Cheah, Julian Chee, Chris Chin, Joelynn Chin, Nam Whue Chin, D Chong, Lee Choong Loong, Catherine & Andy Chopin, S Chowdhury, Francis Chu, Ken Chye, Giancarlo Cittolin, Geoff Clament, C Clark, Linda Clevberger, Christopher Clyde, J M Cochrane, Raymond Coe, Jennifer & Neil Collins, A & M Collinson, Darren Collinson, Basil Condos, Grace Conrad, Iside Constantine, Mary P Conway, Valerie & Rosanna Conway, Bruce Cook, Denis & Aileen Cook, Liane Cook, Fenella Cooke, Stuart Cooke, Linda Cooper, Eric Cordina, Adolf Cortel, Fabienne Cotte, Margaret Coultrup, Diane Cowan, David Cozy, Bridget Craig, Joshua Crane, Daud Creelman, Steve Crocker, Wendy Cronin, Kevin Cunningham, Lee-Ann Cunningham, Susan Curry, Ake Dahllof, A Daley, Franz Dam, Michael J van Dam, Tamatha Darcey, Paisley Davidson, Isobel Davie, Anne Davies, Belinda Davis, Trevor Davison, J Dawson, Hadyn Day, Mike & Jean Day, Derham Daymond, Cynthia De Jager, Johan de Jong, Marco de Lange, Lucien De Prycker, Tom de Smet, Cambina Dean, Anneleen De Boerenkool, A Decalande, Cassie Degnan, Mike DeLarwelle, L den Otter, C B Denning, Peter Derrick, N Deschamps, Lars Dicht, Allan & Naomi Dickinson, Machteld C van Dierendonck, Alex Dittrich, Sheila & Paul Doherty, Matjaz Dolenc, Jan Doms, Ailsa J Donnelly, Suzanne Donnelly, A Donoghue, Tg Dora, Roger Doswell, Colleen Dowie, Susanne Drachmann, Jerry Drawhorn, Uta Dressen, Kirsten Dreyer, Milly Dudley-Owen, G Duffy, Colleen Dulian, Dr R A Duncan, Pat Duncan, Jennifer Dunkley, Richard Durkin, K Duss, R J Dyer, Clare Eaton, Madeline Eaton, Matt Ebiner, Michael Eckert, Gijs Edelbroek, Jeremy Edwards, Sigi Edwards, Marie Ekman Parck, Caroline Ellis, Jonas Engkjaer Christensen, Svend Erik Hansen, Patrik Eriksson, Cathrin Eszbach, Sheila Eustace, Lisa Evans, Ruth & Neil Evans, Derek Ewell, Sybil Faigin, James Farley, Teresa Farrell, Michael Fastenberg, Bruno Fehrenbach, Carlos Fernandez, Rogier Festen, Pam & Alan Fey, Barbara Fielder, Stephen Fine, David Fitzmaurice, Liam Fitzpatrick, Jackie Flanagan, Andy Flemming, Zoe Fletcher, Ed Fogden, Uffe & Henrik Fond, Joseph Fonte, Dr Michael Forster, Paul Fowler, Michael Fox, Alban Franckhauser, Vesa Frantsila, Mary Fraser, Mark Fynn, Gregory Galligan, Kym Gentry, Karen George, Tony Gerber, Boyd Gilchrist, Dave Gile, Deepak Gill, Cath Gillespie, Katrina Gillespie, Sarah Goacher, Charlotte Goedvolk, Tony Goring, Mrs & Mr D Gosnold, Kevin Gover, James Grayson, David Green, Ros Green,

Emilie Gregoire, Iain Grosvenor, Scot Guenter, Paula Guerrein, Ferry C Guijpink, Christina Gustavsson, Rillard Guttmuth, Peter Hackford, Martin Hadley, Duncan Hall, Richard & Jenny Hall, Tanja Haller, Stuart Hamilton, Rowena Harding, Chris Hardy, Timothy Hardy, Hisham Hashim, Tom Haslam, Karen Hatting, Louise Hatton, Rhonda Hawkins, Gaye Haworth, Sister Frances Hayes, Ray Hegarty, Holger Heidersdorf, Tony Helga, Eloise Helme, Mike Hemingway, Beverley Herbert, Monika Hertel, Ruth Heywood, Kavanagh Hilferink, R Hill, Peter Ho, Alicia Hock, Karin Hofland, Paul Hofman, Vincent Hogenboom, Jo'an Hoh, Holger Hojlund, Christine Holike, Robert Hollingworth, Carol Holmes, Karl Holmes, Rebecca Holmes, Marianne Hoornenborg, Heather Hope, Petri Hottola, Nigel Hoult, Toon Huang Yeoh, Jenny Huggett, Thng Hui Hong, Kurt van den Hungen, Hilary Hunt, Russell Huntington, Nazlina Hussin, William I-Ching Sam, Yahaya Ismail, Philippe Jacquot, Gams Jager, Warren Jarrett, Paul Jefferson, J Jegorow, Judy Jere, Jeroen Jeths, Joanna Johnston, Sandra Johnston, Ester & Mike Jok, Alan Jones, Nick Jones, Wally Jones, Kari Jussila, Erik Juul Pedersen, Rachel Kahn, Robert Kalman, Kelly Kaloti, Sudha Kamath, Farid Kareem, Paul & Bev Karlik, Renko Karruppannan, Jan A Kaulfuhs, George E Kavanagh, Alan S Kaye, Jens Kayser, George Kechagioglou, T Keeper, Dave Kelsey, M Kempinga, Alan Kendall, Chi Keng Low, Rosle Khalid, Herb Kieklak, Sebastian Kiesow, Sarah Kilter, Martin Kim, Azman King, Pauline King, Alt Kiren, Hugh Kitchin, L Kitter, Debra A Klein, Steve Knode, Jeff Kok, Lee Kok Piew, Franziska Konitzer, Joke Koppen, Lena Korsnes, Peter Kosin, Susanne Kotner, M Kotvas, Doris Kreit, Geoff Kricker, Maria Kristensen, Marion Kruger, Patty Kruiswijk, Ann Krumboltz, Thommy Kuers, Thomas Kurzc-Zerbe, Hew KW, Simon Kwag Myongjin, Candice Kwok, Jeffery L, Ian Lamont, John Lam-Po-Tang, Guy Langan, Fleur & Tim Langmead, Enrico Lanza, Matt Latham, Cecily Latzell, Paul Lawlor, Lynne Layton, Philippe Le Francios, Isabel Leader, Alan Lee, Auselia Lee, Eileen Lee, Harry Lee, KP Lee, Paulson Lee, E de Leeuw, S Leitners, Manfred Lenzen, Leif Lervik, Rebecca Lesher, Robert Leverton, Dr Cas Liber, Therese Lillieskold, Charles Lim, Lorraine Little, Ruth Littlejohn, Wei Liu, R Liyanapathirana, Eloise Lockhart, Ian Loftus, M Loo, Gabriel Loos, Becky Lou, Peter Lowe, Sarah Luck, David Ludwig, K & J Lumley-Jones, Wai Lun Wan, David Luxon, Mercedes Luzan, Shan Lyn Ma, Chalet Lynchet, Jim MacDonald, Hugh MacIndoe, Penny & Peter MacKay, Vicki Mackay, Daniel Mackey, Margaret MacNeil, Sean A MacPherson, Richard Madden, Bess Mah, John Maidmant, Pat Malone, Stephen Malone, Jay Donald Mann, Stephen & Angela Manthorpo, Johannes Marbert, Nils Marchant, Steve Marcus, Leslie Martin, Lisa Martin, Melanie Martinez, Kristof Masschelein, Sue Masters, Roland Mayer, L J & K P Mazok, Iain McAllister, Ken McAvoy, Meira McBride, Fiona McCarthy, Amy McDonald, Stephen McElhinney, Dudley McFadden, Louise McGarr, Lucy McGilligan, Ms Hilary McLeod, David McMahon, Craig McMillan, Bronwyn McNaughton, Chris Mead, Catherine Medway, Rachel Mellors, Tan Meng Chwen, Alan Merrick, Tony Messanger, Heidi Meyer, Ian Meyeroff, Julie Michalik, Andy Millard, Jon Miller, Nick Miller, Phil Miller, Terry Miller, Shirley Mills, Embong Mohamad, John Moline, Zsolt Molnar, Ron F Monch, M Monteau, Sean Mooney, Gary Moore, Guadalupe Moreno, Lorraine & Bruce Moss, S Mubayi, Andrew Mudge, Doug Muir, Peter Muller, Cristin Murphy, Patrick Murphy, E Naadland, Terry Nakazono, Alessandra Negri, Debby Neiuwenhuizen, Pauline & Jerome Netter, Will Newitt, C Newson, Harry Nichol, Christoph Nieman, Debby Nieuwenhuizen, Nynke Nijkamp, Anita Nogarotto, J & B Norden, Henry Nordstrom, G & B Norheim, Margaret Norman, Achim Nuhr, Rui Nunes, T Nunis, Massimo Nuvina, Mimmo Nuvina, Susan Oakden, Stephan Oetiker, Hakan Olofsson, Deanna Ony, Jan & Gerda Opmeer, Tony Ossendorp, Cristina Osta, Steffen Owen, Patric Paccu, Chloe Paine, Rolf Palmberg, Mark Paluch, Pier Paolo Zenga, Dennis Paradine, Sharon Parsonson, Kate Patane, Jo Pattyn, Lamarque Paule, B R Pearson, Jon Pearson, Michael Pearson, J C & Rev Pearson, Tan Pei Chea, Paul Pelczar, Kaarina Pellikka, Frank Peotzki, Chris Perez, Giorgio Perversi, Michael Petty, Guy Petziall, Tim Phillips, John Phillyes, G & N Phoon, Ram Pillai, Janet & Guy Pinneo, Ricky Pinto, Edo Plantinga, J Plenty, Erik Plugge, Werner Pomwenger, Linden & Adrian Porter, Dr marion Potschin, Jens Poulsen, David Powell, Dale Power, Adam Preece, Sree Prekash, Wilco

Pruysers, Leong Pui Kun, Deanne Purcell, Andy Purdy, Malcolm Purvis, W P Putter, M A Quin, Bob Radke, B L H Ralph, R T Ralph, Anand Ram, Helen Rankin, Sebastian Raum, Petra Rautenberg, Dean Ravenscroft, Nor Razab, M D Reardon, J Rebecca, Ralf Reinecke, Tom Renders, Miro Reverby, Douglas Reynolds, Jenny Reynolds, Eleanor Reza, Antoine Riche, Katherine Rickus, Susan Ridge, Karsten Rimmer Larsen, Rosel Rivera, Jennifer Joy Rizzo, R E Roberts, Lionel Robertson, Yann Roche, James Rodgers, Annette Rodley, Carlos Rodriguez, Ryan Rogers, Andrea Rogge, Jesper Ronngard, Philip Row, Carolyn Rubens, Jarek Rudnik, Frances P Ryan, Wendy S, Isabel Sabugueiro, Haavard Saksvikronning, Nicci Salmon, Sabine Samshuyzen, George Samuel, Helene Sandare, Eric Santoro, Agus Sarta, Christine Sauerwein, Jade Saunders, Julian Scammell, Linda Scharten, Wouter Schik, Michael J Schmidt, Heiko Schmitz, Lawrence Schneck, Frederick Schneider, Gery Schneider, Herman Scholz, Hans Schonockel-Og, Idelette Schuurman, John Sclater, Kevin Scott, Christina & Martin Semler, Chris Sennett, Louise & Philip Shambrook, Tan Shang Wei, John Sharman, Dennis N Sharp, Tim Shaw, Julie Sheard, Norman Shepherd, Alan Sheridan, Kate Shew, Nancy Shilepsky, Yum Shoen Liang, Sven Sielhorst, Gabriele Sigl, Julie Simkins, Art Simon, Lene Simonsen, Amerjeet Singh, Caroline M Skilbred, B J Skiles, Hilde Skogedal, J Slagt, Nathalie van der Slikke, Henny Smit, George Smith, Jeffrey Smith, L Smith, Martin Smith, Nik Smith, Michael Smyth, J & L Snyder, John Soar, Hans Sondern, Marlijn Sonne, Roger & Hilary Southall, Linda Spence, Gary Spinks, Guy Spouge, Rob Spragg, Stephen Sprod, Matthias Staehein, John Standerline, David Steinke, Mikkel Stensgard, Tommy & Agnete Stensletten, Eric Stenson, Jennifer Stepanik, Inge Sterk, Rebecca Stevens, Karen Stevenson, Tim Stewart, Rebecca Stock, Anna Stockley, Debs Stockwell, Jessica Stokes, Gillian Storey, Anita Strand, Tom Stringell, Janis Strom, Amanda Strong, Staisha Stubley, Sheila Su-Borstelmann, June Suh, A Sulkowski, Paul Sundberg, Selvi Supramaniam, R Suurhoff, Eileen Synnott, Nova Tagaro, Emma Tait, Kaname Takada, Mr Kaname Takada, Jesse S J Tan, Lawrence Tan, Carsten Tang, Dave Taylor, Deborah Taylor, Ali Temara, Albert Teo, Victor Teo, Chiel & Eveline ter Laak, Beverly Terry, Anne & Steve Thew, Arleen Thomas, Dr William L Thomas, Nicole Thomas, Peter Thomas, Jean Thompson, Mrs Lisette Thresh, Anders Tihkan, Robette Timothee, Graham Todd, Derek Tokashiki, Alberto Tonti, Hanna Torstensson, Jean-Macr Toussaint, J Trewin, Kevin Troy, Jim Truscott, Jim Tury, Paul G Unterberg, Martin Upham, Anita Utas, Michel Van Dam, Bart van den Broek, M van Dijk, Miranda & Wilfred van Dongen, J W J Van Dorp, Dick van Duijn, Wendy van Duivenvoorde, Sander van Luyn, Rob van Megan, Ab van Peer, Roger & Maureen Vanstone, Jerry van Veenendaal, Paul Vellnagel, Eddy van der Ven, Dave Vicars, Pedro Vilata, Tatiana Visona, Hans Visser, Thijs Visser, Glen Voice, Laszlo Wagner, Wong Wai Cheung, Jay Walder, Janet Walker, Louise Walls, Emily Walton, Ian Ward, Phil Ward, Steven Wassall, S Watts, Jeff & Mau Webb, Nah Wee Kee, Natisha Weissig, E J Weller, Paul Wellington, Jennifer West, Y Wester, Tony Weston, S White, Sarah White, Cattrin & Bob Wickens, Roger Wicks, Karen Widdowson, Marie-Claire van de Wiel, Daniel J Wilgosh, Mark Wilkinson, Don & Teri Wilks, Didier Willemssens, Dylan Williams, L Williams, Peter Williams, Sean D Williams, Holly Williamson, Becky Wilson, Gardiner J Wilson, George S Wilson, F Wood, Simon Wood, Victor Wood, S D Woodhouse, Helen Woodward, Mark Woollett, Lain Wotherspoon, Joyce Wu, Rob Wubben, Paul Wyatt, Bev & Graeme Wyber, Andy Yeates, Foong Yee, Lee Chen Yi, W Zammit, Dr J W Zottnick

# LONELY PLANET

You already know that Lonely Planet produces more than this one guidebook, but you might not be aware of the other products we have on this region. Here is a selection of titles that you may want to check out as well:

**South-East Asia
on a shoestring**
ISBN 0 86442 632 1
US$21.95 • UK£13.99 • 170FF

**South-East Asia phrasebook**
ISBN 0 86442 435 3
US$6.95 • UK£3.99 • 40FF

**Singapore**
ISBN 1 86450 159 6
US$15.99 • UK£9.99 • 119FF

**Mandarin phrasebook**
ISBN 0 86442 652 6
US$7.95 • UK£4.50 • 50FF

**Malay phrasebook**
ISBN 0 86442 463 9
US$5.95 • UK£3.99 • 40FF

**Read This First: Asia & India**
ISBN 1 86450 049 2
US$14.95 • UK£8.99 • 99FF

**Singapore City Map**
ISBN 1 86450 178 2
US$5.99 • UK£3.99 • 39FF

**Healthy Travel Asia & India**
ISBN 1 86450 051 4
US$5.95 • UK£3.99 • 39FF

**Available wherever books
are sold**

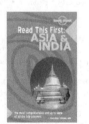

# LONELY PLANET

## Guides by Region

**L**onely Planet is known worldwide for publishing practical, reliable and no-nonsense travel information in our guides and on our Web site. The Lonely Planet list covers just about every accessible part of the world. Currently there are 16 series: Travel guides, Shoestring guides, Condensed guides, Phrasebooks, Read This First, Healthy Travel, Walking guides, Cycling guides, Watching Wildlife guides, Pisces Diving & Snorkeling guides, City Maps, Road Atlases, Out to Eat, World Food, Journeys travel literature and Pictorials.

**AFRICA** Africa on a shoestring • Cairo • Cairo City Map • Cape Town • Cape Town City Map • East Africa • Egypt • Egyptian Arabic phrasebook • Ethiopia, Eritrea & Djibouti • Ethiopian (Amharic) phrasebook • The Gambia & Senegal • Healthy Travel Africa • Kenya • Malawi • Morocco • Moroccan Arabic phrasebook • Mozambique • Read This First: Africa • South Africa, Lesotho & Swaziland • Southern Africa • Southern Africa Road Atlas • Swahili phrasebook • Tanzania, Zanzibar & Pemba • Trekking in East Africa • Tunisia • Watching Wildlife East Africa • Watching Wildlife Southern Africa • West Africa • World Food Morocco • Zimbabwe, Botswana & Namibia
**Travel Literature:** Mali Blues: Traveling to an African Beat • The Rainbird: A Central African Journey • Songs to an African Sunset: A Zimbabwean Story

**AUSTRALIA & THE PACIFIC** Auckland • Australia • Australian phrasebook • Australia Road Atlas • Bushwalking in Australia •Cycling New Zealand • Fiji • Fijian phrasebook • Healthy Travel Australia, NZ and the Pacific • Islands of Australia's Great Barrier Reef • Melbourne • Melbourne City Map • Micronesia • New Caledonia • New South Wales & the ACT • New Zealand • Northern Territory • Outback Australia • Out to Eat – Melbourne • Out to Eat – Sydney • Papua New Guinea • Pidgin phrasebook • Queensland • Rarotonga & the Cook Islands • Samoa • Solomon Islands • South Australia • South Pacific • South Pacific phrasebook • Sydney • Sydney City Map • Sydney Condensed • Tahiti & French Polynesia • Tasmania • Tonga • Tramping in New Zealand • Vanuatu • Victoria • Walking in Australia • Watching Wildlife Australia • Western Australia
**Travel Literature:** Islands in the Clouds: Travels in the Highlands of New Guinea • Kiwi Tracks: A New Zealand Journey • Sean & David's Long Drive

**CENTRAL AMERICA & THE CARIBBEAN** Bahamas, Turks & Caicos • Baja California • Bermuda • Central America on a shoestring • Costa Rica • Costa Rica Spanish phrasebook • Cuba • Dominican Republic & Haiti • Eastern Caribbean • Guatemala • Guatemala, Belize & Yucatán: La Ruta Maya • Healthy Travel Central & South America • Jamaica • Mexico • Mexico City • Panama • Puerto Rico • Read This First: Central & South America • World Food Mexico • Yucatán
**Travel Literature:** Green Dreams: Travels in Central America

**EUROPE** Amsterdam • Amsterdam City Map • Amsterdam Condensed • Andalucía • Austria • Baltic States phrasebook • Barcelona • Barcelona City Map • Berlin • Berlin City Map • Britain • British phrasebook • Brussels, Bruges & Antwerp • Brussels City Map • Budapest • Budapest City Map • Canary Islands • Central Europe • Central Europe phrasebook • Corfu & the Ionians • Corsica • Crete • Crete Condensed • Croatia • Cycling Britain • Cycling France • Cyprus • Czech & Slovak Republics • Denmark • Dublin • Dublin City Map • Eastern Europe • Eastern Europe phrasebook • Edinburgh • Estonia, Latvia & Lithuania • Europe on a shoestring • Finland • Florence • France • Frankfurt Condensed • French phrasebook • Georgia, Armenia & Azerbaijan • Germany • German phrasebook • Greece • Greek Islands • Greek phrasebook • Hungary • Iceland, Greenland & the Faroe Islands • Ireland • Istanbul • Italian phrasebook • Italy • Krakow • Lisbon • The Loire • London • London City Map • London Condensed • Madrid • Malta • Mediterranean Europe • Mediterranean Europe phrasebook • Moscow • Mozambique • Munich • the Netherlands • Norway • Out to Eat – London • Paris • Paris City Map • Paris Condensed • Poland • Portugal • Portuguese phrasebook • Prague • Prague City Map • Provence & the Côte d'Azur • Read This First: Europe • Romania & Moldova • Rome • Rome City Map • Russia, Ukraine & Belarus • Russian phrasebook • Scandinavian & Baltic Europe • Scandinavian Europe phrasebook • Scotland • Sicily • Slovenia • South-West France • Spain • Spanish phrasebook • St Petersburg • St Petersburg City Map • Sweden • Switzerland • Trekking in Spain • Tuscany • Ukrainian phrasebook • Venice • Vienna • Walking in Britain • Walking in France • Walking in Ireland • Walking in Italy • Walking in Spain • Walking in Switzerland • Western Europe • Western Europe phrasebook • World Food France • World Food Italy • World Food Spain
**Travel Literature:** Love and War in the Apennines • The Olive Grove: Travels in Greece • On the Shores of the Mediterranean • Round Ireland in Low Gear • A Small Place in Italy • After Yugoslavia

# LONELY PLANET

## Mail Order

**L**onely Planet products are distributed worldwide. They are also available by mail order from Lonely Planet, so if you have difficulty finding a title please write to us. North and South American residents should write to 150 Linden St, Oakland, CA 94607, USA; European and African residents should write to 10a Spring Place, London NW5 3BH, UK; and residents of other countries to Locked Bag 1, Footscray, Victoria 3011, Australia.

**INDIAN SUBCONTINENT** Bangladesh • Bengali phrasebook • Bhutan • Delhi • Goa • Healthy Travel Asia & India • Hindi & Urdu phrasebook • India • Indian Himalaya • Karakoram Highway • Kerala • Mumbai (Bombay) • Nepal • Nepali phrasebook • Pakistan • Rajasthan • Read This First: Asia & India • South India • Sri Lanka • Sri Lanka phrasebook • Tibet • Tibetan phrasebook • Trekking in the Indian Himalaya • Trekking in the Karakoram & Hindukush • Trekking in the Nepal Himalaya
**Travel Literature:** The Age of Kali: Indian Travels and Encounters • Hello Goodnight: A Life of Goa • In Rajasthan • A Season in Heaven: True Tales from the Road to Kathmandu • Shopping for Buddhas • A Short Walk in the Hindu Kush • Slowly Down the Ganges

**ISLANDS OF THE INDIAN OCEAN** Madagascar & Comoros • Maldives • Mauritius, Réunion & Seychelles

**MIDDLE EAST & CENTRAL ASIA** Bahrain, Kuwait & Qatar • Central Asia • Central Asia phrasebook • Dubai • Hebrew phrasebook • Iran • Israel & the Palestinian Territories • Istanbul • Istanbul City Map • Istanbul to Cairo on a shoestring • Jerusalem • Jerusalem City Map • Jordan • Lebanon • Middle East • Oman & the United Arab Emirates • Syria • Turkey • Turkish phrasebook • World Food Turkey • Yemen
**Travel Literature:** Black on Black: Iran Revisited • The Gates of Damascus • Kingdom of the Film Stars: Journey into Jordan

**NORTH AMERICA** Alaska • Boston • Boston City Map • California & Nevada • California Condensed • Canada • Chicago • Chicago City Map • Deep South • Florida • Great Lakes • Hawaii • Hiking in Alaska • Hiking in the USA • Honolulu • Las Vegas • Los Angeles • Los Angeles City Map • Louisiana & The Deep South • Miami • Miami City Map • New England • New Orleans • New York City • New York City City Map • New York City Condensed • New York, New Jersey & Pennsylvania • Oahu • Out to Eat – San Francisco • Pacific Northwest • Puerto Rico • Rocky Mountains • San Francisco • San Francisco City Map • Seattle • Southwest • Texas • USA • USA phrasebook • Vancouver • Virginia & the Capital Region • Washington DC • Washington, DC City Map • World Food Deep South, USA • World Food New Orleans
**Travel Literature:** Caught Inside: A Surfer's Year on the California Coast • Drive Thru America

**NORTH-EAST ASIA** Beijing • Beijing City Map • Cantonese phrasebook • China • Hiking in Japan • Hong Kong • Hong Kong City Map • Hong Kong Condensed • Hong Kong, Macau & Guangzhou • Japan • Japanese phrasebook • Korea • Korean phrasebook • Kyoto • Mandarin phrasebook • Mongolia • Mongolian phrasebook • Seoul • Shanghai • South-West China • Taiwan • Tokyo
**Travel Literature:** In Xanadu: A Quest • Lost Japan

**SOUTH AMERICA** Argentina, Uruguay & Paraguay • Bolivia • Brazil • Brazilian phrasebook • Buenos Aires • Chile & Easter Island • Colombia • Ecuador & the Galapagos Islands • Healthy Travel Central & South America • Latin American Spanish phrasebook • Peru • Quechua phrasebook • Read This First: Central & South America • Rio de Janeiro • Rio de Janeiro City Map • Santiago • South America on a shoestring • Santiago • Trekking in the Patagonian Andes • Venezuela
**Travel Literature:** Full Circle: A South American Journey

**SOUTH-EAST ASIA** Bali & Lombok • Bangkok • Bangkok City Map • Burmese phrasebook • Cambodia • Hanoi • Healthy Travel Asia & India • Hill Tribes phrasebook • Ho Chi Minh City • Indonesia • Indonesian phrasebook • Indonesia's Eastern Islands • Jakarta • Java • Lao phrasebook • Laos • Malay phrasebook • Malaysia, Singapore & Brunei • Myanmar (Burma) • Philippines • Pilipino (Tagalog) phrasebook • Read This First: Asia & India • Singapore • Singapore City Map • South-East Asia on a shoestring • South-East Asia phrasebook • Thailand • Thailand's Islands & Beaches • Thailand, Vietnam, Laos & Cambodia Road Atlas • Thai phrasebook • Vietnam • Vietnamese phrasebook • World Food Thailand • World Food Vietnam

**ALSO AVAILABLE:** Antarctica • The Arctic • The Blue Man: Tales of Travel, Love and Coffee • Brief Encounters: Stories of Love, Sex & Travel • Chasing Rickshaws • The Last Grain Race • Lonely Planet Unpacked • Not the Only Planet: Science Fiction Travel Stories • Lonely Planet On the Edge • Sacred India • Travel with Children • Travel Photography: A Guide to Taking Better Pictures

# Index

## Abbreviations

B – Brunei                M – Malaysia                S – Singapore

## Text

**Bold** indicates maps.

## Boxed Text

# MAP LEGEND

## CITY ROUTES

| | |
|---|---|
| Freeway | Freeway |
| Highway | Primary Road |
| Road | Secondary Road |
| Street | Street |
| Lane | Lane |
| | On/Off Ramp |

| | |
|---|---|
| | Unsealed Road |
| | One Way Street |
| | Pedestrian Street |
| | Stepped Street |
| | Tunnel |
| | Footbridge |

## REGIONAL ROUTES

| | |
|---|---|
| | Tollway, Freeway |
| | Primary Road |
| | Secondary Road |
| | Minor Road |

## BOUNDARIES

| | |
|---|---|
| | International |
| | State |
| | Disputed |
| | Fortified Wall |

## HYDROGRAPHY

| | |
|---|---|
| | River, Creek |
| | Canal |
| | Lake |

| | |
|---|---|
| | Dry Lake; Salt Lake |
| | Spring; Rapids |
| | Waterfalls |

## TRANSPORT ROUTES & STATIONS

| | |
|---|---|
| | Train |
| | Underground Train |
| | Metro |
| | Tramway |
| | Cable Car, Chairlift |

| | |
|---|---|
| | Ferry |
| | Walking Trail |
| | Walking Tour |
| | Path |
| | Pier or Jetty |

## AREA FEATURES

| | |
|---|---|
| | Building |
| | Park, Gardens |

| | |
|---|---|
| | Market |
| | Sports Ground |

| | |
|---|---|
| | Beach |
| | Cemetery |

| | |
|---|---|
| | Campus |
| | Plaza |

## POPULATION SYMBOLS

| | | | | | |
|---|---|---|---|---|---|
| ✪ CAPITAL | National Capital | ● CITY | City | ● Village | Village |
| ◉ CAPITAL | State Capital | ● Town | Town | | Urban Area |

## MAP SYMBOLS

| | | | |
|---|---|---|---|
| ● | Place to Stay | ▼ Place to Eat | ● Point of Interest |

| | | | | | | | |
|---|---|---|---|---|---|---|---|
| ✈ | Airport | ▢ | Embassy | ▥ | Museum | ▥ | Stately Home |
| ⑤ | Bank | ▥ | Hindu Temple | ▤ | National Park | ◙ | Synagogue |
| ▣ | Bus Stop/Terminal | ✛ | Hospital | ▣ | Police Station | ▨ | Telephone |
| ⌂ | Cave | ▣ | Internet Cafe | ▢ | Post Office | ▮ | Temple |
| ▮ | Church | ※ | Lookout | ▢ | Pub or Bar | ▣ | Theatre |
| ▣ | Cinema | ▲ | Monument | ◙ | Shopping Centre | ❶ | Tourist Information |
| ◣ | Dive Site | ◐ | Mosque | ▨ | Sikh Temple | ▣ | Zoo/Bird Sanctuary |

*Note: not all symbols displayed above appear in this book*

---

# LONELY PLANET OFFICES

**Australia**
Locked Bag 1, Footscray, Victoria 3011
☎ 03 9689 4666  fax 03 9689 6833
email: talk2us@lonelyplanet.com.au

**USA**
150 Linden St, Oakland, CA 94607
☎ 510 893 8555  TOLL FREE: 800 275 8555
fax 510 893 8572
email: info@lonelyplanet.com

**UK**
10a Spring Place, London NW5 3BH
☎ 020 7428 4800  fax 020 7428 4828
email: go@lonelyplanet.co.uk

**France**
1 rue du Dahomey, 75011 Paris
☎ 01 55 25 33 00  fax 01 55 25 33 01
email: bip@lonelyplanet.fr
www.lonelyplanet.fr

**World Wide Web: www.lonelyplanet.com *or* AOL keyword: lp**
**Lonely Planet Images: lpi@lonelyplanet.com.au**